D0516589

Guide to Gale Literary Criticism Series

For criticism on	Consult these Gale series
Authors now living or who died after December 31, 1959	*CONTEMPORARY LITERARY CRITICISM (CLC)*
Authors who died between 1900 and 1959	*TWENTIETH-CENTURY LITERARY CRITICISM (TCLC)*
Authors who died between 1800 and 1899	*NINETEENTH-CENTURY LITERATURE CRITICISM (NCLC)*
Authors who died between 1400 and 1799	*LITERATURE CRITICISM FROM 1400 TO 1800 (LC)* *SHAKESPEAREAN CRITICISM (SC)*
Authors who died before 1400	*CLASSICAL AND MEDIEVAL LITERATURE CRITICISM (CMLC)*
Authors of books for children and young adults	*CHILDREN'S LITERATURE REVIEW (CLR)*
Black writers of the past two hundred years	*BLACK LITERATURE CRITICISM (BLC)*
Short story writers	*SHORT STORY CRITICISM (SSC)*
Poets	*POETRY CRITICISM (PC)*
Dramatists	*DRAMA CRITICISM (DC)*
Major authors from the Renaissance to the present	*WORLD LITERATURE CRITICISM, 1500 TO THE PRESENT (WLC)*

For criticism on visual artists since 1850, see
MODERN ARTS CRITICISM (MAC)

HISPANIC LITERATURE CRITICISM

VOLUME 1

Allende to Jiménez

Jelena Krstović, Editor

Gale Research Inc.

DETROIT • WASHINGTON DC • LONDON

STAFF

Jelena Krstović, *Editor*

Joann Cerrito, James P. Draper, Drew Kalasky, Marie Lazzari, Jennifer Mast, James E. Person, Jr., Joseph C. Tardiff, Lawrence J. Trudeau, *Contributing Editors*

Jeffery Chapman, J. A. Edwards, Judith Galens, Christopher Giroux, Margaret A. Haerens, A. A. Hedblad, Michael W. Jones, Thomas Ligotti, Michael Magoulias, Zoran Minderović, Elisabeth Morrison, Brigham Narins, Sean René Pollock, Anna J. Sheets, Brain St. Germain, *Contributing Associate Editors*

Deron Albright, Pamela Willwerth Aue, George H. Blair, Martha Bommarito, Paul Buczkowski, Thomas Carson, Meggin Condino, Nancy G. Dziedzic, Ian A. Goodhall, Kelly Hill, Kathryn Horste, S. Thomas McCready, Paul Sassalos, *Contributing Assistant Editors*

Jeanne A. Gough, *Permissions & Production Manager*
Linda M. Pugliese, *Production Supervisor*
Donna Craft, Paul Lewon, Maureen Puhl, Camille P. Robinson, Sheila Walencewicz, *Editorial Associates*
Jill Johnson, Elizabeth Anne Valliere, *Editorial Assistants*

Sandra C. Davis, *Permissions Supervisor (Text)*
Maria L. Franklin, Josephine M. Keene, Michele M. Lonoconus, Shalice Shah, Kimberly F. Smilay, *Permissions Associates*
Jennifer A. Arnold, Brandy C. Merritt, *Permissions Assistants*

Margaret A. Chamberlain, *Permissions Supervisor (Pictures)*
Pamela A. Hayes, Arlene Johnson, Keith Reed, *Permissions Associates*
Susan Brohman, Barbara A. Wallace, *Permissions Assistants*

Victoria B. Cariappa, *Research Manager*
Maureen Richards, *Research Supervisor*
Robert S. Lazich, Mary Beth McElmeel, Donna Melnychenko, Tamara C. Nott, Jaema Paradowski, *Editorial Associates*
Maria Bryson, Julie Leonard, Stefanie Scarlett, *Editorial Assistants*

Mary Beth Trimper, *Production Director*
Mary Kelley, *Production Associate*

Cynthia Baldwin, *Art Director*
Mary Krzewinski, *Senior Graphic Designer*
Willie Mathis, *Camera Operator*

ISBN 0-8103-9145-7
Vol 1 ISBN 0-8103-9375-1

Printed in the United States of America
Published simultaneously in the United Kingdom
by Gale Research International Limited
(An affiliated company of Gale Research Inc.)
10 9 8 7 6 5 4 3 2

Contents of Volume 1

literature about himself and his Communist regime.

García Márquez is internationally renowned for his skillful employment of "magic realism" in novels like *One Hundred Years of Solitude*. He was the recipient of the 1982 Nobel Prize for literature.

Introduction

A Comprehensive Information Source
on Hispanic Literature

*H*ispanic Literature Criticism *(HLC)* presents a broad selection of the best criticism of works by major Hispanic writers of the past one hundred years. Among the authors included in *HLC* are such earlier figures as novelist Mariano Azuela, poet Rubén Darío, and essayist Miguel de Unamuno; such acknowledged twentieth-century masters as short story writer Jorge Luis Borges, filmmaker Luis Buñuel, novelist Julio Cortázar, novelist Carlos Fuentes, novelist Gabriel García Márquez, poet and playwright Federico Garciá Lorca, poet Pablo Neruda, and novelist Mario Vargas Llosa; and emerging writers Jimmy Santiago Baca, Sandra Cisneros, Oscar Hijuelos, and Gary Soto. The scope of *HLC* is wide: seventy-one writers representing the United States, Mexico, Cuba, Spain, and many other nations are covered in comprehensive author entries.

Coverage

This two-volume set is designed for high school and college students, as well as for the general reader who wants to learn more about Hispanic literature. *HLC* was developed in response to strong demand by students, librarians, and other readers for a one-stop, authoritative guide to the whole spectrum of Hispanic literature. No other compendium like it exists in the marketplace. Some of the entries in *HLC* were selected from Gale's acclaimed Literary Criticism Series and completely updated for publication here. Typically, revisions are extensive, ranging from completely rewritten biographical and critical introductions to wide changes in the selection of criticism. Other entries were prepared especially for *HLC* in order to furnish the most comprehensive coverage possible. Authors were selected for inclusion based on the advice of leading experts on Hispanic literature, as well on the range and amount of critical material available in English. Coverage is given to important new writers along with to the most studied authors.

Each entry in *HLC* attempts to present a survey of critical response to the author's work. Early criticism is offered, where available, to indicate initial responses. Later selections document any rise or decline in literary reputation, and retrospective analyses provide modern views. Every endeavor has been made to include seminal essays on each author's work along with recent commentary providing current perspectives. Interviews, author statements, and excerpts from the authors' works are also included in many entries. Thus, *HLC* is both timely and comprehensive.

Organization of Author Entries

Information about authors and their works is presented through eight key access points:

- The **Author Heading** cites the name under which the author most commonly wrote, followed by birth and death dates. Name variations, including full birth name when available, are given in parentheses on the first page of the **Biographical and Critical Introduction.**

- The **Biographical and Critical Introduction** contains background information about the life and works of the author. Emphasis is given to four main areas: 1) biographical details that help reveal the life, character, and personality of the author; 2) overviews of the major literary interests of the author—for example, novel writing, autobiography, social reform, documentary, etc.; 3) descriptions and summaries of the author's best-known works; and 4) critical commentary about the author's achievement, stature, and importance.

- Most *HLC* entries include an **Author Portrait**. Many also contain **Illustrations** documenting the author's career, including title pages of works, sketches, or pictures of important people, places, and events in the author's life.

- The **List of Principal Works** is chronological by date of first book publication and identifies the genre of each work. For non-English-language authors whose works have been translated into English, the title and date of the first English-language edition are given in brackets beneath the foreign-language listing. Unless otherwise indicated, dramas are dated by first performance rather than first publication.

- **Criticism** is arranged chronologically in each author entry to provide a useful perspective on changes in critical evaluation over the years. Most entries contain a detailed, comprehensive study of the author's career as well as book reviews, studies of individual works, and comparative examinations. To ensure timeliness, current views are most often presented, but never to the exclusion of important early pieces. For the purpose of easy identification, the critic's name and the date of the critical work are given at the beginning of each piece of criticism. Unsigned criticism is preceded by the title of the source in which it appeared. Within the criticism, titles of works by the author are printed in boldface type. Publication information (such as publisher names and book prices) and certain numerical references (such as footnotes or page and line references to specific editions of works) have been deleted at the editor's discretion to provide smoother reading of the text.

- Critical essays are prefaced by **Explanatory Notes** as an additional aid to readers of *HLC*. These notes may provide several types of valuable information, including: 1) the reputation of the critic; 2) the perceived importance of the work of criticism; 3) the commentator's approach to the author's work; 4) the apparent purpose of the criticism; and 5) changes in critical trends regarding the author.

- A complete **Bibliographical Citation** of the original essay or book follows each piece of criticism.

- An annotated **Further Reading List** appears at the end of each entry and suggests resources for additional study. Boxed information at the end of the Further Reading List directs readers to other Gale series containing information about the author.

Other Features

HLC contains three distinct indexes to help readers find information quickly and easily:

- The **Author Index** lists all the authors appearing in *HLC*. To ensure easy access, name variations and name changes are fully cross-indexed.

- The **Nationality Index** lists all authors featured in *HLC* by nationality or by their professed affiliation.

- The **Title Index** lists in alphabetical order all individual works by the authors appearing in *HLC*.

English-language translations of original foreign-language titles are cross-referenced to the foreign titles so that all references to a work are combined in one listing.

Citing *Hispanic Literature Criticism*

When writing papers, students who quote directly from *HLC* may use the following general forms to footnote reprinted criticism. The first example is for material drawn from periodicals, the second for material reprinted from books.

Albert D. Treviño, "*Bless Me, Ultima:* A Critical Interpretation," *De Colores* 3, no. 4 (1977), pp. 30-3; excerpted and reprinted in *Hispanic Literature Criticism,* ed. Jelena Krstović (Detroit: Gale Research, 1994), pp. 43-6.

Kenneth Minogue, "Che Guevara," in *The New Left: Six Critical Essays,* edited by Maurice Cranston (The Bodley Head, 1970); excerpted and reprinted in *Hispanic Literature Criticism,* ed. Jelena Krstović (Detroit: Gale Research, 1994), pp. 676-82.

Acknowledgments

The editor wishes to acknowledge the valuable contributions of the many librarians, authors, and scholars who assisted in the compilation of *HLC* with their responses to telephone and mail inquiries. Special thanks are offered to *HLC's* chief advisors: Carlota Cárdenas de Dwyer of San Antonio's Tom C. Clark High School; Nicolás Kanellos, founder of Arte Público Press; Luis Leal, acting director of the Center for Chicano Studies (University of California at Santa Barbara); and David Unger, co-director of the Latin American Writers Institute in New York City.

Comments Are Welcome

The editor hopes that readers will find *HLC* to be a useful reference tool and welcomes comments about the work. Send comments and suggestions to: Editor, *Hispanic Literature Criticism,* Gale Research Inc., Penobscot Building, Detroit, MI 48226-4094.

Acknowledgments

The editors wish to thank the copyright holders of the excerpted criticism included in this volume, the permissions managers of many book and magazine publishing companies for assisting us in securing reprint rights, and Anthony Bogucki for assistance with copyright research. We are also grateful to the staffs of the Detroit Public Library, the Library of Congress, the University of Detroit Library, Wayne State University Purdy/Kresge Library Complex, and the University of Michigan Libraries for making their resources available to us. Following is a list of the copyright holders who have granted us permission to reprint material in this volume of *HLC*. Every effort has been made to trace copyright, but if omissions have been made, please let us know.

COPYRIGHTED EXCERPTS IN *HLC* WERE REPRINTED FROM THE FOLLOWING PERIODICALS:

America, v. 128, January 27, 1973; v. 142, March 1, 1980; v. 144, February 7, 1981; v. 163, September 22, 1990. © 1973, 1980, 1981, 1990. All rights reserved. All reprinted with permission of America Press, Inc., 106 West 56th Street, New York, NY 10019.—*The American Book Review,* v. 1, December, 1977; v. 11, October, 1979; v. 4, January-February, 1982; v. 5, September-October, 1983; v. 6, November-December, 1983; v. 11, January, 1990; v. 13, August, 1991; v. 13, February-March, 1992. © 1977, 1979, 1982, 1983, 1990, 1991, 1992 by *The American Book Review.* All reprinted by permission of the publisher.—*Américas,* v. 36, May-June, 1984. © 1984 *Américas.* Reprinted by permission of the publisher.—*The Americas Review,* v. 16, Summer, 1988; v. XVI, Fall-Winter, 1988; v. XVIII, Spring, 1990; v. 18, Summer, 1990. Copyright © 1988, 1990 *The Americas Review.* All reprinted with permission of the publisher, Arte Público Press, University of Houston.—*Anales de la Literatura Española Contemporanea,* v. 8, 1983 for "The Culture Legacy of José Ortega y Gasset" by Blanche de Puy. Reprinted by permission of the publisher and the author.—*The Antigonish Review,* n. 57, Spring, 1984 for "Julio Cortázar's Fiction: The Unfinished Quest" by Amaryll B. Chanady. Copyright 1984 by the author. Reprinted by permission of the publisher and the author.—*AZTLAN,* v. 7, Spring, 1976 for " 'Pocho' as Literature" by Juan Bruce-Novoa. © 1977 The Regents of the University of California. Reprinted by permission of the author.—*Belles Lettres: A Review of Books by Women,* v. 7, Winter, 1991-92. Reprinted by permission of the publisher.—*Best Sellers,* v. 43, April, 1983; v. 45, March, 1986. Copyright © 1983, 1986 Helen Dwight Reid Educational Foundation. Both reprinted by permission of the publisher.—*The Bilingual Review,* v. IV, September-December, 1977; v. XII, September-December, 1985. Copyright © 1977, 1985 by Bilingual Press/Editorial Bilingüe. All rights reserved. Both reprinted by permission of the publisher, Arizona State University, Tempe, AZ.—*Boston Review,* v. XVI, April, 1991 for a review of "The Stories of Eva Luna" by Daniel Harris. Copyright © 1991 by the Boston Critic, Inc. Reprinted by permission of the author.—*Bulletin of Hispanic Studies,* v. XLIII, January, 1965; v. LII, July, 1975; v. LXII, April, 1985. Copyright 1965, 1975, 1985 Liverpool University Press. All reprinted by permission of the publisher.—*Callaloo,* v. 10, Spring, 1987. Copyright © 1987 by Charles H. Rowell. All rights reserved. Reprinted by permission of the publisher.—*Chasqui,* v. XIII, February-May, 1984. Reprinted by permission of the publisher.—*Chicago Review,* v. 17, Fall-Winter, 1964. Copyright © 1964, renewed 1992 by *Chicago Review.* Reprinted by permission of the publisher.—*Chicago Tribune,* December 13, 1992 for "Toward the Deeper Source" by Rockwell Gray. © copyrighted 1992, Chicago Tribune Company. All rights reserved. Reprinted by permission of the author.—*Choice,* v. 13, February, 1977. Copyright © 1977 by American Library Association. Reprinted by permission of the publisher.—*The Christian Century,* v. XCV, November 1, 1978; v. 103, July 2-9, 1986; v. 104, June 17-24, 1987. Copyright 1978, 1986, 1987 Christian Century Foundation. All reprinted by permission from *The Christian Century.*—*De Colores,* v. 3, 1976; v. 3, 1977. Copyright 1976, 1977 by Pajarito Publications. All rights reserved. Both reprinted by permission of the publisher.—*Commentary,* v. 82, July, 1986 for "Ortega y Gasset Revisited" by Richard John Neuhaus. Copyright © 1986 by the American Jewish Committee. All rights reserved. Reprinted by permission of the publisher and the author.—*Commonweal,* v. LXXXVIII, April 12, 1968; v. C, April 26, 1974. Copyright © 1968, 1974 Commonweal Publishing Co., Inc. Both

PHOTOGRAPHS AND ILLUSTRATIONS APPEARING IN *HLC* WERE RECEIVED FROM THE FOLLOWING SOURCES:

Isabel Allende

1942–

Chilean journalist, novelist, and short story writer.

INTRODUCTION

A Latin–American author of fiction, Allende often blends elements of realism and fantasy in her works to examine the tumultuous social and political heritage of South America. She frequently draws upon her own experiences as well as those of her family to emphasize the role of personal memory as a record of the violence and repression that characterizes much of Latin–American history. Despite her recurring use of moral and political themes, Allende maintains that she does not intend to create political fiction. "I write about the things I care about," she has stated; "poverty, inequality, and social problems are part of politics, and that's what I write about. . . . I just can't write in an ivory tower, distant from what's happening in the real world and from the reality of my continent. So the politics just steps in, in spite of myself."

Allende was born in Lima, Peru, where her father served as a diplomatic representative of Chile. Although Allende's contact with her father ceased following her parents' divorce, she remained close to his family—particularly Salvador Allende, her uncle and godfather, who served as president of Chile from 1970 to 1973. As a child in Santiago, Chile, Allende lived with her maternal grandparents, who would later serve as models for Esteban and Clara Trueba, the patriarch and matriarch of the family whose history Allende chronicled in her first and best-known novel, *La casa de los espíritus* (1982; *The House of the Spirits*). After spending her adolescence in Bolivia, Europe, and the Middle East with her mother and diplomat stepfather, Allende settled in Chile and became a journalist, working on television programs and newsreels, as well as writing for a radical feminist magazine. Her life changed abruptly in 1973 when a military coup, led by General Augusto Pinochet Ugarte, resulted in the assassination of Salvador Allende and the overthrow of his socialist government. While she remained in Chile for several months following the takeover, Allende's efforts to assist the opposition of the new regime ultimately jeopardized her safety, and in 1974 she escaped with her family to Caracas, Venezuela. She has since relocated to the United States following a divorce from her husband of twenty-five years and her later marriage to a California lawyer.

Allende's literary career began when she started to write a letter to her dying grandfather, a nearly one-hundred-year-old man who had remained in Chile. "My grandfather thought people died only when you forgot them," the author has explained. "I wanted to prove to him that I had forgotten nothing, that his spirit was going to live with us forever." Allende never sent the letter to her grandfather, who soon died, but her memories of her family and her country were the genesis of *The House of the Spirits*. This work, set in an unnamed South American country recognizable as Chile, spans six decades and tells the story of three generations of a family shaken by domestic and political conflicts. Allende's 1984 novel, *De amor y de sombra* (*Of Love and Shadows*), also takes place in a country where citizens are repressed by the policies of a military regime and concerns two lovers intent on exposing the fate of the *desaparecidos*, people who were "disappeared" by the dictatorship's secret police.

Allende's third novel, *Eva Luna* (1987), relates the passage of the narrator Eva from an illiterate orphan to a successful television scriptwriter. The story of Eva's maturation alternates with that of Rolf Carlé, an Austrian emigré who becomes a photojournalist; when the two meet and fall in love, their separate stories merge into one. *Eva Luna* celebrates the storytelling abilities of the narrator, and in *Cuentos de Eva Luna* (1989; *The Stories of Eva Luna*), Allende transformed into short stories several of Eva's biographical sketches of persons integral to her development. *The Stories of Eva Luna* includes pieces originating in real events as well as episodes from the previous novel. While Allende has acknowledged that not all the stories are told in Eva's voice, the author asserts that "it's her tone" that binds the collection together. Allende has also written a fourth novel, *El plan infinito* (1991; *The Infinite Plan*). Reviewer Nelida Kahan has summarized this work as an account of "the traumatic experiences of an American lawyer raised in a broken family in a Chicano community."

The House of the Spirits has generated a great deal of critical attention, due not only to its merits but also to its likeness to Gabriel García Marquez's *One Hundred Years of Solitude*. Several reviewers have considered Allende's first novel to be closely imitative of the magic realist style introduced by the "Boom," a literary movement of the 1960s whose members, including García Márquez and Alejo Carpentier, tempered realism with mysticism and hyperbole. They cite such similarities between *The House of the Spirits* and *One Hundred Years of Solitude* as their family chronicle structures, magic realist narration, and parallel characters, including Rosa the Beautiful, who greatly resembles García Márquez's Remedios the Beauty. Other critics have contended that while Allende did utilize the technique of magic realism to chronicle legendary occurrences in the history of the Trueba clan, her own voice emerges in her straightforward, journalistic treatment of realistic events surrounding the military coup. Bruce Allen has observed: "Despite its undeniable debt to *One Hundred Years of Solitude*, [*The House of the Spirits*] is an original and important work; along with García Márquez's masterpiece, it's one of the best novels of the postwar period."

Allende's fiction as a whole has received mixed reviews. While some commentators regard her works as derivative or melodramatic, most commend her polished technique, including the lushly detailed prose and compelling images which subtly convey her moral and political themes. Some debate has ensued, however, over whether she successfully combines her political ideas with the fantastic elements in her fiction. Much critical analysis of Allende's work has been devoted to her feminist perspective as well, and her depiction of the patriarchal society of Latin America has been applauded, though some critics charge that her portrayals of Latin males are frequently stereotypically macho and that she at times resorts to other clichés about Hispanics.

Allende's novels and short story collection have been translated into many languages and have achieved international popular acclaim. Moreover, critics have generally come to value Allende not only as a commentator on the turbulent nature of Latin-American society but also as an author of powerful, humanistic fiction. Some have even placed her in the ranks of the "Boom" tradition novelists she resembles. As Alexander Coleman has asserted: Allende is "the first woman to join what has heretofore been an exclusive male club of Latin American novelists. Not that she is the first contemporary female writer from Latin America . . . but she is the first woman to approach on the same scale as the others the tormented patriarchal world of traditional Hispanic society."

CRITICAL COMMENTARY

AMBROSE GORDON

(essay date 1987)

[In the excerpt below, Gordon provides brief commentary on Allende's first two novels, particularly focusing on "what is being said in [*Of Love and Shadows*] about love and shadow, and about their relation."]

The House of the Spirits is not so much a story as many stories, as are all novels in a way, but most of them less so. It is partly, and reflexively, the story of its own inception and creation, beginning in a torture chamber of a modern police state. A young woman, who is the narrator of most of the novel, has been beaten, raped, mutilated, given electric shock, and placed in solitary confinement in a tiny cell called "the dog house," since it is hardly bigger, where she lies in her own excrement and misery, wishing to die. As her mind begins to wander her dead grandmother appears, to remind her that the point is not to die, since that will come anyway, but to survive, which is a miracle, and with the saving suggestion that survival in her case may be accomplished through keeping her mind occupied by writing, in the dark and without paper or pencil, the account of her misery. At first it proves to be almost impossibly difficult; the various characters of her history crowd in and jostle one another for her attention. As she remembers something new she forgets what has just been remembered; but later she develops a key by which she can remember events in order.

The whole comes in her mind eventually to resemble a complicated jigsaw puzzle in which each piece has its own place. "Before putting it all together it seemed to me incomprehensible," she confesses, "but I was sure that if I succeeded in finishing it, a sense would be given to each and the result would be harmonious."

The result *is* harmonious, although how the completed puzzle is to be comprehended remains something of a question. A novel, I think, can be imaginatively rich without necessarily making very clear sense. What comes together in *The House of the Spirits* is not only an often rather jumbled history but also one that is extremely bizarre in detail. Improbability reigns. The point of departure is a young woman with brilliant green hair—naturally that color, not dyed. Although I shouldn't like to go on record that green hair is impossible—if flaming red hair can exist, why not green?—it must be very rare. And if

we dream of green eyes as beautiful, and we do, why wouldn't green hair be even more beautiful? The events of the novel are set in motion when a proud and ambitious, but still poor young man, Esteban Trueba, sees Rosa, *la bella*, in the street, follows her home in a trolley, and from that moment determines that she must be his. Through circumstances beyond their control, she never is. Nine years later, however, Esteban, now wealthy, marries her younger sister, Clara, and builds for her a mansion in the city, with formal gardens, colonnades, and marble statuary, *la casa de los espíritus*, more usually referred to simply as "the big house on the corner." It becomes the haunted setting for much of the subsequent action and supplies the novel with its title.

This is, then, the kind of novel in which strange things are going to happen; in which a girl with green hair may suddenly appear (there is more than one); in which one's mother's head may be kept for years in a hatbox in the cellar after her body has been duly interred—for no very good reason. . . . (pp. 531–32)

The House of the Spirits has no hero, but its central character is Esteban Trueba, whom we follow—intermittently, with interruptions for the various spin-off stories—for more than seventy of his ninety years. Since Esteban is the most purposeful character present, he is also the most intelligible. He is destined for defeat by his willfulness and bad disposition. The constants in his life are love and rage. If Esteban represents pure will, Clara, his wife, appears to be all sensibility. She is a more ambiguous and uncertain character.

Clara is the link with the spirit world. Having known the spirits since childhood, she takes them with her to the great house as a kind of dowry. They bring her messages from the time that is yet to be, or messages from the places where lost things lie. . . . Less trivially, the spirits are an extension of her own clear spirit, or what the author seems to regard as Clara's own clear spirit, her rich and loving femininity.

Nevertheless, for the present reader at least, there is also something a bit spooky and offputting about Clara. She is not entirely healthy and in her own fashion is as stubborn as her husband. Since childhood Clara has used her chronic asthma to have her way and she is given to long periods of silence, in one instance nine years. Esteban Trueba, whom she was scarcely forced to marry, is not a man she ever loves and, after they are married, becomes

Principal Works

La casa de los espíritus (novel) 1982
  [*The House of the Spirits*, 1985]

De amor y de sombra (novel) 1984
  [*Of Love and Shadows*, 1987]

Eva Luna (novel) 1987
  [*Eva Luna*, 1988]

Cuentos de Eva Luna (short stories) 1989
  [*The Stories of Eva Luna*, 1991]

El plan infinito (novel) 1991
  [*The Infinite Plan*, 1993]

a man from whom she increasingly withdraws into the more congenial company of the spirits.

Everything in *The House of the Spirits* spins around the polar opposition of husband and wife, but it spins rather wildly. In a general way, the blighting effect upon the children, a daughter and twin younger sons, who are the offspring of such a mismatched couple is perfectly predictable, even without the aid of the spirits; yet even with their aid it might prove no easy matter to understand why the particular aberrations of this grotesque, although sympathetic, family had to be. The events of their story, or stories, are intriguing precisely where they are surprising, seemingly random occurrences, and finally mysterious.

Moreover, it would probably take more than the spirits to establish any clear relation, other than a proclivity to violence, between the family fate of *los Trueba* and the national fate of their—and the author's—beloved country, never named, under the horrors of a military dictatorship of a previously insignificant general, also unnamed, but whose name few of us would have much difficulty in supplying.

Although the author tells us in an autobiographical note that she was born by chance in Lima, in 1942, Isabel Allende remains loyally Chilean. Her two novels were written in Venezuela, where, according to the flyleaf of *De amor y de sombra*, she went with her husband and two children into an exile "imposed by the overthrow of her uncle, President Salvador Allende." She has told also how she took with her into exile a little bag of earth from her garden in which to plant a forget-me-not, and adds: "During these years it has done nothing but grow and grow. Like my homesickness."

The House of the Spirits has likewise done very well; its sales have also grown and grown. (pp. 532–34)

[The novel's] successor, *De amor y de sombra*—less ambitious and also less in the fashionable mode of domesticated magic—is more to my taste, although I doubt that it will make nearly so big a splash. With one major exception things happen in this novel about the way they usually happen, which, when all is said, is strange enough.

The second novel is considerably shorter. It is carefully plotted and, instead of being diffused over seventy years, is focused on the events of one spring where two rather different things are happening concurrently. A young man and young woman are being drawn together in love as the year waxes, days grow warmer, and a forget-me-not begins to blossom, and the same young man and woman fall increasingly under the shadow of terrible events in a police state which, though again never named, is recognizably the Chile of General Pinochet. They are being drawn step by step nearer to exile and away from their strangely shaped and beautiful land (like a long petal, wrote Neruda) and its suffering people, whom they love more deeply as they are themselves uprooted. The events comprise a single unified action composed about equally of love and shadow, *amor y sombra*, or, more accurately, formed of the interplay of love and shadow. It is a more thoughtful book than its predecessor. As readers we are permitted to participate in the action vicariously, but also we are invited to meditate on it and try to reach some understanding.

It is not by chance that the title suggests from the start an essay: Of Love and of Shadow. It seems reasonable then to inquire what is being said in this novel about love and shadow, and about their relation.

Let me come at this matter somewhat indirectly. If one has recently been reading, or rereading, George Orwell's *Nineteen Eighty-Four*, one has learned from Orwell that love cannot survive the oppression of a police state. Such appears, however, not to be Isabel Allende's view at all. *De amor y de sombra* instead seems to be saying that love can survive even in the shadow of Big Brother steadily watching, can survive physical agony and the threat of death, and perhaps also that love needs the shadow to become most fully love. Lovers can meet and love deep in the shadow, can in time escape and live together in hope of return; moreover, they can help to bring about that day. Provided one thing: that they never forget for an instant either their love or the shadow. The unnamed General-President, speaking from his bunker headquarters, remarks to a worried subordinate that the people have short memories. It is the destiny of Allende's lovers to prove him wrong.

The nasty alternative would be to forget as quickly and often as possible, to submit to group amnesia and a frightened cover-up of the truth. Appropriately, the action begins in the Barrio Alto of what is the capital city in an ambiguous setting, the residence of the heroine's mother, which from the outside is a mansion only slightly less palatial than Senator Trueba's "big house on the corner." Inside, there are surprises. Above the ground floor all is elegance and decorum, but the ground floor of the mansion has been converted into a nursing home for the mostly neglected and nearly forgotten grandparents and great-aunts and granduncles of the sort of people who live in this sort of house, the threatened wealthy who choose to overlook and prefer to forget. (pp. 534–35)

By converting the ground floor, Beatriz Alcántara de Beltrán—who is not exactly a widow and not exactly not a widow—can keep up appearances and manage to live almost in the style to which she was accustomed before the disappearance of her aristocratic and, I fear, somewhat rascally husband, the heroine's father. Beatriz remains uncertain whether he is living or dead and equally uncertain whether her husband simply left her or whether he was "disappeared" by the secret police. She finds the latter explanation intolerable, since she has always accepted the military government's official version that no one has disappeared.

Beatriz lives on with her daughter, Irene, in an unstable amalgam of mansion and geriatric center kept well hidden from sight. She is herself of a certain age and is fighting off the inevitable sagging and wrinkles and flab. . . . So far Beatriz's program has worked beautifully in preserving her body but not so well in preserving her less and less flexible mind in its efforts to maintain a distance between the luxurious and protected upstairs and the dismaying world of the lower floor. By the end of the novel, with the further disappearance of her daughter—the implications of which she is even more reluctant to face—Beatriz has shut herself off from reality almost as completely as have any of the house's pathetic inhabitants. Unwilling to understand, it is as if she were "afloat on a raft with her forgotten and decrepit ancients on an unmoving sea." By that time there is no significant difference between the two levels of her mansion.

Beatriz's daughter, Irene, is at the beginning still partly imprisoned in her mother's world. More than she may have yet come to recognize, she is imprisoned by her professional life as well. Irene is a good, and experienced, journalist committed to presenting the truth; yet she works for a fashion magazine that by its devotion to items of conspicuous display—furs, jewels, the newest fads—is almost professionally blind to poverty and violence under the dictatorship. Irene's own story is the story of how she will free herself from both home and profession with the increasingly loving help of Francisco Leal, a clinical psychologist who has been forced by circumstances to make his living as a fashion photographer. Francisco is a member of the underground and from the start knows at first hand the truth about his country that marble façades and fashion magazines do their best to hide.

Somewhere between truth and the advertisement of whatever is currently in style are human interest stories, which Irene's magazine regards as safe, and it is what begins as no more than a human interest story that sets the events of the novel in motion. . . . [Irene and Francisco] are to investigate a peasant girl who has acquired a reputation as a local saint because of the miraculous cures

that she is said to bring about during a trance that she enters into—or perhaps a seizure that she suffers—each day at noon. We have been told that the parish priest regards her condition as pathological. Although most of the peasants believe, the padre is not alone in his skepticism. Some wise ones have hinted that what the fifteen-year-old Evangelina Ranquileo needs is a man, and perhaps, as it is suggested later, the only man she really wants is her brother. Whichever view is right, the wonders go on.

Less uncertain than the exact nature of Evangelina's condition are Isabel Allende's uses for the crucial scene that takes place in the house of the peasant family a few minutes after Irene and Francisco arrive. This scene elicits our special attention. It is the only place in the present novel where the realm of magic, the spirit world, intrudes upon the action. It accomplishes two things. It permits the author to involve her hero and heroine in events from which they can never afterwards extricate themselves; yet the scene does more in composing a symbolic anecdote of much inclusiveness and vividness. It is as though the pressures and repressions of her country were being reflected in this girl. Hidden forces are coming out through Evangelina, which when fully released might even shake a military dictatorship, forces of love and of life but also of sexual craving and violence. *Amor* and *sombra* meet in Evangelina's extraordinary seizure. Irene and Francisco, the journalist and fashion photographer who are as yet scarcely aware of their own love, are there to see it all. It is *not* a human interest story. (pp. 536–37)

In the scene's blending of the uncanny and unexplained with the violently realistic it seems to me to come considerably closer to García Márquez than anything in the often merely capricious behavior of tipping tables and mobile salt cellars of *The House of the Spirits*. Something powerful (but is it something good or bad?) is taking place inside the girl, but also outside her. As the center of action in this novel, Evangelina has become the vortex of forces too long held in check, which seemingly nothing can withstand once they are released, not even the military, who at this juncture arrive unexpectedly to raid the Ranquileos' house. They get a good deal more than they bargain for when their leader, Lt. Juan de Dios Ramírez, tries to remove Evangelina forcibly from the bed and is instead knocked by her onto the floor, picked up by his tunic without the least effort, shaken like a mop, and deposited outside:

> Through the lens [of Francisco's camera, which she snatched from him,] Irene saw Evangelina tow the lieutenant toward the center of the patio. . . . The officer tried to get to his feet, but she administered a few accurate blows to the back of his neck and left him seated there, while giving him several kicks without anger and ignoring the guards who surrounded her, pointing their guns. . . . The girl snatched the machine-gun that Ramírez held clutched to his chest and threw it far away. It fell in the mud where it sank

in front of the impassive snout of a pig, who sniffed at it before seeing it disappear swallowed up by the filth.

The symbolic anecdote, which is predominantly hopeful, ends there, while (as they say) the force is still with her. The other function of the strange happenings at the Ranquileos, as I have suggested, is to implicate Irene and Francisco so deeply in defiance of the government that they will be forced into flight and exile. When the trance is over, sadly, the soldiers return and Evangelina is carried off without putting up any resistance— later, as it turns out, to be raped and killed. All that her family knows for sure is that she has disappeared. But that is not quite her end. Evangelina is one of the very few disappeared who reappears. What was buried comes to the surface again with a vengeance, and Irene is the principal agent in bringing that about.

A feeling of identity has been growing between the journalist and this girl from a totally different background, the one still alive and the other now dead. A change has taken place. Irene has become now a determined woman with a quest, to find Evangelina or at least to find her body—which proves to be for her a dangerous and, indeed, very nearly fatal activity. She interviews one of the soldiers. She and Francisco visit the morgue. Other avenues are tried. Eventually a tip leads them to an abandoned mine in the hills—for this novel the heart, if not of darkness, then of shadow. On the mine's being opened, what is revealed is not only Evangelina's body but many others in various stages of decomposition, and when the mine at last gives up its dead, outrage spreads through the country. Irene's activities, however, have not gone unobserved by the alarmed authorities.

As events have brought the journalist and the fashion photographer deeper into danger and involvement— deeper into the shadow—their growing love for one another has emerged from what was before hardly more than a close sympathetic friendship. Their first kiss is exchanged in the shocked aftermath of their visit to the morgue. They make love for the first time, in an abandoned cabin, following the nighttime penetration of the mine, with its horrible stench and more horrible discovery. During the act Francisco, who appears to be an articulate lover, calls out to her (perhaps only in his mind), "Irene honey and shadow." A strange but appropriate yoking. Like Persephone, Irene belongs now to both: *amor* and *sombra* are one.

She must enter the shadow more deeply yet. Once the discoveries in the mine have been made public, the pace of the action picks up, as though everything were being hurried along by the forces that have been released. A few days afterward Irene is gunned down in the street. She is badly wounded but not killed. . . . When she is stronger, although under surveillance, the lovers make their escape from the hospital and from the city, and, following country roads and then a path through the woods, they cross the frontier into freedom and exile. But not into oblivion. Irene and Francisco are able to take little with them, but they take what they most need, their love and their memories of the good and the bad, of everything.

Isabel Allende has emphasized all along the cardinal importance of memory. Memory is the matrix where love and shadow meet. Probably among her characters the person who remembers best—not trivially like Borges's unforgettable and unforgetting Funes, but lovingly—is another peasant girl, Evangelina Flores, almost to the minute the same age as Evangelina Ranquileo and, in a rather complicated way, her foster sister. The girl's father and four brothers were among those who disappeared. Although they have now been dead for five years, when the mine gives up its secret she identifies each. . . . She has the love and the courage to remember. Also, before a military court, and without hesitation, Evangelina identifies Ramírez and each of his men who participated in the detention of her family. Consequently she too must seek refuge abroad.

As the novel closes, Irene and Francisco—perhaps reminiscent of Milton's Adam and Eve wandering through Eden—are left by the author moving "toward an invisible line that divided that immense chain of mountains and volcanoes. They felt themselves small, alone and vulnerable." But Irene is strengthened by a talisman; next to her breast under her dress, she carries a little bag of earth from her garden, sent to her by a loyal friend, in which she is "to plant a forget-me-not on the other side of the sea."

On the basis of these two novels, what can be said now, more generally, about Isabel Allende as a novelist? I have already tried to suggest certain of what seem to me the strengths and weaknesses of *The House of the Spirits*. Her chief merit I take to be a certain amplitude of imagination, for Isabel Allende is not a petty writer. There is also more, both good and bad, about *De amor y de sombra* than I have yet had an opportunity to discuss.

One of the things that I find particularly admirable is the book's scope. Although the novel is relatively brief and the action focused on the events of only a single spring, a surprisingly large cast of characters makes its appearance, taken from different classes and conditions of life. Not only are we shown the peasant families Ranquileo and Flores and the aristocratic parents of Irene—her disappeared father apparently genuine and her mother on the whole nouveau riche—but the intellectual middle-class parents of Francisco Leal, themselves refugees from Franco's Spain, and Francisco's brother, José, who combines the roles of priest and plumber while working and living among the urban poor. We are shown also the Cardinal, effectively the leader of the resistance, at close range, and the General-President of the Republic from far off, as if in miniature, comically in scattered glimpses. Among the secondary characters there is a sensitive portrait of a fashionable homosexual hairdresser who began his life as the son of a miner and later became secretly a member of the resistance, without any loss of his hair-dressing skills. Other well-drawn characters could with equal justice be singled out. Assuming the country, despite its anonymity, to be very like Chile, we feel we have come to know it well by the time we reach the final page.

These characters have not been distributed . . . in a random fashion. Instead, they all stand in some important relation to Irene and Francisco. In particular, we are shown, beside the principal pair of lovers, a wide variety of others into whose love the prevailing shadow has fallen. They include among them the married and the unmarried, the rich, the poor, and in one case the incestuous. Their love stories serve as a background for, and at the same time they intermingle with, the central story.

This bevy of lovers, however, points up what seems to me to be the principal weakness of *De amor y de sombra*, something not detectable in the first novel, a certain softness in the writing which is not everywhere apparent but is disturbing when it appears. When Isabel Allende moves in closely upon the act of love—and she seems to enjoy moving in very closely—she tends to lose her restraint and the restraint and the prose becomes over-charged, to say the least. (pp. 538–41)

A friend of mine, a good novelist, asked: "Is there something new to be learned, do I *need* to read this book?" The answer, I think, is a qualified "no" for *De amor y de sombra* as also for *The House of the Spririts*. Unlike certain novels of the [Latin American literary] Boom, *Pedro Páramo, Hopscotch, The Autumn of the Patriarch*, probably others, which enlarge or change our conception of what a novel might be, Isabel Allende has left the novel genre about where she found it. But I am not a novelist and I reflect that novels may also be regarded as weapons. Isabel Allende appears to me to have handled hers with skill to strike a blow for freedom and love against the tyranny that still grips her beautibul country. W. H. Auden once wrote that poems make nothing happen; but novels, less pure, perhaps may. Author and reader alike can live in that hope. (pp. 541–42)

Ambrose Gordon, "Isabel Allende on Love and Shadow," in *Contemporary Literature*, Vol. 28, No. 4, Winter, 1987, pp. 530–42.

ISABEL ALLENDE

(lecture date 1988)

[Here, in a lecture originally presented in 1988, Allende addresses the question of why and for whom she writes.]

Allende on the political nature of Latin–American literature:

I would say that Latin American literature was born with the first Spaniards who arrived in America, discovered the New World, and started writing the Chronicles of the Indies. In the letters they sent to the King and Queen of Spain and to their own families, they recounted what they saw. They came to conquer, they invented a uptopia and spoke with effusive praise of this new continent. Since then, Latin American literature has been marked by political and social restlessness. A major political upheaval resulted from the almost complete destruction of a world on which a foreign culture, religion, and race were imposed. This produced a wave of feelings and emotions that have always been present in our culture and which have affected its political aspects. For five hundred years, we have been exploited and colonized, first by Spain and Portugal, then by other European countries, and nowadays by the United States. The latter is a more subtle form of colonization, but colonization nonetheless. It is impossible for writers to separate themselves from this reality. How could I write without being aware that I come from a society rooted in inequality?

Isabel Allende, in an interview with Marie-Lise Gazarian Gautier, in Gautier's *Interviews with Latin American Writers*, 1989.

In every interview during the last few years I encountered two questions that forced me to define myself as a writer and as a human being: Why do I write? And who do I write for? [In this lecture] I will try to answer those questions.

In 1981, in Caracas, I put a sheet of paper in my typewriter and wrote the first sentence of *The House of the Spirits*: "Barabbas came to us by sea." At that moment I didn't know why I was doing it, or for whom. In fact, I assumed that no one would ever read it except my mother, who reads everything I write. I was not even conscious that I was writing a novel. I throught I was writing a letter—a spiritual letter to my grandfather, a formidable old patriarch, whom I loved dearly. He had reached almost one hundred years of age and decided that he was too tired to go on living, so he sat in his armchair and refused to drink or eat, calling for Death, who was kind enough to take him very soon.

I wanted to bid him farewell, but I couldn't go back to Chile, and I knew that calling him on the telephone was useless, so I began this letter. I wanted to tell him that he could go in peace because all his memories were with me. I had forgotten nothing. I had all his anecdotes, all the characters of the family, and to prove it I began writing the story of Rose, the fiancée my grandfather had had, who is called Rose the Beautiful in the book. She really existed; she's not a copy from García Márquez, as some people have said.

For a year I wrote every night with no hesitation or plan. Words came out like a violent torrent. I had thousands of untold words struck in my chest, threatening to choke me. The long silence of exile was turning me to stone; I needed to open a valve and let the river of secret words find a way out. At the end of that year there were five hundred pages on my table; it didn't look like a letter anymore. On the other hand, my grandfather had died long before, so the sprirtual message had already reached him. So I thought, "Well, maybe in this way I can tell some other people about him, and about my country, and about my family and myself." So I just organized it a little bit, tied the manuscript with a pink ribbon for luck, and took it to some publishers.

The spirit of my grandmother was protecting the book from the very beginning, so it was refused everywhere in Venezuela. Nobody wanted it—it was too long; I was a woman; nobody knew me. So I sent it by mail to Spain, and the book was published there. It had reviews, and it was translated and distributed in other countries.

In the process of writing the anecdotes of the past, and recalling the emotions and pains of my fate, and telling part of the history of my country, I found that life become more comprehensible and the world more tolerable. I felt that my roots had been recovered and that during that patient exercise of daily writing I had also recovered my own soul. I felt at that time that writing was unavoidable—that I couldn't keep away from it. Writing is such a pleasure; it is always a private orgy, creating and recreating the world according to my own laws, fulfilling in those pages all my dreams and exorcising some of my demons.

But that is a rather simple explanation. There are other reasons for writing.

Six years and three books have passed since *The House of the Spirits*. Many things have changed for me in that time. I can no longer pretend to be naïve, or elude questions, or find refuge in irony. Now I am constanly confronted by my readers, and they can be very tough. It's not enough to write in a state of trance, overwhelmed by the desire to tell a story. One has to be responsible for each word, each idea. Be very careful: the written word cannot be erased.

I began to receive academic papers from American universities about the symbols in my books, or the metaphors, or the colors, or the names. I'm always very scared by them. I just received three different papers on Barabbas, the dog. One of them says that he symbolizes the innocence of Clara because he accompanies her during her youth, and when she falls in love, symbolically, the dog dies in a pool of blood. That means the sexual act, it seems. The second paper says that the dog represents repression—the militarists—and the third paper says that he is the male part of Clara, the hidden, dark, big beast in her. Well, really, Barabbas was just the dog I had at home.

And he was killed as it was told in the book. But of course it sounds much better to answer that Barabbas symbolizes the innocence of Clara, so that's the explanation I give when somebody asks.

Maybe the most important reason for writing is to prevent the erosion of time, so that memories will not be blown away by the wind. Write to register history, and name each thing. Write what should not be forgotten. But then, why write novels? Probably because I come from Latin America, a land of crazy, illuminated people, of geological and political cataclysms—a land so large and profound, so beautiful and frightening, that only novels can describe its fascinating complexity.

A novel is like a window, open to an infinite landscape. In a novel we can put all the interrogations, we can register the most extravagant, evil, obscene, incredible or magnificent facts—which, in Latin America, are not hyperbole, because that is the dimension of our reality. In a novel we can give an illusory order to chaos. We can find the key to the labyrinth of history. We can make excursions into the past, to try to understand the present and dream the future. In a novel we can use everything: testimony, chronicle, essay, fantasy, legend, poetry and other devices that might help us to decode the mysteries of our world and discover our true identity.

For a writer who nourishes himself or herself on images and passions, to be born in a fabulous continent is a privilege. In Latin America we don't have to stretch our imaginations. Critics in Europe and the United States often stare in disbelief at Latin American books, asking how the authors dare to invent those incredible lies of young women who fly to heaven wrapped in linen sheets; of black emperors who build fortresses with cement and the blood of emasculated bulls; of outlaws who die of hunger in the Amazon with bags full of emeralds on their backs; of ancient tyrants who order their mothers to be flogged naked in front of the troops and modern tyrants who order children to be tortured in front of their parents; of hurricanes and earthquakes that turn the world upside down; of revolutions made with machetes, bullets, poems and kisses; of hallucinating landscapes where reason is lost.

It is very hard to explain to critics that these things are not a product of our pathological imaginations. They are written in our history; we can find them every day in our newspapers. We hear them in the streets; we suffer them frequently in our own lives. It is impossible to speak of Latin America without mentioning violence. We inhabit a land of terrible contrasts and we have to survive in times of great violence.

Contrast and violence, two excellent ingredients for literature, although for us, citizens of that reality, life is always suspended from a very fragile thread.

The first, the most naked and visible form of violence is the extreme poverty of the majority, in contrast with the extreme wealth of the very few. In my continent two opposite realities coexist. One is a legal face, more or less comprehensible and with a certain pretension to dignity and civilization. The other is a dark and tragic face, which we do not like to show but which is always threatening us. There is an apparent world and a real world—nice neighborhoods where blond children play on their bicycles and servants walk elegant dogs, and other neighborhoods, of slums and garbage, where dark children play naked with hungry mutts. There are offices of marble and steel where young executives discuss the stock market, and forgotten villages where people still live and die as they did in the Middle Ages. There is a world of fiction created by the official discourse, and another world of blood and pain and love, where we have struggled for centuries.

In Latin America we all survive on the borderline of those two realities. Our fragile democracies exist as long as they don't interfere with imperialist interests. Most of our republics are dependent on submissiveness. Our institutions and laws are inefficient. Our armed forces often act as mercenaries for a privileged social group that pays tribute to transnational enterprises. We are living in the worst economic, political and social crisis since the conquest of America by the Spaniards. There are hardly two or three leaders in the whole continent. Social inequality is greater every day, and to avoid an outburst of public rancor, repression also rises day by day. Crime, drugs, misery and ignorance are present in every Latin American country, and the military is an immediate threat to society and civil governments. We try to keep straight faces while our feet are stuck in a swamp of violence, exploitation, corruption, the terror of the state and the terrorism of those who take arms against the status quo.

But Latin America is also a land of hope and friendship and love. Writers navigate in these agitated waters. They don't live in ivory towers; they cannot remove themselves from this brutal reality. In such circumstances there is no time and no wish for narcissistic literature. Very few of our writers contemplate their navel in self-centered monologue. The majority want desperately to communicate.

I feel that writing is an act of hope, a sort of communion with our fellow men. The writer of good will carries a lamp to illuminate the dark corners. Only that, nothing more—a tiny beam of light to show some hidden aspect of reality, to help decipher and understand it and thus to initiate, if possible, a change in the conscience of some readers. This kind of writer is not seduced by the mermaid's voice of celebrity or tempted by exclusive literary circles. He has both feet planted firmly on the ground and walks hand in hand with the people in the streets. He knows that the lamp is very small and the shadows are immense. This makes him humble.

But just as we should not believe that literature gives us any sort of power, neither should we be paralyzed by

false modesty. We should continue to write in spite of the bruises and the vast silence that frequently surrounds us. A book is not an end in itself; it is only a way to touch someone—a bridge extended across a space of loneliness and obscurity—and sometimes it is a way of winning other people to our causes.

I believe in certain principles and values: love, generosity, justice. I know that sounds old-fashioned. However, I believe in those values so firmly that I'm willing to provoke some scornful smiles. I'm sure we have the capacity to build a more gentle world—that doing so is our only alternative, because our present equilibrium is very fragile. In literature, we have been told, optimism is dangerous; it flirts with simplicity and is an insurrection against the sacred laws of reason and good taste. But I don't belong to that group of desperate intellectuals. Despair is a paralyzing feeling. It only benefits our enemies.

My second novel, *Of Love and Shadows*, tells about the *desaparecidos*, "the disappeared ones." It's based on a political massacre that took place in Chile in 1973 during the military coup that put an end to 150 years of democracy. The novel denounces repression and the impunity of the murderers, and it had a warm reception from most readers and critics. But it also drew some strong attacks. Some said it was too political and sentimental and not very objective, as if one could be objective about the crimes of a dictatorship. Maybe these critics would have forgiven me, as other writers have been forgiven, if the book had only been a story of horror and bitterness. They didn't like the fact that in the novel solidarity and hope prevail over death and torture. If the main characters, Irene and Francisco, had died in a torture chamber, or at least if the violent experiences they endured had drowned them in despair and destroyed forever their capacity to love and to dream, these critics might have been more tolerant. Evidently it's hard to accept in literature that love can be stronger than hatred, although it frequently is in life.

If my books are going to be classified as political, I hope readers will find out that they are not political for ideological reasons only, but for other, more subtle considerations. They are political precisely because Alba Trueba, in *The House of the Spirits*, who has been raped, tortured and mutilated, is able to reconcile herself with life; because Irene and Francisco, in *Of Love and Shadows*, makes love in spite of terror; because in my third novel, *Eva Luna*, Eva defeats the odds of her fate with generosity and candor; because these characters search for truth and have the courage to risk their lives.

I suppose I have the secret ambition to become a great writer, to be able to create stories that will resist the passage of time and the judgement of history. Yes, I know, it's terribly pretentious! But I'm more interested in touching my readers—as many of them as possible—on a spiritual and emotional level. To do this from a feminine point of view is a beautiful challenge in the society I live in. The political literature that some women writers have begun to create is so revolutionary that no wonder many critics are scared. Women are questioning the set of values that have sustained human society since the first apes stood on their feet and raised their eyes to the sky. After centuries of silence, women are taking by assault the exclusive male club of literature. Some women have done it before, of course, struggling against formidable obstacles. But now half of the novels published in Europe and the United Stated are written by women. Our sisters are using the cutting edge of words to change the rules we have always had to obey. Until now, humankind has organized itself according to certain principles that are considered part of nature: we are all born (it has been said) with some original sin; we are basically evil, and without the strict control of religion and laws we would devour each other like cannibals; authority, repression and punishment are necessary to keep us in line. According to these theories, the best proof of our perverse nature is that the world is what it is—a round rock lost in the cosmic nightmare, where abuse, war, inequality and hatred prevail.

But a small group of women and yound men are now making the most astonishing statements. Fortunately, most of them work in the best universities, so even if they are only a few, their voices have great impact. These people are questioning everything, starting with our own image as human beings. Until now, men have decided the destiny of this suffering planet, imposing ambition, power and individualism as virtues. (They don't admit this, of course; it is more eloquent to speak of peace and cooperation.)

These values are also present in literature. Critics, most of them men, as you probably can guess, have determined what is good in literature—what is valuable or artistic, according to our aesthetic, intellectual and moral patterns—leaving aside the feminine half of the human race, whose opinions on this or any other matter don't interest them.

I think it's time to revise this situation. But it is not the Old Guard who will do it. It will be done by women and by young men who have nothing to lose and therefore have no fear.

In the process of analyzing books, critics have exalted all kinds of literary experiments, some of them quite unbearable. How many books have you tried to read lately and haven't gotten past page fifteen because they were simply boring? Flamboyant literary techniques win awards even though the subject is deplorable. The worst vices are glorified if the writing is elegant. Lies, bitterness and arrogance are forgiven if the language is original and the author already has his laurels. Pessimism is in fashion.

But many novels that don't fit that pattern are now being written by women and by some brave men, not all of them young—for example, García Márquez, who wrote that incredible and sentimental book *Love in the Time of Cholera*, which is a sort of magnificent soap opera

about two old people who fall in love, and they love each other for eighty years. It's wonderful.

Those writers are shaking the literary world nowadays because they propose a completely new set of values. They don't accept the old rules anymore. They are willing to examine everything—to invent all over again and to express other ethical and aesthetic values; not always to replace the prevailing ones, but to complement them. It's not a question of changing male chauvinism for militant feminism, but of giving both women and men a chance to become better people and to share the heavy burden of this planet. I believe that this is the true political literature of our time.

All political systems, even revolutions, have been created and directed by men, always within the patriarchal regime. Important philosophical movements have tried to change man and society, but without touching the basis of human relations—that is, inequality of the sexes. Men writers of all periods have written political literature, from *Utopia* to parody, but feminine values have been scorned and women have been denied a voice to express them.

Now, finally, women are breaking the rule of silence and raising a strong voice to question the world. This is a cataclysm. It is a new literature that dares to be optimistic—to speak of love in opposition to pornography, of compassion against cruelty. It is a literature that's not afraid of colloquial language, of being sentimental if necessary; a literature that searches the spiritual dimension of reality, that accept the unknown and the unexplainable, confusion and terror; a literature that has no answers, only questions; a literature that doesn't invent history or try to explain the world solely with reason, but also seeks knowledge through feelings and imagination. Maybe, this literature says, it's not true that we are perverse and evil. Maybe the idea of original sin is just a terrible mistake. Maybe we are not here to be punished, because the gods love us and are willing to give us a chance to decipher the clues and trace new paths.

The effect of these books is hard to measure, because the old instruments are no longer useful. Probably the strongest literature being written nowadays is by those who stand unsheltered by the system: blacks, Indians, homosexuals, exiles and, especially, women—the crazy people of the world, who dare to believe in their own force. We dare to think that humanity is not going to destroy itself, that we have the capacity to reach an agreement, not only for survival but also to achieve happiness. That is why we write —as an act of human solidarity and commitment to the future. We want to change the rules, even if we won't live long enough to see the results. We have to make real revolutions of the spirit, of values, of life. And to do so we have to begin dreaming them.

So I will continue to write: about two lovers embracing in the moonlight, near an abandoned mine where they have found the bodies of fifteen peasants, murdered by the military. Or about raped women and tortured men and families who sell themselves as slaves because they are starving. And also—why not?—about golden sunsets and loving mothers and poets who die of love. I want to tell stories and say, for example that I care more for the free man than the free enterprise, more for solidarity than charity. I want to say that it's more important for me to share than to compete. And I want to write about the necessary changes in Latin America that will enable us to rise from our knees after five centuries of humiliations.

Much skill will be needed to write about these things eloquently. But with patience and hard work I hope to acquire that skill. I suppose I'm being very ambitious. Well, most writers are, even women writers.

Now, for whom do I write?

When I face a clean sheet of paper, I don't think of a large audience or of the people who would raise their knives to cut me in pieces. If I did, terror would paralyze me. Instead, when I write, a benevolent image comes to my mind—that of Alexandra Jorquera, a young woman who lives in Chile whom I scarcely know. She has read my books so many times that she can repeat paragraphs by heart. In fact, she knows them better than I do. She quotes me and I don't know she's quoting me. Once she told me that she had discovered in my books the history of Chile that is denied by the official textbooks of the dictatorship—the forbidden and secret history that nevertheless is still alive in the memories of most Chileans.

This is the best compliment my work has ever received. For the sake of this girl I am very demanding with my writing. Sometimes, tempted by the beauty of a sentence, I am about to betray the truth, and then Alexandra comes to my mind and I remember that she, and others like her, don't deserve that. At other times I'm too explicit, too near the pamphlet. But then I step back, thinking she doesn't deserve that either—to be underestimated. And when I feel helpless against brutality and suffering, her candid face brings back my strength. All writers should have a reader like her, waiting for their words. They would never feel lonely, and their work would have a new and shining dimension.

In Latin America today, 50 percent of the population is illiterate. Among those who can read and write, only very few can buy books, and among those who can buy books, very few have the habit of reading. What, then, is the importance of a book in Latin America? None, would be the reasonable answer. But it's not exactly that way. For some strange reason, the written word has a tremendous impact in that illiterate continent. The totalitarian regimes have persecuted, tortured, sent into exile and murdered many writers. This is not an accident; dictators don't make mistakes in these details. They know that a book can be dangerous for them. In our countries most of the press is controlled by private enterprises or by inefficient governments. Eduardo Galeano, the great

writer from Uruguay, puts it bluntly: "Almost all mass media promote a colonialistic culture, which justifies the unjust organization of the world as a result of the legitimate victory of the best—that is, the strongest. They lie about the past and about reality. They propose a lifestyle which postulates consumerism as an alternative to communism, which exalts crime as achievement, lack of scruples as virtue, and selfishness as a natural requirement."

What can writers do against this persistent and powerful message? The first thing we should try to do is write clearly. Not simply—that only works with soap advertising; we don't have to sacrifice aesthetics for the sake of ethics. On the contrary, only if we are able to say it beautifully can we be convincing. Most readers are perfectly able to appreciate subtleties and poetic twists and symbols and metaphors. We should not write with a paternalistic attitude, as if readers were simple-minded, but we should also beware of elaborate and unnecessary ornamentation, which frequently hides a lack of ideas. It has been said that we Spanish-speaking people have the vice of empty words, that we need six hundred pages to say what would be better told in fifty.

The opportunity to reach a large number of readers is a great responsibility. Unfortunately, it is hard for a book to stand against the message of the mass media; it's an unfair battle. Writers should therefore look for other forms of expressing their thoughts, avoiding the prejudice that only in books can they make literature. All means are legitimate, not only the cultivated language of academia but also the direct language of journalism, the mass language of radio, television and the movies, the poetic language of popular songs and the passionate language of talking face to face with an audience. These are all forms of literature. Let us be clever and use every opportunity to introduce ourselves in the mass media and try to change them from within.

In Venezuela, José Ignacio Cabrujas, a playwright and novelist, one of the most brilliant intellectuals of the country, writes soap operas. These shows are the most important cultural phenomenon in Latin America. Some people watch three or four a day, so you can imagine how important that kind of writing is. Cabrujas doesn't elude reality. His soap operas show a world of contrasts. He presents problems such as abortion, divorce, machismo, poverty and crime. The result is quite different from "Dynasty." But it's also very successful.

I tried to put some of that soap opera stuff in *Eva Luna*, because I'm fascinated by that version of reality. The ladies on TV wear false eyelashes at eleven in the morning. The difference between rich and poor is that the rich wear cocktail gowns all the time and the poor have their faces painted black. They all go blind or become invalids and then they recover. Just like real life!

Many of the most important Latin American writers have been journalists, and they go back to it frequently because they are aware that their words in a newspaper or on the radio reach an audience that their books never touch. Others write for the theater or the movies, or write lyrics for popular songs. All means are valid if we want to communicate and don't presume to be writing only for an educated elite or for literary prizes.

In Latin America a book is almost a luxury. My hairdresser calls me Dr. Allende because I usually carry a book, and she probably thinks that a doctorate is the minimum prerequisite for such an extravagance. In Chile a novel of three hundred pages can cost the equivalent of a laborer's monthly wages. In some other countries—like Haiti, for example—85 percent of the population is illiterate. Elsewhere in Latin America, nothing is published in the Indian languages of the majority. Many publishers have been ruined by the economic crisis, and the price of books imported from Spain is very high.

However, we should not despair. There is some hope for the spirit. Literature has survived even in the worst conditions. Political prisoners have written stories on cigarette paper. In the wars of Central America, little soldiers, fourteen years old, write poetry in their school notebooks. The Pieroa Indians, those who haven't yet been exterminated by the genocide being carried out against the aborigines of the Amazon, have published some legends in their language.

In my continent, writers often have more prestige than they do in any other part of the world. Some writers are considered witch doctors, or prophets, as if they were illuminated by a sort of natural wisdom. Jorge Amado has to spend part of the year away from Brazil in order to write, because people crowd into his house seeking advice. Mario Vargas-Llosa directs the opposition to Alan Garcia's government in Peru. García Márquez is a frequent middleman for Central American presidents. In Venezuela, Arturo Uslar Pietri is consulted on issues like corruption and oil. These writers have interpreted their reality and told it to the world. Some of them even have the gift of foretelling the future and put in words the hidden thoughts of their people, which of course include social and political problems, because it is impossible to write in a crystal bubble, disregarding the conditions of their continent.

No wonder Latin American novels are so often accused of being political.

For whom do I write, finally? Certainly for myself. But mainly for others, even if there are only a few. For those who have no voice and for those who are kept in silence. For my children and my future grandchildren. For Alexandra Jorquera and others like her. I write for you.

And why do I write? García Márquez once said that he writes so that his friends will love him more. I think I write so that people will love him more. Working with words is a beautiful craft, and in my continent, where we still have to name all things one by one, it has a rich and profound meaning. (pp. 40–63)

Isabel Allende, "Writing As an Act of Hope," in *Paths of Resistance: The Art and Craft of the Political Novel*, edited by William Zinsser, Houghton Mifflin Company, 1989, pp. 39–63.

E. THOMSON SHIELDS, JR.
(essay date 1990)

[In the following essay, Shields examines how Allende incorporates the element of love and violence in *The House of the Spirits*.]

In an April 1985 address at Montclair State College, "A Few Words About Latin America," Isabel Allende gave her own perspective on Latin American literature: "In these books, written with ink, blood and kisses, reality and fantasy go hand in hand, as they do in real life in Latin America." It would be hard to imagine a better metaphor for Allende's first novel, *La casa de los espíritus*, than "written with ink, blood and kisses." Ink—words, narratives, myths—do not come easily, especially in Latin America, a land of both blood and kisses, of violence, coups, rapes, murder and of love, love-making, family, and ritual. Myth creation, if it aspires to tell as much truth as possible, does not happen with simple strokes on typewriter keys, particularly if the myth must bring together violence and love without glossing over one to emphasize the other. The new myth created cannot conform to old ways, old prejudices—it cannot present a false sense of unity if it wishes to tell more truth than the myths that came before. Therefore, in order to write a new myth for *La casa de los espíritus*, Allende must write a myth based on ink, blood, and kisses. The new myth must find some way to bring together what we usually consider to be irreconcilable elements, violence and love. In other words, the new myth must be a myth of disunity.

Allende portrays the myth of disunity nowhere better than in the scene where *el viejo* Pedro Garcia tells the story of the fox and the hens:

> Un día el viejo Pedro García les contó a Blanca y a Pedro Tercero el cuento de las gallinas que se pusieron de acuerdo para enfrentar a un zorro que se metía todas las noches en el gallinero para robar los huevos y devorarse los pollitos. Las gallinas decidieron que ya estaban hartas de aguantar la prepotencia del zorro, lo esperaron organizadas y cuando entró al gallinero, le cerraron el paso, lo rodearon y se le fueron encima a picotazos hasta que lo dejaron más muerto que vivo.

—Y entonces se vio que el zorro escapaba con la cola entre las piernas, perseguido por las gallinas— terminó el viejo.

But the scene does not end with the old man's folktale of strength through unity. Each of the two listeners— Blanca, the landowner's daughter, and Pedro Tercero, the old man's grandson—reacts to the story in his or her own way:

> Blanca se rió con la historia y dijo que eso era imposible, porque las gallinas nacen estúpida y débiles y los zorros nacen astutos y fuertes, pero Pedro Tercero no se rió. Se quedó toda la tarde pensativo, rumiando el cuento del zorro y las gallinas, y tal vez ese fue el instante en que el niño comenzó a hacerse hombre.

Normally, in a world which emphasizes unity, we would force ourselves to choose one reaction over the other. But Allende does not give us a signal as to how we should react to Pedro García's story. Blanca's laugh is as valid a response to the story as Pedro Tercero's meditations. Instead of editorializing, making one of the two reactions the "accepted" reading, Allende presents both ideas as equal. What Allende gives is a new myth, the myth of disunity. Through ink—through her juxtaposition of the two reactions on equal terms— Allende brings together blood and kisses. For what is more violent than laughing at someone's beliefs, as Blanca does? And what is more loving, as Pedro Tercero eventually does, than to turn someone else's beliefs into the theme song of one's life?

This one scene encapsulates, in good mythic form, the entire argument of *La casa de los espíritus*. The full plot of the novel is too complex to summarize here, but what can be done is to show how this same scene—the uneditorialized juxtaposition of two perspectives on the same action—occurs throughout the work. For example, when Estaban Trueba, the landowner, first goes to his plantation, *Las Tres Marías*, he works hard in an attempt to forget the memory of his dead fiancée, Rosa. However, the memory rests too strongly in Esteban's mind, and he decides—consciously or unconsciously—that only sex will help ease his pain. In order to find the sexual outlet he feels he needs, Esteban rapes a young *campesina*, Pancha García, the sister of his overseer. In this moment, we feel for Pancha as a victim of the master's brutal violations, like her mother before her and her grandmother before that.

Alende could very easily leave the story here, a vulgar Marxist myth of the proletariat victimized by the bourgeoisie and its capitalist values. But nothing happens this simply in Allende's world. Esteban not only victimizes, but he becomes victimized himself through the very same act. Years later, the illegitimate grandson of Pancha's rape returns to cause havoc in Esteban's life. Esteban says:

> Un día estaba en el corredor, fumando un cigarro antes de la siesta, cuando se acercó un niño moreno y se me

plantó al frente en silencio. Se llamaba Esteban Garcia. Era mi nieto, pero yo no lo sabia y sólo ahora, debido a las terribles cosas que han ocurrido por obra suya, me he enterado del parentesco que nos une. Era también nieto de Pancha García, una hermana de Pedro Segundo, a quien en realidad no recuerdo.

Esteban García, the child (or, rather, grandchild) of rape, leads Esteban Trueba into a fight with Pedro Tercero— the same Pedro Tercero who appropriates the story of the fox and the hens—a fight from which Trueba never completely recovers. Trueba fights Pedro Tercero, Blanca's lover, in order to defend Blanca's honor. However, both men end up being brutally beaten by one another. Instead of being the traditional forceful Latin American male, the *macho*, Trueba, from this point on, begins to reform, accepting more and more of his family's liberal ideals even though he himself remains a political conservative to death.

Once again, it would be easy to posit a myth of unity—victimizer becomes victim, and both the individual and the world become better for the lesson learned through the experience. But again, no single unifying myth acts as a static measure for *La casa de los espíritus*. Esteban García returns once more, this time to rape Esteban Trueba's grandaughter, Alba, while she is in prison for political crimes. Ironically, Trueba has sponsored Esteban García's entrance into the police force, where García gains the opportunity to have charge of Alba while she is incarcerated. After the rape scene, the novel ends with the revelation that Alba is pregnant, but because she has also slept with her lover, Miguel, she cannot be sure whose child she carries. "[Estoy] gestando a la criatua que tengo en el vientre," says Alba, "hija de tantas violaciones, o tal vez hija de Miguel, pero sobre todo hija mía." The final result arrived at through this storyline of violence (the rape of Pancha), love (Trueba fights Pedro Tercero over the honor of his daughter), and again violence (Alba's rape) is the "blood and kisses" myth. The child Alba carries is the daughter of either, neither, and/or both Esteban García and Miguel. The child embodies the myth of disunity.

We need to remember, though, how Allende creates her myth. Blood and kisses do not stand alone, but become unified by ink. Ink—words, narrative—serves as the unifying agent by which such disparate elements can be brought together in the same story. For Allende, words have the mystical power to create such transformations. "De manera muy primitiva," writes Allende in her essay **"La Magia de las palabras,"** "le atribuí a la palabra el poder de resucitar a los muertos, reunir a los desaparecidos, reconstruir el mundo perdido." With this in mind, we can look at the novel's overall narrative structure—not the plot, but the manner in which the story is told— and can see how ink transforms blood and kisses into more than just literal acts of violence and love; blood and kisses also become metaphors for the more abstract ideas of the real world and the fantastic.

Allende writes *La casa de los espíritus*, not in her own voice, but through the persona of Alba. Still, as with everything in the novel, the narrative structure cannot be described as simple first-person narrative. In fact, not until the last pages of the book does Alba break into an open presentation of her own voice. Most of the novel, though written by Alba, consists of material she gleans from the notebooks of her grandmother, Clara, interspersed with the memoirs of her grandfather, Esteban Trueba. The difficulty of such a structure occurs in the fact that a variety of voices come together in one history—Clara's notes retold through Alba's "objective" third-person narrative, Esteban's first-person memoirs, and Alba's first-person epilogue. Each voice points the reader in a different direction. Clara's notes concerning her spiritualist friends and their séances point the reader to a world of souls, what Allende (in the opening quotation to this essay) has termed the fantastic element. Esteban's memoirs, on the other hand, concentrate on the political/economic realities of the physical world. Even when he talks about love, Esteban talks about work in the same breath—such as when he works in order to forget the memory of his dead fiancée, Rosa. Finally, when Alba turns to personal narrative in her epilogue, we might expect that the words of a woman who loves both her grandmother and grandfather equally could create some sense of unity. However, no unity appears, at least in the traditional sense. Alba writes:

> Quiero pensar que mi oficio es la vida y que mi misión no es prolongar el odio, sino sólo llenar estas páginas mientras espero el regreso de Miguel, mientras entierro a mi abuelo que ahora descansa a mi lado en este cuarto, mientras aguardo que lleguen tiempos mejores. . . .

Alba can only fill pages with the stories given to her by her grandparents, an activity which fills the days until a better time comes. A traditional myth would tell us who is right and who is wrong, but this new myth does not tell us what to think. Nor does it create a picture of Hegel's thesis, antithesis, and ultimate synthesis. Both Clara's and Esteban's versions of the events have validity, but they are neither combined into some new "correct" point of view nor is either given predominance.

Despite the lack of traditional unity in *La casa de los espíritus*, Allende has not simply recorded stories without giving them some purpose. Her purpose, though, is not the traditional one of judging actions, giving them values, for such a purpose would be exclusive, not inclusive. Exclusionary acts matter to Allende because exclusion occurs first on the fringe. Exclusion disenfranchises those who are not part of a central tradition, and Allende fills *La casa de los espíritus* with people who live on the extreme borders of society— women, *campesinos*, Marxists, spiritualists, and so on. Allende's structure, instead of excluding the fringe element, brings it into focus. With her ink, Allende brings together the extremes—blood and kisses.

To understand how *La casa de los espíritus* brings the fringe into the narrative tradition, a short overview of Roland Barthes' theory of language can be used. In *Writing Degree Zero*, Barthes states:

> We know that language is a corpus of prescriptions and habits common to all the writers of a period. Which means that a language is a kind of natural ambience wholly pervading the writer's expression, yet without endowing it with form or content it is, as it were, an abstract circle of truths, outside of which alone the solid residue of an individual *logos* begins to settle. It enfolds the whole of literary creation much as the earth, the sky, and the line where they meet outline a familiar habitat for mankind. It is not so much a stock of materials as a horizon, which implies both a boundary and a perspective; in short, it is the comforting area of an ordered space. The writer literally takes nothing from it; a language is for him rather a frontier, to overstep which alone might lead to the linguistically supernatural; it is a field of action, the definition of, and hope for, a possibility.

Language, then, is a horizon beyond which people generally do not go. Allende's project, however, steps into the area Barthes calls "the linguistically supernatural." To step into this area can be discomforting, and such a step has the feeling of being a supernatural act; but exploring the linguistically supernatural expands the horizons of language by making what was once considered incomprehensible a part of everyday life. Allende, in **"A Few Words About Latin America,"** says, "In America we are still inventing our own language. . . ." To invent language, Allende must go beyond the accepted limits, the traditional limits, and explore new linguistic areas usually thought to be beyond comprehension. Allende, by positing a world where two linguistic extremes can coexist—violence and love—expands the linguistic playing field, and in the same act, enfranchises what was once only the fringe element.

This expansion of language's playing field I have called the myth of disunity. I do not call *La casa de los espíritus* a pluralistic myth because, again in the traditional sense, it is not. Traditionally, pluralism means that by positing a variety of ideas, by looking at an issue from a number of different perspectives, we will achieve a complete picture of "the truth." But no such truth, no *logos* appears in Allende's novel. Just at the moment we would expect a conclusion, during the last sentences of Alba's epilogue, Allende deprives us of just such an easy satisfaction:

> Clara los escribió para que me sirvieran ahora para rescatar las cosas del pasado y sobrevivir a mi propio espanto. El primero es un cuaderno escolar de veinte hojas, escrito con una delicada caligrafía infantil. Comienza así, "Barrabás llegó a la familia por vía marítima . . . ".

Just when we would expect some form of resolution, Allende takes us back to the beginning of the novel, ending by repeating the book's very first sentence. Instead of closure, which would imply some form of *logos*, the process of ink, blood, and kisses starts again. It may appear that closure comes through the use of a circular process, but not here. When Allende goes back to the beginning of her novel, she gives us a sign that we must rewrite the same story again—a story already lived by the history's characters; a story written by Clara, Esteban, and Alba; and a story rewritten by Alba. The writing of this book never stops, never finds a point of completion because in each return to rewrite the story, readers approach the work with new knowledge—for example, knowing that Alba creates/edits the story. The unity of *La casa de los espíritus* becomes its disunity, its ability and need to contain within its narrative structure those things which cannot be reconciled to one another—violence and love, the fantastic and the real, the various rewritings (rereadings) of its own history.

Finally, the idea of unity in disunity, alongside the idea of the linguistically supernatural, helps to explain Clara's last words to Alba. As she lies dying, Clara is reported as saying, "Cuando ese momento llegara, queria que estuviera tranquila, porque en su caso la muerte no sería una separación, sino una forma de estar más unidas. Alba lo comprendió perfectamente." Through these words, we more completely understand the novel's title—*La casa de los espíritus*. For Clara, death does not mean becoming a ghost—*un espectro, un fantasma*. Ghosts are limited creatures, stuck haunting one place. They are separated from the world, for whatever reason, and are condemned to be seen or felt, but never heard. On the other hand, spirits, *espíritus*, inhabit everything, appropriate everything. Clara, when she dies, will become a spirit. She will live within and beyond the limits of language. As a spirit, she will be everywhere, will become part of the linguistically supernatural. In effect, by leaving her physical body, Clara will embody the myth of disunity in its most complete, its most unified, form. As a spirit, she will be more unified because she will hold more of the universe's irreconcilable elements. And Alba "lo comprendió perfectamente."

Myth, violence, and love. Ink, blood, and kisses. Reality and fantasy hand-in-hand. Latin America. For Allende, taking in the fringes of society—accepting Clara, Esteban Trueba, Esteban García, Rosa, Alba, and all the other characters in *La casa de los espíritus*—means accepting words such as these, even if we do not understand them. "El único material que uso son palabras," writes Allende in **"La magia de las palabras."** All we have to help us understand the world are words. And words control us, not so much by what they say, but by what they do not say. For Allende, only by expanding the horizon of language will we be able to say all that needs to be said. Only by accepting the myth of disunity can language open

itself enough to include all those as equals who now live on or beyond language's borders. Irreconcilable plurality, this is the message, the unity, of *La casa de los espíritus*. (pp. 79–85)

E. Thomson Shields, Jr., "Ink, Blood, and Kisses: 'La casa de los espíritus' and the Myth of Disunity," in *Hispanofila*, Vol. 33, No. 3, May, 1990, pp. 79–86.

DANIEL HARRIS
(essay date 1991)

[In the review below, Harris expresses his admiration of Allende's narrative skills, but unfavorably assesses her treatment of Latin–American characters in *The Stories of Eva Luna*, finding them clichéd and stereotypical.]

By virtue of its sweltering atmospherics and its complex chronicles of entire clans, magical realism has proven to be one of the most enduringly popular literary phenomena of all time. With its indulgence in the supernatural and its permissiveness towards escapist fantasizing, it is also one of the most easily imitated, offering a convenient pretext for writers to evade demands of plot and organization.

The well-crafted stories of Chilean author Isabel Allende elicit both the enthusiasm and the reservations magical realism may inspire in even the most undiscriminating aficionado: enthusiasm about her natural talents as a narrator and her impressive skills as a technician—and reservations about her recklessness and theatricality. She is a gifted opportunist who expertly capitalizes on the mannerisms of South American fiction to create unapologetically derivative and yet eminently readable stories inhabited by quaint eccentrics and sly campesinos. The lush and moody pieces collected in *The Stories of Eva Luna* are some of her finest work to date, their brevity providing a perfect antidote to one of her major failings as a novelist, an irrepressible garrulousness and a narrative style that occasionally tends to be slack and improvisational.

At times, these stories read like raunchy fabliaux, as in **"The Gold of Tomas Vargas,"** in which a wife and her husband's concubine outwit the skin-flint who thrashes them both, or in **"Simple Maria,"** about a cretinous prostitute who attains a kind of innocence through sex, having been battered into a state of sensual Nirvana by a horny Greek sailor. In others, Allende can be elegant and coldly analytic, as in the book's best story, **"Tosca,"** about a quixotic, would-be diva who elopes to the outback with a young medical student where she faithfully plays out her fictions of ministering like Florence Nightingale to his noble mission, grandstanding for an entire life before the credulous yokels of provincial communities.

While it is difficult to resist Allende's undeniable charm as a narrator, both the character of her work and her immense success in the United States raise a number of troubling issues about our attitudes towards the Third World. In stories like **"Walimai"**—about a noble savage from the rain forest who is conscripted into hard labor by heartless white industrialists—or in **"Ester Lucero"**—in which the ancient herbal secrets of a witch doctor miraculously cure a peasant girl who tumbles out of a mango tree only to be skewered on a stake in her backyard—Allende shamelessly sentimentalizes the droll aborigines of primitive society, their purported superstitiousness and irrationality. Nimble and captivating though she is, she ransacks South America as if it were an insipid cache of folksiness and *élan vital*, presenting an Hispanic culture blacktopped into a tropical playground for First World readers, a lost paradise of earthy simplicity. In her hands, the sensuality and passion of magical realism inadvertently become more than just the trite accessories of a literary genre; they are transformed into an ideological indictment of an entire continent.

Allende's notion of herself as a story teller is infused with the populist pipe dreams of a bourgeois Latin American leftist who struggles to recover through literature a lost link with the exotic native culture she somewhat disingenuously claims as her own. In her eyes the act of telling a story is itself political. She associates her craft with the orally transmitted legends of the Indian raconteur, as in **"Two Words"**, about a wise itinerant poet who hypnotizes and unmans a military renegade by means of mysterious linguistic talisman, or in her novel *Eva Luna*, whose ribald Indian heroine, a literary entrepreneur, is the eponymous shadow narrator of the present volume. For all of the genuine pleasure she is capable of bringing politically sensitive readers like myself, Allende's fiction in saturated with a denigrating sort of nostalgia for less complex, preliterate cultures whose childlike spontaneity, wisdom, and harmony with nature she seeks to rehabilitate in her own prose.

If her fiction is political because it harks back to a folkloric world which antecedes the culture imported by the conquistadors, it is also explicitly political in the way in which it "bears witness" to the savagery of South American military juntas. For Allende, story telling is the weapon of the disempowered proletariat against the totalitarian regime, the narrative revenge of a class of people so pitiably subjugated that their only means of retaliation is the spoken word. Virtually all of the pieces in *The Stories of Eva Luna* have a political subtext and function to some extent as informal depositions, like **"Our Secret,"** about two strangers who meet and make love only to discover that they have both been victims of torture, or **"A Discreet Miracle,"** about a radical priest and champion of liberation theology.

The problem with Allende's leftism, as well as with her rich and seductive equatorial settings, is that given the way in which she dishes up a mythopoeic Third World for First World consumption, even the most appaling atrocities in her stories—terrorism, torture, exploitation, avarice, and despotism—are metabolized by the reader not as grave injustices but as cliches and stereotypes. Acts of political violence are only grist for the mill of her incorrigible romanticism, with the vaporous social and historical backgrounds of her fiction aestheticized and trivialized into dreamy confrontations of evil rulers and brave, self-sacrificing heroes. As she lays it on thick about a vital and hot-blooded South America in which characters have "voracious puma eyes" and live "in a dark land beyond reason," the suspicion arises that she performs the old soft-shoe of her lively Hispanic vaudeville for the amusement of gringos. (pp. 28–9)

Daniel Harris, in a review of "The Stories of Eva Luna," in *Boston Review*, Vol. XVI, No. 2, April, 1991, pp 28–9.

EDNA AGUIRRE REHBEIN
(essay date 1991)

[In the following excerpt, Rehbein maintains that Allende manipulates language and the narrator's voice in *Eva Luna* to represent a changing reality in the narrative.]

Cuando escribí *Eva Luna*, por primera vez me senté a escribir una novela y quise escribir una novela en varios niveles. Una novela que fuera como contar un cuento y que fuera la protagonista contándoles a otros el cuento de su propia vida. En *Eva Luna* puse muchas cosas: quería decir, por ejemplo, lo que significa poder contar, cómo a través del contar se van ganando espacios, se va ganando gente, se seduce a un lector. . . . el poder contar cuentos es como un tesoro inagotable. . . [Isabel Allende, personal interview, 5 January 1989]

In *Eva Luna*, Isabel Allende's third novel, the author focuses on two closely linked aspects of story-telling and/or of narrating. On the one hand, she experiments with the *act* of narrating by creating a story in which the roles of Eva Luna, the protagonist, Eva Luna, the narrator, and the role of the character in the soap opera *Bolero* (written by the protagonist) are at first separate, but then seem to converge into *one*. The resulting intertextuality and self-reflexivity create various levels of fictionalization leading the reader to question "reality" within this fictional setting. The other aspect which Allende examines is the *art* of narrating, as she experiments with the text and demonstrates that the slightest manipulation of language can create or transform reality. An individual's adeptness in utilizing language, thus constructs a particular reality. These two aspects of narration, so skillfully crafted by Isabel Allende, are inseparable as they work together to create or change textual "reality" to meet the narrator's liking.

Though at first this work appears to be like many other narratives, it is clear that Allende intends the novel to be more than merely another autobiographical first person account told by the narrator. Allende's intentions for the novel are clearly stated by her protagonist at the end of the novel when Eva states that perhaps all of what has taken place in the story has occurred "de acuerdo al principio de que *es posible construir la realidad* a la medida de las propias apetencias." In the same way that Eva Luna can mold "la Materia Universal" into anything she wishes, Allende and Eva also mold reality according to their liking. In this text, the very act of narrating becomes integrated with the plot of the novel, as the protagonist first learns to tell stories orally, then blossoms from a state of illiteracy, learning to read and then to write, and finally, writes her own story. For Eva, the narrator, and for Eva, the protagonist, the text becomes one long process of learning about the power of expression, be it in written or spoken form.

The importance of revealing or telling about events is seen throughout the novel as other characters also occupy themselves with this activity. Rolf Carlé, the Austrian immigrant who becomes a photo journalist in South America, finds it extremely important to reveal the true story when he reports on political activities. His desire to tell the "official truth" is often frustrated either because the government will not allow it, or because to do so would compromise and endanger the guerrillas' lives. Huberto Naranjo, the guerrilla leader, occupies himself with obscuring the true story, molding it to conform to his needs and even changing his name when necessary. Eva acquires this *gift* of story-telling from her mother, Consuelo, who often engaged in this activity.

Eva's skill is very powerful as it not only serves as entertainment for herself and others, but becomes crucial to her survival. She at times uses it in exchange for food and shelter. Allende explains, "Eva Luna, la protagonista de mi novela cambia sus cuentos por comida, por techo, después por amistad, por amor. . . " Toward the end, this skill becomes her profession when she begins working as a writer. More significant, however, is the fact that throughout her life Eva, the protagonist, relies on her stories to remove her from difficult situations. As she struggles to survive, she relies on their magical power to transport her from the harsh reality by which she is surrounded, to a prettier, more acceptable world which exists only in her dreams or memory. It is through this process, for instance, that as an adult she is able to continue experiencing the "existence" of her mother who died when she was only a small child. Isabel Allende's complex story is a reflection of her own belief in the magical power of the word and the narrative as Eva, the narrator, becomes the active

agent involved in molding reality and consequently the outcome of the novel.

At first glance, the novel appears to be merely another first person account of someone's life: Eva narrates her life story. The first chapter provides background information on Eva's mother, Consuelo, who was orphaned and raised by monks and then went to work for various people; it also tells of Eva's birth. Already in this first chapter Allende introduces the key role played by story-telling and the concept of reality made pliable and changeable through the use of language. Eva's mother, Consuelo, is clearly gifted with the magical powers of story-telling.

> Mi madre era una persona silenciosa, capaz de disimularse entre los muebles, de perderse en el dibujo de la alfombra, de no hacer el menor alboroto, como si no existiera; sin embargo, en la intimidad de la habitación que compartíamos *se transformaba*. Comenzaba a hablar del pasado o a narrar sus cuentos y el cuarto se llenaba de luz, desaparecían los muros para dar paso a increíbles paisajes, palacios abarrotados de objetos nunca vistos, países lejanos inventados por ella o sacados de la biblioteca del patrón; colocaba a mis pies todos los tesoros de Oriente, la luna y más allá, me reducía altamaño de una hormiga para sentir el universo desde la pequeñez, me ponía alas para verlo desde el firmamento, me daba una cola de pez para conocer el fondo del mar. Cuando ella contaba, el mundo se poblaba de personajes, algunos de los cuales llegaron a ser tan familiares, que todavía hoy, tantos años después, puedo describir sus ropas y el tono de sus voces. (emphasis added)

Eva continues,

> Ella (la mamá) sembró en mi cabeza la idea de que la realidad no es sólo como se percibe en la superficie, también tiene una dimensión mágica y, si a uno se le antoja, es legítimo exagerarla y ponerle color para que el tránsito por esta vida no resulte tan aburrido.

At the end of this first chapter, it is also apparent that Eva, like her mother, believes in her own ability to transform reality. She explains, "Una palabra mía y, ichas!, se transformaba la realidad."

The second chapter begins with the life story of Rolf Carlé, a young Austrian boy whose life develops parallel to Eva's. The narrator alternates between a chapter about herself and one about Rolf throughout the remainder of the novel until the last three chapters when their lives intersect and they fall in love. In subsequent chapters, the reader learns about Rolf's own involvement in story-telling through his use of film.

By the third chapter, Eva has actively begun using her story-telling to achieve a number of goals. Eva describes how she told stories to Elvira, her *madrina*: "Me enrollaba junto a Elvira y le ofrecía un cuento a cambio de que me permitiera quedarme con ella." To Huberto Naranjo, the street-wise young boy who helps her survive, who later gets involved in guerrilla warfare, and then becomes Eva's lover, she offers some of her stories as entertainment and compensation for taking care of her: "Me acurruqué entre los papeles y le ofrecí un cuento en pago de tantas y tan finas atenciones." It is through Huberto's insistence that she begins to learn to read.

Eva's ability to create or invent continues to become stonger and more evident. Later, when she finds herself alone again and feeling totally abandoned, Eva resorts to using her imagination to "magically" retrieve her mother who died when she was young.

> Escondí la cara entre las rodillas, llamé a mi madre y muy pronto percibí su aroma ligero de tela limpia y almidón. Surgió ante mí intacta, con su trenza enrollada en la nuca y los ojos de humo brillando en su rostro pecoso, para decirme que esa trifulca no era nada de mi incumbencia y no había razón para tener miedo,que me sacudiera el susto y echáramos a andar juntas. Me puse de pié y le tomé la mano.

And ". . . la presencia visible de [su] madre. . . " continues to accompany her through her troubled days in the streets while she looks for a home.

It is not until she goes to live with Riad Halabí, however, that she actually learns to read and the next phase of her creativity is initiated. Halabí, who finds her on the streets, take her to work with him in his home in Agua Santa. He becomes like a father to her takes a special interest in educating her, finding her a tutor, buying her many books, and teaching her to read. Halabí not only teaches her to read and write, rather more notably, he is the one who makes her an "official" person by acquiring a birth certificate for her. Later Eva reflected on his generosity,

> Riad Halabí me dio varias cosas fundamentales para transitar por mi destino y entre ellas, dos muy importantes: la escritura y un certificado de existencia. No había papeles que probaran mi presencia en este mundo, nadie me inscribió al nacer, nunca había estado en una escuela, era como si no hubiera nacido, pero él habló con un amigo de la ciudad, pagó el soborno correspondiente y consiguió un documento de identidad, en el cual, por un error del funcionario, figuro con tres años menos de los que en realidad tengo.

Her interest in reading becomes a passion and consequently, she begins to write her own stories. She states,

> Yo devoraba los libros que caian en mis manos, . . . mis historias aparecían anhelos e inquietudes que no sabía que estaban en mi corazón. La maestra Inés me sugirió anotarlos en un cuaderno. Pasaba parte de la noche escribiendo y me gustaba tanto hacerlo, que se me iban las horas sin darme cuenta y a menudo me levantaba por la mañana con los ojos enrojecidos. Pero ésas eran mis mejores horas. Sospechaba que nada existía verdaderamente, *la realidad era una materia imprecisa y gelatinosa qua mis sentidos captaban a medias. . .* Me consolaba la idea de que *yo podía tomar esa gelatina*

y moldearla para crear lo que deseara, no una parodia de la realidad, como los mosqueteros y las esfinges de mi antigua patrona yugoslava, sino un mundo propio, poblado de personajes vivos, donde *yo imponía las normas y las cambiaba a mí antojo. De mí dependía la existencia* de todo lo que nacía, moría o acontecía en las arenas inmóviles donde germinaban mis cuentos. Podía colocar en ellas lo que quisiera, bastaba pronunciar la palabra justa para darle vida. A veces sentía que ese universo fabricado con el poder de la imaginación era de contornos más firmes y durables que la región confusa donde deambulaban los seres de carne y hueso que me rodeaban. (emphasis added)

Eva becomes conscious of her own power as the reader of these stories and of the fact that she alone has the power to *create* everything that occurs in her narrative. At times, her imagined environment becomes preferable to the harshness of life itself.

Eva's ability to change her perception of "reality" to her liking continues to become further developed as she gains confidence through reading. Upon moving into an apartment with Mimí, Eva invents an entire family tree for herself by acquiring old photographs of "toda una familia" and placing them on her wall, thereby creating for herself a valid past as well. The hardest photograph to find, however, is that of Consuelo, her mother. She decides on a portrait of a beautiful woman and feels that one is appropriate because the woman in it "era lo bastante hermosa como para encarnar a mi madre." She goes on to state, "así *deseo* preservarla en mi recuerdo" (emphasis added).

Aside from the obvious fact that the previous citation reinforces how Eva is again engaging in molding reality to her liking, this quote represents a pivotal point in the novel because it is one of the first times that the narrator uses the present tense as she relates her life story. Previously, she has been looking back in time at events in her life, in her mother's, and in Rolf's, so she has used the past tenses. It is at this point in the narrative that the lives of Eva, the narrator and Eva, the protagonist begin to converge, and Allende begins to communicate this merging of narrative time and of the protagonist/narrator through her meticulous use of the language. Gradually, in this chapter, and then more suddenly in the next two, there is a shift from the re-telling of events from the past to the recounting of events in the present, as they occur at that moment. This evolution from past to present is seen again just a few pages later as Eva tells of her responsibility for her *madrina*. She explains that upon coming to the capital city, she finds her *madrina*, who has been living in terrible conditions in a public nursing home. With Mimí's help, they move her to a privately run attractive care unit. "Mimí pagó la primera mensualidad," states Eva, adding, "pero ese deber *es mío*" (emphasis added).

Shortly thereafter Eva begins to work as a secretary in the military uniform factory and at night, encouraged by Mimí, she writes stories in her *cuaderno de cuentos*. She begins to see Huberto more, but only when he decides he can come out of hiding. After one of their passionate encounters, Eva reflects on their relationship, once again using the present tense.

> Para Naranjo y otros como él, el pueblo parecía compuesto sólo de hombres; nosotras debíamos contribuir a la lucha, pero estábamos exluidas de las decisiones y del poder. Su revolución no cambiaría en escencia mi suerte, en cualquier circunstancia yo tendría que seguir abriéndome paso por mí misma hasta el último de mis días. Tal vez en ese momento me di cuenta de que la mía *es* una guerra cuyo final no se vislumbra, así es que más vale darla con algería, para que no se me vaya la vida esperando una posible victoria para empezar a sentirme bien. Concluí que Elvira tenía razón *hay* que ser bién brava, *hay* que pelear siempre. (emphasis added)

Whereas previously the narrative has described Eva's life in retrospect, this passage clearly creates the impression that Eva, the narrator is now recounting Eva, the protagonist's life as it is unfolding and developing before her. By merging narrative time in this way, the author dissolves the gap between Eva, the protagonist and Eva, the narrator. At this point in the novel, the *two* become *one*.

This evolution of narrative time is intensified in the subsequent sections as Eva quits her work at the uniform factory and dedicates herself to writing on a regular basis. Mimí, who believes in fortune telling, reads Eva's future and affirms that her "destino era contar." Mimí encourages Eva to begin writing screenplays for the soap opera in which she appears and purchases a typewriter for her. The next morning, as Eva anxiously sits down to write, she is filled with a flurry of emotion and inspiration.

> Desde que la maestra Inés me enseñó el alfabeto, escribía casi todas las noches, pero sentí que ésta era una ocasión diferente, algo que podría cambiar mi rumbo. Preparé un café negro y me instalé ante la máquina, tomé una hoja de papel limpia y blanca, como una sábana recién planchada para hacer el amor y la introduje en el rodillo. Entonces sentí algo extraño, como una brisa alegre por los huesos, por los caminos de las venas bajo la piel. Creí que esa página me esperaba desde hacía veinti-tantos años, que yo había vivido sólo para ese instante, y quise que a partir de ese momento mi único oficio fuera atrapar las historias suspendidas en el aire más delgado, para hacerlas mías.

She explains:

> Se ordenaron los relatos guardados en la memoria genética desde antes de mi nacimiento y muchos otros que había registrado por años en mis cuadernos. Comencé a recordar hechos muy lejanos, recuperé las anécdotas de mi madre cuando vivíamos entre los idiotas, los cancerosos y los embalsamados del Profesor Jones; aparecieron un indio mordido de víbora y un tirano con las manos devoradas por la lepra; rescaté a una solterona que perdió el cuero cabelludo como si

se lo hubiera arrancado una máquina bobinadora, un dignatario en su sillón de felpa obispal, un árabe de corazón generoso y tantos otros hombres y mujeres cuyas vidas *estaban a mi alcance para disponer de ellas según mi propia y soberana voluntad*. (emphasis added)

Allende adds to the text's complexity by allowing Eva to detail the recording of these events which have already been written by the narrator and have been read previously by the reader in this same novel, thereby leading the reader to question the reliability and chronology of the narrative. Eva explains that

> Poco a poco *el pasado se transformaba en presente y me adueñaba también del futuro*, los muertos cobraban vida con ilusión de eternidad, se reunían los dispersos y todo aquello esfumado por el olvido adquiría contornos precisos. (emphasis added)

As she continues to write she begins to speculate about her own future: "Sospechaba que el final llegaría sólo con mi propia muerte y me atrajo la idea de ser yo también uno más de la historia y tener el poder de determinar mi fin o inventarme una vida." It is as if narrative time, the action being retold, has now caught up with the present events and Eva Luna has begun to recount her life as it takes place. The implication, therefore, is that she is now beginning to tell *her* life story as it will transpire in the future, though it has not yet occurred. Eva Luna is now in total control of her destiny: all she needs to do is to write it in order for it to occur in her narrative "reality."

When Eva Luna and Rolf Carlé finally meet at a dinner party, she is asked to supply more of her *cuentos*. Eva's creative powers and the author's utilization of the present tense amidst passages narrated in the past tense are further evidenced. The following passage illustrates Allende's techniques:

> Mimí *dice* que *tengo* una voz especial para los cuentos, una voz que, siendo mía *parece* ambién ajena, como si brotara desde la tierra y me subiera por el cuerpo. *Sentí* que la habitación *perdía* sus contornos, esfumada en los nuevos horizontes que yo convocaba. (emphasis added)

Whereas the early segments of the novel conveyed the idea of a narrator who was telling about her life as it had happened many years back, the interjection of these comments in the present tense make the text seem like a conversation in the present with some momentary descriptions of past events.

In Chapter Eleven, Eva who has become involved in helping the guerrillas with their greatest effort against the government, finds that Rolf, who had previously merely been documenting the events, is also now involved in the struggle. While out in the countryside, waiting for the attack to occur, Rolf asks her to tell a story she has never told before. She willingly begins to tell about "una mujer cuyo oficio era contar cuentos." This unmistakably is a reference to herself, Eva the story-teller. The story she continues to tell, however, is even more engaging and insightful as it seems to correspond very closely to the narrator's/protagonist's life story. She states that the young woman met a man who was very sad and was burdened by his past, so he asks her to create a new history for him. She consents, but after she has told the new story of Rolf's life, Eva comments:

> Por fin amaneció y en la primera luz del día ella comprobó que el olor de la tristeza se había esfumado. Suspiró, cerró los ojos y al sentir su espíritu vacío como el de un recién nacido, comprendió que en el afán de complacerlo le había entregado su propia memoria, ya no sabía qué era suyo y cuánto ahora pertenecía a él, sus pasados habían quedado anudados en una sola trenza. Había entrado hasta el fondo en su propio cuento y ya no podía recoger sus palabras, pero tampoco quiso hacerlo y se abandonó al placer de fundirse con él en la misma historia. . .

The story that Eva tells Rolf is indicative of what has happened in the novel with respect to her own life and Rolf's, for earlier, Eva too had helped Rolf accept his painful past by changing it for him through her *cuentos*. Eva and Rolf have become intertwined just as have the two characters in her *cuento*.

After the guerrillas' successful maneuvers against the government, Eva and Rolf become concerned over how the government will present the news about the occurrence, so they decide to tell the story in the next episode of her soap opera. Eva and Rolf explain that they can avoid any problems with the government censorship because, "siempre se puede alegar que es sólo ficción y como la telenovela es mucho más popular que el noticiario, todo el mundo sabrá lo que pasó en Santa María." Thereby, Eva uses her fictional media to depict a true incident. Eva's soap opera, *Bolero*, becomes very popular and receives enormous attention. Mimí plays herself in the television story, while Eva,

> . . . escribía cada día un nuevo episodio, inmersa por completo en el mundo que creaba con el poder omnímodo de las palabras, transformada en un ser disperso, reproducida hasta el infinito, viendo mi propio reflejo en múltiples espejos, viviendo innumerables vidas, hablando con muchas voces.

At the end of the novel, Eva and Rolf leave the city for a while because they are concerned about possible repercussions from the telecasting of their episode depicting the guerrilla actions. While in Colonia, the couple fall passionately in love. Eva describes their kiss, saying:

> Se acercó a grandes pasos y procedió a besarme tal como ocurre en las novelas románticas, tal como yo esperaba que lo hiciera desde hacía un siglo y tal como estaba describiendo momentos antes el encuentro de mis protagonistas *en Bolero*. Aproveché la cercanía para husmearlo con disimulo y así identifiqué el olor de mi pareja.

The narrator ends the story by stating that they loved one another for a while until their love faded. But then she interjects,

> O tal vez lass cosas no ocurrieron así. Tal vez tuvimos la suerte de tropezar con un amor excepcional y yo no tuve necesidad de inventarlo, sino sólo vestirlo de gala para que perdurara en la memoria, de acuerdo al principio de que es posible construir la realidad a la medida de las propias apetencias. . . Escribí que durante esas semanas benditas, el tiempo se estiró, se enroscó en sí mismo, se dio vuelta como un pañuelo de mago y alcanzó para que Rolf Carlé—con la solemnidad hecha polvo y la vanidad por las nubes—conjurara sus pesadillas y volviera a cantar las canciones de su adolescencia y para que yo. . . narrara. . . muchos cuentos, incluyendo algunos con final feliz.

The novel is a prime example of Isabel Allende's belief in the magical power of words and in the concept that books have their own spirit to exist as they wish. Eva, the narrator, is completely in control of the narrative and capable of molding and defining time and reality as she wishes. Allende demonstrates that the act and the art of narrating consist of the skill and talent to change language in order to achieve the desired textual "reality." (pp. 179–88)

Edna Aguirre Rehbein, "The Act/Art of Narrating in 'Eva Luna'," in *Critical Approaches to Isabel Allende's Novels*, edited by Sonia Riquelme Rojas and Edna Aguirre Rehbein, Peter Lang, 1991, pp. 179–90.

SOURCES FOR FURTHER STUDY

Brosnahan, John. "The Booklist Interview: Isabel Allende." *Booklist* 87, No. 20 (15 October 1990): 1930–31.

> Interview with Allende primarily focusing on her experiences with the short story genre in writing *The Stories of Eva Luna* and on the political nature of her writing.

Hart, Patricia. *Narrative Magic in the Fiction of Isabel Allende.* Cranbury, N.J.: Associated University Presses, 1989, 196 p.

> Discusses the role of magic in Allende's first three novels.

————. Review of *The Stories of Eva Luna. Nation* 252, No. 9 (11 March 1991): 314–16.

> Examines Allende's use of magic realism in *The Stories of Eva Luna* and attempts to clarify her position among such authors as Gabriel García Márquez and Mario Vargas Llosa.

Levine, Linda Gould. "A Passage to Androgyny: Isabel Allende's *La casa de los espíritus.*" In *In the Feminine Mode : Essays on Hispanic Women Writers*, edited by Noël Valis and Carol Maier, pp. 164–73. Cranbury, N.J.: Associated University Presses, 1990.

> Analyzes Allende's portrayal of patriarchal oppression and her "revision of the traditional dichotomy between the sexes" in *The House of the Spirits.*

Rivero, Eliana S. "Scheherazade Liberated: *Eva Luna* and Women Storytellers." In *Splintering Darkness: Latin American Women Writers in Search of Themselves*, edited by Lucía Guerra Cunningham, pp. 143–56. Pittsburgh: Latin American Literary Review Press, 1990.

> Discusses how recent female authors and their fictional narrators create their own reality through words, identifying Allende's *Eva Luna* as an example of this phenomenon.

Rodden, John. " 'The Responsibility to Tell You': An Interview with Isabel Allende." *The Kenyon Review* XIII, No. 1 (Winter 1991): 113–23.

> Interview with Allende about the special political responsibilities she assumes as a Latin–American female writer.

Additional coverage of Allende's life and career is contained in the following sources published by Gale Research: *Contemporary Authors*, Vols. 125, 130; *Contemporary Literary Criticism*, Vols. 39, 57; *Hispanic Writers*; and *Major 20th-Century Writers.*

Jorge Amado

1912–

Brazilian novelist, short story writer, biographer, and dramatist.

INTRODUCTION

*A*mado is a major figure in Brazilian literature and an internationally acclaimed author whose novels have been translated into more than forty languages. The majority of his works are set in the Bahia region of northeastern Brazil and reveal the author's fascination with the rich cultural heritage of Bahia's inhabitants, most of whom are of mixed European, African, and native Indian ancestry. Valued for the insight they offer into rural Brazilian society, Amado's works typically address political and social concerns. His early novels focus on the settling of the region for the cultivation of cacao and on the class conflict which resulted. These works depict a violent, squalid society which the protagonists strive to improve through actions based on communist ideals. Amado's later writings, which have made him a best-selling author worldwide, are more expansive and less overtly political, tempering social criticism with satire, ironic humor, and raucous comedy.

Born in Bahia, where his father owned a cacao plantation, Amado attended a Jesuit boarding school in Salvador where he was introduced to Portuguese literary classics along with the works of Charles Dickens. In 1930 his father enrolled him in law school at Rio de Janeiro. He published his first novel, *O país do carnaval* ("Carnival Land"), the following year and soon became absorbed in literary interests. Amado's second novel, *Cacau* (1933; "Cacao"), was confiscated because of the author's sympathy with Brazil's Communist party, and Amado was briefly imprisoned in 1935—the first of a succession of controversial events that resulted in the banning of his books by the Brazilian government in 1938 and in his exile on two later occasions.

In 1945, when the Communist party gained power in Brazil, Amado was elected federal deputy of Sao Paulo on the party's ticket. Within two years, however, Communism was overthrown in Brazil; Amado traveled to Europe, journeying for the next several years through the Soviet Union and many nations of Eastern Europe. He was awarded the Stalin Peace Prize in 1951, and published his travel memoir, *O mundo da Paz* ("The World of Peace"), in Brazil that same year. The work was quickly seized, however, by Brazilian authorities who objected to the author's idealization of communist society in that work. By the end of the decade, Amado had achieved universal acclaim with the publication of his *Gabriela, cravo e canela* (1958; *Gabriela, Clove and Cinnamon*), a comic novel that heralded what Jon Vincent has described as the author's "diminished faith in the dictates of the Communist party and a diminished exploitation of its icons." Similarly, *Dona Flor e seus dois maridos* (1966; *Dona Flor and Her Two Husbands*) and Amado's other more recent novels have largely eschewed political ideology, presenting instead a more broadly based view of human society. The extraordinary popularity of his novels has made Amado a folk hero in Brazil. As Edwin McDowell wrote in the *New York Times Book Review* in 1988, "the names of characters from various Amado novels adorn everything in Brazil from restaurants and bars to whiskey and margarine."

Amado's first three novels, *O país do carnaval*, *Cacau*, and *Suor* (1934; *Slums*), are generally faulted for being excessively pedantic in expressing communist solutions to social problems. Of these early works the author has commented: "As a young man I sought to put revolution into all my books and I always had a theoretical speech included." *Jubiabá* (1935), Amado's fourth novel, is regarded as his first artistic success. In this work, set in Salvador, Amado details a young black man's struggle against social injustice, infusing the story with elements of Brazilian and African folk traditions. *Jubiabá* was Amado's earliest attempt to capture the multi-ethnic spirit of Brazil's capital city, an endeavor that has evolved into a prominent feature of his artistry. *Terras do sem fim* (1943; *The Violent Land*), considered Amado's finest novel, focuses on the cultivation of cacao in Bahia and the potential for economic prosperity in the region. In this work, rival planters become involved in a violent struggle to gain control of a tract of forest land that will be cleared to produce huge cacao groves. Rich in subplots, *The Violent Land* has prompted praise for Amado's development of a large cast of characters and his deft use of irony—the economic prosperity of the region coming at the expense of tradition, moral values, and human life.

Amado's later work is characterized by an increased emphasis on the individual and on stylistic technique. *Gabriela, Clove and Cinnamon*—a bestselling novel in several countries, including the United States—is a comedy set in the town of Ilheus, in Bahia, after the region has prospered from the cultivation of cacao. Gabriela, a lovely migrant worker, and Mundinho Falçao, a wealthy young man, arrive in Ilheus and are instrumental in overturning restrictive social values and in freeing the town from domination by wealthy landowners. Less polemical than Amado's earlier fiction, this novel reveals the author's increasing focus on such themes as love, sexuality, and friendship, and highlights his growing skill in the use of irony and caricature. *Dona Flor and Her Two Husbands*, another of Amado's novels that achieved widespread popularity, centers on a vivacious and virtuous woman whose roguish husband has died in drunken revelry. Shortly after Dona Flor marries a respectable pharmacist, her first husband returns as a ghost seeking to resume their sexual relationship. Amado focuses on the dilemma of his heroine, who longs for the passionate lovemaking she enjoyed with her first husband, yet appreciates the well-ordered life and social standing provided by her second husband. Like most of Amado's later writings, *Dona Flor* espouses an uninhibited lifestyle free of the constraints imposed by tradition and bourgeois values, employing sensual descriptions of fragrances, food, and sexual activity. The success of this work and Amado's other comedies initiated the republication and translation of such early works as *The Violent Land* and *Jubiabá*; in addition, *Dona Flor and Her Two Husbands* and *Gabriela, Clove and Cinnamon* have been adapted for film.

Although many of his early novels are regarded as little more than vehicles for expressing his political beliefs and many of his later works are denigrated for their overly frank treatment of human sexuality, Amado is widely acclaimed as a masterful celebrant of life and the human experience. The universal appeal of his fiction and his memorable characters have placed him among the most popular Brazilian authors of the modern era. Asked to explain his success, Amado replied: "I write about Brazilian problems from the side of the people and I'm antielitist. I use popular language, I am no James Joyce. And in my works the people always win. I am very proud of that. My message is one of hope instead of despair."

CRITICAL COMMENTARY

DAVID GALLAGHER

(essay date 1969)

[Gallagher is a Chilean-born English educator and critic. In the following review of *Dona Flor and Her Two Husbands*, he notes that the novel is focused essentially on the inner lives of its central characters rather than on the social issues emphasized in many of Amado's early works. Gallagher praises the author's characterizations, but finds the novel excessively lengthy and "often writ[ten] flatly, without discipline or tension."]

For the average citizen of Sao Paulo or Rio, the North-East of Brazil is an area of calamitous suffering he is happy never to have visited. And if this vast, arid region, inhabited by nearly 17 million Brazilians, ever pricks his conscience, it will be to some extent due to the work of three novelists of the North-East, José Lins do Rego, Gracilano Ramos and Jorge Amado.

Amado's early books were renowned for the militant socialist realism he brought to bear, as a member of the Communist party and follower of Luis Carlos Prestes. The relative permissiveness of the Soviet thaw radically altered his writing over the last 13 years. In 1958, he wrote *Gabriela, Clove and Cinnamon*, an ebulliently exotic book in which social postures were abandoned and characters were paraded with more emphasis on their eccentricities than their suffering. *Dona Flor and Her Two Husbands*, a novel about sex and gambling, is in much the same vein.

The problems of the North-East are scarcely mentioned. This time, Amado has nothing to tell us about the dire consequences of mass labor migration to the cities. Nor does he record the agonizing effects of the North-East's droughts, or the fact that less than five percent of the schoolchildren in the North-East finish their primary education. In his new novel, we see the North-East from the inside, through the eyes of its humbler inhabitants, people whose primary interests are the latest film at the local movie house, the prospects of success at roulette or with a handsome *mulatta*, the latest serial on the radio—and, not least, the marriage, widowhood and remarriage of everyone's favorite neighbor Dona Flor Dos Guimarães.

The novel's villain is Dona Rozilda, Dona Flor's mother, and her villainy lies in the fact that she is a scheming social climber. The hero is Dona Flor's reckless first husband, a handsome rogue named Vadinho, whom no *mulatta* has ever been known to resist, who is so charming that no man can refuse to lend him money. Usually, he lavishes the loan on a game of baccarat. If he wins, he throws a party; if he loses, that's too bad; another creditor will be found. When he dies, he dies dancing the samba.

No one who knows Brazil need be reminded that this is an immensely happy country, even in the North-East. Practically everyone in Amado's galaxy of characters exudes a reckless *joie de vivre*. There are innumerable penniless playboys, pranksters and gamblers; dissolute mayors presiding over towns with retinues of voluptuous *mulattas*; lascivious priests; gossiping crones downing glasses of rum at their relatives' wakes. Among them all, Vadinho towers. When he dies, Dona Flor forgets the hours she lived in solitude, while he caroused with any woman in Bahia lucky enough to have him, or squandered money she had painfully saved for a new radio. She can remember only his artistry in bed.

A respected cooking instructress, expert at preparing stewed turtle and fricassee of lizard, she finds her bereavement hard to bear. Erotic nightmares invade her sleep. Widowhood, she finds, is "outwardly all chastity, inwardly a pool of dung." Fortunately the local pharmacist, Dr. Teodoro, is eager to console her, and Dona Flor is glad to accept his proposal of a second marriage.

Dr. Teodoro gives her stability and fidelity. Dr. Teodoro is a solemn man, determined to fulfill his marital obligations, albeit a little predictably: "On Wednesdays and Saturdays, at ten o'clock, give or take a minute, Dr. Teodoro took his wife in upright ardor and unfailing pleasure, always with an encore on Saturday, optional on Wednesday."

Despite which, Dona Flor continues to have lewd visions. Vadinho, a rascal even in death, appears stark naked and irresistible at the foot of her bed. Soon she is forced to yield to his lascivious ghost. For "Coupling is a blessed thing, it was God who ordered it. 'Go and couple, my children, go and have babies' was what He said, and it was one of the best things He did."

In the past few decades the shamanistic traditions of Latin America (usually in countries where there is strong Negro influence or a living Indian culture) have been skillfully exploited in literature. Fantasy in many Latin American novels is a real, active dimension in the char-

Principal Works

O país do carnaval (novel) 1931

Cacau (novel) 1933

Suor (novel) 1934
  [*Slums*, 1938]

Jubiabá (novel) 1935
  [*Jubiabá*, 1984]

Mar morto (novel) 1936
  [*Sea of Death*, 1984]

Capitães da areia (novel) 1937

ABC de Castro Alves (biography) 1941

Terras do sem fim (novel) 1943
  [*The Violent Land*, 1945]

São Jorge dos Ilhéus (novel) 1944
  [*The Golden Harvest*, 1992]

Bahia de Todos or Santos (prose) 1945

Seara vermelha (novel) 1946

O amor do soldado (play) 1947

O mundo da Paz (travel memoir) 1951

Os subterrâneos da liberdade (novel) 1954

Gabriela, cravo e canela (novel) 1958
  [*Gabriela, Clove and Cinnamon*, 1962]

Os velhos marinheiros (novel) 1961
  [*Home is the Sailor*, 1964]

Os pastores da noite (novel) 1964
  [*Shepherds of the Night*, 1966]

Dona Flor e seus dois maridos (novel) 1966
  [*Dona Flor and Her Two Husbands*, 1969]

Tenda dos milagres (novel) 1969
  [*Tent of Miracles*, 1971]

Tereza Batista cansada de guerra (novel) 1972
  [*Tereza Batista: Home from the Wars*, 1975]

O gato malhado e a andorinha Sinhá (juvenilia) 1976
  [*The Swallow and the Tom Cat: A Love Story*, 1982]

Tieta do Agreste, Pastora de Cabras (novel) 1977
  [*Tieta, the Goat Girl*, 1979]

Farda, fardão, camisola de dormir (novel) 1979
  [*Pen, Sword, Camisole*, 1985]

Tocaia Grande: A Face Obscura (novel) 1984
  [*Showdown*, 1988]

---

acters' lives—and, just as the characters themselves ignore the boundaries between reality and imagination, so for the reader, too, real events slip almost imperceptibly into magic. In *Dona Flor and Her Two Husbands* it is the Devil-God Exu who resuscitates the body of Vadinho and restores it to Dona Flor, to distract her from her second husband. "Exu," Amado tells us, "drinks only one thing—straight rum. At the crossroads, he waits sitting upon the night to take the most difficult road, the narrowest, the most winding, the bad road—for all Exu wants is to frolic, to make mischief. . . . Exu, Vadinho's patron deity." As Vadinho explains to Dona Flor, Dr. Teodoro "protects your virtue. He is your outward face, I your inner, the lover whom you can't bear to evade. . . . To be happy, you need both of us. . . . The rest is deceit and hypocrisy."

It is easy to see that the Yoruba deities of Brazil have done a therapeutic service to Dona Flor in resurrecting Vadinho and removing her deceitful inhibitions—a service performed by classical deities in much modern literature. Magic plays another role, that of wish-fulfilling retributions. Just as in Miguel Angel Asturias's novel *Strong Wind* a cyclone summoned by the local shaman levels the exploiting American banana plantations of Guatemala, so in *Dona Flor* the magic of Exu is deployed to avenge the exploitation of the local roulette wheel. During his lifetime, Vadinho lost a small fortune on his favorite number, 17. With magical powers acquired in death, he is able to ruin the casino by causing 17 to come up with miraculous regularity, after whispering to his cronies that they should stake every cent they can borrow on it.

Dona Flor and Her Two Husbands is a remarkable novel for the coolness with which the author is able to impose his extraordinary characters on us. Like them, we learn to take exoticism and magic in our stride. It is a pity that Amado mars his achievement by often writing flatly, without discipline or tension. His refreshing exuberance is diminished by the novel's almost aggressive repetitiveness. Cut to half its size, it would have been a better book.

David Gallagher, in a review of "Dona Flor and Her Two Husbands," in *The New York Times Book Review*, August 17, 1969, p. 33.

L. CLARK KEATING

(essay date 1983)

[Keating is an American educator and critic specializing in the study of Romance languages. In the following essay, he assesses Amado's characterizations in several of the author's best known novels.]

It has been several years since I first read Jorge Amado's novel *Capitaes da Areia*, which tells the story of a gang of Bahia's homeless children, who live on the outer edge of society. Yet I still remember vividly the sense of *déjà vu* that I experienced, as well as my instant conclusion that the characters, who were named The Professor, God's Favorite, Little Pill, The Cat, Two Stumps and Dry Run were the South American counterparts of Damon Runyon's Harry the Horse, Dave the Dude, Phillie the Weeper and other picturesque citizens, as he likes to call them, on the outer fringe of New York's Broadway society. A recent careful rereading of the works of the two authors does not sustain the illusion of similarity. Runyon's ironic objectivity, his pretended refusal to admit any involvement either as writer or thinker for the social consequences of the crimes and misdemeanors that his characters engaged in is a far cry from the passionate involvement of Amado with his characters. Yet there are moments when Amado does not seem too far from the New Yorker. Perhaps the occasional parallels that suggest themselves may excuse me for clinging to the picturesque terminology "guys and dolls" as applied to the characters of Jorge Amado.

For my purpose I shall choose several of the better known works of the novelist in order to see how he approaches the delineation of character. But first some general impressions. As we analyze them several are dominant. In the first place he is a novelist with a definite point of view, who knows exactly what he wants his work to say to his readers. This is as true of his more recent novels where he has ceased to be so preoccupied with reforming society as he was in his earlier ones in which theme and purpose were more plainly insisted upon. Second, he is a passionate novelist, he is *engagé*, which is to say that he cares deeply about what he writes. Third, he makes frequent use of heavy irony in his treatment of character and situation. And if these observations be true, and I believe that they are, the characters that result are molded thereby.

Let us begin our analysis by noticing that although Jorge Amado is bound by affectionate ties to his native city of Bahia, and to the region in which it lies, he is a severe critic of its social organization. Nor is he merely local in his point of view, for as a member of several years of the national congress he had ample opportunity to observe and to experience the mores of Rio de Janeiro. He was not happy about what he saw. Brazilian patriot though he is, he began first and foremost as a Marxist social critic. He saw corruption on every side with nepotism and dishonesty in all walks of life. He perceived the nation's agriculture as dominated by self-styled colonels, who were ruthless in their exploitation of the land and of the people who worked for them, while his sympathies are principally with those who are under the yoke, the proletariat. Therefore, the characters that embody his point of view are starkly tragic. He has told us that *Terras do sem fim (The Violent Land)* is one of his favorite novels,

yet it is in this book that the landowners are most cruel and the peasantry most oppressed. Its date of publication shows plainly that it was written when the social message was uppermost in his mind.

No one who has read this account of the civil war over the possession of new cacao lands to be wrested from the jungle can ever forget the passage where the Negro Damião, a usually docile and never failing marksman, wrestles with his conscience over an assignment to kill a man in cold blood. It is not the first time that he has been assigned to such a task. But for the first time the killer dimly realized the possible consequences of what he is about to do. And when decency wins over habit and obedience, poor Damião runs away to become thereafter a frightened and psychopathic wanderer about the countryside. Certainly other characters in the novel are also memorable. The vicious Colonel Badaro and his equally inhuman opponent, Colonel Horacio, are drawn with a savage pen, while Ester, the cowering child bride of the latter, who is in physical fear of the inevitable bedroom contacts with her husband also presents a pathetic picture.

These are real people whom Amado has created, yet their actions suggest Amado's message concerning social reforms. Is Amado, then, a reformer? He is indeed, particularly during his early phase. Like the Frenchman Zola and the Englishman Dickens he writes not solely as a creative writer but as one who would expose a defective society to his readers. He manages, however, to avoid the pitfalls of the mere theme novelist. His characters, like those of the two foreign novelists just mentioned, may serve a purpose beyond fiction; nevertheless, fiction is always his chief concern. If as a by-product the reader is introduced to a Brazilian society that appears in crying need for change, so much the better. The Brazil that we see in *The Violent Land* is about as enlightened as Czarist Russia, and her peasantry are for all practical purposes serfs as were those of Russia before the emancipation. The question then occurs as to whether Amado has exaggerated his pictures. Anyone who thinks so is hereby referred to the works of the distinguished Brazilian sociologist Gilberto Freyre, who would seem to agree with Amado on all points. We must not be astonished, therefore, if all the characters of this novel are stark, horrible and almost inhuman. The impact on the reader is much like that exerted by a study of Zola's *La Terre*.

From the viewpoint of well created characters perhaps no one of Amado's novels is superior to *Capitaes da Areia*. In this work he has created a band of waifs who inhabit a deserted warehouse on the waterfront. They live by their wits, that is to say, dishonestly, by purse snatching, armed robbery and housebreaking. They are self governing under the leadership of Pedro Bala, an uncharacteristically blond adolescent, son of a labor martyr. Their names and roles have already been alluded to. The evil genius among them is the lame boy, Two Stumps (who is not legless, by the way). For him no deed is too dastardly, for he is sadistic as well as amoral. The Professor is the group's intellect, an avid reader with artistic talent, who plans their campaigns. To mitigate the severity of their place in life the novelist introduces two persons. The first is not a very intelligent priest, Father José Pedro, who makes up in kindness and understanding what he lacks in other ways. His attempts to help the boys go unrewarded by the hierarchy, and there is more than a hint of bitterness in the scene where Amado shows the priest being reprimanded by his superiors for daring to waste his time on a band of outlaws.

The temporary incarceration of Pedro Bala in the reformatory after an unsuccessful coup by the band is an occasion for a lengthy description of the installation and its personnel. The place is unspeakably foul; its personnel inhuman, sadistic and cruel beyond belief. Throughout the book the rich or middle-class persons with whom the members of the band come into contact, are, with two notable exceptions, unfeeling and indifferent. They neither understand nor wish to understand what goes on among the homeless and unfortunate of society. Indeed, they are almost typical capitalists as seen from the Marxist point of view.

A notable chapter is devoted to the struggles of conscience of the pious boy "Little Pill", who aspires to the priesthood, as he tries to resist the temptation to steal a statue of the Baby Jesus from a shop window. And when he succumbs and takes the statue Amado succeeds in convincing us that we have witnessed the triumph of piety over morality. In another chapter we are shown a gang war in all its ferocity, and here we are reminded of *West Side Story*, the Leonard Bernstein operetta based on a story by Damon Runyon.

The climax or chief crisis of the book comes when a couple of members of the gang take pity on an orphan girl, Dora and her young brother. The struggle in this instance is one of lust versus decency. The question is simply whether the gang will admit the girl for the avowed purpose of abusing her sexually or, as Pedro Bala, the leader would prefer, whether they will resolve the issue by sending her back into the streets to die of starvation. Finally a third and decent solution is found. It is decided to allow the girl and her brother to remain. She is to be unmolested by any member of the gang, and this, surprisingly, is what happens. Toward the end of the book, when the girl is dying of fever, she and Pedro Bala are brought together in a passionate union, an episode that is a masterpiece of emotional description unmarred, as I see it, by bathos.

Jorge Amado is never one to end his books hastily, as some authors are inclined to do. His last chapters receive as much care as the first. So it is with *Capitaes da Areia*. As the waifs grow older they must inevitably leave the group to find some sort of place for themselves in the adult world. The places that their creator finds for them [are] consistent with their lives up to the point of their leaving. Pedro Bala goes forth to become a labor leader

in the tradition of his father. The Professor, who had sometimes turned an honest penny by making sketches of passersby, becomes a successful artist who specializes in sketches of the life of the poor. Little Pill achieves his ambition to become a priest. The one truly incorrigible and sadistic member of the group, the lame boy, Two Stumps, commits suicide. But before this resolution of the book's problems comes about we have been held enthralled by a series of adventures in which this gang of outcasts finds our sympathies aroused in their behalf. Incidentally, this novel is probably the outstanding statement by Amado on the subject of social justice.

In an entirely different vein, and an outstanding example of Amado's remarkable gift for irony and satire, are the short story **"A Morte de Quincas Berro d'Agua"**, and the novel *A Completa verdade sobre as discutidas aventuras do comandante Vasco Moscoso d'Aragão*. In the Brazilian edition they are brought together in the same cover under the facetious title *Os Velhos marinheiros*. The opening short story is a marvelous spoof, far from the serious preoccupation with Bahia's orphans, or the fate of the peasants on the land. But in actuality this story, like a number of those of Maupassant, or even like those of Runyon, carries beneath its comical surface a bitter message about the humdrum and hypocritical character of Brazilian middle-class society.

The story of which Quincas Berro d'Agua is the hero tells of the death in a pestilential tenement of a formerly conventional civil servant, married to a dull wife and having dull people for in-laws. This man, at age fifty or thereabouts had simply walked out of his house and moved into the slums. There he became the darling of his new friends, that is to say, the loafers, the pimps, the gamblers, the drunkards and prostitutes with whom henceforth he solely associated. When his death became known the family of Quincas was of course relieved to hear it, and they reluctantly came to sit with the body and to prepare it for burial. Then tiring of their vigil in his dirty and stuffy quarters they made the mistake of leaving the corpse to be watched over by four of his closest and least respectable friends, the ex-army non-com Cabo Martim, the Negro Pastinha, a rogue named Curio, and the fourth a tramp named Pe de Vento. Once alone with the body of the dead man these four proceed to get drunk and—Amado tells this with a straight face—they see to it that the corpse has his share of the rum, which they dribble all over his new suit of clothes. They then swap clothes with him, dressing him in their cast-off rags. They half-carry and half-drag Quincas with them to a party. As a conclusion the corpse, which has shown signs of life, is put into a fishing boat with several of his comrades to sail out to sea, and to die for a second time. This is gross but very good farce. But the inference plainly is that the life that drove Quincas to cast in his lot with the dregs of society was basically as detestable as it was smug; just as the life he lived in the slums while not respectable was as vibrant with life and excitement, as it was unaffected by stuffy morality.

The novel which accompanies this short farce tells the life story of a very different sort of escapist. This tale also has vast quantities of farce and irony in its composition. It relates, or alternately relates and then denies that it is true, the story of the life of a so-called sea captain. As a young man, Vasco Moscoso had cordially despised the commercial success of his grandfather, and, taking after his ne'er-do-well father, he became an idler about town. His chosen associates are a commander in the Brazilian navy, an army colonel, a lawyer, with the title doctor, and a lieutenant. None of these men works very hard at his profession, but all are admired and bitterly envied for their titles by their inseparable comrade Moscoso d'Aragão, that is, by Senhor or Mister Vasco Moscoso d'Aragão. To help him acquire a title of his own his friends, and especially the commander, conspire to have him take the examinations for master mariner. In preparation for it he is tutored and bullied until the examination is taken and passed. Vasco thus becomes in law if not in fact a full-fledged master mariner and entitled to be called Captain. From this moment on Captain Vasco is every inch the sailor. He fills his house with sextants, barometers, chronometers and other naval gear. He is never seen out of uniform, a uniform which bears a decoration which his friends procured for him from Portugal. He lards his conversation with tales of his heroism on the deep and impresses his cardplaying cronies with his salty personality. The crunch comes when circumstances finally force him to take command of a ship on a brief coastal voyage. The prospect both delights and terrifies him. But in uniform he is a hit with the passengers and he solves nautical problems by leaving them to the regular ship's officers. He only comes a cropper when he is required by custom to take personal charge of docking the ship, and when asked how many hawsers to use and how many anchors to drop he shouts desperately "All of them". The laughs are loud and long, for even the passengers can see that the bogus captain has secured his ship as if for imminent arrival of a typhoon. You have guessed it. A typhoon is exactly what occurs and Captain Vasco's ship, alone of all those in port at the time, suffers no damage. He is the hero of the hour and the one skeptic in his neighborhood is so thoroughly cowed that he leaves town. Once again social satire is carefully disguised as fun and humor, but we hardly need a key like that which accompanies the reading of *Finnegan's Wake* to perceive that all is not well in a society where titles are awarded without much care for their meaning. And this is not all. The fact that the captain and his four friends, who occupy places of consideration in society spend much if not all their time in and out of houses of prostitution and that drinking and cardplaying occupy the rest of their time is Amado's way of laughing at Bahia society. At least sinners and grifters have a good time, he says, and that is more than can be said of the straitlaced and so-called respectable elements of society.

Of special interest here is his unique way of telling the captain's story. Two narrators alternate in telling the tale. The first is the novelist himself who is the usual all-seeing, omniscient writer whose attitudes and feelings are revealed only through his characters. The second putative narrator, who alternates with the author, is a fatuous, self-styled poet and historian who tells us a great deal about himself and yet pretends to be open-minded about the truth concerning Captain Vasco's history and adventures. He also provides sardonic comments on the life and character of a certain jurist of scholarly reputation with whom he shares a black mistress. This second narrator, then, becomes an additional character in the novel, and by using him the novelist can indulge in some very rich and ripe humor.

As we leave the adventures of the old sailors we should not fail to remark that these two stories, like all of Amado's fiction, are replete with sensuality. The American Damon Runyon says somewhere that "if you give a woman a couple of children she will let you alone," and one of his characters says concerning a certain beautiful woman something to [the] effect that he would not get involved with any woman no matter how attractive. Such downgrading of sex and the relegating of it to a subordinate place in a man's life is a long way from the whole-hearted acceptance and enjoyment of sexual phenomena that are part and parcel of the philosophy of Jorge Amado. For him a life devoid of women would be no life at all. This is shown everywhere in his work. But two novels illustrate the importance of women in a special way. I refer to *Tereza Batista* and *Gabriela*. The former relates the unhappy adventures of a girl destined by the early flowering of her beauty to be forever a temptation to men. The novel is in fact little more than a paean in praise of Tereza. The same thing may be said of Gabriela, a kind of innocent charmer, the gentle friend of all the men who know her. The American reader must constantly remind himself that none of the sillier aspects of our racist views is relevant in Brazil. Gabriela, like Tereza, is part black and none the worse for that.

Terras do sem fim echoes the same preoccupations, although it may be argued that Amado's women, attractive though they are, have less personality than his men. He is, I believe, a master at portraying men, especially rogues and scoundrels. As for his women, they do not always succeed in becoming individuals, but at times merely represent "woman" or women in general. This is especially true when Amado tries to depict a good woman, from the better classes of society. And although no one can accuse our author of any Puritanical nonsense he does at times seem to be so overawed in the presence of his own decent women characters that they become a trifle inane. Their very respectability deprives them of the ability to display their natural human instincts, and since he does not endow them with any intellectuality they seem frigid and sterile.

The tapestry that Amado's fictions have woven over the years is rich in types as well as in individuals. Each new novel that I read by him, and I make no pretense of having read them all, is sheer delight, for the language, for the descriptions, for the situations and for the people that he creates. If the ability to create living and unforegettable characters is the mark of the great novelist, then Amado is destined a permanent place of honor, among the world's great storytellers. (pp. 340–44)

L. Clark Keating, "The Guys and Dolls of Jorge Amado," in *Hispania*, Vol. 66, No. 3, September, 1983, pp. 340–44.

BERTA SICHEL WITH JORGE AMADO
(interview date 1984)

[In the following excerpt from an interview, Amado offers his views on authorship, the success of his works abroad, his native Brazil, and the socio-political focus of his fiction.]

If Gabriel García Márquez opened the way for Mario Vargas Llosa, Carlos Fuentes, Ernesto Cardenal and many other Latin American writers in Spanish, it was Jorge Amado who did the same for the Brazilian authors. This writer from Bahia, who doesn't like to talk about himself, was the first to tell the world of Bahia, of Brazil and its people. He was the first to demonstrate that Brazilian literature is less homogeneous than that produced in other Latin American countries since it is a product of the cultural diversity of a vast country.

In Brazil they say that Jorge Amado has done more for Brazilian culture than have all the government departments for the advancement of culture in the history of the republic. His work includes 26 titles, 684 Brazilian and 40 Portuguese editions, and 260 translations into over 40 languages. But as he turned 70 two years ago, he merely said of himself that "I am a sensual and romantic Brazilian who lives the admirable life of the Bahian people."

[Sichel]: *Could you give us a brief chronicle of how your works have fared abroad?*

[Amado]: My books have been read in translation for many years. The first, *Cacau,* was translated into Spanish and published in Buenos Aires in 1935. . . . *Jubiabá*, in 1938, was the first French translation. . . . The first into Russian dates from 1937, and the first into English was in 1945. After World War II my books began to be widely translated into the major languages—French, English, German, Russian, Italian, Spanish, Chinese—as well as into more diverse and rare languages. In Russia my books are translated into some ten languages other than Russian. . . . I now am published in 42 languages. There are many pirated editions—in Greek, Arabic, Turkish and Persian, for example. Every now and then I learn that a book of mine has been translated into a rare language like Korean or Mongolian. In some languages I have a strong audience, I'm widely read; in others, literary success hasn't been matched by success in sales, at least for the time being. I think this happens to writers everywhere. (p. 17)

Do you think that the translation of your work can serve a social purpose in the United States or in Europe?

The growing solidarity with our people can help. I think I win friends for Brazil—I know of many who became interested in Brazil after reading my books.

What can a foreigner—a European or a North American—learn about Brazil from reading your work?

I think they can get an idea of Brazilian reality with its immense contradictions, its dramatic poverty and its obstinate, invincible people born from the mix of bloods, races and cultures. My books reflect Brazilian reality and are portraits of my people.

Do you consider yourself a political writer?

Every writer is political, even those who think they have nothing to do with politics, since the mere act of writing is a political act—the writer exerts influence on the readers, and this is a political action. I am a writer who basically deals with social themes, since the source material for my creation is Brazilian reality. . . . [Many of my] novels narrate the life of the people, everyday life, the struggle against extreme poverty, against hunger, the large estates, racial prejudice, backwardness, underdevelopment. The hero of my novels is the Brazilian people. My characters are the most destitute, the most needy, the most oppressed—country and city people without any power other than the strength of the mestizo people of Brazil. They say that I am a novelist of whores and vagabonds, and there is truth in that, for my characters increasingly are anti-heroes. I believe that only the people struggle selflessly and decently, without hidden motives.

Do you believe that literature should have a commitment?

I believe every writer has the right to carry out his own literary work as he sees fit—whether or not he may have a political commitment, take a position on the struggle of the people, write about the social situation or the personal problems of a human being. Each one is master of his own way of existing and creating. Personally, I consider myself to be a writer with a commitment, a writer who is for the people and against their enemies, who develops his work around the reality of Brazil, discussing the country's problems, touching on the dramatic existence of the people and their struggle. I believe that commitment in no way diminishes the quality of the work. However I also believe that the quality of literary work does not depend on the author's degree of commitment.

The only thing of which I totally disapprove is official literature, from any side, for whatever regime it may serve. Literature commissioned as propaganda for governments or political parties will always be limited, momentary, incidental and dogmatic.

As a political writer, could you make a comparison between political literature of the 1930's and that of the 1970's?

I find the political literature of the 1930's was more romantic, broader, less manipulative. The political literature of the present is more limited, conventional, generally more dogmatic, at least as dogmatic as the literature in the 1950's that responded to Stalinism. Of course, there are exceptions. Lately in Brazil some books have been published that are documents of genuine interest; some of them are powerful as well as beautiful, like the books of Gabeira, who is a real writer. It's also worth mentioning with regard to political literature of the 1930's (including early Soviet literature, so free, so strong and spontaneous, in contrast to the later, Stalinist literature) that it was creative literature—poetry, short stories, novels, theater. The current output is inclined to be documentary.

Is Brazil the only Latin American country that has diverse cultural centers? How do you fit into this heterogeneity?

Diverse cultural centers undoubtedly do exist in Brazil, and happily so. But there also exist a very strong national unity that is reflected in our literature. Erico Veríssimo is as Brazilian a writer as José Américo de Almeida, for even though they come from different cultural areas, they exhibit the same Brazilian spirit. It is necessary to understand this phenomenon in order to understand Brazil. I am a Brazilian writer who comes from the culture of Bahia. On the other hand, I don't believe in the existence of what's conventionally referred to as "Latin American literature." What does exist is literature from different countries in Latin America, each with its own characteristics. What the devil does an Argentine writer have in common with a writer from Cuba?

The critics classify your work as regionalist. How do you interpret this view?

Critics can be extremely funny when they're not [offensive]. All of us writers from the northeast have been tagged regionalists. Nevertheless, we are the ones who have had the most general impact.

What do you think of the current output of Brazilian literature?

I look at it optimistically. Much is being written and published. Naturally there are some bad things, but out of it all emerge writers of true quality. They will endure and move our literature ahead.

There is something magical in your work, something that penetrates not only Brazilian society, but also others. To what do you attribute this?

Linda Rabben on Jorge Amado:

It's a mistake to see Jorge Amado as either a great literary artist or a soft-core pornographer, although North American reviewers have characterized him as both. The grand old man of Brazilian letters is, rather, a twentieth-century Charles Dickens: master craftsman, sentimental hack, great storyteller, vulgarian. Like Dickens, he pleases the literary masses while unsettling the elite, who cannot decide whether to hold him in esteem or contempt. One of the last exemplars of a regional tradition whose roots stretch down to the bedrock of classical pastoral, he is also a political novelist in a distinctively modern vein. His protagonists are the wretched of the earth, idealized beyond belief.

Linda Rabben, in her "The Boys from Brazil," *The Nation* (14 May 1988).

The magic of the Brazilian people. Bahia, the principal setting for my books, is a magical land—the city as well as the state. We are a mestizo people, of an intense culture, and every one of us is a magician.

From your point of view, what role does your work play in the Brazilian context?

I influence the mass readership. I am a writer read by a large audience in my country. I transmit a positive message of confidence, struggle, resistance and hope. (pp. 17–19)

Jorge Amado and Berta Sichel, in an interview in *Américas*, Vol. 36, No. 3, May–June, 1984, pp. 16–19.

PAUL WEST
(essay date 1988)

[West is an Anglo-American educator and critic distinguished for his writings in numerous genres, including poetry, the essay, criticism, biography, and the novel. An admirer of Latin American fiction because it "takes risks," West has described the unifying theme of his own writings as the "trauma of being alive, existing, in light of the fact that we're determined by givens out of our control." In the following review of Amado's *Showdown*, West comments favorably on themes, style, and characterization in the novel.]

The only calendar in Tocaia Grande—it was a New Year's gift—hangs outside the dry cacao storehouse, more a toy borrowed from the cradle of time than anything practical.

It pictures a mountain snowscape and a big hairy dog under whose chin hangs a small cask. From the print there dangles a booklet of numbered leaves, a few of which old Gerino now and then peels away, mainly out of gratitude. No wonder life in this verdant riverside shantytown among the cacao groves of South Bahia remains "permanently behind time," thwarting not only those who need to clock the rains and the harvests along the Rio das Cobras, but also Fadul the Turk who owns the canteen and wants to collect punctually on his loans. Nobody even knows which day is Sunday.

That central image in Jorge Amado's new novel suggests that for many years nobody knew which year it was, but the calendar endured, a holy relic. *Showdown* tells how one green and pleasant place grew and died, then grew again, uplifted into squalid village and then suaver town by the grit and vision of successive settlers hell-bent on making a living from those who worked the cocoa crop. So, there had to be a provisions store, a blacksmith and, later on, a dentist, a church and an exclusive club. Indeed, this might be the story of Brazil itself, seen through a dark glass lovingly, honed into a compact metaphor implying a whole nation's tumultuous vigor, its addiction to the life force in hyperbole and, most of all, the capacity for ecstasy of its poor, whose brand of Calvinism has had to let life be bleak and short, so long as it was picturesque. *Showdown* hoists into the light a country whose imagination is its finest crop, but one it cannot eat.

The book abounds in festively elegiac emblems. Each has a powerful effect on that part of the narrative in which it first appears, but all of them resonate throughout the book as well—like the ambush or showdown of the title. It haunts the mind throughout the novel because Tocaia Grande grew near to an improvised hill cemetery dug after a famous ambush in which one of two feuding colonels lost all 27 of his men.

Everyone in the town is to some extent ambushed by time, and by a quaint fecklessness that combines the mood of John Steinbeck's "Sweet Thursday" with that of James Hilton's "Lost Horizon". They all dream and fornicate timelessly, and they are ambushed or "hidden in the bushes" forever, as if Mr. Amado were saying they belong as much to myth as to calendars. Being killed in an ambush by someone in hiding isn't much different from being killed by a deity in hiding too.

"Tocaia Grande" means "big ambush" or "showdown" anyway, and the place has already had more than its share of fame, from events to which there can be no comparable sequel. Or can there be? Mr. Amado's neatly designed chronicle obliges you to wonder which is the worse delusion: a calendar tossed capriciously aside unmarked, or one marked all over with appointments, trips, rendezvous and red letter days. I can think of only one similarly powerful use of this image: in Jean Genet's "Miracle of the Rose," we are told that a man serving a long sentence writes out the calendar of his entire sentence and pastes the sheet to the walls of his cell, thus getting one awful eyeful of his wasted days but at the same time possessing his doom physically, as if it were an artifact or even a person.

But that is not the mood of *Showdown*. Mr Amado gives a portrait of the settlement every bit as beguiling and picturesque as the portrait of a woman was in his *Gabriela, Clove and Cinnamon*. This teeming scene is almost a palette-knife painting of a pioneer nation trapped between the ancient gods of the forest and the new ones of commerce, only to be overwhelmed (for a while) by the sheer force of a river in spate.

Showdown is a vital novel, more complex than it seems at first, written in a long series of ebullient lunges, none of them stylish or notably elegant or eloquent, but in sum haunting and massive. Mr. Amado's prose in his other books sometimes has all the elegance of a badly combed turnip, but here he creates something fecund and funny, tender and burly, as if his lively social conscience, under pressure, had yet again had to take the side of the human race. No doubt *Showdown* would make a compelling movie, but it is essentially a verbal performance. It is only in the words that you can savor Mr. Cicero Moura, a gonorrhea sufferer also known as "Dr Permanganate," who rides "a slow and steady donkey" named Envelope; or such animals as Peba's rheas, seriemas and *currasows*; or woods called *putumuju*, pink peroba and jacaranda; and a conga line of whores named "Dalila, Epifânia, Bernarda, Zuleica, Margarida Cotó, Two-Ton Marieta, Cotinha, Dorita, Teté, and Silvia Pornambuco" (that name teems with both geography and lust). Only Jacinta Coroca, an overworked midwife, is omitted from the catalogue because "she was worth more than all the others put together" and because, when Apagio made to pull his revolver, she kicked him in a place so private that his shriek was heard three and a half leagues away.

The atavistic pleasure in this novel comes from jungle words as well as jungle ways. The characters, almost too many to remember are like revelers from the apocalyptic New Year in which Gerino received the first calender. During a sudden flood the inhabitants save the children by passing them along a chain of prople standing on the 12 wooden beams of the battered bridge, and after the flood they rebuild the settlement. Indeed, the book is almost a chain of tableaux dedicated to human resilience, but you don't mind because Mr. Amado grounds even the most minor character-drawing in anecdotal devotion to detail.

There are enough characters in *Showdown* to allow almost everyone to pick a favorite. Mine include Castor Abdulm the black blacksmith, a horseshoer who turned horse doctor, and then dentist and busybody; Venturinha, the lawyer son of Col. Boaventura Andrade, who is unable to tear himself away from the fleshpots of Rio, where he endlessly trains himself to take over his father's lands; and Jussara, a widow and heiress whose body inflames Fadul the Turk, at least until he realizes she is trying to trick him into marriage, whereupon he thinks of giving her "the amount of money corresponding to the usual payment to a whore for an afternoon in bed."

Mr. Amado reveals Fadul at his most private, by the light of a small lamp counting his money and placing it in a big red bandanna, then putting his copper and nickel coins in two pieces of paper that go into a small leather bag. Off he goes to replace his stock of dried meats, cane liquor, brown sugar and cotton pants at the marketplaces. We get a similarly private view of him out in the woods: "He dove into the river, cleaning off the sweat, the stink of bedbugs and his nighttime visions. He cleaned his teeth by rubbing them with a plug of tobacco; he blew on the embers to revive the coals under the iron trivet, an Asian luxury acquired at cost in payment for a debt in Taquaras." Gazing at the so-called ladies' bidet, a river pool with a waterfall, where the whores bathe and do their laundry, he is "the Grand Turk surveying his empire."

Mr. Amado is not renowned for depicting people at their most intimate, or for intimating the unspoken thought that sinks back uncompleted into the slurry of consciousness where Nathalie Sarraute is queen; but sometimes, as in *Showdown*, he gets the reader close to his characters by observing keenly the externals of mental turnover rather than by probing directly. A mentally handicapped girl who runs after pigs wants so much to be a mother that she shoves clumps of sedge under her dress, at one point pretending to give birth to a piglet. She drowns in the flood, but a sky-blue flower mysteriously appears in her hands. One of the whores, writing to Fadul, inscribes "a number of commas, apostrophes, accent marks, exclamation points, and question marks" under her signature for him to distribute as he wishes throughout her unpunctuated letter.

The delicacy of Mr. Amado in such matters is the perfect foil for a novel whose dominant mode is histrionic and tumultuous. We are dealing as much with easygoing magic here as with psychology: we read that Dodo the birdman barber keeps a dove to pull gray hairs from his head as they appear. Mr. Amado tips the horn of plenty with a practiced swing, not so much copying a world as creating it. And he is not without irony. The last incarnation of Tocaia Grande is a city named Irisópolis, with bungalows and villas, English cobblestones and a Masonic lodge, a social club and a literary society. About all that the narrator's comment is pithy enough: "*isn't worth mentioning, holds no interest.*"

Gregory Rabassa's translation from the Portuguese is nimble and robust. Mr. Amado doesn't give him much scope for subtle wordplay, but Mr. Rabassa's own sense of humor matches exactly that of the book.

The novel's final images of Tocaia Grande are of the "no-name fever" that "reduced the strongest man to a rag before killing him"; Venturinha giving his father a

stroke by heading off for further studies at Oxford and the Sorbonne; the sea on the beaches of Ilhéus (a real town) turning to foam; confessionals being set up in the dry-cacao shed; pigs being shot in the streets with the arrival of law and order; and the final massacre in which Coroca leads the town's defenders against a military force led by a sergeant with a "big old nickel-plated pocket watch."

Much of this ribald, epic novel could not be quoted in this newspaper, but it evinces a compassion as big as Brazil itself. One leaves it as one leaves new, exciting friends, wondering how much of an accident it is that the dying Dodo produces from his bullet-riddled chest a bird. (pp. 3, 37)

Paul West, "Ambushed in the Cacao Groves," in *The New York Times Book Review*, February 7, 1988, pp. 3, 37.

NELSON H. VIEIRA

(essay date 1989)

[In the following essay, Vieira examines the "role of race in *Tenda dos Milagres*' narrative scheme with the aim of clarifying Amado's ideological stance along with his allegorical treatment of this theme."]

Recognized as Brazil's bestselling novelist and acclaimed as a socially-committed writer of the Afro-Brazilian reality in his homeland, Jorge Amado incorporates history, myth and fantasy in his fiction for the purpose of recreating the unique saga and mindset of the Brazilian masses, an economically impoverished but spiritually hopeful people. Also, frequently depicted as a racially as well as politically oppressed group, Amado's *povo* represents an implacable force allegorically interpreted as a manifestation of the nation's irrepressible vitality despite the chronic rise of political regimes of stifling authoritarian power. As a socially-conscious writer of national and international importance, Amado has through his exuberant prose and political derring-do become a national institution in Brazil, where his public statements are scrutinized for their inherent message but, more often than expected, for their political relevancy and accuracy vis-à-vis the country's national reality. Criticized as a writer of lusty and folksy narratives in which the Brazilian poor invariably win daily battles of inspirational but illusory gain, Amado has too often been misinterpreted in his concommitant roles of novelist, political activist and outspoken national figure. As a result, Amado over the years has managed to be the source of many polemics where his use of fact and fiction, history and allegory, is easily misunderstood by those desperately searching for concrete answers to national problems. Such a controversy has been sparked by Amado's conceptual depiction of racial mixture in Brazilian society.

In an interview for the American press on the occasion of the English translation of his novel *Tenda dos Milagres* [*Tent of Miracles*], Jorge Amado was quoted in the daily *O Estado de S. Paulo* (Oct 9, 1971) as saying the following: "Meu país é uma verdadeira democracia racial. . . " [My country is a true racial democracy. . . .] That comment, considered a well-known and convenient platitude disseminated by the State and by those who professed the absence of racial prejudice for purposes of creating a positive international image of Brazil, supplied more material to the plethora of criticism already aimed against Brazil's internationally known storyteller. The myth of a racial democracy, implying equality for all races in Brazil, has long been contested by many Brazilian scholars and "Brazilianists," particularly since the landmark work of the Brazilian sociologist Florestan Fernandes. This Brazilian myth of racial equality, based upon Brazil's history of racial mixture and promoted in the 1930's by famous sociologist Gilberto Freyre with his "Luso-Tropicalist" theory, lost some credibility against other arguments and studies which black activists such as Abdias do Nascimento have championed. By pointing to the lack of political representation and socio-economic justice for Brazil's 35–50% black plurality, Abdias and others have helped to unmask the insidious aspects of the racial situation in Brazil. Famous studies by Degler, Skidmore, Brookshaw, and others have implied that racial equality was indeed a myth that the State was suspected of promoting. Over the years this issue has continued to spur a series of bitter debates and polemics, one of the most provocative being the "in-house" battle reactivated in 1983 by Abdias do Nascimento, who called Jorge Amado a racist because he interpreted the Bahian novelist's use of the term 'racial democracy' as an indication of his refusal to acknowledge the existence of racial prejudice in Brazil. As a writer, but especially in his role as a Federal Deputy (PDT-RJ), Abdias do Nascimento publicly protested the motion of support accorded to Jorge Amado by the Legislative Assembly of Bahia.

Given this heated controversy and impassioned discussion, how does one then reconcile Jorge Amado's detailed depiction of Brazil's racial bigotry and repression in his works with the afore-mentioned quote and accusation? Particularly, how are we to read the novel *Tenda dos Milagres,* which is recognized as *the* one novel of his more-than-twenty titles which most directly addresses the issue of race relations in Brazil while enthusiastically defending Afro-Brazilian culture, a narrative that appears to be in clear opposition to the "public" statement made by Amado? Not surprisingly, the validity of Amado's ethics and advocacy regarding Afro-Brazilians, so flagrantly and consistently portrayed in his narratives, is, in the face of such a statement, questioned by such activists as Abdias do Nascimento.

In light of the above observations, this study proposes to examine the role of race in *Tenda dos Milagres'* narrative scheme with the aim of clarifying Amado's ideological stance along with his allegorical treatment of this theme. Attention will also be given to the work's sense of history via its temporal structure, the technique used by Amado to present, above all, the history and issue of racial, and on equal footing, political repression in Brazil—a reality which finds its objective correlative mirrored here in the violence and persecution perpetrated by authoritarian whites against an economically oppressed Afro-Brazilian population. In fact, the issues of social, political and/or economic repression have become the cornerstone of every novel written by Marxist-inspired Amado, with the oppressed *povo* being the victims, frequently embodied by the nation's Afro-Brazilian population. This personification is most evident in such works as *Jubiabá, Gabriela, Os Pastores da Noite,* and *Tenda dos Milagres.* However, it is the latter, published in 1969, which provides the most incisive and multi-dimensional portrayal of the authoritarian proclivities emanating from political and racial repression in a society where the various elites are fraught with the preoccupation of appearance and maintaining the status quo. Written and published during the darkest hour of Brazil's former military rule—known colloquially as the *sufoco*—, this novel must be read within that historical timeframe, since allusions to Brazilian history in the novel's complex temporal structure continually serve as insightful clues to Amado's allegorical reportage and testimony of the repressive 1968–69 period, a time when explicit statement always ran the risk of being censored.

Evaluating Brazilian literature written in the 60's and 70's, critics such as Silviano Santiago, Roberto Schwartz, Flora Sussekind, and Heloísa Buarque de Hollanda have repeatedly referred to the allegorical nature of works which reported the reality of that period in a para-journalistic fashion. Among the myriad writers using allegory, Jorge Amado comes to mind because he draws heavily upon this form of symbolism to recreate his unique view of Brazilian life. If we consider one of Northrop Frye's more obvious definitions of allegory [in his *Anatomy of Criticism*, 1968], its applicability to Amado as well as to many other writers is immediately apparent: "A writer is being allegorical whenever it is clear that he is saying 'by this I *also* (*allos*) mean that.'" In a related sense, Frye also states: "Commentary thus looks at literature as, in its formal phase, a potential allegory of events and ideas." Since Amado's works are frequently supercharged with historical events and ideas which reflect, via his dynamic personages or figures, social history and, moreover, a Brazilian "intrahistorical chain of events," we shall also consider Eric Auerbach's view on allegory [in his *Mimesis*, 1946] for a related theoretical framework. Auerbach's use of "figural interpretation" for allegory, in terms of his reference to the antique conception of history, provides us with a working premise for understanding Amado's keen perception as to the inter-related patterns of events in Brazilian history and their mutual allegorical potentialty. According to Auerbach:

> Figural interpretation establishes a connection be-tween two events or persons in such a way that the first signifies not only itself but also the second, while the second involves or fulfills the first. The two poles of a figure are separated in time, but both, being real events or persons, are within temporality.

It is this figural treatment of history that pervades Amado's narrative.

In *Tenda dos Milagres*, the juxtaposition of various time periods enables Amado to draw upon the intercon-nections between events or situations that manifest racial and political repression. With such a structure, Amado demonstrates that the recurring paradigm of repression and authoritarianism is an inherent part of Brazil's social history. In other words, the Afro-Brazilian experience of racial oppression also becomes an extended metaphor for identifying and condemning socio-economic inequality and political repression as a repeated practice on the part of Brazil's ruling elites. Or, as Joan Dassin stated in her 1979 study ["Tent of Miracles: Myth of Racial Democ-racy," Jump Cut, No. 21, November 1979] of Nelson Pereira dos Santos' film version of Amado's novel: "...the rule of force endured by white Brazilian society since the military seized power fifteen years ago has *always* been the norm for black Brazilians." It is therefore our con-tention that the allegorical or figurative relationship be-tween racial oppression and political repression within the scope of History is crucial to understanding Amado's view of Afro-Brazilians in Brazilian society. This allegory also has implications for his use of the term 'racial democ-racy'. However, it is obvious that the above relationship does not immediately clarify Amado's motivation or in-tent behind his public statement on racial democracy. As a matter-of-fact, it appears to confound the issue even more.

If, on the one hand, Amado, within his novels, de-picts rampant racial discrimination in Brazil, how can he refer to the existence of a racial democracy on the other? Is he being a hypocritical racist as some would like to be-lieve? Is this another example of the ambiguous nature of Brazilian race relations or merely one more blatant contra-diction for "Brazilianists" to deride? Perhaps the answer lies somewhere within the very complex problem of un-derstanding Brazil's race relations and Brazil's historically problematic political scene. In this vein, *Tenda dos Mi-lagres* may serve as a possible key to Amado's meaning of a racial democracy, and by extension, may perhaps of-fer a preliminary clue to the rationale behind his public statement.

The novel's mulatto protagonist, Pedro Archanjo, a runner/messenger at the university medical school, is a self-taught anthropoloigist, bon-vivant and cult priest who documents and writes about the customs and tra-ditions of Afro-Brazilian life in Bahia. Much to the dis-pleasure of the European-oriented antagonist, Professor Argolo—a white supremacist who wants to rid Bahia of all its mulatto population—, Archanjo becomes a spokesman and leader for the Afro-Brazilian community. Publishing his studies with the help of his friend's printing press, housed in the Tent of Miracles, where the devout come to order miracle pictures as an expression of gratitude for having their prayers answered, Pedro Archanjo, a form of divine messenger as suggested by his family name and his nickname, the "Eyes of God," spreads the word about the extensive effect of racial blood mixture across all lev-els of Bahian society. When the first page of messenger Archanjo's first book on Bahian life is printed, the very first sentence is seen as "seu clarim de guerra, sua palavra de ordem, resumo de seu saber, sua verdade" [his mar-tial buglecall to arms, his truth, the sum of his knowl-edge]. This first sentence reads as follows: "É mestica a face do povo brasileiro e é mestica a sua cultura". [The face of the Brazilian people is a mestizo face, and its cul-ture is mestizo]. Emphasis should be placed upon the word "face" because reference is made to Argolo's and his colleague's faces as being mestizo like Archanjo's and his humble friend's. However, while *all* Bahians may be racially mestizo (including the racist Professor Argolo), it is obvious that not all are *culturally* mestizo: "São mesti-cas a nossa face e a vossa face: é mestica a nossa cultura, mas a vossa é importada, é merda em pó" [Our faces are mestizo faces, and so are yours; our culture is mestizo but yours is imported. It's nothing but powdered shit]. Here, Amado is making a sharp distinction between racial mixture and cultural differences, the latter possibly har-bouring culturally instilled discrimination and the former being an irrefutable fact, despite the circumstances of its origins. Consequently, the racial democracy he alludes to draws upon the actual mixed racial composition of Brazil-ians who may or may not be racial bigots. However, as we shall see, Amado also uses this term within a political context, one that will be explained once our allegorical premise is further delineated.

With these considerations in mind, discussion will now focus upon how the novel recreates a sense of Brazil-ian social history via allegory and the sophisticated juxta-position of different timeframes and different narrators. In terms of Amado's deft use of structure and point of view, Earl E. Fitz states the following: ". . . *Tenda dos Milagres* goes a long way toward dispelling the enduring and pernicious myth that Jorge Amado is not as tech-nically brilliant as he should be." From this stance, we propose to demonstrate how Amado's technical dexterity dramatizes the dynamics of multiple and contradictory perspectives within a given culture, while providing an historical sway and panorama vis-à-vis the relationship be-tween racial oppression and political repression in Brazil. At the same time, we intend to single out *Tenda dos Mila-*

gres as a powerful narrative of socio-political reference to the Brazil of 1968, one in which Amado's documentary-like reportage on race relations and violent political repression stands as testimony of that period.

Regarding the novel's time construct, the storyline begins in 1968, exactly one hundred years after the protagonist's birth, and is narrated by the somewhat unreliable but sympathetic Fausto Pena, a struggling young poet. Fausto Pena is hired by the handsome, blond American scholar/Nobel prize winner and distinguished Professor at Columbia University, Dr. James D. Levenson, to do research on Pedro Archanjo for an introduction to Levenson's English translation of the mulatto's works. Pena's 1968 first-person account, narrated in the present and interspersed throughout most of the novel, occupies approximately one-fourth of the book. The rest of the narrative, told by an omniscient voice, contrasts with that of the dramatized narrator by its more historically "objective" stance and its primary purpose of telling the actual truth about the past and the contradictions in Pedro Archanjo's life. Unknown to Brazil's literati until Levenson's discovery, and consequently a blank page of cultural history for the rest of the population, Pedro Archanjo's life and works are soon praised and consecrated as though the famous American's mere recognition of their overall ethnological merit justified this sudden interest and attention; this reaction being indicative of Brazil's need for approval from the outside, something Amado criticizes. Considered by Levenson to be indispensable reading for understanding the racial situation in Brazil, these acclaimed works quickly receive commercial attention that ultimately leads to local and national campaigns which, on inauthentic grounds, bombastically institutionalize Pedro Archanjo as a Brazilian hero. The hype and fanfare surrounding the created myth of Pedro Archanjo are described in the young Pena's narrative, which in turn conveys his own frustrated attempts as a failed scholar and poet in the face of the authoritarianism implicit in the establishment's sense of supremacy, nepotism, justice, and the status quo, a situation that hasn't varied very much since Archanjo's time and one that, moreover, has universal relevance:

> Para obter-se pequeno aplauso, nome nas colunas, citação em jornais e revistas, vasqueiros bafejos do sucesso, paga-se alto preço em compromissos, hipocrisias, silêncios, omissões—digamos de uma vez a palavra exata: baixezas. Quem se nega a pagar?

> [To earn a smattering of applause and to get one's name in the newspapers; to be quoted by columnists in magazines; in fact, for any slightest puff of success, one pays a high price in entangling commitments, hypocrisy, silences, omissions—in vileness, let's call a spade a spade. And who among us scorns to pay the price?]

Except, however, for his own short narrative, Pena

gives up the fight for getting at the truth and pulls out before telling the rest of Archanjo's story: "Não vejo por que recordar momentos maus e tristes quando a glória finalmente ilumina a figura do mestre baiano" [I see no reason to call to mind those bad, sad times, now that glory mantles the face of the great Bahian]. As a weak and cuckolded figure with good intentions, Pena represents the ambivalent artist or intellectual who in times of social and political crisis sells out in order to save his own skin. The following acknowledgement made during his last pages reveals more than he intends—ergo the reader's double perspective:

> No fundo do meu ser dorme um inconformado, um marginal da sociedade, um radical, um guerrilheiro e disso faço praça nas ocasiões devidas (atualmente vasqueiras e perigosas, não preciso explicar os motivos, estão na cara, como se diz).

> [In the depths of my ego there is a rebel, an outlaw, a radical, a guerrilla; and I don't hesitate to say so on suitable occasions (there aren't too many of those just now; it's hardly necessary to explain why not, the reason is staring us in the face, you might say).]

These thoughts may reflect the dilemma of many who are not part of this society's mainstream—the marginal poor, the political left and the mestizo. In this instance, the marginal position is embodied by a young, impoverished artist, intellectual and leftist who cannot overcome the establishment's economic and socio-political hurdles. This view of the 1968 period is epitomized by Pena's choice of words —*marginal, radical, inconformado* and *guerrilheiro*. The 1968 period and its repressive and authoritarian features are further evoked allegorically by such contemporary items as the greedy and unscrupulous advertising company, Doping Promoção e Publicidade S. A., and its financial supporters—SNI (Serviço Nacional de Informações) and the Police—obvious references to DOPS (Departamento de Ordem Política e Social), General Golberry and the Doctrine of National Security and Economic Development, important elements of the repressive state in 1960s. Preoccupied with the State's image and legitimacy, these groups and individuals dictated from 1964-73 a national rightist ideology based on authoritarianism. Other repressive measures of this period, reflective of the above ideology and manifested by such groups as the IPMs (Inquéritos Policiais Militares), the rightist TFP (Tradição, Família and Propriedade) and such paramilitary, vigilante elements as the Squadrons of Death, are mirrored respectively and allegorically in terms of political, racial and religious repression, with references being made to their existence within the respective historical period as well as across both Archanjo's and Pena's times. For example:

> . . . por ocasião da Assembléia Constituinte de 1934, houve quem desentranhasse dos arquivos da Câmara

as prospostas contidas na plaquete do professor Nilo Argolo: "Introdução ao Estudo de um Código de Leis de Salvação Nacional."

[On the occasion of the Constitutional Assembly of 1934 there were those who pulled out of the depths of the Chamber's archives the proposals contained in Professor Nilo Argolo's leaflet: "An Introduction to the Study of a Code of Laws for National Salvation."]

O professor Batista assumira recentemente a presidência da benemérita Associação de Defesa da Tradição, da Família e da Propriedade, sentia-se responsável pela segurança nacional.

[Professor Batista had recently assumed the presidency of the worthy Association in Defense of Tradition, the Family, and Private Property, and he felt a personal responsibility for the national security.]

. . . quatro membros da "escolta de facínoras" decantada nos jornais da oposição: "malta de assassinos promovidos a agentes de polícia pelo atual Governo do Estado. . . "

[four members of the "gangster bodyguard," as an opposition newspaper described them: "A gang of thugs promoted to police agents by the state government tries to destroy our presses."]

Also, the philosophy formulated in the early 60's at the Escola Superior de Guerra (The Brazilian War College) was, according to Maria Helena Moreira Alves, one of on-going war to protect the nation from the "enemy within." As a recurring cultural paradigm, this paranoid paternalism on the part of the military and civil authorities of the 60's is symbolized by Amado's depiction of the earlier timeframe of the 20's when the religious persecution of Afro-Brazilian priests and cult followers was carried out by the despotic District Police Chief, Pedrito Gordo. This earlier period is resurrected in order to illustrate the continuous authoritarian proclivities within specific elements of Brazilian society:

Ouvida pela imprensa governista a propósito da campanha da polícia, o professor Nilo Argolo a definiu com justeza e elogios "Guerra santa, cruzada bendita, a resgatar os foros de civilização de nossa terra conspurcada." Entusiasmado, comparou Pedrito Gordo a Ricardo Coração de Leão.

[In an interview in the government press *à propos* of the police campaign, Professor Nilo Argolo described it as righteous and praiseworthy: "a holy war, a holy crusade to recover the citadels of civilization in this besmirched city of ours." He enthusiastically compared Pedrito Gordo to Richard Coeur de Lion.]

By juxtaposing Pedro Archanjo's frustrations with those experienced by Fausto Pena in the late 60's, Amado establishes a historically figurative framework for his thesis on the insidious and never-waning nature of authority and repression as these bear upon race, politics and Afro-Brazilian religious beliefs. Consequently, besides serving

as a device for Amado's statement on cooptation, admittedly for some Brazilians an understandable reality and by-product of the 1968 period (see Flora Sussekind, *Literatura e Vida Literária*, 1985), the young Fausto Pena's situation, as he faces the economic and socio-political repression of the late 60's, also mirrors in part Archanjo's experience in the 20's and 30's, the latter's being a more noble struggle for racial and religious equality against the authoritative forces of oppression during his own age. (An allegorical evocation reverberating up to our own times is the parallel seen in the persecutions of the fictional priestess Mãe Majé Bassan and the real Mãe Menininha do Gantois, a victim of religious intolerance and misunderstanding, even up to her death in August, 1986.) Reflecting both negative and positive qualities, Fausto Pena's role also suggests the need to avoid judging all people in simplistic black and white terms. In so doing, Amado hints at the complex nature of the Brazilian and the human predicament. Given the feelings of ambivalence the reader may entertain toward Fausto Pena, as his two names appropriately evoke via his Faustian psyche of self-pity, Amado's decision to exit him prior to the novel's ideological finale is in concert with his program of establishing the true heroic nature of Pedro Archanjo. Disciple/archangel/messenger, Archanjo communicates to the reader by his example as role model. From his own experience in difficult socio-political times, he manifests an unwavering commitment to his beliefs. In the process, he points to his interpretation of racial mixture and repression in Brazil.

The parallels between racial oppression and political repression are enhanced even more within the omniscient narrator's wide timeframe, which offers a full account of Pedro Archanjo's life by differentiating between its facts and fictions. Here, the hero's humble beginnings are traced from 1868, when his black father, forcibly recruited to fight in Brazil's War with Paraguay, is killed—the violence of the 1868 war finding its contemporary counterpart, exactly 100 years later, in the severe repression and violence of 1968. The story follows Pedro to his position as messenger in the Bahian School of Medicine in 1900; and also during the time of his major publications (1904–1928) which cause a reactionary polemic by the racist Professor Argolo with his theories of Aryan superiority. Argolo is eventually discredited when Archanjo's research shows the "white" professor to be the "mulatto's" distant relative. This ironic situation points to the haughty pedant as the epitome of the prejudice and hatred engendered by a black/white dichotomy that can provoke divisiveness across *all* levels—racial, religious, economic, social, and political. Archanjo's defense of racial mixture, as a vehicle for achieving more social justice, leads to his imprisonment and to the destruction of the Tent of Miracles by the police. Later, this persecution takes on the Afro-Brazilian *terreiros* of worship, which are also destroyed by the police under the sanctified pretext of protecting the Brazilian nation and culture from the crime and corruption of pagan forces, i.e., non-Christian, non-Latin and non-European elements.

While Fausto Pena's narrative closed with Archanjo's imprisonment, the omniscient narrator resumes the rest of the story, paralleling the indigent mulatto's poverty and death in 1943 with background allusions to Naziism and Hitler's genocide program, thereby showing one of the dangerous results of belief in Aryan supremacy. Before dying, Archanjo, always the messenger/crusader, reminisces over his lifelong battle against the evil forces of bigotry and exhorts those who are to come after him to close the "gates" of division between the races by making the mixture of blood more complete. In short, he advocates the "browning" of Brazil. After the omniscient narrator describes the hypocritical pomp surrounding the 1968 commercialized centennial celebration of Archanjo's birth, promoted by Bahia's politicians, businessmen, the State, and puffed-up academicians, the novel ends a few months later with the 1969 *Carnaval* where Archanjo's glory is celebrated honestly and in true popular fashion. More authentic to his life and more festive than the centennial, this popular tribute in the colorful streets of Bahia, in the form of a samba school's musical theme and allegorical floats, symbolizes the mulatto Archanjo's victimization and tribulations, but also his humane and *democratic* sense of life.

The symbol of racial mixture as a possible solution to minimizing Brazil's cultural and political divisiveness is the novel's main motif, reflecting the perspective which emerges from Pedro Archanjo's studies and teachings. A passage from his book, *Influências Africanas nos Costumes da Bahia*, however, demonstrates the truly profound character of Archanjo's vision—one which does not limit mixture to race alone but to culture as well. In other words, racial mixture is seen as a vehicle for eventually *overcoming*, in the future, such existing cultural barriers as social, political, religious, and economic prejudices which operate from top to bottom and are passed on from one generation of elites to the next:

> Formar-se-á uma cultura mestiça de tal maneira poderosa e inerente a cada brasileiro que será a própria consciência nacional e mesmo os filhos de pais e mães imigrantes, brasileiros de primeira geração, crescerão culturalmente mestiços.

> [A mestizo culture is taking shape, so powerful and innate in every Brazilian that in time it will become the true national consciousness, and even children of immigrant fathers and mothers, first-generation Brazilians, will be cultural mestizos by the time they are grown.]

Unfortunately, this "cultural" (read class) mixture will take longer to materialize than the racial (read biological). Never blindly idealistic, Pedro Archanjo recognizes the difficulty in reaching "cultural" equality. He articulates this perception toward the end of his life after the disappointing experience with his own son, Tadeu Canhoto, a mulatto engineer who "sells out" by marrying a white girl from a rich, traditional family. Tadeu's marriage represents a further step in the mixing process; however, as Archanjo realizes, it is done at a price, the maintenance of the status quo: ". . . no Corredor da Vitória o dinheiro embranquece, aqui miséria negra" [In the Corredor da Vitória money makes you white, and here in Tabuão Street poverty makes you black]. Consequently, the cultural "browning" of Brazilian society is sacrificed to the supremacy of economic "whitening". As a young man climbing the financial ladder to success, Tadeu gives up his role and life in the Tent of Miracles and effects no change except for that related to his own self-interest. Despite his "success", as other readers and critics have noted, Tadeu, considered to be a good boy, is, nevertheless not portrayed as an exemplary figure, as is his father. In fact, Tadeu is, in the eyes of his father as he takes his leave for the last time, "circunspecto e distante." In the eyes of the implied author, the irony in the different fates of father and son is further emphasized by the ambivalence implied in the names for the son. Tadeu, for the good Saint Jude, contrasts with Canhoto which, besides meaning left-handed, is also used as a nickname for the devil. Ergo, the implication of possible betrayal, or at least of being non-committal. While Pedro is incapable of renouncing his son, it is clear that for change to take place, racial mixture alone is not enough—cultural and economic divisiveness still exist. This attitude is implied at the close of the above scene when Pedro discusses Tadeu and racial mixture with his close friend Lídio Corró:

> A divisão de branco e negro, meu bom, se acaba na mistura, em nossa mão já se acabou, compadre. A divisão agora é outra e quem vier atrás feche as cancelas.

> [The dividing line between white and black, *meu bom*, will end when the mixing is complete; and we've done out part, *compadre*. Now there is another kind of dividing line, and whoever comes behind has to close the gates.]

Although Pedro and Lídio have done their part to generate the mixture while they were young—the randy Archanjo even having fathered a son with the white Finnish woman Kirsi—the division or separation of the races still goes on. It is up to the next generation to carry on the struggle and close the gates of cultural and class divisiveness. Until the image and reality of economic success reach the *mestizo*, the prejudices will continue. This allusion to the division among the races in Brazil is repeated at the close of the novel, just before Pedro Archanjo dies on the streets in the Pelourinho, the neighborhood which symbolizes the old system of punishment and authority frequently imposed upon slaves.

Thus, to suggest that Amado is racist or ambiguous with regard to race relations in Brazil is to misread this novel's underlying theme as well as to misunderstand his public statements. While Amado is professing racial mixture via Pedro Archanjo's voice, he is not implying that the mixture of blood alone will solve the problems. There are too many incidents in the novel that suggest otherwise and which demonstrate Amado's acute awareness of the existence of racial prejudice in Brazil. For example, when trying to pursuade Tadeu's future father-in-law to disregard the young man's skin color, a lawyer friend affirms the following: "O que lhe impressiona, prezado coronel, é a cor não a raça" ["What appears to weigh most with you, my dear Colonel, is color, not race"]. This statement also calls to mind Anani Dzidzienyo's monograph on the Brazilian criteria of 'boa aparência' (good appearance) in color as the means of categorizing individuals according to race and class. By also addressing the issue of appearance, Amado strikes at the core of racial strife in Brazil, as have writers such as, among others, Aluísio Azevedo in *O Mulato* (1880), Lima Barreto in *Clara dos Anjos* (1904–05), and Mário de Andrade in *Macunaíma* (1928). However, Amado goes one step further by insisting on the existence of prejudice within an historical and socio-political context. He refers to the prevalent racial mixture as a racial democracy because mixed blood like political democracy, may someday touch *all* Brazilians. Amado further accentuates the political context by having Archanjo praise the mestizo as the representative of the majority of the poor in Brazil, i.e., those who *miraculously* manage to survive against the worse socio-economic and political conditions:

Assim sendo, a preservação de costumes e tradições, a organização de sociedades, escolas, desfiles, ranchos, ternos afoxés, a criação de ritmos de dança e canto, tudo quanto significa enriquecimento cultural adquire a importância de verdadeiro milagre que só a mistura de raças explica e possibilita. Da miscegenação nasce uma raça de tanto talento e resistência, tão poderosa, que supera a miséria e o desespero na criação quotidiana da beleza e da vida.

[. . . For this reason, the preservation of custom and tradition, the organizing of societies, samba schools, parades, carnival parades, bands, and *afoxés*, and the creation of new dance rhythms and songs—all that signifies cultural enrichment—takes on the character of a veritable miracle which can only be explained by miscegenation. The mixture of races has given birth to a new race of so much talent and endurance, of such power, that it is able to rise above misery and despair in a daily creation of beauty and of life itself.]

Although considered to be idealistic and mythical, this thesis of the resiliency of the poor, a strong motif in such novels as *Pastores da Noite* (1964) and *Tereza Batista Cansada de Guerra* (1972), also refers to the "miracle" inherent in the novel's title, implying that true miracles, economic or otherwise, go on every day with no help from the State. Of course, at the time of the

novel's publication the military regime's "Economic Miracle," underway since 1967, was giving very low priority to socio-economic programs benefiting the poor. As a parody of that economic program, Amado's novel strikes another allegorical blow against the military State and its elites. By juxtaposing racial oppression with political repression within and across historical time periods, he calls attention to the source of this injustice and violence, i.e., military and civil authorities who see these as a threat to the status quo. Ergo, the repression of these issues, their *sufoco*, is but another affirmation of the lack of democracy in the Brazil of that period as the following passage clearly demonstrates:

. . . na presença de autoridades civis, militares e religiosos, o orador oficial da cerimônia, o doutor Saul Novais, funcionário responsável por assuntos culturais, advertido a tempo sobre os inconvenientes de referências a democracia racial, mestiçagem, miscigenação, etcetera e tal, temas subversivos. . .

[. . . in the presence of civil, military, and religious authorities, the official orator of the ceremony, Dr. Saul Novais, the municipal functionary responsible for cultural affairs, forewarned that references to racial equality, miscegenation, etc. and so forth, subversive themes, might possibly be inopportune]

As subversive, the interrelatedness and relationship of these issues to equality and human rights affirm Amado's awareness of how volatile the term 'racial democracy' can be within a repressive state, especially if emphasis is placed upon the word "democracia." Amado's public usage of this term serves to call attention to its subversive character in an authoritarian society. The more he employs this term in a literary, political and public context, the more he hopes to contribute to its gradual realization. Ironically, the State's eventual willingness to use the term "racial democracy," to project a positive international image of Brazil, in fact pointed to the State's inauthentic motives which exploited this term as a smoke-screen for covering up the actual lack of racial and socio-political equality in Brazil. The absence of democracy during the historical periods in the novel is further emphasized by the long discussion of the Naziism of the Second World War and the plight of the Jews. In the following passage, reference is made to an anti-Hitler writer who makes a vituperative speech in which ". . . atacou as limitações à liberdade, produtos da ditadura, reclamou democracia, 'em defesa da democracia os soldados empunham as armas contra o nazismo' " [. . . he attacked the restrictions on freedom that dictatorship had brought with it and called for democracy: "Soldiers are bearing arms against Naziism to defend democracy."] The novel's historical references and allusions to such past events as religious prejudice, censorship, political repression, student uprisings, and *passeatas*, as well as characters who by implication embody real historical personages such as the black crusader, Manoel Querino, the historical inspiration for Pedro Archanjo, not to mention the direct use of real people's names such as that of the turn-of the century sociologist Nina Rodrigues, contribute to Jorge Amado's strong sense of historical reality. Also, Amado symbolically alludes to the considerable socio-political impact of Brazilian Popular Music (MPB) in terms of the 67–68 *tropicalista* countercultural movement. By giving the combined name of Caetano Gil to a young "bravo e rebelde trovador, tirando verso e música na viola" [a brave rebel of a balladeer. . . drawing verse and music out of his guitar], Amado pays historical and cultural tribute to such iconoclastic composers and popular singers as Caetano Veloso and Gilberto Gil, who were strong political activists in that period. According to Hollanda and Gonçalves [in their "Política e líteratura: a ficção da realidade brasileira," *Anos 70*, vol. 2, 1979], Amado's symbolic references explain his use of allegory as a means of reporting the truth during periods in which his country was subjected to oppressive authoritarian regimes. In a recent interview appearing in *Leia* [April 1986], Amado reiterates this stand and explains how, by figurative history and extended allegory, he recreates life:

> Mal e mal eu aprendi esse ofício de recriar a vida. Eu escrevi um livro, *ABC de Castro Alves*, porque eu achei que era uma necessidade naquele momento (1941), no Estado Novo, quando havia uma grande corrupção na vida intelectual, mostrar o exemplo de um escritor que foi consequente e fiel toda a vida. . . Escrevi *O cavaleiro da esperanca*, sobre Luís Carlos Prestes, num momento em que eu julguei necessário, que podia dar uma ajuda na luta pela anistia e pela redemocratização do país. . .

> [I had barely learned this art of recreating life. I wrote a book, *The ABCs of Castro Alves* because I thought it was a must at that time (1941), during the dictatorship of the New State when intellectual life had deteriorated, to show the example of a writer who was coherent and loyal all his life. . . I wrote *The Knight of Hope* about the Communist Luís Carlos Prestes during

a time which I judged to be important, a book which could give support to the struggle for amnesty and the redemocratization of the country.]

Through the use of fact and fiction—history and allegory—Jorge Amado strives for a measure of social truth that only literature can provide. As a form of conclusion and statement on Amado's historical and allegorical vision, another passage from the above interview offers an insightful self-commentary on the relationship between his vivid and trenchant grasp of Brazil's social history and his skilled craftsmanship as a writer of fiction:

> Vivi os grandes acontecimentos do meu tempo, conheci os homens importantes do meu tempo, convivi com eles, fui amigo de muitos deles. Enfim, ganhei uma experiência de vida como pouca gente ganhou. Ao lado dessa experiência de vida, evidentemente ganhei experiência literária. Se você exerce honradamente o seu ofício, e eu exerço o meu ofício honradamente, você melhora. Mas eu respondo definitivamente dizendo que não sou um literato. O literato procura escrever bonito, com graça. Sou um escritor e o escritor recria a vida.

> [I lived through the great events of my time, I got to know the important men of my time, I lived with them, I was a friend to many of them. In short, I gained a life of experiences as few people have. Along with that life experience, I evidently gained some literary experience. If you practice your craft honestly, and I do practice my craft honestly, you get better. But I can say definitively that I am not a man of letters, a highbrow. The man of letters tries to write prettily, with flair. I am a writer and the writer recreates life.]

(pp. 6–21)

Nelson H. Vieira, "Testimonial Fiction and Historical Allegory: Racial and Political Repression in Jorge Amado's Brazil," in *Latin American Literary Review*, Vol. XVII, No. 34, July–December, 1989, pp. 6–23.

SOURCES FOR FURTHER STUDY

Ellison, Fred P. "Jorge Amado." In his *Brazil's New Novel: Four Northeastern Masters*, pp. 83–108. Berkeley and Los Angeles: University of California Press, 1954.

> Surveys Amado's fiction, commenting on the author's themes and technique. Ellison concludes that "serious defects in [Amado's] artistry are overcome by the novelist's ability to weave a story, to construct vivid scenes, and to create fascinating characters."

Krueger, Robert. "Abertura/Apertura: A Political Review of Recent Brazilian Writings." In *The Discourse of Power: Culture, Hegemony, and the Authoritarian State in Latin America*, edited by Neil Larsen, pp. 172–93. Minneapolis: Institute for the Study of Ideologies and Literature, 1983.

> Brief discussion of politics in Amado's fiction, focusing on *Farda Fardão* as "a continuation of Amado's well established fetishism of race, nation, and sex in which the

Brazilian working class disappears behind its pseudo-lyrical image."

Silverman, Malcolm. "Allegory in Two Works of Jorge Amado." *Romance Notes* XIII, No. 1 (Autumn 1971): 67–70.

Presents allegorical interpretations of *Jubiabá* and *Shepherds of the Night*.

———. "Moral Dilemma in Jorge Amado's *Dona Flor e Seus Dois Maridos*." *Romance Notes* XIII, No. 2 (Winter 1971): 243–49.

Examines the eponymous heroine's struggle to repress her sexuality following the death of her "sensualist" husband.

Thomas, J. C. "Jorge Amado." *Publishers Weekly* 207, No. 25 (23 June 1975): 20–1.

Basing his comments on an interview with Amado, discusses the author's views on such topics as women and native culture.

Vieira, Nelson H. "Myth and Identity in Short Stories by Jorge Amado." *Studies in Short Fiction* 23, No. 1 (Winter 1986): 25–34.

Examines a sampling of Amado's short stories, pointing to themes and techniques common to all of his fiction.

Wolfe, Bertram D. "Panorama of a Tropic Frontier." *New York Herald Tribune Weekly Book Review* (17 June 1945): 4.

Positive review of *The Violent Land*. Wolfe asserts that this novel, which focuses not on the individual but rather on "a society, a region and an industry," is "one of the most important novels to have come North in some time, and, because of its frontier character and crowded action, one of the most accessible to the American reader."

Additional coverage of Amado's life and career is contained in the following sources published by Gale Research: *Contemporary Authors*, Vols. 77–80; *Contemporary Authors New Revision Series*, Vol. 35; *Contemporary Literary Criticism*, Vols. 13, 40; *Dictionary of Literary Biography*, Vol. 113; and *Major 20th-Century Writers*.

Rudolfo Anaya

1937 –

Chicano novelist, short story writer, and playwright.

INTRODUCTION

One of the most influential authors in Chicano literature, Anaya is acclaimed for his skillful mingling of realism, fantasy, and myth in novels exploring the experiences of Hispanics in the American Southwest. Stemming from his fascination with the mystical nature of Spanish-American *cuentos*, or folk tales in the oral tradition, Anaya's works often address his loss of religious faith. As Anaya has explained, his education caused him to question his religious beliefs, and that, in turn, led him to write poetry and prose. "I lost faith in my God," Anaya has stated, "and if there was no God there was no meaning, no secure road to salvation. . . . The depth of loss one feels is linked to one's salvation. That may be why I write. It is easier to ascribe those times and their bittersweet emotions to my characters."

Anaya was born in the village of Pastura, New Mexico. There, and later in nearby Santa Rosa, where Anaya spent the majority of his childhood, people gathered to hear and tell stories, anecdotes, and riddles. Anaya has commented: "I was always in a milieu of words, whether they were printed or in the oral tradition. And I think that's important to stimulate the writer's imagination; to respond to what is going on around him, to incorporate the materials and then rehash them and make fiction—to start at a point of reference which is close to one's being and then to transcend it—that's important." The author was profoundly affected by the old storytellers, the myths of his Mexican-Indian ancestors, and the land itself; the plains in which he was raised provide the setting for most of his novels and short stories.

In 1955 Anaya graduated from Albuquerque High School. He then attended Browning Business School for two years before entering the University of New Mexico, where he received his master's degree in English in 1968. At the University Anaya studied such novelists as Thomas Wolfe, William Faulkner, Ernest Hemingway, and John Steinbeck; aspiring to become a writer himself, he attempted to imitate their style and technique but was unsuccessful. "I made a simple discovery," Anaya has related. "I found I needed to write in *my* voice about my characters, using my indigenous symbols." Thus, he began writing *Bless Me, Ultima* (1972), a novel about a boy growing up in New Mexico shortly after World War II. Anaya spent nearly seven years writing and rewriting this first novel. Completed in 1972, *Bless Me, Ultima* was a resounding success, earning Anaya the second annual Premio Quinto Sol prize for literature. His two subsequent novels, *Heart of Aztlán* (1976) and *Tortuga* (1979), consolidated Anaya's reputation as an important American author of fiction. In addition to writing novels, Anaya has taught courses in creative writing and Chicano literature at the University of New Mexico, edited several books on Chicano literature, experimented in drama and script-writing, published a collection of short stories, and contributed many articles to literary periodicals. He also received the 1993 PEN Fiction award for his *Albuquerque*.

Centering around the dilemmas of young Spanish-Americans, *Bless Me, Ultima*, *Heart of Aztlán*, and *Tortuga* form a loose trilogy, embedded in myth and bound by common themes that focus on the deterioration of traditional Hispanic ways of life, social injustice and oppression, disillusionment and loss of faith, and the regenerative power of love. *Bless Me, Ultima* features a young boy named Antonio whose maturation is linked to his struggle with religious faith and his difficulty in choosing between the nomadic life of his father's family and the agricultural lifestyle of his mother's. Necessary to Antonio's development is Ultima, the *curandera* ("healer") who comes to live with Antonio's family and acts as a spiritual guide. Her teachings from Native American mythology and her unconditional love for Antonio nurture and sustain him, enabling him to recognize his own strength and ability to overcome life's disappointments. *Heart of Aztlán* relates the story of a Chicano worker who, due to financial difficulties, is forced to move his family from their rural home to the city, where he has obtained employment in the railroad factories. A sociopolitical work, the novel examines life in a Chicano ghetto, addressing the exploitation of poverty-ridden laborers by corrupt elements in religion and industry. Oppression is also prevalent in *Tortuga*, wherein the plight of the title character—a young boy suffering from paralysis—dramatically emphasizes the need for healing in what Anaya has described as "a society that was crushing and mutilating" people. Tortuga's recovery, hastened by the emotional well-being that results from his love for a nurse's aide, exemplifies the healing power of love and the inextricable link between emotional, spiritual, and physical health.

Bless Me, Ultima has generated more critical review, analysis, and interpretation than any other novel in contemporary Chicano literature. Critics of this work have found Anaya's story unique, his narrative technique compelling, and his prose both meticulous and lyrical. The reception of *Heart of Aztlán*, however, has been less enthusiastic. Although many critics have approved of the novel's mythic substructure, some commentators have found Anaya's intermingling of myth and politics confusing. Juan Bruce-Novoa has noted that "*Ultima* produced expectations that *Heart of Aztlán* did not satisfy. Not that the introduction of blatantly political topics is a fault in and of itself—no, it is a matter of the craftsmanship, not of the themes, and *Heart*, for whatever reason, is less polished, less accomplished." *Tortuga* has also prompted a mixed critical response. Some commentators, extolling the novel's structural complexity and innovative depiction of Chicano life, have proclaimed *Tortuga* Anaya's best work; others, however, have denigrated the novel as melodramatic and unrealistic. For instance, Cordelia Candelaria has asserted that the characters presented in *Tortuga* are "lacking in human vitality and motivation" and "perform like mechanical metaphors."

Anaya's novels continue to be studied and analyzed with an intensity accorded to few other Hispanic writers. Praised for their universal appeal, his works have been translated into a number of languages. Of Anaya's international success, Antonio Márquez has written, "It is befitting for Anaya to receive the honor and the task of leading Chicano literature into the canons of world literature. He is the most acclaimed and the most popular and universal Chicano writer, and one of the most influential voices in contemporary Chicano literature."

CRITICAL COMMENTARY

SCOTT WOOD

(essay date 1973)

[In the following excerpt from his review of *Bless Me, Ultima*, Wood praises the novel as "a rich and powerful synthesis for some of life's sharpest oppositions."]

The mainstream American novel has consistently revealed at least one common truth about life in this country: it is filled with contradictions and extreme ranges of experience which cannot be reconciled. (p. 72)

Bless Me, Ultima is a unique American novel. Living apart from the mainstream, a young New Mexican Chicano has offered in this, his first novel, a rich and powerful synthesis for some of life's sharpest oppositions. Perhaps Rudolfo Anaya would object to my calling his novel "American," even though it is the story of a young boy growing up in New Mexico during and immediately after World War II, a war in which his three older brothers fight. Despite Anaya's reflections on the effect of the war on American communities, the alienation of sons and their flight to the city, deeper themes are at the book's heart. (pp. 72–3)

In the course of the novel, throughout three years of spiritual genesis, the boy [Antonio] is torn between maternal forces: the earth, Catholic ritual, family ties; and the opposing powers; the flowing river, the golden carp (its god), the dream of nomadic liberation. His mother would have him be a priest. She is a Luna, a descendant of the Spanish priest who settled the farming valley. But Antonio has the blood of the Marez, of the changing and inconstant sea. His father's primitive roots are Antonio's connection to older myths; he cannot embrace the Catholic faith without struggle and ambivalence. Anaya builds this opposition with admirable skill; he develops a complexity of natural symbols and mythic anecdotes in a simple lyric style which becomes, finally, an inexorable power beneath his plot.

The plot begins with the coming of Ultima to the household of Antonio Marez. She is a *curandera* (one who cures with herbs and magic). This old woman, so strange and wonderful, was midwife at Antonio's birth; she becomes so again as he struggles to give birth to his soul. The events of Antonio's young life are violent and incomprehensible; three violent deaths, diabolic possessions, his brothers' moral collapse, cruelty and bigotry in his childhood friends. Through each shattering event

Antonio is accompanied by the wise and tender force of Ultima; she blesses him with a vision of life neither Christian nor pagan, but a melding of both and, somehow, deeper than either.

This is a remarkable book, worthy not only of the Premio Quinto Sol literary award for which it was selected, but worthy in other respects, as well. To wit: for its communication of tender emotion and powerful spirituality without being mawkish or haughty; for its eloquent presentation of Chicano consciousness in all its intriguing complexity; finally, for being an American novel which accomplishes a harmonious resolution, transcendent and hopeful. Anaya offers a valuable gift to the American scene, a scene which often seems as spiritually barren as some parched plateau in New Mexico. (pp. 73–4)

Scott Wood, in a review of *Bless Me, Ultima* in *America,* Vol. 128, No. 3, January 27, 1973, pp. 72–4.

ALBERT TREVIÑO

(essay date 1977)

[In the essay below, Treviño examines *Bless Me, Ultima* from the perspectives of "the realist, the moralist, the expressionist, and the structuralist." Treviño also comments on character and symbol in the novel.]

In her essay "The Necessity of Teaching the Nature and Function of Literature," Audrey Renwicke Gibson states:

> Literature is man centered. It is the attempt of the human imagination to come to terms with an alien universe, that which is out there, set over against ourselves. Literature doesn't so much describe this world as try to allay our anxieties about it by associating our minds with it in two ways, by analogy and metaphor. Freud said that an analogy proves nothing but it makes us feel more at home. This is what literature attempts to do; it makes us feel more at home in a hostile environment.

The novel *Bless Me, Ultima.* By Rudolfo Anaya, not only attempts but accomplishes this goal to make us "feel that the strength within the human heart can overcome the tragedies in life. Thus, in the end, he is able to accept Ultima's death as part of the great design of things. A wiser person due to Ultima's influence, Antonio is able to at least partially resolve his questioning of God, with the intent of someday forging a new religion which could "answer the questions of the children."

Antonio's second area of development involves the resolution of his inner conflict regarding his personal destiny. Throughout the novel Antonio is torn between the wish of his father, a Márez, that he be a man of the *llano*, a *vaquero*, and the wish of his mother, a Luna, that he be a priest of a farmer. With the help of both his father and Ultima, however, he is able to resolve his conflict and think about creating his own dream. Near the end of the novel his father admits to the need for reconciliation of differences within the two factions of the family and for a reform of the old ways. From Ultima Antonio learns that each person must be the author of his own destiny and that human destiny can only be realized upon the acceptance of reality and through the understanding that comes with life.

The primary concern of the realist is how well the novel mirrors reality. *Bless Me, Ultima* is an accurate and realistic look at one young member of a rural Mexican American family. The work is not designed to be saga of the collective Mexican American experience nor is it specifically a comment on the social problems faced by the Mexican Americans in the Southwest. To critique the novel from such a viewpoint would ignore the author's intent.

In the novel Anaya takes advantage of the two opposing forces of the *bruja* and the *curandera* and what they traditionally represent to illustrate the relativeness of Good and Evil. While Ultima is referred to as a *curandera*, there are those who consider her to be a *bruja* as are Tenorio's three daughters. Though she is put to the test for witchery, the results do not leave the reader with the clear impression that she is a symbol of goodness. Her use of evil to combat evil and her admission that she has interfered with man's destiny, thus upsetting the natural harmony within the universe, seem to indicate the blending of the two seemingly opposite forces.

There are other folkloric references within *Bless Me, Ultima*. The owl, which comes to represent Ultima's spirit, is Antonio's protector in the novel, though in folklore it is normally a symbol or sign of evil or witchery. Anaya again takes advantage of this seeming contradiction to illustrate the relative nature of what we normally consider the diametrically opposed forces of Good and Evil and to warn the reader that what has traditionally been the case isn't necessarily true.

In writing on Antonio's childhood experiences, Anaya naturally reflects on Antonio's schooling, painting a realistic picture of the embarrassing experience of

---

Principal Works

Bless Me, Ultima (novel) 1972

Bilingualism: Promise for Tomorrow (screenplay) 1976

Heart of Aztlán (novel) 1976

Tortuga (novel) 1979

The Season of La Llorona (drama) 1979

Rosa Linda (drama) 1982

The Silence of the Llano (short stories) 1982

The Legend of La Llorona (novel) 1984

The Adventures of Juan Chicaspatas (verse) 1985

A Chicano in China (nonfiction) 1986

Lord of the Dawn: The Legend of Quetzalcoatl (novel) 1987

Albuquerque (novel) 1992

---

more at home in a hostile environment." The novel is a statement about man and his relationship to the universe.

This study offers a critical interpretation of *Bless Me, Ultima*. The novel will be briefly examined from four viewpoints—that of the realist, the moralist, the expressionist, and the structuralist.

Bless Me, Ultima is basically a maturation novel, tracing the development of Antonio Márez, the main character, from a young, inquisitive, and immature boy to a more understanding and knowledgeable one. Rudolfo Anaya uses the first person point of view in the novel as the narrator, Antonio, reflects on his life beginning at the age of seven when he first comes under the influence of Ultima, an elderly *curandera* who is invited to live with his family. The story is set in the little town of Guadalupe, New Mexico during the 1940's and covers a period of two years. Antonio matures in two basic ways. Perhaps his most significant development is his ability to come to some understanding and acceptance of life which for him poses numerous questions about Good and Evil. As the novel opens, Antonio is at the stage of entering school and beginning catechism in preparation for his first holy communion. Lacking an understanding of the world around him, Antonio goes through periods of insecurity, fear, guilt, and disbelief when he is unable to comprehend the forces larger than himself which influence and control his life. He encounters evil and violence and comes to question both the power of the Church to effectively deal with Evil and God who allows the good and innocent to suffer while the evil goes unpunished. From the wise and loving Ultima, however, he comes to realize his inability to see the great cycle of life, the harmony within the universe, that binds everyone. He learns from her to see the good and strong and beautiful in life and to realize

the non-English-speaking Mexican American first grader. A related yet more important concern of Anaya is his depiction of the Church as an institution that fails to answer the questions asked by children, depends on the parishioner's fear of a God that punishes, and provides traditional rituals which are void of meaning.

The moralist views *Bless Me, Ultima* in terms of Antonio's maturation into a wiser and more understanding person who is able to gain strength from life and who sees the need to determine his own destiny. The central theme that Anaya is conveying to his audience is that maturation involves understanding and understanding comes only with life. Without understanding we fear, and what we fear we call evil. Thus, what may be good, because it is a natural part of the universal harmony, we may call evil simply because we see only the parts and not the great cycle and thus fail to comprehend. This is exactly Antonio's problem. He experiences evil and violence which go unpunished, and he wants immediate explanations. When neither the Church nor God, after he takes holy communion, provides him with answers, he seriously questions God to the point that he considers other gods such as the pagan golden carp.

Another important lesson presented by Anaya is that man must accept life and build strength, not despair, from it. The author conveys this message in several ways. It is Antonio who is awed by the perseverance of the carp in its battle to swim upstream in an effort to avoid the subsiding waters. He expresses his belief that the life struggle is a beautiful sight because each year the drama repeats itself. Also, a voice in one of Antonio's dreams states that creation lies in violence. Anaya seems to be saying that suffering, tragedy, adversity, can be both productive and beautiful in a sense if it makes us stronger, wiser, and more sympathetic human beings.

In emphasizing man's search for his own destiny, Anaya constantly makes the point that man must not interfere with the destiny of any man for this would create a disharmony. The most significant illustration of this is Ultima's comparison of man's destiny to an unfolding flower which, free from any outside meddling, takes only sun, earth, and water to blossom.

The expressionist views *Bless Me, Ultima* from the standpoint of the author's projection of himself into the literary work. The reader can readily see that Anaya intimately understands the Mexican American culture and the people he describes. Obviously, Anaya is influenced by his background, having been born and educated in the little rural town of Santa Rosa, New Mexico. The novel is undoubtedly strengthened by the author's personal memories, experiences, and observations. On the basis of plot, theme, and the portrayal of characters in the novel we can assume certain feelings, values, and beliefs on the part of the author. For example, the reader might reasonably speculate that the character of Antonio in certain respects expresses the feelings and thoughts of Anaya himself. Or,

from Anaya's mention of the numerous hardships faced by the people of Las Pasturas one gets the impression that Anaya sympathizes with them even though María dislikes them. However, as to Anaya's exact values, thoughts, and emotions, the reader can only conjecture. Anaya's characters are individuals, not stereotypes. They do not role play and thus they speak only for themselves.

From a structuralist viewpoint, *Bless Me, Ultima* is an effective, well-written work. Anaya has a simple style, free from affectation, interspersed with some perceptive images which illustrate his keen observation of people and rural life. The author also does an effective job of characterization. All his characters emerge as real, believable people whose actions are consistent with their personalities. As previously stated, the novel revolves around the character of Antonio, a dynamic character who changes and matures by the actions through which he passes. By observing the impact of these actions on Antonio's inner self, the reader gains an understanding of his character and is able to trace his development throughout the novel.

Since *Bless Me, Ultima* is mostly a novel of character, the function of plot in the novel is primarily to translate character into action. The incidents spring naturally from the characters, and these actions are all interrelated in some way to relate to the character development of Antoniao. The novel relies on the physical, external conflict between Ultima and Tenorio and between Antonio's father and mother to develop Antonio's internal, spiritual conflict. The climax comes in the final chapter when Antonio comes to his realization about his personal destiny and religious beliefs. The only consistent plot technique utilized by Anaya is that of foreshadowing. Occasionally his characters say things which foreshadow coming events, but it is usually in Antonio's dreams that Anaya gives the reader some warning or indication of what to expect.

Bless Me, Ultima is a very symbolic novel, making use of universal symbols to hold the novel together and reinforce theme. The bridge operates as a symbol of Antonio's maturation, the transition from childhood to manhood, from innocence to understanding. It is at the bridge early in the novel where the innocent Antonio, hiding in the reeds, experiences the killing of the war-crazy Lupito and undergoes his initial questioning about God's punishment. At the end of the novel it is also at a bridge where the evil Tenorio tries to kill Antonio. Here Antonio realizes the meaning of "sacrifice of commitment" as he courageously attempts to warn Ultima of Tenorio's evil plans.

The river is also used as a symbol, though its meaning is initially more ambivalent. It separates Antonio's house from the town, and comes to symbolize or signify the dividing line between the innocence of the llano and the evil of the townspeople. Throughout the novel, the river becomes both a creative and a destructive force. On the one hand, it provides water for the fields of the Lunas as it provides a home for the golden carp. On the other hand, the river takes the life of Antonio's friend Florence and flows with the blood of the murdered Lupito. With the blending of these two forces, the river becomes a symbol of the irreversible passage of time and man's journey to his final destination. The waters of the river move toward the sea where they are in turn acted upon by the moon as part of the continuous cycle within nature. With the use of the surnames Márez, sounding like *mares*, or "seas," and Luna, meaning, "moon," Anaya makes an effective connection to Antonio's journey through life. In this way Anaya combines plot, theme, and character into a well structured literary work.

In conclusion, regardless of what critical approach we take to analyze *Bless Me, Ultima*, we must consider this novel as an exemplary one—one whose simplicity of style, yet depth of meaning, should be carefully examined by future Chicano novelists in their effort to write Chicano novels. (pp. 30–3)

Albert D. Treviño, "*Bless Me, Ultima*: A Critical Interpretation," in *De Colores*, Vol. 3, No. 4, 1977, pp. 30–3.

RUDOLFO ANAYA

(essay date 1982)

[In the following essay, written in 1982, Anaya discusses the ideas and events which inspired the stories in his collection *The Silence of the Llano*, while commenting generally on the art and method of storytelling.]

The process by which a literary work is created intrigues us. Some readers feel that if we can understand something of that process we might understand the very origin of the spark of creativity. A complete understanding of the writer's creative impulse will always elude us, but perhaps we can catch intimations of that creative drive as we read the individual notes and works of writers. In these notes I would like to share with the reader part of the process and the circumstances which went into the writing of the collection of stories, *The Silence of the Llano*. This, I hope, will provide a broader setting for the stories and at the same time allow me to speak of my interest in the craft of writing.

My main objective in writing fiction during the last ten years was the creation and completion of the trilogy comprising three novels: *Bless Me, Ultima, Heart of Aztlán*, and *Tortuga*. However, during the course of those years I also wrote a number of short stores. I have discussed the creation of the novels in various interviews and lectures; here I would like to share some observations and thoughts about my short stories.

The short story when prsented in the oral tradition can be a simple but compelling form. It can also be made to move beyond its reginal arena to engage language and form in the expression of a vision which reflects the writer's sense of life. A writer is an artisan who works with words, and so he must possess the language he uses. But he must also seek his "inner voice"; he must experiment with and use many variations of the craft; he must write toward the "truth inherent in the story"; and he must be keenly aware of style and form.

In these notes I would like to discuss each of the stories included in *The Silence of the Llano*. But first some background.

I was born on the high plains of eastern New Mexico, a land which drops from the Sangre de Cristo Mountains to form the Llano Estacado. I grew up along the Pecos River valley in a small town by the name of Santa Rosa. Once, this land belonged to the nomadic Indians; later, Spanish and Mexican settlers moved into the region from the Taos and Santa Fe area. Sometime during the mid-nineteenth century Anglo-Americans began to fill the range land.

The history of this land and the different cultural ways of the people were depicted in many of the stories I heard as a child. Those people who moved in and out of my childhood came to tell stories, and it was the magic of their words and their deep, humble humanity which must have sparked my imagination. A writer must be a listener and an observer before he can be a writer.

I feel fortunate to have been born on the llano. The wild, nomadic vaquero ways my father, sheepherders were my old *abuelos*, and a woman from the river valley was my mother . . . but in an extended family, all of the people I met while growing up nurtured me and I had the need even then to put into words the magic I felt. The land was a mystical force, and so were the Hispanic people with their unique Mediterranean world view, a value system formed in the old world, infused by the Moorish and Jewish influence, and renewed in the Americas by the native religious spirit of the Indians. Those people and their view of the world has influenced me greatly, and so I often return to the llano for my inspiration. "**The Place of the Swallows**," "**The Road to Platero**," and "**The Silence of the Llano**" all draw from the land that I knew as a child.

There is something very positive to be said about a writer's sense of place, that is, that place he knows best, that place where his stance as a writer is most solid. "**The Place of the Swallows**" was one of the earliest stories I wrote, and it reflects my concern with the primary mystery of the river, water, birth, regeneration, and the subconscious. As a child I wandered up and down the river, sometimes alone, most often with the Chavez boys who were my closest neighbors. Adventures and escapades filled our days, but in addition to that, there was always for me the deep sense of the mystery of life which pulsed along the dark green river. Romantic? Perhaps, but I wouldn't trade that place of my child-hood for any other.

"The Place of the Swallows" was a story written under the strong influence of *Bless Me, Ultima*. I used the group of young boys as a tribal group, and within the group the person which interested me the most was the storyteller. The story is really about the art of storytelling and the role and function of the storyteller within his tribe, his social group. The tribe of boys reflects mankind, but in the story they have moved away from the town and the neighboring farms to enter the river valley, and so in their game they undergo an atavistic metamorphosis and actually become the hunters of the cave. When they sit around the fire at the end of the day they need the storyteller to recount their exploits. The storyteller records, in oral history and song, the entire history of the tribe, but as every writer discovers, it is also imperative that the storyteller be true to himself.

Was I—as I roamed the river valley with my child-hood friends, moving back and forth between the civilized world of my Catholic heritage and the pagan truths which seemed so evident in the world of raw, primal nature— becoming the storyteller? I know the condition of child-hood innocence has interested me intensely, for it was the innocent child in the novel *Bless Me, Ultima* who peered directly into the dark waters of the river and saw the primal (and therefore innocent) archetypes of the collective memory. The child is capable of becoming aware of and accepting the illumination of truth and beauty. The archetype, as a perfect symbol which communicates a truth, is obvious to the child. But the child can also see the ghosts of the past, the ghosts of the bush, the shadows of the cave which are a projection from within, and he is also aware of the demons we have created to haunt us since our first dawn on earth. Because the child is open to the presence of the primal mode, he is most in touch with the tribal memory and the truth latent in the archetypes, and this awareness can produce both fear and illumination.

As I have said, I was greatly influenced by the oral tradition of story-telling. The visits of neighbors or family were exciting and anticipated events. The visitor always brought a story. At night, after our supper, we would sit around the kitchen table, near the wood-burning stove to listen to stories. If it were summer we would move outside to the cool, evening air, and there would often be a special treat of a watermelon, cold from being in the icy water of the well all day, and the storytelling would begin. There is a special atmosphere which develops when a story is told. I feel an aura envelops the teller and his audience, and it is that same aura which now envelops me when I write, an aura which is a dimension of "the time of the story." That is, the time which the story itself can create, a time which destroys strict, linear time and creates a continuous, cyclical time which is harmonious.

A storyteller is effective in his craft if his voice, style, delivery, and movements create this aura of time. It is more than just mood. The mood is the total feeling or intensity which the story creates, a total unity of atmosphere which tense then releases. But aura is mood plus time, it is the achievement of a story which completely engrosses the reader. Being in that time of the story changes the listener or the reader forever. Once one has lived in the magic moment which the words bring to life, once one has stepped into the reality of the story, one is never again the same. This is the power of the storyteller; he can create new visions of old realities. The aura of the story is the vibration of time and truth inherent in the new reality that the story creates. The young boy who is the storyteller in **"The Place of the Swallows"** learned that during the telling of his story.

In much of my writing I refer to the llano, the open plain country where I was raised and which I use as the setting for some of my stories. The llano is generally flat; arroyos and mesas dotted with piñon and juniper carve the land, and the muddy rivers move south to empty into the Rio Grande. My forefathers moved there to raise sheep and cattle, ranches became haciendas and were given names, and some of those became small villages. Later the Texans came, hungry for land, and the two cultures which had already met in northern New Mexico and in the borderlands of Texas met on the Llano Estacado of New Mexico. There was the obvious shock and turmoil which is always present when two different cultures meet; sometimes there was a sharing, many times bloodshed. It was a time of change, and a time of heroes.

But it is people who are at the center of every story. I knew the vaqueros, the farmers, the people of the small villages. I listened, and their stories were a magic potion, a rendering of the everyday life where it was possible for small joys to lift us in exultation, where men and women I knew became heroes and heroines. Life could be made bigger than the sum of its parts when the storyteller spoke.

"The Road to Platero" and **"The Silence of the Llano"** are stories which obviously use the llano as a background, but allow me a short digression which I believe will shed some light on those stories. Some years ago while reading through old Mexican corridos, the ballads of the people, I came across the "Ballad of Delgadina." The story is about a man who falls in love with his daughter. He asks for her love, but she refuses, citing all the moral reasons why such a love cannot be. In a rage he has his servants lock her in her room, and she is allowed to drink only salt water until she changes her mind. By the time the father realizes his wrong, it is too late, she is dead. The ballad ends with the moral: Delgadina rests in heaven surrounded by angels, her father dies and receives the torment of hell. I took the outline of the story and wrote a drama which I call *Rosa Linda*.

I have been writing and revising that drama for a number of years, and so it is natural for the theme of the father/daughter relationship I am exploring in that drama to find its way into some of the stories I was writing at the same time. The theme begins to appear in **"The Road to Platero"**. In a sense, the story is almost a warming-up exercise for the bigger and more challenging story in the play. This theme of incest is as old as mankind, and it has been the subject of many literary works, but the subject is still taboo, and it is a theme which is difficult to treat.

I like to use the term "the writer's stance" to describe or suggest the position the writer takes in relationship to the story, that is the position and the distance of the writer in relation to the characters about whom he is writing. It is from that stance that the writer will relate the story. As the story develops he may move into the story itself, his voice may decrease or intensify, as he wishes, but for the beginning writer sometimes a fixed, solid stance can help clarify the point of view. Because I like to use a first person narrative, I often find myself too close to the story. In the first version of **"The Road to Platero"** the story was related in first person, and the narrator was the fetus in the womb of the woman. That's how I first thought out the story, and it was a unique and challenging view, but it compounded my problems. There was something surrealistic to the story, but it was too much for the story to carry. At any rate, the story set out to create a mood, to intimate a set of circumstances which culminate in story, so it didn't need much extraneous experimentation to achieve the mood. It was the "voice of the narrator" which would sketch out the village, the hot days in the llano as the women awaited the return of their men, the torture which men often inflict on women, and the hint of old relationships and murder. That "voice of the narrator" becomes the writer's stance, it becomes a story.

In the novel *Tortuga* the protagonist is a young man who is encased in a body cast; partially paralyzed, he cannot move about, and yet he relates the story. Other points of view are developed as we learn the stories of other patients in the hospital. Point of view when confronted and used correctly can make for unique style, but like time in a story, it can be fragmented, and beyond a certain point the unity of narration breaks down and the very time the writer seeks to make continuous in the story becomes discontinuous. Some will argue that the thought process, dreams, and perhaps the neurosis of contemporary time all occur in discontinuous time, but I suggest that the mind seeks to give coherence and pattern to time in order to understand what thought and dream and neurosis have to reveal to us. To give in to discontinuous time is to give in to chaos.

Perhaps the fragmentation of time and of the soul are at the core of contemporary writing. As there is turmoil and unrest in the individual and in the world, then the more reason why the story becomes a new ordering of the mundane world. The laws of the cosmos are not out of kilter, and they have influenced our evolution as humans since the first day of creation. Deep within each one of us lies the integrated self which seeks unity and harmony, and stories are a way to reflect aspects of that search.

One of the most frequent questions a writer is asked is: Where did you get the idea for your story? The second most-asked question is: Did it come from "real" life? I don't have a conclusive answer, but perhaps the writer is tuned in to some sensibility of life's vibrations which allows him or her to pick up a word, an idea, a character or theme, or an incident which strikes a chord in his subconscious. All of life, real or imagined, has the potential to be the spark which ignites the creative imagination.

Stories have come to me in dreams, while walking or watching television, from incidents in the past, from the people I meet everyday, what they say and do, from memories moving into consciousness. Whatever suddenly rings with the tone and pitch which I have come to sense as a story is the "germ of the story." Once that small seed or germ is deposited, I have to write the story. Life provides us with the seed, the writer as artisan must give it form.

But a writer just doesn't sit and wait for the story to begin. One learns to think continuously about stories; in fact, one's thought process becomes that of reinterpreting life as story. I call this process "story-thinking." In my mind are the characters, dialogues, settings, and themes of many stories, of which only a very few will ever be written. "Story-thinking" is part of the creative process, the dialogue with the world. It is an exhilarating process.

One day I was telling my wife the story of a sixth grade friend I had, and how he came up with the devilish idea of pasting small mirrors to the tip of our shoes so we could slip them under the girls' skirts and thereby solve the mystery of sex, a mystery that was bothering all of us about that time. I told her the story and we laughed and suddenly I realized the idea was unique enough to be a written story. From that idea **"The Apple Orchard"** emerged, a story based on a real incident.

Perhaps the ending of **"The Apple Orchard"** stretches the reader's acceptance of what is believable. Even in fiction we have to deal with what is believable, by which we mean: given the total context of the story, how far can you stretch the pattern of consistency so that it fits a "realistic mode?" The reader will ask: Would a young teacher really do what this teacher does for Isador ? This is not a "real" teacher; she is a character. Maybe we have never met a single teacher who would do what this teacher does, but within the context of the story, does it work? If I have convinced the reader that the story is not about sex but about love and beauty as they might be in a pure and sharing realm, then, the ending works; it is believable. The young teacher is willing to give of her love and beauty (only at this time and place) so that Isador can progress in understanding love and beauty as forms which flower, grow to fruition, then change into the gnarled form of the winter branch. A friend of mine who read the story said, "I wish I had had a teacher like that when I was young." He meant, how simple and courageous it might be to teach the beauty of the body in an honest and direct manner.

This story, **"The Apple Orchard"**, is also the story of the artist. Isador represents the young artist. A number of my stories are concerned with the development of the artist, his rites of passage from innocence into adulthood, the vision of truth to be learned. Isador says at the end of the story that has glimpsed a truth in beauty, but it is a fleeting thing. The important commitment he makes is to continue to explore truth and beauty. He has had his eyes opened for a moment; now it is up to him to learn to "see". Life and the universe are changing around him and if he is to espouse a vision of truth on which to build the foundations of his world, he must keep in touch with life. The writer opens himself up and reveals his deepest secrets and feelings and thoughts. He is constantly open to the awesome mystery of life; he is exhilarated by its profound joys, and he feels the deep sorrows. One suffers less if one protects his inner self, if one shuts himself away from hurt, but I know few writers who can do this and write. The writer is an adventurer who is constantly exploring and observing the entire range of unpredictable human behavior and the constant unfolding of creation.

Now we come to that strange tale, **"The Village Which the Gods Painted Yellow."** I was there in Uxmal, and when I returned I told parts of the story to my wife, and later, I sat down one January day and wrote the story. I wrote the story in the first person because I was more or less convinced that I had experienced the story. I had met Gonzalo, I had been there, I had rambled alone around the magnificent ruins of Uxmal on that day of the winter solstice. So where did one reality leave off and a new one start? Is it possible that the writer can get too drawn into the story? This is a real concern of a writer. The story wasn't working because I was too close to it, I was too deep in it. How was I to extricate myself from being bound with the life of the character? I changed to third person, created more distance between me and the story, and gave up the idea that the story had happened to me. I created Rosario and the story became his. The story is not built around depth of character; it is built around an adventure and a theme. In the story, time and legend and the strength of belief are more important than the actual characters. For me, **"The Village Which the Gods Painted Yellow,"** will always be a story which I entered too deeply.

I know I shall return to those ruins, and to the other ancient cities of the Yucatán and Guatemala. There are very powerful places there, good vibrations for the person who is in search of truth. But one should not tamper with the power of the earth and the power of the people unless one is very committed and very strong. I do not wish to remain lost in the stories waiting there for me, and so I will walk lightly, armed with magic.

The Southwest, this place I call my home, a place called Aztlan in the legends of the ancient Aztecs, is the same kind of place, a place of power. Perhaps that is why it attracts so many writers and artists. Power flows through the land and the people, dimensions of reality quickly evaporate under our sun, the visions and the dreams compel as much as any other force.

"The Silence of the Llano" is a story which creates its own aura and ambiance. When I wrote that story I felt myself returning to the llano, I saw and felt it again as I knew it when I was young and growing up. The aura became very real for me. It became palpable. It is one of my longer stories, but I think it can maintain its mood for the reader.

The llano is a lonely place. One comes upon lonely, isolated ranch houses. Faces peer from behind parted curtains. How do these people live? What do the women feel? I had seen the face of the young girl in the story peer at me, so many times. I began the story in the oral tradition: "This man's name was Rafael . . . " This is the way an old storyteller from the llano might have begun a story as he sat around with his compañeros, on a dark night in a sheep camp miles from the nearest village, with only the fire and the sound of words to give the hint of the human presence in the deep and dark of the lonely llano. That's how I wanted to tell this story, a story of a tormented man, a story of the cycles of time and the seasons which leave their imprint on the people.

One day the face of the young girl appeared again, and I sat down and wrote the story. It was as if over the years that young girl had been living in my memory, and suddenly she came with such force that I had to write the story. What a girl were born without access to language, to the companionship of other women, what would her thoughts be like, what would she feel? If there ever was magic to the word it is real magic to the girl in this story, as she lives in silence. The story is about silence, what it can do to people; it is about the sacredness of the word, spoken and unspoken, and it is also about the vast gulfs which can separate people when the word is not present between them.

What interested me greatly was the aura of the story. I wanted actually to move the reader into the llano, I wanted the reader to be at Rafael's side during the telling of the story. If every writer has a "voice," a personal, internal rhythm and language which is unique to him as a storyteller, then my voice is what I hear in **"The Silence of the Llano."** Writing is a search for that voice.

The most recent story in the collection, **"B. Traven is Alive and Well in Cuernavaca,"** is a story which takes a number of experiences and incidents which happened over the course of a summer and brings them together as one story. Let me first say that I have been going to

Mexico for many years, and most recently I have been going to Cuernavaca, to write and rest, and to communicate with the people and the earth of Mexico. I travel, wander through the *mercados*, visit ruins and museums, read, but mostly I just observe and listen. We have a dear friend in Cuernavaca, Ana, to whom the Traven story should be dedicated, for if there was ever a woman with much power and a fascinating life, it is she. Anyway, one recent trip to Mexico turned out to be a nightmare of sorts, a journey in which we used every type of transportation imaginable, and experienced the strangest incidents. A few months before the trip I had read B. Traven's *Macovio*. Then in Cuernavaca I met a gardener, *el jardinero,* who loved to tell stories. We got along very well, always trying to outdo each other in the stories we told each other. All these separate incidents are not a story, but they began to clamor to be put into a story.

During this time of germination, I am in a state of tension. I cannot share the story until the time is ripe. Nothing must touch the forming story. I think that is what the *jardinero's* treasure represents, the story in the subconscious of the writer. And it is the writer who must journey into that darkness to bring forth the final form, the truth of the story.

It was only after I finished the Traven story that I read completely the works of B. Traven, and also read a biography of him. I was surprised to find how close I was to the man's character in the story. Actually, even if that revelation were not correct, it would make little difference to the story, because the story is not really about B. Traven. It is a story about a story being born. It also relates something of what I feel in Mexico.

The Traven story also relies on a series of events, or what is often called plot. In some cases the events begin to predict the development and ending of a story. As the events unfold, or as the lives of the characters change, the reader should enter the story and become part of the story. Then the story is dynamic and alive. If that doesn't happen the story remains at one level. In the Traven story the series of events, or the plot, which finally jell for me as the writer, are only the skeleton on which to hang the themes which the story develops about life.

Finally, I have included in this collection three excerpts from previously published novels. I think they illustrate how stories work (or are told) within stories. And the excerpts stand as stories within themselves. It may interest the reader to know that **"The Christmas Play"** from *Bless Me, Ultima* is actually a separate story I wrote as relief for the murder which is to follow that scene in the novel. Readers have liked its humor. Others have asked why isn't there more humor in my writing. The life of the Mexicano, the Chicanos of the United States, is full of witty anecdotes, jokes, a rich picaresque word play, in short, a lively sense of life. When we gather together around the kitchen table, at weddings or funerals, at fiestas or community affairs, humor is an integral part of the

occasion. Lack of humor in my work says more about my character than the character of the culture. In the face of a dominant and often oppressive culture, humor acquires aspects of cultural survival and resistance. We have our storehouse of jokes about the Anglo-American, as he has jokes about us. In the recent development of *teatro* in the last few years, that humor has been used effectively, and a few Chicano fiction writers are also using it effectively. But I have been preoccupied with a world view which is serious, and not much humor has found its way into my writing. Perhaps in the future I will attempt more humor, as I did in **"The Christmas Play."**

"El Velorio" is the wake scene from *Heart of Aztlán*. *Velorios* are an integral part of the Hispanic culture, but as the culture becomes more urbanized, *velorios* are seldom held. In the villages and barrios, however, they are still a part of the grief and outpouring of sentiment which comes with death. I think the scene is self-contained, as it explores a theme of life and the characters which revolve around a wake. This scene was written to honor the dead and the *resador*, the man who comes to pray and guide the departing soul, and to guide the community of people who gather to perform one of the most human endeavors, the burying of the dead. The scene also allows me to combine the New World myth which I explore in much of my work with the Christian sense of death.

"Salomon's Story" is a story which Salomon tells in the novel *Tortuga;* as mentioned above, it is tied to **"The Place of the Swallows,"** and someday will be tied to an entire series of stories I want to write about this tribe of boys at the river. I hunted, during my younger years, with Cruz, an old man from Taos Pueblo. He taught me many things about the hunt. The deer is a brother, and if the hunt is not executed correctly then the forces, which balance life, are disturbed. Not only the unwise hunter may be hurt, but the entire pueblo may suffer. Perhaps the same is true of writing: tell a story which is not true—not consistent with the internal working of one's world view—and some may suffer. Of course I had hunted long before I met Cruz; along the river with the tribe of boys of the story, we roamed up and down the dark river valley in search of prey, driven by the instincts which told us we were hunters. But instinct and the dark blood in which it dwells, must come to light. That is what Salomon is saying in his story; not only must the relationship with nature be in balance, but the internal balance of each person must be a goal, and the symbol for that is the light which must be shed on the history of the tribe and the individual.

The storyteller tells stories for the community as well as for himself. The story goes to the people to heal and re-establish balance and harmony, but the process of the story is also working the same magic on the storyteller. He must be free and honest, and a critic of things as they are, and so he must remain independent of the whims of groups. Remember, the shaman, the *curandero*, the mediator do their work for the people, but they live alone. They embody the recluse of the society, but they accept their roles; they learn to live an independent existence. So the writer is the focus and the mirror of the community from which he takes his material, and yet he is apart from them. In the end of greater community is always humanity, and the individual has always been, at the same time, a single being within the community and a part of the whole. (pp. 47–57)

Rudolfo A. Anaya, "'The Silence of Llano': Notes from the Author," in *MELUS*, Vol. 11, No. 4, Winter 1984, pp. 47–57.

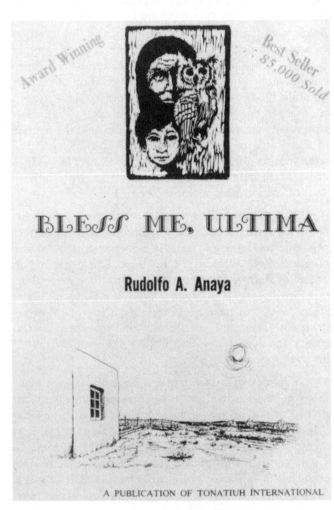

Cover for Anaya's first novel.

ANTONIO MARQUEZ

(essay date 1982)

[Below, Márquez reviews the trilogy *Bless Me, Ultima*, *Heart of Aztlán*, and *Tortuga*, focusing on Anaya's style, themes, critical reputation, and overall contribution to Chicano literature.]

The homage to Rudolfo Anaya comes at an appropriate time. Recently, the *New York Times Book Review* belatedly granted him national status. Moreover, Anaya's work is on the verge of international recognition. The growing interest in Anaya and other Chicano writers in Latin America and Europe, attended by the expected translations of *Bless Me, Ultima* into German and Polish, opens new vistas for Chicano literature. Just as *Bless Me, Ultima* (and Tomás Rivera's *Y No Se Lo Trago La Tierra*) formed the vanguard of modern Chicano prose, Anaya's work is at the vanguard that promises to liberate Chicano literature from the confines of "ethnic" or "regionalist" literature. It is befitting for Anaya to receive the honor and the task of leading Chicano literature into the canons of world literature. He is the most acclaimed and the most popular and universal Chicano writer, and one of the most influential voices in contemporary Chicano literature.

Anaya's literary career has been energetically diverse: novelist, essayist, folklorist, short-story writer, and playwright. Not slighting this admirable diversity, Anaya's major contribution has been as a novelist, and his reputation and achievement largely rest on *Bless Me, Ultima*, *Heart of Aztlán*, and *Tortuga*. Therefore, this survey focuses on Anaya's novels. It is a conspectus that will exclude critical examination of the plots, characters, folklore, legends, extensive symbolism, and other particulars that animate his novels. Concomitant with his role as the most acclaimed Chicano writer, his work (especially *Bless Me, Ultima*) has inspired the largest body of criticism in contemporary Chicano literature. This essay, then, is a general assessment of Anaya's position in Chicano literature, the critical reception of his work, and the nature of his achievement and reputation.

It was *Bless Me, Ultima* (1972) that vaulted Anaya to a stellar position in Chicano literature and a significant place in American literature. The subsequent novels, *Heart of Aztlán* (1976) and *Tortuga* (1979), solidified his reputation. To assess the significance of Anaya's work one must first consider its place in Chicano literary history. The appearance of *Bless Me, Ultima* was auspicious and rather startling. It stood in stark contrast to the shrill polemics that emerged from the political cauldron of the 1960s and attempted to pass for literature. *Bless Me, Ultima*, a muted and subtle work that dissuaded politics, projects reams of symbols and archetypes, and fused realism and fantasy, demonstrated that it was a painstakingly crafted novel. There appeared in the often woolly perimeters of Chicano fiction a singularly accomplished novel. To appreciate this accomplishment one only has to view his predecessors. José Antonio Villarreal's *Pocho*, Raymond Barrio's *The Plum Plum Pickers*, and Richard Vásquez's *Chicano*, for example, were important literary expressions of Chicano life, but they were marred as novels. All too often stilted and amateurish, they lacked novelistic invention or artistry. In the early 1970s two works appeared that marked a significant break from formulaic "social protest literature." These two works, Rivera's *Y No Se Lo Tragó La Tierra* and Anaya's *Bless Me, Ultima*, initiated the maturity and diversification of contemporary Chicano fiction. Quite different in theme and form, they were distinguished by their structural complexity and innovative exploration of Chicano life. Informed with the experimental techniques of William Faulkner and especially of Juan Rulfo, Rivera brought an eviscerating realism and existentialist thematics to Chicano fiction. On the other hand, Anaya's novel opened new vistas with its richly poetic vein and mythic configurations. Equally important, they brought a greater honesty and authenticity to the portrayal of Chicano life and countered stereotypic literature on the Chicano. *Bless Me, Ultima* forcefully dramatized that "Chicanos are not simple, fun loving, tradition-bound, lovable non-achievers or other mythical stereotypes such as those produced by John Steinbeck, but, rather, complex individuals like those found in any society". [Rolando Hinojosa, "Mexican-American Literature: Toward An Identification," *Books Abroad* (Summer 1975)]. In a similar vein, Daniel Testa, who has provided the most astute criticism on *Bless Me, Ultima*, concluded his critical study with praise for Anaya's large accomplishment and promising talent: "As a creative writer and spokesman for the Hispano-mestizo minority, who for too long has struggled in the backwaters of American life, Anaya gives every indication of invigorating the cultural growth of his people and verifying the existence of an inner force and power in their daily lives" [Daniel Testa, "Extensive/Intensive Dimensionality in Anaya's *Bless Me, Ultima*," *Latin American Literary Review* (Spring-Summer 1977)].

Although some critics were irritated by its "affectations" and "artistic naivete," *Bless Me, Ultima* was generally well-received and enthusiastically acclaimed in some quarters. It was deservedly praised for its fine storytelling, superb craftsmanship, and the artistic and philosophic dignity that it brought to Chicano literature. However, the joy of discovery often took injudicious turns; some critics celebrated *Bless Me, Ultima* as "an American classic" and carelessly and erroneously placed Anaya among Faulkner and Joyce. Fortunately, most assessments of *Bless Me, Ultima* were sensible and gave the work and its author their due worth. Martin Bucco emplifies the judicious criticism:

To be sure, if Anaya is not a world voice, he is at least a valuable new one, gifted and youthful, his creative consciousness suggesting, establishing, creating . . . the serious Mexican-American regional novel need not atrophy simply because it does not coincide with mass taste or with the complex art of Joyce, Gide, and Faulkner. [Martin Bucco, "A Review of **Bless Me,**

Ultima," *Southwestern American Literature* (Winter 1972)].

The most common refrain was that **Bless Me, Ultima** "achieved something that few pieces of Chicano literature have; that is, simply, that it stands by itself as a novel, with the 'Chicano' added later . . . " [Dyan Donnelly, "Finding a Home in the World," *Bilingual Review* (January–April 1974). The emphasis on **Bless Me, Ultima's** primary achievement as a novel and its secondary trait of ethnicity is an appropriate criterion. Ultimately, the novel's success rests on Anaya's imaginative mythopoesis and his careful and loving attention to the craft of fiction. The latter quality leads to a larger issue. Anaya from the start has seen himself, and rightly so, as an artist. He has vigorously made clear that he is not an apologist, polemicist, or literary ideologue, and he has frequently spoken out against the "politicization" of art: "I think any kind of description or dictation to the artist as a creative person will ruin his creative impulse. . . .The best writers will deal with social responsibility and the welfare of the people indirectly—as opposed to direct political statement or dogma." [David Johnson and David Apodaca, "Myth and the Writer: A Conversation with Rudolfo Anaya," *New America* (Spring 1979)].

Anaya's aestheticism and his avoidance of doctrinaire politics have been the major targets of his detractors. And his detractors, mostly academic critics and ideologues of the marxist stripe, found ample ground in **Heart of Aztlán** for their contentions. The general attack is that Anaya's archaism and myth-making are vague abstractions that have no bearing on existing and pressing issues. In a recent panel discussion with other Chicano writers and academics, Anaya offered this explanation of his mythopoesis:

I define myth as the truth in the heart. It is the truth that you have carried, that we as human beings have carried all of our history, going back to the cave, pushing it back to the sea. It seems to me that what happens at a certain time with people is that in order to come to a new conscious awareness they need to separate necessarily from a social, political context. ["**Mitólogos y Mitómanos**", *Maize: Xicano Art and Literature Notebook* (Spring–Summer 1981)].

Anaya subsequently took the critical brunt of the colloquium. One participant voiced a common complaint about Anaya's fiction: "I think that his idea of truth in the heart is very, very abstract." Another participant was rankled by the lack of practicality in Anaya's myth-making: ". . . looking back to the man with ultimate wisdom . . . won't answer the problem that's facing us directly and that's never answered." Alurista, a major Chicano poet and Anaya's most testy adversary in this exchange, questioned Anaya's archaism and concluded: "Necesitamos un mito más racional que confronte las necesidades comtemporáneas, y que confronte el enemigo del espíritu del hombre [We need a more rational myth that will confront contemporary necessities, and that will confront the enemy of the human spirit.]" This confrontation is used as an example of the numerous occasions where Anaya has been taken to task and prompted to defend his work. One can plausibly assume that Anaya by now is weary of these polemical confrontations and indifferent to the criticism that argues that he has failed to become a "committed" and "relevant" Chicano writer.

The controversy found specific grounds in *Heart of Aztlán*. The critical reception was divided and often delusive: its champions were charmed by the mythic substructure and poetic correspondences, but ignored its technical discrepancies; its detractors damned the confusing mixture of politics and metaphysics, but ignored the frequent moments of lyrical and poignant introspection. Some readers cloyed the novel and made heady assessments: "In *Heart of Aztlán* a prosewriter with the soul of a poet, and a dedication to his calling that only the greatest artists ever sustain—is on an important track, the right one, the only one". [Karl Kopp, "A Review of *Heart of Aztlán*," *La Confluencia* (July 1977)]. On the other hand, some critics were vexed by the novel's diffused narrative line and vague morality:

> Can insight into the existence of a spiritual bond destroy oppression and end exploitation? Can the feeling of a shared communal soul destroy the chains of steel that bind the people? Is there not some other ingredient necessary in addition to a spiritual feeling of love? Has contact with the myths provided a real tool to correct social injustice? [Maria López Hoffman, "Myth and Reality: *Heart of Aztlán*," *De Colores* (1980)].

There was much blather over Anaya's exotic metaphysics and fuzzy political notions, but very few readers pinpointed the chief failing of *Heart of Aztlán*. the crux of the matter was suggested by Bruce-Novoa in a brief preface to an interview with Anaya: "*Ultima* produced expectations that *Heart of Aztlán* did not satisfy. Not that the introduction of blatantly political topics is a fault in and of itself—no, it is a matter of the craftsmanship, not of the themes, and *Heart*, for whatever reason, is less polished, less accomplished" [Bruce-Novoa, *Chicano Authors: Inquiry by Interview*, 1980]. Precisely, the novel's detriment was its lack of craftsmanship. *Heart of Aztlán* stands out as a blemish in the Anaya canon because its disjointed and amorphous style contrasts with the meticulous, controlled, and carefully executed prose of Anaya's other works. Ostensibly, it was an experiment that sought to combine mythic elements and a socioeconomic theme. It attempts to balance and form a correlation between the myth of Aztlán (presented in numerous symbols and archetypes) and barrio life in Albuquerque in the 1950s (presented in realistic details of socioeconomic conditions and the labor struggles of the time). But it is a literary mixed-bag rather than a cohesive work of fiction. Apparently, Anaya placed himself in a difficult novelis-

tic stratagem in trying to work two discordant plots and themes. Anaya has commented on the technical problems involved in transforming Clemente from a drunken wastrel to a spiritual visionary that leads a labor struggle armed with love and mysticism:

> It's most difficult, because he's caught up in a very realistic setting and then how in hell do you take him into his visionary trip that I attempted to do with Clemente. I suppose I could have done it in a dream, I could have done it in some kind of revelation, and I chose to do it instead through Crispín and the old woman, the keeper of the rock "[Myth and the Writer: A Conversation with Rudolfo Anaya"].

Anaya's telling comments on the "visionary trip" that leads to the novel's rather forced resolution suggest that Anaya was not confident or totally clear about the execution of the novel. Culling this candid moment of auto-criticism, Anaya offered a more telling admission that shed light on his most common liability: his occasional rhetorical excesses and cutesy mannerisms. He explains his playful manner:

> I get a kick out of doing things that I know people will respond to, especially critics. In *Heart of Aztlán* I did something that was really too cutesy . . . 'The sun sucked the holy waters of the river, and the turtle-bowl sky ripped open with dark thunder and fell upon the land. South of Aztlán the golden bear drank his fill and tasted the sweet fragrance of the drowned man's blood. That evening he bedded down with the turtle's sisters and streaked their virgin robes with virgin blood . . . Oh wash my song into the dead man's soul, he cried, and soak his marrow dry.' That's part of that. I get carried away.

Apart from the convoluted narration, Anaya touches on a pointed issue. All too often, he is "cutesy" and "gets carried away" in purple prose.

The critical reception of *Tortuga* is less defined. At the present, The criticism on Anaya's third novel consists of a scattering of reviews. So far the reception of *Tortuga* has been favorable. The cursory reviews have noted the strong narrative line, the striking realism, and the novel's powerful theme. However, the connecting elements in the trilogy and Anaya's maturation have not been considered. Foremost, there is an integrity and cohesiveness to *Tortuga* that were lacking in *Heart of Aztlán*. Apart from containing the rudiments of Anaya's fiction—a mythopoeic cluster of images and symbols, it discloses sharper insight and accommodation of realistic situations. Notably, Anaya returns to first-person narrative point of view, which seems to be more conformable to his style. We can gather that Anaya in *Heart of Aztlán* was stretching out and experimenting with new ways of telling a story. The return to the narrative technique of *Bless Me, Ultima* makes *Tortuga* a smooth and lucid novel which is free of the vagaries that made *Heart of Aztlán* less than successful. It can also be noted that Anaya returns to the exploration of "memory and imagination." These two elements gave *Bless Me, Ultima* a magical resonance. *Tortuga* achieves a similar effect with its Proustian overture and memory-laden images: "I awoke from a restless sleep. For a moment I couldn't remember where I was . . . Upon waking it was always the same; I tried to move but the paralysis held me firmly in its grip." And later: "The words struck chords and a remembrance of things past would flood over me and in my imagination I would live in other times and other places. . . ."

Tortuga, which has neither achieved the popularity and critical acclaim of *Bless Me, Ultima*, nor received the brickbats leveled at *Heart of Aztlán*, is in several respects Anaya's most accomplished novel. True, there are still rhetorical excesses and inconsistencies in the lyrical voice. When measured and used to enlarge a character's sensibility, the lyricism is quite effective: "I followed her gaze and through her eyes I saw the beauty she described, the beauty I had not seen until that moment. The drabness of winter melted in the warm, spring light, and I saw the electric acid of life run through the short green fuses of the desert plants and crack through the dark buds to brush with strokes of lime the blooming land." Here Anaya magically employs his poetic gift to catch an expressive moment. In the lesser moments, the lyrical manner is too self-conscious and rhapsodic. For example, at one point Anaya indulges in hackneyed Homeric metaphors:

> The daughter of the sun awoke to weave her blanket with pastel threads. Her soft, coral fingers worked swiftly to weave the bits of turquoise blue and mother of pearl into the silver sky. She had but a moment in which to weave the tapestry that covered her nakedness, because behind her the sun trumpeted, awoke roaring alive with fire and exploded into the sky, filling the desert with glorious light and scattering the mist of the river and the damp humours of the night. Dawn blushed and fled as the sun straddled the mountain, and the mountain groaned under the welcomed light. The earth trembled at the sight.

At such moments, one wishes that Anaya had been more restrained. Happily, such passages are few and the greater part of the narrative is enriched with vibrant lyricism.

Moreover, *Tortuga* is the product of Anaya's increasing prowess as a novelist, and one can conjecture that Anaya esteems it as his best work. His third novel demonstrates, notwithstanding the discrepancy noted above, that Anaya has conscientiously worked at his craft. In brief, it is a more disciplined and carefully executed novel. And it presents a stronger correspondence to the "real world" of human suffering and failure. The intention was stated even before the novel was finished: ". . . It will deal with the kind of crippling of life that we have created in our society, where love is no longer the predominant feeling that we have for one another. Once love

is not the feeling that dictates our social interaction with each other, then we cripple people." *Tortuga* intensely dramatizes this condition. The novel is set in a children's hospital, and it relentlessly and graphically describes horrible diseases, amputations, and the nerve-shattering cries of pain and despair. Appropriately, it also extensively explores the battered psyches of society's "throwaway children." By far, it is Anaya's most sober work and it discloses a compelling tragic sense. Whereas the tragic sense was often weakened by obtrusive sentimentality in the earlier novels, in *Tortuga* it is sustained and rivets a truth about the unconscionable disposal of human beings. This is not to suggest that the tragic sense overwhelms the novel and renders it a dark and pessimistic work. To be clarified later, Anaya's mythopoesis and his faith in the regenerative power of love deny victory to the forces of death. Rather, it is meant to emphasize Anaya's large compassion for human suffering and to credit his moral vision—which refuses to tolerate the absence of love and humaneness in the world.

Mythopoesis—myth and the art of myth-making—is the crux of Anaya's philosophical and artistic vision. Precisely, Anaya's archetypal imagination is rooted in an archaism that reveres the wisdom of the past and sees this ancient wisdom as a means toward the spiritual fulfillment of humanity. It is also informed by the conviction that myth is an eternal reservoir that nourishes the most creative and the most universal art. Anaya's aesthetic credo is in accord with Northrop Frye's distinction that "myth is a form of verbal art, and belongs to the world of art. Unlike science, it deals, not with the world that man contemplates, but with the world that man creates," [Northrop Frye, "Myth, Fiction and Displacement," *Myth and Myth Making*, ed. Henry A. Murry, (1960)]. Anaya, well-versed in mythic literature and the theory of archetypes, has repeatedly defended the validity of myth and archetypes:

> One way I have of looking at my own work. . . is through a sense that I have about primal images, primal imageries. A sense that I have about the archetypal, about what we once must have known collectively. What we all share is a kind of collective memory. . . . It simply says that there was more harmony, there was more a sense that we knew we are dust. That we had been created from it, that we were in touch with it, that we danced on it, and the dust swirled around us, and it grew the very kind of basic stuff that we need to exist. That's what I'm after. My relationship to it. ["Myth and the Writer: A Conversation with Rudolfo Anaya"].

Anaya's comment, of course, echoes Jung's "collective unconscious," and there are striking similarities to Jung's thoughts in *Modern Man In Search of a Soul:*

> . . . there is a thinking in primordial images—in symbols which are older than historical man; which have

been ingrained in him from earliest times, and, eternally living, outlasting all generations, still make up the groundwork of the human psyche. It is only possible to live the fullest life when we are in harmony with these symbols, wisdom is a return to them.

Similarly, Anaya shares with Jung, Mircea Eliade, and other contemporary exponents of mythopoetics a concern for the demythicization of human consciousness and the fragmentation of the human psyche. Anaya gives emphasis to terms like *polarity, duality*, and *dichotomy* in describing the spiritual and psychic debility which he sees as characteristic of modern existence:

What did archaic men do that we cannot do? Archaic man could communicate with both worlds. Where does dualism and polarity come from? We can say it comes from social reality and the dialectic. I disagree, I say it comes from our spiritual self, a disharmonizing force. Our civilizing and socializing influence has made us not as unified, not as harmonious, as archaic man. To go back and get in touch, and to become more harmonious, we go back to the unconscious and we bring out all of the symbols and archetypals that are available to all people. [**"Mitólogos y Mitómanos"**].

Anaya's conviction that harmony and the reconciliation of elemental forces are needed for spiritual fulfillment leads to the holistic philosophy that forms the thematic core of his three novels. His trio of seers—Ultima in *Bless Me, Ultima,* Crispín in *Heart of Aztlán*, and Salomón in *Tortuga*—are agents of reconciliation and harmony. The oneness of things is repeatedly stated in multiple images and thematic motifs. In *Bless Me, Ultima*, a parable of good and evil in which discordant elements create dissension and violence, harmony is the greatest good. It is noteworthy that Anaya, through mythopoesis, encompasses the particular and the universal. In Antonio, the narrator and central character of the novel, Anaya projects the immemorial struggle for identity and self-knowledge. Antonio endures the rite of passage that takes him from childhood to adolescence, from innocence to incipient knowledge, and into the complex world of human affairs. His passage leads him to experience *la tristeza de la vida,* the truism that human existence is often a sad and tragic enterprise. The spiritual source that enables Antonio to overcome the disillusionment and the tragedies of life is Ultima. She brings to Antonio a holistic creed and the ultimate truth (the pun on *ultima,* the last and the ultimate of things, is charming and unobtrusive) that the greatest wisdom resides in the human heart. In a dream sequence, Ultima whispers to Antonio the direction that he must take toward true knowledge: "You have been seeing only parts, she finished, and not looking beyond into the great cycle that binds all." Through Ultima's teachings and example, Antonio finds the moral and spiritual strength to reconcile the familial differences, the religious contraries, and the other polarities that serve as the novel's thematic conflict. The dichotomies are unified and the narrative

converges in ringing affirmation: ". . . I made strength from everything that had happened to me, so that in the end even the final tragedy could not defeat me. And that is what Ultima tried to teach me, that the tragic consequences of life can be overcome by the magical strength that resides in the human heart." The novel ends with a celebration of love—the unifying principle of human existence.

The conclusion of *Bless Me, Ultima* is unabashedly sentimental, and introduces an ethical prescription that is reiterated and intensified in *Heart of Aztlán* and *Tortuga*. Starting with the novel's title, *Heart of Aztlán* works the same thematic metaphor to describe the inner force that will lead to the discovery of an ancient and profound truth. The quest for *Aztlán* is, in effect, a search for the peace and harmony that have been lost throughout history and that loss has removed Chicano people from their identity and purpose. The pristine truth is that the Chicano can *return* to Aztlán; it has always existed, but people became blind to its magical presence. In an epiphany (one of Anaya's favorite devices), Clemente, like Antonio in *Bless Me, Ultima*, discovers the mythic power of Aztlán:

Time stood still, and in that enduring moment he felt the rhythm of the heart of Aztlán beat to the measure of his own heart. Dreams and visions became reality, and reality was but the thin substance of myth and legends. A joyful power coursed from the dark womb-heart of the earth into his soul and he cried out I AM AZTLAN!

True to the holistic concept that nerves Anaya's fiction, Clemente sees his place in the cosmic scheme of things and unifies the elements that previously had created alienation and confusion. Again it leads to the recognition of the superior force of love and the rejection of hatred and violence: "The real fire of heaven is not the fire of violence, it is the fire of love!" The sentimental conclusion was effective in *Bless Me, Ultima*, but in *Heart of Aztlán* it is close to being a platitude. And here is where Anaya risked critical fire in suggesting that love is the answer to the oppression and injustice suffered by Chicanos.

Laced with mythopoeic images and symbols, *Tortuga* works similar metaphysical and ethical themes. Centered on a sixteen-year-old boy nicknamed "Tortuga"—due to his crippling paralysis and the "turtle cast" which he has to wear, the novel amplifies his anguish and alienation as he bitterly turns away from life and loses faith in divine providence—and himself. The resurrecting agent is Salomón, a seer and mythic figure who discloses *the path of light* (the way to reconciling wisdom and the spiritual fulfillment of the individual). Although he is a terminally-ill patient (and dies like Ultima in a similarly poignant scene), he is an abundant reservoir of spirituality and is the force that leads Tortuga to the recognition of life's value. He instructs Tortuga to appreciate and affirm the

---

Anaya on the future of Chicano literature:

The future is bright. The de-emphasis will be on merely mirroring the cultural, in the sense of a representational or realistic mirroring of the culture, the trend is to a more personal work which will carry the culture in it, but will have a concern with experimentation, with style, and perhaps character. Maybe I'm saying this because I feel this is where my work is going. Somehow I never set out to mirror the culture, to hold the espejo [mirror] up to the culture. Many people have said this is what is in my work, but that is not a primary intention of the work. I have always thought that the background—which is the background of my own personal life—will normally fit itself into whatever my concern happens to be. In a sense I think this is repeated in the whole scene of Chicano literature.

Rudolfo Anaya, in *Chicano Authors: Inquiry by Interview,* by Juan D. Bruce-Novoa, University of Texas Press, 1980.

---

beauty of life: ". . . life is sacred, yes, even in the middle of this wasteland and in the darkness of our wards, life is sacred. . . ." Like his predecessors, Salomón embodies a holistic metaphysic and celebrates the oneness of life: ". . . we're all bound together, one great force binds us all, it's the light of the sun that binds all life, the mountain and the desert, the plains and the sea." The expected truism that love is the force that binds human life is dramatically (perhaps melodramatically) announced: "That's what Salomón had said. That love was the only faith which gave meaning to our race across the beach. The path of the sun was the path of love. I needed to love!" Culling tropes from Eliot and other modern poets who have metaphorically described the spiritual sterility of our times, Anaya dovetails the narrative to Tortuga's realization that Salomón had left him a legacy of regenerative mythopoesis: "We must create out of our ashes. Our own hero must be born out of this wasteland, like the phoenix bird of the desert he must rise again from the ashes of our withered bodies . . . He must walk in the path of the sun . . . and he shall sing the songs of the sun." Tortuga nobly meets the task. Like Antonio in *Bless Me, Ultima,* he becomes a singer of songs; he will become a poet that will transmit the magical wisdom inherited from Ultima, Crispín, and Salomón. And, of course, he will sing songs of love. The concluding sentences of the novel describe Tortuga's homeward bound journey. His singing voice fills the bus and streams across the majestic expanse of the New Mexico desert. And Salomón's loving encouragement reverberates across the closing page: "Sing a song of love, Tortuga! Oh yes, sing of love!"

The avenue for Anaya's accomplishment in expanding and invigorating the Chicano novel has been myth and the mythopoeic art. Here lies the core of his novelistic invention. His archetypal imagination richly mines

indigenous materials, fuses them with poetic images and symbols, and connects the past and the present to make something new from the old. On a smaller scale, Anaya possesses the gift and achieves the art credited to one of the twentieth-century exemplars of mythopoesis, Thomas Mann: "In a narrative tone that recalls the past, he reveals what we find disturbing in the present. He is at once old and new, and his gift is the mingling of the mythic and the present moment" [Wright Morris, *About Fiction,* 1975)].

At one point in *Tortuga,* Salomón explains the mythologizing behind his stories: "Each carries a new story, but all these stories are bound to the same theme . . . *life is sacred.*"

Similarly, each of Anaya's novels presents a new story, but they are bound by one central theme: life is sacred and the love of life is the greatest human accomplishment. Anaya cherishes the kinder moments of the human race and sings a song that seeks to bind humanity. There is much truth in his song, and there is a largeness of heart in the man and his work. Anaya's work is eloquent testament that art can teach us to recognize our humanity. It is an exemplary achievement. (pp. 33–52)

Antonio Márquez, "The Achievement of Rudolfo A. Anaya," in the *Magic of Words: Rudfolfo A. Anaya and His Writings,* edited by Paul Vassallo, University of New Mexico Press, 1982, pp. 33–52.

CORDELIA CANDELARIA
(review date 1983)

[Candelaria is a noted Chicano poet, educator, and critic whose works include *Chicano Poetry: A critical Introduction* (1986). Below, she surveys the stories of Anaya's *Silence of the Llano,* assessing their strengths and weaknesses.]

As a title *Silence of the Llano* has a compelling lyrical beauty about it evocative of the profound stillnesses captured in Japanese watercolors where calm exteriors seem to mask all the exuberant complexities of life. As a book-length collection of short fiction, *Silence* does not, unfortunately, sustain the lyricism throughout the ten stories. Instead, the book contains flashes of Anaya's best style—remembered from *Bless Me, Ultima*—and aspects of his worst.

To get the harshness out of the way, this work is weakened by two problems, one major and one minor. Starting with the latter, the title is misleading because fifty percent of the stories do not fall within the theme or modality suggested either by the title or the title story, and, in fact, pieces like **"The Christmas Play"** (out of

Bless Me, Ultima) and "The Apple Orchard" are decidedly out of harmony with "the silence of the llano" motif. Normally, the simple addition of "and other stories" to a title signals that a collection, like this one, is wide-ranging and not intended to be part of a thematic set. The much more serious drawback, however, is the difficulty the author has with effective characterization, a persistent problem for Anaya. To begin with, Anaya's tendency to rely on character *types*—i.e., people as symbols and not people—is well-represented here. For example, the mother and the daughter in the title story and the father in "**The Road to Platero**" are drawn as figures representing, respectively, feminine docility and the tyranny of love. Rather than developing these (and other) characters through the psychological nuances of their conduct in a variety of human relationships, Anaya presents them in one dimensional perspective understood primarily through the narrator's description of them and only secondarily through their words and actions. This device worked in *Bless Me, Ultima* because neither the heroic *curandera* nor the boy/quester figures were limited to these patterns but were, instead, developed characters engaged in a wide array of activities and experiencing a variety of subjective states. Quite oppositely, Anaya's use of this allegorical device seriously undermined *Heart of Aztlán* his second novel, and ruined his third, *Tortuga*, where the characters, lacking human vitality and motivation, perform like mechanical metaphors.

Related to this is another difficulty with characterization in the book, one that appears chronic for the author. Except for Ultima, who was enlivened by the force of her particular personality in conjunction with her symbolic value, Anaya's female characters have been predictable idealizations of feminity (e.g., Cristina in *Heart of Aztlán* and Ismelda in *Tortuga*) or predictable renderings of feminine undersirables (e.g., the Trementina sisters in *Ultima* and the hospital board matrons in *Tortuga*). What is grating in this work is not that women do not appear in two stories nor that they are inconsequential in most of the rest, but, rather, that they are consistently referred to in sexist terms. For instance, we expect that Miss Brighton in "**Apple Orchard**" will be described in the narrow terms associated with an adolescent boy's sexual awakening, for the story is about Isador's pubescence and she is central to it. But it is totally implausible and unrealistic *in terms of the story itself* for her to disrobe in the classroom to provide the hero with his first serious sexual encounter. The *deus ex machina* quality of the scene turns the story into a facile sexual fantasy where woman once again functions as mere sex object. Similarly, Justino's "big, luscious women" in "**B. Traven Is Alive and Well in Cuernavaca**" and the "hot and lonely and ready for company" European women in *"The Village which the Gods Painted Yellow"* are taken from the same stereotypic pattern, and the author gives no suggestion that the stereotype is employed with any irony.

Notwithstanding these shortcomings, *Silence of the Llano* has its strengths. Indeed, these strengths make the important problem with characterization all the more poignant, for Anaya does have an artist's eye and a wealth of wonderful material, and his experiments with subject and theme from book to book indicate that his artistry is still vital and energetic. Perhaps all he needs is a tougher editor. At any rate, some of the best features of this collection are the inclusion of details from the *raza/mestizo* experience and imagination, the treatment of preindustrial autochthonous life, and the focus on the theme of fictivenes in life vis-a-vis the essence and value of fiction.

When Anaya taps his vast reserves of information and insight into Chicano culture and heritage, his writing seems effortless and, often, inspired. Certainly, a good part of *Ultima*'s success derives from this, just as in the present work the title story and "**B Traven . . . in Cuernavaca**" work best when Anaya evokes his theme in the context of *raza* life and symbols. In the same way, "**El Veloria**," the excerpt from *Heart of Aztlán*, succeeds as an independent story unit because it centers on the rich customs and rituals of a Southwestern wake, and that center makes the story as powerful as Rufus' need to have "a proper velorio" for his son.

For the most part, *Silence of the Llano* is similarly effective in its presentation of preindustrial images and values—both those with an historical basis in the past and those conjured up in Anaya's imagination. Anaya's fascination with the pre-American past is defining characteristic of his aesthetic vision, and though it sometimes undercuts his work (e.g., the Billy Jack philosophizing by Clemente in *Heart of Aztlán* and Salomón's sentimentalism in *Tortuga*), it more often has an uplifting effect. Concerned with demonstrating the efficacy of a preindustrial, primitive worldview to contemporary society, Anaya employs this theme in half of the stories here. It works particularly well in "**The Place of the Swallows**" where a tone and atmosphere of solemn isolation is sustained throughout the story. It works less well in "**The Village which the Gods Painted Yellow**," where Gonzalo's quest and Rosario's motivations are not always clear. Still, the jungle scenes in that piece evince a mystery and drama that produce their own special effect on the reader.

The most exciting element for me in *Silence of the Llano* is the emphasis Anaya gives to the theme of fictiveness and fiction—their essence, meaning, and purpose—and their relationship to lived experience. Several of the stories are developed around this theme, and they are the most creative, provocative, and interesting pieces contained in the collection. "**Place of the Swallows**" for example, deals with the transformation of shared experiences when they are re-created as stories for recreation.

   . . . there is a special time which the telling of the story creates, a time and place which become more important than the adventure lived. Why? I ask myself. What do the words create? In the story the marsh becomes a swamp, slipping into mud becomes a near-fatal fall into the quagmire, and the stoning of a harmless garter snake becomes the killing of a poisonous viper. In the shadows of the river I make them see giant monsters, unknown enemies, which I know are only reflections of the words I use. I choose details carefully and weave them all into images; they see themselves as heroes and nod their approval.

In its description of the power of language and fiction to reify and, even, to transmute shared experience, the passage conveys the dynamic relationship between "real" life and fiction. Fiction vis-a-vis reality also forms the thematic nub of **"A Story"** and **"B Traven. . . in Cuernavaca."** In both works the very making of a story—any story as well as the writing of these two stories themselves—provides the framework for the plot, thus allowing Anaya to achieve a Pirandellian irony aspiring to the magic realism of Garcia Marquez. In **"A Story"** the writer (i.e., Anaya's narrative persona) appears as The Writer (i.e., a character) whose encounters with both "actual" characters in his fictive life and imagined ones trying to charm their way into his fictional writing call attention to the *act of* the art of fiction. The acting part is underscored by the story's dramatic elements (e.g., the cast of characters and the stage directions)and by the theatrical behavior of the characters. In the same way, the fictiveness theme is succinctly captured in the title **"B Traven Is Alive and Well in Cuernavaca."** By referring to Traven, pseudonym of Mexico's most elusive and mysterious writer, the expatriate European Berick Torsvan, Anaya immediately calls into question the nature of the reader's and writer's shared reality. The story itself reveals that what keeps Traven "alive and well" is his art, the canon of fiction that constitutes his life's work, *not* his life, for no biography would be definitive of such a private man.

[B. Traven] has become something of an institution in Mexico, a man honored for his work. The cantineros and taxi drivers in Mexico City know about him as well as the cantineros of Spain knew Hemingway, or they claim to . . . if the cantinero knows his business, and they all do in Mexico, he is apt to say, "Did you know that B. Traven used to drink here?". . . if you don't leave right then you will wind up hearing many stories about the mysterious B. Traven . . . Everybody reads his novels, on the buses, on street corners, if you look closely you'll spot one of his titles. One turned up for me, and that's how this story started. I was sitting in the train station in Juarez, waiting for the train to Cuernavaca, which would be an exciting title for this story except that there is no train to Cuernavaca.

After a series of encounters with the picaresque Justino and a number of episodes in Mexico City, the I-narrator finds the inspiration which has been eluding him throughout the story. "I quickened my pace be-

cause suddenly the story, was overflowing and I needed to write." The start of his writing marks the end of the story. Despite Anaya's occasional faulty rhetoric and his didactic tendency to tell stories along with **"Place of the Swallows"** disclose a freshness and depth not seen in the last novel. Like our first experience with *Ultima*, these qualities leave one looking ahead to Anaya's next publication.

Cordelia Candelaria, "Problems and Promise in Anaya's *Llano*," in *The American Book Review*, Vol. 5, No. 6, September–October, 1983, pp. 18–19.

RUDOLFO ANAYA WITH JOHN F. CRAWFORD
(interview date 1986)

[In the following interview, conducted in 1986, Anaya discusses his Chicano heritage and its impact on his works, focusing particularly on his *Bless Me, Ultima*, *Heart of Aztlán*, and *Tortuga*.]

[Anaya]: One of the most interesting experiences about coming to Albuquerque in the fifties was coming from a very small rural town into a big city *barrio* and being thrown into a completely different life-style. Recently, while attending the Writers of the Purple Sage Conference, it occurred to me that almost every writer there had shared a similar experience. No one lives in a small town any more; nearly all of us are city writers. Although I had all my upbringing in that small town, the majority of my life has been spent in the big city now. That's kind of shocking—we write about our roots that are close to the land, and then we get slapped with this new reality.

[Crawford]: *In your novels there's a double move, from the llano to the small towns and then to the big city.*

I think it's a progression that has happened in New Mexico. Historically, after World War II you have that exodus from the small towns into the metropolitan areas, especially from the Mexican working community. The new professions were being opened up, the GI Bill was sending some of the veterans to the university, and my writing reflects that historical pattern.

*In **Heart of Aztlán** it sounds like the small factories were opening up in New Mexico and they were exploiting cheap labor where they could find it, and that would be a reason also.*

Absolutely.

One particular way I remember you writing about the space you grew up in had to do with interior space: the public library in Santa Rosa.

I would visit it periodically, starting at an early age, when I was in grade school. It was a little one-room library actually placed on top of the fire house on the first floor, where there was an old beaten up fire truck used on a volunteer basis when there was a fire in the town. We climbed up those rickety steps to the little room that was the library. That interests me too, you know, looking back at what was formative in my love of books.

In your novels the formative influences seem to be the figures who represent wisdom and knowledge, like Ultima and Crispin. Were there real people like that in your life who would serve such a function, or are those characters a sort of metaphor or composite?

I think it was a little bit of each. In our Hispanic culture there is a great deal of respect given to older people—and growing up in the forties as I did, the relationships that we had with older people were ones of trust. We listened to what they said and we learned from them. And there were specific people that I knew and held in awe. These fabulous *vaqueros* would come in from the llano and my father or brothers and I would visit them; to me, they were almost mythological figures, bigger than life. I think I felt the same way about teachers, because it was normal in our culture to be taught by anyone who was older and to give him or her respect. So when I came to write my novels, which basically have to do with a search for meaning or an archetypal journey, the person who can guide the hero turns out to be the older person not only out of the structure of myth as we know it but out of my background, out of my life. Those older people played very important roles. We believed that *curanderas* could cure; we saw them do it. We believed that there were evil powers that came to be represented by witches, because we lived in the universe where we saw those powers work.

And also that things were animated with life, like Tortuga the mountain. There were places that had power.

Most definitely. I think it's Clemente in **Heart of Aztlán** who recalls, "I remember there were times and certain places in the llano where I grew up where I would stand at this place and have a feeling of elation, a feeling of flying"—that's interesting, because there are *cuentos* or folk tales where you get these little stories about people who can fly—so in your mind you think, where does this power come from? Is it the power of imagination that we as a communal group are given by those older, wiser people, or can it actually be? So it was very interesting to deal with the power that the earth has to animate us—we *are* animated by the power of the earth—it is in Native American terms our Mother—it nurtures us, it gives us spirit and sustenance, and I guess if we're attuned enough or sensitive enough it can give us different *kinds* of powers. And so, coming out of that kind of complex universe where I grew up thinking of all these places, the river and the hills, having this life to them, this animation, it was very good not only for my growing up but for the imagi-

nation, getting fed by that very spiritual process that was in the natural world around me.

That must have come to you first in the cuentos *themselves, the stories you would have heard while growing up. When did you start taking an interest in myth outside your own culture—was that in college—and where did this interest lead you?*

It was probably when I was an undergraduate here at UNM. We were guided to read Greek mythology. I wasn't really making the connections because I was looking at it as stories that had to do with another time and place. I think it wasn't until I turned more toward Native American mythology that I began to see that there are these points of reference that world myths have, that somehow speak to the center of our being, and connect us—to other people, to the myth, to the story, and beyond that to the historic process, to the communal group.

You have a way of making the myths take on very specific roles in the novels. I'm thinking of the incredible way that the mountain and the boy interplay at the beginning of Tortuga, *where the mountain actually moves and something in the boy moves. It must have taken a great deal of trial and error to find out artistic ways to make the myths connect up with the plots of the stories you were working. They seem highly integrated in* Tortuga *especially.*

I would hope that by **Tortuga** they would seem integrated, because it was my third novel and I had been consumed by that process long enough, and possibly also had learned a little bit about how to write a novel.

I have been told, when I travel around the country and read, that there haven't been that many American writers interested in the role of myth and in making myth work in contemporary settings—but I think now we see more and more writers doing that. All the Native American writers tend to do that, fuse their sense of myth into their stories, but at least awhile it's been rather new to people.

The other thing that people seem to remark on is that not too many writers are lyrical novelists—you know. *Ultima* opens with a great deal of lyricism, a song of invocation almost, if not the Muse then to the Earth, because Antonio says, "In the beginning she opened my eyes and then I could see the beauty of my landscape, my llano, the river, the earth around us." There are other examples in American literature when that happens, but certainly it's been one of my preoccupations. I think the sense of diction and syntax and rhythms of language that come out of having grown up in a Spanish-speaking world, and the act of transferring that to English, creates a "fresh ripple" in people's sensibilities as they read this new language, this conversion of Hispanic language and world view into English. They may be a little shocked at the onset, but most people who get past it find it's refreshing, it's new.

I was especially struck by the freshness of the language in the Christmas play scene in Ultima and when the chil-

dren go to the theater in **Tortuga**—*partly, I think, because these are scenes of rebellion against the norms of authority and partly because these are children in their spontaneity. There is such vitality in these scenes, where one set of cultural and social expectations crosses another. I suppose when you were writing* **Ultima** *there wasn't much like that in prose, even in Chicano prose.*

No, there wasn't—actually, I had read absolutely no Chicano prose during all my school years, including my university years. There were a few novels out there, and I suppose if you were into research you could have found diaries and newspapers, or in folklore you could have read the *cuentos,* but contemporary Chicano prose wasn't born until the mid-sixties during the Chicano movement, and so I think in a sense what we did in the sixties was to create the model itself, or as I have phrased it elsewhere, we set about to build a house and in the sixties we build a foundation. From that comes what we're seeing now in the eighties, an incredible amount of production and writing and unique forms and styles of writing. But all of that was new; it was new to me. In fact, in the sixties when I first began to work, I used Anglo American writers as role models. But I really couldn't get my act together until I left them behind. They had a lot to teach me and I don't underestimate that—you're learning whether you're reading a comic book or Hemingway or Shakespeare or Cervantes—but I couldn't tell my story in their terms. And it wasn't until I said to myself, let me shift for myself, let me go stand on my earth, coming out of my knowledge, and tell the story then and there—that's where Ultima came in. She opens my eyes as she opened Antonio's eyes at the beginning of the book, for the first time; so I sat down to write the story **Bless Me, Ultima,** thinking in Spanish though I wrote it in English. And it worked, because I was creating what to me was a reflection of that real universe that I knew was there.

It seems tremendously integrated—not only as to myth and plot, as we were just discussing, but the style. I know you said you put it through several drafts; it looks as if it just sprang out of heaven that way. That must have taken an enormous amount of work.

At least seven drafts *is* a lot of work. And then there is a concern for what you just said, that integration, that consistency that you don't want to give up in any one place, and a kind of conscious/subconscious working and interrelating of the myths and the symbols so that they all make a consistent pattern, like weaving a beautiful Navajo rug, you know? It's consistent because it reflects not only the particular person who does the weaving, but all the communal history that went into those symbols and those colors.

There also you have the sense of the llano, probably best described there of the three books—and also the farming communities and the towns. And there's a juxtaposition of one against the other, shown in the conflicts of the two

families. Was that from your own background? Were both sides of that conflict present within your own family?

Yes, in fact, my mother is from a farming community and my father did most of his work as a *vaquero*—what you would call a cowboy or a sheepherder—out on the llano in the ranches; so there was the antagonism between the *llaneros* and the farmers in my family.

I love the way the farmers are people of few words. When they are talking to Antonio they will communicate in a few sentences what they have been thinking about all day. That seems to be true of farmers everywhere.

Yeah, I think it is a characteristic, isn't it, of people who work with the earth to have imbued in them a sense of patience. On the other hand, they also have their own storytelling, and I remember visiting those farms along Puerta de Luna, where my grandfather had a farm, and late at night people would gather around and begin to tell stories. But the tradition was kind of different. The *llaneros (vaqueros* to me) would always be the loud men; they made a lot of noise, they were rough, they were gruff, they laughed more and probably drank more, so what you learned from the respective groups was very different, had its own flavor. . . .

There's a strong sense in **Ultima** *that the life experience cuts against some of the aspects of traditional Catholicism, so that there seems to be a sort of striving to supplant or transform it into a kind of world religion based on experience, especially mystical experience. Am I right about this? And did you encounter resistance from traditional Catholics for that message in the book?*

I've never felt there was any resistance or opposition. I think quite the contrary, a lot of readers who are Catholic have seen an accurate portrayal of the church at least as it was in those times—you're talking now about forty years later, and things have changed. But I think it's fair to say that what goes on in the novel also reflects my attempt to get an understanding of the Native American tradition and those other religions that are not Catholic and not based in the Christian mythology.

Especially from the indio.

Especially from the *indio.* And again, not to give up the one tradition for the other, but to see if those points of reference I talked about can be reached, whether from my Catholic world I knew as a child or my exploration of the Native American world that is also part of me or the worlds that I read of in other mythologies, such as Buddhism. And so I think for me to look only in my Catholic background was too limiting, and **Bless Me, Ultima** begins to explore new ground.

I was struck by the richness of choices that Antonio has at the end of the novel. He has many things to think about, reconcile, bring together.

Well, his universe begins to get constricted. I think Antonio's life is—as he begins to see that he is losing the innocence of childhood—it possibly reflects the life of the Hispanic community in New Mexico, in the sense that we too began to lose that age when the only thing that affected us happened within our family or our village. The world was changing around us and was going to bring a lot of new and positive things to us, but also some threats. And we had a lot of decisions to make. Pretty quick.

There's a thread of continuity in the books—literally, the same family is mentioned first in Ultima, *is the whole subject of* Aztlán, *and the boy carries on in* Tortuga—*but also, there is the thread of another kind of continuity. It seems to me that the three books are a trilogy, and in the third book is an overall interpretation you can bring—what the boy is going through personally somehow involves the whole culture, and his success, his survival, is a very important thing: an achievement for everyone.*

It's strange that no one has ever said that, you know. And I agree with your interpretation, because it seems to me that one of the important things I was doing in *Tortuga* was taking the main character and trying to make him well again after he had been crippled by life, by the circumstances that occur in *Heart of Aztlán*. And I felt that as much or more than any other character I had ever created, Tortuga was Everyman of the Chicano culture, that indeed the culture was under assault, and that the paralysis reflected in Tortuga was that paralysis that had set on the community. Tortuga has not only to get well, he has to perform still more heroic tasks in the future; not only that, the Mexican American community has to find ways of breaking out of its bondage, its paralysis.

It's also true that there are people from other cultures in the hospital who are also afflicted. . . .

Yes, and in this respect I think the novel should acquire some kind of universal meaning, because what we have created of our modern society can paralyze all of us—those of us from minority groups get displaced more and used more, but I think if we are not careful the same forces that cripple us can do it everyone. So you have in the hospital, even if they are never completely identified by ethnic group, representatives of all of them.

In all three novels, the power of love is the redeemer in some sense. In Tortuga *it's very much a literal one: It's sexual love, it's also working together—there's a wonderful sense of the people pulling together in a more collective spirit within the room he's in; there's real affection between the boys there—in fact, that seems to be the dominant message that your novels carry . . . .*

I think you're right. Though I have lived in and explored the existential universe, I have come back to a communal universe. I grew up in that tradition, I left it in some of my wanderings, and I returned to it; and what the tradition of the community has to teach us is what I've already alluded to—respect, love for the family and for the village that is the community. I think that's where the power of love comes in. I feel it has sustained

all those Indian and Mexican pueblos that have occupied this region for such a long time; they must have had it as they came together and formed their bond—a bond not only of tradition and language and culture and heritage, but of love. That's how they were able to survive, and that's how they will be able to survive in the presence of all those powers that can cripple and kill us, you see.

In Heart of Aztlán *there is also that spirit of coming together, within the community established in Albuquerque, in the various parts of the* barrio *whatever the difficulty of the circumstances.*

One of the things that some critics have viewed as a failure in *Heart of Aztlán* has been that no structure, no political structure with a given political ideology, is put into place. But I guess my feeling is that while those structures may come into being, if they're not shored up by some common respect and a common goal that we have as human beings, they don't last long. And I do see their importance—they're the way we get things done in today's world. But I was more interested, I guess, in following the other side of that coin, and that is can we really get together as a community—not because of what's in it for me, but because of that old sense of value that has sustained all communities on earth throughout history. And to me, the element of love must play a large role in it.

That brings me to a political question. You had clearly stated ten years ago that you didn't feel Chicano literature was strongest when it was narrowly addressed to political struggle and resistance. Ten years ago, the climate was very politically charged. What do you think about this now?

What I have come to see is that there is even more need now for what we call a political stance, in our poetry and our novels. That seems to be a big change from where I was ten years ago. I guess I thought then that the literature we were writing would be very good for our community, one more place where we could reflect on our history and our identity and move on from there, and that we didn't have to overwhelm the reader with "message," so to speak; we didn't have to hit the reader over the head with ideology. I think that's principally the reason I wasn't in tune with the political writings of the Chicano movement at the time. I felt all too often that the ideology came up short—all too often it was only a Marxist ideology—and, too, I tended to see in writers whose main concern was message a lack of aesthetic attention to what they were practicing, what they were learning to be. They didn't really want to be writers whose main concern was message a lack of aesthetic attention to what they were practicing, what they were learning to be. They didn't really want to be writers, they wanted to be politicians, and I think there's two different animals there. Can you get those two together in the same work? Can a very good writer who has learned and paid attention and practiced his craft communicate his political feelings about the society? I think yes; I feel stronger about that now than

I did then. I still think it's probably the hardest kind of writing to do, because you tend to put the reader off. The reader wants story and you're talking message; the reader may quickly leave you. But it is important in this country, especially when you speak of our community, the Southwest. We have not only the story to write, we also have to remind our people about their history and their traditions and their culture and their language, things that are under that threat that we talked about right now, and liable to disappear if we don't look closely at ourselves in a historical process—and part of analyzing that historical process is not only story and myth and legend and tradition, it's a political space we occupy. How have we occupied it? How have we been used in that political space?

Recently I've played around with an essay in which I talk about writing in colonial space, which is a political concept, right? How do we feel as a minority group, a clearly recognizable ethnic group, when we have to respond to colonial space—how do we carve out our own identity? This is what the Chicano movement was all about, trying to create within colonial space the space for our own community, our literature. And that process is tied into the political process.

So in a sense you're always tied into it—I think my three novels are. The fact that they don't clearly call for one specific ideology may be interpreted as a critical fault in a political novel, but I didn't set out to write political novels. Though I do see their importance.

I think probably the novel that I'm writing now, which is again set in Albuquerque, is my analysis of my contemporary world, the present, today: What role do the different cultures of New Mexico play vis-á-vis each other? how is the Southwest changing? what is the concept of the Sunbelt all about? who is coming here and why are tremendous investments being made across the South west? what do they mean to our communities that have been here a long time? I think probably the only way we respond to some of these questions, critical questions if we're going to exist as a culture, *is* in novels that carry that social-political impact and perhaps allow the public to think on those questions that are crucial. But I'm still of the opinion that you do that through a well-told story.

I've noticed there seem to be affinities between the ideas you're expressing and the writings of magic realism in Central and South America—being political in the broadcast sense, describing what is happening in the Americas, and doing it with art—not leaving it to rhetoric. Do you have any direct relationships with Marquez or Fuentes or. . . .

No, I haven't. If I were more inclined to go around visiting with writers, I would have found ways, but I'm not. I have one short story called **"B. Traven Is Alive and Well in Cuernavaca"** which begins something like this: "I don't go to Mexico to meet writers; I go to write!"

*I want to go back to **Tortuga**. It seems to me it's the most political novel you've done because it's the most concen-*

trated on this extended metaphor we've been talking about—because that hospital is also a prison. The Indian boy that gets out dies very soon. It's as if people have been cut off from the land so that in going back to it, it becomes dangerous.

Yeah . . . the idyllic and pastoral llano and river valley of **Bless Me, Ultima!** becomes the cancerous desert, the blinding sandstorms that you have to cross to get back home, the frozen mountain in midwinter that the Indian boy has to cross and that kills him. So even the land has almost become an antagonist, whereas before it was the nurturing mother. We get the sense of the unnatural storms, radiation, death in the desert, grasses described as brittle, and that's all part of the extended metaphor, the reflection of what we are doing to ourselves, what we are doing to our earth.

One thing you did in that book struck me in a very personal way, because I spent some time myself in children's hospitals. It's where you talk about pain. You say that for someone who's had a great deal of pain, it's very hard to avoid things like drugs and alcohol later, because pain is a high and you get used to it. That's a very clear insight. When I read that I thought, "This guy has been there." You must have known something about that experience to be able to write that way.

Yeah, well, I spent a summer in one of those hospitals and that's where the germ of the novel comes from—the experience, some of the characters, and some of the things that he went through. Around that is the reflection of what we are doing to ourselves and to the earth. It does have the hope in it that my characters seem to keep looking around—there must be *somebody* out there who I can make contact with—like the persons I knew in childhood who were a little wiser and more solid because they were sharing themselves. And even though the rest of the landscape alternates between the dead desert with the sandstorms and the frozen mountains around the hospital on the west side, the springs of the mountain are still running, there is still hope, it's not too late, and you can go there and you can bathe and be made whole. But there's very little of that left, you know. And we've got to touch base with it pretty quick. Otherwise, living in this region that has so much potential to it, because it's a very special corridor in this country, the Rio Grande Valley and the cultures that have been here for thousands of years—it's a very special place—if we don't realize that, we're going to lose part of the hope that this region has to offer us and the people in it.

We might end with one other question about that. It seems to me that some of the most responsible writers, as well as some of the best, from the three cultures here have written about this sense of place in one way or another—I'm thinking of Edward Abbey, who's really a westerner; Leslie Silko and Simon Ortiz; certainly yourself; and several others who have addressed it in a big way, in novels. What do you think the prospects are for this multicultural work becoming a national forum that people can begin to see as a model for such statements?

I think that has already happened. I see any number of regions around the country that are in a sense turning inward and looking at themselves and producing wonderfully gifted writers. I'm not sure that we in the Southwest caused that forum; the times themselves are calling for a truly representative speaking to each other, letting down some of these false borders that we've had between us. I think that's very positive thing. What's happening in this country—if we are part of it, much more power to us—is that if we are able to take our different perspectives of how the world ought to be—alerted to the fact that there are people out there who thrive on destroying—and share these perspectives, you know, communicate among groups, then we have something to offer the whole country and the world. The world *is* interested; that's one thing that is conveyed to me every time a visitor comes through here. They've locked into the Southwest as a place going through a very interesting experiment—it has to do with how people can live with each other, can share—and this is as important to the whites and the Maori of New Zealand as it may be to the Catalonians and the Basques, the Nicaraguans and the Misquitos, you know what I mean? It's important to us to realize that we are center of focus—a lot of people are looking at us, and we can do something very positive with all the changes that are coming across this land, or we can blow it. And I tend to want to work more on the positive things that are going on here, so that we can learn from each other. (pp. 85–93)

Rudolfo Anaya and John Crawford, in an interview in *This is about Vision: Interviews with Southwestern Writers,* William Balassi, John F. Crawford, Annie O. Eysturoy, eds., University of New Mexico Press, 1990, pp. 83–93.

SOURCES FOR FURTHER STUDY

Anaya, Rudolfo A. with Ray González. "Songlines of the Southwest: An Interview with Rudolfo A. Anaya." *The Bloomsbury Review* 13, No. 5 (September–October 1993): 3, 18.
> An interview with Anaya following his retirement from teaching at the University of New Mexico.

Bruce-Novoa, Juan D. "Rudolfo A. Anaya." In his *Chicano Authors: Inquiry by Interview,* pp. 183–202. Austin: University of Texas Press, 1980.
> Interview in which Anaya discusses his background, his early novels, and Chicano literature.

Cazemajou, Jean. "Mediators and Mediation in Rudolfo Anaya's Trilogy: Bless Me, Ultima, Heart of Aztlán, and Tortuga." In *European Perspectives on Hispanic Literature of the United States,* edited by Genviere Fabre, pp. 55–65. Houston: Arte Publico Press, 1988.
> Examines Anaya's ability to synthesize–through character, language, and structure—the many elements of his Chicano heritage in his fiction.

Daghistany, Ann. "The Shaman, Light and Dark." In *Literature and Anthropology,* edited by Philip A. Dennis and Wendell Aycock, pp. 193–208. Lubbock: Texas Tech University Press, 1989.
> Compares and contrasts Ultima, the spiritual guide from *Bless Me, Ultima,* with other priest-like figures in world literature to elucidate the archetype of the shaman.

Elías, Edward. "*Tortuga*: A Novel of Archetypal Structure." *Bilingual Review* IX, No. 1 (January–April 1982): 82–7.
> Asserts that *Tortuga* transcends its Chicano worldview "by being structured in its entirety around stock, archetypal myths."

Jung, Alfred. "Regionalist Motifs in Rudolfo A. Anaya's Fiction (1972-82)." In *Missions in Conflict: Essays on U.S.-Mexican Relations and Chicano Culture,* edited by Renate von Bardeleben, Dietrich Briesemeister, and Juan Bruce-Novoa, pp. 159–68. Germany: Gunter Narr Verlag Tübingen, 1986.
> Illuminates the many New Mexican motifs in Anaya's fiction.

Lamadrid, Enrique. "The Dynamics of Myth in the Creative Vision of Rudolfo Anaya." In *Pasó por Aquí: Critical Essays on the New Mexican Literary Tradition, 1542-1988,* edited by Erlinda Gonzales-Berry, pp. 243-54. Albuquerque: University of New Mexico Press, 1989.
> Explores the function of myth in Anaya's fiction.

Lattin, Vernon E. "The 'Horror of Darkness': Meaning and Structure in Anaya's *Bless Me, Ultima*," *Revista Chicano-Riqueña* VI, No. 2 (Spring 1978): 50-7.
> Maintains that *Bless Me, Ultima* presents a spiritual journey "structured by four deaths Antonio witnesses and by ten mythic dreams he has before awakening a man."

Mitchell, Carol. "Rudolfo Anaya's *Bless Me, Ultima*: Folk Culture in Literature." *Critique* XXII, No. 1 (1980): 55-64.
> Analyzes provincial Spanish-American culture in *Bless Me, Ultima,* focusing particularly on "*la familia*" and the roles of children, adults, and the aged; the conflicts in a traditional patriarchal family between the roles of women and men; the roles of and attitudes toward the *curandera* and the *bruja;* and the close ties between the sacred and secular life in traditional society."

Tonn, Horst. "*Bless Me, Ultima*: A Fictional Response to Times

of Transition." *Aztlan* XVIII, No. 1 (Spring 1987): 59-68.
   Examines the "extraliterary context" of Anaya's first
novel, asserting that *Bless Me, Ultima* promotes reconciliation between past and present cultural conflicts in
Spanish-American literature.

Additional coverage of Anaya's life and career is contained in the following sources published by Gale Research: *Contemporary Authors,* Vols. 45-48; *Contemporary Authors Autobiography Series,* Vol. 4; *Contemporary Authors New Revision Series,* Vols. 1, 32; *Contemporary Literary Criticism,* Vol. 23; *Dictionary of Literary Biography,* Vol. 82; *Hispanic Writers; Major 20th-Century Writers.*

Reinaldo Arenas

1943–1990

Cuban novelist, poet, essayist, playwright, and short story writer.

INTRODUCTION

*A*renas is among the most widely read authors of Cuba's post-revolutionary generation. Well–regarded for the group of novels that he refers to as his "pentagony," Arenas relates in his writings experiences that reflect the turbulent political atmosphere of his homeland. His works are distinguished by imaginative embellishment of history and reality with surrealistic images and fantastic elements. Lauded for their vivid imagery and psychological complexity, Arenas's novels passionately depict the emotional turmoil of life in a totalitarian state.

Born in Cuba, Arenas was abandoned by his father at an early age and was raised by his mother and maternal grandparents in a poor, rural environment. At the age of fifteen, he joined the rebel forces that fought against the army of president Fulgencio Batista. When Fidel Castro's new revolutionary government awarded him a scholarship to study agricultural accounting in 1962, Arenas moved to Havana and enrolled in the university there. The following year he entered a contest in which he had to tell a famous children's story in five minutes; since he could not find any that he liked, Arenas composed his own. He so impressed the judges that he was given a job in the National Library. While employed there, he began writing short stories and working on his first novel, *Celestino antes del alba* (1967; *Singing from the Well*). Although the work was awarded a prize and published in Cuba, civil authorities viewed it unfavorably for its discussion of the struggle between the writer and the forces of oppression. Consequently, Arenas was forced to smuggle the manuscripts of his next two novels, *El mundo alucinante: Una novela de aventuras* (1969; *Hallucinations: Being an Account of the Life and Adventures of Friar Servando Teresa de Mier*) and *El palacio de las blanquísimas mofetas* (1975; *The Palace of the White Skunks*), out of Cuba in order to have them published. These novels were subsequently translated into French and several other languages, establishing Arenas as an international literary figure. In 1973 he was charged with the crimes of homosexuality and "ideological deviation" by Castro's regime. The author tried to escape imprisonment, but was captured and sent to jail and later to a rehabilitation farm, where he was confined until 1976. Following his release, Arenas remained in Havana performing menial jobs and writing clandestinely. He was one of approximately 140,000 Cubans who emigrated to the United States in the Mariel boatlift in 1980. Arenas settled in New York City and completed several novels, poems, short stories, and his memoirs over the next decade. Having contracted AIDS, Arenas committed suicide in December 1990. His autobiography, *Antes que anochezca* (1992; *Before Night Falls*) was published posthumously in English in 1993. Prior to his death, Arenas designated Princeton University's Firestone Library as the repository for his unexpurgated memoirs; the manuscript is sealed until the year 2010, according to curator Donald C. Skemer, because "that's where [Arenas] bared all. . . . Some of the people involved might be killed."

In an interview conducted shortly before his death, Arenas referred to his books as a collective "pentagony" that imaginatively depicts the reality of life in Castro's Cuba. *The Palace of the White Skunks*, described by Ilan Stavans as "an intriguingly baroque, polyphonic study of despair," is a family saga that relates the misadventures of a fierce and erratic clan living in rural Cuba. The work is replete with an array of bizarre and unhappy characters who want either to hide or escape from their impoverished and brutal world. The story's protagonist, an adolescent named Fortunato, manages to flee his family's madness by joining the revolutionary guerilla forces fighting against the government. In a narrative that alternates between the first and third persons, Arenas gives the reader access to the thoughts of the desolate family members, thereby showing, from a variety of perspectives, how poverty can fragment families, shatter dreams, and strangle hopes. Another of Arenas's novels, *Hallucinations*, is presented in the form of a fictionalized biography. The novel recounts the life and adventures of a nonconformist Mexican monk, Friar Servando Teresa de Mier, who suffers persecution at the hands of the church and the state in his fight for Mexico's independence from Spain. Described by Helen R. Lane as "wildly unpruned" and "cluttered," *Hallucinations* is generally viewed by commentators as a spiritual autobiography, the story of one person's quest for liberation and perfection in an often contradictory and complex world.

The "pentagony" also includes a fictionalized retelling of Arenas's own struggle to mature artistically despite restrictions imposed by totalitarian rule. *Singing from the Well* poignantly depicts how creative imagination suffers in a closed society. The novel is an evocation of the fantastic visions experienced by a mentally impaired boy growing up in Cuba's rural poverty. Illegitimate and raised by cruel and ignorant grandparents, the peasant boy imagines, among other things, that he can fly to the safety of the clouds when threatened by his ax-wielding grandfather. The desperately lonely boy finds solace in his relationship with a cousin (or alter ego), a poet named Celestino, who carves verses on trees. Alienated from the world, they hide together inside a hole in a tree trunk where they remain secluded for a thousand years. *Otra vez el mar* (1982; *Farewell to the Sea*), which Arenas described as a depiction of "the secret history of the Cuban people," relates Cuba's tumultuous political events and their impact on the nation's citizenry. In the novel, set at a seaside resort in Havana, a depressed homosexual poet and his wife reflect on their hopes and disappointments in view of the fall of Batista's government. The first portion of the book is a lengthy interior monologue in which the woman laments both living in Castro's Cuba and enduring a passionless marriage. Cognizant that her husband will never be able to return her affection, she cries: "Somewhere there must be more than this violence and loneliness, this stupidity, laziness, chaos and stupor. . . . Somewhere someone is waiting for me." The second part, a long poem in six cantos, documents Hector's thoughts regarding Cuba's failed revolution, and his own homosexual longings. Seated on the beach and gazing upon the sea, Hector and his wife painfully realize that the ocean surrounding Cuba is both their liberator and their jailer.

Many commentators laud Arenas's novels as piercing studies of human emotion. As Jay Cantor has observed, "Mr. Arenas is not interested in ordinary realistic drama. He wants to give the reader the secret history of the emotions, the sustaining victories of pleasure and the small dishonesties that callous the soul." Although some critics object to the strong anticommunist demeanor in his books, virtually all extol the power and beauty of his prose. Scholars also regard Arenas's novels as excellent examples of the Spanish-American "neo-baroque" style in which illusion, history, and philosophical ideas are joined in an organic unity. Hailed by critics as one of the most significant figures in contemporary Latin-American literature, Arenas is, in the words of Emir Rodríguez-Monegal, "the only voice to come out of Cuba in recent years that truly questions the official version of reality, political or otherwise."

CRITICAL COMMENTARY

THE TIMES LITERARY SUPPLEMENT
(essay date 1970)

[In the following review, the critic praises *Singing from the Well*, particularly noting its fantastic and incongruous imagery.]

Cuba is a country which, unlike most others in Latin America, has had a singularly fertile and imaginative literary tradition, and although the Cuban revolutionary authorities are more eager to encourage experimental writing by foreigners than by Cubans, Reinaldo Arenas's *Celestino antes del alba* is evidence that the limitations imposed on Cuban writers are not always excessively dour ones.

The novel depicts the vision that a retarded, hallucinated child has of a cruelly aggressive and arid rural environment in Cuba. The son of an unmarried mother, he is brought up in the house-hold of his grudging and violent grandparents. The child cannot easily distinguish between fantasy and reality, and whenever the grandfather pursues him with an axe, he is able to fly off and escape into the clouds. At one point he is devoured by ants; on the next page he is safely in bed, having nightmares. . . .

In many ways the child's madness is an excuse for Reinaldo Arenas to indulge in a surrealist romp, a point easily made when the child blithely quotes Arab and Chinese poems which his retarded and provincial mind could scarcely have encountered . . . . [One] of the merits of this novel. . . is the lively and convincing manner in which the fantasies are sustained. But there is also a great deal of human and social significance in the child's pathetic longing for affection in so unsympathetic an environment.

Celestino antes del alba is a distinguished first novel in what has now become an eminent tradition of fantastic literature in Latin America, and it deserves the considerable publicity it has received in the Spanish-speaking world.

"Double Vision," in *The Times Literary Supplement*, No. 3557, April 30, 1970, p. 485.

HELEN R. LANE
(essay date 1971)

[In the following review of *Hallucinations*, Lane describes the novel as an "imaginary biography" that explores the human quest for "authentic liberation."]

To the gallery of enduring universal types, the Spanish literary tradition has contributed the *picaro*, that roguish wanderer as untrappable as wind who outwits a wicked world that would enchain his very uvula. Reinaldo Arenas, a young Cuban author obviously taken with this figure of untrammeled freedom as Latin America's only hope of authentic liberation, has chosen as the hero of his *Hallucinations* an amazing real-life adventurer: Father Servando Teresa de Mier.

Americans may recognise this name only as that of a street not far from Sanborn's in Mexico City, but any Mexican schoolchild knows that Father de Mier was a friar, born in the humblest of circumstances in Monterrey 200 years ago, who shut himself up in his monastery cell with heretical books from abroad and emerged to preach to his colonialized fellows the subversive notion that the Virgin of Guadelupe was a Mexican deity, not a Spanish importation.

History records that he thereby incurred the wrath of the church, escaped from an almost mythical number of jails in Mexico and Spain, wandered on foot throughout the capitals of Western Europe, where he met such figures as Napoleon, Madame de Staël, Chateaubriand, and von Humboldt. Later, he returned to Mexico to fight for independence, forthrightly proclaimed to his compatriots that the quisling Emperor Iturbide was "worse than a whore from Pistoja," and ended his long life of authority-baiting as a hero of the new Mexican Republic—a guerrilla in a cassock venerated for his withering scorn for vulgar revolutionary practices that were no more than disguise for greed and bad manners.

Arenas calls his imaginary biography of Friar de Mier "simply a novel," but his impenitent amalgam of truth and invention, of historical fact and outrageous make-

Principal Works

Celestino antes del alba (novel) 1967
[*Singing from the Well*, 1987]

El mundo alucinante: Una novela de aventuras (novel) 1969
[*Hallucinations: Being an Account of the Life and Adventures of Friar Servando Teresa de Mier*, 1971; newly translated as *The Ill-Fated Peregrinations of Fray Servando*, 1987]

Con los ojos cerrados (short stories) 1972

El palacio de las blanquísimas mofetas (novel) 1975
[*The Palace of the White Skunks*, 1990]

La vieja Rosa (novel) 1980
[*Old Rosa and the Brightest Star*, 1989]

El central (poem) 1981
[*El central: A Cuban Sugar Mill*, 1984]

Termina el desfile (short stories) 1981

Otra vez el mar (novel) 1982
[*Farewell to the Sea*, 1985]

Arturo, la estrella más brillante (novel) 1984
[*Arturo, the Brightest Star*, 1989]

Necesidad de libertad (essays) 1986

Persecución (plays) 1986

La loma del ángel (novel) 1987
[*Graveyard of the Angels*, 1987]

El portero (novel) 1989
[*The Doorman*, 1991]

El asalto (novel) 1990
[*The Assault*, 1993]

Color del verano (novel) 1990

Antes que anochezca (autobiography) 1992
[*Before Night Falls*, 1993]

believe is also a philosophical black comedy. It is also a sweeping fresco of an age of unbelievable injustice, and an implicit call for more Third World *hombres formidables* of this friar's incredibly incorruptible stamp. (This novel, incidentally, has been forbidden in Cuba, where there seems to be no room for Father de Mier's brand of home truths about institutionalized revolution.)

Hallucinations has been aptly named, for Arenas works in the sardonic nightmare tradition of Quevedo and Goya, and images of human cruelty as sharp as slivers of glass and as penetrating as a scream fill its pages. But this *picaro* proceeds through a world of blood and bayonets and breaking bones with the equanimity of an armored tank. The unremittingly utopian Friar escapes one dreary prison after another, aided variously by his wits, an umbrella, "the juice of his fingernails," and pure poetic invention. He meets the onslaughts of rats and

lice, a marriage-bent female, bloodthirsty inquisitors, a slaveship captain, and a plantation overseer in the cotton fields of the American Deep South with the same crusty soul-saving irony and skin-saving presence of mind.

He encounters on his travels not only cynical revolutionaries in the French capital and venal priests all over Western Christendom—but also such figures from a country of the mind as Virginia Woolf's hermaphroditic Orlando. In the end, the historian's fact and Arenas's fiction blend into a surrealist fantasy of sheer freedom versus sheer power that breaks every earthbound canon of conventional fictionalized biography.

This is a wildly unpruned *ficción*, often as cluttered as a Churriguer-esque Mexican cathedral and suffering on many pages from Latin logorrhea. It is definitely not a book for readers who get queasy at leaps of dream-logic and trapeze acts of the imagination.

Pedestrian spirits will be disturbed to see that Friar de Mier arrives in Cadiz on the back of a great whale after a mid-Atlantic shipwreck, that he magically floats over Pamplona as if launched from a catapult of the devil, that he paddles in hallucinatory lakes of sperm on a phantasmagoric tour of the royal hunting preserves, personally conducted by the dissolute King of Spain. This book is a very Spanish vision of the chaos of life itself, a sleep of reason where moral miracle and monstrousness cohabit, where humor is warp and horror woof, where even such irrepressible spirits as Father de Mier are doomed to become only echoes' bones.

It is said that after his death the Friar's mummified body was exhibited for years in a traveling circus. Hagiography, the celebration of death-defying acts of faith, is thus closer to the fundamental plot of the human dreamplay than the tidy-ant conventions of the chronicler. The reader who lets himself be swept away by the force of Arenas's vision will find it not at all strange that the laws of the probable in this moral fable have no more bearing than in a medieval legend. Thanks to his verbal prodigies (at once savory and soaring) Friar Servando Teresa de Mier joins the roll of picaresque saints a lay age can light a candle to. *Hallucinations* becomes a spirited demonstration that, as Don Quixote told Sancho, "the high road is far better than the inns." (pp. 4, 20)

Helen R. Lane, in a review of *Hallucinations*, in *The New York Times Book Review*, August 29, 1971, pp. 4, 20.

REINALDO ARENAS WITH F. O. GIESBERT

(interview date 1981)

[In the following interview conducted in New York

City in 1981 Arenas discusses his imprisonment as well as the oppression of homosexuals and intellectuals in Castro's Cuba.]

[Giesbert:] *How does Reagan's America strike a Cuban dissident?*

[Arenas]: Me, a dissident?

You did get out of Cuba.

That's true, I got out of Castro's paradise along with 125,000 other people. But was there a single dissident among us? That remains to be shown. . . .

Let's not quibble.

I was no more or less a dissident than any writer is.

Isn't any writer a potential dissident?

Maybe. But I'm no political militant, anything but. I'm no Kravchenko.

Then why did you leave Cuba?

Quite simply, because I was a writer; and a homosexual too, which didn't help.

How has it affected you to be suddenly deposited in New York?

I love this town, and it's much more cosmopolitan than it is American. It is marvellous to be able to melt into the crowd. But the "American dream" I've woken up to is fairly mind-boggling for somebody in my position, coming from a system where all the decisions are made for you. For twenty years or more it was the State that fed my belly and stuffed my head. I was its slave really, like the whole Cuban nation. That has its drawbacks, but there are also advantages—there you can let things slide, not in America. Here you have to get a grip on yourself, otherwise you'll be carried away. So I'm learning how to choose, and refuse, and how to struggle. Not so easy.

You arrived on the Florida coast with all the "dregs" of Cuban society—what they called "the flotilla." Were you all alone with just a suitcase, like someone out of an old newsreel?

No suitcase—and just dressed in pyjamas. Because I was in bed when the police came looking for me to take me to the boat. It happened very fast, and I had to leave all my manuscripts behind— naturally they were confiscated. When I set foot on American soil on 5 May 1980, all I had in the world was one spare shirt.

You were one of the few writers who managed to get out last year. Why was that?

Because I had admitted my "errors," and so the regime considered me a broken reed. It's true I'm no hero. Nothing like a man like Armando Valladares, for instance.

Who is he?

The poet Armando Valladares has been in jail since 27 December 1960, and he's been treated so brutally that he is now paralysed in both legs. He refused to submit to his jailers' "rehabilitation plan," and even dared to go on writing. There's something of the Spanish Inquisition in Castroism—the heretics must always retract, you know. I admire the ones who resist by refusing to say their *mea culpa*. Frankly, I didn't have the nerve.

But you had enough nerve to go into exile.

Along with the poets Reinaldo Garcia and Roberto Valero, I was one of the first who asked to leave last year when the regime started its spring-cleaning. As a matter of fact I'd been trying for years to get out. As a writer I often used to get invitations to go to France or other countries. When I saw that Castro was letting his "social deviants" play truant, I immediately rushed down to the commissariat of police and showed them my identity book. Everybody has one over there—it contains your entire life story, in great detail. The cops saw that I was "anti-social" and that I'd been in prison —in other words I was a piece of genuine "garbage," suitable for dumping on to the American mainland. Two days later they shoved me on board an old hulk leaving for Florida. I don't mind admitting that my heart was in my mouth all through the crossing. They'd split the leavers into three groups— detainees, the mentally ill, and "misfits" of my kind. They had things arranged so that every sailing contained a third of each category. The boat itself was falling apart. Still, we made it. It was after I left that the government took its precautions to prevent "*déclassé* intellectuals" from bolting.

Is it because you were a "declassé intellectual" that you were kept mouldering in Castro's prisons from 1974 till 1976?

Literature is very dangerous activity over there. I published three novels abroad—particularly in France and the United States— because they had been rejected by Cuba's only publishing house, the Union of Writers and Artists. Crime number one. And I occasionally held little get-togethers, strictly literary, where my friends and I would read some "work in progress." Crime number two.

Are you saying that you were imprisoned solely for those two reasons?

Not those alone; actually there's a whole context to the thing. My second book, *Hallucinations*, could be interpreted as some sort of act of resistance, but it wasn't specially getting at Castroism. It even received honourable mention in the National Literature Competition in 1966. The truth is that in Cuba the writer always has to think the correct thoughts, and scrupulously follow the directives of the Communist Party. If he doesn't, he's persecuted. I myself have never gone in for any particular political activities, and my origins are not the least bit suspect. I'm a peasant—a genuine little peasant with horny hands who believed in the Revolution. Frankly, I've come round a bit since then. And when they did get round to arresting me, it wasn't because I was fighting against the regime, but because I had no respect for the rules of the official literature or of conventional morality.

What happened when they arrested you?

It was while I was sitting on a beach with some friends, reading a manuscript. The previous day, my lawyer had told me that my case was hopeless: the police had a stainless steel dossier on me. It was all there—every least action for the last few years, almost to the minute. At that time I was married. Well, State Security had in their files even the poems and one play that my wife had written.

What was the indictment?

On the lines of "Homosexual . . . and Enemy of the Revolution."

Is that a serious crime, homosexuality?

Very serious. But there's a whole compendium of crimes in the field of public morality. In Cuba, for instance, it isn't a good idea for lovers to kiss on public benches. It happens, but it's risky . . . they call that sort of thing "public scandal." The police will ask a man whether it really is his wife he's kissing. If it isn't, he's in trouble. Wearing your shirt open is also very much frowned on. And it's all perfectly logical: tyrannies are always hyper-moralistic because love and sex are expressions of freedom—so they have to be got rid of.

What is it like to be homosexual in Cuba today?

An outsider in danger. Because Castroism is really a very *macho* system, and it has taken over the most reactionary prejudices of old Spanish morality. Cuba is ruled by bourgeois types of the kill-joy persuasion, and they've written all of their ancestors' little hang-ups into the law. So you get a law like the one called "*peligrosida*," which defines everything which may be "harmful" to society. Homosexuality and prostitution fall into this category, adultery too; and a taste for American pop music as well. And the regime isn't kidding. I had a friend who fixed up a receiver to listen to radio stations broadcasting from the United States. Six years inside.

Castroist legislation is thoroughly repressive in its morality. Homosexuals are supposed to be "re-educated," which means that they can sometimes be sent far away from the towns, on forced labour. They can't go to university; artistic careers in the cinema or the theatre are closed to them. Castro himself put it very clearly: "It is not permissible that homosexuals, in spite of their artistic qualities or reputation, should have influence over the cultural upbringing of the young."

But you yourself did have a job?

Until my arrest, yes, I did. I was a reviewer for an official monthly literary magazine, the *Gazeta de Cuba*.

How did your stretch in jail turn out?

First of all I spent four or five months in a small windowless cell in a State Security prison. I lived there alone and deprived of all rights, like many other Cuban detainees. No lawyer and no visitors. If you don't confess, there's a chance you'll never get out. You can be tortured too; for instance, they'll shut you in a room and feed steam in till you pass out. So eventually I just quit and signed, and then I was transferred to El Morro—a 16th-century fortress built by the Spaniards, overlooking the port of Havana. It was Batista's big prison once, and now it is Castro's. I was in an enormous room with more than 300 people crammed into it. There are seventeen such chambers. For a lavatory we had a little hole where you generally had to queue. There was no air, the floor was caked with filth, and there were also rats, tarantulas and fleas.

Tell me about an ordinary day in El Morro.

The light is kept on all the time, and there's a hellish roar of sound, constantly. Often brawls break out between detainees. We had nothing to do, in fact, and not much to eat, but the prisoners could be pretty ingenious like the one who tied a hook on the end of a piece of cotton, stuck on a lump of bread, and flicked it out through a loophole. He was catching birds. I set up as a public scribe, and everybody came to dictate their tale to me. I met a lot of really good people there, and you'll see them in the books I'm going to write, I think.

After the penitentiary, you were sent to a "rehabilitation camp". . .

Concentration camp is more like it. It was called *Reparto Flores* (the flower quarter). We were building houses for the Russians. There are plenty of camps like that, in Cuba. They always have tasteless names like "New Dawn," or "Free America." You can't help being reminded of the mentality behind that Nazi slogan for labour camps—*Arbeit macht frei*. Work didn't make me free though, because they could sweat us as long as they liked—a work day might be fifteen to eighteen hours long—and we had to recite Castro every morning. That wasn't the softest job, believe me. Everybody stood there with a copy of the Head-of-State's latest speech: and he seems to make one practically every day.

One day a young prisoner refused to read the Gospel According to Castro—he was a Jehovah's Witness. The warders laid into him with boots and gun-butts, and left him for dead on the ground. The next man—he was another Jehovah's Witness—gave way in tears. That was the kind of humiliation they inflicted on us. We were on a strict diet of daily "socialist" prayers. But even the man in the street is obliged to recite his thanksgiving to the great man, you know—at least once a week.

How is that done?

Through what they call the "study circle." The Committee for the Defence of the Revolution (CDR) calls a weekly meeting for the local people to say their

Castro. It usually happens on a Wednesday, and if you skip your lesson, they make trouble for you. For instance, if you want to buy a transistor radio, you need authorisation from Committee. Absentees or truants don't get it.

Did you still go to the "study circle" after doing your tour of the Cuban jails?

Of course. It's very much in your interest to be in these people's good books, because they can mess up your life. They have all sorts of powers over you. In your building, for instance, there is always a concierge who keeps an eye on everything, what time you go out, when you come back. You can't hide anything from your concierge; and that is how the Committee becomes the master in your own house. You need its permission to have a friend or relation to stay with you; you have to buy the forms, fill them in, and then hand them over to the proper authority. And your guest will have to produce his identity book and get it stamped. It's an absolute tangle every time you want to have a little get-together. . . even to make music, even for a family reunion. I lived in Havana. Well, each time I wanted to see my family, at the opposite end of the island, I had to negotiate a whole cordon of red tape and bureaucratic procedure.

Where are your personal roots?

In Oriente province, a little village miles from anywhere. My grandparents and my mother are sun-burned peasants—scholars of the things of nature, who grow maize and rear livestock. They taught me magic of trees, herbs and spices. It was while going to draw water from the well that I started dreaming up stories or making songs. I had the time: the well was a long way from our house. In my family we have always been very poor, desperately poor.

In the late 1950s, you were a Castroist then?

Yes, because I fought against Batista, like all the peasants. At fourteen I had joined the resistance, in the Velazco region. But I was a guerrilla without a revolver, because of my age; and my role amounted to doing the cooking and washing for the fighting men. Occasionally I would act as a guide in the mountains. I don't want to look as if I'm rewriting history, but it seems to me that in those days the people were against the tyrant in power, rather than in favour of Fidel Castro. And it was the people who brought down the last regime. Don't forget that when Batista gave up and fled, Castro and his men were still hiding in the Sierra—he didn't come down from his mountain-top till a few days afterwards, when it was all over. And that is how one dictatorship replaced another.

All the same, surely this one isn't worse than the last?

It is. This dictatorship is total, systematic, scientific. Some tyrannies leave little chinks of social space where some freedom can slip between. Not Castroism. Everything is monitored in Cuba: your house, your street, your workplace.

The regime still gave you your education.

True. Like all the young peasants, I believed that the Revolution would be a tremendous cultural liberation. I studied accountancy and worked on a collective farm, and I devoured all the books I could lay my hands on—my first literary excitement was, I remember, Pablo Neruda.

You, the peasant, may also want to concede that this system has put food in the mouths of the small farmers.

I'm not so sure. It seems to me more as if they're still starving to death, still as wretched as ever. The difference is that the foreign press is no longer in a position to know about it, because it can't see what people would be eager to disclose. The regime has taken their land away from the small peasants, and Cuba has turned into one big farm—less productive, naturally—where everything really belongs to Fidel Castro. He jumps into his helicopter, looks at the fields, and issues his orders: "Plant me some sugar-cane here—cut down those palm-trees there." And the result is that the island is just a huge plantation in a shambles, where in the end the people haven't got any more bread than they've got freedom. Because nothing has really changed. Nothing. Batista's private beach, the Miramar Yacht Club, still hasn't been opened to the public, for example.

Why not?

Because it's reserved for Castro's leadership elite, that's why not!

Are there still executions?

A lot of people "disappear" in prison, much as in Argentina. In Havana we have a custom that goes back to the Spanish era: every night, at nine o'clock, a nine-gun salute is sounded to tell everybody it's time for bed. They say on the grapevine that that's when the executions are held, in the penitentiaries. The sound of the salute, they say, drowns the sound of the execution squad. There's no proof that the rumour is true, but I think it's plausible.

Would they also kill the "politicals"?

Obviously. Anyway, it's sometimes awkward to distinguish between them and the "common law" criminals: there are more politicals than people think. After all, if you take a stroll with your shirt unbuttoned in Cuba, isn't that basically a political gesture?

Wouldn't you say this regime has some extenuating circumstances, being so much under pressure from the United States?

No. If the United States had really wanted to overthrow Castro they would have done it long ago. As a matter of fact I wonder whether, in a way, it doesn't suit them. It's a kind of vaccine for Latin America. Who could possibly want to imitate a country that is on its last legs economically, and sold its national independence to the Kremlin? It makes an ideal warning sign.

What do you think of Castro?

There's a Napoleonic spirit about him, but he isn't really a Bonaparte. Just a Narcissus of the mass media age. . . . When he came into government he announced that he'd "soon" get out—that was 22 years ago. And still he hangs on as always, with his delusions of grandeur and his lust for power. Domestically speaking, his experiment has been a fiasco: and it's the Russians who are propping up the Cuban economy, with a subsidy of at least five million pounds a day.

Wasn't it the Americans' own policy that threw Castro into the Soviet camp?

It is a deliberate choice on Castro's part. The United States don't lose sleep about supporting right-wing dictatorships, it's true, and they detest the left-wing ones. But they would have taken a much more friendly line if the great *Lider Maximo* had joined the non-aligned countries—the genuinely non-aligned ones. Only that wasn't Castro's plan: he'd lost all idea of bringing our island liberty, equality and fraternity, even though it was possible to think so in his first few years. In fact his ambition was to become a world-famous figure, and the Soviet Union was ready to support him. It enabled the Cuban army to send an expeditionary force of tens of thousands of soldiers into Africa, and it made Cuba a rather impressive military fortress. If Fidel Castro hadn't made a present of himself and his country to the USSR, he wouldn't have the weight and influence he has today.

Are the Cubans proud of their international role in Africa?

You know, wars are often made as a sop to hungry people.

Do Cubans readily accept the some tens of thousands of Eastern-bloc advisers who live in their country?

The Russians and their allies live totally apart from Cuban society. They don't live with us. They have their private beaches, their exclusive shops, special buses, and needless to say, all kinds of privileges. In Cuba we call them *bolos*—hayseeds. We say they smell bad, and there's a continual flow of anti-Soviet stories. For instance: "A big tombola session is organised. First prize: a week in the Soviet Union. Second prize: three months." Before watching television at night, people ask: "Is it a good film, or is it Russian?" Apparently the graft hasn't taken. When a cinema is showing a Russian film, no one goes—even if it's a masterpiece. But as soon as they advertise an American film, they're packed. Not long ago the government decided to show *King Kong*, after a big press campaign against its "cretinism." The film was a smash hit. That's one country where the American model is wearing well.

What do you think of cultural activities in Cuba, apart from the showing of Soviet films?

Culture is really nothing but bourgeois art now. They publish all the novels that were in vogue in Franco Spain, for example—from Paul Bourget to the usual old Spanish type, with stories about women totally devoted to their husbands—you know the sort of thing.

Are the cultural establishment all prudes, then?

Exactly. In Cuba, I'll say it again, the entire superstructure is in the hands of a bourgeoisie. And this is no advanced liberal bourgeoisie—it is totally reactionary. So the congresses on education and culture are all completely surrealistic. Everybody wears the same strict dress, and even long hair is forbidden. The Castroists have, actually, a real poor-white mentality. Do you know what category of Cubans is getting the worst treatment nowadays? The blacks. It's no accident that they always do the dirty jobs, cut the sugarcane and fill the prisons. Every time the police do a street check, they always start by arresting the blacks with no questions asked. In other words, with Castro you'd better not be "different"—meaning a black, or a prostitute, or a hippie, or a homosexual, or an intellectual.

Or a novelist?

Then you become a potential condemned man. First you have to struggle, like all Cubans, inside a totally bureaucratic world. It is always in the right. That is how I came to have all my work published abroad—where I had never set foot! Yet in Cuba nothing came out. The publishing machinery is implacable. The Union of Cuban Artists & Writers—for which I worked—issues a favourable or unfavourable verdict on the publication of your manuscript. Then the Ministry of Culture has the final word, and there is no appeal. The minister there is Alfredo Guevara, who is very bright and very personable, and covers up for all of Castro's exactions. In fact he has put his charm into the service of repression. To complicate things further, he's probably a homosexual himself; they use him to sell the Cuban cultural image abroad, and he excels in that. He has managed to hide his devil behind a sweet angelic smile.

Do you say that because he refused to publish two of your novels, and they've been published everywhere but Cuba?

I say it because Guevara is one of the people who are doing their utmost to banish art from Cuba. So many despotisms have perished from touching it! Well, Castroism is not going to take that chance, that much is clear. Because writers are supposed to spread ideas—and for ideologues, there's nothing more dangerous than new ideas—they are to be Public Enemy Number One. They must be watched night and day; their manuscripts must be ceaselessly confiscated. Some time before I left, for example, I wrote a text which I hid in a plastic bag, under a tiled floor in my house. One day it vanished.

You must get paranoid pretty quickly when you work in conditions like that, don't you?

Extra careful, more like. Between two fits of discouragement, I used to try to memorise all my works, because the police make off with anything that's unlucky enough to be written down.

Even poems where the sky is blue and the sea is tranquil?

Even that. Everything is disappearing. For instance, Cuba had one fine writer, Virgilio Pineira, who at the end of his life had completed several novels and a few plays—but naturally it had not been possible to publish anything. When he died, two years ago, the police seized all his manuscripts. Ten years of work wiped out at a stroke.

What could upset the regime in a few pages of pastoral verse?

The fact that they are not written in praise of regime. That is called "ideological deviationism," and it's a crime. If you don't touch your forelock to the system, it's because you have subversive motives.

What about foreign writers who are banned?

We always suffer by comparison with writers who are either foreign or dead-and-gone. Because what they write can't possibly be interpreted as attacking the system. But the Castro censorship keeps a long pair of scissors. In the National Library's section of books forbidden to the public there are even Pablo Neruda's Memoirs, and books by Sartre, Carlos Fuentes, and Borges. But it gets worse: once I helped somebody to stage *La Celestina*, a picaresque piece by Fernando de Rojas and a great classic of Spanish literature. Even the Inquisition didn't stop it being published. Well, the play was banned in Cuba. Why? Because one of the characters is a tart. Torquemada was less squeamish than Castro.

Did the police take many manuscripts of yours?

Some poems, some short stories, and also a long novel of a thousand pages. I first wrote it fifteen years ago; then it was confiscated. I'd given it to someone to look after, and one day he said: "Sorry, police came and took it away." So I rewrote it from memory. When State Security arrested me in 1974 they took the new version, along with all the unpublished manuscripts I had hidden at home. But that time I had taken precautions by photocopying some passages and stowing them somewhere safe. In jail I tried to reconstruct it all in my mind, but when I came out, I was too desperate to feel like reworking it. It was in New York that I resurrected it for the third time. From the day I reached the United States I couldn't get it out of my mind, as if it had to be finished before I could start to exist again.

What is the theme?

A man and a woman sitting by the sea and thinking about what has happened to them since the revolution of 1959. My novel is called ***Once More the Sea***, and tells the secret history of the Cuban people, the people who swarm behind the official phoney history, with its military processions and mass meetings, and also the back-scratchers.

Who are you referring to?

I'm referring to all those people who make their little trip to Cuba, sing their song of praise, then fly away. They're happy just to parrot what the officials tell them, without even opening their eyes. It's always the same old story, like Andre Gide's visit to Moscow. Still, we console ourselves with the thought that the same people will probably come back and be disenchanted in a few year's time.

But in the light of what you're saying, how do you explain Castro managing to remain so popular with all the radicals in the Third World?

It's precisely because Castro's press never allows the Cuban people to speak, the ones in the concentration camps, or the ones in the old Havana, who are just as destitute as they were under Batista.

All the same, Castroism has had some influential supporters—take Alejo Carpentier, for instance.

What does that prove? I like Alejo Carpentier's books a lot, and he was kind enough to admire *Hallucinations*, and even to stand up for it. But he was a sort of official writer who came to Havana as a tourist. He lived in France, not Cuba. So. . . .

What are you living on now?

I am a professor of Cuban literature at the International University of Florida. And I try to keep on writing.

Is it easier in New York than in Cuba?

In Cuba the writer is liable to suffer hardship and oppression. Here you have to be on your guard against the excesses of liberty. It is not so easy to resist that, especially when you arrive, as I did, with a culture gap of several centuries. But I have the impression that suddenly there is a lot to say, and I can say it without having State Security breathing down my neck. I'm starting from scratch, in fact. The French Revolution has that story of the Abbé who was asked what he had done during the Terror, and his answer was:"*J'ai survécu.*" That's what I've done, "survived," and so have ten million other Cubans. But today, after all these years, I feel I am finally starting to live. Sometimes it's a mixed feeling. Do you know that I'm taking a risk right now?

What do you mean?

Castroism doesn't like its opponents to talk freely, you know. Even in New York. . . . (pp. 60-2, 64-7)

Reinaldo Arenas and F. O. Giesbert, in an interview, in *Encounter*, Vol. LVIII, No. 1, January, 1982, pp. 60-2, 64-7.

Dust jacket for Arenas's 1988 novel, *The Doorman*.

ENRICO MARIO SANTÍ

(essay date 1984)

[In the following excerpt, Santí provides an overview of Arenas's life and literary career.]

"*But what made me saddest was not having a good book to read, or pen and paper to write down all the ideas that were burning inside.*" Fray Servando's lament about his fate in the last of the string of imprisonments that he endures throughout *El mundo alucinante, Una novela de aventuras* (1969), Reinaldo Arenas's imaginary biography, reads today like an eerie prophecy about the fate of its author and of an entire generation of writers fallen from grace with the Cuban revolution. Up until four years ago, when Arenas arrived in Key West in the Mariel boatlift, little if anything had been known of his whereabouts for the last decade. Though praised abroad for two prize-winning

novels, a collection of short stories and a series of perceptive essays, inside Cuba Arenas had become a non-person, ostracized since the Revolution's Stalinist turn in 1970. A victim of trumped-up charges of corruption, stripped of his right to a job, his first (and only Cuban-published) novel banned, forbidden to write, Arenas was forced successively to spend time cutting cane in a sugar mill, to serve a year-and-a-half prison sentence, and to live an additional four years under virtual house arrest. Inquiries about him from visitors to the island were met either with blank stares or firm denials of his existence. Invitations to lecture abroad never reached him. In 1975, the French translation of Arenas's third novel, *El palacio de las blanquisimas mofetas*, appeared in Paris without any comment about the Spanish original. Little did Parisian readers suspect that at the time of the novel's release its author was languishing in a Havana prison, punished in part for smuggling out the manuscript. (p. 227)

In 1965, when Arenas's first works began to appear in Havana, he was very much a writer of the Revolution. Not that those early works extol the new regime, but that his very emergence as a writer was made possible by the liberal cultural policies of the Revolution during its first few years. Born in 1943 (July 16) of unmarried peasant parents in Cuba's rural, easternmost Oriente province, Arenas was raised in Perronales, a small town on the outskirts of Holguín, by his mother, grandparents and ten aunts. (The father abandoned the family shortly after his son was born.) After attending local public schools and a brief involvement with the anti-Batista rebel forces, Arenas won a scholarship to study accounting under the Revolution's new agrarian reform program. A second accounting scholarship sent him to Havana for the first time in 1962, when he began to take courses at the university.

Havana in the early 1960s was a cauldron of politics and culture. Castro's proclamation of a Socialist revolution in 1961 involved an aggressive cultural policy that attracted the support of Latin American and European writers. For example, that year Castro's famous "Meetings with the Intellectuals" led to the creation of the Cuban Writers' Union. It did not take Arenas long to get caught up in this whirlwind and abandon accounting for a career as a writer, until then a secret ambition. By the time he arrived in Havana, Arenas had produced a considerable body of *juvenilia*: three extravagant "novels" (*Oué dura es la vida, ¡Adiós, Mundo Cruel!, El Salvaje*) mostly inspired by B-rated Mexican films, and three poetry notebooks. The spark came in 1963 with Arenas's entry in a children's story contest sponsored by the National Library. In an interview with Cristina Guzmán, Arenas has described how the contest required the retelling of a famous children's story in exactly five minutes. Unsatisfied with the ones he read, he decided to write one himself and memorize it. "The stern jury heard it, liked it and asked me who the author was. I told them I had written it myself and then handed them the manuscript. The next day

I got a telegram from Eliseo Diego, a writer who worked in the children's collection . . . offering me a job in the library."

Arenas's story, later lost, was **"Los zapatos vacíos"** (**"The Empty Shoes"**) about a country boy who on Christmas morning is forgotten by the Three Wise Men but is later rewarded by Mother Nature. Both the recognition implied by the award and the free time afforded by his new position encouraged Arenas to write a whole book of children's stories, a losing entry in the 1963 Casa de las Américas contest. Although five of the stories eventually made it into print, most of them would not be published in book form until much later. Arenas's three earliest vignettes are epiphanies, brief chronicles of the loss of innocence: one child discovers the world of illusion, another awakens to the cruelty of material survival, a third one confronts time and death. The importance of these early stories can hardly be exaggerated. Arenas's interest in the child's point of view, here and in later works, allows him to juxtapose the worlds of naive fantasy and vulgar reality. This technique reaches its most daring form in *Celestino antes del alba* (1967), his first novel, which Arenas conceived while writing a similar children's tale, and in **"Bestial entre las flores,"** the 1966 story that concludes this first "naive" cycle. Set in rural Cuba and narrated from the point of view of a mentally retarded boy, *Celestino* tells the story of an *alter ego* who writes poetry on tree trunks which the boy's grandfather promptly chops down. The difference between the novel and the earlier stories is slight but important. Whereas the stories belong to children's literature, the novel belongs to fantastic literature, told *from* the experience of childhood, recreating the frightened incoherence of a child's discourse. More importantly, *Celestino* is the first installment of a projected five-part, semi-autobiographical *Bildungsroman*. *El palacio de las blanquísimas mofetas* (1980) and *Otra vez el mar* (1982) are sequels to *Celestino*.

Celestino won a first honorable mention award in the Cuban Writers' Union's inaugural "Cirilo Villaverde" contest in 1964, losing out to Ezequiel Vieta's *Vivir en Candonga*, about a naturalist who discovers the meaning of the Revolution while searching for a rare species of butterfly. Arenas's response to the apparent ideological bias behind the jury's decision came three years later, when the novel was finally published, in the form of an essay titled **"Celestino y yo."** In that essay, Arenas took to task what he called the doctrinaire realism upheld by "99 percent of our critics" and defended the writer's duty "to express the different types of reality that lie under an apparent reality." And Arenas's battle seemed to have been won when poet Eliseo Diego, in his review of *Celestino*, hailed it as "one of the few Cuban books where the old anxieties of rural man reach us movingly, making of their simple exposure an outcry far more terrible than any explicit protest."

Barely a year before the release of *Celestino* in 1967

Arenas had already written *El mundo alucinante: Una novela del aventuras*, his second and better-known novel about the life of Fray Servando Teresa de Mier (1765–1827), and the rest of the stories collected in *Con los ojos cerrados*. (These books won honorable mentions in the 1966 and 1968 Writers' Union contest, respectively.) The idea for Fray Servando's "imaginary biography" had come to Arenas, as the novel's letter/preface states, while reading "an awful history of Mexican literature" for a lecture on Juan Rulfo. It was in fact while working at the National Library, where he had read everything from Dostoyevsky to Virginia Woolf, that Arenas researched Fray Servando's life and works. The result, after an intense year of writing, was his "biography" of the famous Mexican priest and revolutionary "such as it was, and could have been; such as I should have liked it to have been".

It was the publication of *El mundo alucinante* in Mexico in 1969, along with that of *Con los ojos cerrados* in Montevideo three years later, that established Arenas's reputation *abroad* as a first-rate writer. One must underscore abroad because neither book was ever published in Cuba. Because both had won honorable mentions, publication was only optional under Writers' Union rules; and by the time the Union exercised that option it was refused. (In the case of *El mundo alucinante*, it was argued that some of the novel's erotic passages would have been too controversial.) In exchange, the Writers' Union offered to publish *La vieja Rosa*, a *nouvelle* that Arenas had written several years before. The offer, however, never materialized. Thus in answer to seperate requests from editors Emmanuel Carballo and Angel Rama, both of whom visited Cuba in the late 1960s as jury members of the Casa de las Américas Prize, Arenas handed over his two manuscripts for publication abroad.

These publishing tribulations not only explain why Arenas is known mostly as the author of *El mundo alucinante* (*Celestino's* single run of 3,000 copies was designed for local consumption only), but also reflect the increasingly dogmatic values of Cuba's developing cultural policy. Although by 1968 Arenas was one of the editors of *La Gaceta de Cuba*, the arts tabloid of the Writers' Union where he had started working in 1967, the only texts he was able to publish were a series of literary essays and reviews. It was in 1968, we should recall, that the first Padilla "affair," over the merits of *Tres Tristes Tigres* (1967), the novel by exiled writer Guillermo Cabrera Infante, erupted on the Cuban cultural scene. Two years later, Heberto Padilla himself was imprisoned, for an alleged conspiracy against the state, and forced to recant his "bourgeois attitudes" publicly. Padilla's recantation soon made the liberal left of Europe and Latin America, until then loyal supporters of the Revolution, break openly with Castro. In response, Castro himself called for a Cultural Congress which he used to denounce his former allies and to place greater restrictions on intellectual activity on the island. But neither Padilla's trial nor the mock Congress could conceal the real reasons for both. That same year, the failure of the "ten million ton" sugar harvest had brought on a political and economic crisis of such proportions that the Soviet Union had to step in with increased aid. In exchange for aid, the Cuban government became "institutionalized" by creating a Communist Party and a People's Congress. For Cuban intellectuals "institutionalization" meant even greater restrictions on cultural activity.

The effects of these new cultural policies on a good number of Cuban writers whose works did not fit the newly-imposed ideological strictures have been devastating—either a harsh ostracism for some (poets José Lezama Lima and Virgilio Piñera died victims of this treatment) or exile, internal and external. As part of the government crackdown, Arenas, along with the entire staff of *La Gaceta de Cuba*—including well-known writers Reynaldo González, Miguel Barnet, and Belkis Cuza Malé—was dismissed from his job at the Writers' Union and sent off for "reindoctrination" to the Manuel Sanguily sugar mill in Cuba's westernmost province of Pinar del Río. During the six months of forced labor spent there Arenas wrote secretly *El central*, a long visionary poem, highly critical of the Revolution, which he managed to smuggle out three years later. Not until Arenas reached the United States, was the poem published. As in *El mundo alucinante* which incorporates the texts of the real Fray Servando into the stuff of the narrative, in *El central* historical texts such as López de Gómara's *Historia General de las Indias* and Novas Calvo's *El negrero*, chronicles of past periods of slavery in the island, support a vision of contemporary suffering and repression.

One can only assume that it was the publication abroad of *El mundo alucinante* as well as that novel's quick success that angered Cuba's cultural commissars and caused Arenas to become increasingly marginalized at home. Returning to his job in early 1971, Arenas found himself demoted to the rank of proofreader, receiving a salary from the Writers' Union for *not* writing. Thus, secretly again, he began working on *El palacio de las blanquísimas mofetas* as a sequel to *Celestino*, developing the character of the wild child poet into an adolescent. Whereas in *Celestino* there is a dateless world of fantasy that corresponds to the child's perception, *El palacio* gradually presents a historical context (the late fifties in Cuba) as a counterpart to the poet's awakening to the world of desire. Organized around five "agonies" or dramatic visions which the protagonist (now called Fortunato) projects on his deathbed, *El palacio* constitutes Arenas's most experimental work to date. But by 1972, when Arenas completed the manuscript, he had given up on ever being able to publish his works in Cuba. In late 1973 he managed to smuggle *El palacio* to France along with the manuscripts of *El central* and of several short stories and poems. Also among those works was the second version of *Otra vez el mar*, the second sequel to

Celestino. The first version of *Otra vez el mar* had been "lost" by a close friend to whom Arenas had entrusted his single copy. When in June 1974 the Cuban Security Police arrested Arenas on charges of corruption and public disturbance, the evidence produced by the government against him included not only proof that he had smuggled his manuscripts, but that same "lost" copy.

Only recently, with Arenas's arrival in the US, have the circumstances of his arrest and imprisonment been discussed publicly. The Cuban government has only issued an oblique statement on the matter, its reticence reflecting the view perhaps that there never was an "Arenas affair," as there was a "Padilla affair," and that whatever "problems" Arenas may have had were of a moral and not of a political nature. For a time rumors circulated about his being arrested on charges of corrupting a minor. But in at least two separate interviews Arenas has given a different version of the facts. While admitting that he was charged with being "Homosexual and enemy of the Revolution," Arenas describes the incidents that led up to his arrest as follows:

> I was with a friend at Guanabo Beach when I discovered that our clothes and some poems I had left at the shore had been stolen. When we got to the station, where we'd gone to report the thieves, they were there holding our things, and they and the police began accusing us of causing a "public disturbance." They finally let us go, but a couple of months later my attorney was handed the government's case against me. My dossier included, among other things, the copy of the novel that my other friend had "lost" a year before, the poems that had been stolen from me at the beach, a report from my supervisor at the Writers' Union accusing me of being an "immoral employee," plus charges of smuggling out my manuscripts and of publishing two of them abroad. It was, in short, a criminal record, and the bottom line was an eight-year prison sentence. . . . My attorney painted a grim picture, so I began to make my plans to leave by boat. . . . I told my plans to the friend who had been with me at the beach (strangely enough, no charges were ever brought against him), but a few hours later I had the State Security Police at my doorstep. They ransacked my apartment and confiscated all my belongings, including a copy of the second version of *Otra vez el mar* that I had kept. I was taken to jail to await trial for the next eight months. During that time I was threatened several times with ten and twenty-year sentences. . . I was then tried and sentenced to a year and half in prison.

Whether or not Arenas ever corrupted a minor seems to have played a small role in his problems with Cuba's Security Police when compared to the list of more plausible "crimes" which he claims to have been charged with—especially the publication abroad of two prize-winning works that the Cuban government had refused to publish. More important than the charge of homosexuality, then, seems to have been the government's fear of having a second version of *Otra vez el mar*, which deals critically with life in contemporary Cuba, smuggled and published abroad, to its further embarrassment. And whether or not the charges that were brought against Arenas were justified, the point remains that he began to be punished much earlier, in 1968, when *El mundo alucinante* was censored, and continued to be punished for several more years, after having served his sentence, by being forbidden to write. The distinction, drawn frequently by apologists of Cuba's repressive cultural policy, between a writer's moral and political crimes, seems morally attractive but politically naive.

After his release from prison in January 1976, and as part of his sentence, Arenas worked as a carpenter in a construction squad assigned to the Reparto Flores "rehabilitation camp," building homes for Soviet soldiers and their families. During the next four years he survived doing odd jobs, sharing a room in a rundown hotel in the old section of Havana. Cristina Guzmán, a Venezuelan editor who during this difficult time went to Cuba to interview Arenas, has described how nobody in Havana "seemed to be able to or to want to remember his name, much less his address," and how, after several days of inquiry, she finally found his "minimal room, a couch that barely fit two people, a pair of chairs and a square table. On the left, a makeshift stairway that leads to what looks like a bedroom." Arenas's wretched quarters were a reflection of his nonperson status. Because the Cuban Security Police had kept the two copies of *Otra vez el mar*, he was placed under virtual house arrest, forced to pretend that he had lost all interest in literature and to play the role of a reformed citizen. His only hope was to emigrate, but paid invitations to lecture abroad from Editions du Seuil (Arenas's French publisher) and Princeton University never reached him. Several attempts to escape by boat failed. Only in April 1980, with the crisis precipitated by the forced entry of 10,000 Cubans into Havana's Peruvian Embassy, did the possibility to emigrate become real. Taking advantage of the government's decision to grant safe passage to all the "anti-socials" who wished to leave the island, Arenas applied for an exit visa, slipped through unnoticed, and eventually became one of the 140,000 people who made it through the Mariel-Key West boatlift. According to at least one report, when news of Arenas's departure reached Cuba's Culture Ministry its agents rushed to Mariel Harbor to "rescue" him, only to find that the dinghy to which he had been assigned had left moments before. The agents then turned to the inquisitive foreign news correspondents to give assurances that Arenas could have left in a more normal fashion had he only requested it.

Following his arrival in the US, on 6 May 1980, Arenas arranged for publication of the first Spanish edition of *El palacio*, nearly ten years after completing the manuscript, and for publication of *El central*. After a sum-

mer lecture tour in Florida, New York, Puerto Rico and Venezuela, he taught a course on Cuban poetry at Florida International University in Miami. In December of that year he moved to New York City. During the last three years there has been a flurry of writing and publishing. In addition to the release of a new edition of *El mundo alucinante*, a second edition of *Con los ojos cerrados*, now retitled *Termina el desfile* has appeared in Spain. The new story that closes the volume (and gives it its new title), deals with the events surrounding the entry into Havana's Peruvian embassy and provides an ironic contrast with the first story, **"Comienza el desfile"** about the first day of the Cuban Revolution.

Had Arenas's been the only case of a Cuban writer's disaffection with the revolution, perhaps there would be cause to cast doubt on his version of the facts relating to his case. But Arenas joins the ranks of a considerable number of distinguished Cuban writers—Antonio Benítez Rojo, Edmundo Desnoes, César Leante, Heberto Padilla, José Triana, and others—who in the past six years have chosen exile over aesthetic or moral self-betrayal. It remains to be determined, at least for the purposes of the literary historian, what common objective circumstances, if any, have prompted the recent exile of such prominent literary figures. But that could only be done, I suggest, through a detailed comparative study of Cuban literature and cultural policy since 1970, which we still lack. (pp. 228–35)

Enrico Mario Santí, "The Life and Times of Reinaldo Arenas," in *Michigan Quarterly Review*, Vol. XXIII, No. 2, Spring, 1984, pp. 227–36.

JAY CANTOR

(essay date 1985)

[Here, Cantor reviews *Farewell to the Sea*, describing Arenas as an author primarily interested in revealing "the secret history" of his characters.]

Reinaldo Arenas, a Cuban writer, made his way to the United States as part of the Mariel exodus in 1980. But the rigors that implies are rarely directly realized in *Farewell to the Sea*. . . . Oppression here is a pounding, omnipresent but also somewhat abstract fact, like the sea of the title itself.

The scant story of Mr. Arenas's novel . . . is of a couple's week at the seaside. The husband has a brief affair with a boy staying with his mother in a cabin nearby. The boy commits suicide. The couple return to the city. The book's action takes only slightly longer in the novel's telling than it does here. The boy's personality is almost

---

Emir Rodríguez-Monegal on the Cuban rejection of Arenas:

It is easy to understand why a progressive and historical regime such as the Cuban could not accept Arenas, the writer. He is truly counter-revolutionary because his texts undermine the official ideology of the regime, mock the progressive view of history and deconstruct our views of reality. More dangerous than Lezama Lima (with whom he has many literary and poetic affinities), more effective than Padilla (an easier target for the regime because he uses the same bureaucratic language), Reinaldo Arenas is the only voice to come out of Cuba in recent years that truly questions the official version of reality, political or otherwise.

Emir Rodríguez-Monegal, in *Latin American Literary Review* (Spring, 1980).

---

nonexistent, the motivation of the suicide unmentioned. The responses to the drowning are the work of a few pages. Mr. Arenas is not interested in ordinary realistic drama. He wants to give the reader the secret history of the emotions, the sustaining victories of pleasure and the small dishonesties that callous the soul.

The first third of the novel is a long monologue by the wife that unfolds during the week's vacation. Punctuated by her dreams and fantasies, this section is pervaded by the dreary monotony of life under Fidel Castro, the silence and seperation between characters. The revolution declines in rhythm with the wife's recognition of the hollowness of her marriage. . . .

This appropriately unnamed wife's plaint is tightly strung along its theme—her longing for her husband. She speaks of the terror of the regime, under which "the obligatory adoration of a single person. . . is raised to dizzying heights, and persecution and absolute enslavement are the order of the day." Yet she herself seems in thrall to Hector, her husband, and has few thoughts that are not formed by her adoration of his body, her yearning for him. Even her dreams of escape are dreams of love. "Somewhere there must be more than this violence and loneliness, this stupidity, laziness, chaos, and stupor. . . . Somewhere someone is waiting for me."

It could hardly be called ethically wrong—except by the same sort of mentality that leads to the jailing of writers in Cuba—that her political urgency here ends in the necessarily always unrequited refrain of a love song. It is part of Mr. Arenas's strength that he does not give his characters' unhappiness a simple political explanation. . . . It is the necessity of art to complain endlessly, to say—as if pointing to the sea—that beyond the confinement of the state there is another confinement, beyond this freedom there is another freedom, so large as to be unbearable.

The book asks the questions of art, but one feels it could do it more artfully. For each point is repeated and after a while the wife's obsession feels like a limitation not of history, or the human condition, but of the author, who might have granted her a wider life, given her a name.

The last two-thirds of the novel, Hector's portion, which covers the same week at the beach, is almost entirely phantasmagorical, with long portions of poetry that sometimes show flashes of brilliance. One section is a wonderful refutation of Whitman's optimism, done in Whitman's style. But the poetry frequently gives the feeling of hysterical wordplay, of a mind maddened by slogans and enforced silence, clearing itself of static and lies before sleep. The poetry often fails, too, from a gauzy insubstantiality: "Remember, we are nothing but some passing terror, an angry/impotence, an insatiable, ephemeral flame."

Hector's personality, openly and honestly presented, can be unattractive, selfish, unfeeling. He uses as accusation toward others the very sorts of sexual politics that are used to condemn him. . . . His fantasies of monsters, mass executions and cruising are sometimes powerful in their perception of political degradation as physical degradation, but they are also often wearing in their length and repetitiveness.

One feels within the silence that surrounds these characters the power of the regime, of Mr. Castro's voice, which has perhaps monopolized and subverted the possibilities of speech, made itself the limit even of fantasy, causing Hector to turn within himself in a solipsism so extreme that it is almost a self-immolation. Maybe that is as close as he can come to power over his own life. But it would be awful to think that the regime need inevitably triumph over the demands of the novel, its possibilities for variety, for an involving verbal texture and for the imagination of others.

Jay Cantor, "Dreams of Escape, Dreams of Love," in *The New York Times Book Review*, November 24, 1985, p. 31.

D. KEITH MANO
(essay date 1986)

[Mano is a distinguished American novelist whose works deal with the relationship between Christianity and the modern world. Below, he offers a mixed review of *Farewell to the Sea*, censuring it as "distasteful and invariably difficult," while praising it as a powerful denunciation of Cuban totalitarianism.]

[*Farewell to the Sea*] has the rainbow sheen, the deceptive lusciousness of rotted meat. It is, for Cuba, what surgical drains are for heavy, abscessing flesh. Twice *Farewell to the Sea* was confiscated by Castro. Twice it was rewritten from memory. In 1974, at last, Reinaldo Arenas smuggled his manuscript out to Spain. It is the conclusive indictment of Cuba under Castro, vicious as *sjambok* blows across an open mouth. If you thought Cuba couldn't be worse than Russia (at least it doesn't get cold), reconstitute your thinking. Repression there, per capita, is even more thorough, *attentive*. The Cuban people didn't have any comfortable, Old World acquaintance with totalitarianism. They had to be broken, then taught again from Lie One. And Cuba, remember, has no permeable border. "Our unavoidable, clear condition of slavery, the fact of having been born into the muted crowing of an island, the terrifying helplessness of an island, the prison-prison-prison that is an island."

Yet, yes, I'm ambivalent. *Farewell to the Sea* is sometimes distasteful and invariably difficult. It has a sordid, old-queenish homosexual mattress stink to it: direct descent from *Our Lady of the Flowers* by Genet. This is, in a sense, Whitman gone putrid—singing the body unelectric and cynical and sold. Castro has put on his biker gear and stomped the gay populace in Cuba. There are, apparently, homosexual concentration camps. Of course Communism has long been associated with a repressive attitude toward free sexuality. And this isn't mere prudishness. Totalitarian mind-managers understand that sex can provide fierce competition. With gay love, in particular, passion is often as obsessive and total as the dialectic itself. And you can't reeducate a homosexual. Arenas's estimable courage, his mad, beautiful prose-poetry, is, I sense, glandular in part. The anti-Communist freedom fighter as chickenhawk.

Arenas begins with a paragraphless 168-page narrative passage. Talk about undying prose. You couldn't kill this with an Irish press gang. But once you accept his premise—that your eye will never be allowed to rest—then literary nervous collapse occurs. In fact, this narrative portion is the precise syntactical analogue of totalitarianism—stopless, paranoid, over-officious. Communist government can operate only by leaving a subject mind no leisure for doubt or introspection. Husband and wife, both minor officials in the Castro regime, are on vacation. Their safety, they know, is precarious. Betrayal and collaboration with a repressive state have choked love off. Nonetheless, the meticulous horror of totalitarianism, the sheer, dull *momentum* around it will keep them in moral paralysis. This striking and effective portion is followed by six long canto segments. Arenas has often written impenetrably here, half brilliant, half show-offish (in a bravura translation by Andrew Hurley, who must be certifiable after that effort). Much material, I suspect, was culled from Arenas's poetic storage hamper. Ultimately you don't read either for understanding or for pleasure, but for the cumulative, avalanchine weight of his case against Castro.

Forced labor, torture, concentration camp—those are the *good* parts. They, at least, might inspire a serviceable passion or two: anger, fear, courage, the stuff of revolt. But Communism is essentially rule by nitpicking and attrition. It cripples the sense of self esteem. Civil interchange reduced to desperate and niggardly arithmetic. Friendship sold for pitiful advantage. "The price of a sink—never to write the poem. . . Every chair an act of cowardice." Not to mention youth—a time with no franchise under totalitarianism.

> Look at the boys, look at them move
>   now.
> It is almost heartbreaking, how much
>   they want to exist.
> Long sideburns, barely sprouting
>   beards, hair
> kept secretly long
>   (hidden for now under their caps).
> See how desperately they try to
>   find their place.
> They have ceased to exist.

There is no more dispiriting attribute of Communism, that its children are born into a sardonic and immediate middle age.

Farewell to the Sea is afflicted with terrible gigantism. It can exasperate: overblown, encyclopedic, compulsive. But this is also the stylistic demeanor of Communist government. For just that reason, I suppose, poetry has always been much more vital in Russia and Cuba. It is a sort of secret code. People learn to be allusive, oblique: they communicate by symbol and dubious reference. The clarity expected of narrative fiction is dangerous: evidence that can be held against you. Minds become isolate within the totalitarian ambit. Set apart by mistrust and fear, they turn inward to create monstrous, antisocial fantasy.

Nonetheless, Arenas's documentation, overwrought as it may be, is both stunning and unanswerable. More so, because the liberal establishment will be hard put to repudiate it. Homosexuals, after all, are an accredited Left minority. Women on sexual harassment. Blacks on South Africa. Homosexuals, now, on Castro. It is decisive. We should've sent an all-gay force to the Bay of Pigs. (pp. 54–5)

D. Keith Mano, "Totalitarian Ambit," in *National Review*, New York, Vol. XXXVIII, July 18, 1986, pp. 54–5.

REINALDO ARENAS WITH PERLA ROZENCVAIG
(interview date 1990)

[The following interview was conducted in New York City two months prior to Arenas's death. Here, the novelist reflects on his literary career, discussing themes and symbols that recur frequently in his writings.]

[Rozencvaig]: *Reinaldo, it was exactly 10 years ago this month that we met. You had only arrived a few months earlier via Mariel, and you immediately granted me an interview. What has this time spent in New York meant to you as a person and as an artist?*

[Arenas]: Put simply, living in New York meant that I could write. I have almost been able to finish a narrative cycle that I had been dreaming of writing since I was 18 years old in Cuba. In Cuba, carrying out this project would have been very difficult because of censorship. Not only would it have been impossible to publish any of it, but it would have been almost impossible to find a place to store the manuscript. Besides, working under those conditions wouldn't have been particularly stimulating. New York gave me the chance to finish my work, and that's given me immense satisfaction. When I left Cuba, I had only published three books: *El Palacio de las blanquísimas mofetas* (*The Palace of the White Skunks*), which came out in Spain just as I was leaving, *Celestino antes del alba* (*Singing from the Well*), the only book I actually published in Cuba, and *El mundo alucinante* (translated in 1971 as *Hallucinations*; retranslated in 1987 as *The Ill-Fated Peregrinations of Fray Servando*), which came out in Mexico.

What about your collection of stories **Con los ojos cerrados** (**With Closed Eyes**), *which came out in Uruguay before those others?*

You're right, I'd forgotten about that. Probably because I wrote another story when I got here, *Termina el desfile* (*The Parade Ends*), which I used as the title piece for a new edition of my short stories. But, going back to your first question, I would say that by being here I have been able to finish a cycle of five novels about Cuban reality, starting with a period prior to the revolution and ending with the end of Castroism—a really hallucinated world where repression and the fight for freedom are completely enmeshed.

Of the five novels in your pentagony, as you call it, the three published texts, **Singing from the Well, The Palace,** *and* **Farewell to the Sea** *are well known. Could we talk about the two unpublished novels,* **El color del verano** (**The Color of Summer**) *and* **El asalto** (**The Assault**)?

Certainly. Just let me say that both will soon be published, in Spanish and in English.

In **El color del verano,** *we see that gloomy skunk again, the writer who hides behind several different masks—which is appropriate in a novel that contains a carnival. I wonder if that skunk is the link between this novel and its predecessors.*

Up to a point. The gloomy skunk undergoes a metamorphosis, so he can extend his existence through that of various characters. He is a homosexual who lives in Cuba, the victim of all sorts of persecution. In spite of it all, he's trying to write a novel which the government is trying to find and destroy. He's got a double in the United States, Gabriel, who's just come back from a trip to Havana. That's where his mother is, and because of all that, Gabriel has a series of complexes he can't overcome.

Do those complexes derive from his sexual orientation?

Yes, and also because he didn't fulfill his mother's dream. The gloomy skunk also turns into a character who incessantly writes letters to Cuba. Those three characters fuse into one by the end of the novel.

At the end of **Farewell to the Sea,** *something similar happens when the reader realizes that the feminine character is Héctor's invention, that he's been alone the whole time.*

Right, because in many of my novels the characters create other characters, create doubles that complement them, or show other aspects of their personality.

This mirroring or doubling of the creative process within the text makes your characters extremely complex. They all have vivid imaginations, but they are marked, even conditioned by the autobiographical element that slips into almost all your writing.

That's true. The novels depend on lived experience, from personal things to politics. The pentagony is a literary, that is, fictionalized retelling of all those experiences. Celestino in *Singing from the Well* is the poet's childhood; Fortunato in *The Palace* is his adolescence; Héctor in *Farewell to the Sea* is the young adult. In the fourth novel, *El color del verano*, which I began and finished in New York, the gloomy skunk/Gabriel represents maturity. He's experienced every kind of suffering. The only consolation left to him is to finish his book which, ironically, he can't. So each of the books, including the last, *El asalto*, contains elements which, even if they're not absolutely autobiographical, are closely related to me.

What exactly are those elements?

The quest for freedom, the love/hate relationship with the mother, and repression. In *El color del verano*, that repression is heightened because we see it through the eyes of Fifo, the decrepit tyrant who's been in power for 40 years.

Was **El color del verano** *harder to write because of Fifo?*

Let's say that *El color del verano* is my most ambitious novel as well as the one that synthesizes all my themes. It doesn't have one or two characters—it's got hundreds: the dictator, the mother, a slew of rather goyesque figures, the people, the military men, and the foreigners who come to the dictator's gala celebration. The party ends in a carnival that precipitates the collapse of the dictator's state.

Should we be thinking of Proust's Cities of the Plain *when we read* **El color del verano**?

Let me put it this way. Proust gives us a vision of a universe through a character who doesn't tell the author's autobiographical truth. That is, Proust does not appear in his novel as a homosexual character. Instead, he appears as a seducer of women. Sodom he leaves to other characters. I think people make a mistake when they think that in *Cities of the Plain* Proust's character is homosexual. The author might have been, but his character isn't. In my case, well, I've always been very irreverent, as I hope to be until the end. In my last novel, the character is named Reinaldo.

Which is something you did in your earliest stories, "Los dos Reinaldos" ("The Two Reinaldos") for example.

Proust also includes childhood, the life of the writer, and no question about it, the homosexual world which I, too, have wanted to describe in my novel. The difference is that I could be more uninhibited, more ironic, and a bit funnier. That's the world I lived in, a world that would disappear if it weren't caught up in a book. After all, the place where it all happened, Cuba, doesn't exist in the same way—it doesn't exist in New York either. So, my novel is a bit like Proust's *Cities of the Plain*, but filtered through my imagination, my irony, and my desolation.

The strange thing about **El asalto** *is that it can be read as a detective novel, although the way you manipulate the detective-novel structure reflects that irreverence you mentioned before.*

I never thought about the novel in that way. But you're right: It is a sort of detective novel. A detective chases a character who turns out to be the supreme detective. But the detective on the hunt doesn't realize it.

You make it sound simple! The tension really mounts when we find out who the hunted man is.

Sure, but that's like all my novels: masks and carnival, where the object of the chase reveals its double identity when captured. That's how the pentagony was supposed to end.

This double identity concept derives from one of the constants in your writing: the love-hate relationship with the mother.

The mother in my novels is a symbol—of love and even of sex. The mother image fuses with that of the moon, which for me is one of the most maternal—and mysterious—symbols. It's also a symbol of the repressive *machismo* we've all suffured. So the fury the protagonist feels in *El asalto* is that of frustration, of thinking that the person to blame for that frustration is his own mother. Ironically, he looks more and more like her every day.

Thinking now about your life in New York, which enabled you to write—paradoxically—about your life in Cuba, your novel **El portero (The Doorman)** *must have a special place in your oeuvre.*

It does. *El portero* begins what I call my New York cycle, which also includes *Viaje a la Habana* (Journey to Havana). It's a quest series, a quest for a world we did not leave behind in Cuba but which we haven't found in exile either. The doorman is looking for a door, a happiness, a kind of good fortune that doesn't exist. It's a book about uprootedness and desolation.

It sounds like the quintessence of exile.

That's just what it is. It deals with exile as a general idea. Look, the doorman is a character whose life sums up the lives of a million people. He's looking for a door, not the door to economic prosperity, but a door that opens to the happiness and peace he didn't find in Cuba and which, of course, he doesn't find in Yew York.

Could you tell us more about that door?

It's a symbolic door. Someone who's been uprooted, exiled, has no country. Our country exists only in our memory, but we need something beyond memory if we're to achieve happiness. We have no homeland, so we have to invent it over and over again. That door the protagonist, Juan, invents is something like the irrecoverable homeland and the lost time that is also irrecoverable. All the animals in the novella can return to their homelands—the country, the lake, the river—but for man, above all the exile, there is no return. That's one of the doorman's messages.

Would you say the animal closest to the doorman is the dog Cleopatra?

Both of them are like fossils from some remote era, totally anachronistic beings who do not exist in this commercialized world of ours. They want to live in their own worlds. The other animals play along with their owners but Cleopatra doesn't. She will not lower herself. Neither does the doorman. That's the affinity they share. At the end of the book, all of the characters find a door and leave, but those two can never find their doors.

Doesn't all of this meditation on exile ultimately relate to your major concern, Cuba?

Of course, I'm concerned with everything that happens in Cuba, which is perhaps why living here I feel like a shadow whose spirit, whose real being is there. In 1988, I was in Spain, hidden away from the world and its pain, with a friend—more than a friend, a brother for almost 30 years—the painter Jorge Camacho, when the plebiscite took place in Pinochet's Chile. I didn't know if Pinochet would win or lose, but I suggested to Jorge that we ask Fidel Castro to have a plebiscite of his own. Camacho thought it was a great idea and told me to write the letter immediately. Jorge, his wife Margarita, and I composed a short, blunt letter which we all signed. We knew, of course, that Fidel Castro would never hold a plebiscite, and all we hoped to do was to shame him.

But the letter went around the world. . .

Well, we sent copies to Vargas Llosa, to Octavio Paz, and to a series of distinguished writers and intellectuals. We thought that if they helped us we could gather more and more signatures. We knew that for people to take the letter seriously, it would have to be signed by persons of standing. We were pleasantly shocked at the number of signatures we got, especially because we had so little time. It was the end of October, and we wanted the letter to appear before January 1, 1989. In those few months we received hundreds of signatures, so the letter now is a kind of historical document, signed by 10 Nobel laureates.

And it made quite a splash.

It appeared in more than 50 newspapers, including *The New York Times.* Soon the letter and related documents will come out as a book. So we had a remote dream in a remote place, and it became one of the most effective protests against Fidel Castro's Tyranny. It would have been impossible if we didn't have Vargas Llosa, Octavio Paz, Fernando Arrabal, Elie Wiesel, and many others who gave us their unconditional support and their sound advice. They were the ones who really made the letter possible and made it as convincing as it was.

Compiling the documents must have been a nightmare.

It was an incredible amount of work, especially because we somehow lost the original manuscript. What happened was that I gave all the papers to Orlando Jiménez, the cineast, who had been invited by the Socialist party to give a lecture in Italy. On the way, he lost everything. So I had to start over from scratch, relocate all the relevant documents, including the letter in all its various forms, the various responses to it, and the newspaper articles about it.

You took part in another kind of anti-Castro protest, the documentary film **Havana.** *Tell us about it.*

I was in Paris for the presentation of the French translation of **La loma del ángel (Graveyard of the Angels)** and by chance met Czech filmmaker Jana Bukova, who'd been in exile for 20 years. She told me she was going to Cuba to make a film.

But the film is structured around your work. It begins with **Empieza el desfile (The Parade Begins)** *and ends with* **Termina el desfile (The Parade is Over).**

Jana Bukova had been interested in my work before meeting me, as was her literary assistant Walberto Ferrari. I helped her as much as I could and told her that it would be virtually impossible to go to Cuba to make a film about Cuban reality. But she did it.

The film shows the dire poverty of those who supposedly benefit from the revolution.

I told her where she should go so she wouldn't be tricked. She had to see the Cuban tenements and speak with real Cubans, especially black Cubans so they could tell her about their living conditions. She did just that and then used literary texts—some fragments of mine and pieces by other Cuban writers—to make a kind of historical framework. At the beginning I didn't think it would

turn out well, but when I saw the picture I thought it was a masterpiece.

I agree. It's not only a documentary but a work of art.

It's the most complete documentary ever made about Cuba because it contains music, Cuban tradition, landscape, literature—everything. I'm happy I had the chance to collaborate because the film gives a complete picture of Cuba as Hell.

Reinaldo, when you write, do you have a specific reader in mind?

Only in the sense that the reader I have in mind at first is myself. I read the texts, and if I don't like them, I destroy them. If I like them, I split into two readers and so on until I am a multitude. I think every work of art is an act of complicity between the artist and the public. What we writers produce, I think, is almost totally absorbed by the writer. Readers assimilate whatever they can or want to assimilate according to their sensibility, which means that a book is constantly changing, inexhaustible. Each reader invents his own novel. We provide a series of symbols and signs, pains, hopes, and fears which the readers organize according to their own criteria.

You've created a lot of unforgettable characters, but I think that of all your characters the most incredible is you.

Thanks Perla, because that character I've left in my books is the meaning of my life. I feel very happy that I've been able to finish, or almost finish—because we never finish, not even when we die—the literary cycle I'd laid out for myself. Perhaps a future reader of mine will say: How these people suffered! What a world they had to live in! How sorry we feel for them! (pp. 78–83)

Reinaldo Arenas and Perla Rozencvaig in an interview in *Review,* No. 44, January–June, 1991, pp. 78–83.

ILAN STAVANS
(essay date 1991)

[In the following review of *The Palace of the White Skunks,* Stavans describes the novel as "an intriguingly baroque, polyphonic study of despair."]

A talented writer persecuted by Fidel Castro's regime because of his homosexuality and his rebellion against social realism, Reinaldo Arenas left Cuba in 1980 in the Mariel boatlift. Arenas—whose experimental prose marked him as a follower of the Cuban poet and novelist José Lezama Lima as well as James Joyce and Laurence Sterne—had been imprisoned by the Cuban Government when his work, smuggled to the outside world, began to circulate in French and Spanish in the late 1970's. After his arrival in America, he maintained a precarious existence in Manhattan's Hell's Kitchen, only achieving some measure of security with the publication of an English translation of his novel *Farewell to the Sea*. But this security was to be short-lived. Suffering from AIDS, Arenas committed suicide, at the age of 47, in December of last year.

At times in his demanding, idiosyncratic fiction, Arenas openly set forth to rewrite a classic. At others, he created haunting, original images of death, repression and escape through his admirable use of unconventional narrative techniques. Not surprisingly, his characters are marginals in society at large—fools, suicides and hysterics.

Today, some might find Arenas a bit outmoded. After all, we have outlived the nouveau roman and are slowly returning to straightforward realism. But we should. Remember that *The Palace of the White Skunks* first appeared in Spanish in 1975 and that Andrew Hurley's English translation, a faithful rendering of the eccentricities of the original, is but an overdue rediscovery. The novel is part of what Arenas called a *pentagonía*, a series of five semiautobiographical "agonies"—two other sections of which, *Singing From the Well* and *Farewell to the Sea* have already appeared in English—in which the hero is the same person, despite the fact that he carried different names and suffers different fates.

In this carnival of a novel, a family saga of sorts that recounts the misadventures of a cruel and erratic clan, the protagonist, called Fortunato, is an adolescent living in Holguín, a town in Cuba's Oriente province. The year is 1958, and the revolution is taking shape. The bizarre cast of characters includes Fortunato's unmarried mother, Onerica, an émigré working in the United States; his aunt Digna, who won't forgive or forget Moisés, the husband who left her; his cousin Esther, who poisons herself to death at the age of 13 and whose mother, Celia, is crazy; and his grandmother, Jacinta, who seems to spend most of her time on the toilet.

Some characters share incestuous desires. Others live in a self-inflicted silence, while everyone around them engages in aggressive verbal outbursts. Brutality is the prevailing mode of behavior. No one is happy. Everyone wants to hide, to escape. Eventually, Fortunato manages to do so, almost accidentally, by trying unsuccessfully to join the guerrillas who are rebelling against the Government.

What never appears in the novel is the palace of skunks—be they white, green or translucent. But then, this seems fully in keeping with Arenas's notions about the unreality of "real" life. This liberating spirit is first suggested in the table of contents, where the prologue and epilogue are placed together. Afther that, we expect further surprises, which Arenas duly delivers. Part Three, for instance, is a brief play. One also finds, placed alongside the main text of the novel, quasi-encyclopedic essays about flies, which have nothing to do with the plot. And

there are press clippings, as well as isolated paragraphs in smaller type that provide historical or personal information.

Fortunato and most of the other characters in the book are fatherless; thus the absence of an authoritative narrator seems a formal reflection of the psychological imbalance of the cast. An anarchic, free-flowing voice, constantly oscillating between the first and the third person, takes us into the protagonist's mind and the minds of his family members—and into reality itself. What emerges is an intriguingly baroque, polyphonic study of despair. Reinaldo Arenas's characters, like those of William Faulkner, are irredeemable, destined to suffer. They are possessed and suffocated. In scene after scene, we hear their tormented screams as they succumb to the perverse joke that has been played upon them by fate.

Ilan Stavans, "An Irredeemable Clan," in *The New York Times Book Review*, January 20, 1991, p. 20.

MICHAEL WOOD
(essay date 1991)

[In the following excerpt, Wood examines *Old Rosa* and *The Palace of the White Skunks*.]

Skunk hour, in Robert Lowell's well-known poem, is a time of jaunty, disreputable defiance. The skunks march up Main Street, ready to take over the town. They are the scavenger's answer to the poet's Miltonic despair. "My mind's not right," the poet says, and "I myself am Hell." The skunks don't say anything, they just dive into the trash, making both mind and Hell seem irrelevant, almost an indulgence. The human skunks in the work of the late Cuban writer Reinaldo Arenas are too depressed and depleted for any such bravado. Survival for them is not defiance, it is part of the penance, what they are condemned to. For the torment of Hell is not its pain or disorder, but its obdurate sameness. Even another Hell would be a comfort, but there is no other.

> Another hell, another hell, maybe more monotonous, maybe even more suffocating, maybe even more disgusting and reprehensible than this one, but *another* one, at least.
>
> Now I see that hell is always what you can't reject. What's just simply *there*.

And yet there is a lurid life in the writing of these disasters, a genuine exuberance in the detailing of miseries. It's as if a Cuban version of Buñuel's *Los Olvidados* had been shot in brilliant Technicolor. (p. 21) [Arenas] was a profuse, imaginative, well-read, and disturbing writer, a traitor to silence, as he says of one of his characters; a novelist who sought to give voices to the voiceless, and not only the obviously voiceless, the visibly suppressed, but also those victims and sufferers whose distress eludes us, perhaps because they are too many or because we can't read their muted style. In Arenas's fiction even the most cramped or muffled minds are lent a fabulous fluency: no sorrow is left unturned.

Old Rosa, composed of two novellas written in 1966 and 1971, is described as a novel in two stories, and this is, in miniature, a good definition of Arenas's whole fictional opus: consciousness flows from book to book, characters change, die, disappear, but the story continues. The Cuban writer Severo Sarduy writes of Arenas's "recurrent and musical" narrative, of his novels as one "long uninterrupted sentence," but also insists on the play of different voices, each character having his/her own rhetoric and images and obsessions. The author is a ventriloquist, projecting his life into a tissue of other, imagined minds, but those minds are possibilities, extensions of a plight, not mere duplications in another key. One thinks of Lorca depicting a house full of desperate women in *La Casa de Bernarda Alba*; the desperation was theirs and his, and indeed in one register the desperation of a whole country. It is in this sense that Arenas's claim that he is writing "the secret history of the Cuban people" is not as extravagant as it looks. The secret is not in the events but in the mentalities. Similarly, when Arenas says his novel *Hallucinations* recounts the life of the Mexican monk Fray Servando Teresa de Mier "as it was, as it may have been, as I should have liked it to have been," he is not offering those perspectives as alternatives. The books aims for all three, and this is why Arenas can say he wants it to be, rather than a historical or a biographical novel, simply a novel. His pentagony is both a sequence of autobiographical novels and a sequence of . . . novels.

The Old Rosa of the title story is a landowner who sets fire to her house and herself in a rage of frustration at a world which has escaped her control. Rosa is tough and pious. She drives her husband to suicide by rejecting after her third child, all his sexual approaches; her very prayers are said to sound like orders. But now the Cuban revolution has taken her fields and her elder son; her daughter has married a black and gone to live in the city; her younger, favorite son is homosexual. She meets, in the shape of an encroaching hallucination, an angel who represents all the desire and grace and happiness she has refused in her life, and refused, she now sees, for nothing. She thinks the angel maybe the Devil come to mock her, feels she has "been swindled all her life," grasps "the dimensions of an immeasurable solitude." But then she recognizes the rigidity and hollowness even of her renunciation, the way her religion has allowed her to deceive herself. The angel is a more intimate, less official enemy, a Catholic's version of Henry James' beast in the jungle: "But you're not the Devil, she said finally, and now her

words seemed to stumble upon the terrifying answer. You are something worse. You are nothing." At this moment the house begins to burn and Rosa and the angel are consumed together: "The two figures. . . no longer were distinguishable."

The opening of *Old Rosa* affords a very good glimpse of Arenas's style:

> In the end she went out to the yard, almost enveloped in flames, leaned against the tamarind tree that no longer flowered, and began to cry in such a way that the tears seemed never to have begun, but to have been there always, flooding her eyes, producing that creaking noise, like the noise of the house at the moment when the flames made the strongest posts totter and the flashing frame came down in an enormous crackling that pierced the night like a volley of fireworks.

There is quite a bit more than we need here—the fireworks weaken the picture rather than strengthen it, and the "enormous crackling" seems mere bombast compared to the discreet, domestic "creaking noise"—but the ancient weeping and the transfer of the creaking from fire to tears, masked as a simple simile, are very powerful, and Arenas prolongs this scene with a string of conditional, bifurcating notions which place us both inside and outside it. Rosa looks like a little girl in the sort of story "she had never read", if a neighbor had passed, he/she would have seen that this was Old Rosa; but if Rosa had screamed, no one would have heard her for the sound of the fire. Rosa might have thought, *My God, this is hell,* and she might have prayed, but she didn't. The effect is to set up fleeting, parallel fictions, other Rosas; to make writer and reader Rosa's allies but also to remind them of their difference from her, the books they have read, what they themselves might have thought, their safety from the fire.

Arturo, in the second story in the book, is Rosa's youngest child, now in a Cuban camp for homosexuals. Like Rosa, he is dying as the story begins and ends. He has been shot while trying to escape, and the text recounts his various strategies for survival in the camp, and meditates on the strange collusions that power exacts from weakness. Arturo separates himself mentally from the other prisoners, from what he sees as "*their* world. . . *their* repulsive lives. . . their endless, stupid conversations, with their exaggerated, effeminate, affected, artificial, false, gross, grotesque posturings," but the very language suggests the fragility and anxiousness of the separation, and we learn that Arturo has become an expert mime of every stereotyped homosexual gesture, because he thinks "it's easy to fit in anywhere, slip into any reality at all, as long as you don't take it seriously, as long as you secretly scorn it":

> Arturo did begin to use that affected, dizzying slang of theirs, begin to cackle and howl with laughter like any ordinary queen, to sing, pose, shadow his eyes and dye his hair. . . until he had mastered, come to possess, all

the cant, every typical movement and feature of the imprisoned gay world. . . .

But does Arturo scorn this world? Can he, should he? What bothers him about "them," the other prisoners, is their agile complicity with the system that persecutes them, their ability to "trivialize the pain":

> They would do anything, suffer any terror, turn the other cheek to any insult, and immediately incorporate it into the folklore, the customs, the daily calamities, yes, they had a gift for transforming terror into familiar ritual.

One hardly knows whether to admire or despair of such a gift. "Leopards break into the temple," Kafka wrote in a parable Arenas is perhaps thinking of here, "and drink to the dregs what is in the sacrificial pitchers; this is repeated over and over again: finally it can be calculated in advance, and it becomes part of the ceremony."

Like Rosa, Arturo sees an angel, only this is a benign figure, an ideal future companion, the prince who will one day redeem all the dross and mess of ordinary, disfigured life. Arturo has found an escape in writing, in imagining a fabulous alternative world where there are brilliant, precious palaces and fountains and music, and rows of stately elephants; a dwelling worthy of an angel. But is this an escape? Don't all such escapes confirm the very prison they seek to deny? Where else but in penury would one dream up such riches?

These are the questions the story is designed to pose. Is it true, for example, that "reality lies not in the terror one feels and suffers but in the creations that overpower that terror, and wipe it out," and who could answer this question for us? Or is the dead, tortured body of a fellow prisoner the ultimate absolute real, erasing all found fantasies and visions? Is time another such reality, "aggressive, fixed, unyielding, unbearable"? We can't deny the second, harsher reality; can't want to undersell the power and freedom of the imagination, even harassed, even imprisoned. Not too long before his internment Arturo was "still convinced that a cluster of signs, a cadence of images perfectly described—*words*—might save him. . .". The tense suggests he is no longer convinced, but the signs are what he has, and he dies having "reached the monumental row of stately, regal elephants" which frames this story like a frieze formed of Arturo's writing. He has died, that is, into his fantasy; not saved but not simply canceled.

The two stories make a novel not just because they narrate the final days of two members of the same family, and not just because Arturo, about to be killed, confuses the brutal camp lieutenant with his mother, and places her at the head of the shooting party. She is "the only person who had ever loved him" but she had also tried to kill him on discovering his sexual preferences. She is the unavoidable, the prison behind the prison. But the novel puts the two characters together on another plane outside the particular events of their lives. They meet different angels, but embody the same despair, the same feeling of being "condemned to live in a world where only frustration made sense and had a place."

This world is historical, not some eternalized human condition; but it is not simply Cuba in the 1950s and 1960s. It is every (historical) world which regularly resorts to repression and makes difference and deviance routinely punishable. Some of the contributors to the Hernández Miyares-Rozencvaig collection [*Reinaldo Arenas: Alucinaciones, fantasía y realidad*, 1990] rather cheerfully insist on what they see as the counterrevolutionary, antiprogressive tendency of Arenas's writing, as if it was all right to be a reactionary as long as you were against Castro. But it is the subversive quality of the writing that seems to me most notable, its refusal not of progress or revolution but of a rigid correctness, of sentimentality and bullying. It is writing that seeks to construct, as Juan Goytisolo says, "a habitable mental space" against the political and moral odds. The mere possibility of such a space is enough to make many people, on the left and on the right, want to invade it, abolish it.

All of Arenas's skunks dream and some of them dream novels, pour their imagination on to paper. Their minds are not right, but their world is not right either, their very unhappiness is a form of protest. At the center of *The Palace of the White Skunks* is Fortunato, a boy who, like Arenas, runs off to join the rebels in 1958. Like Arturo, Fortunato has discovered in writing a promise of salvation; but not only for himself. He is "like a lightning rod for terror," he thinks, "for terror in all its variety," and he insists that he *has been* all the members of his desolate family, that he is the emissary of their song, their isolation. Thus he has been his bitter grandfather; a Spaniard who emigrated to Cuba from the Canary Isles; his pious, crazed grandmother, his spinster aunt, interminably locked in the bathroom; his married aunt, abandoned by her husband and forced to return home with two children to care for; those two precocious misbehaving children themselves; his other aunt, haunted by her dead daughter, who committed suicide at thirteen; that daughter too.

> Many times—all the time, really—he had been all of them, and he had sufered for them, and perhaps when he had been them (for he had more imagination than they did, he could go beyond the mere here-and-now) he had suffered more than they, deep within himself, deep within his own, invariable terror.

The one person he hasn't been, can't be, is his mother, who has gone off to work in the United States; she is Fortunato's betrayer and only fixed resource, he would love her if his resentment would let him.

"All the time really" is a Nabokovian gag, reminding us that all these creatures are *written*, inhabitants of the imagination of Fortunato/Arenas, since he is, doubly, the only voice they have: because their pain would otherwise go unrecorded, and because they are fictional anyway. Fictional, but not without live counterparts, and most of them drawn, I assume, from models found in Arenas's childhood in the Cuban countryside and in the town of Holguín. Like Arenas's Mexican monk, Fortunato's family is both inside and outside the mind of the memorialist: as it is, as it might have been, and as he revamps it. There is of course something self-serving and self-deluding in Fortunato's sense of his mission: how could he suffer more than the others do? He is too much in love with his job as scapegoat, and his "deep, invariable terror" seems overwritten, however genuine and constant the terror might basically be. But then he is young, and Arenas hasn't written about him ironically.

He hasn't written any of this book ironically; he has written it lyrically ("The moon moistened its cold embittered face in the clouds"), making excess and stylistic risk a kind of signature. Certainly there has to be a danger of coyness in a novel that begins, "Death is out there in the backyard playing with the wheel off a bicycle." What staves off the coyness, leaving us with just the danger, is the intensity and detail of the evoked reality (the broken, once much-ridden bicycle rather than the allegorical reaper), and the intelligence of the narrator's reflections on what is happening, the sense of a mind trying to make sense of miserably fragmented lives, battered by poverty and strangled desire.

> But what was God for them? God was above all the possibility of crying their lamentations, their only real possibility. God offered them the occasion, which all men and women need if they are not to become absolute monsters, of being children from time to time, with their whining and their complaints, their anger, their fits of tears. . .

There are grim jokes too, as when the grandmother is described as "screaming 'I can't take it anymore' till you can't take it anymore." Arenas has been reading Joyce and Rimbaud and he makes an entire section of the work a phantasmagoric play in the manner of the "Circe" chapter of *Ulysses,* and echoes the prose poems of *Illuminations.* He plays with the layout of the page, inserting paragraphs of comment from the characters in small corners of different print. He quotes film announcements and beauty advice, as well as revolutionary bulletins from the late 1950s.

Fortunato also has the nightmare I have associated with Henry James— "the certainty that nothing, not even something terrible, would ever truly happen to him"— and one of his aunts longs for "the consolation of some terrible disgrace, some awful misery, some unbearable bad luck." Fortunato/Arenas grants her wish, sends her patrolling the streets looking in vain for a man and has her beaten, robbed, thoroughly humiliated. And Arenas saves Fortunato from his nightmare by having him arrested by Batista's troops, tortured, allowed to run free, and then shot and hanged. This is a place where "the interpreting ceases," Fortunato thinks. "And all the games vanish, and all the fights, all the escapees crash into each other and fuse, burst, and form a hard brick wall." Except that they don't, at least not in fiction, and not in the mind of anyone prepared to remember or imagine the missing. Everyone dies many times, and Arenas allows Fortunato and his young cousin a talkative life after death, so he knows that something terrible has happened to him; and will go on happening to him, since hell is all there is and ever was. Even happy or beautiful moments feed the horror. "Everything becomes golden, fleeting, glorious," the narrator reflects, "so that one would think the world was made to be lost." But then it is made (again and again) before it is lost, and Arenas's writing—impeccably translated here, as I hope my quotations may suggest—offers us the drama of the making as well as the document of the ruin. (pp. 21–3)

Michael Wood, "No Sorrow Left Unturned," in *The New York Review of Books,* Vol. XXXVIII, No. 5, March 7, 1991, pp. 21–3.

FRANCISCO SOTO

(essay date 1991)

[In the following review of *The Palace of the White Skunks,* Soto judges the novel a complex, penetrating study of human existence.]

Singing from the Well, The Palace of the White Skunks, and *Farewell to the Sea* constitute a unique intradependent unit within Arenas's total novelistic production. These three novels form part of a five-book "secret history of Cuba" that will be completed once *El color del verano* and *El asalto* are finally published (these last two texts, which the author finished shortly before his death last December, are already under contract by Viking; the Spanish editions are expected out later this year from Universal, Miami). This pentalogy, which Arenas insisted on calling a "pentagony"—a playful but revealing neologism that underscores the despair and agony suffered by the characters in each novel—reflects different historical periods and provides a futuristic vision of Cuban society: the Batista era (*Singing from the Well*), the revolutionary guerrilla struggle (*The Palace of the White Skunks*), the institutionalization of the revolution from 1958 until 1970 (*Farewell to the Sea*), the summer of 1999 (*El color del verano*), and an even further look into the future of an alienated and tyrannized society (*El asalto*). In each novel of the pentalogy the main character is destroyed, only to be resurrected under a new name in the subsequent text, where he suffers a whole new set of ordeals.

The Palace of the White Skunks covers the adolescent stage of the protean main character of the quintet. Fortunato, a sensitive and restless young man living through a turbulent political period in Cuban history, the insurrection against the Batista regime, is desperate to escape the cruelties of his family (he calls them wild beasts), as well as to escape from Holguín, a small rural town "of symmetrical streets and townsfolk inalterably practical." Eventually, Fortunato escapes and attempts to join Castro's revolutionary forces. However, his flight for freedom ends tragically with his arrest, torture, and execution by the Batista police.

The story of *The Palace of the White Skunks* is not just the story of Fortunato, it is also the story of Fortunato's eccentrically cruel and obsessive family: Polo, the grandfather who considers himself cursed for having engendered only daughters; Jacinta, the superstitious and blasphemous grandmother who spends her days compulsively going to the bathroom; Aunt Celia, who is driven to madness after her only daughter Ester commits suicide; Aunt Digna, abandoned by her husband Moisés and left to raise the mischievous Tico and Anisia; Aunt Adolfina, a spinster desperate to lose her virginity; Onérica, Fortunato's mother who abandons him and goes to the United States in search of her own "fortune." These characters, or rather "voices" (for the text is constructed as a cacophony of voices), are given the opportunity to recount their own obsessive stories of despair. Yet, in this Tower of Babel where no one understands any one else, personal agonies are fated to (re)echo within the chambers of the novel. That the characters, prisoners of their own suffering, yearn in desperation to find a receptive listener only underscores their alienation.

The ironic and ludicrous title, *The Palace of the White Skunks,* already alerts the reader to the unconventional story that is to follow. In this novel, the notion of a well-structured plot is subverted by the presentation of a narrative time-space of multiple possibilities that invites the reader to sort out the various narrative threads and, thus, to work out a larger meaning. This is a text that requires a more flexible approach to reading—letting go of traditional expectations and following the creative detours and interruptions in the narrative. The reader is asked to make the text intelligible in spite of its violations and transgressions, to accommodate the shifting codes of a multifarious "reality." In this way, the initial image of death riding on a bicycle around the family home is "real" within the text as the protagonist's frustrated attempt to join the revolutionary struggle. Fortunato's walking on the roof while stabbing himself, Ester and Fortunato's chats beyond the grave, demons and spirits dancing in the living room, the extreme poverty of the rural town, the struggle against Batista, the grandmother's blasphemies and insults, Adolfina's sexual frustrations—all have equal

credibility and contribute to the novel's textual validity.

The Palace of the White Skunks is divided into three parts: "Prologue and Epilogue," "The Creatures Utter Their Complaints," and "The Play."

In part one, the crisscrossing of voices is so tangled that it is nearly impossible to decipher what is going on. Narrative continuity is undermined as words appear to be little more than muffled echoes reverberating on the written page. However, all of the book's themes and narrative levels (imaginary, poetic, and historical) are concentrated in this section, which paradoxically (con)fuses what is traditionally the first (prologue) and last words (epilogue) of a traditional text. In *The Palace of the White Skunks* there is no first or final word on any given matter; discourse is presented as an open-ended and simultaneous verbal game that transgresses the traditional novel's regard for causality/linearity.

The second part constitutes the major portion of the novel. This section is divided into five "Agonies" in which each family member attempts to articulate his or her intimate sufferings. But the intermingling of voices ofen conceals the identity of the speaking subject. The text also contains newspaper accounts, bulletins of guerrilla activity, advertisements, film announcements, and beauty magazines mixed in with the babel of voices. In the "Fifth Agony" there are 12 "versions" of the novel's two most significant episodes: Fortunato's decision to run away from home to join the guerrillas and Adolfina's unsuccessful attempt to lose her virginity during a night on the town. The contradictory version of these two fruitless quests reveal the insurmountable complexity in any attempt to record "reality" faithfully.

Part three is a play within the novel. With this shift in genre (from novel to drama) comes another significant change, a shift from interior monologue to dramatic dialogue. In this phantasmagoric theatrical representation the family members become performers who reenact their own lives and obsessions. Immediately following the play is a "Sixth Agony," which recounts yet another "version" of Fortunato's escape. The omniscient narrator of this last "Agony" describes the young man's torture and death at the hands of the government soldiers. However, in "version" seven of the previous section this same omniscient narrator, a traditionally reliable voice, expresses doubt about whether Fortunato joins the rebel forces. Whatever the truth is, no version denies Fortunato's basic reasons for wanting to leave, or escape, his home: hunger, poverty, repression, lack of opportunities, and the suffocating "realities" of his family life.

With its narrative strategy that fragments the story, *The Palace of the White Skunks* invites the reader to recreate a bewildering collage that may at first disorient but ultimately reforges the connection between life and art at the level of the imaginative. In this third novel, Arenas paints a disturbing portrait of the poverty and misery of rural Cuba shortly before the triumph of the revolution. While many Cuban novelists of the 1970s were writing realistic works that presented the revolution idealistically as the moment that radically transformed Cuban society for the better, Arenas portrays the revolution as the catalyst in the death of his protagonist and in the emotional destruction of a family. Although Fortunato is destroyed in *The Palace of the White Skunks*, he, like the phoenix, is resurrected in *Farewell to the Sea* as the adult Héctor. Yet Héctor, living under an institutionalized revolution, is condemned by the same fate to continue questioning his tortured existence and marginality. (pp. 90–1)

Francisco Soto, in a review of *The Palace of the White Skunks*, in *Review*, No. 44, January-June, 1991, pp. 90–1.

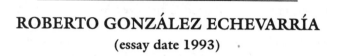

ROBERTO GONZÁLEZ ECHEVARRÍA

(essay date 1993)

[González Echevarría is a noted Hispanic scholar and author. In the following excerpt from his review of Arenas's posthumously published memoir, *Before Night Falls*, he discusses some of the main threads of the work, calling it "an absorbing book, with the fascination one finds in stories by survivors of death camps or in lives of the saints."]

[Arenas] was raised amid the most desperate want, first by his jilted mother, then by a host of similarly betrayed young women and by his maternal grandparents. His absent father makes only one appearance in his book, but it is a memorable one:

One day my mother and I were on our way to visit one of my aunts. As we walked down to the river, a man came toward us; he was good-looking, tall and dark. My mother fell into a sudden rage; she began picking up stones from the riverbank and throwing them at his head, while the man, in spite of the shower of rocks, kept coming toward us. When he was close to me, he put his hand into his pocket, pulled out two pesos and gave them to me. He then patted me on the head and ran away to avoid being hit by one of the stones. My mother cried all the way to my aunt's house, where I found out that the man was my father. I never saw him again, nor the two pesos; my aunt asked my mother to lend them to her and I do not know if she ever paid them back.

That is a revealing anecdote, showing Arenas's bewilderment in a world where even those who love him harm him. The tall, dark and handsome father will pursue Arenas throughout his life, marking indelibly his relationships with men and women. The aunt who pilfers his meager legacy will also reappear in the shape of another

aunt, a hypocrite who denounces his sexual activities to the police while she carries on a dissolute life of her own.

To say that Arenas grew up close to nature may sound like a cliché, but in his case the phrase could not be more literal. Among his favorite childhood pastimes were eating dirt, from which he got a big belly full of worms, having sex with various animals and playing with mud in the falling rain. So was running through fields shouting hymn-like poems of his own invention, listening with rapture to the stories told by his grandmother and following the soap operas the women heard on their dilapidated radio. This was Arenas's sentimental and literary education, one from which he would draw much of his inspiration later. An even harsher lesson was to discover and be forced to conceal from the neurotically macho Cuban society his attraction to men.

Before Night Falls is an autobiography that covers the span of Arenas's life, from early childhood to his suicide letter blaming Castro for all of his calamities, including his death. It is an absorbing book, with the fascination one finds in stories by survivors of death camps or in lives of the saints. Arenas is betrayed by friends, spied on by fellow writers working for state security, beaten by lovers and jailers, coerced into signing vile confessions, forced to labor in stifling cane fields and compelled to "reform" sexually and politically. He is such a pariah that he must seek escape in the most spectacular ways, from an attempt to swim across Guantánamo Bay to reach the United States naval base there to braving the Florida Straits in an inner tube. All his tries are thwarted by vigilant authorities and informers. Once, fleeing the police, he hides for weeks in Lenin Park, a Communist theme park on the outskirts of Havana. There he spends his time writing the first version of these memoirs (his manuscript is later confiscated) and reading Homer, a flight from reality that necessarily ends every day as night falls (hence the title of his book). To lure people into turning him in, the police announce that a C.I.A. agent and rapist is on the loose. Arenas is careful not to be seen by anyone, but is eventually caught and barely saved from a lynch mob. In episodes such as these Arenas appears as a kind of Jean Valjean, and his book reads like a romantic adventure novel.

In prison, from December 1974 until early in 1976, Arenas finds a mirror image of Cuban society, except that this mirror not only reflects but magnifies too. Months pass before he is brought to trial on a morals charge. In the meantime he is sexually abused, forced to live in the most degrading and unsanitary conditions, reduced to a subsistence diet that he supplements by eating, among other things, sparrows that another inmate has taught him how to capture. When the morals charge does not hold up—mostly because the Government's key witnesses, two youths, refuse to testify they had sex with him—he is forced to confess to counterrevolutionary activities, including sending his manuscripts abroad. Arenas is also made to promise that he will write optimistic novels and refrain from homosexual activity. He is then sent to a rehabilitation camp, from which he at last emerges, bereft of work or sustenance and closely watched by his aunt and the authorities.

As strange as it may seem to speak of innocence in dealing with a work so redolent of the violence (symbolic or real) of sexual exchange, there is in Arenas a sense of liberation attached to lovemaking that seems pre-Freudian in its candor. The punishment that usually follows a seduction catches him full of surprise or outrage, as if he were the first to be expelled from Paradise. The same is found in his descriptions of the labyrinthine intrigues, back-stabbing and betrayals among writers and other co-workers. It is as if on some deep level Arenas had innocently believed in Castro's rhetoric (a good deal of it derived from Jose Martí, the Cuban poet and patriot), and could only measure imperfect human performance against absolute standards of purity.

In this he is like a true son of the revolution and of Castro, who inevitably assumes in this book the role of the evil father who rejected his mother, condemning her to a life of shame and lack of love. Characteristically, Arenas's retaliation is through seduction: "Many of the young men who marched in Revolutionary Square applauding Fidel Castro, and many of the soldiers who marched, rifle in hand and with martial expressions, came to our rooms after the parades to cuddle up naked, and show their real selves, sometimes revealing a tenderness and true enjoyment such as I have not been able to find again anywhere else in the world."

Castro, of course, sets himself up for such a role in ways that sometimes appear too crass to be true. When asked last year in Spain if he felt compunction about having had to fire his eldest son from an important position, Castro answered, much as would have Gabriel García Márquez's aging dictator in "The Autumn of the Patriarch," that all Cubans are his children. *Before Night Falls* is a narrative linking poignantly the personal and political levels of this family romance, told from the point of view of the abandoned son. (pp. 1, 32–3)

Arenas was fascinated by the infinite: by the sea, the stars, the expanses of the mind. He was always testing himself against such unreachable horizons. In his private life, erotic passion drove him to probe the limits of the social and the political. Arenas figures that by 1968 he had participated in around 5,000 sexual encounters. His arithmetic on these matters would make Leporello's voice break in shame. Arenas was disappointed by the way in which homosexuals in the United States band together and seek one another for satisfaction, whereas his passion was to seduce men (to play the active role does not define one as a homosexual in Cuba). It is clear in *Before Night Falls* that Arenas saw in sexuality, as in writing, a way to freedom, but a freedom conceived in risk rather than community. Even among the oppressed, Arenas had to be a pariah.

Reading Arenas is like witnessing a bare consciousness in the process of assimilating the most universal, but powerful, human experiences and turning them into literature. Because of this, *Before Night Falls* is crucial to understanding his works. But, more important, it is a record of human cruelty and the toils of one individual to survive them. Anyone who feels the temptation to be lenient in judging Castro's Government should first read this passionate and beautifully written book. (p. 33)

Roberto González Echevarría, "An Outcast of the Island," in *The New York Times Book Review*, October 24, 1993, pp. 1, 32–3.

ALASTAIR REID

(essay date 1993)

[In the following excerpt from a review of Arenas's *Before Night Falls*, Reid points out "a noble and imperturbable dignity" about the work and claims that "it is a book above all about being free."]

[Arenas's] books are demanding. The five novels of his *pentagonía*, the recreation of his Cuba, are not novels in any conventional sense. In them, separate stories crowd in on one another, hallucinatory passages give way to disembodied conversation, in the first person and in the third person. There are long passages of pure lyrical writing in which the distinction between poetry and prose is blurred. Meditations are sometimes juxtaposed with official documents—reality is multifaceted, contradictory, labyrinthine. Yet throughout, the books show a high literary intelligence and a voluptuous command of different modes of language, from hallucinatory flight to science fiction. Also, his books appeared in irregular order in other countries, while he remained in Cuba, out of reach. After he died at the end of 1990 he left behind for his readers, in the form of a memoir, a map of the reality from which they were made, *Before Night Falls*.

Before Night Falls is an extraordinary book, extraordinary in its restraint and its dignity, particularly in view of the tribulations that seemed always to dog him. He had every reason in the world to write his book of "vengeance against most of the human race". . . ; yet the tone of the book, while not without its sardonic asides, is calm, dispassionate, spare. It makes no argument; instead, it recreates a life that, so passionately lived and so desparate to find space for itself, is beyond argument. The face of Reinaldo Arenas that fixes the reader from the book jacket has a gaze, wary and relentless at once, that has to be met. It is the face of an Ancient Mariner, come to tell his tale. . . . What is most affecting about his memoir is

Arenas's account of his fierce struggle to secure that minimal freedom, his insistent search for that very space and time to write in a Cuba that increasingly denied it to him. He claimed the same freedom for himself sexually, to a point of recklessness. . . .

Readers of Arenas's novels will find in *Before Night Falls* the sources of many of his stories and the events in them; what they will not find, however, is their stylistic brilliance, their flights of language. The language of the memoir is stark, the sentences short and staccato, with an urgency of forward movement. He is recalling his life, ticking it off in sharp, remembered moments, against the clock, with death waiting at his elbow. (p. 23)

Inasmuch as he always refused to be a pawn in other people's games, his memoir by its nature remains a purely personal accounting, not a weapon for the use of others. If anyone was entitled to his rage, it was Arenas. *Before Night Falls* might well have been a long cry of anger, a diatribe, but it is marked much more by its fierce determination to describe his experience honestly and incontrovertibly than by anger or self-pity.

There can be a vast distance between those who proclaim human rights and those who return, like the Ancient Mariner, with their tales and evidence of human wrongs. A bent for writing like that of Arenas would have been recognized in many other countries and given ample room in which to develop; but since he was never given any room he could count on, his enormous energy was compressed to an explosive degree. He was forced into defiance, into attitudes and actions he would never have chosen. He claimed, after all, to be no more than a writer and a chronicler: his cause was his own. Like most writers, all he wanted was to see his books published; they were his justification. He ends the memoir with a luminous meditation on being freed from the past, with death waiting. "Now, the state of grace that had saved me from so many misfortunes had come to an end." There is a noble and imperturbable dignity about *Before Night Falls*; it is a book above all about being free.

Alastair Reid, "Troublemaker," in *The New York Review of Books*, Vol. XI, No. 19, November 18, 1993, pp. 23–5.

SOURCES FOR FURTHER STUDY

Borinsky, Alicia. "Rewritings and Writings." *Diacritics* IV, No. 4 (Winter 1974): 22–8.
> Views *Hallucinations* as a work in the tradition of the Hispanic antirealist and French symbolist literary movements.

Olivares, Jorge. "Carnival and the Novel: Reinaldo Arenas' *El Palacio de las blanquísimas mofetas*." *Hispanic Review* 53, No. 4 (Autumn 1985): 467–76.
> Maintains the *The Palace of the White Skunks* is informed by an inverted, "carnival logic," masterfully blending humor and pathos.

Rodriguez–Monegal, Emir. "The Labyrinthine World of Reinaldo Arenas." *Latin American Literary Review* VIII, No. 16 (Spring 1980): 126–31.
> Argues that Arenas's works are purposefully complex in structure and characterization to deride a progressive view of history, to challenge fixed notions of reality, and to undermine Castro's political ideology.

Wood, Michael. "Broken Blossoms." *New York Review of Books* XXXIII, No. 5 (27 March 1986): 34–8.
> Scrutinizes *Farewell to the Sea* as a literary and political work, paying particular attention to the character of Hector.

Additional coverage of Arenas's life and career is contained in the following sources published by Gale Research: *Contemporary Authors*, Vols. 124, 128, 133; *Contemporary Literary Criticism*, Vol. 41; and *Hispanic Writers*.

Ron Arias

1941–

(Full name Ronald Francis Arias) Chicano journalist, novelist, and short story writer.

INTRODUCTION

A distingushed contributor to contemporary Chicano fiction, Arias is known principally for his widely acclaimed debut novel, *The Road to Tamazunchale* (1975). Critics have cited the work as an outstanding example of "magic realism," a literary form popularized by Colombian author Gabriel García Márquez that blends reality with fantasy. Arias's own style of magic realism has been described as a mixture of precise, journalistic descriptions, and stream-of-consciousness writing that often centers on magic figures who can manipulate reality. Noted Chicano author Juan D. Bruce-Novoa has commended Arias as "a skilled, patient craftsmen, with a healthy sense of irony about himself and the world."

A Los Angeles native, Arias, whose stepfather was a career Army officer, relocated frequently during his childhood. He spent much of his youth with his maternal grandmother, who acquainted him with Chicano culture and encouraged him to record his thoughts and observations in a notebook. Arias wrote for school newspapers while attending high school and college and, in 1962, was awarded an Inter-American Press Association Scholarship to Buenos Aires, Argentina. There, he worked as a reporter for the *Buenos Aires Herald* and sent numerous exclusives on the outbreak of the Argentine Neo-Nazi movement to American newspapers in New York and Los Angeles. That same year, Arias joined the Peace Corps, spending a year in a small village in Peru where he witnessed a government massacre of recalcitrant peasants. These experiences were, in Arias's own words, a "true education—at least where writing is concerned." Returning to the United States in 1967, he studied Spanish and journalism at the University of California. For the next four years, Arias continued to write for various publications both at home and abroad. His reputation as a prominent Chicano author was established with the publication of *The Road to Tamazunchale*. Arias also contributed several features on barrio identity and the education of Chicanos in Anglo schools to *Nuestro*, a popular Hispanic journal. In 1989, he wrote a nonfiction novel *Five against the Sea* (1989), which recounts the terrifying odyssey of five fishermen blown offshore during a fierce storm. The author currently resides in Stamford, Connecticut, where he is engaged in a variety of literary projects, including scriptwriting for film and television.

Nominated for a National Book Award in 1976, *The Road to Tamazunchale* chronicles the final days of a retired encyclopedia salesman named Fausto Tejada. In order to understand and accept his impending death, Fausto makes an imaginative journey to Tamazunchale, a Mexican village symbolizing the final resting place. The story opens with an ailing and despondent Fausto peeling off his skin; not until his niece Carmela enters the room does the reader learn that Fausto has actually been playing with a wad of tissue paper. The incident functions as the first in a series of events wherein the boundaries between reality and illusion, past and present, and life and death are deliberately obscured. Later, Fausto travels to sixteenth-century Lima; he helps an Incan shepherd move his flock off the Los Angeles freeway; he leads hundreds of men across the Mexican American border; he finds himself in a play called "The Road to Tamazunchale"; and, finally, he joins his friends and neighbors on a cosmic picnic where he is reunited with his deceased wife. The novel culminates with Fausto accepting his inevitable demise, though exactly when this occurs is ambiguous. As Vernon Lattin has explained, even after Fausto dies "the novel continues for one more chapter without suggestions of distortion or logical violation. Fausto and his friends continue as in the past: there is no funeral or burial; the logic of the world and the dichotomy of life and death have been transcended, and the road to Tamazunchale has become a sacred way for Everyman to follow."

Critics concur that the primary concern of *The Road to Tamazunchale* is the universal human need to rationalize and find peace with the mystery of death. The central character, Fausto, is based, in part, on the protagonist in the Faust legend. Like his namesake, Fausto wishes to experience life fully and to extend his existence so that he might complete unfinished business and attain his loftiest goals; the quest, however, simultaneously forces him to face his own hitherto overlooked mortality. For example, when Fausto in a dream seeks to save some *mojados*, or "wetbacks", by leading them across the desert to freedom, he is shaken out of his reverie by Carmela's death-bed conversation with friends about her uncle's fever and delirium. Scholars have also observed that Arias's protagonist shares an intellectual affinity with Miguel de Cervantes's Don Quixote, a prototype of idealism and redemptive imag-

ination. Arias depicts Fausto as foolishly impractical in his pursuit of ideals, diverting himself from death's nearness through his imaginative labyrinthine wanderings in Peru and engaging in extended bedside conversations with his dead wife. Arias highlights the novel's quixotism in several comedic episodes, for example, in scenes where bizarre associations are made between Fausto's epidermis and chicken skin, nylon hose, and tissue paper, or in the episode in which Fausto and Marcelino Huanca, a Peruvian alpaca-herder reminiscent of Sancho Panza, stumble onto a Hollywood motion picture set and are mistaken for acting extras. Although some critics, such as Mariana Marín have argued that *The Road to Tamazunchale* is a superficial parody of Cervantes's *Don Quixote* (1605) and a "feeble and futile attempt to juxtapose the realms of fantasy and reality," most agree that Arias's novel is one of the finest interpretations of that work in contemporary fiction. Critics also note that *The Road to Tamazunchale* incorporates modern Latin-American narrative structures and strategies. Arias's conceptualization of death as a presence among the living, for example, is borrowed from Hispanic writers Juan Rulfo and Carlos Fuentes. Howerver, Arias was most deeply indebted to García Márquez—as he explained to Bruce-Novoa, "I'll always remember my sense of pleasure and wonder when I first discovered, page-by-carefully-page, [García Márquez's novel] *Cien años de soledad* (1967; *One Hundred Years of Solitude*) transformed, *deepened* reality in so many of its aspects—tragic, humorous, adventurous, wondrous." Chapter seven of *The Road to Tamazunchale*—the story of a drowned man who is restored to life by Indian magic and eventually adopted as a husband—bears a striking resemblance in outline, tone, and detail to García Márquez's short story "The Handsomest Drowned Man in the World: A Tale for Children" (1971). Further, the scene in which Fausto is nearly buried after he interrupts a funeral procession suggests an affinity to García Márquez's "The Other Side of Death" (1948), a firsthand description from the grave of postmortem sensation. Critics have also noted that Arias's humorously ironic narrative tone resembles García Márquez's. This influence is apparent in several scenes in *The Road to Tamazunchale*, especially in Arias's description of Fausto hiding an Incan shepherd in the coffin of a passing funeral procession and the introduction of members of a barrio community that follow a little cloud that moves about the neighborhood like a stray dog, dropping snow here and there. While certain scholars point to the difficulty of following the interplay between the real and fantastic in *The Road to Tamazunchale*, most commentators have agreed with Willard Gingerich, who asserted that the novel "is not a free-floating 'fabulist' narrative of the avant-garde sort practiced about New York. . . . It is a fable, but one which extends itself out of the roots of suffering and death, a fable of human emotions, not limited to the exhausted formulas of 'realism' or deformed by misapprehended techniques of new masters."

While Arias's other works, his short stories and *Five against the Sea*, have gotten very little critical attention, reviews of *The Road to Tamazunchale* have been almost universally favorable. Early analyses centered on Arias's adaptation of the modes of the "new Latin American fiction," focusing on the novel's contradictory and ambiguous characters, thematic overlapping of illusion and reality, attention to the rhythm and idioms of Chicano speech, and vivid descriptions of Mexican-American life. Carlota Cárdenas de Dwyer has drawn attention in particular to two "levels of interest"—

the phenomenon of the aging physical Fausto and the allegorical excursions into the inner world, while other critics have highlighted the book's exploration of such broad themes as the *mojados* and the search for Paradise. Although some critics, such as Gingerich, have faulted Arias for failing "to trust the fictive imagination to its fullest," censuring his reduction of fantastic imagery to a function of Fausto's feverish mental activity, most assert that *The Road to Tamazunchale* is a masterful novel which utilizes in the the words of Eliud Martínez, "the artistic resources of the modern and contemporary novel (and the arts) in a comparable way, deliberately and intuitively."

CRITICAL COMMENTARY

RON ARIAS WITH JUAN D. BRUCE-NOVOA

(interview date 1975)

[The following interview was conducted in the summer of 1975. Here, Chicano poet and novelist Bruce-Novoa probes Arias's background, experiences, and attitudes toward contemporary Chicano literature.]

[Bruce-Novoa]: *When and where were you born?*

[Arias]: November 30, 1941 in Los Angeles, California.

Describe your family background.

My parents are from El Paso and Nogales; grandparents from Chihuahua and Durango. The only line I can follow back is my maternal gradmother's; she was a Terrazas from Chihuahua, and of course in the last century they pretty well dominated politics and power in the state. Also, right after the conquest in the 16th century, New Spain's first known poet writing in Spanish was a Terrazas.

What is your present situation?

I am now an English composition, journalism and creative-writing teacher at Crafton Hills college, a junior College in Yucaipa, California. My wife teaches Spanish at another college; and we have two boys, six and eight.

When did you first begin to write?

I first began to write fiction seriously several years ago, just past the age of thirty. However, I had worked for about seven years as a newspaper reporter, Latin American

stringer and technical writer, living for good stretches in Buenos Aires, Cuzco, Caracas, Washington, D. C., and Los Angeles.

What kind of books did you read in your formative years?

Mostly comic books and historical novels.

What is the extent of your formal education?

I have a B.A. in Spanish and an M.A. in journalism.

How much has formal education aided or hindered you as a writer?

It's hard to say. All I can say is that I liked my senior year in high school and the first year and a half of college; the other years, especially college,were a frustrating bore.

Which was the predominant language in your home as a child and which do you speak more fluently now?

With my parents, English; with my grandmother, Spanish, and I spent a lot of time with her when I was very young. I'm more fluent in English, although sometimes not as comfortable.

Do you think that Chicano literature has a particular language or idiom?

Yes, but I think it goes beyond the language and words themselves. Perhaps it's a matter of attitude, of certain feelings conveyed. For example, most of my dialogue is written in English (because that's what I can write with more skill) but I'm translating from the Spanish in my mind—that is, the characters are often speaking Spanish. One of these days I'll put *Tamazunchale* and some of my stories into Spanish, then see if my theory holds.

Principal Works

"El mago" (short story) 1970

"The Interview"(short story) 1974

"A House on the Island" (short story) 1975

The Road to Tamazunchale (novel) 1975

"The Story Machine" (short story) 1975

"The Wetback" (short story) 1975

"The Castle" (short story) 1976

"Chinches" (short story) 1977

"The Boy Ate Himself" (short story) 1980

Five against the Sea (nonfiction) 1989

How do you perceive your role as a writer vis-a-vis: a) the Chicano community or movement, b) U.S.A. society, c) literature itself?

a) I hope to hell I'm part of it, wherever we may go. When you say Chicano movement, I think of pride, strength and a tremendous creative voice that is just now becoming popularized. If we are good enough I don't believe our creations will be trivialized like so much else in this country.

b) Close to indifferent.

c) With the head I've got and the remaining years ahead, I hope I can do some original things. Otherwise, I wouldn't (couldn't) write.

What is the place of Chicano literature within U.S. literature?

Practically speaking, that's for New York to decide. If it helps them, big publishers will exploit us, and maybe we'll be lucky to slip in a few pearls; maybe these will survive.

What is the relationship of our literature to Mexican literature?

Close, especially with Rulfo among the moderns and Nahua expression in the 16th century and before.

Does the Chicano author have anything in common with the majority group writers?; what differences?

Lots. We write, we hustle, we claim certain places in the mind, more often than not we take ourselves too seriously. Traven makes this statement better than anyone else I've read. The differences are many if you're speaking of cultural attitudes. In this regard, I think Chicanos have one of the shortest umbilicals, and for our art's sake I hope we can keep our pretentions in check.

Does our literature share common ground with Black literature?

I assume it does, but I haven't read that much by Black authors to give an answer I trust.

Is there any relationship with the literature of other Spanish-speaking groups.

I can only speak for myself, and I would say yes, there is some connection, a not too-studied preference for the style of certain pieces-Quiroga's jungle stories, Roberto Juarrez of Argentina, Ciro Alegría, Ricardo Palma, José Eustacio Rivera's *La vorágine*, Donoso, Benedetti, Naipaul and Machada d'Assis, if I'm permitted, and of course *Cien años de soledad*. In the end, though, what most excites me are the early chronicles.

Do you perceive yourself and your work as political?

What isn't political?

Does Chicano literature have a distinctive perspective on life and if so, what effect does it have on the literature?

Two crazy questions. I only hope the answers become evident in the work of Chicano writers.

Does our literature improve communication between Chicanos and Anglo-Americans?

I'd like to think so.

Does Chicano literature reevaluate, attack or subvert the value system of the majority society? Is it revolutionary?

It's too soon to say.

What problems have you encountered in publishing? Have they been racially founded?

Many—and I think I've been lucky so far. I send my stories mostly to *Revista Chicano-Riqueña, El Grito, Bilingual Review, Caracol* and other "ethnic" outlets, with an occasional crazy gesture to places like *Ms., Atlantic Monthly* and *Paris Review* (rejections). I know I'll be read with understanding by the first group, but who knows about the slick and quality "outsiders" magazines? About the efforts with my book, I tried two big houses—Doubleday and Farrar-Straus-Giroux. They both liked it, but predictably saw little sales potential and of course no movie possibilities. So I went to a small press that's done some excellent books by all kinds of people (Kostelanetz, Anderson-Imbert, William Stafford. experimentalists, traditionalists, science fiction, you name it). But now that I've gotten some reaction on the book, I find that non-Chicano or non-Hispanic readers like *Tamazunchale* usually for different reasons than Chicanos, and this goes for the Anglo publishers.

Are Chicano writers at a disadvantage in trying to practice the art of writing?

Of course. It's easy to pigeon-hole us. In the U.S. everyone is inevitably reduced to an epithet. So when the market becomes overstocked with "ethnics," as if we're all figured out and we have little more to offer, we as writers will just have to dig in and produce even finer work, whether in books, film, T.V. or theater.

What are the most outstanding qualities of Chicano literature? Weaknesses?

Again it's too soon to answer.

Which are the most important milestones so far in Chicano literature?

I haven't yet read *Peregrinos de Aztlán* [Miguel Méndez], but in the prose fiction I've seen I would say Tomás Rivera is a tremendously careful and perceptive writer, often saved by his wonderful touch for humor. In theater, the Teatro Campesino's *La carpa de los rasquachis* and some of the more popular actors wake a lot of people up. Of the poets, Alurista *must* be heard, not read, to realize the unique strength of his creation. Of the poets best read I like Omar Salinas and Leonard Adame. About "milestones," I don't know. I just know what I like.

What future do you see for Chicano literature, the retention of distinctiveness or the deemphasis of its distinctive characteristics?

I can't answer this, and I'd be very interested to know who of your interviewees can.

Who are the leaders among Chicano writers and why?

I could easily say who is not, but that would't mean that the left-overs would be at the "top." In other words it's too soon to say. With a dozen or so writers each with one or two books to their name, how can you ask, Which of you is the big chingón? Give us a while more to develop, then some of us might raise a hand and say, "me!" Maybe some have. But I'd like to think of us all writing in a collective effort, adding our best talents to an entire body of Chicano expression. (pp. 70–3)

Ron Arias and Juan D. Bruce-Novoa, in an interview in *The Journal of Ethnic Studies*, Vol. 3, No. 4, Winter, 1976, pp. 70–3.

TOMÁS RIVERA

(essay date 1975)

[Rivera was a distinguished Chicano poet and novelist. In the following essay from his Forward to *The Road to Tamazunchale*, Rivera points out that dying—not death—is the novel's principal concern.]

In 1970 when I received the First National Premio Quinto Sol literary Award for "... y no se lo tragó la tierra," I was asked my thoughts concerning the Chicano literary movement. Ron Arias' *Road to Tamazunchale* reminded me of what I had said and still believe:

I think it is imperative that those Chicanos who need it, immerse themselves in the profound and satisfying intent of finding their identity. I do not think that the search has to manifest itself as dogma for those Chicanos who do not demand this search from their own lives. Chicanismo to me represents the rebirth of a

spirit which now . . . begins to manifest itself in different forms. One of these is of course, literature. I believe that the most important thing for art and literature is to liberate itself from dogmas and to express freely not only the suffering, the injustice, but rather the totality of the Chicano. We have always been complete people and now that we search the abstract, imagined, forms to represent this reality, we need to represent and make concrete every angle and side of the Chicano. Our intent in literature, then, has to be totally human.

Death is not an uncommon element in literature; it is one of the original elements. I shall never forget reading about Poe's deliberateness in writing *The Raven*:

Of all melancholy topics, what, according to the universal understanding of mankind, is the most melancholy? Death—was the obvious reply. And when, I said, is this melancholy of topics most poetical?—When it most closely allies itself to Beauty: the death, then, of a beautiful woman is, unquestionably, the most poetic topic in the world.

Ron Arias also reminded me of this passage. For in a very deliberate way he chooses to develop a complex creative attitude within the concept of not death but dying. It isn't really the same. Arias tells the reader that dying as living is a creative ambient and attitude. As a Chicano piece of literature, it reveals the main character not in contemplation of Death as some social anthropologists would have Chicanos do as part of their cultural traditions, but rather in the creation of Death. *The Road to Tamazunchale* is, then, a creation of death, a most acute, at times humorous, approach to the unapproachable. In this novel, Chicano Literature gains a most creative dimension.

Tomás Rivera, in a foreword to *The Road to Tamazunchale: A Novel* by Ron Arias, WCPR, 1975, p. v.

JUDY SALINAS

(essay date 1976)

[In the following review of *The Road to Tamazunchale*, Salinas praises Arias's style and characterization, lauding the novel as a "Chicano masterpiece."]

With [*The Road to Tamazunchale*] Ron Arias won the 1974–75 University of California/Irvine Chicano Literary Contest. The novel is a Chicano masterpiece because Arias handles style and characterization as magically and masterfully as his Hispanic contemporaries' classic, such as Mexico's Juan Rulfo in *Pedro Páramo*, Cuba's Alejo Carpentier in "Viaje a la Semilla" ["Voyage to the

Seed"], Argentina's Julio Cortázar in "Axolotl" and "Todos los fuegos el fuego" ["All the Fires One Fire"], Mexico's Carlos Fuentes in his short stories from *Los días enmascarados* [*The Masked Days*], and Columbia's Gabriel García Márquez in his novel, *Cien años de soledad* [*One Hundred Years of Solitude*]. This short novel is, indeed, as Chicano novelist José Antonio Villarreal called it, "a small. . . jewel," while at the same time demanding its merited place and that of the author among the internationally recognized works and writers listed above. In the *Forward* to the novel, Tomás Rivera, prize-winning author of . . . *y no se lo tragó la tierra* [*And the Earth Did Not Part*], states that it is "a creation of death, a most acute, at times humorous, approach to the unapproachable. In this novel, Chicano literature gains a most creative dimension." With *The Road to Tamazunchale* Ron Arias reaffirms that Chicano literature no longer needs a justification to be included as a universal literature, with Arias carrying on the tradition of literary excellence established in Rivera's novel and in those of *Casa de las Américas* prize-winning Chicano novelist, Rolando Hinojosa.

From the first page, Arias captures the reader in a whirlwind of narration that does not let him withdraw until long after the end of the novel. The main character, Fausto, a bookseller by trade, and Arias' Chicano counterpart to Göethe's Dr. Faustus, creates his own Death and the reader shares in that creative process. From the beginning, the reader is not sure that Fausto is alive or dead. However, on the basis of chronological time, events, characters and places which appear in the work, there is little doubt that Fausto is outwardly expiring while inwardly prolonging the dying process which Arias ably presents as a renewal of life. Thus, in an ironic way, the novel merges death and birth in an eternal blend. While apparently still alive, this seller of the *Books of Knowledge*, dictionaries and all other books offering wisdom, draws the reader into his own encounters with people from his barrio existence— Carmela, his niece; Evangelina, his dead wife to whom he refers to as Eva, as though he were the first Adam; and Mario, a young man who dresses in black and symbolizes Death. Mario chauffeurs him around Los Angeles in a stolen Chevy Impala while searching for Marcelino, a lost Inca shepherd driving a herd of Alpacas, who is to aid Fausto in his transition from life to his rebirth through death. The reader does not desecend into the world of the living dead spirits, as he must do in *Pedro Páramo*, but rather he lives with them on an equal plane and then ascends or passes with Fausto and Evangelina upwards through Death, as in the birth process. In the first two pages of the novel, Fausto, like Xipe Totec, the ancient Aztec god who sheds his skin each Spring and thus represents the renewal of life, removes his outer garment of skin, the outward manifestation of "life". Fausto, a modern-day Xipe Totec and Don Quixote of the Chicano Barrio, wanders through Los Angeles, Lima and other points and walks, talks and dines with the dead of

the recent past as well as those of the Aztec, Incan and Mayan past. He brings to the United States a contingent of wetbacks dressed as Marines, who can easily cross the border from Mexico, so that they might reap the bountiful fruits of this Paradise. They march across an exclusive golf course in one of the most humorous moments of the novel while the Anglo ladies in their golf carts oooh and aaah over them. However, they all end up in the Los Feliz theater and barber shop, along with Fausto and his friends, where they see a presentation of "The Road to Tamazunchale", which is the road to Death. For Fausto, the wetbacks and for David, another character who has drowned in the barrio's dry riverbed, there is redemption and perfection that all achieve in their vision of Death which they failed to obtain in Life. Instead of dying of neglect and the harshness of life as in reality, David dies in the novel of too much love. A lonely spinster honeymoons with David's perfect cadaver, Arias' literary ironic counterpart to Michelangelo's statue. In fact, David is more beautiful in death than in life with his scars, gold teeth and a tick imbedded in his thigh. David symbolizes for the spinster, Mrs. Rentería, and for the Chicano community, a little hope and satisfaction in Death, for it treats them more humanely than Life.

In Rivera's introduction, he refers to the necessity of the Chicano author to find an identity for the Chicano as well as the author himself. And so in *The Road to Tamazunchale*, Ron Arias promises further excellence for himself in particular and for Chicano literature in general. (pp. 111–12)

Judy Salinas, in a review of "The Road to Tamazunchale," in *Latin American Literary Review*, Vol. IV, No. 8, Spring-Summer, 1976, pp. 111–12.

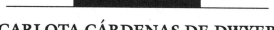

CARLOTA CÁRDENAS DE DWYER
(essay date 1977)

[In the following essay, Cárdenas de Dwyer analyzes the major themes of *The Road to Tamazunchale*, identifying two prominent motifs: the phenomenon of the aging Fausto and his imaginative excursions into the inner world.]

The work of Jorge Luis Borges is a species of international literary metaphor. He knowledgeably makes a transfer of inherited meaning from Spanish and English, French and German, and sums up a series of analogies, of confrontations, of appositions in other nations' literatures. His Argentinians act out Parisian dramas, his Central European Jews are wise in the ways of the Amazon, his Babylonians are fluent in the paradigms of Babel [Anthony Kerrigan in the Introduction to Borges' *Ficciones*, 1962].

These remarks about Borges seem pertinent as one prepares to approach an unpretentious, slim volume bearing the label "*The Road to Tamazunchale*—a novel by Ron Arias." While it is not the point of this discussion to establish Arias as a second Borges, consideration of this passage does highlight the degree to which this young Chicano writer echoes and reinvents a variety of previous literary antecedents in a process aptly named "international literary metaphor" by Anthony Kerrigan in his introduction to Borges' collection of stories entitled *Ficciones*. For one might as easily write of Arias that his Chicanos parody a German *Faustbuch*, a chivalric romance, and a picaresque novel; that his *vatos* are as sagacious as any Central European Jew; and that his East Los Angeles *barrio* is as various and as complete a complex as cosmopolitan Buenos Aires.

Yet, in spite of his far-flung associations, Ron Arias is thoroughly recognizable as a "Chicano writer." His narrative of the last peregrinations of a dying old man is full of realistic detail from contemporary Chicano life. From the devoted niece Carmen with her unrelenting patience and the self-styled curer Cuca with her salubrious *ponche* to the street-smart Mario and the respectful Jesús, who prefers to be called "Jess," from the Cuatro Milpas restaurant and Los Feliz theatre to the vintage *mariachi* records and the mute parakeet called Tico-Tico, everything rings true to the Chicano reader who shares memories of a corresponding familial and social structure.

While the authentic detail of Chicano life is vividly captured by the author, that is not what is most intriguing to the modern reader. This tale of Fausto Tejada, seemingly more of a novella in many ways, engages the reader's concern on two basic levels of interest. The first level of interest focuses on the aging Fausto as he embarks on a series of imaginative forays into the world of his inner-conscious in order to explore various stages of post-terrestial existence. In each successive encounter with an aspect of his approaching death, i.e., wake, burial, etc., Fausto confronts and dispels the frightening and threatening qualities of death. At the end, his journey complete, all his anxieties are resolved and he is able to rest in peace: "Fausto set himself down beside his wife, clapped some life into his cold hands, then crossed them over his chest and went to sleep." Yet, the reader follows the peripatetic old man to this point of peaceful and perdurable reconciliation only after a series of bizarre and sometimes baffling experiences. These excursions into the inner world, with their fusing of the local and the exotic, the literary and the historical, furnish the second basic level of interest. Within this elaborate narrative structure, the character of Fausto Tejada and his overriding concern about his impending death are of major thematic significance and furnish the essential lines of coherence and continuity.

Fausto Tejada, with a tenacious grip on his fail-

ing/fleeing mortality, sports many guises as he ventures forth. At one moment he is a shabby Doctor Faustus, a retired door-to-door book salesman rather than the Old World scholar, but nonetheless seeking experience itself as much as knowledge of truth. However, like his namesake in the early *Faustbuch*, the German store of Faust legends from which sprang the Faust of Marlowe and Goethe, he conjures images and exploits to satiate his thirsting imagination. At the next moment Fausto proclaims himself "Don Fausto Tejada," and donning cape and staff he pursues with unwavering commitment his quests, both minor and major. At times, he seems to follow in the irregular footsteps of the first quixotic knight as he marshals alpaca instead of armies and when his staff is described as a rusty hoe. Yet, his picaresque journey contains many elements of the pure Romantic, as he nobly befriends and harbors the displaced Peruvian shepherd, Marcelino Huanca.

Fausto, with his flickering shades of Doctor Faustus and Don Quixote, is Everyman now quaking before the apparent nothingness of death. He is also a contemporary, urban Chicano surrounded by *curanderas* and *vatos*. Additionally, the very form of the narrative establishes him as a modern man, liberated from the confining categories of nineteenth-century realism. Just as Fausto shares the traditions of the Germanic legend, the medieval romance, and the Spanish picaresque, so is Ron Arias, as a modern Chicano author, wedged between the parallel traditions of modern United States writers and the so-called magic realists of contemporary Latin-American fiction.

Here in *The Road to Tamazunchale* one may observe many of the implicit attitudes and explicit qualities common to the writings of Kurt Vonnegut, William Burroughs, John Barth, and Thomas Pynchon, as well as to Alejo Carpentier, Jorge Luis Borges, Juan Rulfo, Carlos Fuentes, Mario Vargas Llosa, and Gabriel García Márquez. For writers in both groups display the same genius for creating a glittering jewel-work of intricate narrative pattern, underpinned, in some ways also undermined, by a fundamental ontological dilemma. The ambiguous conflict in Alejo Carpentier's *El reino de este mundo* (1949) between the perspective of the European imperialists who view Mackandal as a vanquished renegade and that of the indigenous inhabitants who perceive him as triumphant messiah is not unlike the unresolved question in Thomas Pynchon's *The Crying of Lot 49* (1965) of whether Oedipa's theory of the Tristero conspiracy is delusion or discovery, insanity or insight. Despite their many differences, the works of all these writers move in concert to challenge seemingly rational approaches to the absurdities and tragedies of twentieth-century life and to voice disdain for simplistic solutions.

Because the personality of Juan Tejada and his pervasive concern about his impending fate are of major thematic significance and furnish the essential lines of continuity and coherence in the narrative frame, it is possible, in the last analysis, to separate the pathways of his spiritual odyssey from those of his fabulous journeys, for the events of the latter produce the terms of the former. Therefore, it is necessary to examine carefully the entire text of the work to apprehend its unified literary dynamics. While a complete exegesis of the novel would be rather lengthy to include in this discussion, a close reading of the first two chapters is offered here to illustrate precisely the nature of the interplay between the spiritual odyssey and the corresponding series of fabulous journeys. From the first moment, the template of Fausto's mental activity provides the associative pattern of his various wanderings. Fausto's disassociation of his psychic powers from corporeal confines is dramatized with startling intensity in the opening scene when he, in effect, disengages himself from his "human coil."

The first chapter begins with a matter of fact description of Fausto quietly and deliberately removing a layer of skin from his infirm and wrinkled body. The procedure is conveyed in precise terms and likened to such a mundane and unnoteworthy occurrence as the removal of nylon hose. "It bunched at the knuckles, above the fingernails. Carefully he pulled each fingertip as he would a glove." Yet while Fausto's removal process and even the neatly folded "wad of skin" are of seemingly convincing veracity, Fausto's niece Carmela enters and perceives nothing unusual about the old man, indicating concern solely about his relative well-being. Then, after unfolding the dry tissue and displaying the "feather-light suit" on the bedding, Fausto is disappointed when his niece registers no surprise. Indeed, she seems to notice nothing unusual at all. Oblivious to her uncle's grotesque design to call her attention, Carmela only recalls his previous attacks in the past. The disconcerting image she remembers is that of him in the hospital, "straining to speak, with a tube in one arm and another up a nostril."

It is morning and Carmela is looking in on her uncle before leaving for her job. Assured that he is comfortable, she leaves him, telling him that his breakfast is on the table. Fausto arises and reminisces briefly about his life since his retirement:

For six years he had shuffled to the window, to the bathroom, down to the kitchen, through gloomy rooms, resting, listening to the radio, reading, turning thin, impatient, waiting for the end. Six years ago she had convinced him to stop work.

Abruptly, with no introduction or preparation, Carmela's voice from that scene in the past is heard. In fact, the entire short scene between the two is given as if it were being replayed in the present. Fausto's compliant and slightly resigned "I'll stay" in response to her plea that he retire and stay home echoes with almost ringing clarity.

Then, a transition to the present is provided—"Now, years later. . . ."—and Fausto is overwhelmed with the awful sensation of his body becoming a decaying and dying thing: "He felt as if his muscles were finally turning to worms, his lungs to leaves and his bones to petrified stone." He responds to this thought of death with fury and outrage. For the first time Fausto is seen involved with the unavoidable present and the unwelcome anticipation of his eventual, if not imminent, death:

Suddenly, the monstrous dread of dying seized his mind, his brain itched, and he trembled like a naked child in the snow. No! he shouted. It can't happen, it won't happen! As long as I breathe, it won't happen. . . .

Fausto's desperate yearning for an alternative to his fated demise answered by what he perceives as "the song of life." The mysterious sound "beckoned with the faint, soft sound of a flute." The chapter closes with the dying end of the enticing sound.

Chapter two begins with Fausto's firm conviction that he will embark immediately—his destination Peru, his armament a sword with buckler. Meanwhile, before going down to the kitchen, he dresses himself in his customary smoking jacket and khaki trousers. Hurrying toward the stairs, his thoughts roam excitedly to his imagined journey to Peru. His mind fills with thoughts of an Old World viceroy, a garrison, and his goal, Cuzco, heart of the Inca civilization. Steadying himself on the bannister, he considers various means of transport and finally decides on the bus, concluding reasonably that "he was never the best of horsemen."

At this point Fausto seems to be overcome by his own emotions and collapses on the floor: "Excitement rose in his throat, and suddenly his fingers had sunk into the carpet." With his physical collapse his fantastic journey begins as he hurries through Lima toward a bus. After arriving in Cuzco and settling in a hotel, he is surprised to find Carmela in his room in a very uncharacteristic attitude: "At first her beauty left him speechless. She sat on the edge of the bed with her back to the afternoon light, her long black hair spread over her shoulders." However, when Fausto addresses this beguiling figure as "Carmela," she maintains that her name is Ana. She promises to take him to a mountain visible in the cloudy distance. They set off by train, but soon are walking through a steamy Amazon valley.

Becoming increasingly fatigued, Fausto begins to lose consciousness. Seeing a vague but menacing figure in the thick brush, he charges, like Don Quixote toward the windmills. The unarmed Fausto speculates, "If it were death, he would impale the monster to the hilt." Succeeding only in entangling himself in the vines of a tree, he is rescued by Ana, who cuts him free with a machete.

The two continue their journey through an exotic and lush valley, halting briefly at a pool to bathe and refresh themselves. They resume their trek again, now moving upward toward the barren promontory above the valley. Passing through a "cloud-forest of weird, root twisted shrubs and moist, darkened hollows," the strange and unreal atmosphere gives way to an eerie one, slightly gothic in its threatening undertones. "The gnarled branches of these stunted phantom trees seemed to reach out and block the trail." The extraordinary and preternatural character of the area is further defined when Ana asserts that stranded travelers live on here "as insects, bats, even rocks."

With the gradual descent of nightfall, the two approach a torchlight processional that is ascending the mountain. Ana rushes ahead. Clutching his chest in a spasm of pain, Fausto calls out, but he is responded to only by a child's beckoning gesture. Dragging himself forward, Fausto observes people engaged in ritualistic ceremony. The men dance, "their ponchos whirling in one great circle around the women who kneeled in the center, sending their wails to the rocky crags above." Nearing a "crude platform" with Ana's assistance, Fausto reclines and becomes the object of the mourning rite. "Too tired to refuse their grief," Fausto nonetheless questions and, in effect, refuses the role of corpse assigned to him.

At this point Fausto's two frames of reference converge as he addresses Ana and is answered by his niece, Carmela. The "crude platform" is now his own bed and he is, once again, at home.

After suffering a physical collapse and imagining himself as the central figure in a wake ceremony, Fausto maintains his staunch refusal to capitulate his spirit to the forces of death, and he hears again, while lying prostrate on his bed, the mysterious flute with its tantalizing song of life. He remarks to Carmela, "It's beautiful. . . I can't think of anything more beautiful." Like Juan Dahlman in Borges' "The South," who escapes from spending his last moments in the boring dreariness of an antiseptic institution by virtue of his imagination and memory, so does Fausto here flee from inglorious collapse. Weakened but not overcome, he withstands the shock of near death and is able, in the next chapter, to play-act at death.

While the exploits of Juan Tejada may initially exhibit a dazzling display of technical mastery and creative virtuosity, there lies beneath the glittering surface of this imaginative account a profound and substantive core. Although some of the seemingly incongruous and unexpected elements may appear arbitrary, none is without its ideational justification or relevance. From start to finish, Fausto doggedly pursues the spectres of his own subconscious. Traversing borders of consciousness as well as of geography in the first eleven chapters, he repeatedly returns to the Elysian Field near his own backyard. Finally forgoing his struggle in chapter thirteen, he declines, for the first time, to participate in the climactic fantasy of metamorphoses in which movement is not from one area to another but from one form of being to another.

In conclusion, it is important to note that the character of Ron Arias' realism is deep and thoughtful. Unlike the short-lived Realists of the nineteenth century, Arias strives to portray not the slick surface of experience, but the varied texture of inner response to that experience. Closer to *Tristram Shandy* than to many of its Chicano predecessors, *The Road to Tamazunchale* reveals, as in Fausto's incident with the filmmakers, that after the revolution is over, life and the universal search for psychic survival persist. (pp. 229–33)

Carlota Cárdenas de Dwyer, "International Literary Metaphor and Ron Arias: An Analysis of 'The Road to Tamazunchale'," in *The Bilingual Review*, Vol. IV, No. 3, September–December, 1977, pp. 229–33.

Dust jacket for the 1978 edition of Arias's novel.

MARIANA MARÍN

(essay date 1977)

[In the following essay, Marín examines the interplay between the real and fantastic in *The Road to Tama-*

dividing the fantastic and the real worlds.

Vernon E. Lattin on Fausto Tejada's search for an integrated life in *The Road to Tamazunchale*:

[In] Arias's Chicano novel, *The Road to Tamazunchale*, the quest of the protagonist, Fausto Tejada, ends with a rediscovered sense of the sacred continuity of life. Combining the Germanic Faust and the Spanish Don Quixote, Arias creates a Chicano who can transcend the boundaries between illusion and reality, between imagination and fact, between life and death. Through a series of simulated death scenes, fantasies, and dreams the logic of time and space is dissolved, and, unlike his legendary European namesakes, Fausto Tejada escapes disillusionment, death, and damnation. Whereas at the beginning of the novel the dying Fausto is picking the rotting skin off his body and seeking pity, by the end of the novel, having seen the deficiencies of Christianity in a series of comic episodes, and having teamed up with a mephistophelian Pachuco (Mario) and a Peruvian Shepherd (Marcelino Huanca), he forgets his own dying and looks outward to help others. He has learned from the Peruvian shepherd of his Indian past, and he has developed a sense of pastoral wholeness and the continuity of past with present. After Fausto's death the novel continues for one more chapter without suggestions of distortion or logical violation. Fausto and his friends continue as in the past: there is no funeral or burial; the logic of the world and the dichotomy of life and death have been transcended, and the road to Tamazunchale has become a sacred way for Everyman to follow.

Vernon E. Lattin, in his "The Quest for Mythic Vision in Contemporary Native American and Chicano Fiction," *American Literature* (January 1979).

The thirteen chapters of the short novel narrate the adventures, some real and some imaginary, that occupy the last four days of the life of the protagonist, Fausto. In the face of his physical deterioration and agony, the challenge that the process of dying poses for Fausto permits him, as his name suggests, to momentarily recover aspects of youthfulness and to fabricate solutions to his various dilemmas.

The opening scene, graphically and not without a tinge of grotesqueness, presents Fausto attempting to divest himself of his skin, which in a very physical and material way shackles him to and acts as a reminder of his impending death. The "feather-light suit" of skin he wads in his hand, is not visible to his niece, Carmela. Not only is there a clear difference for the reader between what the old man and Carmela perceive but Fausto himself is aware of the discrepancy: "She must be blind, she didn't even notice." Because the description of the first paragraph is written from Fausto's point of view, during this episode the reader shares in Fausto's illusions, while by means of Carmela, who does not participate in his fantasy, the reader is able to recognize that Carmela and Fausto still live in a world governed by the laws of Nature.

On the other hand, in the second chapter, once the reader is forced without any warning to be witness to a dream-like excursion, to be deceived by dream mechanisms and to experience the selective distortions of everyday life that make up dream material, one is no longer asked to witness a discrepancy in perception, our focus must change if we are to follow Fausto in this venture. At the sound of a train's whistle the scene abruptly changes to a dream of Peru. However, upon the reader's introduction to it, it would seem we were witnessing a flashback to a trip Fausto might have taken to Peru. But quickly, at the mention of Fausto's composition of a report to a colonial viceroy, the reader can only assume Fausto is dreaming. For nearly seven pages Fausto's perceptions, which in the first chapter are revealed to be illusions, guide the reader through an incestuous relationship with a beautiful substitute for Carmela: Ana. The chapter ends with the intruding presence of his niece, and once again Fausto and Carmela are back in the real world.

With different modes of narration continually interchanging throughout Fausto's on again, off again struggle with death the consequent disorientation the reader suffers is also a constant throughout the novel. The changes in modes not only jar the flow of the narration, but the reader is desultorily asked to alter, in varying degrees, the very conventions (s)he has accepted in other episodes, conventions which the text needs for the narration to continue to be intelligible and which the reader needs for even a basic understanding of the work.

zunchale, arguing that the novel is not a moral parody of satire in the manner of Miguel de Cervantes's *Don Quixote* (1605) or the Faust legend.]

Tomás Rivera in the "Forward" to *The Road to Tamazunchale*, a first novel written by Ron Arias, proposes it as the novel in which "Chicano Literature gains a most creative dimension." However, if creativity means the ability to conjecture visions of a realm where fantastic events are common place while not losing sight, at the same time, of the concrete realities that condition such imaginative projections, then *The Road to Tamazunchale* is not the novel Rivera contends it is. To achieve the postulated creative effect, the novelist could have blurred the horizon separating fantasy from reality, permitting the characters to leave and reenter the real world. The fantastic adventures, thus, could illuminate the complexities of the specific and real social issues and situations upon which the fantasy comments. As a close look at the novel will clearly demonstrate, instead of continuing the interplay between the fantasy and reality elaborated in the initial chapter, Arias obliterates, not merely makes nebulous, the border

During Fausto's second excursion from his home, his first real one, Mario, his new-found side-kick, sees wandering about the streets of Los Angeles the herd of alpacas which in the previous chapter had been an element in the Peruvian dream. As the novel progresses, Fausto's altered Perception of reality and fantastic experiences are shared by the other characters Marcelino, the errant shepherd, is visible to one and all, from Marlon Brando to Carmela's once skeptical boyfriend, Jess; the children who jokingly call Fausto "Toto" play in the snow brought to the barrio by a mysterious cloud; Mrs Renteria, the neighborhood virgin, "honeymoons" with a dead wetback, much to the community's satisfaction and approval; a group of Mexicans, bullied by Fausto during his dream to follow him from Tijuana to California, form an army of undocumented workers and magically disappear ascending "a plywood ramp leading up to the sky"; and finally, with an audience of friends and neighbors who instead of attending his funeral or burial watched him acrobatically transcend death. Fausto, after gliding out over the sea, vanishes into a cloud, only to reappear at his wife's side and fall asleep. By having the characters participate in Fausto's demented fantasies, the initial interplay between and juxtaposition of the fantastic and real worlds is forsaken for the unquestioned dominance of the former, much unlike the novel which *The Road to Tamazunchale* seeks to parody: *Don Quijote*.

Although the name of the modern faustian caricature and the theme of death and rejuvenation might immediately suggest a strong association with Faust, *Don Quijote* is, though at a superficial level, the most influential precedent and model for *The Road to Tamazunchale*. The superficiality of Arias' parody of *Don Quijote*, as evidenced in his feeble and futile attempt to juxtapose the realms of fantasy and reality, is limited to mediocre imitations of characters (Don Quijote/Fausto, Sancho Panza/Mario, "the Niece"/Carmela), especially Don Quijote. Cervantes succeeds in counterposing Don Quijote's illusions and Sancho Panza's realism, but Arias has Mario relinquish his possible realistic posture when he actually sees alpacas in the streets of Los Angeles. Just as Don Quijote imagines his ridiculous regalia to be the armaments of a knight, Fausto distorts his straw garden hat and hoe into a pith helmet and staff, which along with his long-deceased wife's pink cape make up the finery he flaunts during his escapades. While Don Quijote's reading of chivalric novels inspired his jaunts, the Books of Knowledge Fausto sells provide only bits of information which, if they provide local color in his dreams and in one instance are even used to appease the suspicions and intimidations of "la migra," foment Fausto's inclination to align himself with the masters. Although this alignment is first seen in the second chapter where Fausto imagines or dreams, he trudges through Peru as a *conquistador* in pursuit of the viceroy. In no other episode as in the one in which he commands the Mexicans to trail after him into California is Fausto's proclivity towards playing the role of the master clearer. Reappearing in this dream,

his wife ironically tells him: "You are the one-eyed man leading the blind—el rey Tuerto." While Don Quijote's encounter with the gang of galley slaves is instigated—as supposedly is Fausto's with the Mexicans—by the desire to come to the aid and succor of the downtrodden and the offer of freedom from an oppressive existence, it ends with the galley slaves stoning, hitting and leaving their would-be patron naked. The galley slaves, unlike Fausto's acquiescent army, recognize that however tempting this idealistic offer of freedom appears, it is nonetheless the product of a demented mind which lacks the power and means of fulfilling high-sounding promises.

Poor imitation of Sancho Panza that he is, Mario does not even quite suggest an authentic *pachuco* (only a caricature of one), although he sports the traditional attire of the East Los Angeles's *pachuco*, stereotypically thieves whenever the opportunity presents itself and cruises in low-rider style. Arias's characterization of the *pachuco* breaks down at the very basic level of language: Mario's Spanish is limited to the typical and common one word bursts and short phrases like "vato," "ese" and "allí te watcho." Missing is the rich word play by which the *pachuco* demonstrates a dexterity in speaking both English and Spanish, and this seriously handicaps Arias' *pachuco*.

The sparse use of Spanish also affects other characters in the novel. For all her renown as the barrio practitioner of shamanism and soothsaying, folkloric arts indicative of traditional Mexican and Indian origins, Cuca pronounces only the interjectional "al cabo" while practicing her powers at her "compadre's" bedside. Having spent part of his early life in the border town of El Paso, where even sales in major department stores are transacted in Spanish, Fausto's slight use of Spanish is uncommon. The language shifts that do occur in the novel are scarce and minimally draw upon a repository of perhaps, at best, one hundred Spanish words and phrases. Arias's own reticence towards Spanish is made transparent by phrases like "Although Fausto's Spanish wasn't the best. . . " and ". . . although the Spanish words were spoken rapidly. . . ." To qualify Fausto's or anybody's for that matter, Spanish as less than "best" is to adhere to the verbal deficiency theory often proposed by the dominant class in describing the language of the lower class. Given the existent social hierarchy, language varieties of dialects will also be stratified and it is Arias' lack of concern for this fact that makes him sustain here the biases and linguistically incorrect notions about the Spanish of Chicanos. The second cited phrase demonstrates the typical attitude of non-native Spanish speakers of monolingual English speakers who perceive native speech patterns as rapid.

The gravity of Arias' reticence is accentuated because, with the exception of the policeman, the two Forest Lawn representatives, the muscle-flexing "Mr. America," the "people, mostly black" who are at the movie location, the border guards, the two surfers, the golfers and the golf course manager, the other—far more numerous—characters in the novel are all Mexicans, Mexican immigrants or Chicanos. Further on the novel abounds in dialogue. Obliged to rely solely on English, the characters are kept from expressing themselves bilingually. Hence, the stilted, at times, nature of their conversations. A short question and answer exchange between Fausto and Mrs. Rentería is a good case in point:

"Is it still there?"

"It's melting."

"I mean the cloud."

"No sé. I dropped everything and ran."

An even more revealing repartee takes place between Carmela amd Mario:

"Shh! Keep It down."

"Hey, man. . . "

"Don't call me man."

"Alright, esa. . . "

"Stop it! You think you're a *pachuco* or something?"

As is evident from the above two examples, the linguistic interchanges tend to be dominated by short retorts, commands and queries with little discussion or discourse.

The twelfth chapter, almost entirely all dialogue, exemplifies in an extreme manner the consequences this generally has on the tone of the novel. Although Fausto is lying on his death bed, the dialogue abounds in jokes, one-line wisecracks, story telling and the scene culminates in a party. Though this scene is entertaining for the characters (with the exception of the near-dead Fausto), and though it may be intended to be entertaining for the reader, the humor is completely nullified by the characters', and Arias', own lack of scruples. Undermining the reader's entertainment are Jess' expression of avaricious concerns, the drinking of Coors beer without the slightest mention of or concern for the boycott against this beer and a lack of realism on the part of the characters in this rare (for the novel) realistic scene. It is precisely this lack of realism, for instance, that motivates Mr. Rentería to send the moribund Fausto a pineapple upside-down cake "in case he was hungry" and it also explains the record player being brought into Fausto's bedroom where the party then took place.

Just as Arias lets slip by the opportunity to make known Coors' discrimination against Chicanos, so too does he narrate the "coyote" activities of Fausto and other injustices without taking the side of the victimized. Of the hypocritical characters who would seem to deserve either ironic or satirical treatment, Arias chooses to try to entertain the reader by poking fun at the innocent and least deserving. Although it is only once that Arias uses a parenthetical and ironic expression to overtly reveal his presence in the novel and thereby his attitude towards his characters, it is not rare that specific words, usually in the form of similes and metaphors, allow his biases to surface for the reader's attention. Mario is repeatedly called a boy while the two young women waiting for the bus are not called girls. (This makes one wonder if Arias' linguistic tokenism is limited only to the women question.) By implying that Mario is less than a young man, Arias, in his lack of understanding of the *pachuco*, demeans him, as does the dominate class in society, to the status of a second-class citizen. In the Keystone Kops episode, Mario and Fausto are named "prisoners." They had not been arrested, tried, convicted nor imprisoned and, if anything, they might be called suspects, unless Arias is acting as prosecutor, judge and jury. Tiburcio, in a flashback scene, is detained and incarcerated with Mexicans who are suspected of not having the permission of the immigration authorities. A few sentences before, the reader had been told Tiburcio had been "mistakenly" picked up. Yet, instead of sympathizing with this injustice, Arias strips Tiburcio of his humanness and likens him to a baboon. Once again Arias demonstrates his lack of comprehension of the Chicano experience. This blindness is shared by Fausto, who likens to "wild dogs" the undocumented Mexicans who come to work in the United States. But it is not only the victims of injustice who are subjected to Arias' disdain. Mrs. Noriega's granddaughter is described as having "made a claw with her free hand and raked over (David's) black hair." Certainly the requirements of literary consistency can be invoked to explain the use of the word "claw," the forked end of a tool and an animal's appendage; but the word "comb," though not as effective metaphorically, would have retained the girl's humanness.

Just as Arias uses denigrating metaphors and images to characterize the innocent and the victimized instead of using these literary devices to denounce those guilty of condemnable behavior, he is also far from satirizing either those characters and situations which maintain the oppression of Chicanos or (with the exception of Evangelina) the hypocritical attitudes and behavior of which Chicanos are capable. Any possible satirical statement *The Road to Tamazunchale* could hope to make is vitiated within the novel itself by the other Chicano characters' approval of Fausto's demented and exploitative behavior and the aid these characters provide for its accomplishment. In addition, both Arias' own exaltation of these kinds of activities and the sympathy with them this implies, impair him from taking the critical stance necessary to satirize them from a perspective informed of and sensitized by a criticism of the exploitation suffered by Chicanos.

Nonetheless, Bernice Zamora in a review of the novel argues it is a satire and a successful one (". . . Arias successfully sustains his satire mainly through theme . . . "). Though there are moments of attempted ridicule, they border more on the farcical than on the satirical. The most noteworthy of these, because of the slapstick quality the writing conveys, occurs near the end of the third chapter, just after Fausto and Mario have become friends. Mario scurries over an embankment of ice plant to pour milk into the gasoline tank of a policeman's motorcycle, while the officer slips and slides in Peruvian alpaca excrement. Reminiscent of Keystone Kops, as Bernice Zamora aptly points out in her article, this scene portrays a member of the forces of oppression as inept and, along with the ironic association of the police officer with the excrement, it is this ineptitude that provokes the reader's laughter. If the reader is typical of the majority of Chicanos, that is if (s)he is a working person who earns a modest or less income and whose encounters with the police are far from funny; and while for the typical Chicano reader the scene may evoke only echoes of police brutality and harassment, their everyday occurrence is, we know, all too real for more than a brief release of the reader's hostility towards the police. The result of any humor this scene may produce is the blunting of the gut-level hostility towards themselves that police brutality and other forms of oppression and injustice necessarily provoke.

If the novel were to function as satire and not just as an attack for the sake of attack, the characters' antics would not only be ridiculed but there would also be an ensuing plea for rational, if not just behavior. Such behavior would uphold an existing or proposed societal norm. By accepting the dominant class' view of the *pachuco* as a second-class (or worse) citizen, by not challenging Fausto's delusions of grandeur and exploitative leadership, by losing sight, at best, of the social issues and problems that condition imagination and fantasy, by characterizing Mexican workers as "wild dogs," by seeking to trivialize the injustices Chicanos suffer and by not aligning himself with the victims of those injustices, Arias failed to write a satire and, further, grossly failed to advance the "creative dimension" of Chicano literature. (pp. 34–8)

Mariana Marín, "The Road to Tamazunchale: Fantasy or Reality?" in *De Colores*, Vol. 3, No. 4, 1977, pp. 34–8.

WILLARD GINGERICH
(essay date 1977)

[In the following essay, Gingerich offers a favorable assessment of *The Road to Tamazunchale*, particularly the character of Fausto, but faults Arias for "his hesitation to trust the fictive imagination to its fullest."]

"The Skin Drew Tight at the elbow. Slowly it began to rip, peeling from the muscle. No blood. The operation would be clean, like slipping off nylon hose. He always had trouble removing chicken skins, but this, he could see, would

be easier." So are we introduced to old Fausto, the dying hero (yes, hero) of Ron Arias's first novel, peeling off his own liver-blotched skin with all the sacred nonchalance of an Aztec priest stripping himself of the stinking skin of a sacrificial offering to Xipe Totec. Fausto's maternalistic niece doesn't notice the folded skin he shows her: "She must be blind," Fausto thinks. Like the pre-Columbian serpent of wisdom, the old man puts off his mortality to begin taking on something else.

This masterful narrative is the account, pathetic, fantastic, glorious, and transcendent, of an old Chicano's preparation for and passage into death, somewhere in the barrio of Los Angeles (the places are all there, but I don't know L.A.). It is and is not a passage to Tamazunchale, a very real "former Huastec capital, a tropical village" of Mexico, as a postscript from *Toor's New Guide to Mexico* informs us. The novel's title appears in the novel itself as the name of a makeshift play some impoverished barrio people improvise for their own entertainment in a broken-down theater. "You see," explains the MC, "whenever things go bad, whenever we don't like someone, whoever it is, . . . we simply send them to Tamazunchale. We've never really seen this place, but it sounds better than saying the other, if you know what I mean. . . . Everyone," he adds, "is on that road, Sí, compadres, everyone! But as you'll see, Tamazunchale is not what you think it is." And it never is. As Fausto tells a little girl who asks him in the play, "Are we going to die?" "No one dies in Tamazunchale." "No one?" "Well, some people do, but they're only pretending." And in the play's finale actors, audience (including one boy who really is from Tamazunchale), and all but Fausto march up a ramp from the stage and out into the stars.

Of course, it is all in the dying mind of Fausto, or in the dreams of the poverty-stricken wetbacks, or in the mind of Arias—or perhaps even in that fine fictive space which a whole generation of Latin novelists have reinvented, mastered, and recovered our belief in, a space where the names "realist," "surrealist," "fabulist," and "social historian" all meld into one: magician of the imagination. The "boom" of fiction in Latin America has met little true understanding among the writers of the north, despite the best efforts of John Barth, but Arias has served a full apprenticeship with the best. Apropos of Borges, Fausto goes shopping with some friends to prepare for his death. He buys diaries, journals, crates of paperback, encyclopedias in five languages, a Nahua grammar, a set of Chinese classics, a few novels by a promising Bulgarian author, a collection of Japanese prints, an illustrated Time-Life series on nature (this is L.A., remember), an early cosmography of the known and unknown worlds, a treatise on the future of civilization in the Sea of Cortez, two coffee-table editions on native American foods, an anthology of uninvented myths, and three boxes of unwritten books. "But Tio, look nothin's in them. It's all blank pages." ". . . I want these." "What for?" "Some people might want to write their own books. If I'm going to own a store, I want to have everything." Arias knows the irony and fantasy of García Marquez, the narrative devices of both Faulkner and Cortazar, the violence of Vargas Llosa, the visionary death-knowledge (essential to his entire plot) of Juan Rulfo and Carlos Fuentes, and the indigenist magic-realism of Asturias. But this novel is in English, and Arias leaves no doubt of his acquaintance with the genre in that language.

He does not enclose himself in technique, however, and perhaps the surest sign of his promise is the ability to use technique as a lens, a scalpel, in laying bare the glory and desperation of the wetback, not as a social commentary but as a human paradigm. This is not a free-floating "fabulist" narrative of the avant-garde sort practiced about New York, for which Tom Wolfe has justly expressed little hope. It is a fable, but one which extends itself out of the roots of suffering and death, a fable of real human emotions, not limited to the exhausted formulas of "realism" or deformed by misapprehended techniques of new masters.

If Arias can be faulted in any major way, it is perhaps in his hesitation to trust the fictive imagination to its fullest. In his ambivalence between a rationalist reductio of all things fantastic to a function of Fausto's feverish brain chemistry, a realist reductio, and a commitment to the resonant mystery of Fausto as image of the imagination itself. If this ambivalence were calculated to pose the equivocal nature of death and experience themselves, it would provide additional levels of narrative harmony; but I don't believe Arias is working for that juxtaposition. When he implies, for example, that Fausto's trip to Cuzco has been a dream, it is clear that he means the "dream" of the psychologists, a quantity of psychic material which, with the correct rational terminology, may be shown to originate into conscious, linear, everyday experience. But, on the other hand, the quality itself of that narrative event reveals Arias's awareness of an ineffable otherness within Fausto's dream, providing a surpassing escape from self, psychology, and even death, an escape which is the figure of Arias's own dream of imagination in which Fausto is artist, and hence reader. Arias equivocates, in other words, between a conviction of the rational "Thomas and Charlie," as one character calls the mythic Mexican town, and the true Tamazunchale of liberated fictive imagination.

Tamazunchale is a serious critique of the infra-culture which has consumed Fausto (one of his last acts is to lead a ragtag band of wetbacks into the interior to food and shelter), but only by reflection. It is not Fausto's experience of oppression which lends him finally a social and moral transcendence; it is a chicanismo of spirit, having nothing to do with race, which finally liberates his imagination to swallow up the Santa Monica Freeway, the A & P shopping carts, and the black Chevies with glass-packs. Tomás Rivera, in a foreword to *Tamazunchale*, says:

Chicanismo to me represents the rebirth of a spirit which now . . . begins to manifest itself in different forms. . . . I believe that the most important thing for art and literature is to liberate itself from dogmas and to express freely not only the suffering, the justice, but rather the totality of the Chicano. We have always been complete people and now that we search the abstract, imagined, forms to represent this reality, we need to represent and make concrete every angle and side of the Chicano. Our intent in literature, then has to be totally human.

Rivera believes, and he is correct, that Arias has achieved that intent at the very introduction of his career. But there is a further dimension to the chicanismo of this book, a dimension which occurs as function of its antecedents and its accomplishment, both well beyond the concerns of ethnic or political identity. There is at this point in the literary history of North America no consciousness more resonantly symbolic of all its fiction could become than the liberated Chicano consciousness. Combining all the currents of indigenous, colonia (Spanish and Anglo), and modern Yankee identities into one being, it appropriates all that is American in experience for itself, free to more at will among genres, languages, and techniques (in one of the richest literary geographies in the world) and feels no obligation to reject anything by reason of blood or tradition. In this first work, Arias shows the promise of such a consciousness.

The indigenous permeates the narrative, from its epigram (taken from one of the Nahuatl poems of King Nezahualcoyotl) to the last rest of Fausto in the lap of his already dead wife, primarily in the form of a Peruvian named Marcelino who first insinuates himself into the story only as the distant sound of a flute in Fausto's mind. When Marcelino appears, he is a herder of alpaca, leading his animals right up onto the freeway in the midst of a funeral procession. In his poncho and flop-eared cap, he wanders in and out of Fausto's L.A., at one point revealing a secret cure for all sickness: he tells Fausto to build a small pile of stones as high as he can. "Then, and this is the hardest part, . . . if you truly believe you can, you place one more stone on top. If it stays and does not fall, you will be as strong as that last stone. Nothing can make you fall." Together the old Chicano and the Peruvian herder wander through a movie set in what must be one of the finest echoes of Don Quixote and Sancho Panza in contemporary fiction.

It is Fausto himself who takes the burden of Spanish consciousness, the second quotient of Chicano imagination, playing (and being) conqueror of Peru and acting the picaro for this entire improbable adventure. The yankee figure is a sleek, young, goateed "vato" named Mario who picks up Fausto on a bus because he thinks the old man will make a good distraction while he filches radios, jewelry, or "anything he can fit under his jacket." Mario has completely absorbed Emerson's lamented sense of "commodity" and Jay Gatsby's lust for success. He vows he will not end up like his father who couldn't wait to die, "cause I ain't gonna work." In a stolen car they cruise in and out of trouble and reality.

The reviewer for *Plural*, Mexico's most prestigious literary journal, called Fausto a "Don Quixote of the wetbacks," and one cannot imagine a better term to describe the irony, pathos, gnarled idealism, wryness, and glorification of this broken-down senior citizen of the L.A. suburbs. This novel is more than the completion of an apprenticeship, and the novelist who can fulfill its promise will be one to reckon with in the broadest spectrum of American fiction. (pp. vi–vii, 302–04)

Willard Gingerich, "Chicanismo: The Rebirth of a Spirit," in *Southwest Review*, Vol. 62, No. 3, 1977, pp. vi–vii, 302–04.

EVA MARGARITA NIETO

(essay date 1986)

[In the following essay, Nieto indicates Arias's reliance on established Latin-American narrative structures and strategies in *The Road to Tamazunchale*, noting the author's refinement and enhancement of such devices.]

Ron Arias' short novel *The Road to Tamazunchale* (1975) experiments with a number of established narrative structures, all of which are familiar to readers of Hispanic literature. These experiments, which create a mental (internal) and representational (external) simultaneity in the work, have been likened to the novelistic techniques employed by Gabriel García Márquez and Carlos Fuentes. What has not yet been analyzed is the similarity of their readership and the presence of what has been traditionally called "influence" and "tradition" in this readership. Critics have, on the contrary, referred to the direct influence of the contemporary Latin American narrative on Arias' work and his acknowledged acquaintance with that body of narrative. Yet it is evident that Arias shares a much broader and deeper understanding of narrative structures with that group of writers. It is this shared understanding that creates a type of dialectic between the texts and structures that Arias has drawn on and the text he has produced.

The presence of interpolations and intertextualities has already been established with regard to the works of the Latin American authors. It is still an undetermined factor with regard to the established group of Chicano authors, despite their presence in academic circles and their obvious readership. What I propose to analyze in this brief study is the use of these structures in this novel, for I think that *The Road to Tamazunchale* can be read

both as a sampler of narrative structures and as a key to Ron Arias' readership. Most importantly, I think that the analysis of these techniques can cast new light on the novel and its relationship to its readers.

Arias' studies in literature at the University of California, Los Angeles, and his continuing friendships with academicians and critics are evidenced both in articles on his work and by interviews. In this, I again assert, he is not unique among Chicano writers. The relationship of the Chicano movement to the university has long been understood. Yet the relationship between that experience, the readership, and the text produced has been a factor too long ignored by critics of Chicano literature. Although Latin American critics and readers understand the literary background of a Mario Vargas Llosa or a Carlos Fuentes, the emphasis on the sociopolitical context and circumstances of Chicano literature has created a false impression of social popularity that has limited its readership.

I do not pretend to suggest that these works are lacking in social commentary or meaning. As narrative, as novels, their relationship to the reader involves a commitment to social reality. In another place, I will analyze the functions of the structures that I propose to read in the text with regard to that very important issue. For now, I would like to refer to that very text in order to elucidate my contentions.

The Road to Tamazunchale is a short novel set in Los Angeles, with abrupt place changes to the Peruvian Andes (Cuzco), trips to Tijuana and the Coast, and a protagonist who is an old, lonely, retired door-to-door book salesman. Fausto Quiroga, the protagonist, lives with his niece, Carmen, in the Lincoln Heights barrio. Fearing the nearness of death, he decides to make his final days meaningful. With the acquaintance of Mario, a *vato* from the barrio, he sets off to activate his sedentary existence. A series of real and imagined episodes concludes with the characters jumping into a television screen that someone forgetfully turns off.

Within the context of this plot and structure, the title itself, "The Road to Tamazunchale," becomes an introductory metaphor. The road that Fausto follows is an apparent simulation of life, formulated through action and episode and creating a type of exemplification through mimetic devices. The concept of text=road=life is an established literary tradition, not only as a narrative in the modern sense, but in the didactic and prenovelistic traditions of England, Italy, and Spain. In avoiding the more common "historia," "vida," or even, in contemporary terms, "muerte," Arias seems to return to the structures set forth by Juan Ruiz in his *Libro de buen amor* (1350), in which the narrator explains that his book is a type of road-life and that the reader-traveler should embark upon it as one would on a journey. The remarkable thing is that Juan Ruiz' work is also a sampler of poetic form and meter, a concept that *Tamazunchale* seems to share on a narrative level.

There is still another aspect that the two works have in common. The medieval example ends with the narrator suggesting that the reader carry on with the text-road-life, thus passing the wand of creation on to him. In *Tamazunchale* the characters pass from the narrative/novelistic structure into the visual and dramatic structure of the television screen. I will not comment on the ominous meaning of this episode with regard to the written text's demise, but what does seem apparent is that this kaleidoscopic ending correlates to some extent with the open-endedness of Juan Ruiz' text.

Passing on to the pretextual quotation, which is taken from López de Gómara's history of the conquest of Mexico, the question of "historia" again comes up, for it is this version precisely that Bernal Díaz del Castillo refers to consistently. The author of *La verdadera historia de la conquista de La Nueva España* (1569) contends that he writes this "true" history to refute the lies and exaggerations that appear in the López de Gómara version. By using this quotation, the tone of *Tamazunchale* takes on new dimensions; not only are we involved with the word "historia" in terms of a personal history or account, but the question of fictional narrative versus history is also being raised. By alluding to the chronicle genre (moreover, a historical genre that is generally accepted as the first European literary documentation in America), the invention of history, the fictionalization of "truth," becomes a part of the problematic structure within the work. It is a question that consistently appears in the Latin American narrative of the sixties and seventies.

One has only to turn to Gabriel García Márquez' *Cien años de soledad* (1967) and Carlos Fuentes' *Terra Nostra* (1975) to find two immediate and viable examples. It is a problem, moreover, that extends throughout Arias' work, appearing again in the posttextual quotation, the description of Tamazunchale taken from Frances Toor's guidebook to Mexico. In inserting the mispronunciation of "Tamazunchale" in the theatrical representation toward the end to the novel ("Thomas and Charley"), the ironic dimensions of definitions per se are maintained. By questioning the function of valid historical data in the first quotation and geographical references in the second, Arias questions the relationship between stable and solid, temporal and spatial values.

If these phenomena already suggest a knowledgeable interplay of narrative experiments, the chapters themselves, separated as they are into episodes, also suggest prior structures. The novella, the collection of tales, the picaresque, the pastoral, and the novel of chivalry are all episodic; so for that matter is the *Quijote*. These genres also have in common a concept of hero (or antihero), a form of narrative, and some sense of spatial and temporal representation.

The first chapter of this novel, the reader's introduction of Fausto, sets into motion the series of choices he will put into action in order to determine his own novel or life. In the opening paragraph, the omniscient third-person narrator describes him carefully removing his entire skin, like a finely knit suit. The sense of shock the reader experiences is somewhat mitigated where that action is viewed within a broader context. A "change of skin" in Nahuatl terms corresponds to a change of life. The parallel between this representation and the presence of the same phenomenen in Carlos Fuentes' *Cambio de piel* (1972), in which the characters are caught in the sententious repetition of the lives and frustrations of their ancestral counterparts, the pre-Hispanic inhabitants of the Valley of Mexico, extends Arias' readership toward both ancient and contemporary Mexico. Fuentes' novel refers directly to Xipetotec, the Nahuatl diety who suffers flagellation in order to change skin and thus undergoes a transformation into a new life.

Fausto's symbolic change of skin begins with a mimicry of this ancient rite and also corresponds to the change of name in the classic European structural model, *Don Quijote*. For just as the taking on of a name and the rites of knightly ordination (with the subsequent humiliation and physical abuse) correspond to a baptismal rite for Cervantes' character, the stripping off of the old skin, which also embodies anguish and pain, renews Fausto for his initiation into a new life.

At the end of the first chapter, the opening ritual and the reader's realization that the act has been entirely imagined also open up new dimensions of Fausto's personality. The imagined act, for instance, has been made up to try to attract his niece's sympathy and attention. Her reaction, which is ordinary and mundane while still somewhat loving, serves to notify the reader that Fausto's grisly act has been imaginary and that Fausto is lonely and in need of love. The far-off sound of a flute at the end of the chapter is the device that opens up the old man's closed and lonely world to a reality of action and dialogue. Through it the narrator begins the next structural experiment, the invention of a strange combination of Fausto's contemporary world view and the active ideal world of the fifteenth century conquistador.

This combination of the pastoral, the novel of chivalry, and the *crónica* also serves to introduce one of the mainstays of the novelistic experiment within the novel. Marcelino, the Andean shepherd, is the shadowy and mysterious figure whose flute was heard at the end of Chapter 1. His name as well as his existence conjure images of Cervantes' interpolated novel. Rather than telling his story, Marcelino intertwines his existence into that of the characters living in Los Angeles. His presence then serves to transform their reality, their space; Elysian Park becomes the Elysian Fields.

Yet, as in the narrative models that precede Cervantes, the predominance of narrative over dialogue, the need for a dialectical opposite, creates a search for a counterpart. The archetypical duo of the knight-squire is realized when Fausto meets Mario, a lowrider *cholo* from the Frogtown barrio of Lincoln Heights. Like Don Quijote and Sancho, Fausto and Mario represent harmonic opposites in terms of their socioeconomic circumstances. By creating the harmonic duo on a conflictive level, Arias puts into motion the process of character dynamics and interaction through the use of dialogue. Communication and growth can now happen.

The blend of elements, models, modes, and narrations, drawn as they are from European and American sources, defines the rich and original dimensions of this novel. When it focuses on the dynamics of the knight-squire archetype, the process of dialectic (and dialogue) rather than narration also comes about. The knight-squire focus also begins to draw the novel closer to the *Quijote* in its strong parallels in characterization and dynamic process. Like Don Quijote, Fausto begins his novel-life-road-search just before his death. The process of becoming becomes *materia* through the process of writing and retelling, through mimesis and re-creation. The apparent absurdity and comical deeds of an imaginative old man draw on similar models in Cervantes' masterpiece. In this melange of the comic and the ideal, Fausto moves on, however, toward his own destiny, toward the formation of his own reality. Thus, despite the taking on of a "Faustean" name—thus implying the generic definition of Goethe's work as yet another feasible model—the selection of the young counterpart, the process of dynamic action through dialogue, and the idealism that pervades the novel also set its course.

This narrative experimentation probably reaches its climax in the middle of the novel with the interpolation and retelling of an episode that bears a strong resemblance to a short story by Gabriel García Márquez. In the seventh chapter of the novel, the barrio children, playing in the dry riverbed, come upon the body of a drowned *mojado*. The subsequent succession of events, the "baptism" (taking on of a name) of the drowned man, his integration into the society that functions in the novel, the night of passion between Mrs. Rentería, the old woman, and the beautiful corpse-lover, are all, except for the latter, variations on García Márquez' short story "El ahogado más hermoso del mundo."

As is the case with the other examples cited, this interpolation should be seen as yet another novelistic experiment that Arias undertakes. Yet, because it is so clearly tied to the model that precedes it, it deserves some reflection on the mythopoetic meanings it arouses.

The differences that exist between the two examples lie in the setting, the languages (Spanish, English), and Arias' insertion of the night of love that takes place between the spinster and the dead man (hinted at in the García Márquez model). The similarities consist of the following; the initial discovery of the corpse by the children (in both cases, a drowned man); the women's admiration of the physical beauty of the corpse and the envy and desire the corpse arouses; the bestowal of a name,

and thus an identity, on the corpse; the transformation through death (transfiguration) that takes place in the barrio (village), that is, the new sense of purpose through the presence of death.

What the reader initially questions, however, is the function of this interpolation in Arias' novel. What is accepted with regard to the other examples of novelistic experimentation I have already mentioned here becomes a puzzle. Moreover, one remembers that the preceding model (and I purposely do not use the word "initial" or "original") is a short story, complete in itself. This example, however, appears within the structure of the novel, directly in the center. I must elaborate once again on the techniques I have referred to at the beginning of this study.

I have already spoken of the dynamic process behind the formation of Fausto's character. I observed that the road of the novel is akin to life itself, that the first chapter sets into motion the process of exploration and selection that creates meaning out of the old man's life. The complication occurs in the emphasis on old age as a factor in the novelistic process. Like his model and archetype Don Quijote, Fausto seeks the meaning of human purpose in this twilight stage of life. Significantly, in terms of this novel's structure, that process becomes more insistent from the seventh chapter on. The passage from one life to the next becomes more and more the *materia prima*, whereas the search for the narrative form, the election of one form of novelizing over another, had been the novel's preoccupation up to Chapter 7.

As the novel's mainstay, then, this interpolation merits some discussion. Certainly, the theme itself, which focuses on transfiguration through death, is familiar enough; what is far less familiar are the circumstances of the death, which make it difficult to accept if one has a traditional Western perception of this event. Both narratives, first of all, place the event within a familiar, ordinary framework of time and space. Moreover, the cause of death is not known; the identity of the corpse is also unknown. Consequently, neither violence nor tragedy, those two great poles of literary distance, are present to create a sense of pathos or anguish. The question of an initial detachment is important to both narratives, for the absence of knowledge about or familiarity with the person the corpse once was allows for the imaginative dimensions of growth, wonderment, and invention.

There is in Arias' example, moreover, a difference as to the circumstances surrounding the death; the corpse is found in a dry riverbed; still, he is David, the "drowned mojado," and reference is made to someone being swept downstream several winters ago. The invention of the cause of death by drowning is important in that the discrepancy between fact and invention lies in the reader's interpretation of the event, but not in the neighborhood's collective belief in it. Moreover, David is a "mojado," a wetback. Is David's death related to his "mojado-ness"?

That is to say, is death in the dry riverbed a symbol of the anguished death of the exploited Mexican undocumented worker? Since the answer to that question lies only in our "reading" of the narrative, I would point out that one of Fausto's ensuing preoccupations after this episode involves protecting undocumented workers and that it becomes a raison d'être for him. It is also significant that this ambiguity does not exist in the García Márquez example. Since the corpse in that version is found on the beach and reference is made to waves and to seaweed, the sense of wonder has a different focus; the question of the corpse's origin becomes important.

Still, the distance between what I have called the Western perception of death and the familiarity with it in the context of Arias' novel rests on the use of the following devices: the children playing with the corpse; the perception by the older participants of the "normalcy" of that act; and the acceptance of the corpse by the society of the narrative to the point of baptizing it, dressing it, and elevating it to the role of a person, thus giving it an identity. The sense of familiarity and innocence projected in these two examples nonetheless has a parallel in the mythic structures of the Western tradition.

What has seemingly been lost by Anglo culture is the Hispanic belief in the marvelous. What I mean by this concerns the importance of the Christian belief in resurrection as demonstrated in the Gospel narration of the death of Christ and in the legend of St. James the Elder (Santiago de Compostela). In the Gospels, the function of belief lies in its power to convince that even physical death through the crucifixion does not deny the possibility of resurrection. It is thus basic to the belief in death and transfiguration. Still, as a myth, it relies on distance—a time and place far enough removed from our daily lives so as to create either a chasm of disbelief or a permission to believe. Furthermore, the distance between that event and our present lies in the language of narration. Even contemporary translation of the Bible cannot overcome that distance.

The legend of St. James of Compostela offers other possibilities. It begins with the arrival of a corpse borne on a small boat or raft that is deposited on the beach near Santiago in Spain, and from that point on the legend develops, for this body is the body of St. James, an apostle of Christ. The result of that event is the cult of St. James, one of the most powerful social and artistic manifestations of the European Middle Ages. More importantly for my intention here, the legend of Santiago is one of the most powerful myths functioning in the Hispanic tradition; hence, its retelling here, its participation in the infinite textures and texts that make up literature.

What is compelling about the levels of meaning in Arias' novel, however, concerns the manner in which it constructs a dialectic between the reader and itself. I interpret this demand on the reader as an intention toward participation, not on an elitist level of meaning that rejects one group of readers for another, but as a challenge toward understanding, toward developing perceptions about the bridges and chasms, the fragments and traditions that make up Chicano culture. The novel focuses on an ordinary reality, but episode after episode of marvelous daily occurrences (for example, the snowstorm that falls only within the barrio) function as transformations of Fausto's ordinary existence, and through him and with him they transform that reality and that life into the extraordinary. The novel focuses on death, from the anticipation of death at the beginning to the novel's structural apex, the seventh chapter, and finally to its culmination, Fausto's passage from the narrative into the television screen (I repeat, a new "visual" dimension, perhaps?). Death and its transformation embody the meaning of Fausto's life and the mythopoetic levels of the novel. Both are an affirmation of the ordinary in the marvelous. What we share in that process is a unique experiment within the space of the Chicano narrative, a shared reading into broader areas of ourselves and of human understanding. (pp. 239–46)

Eva Margarita Nieto, "The Dialectics of Textual Interpolation in Ron Arias' 'The Road to Tamazunchale'," in *Contemporary Chicano Fiction: A Critical Survey*, edited by Vernon E. Lattin, Bilingual Press / Editorial Bilingüe, 1986, pp. 239–46.

SOURCES FOR FURTHER STUDY

Latin, Vernon E. "The 'Creation of Death' in Ron Arias's *The Road to Tamazunchale*." *Revista Chicano-Riqueña* X, No. 3 (Summer 1982): 53–62.
    Explores how the concept of death shapes the structure, themes, symbols and characterization of *The Road to Tamazunchale*.

Lewis, Marvin A. "On the Road to Tamazunchale." *Revista Chicano-Riqueña* 5, No. 4 (Fall 1977): 49–52.
    Investigates how Arias interweaves the themes of the *mojados*, or wetbacks, and the search for Utopia in *The Road to Tamazunchale*.

Martínez, Eliud. "Ron Arias's *The Road to Tamazunchale*: A Chicano Novel of the New Reality." *Latin American Literary Review* V, No. 10 (Spring-Summer 1977): 51–63.

Examines *The Road to Tamazunchale*, asserting that the novel "is a pace-setter and marks a new direction for Chicano literature."

Saldívar, José David. "The Ideological and the Utopian in Tomás Rivera's . . . *y no se lo tragó la tierra* and Ron Arias' *The Road to Tamazunchale*." In *Missions in Conflict: Essays on U.S. Mexican Relations and Chicano Culture*; edited by Renate von Bardeleban, Dietrich Briesemeister, and Juan Bruce-Novoa, pp. 203–14. Tübingen, Germany: Gunter Narr Verlag Tübingen, 1986.

Understands the novel as a revolutionary work heralding the advent of a new world order that resulted from "human intervention and labor."

Additional coverage of Arias's life and career is contained in the following sources published by Gale Research: *Contemporary Authors*, Vol. 131; and *Dictionary of Literary Biography*, Vol. 82.

Roberto Arlt

1900–1942

(Born Roberto Godofredo Cristopherson Arlt) Argentine novelist, playwright, essayist, and short story writer.

INTRODUCTION

*L*auded by critics for exploring innovative themes in his narrative and theater, Arlt was one of the most influential figues in Argentine literature during the first half of the twentieth century. He is chiefly remembered for the novels *Los siete locos* (1929; *The Seven Madmen*) and *Los lanzallamas* (1931), whose plots explore the tension between illusion and reality, focusing upon the metaphysical anguish of the alienated individual in twentieth-century society. Arlt treated similar themes in dramas such as *Trescientos millones* (1932), *El fabricante de fantasmas* (1936), and *Saverio el cruel* (1936), in which imaginary life becomes indistinguishable from real life for the protagonists. Premised on what he considered a breakdown of the philosophical and religious values of Western civilization, his fiction and dramas concern the plight of individuals contending with "the inevitably crumbling social edifice," frequently depicting social unrest, urban alienation, deviant behavior, sexual maladjustment, and class hostility. Arlt is also noted for his "Aguafuertes porteñas"—"etchings" of Buenos Aires life: collected essays whose language and tone are still admired by Argentine writers.

The son of German immigrants, Arlt was born in Buenos Aires in 1900. Although he received little formal education after leaving school in the third grade, he read a great deal during his childhood and youth. As a young man Arlt attended the Naval School of Mechanics; in the following years he worked at many jobs and served as secretary to the novelist Ricardo Güiraldes from 1925 to 1927. He published his first major work, the novel *El juquete rabioso* (1926), during his association with Güiraldes. At this time, most Argentine writers were identified with one of two groups, the Boedo street group, known for social realism and proletarian concerns, and the Florida street group, known for avant-garde modernism. Reviewers of *El juquete rabioso*—most of whom found fault with Arlt's undisciplined, journalistic style—associated the realistic tone and lower-class setting of the novel with the Boedo street group. Arlt strengthened this association by spending much of his time in La Puñalada, a cafe frequented by underworld types, and writing sketches about its disreputable habitués. The individuals portrayed in these sketches served as prototypes for the characters of his next novel, *The Seven Madmen*. Beginning in 1929 Arlt wrote a column, "Aguafuertes porteñas," for the newspaper *El mundo*. "Aguafuertes" drew a wide readership, and Arlt continued to support himself by newspaper work untile he died of a heart attack in 1942.

Arlt believed that literature, if it is to express human experience, must not present a world more ordered than reality, which he saw as essentially chaotic and irrational. He therefore rejected the conventions of social realism, then popular in Argentina, to create a complex fusion of fantasy and reality in works replete with grotesque imagery and logical inconsistencies. Arlt's novels thus mingle the realistic with the absurd to violate the reader's expectations of conventional verisimilitude. His most famous novel, *The Seven Madmen*, and its sequel, *Los lanzallamas*, concern an unemployed bill collector, Remo Erdosain, who joins a group of eccentrics who plot a revolution led by a man known only as the Astrologer. Appearances prove recurrently deceptive; in fact, the long-waited revolt proves to be largely illusory: after a few random acts of violence, most of the group, including Erdosain, perish. Only the Astrologer and his lover Hipólita, who have proven their abilities to see beyond and even to manipulate illusions, survive. Critics suggest that Arlt used these characters to demonstrate that self-reliance is essential to establish and preserve personal identity. Arlt located the true source of his character's suffering not in personal misfortune but in a spiritual crisis afflicting twentieth-century society as a whole. Describing Erdosain and his partners, the author wrote: "These individuals . . . are tied or bound together by desperation. The desperation in them originates, more than from material poverty, from another factor: the disorientation that, after the Great War, has revolutionized the conscience of men, leaving them empty of ideals and hopes."

Like his novels, Arlt's dramas also explore the effect of twentieth-century society upon the individual and the tenuousness of human perception. Often the fantasies of his characters intertwine themselves with everyday life in a way which weakens the traditional boundaries between the conceptions of the author and the drama. Some critics compare this aspect of Arlt's work to similar displacements of roles in the works of the Italian playwright Luigi Pirandello, especially the latter's *Sei personaggi in cerca d'autore* [*Six Characters in Search of an Author*]. For instance, in *El fabricante de fantasmas* a dramatist who has murdered his wife is pursued and ultimately executed by characters from his plays, and in *Trescientos millones* a servant girl escapes her harsh existence by dreaming of a romantic and exciting life which becomes increasingly more real until, after her death, the characters she has imagined dance about her corpse, rejoicing in their new freedom from her control. Critics suggest that Arlt expressed a perception of life as being essentially meaningless and cruel through his characters' lack of definite knowledge and ultimate control over their lives. Sometimes the unkindness of life is linked to social status; his plays *Saverio el cruel* and *Trescientos millones* feature poor protagonists who are abused by the wealthy. This has led some Argentine writers to view Arlt as a socialist, though other students of theater state that while Arlt's concern for the poor is obvious, his main interest was the examination of consciousness. As is the case with all of Arlt's literary work, the underlying purpose of his dramas is to subvert any attempt to evaluate them according to rationalistic criteria of aesthetic, intellectual, or moral worth. Arlt sought to prevent the reader from relying on a rational interpretation of his words and, in the words of Naomi Lindstrom, to "persuade him to accept the irrational, the unexplained and the anomalous as predominant features of human existence. . . ."

Arlt's "Aguafuertes" offer sympathetic portraits of characters representing the lower and working classes of Buenos Aires. Generally realistic, the "Aguafuertes" also feature humorous exaggeration and irony: Jack M. Flint remarks that Arlt's "realism often spills over into the grotesque." The essays present a wide variety of human types, and even criminals and other characters who might normally prove unattractive to readers become interesting and appealing because of Arlt's understanding depictions of them. Critics indicate that part of the vitality of the "Aguafuertes" derives from Arlt's convincing use of slang and local colloquialisms to evoke a sense of place and time. Arlt was one of the first Argentine writers of note to write in the national idiom rather than in the Spanish of Spain, just as he was one of a small group of authors who rejected traditional Argentine romanticism and emphasized lower-class urban language and settings.

Although only *The Seven Madmen* and a few of his stories and essays have appeared in English, Arlt's works continue to enjoy a wide readership and much critical attention in South America. Argentine novelist Julio Cortazar acknowledged Arlt as an important influence on his own fiction. Indeed, critics have evaluated his work in light of the literary innovations of modern Latin American writers and have found in Arlt's work the seminal development of many of the ideas that would preoccupy the literature of his continent after his death. Scholars find Arlt difficult to characterize: some feel that he was a pioneer of Argentine Modernism for his exploration of consciousness; in addition critics sometimes view him as the forerunner of later movements such as Existentialism, in his suggestion of a lack of absolute value or knowledge, and Magic Realism by his presentation of illusion and fantasy which impose themselves on reality. Assessing the significance of his in-

novations, Jorge Lafforgue designated Arlt's works, with those of Juan Carlos Onetti, as "the beginnings of current Argentine-Uruguayan fiction"; Lafforgue's appreciation was echoed by Onetti himself, who stated: "If any inhabitant of our humble shores managed to achieve literary genius, his name was Roberto Arlt."

CRITICAL COMMENTARY

ROBERTO ARLT

(essay date 1933)

[In the following excerpt, which originally appeared in 1933 in Arlt's newspaper column "Aguafertes porteñas," Arlt responds to an editorial by the Argentine academic Monner Sans in which Sans criticized the common use of slang and ungrammatical constructions in Argentine Spanish.]

Dear Mr. Monner Sans: Grammar is much like boxing. I'll explain it to you:

When a man takes up boxing and has no feel for it, all he does is copy the moves his teacher shows him. When another man takes up boxing and has it, and puts up a magnificent fight, sports writers exclaim: "He came at him from all sides!" Meaning, he's bright, so he finds a way around the textbook grammar of boxing. Needless to say, the one who finds a way around the grammar of boxing and lets fly "from all sides" wipes up the floor with the other guy, and that's how this phrase of ours got started: "European or show boxing," that is, boxing that's fine for show, but for fighting is no good at all, at least against our agrammatically boxing boys.

With peoples and with languages, Mr. Monner Sans, the same goes. Peoples with no brains keep reusing the same language forever, because, with no new ideas to express, they don't need new words or ways to say things; but, on the other hand, peoples that, like us, are continually evolving, come up with words from all sides, words that give schoolteachers fits, just as a European boxing teacher has a fit over the inconceivable fact that a kid who boxes all wrong wipes up the floor with one of his students who's technically a perfect boxer. All right: I see why you'd get upset. Go right ahead. . . .

A nation imposes its art, industry and business by

imposing its language. Take the U.S. They send us their products with the labels in English, and we get used to a lot of English words. In Brazil, a lot of Argentine words (slang words) are popular. Why? It's the superiority of language imposing itself.

"Last Reason," Felix Lima, Fray Mocho and others [folk humorists] have had a lot more influence on our language, than all the philological and grammatical flim-flam of a Mr. Cejador y Frauja, Benot and that whole dusty, cranky gang of bookworms, who just grub around in files and write memos that not even you, illustrious grammarians, bother to read, because they're so boring.

This phenomenon more than proves the absurdity of trying to straight jacket in a prescriptive grammar the constantly changing, new ideas of a people. When a crook who's about to stab his cohort in the chest says: "I'm gonna stick you but good," it's much more eloquent than if he had said: "I shall insert my dagger in your sternum." When a hood exclaims, when he sees a band of cops coming, "I had 'em eyeballed!" it's much more graphic than if he said " I had surreptitiously observed these officers of the law."

Mr. Monner Sans: if we paid attention to grammar, our great grandparents would have had to respect it, and so on backward, so it follows that, if our forebears had respected grammar, we, men of the radio and the machine gun, would still be using caveman speech.

Roberto Arlt, in an excerpt from "The Language of Argentines," translated by Naomi Lindstrom in *Review*, No. 31, January–April, 1982, p. 31.

Principal Works

El juquete rabioso (novel) 1926

Los siete locos (novel) 1929
   [*The Seven Madmen*, 1984]

Los lanzallamas (novel) 1931

El amor brujo (novel) 1932

Trescientos millones (drama) 1932

Aguafuertes porteñas (essays) 1933

El jorobadito (short stories) 1933

Aguafuertes españolas (essays) 1936

El fabricante de fantasmas (drama) 1936

Saverio el cruel (drama) 1936

La isla desierta (drama) 1938

La fiesta del hierro (drama) 1940

EL criador de gorilas (short stories) 1941

*El desierto entra en la ciudad (drama) 1953

Nuevas aguafuertes porteñas (essays) 1960

Novelas completas y cuentos. 3 vols. (novels and short
   stories) 1963

Teatro completo. 2 vols. (dramas) 1968

Obra completa. 2 vols. (novels, dramas, essays and
   short stories) 1981

* This work was written in 1942.

JEAN FRANCO
(essay date 1969)

[Franco is an English critic and educator who has written and edited numerous studies of Latin American literature. In the following excerpt, she discusses Arlt's novels of alienation, in which he portrays the city as a place of robbery, murder, and predation.]

Roberto Arlt was the first serious explorer in Spanish America of the urban complex and its nightmares. He himself was the son of an immigrant who had found the struggle for life hard in the 'promised land' of America. Thrown at an early age on to his own resources, Arlt was forced into a variety of jobs. He had an intelligence that was dazzled by scientific inventions, but these talents could not be developed for he left school at an early age. He finally found his way into journalism, was associated with a socialist realist school of writers, the 'Boedo

group' (which was named after the street in which they met), and like them felt a strong sense of identification with the poor and a distrust of élitism in literature. Yet his own work could not be contained within the limits of realism. His first novel, *El juguete rabioso* [*The Angry Toy*] was, however, strongly reminiscent of Gorky whose writings the Boedo group greatly admired. This black account of poverty and delinquency, based on his own childhood and youth, was long in finding a publisher and totally failed to make an impression on an Argentine literary scene that was dominated by the fashion-conscious élite. Yet Arlt told a powerful story of boys in the slums whose poor home backgrounds offered no food for the imagination except for the lurid adventures of bandits, those legendary figures of the 'penny dreadfuls'. The boys grow up dreaming of crime as the weapon that will liberate them both from poverty and from spiritual starvation. Real life, on the other hand, is a constant chain of frustration. The protagonist, Silvio Astier, works first as a shop assistant, in which job he is pitilessly exploited and then having joined the army in order to find an outlet for this scientific curiosity, finds that intelligence is superfluous. He is demobilised and sent back to the slums. Only the ending mars the book. Arlt, whose personal experience formed the background of the story, did not know how to bring it to a close. He has his protagonist betray some criminal associates and thus redeem himself in the eyes of society. Even so, the redemption is sour. Silvio Astier can only become a part of society through treachery.

Arlt's two outstanding novels are *Los siete locos* [*The Seven Madmen*] and *Los lanzallamas* [*The Flame Throwers*]—these being two parts of a single narrative. Once again, the protagonist, Erdosaín, is based on Arlt himself, but this time the novelist breaks the bonds of realism and writes a fantasy which is a crushing condemnation of modern society. Erdosaín is an embezzler whose wife leaves him in desperation at her life of poverty and who is threatened with prosecution unless he repays the money he has taken from his firm. He falls in with a group of madmen who conceive the plan of kidnapping the rich Barsut and raising money from him to start chains of brothels. The money they make is to be devoted to the destruction of society. The plot is less important, however, than the fantastic gallery of characters such as the Astrologer, the Melancholy Pimp and the Gold-Seeker, whose madness is only the desperate reaction of men whom society has rejected and who live in a state of anguish which is inseparable from modern life:

Esta zona de angustia era la consecuencia del sufrimiento de los hombres. Y como una nube de gas venenoso se trasladaba pesadamente de un punto a otro, penetrando murallas y atravesando los edificios, sin perder su forma plana y horizontal. . . .

[This zone of anguish was the consequence of the suffering of men. And like a cloud of venomous gas it moved heavily from one point to another, penetrating walls, passing through buildings, without losing its flat and horizontal shape. . . .]

Escape into fantasy leaves man in a sorrier dilemma than before. Erdosaín has the purest ideals of love but invariably finds himself with prostitutes. The constant process of disillusionment leaves him in a state of total alienation:

El no era ya un organismo envasando sufrimientos, sino algo más inhumana. . . quizá eso. . . un monstruo enroscado en sí mismo en el negro vientre de la pieza. Cada capa de oscuridad que descendía de sus párpados era un tejido placentario que lo aislaba más y más del universo de los hombres. Hasta la conciencia de ser, en él no ocupaba más de un centimetro cuadrado de sensibilidad.

[He was no longer an organism containing sufferings, but something more inhuman. . . perhaps this. . . a monster coiled round itself in the black stomach of the room. Each layer of darkness which descended from his eyelids was a placenta-like web that isolated him more and more from the universe of men. Even the consciousness of being did not occupy in him more than a square centimetre of sensibility.]

These states of alienation are characteristic of *urban* man, of man caught in the iron net of capitalist society which has systematised exploitation, robbery and murder. The seven madmen, in their plot to destroy 'this implacable society', employ society's own weapons of murder, prostitution and robbery. Arlt's account of the mad fantasies of his characters is interspersed with reports of real contemporary events—war in China, strikes, etc. Reality, in fact, outstrips fantasy.

Arlt was a pioneer in a field which few European novelists had entered successfully, and he conveyed a personal and nightmarish vision of a world in which the city itself was the main enemy. His point of view was that of the anarchist who sees a return to a simpler rural society as the only effective solution. So the Gold-Seeker believes that in the solitude of nature man regains the sense of his own identity:

Desafiando la soledad, los peligros, la tristesa, el sol, lo infinito de la llanura, uno se siente otro hombre. . . distinto del rebaño de esclavos que agoniza en la ciudad.

[Defying solitude, dangers, sadness, the sun, the infinity of the plain, one feels oneself another man, different from the flock of slaves who agonise in the city.]

Arlt wrote two other novels, *El amor brujo* [*Bewitched Love*] (1932) and *El jorobadito* [*The Little Hunchback*] (1933) and published a collection of short stories, *Aguafuertes porteñas* [*Buenos Aires Etchings*] (1933). (pp. 303–05)

Jean Franco, "The Contemporary Novel and Short Story," in her *An Introduction to Spanish American Literature*, Cambridge at the University Press, 1969, pp. 300–56.

PAUL GRAY
(essay date 1984)

[In the following review, Gray discusses *The Seven Madmen,* hailing Arlt as "an entertaining pioneer in the new world of South American fiction."]

It has taken a while for this novel to find its way into English. *The Seven Madmen* was first published in Argentina in 1929. Its author, Roberto Arlt, was a disheveled Buenos Aires journalist who defiantly disregarded the rules of Spanish grammar and the finer sensibilities of critics. They in turn hooted at his work, which included four novels, two collections of stories and eight plays. The author once mordantly mimicked the typical response of his detractors: "Mr. Roberto Arlt keeps on in the same old rut: realism in the worst possible taste."

If anyone ever actually believed that this novel was realistic, then life in the Argentine capital must once have been unimaginably weird. True, the trappings of proletarian fiction are all roughly in place—lowlife taverns, brothels and urban rot: "The setting sun lit up the most revolting inner recesses of the sloping street." But the anti-hero who stumbles through this landscape is a perversely comic invention. Remo Erdosain collects bills for a sugar company and engages in petty embezzlement. He also writhes in noisy anguish at a world that can ignore his true genius. "Didn't they call me crazy," he asks an acquaintance, "because I said they should set up shops to dry-clean and dye dogs and metallize shirt cuffs?" One day, everything gets even worse. His employer tells Erdosain that he must repay the money he has stolen or face jail, and his wife informs him that she is running off with another man. He luxuriates in grief raised to a higher power: "If he had had the strength, he would have thrown himself down a well."

Instead, Erdosain joins a mysterious figure called the Astrologer in a plot to take over the world. It goes something like this: Give the masses a new religious symbol to believe in ("harness the madman power") and then exploit their zeal to create wealth, in this case by mining gold in a remote area of Argentina. The Astrologer explains: "See? We'll lure the workers in with false promises and whip them to death if they won't work." Erdosain feels flattered to be included among the brains of this organization. His invention of a copper-plated rose, once perfected and put into production, will provide capital for the fledgling revolution, as will the string of bordellos the Astrologer plans to establish. Anticipating power, Erdosain dreams himself in a chamber at the bottom of the sea: " On the other side of the porthole, one-eyed sharks were swimming about, vile humored because of their piles. . . . Now all the fish in the sea were one-eyed, and he was the Emperor of the City of one-Eyed Fish."

Such surrealistic touches, largely unappreciated during his lifetime, now mark Arlt as an entertaining pioneer in the new world of South American fiction. Despite his ineptitudes, Erdosain is astute enough to sense that "on a deeper level than consciousness and thought, there's a whole other life, more powerful and vast." *The Seven Madmen* staked Arlt's claim to a terrain that others, including Borges and García Marquez, continue to explore.

Paul Gray, "Dyed Dogs," in *Time*, New York, Vol. 124, No. 9, August 27, 1984, p. 58.

JACK M. FLINT
(essay date 1985)

[In the excerpt below, Flint considers the views of society and the individual expressed in Arlt's novels and his "Aguafuertes porteñas, " noting in particular thematic similarities between *The Seven Madmen* and Dostoevsky's *The Devils*.]

[Politics and Society] is one of the most contentious areas of Arlt's writing. Since his death in 1942, his reputation as a "political" novelist has grown consistently amongst certain sections of Argentine society, largely, in our opinion, without due regard to what he actually wrote. He has been raised as a standard against bourgeois reaction by the left wing, who have claimed him amongst their ranks. He has been ignored by many intellectuals who have carped at his "bad writing". He has been read by rebellious youth for his spirit of revolt. His ambiguous relationship with Florida and Boedo suggests that by his mid-twenties he was not prepared to make a definite commitment either in artistic or political terms. By the outbreak of the Spanish Civil War, following his visit to Spain and North Africa, he was following the Communist line, according to his contemporary Juan José Gorini. However, in the polarization of opinions precipitated by that war, liberal intellectuals of all kinds did likewise throughout Europe and America. The disputes about Arlt's politics, like those about his style and the influence of Dostoevsky on his work, seem to have been founded on a lack of evidence and close knowledge of what he actually wrote. One would

be hard taxed to reconcile the anarchic, individualistic rebellion of his two major novels with the hard lines of left-wing thinking. Arlt's view of the world as an appearance in which reality sometimes outstrips fantasy is far removed from the deterministic theories of left-wing ideology. Arlt would doubtless have welcomed many social improvements but not on the political basis proposed by many of his contemporaries.

It can readily be appreciated from a reading of the novels that his political ideas and attitudes hardened during the crumbling economic situation of 1929–32. Sebreli is right to claim that his characters are, in this sense, dateable. ["Inocencia y culpabilidad de Roberto Arlt", *Sur*, no. 223 (1953)]. He adds that without the economic conditions of the time, his characters' anguish would have been of a different kind. All this is very true, but it is this fact that has misled Arlt's more deterministic critics. It is the ability of Arlt's characters to assume universal stature that makes him worthy of our attention today. Writers like Castelnuovo and Mariani were also faithful representers of the social stress of the period, but they were incapable of rising to the metaphysical heights that are achieved in Arlt's fiction. Sebreli seems to be more to the point when he adds that Arlt was too preoccupied with his own relations with the world to be bothered about those in society. Ghiano feels that Arlt disdained the puerile optimism of some writers of his generation for whom the solution lay solely in political change. This is surely the real key to Arlt's position. There are moments in the Astrólogo's disquisitions on revolution and society when it is in doubt whether society's follies are under attack or those of the Astrólogo himself, such is the ambiguous cloak under which the author hides. In Arlt, as in Dostoevsky, the optimism of the revolutionary is meant to be seen as yet another part of, and not an answer to, social problems. It is therefore understandable that he should have been drawn towards the Russian's stance in *The Devils*, as more recent criticism has shown, for they both seek to reveal social ills but mock at solutions based on collective action at the expense of the individual. Even in his first novel, Silvio dreams, not of revolution or indeed social change, but of how his inventions might lift *him* out of the degradation of his social background. Erdosain and Balder have little or no sense of solidarity; they merely sneer at all those who suffer "el servilismo del cuello duro", those who squirm under a boss. There are later glimpses of solidarity in *El amor brujo*,—written during the worst effects of the depression—when Arlt criticizes young office-girls who "en vez de pensar en agremiarse para defender sus derechos, pensaban en engatusar con artes de vampiresas a un cretino adinerado que las pavoneara en una voiturette." Even here, it is obvious from the tone that what worries him is not really the lack of union solidarity but the vampire habits of the young women. As Masotta says [in his *El sexo y traición en Roberto Arlt (1965)*]: "Un crítico de izquierda tendría razón de definirlo así: el hombre de Arlt, que viene de la masa, no apunta a la clase social. Esto a pesar de que su búsqueda es una empresa de *desmasificación*, en tanto quiere dejar de ser el oscuro individuo anónimo, para convertirse, en un relámpago, en sí mismo." This process of "demassification", which aims to restore the individual's rights and consciousness of self, is what fundamentally distinguishes Arlt from standard centralist left-wing ideology. It would be unwise to ignore the possible influence of anarchist thought, however, which always had a strong grip in Argentina. (Much of Boedo's thinking was culled from Kropotkin and Bakunin.) Communist and socialist efforts, on the other hand, are directed at the restoration of the individual's rights in a reformed social framework directed from the centre, whilst Arlt's characters are always busy opting out of any framework at all. (pp. 72–3)

Arlt was obviously aware of the broad lines of left-wing ideology. The hotchpotch of political thought advanced by his characters shows a general, if unsophisticated knowledge. He had lived through a period of acute change during which the theories of Bolshevism were speading round the world, following the 1917 Revolution. We may assume that he had heard endless debate and argument during his adolescence and early manhood. Nevertheless, a reading of his works would not allow any specific conclusions as to his allegiances. . . . Knowing his sombre view of human kind, it is time to see the proposals in his fiction for what they are: an extended irony aimed at simplistic revolutionary ideology. Too little has been made of the distinction between sincere social comment and ironic, black humour. The revolutionary "proposals", in our view, belong to the latter, whilst the compassionate observation of human beings and society in parts of the novels and many of the *Aguafuertes* belong squarely to the former. Like many of his contemporaries, under the pressure of the new existential thinking of his time, Arlt believed that the real revolution was to be achieved in the individual and not in the mass.

Admittedly, as his writing progresses, there is a noticeable shift from fantastic reactions to social inequality and injustice towards more concrete social observation. At the beginning of *Los siete locos*, as in its predecessor, the protagonist dreams of solutions to his oppressed condition which are engendered in his fantasy. As he wanders through the wealthier areas of the city, his reaction to the splendour he comes across is not one of rejection or revolt; he merely wonders how quickly he can join it. . . . As the novel advances, more serious social comment makes its intrusion. The Astrólogo becomes Arlt's mouthpiece not only for harebrained revolutionary schemes but also for soundly-based strictures on society. He proposes a revolution centred on a great lie, with an electric chair on every street corner, or a guillotine from which the heads will roll like grapes at harvest time, innocent and guilty alike, to satisfy the people's craving for sensation. To this satire of degraded human nature belong his ideas for fi-

nancing the revolution by a chain of brothels (perhaps not so outlandish if one bears in mind the horrifying facts and figures) and the search for some symbol to inflame the plebs. . . . It is not only the thoughtless populace that comes in for such treatment. When the revolutionaries assemble, the Mayor (a spurious Major who turns out to be real after all) seizes the opportunity to spread the criticism to the Cámara de Diputados, accusing them of being sold to foreign companies, whilst the Communists, too, receive their share of lambasting, being qualified as "un bloque de carpinteros que desbarran sobre sociología en una cuadra". The whole thing is a romp with Arlt enjoying himself mightily. However, by the time he composes *Los lanzallamas*, following the conservative *pronunciamiento* of 1930, the satirical and bantering tone gives way to harder reactions. Capitalist society, in complicity with atheism, has turned man into a sceptical monster. . . . And yet, the Astrólogo's ideas for the promotion of the revolution change not one whit throughout the two volumes: the great "mentira metafísica" which will satisfy man's hunger for belief. But comments on society become more astringent and more pertinent. His philosophy is an amalgam of megalomania (which would like to shake the world by the ears) and sensible social criticism. His lunacy, which would put to death those who constitute a danger to the revolutionary cause—and many who do not—provides Arlt with a splendid cover for his anarchistic attack on society. If we were to sum up this aspect of Arlt's thinking, we might say that his social strictures are always valid, or at least meant to be taken seriously, whilst the political solutions put forward belong to his world of fantasy, in which death-rays, phosgene factories, guillotines and electric chairs abound. He slips quick-footedly from one to the other; woe betide the reader who fails to notice the change in step. It was his inability to control this process that finally aborted *Los lanzallamas*. Death-rays and poisonous gases overwhelm the social awareness; destructive adolescent fantasies take over. Too much attention is given to daydreams towards the end of the work and too little to the sharp-edged satire in which he excelled.

Returning to Dostoevsky, we may now establish certain further textual parallels. In *The Devils* Verkhovensky's "group of five" assembles at Virginsky's house. "The five chosen ones were sitting now at the general table and very skilfully assumed the air of ordinary men, so that no one would notice them." (A noteworthy detail; with Verkhovensky's group, but not part of it, is an army major. Arlt, too, includes the Major amongst his *seven* conspirators. Haffner, looking ordinary like Dostoevsky's revolutionaries, "está leyendo unos papeles en blanco"!) The dynamic for the Russian group consists in the murder of Shatov by the rest, an idea first proposed by Stavrogin. Similarly, Erdosain proposes the murder of Barsut to the Astrólogo, who readily accepts the plan. The motive is different, however; Shatov is to be killed in order to bind the conspirators together in secrecy, whilst Barsut is to be sacrificed ostensibly for his money. Shatov is in fact killed; in Arlt's novel, the Astrólogo deliberately contrives a mock murder, deceiving Erdosain and producing one of the most hilarious black scenes in Arlt's writing. So much for the general framework.

The ravings of the Astrólogo derive directly from those of Verkhovensky, in their combination of millenarian belief and political cynicism. The Russian proposes to use the aristocratic Stavrogin as a figurehead for the cause; he will be wheeled on to the stage to satisfy the mob's need to identify with some eminent personage. The Astrólogo proposes a figurehead like Krishnamurti, taken from Theosophy, some boy-god who will dazzle the multitudes. "We shall say he is in hiding", Verkhovensky said quietly, in a sort of amorous whisper, as though he were really drunk. "Do you know what the expression in hiding means? But he will appear. He will appear. We shall spread a legend which will be much better than that of the sect of castrates. He exists, but no one has ever seen him. Oh, what a wonderful legend one could spread! And the main thing is—a new force is coming. And that's what they want. That's what they're weeping for." This cynicism finds its reflection in the Astrólogo's boy-god. . . . The Astrólogo proposes *autos de fe* in the streets to inspire the latent madmen in society. So, too, Verkhovensky relies on the hidden resentment and irrationality of the populace. Schoolboys who kill a peasant for the sake of a thrill will swell their ranks; juries who acquit criminals without distinction, administrators, authors,—"oh, there are lots and lots of us, and they don't know it themselves", he cries. Examples of this kind might be multiplied, but the foregoing will certainly show that Arlt dipped more than carelessly into Dostoevsky's novel. Nor would it be exaggerating a point to see in Stavrogin's perverse marriage to the *crippled* Miss Lebyatkin a parallel with Ergueta's marriage to Hipólita, whom he insists on calling "la Coja". There is also a fundamental theme running through both works: that of man's aspirations to become God. In *The Devils*, Kirilov's argument leads to the belief that through suicide he himself will become God. The only real aspiration for man, the Astrólogo tells Barsut, is to wish to become God, "querer ser Dios, confundirse con Dios". Dostoevsky not only worked out his own religious problems through his novels but he reconstituted this exercise in exciting narrative. Arlt could not be accused of novelizing his religious feelings, but the ravings of characters like Ergueta, the religious fanatic, in conversation with Barsut, are wholly reminiscent of the Russian's lengthy dialogues on religion. We do not mean to belittle Arlt by these references to Dostoevsky, nor to detract from the power of his characters. They are not transplants from Russian literature by any means. They are indigenous creations growing out of Arlt's experience of people he met in Buenos Aires, as he himself maintains. "Son individuos y mujeres de esta ciudad a quienes yo he conocido."

But it is pointless to deny, as some have done, that these affinities and influences exist. No literature grows out of the void; it sinks its roots in what has gone before. If it did not, it would be the worse for that.

Arlt's "revolution" is, then, a protest, a cry against the dehumanizing forces in the society of his day, a cry against not only the governing classes but against the proletarian hordes who condone their influence. . . . (pp. 74–7)

His exhortation is to personal rebellion, not to planned revolution. In his novels the real battle is joined in the individual; in an Erdosain grappling with his anguish or a Balder with his disgust or a Hipólita with her poverty—all struggling to escape from the "rebaño de esclavos que agonizan en la ciudad". The solution to these creatures' anguish does not lie in collectivity; there is nothing in Arlt to suggest such an outcome. It is towards individualization that he aims. The solution is personal and existential.

Under no circumstances can Arlt's solutions for the ills he recognizes around him be interpreted as socialistic. There are times when they are anarchistic, even nihilist, with the total destruction of society as an immediate goal. But Kropotkin, one of the theoretical fathers of Argentine anarchism, never advocated the attack on mechanized society which is a kingpin of Arlt's ideology. The latter's view of technological society as destructive of individuality belongs foursquare to the contemporary polemic against scientism, to the existential revolution of the day. . . . Arlt sought to make the individual aware, not to reform him.

If one reads only Arlt's novels, with their undiluted pessimism and lack of constructive solutions, one would take away a sombre picture indeed. They are not even redeemed by their humour in the final analysis, for this, too, is black in the extreme. Fortunately, they are not the whole Arlt by any means. We have been concerned so far with his ideology and have perforce stayed within the realm of his fictional prose. But he lived by the pen, as so many Argentine writers have done, not only as a reporter but as an *aguafuertista*. It is to his *Aguafuertes porteñas* that we turn finally, for, although they carry no specific ideology, they offer a social documentation of the Buenos Aires of the 1930s in which their author's love of humanity and his compassion for its distress and follies is never far below the surface. They provide a valuable and often humorous antidote to the grey tones of the novels and will allow us to put a gloss on some of the ideas that have emerged so far. . . . Since their original publication in the 1930s there have been three editions in book form in 1950, 1960 and 1969 and, subsequently, a series of re-editions during the 1970s, a fact which is testimony to their continuing popularity and relevance. Arlt wrote them from day to day in an haphazard fashion but later editions have sought to impose some order by re-classifying them into, for example, articles on women, *porteño* types, the social crisis. This zeal for order was never very apparent in their author, who worked as the inspiration moved him, now prompted by some picturesque *lunfardismo*, as in "Divertido origen de la palabra 'squenum' ", or some colloquialism as in "Apuntes filosóficos acerca del 'hombre que se tira a muerto' ", now pinning down a whole social class by an apparently insignificant detail. To classify the *Aguafuertes* is to detract from their spontaneity. A number of articles collected together on the theme, say, of *porteña* womanhood and their charms and vices is to assume a continuity of thought that Arlt never enjoyed. Whilst we have chosen to classify his ideas, perhaps arbitrarily at times, it seems inadvisable to impose such a strait-jacket on these delightful cameos of Buenos Aires life. An important feature is their use of *lunfardo*, an important component of his style. It is fair to conclude that, whilst his call in his political ideas is to individual rebellion, in the *Aguafuertes* his linguistic technique relies largely for its appeal on class solidarity, often summed up in one or two typical *lunfardo* terms which act as "in-group" indicators. . . . In the novels, man and his environment are at odds and the anguish of one and the other interpenetrates. In the *Aguafuertes*, the city and its dwellers are at one, in harmony. Not that life is ever depicted as easy; the time is 1930 and the depression is upon us. But the bitterness of the fictional works is absent here, a gentle irony replacing the spleen. (pp. 77–80)

Figures from the novels appear here and there, like the prospective *suegra* who dispatches the younger son to keep an eye on the doings of her daughter and the *novio;* the child must be bought off by frequent greasing of the palm. But normally the gallery of *porteño* types exists in its own right, like the *curanderas* who are "unas furbas de más de treinta años. Gastan lutos y en la garganta una cinta de terciopelo negro, que agrisa el polvo de arroz y la natural grasitud de sus pescuezos de gallina". Arlt had a Quevedo-like eye for the detail with which to transfix a whole character and, as with Quevedo, realism often spills over into the grotesque. Perhaps this was essential to his success. . . . [The] Turkish carpet-seller, the woman who overspends on the *quiniela*, the bachelor, the liar, the persistent malingerer, the peeping Tom who spies into houses from his flat roof, and a hundred others, are all the subject of well-aimed but indulgent censure. The only figure for whom there is no compassion, as in the novels, is the bourgeois. Arlt's bitterness is consistently turned against the small property owner and shopkeeper in his fiction, as we have seen, because in their greed they have "taken their eyes off the stars". But in the *Aguafuertes* the loathing is muted. Nowhere does one find the nauseous reaction of Erdosain against "los tenderos que desde el fondo de sus covachas escupían a la oblicuidad de la lluvia". His gall is now tempered by understanding, as in his depiction of the café owner who is torn between saving eighty pesos a month by having his comely wife attend to the phonograph and his jeal-

ousy at the avid eyes cast over her anatomy by his clients. In all these cases, Arlt's regard for his fellow-man, even in the most ridiculous plight as with the café owner, is paramount and assuages the rancour that invests the fictional works. The *Aguafuertes*—human, subjective and ironic—are an equally valid attempt to come to terms with the realities of the great city as are the novels. They display a compassionate facet of their author's temperament that the novels would never suggest. These qualities are acutely seen in "Atenti, nena, que el tiempo pasa", in which Arlt takes the *carpe diem* theme and makes it his own, couching it in thoroughly *porteño* terms. The irony and grotesque exaggeration would not be out of place in Quevedo. Arlt has seen a young woman on the tram playing haughty to her unprepossessing boyfriend. His hatred of sham and conceit leads to a piece of compelling popular philosophy. . . . This amalgam of gentle censure and compassionate observation, allied to the deft handling of *lunfardo* and other slang terms, reveals a very different Arlt from that of the fictional works. Where the novels and the *Aguafuertes* find common ground is in their moral stand against all who satisfy their own desires at the expense of others, those who damage illusions and destroy the gentleness of life. For, in spite of his caustic remarks and hatred of so much that society had created around him in an implacable city, his was a gentle and receptive soul. As one of his characters says: "Yo te amo, vida, a pesar de todo lo que te afearon los hombres". (pp. 80–2)

Jack M. Flint, in his *The Prose Works of Roberto Arlt: A Thematic Approach*, University of Durham, 1985, 93 p.

NAOMI LINDSTROM

(essay date 1985)

[Lindstrom is an American critic who has written extensively on Latin American literature and has translated Arlt's *The Seven Madmen* into English. Below, she examines both the ways in which male characters define the identities of women and the development of Hipólita's sense of self-determination in *The Seven Madmen* and *Los lanzallamas*.]

This paper looks at how one author, the Argentine, Roberto Arlt, makes society's mythification of woman one element of his fictional representation. It should be emphasized that I am not accusing Arlt of falsely mythifying woman. On the contrary, Arlt invokes the mythification process precisely in order to expose and to reveal its mechanisms and thus deconstruct it. This exposition is effected through the creation of a female character, Hipólita, who appears in Arlt's novel *Los siete locos* [1929; hereafter abbreviated *SL*] and its sequel, *Los lanzallamas* [1931; hereafter abbreviated *L*]. Hipólita is notable for, among other things, her power to provoke men to feats of extravagant mythmaking.

Reading the novels, one receives remarkably little reliable information about the "real" Hipólita, although this fact has not stopped critics from characterizing her in definitive terms. As any reader must immediately note, the novels lack a reliable central narrator. To read, one must continually heed the distortions and falsifications of the unstable Arltian characters. Thus, Hipólita herself is not in the foreground, either as individual or as representative of her sex. What claims attention is the mythic mechanisms by which men seek to make sense of her. Hipólita's femininity is only significant in that it elicits this paradigmatically—and appallingly—human behavior. Arlt is by no means writing feminist literature, but his utilization of Hipólita confirms Beauvoir's statements about woman's treatment.

One sees Hipólita mythified by two different men. The process begins with her husband, the deranged Ergueta. Ergueta succeeds in communicating his mythmaking ardor to Erdosain, the unhappy antihero of the two novels. Between the two men's efforts, Hipólita is re-elaborated into three separate versions of womanhood.

Ergueta's account of Hipólita is the most suspect, for the man is unmistakably insane. When Ergueta first appears, he has met Erdosain in a café in order to give an account of his recent actions. As Erdosain already knows, Ergueta has met a prostitute in his low-life wanderings and subsequently married her. To transform this sordid anecdote Ergueta relies on his private apocalyptic mythology. In his scheme, the seedier milieux of Buenos Aires have become an eschatological backdrop against which he and Hipólita play out a drama of sin and redemption. Through a system of paradoxical relations, Ergueta is both a redemptive prophet and a sharpster. Hipólita is both a virginal creature, a *donna angelica*, and a streetwise whore.

The first part of this conversation goes badly. Ergueta's discourse is clearly a mythic one, but Erdosain persists in attempting to engage him in rational discourse. Erdosain points out that Hipólita cannot be the Lame Whore of the Apocalypse since she is an able-bodied young woman. This literal-mindedness has no effect on Ergueta, who continues to fit experience to myth: "pero ella es la descarriada, y yo el fraudulento, el 'hijo de la perdición' " (but she is the woman gone astray, and I am the deceiver, the "son of perdition") [*SL*]. Particularly baffling to Erdosain is Ergueta's inclusion of very worldly realities in his apocalyptic elaboration. For example, Ergueta is proud of his astuteness in marrying under Uruguayan law, thus rendering divorce possible.

At midpoint in the conversation, Ergueta produces a photograph of Hipólita. This image corresponds to Er-

gueta's exaltation of Hipólita as a divine creature. Overwhelmed by this pseudo-objective documentation, Erdosain abandons his rationalistic approach to the woman. Now he begins to work out his own myth of Hipólita as a pure being. In effect, he accepts Ergueta's account with only one alteration: Ergueta now appears as Hipólita's beastly oppressor. The narrator exposes Erdosain's mental processes: "Pensó en la deliciosa criatura y se la imaginó soportando a este bruto bajo un cielo oscurecido por grandes nubes de polvo e incendiado por un sol amarillo y espantoso. Ella se marchitaría como un helecho transplantado a un pedregal" (He thought of the delicious creature and imagined her suffering under that great brute beneath a sky dark with dustclouds and set ablaze by a dreadful yellow sun. She would wilt like a fern planted into lava rock) (*SL*).

This goddess like image of Hipólita, the "deliciosa criatura" (delicious creature) of "gran sensibilidad" (deep sensitivity) is short-lived. It is shattered when the "real" Hipólita shows up on Erdosain's doorstep, seeking aid. The man immediately notes features incompatible with Hipólita's supposed ethereality: her freckles, her red hair, her sharp features, her seeming unconcern over her husband's descent into madness. Consequently, Erdosain spends the first part of their encounter questioning the woman about key elements in her *donna angelica* myth. In Ergueta's elaboration, one proof of Hipólita's spiritual purity is her history of self-abnegating and charitable acts. Now Hipólita denies this history: "pero, ¿así que a usted le dijo que yo había regalado mi collar a una sirvienta?. . . ¡Qué hombre!" (but, so he told you I gave my necklace to a servant? That man!) (*SL*)

In response to the new situation, Erdosain remolds his perception of Hipólita. He now perceives her following a pattern [Kate] Millett discusses [in *Sexual Politics*] as the "vagina dentata." Whereas before Hipólita's gaze seemed otherworldly and spiritual, it now appears as a "malévola mirada verdosa" (malevolent green gaze) attacking Erdosain with "haces de mirada" (a host of bolts streaming from her eyes) (*SL*). Hipólita's thin facial features before signaled refinement and delicacy; in the new version, they are harsh and sharp. After reorganizing his perceptions of the woman, Erdosain concludes that she must be "fría. . . una mujer perversa" (cold. . . a perverse woman) (*SL*). In a complete inversion, Hipólita has moved from being the pure and vulnerable girl to the callous predator.

This highly unfavorable mythic treatment is not Erdosain's final version of Hipólita. Another alteration begins to take place when the man notices the woman's fatigue. This small sign is an indication for Erdosain to incorporate Hipólita into another of his mental categories, the world's "insulted and injured." He begins to imagine a pathetic scenario for her: "[Hipólita] lo miraba con fijeza, pero la dureza de lineas que estaba rígida bajo la epidermis de su semblante como una armadura de voluntad se descompus de fatiga. Con la cabeza inclinada a un costado, a Erdosain le recordó a su esposa. . . quizá fuera a parar en un hotel de muros sucios, y entones, apiadado, dijo:—Discúlpeme" ([Hipólita] stared at him steadily, but the hardness of the lines held taut under the skin of her face like an armor of will broken down under the strain. With her head tilted to one side, she reminded Erdosain of his wife. . . maybe she'd end up in a hotel with dirty walls, and then, seized with pity, he said, "I'm sorry") (*SL*).

When Erdosain has fully integrated Hipólita into his mythic race of suffering souls, he engages her in a rather bathetic ceremony in which they confess their respective histories of personal humiliations and degradations. Erdosain is moved to tears by this ritual and declares the couple profoundly united as two of life's losers. Willing to accord Hipólita favorable treatment, he once more perceives her gaze as attractive, emanating "un calor súbito" (a sudden warmth) (*SL*). Exhausted by his efforts to remold the woman's image, he drifts into a state of half-sleep.

As Erdosain falls silent, the reader becomes privy to the woman's thoughts on the recent events. "These reflections show exactly how unproductive and false Erdosain's mythmaking has been. The man has assumed that the woman would be pleased to figure as one of the world's noble underdogs. In fact, Hipólita rejects this image of herself and the maudlin scheme that supports it. She sees Erdosain as "un débil y un sentimental" (weak and sentimental) (*SL*). Moreover, she knows that he cannot establish an adequate relation with her, but will always remain dependent and irresponsible, substituting sentimentality for much-needed "empuje"(drive) (*SL*).

Erdosain's relations with Hipólita largely repeat Ergueta's failure. Both men exhibit a lack of interest in knowing the woman as an existent human being, capable of reacting, choosing, and changing. Rather, they seek to impose upon her a fixed pattern that will satisfy their private world schemes. Hipólita offers herself as the *materia prima* of men's private myths because she finds financial benefit in this practice. However, the procedure is unsatisfactory to all concerned. Hipólita can please Ergueta by playing along with his apocalyptic myth, yet his obsessions destroy him and he ends up reviling her. Erdosain makes a fool of himself in front of her and nearly kills her later. Hipólita, meanwhile, feels a growing revulsion for men: "Todos son así. . . . Los débiles, inteligentes e inútiles; los otros, brutos y aburridos" (That's how they all are. . . . The weak ones, intelligent and useless; the rest, a lot of boring animals) (*SL*).

Given Hipólita's history of failures, one takes special note when a new man succeeds in his relations with her. This individual is the Astrologer, an enigmatic revolutionary. His ability to reach the alienated young woman helps reveal Ergueta's and Erdosain's inadequacy.

Immediately upon meeting Hipólita, the Astrologer submits her to a bizarre process of testing and evaluation. Among other things, he refuses to admit her to his house, conducting their initial interview on the lawn. There, he bombards her with a curious and trying set of utterances. Miscellaneous hostile remarks, impertinent questions, and reflections on the human condition force Hipólita to react to the man.

While Hipólita's initial response is one of disorientation, she soon enters into the Astrologer's type of irrational discourse. She begins to reveal some of her most disturbing experiences "sin poder explicarse el porque" (for reasons she couldn't figure out) (*L*). This spontaneity is a departure from Hipólita's previous habit of calculating her remarks to fit the man's fantasies.

Eventually, the Astrologer is satisfied with Hipólita's potentialities as revealed by her behavior under his peculiar interrogation. Subsequently, she becomes a member of his inner circle and the person he most confides in. When disastrous events overtake the Astrologer's band of revolutionaries, Hipólita is the one he chooses to take with him into underground exile.

The relation between the Astrologer and Hipólita is no idealization of the man-woman bond, for many reasons. Both partners remain engaged in trickery, criminal activities, and manipulation of others, yet the Astrologer does keep in mind that woman is a being who can make decisions and alter herself willfully. One might describe his intervention by saying that he lends support to Hipólita's labors to work out her own myth, a system that can give direction to her vital energies and provide existential satisfactions. In this sense, the Astrologer meets Beauvoir's requirement that, just as "man is defined as a being who is not fixed, who makes himself what he is," woman must receive the same treatment. He forces Hipólita to confront her past actions and to start seeing herself as a unique being, not just the malleable stuff of men's mythmaking. At the least, one can say that he allows her to glimpse what she is capable of becoming:"a human being in quest of values in a world of values."

As Hipólita ceases to be the object of mythmaking and learns to collaborate in the creation of an archetype, what must change in her behavior and in that of the men around her? [Simone de] Beauvoir, can suggest an answer. The *Second Sex* contains a strong implicit statement that discourse, verbal behavior, is the realm in which woman wins or loses her "authenticity." Although Beauvoir does not claim to be working in the area of discourse analysis, she frequently carries out just such investigation. She scrutinizes a large corpus of female utterances and writings, including remarks made in casual conversation as well as on more formal occasions, private diaries and letters, confessions, and testimonial statements. She also examines men's habits in speaking with or writing to women as well as the fictional representations of female or female-male discourse situations. Her purpose in bringing together and analyzing this mass of examples is twofold: (a) to see how women gain, or lose, the ability to formalize their life experience in words, even if those words are only addressed to a diary or an intimate confidant; and (b) to examine women's ability to "make their voices heard," to participate efficaciously in verbal exchanges.

When the reader first learns about Hipólita, the woman has been entirely "robbed" of her own discourse. This figurative theft occurs as her mad husband, Ergueta, insists on forcing her to fit a preexisting text, the Book of Revelation. If Hipólita is to be "her own woman," then the discourse that defines her must be the speech she herself produces; but that discourse has been entirely displaced by the words of St. John and Ergueta.

Gostautas has pointed out the most important device operant in this displacement. To use Gostautas's example, Ergueta narrates to Erdosain a beatific vision supposedly related to him by Hipólita. What is immediately striking is the lack of correspondence between the woman's story and everything else one learns about her. The visionary tale has manifestly grown out of Ergueta's beliefs and experiences, not his wife's.

The incongruity becomes even more apparent when Ergueta cites his wife "verbatim." These reported utterances stand out for their highly figurative, emotive language—for example, "Entraré en tu case desnuda" (I will enter your house naked) (*SL*). Such expression is identical to Ergueta's more lyrical flights of speech, based on a scriptural paradigm, but bears no resemblance to the remarks made by Hipólita.

Perhaps most curiously of all, the madman reports verbal actions Hipólita has allegedly used to disrupt conventional situations. For example, he claims that she declared herself a prostitute in front of her ultrarespectable in-laws and that she rejected worldly wealth in front of her demimondaine associates. The use of inappropriate speech acts to disturb and disorient is very much a characteristic of Ergueta, but one does not see Hipólita perform such disorderly actions.

A systematic pattern governs Ergueta's crazed insistence on "misquoting" his wife. The madman has devised an entire set of verbal practices that he considers suited to the Whore of the Apocalypse, a corrupt-virginal creature living in the last days of sinful man. Whatever the real, noneschatological Hipólita may have said is entirely accidental and can safely be discarded as insignificant. This substitution of invented discourse for a woman's real remarks is a crude myth-creating device, but an extremely powerful one. Confronted with the evidence of its falsity, Erdosain can only wonder at the hold it exercised upon him:" Yo le creía en estas circunstancias" (I believed him when I was there) (*SL*). Ergueta's very persuasiveness suggests that he is only carrying to a deranged extreme a pattern already present in male-female verbal interactions.

Erdosain is considerably saner than his Bible-reading friend. Therefore, his practices more closely approximate those of "normal" speakers. Such a move toward relative sanity is noticeable in his early exchanges with Hipólita. He confronts the woman with the image of her discourse that Ergueta supplied; she rejects this image as alien and unrecognizable, unrelated to anything she ever said or might say. The two agree that Ergueta's distortion of his wife's speech is simply a sign of his madness. Neither seems to note the organized, purposeful character of this eccentric behavior.

Erdosain may dismiss Ergueta's outlandish procedures as lying and madness, but he, too is eager to supply Hipólita with a discourse suited to his mythic image. Their first encounter goes badly because the woman unwittingly violates the man's notions of how she should speak. Erdosain finds profoundly disturbing those aspects of Hipólita's language he deems" impestivo y prostibulario" (rough bordello talk) or "canalla" (gutter language) (*SL*, p. 158). He can only accept her as the long-suffering, great-spirited female, the *donna angelica* who loves and shelters men even at the cost of great personal suffering. He cannot allow such a creature to coarsely address him as "m' hijito" (kid) or to employ such a vulgar proverb as "Paciencia, mala suerte" (That's the way the cookie crumbles) (*SL*).

During this exchange, Erdosain gives Hipólita clues to indicate how she should express herself. He complains that her words sound too cold and unfeeling: "me habla de tode este drama con una tranquilidad que asombra" (you're telling me this whole drama so coolly it's unnerving) (*SL*). When she still fails to speak as the emotive, sweet woman he has in mind, he prompts her with less and less subtlety: "dígame. . . ¿sufrió mucho al lado de él?" (tell me. . . did you suffer much with him?) (*SL*). Hipólita's unresponsiveness to this prompting disgusts Erdosain so deeply he is driven from her presence.

However, the next interaction between Erdosain and Hipólita proceeds much more smoothly because the man has replaced the real Hipólita with an imaginary simulacrum of her, an "interlocutora hipotética" (imaginary conversation partner) (*SL*). Unlike the original, the fantasized Hipólita satisfies Erdosain. Now he enjoys Ergueta's privilege: he can control both what he says and what his female companion "says." This conversation in fantasy restores the completeness of Hipólita's "sweet creature" myth, which was severely damaged by the woman's autonomous verbal behavior.

Erdosain eventually attempts to reestablish contact with the real Hipólita. During this interchange, Hipólita is much more able to supply the man with the type of speech he demands of her. After her initial clumsiness, she appears to have mastered the key elements of this expression: she must speak a great deal about suffering, both hers and his; she must express abundant, even maudlin, compassion for the wretched; she must continually sweeten and soften her discourse.

Now Hipólita, who formerly insisted upon a stoical attitude encourages the man to pour out his tribulations to her: "¿Por qué está triste?" (Why are you sad?) (*SL*). Formerly, she had distressed Erdosain by the tart, cynical tenor of her remarks. Now she tells him that he must never commit suicide because "Eso está en manos de Dios" (That's in God's hands) (*SL*). Erdosain responds with warm enthusiasm to this sentimentalized mode, encouraging Hipólita to tell him the story of her misfortunes. Here, he pushes her toward bathetic expression through small clues and promptings. When her story strikes him as too detached and neutral, he reminds her, "Debe ser triste" (It must have been sad); Hipólita, willing to follow these signals, responds, "Sí, es muy triste ver felices a los otros y ver que los otros no comprenden que una será desdichada para toda la vida" (Yes, it's very sad to see other people happy and see how other people don't understand that you're going to be unhappy your whole life long) (*SL*). In this way, she produces an account of her life virtually to order. The reader will find this impromptu autobiography mawkish and improbable-sounding, but for its intended consumer it is a source of enormous listening pleasure. "Cuente, la deliciosa criatura" (Tell me, delicious creature), he says, rewarding her with immoderate praise for her absurd and disjointed narrative efforts.

Arlt's text indicates the inauthenticity of such speech through both Hipólita's disgust as soon as she is able to disengage herself from the encounter, and the fact that Erdosain elicits from Hipólita a verbal response largely identical to the one he earlier had obtained from his wife, Elsa. Since the two women are otherwise quite unlike, this last circumstance is especially striking.

To look at this parallelism, one may turn briefly away from the consideration of Hipólita and toward an examination of Erdosain's most important exchange with Elsa. Here, Erdosain has cause to be offended, for his wife is leaving him in the midst of his misfortunes; moreover, she is accompanied by a man who appears to be her lover. Elsa manages to distract her husband from these unhappy facts by allowing him to engage her in a melodramatic conversation about suffering. First, she impresses upon him the personal sacrifices she has made as his wife. Apart from her obvious argument that the man has been "a poor provider," Elsa is using a calculated strategy. She knows that Erdosain is unable to resist his own myth of the wretched, self-abnegating female.

The sentimental element in their talk grows stronger until Erdosain and Elsa finally move into a totally bathetic exchange. A sample of this dialogue shows the extreme point of Erdosain's "heart-wrenching" male-female discourse :

—Mirá. . . esperame. Si la vida es como siempre me dijiste, yo vuelvo, ¿sabés?, y entonces, si vos querés nos matamos juntos. . . ¿Estás contento?

Una ola de sangre subió hasta las sion es del hombre.

—Alma, que buena sos, alma. . . dame esta mano— y mientras ella, aún sobrecogida, sonreía con timoez, Erdosain se la besó—. ¿No te enojás, alma?

Ella enderezó la cabeza grave de dicha.

—Mirá Reme. . . yo voy a venir, ¿sabés?, y si es cierto lo que decís de la vida. . . sí, yo vengo. . . voy a venir.

—¿Vas a venir?

—Con todo lo que tenga.

—¿Aunque seas rica?

—¿Aunque tenga todos los millones de la tierra, vengo. ¡Te lo juro!

—¡Alma, pobre alma! ¡Qué alma la tuya! Sin embargo, vos no me conociste. . . no importa. . . ¡ah, nuestra vida! (*SL*)

("Look, wait for me. If life is the way you always told me, I'll come back, see?, and then, if you want, we'll kill ourselves together. . . Are you happy?"

A wave of blood suffused his whole face in warmth.

"Dearest, how good you are, you sweet soul. . . Give me your hand," and she, though startled, smiled shyly. Erdosain kissed it. "You're not mad at me, darling?"

She raised her head, somber with happiness.

"Look Remo. . . I'm going to come, see?, and if it's true what you say about life. . . yes, I'll come. . . I'm coming back."

"You'll come? "

"With everything I've got."

"Even if you're rich?"

"Even if I have all the millions in the world, I'll come. I swear!"

"Poor, dear, sweet soul! What a soul you have! But still, you never knew me. . . it doesn't matter. . . ah, our lives!")

This ridiculous verbal performance, which continues far beyond the transcribed fragment, shows Elsa soothing her husband with an abundant supply of the talk he craves. It is certainly not the speech of a " human being in quest of values," as Beauvoir would say, but of a woman seeking to conform to a myth of woman.

The end of these oppressive patterns comes when Hipólita meets the Astrologer. This significant encounter occurs as the first episode of *Los lanzallamas*, the second book of the Erdosain story. This segment is entitled "El hombre neutro" (The Neuter Man); the obvious reference is to the Astrologer's castrated condition, revealed in the course of the exchange. However, one must note that the Astrologer is also neuter and neutral in much of his verbal behavior toward Hipólita. With his extraordinary insight into human nature, he correctly guesses the essential fact of the Erdosain-Hipólita encounter: an impulsive man has imprudently poured out too much of his story to a designing woman. The present intention of Hipólita is, clearly, to practice her Delilah-like wiles on the Astrologer. The latter, however, is already on his guard; he refuses to react to Hipólita and subjects her behavior and remarks to careful scrutiny. In a very short time he has accurately diagnosed her new strategy: "El Astrólogo sin mostrarse sorprendido la miró tranquilamente. Soliloquió: 'Quiere hacerse la cínica y la desenvuelta para dominar' " (The Astrologer, showing no surprise, looked at her coolly. He mused to himself: "She wants to come across the tough dame to get the upper hand") (*L*).

The first counterstrategy of the Astrologer is simply to break with the major conventions governing conversation. For some time, he refuses to show any reaction to Hipólita or to respond to her "tough" remarks. The woman becomes increasingly flustered, speaking more and more pointless words in a futile attempt to display self-possession. When the man does speak, a further rupture with norms occurs. Though her identity is perfectly evident to him, he subjects her to redundant inquiries about it. All this anomalous behavior finally succeeds in causing the woman to abandon her conversational role of "tough cookie":

—¿Así que usted es amiga de Erdosain?
—Va la tercera vez que me lo pregunta. Sí, soy amiga de Erdosain. . . pero, ¡Dios mío!, qué hombre desatento es usted. Hace tres horas que estoy parada hablando y todavía no me ha dicho: "Pase, ésta es su casa. . . " (*L*).

("So you're Erdosain's friend?"

"This is the third time already you've asked me. Yes, I'm Erdosain's friend. . . but, my God, what a rude man you are! Here I've been standing for three hours talking and you still haven't said to me, 'Come in, make yourself at home'.")

Hipólita's disconcerted state allows the Astrologer to speak to her more freely. He further breaks down her defenses by telling her he considers her "una charlatana" (a bluffer) (*L*) and by making sport of her plan to blackmail him.

The conversation now enters a second phase in which the Astrologer actually seeks to communicate with Hipólita. Here, too, he is exceptionally cautious not to allow her to slip back into her old discourse habits. The woman is accustomed to listen to men's talk for signs of personal involvement, which she can then use in devising a response. She habitually responds as a woman to a man. The Astrologer frustates this practice by keeping her discourse severely impersonal and abstract, almost like a lecture addressed to an anonymous public. The woman has no idea how to deal with such dehumanized expression of ideas and information: "Hipólita asintió, presa de malestar. Todo aquello era innegable, pero ¿con qué objeto le comunicaba tales verdades?" (Hipólita agreed, full of misgivings. All that was undeniably true, but what was he doing telling her all this true stuff?) (*L*).

The barrage of cold, general talk is a test to which the Astrologer is subjecting Hipólita. Now she must re-

spond without recourse to her "female wiles," with no fixed mythic pattern to guide her. The Astrologer places the burden of the conversation on her by demanding abruptly that she show she has been following the ideas he has been setting forth.

Given the novelty of this task, Hipólita performs well. Her impromptu speech brings together abstract meditations, reminiscences, and reflections on her experiences. The narrator reports not only Hipólita's words but also the reactions of the Astrologer. In every case, the man is pleased with the freshness and vividness of the woman's expression. "El Astrólogo asienta con la cabeza, sonriendo de la precisión con que la muchacha roja evoca la llanura habitada por hombres codiciosos" (The Astrologer nods his head yes, smiling at the accuracy with which the red-headed girl evokes the plains inhabited by greedy men) (*L*). While his response to her attempts to "decipher" and exploit him was an impassive coldness, he greets her efforts toward independent expression with enthusiastic smiles and verbal encouragement.

The myth of woman has been an implicit issue throughout the dialogue: first, because of the Astrologer's refusal to let Hipólita speak as a myth; and second, because of Hipólita's remarks concerning the role of woman in society. Only toward the end of the interchange does the issue of the mythification of woman in society become an explicit topic.

At this juncture, the Astrologer must meet the challenge of describing woman's mystical-magic potential without reverting to the old, confining patterns. He does so by couching his thoughts in an "open" language, a mythical-sounding, highly ambiguous language that invites multiple interpretations and amplifications. For example, when Hipólita asks him to justify his belief in woman by giving a reason, he replies, "Porque ella es principio y fin de la verdad" (Because she is the beginning and the end of truth) (*L*).

This "open" discourse is, in a certain sense, an answer to Beauvoir's complaint. Beauvoir denounces the discussion of woman when it relies on the concept of myth and on a mythic mode of expression. Her point is that myth has traditionally been used to constrain woman to a limited number of fixed roles and images. The authors she examines speak of woman in such a way as to cut off some of her possibilities—most notably, the possibility of full autonomy. The Astrologer's mystical speech emphasizes the diversity of individual women, their need to choose their own existential paths. He is certain that such authenticity can occur within a mythic conception of womanhood.

Hipólita, who serves as questioner and examiner, offers an argument impressively similar to Beauvoir's. She points out how little benefit women have enjoyed from the cosmic lifeforce that mythifiers attribute to them "hasta ahora no han hecho más que tener hijos" (up till now all they've done is have children). The Astrologer insist that his dynamic, utopian vision of woman contains a fundamental difference: "Deje que [las mujeres] empiecen a despertar. A ses individualidades" (Let [women] begin to awaken. To be individual beings) (*L*).

During this exchange, Hipólita displays unaccustomed and surprisingly vivid speech. Yet, she is still under the guidence of a male sponsor, even if that male sponsor insists on her individuality. It still remains for Hipólita to speak on her own. This is the particular importance of the woman's lengthy interior monologue and soliloquy, transcribed in the chapter "Hipólita sola" (Hipólita Alone) (*L*). The narration here relies on varying techniques for rendering the changes in the woman's consciousness resulting from her conversation with the Astrologer. Direct and indirect interior monologues give the reader access to a process of self-definition in its earliest stages. Hipólita, though chaotic in her organization, comes closer and closer to affirming her right to self-determination. When her thoughts on this subject are most fully formalized, she literally gives voice to them in an assertive statement of her need for individualistic fulfillment and choice.

The fact that Hipólita has no audience for her personal declaration of independence does not indicate the defeat of communication. Rather, it shows that she can now speak without relying on the cues provided her by a male interlocutor to whose needs she must cater. The lengthy interior monologue and soliloquy constitute Hipólita's last significant appearance in the work—significantly so, for her story here reaches a point of closure. By assuming "her own voice," by effectively articulating her need for choice, the former prostitute also pronounces an end to her old, myth-governed discourse and a beginning to the elaboration of a new mythic self. (pp. 152–66)

Naomi Lindstrom, "Arlt's Exposition of the Myth of Woman," in *Woman as Myth and Metaphor in Latin American Literature*, edited by Carmelo Virgillo and Naomi Lindstrom, University of Missouri Press, 1985, pp. 151–66.

DAVID P. RUSSI

(essay date 1990)

[In the following excerpt, Russi discusses Arlt's plays *Trescientos millones*, *Saverio el cruel*, and *El fabricante de fantasmas* as examples of metatheatre, which Lionel Abel characterized as "theatre pieces about *life seen as already theatricalized*. By this I mean that the persons appearing on stage in these plays are there. . . *because they themselves knew they were dramatic before the playwright took note of*

them. What dramatized them originally? *Myth, legends, past literature, they themselves.*"]

The interplay of two levels of reality in Roberto Arlt's dramatic production has been well studied. Raúl Castagnino [in *El teatro de Roberto Arlt*, 1964] finds that "dualidad de planos, sea sueño o vigilia, realidad o fantasía, donde aquellas tramas se alternan y complican" is one of the characteristic traits of his work. However, this "duality of planes" is also a basic characteristic of theatre itself. While on the one hand we, as readers or spectators, witness the unfolding of events that we know not to be real, we are willing to allow the fictional world to be our reality for a while. Thus viewed, the fiction of drama becomes reality. That the public accept the fictional reality being presented to it was, in traditional theatre, considered the norm. But this view of drama as a reality to be accepted for only a short while has come under serious question, especially in our century, as new theatrical forms were proposed and implemented which rejected the passive role of the audience and attempted to invite the spectator to see theatre for what it really is: fiction, played out on the stage by actors: who may or may not be trying to portray reality.

Brecht and Artaud were, of course, the main expositors of the practical and theoretical basis on which such types of theatre have been developed, along the lines of the epic and the absurd, both of which have had a great deal of impact on contemporary stage production. These are, however, global views of theatre and they are deeply bound with an ideology or philosophy of man that conditions, or should condition, in their opinion, the very essence of all theatre. And we must keep in mind that Arlt lived before these forms of theatre came to exert their full influence on dramatic production. What we do know, as James Troiano has shown [in "Pirandellism in the Theatre of Roberto Arlt," *Latin American Theatre Review* 8.1 (1974)], is that "there are obvious direct influences in Arlt's plays" of Pirandello's theatre, and that they are such that rather than merely reproduce the Italian's themes and techniques, these "are transformed and thus integrated into Arlt's own bizarre literary style and *Weltanschauung*." Arlt himself denied this influence on his theatre, but the very fact that he himself was not willing or able to see it points to the originality with which he adapted it, created it, creating a form strictly his own.

Arlt's theatre will not let itself be bound by the limits of a simple category. While not necessarily falling into any one particular current, his theatre shares individual traits with several theatrical tendencies and also stands apart in a unique and unmistakable way with respect to its audience, a theatre that is both aware of its own theatricality and of the existence of the duality inherent in its expression. Lionel Abel states [in *Metatheatre: A New Voice of Artistic Form*, 1963] that "only certain plays tell us at once that the happenings and characters are of the playwright's invention," and that to this type of theatre belongs a "whole range of plays" which still enjoy a commonality:

> All of them are theatre pieces about *life seen as already theatricalized.* By this I mean that the persons appearing on stage in these plays are there. . . *because they themselves knew they were dramatic before the playwright took note of them.* What dramatized them originally? *Myth, legend, past literature, they themselves.* They represent to the playwright the effect of dramatic imagination before he has begun to exercise his own. . . . they are aware of their own theatricality.

Elaborating on this idea and dealing specifically with the character as a fictional entity, June Schlueter speaks [in *Metafictional Characters in Modern Drama,* 1979] in terms that are particularly appropriate to this study:

> By its very nature, the dramatic character is twofold: it is simultaneously both actor and character. . . . Normally we willingly accept this convention. [But in the plays to be studied here, the playwright] is asking us not to forget the fictive nature of the *dramatis personae,* have instead created a situation which may be more demanding intellectually and confusing emotionally, but which ultimately is truer to the conception of drama than the conventional absorption in illusion. For by insisting that the audience cognitively maintain bifocal vision, the playwright is constantly and overtly sustaining the dialectic which exists between reality and illusion.

Arlt insists on making us maintain this "bifocal vision" alert as we experience the world of his theatre, a world that is the result of the hermeneutical relationship between the conventions of literary fiction past and present, and Arlt and the world that surrounds him. By calling attention to the fictional nature of his characters, Arlt forces us to consider the possibility of fiction in the reality we live. By presenting imaginary characters that are not only aware of their fictional nature, but also examples of characters affected by other fiction who are struggling to interpret various levels of reality, he is also giving us a look at the insidious ways in which we can be affected by literary conventions in everyday life as well as in our dreams.

It will be our purpose here to show how three of Arlt's best known plays *300 millones* (1932), *Saverio el cruel* (1936) and *El fabricante de fantasmas* (1936), develop along the lines of metatheatre to present an ambiguous picture of "reality" subverted by another reality which, while being the product of fiction, of imagination, comes to be just as real, to the character or characters experiencing it, as the reality within which it was created. In so doing, Arlt is trying to address the problem of literary conventions and of their general effect on people as instruments of self-inflicted victimization, and, eventually, to the need for revitalizing Argentinean theatre of his time.

300 millones, Arlt's first play written for the independent theatre of Buenos Aires, offers us a look at a world of fantasy and illusion which is completely constructed of conventions that in themselves have come to constitute a reality while coexisting, though on another plane, with Silvia's reality. As a maid in an upper middle class home, Silvia creates and then lives in a world populated by *fantasmas,* which is the world of her dreams; here she is able to escape and find relief from the other world she exists in, the "real" world, which keeps intruding, disrupting her dream world.

Silvia acts out conventions, and the entire action of the play is made up of them, as one can see by giving a quick synthesis of it: an inheritance of "trescientos millones" makes her instantly rich, fulfilling a commonplace dream she then falls in love with the Galán while on a cruise vacation and gets married. She and the Galán have a baby, but even in the world of dreams things go wrong and the baby is kidnapped by a gypsy, while the Galán is killed in the process; Rocambole, the good guy, vows to find the child. Many years later he does: as Cenicienta she is being abused every way except sexually by the nasty Vulcán, and Rocambole steps in to save her from a fate worse than death just as she is about to be sold off to an old man, who has some obviously lewd plans in store for her. Justice is done and happiness reigns once again. Finally, the daughter, who also has dreams, brings home her own hyperconventional Galancito, whom she plans to marry, and just as Silvia is about to give her blessing, reality intrudes once more in too shocking and grotesque a way to cope with and the only unconventional act of the play takes place: Silvia takes her own life. Her suicide in the real world is a dual expression of rebellion and defense: from the real world she cannot cope with and from the world that she created that is so bound up with the conventions of the fiction of the other as to make it, too, unbearable.

This is a storyline that is completely made up of literary conventions, portrayed here as forming an alternative reality created by a fictional character who, not able to cope with the fictional reality within which she existed, had to escape to another level of existence, a dream world. The dialogue that the *fantasmas* have in the prologue shows both their conventionality and their consciousness of this situation. The Galán that says to Rocambole that "el hombre es esclavo de su sueño. . . es esclavo nuestro" is acknowledging the terrible position of people that are so affected by conventions as to become victimized and enslaved by them, and this is exactly what has happened to Silvia. She is conscious of the fact that she is acting and that the others are as well, and they are just as conscious of this fact as she is. (pp. 65–8)

But in the end she ends up accepting the convention, a convention that both she and the Galán have rejected as ridiculous throughout their conversation.

The observations of the *fantasmas* themselves during the brief moments in which the dream action is interrupted by reality reveal the truly tragic point that Arlt proposes. Not only are men slaves of conventions but "debería prohibírsele soñar a los pobres," because "por falta de cultura" they imagine "los disparates más truculentos." The poor, then, not only live a reality that is unacceptable, but they should not be allowed to dream because they do not know how. They are the ones that are most affected by what they read in order to escape, and that is what they draw upon to fill their dreams. Of course it is absurd that the *fantasmas* who are protagonists of the dream of conventions that Silvia has been making come to life should complain about her "disparates más truculentos," especially when one considers that "la autora es ella." But it is precisely with this absurd play between the two levels that Arlt is making his audience aware of the point he wishes to make, and he is able to do it by creating characters that, by reminding us constantly of their fictional nature within the action, force us to look at the issue more clearly.

In the words of Patricia Waugh, "in showing us how literary fiction creates its imaginary worlds, metafiction helps us to understand how the reality we live day by day is similarly constructed, similarly 'written'." Arlt is able to do this and to achieve great dramatic effect and tension in *300 millones* while doing it. In *Saverio el cruel,* which has been regarded as Arlt's best play, the playwright was able to heighten the dramatic tension produced by the dialectic relationship of reality and fantasy and to surprise his audience completely by presenting us with a performance within the performance. Susana has convinced some friends to play a trick on Saverio, a local butter distributor, making him think that she has gone mad and that the only cure would be to destroy the evil colonel that is pursuing her in the world of her madness. Saverio, convinced in his simplicity, agrees to take on the role of the colonel, and as he does so he begins not only to create the personality of his character from his own stereotyped view of the general category "colonels," but also to believe in the reality of his role. Unlike *300 millones,* the story limit itself is not constructed with conventions; however, the development of the farce that constitutes the trick against Saverio is, and it is here, in the context of the play within a play, that we see them and their effects.

All the characters are aware of their own theatricality, as they rehearse their roles (Saverio does so in the first three scenes of Act II) and congratulate each other on a performance; the first three scenes of Act III portray the environment backstage just before a performance. In Act I, Pedro, Luisa and Saverio are spectators to Juan and Susana's performance, but at the same time the first two are also characters within the performance, their role being to convince Saverio of the reality of the farce, while all of them are performing the play that Arlt created. This situation of characters that are aware of themselves as characters and of the theatricality of their world points up the

theatricality of life in general. We wear masks, according to Pirandello, and do we ever know when the mask is off? Arlt is, in this play, making us aware of this kind of problematic, forcing us to consider just how much of life is actually role play, theatre nested in the performance of life.

And just how much is life affected by certain types of conventions, especially those we get in our literature? This is a question that Arlt also deals with here, as he did in *300 millones.* The characterization and plot in the farce that is created in order to trick Saverio is really a composite of literary conventions of the past. Susana says that she is a "fugitivea de la injusticia del colonel desaforado," but characterizes her role as "semejante a la protagonista de la tragedia clásica," while at the same time she sets up an environment and uses a language the similarity of which to that of the opening scene of *La vida es sueño* by Calderón de la Barca is rather easy to see, and her statement that "parece un sueño todo lo que sucede" makes this all the more obvious. Juan, who is characterized by Susana as a shepherd, brings in elements of pastoral literature, but when she realizes that he "deja mucho que desear como pastor" she sees him for a moment as a Tarzan. She is, she tells Juan, Queen Bragatiana, "fugitiva a la revolución organizada por un coronel faccioso," and here the literary convention is mixed up with something of the everyday reality of the contemporary world. All this is the product of Susana's imagination which, conditioned by her readings, has been improvising a story line. She, or rather her "ingenio," is the source of the idea and thus is the author, while she is also the actress of the farce which, rather than trick Saverio, will lead to her own derangement.

Although we do not ever really suspect Susana of being insane, we are given subtle clues throughout her appearances in the play, which are limited to the first and the last act, that Susana is really not sure as to which world is real. (pp. 68–70)

These clues are subtle, woven in the dialogue so that we do not really see them because we are not able to distinguish well to what point Susana has taken on her role. Meanwhile, Saverio has been convinced to play the part of the colonel and he dives into his role with an enthusiasm that betrays his need to create a more meaningful world for himself. Such is his enthusiasm that we are led to believe that it is he who is losing touch with reality. Act II begins with the ludicrous rehearsal of his role as a colonel, a role that he is rehearsing according to the context of his own time, within which it more properly exists, thereby pointing out some rather hard realities of contemporary world, such as the fact that "se toma el poder por quince días y se queda uno veinte años." His dream of a weapons salesman who, masked, offers him the latest in weapons technology, contrasts with his decision to buy a guillotine. Though as a colonel he thinks in contemporary terms, Saverio is influenced by conventions of other times, and thus has to have a throne. Here, again, we see various levels of influence of literature on the imagination that, when coupled with reality, produce an incongruous picture. (pp. 70–1)

La "burla cruel," as Juan categorizes it, is carried out to the end, but Saverio, who has been told of the trick that was being played on him, confronts Susana with reality, a reality that has shattered his dream. And it is only now that we see that Susana is the one who is really trapped in her world of fantasy and cannot escape. And we know, because we have been told by Pedro, what has caused Susana's derangement, "probablemente. . . exceso de lecturas. . . una gran anemia cerebral." Was this not, after all, the cause of Don Quijote's "locura"? But Susana, unlike him, is not able to let go of the world of conventions that her imagination conjured up and, convinced that Saverio is the Colonel, she shoots him. (p. 71)

The surprise that the ending of *Saverio el cruel* has in store for the spectator has a great dramatic effect and it forces him to become aware. Susana's "locura" is, of course, an extreme example of fiction's effect on us, but it does drive home a point: the dry, sterile repetition of conventions which have caused us to formulate a stereotyped idea of the ideal world are just that, dry and sterile; and they can be dangerous as well, because if we build our dreams on them we ourselves become, in effect, expressions of these same conventions which, as we saw in *300 millones,* may not be any better than the reality from which we were trying to escape through them.

In *El fabricante de fantasmas,* which Arlt brought to the public on the professional stage, he maintains his concern with a theatre aware of itself, but the focus is on the creative process and on the relationship between the author, his creation and the public. A playwright, Pedro, is the central character, and at the outset he kills his wife Eloísa by pushing her out of a window. Soon after the murder he begins to write plays which make use of threatre as "un medio de plantearle problemas personales a la humanidad. . . en ese caso, mis problemas," projecting unpleasant aspects of reality onto his stage production. His first play so closely resembles the circumstances of the crime he has committed as to prompt a visit from the judge who had reviewed his case after Eloísa's death. As he continues to write, Pedro develops a series of grotesque characters for his dramatic production, fictional representations of the vision of reality he wishes to bring to the public. But his reality is Arlt's fiction, and in it the dividing line between fantasy and everyday existence, as we have seen already, is not at all clear-cut: Pedro's creations come to life, transcend their fictional existence to the point of invading the "real" world.

As in other plays we have examined, there is a purposeful effort on the part of some of the characters to stress their fictional nature and make it evident to the reader or spectator. Most notably, when Pedro tells Martina " *(Con intimidad)* Aunque no lo crea, soy un personaje verídicamente teatral," he is not only pointing out

his fictional nature on the stage, but he is also implying a fictional level of existence within the mark of reality that constitutes his world, the expression of the roleplay that is part of life. However, Pedro is not able to recognize the same situation, that of fiction acquiring a place within "reality," as regards his own fictional creations.

The fact that a Criado introduces the *fantasmas* to the scene in Act II contributes to breaking down the separation between reality and dreamworld, bringing the two levels together and allowing these creations of Pedro's imagination to claim their own existence: "Duda de nuestra legitimidad después de fabricarnos." They carry their complaint even further, telling Pedro that he has not shaped them as he should have. . . . (pp. 71–2)

The relative nature of what is "real" pervades this play. Even the *fantasmas* have a life of their own that refuses to be obliterated by the fiction of representation. They, his *hijos,* assert it by coming back to Pedro, their "creator," who finds himself haunted by them to the point of being driven to suicide: he is victimized, justly, by his own fiction become real. The audience is forced to become aware precisely of the status of the *fantasmas* as fictional characters who could just as easily be taking on another role, and also to see that fiction can not only affect reality, but became an active and dangerous part of it. Further, by showing fiction that so consistently affects even its own author, Arlt is causing the public to consider the effect of fiction on itself and its own reality.

Arlt has not forgotten about literary conventions in this play, and we see them specifically in the sixth scene of Act I, where Pedro has a Substituto of himself and the shade of Marina rehearse a scene which he creates, directs and corrects as it is taking place. Much of the dialogue that takes place between them has an openly *folletinesco* flavor, and reminds us of the scene between Silvia and the Galán in *300 millones.* However, Arlt's concern here is more deeply rooted in the *creation* of conventions, and he is addressing those conventions peculiar to established Argentinean theatre, looking at their effects on their "creator" and on the receptor, the audience.

Writing about metafiction, Linda Hutcheon makes a statement which can easily be extended to the metatheatrical mode we are considering; she says that "the point of *meta* fiction is that it constitutes its own first critical comentary." In *El fabricante de fantasmas,* Arlt is providing a critique not only of theatre in general, as he has done in the other plays we have seen, but, more specifically, of Argentinean theatre of his time. Pedro, the author, is shown in his relationship with the public. (pp. 72–3)

[In one long, significant quotation by Pedro, we see expressed] the dilemma of the playwright who cannot know beforehand how to please the public and who has to produce without any possibility whatsoever of certainty as to the ability of his work to entertain an audience. But we also see. . . the pitfall that brings an art form, to a point of stagnation that threatens to kill it: the trite repetition of the "ramilletes de doradas mentiras," conventions, motifs and devices that have worked in the past and which offer the author a measure of security in terms of the public's acceptance of the product. And Pedro is for Arlt precisely the paradigm that shows us how *not* to make theatre, because he does not respect his public: rather than challenging it by presenting new forms in his theatre, he is willing to feed it the same used-up conventions of the past which entertain it but which in fact are causing a stagnation which is ultimately damaging to the art form. (pp. 73–4)

Pedro's attitude leads him to write plays that will attract viewers and be successful by creating a series of extreme *tipos* obviously taken from the lower strata of society which aim to appeal to the test of a middle or upper class drawn to plays that deal with the tragic situation of the poor. Although the theatre that Pedro is shown as producing for his stage is composed of a series of grotesque exaggerated characters (Jorobado, Prostituta, verdugo, Coja, Ciega), we can see a parallel between this and the kind of theatre that had developed in the region of Río de la Plata, which stressed *criollo* and costumbristic elements. The presentation of certain character types, such as the Italian immigrant, for example, continued to be repeated until Argentinean theatre found itself stagnant and in need of rejuvenation.

It was not by accident that Arlt should have found an audience for his critique in the teatro independiente; these characters of costumbristic presentation of life had, by Arlt's time, become completely overused. The commercial overuse of theatrical forms in an effort to compete for survival in a changing society with new media aimed at entertaining the public is evident in this play, which presents a small-scale parody of the growth of Ar-

gentinean theatre in the development of Pedro's dramatic production. It is ironic, and rather sad, that the reaction of the public to this play should have been a reflection of the very criticism that is contained in it, since by rejecting it, the public reacted precisely in the same way as Pedro's public would have: spoon-fed for years, it was unable to appreciate a new form of theatrical expression bold enough to criticize itself.

The three plays we have considered make clear use of metatheatrical techniques to bring the audience to awareness of the state of the medium it is participating in by being spectator to a performance. We have been able to discern a progression in them from laying bare the conventions of fiction and the theatricality of theatre itself in *300 millones* and *Saverio el cruel,* to a direct critique of the state of Argentinean theatre of Arlt's time in *El fabricante de fantasmas.* He first forced the spectator to become conscious of the fact that the influence that fiction exerts on reality can be just as great as that of reality on fiction, if not more. This in turn leads one to consider that fiction, just as reality, can acquire a trite, humdrum characteristic if it is not rejuvenated and changed. This Arlt does in such a way that, while his meaning can be seen as specific to Argentinean theatre, it may also be seen in a more general sense as referring to states anywhere. He is warning us as human beings to be conscious of both the great influence of fictional conventions on our dreams and fantasies, as well as of their danger to the theatre of his time—and ours—when constructed of trite, stagnant conventions which may make it of an empty form of expression. (pp. 74–5)

David P. Russi, "Metatheatre: Roberto Arlt's Vehicle toward the Public's Awareness of an Art Form," in *Latin American Theatre Review*, Vol. 24, No.1, Fall, 1990, pp. 65–75.

SOURCES FOR FURTHER STUDY

Foster, David William. "Roberto Arlt's *La isla desierta:* A Structural Analysis." *Latin American Theatre Review* 11, No. 1 (Fall 1977): 25–34.

> Examines how the structure and language of the play serve to express its principal theme: the instability of reality.

Lindstrom, Naomi Eva. "The World's Illogic in Two Plays by Argentine Expressionists." *Latin American Literary Review* IV, No. 8 (Spring-Summer 1976): 83–8.

> Contends that a thematic affinity exists between Arlt's play *El desierto entra en la ciudad* and German Expressionist drama, both of which demonstrate the failure of reason to serve as a panacea for the ills of humanity.

——. Introduction to *The Seven Madmen,* by Roberto Arlt, translated by Naomi Eva Lindstrom, pp. v–ix. Boston; David R. Godine, 1984.

> Describes the changing critical reception of *The Seven Madmen* and notes the tone of uncertainty that pervades the novel.

Review: Latin American Literature and Arts 31 (January-April 1982): 26–41.

> Section devoted to Arlt which includes the following: a chronology of Arlt's life and works by Lee Dowling; "Arlt: The Maverick" by David William Foster; translated excerpts from "Aguafuertes porteñas"; "Preface to *Los siete locos*" by Juan Carlos Onetti; a translated excerpt

from *The Seven Madmen*; and "Live Language against Dead: Literary Rebels of Buenos Aires" by Naomi Lindstrom.

Troiano, James J. "Pirandellism in the Theatre of Roberto Arlt." *Latin American Theatre Review* 8, No. 1 (Fall 1974): 37–44.
　　Traces the influence of Luigi Pirandello on Arlt's plays.

———. "Literary Traditions in *El fabricante de fantasmas* by Roberto Arlt." *Inti* XXIV–XXV (Fall-Spring 1986–87): 163–72.
　　Traces the literary traditions adapted and parodied by Arlt in his *El fabricante de fantasmas*.

Additional coverage of Arlt's life and career is contained in the following sources published by Gale Research: *Contemporary Authors*, Vol. 123 and *Twentieth-Century Literary Criticism*, Vol. 29.

Juan José Arreola

1918–

Mexican short story writer, novelist, dramatist, and essayist.

INTRODUCTION

*A*rreola was outstanding among the generation of young writers who transformed the Mexican short story in the mid-twentieth century. He wrote satirical and boldly irreverent Modernist works that treat themes of universal consequence, breaking with the Mexican tradition of realistic literature that focuses on native themes and subjects. In his writings Arreola comments on the absurdity of life and attacks hypocrisy, complacency, religiosity, commercialism, and materialism, as well as the possibility of harmony between the sexes. His point of view has been described as existential—emphasizing the emotional isolation of human beings and the irrationality of human existence—and decidedly modern; his friend Seymour Menton has called him "a true man of the twentieth century, an eclectic who at will can draw upon the best of all who have preceded him in order to create truly masterful works of art which in turn will be seized upon by others."

Arreola was the fourth of fourteen children born to a deeply religious family in Zapotlán el Grande (now Ciudad Guzmán), in west central Mexico. As a child he demonstrated an excellent memory and an interest in literature, but he was forced to end his formal schooling at the age of twelve to become a bookbinder's apprentice. He worked a series of jobs in Zapotlán before moving to Mexico City, where he enrolled in the Instituto de Bellas Artes to study acting in 1939. He was also writing during his time in the capital and becoming acquainted with a group of young Mexican writers. He collaborated with Juan Rulfo in the creation of the short-lived literary journal *Pan* in the early forties, and in 1943 published his first nationally recognized story, "Hizo el bien mientras vivió." His acting provided the opportunity to travel to France on a fellowship in 1945, but Arreola's stay in Europe was brief, cut short by symptoms of a nervous disorder. He was back in Mexico City the following year, working in an editorial position at the Fondo de Cultura Económica. Arreola continued his writing during this period, publishing *Varia invención*, a collection of stories, in 1949. The work elicited almost no response from critics, although it was noticed and read in the literary circles of Mexico City. However, his next collection of stories, *Confabulario*, published three years later, inspired generally positive comment. *La hora de todos*, his first play, was performed in 1953 and published the next year, followed by a series of prose sketches called *Punta de plata*, together with illustrations by artist Héctor Xavier, in 1958. This latter work was expanded and renamed *Bestiario* and appeared, along with almost everything else he had previously published, in the *Confabulario total* (*Confabulario and Other Inventions*) of 1962. Arreola wrote his only novel, *La feria* (*The Fair*), in 1963. Eight years later he completed *Palindroma*, which includes his second play, *Tercera llamada ¡tercera! o empesamos sin usted*. Arreola's production of new fiction dropped off after *Palindroma*, as he focused his attention on lecturing and became involved in television.

Although he wrote in a variety of genres, Arreola is best known for his short stories and sketches, which have been praised for their stylistic originality and philosophical sophistication. Ranging from one-page vignettes and brief, comic pieces to apocryphal biographies of historical figures and existential short stories, Arreola's works demonstrate his wry and satirical humor, as well as his deep cynicism and pervasive sense of absurdity. The vignettes of his *Bestiario* combine these elements, discovering human foibles in a series of animals—among them a rhinoceros, a boa constrictor, and a hippopotamus. His tone in these works, ostensibly that of an objective naturalist, masks a clever allegory, which satirizes human vanity, destructiveness, and insensitivity and criticizes the state of sexual relations between women and men. Of this bestiary, Margaret Mason and Yulan Washburn have written, "[Arreola] regards animals as a mirror in which man sees himself reflected. Man's qualities and defects, both spiritual and physical, are accentuated in beasts." The allegorical nature of Arreola's writings is also evident in one of his most famous short stories, "El guardagujas" ("The Switchman"). In this tale the traveler X—— attempts to make his way along a national railroad system that seems to obey no laws of rational order. The switchman who explains the workings of the railroad describes areas where one of the rails does not exist, false facades of stations, chasms without bridges and the unlikely chance of X—— ever reaching his destination, the town of T——. The work is seen as a comment on the inadequacy of Mexico's transportation system, as well as an exploration of the inescapable absurdity of human existence.

The Fair, Arreola's sole novel, shares certain affinities with his other writings. Like many of his shorter works, *The Fair* lacks the well-defined characters and plots of conventional fiction. Instead, the novel develops from related and unrelated scenes, partial conversations, and portions of letters and diaries; it suggests plot and character instead of depicting them directly. "Yet the totality of the work has body, literary development, and novelistic scope," suggests Joseph Sommers. The novel's fragmented parts coalesce, Sommers explains, to portray the life-cycle of a Mexican village, from its founding in colonial times to its deterioration in the present age. *The Fair* concludes with a fabulous display of fireworks set off by vandals, which, instead of providing harmless entertainment, kills several onlookers. "If this symbolism implies anguish and cynicism," writes Sommers, "these qualities are mediated by the author's understanding and sympathy for the complexity of human problems. Arreola's sensitive use of language. . . and his wry tone of bitter humor are the basis for the literary unity of this novel."

Although early reaction to *The Fair* was mostly negative, the novel's publication did much to address a stereotype from the mid-fifties that labeled Arreola an overly cosmopolitan writer uninterested in Mexican themes. Over the years, however, the novel has achieved greater esteem. Arreola's dramatic works, critics generally agree, demonstrate only an attenuated version of his literary skill; and, although his *Moment of Truth* was awarded best play of 1953 by the Mexican National Institute of Fine Arts, that year saw its only performance. Critics have more often responded positively to his short stories—succinct, universalizing pieces that have evoked comparisons to those of Argentine writer Jorge Luis Borges. In his shorter works are found the finest examples of "Arreola's fertile imagination and his sense of form and humor," which according to Russel M. Cluff and L. Howard Quackenbush "have immortalized him as one of Mexico's foremost writers of prose."

CRITICAL COMMENTARY

DONALD A. YATES
(essay date 1964)

[Yates is an American educator, editor, translator, and critic specializing in Spanish literature. In the following review, he appraises the English translation of Arreola's *Confabulario total*, noting that the work satirizes "man and his entanglements with logical absurdities."]

In 1962, Juan José Arreola published in Mexico City his *Confabulario total*. It was, in a sense, his "Collected Works," since it brought together most of his short stories, including some of the earliest, which date back to 1941; his latest short sketches or fables (from which the book takes its title); his *Bestiary* of 1958, a satirical, anti-U.S. play, and all of his most recent prose pieces.

The present translation of *Confabulario total,* as the newest title in the Texas Pan American Series, confers a certain distinction on the forty-six-year-old author, for probably more of Arreola's over-all literary production is now available in English than of any other Spanish-American writer. The intellectual sophistication and imaginative virtuosity of this collection suggest that he is in many ways worthy of the honor.

The most polished and the most given to verbal and conceptual play of his "generation" of Mexican writers—a group that includes Agustín Yáñez, Juan Rulfo, and poet Octavio Paz—Arreola performs generally in the guise of satirist—a curious type of satirist whose professed pessimism is more cultivated than convincing. The piece that deals with the hyena in his *Bestiary* is a descriptive gem: "The limner boggles and sketches only with difficulty the gross mastiff head, the hints of pig and degenerate tiger, the sloping line of the body, slippery, muscular, dwindling." But the bite of the final line penetrates only the flesh and not the bone: "He is perhaps the animal that has made the most converts among men." The observation amuses, as does the previous description of the boa as nothing more than a digestive process.

Arreola's target is man and his entanglements with logical absurdities; but the paradox inevitably interests him more than the plight. **"The Switchman,"** wherein the fantastic mismanagement and downright arbitrary deceptiveness of an imaginary national railroad system acquires, over the space of a few pages, the stature of a magnificent allegory of the human condition, is possibly his finest short story; it also happens to be one of his gaiest. The originality of Arreola's satire provokes surprise together with delight: he suggest that if all the rich men of the world were to pour their joint wealth into the construction of an inconceivably complicated and expensive machine designed to disintegrate a camel and zip him through the eye of a needle, then they would indeed most likely come to pass through the gates of Heaven.

Arreola shapes up as a better stylist than moralist: beauty of form often eclipses the substance of an idea. Consider the opening lines of his short story **"Liberty"**:

Today I proclaimed the independence of my acts: Only a few unsatisfied desires and two or three worn-out attitudes gathered together at this ceremony. A grandiose proposal that had offered to come sent its humble excuses at the last minute. All took place in a frightful silence.

I believe the error consisted in its noisy proclamation: trumpets and bells, firecrackers, and drums. And to finish off, some ingenious pyrotechnical stunts concerning morality which burned only halfway through.

The excellence of the translation by George D. Schade is evident in these lines. He has done Arreola a humble and faithful service. Schade has taken certain liberties with the organization of the original *Confabulario total,* some of which he acknowledges. He has mysteriously shuffled a few of the stories about, but has wisely excluded the undistinguished play *La hora de todos*.

The most disconcerting feature of this book, however, must be charged to Arreola himself, who arranged the contents of the Mexican edition in such a way that his most recent fiction comes first in the book and his earliest, least controlled, and least impressive work appears last.

The reader gets the odd impression that he is witnessing a gifted writer irrevocably and unaccountably losing his touch right before his eyes.

Donald A. Yates, "Caught in Our Logical Absurdities," in *The Saturday Review,* New York, Vol. XLVII, No. 31, August 1, 1964, p. 32.

GEORGE D. SCHADE
(essay date 1964)

[In the following excerpt, Schade surveys the collected pieces of Arreola's *Confabulario and Other Inventions,* noting the author's stylistic gifts and deft use of humor and satire.]

Arreola, who has lived for many years in Mexico City, was born in Ciudad Guzmán in the state of Jalisco, Mexico in 1918. His stories first appeared in little magazines in Guadalajara in the early 1940's—one of them called *Pan* he edited with his friend Rulfo—and his first book, *Varia Invención*, came out in 1949. *Confabulario* followed in 1952, and in 1955 was published in a second edition together with *Varia Invención* in one volume. His bestiary appeared in 1958 under the title *Punta de Plata*. In 1962 these books, together with the addition of a large number of new pieces, were all brought out under the title *Confabulario Total, 1941–61.*

This book is difficult to classify. Some of the pieces—like **"The Switchman," "The Crow Catcher," "Private Life"**—are clearly short stories in a modern mode, ranging widely in technique and style; a great many others, as the title would indicate, are fables; still others are sharp, satiric, one-page vignettes, and can hardly be called short stories. The tone and language vary considerably according to the subject. For example, in **"Baby H.P."** and **"Announcement"** Arreola parodies the commercial world of advertising, using jargonistic terms and breathless tone with excellent effect. But the same marvelous invention and wit, the same trenchant satire, and impish, impudent humor run throughout the collection.

In an age when many writers take themselves so seriously as to be solemn, it is refreshing to come across an author like Arreola, who laughs gleefully and wickedly at man—and by implication, at himself—puncturing all the foolishness he indulges in and cutting through the glaze of manners society sets so much store by.

Arreola is an accomplished satirist. He is very good at finding chinks in the armor, attacking his subjects in their most vulnerable spots and sometimes in places where they probably did not realize they were vulnerable. Bourgeois society and all its false values, rampaging twentieth-century materialism, the bomb, the cocktail party are just a few of his targets. With mordant descriptions, pungent attacks, or sly irony, he shows how silly mankind is, how outrageous man's behavior and antics are, how one is at the mercy of a world and society that more often seems to care for what is trivial and ephemeral than for what is essential. Arreola jabs at complacency and ruthlessly exposes pompous and hypocritical attitudes.

He takes a depressing view of most human relationships, and in a large number of his stories and satires he chips away at love and its illusions. Like the celebrated seventeenth-century Spanish satirist Quevedo, Arreola is particularly hard on women and marriage. According to him, women are given to treachery and adultery, and the impossibility of finding happiness in marriage is a recurring theme and echo in his work. Whatever the subject of his satire, Arreola most often achieves his effects by a deliberate jumbling of phantasy and reality, a mingling of the logical and the absurd, a blend of imaginative frivolity and Orwellian grimness.

Arreola's range includes not only the present, but much of the past. He has a special penchant for medieval times, attested in such pieces as **"The Song or Peronelle," "Sinesius of Rhodes,"** or **"Epitaph,"** a short, sympathetic biographical sketch of the poet Francois Villon. Erudite allusions from other literatures and history crop up often in his prose, as well as learned references to writers and their works in other fields—anthropology, psychology, science. And he seems astonishingly knowledgeable about a variety of esoteric subjects, for example, Roman and other ancient war machines, which he describes in an hilarious story called **"On Ballistics."**

One of the most ingratiating and delightful parts of Arreola's collected works is his *Bestiary,* consisting of twenty-six brief sketches. Here Arreola harkens back to that form which was so fashionable in medieval times with moralists and allegorizers, where certain virtues or characteristics were popularly attributed to certain beasts, real or imaginary. All of Arreola's beasts are real, their human-like foibles and defects uncomfortably real too. Though Arreola's general outlook and some of the details in his bestiary will probably horrify the overly sentimental, still there are lyrical and poetic touches to offset to some degree the refined savagery of his satire.

Endowed with a resilient mind that skims swiftly from point to point, Arreola is also a gifted stylist. His imagery and language, except in some of the earliest stories, are tart and fresh, his choice of words sometimes startling the reader, at other times stinging him, frequently delighting him. His writing is crisp with sentences that tend to be short and closely packed, yet there is no jerky or jolting effect; it is all perfectly under control, balanced and rhythmic. Anyone whose ear has become somewhat dulled by the monotone of much present-day literature will probably be charmed by the banquet in store for him in word and image in Arreola's prose.

Arreola has his quota of enthusiastic admirers; he has also his blinkered critics who upbraid him for turning his back on so-called Mexican themes. Of course, it is his enormous sophistication and universality that should attract readers of English, though he has done a few pieces

Principal Works

Varia invención (short stories) 1949

Cinco cuentos (short stories) 1951

Confabulario (short stories) 1952

La hora de todos: Juguete cómico en un acto (drama) 1953

Punta de plata (short stories) 1958; also published as *Bestiario*, 1972

*Confabulario total (short stories) 1962
[*Confabulario and Other Inventions*, 1964]

La feria (novel) 1963
[*The Fair*, 1977]

Palindroma (short stories and drama) 1971

Inventario (essays) 1976

Confabulario personal (short stories) 1979

**Includes *Varia invención, Confabulario,* and *Bestiario.*

very Mexican in theme and setting like **"Ballad"** and the impressive and touching story **"The Crow Catcher,"** which should have an exotic appeal for the foreign reader.

Obvious attractions abound in these satires, but there are also subtle delights often lurking below the surface. One will find, for example, several levels of meaning in a story like **"The Switchman,"** where the inadequacies of the Mexican railroad system are satirized on the obvious level; on a more symbolic level various interpretations of this story are possible.

If we wish to seek them, parallels to Arreola elsewhere are not difficult to find. **"Small Town Affair"** with its psycho-zoological tendency—a man assuming the attributes and horns of a bull—is somewhat reminiscent of Kafka's wretched character in "Metamorphosis" who awakens one morning to discover himself transformed into a gigantic insect. As the Mexican writer and critic Emmanuel Carballo has pointed out, several of Arreola's distinctive apocryphal biographies, including **"Nabonides,"** **"Balthasar Gérard,"** and **"Sinesius of Rhodes,"** are inspired by Marcel Schwob's *Vies Imaginaires.* A contemporary author with whom Arreola is frequently compared is the Argentine Jorge Luis Borges, with his playful, extraordinarily penetrating intellect, brilliant imagination, and phantasmagoric stories (he has written a bestiary too). Going further back in time, we can cite other similarities: the icy wit and coarse, bawdy, macabre humor of Quevedo, or the cleverness and cynicism of Voltaire. But though we detect reminiscences of one writer and echoes of another in Arreola's work, there is no doubt that he has a voice of his own, an inimitable style of utterance.

With such a large number of stories, fables, and

sketches—almost one hundred—some unevenness is bound to occur, but in my opinion, the shadows recede before the lights. There are brilliant pieces in *Confabulario* and the other books which really dazzle. (pp. vii–xi)

George D. Schade, in an introduction to *Confabulario and Other Inventions* by Juan José Arreola, translated by George D. Schade, University of Texas Press, 1964, pp. vii–xi.

KESSEL SCHWARTZ
(essay date 1971)

[Schwartz is an American educator, editor, and critic who has written extensively on Spanish literature. In the following excerpt, he discusses Arreola's focus on morality, absurdity, and irrationality in his short stories and his novel, *The Fair*.]

Juan José Arreola, the fourth of fourteen children, was unable to attend school. He undertook a variety of physical and intellectual positions in a bank, on a newspaper, and in the theater, partly through the efforts of Louis Jouvet who met him in Mexico and took him to Paris. On his return he became a member of the publishing house Fondo de Cultura Económica, where he was able to continue the close association with books and reading which he loved so much. In 1952 he founded the publishing house Los Presentes, through which Carlos Fuentes first came to public attention, and he has continued to inspire young writers through his "Taller literario" and his review *Mester.* In 1961 he was named coordinator of literary publications for the Presidencia de la República. In the 1950s a polemic took place between his supporters and those of Rulfo about the relative merits of a national novel as opposed to the novel of special stylistic techniques. Because he eschewed an hermetic nationalism Arreola was considered heir to the traditions of the Contemporáneos and similar groups. Arreola found many new Mexican novelists to be vulgar and extreme and longed for a return to classic perfection. Less regional than Rulfo, Arreola, for all his universal and intellectual pretensions, superficially foreign to Rulfo's elemental problems of daily life, is as intensely Mexican in many ways. Primarily a short story writer, he has been called "el cuentista más rico, extraño y singular de los que escriben en nuestro idioma." Seymour Menton, a friend of Arreola, shows [in *Hispania*, 1959] how the latter moved from anguish, despair, and the struggle of lonely individuals to "the placid skepticism of magic realism." Menton also insists that Arreola, beyond any cosmopolitan intellectualism, exhibits a very definite "Mexican spirit whose roots go as far back as Lizardi."

In Arreola, who concentrates on the sexual, the ethical, and the aesthetic, one sees in varying degrees the interplay of moralism, universalism, and magical realism. He fancies himself a modern day moralist who is concerned with social justice, and he is not reluctant to expose the evils of Occidental materialism. More importantly, he carries on the tradition of fantasy in Mexican fiction established by Alfonso Reyes (an intimate friend) and others. Arreola stresses throughout the importance of formal beauty and his preoccupation with literary structures. In these he has tried to combine letters, diaries, commercials, biography, and the medieval fable.

Arreola's first collection of stories, *Varia invención* (1949), is varied, as the title implies, in both theme and techniques. All nonetheless seem to involve "sutiles casos de conciencia, intrincados problemas intelectuales. Le preocupa la teología, el infinito, en general los problemas metafísicos." Arreola identifies with famous historical characters and fuses reality and invention to give us animal fables whose protagonists are either humanized animals or men with animal qualities. Of his twenty-three short stories comprising the section called "Bestiario," each has a name of the significant animal. Arreola reveals an unusual sense of humor, tinged at times with sarcasm and at others with pity for man's foibles. In 1952 his second collection, *Confabulario*, appeared. More obscure, existentialist, and fantastic than his first volume, with its magic realism and irrational universe it reminds one of Kafka in its reflection of the depersonalized and mechanized life of the twentieth century.

In 1955 the two books were combined to form one artistic unit, having a third edition, *Confabulario total* (1962), and still another in 1966, in whose prologue Arreola states: "De hoy en adelante me propongo ser un escritor asequible, y no sólo por el bajo precio que ahora tengo en el mercado, sino por el profundo cambio que se opera en mi espíritu y en mi voluntad estilística." Aware of the absurdity of life, he tells us about lonely individuals, examines Golden Age literature and the function of creative artists, and gives us a general criticism of American society. Typical of one phase of his work is **"El silencio de Dios,"** where a man must choose between good and evil and tries to establish a dialogue with God in order to relieve himself of the doubts, anguish, and despair he feels at his own life and those of fellow human beings. Choosing good over evil naught availeth, as God tells him to accept what life brings. Man cannot understand God's designs and must face the future with hope. Arreola continues variations on his evangelical themes in stories like **"En verdad os digo,"** where rich men may enter heaven, as camels, through the use of modern electronic and atomic science and so find themselves able to pass through the eye of a needle. Other stories involve everything from adultery to science fiction. Arreola illuminates his stories with suggestive imagery and makes one wonder at the subtleties of the human mind and at organic existence.

Arreola's first and to date only novel, *La feria* (1963), winner of the Villaurrutia prize, is made up of bits and pieces as varied as his stories, parts of which he inserts into his longer narrative. He uses monologues, flashback, counterpoint, a diary form, and dreams. Biblical texts, memoirs, social commentary, history, and experiences from his youth, intermingled with allegory, fable, apologues, sociology, philosophy, the absurd, and the logical, are superimposed on the life stories of people in an imaginary town of southern Jalisco. Compassionately yet skeptically, Arreola views man's insistence on moving towards his own self-destruction. The true protagonist seems to be the town of Zapotlán itself. Its multiple dwellers give us an accurate picture of the religious and social life, the humdrum of daily living, and the semi-anonymous inhabitants, who number thirty thousand more or less. The Mexican Revolution has neither helped nor changed their languid and stagnant town, left largely unmoved also by Indian attempts to recover their land and by the cristero revolts. The town's economy is based on corn. Through a shoemaker and would-be writer and agriculturist, we learn about the sowing, cultivation, and reaping involved. Arreola includes a number of legends about corn, combining the telluric theme with those of religion and sex, the latter done as a series of confessions and involving onanism, the reading of pornographic literature for sexual excitement, adultery, and homosexuality. In man-woman relationships the former seems superior, but both need love and suffer from sensual frustrations and the loss of ideals. Poor Concha de Fierro, a prostitute, cannot lose her virginity in spite of her best efforts, until the ragged bullfighter, Pedro Corrales, makes good use of his sword. During an earthquake the frightened town residents indulge in a general confession which overburdens the priest's capacity.

Religion and humor seem to be two of the constants in Arreola's novel. The town's patron saint is Saint Joseph, brought there in 1745 by a mysterious muleteer. Every year a fiesta is celebrated in his honor, and this year several prelates will crown Jesus, the Virgin Mary, and poor Saint Joseph, who for all his importance, is outranked in his own town. The town lives almost by its saint's calendar rather than by historical event. The fair, a transitory event as man in the world is a transitory being, is burned to the ground at the end, and so man will disappear also. Arreola seems obsessed by man's inexplicable need to pervert, corrupt, and destroy, not only others but also himself. Man has become a victim of his own rhetoric and incredible inventions. He foolishly substitutes words and machines for harmony, love, and reinforced human values—the only hope for survival in an increasingly dehumanized and absurd world in which man has refused to accept responsibility for his own self-destructive tendencies. (pp. 292–95)

Kessel Schwartz, "The New Novel, IV: Juan José Arreola," in his *A New History of Spanish American Fiction, Volume II*, University of Miami Press, 1971, pp. 292–95.

ROSS LARSON
(essay date 1977)

[In the following excerpt, Larson discusses several of Arreola's short stories, describing them as efforts to expose "the moral conscience of the individual."]

Perhaps the most obvious features of Arreola's stories are their stylistic elegance and the extravagance of their action, either of which would be enough to set them apart from the course of the Mexican narrative so long subject to evaluation according to ethical and not aesthetic criteria. Socialist realism values content above form, and encourages direct expression of an impersonal conception of reality. Arreola acknowledges the artist's social responsibility, but he contends that documentary fiction is merely a useless repetition of life and that its task could much more effectively be performed by the newspaper, radio, cinema, or television.

If art is the transformation of exterior reality into aesthetic experience, Arreola is the consummate artist with absolute control over the word—which is for him the material concretion of an emanation from the human soul. He rejoices in the constant accusations that he is *manierista, amanerado, filigranista, orfebre,* but he rejects the serenity of the ivory tower and specifically urges

> una lucha honda y constante en pro de la paz universal. Nadie mejor que el artista para emprenderla y proclamarla. Porque ser artista, no es una disculpa para la inacción, sino más bien un compromiso grave y profundo que no debe ser eludido.

Instead of directing his criticism against obvious national symptoms—poverty, illiteracy, and political corruption—Arreola attacks the malady at its source: the moral conscience of the individual. His story **"Informe de Liberia"** (1959) deals with unborn children who refuse to enter this world. **"Flash"** (1955) reports on a mad scientist whose patriotic invention, an atomic "absorber," has ingested a large number of his fellow countrymen together with the railway train in which they were traveling. **"En verdad os digo"** (1952) presents us with another scientist whose power of invention is greater than his sense of morality. He earns a fortune with an ingenious project to construct a machine capable of passing a camel through the eye of a needle. **"Baby H. P."** (1952) is a sort of Leyden jar fitted with a harness, which is designed to convert a baby's tremendous energy into electricity. The idea seems both grotesque and frivolous, but at bottom it is quite serious. What Arreola wants to suggest is, first, that the baby could electrocute itself (physical

annihilation) and, second, that blind utilitarianism will annihilate man spiritually.

Such a depreciation of moral values necessarily implies the failure of religion and, in **"De L'Osservatore"** (1962), we have a notice from the Vatican newspaper advising us briefly that, at the beginning of our Era, Saint Peter's keys were lost in the suburbs of the Roman Empire. The finder is asked kindly to deliver them to the reigning Pope because for more than fifteen hundred years no one has been able to enter the Kingdom of Heaven. The concrete indications of the period (more than fifteen centuries ago), the setting (in the suburbs of the Roman Empire), and the religious context when taken together suggest Constantine, who established himself in Byzantium in A.D. 313. It will be recalled that, following his conversion, Constantine proclaimed Christianity the official state religion. Thus penetrating below the surface of the (apparent) caprice, we can discern some aspect of Arreola's personal vision; in this case, his conviction that, at the moment of instituting the Church, Christianity lost its validity (the keys were lost). Arreola returns to this theme in a recent story, to which he gives an English title, **"Starring: All People"** (1967), and which he offers in homage to Cecil B. De Mille. Here the history of the world is presented as an incomplete and mediocre movie that failed with both the public and the critics. The star actor, Jesus Christ, reveals to us in an interview that he is dying to go back to remake the film and give it a happy ending, but his father is still withholding his permission.

Arreola's philosophy of life is most adequately expressed in **"El guardagujas"** (1952), a Kafkaesque story concerning a fantastic railway system with only some sections completed, but where it is possible to buy tickets for any destination. No one knows what trains are running or where they are going. At any moment a train might arrive at the edge of an abyss where no bridge has been constructed. In such a case, the passengers dismantle the train and carry the parts to the other side, there to rebuild it and continue their journey. According to Arreola, this is what life is like: a series of absurd chance occurrences to which every man should surrender himself. In the same way, the moles of **"Topos"** (1952) yield to the attraction of death, leaping into the holes that lead to the fiery center of the earth. **"La caverna"** (1952), where one wanders in fear and trembling, is a vision of the final unknowable nothingness. But even as we are drawn to the universality of death, so we seek to lose our individuality in woman. Hence **"Topos"** and **"La caverna"** can also be interpreted satisfactorily as symbolic of the sexual experience.

For the existentialist, nothing matters more than the authenticity of his choices and the personal relationships he achieves. The natural hope that through sex a complete communion is possible becomes an obsession in Arreola. He confesses that *"la percepción de la mujer. . . ha sido el leitmotiv de mi existencia."* Recently he composed a list of the women who have played a decisive role in his life, not just lovers but also teachers, relatives, and writers. The list stands at seventy-two names. On the subject of woman, Arreola has always expressed himself with bitterness, an attitude which his one great love affair (1953–58) served only to reinforce.

"El soñado" (1949) is a narration in the first person by what seems to be an imaginary or unborn child, but is in fact the monstrous thing that two people engender just by living together. It is not literally a child but a presence, an ill feeling, an animosity, an indifference. Arreola does not conceal his resentment and disillusion. Reluctantly he acknowledges the impossibility of love, but he attaches part of the blame to man for he falsifies the nature of woman. **"Una mujer amaestrada"** (1955) gives us a tragic vision of marriage; a mountebank grotesquely exhibiting his wife to the public and making her perform clumsy dances and feats of simple arithmetic as if she were a trained bear so that the spectators will share his opinion of this marvelous woman. The female plastic robots of **"Anuncio"** (1962) **"Parábola del trueque"** (1955) represent woman as a mere tool for the sexual satisfaction of man. But it is woman herself who accepts all these conflicting roles that man invents. At one moment she is asked to be a goddess, then she is a maid, then a devil, and then a mother. . . Arreola is not anti-feminist and his conclusions distress him since they blasphemously attack his scared concept of woman, which is more or less as follows:

> Necesito abrazar en la mujer el árbol de la vida, creer que estoy ligado a la vida universal, que ya no hay individuación; que la mujer es, en este momento, la puerta de escape hacia el todo. La mujer que nos trajo de la universalidad a la individuación, es también la puerta del paraíso. Reingreso de la individualidad al todo. Por eso en el amor existe ese perderse, dejarse derivar como en un río.

It is worth noting parenthetically that Arreola is overcoming his disillusionment with woman. He sees the history of civilization thus far as characterized by its masculinity and he considers it a failure. The only possible salvation for humanity, he now believes, is through woman and a new feminine orientation in life.

Because Arreola's work is full of humor and irony, he has been regarded as a jester interested only in novelty and in amusing or scandalizing the reader. Indeed Arreola is a formalist and a virtuoso of the Spanish language, but almost never is he trivial or gratuitous. On the contrary, his themes are profoundly human. He employs elements of his own personal drama to express, in fragments, a vision of man's existence. Arreola's concise style together with his intuitive technique produce incomprehension on the part of the public. His meaning is never obvious or easily accessible, but it always exists—between the lines.

The famous polemic, then, which arose from the in-

dignation and outrage surrounding the publication of his first works misrepresented Arreola's position, but it did serve to vitalize Mexican letters for more than a decade. The *arreolistas* proclaimed the supremacy of art, an essentially intuitive faculty, over all national and political considerations. Their mentor taught respect for aesthetic values and demonstrated how literature could be raised above the merely regional and circumstantial. (pp. 79–82)

Ross Larson, "Expressionism," in his *Fantasy and Imagination in the Mexican Narrative*, Arizona State University, 1977, pp. 77–88.

Arreola circa 1959.

YULAN M. WASHBURN

(essay date 1983)

[In the following excerpt, Washburn discusses Arreola's *Palindroma*, observing that its contents are presented with a bluntness and cynicism that departs from the author's earlier style.]

In 1971 [Arreola] published his first completely new title in several years, *Palindroma* [*Palindrome*]. In general

Palindrome is similar to Arreola's previous books: there is the same distinctive style, the same variety of subject matter and form, and—despite Arreola's good intentions in his 1966 prologue—a preponderance of works outrageously scoring the man-woman relationship. There are also some major differences between *Palindrome* and the bulk of his previous work. Most of the volume is occupied not by short prose creations, but by a one-act play. Moreover, Arreola's malice and cynicism, which previously had been held in check and merely simmered beneath the surface of his writing, are at times escalated to a pitch beyond that of any previous work. Some of the entries have the character of dirty jokes or leers in an all male barbershop, leers loftily couched in the refinements of scholarship and high, prose art. **"El himen en México"** [**The hymen in Mexico"**] purports to be a medicosociological treatise on the indurate hymen of Mexican women, and concludes with a mocking rhapsody to the "secret membrane," in which the supposed researcher, now aging, laments that he has not been able to verify personally all of his data. **"Receta casera"** [**"Household recipe"**] portrays Arreola's view of the overweening vanity of women and gives suggestions for playing on that vanity to lure them to one's home, where they can either be suffocated or seasoned to taste. **"Para entrar al jardín"** [**"Entering the garden"**] begins with an erotic passage—the most suggestive part of which is archly printed on the outer jacket of the volume—which seems to come from a sex manual. At first it reads like a startlingly bold description of how a male should begin sexual penetration of the female, but by the second paragraph it turns into detailed directions for murdering the woman and disposing of the body. Many of the selections scathingly satirize the grow-

ing openness about sex that has become modish in recent years and is now one of the focuses for best-sellers and erotic mass magazines; taken as a whole, however, such selections also bitterly mock the unexamined assumption that a fuller sex life will lead ineluctably to fuller happiness.

The change in manner in the short pieces is perhaps what Arreola was referring to when he spoke of a "change in spirit" in his 1966 prologue. Gone is the glancing innuendo, the light stroke of irony. It is as if Arreola had suddenly become a prophet with his eyes flashing on the idolatries of our time. In many of these pieces he plunges into muscular, roundhouse burlesque that is bludgeoning and uncompromising. He sneers at mass values as expressed in athletics, racial prejudice, the movies, the omniscience of science, and sex as a commodity. In a sense, then, Arreola keeps his promise of the 1966 prologue. He is at times more blunt and less subtle in the Palindrome fictions; yet the recondite allusions and provocative obscurities still abound in this anthology.

Arreola's love of words comes out strongly in the palindromes that dot the work. A palindrome, technically, is a bit of language play in which sentences are constructed that read the same forwards or backwards. "Madam, I'm Adam" is perhaps the most familiar and ignoble one in English. Most palindromes merely display verbal skill. Arreola's palindromes, however, toy with a concept as well, usually having to do with women. These palindromes are used to separate the sections of the book—much like the woodcuts in The Fair—and are related to the contents of each section. The palindrome which precedes the play, for example, is "Adán sé ave, Eva es nada." Utterly unreproducible in English, this palindrome means something like "Adam, be a bird, Eve is nothing," and encapsulates Arreola's view that man is a spirit whose nature it is to soar, even though he can take flight only against the temptation to bury himself in the illusory flesh of woman. The palindrome which precedes the section called "Syntactical Variations" is astonishingly complex. It consists, in fact, of two palindromes and is an invitation from one girl to another that would have fit well into the Greek Anthology.

Sofía Daífos a Selene Peneles:
Se van Sal acá tía Naves Argelao es ido
Odiseo alégrase Van a Itaca las naves
(Sofía Daífos to Selene Peneles:
They're leaving   Get it over here, Baby
    Naves Argelao has gone
Odysseus is delighted   the ships are going
to Ithaca)

The final palindrome—standing by itself at the bottom of an otherwise blank page at the end of the book—is ". . . eres o no eres . . . seré o no seré" ("You are or you are not . . . I will be or I will not be . . . "). It seems to be a play on Shakespeare's "To be or not to be," and is followed by the exclamation, "*That* is the real palindrome!" which for Arreola sums up all the striving of human life.

The major portion of *Palindrome* is occupied with a new theatrical piece by Arreola, *Tercera llamada; tercera! o Empezamos sin usted* [*Last call, last call! Or we'll start without you*]. The play itself is a kind of palindrome in that it begins and ends in roughly the same way, and also works back in time by employing several of Arreola's earlier works. The work is a spectacle depicting in unsubtle fashion (Arreola subtitles it a circus farce) his vision of the agonies of the man-woman relationship, especially in its domestic aspect. The male character is called *Marido* ("Husband") and is depicted as a feckless, ineffectual person who is systematically duped by the other characters and by his own confused yearning for the ineffable. Blanca, the female protagonist, is promiscuous, flighty, earthy, and cunning, but she has an occasional hankering for the ineffable herself. Angel, a demonic changeling who plays seven distinct roles, toys with the man and woman. The play strives to present Arreola's version of the man-woman dilemma dramatically, but it is not surprising to learn that up to now the play has been performed but once, and then by an amateur group in Arreola's home state of Jalisco. Even though the work sums up Arreola's consistent views on woman more clearly than any other one work, it is essentially a weak vehicle and indicates that drama is not one of Arreola's strengths. (pp. 33–5)

Yulan M. Washburn, in his *Juan José Arreola*, Twayne Publishers, 1983, 143 p.

PAULA R. HEUSINKVELD
(essay date 1984)

[In the following excerpt, Heusinkveld examines Arreola's "El guardagujas," "Autrui," and "El mapa de objetos perdidos" as modern, existential allegories.]

In this century we have seen radical changes in the genres of literature. The Theater of the Absurd breaks theatrical conventions, and the New Novel differs radically from the traditional novel. This article considers a contemporary Mexican writer whose brief prose fiction, like much literature of this century, defies easy classification. The artistic purpose of Juan José Arreola is clearly not that of a traditional short story writer, who keeps the reader's attention with plot development, suspense, climax and denouement. In many of the brief fictional pieces in his *Confabulario*, Arreola presents only a static situation, usually of a bizarre or fantastical nature, that leaves the reader groping for meaning. In the absence of a traditional story line, the reader may be only minimally interested in finding out what will happen, if indeed anything will happen at all. The more urgent question becomes: "What can it possibly all mean?"

As George Schade pointed out in the introduction to his English translation of *Confabulario*, the very title of Arreola's famous volume suggests a collection of fables. Although some early reviewers of Arreola's work interpreted his bizarre fictional creations as mere flights of fancy, critics generally acknowledge a deeper significance in these texts. Seymour Menton was the first to explore beneath the surface of Arreola's fantasies and subsequently discover serious underlying themes, ranging from existential anguish to a warning against modern man's self-destructive potential. Thomas Tomanek has convincingly demonstrated Arreola's indebtedness to Franz Kafka, whose own bizarre fictional creations have been described as modern allegories.

Largely due to the influence of the works of Franz Kafka, critics have begun to re-examine the nature of allegory and to recognize the range of artistic possibilities for this symbolic form in twentieth century literature. "Allegory" has in fact gained acceptance as a critical term applicable to a particular kind of modern symbolic literature— literature which closely resembles the tales of the *Confabulario*. Despite the widespread acknowledgement of symbolic meaning in many of Arreola's texts, however, no one has yet ventured to study Arreola's works in terms of allegory. This [essay] proposes that indeed most of Arreola's stories can best be understood as modern allegories. (pp. 33–4)

To convey his skeptical vision of the world through allegory, Arreola repeatedly uses symbols that represent human limitations and failures rather than human potential. As symbols of mankind, he chooses animals (as in the selection of *Bestiario*) and nameless anti-heroes who lack control of their circumstances. Supernatural antagonists and nightmarish situations throughout the *Confabulario* symbolize the existential dilemmas that modern man must confront. Unlike the heroes of classical allegory, Arreola's anti-heroes never have a chance. In **"Uno de dos,"** the narrator is overpowered by a maleficent angel who is portrayed as an aggressive boxing adversary. In **"Autrui,"** the narrator is overcome by a mysterious antagonist with supernatural powers. The narrator of **"La migala"** is terrorized by a surrealistic insect. The inability of Arreola's characters to overcome these antagonists or supernatural forces represents the impotence of man in all spheres of human existence.

The broad expansive panoramas of classical allegory are replaced in the stories of Arreola by symbolic settings of limited dimensions which confine the helpless protagonist. In **"La trampa,"** for example, the narrator is an insect trapped in the web of a female spider. In **"Luna de miel,"** the narrator is trying to escape from a sticky sea of honey. The narrator of **"El rey negro"** is a black king trapped into the corner of a chessboard. The poet-narrator of **"Interview"** is confined with the rest of humanity in the belly of an enormous female whale who is drifting toward nothingness. These and other symbols of confinement throughout the *Confabulario*, convey a vision of man as an impotent creature lacking control of his life or destiny.

Compared to allegories of the Medieval and Renaissance periods, Arreola's stores have a minimal amount of action. The only development in many selections is the protagonist's eventual acknowledgement of his inability to act and his acceptance of an impossible situation. In classical allegory there was no place for inaction, since inaction meant impotence. In Arreola's allegories, however, impotence is in fact the message—man's impotence in an alien world. (pp. 35–6)

Arreola's use of allegory can best be understood through careful examination of his treatment of a symbolic journey, a struggle between antagonists, and a quest. These symbols appear in three stories in the *Confabulario*, "El guardagujas," "Autrui," and "El mapa de objetos perdidos," respectively.

In "El guardagujas," Arreola addresses the theme of the inherent limitation of the human condition. In this story we find the traditional symbol of life as a journey. This train trip, however, is very different from the journeys of classical allegory in which the hero proceeded confidently of his own free will across expansive panoramas toward a definite goal. The passengers on Arreola's train do not travel under their own power but rather are confined within the enclosed space of a vehicle whose speed, direction, and ultimate destination they cannot control, or even know. The journey on Arreola's train suggests a restrictive view of life: man, like the passengers on the train, is unable to control his own life or destiny.

The protagonist in this story, the stranger, resembles K. in Kafka's *The Castle* in that he initially declares a specific goal, only to be confounded and frustrated by a bizarre system. From the moment the would-be traveller arrives at the deserted train station, he begins to sense that he is on unfamiliar ground where logic and order have no place.

The stranger seems to be an ordinary man with the logical, realistic expectation of being able to board a train that will carry him to his destination. His dilemma seems realistic enough for the reader to identify with it. Yet Arreola provides no information whatsoever about this character, not even a name. This deliberate vagueness invites abstraction. The stranger could be anyone striving toward a goal.

The odd little switchman, who appears out of nowhere, provides a counterpoint to the realistic expectations of the stranger. While the clear, pointed questions of the stranger represent man's attempt to find reason, the preposterous rambling responses of the switchman suggest the futility of man's efforts to impose logic on an absurd world.

The switchman has never boarded the train. His purpose in the story seems to be that of an ironic observer who must convince the stranger of the necessity for accepting the absurd. (As George McMurray has pointed out [in the *Latin American Literary Review*, 1977], the switchman must switch the stranger away from his one-track, logical expectations and put the stranger's mind on a different track!)

The railroad company, known as "la empresa," repersents the outside force or absolute power that supposedly directs human lives. The utter unreliability of the company reflects a twentieth-century world view—that our lives are totally dictated by chance.

Like Kafka's characters, the stranger gradually realizes that he has no control over the direction of events in his life, that he has only one option—to accept or deny his inability to decipher or control this illogical system. In "El guardagujas," the stranger makes the positive decision to board the train. By the end of the story, he has lost sight of his original goal, T., and has decided to journey toward the unknown X. Arreola implies that we do have one important choice. We can either stand on the station platform, forever, frustrated, or we can follow the stranger's example and board the train, that is accept the absurdity of the human condition and embrace life such as it is.

The noisy arrival of the train and the simultaneous magical disappearance of the switchman provide an appropriate ending for a story that has maintained a delicate balance between the plausible and the fantastic. By blurring the distinction between the plausible and the impossible, Arreola forces the reader to step back, like a detached observer, to seek an explanation for the apparent absurdity. At this point the reader should be able to discover other levels of meaning.

One critic, Luis Leal, has observed that "El guardagujas" can be interpreted simultaneously on at least three meaning levels: as a brilliant satire of the Mexican railway system, a biting commentary about Mexican government and society, and as a philosophical statement about the human condition. This juxtaposition of apparent realism and fantasy is Arreola's primary method of hinting at multiple meaning levels in texts throughout the collection.

Arreola's symbols become much more negative when he focuses on the human limitation that he considers to be most responsible for unhappiness on this earth, man's inability to relate to his fellow-man and his consequent isolation. In "Autrui," which Arreola has cited in an interview with Emmanuel Carballo as a key story of the collection, our fellow-man is represented as a terrifying, omnipresent foe. The narrator of this story (who symbolizes mankind) relates in anguished tones his persecution by Autrui, an insidious, undefined presence which exercises supernatural powers to confine the narrator within an ever-diminishing space. As a result of Autrui's pernicious designs, the helpless narrator finds himself in a surrealistic maze of blind alleys and is later mysteriously trapped in a room which seems to be shrinking. Unable to defend himself against his invisible foe, the narrator comes to an ignominious end without ever asserting his own identity. He ultimately finds himself boxed inside a hexagonal capsule no larger than his body, at which point be begins to putrefy.

The blind alleys, the tiny room, and the hexagonal capsule in this story are all powerful images of confinement. Like Sartre, Beckett, Kafka and others, Arreola has placed his anti-hero within a constricting space, a graphic protrayal of man's entrapment within certain limitations.

The name "Autrui," from the French "autre," or "other," is the key to the story's meaning. As Arreola explained during the same interview with Carballo, Autrui's dogged persecution of the narrator represents the unavoidable imposition of our fellow-man upon each one of us and the consequent restriction of our freedom of movement:

> Se trata de la acotación de nuestro espacio vital por parte de nuestros prójimos, que nos ciñen hasta que nos dejan reducidos a la cápsula física de nuestro cuerpo. El único espacio de que disponemos verdaderamente es el espacio de nuestro cuerpo. Y por esto, este hombre que pensabe en cosas grandes se pudre dentro de su cápsula. Se le pudre el yo.

The story reaffirms Sartre's existential dictum that "hell is other people" and conveys the paradoxical dilemma that, because of man's inability to communicate with his fellow-man, he withdraws into himself, only to be consumed by self-destructive alienation. The story implies that man's alienation is devastating to the self and causes even more anguish than the lack of free will or human mortality.

In this story, just as in **"El guardagujas,"** Arreola blends realism with fantasy. In this case, however, he uses a realistic format—that of a diary—to convey totally surrealistic events. The diary form in itself inspires belief. The precise language and the frequent use of preterite verbs reinforce the impression that the narrator is presenting an accurate account of his daily activities.

Yet the narrator implies that the physical, day-by-day persecution described in his diary is symptomatic of a longer-lasting, insidious persecution of a non-physical nature. In the opening lines of the story, the narrator expands the time frame to include his entire life, thus facilitating allegorical interpretation:

> Sigue la persecución sistemática de ese desconocido. Creo que se llama Autrui. No sé cuándo empezó a encarcelarme. Desde el principio de me vida tal vez, sin que yo me diera cuenta.

These clipped sentences, almost spit out as if the narrator has been running, create the impression that the

life-long metaphysical persecution of Autrui is just as devastating as the immediate persecution described in the diary.

The total effect of this incongruous use of a diary to relate surrealistic experiences is unsettling. In **"Autrui,"** as in **"El Guardagujas,"** the reader is left hovering uncomfortably between the realistic and the impossible. Once again, Arreola has presented realistic and fantastic elements in a juxtaposition which creates tension and forces the reader to seek an underlying meaning.

Both **"El guardagujas"** and **"Autrui"** use symbols common in traditional allegory—that of a journey and a struggle between two antagonists, respectively—to convey negative ideas. The stranger in **"El guardagujas"** has no control over the direction of his life. The narrator of **"Autrui"** is consumed by alienation from his fellow man. A third symbol common in traditional allegory—that of the quest—also appears in the *Confabulario* to convey a message typical of a twentieth century world view.

In **"El mapa de objetos perdidos,"** the narrator, representing mankind, purchases a magical map which helps him to find lost objects. His searching, however, scarcely resembles the purposeful quests of classical allegory. To begin with, the narrator's quest is begun in indifference, since he agrees to try the magical map merely because "era domingo y no tenía qué hacer." His quest, then, is not directed toward any particular goal. Throughout the brief story, his attitude suggests a certain amount of boredom and disinterest. The map itself does not supply directions leading to any specific destination. Instead, it leads the narrator to lost or discarded objects, cheap trinkets which he in turn sells to make a miserable living. The implication is that any ideas, concepts, or beliefs which questing modern man may stumble upon have already been handled and then discarded or forgotten. The occasional "mujer perdida" which the map reveals is of a quality as low as that of all the other objects, worn-out and ordinary.

Although the search is unmotivated and lacking in direction, the map continues to reveal more objects. The narrator speaks of the first trinket he found, an old plastic comb, as "el primer eslabón de una cadena." The image of the chain suggests continuance, perhaps bondage. Even though the quest leads to nothing of consequence, it draws the narrator almost against his will into a perpetual activity of searching.

Arreola's technique in **"El mapa de objetos perdidos"** is quite different from that used in **"Autrui."** The magical nature of this story is not immediately apparent. The narrator provides very little detail and avoids any sensational description of the supernatural qualities of the map. Yet his repeated denial that the map vendor is unusual alerts the reader, ironically, that something about the map may be extraordinary: "El hombre que me vendió el mapa no tenía nada de extraño. Un tipo común y corriente, un poco enfermo tal vez. Me abordó sencilla-mente, como esos vendedores que nos salen al paso en la calle." This introduction to the map vendor is not visually specific enough to indicate a comfortable realism, nor is it fantastic. It simply creates an aura of mystery and draws the reader on.

Even in the absence of blatantly impossible events, this neutral language confronts the reader with a strange world which has an unsettling combination of "elusive-ness and familiarity." To quote Gay Clifford (in reference to a different allegorical work):

> The passage's strangeness derives not from exoticism, but from the fact that is so neutral, so indefinite, and yet immediately suggests that it means something important. . . Part of the urgency comes from the neutrality of the vocabulary . . . we accept that these things are familiar in some way, even while we sense that they are also remote. . . We are compelled to read on in order to understand this enigmatic lack of congruity. The worlds of allegory are only half-familiar and they are rarely safe.

In short, when the characters or the action of a story are obviously supernatural, as in **"Autrui,"** Arreola uses a realistic style. When the characters are somewhat plau-sible as in **"El mapa de objetos perdidos,"** the language is vague and unsettling. In both stories, Arreola hovers on the line between apparent realism and fantasy. In both cases, the incongruity between realistic and fantastic el-ements creates tension and forces the reader to seek a meaning beyond the obvious. He hints at the presence of another meaning but does not reveal what it is.

The three stories discussed here share a number of important characteristics. Each one sustains at least two levels of meaning from beginning to end, and each presents fictional elements to symbolize a set of related ideas. In this sense these stories may be considered alle-gorical.

At the same time, Arreola's stories convey a negative world view characteristic of this century. On the basis of these representative stories, we may hypothesize that the allegories of the **Confabulario** have the following char-acteristics: (1) a skeptical, pessimistic view of the world; (2) an anti-hero who lacks control of his circumstances; (3) symbols that convey man's limitations rather than his potential; (4) a lack of overt didactic intent, and (5) an absence of explicitly stated correspondences between fic-tional and real meaning levels. Surely these works may be considered as modern allegories.

The stories of Arreola's **Confabulario** do reveal negative aspects of modern man: existential anxiety, alien-ation, estrangement, and dehumanization. Yet Arreola's stories lack the bleak despair characteristic of other mod-ern allegories such as Kafka's. Through symbolic char-acters who accept their circumstances, Arreola obliquely

conveys his own acceptance of human limitations. Fur-thermore, he often lightens his pessimistic message of creating inherently humorous symbols. The absurdity of a railroad company's asking passengers to carry a disas-sembled train across a gorge makes the reader smile and softens the message about the seemingly insurmountable obstacles in life.

Taken as a whole, the allegories of the **Confabulario** show tremendous creative imagination, stylistic versatil-ity, and Arreola's own poetic vision of the world. They represent a skeptical vision of mankind characteristic of this century, yet bear Arreola's personal stamp, an abid-ing humor combined with a benign acceptance of man's absurd condition. (pp. 36–41)

Paula R. Heusinkveld, "Juan José Arreola: Allegorist in an Age of Uncertainty," in *Chasqui*, Vol. XIII, Nos. 2–3, February–May, 1984, pp. 33–43.

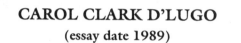

CAROL CLARK D'LUGO
(essay date 1989)

[In the following excerpt, D'Lugo applies reader-response theory to Arreola's *The Fair*, commenting on the reader's role in unifying the fragmentary novel by assimilating its multiple points of view.]

Juan José Arreola's *La feria* is a unique blending of re-gionalism and universality, to the detriment of neither. Its regionalism is most evident in the content: an array of Mexican characters particular to Arreola's native Ciudad Guzmán, formerly Zapotlán el Grande; language replete with *mexicanismos* so crucial to the text that the trans-lator for the English edition could not bring himself to mutilate the novel by translating certain of them; refer-ences to rural life which, although not specific to Mexico in theme (concern for the land, emerging sexuality, local literary groups), in treatment become the quintessence of Jalisco. *La feria's* universality, on the other hand, can be traced directly to form, for its creative use of fragmenta-tion links Arreola to a family of twentieth-century authors who, through innovative narrative strategies, force their readers into an awareness of the need to work actively with the given text.

Any examination of *La feria* must take into consid-eration its fragmented status, for Arreola's treatment of this technique cannot be ignored. While some critics have addressed the issue of fragmentation, however, what has not been fully explored is the special relationship between story and discourse, and the manner in which these two aspects of the novel are reflective of a desired reader response. In *La feria*, diegetic and discursive elements consistently point toward a designated process for an active reader's role. Throughout the novel, whether reflected in actions, images, or language, one perceives a movement from the individual to the collective, from the microcosmic unit to the whole, thus drawing the reader's attention to the process of unification. As a consequence of the repetition of this technique, one becomes aware of the dramatization of a possible cohesiveness attainable by responding to the author's inducing the reader to work with the fragments to forge a whole, to construct and/or complete the novel that is *La feria*. To reinforce this notion, Arreola offers his readers a negative example of potential response. He includes as a model of a reader-in-the-text one who remains distanced from that which he would understand. At the same time, this character voices the contrast between an active and a passive reading of circumstance, hence of narrative. While the active reading not only takes more effort, but also reveals a more painful reality, it is, finally, the more satisfactory and fulfilling. It offers a complete experience that provides multiple levels of significance for the reader.

By its fragmentation, *La feria* calls attention to its status as a non-whole. Yet through elements of story, the text offers its readers an example of a role which will fulfill the novel's potential through their active involvement with the segments. The fragments cry out for unification. Indeed, one might say that in Arreola's novel, on various levels, story represents the dramatization of the desire of its discourse.

John Upton calls *La feria* "a gallery of voices," a complimentary phrase as used by the translator, yet also the source of initial disorientation for the reader. In this novel a wide variety of characters speak out in an ample spectrum of discourses. Generally the narration is in the first person, although there are exceptions. The reader is exposed to, among others an Indian *tlayacanque* who comments on the indigens' claim to the land; a shoemaker who decides to try his luck at farming; a preadolescent experiencing sexual feelings and confessing all; a ladies' man flaunting sexual prowess; a few prostitutes and their madam; a poetess who sells cosmetics as a complement to her erotic verse; assorted shopkeepers; a budding poet recording his efforts to court a young girl; and San José, the patron saint of Zapotlán. One meets the rich and the poor, the educated and the ignorant, the experienced sexually obsessed and the innocent sexually obsessed. Characters either speak out themselves or are spoken about; rarely do they speak to each other. Some voices appear with frequency, others surface but once; some are identified, others are left anonymous. Frequently the readers must make their own identification through the content of the speech: references to the narrator's profession; certain peculiar characteristics traceable to one personage; an indication of reciprocity in a relationship about which the reader has been informed from the other point of view; reiteration of language or theme. Complicating matters even further is the inclusion of recorded voices from historical documents, newspapers, even the Bible. The reader's initial reaction is very likely to be that the fragments have been thrown together haphazardly, as Raúl Chávarri comments: "puestas una tras otra, al azar."

Arreola divides his text into 288 fragments, a self-referential strategy flaunting non-linearity, a lack of respect for traditional norms of narrative continuity. He then further calls attention to this truncated discourse by inserting a variety of vignettes, one for each space between fragments. (pp. 57–9)

Contiguous fragments at times demonstrate the use of perspectivism, that is, different points of view in relation to the same occurrence. Frequently, however, contiguity yields nothing more than spatial concurrence, as the segments seem totally unrelated. In addition, one finds sections dating from Colonial times, the *Reforma*, and the Revolution intercalated into those of the "present," the latter not identified by a year, but clearly established as a linear movement from the spring sowing to the autumn harvest and October fair, as reinforced by the farmer's notes and the young poet's diary.

Certain linear coherence within an apparently otherwise unordered discourse, in fact, soon lessens the reader's initial disorientation. For, despite a great variety of narrative voices and forms, certain definite linear episodes are clearly discernible. Arreola himself has identified five: "Los fragmentos componen cuatro o cinco series bastante evidentes. Ellas son las labores agrícolas, la lucha por la tierra, las veladas de los miembros del Ateneo, las confesiones del niño, los amores del joven poeta. . . ." To this I would add the Licenciado's funeral, important not only for its linear development, but also for its bringing together of story, discourse, and reader's role, as shall be demonstrated below.

Arreola confesses to having had the intention of writing a novel in the traditional manner or, in his words: "puro y extendido, esto es, continuo." Soon, however, he found himself disillusioned with what he had written; it lacked the rhythm he desired. Recognizing the quality of some shorter sections and relating them to his earlier works consisting of brief pieces led Arreola to an idea for a new approach: ". . . una idea que se ha vuelto convicción: la de captar mis impresiones del mundo y mis estados anímicos, esto es, las reacciones ante lo que moralmente me acontece, en pequeños textos o relatos que tratan de resumir mi concepción del mundo." Arreola mixed his creative sections based on his experiences in Ciudad Guzmán with the aforementioned written excerpts from actual documents plus biographical information requested from some of his fellow-citizens and incorporated almost verbatim. The sections are all brief and evocative in some way of life in Zapotlán, with special emphasis on language.

In an interview with Gustavo Sainz, Arreola in a sense justifies his selected discourse by contrasting the twentieth-century author with his nineteenth-century counterpart. As paraphrased by Yulan Washburn [in his *Juan José Arreola*]: "Arreola says that the twentieth-century writer's mind is simply not the same as that of the earlier writers who developed so many of the techniques that have come to be associated with the novel. The interior of the mind and memory are not made up of long discourses." Washburn goes on to compare Arreola's fragmented discourse to the sensorial impressions one would experience in a stroll through an actual fair:

> He . . . put his novel together so that it entered the readers' mind in much the same way that the readers would perceive reality if they were walking through a fair: they would encounter people they did not know and would never get to know; they would hear passing scraps of conversation, exclamations, and tones of voice; they would see faces at one point and reencounter them at another, never knowing their names. If the readers were attentive they might learn the stories of a few passers-by. In a sense everything would be a confusion, but it would be a confusion familiar to every reader in life as it is actually lived every day by the consciousness.

Arreola's analogy of the same process is even more provocative, as he makes a comparison between his novel and: ". . . un archipiélago de pequeños islotes que al fin y al cabo suponían bajo la superficie de los hechos narrados una masa continental. Esto es, la novela probable de la cual sólo he querido dar, finalmente, una serie de puntos o de situaciones agudas."

Here, without mentioning it explicitly, Arreola touches upon the reader's role, for to reach the "continental mass," the probable novel requires movement, activity. It is important to note that the author does not impose strict limits on his readers: the outcome is *la novela probable*, not a clearly defined construct. Arreola does, however, incorporate through story and discourse a suggestion of what type of activity or movement on the part of the reader will initiate the process, beginning with a subtle indication of grouping in the fragments related to the Licenciado's funeral.

Although manifesting multiple narrative voices, segments sixty-four through eighty-three all relate to one occurrence: the death and burial of the usurer. Until this point in the novel, the voices, although possibly speaking about the same theme (land, for example), did not reach out to each other in communication but, instead, spoke in isolation. Speakers were as disconnected as fragments. Beginning with section sixty-four, one finds for ten pages communication among characters as well as cohesiveness among fragments, since each successive segment yields more information. As the multiple perspectives are combined by readers to form a more ample vision, they begin to understand the inadequacy of one point of view. Char-

acters group together, either to bury the Licenciado or to gossip about him; fragments are united into a cohesive whole; finally, readers have illustrated before them tangible evidence that combining certain parts can produce a unit. This piece of story reflects both discourse and reader's participation, making readers aware of the attempts at grouping they have already made in response to the initial incoherence of the fragmented text. The Licenciado's funeral is, in effect, a dramatization of the reader's activity and a confirmation of the positive results attainable through involvement with the text.

Significantly, there are other pieces of story subsequent to the Licenciado's funeral which reinforce the notion of grouping, of going from the individual to the collective. Those who owe money to the deceased speak of forming a debtors' association; some with literary leanings decide to form the Ateneo for cultural exchanges. Gradually, following the story-induced impetus, the reader moves beyond the more superficial level of grouping individual stories (all the confessional scenes; the farmer's notes) to a more profound stratum of artistic composition where other aspects of Arreola's masterfully controlled unity are waiting to be discovered.

Once readers allow themselves to move in and among the fragments, they find that the movement from the individual to the collective is reflected throughout the novel, giving it a cohesiveness which could not be appreciated from a more distanced view. In this sense, the reader's role can be seen in contrast to the vision of the whole reflected by the priest's ascending a nearby hill to view Zapotlán:

> Veía el valle como lo vio la primera vez Fray Juan de Padilla, sólo por encima: "Pero yo, Señor, lo veo por debajo. ¡Qué iniquidad, Dios mío, qué iniquidad! Un río de estulticia me ha entrado por las orejas, incesante como las aguas que bajan de las Peñas en las crecidas de julio y agosto. Aguas limpias que la gente ensucia con la basura de sus culpas . . . Pero desde aquí, desde arriba, qué pueblo tan bonito, dormido a la orilla de su valle redondo, como una fábrica de adobes, de tejas y ladrillos.

It is true that the priest's vision unites Zapotlán spatially and serves as a temporal unifier, joining the priest and Fray Juan de Padilla. The priest's own words, however, indicate the inadequacy of such a distanced vision. From afar, one can appreciate the picturesque quality of the sleepy town. But such a vision is a distortion of reality as the priest knows it; reality, for him, involves the souls of the people, and to know the people, one must be among them and interact with them.

The priest is, in effect, a dramatization of the reader-in-the-text. Contrasting his two visions, one passive from above, the other active and involved, one perceives a direct parallel with the reader's role. Readers of *La feria* cannot remain distanced from its fragments without sacrificing the dynamism of the novel. They must move mentally among the segments relating the pieces of discourse, characters, and images.

Readers who undertake such involvement will appreciate the unity of *La feria*. As a specific example, movement from the individual to the collective transcends fragments to yield a cohesiveness indicative of Arreola's controlled artistic vision, both of the novel and of the suggested reader's role. I will examine the more important indicators of collectivity giving special attention to imagery and language. Instead of two hundred candles costing one peso apiece, don Fidencio is asked to construct one massive candle at the price of two hundred pesos. Because of inclement weather, the private funeral oration will instead be published in the newspaper for all to read. The farm laborers join the majordomo is tossing their hats to the ground, where the individual units fall into the shape of a cross. Even sexual pecadillos are spatially unified in the infamous *Zona de Tolerancia*. Through language Arreola reinforces the reader's awareness of unification, as he has a character comment on the new arrangement: "Más vale tener un lugar de a tiro echado a la perdición, que no todas esas lacras desparramadas por el cuerpo de Zapotlán."

Wording once again emphasizes movement from the individual to the collective with regard to the confessional scenes. At first, the young boy confesses, on an individual basis, to having had thoughts about sex. Quickly the reader is brought to associate the words, "Me acuso Padre," with the boy's part and thus should be well prepared for the collective confession after the earthquake which begins: "Me acuso Padre de Todo." The rest of the fragment, the longest of the novel, details a chaotic series of confessed sins which pulls together the townspeople to such an extent that the priests decide a single *Ego te absolvo* will suffice. Circularity within the mass confession reinforces its unified status: it begins and ends with "Me acuso Padre de que me robé una peseta." Even more impetus to consider the unity of the confession section is provided by the infrequency of periods of provide closure. Generally, individual voiced confessions are joined by commas, with occasional suspension points or exclamation marks. Mauricio Ostria notes the paradoxical nature of fragmentation's producing unity, precisely in the lengthy confession:

> Cada frase es una voz; cada voz un narrador que se relaciona de modo personal—y por lo tanto original—con los sucesos a que se refiere y con el interlocutor. La fragmentación ha llegado, pues, a su máxima expresión. Sin embargo, mágicamente, los fragmentos narrativos se han unido indisolublemente hasta dar origen a un nuevo ser; el ser del pueblo: acontecer colectivo coreado por la comunidad, vinculada en un solo acto, acto de fe personal y comunitario: todo el pueblo es el acontecer, el narrador y el interlocutor. Es ésta una nueva forma narrativa que no ha sido todavía suficientemente apreciada.

Finally, language alone is capable of fostering a sense of collectivity. A reference within the text to "la gran familia mexicana" during the annual celebration of independence may not seem unusual enough to call the reader's attention, but the beginning of the novel clearly announces a sense of collectivity: "Somos más o menos treinta mil. Unos dicen que más, otros que menos. Somos treinta mil desde siempre." In its privileged position, the first word of *La feria* is a signifier of plurality: *Somos*. Significantly, Arreola has stated: "El pasaje que condensa el espíritu del libro es el primero."

With such an emphasis on the movement from the individual to the collective with people, with objects, and with fragments, it comes as no surprise that there is also unity in theme. Chávarri gives particular mention to death, which he considers a classic theme for recent Mexican novelists. Death is not the most pervasive thematic unifier, however; it does not unite enough of the characters. By far the most thorough and persuasive treatment of theme in *La feria* is that of Luis Leal, who clearly demonstrates that the thematic unifier for individuals, collectives and institutions is *el fracaso:* failure. (pp. 59–63)

Leal sums up the multiple failures, linking them with what he considers the critical motif of the novel, the fair: "Todos estos personajes fracasados, todas estas instituciones fracasadas, todos estos santos, reyes virreyes, curas, señores y monseñores impotentes para detener la marcha hacia el fracaso, han sido hábilmente integrados, como en un mosaico, en obra narrativa cuyo motivo central es la feria." The novel culminates in the fair, and it, too, is a failure. Vandals spill kerosene about the bases of the *castillo's* platform, then quickly ignite them. Interestingly the final narrative voice combines audience (reader) response with the by now predictability of another failure: "En vez de arder parte por parte y en orden previsto por don Atilano, ya se imaginarán lo que pasó. El estallido fue general y completo, como el de un polvorín." The passage is also strikingly evocative of a reading of *La feria*. It is hard to read this novel, fragment by fragment, without having one's mind actively attempt to relate parts. This penultimate image would seem to suggest a source for the following description by Arreola: "*La feria* pertenece al género de los apocalipsis del bolsillo, y por lo tanto es natural que sus páginas recojan fragmentos, textuales o deformados, de la más variada tradición oral y escrita. . . ."

Arreola moves the reader beyond the fragments through grouping, through imagery, through themes which transcend the segmented discourse. Readers combine and contrast the multiple narrative voices for, to whom are these voices speaking if not to them? There seems to be little consensus among characters, even less communication. The reader must unite these limited, isolated visions (fragments), joining the characters efforts, opinions, emotions, and failures to form a fuller vision of

Zapotlán past and present. There is a reality beyond these fragments, alluded to in epigraph:

> Amo de moun pais, tu que dardais manifesto
> E dins sa lengo e dins sa gesto
> F. Mistral

This exerpt in modern Provençal from *Calendau* by Frédéric Mistral evokes the ultimate reality as the soul of one's country, here used in the Spanish sense of *patria chica*. Even more crucial in relationship to *La feria*, however, is the revelation of soul through words and deeds. From each narrative voice the reader is directly exposed to a perspective of it in Zapotlán. There is no intervention, no extraneous person to color the reader's interpretation. To be sure, no one voice, no one character is capable of a true vision of the whole. The only character who attempts to conceive a whole from a singular perspective forms a distorted vision from afar. Not even the author can capture the total reality of Zapotlán, not in narrative description. Arreola must evoke that reality through fragmentation, through pieces of life as represented by words and deeds, and allow the readers to construct their version of Zapotlán. The totality of these constructions might approach the real.

One reviewer has written of *La feria* that it cannot be told to someone else, it must be read: "*La feria*, como tiene el mérito de ser obra para ser leída, no puede contarse. En su corriente de opinión estriba el argumento para cada pasaje. Paso a paso con la vida pueblerina hay que hacer anales para explicarse el espectáculo." The work is to be experienced. The reader must move in and among the fragments to sense a whole. There really is no need to make a chronological ordering of all events, as the second portion of this passage might suggest. To do so is tantamount to mutilating the text. . . . (pp. 65–6)

Nor could the author of *La feria* change discourse without doing irreparable damage to his conception. Arreola has spoken with some frequency of his work as a manifestation of poetry in prose. His reader must therefore be able to receive the work in the same spirit. Any reader who remains passive, waiting to be told a full story, will either give up or dismiss the work as a bad novel, as at least one critic has done: "Arreola ama la vida y ama la literatura. Le falta la idea que le arrastra a escribir la obra que espera, que necesita. Por eso, frente al compromiso editorial, escribe la mala novela, pero honrado, toma las tijeras y corta y recorta hasta dejar el manuscrito en una serie de cuadros sobre la realidad mexicana" (Martínez Palacio).

But this is to remain passive before a very evocative text, to ignore poetic stimuli of this prose. Arreola's own words defend him best. In an interview with Mauricio de la Selva, Arreola comments on poetry but with a clear linkage to his literary production and notion of reader response:

> . . . el poema es una estructura verbal que dizque encierra la poesía, y yo siento que ese hueco formal, por dentro, nos da la sensación, y nos da la sensación porque nosotros lo llenamos, nosotros lo colmamos. El poeta en realidad crea el vaso. Y aquí si hay que citar la *boutade* de André Gide, que decía: "crea una forma bella, porque una idea más bella todavia vendrá a habitarla"; y esa "idea más bella todavía" es lo que nosotros formamos.

Arreola's appreciation of the poetic nature of his prose becomes even more apparent when he speaks about language:

> . . . ese lenguaje al que aspiro y al que me he acercado alguna vez el lenguaje absoluto, el lenguaje puro que da un rendímiento mayor que el lenguaje frondoso, porque es fértil, porque es puro tronco y lleva en sí el designio de las ramas. Este lenguaje es de una desnudez potente, la desnudez poderosa del árbol sin hojas. . . Tal vez mi obra sea escasa, pero es escasa porque constantemente la estoy podando. Prefiero los gérmenes a los desarrollos voluminosos, agotados por su propio exceso verbal . . . El árbol que desarrolla todas sus hojas, hasta la última, es un árbol agotado, un árbol donde la savia está vencida por su propia plenitud.

Arreola sows so that the reader might reap. His work is suggestion, evocation, and the fragmented structure of *La feria* serves his stated purpose well. Instead of burying readers in excessive verbiage, trying to relay everything about life in Zapotlán, he shows enough respect to allow them to supply the leaves for the tree in an individualized arrangement of a whole. Arreola achieves a shaping of reader response in an inobtrusive way, letting diegetic and discursive elements function within the text in such a manner so as to dramatize for the reader a potential process for unification without an overtly intervening authorial presence. Readers of *La feria* are indeed privileged: respected for their competence, allowed their artistic freedom, and privy to the experience of Zapotlán through a joint creation. (pp. 66–7)

Carol Clark D'Lugo, "Arreola's 'La Feria': The Author and the Reader in the Text," in *Hispanofila*, Vol. 33, No. 1, September, 1989, pp. 57–67.

SOURCES FOR FURTHER STUDY

Burt, John R. "This Is No Way to Run a Railroad: Arreola's Allegorical Railroad and a Possible Source." *Hispania* 71, No. 4 (December 1988): 806–11.

> Investigates affinities between Arreola's "El guardagujas" and Nathaniel Hawthorne's "Celestial Railroad."

Gilgen, Read G. "Absurdist Techniques in the Short Stories of Juan José Arreola." *Journal of Spanish Studies: Twentieth Century* 8, Nos. 1–2 (Spring-Fall 1980): 67–77.

> Analyzes several stories contained in Arreola's *Confabulario* as expressions of absurdist literature, as outlined by Albert Camus in his *Myth of Sisyphus.*

Herz, Theda M. "Continuity and Evolution: Juan José Arreola as Dramatist." *Latin American Theatre Review* 8, No. 2 (1975): 15–26.

> Discusses the plays *La hora de todos* and *Terceran llamada*, noting Arreola's development as a dramatist in the seventeen-year interim between the two works.

——. "Artistic Iconoclasm in Mexico: Countertexts of Arreola, Agustín, Avilés and Hiriart." *Chasqui* XVIII, No. 1 (May 1989): 17–25.

Identifies Arreola as a pioneer of Mexican literature whose works of the 1960s and 1970s transgressed literary traditions.

Leal, Luis. "The New Mexican Short Story." *Studies in Short Fiction* VIII, No. 1 (Winter 1971): 9–19.

> Outlines Arreola's involvement in the evolution of the modern Mexican short story.

Mason, Margaret L., and Washburn, Yulan M. "The Bestiary in Contemporary Spanish American Literature." *Revista de Estudios Hispanicos* 8, No. 2 (May 1974): 189–209.

> Explores Arreola's symbolic depictions of human nature in the animal sketches of his *Bestiario.*

Menton, Seymour. "Juan José Arreola and the Twentieth Century Short Story." *Hispania* XLII, No. 3 (September 1959): 295–308.

> Comprehensive overview of Arreola's short stories.

Washburn, Yulan M. "An Ancient Mold for Contemporary Casting: The Beast Book of Juan." *Hispania* 56, Special Issue (April 1973): 295–300.

> Examines Arreola's *Bestiario*, featuring an analysis of the vignette called "El Rinoceronte."

Additional coverage of Arreola's life and career is contained in the following sources published by Gale Research: *Contemporary Authors*, Vols. 113, 131; *Dictionary of Literary Biography*, Vol. 113; and *Hispanic Writers.*

Miguel Asturias

1899–1974

(Full name Miguel Ángel Asturias) Guatemalan novelist, short story writer, poet, playwright, and journalist.

INTRODUCTION

*A*sturias, a career diplomat and one of Guatemala's most renowned writers, is especially known for his extensive use of both ancient mythologies and socialist political themes in enigmatic and unique literary works. He received wide recognition for his first novel, *El señor presidente* (1946; *El Señor Presidente)*, a realistic political novel; however, his subsequent novels—*Hombres de maíz* (1949; *Men of Maize*) and *Mulata de Tal* (1963; *Mulata)*—conveyed his new "cosmovision," a transcendent vision of the world expressed through the blending of the mythical and timeless with the material world and its events. Indeed, Asturias's work has been especially praised and studied for his "magic realism" technique, which seamlessly synthesizes the fantastic and magical with real-life images and events to present a unified vision of life and truth.

Born in Guatemala City, Asturias was the son of a prominent supreme court justice. When Miguel was young, his father fell out of political favor and was forced to move with his family to Salamá, a town in the heart of Guatemala's Mayan Indian interior. After graduating as a lawyer from the Universidad de San Carlo in 1923, Asturias founded *Tiempos Nuevos,* a newspaper critical of Gautemala's militarist government. The newspaper's viewpoint made enemies for Asturias, who left Guatemala after his life was threatened and moved to Paris. There he studied oriental mythology at the Sorbonne (1923-28). After working for a time as a journalist in Europe, he returned to Guatemala in 1933, becoming increasingly involved in governmental affairs. He was elected to the national congress in 1942, named attaché to Mexico in 1946, minister-counselor to Argentina in 1947, diplomat to Paris in 1952, and ambassador to El Salvador in 1953. With the advent of a rightist regime in Guatemala which he publicly opposed, Asturias lost his citizenship and worked as a journalist in Venezuela and other countries. By 1966 he had regained his citizenship and was named ambassador to France. While engaged in these wide-ranging political roles, Asturias continued his ambitious writing career which embraced several novels, short stories, books of poetry, and plays. He died in Madrid in 1974.

Asturias first received literary recognition with his collection of short stories *Leyendas de Guatemala* (1930), based upon a series of ancient Mayan legends. Subsequently, he published two volumes of poetry, finally winning widespread acclaim with his novel *El señor presidente*. Written in 1932-33 but not printed until 1946 for political reasons, the novel was loosely based on the career of Guatemalan President Manuel Estrada Cabrera, and incorporated the ancient Babylonian Ishtar-Tammuz myth. It tells of the machinations of a ruthless president who acts without reference to the moral norm, causing even his closest associates to suffer from his cruelty. Asturias's next major novel, *Men of Maize*, relies heavily on Mayan mythologies. The story opens with Gaspar Ilóm and his fellow corngrowing Indians, who believe the corn to be sacred, battling a modern society which grows corn solely for commercial reasons. Colonel Godoy and the army destroy Ilóm, the Indians, and the sacred mythology of the corn, and for that they are cursed. The rest of the novel concerns the curse's implications and various characters' elusive encounters with the sacred, entwining the mythic and the real to express Asturias's "cosmovision." Asturias's next novel was *Viento fuerte* (1949; *Strong Wind*), the first part of what came to be called the *Banana Trilogy*, which also includes *El papa verde* (1954; *The Green Pope*) and *Los ojos de los enterrados* (1960; *The Eyes of the Interred*). Together the novels of the *Banana Trilogy* illustrate the effects of the coming of the American Fruit Company to Guatemala. As the company clears the tropical forests and establishes the banana fields, many economic hardships affect the Guatemalan people and those independent farmers who need to sell their crops to the American company. In the third book, *The Eyes of the Interred*, a massive strike is underway and violence is expected. The protagonist, Sansur, convinces the people to seek a nonviolent solution to their problems. In the end the people achieve a modest, yet optimistic victory: the establishment of a labor union for the protection of their rights and dignity. Another political work, *Weekend en Guatemala* (1956) is a collection of critical short stories focusing on the American invasion of Guatemala and the overthrow of President Jacobo Arbenz. Asturias's last major work, the novel *Mulata*, extensively utilizes both Mayan and

Greek myths to explore the clash between the spiritual and material in modern life.

Critics have generally focused on Asturias's liberal incorporation of Greek, Aztec, Babylonian, and Mayan mythologies into his works, attributing such an approach to his upbringing in a remote Mayan town, his studies in oriental mythologies, and his translation of the Mayan *Popol Vuh*, a collection of ancient, sacred Mayan scriptures. Many scholars contend that because of his broad use of myth, his writings are often inscrutable and they evidence an apparent lack of structure and cohesion. While some commentators point out that Asturias's unique blending of the mythical with the real world creates his own peculiar view of what is real and true, others contend that many of Asturias's works have a blatantly socialist agenda which detracts from the power of his story lines. Furthermore, critics have faulted Asturias for his lack of true characterization, or sacrificing the character for the broader aims of his mythologized vision of society and the world. This approach, critics have said, tends to make his characters flat and somewhat unrealistic. Then too, some describe Asturias's writing style as baroque because of its bold and startling, yet logically ordered aspect, while others stress the existential and surreal elements in his writings, wherein the ultimate meaning and truth of events in the here and now are couched in magical and mythical terms. Commentators have also pointed out that several of his works, notably *Men of Maize* and *Mulata*, successfully explore themes such as the search for the lost feminine element in modern society, the role of love in life, the understanding of the self, and optimism and zest for living.

Asturias's works, though widely read in Guatemala and France for their eloquent explorations of and uniquely crafted statements about the unbalanced psyche of modern humankind, are not well known to North American audiences. Nevertheless, Asturias has received many literary accolades, including the Prix Sylla Monsegur in 1931 for *Leyendas de Guatemala*; the Prix du Meilleur Roman Estranger in 1952 for *El señor presidente*; the Lenin Peace Prize in 1966 for the *Banana Trilogy*; and the Nobel Prize for literature in 1967. In an interview with Günter Lorenz, Asturias said that his readers "should be conscious of the fact that . . . [my] works constitute the response to this living and changing reality. One must see not only with the eyes. One must penetrate this green world, this land of tigers and eruptions. One must familiarize oneself with this cosmic world, with this world of telluric struggles, with this world in which the struggle for survival still goes on."

CRITICAL COMMENTARY

ARIEL DORFMAN
(essay date 1967)

[A Chilean author and critic, Dorfman's writings often examine the influence of culture on social and political values. Below, Dorfman examines Asturias's blending of Mayan myth with reality in a close reading of *Men of Maize*, contending that "time becomes eternal and eternity becomes mortal" in the author's 'new cosmovision' of the world. This essay was written in 1967.]

A strange fate has befallen Miguel Angel Asturias's masterpiece, *Men of Maize*. Along with Alejo Carpentier's remarkable *The Kingdom of This world*, which was also published in 1949, it could well be said to inaugurate the extraordinary renaissance of the contemporary Latin American novel. And yet it has been consistently underrated by critics and neglected by readers. (p. 1)

Even those few critics who recognize *Men of Maize's* outstanding qualities, have had to accept the arguments of its detractors, affirming its greatness in spite of its defects. Giuseppe Bellini [in *La narrativa de Miguel Angel Asturias*, Milan, 1966], for instance, who has given in the most affectionate consideration, asserts that its unity is not to be found in the plot but rather in the "climate." In order to transmit the "spirit of Guatemala," he suggests, or because it is a "symphonic poem" which mixes the social and mythic spheres, its structure is inevitably dispersed.

If we are to rescue a work that has contributed so significantly to the founding of a new dynasty in Latin American fiction, a new way of transmitting and understanding our reality, we must go beyond such vague generalizations. Only a close reading of its six parts, attempting to find the novel's hidden unity, will allow, I believe, a real understanding of the significance and originality of *Men of Maize*, the reason why it should be considered a major source for the new forms of fiction that were to be written on our continent in the following decades.

The first chapter tells how Gaspar Ilóm, the chief of the lands of Ilóm, begins a war against those who plant corn for commercial reasons. Señor Tomás Machojón, instigated by his wife, poisons the chief, and the latter, abandoned by his wife, la Piojosa Grande, drinks the river to pacify his guts, thus saving himself. But he gains nothing thereby, since Colonel Chalo Godoy has taken advantage of his absence to kill the Indian fighters. Gaspar throws himself into the river so as not to have to survive his warriors.

This action must be deciphered by the reader, who will find himself submerged in a buzzing swarm of words that float dream-like between the real and the fictional. One must interpret, break the linguistic spells, and uncover within that flowing cavern the profile of a meaning. This narrative method serves to indicate that we are confronting a moment, at the beginning of the book, in which dream and reality cohabit, in which the mythic is still fully incarnate in man, in which the human and the natural worlds are interchangeable.

Using certain magical, iterative formulas, the "ground" tries to awaken Gaspar Ilóm, who is sleeping, buried, "unable to break away from a snake of six hundred thousand twists of mud, moonlight, forests, springs, birds and echoes which he felt around his body." The earth "falls dreaming," but he cannot go on sleeping because there is no shade, no vegetation, "he awakens among what were once mountains, but are now the bare hills of Ilóm"; it (the earth) has been violated, snatched from its natural, sacred, state, thus making impossible the magical union of man and nature, the primordial link that is possible in a prelogical, unreal stage, where everything sleeps and everything dreams, not like now, a present in which there exists "corn-growing land filled with stagnant water from being awake so much." Provoked by the action of the corn growers who burn the vegetation in order to be able to grow corn for sale, offended by the destruction of her shade-filled forests which are converted into useless gold, desperately needing to go back to sleep and to make magic, nature orders Gaspar Ilóm to destroy the sowers, to install a symmetry of retribution, doing to them what they have done to the earth: "chop out the eyebrows of those who put axe to trees, burn the eyelids of those who burn the forest and freeze the bodies of those who stop the water." The cleansing from evil is proclaimed, and the return to balance, and revenge upon those who have separated man from nature. This loss of origin, a theme that runs throughout Asturias's work, necessarily brings oppression and exploitation in its wake, whether it comes from a local dictator, a Spanish conquistador, or the North American Empire. Corn "sown to be eaten is the sacred nourishment of man, who was made of corn. Sown for business it is the hunger of man who was made of corn." There are two types of

Principal Works

Leyendas de Guatemala (short stories) 1930

*El señor presidente (novel) 1946
   [*The President*, 1963; also published as *El Señor Presidente*, 1964]

Hombres de maíz (novel) 1949
   [*Men of Maize*, 1975]

Poesía sien de alondra (poetry) 1949

†*Viento fuerte* (novel) 1950
   [*The Cyclone*, 1967; also published as *Strong Wind*, 1968]

†*El papa verde* (novel) 1954
   [*The Green Pope*, 1971]

Weekend en Guatemala (short stories) 1956

†*Los ojos de los enterrados* (novel) 1960
   [*The Eyes of the Interred*, 1973]

Mulata de Tal (novel) 1963
   [*Mulata*, 1967; also published as *Mulata and Mr. Fly*, 1967]

*This work was written in 1932–33.

†These novels constitute the *Banana Trilogy.*

men of maize, those who live in the magical plenitude of a sensual continuity with nature, the forms of a dream, of a sleep, and those who live in wakefulness, hunger, and death. The latter are uprooted, lose their roots, not only in a metaphorical sense, but also really and literally, becoming vagabonds upon the earth, deniers of the sacred vegetable growth. Therefore, the picaresque is ever-present in all of Asturias's production and in this work in particular: the directionless wandering in search of food, the absurd pilgrimage, a wind which passes again and again and brings ruin, which "will diminish the land and the corn grower will leave, taking his seed elsewhere, until he himself is finished, like a faded ear of corn in the midst of rich lands," with the nostalgia of rest in the wind of his eyes, the memory of the primal immobility that Gaspar Ilóm imitated and that is the equivalent of the lost paradise. (pp. 1–3)

In his struggle, Gaspar has the aid of cosmic forces, the yellow rabbits for whom "there is no secret, no danger, no distance," the spirit of the fire which does battle beyond the death of the chieftain himself and is an emanation of the natural order seeking permanence in its being. Everything that refers to Gaspar is seen through whiffs of apparent chaos, which vibrate nevertheless with the secret vertebration of ritual. The exaggerated language, its serpentine, baroque syntax, a world that slithers forward like a snake, the union of dissimilar elements, transfiguration by means of the word, sacred, solemn, and distant, the

inner vision of what is happening: it all produces in the reader's mind the process of enveloping primitivism that the character himself is living, and forces the leveling of dream and reality, leading the reader to mix fiction and fact without being able or wanting to separate them. The main theme of the novel, the relationship between myth and reality, has its narrative and linguistic correlation in this fusion, but it is only revealed fully in the first chapter, where the mythic impulse transfixes everything. The fact that legend and reality, word and deed, are the same experience for the reader and for the character, will contrast with the remaining chapters, where it is precisely the relationship between these dimensions, how near to or far from each other they are, that is made problematic.

Take the poisoning of Gaspar Ilóm, at the beginning of the novel. If we were to try to give a chronological or merely logical order to this chaotic moment (Gaspar is poisoned, the poison is made from two white roots, la Piojosa Grande flees), we would find two successive, and perhaps parallel, sequences which coincide in certain recurrences but whose linkage does not allow us to exactly place each event nor to impose any order upon that rush of images, prophecies, and foreshadowings. One of the two sequences (Which of the two? And what if it were both?) is a premonitory dream (or memory dream) of a la Piojosa Grande. The repetition, once in dream, again in reality, without being able to define which is which, blurs and clouds the habitual way in which things occur in this world. The reader must simply absorb what happened, must interpret it, he or she suddenly transformed into a magician. What is dreamed and what is lived are inextricably bound together, and this means that any effort by the reader to order that world will falsify it and end up in failure. Just as his characters struggle against civilization and against cold, everyday reality, Asturias will in the rest of the work, albeit in a more subdued manner, continue to destroy all rational mentality, using, although in a less exaggerated fashion, every viable means to make his language boil: tossing out time shifts, interweaving impersonal and subjective points of view, confusing colloquialisms and the thoughts of his characters with the supposed objectivity of actions, silencing men and personifying the animal and plant kingdoms, detaching all points of reference, sweeping away conventions. Fire, one of the protagonists of the novel, is also its formal principle: words are flames, they sputter, they refuse to be enclosed, they hop like gleaming yellow rabbits, they die down and then rise up again with an uncontainable rhythm of revenge, the consummation by the fire-grandfather-son, punishment, and we have reached the second chapter which narrates how those who betrayed Gaspar Ilóm are punished.

When the chief died, the witch doctors of the fireflies had foretold the death of all the poison carriers and of their children, indicating that "su semilla de girasol sea tierra de muerto en las entrañas de las mujeres. . . "

("their sunflower seed will be a dead man's earth in the wombs of women. . . "). The curse begins to be fulfilled in the second chapter with the death of Señor Tomás and of his son Machojón, as also with that of Vaca Manuela.

The first to disappear is Machojón, who was on his way to ask for the hand of his girlfriend, Candelaria Reinoso, in marriage. No one knows what happened to him; only we, the readers, directly sense the supernatural wonder of his absorption by the fireflies, that fire that leaps from the words of the witch doctors: "From his hat behind his ears, along the collar of his embroidered shirt, down the sleeves of his jacket, along the hairy ridges of his hands and between his fingers, like a cold sweat the flickering gleam of the fireflies coursed, a light like the beginning of the world, in which everything was seen without any clear shape."

Suddenly the rumor spreads that Machojón rides each time the land is burned off, just prior to the sowing of the corn. This version originates in the visit of a mysterious woman to Candelaria Reinoso. Everything indicates that the woman is a semi-imaginary creature: we do not know who she is nor where she comes from; she is referred to as "ghost woman"; another customer does not see her; several times there is mention of her "teeth as white as lard" and "lard-like clothing," which is significant when we remember that it is precisely lard that Candelaria sells. What the woman affirms is also vague: "Yes, child, who would believe it, but the men who went out to burn off the land saw Don Macho mounted on his horse among the flames; they say he was dressed in gold." Lost in the gossip of others, anonymous, unknown, coincidental with what the narrator has already revealed, the legend of Machojón is born into reality. Immediately, "Candelaria Reinoso closed her eyes and dreamed or saw that Machojón was riding his wild stallion down from the top of the hill they were burning. . . " We are left in suspense as to whether she actually saw him or dreamed him.

In her turn Candelaria will transmit what she has heard, or what she has desired, or what she has imagined, to Señor Tomás, who will begin to give up lands for clearing, just to see his son who "appeared in the middle of the best fires, riding his stallion, bathed in gold. . . his spurs sparkling like stars and eyes gleaming like sun." Señor Tomás consolidates the legend, trying to provoke the presence of the supernatural, while the corn growers take advantage of his weakness, since it is in their interest to obtain lands for their seed "without any formal arrangement"; they feed his madness, assuring him they have seen Machojón galloping among the flames, repeating the same words already on everyone's lips. Thus, this legend, which is of human origin and which has been invented out of the daily needs of each man and woman, will increase the action of the fire, more and more, until the night arrives when Señor Tomás, hearing the truth from the mouths of the children and the fools (who make fun of the story and transform Machojón into a scarecrow),

decides to disguise himself as Machojón and imitates the appearance of his son as it is described in the popular tale; he sets fire to the dry corn field "in order to ride among the flames mounted on his stallion so they would believe he was Machojón." He wants that golden Machojón to exist (despite the fact that he cannot see him, he knows that he is real), and he wants the corn planters (who say they can see him, but do not believe in his reality) to be his witnesses. In a little while the fire spreads, the tone of the first chapter returns; Señor Tomás's fire becomes the mythic flame of the fireflies, the avenger who flows from the words of the witch doctors: "An immense firefly, as immense as the plains and the hills." First it is said that it is "like (igual a) the ears of yellow rabbits, in pairs, by the hundreds, baskets full of yellow rabbits, fleeing the fire, a round beast that was all face, no neck, a face rolling on the ground, a leathery-faced beast with an angry eye, among the heavy brow and the thick beard of the smoke." From the comparison "like" he goes to the metaphor and from there to the full and real narrated presence of the yellow rabbits, the mythological element: "the ears of the yellow rabbits moved among the sandy, deep-water streams without being extinguished." Thus, in one simultaneous instant, men create an action (setting a fire) and effectively provoke another (the revenge of the yellow rabbits); they are the servants of the fire and of the legend that has become reality. The origin of the fire and of the myth is found in human actions, but it has its foundation, its raison d'être, in the magical world, in the fulfillment of a curse. Señor Tomás, the corn planters, and also Vaca Manuela, are consumed by the fire that they themselves set, which is at the same time the cosmic fire punishing their betrayal.

It comes from Gaspar Ilóm who "had managed to hurl the lasso of his word around the fire that wandered freely in the mountains of Ilóm, and then to take it home and tie it up in his house, so that it wouldn't destroy all the trees, so it wouldn't work in collusion with the corn planters and merchants." The Indian's death means freedom for the fire, because "fire is like water when it is spilled. There is no way to hold them back." Men are transformed into "little fingers of a dark will that struggles, after millenia, to free the captive of the white hummingbird, prisoner of the man in the rock and in the eye of the grain of corn," the fire that sleeps there, ready to burst forth: "the captive can escape from the guts of the earth, into the heat and the light of the clearing fire and of war." When there is war (men destroy men) or there is clearing of land (men destroy earth), fire can escape, infected by human action, aided by the gestures of those beings who, without understanding the unlimited mythic power of their instrument, use it for their own ends, freeing the great, universal fire that seeks to wander free and destroy. "Its prison is fragile, and if the fire escapes, what brave, virile soul can struggle against it, when all flee in terror?" Therefore, because it is magical only the *word* could bind the fire "so that it could do no damage." The supernatural cannot intervene arbitrarily; it must be invoked from the world of the human; it must originate in everyday events, just like the legend, that has its origin in small human words, and becomes gigantic because once man has hurled it out it begins to grow, to swell, on its own account. Myth, like fire, is held by fragile bonds, and it only requires a tiny spark to produce the final conflagration, a single word in an unknown mouth, a nothing that speaks, so that a story goes out victoriously to move around the world and take over reality. The words of the witch doctors are fulfilled. The legend of Machojón ends up being real, creating a fire, provoking an imitation that leads to the desired revenge.

It has been affirmed [by José Antonio Galaos] that Asturias's fundamental theme is freedom. It seems to me, on the contrary, that what most concerns him is tyranny, alienation, the grotesque presence of punishment in any of its forms, in a decaying world. Dictatorship, which in *El Señor Presidente* manifested itself in the political realm, is now a dictatorship of fire and of the word, but always a tyranny that men themselves ask for, adore, and help to build. Just as el señor Presidente can exercise his mandate because he is sustained by fear and by the conscious or involuntary support of others, the legend is able to impose itself upon reality because men live it fully as a way to make sense of their humanity, and thus the cosmic fire can break out because men concur with its effort and thus free it. The "little human bundles" of Asturias's world end up destroying themselves, being disintegrated by the very forces they themselves released or supplanted by the words they themselves spoke. This tyranny of language perversely parallels the political oppression which is omnipresent in Asturias's world. Magic and the law both are born in that primitive universe from an original curse, an order which men cannot deny. The phantom of inhuman powers entangling mankind runs throughout Asturias's work, from *El alhajadito* to the victimization suffered by the characters in Tierrapaulita, that magical and Pantagruelian dominion of *Mulata de Tal*. The consolation which Asturias leaves us is that human beings are responsible for their own condition.

And the revenge goes on.

The brothers Tecún kill all the Zacatón family. Ostensibly, they do so to put an end to the spell by which the Zacatóns have harmed Señora Yuca, by "putting a cricket in her navel"; but in reality it is a matter of punishing the Zacatóns for having been the pharmacists who sold the poison used against Gaspar, as we will learn in the last chapter. Once again, a supernatural action is channeled through human hands. In order to discover who had caused the damage, according to the healer, the brothers needed "a fire of living trees so that the night would have a tail of fresh flames, the tail of a yellow rabbit," and we can guess that the Tecún will be the voice of the fire, the instrument of revenge. "The healer wedged himself in the doorway, bathed in crickets, a thousand tiny hiccups outside that answered the sick woman's hiccuping inside, and there he counted the fleeting stars, the yellow rabbits of the witch doctors who lived in the hide of virgin deer, those who offered and took away eyelashes of breath from the eyes of the soul." The hiccups and the crickets that the mother of the Tecúns has are, in fact, a part of nature, provoked by the healer in conjunction with the yellow rabbits. And the decapitated heads of the Zacatóns will be burned, consumed by the words, the verbal flames, of the witch doctors: "The flames, with the scent of human blood, stretched out, slipping away in fear, then they crouched for the attack, like golden tigers."

As a second part of the chapter we have the narrative of the death of the deer of the seven clearing fires, who in reality is the healer himself. It is the start of the theme of animal and man as a single entity: "They were one. The healer and the deer of the seven clearing fires, like you and your shadow, like you and your soul, like you and your breath."

But there is another focus of interest in this brief chapter. Seven years have already passed since Gaspar's death. Asturias has slowly distanced us from that moment, opening up a breach of time which will permit the creation of the legend. The entire book is full of dialogues in which the past is discussed and an event is ritualized as a way of molding its linguistic permanence. At times this event, already witnessed by the reader, is repeated just as it was before, word for word, narrating once again what happened. At other times, the exchange that comments on this previous event gradually deforms it, changing its meaning. In any case, the thrust of these dialogues is clear: the legend is created not just in its founding moment, in human action, but also in its transmission, which will determine what can be forgotten and what remembered of that instant. As the pages unfold, intermingled with the life of the men of maize, stitched into imperceptible time, the myth gradually becomes residual, it becomes dynamic in the present and the future, it is remade slipping into the future. And it is this presence of time, this basic dimension of all current Latin American narrative, which is going to change the interrelationship, distance and nearness, between myth and reality. For Asturias, time passes in the essential site where man becomes man, the fount of all lies and of all knowledge, the place where imagination and history touch: language.

In that world populated by saying, by "the whys and wherefores of ancient speech," by events in process of becoming memories, the words of the witch doctors weigh ever more upon the memory of the last recipient of the curse, Colonel Chalo Godoy. During the entire horseback ride on the last day of his life, the light is playing with him, slowly surrounding him with signs of his approaching disappearance, worms of fire, "splendor of chaos," that he does not know how to interpret, until he is burned alive.

The way in which his death is narrated is striking and indicates another step in the evolution of the myth and of reality. We never see Godoy's agony as an objective fact; we are never sure how it happened; we are not supported by the omniscient knowledge of the narrator, who refuses to describe that death, surrendering his voice to one of his characters, Benito Ramos, who, because he has made a pact with the Devil, has the necessary prophetic gifts to tell us, even though he is far from the events themselves, how the Colonel died (or how he is dying at that moment, far from the place where Benito is riding). That event, at least in so far as we are concerned, never exists except in Ramos's words. The event becomes memory before it happens; it is an echo before it is a voice; and a legend before it is reality. The fantastic element, as it becomes more distant from its mythological origins with the passage of the years, fading into a post-arcadian world, becomes plausible, a full and integral part of reality, constructed from the perspective of a character. Immersed in everyday events, exiled form the realm of the magical, but still able to invoke its presence, the men of maize shape the legendary sphere that is always with them, as a continuous creation

Through his version, Benito turns out to be a collaborator in the act of revenge. Those events could have originated in any of a number of human events that are mentioned, as if in passing, with hardly any attention given to them: Godoy's cigar was lit, the Tecúns trapped the Colonel and burned the forest where he took refuge and many years—many pages—later we will learn: "In the report which the government made it said only that Colonel Godoy and his troops, while returning from an investigation, died in a forest fire."

And once again the fire is the center of the revenge, the element that unites reality and fiction: one of the circles that surrounds the Colonel and kills him "looks like a boiling pot, and is formed by an uncountable number of bear grass rounds of daggers made bloody by a fire. . . Their bodies are formed of fireflies and therefore, in the winter, they are everywhere, flickering their existence on and off." It is the seventh clearing, the epoch prophesied for Godoy's death: "and the seventh. . . will be of the fire of the golden owl which hurls owls from the depths of the pupils of its eyes." And this fire, creating a myth of itself from the inner eyes of man, from the tongues that slip like smoke and embers around its essence, is simultaneously the same fire with which the land was burned, the fire that was and is used to destroy and to make commerce, revenge of the fire that was the death of the land and now is the death of the man who betrayed Gaspar: "nevertheless, the smell was now that of fire in the air, the fire for clearing the land, for burning off the forest." This death is even more ironic when we realize that the Colonel was playing with the fire: "Fighting with guerrillas— he said a few moments before dying—is like playing with fire, and if I could do Gaspar Ilóm in, it

was because from the time I was a child I learned to jump over fires, on St. John's Eve and the Eve of Immaculate Conception." His death coincides with the momentary resurrection of the healer, whose presence is necessary for the deadly fire to begin: "I revived and only to get rid of the one who had also reached his seventh fire." The fire is identified with time, it becomes ubiquitous, an element by which one measures life: instead of years, clearing fires.

The first four chapters, therefore, demonstrate an evident cohesion, unfolding around Gaspar Ilóm's death and the revenge taken upon his executioners, a punishment that is carried out by human hands for superhuman reasons, a destruction that is at one and the same time reality and legend. The passage of time will allow each episode to be consolidated in a story, made myth for every succeeding generation. The fifth chapter, nevertheless, seems to escape this unity. Called a jewel within itself, it has been repeatedly affirmed that we are dealing with an independent episode, bearing no organic relationship with the rest of the book.

At first glance it would seem that the critics are right. What possible relationship between what precedes it and this story of the blind Goyo Yic, who recovers his sight in order to be able to find María Tecún the woman who has abandoned him? Only vague threads of plot unite this episode with the four preceding ones; it seems to unfold in another period of time, almost in another geographic space.

Nevertheless, this story is essential to the profound development of the book. In fact, the chapter narrates a process of forgetting, the progressive loss of a woman along the pathways of memory.

The herb seller operates on Goyo Yic so that he can undertake the search for María Tecún but when he recovers colors and shapes and distances and light, he realizes that "his eyes were useless to him," because María Tecún was his "rubber plant blossom. . . a blossom invisible to the eyes that see outside but not within, flower and fruit of his closed eyes, in his loving darkness that was sound, blood, sweat, escape, a vertebral jolt," and the everyday world, which comes in through the eyes, subtitutes his inner, imaginative vision, his original relationship with that woman who abandoned him. He had created her within himself, in the conjunction of all his senses; as he becomes more like all other men, he loses that experience that had connected him with María Tecún. We see how he involuntarily betrays that real image, how as the days slip by, he loses his connection with that first vision, the one he had when he was still blind, when his world was still created like a ghostly but secure dream. "He was searching for María Tecún but in the remotest depths of his consciousness he no longer looked for her. He had lost her."

One night he sees his shadow in the moonlight. It is the shadow of a *tacuatzín,* "with a pouch in front in which to carry its offspring," his *nahual,* his protector animal, but more than that, it is his guardian essence, the fundamental aspect of his magnified soul, in animal form. Just as the deer for the healer, the tacuatzín is Goyo Yic's double, and the dominant passion of his personality: "You know that human beings carry their young in pouches like the tacuatzín." This little animal, which accompanies him everywhere, is the symbol of his need to find María Tecún and his children, so much so that "Goyo Yic was known more by the nickname Tacuatzín than by his own name." But when he has sexual relations with another woman, the tacuatzín disappears, along with the possibility of finding his wife in spite of having lost the Amate flower: "The Amate flower, transformed into a tacuatzín, had just left its empty fruit, escaping so that the blind man would no longer see it, just as he could not see María Tecún, the blind man who was now seeing other women. A truly beloved woman cannot be seen; she is the Amate flower, seen only by blind men, the flower of the blind, of those blinded by love and by faith, of those blinded by life." After the flight of his guardian animal, Goyo Yic wanders the land, falling into a state of oblivion tinged by memories, like doves in the smoke: "Only when he heard other women's voices did Goyo Yic remember that he was looking for María Tecún. Finally he didn't think about her much at all. He did think of her, but not as before, and not because that was his intent, but simply because. . . he wasn't thinking." It is time which is digging a pit between the woman and his memory: "He was gradually shrunken, to the point where there was almost nothing left, by the years and the grief that hangs a man without a rope, but hangs him nonetheless, and by the bad climates in which he had been living, in his wanderings, searching all the towns and villages along the coast, and from drinking so much liquor to raise his spirits a little and to get rid of the bitter taste of his absent woman, until he became no one and nothing." And at the end of the chapter he will confess to his friend Domingo Revolorio, with whom he will go to jail as a supposed smuggler: "But so much time has passed that I no longer feel anything. Before, my friend, I searched for her in order to find her; now I search in order not to find her."

In fact, every human being lives the experience of Goyo Yic, his erased past, his necessary deformation of his life experience, his distancing from some obscure initial moment, and all of us, like him, go in search of that earlier purity, losing all trace of it, first drop by drop and then in cascades, as time intervenes. Goyo Yic gradually leaves behind his original identity, just as the other characters were separated from the events prior to their presence, those moments that they have not lived personally, but which they have heard about, that have remained in the form of the word, of spoken memory. Goyo Yic bids farewell to the first image he had of María Tecún; he loses the Amate flower, loses his blindness and the tacuatzín; he loses his archaic self, chews up his past and dimly remembers something that happened to another Goyo Yic, far

from himself, and between one and the other there has been an accumulation of picaresque adventures, women, and roadways, all of what turns the men of maize into vagabonds. This inability to go on being himself, the break from his own continuity in time, simultaneously allows his life to become separated from the way in which it happened; that is the first step toward his deformation, his essentialization in the popular mind. What he does with the old Goyo Yic and with the old image of María Tecún is what the people will do with the story of his life; they will transform it into legend, and his mythification is possible and even necessary because it is the only way to recover through memory and through the word that original but lost self.

Thus, Goyo Yic experiences the same phenomenon that is presented in the rest of the novel, the same process of distancing from and loss of an earlier deed, except that here it is embodied in a specific man, in whom the psychological roots of a reality that seemed to be only social are examined. Goyo Yic lives a specific experience of forgetting, all subjectivity being absorbed by the picaresque action of time. It is the same thing that happens in the rest of *Men of Maize*, where something is lived through so that later it may remain encapsulated in the future word, distancing itself from its true form at the same time that it reflects it, a carnival mirror that deforms, but captures none the less the trembling essence of things through legend, thus transcending the sad certainty of everyday events. This chapter, therefore, allows us to discover how the foundation of legends is rooted in the individual human beings's experience of time and in the internal disintegration that all human beings suffer. What happens to Goyo Yic in his mental transformation is what happens to humanity in its historical transformation. The ex-blind man's distancing from himself, this separation between reality and fiction in the life of the man who is depositary of that experience, is the first step toward the later legend. The first one to disturb reality and to transmute it is the subject himself, who becomes an accomplice in the process of conversion. In the earlier episodes those who deformed the original event were beings who had not lived that experience, beings who were not witnesses, but mere bridges of communication for that which they had not seen.

Of course, the psycho-biographical roots of the fictive do not occur just in this chapter, but are found throughout the novel. Uperto, one of the Tecúns, experiences a similar phenomenon: "With the eyes of his imagination he saw the deer killed by Gaudencio, in the darkness of the forest, yet far from the forest; and with the eyes of his face, the body of the healer, lying there before him." This difference between the eyes of the imagination and those of the face sustains the relationship, whether conflictive or cooperative, between what is real and what is imagined. In the case of Goyo Yic the eyes of the face displace the eyes of his imagination, an implacable corruption of his origin, the fount of all future truth, the window which will allow the world of myth to breathe into the vital center of every man. We can observe something similar in Señor Tomás: he doesn't see Machojón with his physical eyes, but he does see him with the eyes of his fantasy. He sees the profound truth, his punishment; he creates his destiny and his own death in accordance with that truth; he goes beyond the surface and forever after places the legend of his son in the trembling nucleus, the process of eternalization, which is everyday conversation, what people will say about him and his life.

By making the mythic phenomenon individual and personal in this chapter, by making it coincide with the life cycle of every man, his irremediable distension and loss of himself, Asturias has explored, now from a new, oblique angle, the creation of the legendary, insisting upon using as his point of departure the concrete minute hand of the clock that tick-tocks away our lives, that which destroys by shaping the myth, a happening that goes beyond ourselves, a touching upon others from mouths which reproduce us and tongues that repeat us.

We have established that, for these legends to acquire reality it is crucial that time pass, that men move away from that past, so that the action that occurred will not belie the word that transmits it. In this last chapter, many years have already gone by. One character mentions that "One of my grandparents used to say that he had plainly seen a healer who changed himself into the deer of the seven clearing fires; but all that happened so long ago. . . " and "There are more and more pieces of land being ruined by the corn growers." Always, when speaking of the past, when reestablishing the location and recounting the legends of Gaspar, of Machojón, and of Chalo Godoy, the characters try to give the impression of a vast distance, stretching backward in time, an uncrossable, irreversible abyss. The transformation of the past into myth hurls the characters into an incommensurable confusion of chronologies and distance from points of reference. The habitual duration of things is destroyed or ignored. The story of Machojón, for example, is not only spread from mouth to mouth, autonomous, altered ("He thought he saw fireflies, his memory of that horseman Machojón, who became a light in the heavens when he was on his way to lay claim to the future, was so vivid,"—a story that is repeated, with variations, some six times in the chapter), but also it has been fused with the popular vocabulary that is used to interpret reality, a word that automatically crops up when its use is suitable, a mental structure that man applies from his unconsciousness until the events that the readers witnessed persist only in popular sayings, that dictionary that is born out of everyday conversation: "transformation into a Machojón of hail" and a character goes through a harness shop where he sees horses "that move almost like fireflies. . . He thought he saw El Machojón the way they say he can be seen when-

ever they are burning off the land. A pure light in the sky."

This incorporation of the past into the imagination of each present moment is emphasized by the frequent dialogues, as we have already noted, in which the legend is being formed from the words exchanged by men. That which seemed to be past is lived again, but changed ("hearing everything that happened before as if it were happening now"), in order to evade the prison of regular time ("maybe history has been invented for that reason, to forget the present"). It is the metamorphosis of the impersonal into an individual human voice: the event, which before existed as word on the level of the narrator, becomes a word in the mouth of the character. The "objective" knowledge, to which the reader had access while the characters suffered the tyranny of events, is integrated into the world, digested by a thousand anonymous bodies, returned to the realm of the concrete so that it can go on spinning. It has become independent of its factual situation and is living only in its linguistic situation, thus acceding in some way to the realm of the timeless.

But time is necessary in order for this other dimension, this realm beyond a communicative context which deceives the clock, to exist. In this sense, Asturias connects with Proust, Mann, and Joyce, who have demonstrated the appearance of the eternal, of the mythic, in the corrosion of each moment, in the minuscule death of each object.

It is therefore not at all paradoxical that in the face of that vague chronology and that shipwrecking of dates, there also appear concrete mentions of a regular, measurable time, just as in the face of magical and associative language we find the prosaic usages of everyday speech. It is in the great mosaic of what grows by aging, of unfolding lives, where legend can appear and be transformed. Between the first page of the novel and the last no more than fifty years have passed, although they also seem separated by an eternity. Candelaria Reinoso, the girlfriend of Machojón is still of marriageable age at the end of the novel; Benito Ramos (who married María Tecún) is about to die; Musús, another of the Colonel's companions, has gotten married; María Tecún, who was only one year old when the Zacatóns died, is by now a mature woman with adult children; the blind Goyo Yic has been in prison for three years and seven months. Many of these statements contradict each other and would apparently even impede the establishment of the legend (for example, in the case of María Tecún, who is almost transformed into the word before she has lived), but they help us to enclose the characters within fixed, albeit fluctuating, limits, within which the mythic becomes at the same time both close and distant. This contrast between two kinds of time, living between one and the other dimension, which can also be seen in *El Señor Presidente* (as Ricardo Navas Ruíz has shown) and in Austrias's other works, this thirst for eternity and this subjection to the present moment draw fiction and reality even closer together, duplicating the fundamental planes of the novel.

On the other hand, this sweeping prison in which the characters mature and decay is their punishment for having broken the repose in which the earth dreamed it was one with man, and became commercial men of once-divine corn. Theirs is a degraded world, replete with sickly beings, beggars, blind men, like so many others in Asturias's other books. Thus, the deformation of the world through language, the vortex of metaphors which press objects beyond all recognition, the grotesque mirror wherein time and the word come together in a monstrous copulation, is much more than a literary recourse or an influence of European Surrealism. It expresses the desire to shape the horror caused by the loss of the magical, so that a demoniacal reality can be shown through twisted, bestial lenses. Or perhaps it is a way of dealing with mysterious forces that control us, a spell that replicates the image of the hell it would like to exorcize.

Magic still reigns in that world where the exiled wander without rest and with little hope, but it no longer shows any evidence of the primitive and benificent power which sustained the dream of Gaspar Ilóm. If, earlier, everything was linked by a great primordial and coherent animism, now it is the union of the dissimilar, the caricaturesque presence of missed meetings and howling, a zone where the merely diabolical seeks to manifest itself. And nevertheless, in that continuing vestige of the magical, revenge on time which corrupts, decomposition of forms, death of the origin in the mouth without teeth, in the shadow left by the sun as its light is extinguished, in this punishment, man finds, at the same time that he finds his nothingness, his freedom. Myth, nostalgia of what has been lost, the falsification of what is original, is also a means of recuperation, a recovery perhaps for something better.

Is it possible, that this myth, which changes and rips apart what happened at the beginning, could at the same time be the depository of human truth? Can time and eternity meet in legend?

The answer Asturias gives to these questions can be clarified through an examination of the two most important episodes in the sixth and last chapter of *Hombres de maíz*.

The wife of Nicho Aquino, the postman of San Miguel Acatán, has abandoned him. Thus we see repeated the basic situation of Goyo Yic, whose story, now made legend, has undergone several variations. Any woman who runs away is called "tecuna," (just as in the case of Machojón, the proper name has become a common noun) and every abandoned husband is a "blind man": "remember what they say happened to the blind man who insisted on going in search of María Tecún. He heard her talking and at the moment when he was going to catch up with her, he recovered his sight, only to see her changed into stone and forgetting that she was on the edge of a precipice." This same version, adorned in one way or another, is repeated by many other characters, demonstrating that very little is left from the original story of Goyo Yic and María Tecún. The popular imagination has snipped away what was useless, the surface which does not represent the essential truth of the human experience and has left what can be remembered, although the final version (which will also change with time) is far from corresponding exactly with the actual facts. Man, in his turn, becomes trapped in the legend: his behavior is oriented by that story and he is attracted by it, until reality begins to imitate fiction.

We can see the most typical example of this in the survival of the witch doctors' curse. They had said that those responsible for the death of Gaspar Ilóm would be unable to have children. But what is significant is the form in which this is fulfilled: if the wife of Benito Ramos has a son, the only possible explanation is that she deceived him; when Musús has one, "it is his child by another." The legend cannot be placed in doubt, for its has become so real that is shapes men's conduct and their interpretation of it. By the mere fact of having been uttered, the curse produces its effect: given credence, it has already achieved its end. Everything that happens will take on certainty or will be invalidated according to the a priori conviction of men. "Those people sacrifice themselves to keep the legend alive," says don Déferic, and he adds: "The victims matter little as long as the monster of popular poetry is fed." Every archetype, which begins with an individual, almost insignificant situation, grows toward its justifying echo.

But this dictatorship ("The gods disappeared, but the legends remained, and the latter, like the former, demand sacrifices; the obsidian knives to tear the heart of the sacrifice victim from his chest disappeared, but the knives of absence, which wound the victim and drive him mad, remain") is possibly due to the existence of an internalization of that imaginary dimension, a fall toward deeper, universal regions of what is human: "The cry (of María Tecún) was lost with her name beneath a storm of accents in the depths of her ears, in the canyons of her ears. She covered her ears but she kept on hearing it. It did not come from outside, but from inside. The name of a woman that everyone shouts to call that María Tecún they carry lost in their consciousness." The supposedly arbitrary development of the legend is in reality a movement toward what is endearingly human; it gradually models what man should be, and through its imitation it sheds any contingent form that is not useful: "Who has not called? Who has not, at some time, shouted the name of a woman lost in his yesterdays? Who has not, like a blind man, pursued that being who abandoned his own being, when he was present, who went on leaving and who goes on leaving his side, fugitive, 'tecuna,' impossible to hold back, because if she stops, time will turn her to stone?"

And at the end of the novel, after Nicho has descended to his nahual (the coyote) in search of his wife, the healer (deer of the seven clearings) will explain that the stone of María Tecún is in reality María la Lluvia, la Piojosa Grande, who "standing erect, will be present in the time that is to come, between heaven, earth and emptiness." Suddenly, we remember that other woman, the first to run away from her husband, Gaspar Ilóm; the same situation has circulated through the novel three times, in a different, disguised form each time, each time contributing to the legend, to the need to relate, in an atemporal form, the fact of separation, the loss of the past and of one's origins, the need to make oneself a stone against time.

One character, nevertheless, does not believe in the **"tecunas"** and in this way we come to the second sequence of the last chapter: the muleteer, Hilario Sacayón, has invented a legend, which has become independent of its creator, spreading on its own, objectified by the people. "Who hasn't repeated that legend that he, Hilario Sacayón, made up in his head, as if it really had happened? Wasn't he present during a prayer in which they asked God for relief and rest for Miguelita de Acatán? Haven't they searched in the old books of the parish registry for the baptismal certificate of that marvelous child?" It is the famous Miguelita, "whom no one knew and about whom everyone was talking because of the fame she had been given in places where mules and muleteers gathered, inns, taverns and wakes, by Hilario Sacayón." Here, for the first time, Asturias focuses on the problem of the legend from the perspective of the inventor drawn from a state of anonymity in order to confront him with the extreme and autonomous growth of his own lie, the product of drunken sprees and highs. It is yet another angle for the binomial myth-reality. Hilario Sacayón does not accept the voracity of the stories that surround him because he knows that the origin of each legend (whether it be that of Machojón, or of a nahual, or of Gaspar Ilóm, or María Tecún, or Miguelita) resides in false clouds of alcohol.

It is in vain that Na Moncha explains to him that "one often believes he is inventing what others have forgotten. When someone tells what is no longer being told, he tells himself, I invented it, it's mine, this is mine. But what he is really doing is remembering what the memory of his ancestors left in his blood. . ." Hilario refuses to be the verbal bridge to communicate with a pre-existent past; he refuses to be the one who "saved (that story) from oblivion," so that it could "go on like the rivers." But one of the legends in which he does not believe will take control of his being, and will make him admit the reality of certain myths.

Nicho Aquino has left for the capital with the mail. Don Déferic, fearing that the former will fall over the legendary stone of María Tecún, contracts Hilario to catch up with him and to accompany him until he crosses the difficult area. Hilario does not find him, but he sees a coyote when he goes past the stone: "Therein was the doubt, because he saw it clearly, and saw that it was not a coyote, because when he saw it he had the impression that it was somebody, and somebody known to him." And the idea that it is Nicho whom he has glimpsed gradually sinks into his being like a parasite, little by little, against his rational will, the realm of the magical takes over his mind and obsesses him with its possibility: "He almost knew it now and was now convinced of what he did not want to be convinced, of what his human condition completely rejected, that a being like that, born of a woman, nourished with a woman's milk, bathed in a woman's tears, could turn into a beast, could become an animal, put his intelligence into the body of an inferior being, stronger, yes, but inferior." Thus, the one who invented a legend must recognize that the imaginary or the impossible is true; he must in his innermost being accept the fact that he has not invented "his" legend, but rather that it belongs to other men and that no individual can deny his magical link with another world, not the everyday world, since the deep and authentic sense of history will correct that invention and man will use it to explore his own destiny. Hilario accepts, speaking for the author himself in a sort of *ars poetica*, being one link in a minute chain of true fictions: "he knew it, with all the powers of his soul that were not found in the senses, he knew it; his conscious mind had irremediably accepted as real what before, for his intelligence and conduct, had been a story."

The truth for Asturias is not found in the correspondence that can be established between a story and the factual events that it relates and that gave it its origin, but rather that something is more real when it more profoundly transforms those events in the direction of the unforgettable; it rescues the myth from its circumstantial beginnings, even though in order to do this, it must destroy and forget part of what apparently happened. Human beings, blind, lost in an under world, possess their myths only in order to orient themselves in the darkness, to understand their essence which is scattered in time. Reality begins to imitate that legend; man is transformed into the instrument which prolongs other beings, that touches other ears. Thus, in the poetic act, that of Asturias and that of his characters, the individual encounters his social self, he touches what is real and what is imaginary; time becomes eternal and eternity becomes mortal; there is a reconciliation of both kinds of men of maize, whose opposition and struggle have been shown at last to be an intense and solidary synthesis, two dimensions of one, unique irreducible human being. Myth and movement mutually support each other; they need each other in order to be able to exist: eternity feeds on the wandering mobility of human beings, imperfect fluctuations in the veins of time, and that movement is possible because it is supported by the enduring accompaniment of the imaginary.

This unity between men of maize has its correlative

in the unitary evolution of this text: what seemed to be chaos is a deeper order; what was scorned as narrative irregularity is the inauguration of a new cosmovision; what seemed to be dispersed is really the temporalization of realities becoming words. Asturias narrated this experience (time, myth, reality, language, the interiorization of the social, the new ways of expressing our Latin America) in the only possible way in which it could have been narrated. Na Moncha never spoke so truthfully (and she was speaking with Asturias, who invented her as Hilario invented Miguelita) as she did when she explained that "If it hadn't been you, it would have been someone else, but someone would have told it so that it wouldn't be forgotten and lost completely, because its existence, fictitious or real, is a part of life and of nature in these parts, and life cannot be lost; it is an eternal risk, but it is not lost eternally." (pp. 3–23)

Ariel Dorfman, "'Men of Maize': Myth as Time and Language," in *Some Write to the Future: Essays on Contemporary Latin American Fiction,* translated by Ariel Dorfman with George Shivers, Duke University Press, 1991, pp. 1–24.

Drawing by Salazar from Asturias's book of poems.

MIGUEL ÁNGEL ASTURIAS WITH GUNTER W. LORENZ

(interview date 1970)

[In the following interview, originally, published in the journal *Mundo Nuevo* in 1970, Asturias discusses the influence of his Guatemalan heritage and his political views in his *Banana Trilogy, El Señor Presidente,* and *Leyendas de Guatemala.*]

[Lorenz]: *The theme of* **Strong Wind** *has been the central theme of your life. What is your attitude toward this novel and its contents today?*

[Asturias]: For me, the novel **Strong Wind** marks the beginning of a new method of writing novels. Let me explain. I wrote *El Señor Presidente*, a political novel, without a social commitment. In writing *Leyendas de Guatemala* (**Legends of Guatemala**) and **Men of Maize,** I concentrated on Guatemalan myths and traditions. But it seemed to me that those works were not coming to grips with Guatemala's real problems. In 1949, I went to Buenos Aires as part of the Guatemalan diplomatic mission. Later, shortly after writing **Men of Maize,** I had an opportunity to get to know some parts of Guatemala better, especially those regions where the United Fruit Company was operating. My visits to those plantations, my conversations with the poor workers and their families who had to live in those miserable camps as if they were convicts—all this provided me with the basic elements of **Strong Wind.** That is how the first of my novels came about which was not primarily concerned with politics, as *El Señor Presidente* was, or with myth, as were **Leyendas** and **Men of Maize**; it dealt instead with the reality of Guatemala as reflected, of course, in my temperament and manner. If we speak of the motivation, the inspiration, or better still, of the urge that moved me to write that book, I should mention, first of all, the impact—cutting through me like a whiplash—made upon me by the living conditions of these people who worked under a merciless tropical sun and who were consumed with disease. Their spiritual horizon was purposefully restricted so that their physical strength might be more easily exploited; consequently, they were brutalized to such a degree that their aims in life did not go beyond alcohol, women and dance. The result of this frightening insight was the birth of **Strong Wind,** which was, in a certain sense, an outcry against injustice. And I myself underwent a transformation like that of Paul who, as Saul, had kept his eyes closed to the reality before him. . . .

I believe that **El Señor Presidente** *is your most important work, that the trilogy and* **Week-end en Guatemala** *testify to your sincerity but do not reflect a great literary transformation of materials.*

Naturally that is a matter of opinion. There is no need for us to quarrel about it, for you are not the only person who thinks this way. But you forget something very important. In literature, for the author who writes it and in a certain sense fathers it, every book has the same meaning as a strictly personal confession. The trilogy means a lot to me because there was an existential conscientiousness in its origin that I hadn't previously taken very seriously. When I faced the reality of the plantations, my conscience awoke. And that was the reality of my country, not an invention of mine; it was in no way imaginary. I repeat: it was the reality of my country that reduced me to a state of despair and forced me to tell myself and others what is contained in these novels. Whenever I reread *Strong Wind* today from this vantage point in time, I know that it contains a great deal of what makes up the destinies of the men who inhabit the countryside of Guatemala. It shows, for example, how the small farmers grow poor in the suburbs of the metropolis; how they lose their sustenance, and how in the squalid and miserable slums their lives flicker and die out like pieces of charcoal. And so, finally, they have to migrate from the highlands to the plantations in the tropical coastal region where they soon become ill, die, or vegetate as consumptives, syphilitics and alcoholics. To understand this you ought to read *Strong Wind.* Interpreting it as my personal reaction to these living conditions. On the other hand, I would have to say that I have not completely moved away from everything having to do with myth. I have often been criticized, especially in socialist countries, for retaining the mythical aspect, which, say the communists, weakens my social criticism and the depiction of reality. I answer that, for my part, I do not know what to do with the impotent production of "socialist realism." I tell everyone that my novels are realistic because they take into account the mythical aspect, because the magus, or the god Huracán, shapes a reality in the minds of the men of my country—he is omnipresent. Although the wind that destroys the banana plantations in *Strong Wind* is very real, to the Indians it is a magical event, for this way of thinking of it is profoundly natural to their minds.

Reportage or documentation dominates, and this has damaged the trilogy, I think, as a literary work.

Naturally, I cannot evaluate this as an outsider; nevertheless, the trilogy continues to be important to me. There is something else I want to say: taking into account the predominance of psychic reality and the magical qualities of the world around me, I cannot resort to a simple form of realistic representation; one must take into account the characteristics of reality from a stylistic point of view as well. Because of this, I think it is stupid for some communists to accuse me of betraying the anti-imperialist struggle, the struggle against colonialism and

for having included in my work all this reality instead of a middling reality. In the trilogy, as in all my other works, I have written about the men of my country, who suffer and who are in great need. You cannot speak or write about these men without the proper respect for what they believe, which, for many of them, is something more than a dream or imagination—it is an irreducible reality. Thus, *Strong Wind* combines social reality with the element of magic.

The theme of **Strong Wind,** *so timely for all of Latin America, is a political theme, if we take "political" in its broadest sense as a concern for* polis, *for community.*

I think the Latin American writer has one essential and permanent function: to reflect in his work the reality of his country. In Latin America there have always been writers who have locked themselves up in ivory towers; there have always been writers among us who have neglected their duty and tried to forget about the reality of their country. I believe that Borges is a great writer, a great European writer. He in no way resembles a Latin American writer. Born in Argentina, he has several times called himself an exile in his own country. To some extent this is an attack on Borges' writing which disregards its value. But I believe that Borges ought to be viewed as a European writer. No doubt we have very different concerns in our two literatures. Our world is very different from that of Borges. Our works are composed of different feelings and thoughts. There exists an abyss between that literature of abstention and ours, which I don't like to define as committed literature—this concept has been misused so much—but rather as a literature of commitment, a literature of struggle written by authors who feel committed to their world. I should add something else here I have often heard the opinion, especially in Europe, that committed literature—or, as I call it, the literature of commitment—is not very fertile because it restricts itself documentation, but that is a gross error for our literature has never been limited simply to documentation but has always been a literature of combat. It has always been a literature of active participation in the struggle of our people against the oppressor. It seems to me that this is quite different from mere documentation. We do not restrict ourselves to determining the facts, but we try to modify the facts, to improve them, to submit them to the rule of justice. Latin American literature is a literature that is committed to life; it demands of us that we know our jungles, our pampas, our mountains and the enormous problems we suffer from. I do not believe that anyone who goes about it sincerely can write without listening, even while closed up in his room, to the thunder of the Orinoco, the Paraná, or the other important rivers in Latin America. I don't believe that a writer can restrict himself simply to the manipulation of words, to the arrangement of capitals and lower-case letters, to a repetition of the beautiful and educated formulas of the nineteenth century. Anyway, you have to be able to do all these things if you want to be a good writer, for good intentions alone are no substitute for ability. This has frequently bothered me about committed authors.

You defend a committed literature which is not restricted to formulaic expression.

Exactly. That is what I meant to say. Literature arises only when two important conditions are met: theme and form. I do not believe that many of today's attempts at so-called experimental literature are yielding very unique results, for this writing is generally lacking in great human themes. My God, I experimented, too, in my youth: in those days we had ultraism, surrealism and movements that were given various names.

Do you believe that influences from that period have affected your work?

Well, surely some have. Perhaps it is not so noticeable in my case as in others. I was unable to dissociate myself from my heritage. In my poems, especially in those from that period and in *El Señor Presidente*—perhaps in *Leyendas* as well—there are reminiscences. There are, possibly, surrealistic reminiscences in *El Señor Presidente*. But I would say that those literary experiences, in my case, have passed through a magic philter.

But don't you see that literary experiment and commitment are basically opposed to one another?

No. Why should I have to see it? What matters is that there are two poles. One cannot say "form is everything" and forget theme, or "content is everything" and leave aside form. The committed author is also committed to demonstrating greater mastery, greater artistic talent. But artistry alone—and this is my rule, the credo of my commitment—is not enough. But let us speak of Latin America again: without listening to the outcry, without the voice of our farm workers, without listening to the lament of the *mestizo*, without listening to the white man who arrived in our land expecting something different from what he found, without seeing this whole trembling, suffering, struggling world—without all this, we cannot write literature. Since 1920, our novels have been opening the gates to this world and thanks to them, the European public has begun to know us. These are not in any way definitive works. But our literature will not stagnate at this stage in the descriptions of these cruelties, these landscapes, Indians, Blacks, Whites, of the sweat and blood, the fear and pain—no, no. Our literature has its own logic and will develop in the future. The day will come when it will produce works like those that are well known in Europe, such as the psychological novel. But at present our principal duty is to be witnesses. Witnesses, accusers, and protestors all at the same time. We should bear witness in our works to the inhuman situation that prevails in our society. And we should change it. That is our duty.

Did the changes in your social status, your way of life, after 1966—more exactly, your transformation from an em-

igrant into a diplomat—modify your politico-sociological concept of literature?

I do not believe that these changes have modified my thinking in any way. Certainly, I said it all at the outset. You see, I wrote **Strong Wind** when I was in charge of my country's embassy in Argentina. I already had diplomatic obligations during the period in which I was writing that book, so it is logical to think that I would later drift away from these themes—whether myths or social relationships—simply because I got involved in diplomacy again? The charge that I sold out and was a traitor to the cause is as stupid as it is crude. I have lived and suffered a lot in my life, and I do not believe that a group of stupid boys incapable of drawing distinctions, a special group of communists or anarchists, will be able to achieve any results by attempting murder and throwing bombs beyond that of providing the enemy with a good excuse to smother our recently born and minimal freedom.

Perhaps at this time we can say something about the biographical element which plays such an important role in your work.

I was born in Guatemala City. My father was a *mestizo*, by profession a lawyer. My mother, an Indian—a Mayan—was a school teacher. I am Latin American. This does not mean that I am not proud of the Indian blood I have inherited. I am a *mestizo* with a lot of Indian blood, which shows up in my face. But I consider myself *mestizo* because the future of Latin America depends on *mestizaje*, which is a sign of balance and mutual understanding. As a teacher, my mother accomplished a great deal in the Indian schools, while my father, as a lawyer, was also concerned with this poor and defenseless people who were exposed to the harshness of the power wielded by the whites and the *mestizos*.

Do you see in mestizaje *something like a spiritual force for the betterment of the Indian in face of the whole social problem, as you put forth in your doctoral thesis of 1923?*

When I was born, Guatemala was in the hands of the dictator Estrada Cabrera, who had come to power with North American aid and had sold his country to the Yankees. At that time, my father was the President of the Supreme Court of Justice, and because he refused to obey the wishes of the dictator, who tried to force him to pass the death sentence on students who had participated in an organized demonstration against him, my father had to resign from his position. We moved to my maternal grandparents' house in a small Indian village in Bajo Vera Paz, and there I came into contact with the world of the Indians and got to know their legends and songs. This was the beginning. When my father was pardoned, we returned to the city, and I had to prepare myself for a profession. I had wanted to be a composer. Even today that is what I would like to be, if I weren't a writer. But my father did not agree, and so, following family tradition,

I took up the study of law. I never did become a good lawyer. . . .

Aren't you underrating this aspect a little? Your thesis was awarded "summa cum laude" and it was published.

That's right, but I didn't have my heart in it, and I did not write a "juridical" work. I wanted to be a writer, and I became one when the great earthquake destroyed Guatemala City. During that period I wrote my first poems and my first short stories. Someone even saw fit to publish them. Later, my father sent me to London to study international law, but I escaped and went to Paris to study anthropology with the great Reynaud, who was my teacher there. I translated the old Mayan texts of the *Popol Vuh* and the *Anales de los Xahil* into Spanish in order to write *Leyendas de Guatemala*. . . .

Which were highly praised by Paul Valéry.

That's right, and you know what came after that. So that we don't misunderstand one another, I would like to point out that in my opinion, *mestizaje* represents a natural, logical and unique form in Latin American life. . . I'm *mestizo*. This does not mean that I want to deny a single drop of my Indian blood or that I am not proud of it. I have no reason to be ashamed of it. On the contrary, I am proud to know that there is a lot of Indian blood running in my veins. Our Indians have not had to be ashamed of their past. But I am a *mestizo*. I feel and react to things as an American does, and therefore I am *mestizo*. The future of our America is a *mestizo* future. The meaning of American life has been determined by the mixing of Europeans with American Indians. No one can change that. For us, the problem is not the Indian, but what has happened to him in the past and in many cases what is happening to him now.

When you received your doctorate, the Mexican program of assimilation was not even a topic for discussion. . .

The subsequent direction of events in Mexico has confirmed my ideas in this regard. To be exact, my second book, *La arqitectura de la vida nueva* (**The Architecture of the New Life**, 1928) deals with the subject. How we resolve this problem has a bearing upon the American of the future, as I said in that work. The majority of Indians today, but not all, are poor. They have no education and are apparently unable to be assimilated into the twentieth-century way of life. They are not to blame but that is the way it is. Although not altogether. They are poor, it is true; they lack civilization, but they are men with a great deal of culture, which I am well aware of. Only by living among them for a time can you realize that they should not be left to themselves, as the whites left them in spite of their poverty. They have many good qualities: they are loyal, sensitive. What they need is forming, that is to say, the forming of our age in order to be able to participate in it. I say today, as I did in 1923: give them schools, work that they can perform, and then what

is in them can be appreciated. This was demonstrated in Mexico. . . .

You should add that you have been a university professor, a newspaper editor, a doctor of philosophy, founder of the first Guatemalan political radio station, founder of the people's university for Indians, politician, diplomat and several times an emigrant. How many times did you have to live in exile?

Altogether I have spent almost half of my life in internal and external exile. Anyone who writes and thinks about politics in Latin America, especially in Central America, has to become accustomed to that.

And your books? How were they conceived? You have mentioned a frightening tragedy, the beginnings of which it was your lot to live through and which you later decided to write about.

Yes, at 10:20 p.m. on the 25th of December in 1917 an earthquake destroyed my city. I saw something like an immense cloud conceal the enormous moon. I had been placed in a cellar, in a hole, a cave, or some place else. It was then that I wrote my first poem, a song of farewell to Guatemala. Later, I was angered by the circumstances during which the rubble was cleared away and by the social injustice that became so bloodily apparent. As a result, I wrote a short story. I had already written some insignificant short stories earlier. But this one—**"Los mendigos políticos"** (**"The Political Beggars"**)—was very important to me. From it would later come *El Señor Presidente*.

The story behind the genesis of this novel is very funny. It was recited aloud before it was written down?

That's right. When I arrived in Paris I met Neruda and Arturo Uslar Pietri. We went around together every night elaborating our great plans for the future. One day, one of us—I believe it was Uslar Pietri—had the idea of placing a bet, the terms of which stipulated that each of us, during our evening meetings, would have to tell a story. I remembered *Los mendigos políticos,* and every night for weeks I told this story, as a kind of novel in installments. Since on each occasion new material was needed, the story grew and grew. I felt like Scheherezade, and my friends encouraged me to write the story down. I don't recall well now, but I believe that I wrote that text at least nineteen times before it satisfied me.

That was around 1930, but the book was not published until much later.

When Ubico's dictatorship ended in 1945, sixteen years after it had been written. The dictator had prohibited its publication because his predecessor, Estrada Cabrera, was my "*Señor Presidente*," which meant that the book posed a danger to him as well.

Since you are regarded as the inventor of "magic realism" and are presently thought of as its most successful practitioner, would you define its characteristic and clarify it once and for all?

I will try to explain to you in very simple words what I understand as "magical realism." An Indian, or a *mestizo,* someone who lives in a small village, tells of having seen how a cloud or an enormous stone changed into a person or into a giant, or how the cloud became a stone. All these are hallucinatory phenomena frequently found among the people of small villages. Of course we laugh at the story and do not believe it. But when you live among these people, you begin to perceive that these stories have importance. The hallucinations and impressions a man gets from his surroundings tend to become realities wherever there is a definite religious or cultural basis for it, as in the case of the Indians. It is not a concrete reality but a reality that arises from a definitely magical imagination. Because of this, and because of what it expresses, I call it "magical realism." There is more: a woman getting water from a well falls in, or a rider falls from his horse or there are other daily accidents—these *faits divers*, we might call them, are subsequently transformed into magical events if there exists a suitable rationale for it. For the Indian or the *mestizo,* the woman doesn't fall into the well; rather, the well attracts her because it needs her to transform her into a serpent, a spring, or into anything else you might imagine. And the rider does not fall from his horse because he has had one too many but because the rock upon which he struck his head in the fall "called" him. This is how the stories we call legends arise. I doubt that they are limited to Guatemala or to the Indians. There is a religious motive, or principle, present in everyone. This is certain. But what is characteristic of my country is what arises as a consequence of this motive. The ancient Indian literature, the Indian books that were written before the European conquest, before Columbus—for example, the *Popol Vuh* or the *Anales de los Xahil*—are distinguished by this intermediate reality. Between the reality which could be called the "real reality" and the magical reality such as that which these men live is a third reality, which is not only a product of the concrete and the visible, not only hallucination and dream, but is the result of the fusion of the two. It is a bit like what Breton and the surrealists attempted; it is what we could call "magical realism." Magical realism in all certainty, has a direct relationship to the original mentality of the Indian. The Indian thinks in images. He does not see things in process, but he always displaces them into another dimension, in which we see the real disappear and the dream emerge, in which dreams are transformed into tangible and visible reality.

Do you believe that your novels can be translated?

In order to translate Latin American novels there must be a poetic potential in the translator. If the translators of our works are not basically poets and cannot translate our books with good sense, they will not communicate, not even remotely, what is in them. To do this, the first and most important criterion for the translator is,

in my opinion, the answer to this question: Can he translate the poetic aspect of the book? In the second place, it requires an absolute command of the two languages, but most of all of the other, since Spanish is a language that covers an immense spectrum, and this spectrum of words, which is transformed at moments, of feeling, thinking, and intuition, has to be translated as it is expressed in the original. This is not my whim but a principle. I understand something of the job because I have translated Indian texts, Sartre, Anouilh and many others. The translator should be able to repeat everything that the author meant, including what is between the lines and in the images. To do it, the translators of our novels ought to be persons who are conscientious, who know exactly what is happening in Latin America, who know that everything is changing, that the problems are also changing, and that new ones are emerging. They should be conscious of the fact that our works constitute the response to this living and changing reality. One must see not only with the eyes. One must penetrate this green world, this land of tigers and eruptions. One must familiarize oneself with this cosmic world, with this world of telluric struggles, with this world in which a struggle for survival is still going on. The translation should emerge from all this, it should be faithful to all this. It should not be just another commercial venture. Whoever thinks it should be will fail. I have especially good reasons for underscoring this aspect. Certainly this is where Germany, in contrast to France and Italy, has committed so many errors in the translation of my works and of those of other Latin Americans. The translation was left to persons who know Spanish well—I have no doubt—but they do not know our Spanish, and for this reason they do not know our spirit and our feelings. So they translate books from "Spanish," that is, they treat them as if they had originated in some region of Spain, which is far removed from our temperament, from our way of life, from our character and from our way of talking. (pp. 5–11)

Miguel Ángel Asturias and Gunter W. Lorenz, in an interview, translated by Tom J. Lewis, in *Review*, No. 15, Fall, 1975, pp. 5–11.

JOHN WALKER
(essay date 1970)

[In the following essay, Walker explores the significance of the idiot Pelele in molding the plot of *El Señor Presidente*.]

In previous studies of *El Señor presidente* critics have tended to concentrate on the black shadowy figure of the president, who, though he provides the title and pervades the novel, appears only briefly, or the real protagonist, the ambivalent Cara de Ángel ("bello y malo como Satán"). These two overshadow a whole host of minor figures like Camila, Canales and Carbajal, the Auditor, Lucio Vázquez, etc.

One key figure, however, who has received little attention from the critics is the mute idiot *el Pelele,* who appears in only the first four chapters and at the end of chapter seven (Part 1). In spite of the paucity of his appearance, the brevity of his fictional life, and his non-contribution to the spoken side of the novel, *el Pelele* has a major role to play, not only by his action which sparks off the whole plot of the novel (chapter 1), and his link with the protagonist Cara de Ángel (chapter 4), but also by the ambience which he in particular helps to create in chapter 1, which sets the tone of the novel, the nightmare atmosphere of his flight in chapter 3, and the dream-fantasy world of chapter 4, before disappearing from the scene at the end of chapter 7.

In the opening chapter, Asturias, with great economy of description, sets the scene for the novel, conveys the atmosphere, and introduces the catalytic action which sets the plot in motion. In each of these three aspects the idiot is centrally involved. In a vivid portrayal of the dregs of humanity, the grotesque inhabitants of the gutter (ironically gathered in *el Portal del Señor* in the shadow of the cathedral), Asturias introduces a gallery of Goyesque characters, drawn from the depths of degradation, "sin más lazo común que la miseria, maldiciendo unos de otros. . . " ranging from the blind woman who dreams she is covered with flies and hanging from a hook like meat in a butcher's shop, the pregnant deaf-mute and the degenerate mulatto to the legless blind man. Amidst the sobbing, the moaning and the weeping of this "familia de parientes del basurero" the cry of the idiot is the saddest: "Partía el cielo. Era un grito largo, sonsacado, sin acento humano" Choosing the idiot as a representative of the innocent, the a-political, who suffer the abuses of a totalitarian regime, Asturias underlines the point by showing how dictatorship corrupts a people and destroys its values to the extent that even compassion for one's companions in distress ceases to exist. In this infernal atmosphere the idiot's only happiness resides in the memory of his dead mother somewhere in the distant past. In the unnatural, inhuman atmosphere that Asturias tries to establish in the opening scene, the word "madre" is a curse, a torment in the mouths of *el Pelele's* fellow-sufferers, who use it to incite him to fits of uncontrollable hysterics. In his attempts to escape the taunts of the rabble, "entraba a las casas en busca de asilo, pero de las casas le sacaban los perros o los criados. Lo echaban de los templos, de las tiendas, de todas partes, sin atender a su fatiga de bestia. . . " Amongst these brutalized people pity and respect have been replaced by obscenity and scorn for maternal values—"Pelelito, el domingo te casás con tu madre. . . ."

As well as using the mute idiot as a symbol of the silent masses who have no voice under despotism, Asturias introduces the subtle portrait of the mother-loving figure suffering at the hands of those who, long under the domination of the over-aggressive father-figure (the president), lack love and pity—the result of maternal deprivation. The one son who is not *dénaturé* suffers the insults of his brothers and finally dies, innocent of his crime. Denied refuge, comfort and compassion, he finally falls asleep after countless nights of insomnia, only to be startedly wakened by the raucous taunt of "madre"—enough, given the idiot's physical and psychological condition, for *el Pelele* to destroy his tormentor with an attack of uncontrolled fury—". . . le enterró los dedos en los ojos, le hizo pedazos la nariz a dentalladas y le golpeó las partes con las rodillas hasta dejarlo inerte." Only after *el Pelele* escapes like a mad thing do we realize in the closing punch line of the chapter that the murdered man is Colonel José Parrales Sonriente, one of the president's important agents. Thus Asturias skilfully blends the atmosphere of degradation and cruelty in which he situates the idiot whose one instinctive reaction, springing from his mother-love, initiates the whole chain of events that form the plot of the novel—a simple action that enmeshes all the characters from the president downwards, and yet is prompted by innocence and mother-fixation. It is further ironical that, in an atmosphere of lies, corruption, conspiracy and deceit, an uninvolved, ingenuous figure, without political motivation, should be the one to strike out again the dictator and his henchmen.

Having introduced the background that produces figures like *el Pelele* and having used him as the catalyst to spark off the action of the novel, the author, in one of the finest chapters of the book, worthy of Dostoievsky's *The Idiot,* describes vividly the flight of *el Pelele* from the scene of the crime (chapter 3), and adds further to the atmosphere, hammering home the ghoulish nightmare ambience of life under a despotic regime. He effects this in two ways:—first, the description of the nightmare flight as witnessed through the tormented mind of the idiot, highlighting the atmosphere of fear, terror and darkness; second, through the dadaistic incoherence of meaningless language, and the onomatopeic descriptions of the sounds and noises that go through his deranged mind. With a Kafkaesque description of "las calles intestinales, estrechas y retorcidas" and the constant repetition of *sombras* and *subterráneas,* the author creates the atmosphere conducive to the future events of the novel. Againts this surrealistic background "medio en la realidad, medio en el sueño," the idiot pursues his crazy, aimless way "medio despierto, medio dormido" passing an infinity of doors and windows, as he defends himself from the hostile telegraph poles, whilst the buzzards perform a *danse macabre* in anticipation above his head. Asturias brilliantly portrays the atmosphere for the whole novel through these cinematographic shots in black and white, reminiscent of the opening scene of Cervantes' *novela ejemplar, El coloquio de los dos perros*—both taking place in that foreboding half-light between night and day. With the aid of the *desproporción fantástica* of the vertiginous flight and the disassociation of ideas which he uses to describe the idiot's wanderings, he succeeds in coveying the confused social state of the country itself. Asturias employs also surrealistic techniques of language in his treatment of the hopeless wandering of the idiot to emphasize the nightmarish, meaningless world of oppressed Guatemala, or any country under dictatorship. Here Asturias transcends the national level and reaches truly universal heights. The constant repetition of the senseless "erre, erre, erre. . . ." interspersed with the tragic chorus of "madre," supported by the typical Asturias technique of piling up words "Curvadecurvaencurvadecurvacurvadecurvaencurvala mujer de Lot" and accumulating sounds—"¡Ta-ra-rá! ¡Ta-ra-rí!/¡Tit-tit!/¡Tarará Tararí!/¡Simbarán, bún, bún, simburán!. . . " all add to the general confusion and to the idea that he tries to convey i.e. it is better to be dead than alive: "El cementerio es más alegre que la ciudad, más limpio que la ciudad! ¡Ay, qué alegre que los que van, ay, a enterrar!" The crashing crescendoes (ta-ra-rá, bún, bún, bún) are intended to portray the confusion and the noise in the tormented mind of *el Pelele* who, stricken with pain, "dentro de los huesos, sentía un labertino." In the confused world of his mind, and for all oppressed people, there was no escape. Imprisonment was their norm. Even when he dreams of taking the train to leave the city, it keeps coming back to the point of departure like a toy on a string. Confusion, imprisonment, alienation were the everyday features of their life.

Bleeding profusely from the buzzards' attacks and suffering excruciating pain from his broken leg, the idiot finds no help from his fellowmen nor any escape in this world. His only means of evasion, therefore, is in the dream world of fantasy, where he re-creates, by compensation, the beautiful mother-figure that he lacks in real life. Through this dream world Asturias shows his capacity for portraying fantastic beauty as opposed to the nightmare ugliness of *el Pelele's* flight. With the surprisingly lovely image of the *Manzana-Rosa del Ave del Paraíso* that the exhausted idiot manages to conjure up in his limited mind. Asturias merely highlights the sordidness of reality. In this escapist world of surrealism (ironically against the background of the rubbish dump) the author compassionately introduces the Mother-Virgin figure who takes the forsaken idiot by the hand "a un estanque de peces de colores y le dio el arco-iris para que lo chupara como pirulí." The complete happiness of the idiot in this make-believe world is an obvious portent of his imminent death, and a biting indictment of the harsh world of reality.

The real world soon re-establishes itself under a blue sky "adornado como una tumba altísima por coronas de zopilotes que volaban en círculos dormidos." A simple woodcutter finds the idiot and, whilst he tries to help him, he is joined by another good Samaritan, who proves to be the protagonist (hero?) Cara de Ángel. It is significant that this first appearance of the hero links him with *el Pelele,* the murderer of the president's powerful agent. Even more significant is that in this first appearance he performs an act of charity—probably the first one in his political life, as we know he has had a shady past as hypocrite, liar, crook and the dictator's sycophantic favourite. This first act of charity, on behalf of *el Pelele,* a prelude to his relationship with Camila and his spiritual salvation through love, is his tragic flaw. When he reports late to the presidential palace he apologizes for his delay, explaining that he stopped to help a wounded person, but ". . . no se trataba de persona conocida, sino de uno así como cualquiera!"—a remark that reinforces the tragic irony, since now the idiot is a very important person indeed, completing the fatal link with Cara de Ángel and the president. The president, cunning as ever, decides to make use of the agent's murder to rid himself of two political opponents, who can be accused of the crime, one of them being General Canales, the father of Camila with whom Cara de Ángel later falls in love. It is clear, then, that with his instinctive reaction the idiot has set in motion the whole chain of events that will link with Cara de Ángel and all the other characters in the novel. Before the political undesirables can be liquidated, however, the authorities have to remove the real assassin, *el Pelele,* who is murdered on the pretext that he is "un hombre con rabia." After crawling up the steps of the *Portal del Señor* like a dying cat, he is brutally shot and killed by the president's thugs. As always, no one sees anything—except a shadowy figure in the episcopal palace who absolves him from his "sins" at the moment of death.

The scene having been set, and the action initiated, *el Pelele* can now be dispensed with, as he has fulfilled his key functions in the novel i.e. to set off a chain of political events that form the material of the rest of the novel, and link him with the hero; also, to create the atmosphere of a nightmare world by means of surrealistic imagery and language. With the death of the idiot the fantasy world ends and **El señor presidente** becomes merely a political novel of social protest. It is the funciton of the idiot to link these two levels of Asturias' writing—the realistic and the fantastic. That Asturias was able to do this through the figure of a dumb idiot is a tribute to his characterization, his ability to create atmospheres, and his skill in weaving plots. His astuteness in selecting such an unusual figure for a key role is one of the features that makes **El señor presidente,** if not his most artistic, at least his best known, novel. (pp. 62–7)

John Walker, "The Role of the Idiot in Asturias' 'El Señor Presidente'," *Romance Notes*, Vol. XII, No.1, Autumn, 1970, pp. 62–7.

SUSAN WILLIS
(essay date 1983)

[In the essay below, Willis explores Asturias's *Mulata de Tal,* suggesting that it "is a book where masks and metamorphosis are the norm: punning, the lingua franca; and sexual fantasy and farce, the common denominator of all relationships."]

Miguel Angel Asturias' *Mulata de Tal* is carnival incarnated in the novel. A ribald bacchanalia, it represents a collision between Mayan Mardi Gras and Hispanic baroque. This is a book where masks and metamorphosis are the norm; punning, the lingua franca; and sexual fantasy and farce, the common denominator of all relationships. What better model for the application of Bakhtin's notions about carnival?

This is where a problem arises. Even though the *Mulata* appears to be a made-to-order Bakhtinian text, it must be more than demonstrative festival. Rather, its use of carnival must reverse societal norms. In the *Mulata* where everything appears to be caught up in the world of masquerade, the task of distinguishing the social ground seems difficult at best. This is a crucial point. According to Bakhtin, "once a sign has been withdrawn from the pressures of social struggle, it loses its force" [in V.N. Voloshinov, *Marxism and the Philosophy of Language*, 1973] and becomes an empty signifier, something of a literary commodity. Thus, the project of reading the *Mulata* historically will depend first of all upon defining its social ground.

One way to do so is in relation to the entire corpus of Asturias' writing where mask and metamorphosis are often used to articulate rebellion in class society. One such text is the story, "**Torotumbo**" in Asturias' collection *Week-End En Guatemala,* written as the author's testimony of support for Arbenz shortly after invading forces had toppled his progressive left government. In the story, the lines of class conflict are clearly drawn: on the one hand, the Anti-Communist League, composed of Archbishop, the reactionary President of the Republic, and a strongarm yanqui advisor. These are opposed by the Indians and their more revolutionary class allies: the intellectuals and urban guerrillas. The historical allegory is set in motion when a member of the Anti-Communist League, who, in his public life keeps a costume shop, dons the mask of "carne cruda" (the devil) and rapes and murders a young Indian girl. This reenactment of the Conquest concludes with a popular uprising during which the costume shop is blown up with the whole of the Anti-Communist League inside. When it becomes known that

the President of the Republic has perished, the army lays down its arms and the revolution is achieved.

What makes "Torotumbo" an enactment of Bakhtin's theory of the subversive function of carnivals is the way the social ground of class conflict is defined within and against festival. "Torotumbo" is both a day of carnival and revolution where it is very difficult to distinguish dancing from fighting in the streets. Masquerade is the means of demasking authority. When the devil blows up in the costume renter's shop so too do the perfect renditions of President, Archbishop and yanqui. As the wave of dancers, i.e. revolutionaries, pass through the streets, filling them, seizing them, the police step out of their uniforms, leaving them and their former identities behind as if both were temporary disguises: "se arrancaban los uniformes y los dejaban botados como disfraces." The image is transformational as is the whole story for it suggests more than a simple substitution of a new humanized reality for a former oppressive illusion. That oppression, like the costumes, must be worked through, used up (botado) and torn off (arrancar).

Another magical strategy used by Asturias to create the carnivalesque reversal of history is metamorphosis. His novel *Hombres de Maíz* offers a good example. Like *Mulata de Tal,* it portrays a world where myth and history collide. The centuries of unresolved conflict between Indians and the conqueror is enacted in this Twentieth Century version as a clash between a highland Indian hamlet and the army. The novel depicts the massacre of an Indian band followed by the retaliatory slaying of an army patrol. These are the political historical events; their translation into myth yields a more complex tale. When Gaspar Ilom, the Indian leader, discovers all his men have been killed and that their struggle can no longer be waged on the world historical level, he throws himself into a river "like a stone." Swimming, he metamorphoses into "a cloud," then a "bird" and finally a "shadow of his shadow in the water." From there he goes on to join the realm of spirits where he is able to communicate with the "nahuales," the animal protectors, who, as the Indians believe, guide the daily lives of humans.

Meanwhile, to world-historical eyes it appears the soldiers were caught in a box canyon where they perished when the Indians sent a wind-driven fire down upon them. The mythic version which weaves its way in and out of Asturias' novel is more complex and iconographically more interesting. The coronel at the head of the patrol was "neither burned nor did he die fighting." Instead he was struck down by magic and turned into a small wooden figurine, a toy soldier:

Los brujos de las luciérnagas, después de aplicarle el fuego frío de la desesperación, lo redujeron al tamaño de un muñeco y lo multiplicaron en forma de juguete de casa pobre. . .

The question posed by *Hombres de Maíz* as with

all mythic texts from the colonized world is not which version is most credible, but how these polysemous interpretations mobilize the conflicts and contradictions of history. Against the ground of history, metamorphosis, as a carnivalesque strategy, permits the expression of more than one collective fantasy. The Indian chief's final integration with the spirit world—his community of plenitude—while it derives from Indian cosmology, also articulates the white world's expectations. Similarly, the coronel's transformation into a wooden toy—a poor man's commodity—is exactly the way the white world is perceived by Indians.

What sets the *Mulata* apart from these other texts is that the social and historical ground against which the world of myth emerges is already extensively absorbed into the mythic register. A schematic outline of the novel's events will reveal the deep mythification of history:

The story begins when Celestino Yumí, a poor and childless wood-cutter, makes a pact with the devil to obtain lands and wealth. In exchange, Celestino must parade about at fairs and in church with his fly open (to maken women sin), and he must also give the devil his wife (Catarina Zabala). Appearing in the form of a corn husk demon, the devil is already a melange of Christian and pagan iconography. Yumí completes his part of the bargain; becomes the wealthiest man around; and with his wife gone, eventually meets and marries the Mulata, a tempestuous libertine, who takes pleasure in pain and delivers both abundance and destruction upon Yumí and all his possessions.

The source of Yumí's wealth is a small box filled with tiny clay objects given him by the devil. Each time Yumí removes a miniature hen house or stable from the box, that object instantaneously appears in full size on his property. Finally only one object remains: a miniature clay shepherdess, his wife. Deciding she will never be noticed amongst his abundance, Yumí removes the shepherdess only to discover that his wife is now a dwarf. As a dwarf, she is both the child that she and Yumí longed for but never had, and she is also a plaything for the Mulata who dresses her in doll's clothes. Able to roam the house at will, Catarina, whose dwarf name is Lili Puti or Juana Puj (throughout the book names are often puns and correspond with changes in identity), discovers that the Mulata, notwithstanding her sumptuous breast, coltish legs and waspish waist, is sexually "neither a woman or a man." Actually Yumí might have guessed his wife's hermaphroditism as she has consistently only offered him her backside.

Yumí's good fortune comes to an abrupt end when the dwarfish Catarina imprisons the Mulata in a cave, only to have her escape, at which point all of Yumí's possessions are levelled by a tremendous earthquake and covered over with an immense sheet of lava. Reduced to poverty, Yumí hits the road with his miniature wife and a dancing bear—

the trio determined to earn their living as a traveling road show.

At this point, Yumí meets the "sauvages," erstwhile humans, who, as drunken revelers, stayed in their wild boar's costumes too long and so became wild boars. The "sauvages" accept Yumí into their community, renaming him Hayumihaha and his wife, Hazabalahaha. (Notwithstanding the linguistic "ha has" the "sauvages" have lost the ability to laugh).

In Yumí's next confrontation with the devil, who appears as a man capable of becoming a stone, Yumí, following the advice of the grandmother "sauvage," succeeds in getting his wife back to normal size. This he does when the devil attempts to make off with Catarina by hoisting her upon his pitch-covered back. With Yumí holding tight to Catarina's legs and the devil dragging her off, Catarina is stretched to her proper height.

Yumí and his wife now decide to become great sorcerers and set off for Tierrapaulita where they will undergo their apprenticeship. They have packed Tazol, the corn husk demon into one of their bags, having fashioned him in the shape of a cross to neutralize his powers. The tactic fails, however, and Tazol impregnates Catarina through her navel. This makes Catarina something of a powerful demon-sorceress, renamed Giroma. Out of revenge for her own previous endwarfment, she has Tazol turn her husband into a dwarf. For Yumí, small stature does not mean inferiority as he dons a pair of stilts and becomes the dance wizard, Chiltic. Giroma, not to be out done, exploits both devilish child and dancing husband by commanding them both in an acrobatic road show.

At this point, Huasanga, a spidery dwarf woman, appears on the scene and is married to Chiltic by the priest of Tierrapaulita. It should be noted that Tierrapaulita is beseiged by pagan gods, including the mightly Cashtoc, and the village priest is all but powerless. As living testament to the deformation of religion and the destruction wrought by nature, Tierrapaulita and its inhabitants are all twisted and misshapen.

In a fit of jealousy over her husband's marriage to the dwarf woman, Giroma orders Tazol to turn Chiltic into a giant, thus placing him out of Huasanga's reach. This he does and the now gigantic Yumí joins the earthquaking dance of the giants, Huracán and Cabracán. Huasanga, out of revenge, then pulls off and runs away with Giroma's sex, making her something of an asexual equivalent to the hermaphroditic Mulata. In the mean time, the priest is attempting to smuggle in a shipment of Holy Water, hidden inside a number of coconuts. The demons get wind of the plan and cover each of the coconuts with a woman's sex, Giroma's among them. This creates the most obscene image in the book when the priest, attempting to open a coconut, beholds "a woman taking a leak."

With all of Tierrapaulita rocking to the rhythm of the dancing giants and the Holy water turned to corruption, Cashtoc gathers up his mighty caravan and marches off into the moutnains. The priest, too, abandons Tierrapaulita, leaving behind the lesser witches and demons (Yumí and his wife among them) to do battle with a new demon: the Christian devil, who goes by the name, Candanga, and whose edict: "Breeding time" is heralded throughout the streets of Tierrapaulita.

Now a new priest and Sexton arrive in Tierrapaulita to do battle with Candanga. When Father Chimalpín throws down his glove as a challenge to the devil, it is picked up by Yumí, now a pock-marked Indian who says his name is Quiquín and whose body also offers an earthly home to the devil Candanga.

Meanwhile the Mulata has turned up again, taken over the body of the Sexton, and is attempting to seduce Yumí as a way of unmasking Candanga because the Mulata also harbors the pagan deity, Cashtoc. This puts the confrontation on three levels: Yumí/Mulata, Quiquín/Sexton, and Candanga/Cashtoc. It is important to note the iconographic cross-fertilization as the Indian includes the Christian devil, while the Sexton the pagan one. Their seductive sparring comes to an end when Yumí sprouts eleven thousand hedgehog quills at the site of each of his pock marks. The Mulata leaves the body of the Sexton and the Yumí hedgehog turns to do battle with the priest who has sprouted eleven thousand arms and looks like a many legged spider in order to grasp each of the devil's horns (quills). The battle reaches a new level when the priest marries Yumí to the Mulata in a Requiem mass "for all of death" and the husband takes his bride, much to the Mulata's masochistic delight, by piercing her body with his many quills. At this point both former spouses, Giroma and Huasanga, jealously attack the Mulata—Huasanga snatching her sex, and Giroma taking away half her body so that the Mulata becomes something of a snake woman, possessing one arm, one eye, one lip, one leg, etc.

Giroma and Yumí, who has become a paralytic with a skeleton of gold, retire to their sorcerers' castle where Giroma casts the Mulata's spare parts into a pond, leaving them there to float before her husband's admiring gaze. Meanwhile, the devil reigns in Tierrapaulita, demanding that the population breed, and Father Chimalpín awakes to find his whole body covered with small pox scars, the cure for which involves riding a bucking meat-eating mule. During this time the Mulata manages to retrieve her sex and body parts, having invaded the sorcerers' castle in a dress she shares with a skeleton woman.

The tale comes to an end when all of Tierrapaulita shakes to the ground to the rhythm of the bucking meat-eating mule. Yumí is discovered dead and quartered (his bones really weren't made of gold). The once powerful Giroma settles to the ground and is gradually covered over with dust and rubble. And the Mulata—well, she remains, having undergone a miraculous rebirth during which she is stripped of all her powers but emerges as her own daughter. ("I am the daughter of the one I am"). And the priest—having shook off his pock marks during the wild ride, awakes to find himself in a modern hospital where he is slowly and relentlessly growing into an elephant.

These are the novel's skeletal events. Actually, there are many more tangential characters and incidents, like a skull-eating demon who breaks his teeth on a plaster head of John-the-Baptist and angrily lashes out at the Sexton, whom he has previously endowed with a mighty bridge-like arm, causing that arm to wither just when the priest is attempting to escape from Tierrapaulita over the Sexton's arm. For its complexity and inventive imagination, Asturias' novel captures the essence of Latin American mythic storytelling. This is a tradition as humorous and deeply textured as the marvelous Brazilian myth: *Macunaíma*, and as old as the great Mayan myth of creation: *Popul Vuh*. As the Spanish translator of the latter, Asturias was well schooled for the project of bringing the mythic world into modern narrative settings.

The *Mulata* demands an historical reading. This is true not only because its author was, during the time of global cold war and in the face of more than one anti-dictatorial struggle in his homeland, a staunch supporter and spokesman for left politics; but also, as every student of Lévi-Strauss knows, because myth is the way primitive societies explain history. For contemporary readers reared to expect causality in narrative, the project of reading myth historically necessitates a new way of thinking and requires three operations: interpreting the images or icons themselves, defining the relationship between these icons, and examining the overall process within which the icons are defined.

The task is demanding if only for the historical density of the icons themselves. Each is a tightly packed unity of conflicting historical material. For instance, the "sauvages," whose language involves placing a "ha" before and a "ha ha" after a name (Hayumihaha), have ironically lost the ability to laugh. This is Asturias' way of punning Pope Paul III, who, in the midst of a heated debate over whether or not the Indians could be pressed into tributary labor in exchange for salvation, declared that the Indians were indeed human because they could laugh. The iconographic analysis does not end here. For the "sauvages," as Yumí discovers, who not only laugh and have a language, but a community, folklore and kinship system as well, represent an extended metaphor of the way primitive peoples have been portrayed by anthropologists. As pagan wildmen, they satisfy the white Christian world's need for a primitive order. (pp. 46–51)

Susan Willis, "Nobody's Mulata," in *I & L*, Vol. IV, No. 17, September–October, 1983, pp. 146–62.

SOURCES FOR FURTHER STUDY

Brotherson, Gordon. "The Presence of Mayan Literature in *Hombres de Maiz* and Other Works by Miguel Ángel Asturias." *Hispania* 58, No. 1 (March 1975): 68–74.

> Explores Asturias's use of Mayan mythology in *Men of Maize.*

Callan, Richard J. "The Quest Myth in Miguel Ángel Asturias's *Hombres de maíz.*" *Hispanic Review* XXXVI, No.3 (July 1968): 249–61.

> Assesses Asturias's use of Greek/Mayan/Aztec mythological archetypes, and of the "search for the Feminine component" in *Men of Maize.*

——. *Miguel Ángel Asturias.* New York: Twayne Publishers, 1970. 182 p.

> Surveys Asturias's life and many of his major works.

Campion, Daniel. "Eye of Glass, Eye of Truth: Surrealism in *El señor presidente.*" *Hispanic Journal* 3, No. 1 (Fall 1981): 123–35.

> Discusses Asturias's use of surrealism to explicate his political and social themes.

Díaz, Nancy Gray. "Metamorphosis as Integration: *Hombres de maíz.*" In her *The Radical Self: Metamorphosis to Animal Form in Modern Latin American Narrative,* pp. 34–50. Columbia: University of Missouri Press, 1988.

> Assesses Asturias's use of the Mayan concept of "metamorphosis to animal form" for several of the characters in *Men of Maize* as a "key to an understanding of. . . the ending of the novel."

Himelblau, Jack. "Love, Self, and Cosmos in the Early Works of Miguel Ángel Asturias." *Kentucky Romance Quarterly* XVIII, No. 3 (1970): 243–64.

Examines Asturias's early poems and the themes of love and self which are coupled with his cosmovision of the world.

Irving, T. B. "The Hero in Asturias's Novel: *The President.*" *University of Toronto Quarterly* XXXVIII, No. 2 (January 1969): 192–206.

> Explores Asturias's political focus in *El señor presidente,* and how it presents dictatorship as "a grotesque and almost asphixiating concept of the total state. . . ."

Martin, Gerald. "Miguel Ángel Asturias: *El señor presidente.*" In *Landmarks in Modern Latin American Fiction,* edited by Philip Swanson, pp. 50–73. London: Routledge, 1990.

> Explores the structure, content, and character development of Asturias's *El señor presidente,* illustrating how they contribute to the novel's political and social themes.

Mead, Robert G., Jr. "A Myth for Mankind." *Saturday Review* L, No. 44 (4 November 1967): 32.

> Examines how Mayan myths "cross geographical and cultural barriers" in Asturias's *Mulata.*

Peréz Galo René. "Miguel Ángel Asturias." *Américas* 20, No. 1 (January 1968): 1–5

> Illustrates how Asturias portrays his concern "for man's problems" and his agony over "his mutilated rights" through the character of the idiot Pelele in *El Señor Presidente.*

Prieto, Rene. "The New American Idiom of Miguel Ángel Asturias." *Hispanic Review* 56, No. 2 (Spring 1988): 191–208.

> Details the extensive use of Mayan mythology in *Men of Maize.*

Additional coverage of Asturias's life and career is contained in the following sources published by Gale Research: *Contemporary Authors,* Vols. 25–28, 49–52; *Contemporary Authors New Revision Series,* Vol. 32; *Contemporary Authors Permanent Series,* Vol. 2; *Contemporary Literary Criticism,* Vols. 3, 8, 13; *Dictionary of Literary Biography,* Vol. 113; *Hispanic Writers;* and *Major Twentieth Century Writers.*

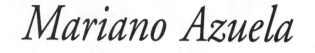

Mariano Azuela

1873–1952

(Also wrote under the pseudonym Beleño) Mexican novelist, short story writer, and biographer.

INTRODUCTION

Noted for his use of colloquial dialogue and simple plots, Azuela was instrumental in shaping the development of the modern Mexican novel. His works generally focus on the Mexican Revolution, social reform in Mexico, and the plight of the common citizen. Inspired by the writings of French social activist Émile Zola, Azuela joined the revolutionary movement, and it was during those war years that he wrote his most famous novel, *Los de abajo* (1915; *The Under Dogs*). The novel is replete with pessimism and irony, and it shows how the ideals of social reform which fuelled the revolution were ultimately subverted by the revolutionaries themselves. Azuela's disillusionment with the aftermath of the Mexican Revolution led him to continue writing about those same themes for much of his literary career. Today Azuela's works are viewed as insightful and colorful glimpses into a major moment in modern Mexican history.

Azuela was born in Lagos de Moreno, Jalisco, Mexico, in 1873. He attended preparatory school in Lagos, and then studied at the University of Guadalahara, where he graduated with a degree in medicine in 1899. Azuela joined the Mexican Revolution when it began in 1910, and three years later became a member of Pancho Villa's rebel forces, whom he served as an army physician. After the revolution, Azuela settled in one of the poorest neighborhoods in Mexico City and opened a medical practice for the indigent population. He also continued his writing career, earning the prestigious National Prize for Literature in 1949. Azuela died in 1952 and was buried in the Rotunda des Hombres Ilustros in Mexico City.

In the years before the outbreak of the Mexican Revolution, Azuela wrote *María Luisa* (1907), *Los fracasados* (1908), and *Mala yerba* (1909; *Marcela: A Mexican Love Story*)—novels that championed the poor and downtrodden classes in their struggle for justice against the dictatorial Mexican government of Porfirio Díaz. Written while Azuela was in exile with Pancho Villa in Texas, *The Under Dogs* was initially published in serial form in the newspaper *El Paso del Norte* in 1915, and then as a book in the following year. The novel attracted little attention among contemporary readers and critics. It was not until 1924 that the work was "rediscovered" by the Mexican literati and hailed as the quintessential novel of the Mexican Revolution. As the conflict drew to a close, Azuela's focus shifted to its effects on the people of Mexico in *Las tribulaciones de una familia decente* (1918; *The Trials of a Respectable Family*), which traces the tragic decline of a dispossessed estate owner's family as it seeks a new life in postwar Mexico City. In succeeding years, he incorporated into some of his novels the stream-of-consciousness technique that was in vogue in Europe at the time: these include *La malhora* (1923), *El desquite* (1925), and *La luciérnaga* (1932; *The Firefly*), all of which depict the psychological effects of the revolution on the individual. Many critics have argued that these works are couched in such obscure and abstract symbolism that they are unappealing and difficult to read. Azuela's next major novel was *Nueva burguesía* (1941), which explores the advent of a new social class in Mexico made up of revolutionaries who had abandoned their political and social ideals. Three more of Azuela's novels were published posthumously: *La maldición* (1955), about a family that is forced off of its provincial farm and emigrates to Mexico City, where it is virtually destroyed by city life; *Esa sangre* (1956), which continues the story of *Mala yerba* and relates the psychological struggle between farm owners and farm workers in post-revolutionary Mexico; and the biographical novel *Madero* (1958-60), which is about the life of the first elected president of Mexico following the Díaz regime, and which had been left unfinished until it was completed by Alí Chumacero.

Critics generally agree that Azuela's *The Under Dogs* stands as the most important of the novels that document the events of the Mexican Revolution. Combining rural dialogue, familiar countryside and town settings, and a simple plot that focuses on the revolution itself, *The Under Dogs* provides the reader with a remarkable insight into the goals and aspirations of the Mexican people and the revolutionaries who fought in the war; but the novel also expresses the disillusionment which resulted from Azuela's realization that in the aftermath of the conflict the revolutionaries, in whom he had placed his hope for social reform, had virtually lost sight of their aims. Commentators have also contended the Azuela's pessimism toward the revolutionary movement extended to his later novels, maintaining that in these works he continued to be highly critical of the Mexican government and social conditions. They have further asserted that a key element in all of Azuela's works is the role of the common person, who is always at the mercy of the political and social forces over which there is no control. From the rebel peasant Demetrio in *The Under Dogs* who is caught up in the flow of events and thrust into the revolutionary spotlight, to the aristocratic farm owner Julián Andrade in *Esa sangre*, who tries to deal equitably with his workers, Azuela generally focuses on the fight of individual Mexican citizens for social justice, freedom, and security. Commentators have pointed out that Azuela modified his main theme throughout his literary career, gradually replacing the physical revolutionary struggle with the postwar psychological struggle.

Azuela is remembered as a novelist whose solid personal convictions and sense of purpose regarding social reform in Mexico guided the characters and themes of his principal writings. Of this approach to writing novels, Azuela stated: "If I put passion in the pages, I included no lie or unfounded judgement. . . . Of all of which I may be accused, the least is having deformed the truth."

CRITICAL COMMENTARY

WALTER M. LANGFORD
(essay date 1971)

[In the excerpt below, Langford presents a comprehensive overview of Azuela's major novels, commenting on the revolutionary themes of his early works and the disenchantment inherent in his later novels.]

Not only was Mariano Azuela the first [Mexican novelist] to write about the Revolution and its effects, but in

Principal Works

María Luisa (novel) 1907

Los fracasados (novel) 1908

Mala yerba (novel) 1909
  [*Marcela: A Mexican Love Story*, 1932]

Andrés Pérez, maderista (novel) 1911

Sin amor (novel) 1912

*Los de abajo (novel) 1915
  [*The Under Dogs*, 1929]

Los caciques (novel) 1917
  [*The Bosses*, 1956]

Domitilo quiere ser diputado (novella) 1918

Las moscas (novella) 1918
  [*The Flies*, 1956]

Las tribulaciones de una familia decente (novel) 1918
  [*The Trials of a Respectable Family*, 1963]

La malhora (novel) 1923

El desquite (novel) 1925

La luciérnaga (novel) 1932
  [*The Firefly*, 1979]

El camarada Pantoja (novel) 1937

San Gabriel de Valdivias, comunidad indigena (novel) 1938

Regina Landa (novel) 1939

Avanzada (novel) 1940

Nueva burguesía (novel) 1941

La marchanta (novel) 1944

La mujer domada (novel) 1944

Sendas perdidas (novel) 1949

La maldición (novel) 1955

Esa sangre (novel) 1956

Obras completas (novels, short stories) 1958

Madero: Biografía novelada (novel) 1958–60

*This work was originally published in serial form in 1915, and as a novel in 1916.

doing so he broke with the novelistic tradition so long in vogue in his country and initiated a new treatment of the novel. In *Los de abajo (The Under Dogs)* Azuela etches an approach and a style that will characterize the cascade of works comprising the Novel of the Mexican Revolution, an output which rather completely dominated the novel from 1925 until about 1945. Attuned in remarkable degree to the military struggle and the social upheaval it attempts to mirror and interpret, *Los de abajo* is of course set in the historical reality of the Revolution and is narrated in terse, simple, colloquial language.

Uncomplicated both as to style and to plot, this novel truly reflects the Revolution as it was. And all of the novelists of the Revolution who came after Azuela have continued to tell it the same way.

Action takes precedence over description and characterization, conciseness and directness replace the verbosity and sermonizing of the past. As a result, the twentieth-century Mexican novel emerges with legitimacy and is able to stand on its own feet.

Not often does one man and one work exert such influence on the literature of a country. While Azuela was to produce more than twenty novels, it is safe to affirm that his influence on other novelists of the Revolution would have been much the same had he written only *Los de abajo*. And this is not at all intended to downgrade the value and importance of some of his other works. It is simply that *Los de abajo* stands forth from the outset as the bellwether of the novel of the Mexican Revolution. (pp. 16–17)

[Azuela's] *Andrés Pérez, maderista*, 1911, [is] at once the first novel of the Revolution and a remarkable document but in no sense a great novel. It seems to have been hastily constructed, the minimal development of an outline. The style is simple; almost journalistic, and the few important characters do not come to life as real individuals but personify types.

The action line of *Andrés Pérez, maderista* is not complicated and the novel covers little more than one hundred pages in any of its editions. Andrés Pérez, a young newspaperman in Mexico city, receives an invitation from his former classmate Toño Reyes to visit him and his wife, María, at their hacienda. On an impulse Andrés quits his job and goes. Toño shows immense interest in the rumors of a possible revolution and queries Andrés, who describes the restless spirit in the country and ends by saying, "One has the presumption that something serious is going to happen." Thereafter he indicates clearly his lack of interest in revolutionary talk and activity.

Shortly thereafter the Revolution breaks out. Toño is disillusioned with the attitude of Andrés, who decides to return to the capital. But before he can leave an order comes from the district political leader for his arrest as a "revolutionary agent of Francisco I. Madero who has gone to the hacienda to arouse the people." Despite the denials by Pérez, Toño—and soon everyone in the area—comes to believe that he really is an undercover agent for the Madero uprising. They even gather money to aid the cause and hand over to Andrés a thousand pesos. A sleepless night brings him to the decision to skip town with this windfall and go to the U.S. for a few months.

Picked up by the police on his way to the train station, Pérez in jail becomes an ever larger hero. Toño Reyes leads a successful local uprising but is killed in the skirmish. Andrés Pérez is of course released when the rebels take control of the area, He is almost alone in recognizing the cynicism and opportunism of various figures who embrace the revolutionary cause only to save their own hides and their fortunes. The last lines are the final cynical touch. Once more on his way to the train, Pérez passes the doorway of Toño's widow, María, who has clearly been attracted to Andrés from the beginning. He pauses, thinks a moment, and then turns into the doorway.

The most interesting thing about *Andrés Pérez, maderista* is the stance Azuela takes toward the Revolution. He is asserting that some of the most committed and idealistic revolutionaries are either killed off in the fighting or are so lacking in the practical realm that opportunists and revolutionaries in name only are able to gain control of the operation (especially on the local level), with the result that there is really no revolution but only a change in bosses. Actually, this disenchanted view is not at all unique. It is an attitude quite common throughout the literature on the Revolution. The amazing part is that Azuela, in the very first months of the Revolution and in the full flush of victory, perceives clearly what was to become evident to many others only with the passage of time, namely, that the Revolution from the outset was infiltrated, adulterated, and undermined by large numbers of antirevolutionaries who shrewdly protected their power position merely by proclaiming loudly and insistently their adherence to the cause. (pp. 17–19)

Los de abajo breaks sharply and abruptly with the Mexican novelistic tradition. True, it is strongly anchored to historical fact, but in this it is not innovative, since the historical novel had previously been cultivated in Mexico. Also, it is decidedly realistic and again this is nothing new, for realism was already established as a strong current in all of Spanish-American literature. What is new about *Los de abajo* may be summarized as follows:

1) It plants the Revolution firmly in center stage as the overriding theme. In fact, one can correctly say that the Revolution itself is the true protagonist of *Los de abajo*. In this respect it goes much farther than *Andrés Pérez, maderista*, which, though it was the first novel of the Mexican Revolution, still revolved on the outer periphery of the Revolution itself.

2) In style *Los de abajo* abandons the former cult of verbiage. Instead, Azuela rides the pendulum almost to the other extreme and initiates a new tendency toward brevity, terseness, and suggestion. Sentences usually are short, sometimes piling upon one another in staccato manner. A few words, through the device of suggestion and projection, do the work of many. Description is sublimated; dialogue assumes a prime role.

3) The speech of the Mexican peon is highlighted. Nothing on this same scale had been attempted in earlier Mexican novels. For the uninitiated, the use of the highly colloquial language of the common man may pose a slight problem in comprehension, but undeniably it imparts a distinct and genuine flavor to the conversation and the work as a whole.

4) Plot gives way in considerable degree to episode and incident. There is progression from start to finish, and the loosely linked episodes do lead to change and eventual resolution, but of greater concern seems to be the creation of the *ambiente* (atmosphere), of a mood keenly attuned not so much to the specific incident as to the whole Revolution itself. *Los de abajo* is an admirable example of how style, speech, action, attitude, and thought create a pervasive atmosphere that reflects faithfully the spirit of the moment, the spirit of the Mexican Revolution as it was.

It is a tribute to Azuela that each of these features became characteristic of the flood of novels about the Revolution, an outpouring triggered by Azuela and later to become the most widely cultivated cycle in the history of the Mexican novel. If imitation is the highest form of flattery, then Mariano Azuela is a most flattered person.

As already mentioned, *Los de abajo* is a direct outgrowth of Azuela's own participation in the Revolution. Written partly in the very heat of battle and finished as soon as the author reached safety in El Paso, this work understandably carries the trademark of authenticity. It would be difficult to imagine a set of circumstances more favorable for capturing the intimate mood of a given time.

The story of *Los de abajo* is built around the revolutionary activities of Demetrio Macías and his followers. Demetrio, modeled somewhat on General Julián Medina, finds himself in the Revolution not through any conviction whatever but through personal differences he has had with the *patrón*, don Mónico. Demetrio is a simple peasant, unable to read and not intellectual enough ever to understand the political ideals, nuances, and aspirations of the revolutionary movement. Demetrio leaves his wife and small son and, with his little band of twenty-five men, all of the same background as himself, ambushes a larger federal force in a canyon close to his home, inflicting heavy damage on them but being rather seriously wounded himself.

He and his men find shelter and a warm welcome in a "rancho" or tiny village in the mountains. Here Demetrio recuperates for two or three weeks, treated by one of his principal followers, Venancio, who has been a barber and is easily the best educated and most intelligent of the group. A girl of the village, Camila, serves as nurse for Demetrio, who comes to look upon her with fond eyes. But Camila has fallen completely for Luis Cervantes, a sort of dandy who has been picked up and brought in by one of the sentries.

Cervantes is intelligent and educated (he has studied a bit of medicine and has been a journalist), but the reader quickly tags him as an opportunist. Drafted by the federals, he has deserted and when caught by Demetrio's men insists that his one ambition is to serve the Revolution. His colors begin to show when he keeps hands off the willing Camila because he senses that Demetrio will want her. But Cervantes is a good one with words and articulates all the right phrases about the Revolution, its aims, ideals, and principles. Thus, he entrenches himself as Demetrio's "brain truster" and idea man.

Although Demetrio's forces continue to grow and to win a few skirmishes with the federals, Cervantes convinces him that he must align himself with one of the important generals if he is really to amount to anything and contribute much to the cause of the Revolution. The decision is taken to join up with General Pánfilo Natera, who in turn forms part of the army of Pancho Villa. As the townsfolk express their fond good wishes, they depart from Camila's village, leaving her behind to pine for Luis.

After winning along the way a fierce encounter with the federals, Demetrio with a hundred men meets Natera in Fresnillo. Cervantes and Captain Solís of Natera's command recognize each other from former days and engage in a most interesting dialogue about the Revolution. Solís, once imbued with the fire and enthusiasm which Luis now has (or pretends), admits to much disillusionment: "There are deeds and there are men who are nothing but pure gall. And that gall keeps falling drop by drop into the spirit, and it embitters everything, it poisons everything. Enthusiasm, hopes, ideals, joys. . . nothing ! Then one has nothing left but to become a bandit like the others or to disappear from the scene, hiding himself behind the walls of a fierce and impenetrable egotism." And a little later: "I ask myself why I keep on fighting. The Revolution is a hurricane, and the man who goes into it is no longer a man, but just a miserable dry leaf driven by the wind." Some time later, during the course of a battle, Solís exclaims: "How beautiful the Revolution is, even in its very barbarity!" Then he adds: "What a disappointment, my friend, if those of us who offered all our enthusiasm and our very life to overthrow a miserable assassin should turn out to be the builders of an enormous pedestal on which a hundred or two hundred thousand monsters of the same species might place themselves. . . . What a waste of blood!" A moment later Antonio Solís is hit and adds his own to all that other wasted blood. Azuela almost certainly is speaking his own thoughts and feelings through the words of Solís.

When Demetrio is made a colonel in Natera's forces the tempo picks up, though what is revealed is the gradual demoralization of Demetrio and his followers. He decides he wants Camila with him and Cervantes goes back for her, letting her think he has come to take her for himself. Later Camila is stabbed to death by la Pintada, a gross and brassy camp follower. There is a lot of drinking between battles, much boastful talk, some seducing of young girls, and a few fatal arguments. The taking of any town triggers unrestrained looting and pillaging.

Inexorably, the fortunes of Demetrio and his men follow the fate of Pancho Villa's army. A high point is reached and then the tide turns. As they give ground and move back toward the north, morale falls and desertions increase. They meet stony aloofness in villages which a year before had embraced them warmly. Among the deserters is Luis Cervantes, who has made off with a good bit of plundered loot to El Paso, from where he writes to Venancio to relate how he is prospering. By now Demetrio is a general, but he commands few more than the small band with which he started.

They return for the first time to where Demetrio had lived. His wife is beside herself with joy. His little son, terrified, doesn't know him. The woman begs him not to leave again and asks why they must keep on fighting. Tossing a stone down the side of the canyon, Demetrio answers, "See that stone, how it can't stop. . . ." As he departs with his few men, they are ambushed in the same spot where he had won his first victory. Though hopelessly trapped, Demetrio is possessed for a moment with the wild joy of battle, of his own fabulous marksmanship ("where he puts his eye, he puts the bullet"). "And at the foot of a crevice as enormous and sumptuous as the portico of an old cathedral, Demetrio Macías, with his eyes fixed forever, keeps aiming with the barrel of his rifle. (pp. 20–3)

Soon [Azuela] had produced several more works with revolutionary themes: *Los caciques* (*The Bosses*), published in 1917, and *Las moscas*, (*The Flies*), *Domitilo quiere ser diputado* [*Domitilo wants to be a congressman*], and *Las tribulaciones de una familia decente* (*The Trials of a Respectable Family*), all published in 1918. Except for *Las tribulaciones de una familia decente*, these works are so short they can barely be called novels. In each of them Azuela continues his mordant analyses of the Revolution and its effects and with sarcasm and irony restates and reinforces his deep disappointment with the venality and unprincipled actions of many self-proclaimed leaders and supporters of the Revolution. *Las tribulaciones* the longest of these works, is also the strongest.

As the title indicates, this novel is the story of the hardships suffered by a formerly well-to-do provincial family after the Porfirian regime gave way to the Revolution. Moving to the capital from Zacatecas, the Vázquez Prado family hopes somehow to cling to its accustomed social and economic position. At least this is the driving motive of Agustinita, the mother, who until now has ruled the family by virtue of having been the source of its wealth. The father, Procopio, at the outset appears henpecked and somewhat insecure. Of the two daughters, Lulú comes through a bit colorless, while Berta is headstrong and ambitious. One son, Francisco José, has no great part in the novel, whereas his brother César, having set himself the task of writing the family history, narrates the first half of the story.

Known to be opponents of Carranza, the Vázquez Prado family sees its fragile hopes of rehabilitation disintegrate with the triumph of the Carranza forces. Berta provides a momentary ray of hope by marrying Pascual, a thoroughgoing opportunist and hypocrite whose complete lack of principles allows him to insinuate himself into high office in the new regime. But before long Pascual provokes his own downfall, and this time the social and economic ruin of the family seems complete.

Procopio, no longer in the shadow of Agustinita's money, now moves into command. He takes an ordinary position with a business firm, something which, back in Zacatecas, custom and the "right thing" would not have permitted him to do. Procopio's genuine and Christian qualities emerge as he organizes the life of the family around its new and humble yet honest and decent orientation, and furthermore he claims the respect—even from Agustinita—which is his due as head of the household. He then sends for Archibaldo, erstwhile suitor of Lulú, who has been scorned for his humble origins, and invites him to come to claim the hand of the daughter.

In *Las tribulaciones de una familia decente* Azuela is again displaying his revulsion toward hypocrisy and opportunism, and he leaves us with the moral that money brings no assurance of happiness. He likewise says to the rich that plain, honest work—even manual labor—is dignifying and can bring true peace of mind.

The influence of Emile Zola is perhaps more noticeable in this novel than in any other of Azuela's works. The naturalistic tendencies in *Las tribulaciones* drew these comments from one observer [Manuel Pedro Gonzalez, *Trayectoria de la novela en México*, 1951]:

> The concept of the novel as a laboratory, of the 'experimental novel,' on which Zola's theory rests, is here employed with a fidelity and a mastery never achieved by Federico Gamboa, the most loyal and tenacious disciple which the French master was to have in the Spanish tongue. The changing fortunes of the Revolution and economic misery serve here as reagents or tests to 'experiment' with the characters and observe their reactions, through which they come to define themselves.

Furthermore, the characters as a group are as fully delineated in this novel as in any other Azuela work. Procopio in particular, and also Agustinita, Berta, and Señora de Tabardillo (a family friend) emerge as truly human and individual personalities. Agustinita can claim the added distinction, in the opinion of one critic, of being the first well-drawn female in any Mexican novel who plays a prime role in the plot.

One thing which weakens the overall effect of *Las tribulaciones* and puzzles all observers is that in the middle of the story Azuela shifts the vantage point from which the action is related. The first part of the book is narrated by César, who then is permitted to die. Thereafter the author himself takes over in the guise of the omniscient observer. The reader finds no reason for this unusual technique, which, if nothing else, is disconcerting at the time it occurs. Nevertheless, the novel is one of the three or four best among the score or more which Azuela published.

Following the appearance of *Las tribulaciones de una familia decente* in 1918, Azuela gave us no new novel until 1923. Looking back over his literary career, one must conclude that this was a truly difficult period for Mariano Azuela, perhaps even a crucial one. It is my own conviction that during this time he was frustrated and disheartened, and that the underlying cause for this state of mind was the poor reception given his works by both readers and critics. It may be a bit unfair to blame the readers in this matter, for in those days comments and reviews by critics in the public press constituted the principal means of publicity for any newly printed work. And the critics remained almost 100 percent silent in the face of the ten novels and novelettes which Azuela had published by the end of 1918.

Manuel Pedro González has documented the nearly complete refusal, or at least failure, of the Mexican literary critics to discuss Azuela's works between 1907 and 1923. Indeed, González sees the whole thing as almost a conspiracy on the part of the critics to keep his books from becoming known. While it may be overreacting to see such a conspiracy, the attitude of the critics does seem fairly transparent. In their eyes his revolutionary theme and style represented a disturbing departure from the comfortable norm they had known and cultivated. They felt threatened by this new novelist and since they did not have Azuela's vision, nor had they shared his involvement in the epochal events of the Revolution, they completely ignored him.

In any case, when Azuela began writing again things had changed. The Revolution as such was no longer his theme, nor did he employ the sincere, straightforward style which had helped break the spell of the nineteenth-century novel. Deciding, as one critic puts it, to see if he too couldn't "dar gato por liebre" (pass off a cat as a rabbit), Azuela began experimenting generously with cubist techniques and published three novels which he later admitted were written with tongue in cheek [F. Rand Morton, *Los novelistas de la revolución mexicana*, 1949].

These three novels are *La Malhora* [*Evil woman*], *El desquite* [*The retaliation*], and *La luciérnaga* [*The Firefly*], published respectively in 1923, 1925, and 1932 (though apparently this last work was written in 1926). These are often called hermetic novels, in contrast to the open and easily understood works which Azuela produced earlier. They are avant-garde, tinged with surrealism, at times difficult to comprehend.

La Malhora misses—though not by too much—being a fine novel. Certain things about it make it both interesting and important. It is one of the earliest of the

Mexican novels to depict with stark realism and shattering pessimism the subhuman existence of degraded individuals in the poorest parts of Mexico City. When the protagonist, la Malhora, has sunk about as low as humans can, she is regenerated by an unstable doctor and is taken in by three overly pious women, until one day her past suddenly confronts her again and she reverts to type. Environment has played a determining and disastrous role in her life.

It is in the narrative techniques employed by Azuela that *La Malhora* holds the most interest for us. Here there is generous use of confused and unexpected images, elliptical sentences, tricky metaphors, single words expected to do the work of many. Yet the author's most significant innovation lies in his entering the subconscious thoughts of one of his characters. When the demented doctor indulges in an interior monologue, Azuela is anticipating by two decades the utilization of this and other techniques by Agustín Yáñez in his *Al filo del agua*, which . . . is to take the Mexican novel around a sharp turn into new paths. Azuela's role as a precursor of the trend which now dominates the novel in Mexico, and elsewhere, is generally overlooked because it was but a momentary experiment on his part, one which found no echo in the style and technique of his fellow novelists until Yáñez came along.

Another unusual feature of *La Malhora* is that almost no one really understood its conclusion. On the final page la Malhora goes looking for her two mortal enemies, la Tapatía and Marcelo, who have been the cause of most of her grief, with the intent of killing them. When it appears that she is about to carry out her purpose, we come to the closing words of the story: "La Malhora talló dos cristales que corrigieran su astigmatismo mental." This says that la Malhora ground two lenses to correct her mental astigmatism.

This puzzling finish confounded even the best critics for some time. Those who commented on it interpreted it as saying that she had indeed killed la Tapatía and Marcelo. After nearly twenty years of this guesswork, Azuela himself gave this clarification: La Malhora "saw clearly the true situation of her enemies, now old and beaten down by life, and she forgave them with the most profound contempt. She didn't kill either la Tapatía or Marcelo. Her vengeance was in scorning them" [Quoted in Bernard M.Dulsey, "Azuela Revisited," *Hispania* XXXV (1952)].

While *El desquite* is of small consequence, the last of these "untypical" Azuela novels, *La luciérnaga*, ranks high among his total output. In fact, it probably stands, along with *Los de abajo* and *Las tribulaciones de una familia decente*, as one of Azuela's three best works. *La luciérnaga* is a psychological study in some depth of three characters who, while they come through quite clearly as individuals, at the same time represent three rather common types in Mexican society.

José María personifies the miserliness and narrowness of one so self-centered and self-righteous in his provincial existence that he sees nothing of value in big-city life. His brother, Dionisio, is one tabbed by destiny for a lifetime of failure. He is a middle-class provincial who rushes to the metropolis completely confident of conquering, only to suffer unrelieved disaster. The lesson nevertheless is lost upon him. Conchita is the exemplification of the best in Mexican motherhood. Long-suffering, compassionate, and understanding, her strength and integrity serve to redeem the shortcomings of her husband, Dionisio, and her brother-in-law, José María. She is the strongest female figure in all the Azuela novels indeed, these three are among the most clearly depicted characters of the hundreds created by Mariano Azuela.

La luciérnaga is also a study in contrasts between the urban capital and the provincial town. In this it has a close kinship with *Las tribulaciones*, though the contrast here is more effective because it is in evidence from start to finish.

The story narrated in *La luciérnaga* is not complicated. On the death of their father the two brothers inherit a modest fortune. Despite the opposition of José María, Dionisio takes his wife and children to Mexico City, with the announced intention of giving his family a better education and of multiplying his fortune. But he proves a soft touch for the city slickers, who fleece him at every turn. As everything goes wrong, the reader is witness to the gradual degeneration of Dionisio—physically, economically, and morally. With the last of his money he buys an old bus and then, while under the influence of drugs, drives it into the side of a streetcar, killing some passengers and demolishing the bus.

It is this scene which opens the story, and Dionisio's subconscious thoughts and recollections as he lies stupefied fill in for us much of the background. Desperate now for means of feeding his family, Dionisio writes to José María for help. The story turns then to the stingy brother back in the little town of Cieneguilla. José María, a most complex personality, is dying of tuberculosis. He is withdrawn, and through his inner thoughts we see the aridness of his heart and his soul. He justifies his refusal to send any money by saying he cannot contribute to Dionisio's sinful existence.

Things continue to go downhill for Dionisio's family in Mexico City. The oldest of the children, the teen-aged María Cristina, gets a job to help out—and also gets in with the wrong sort of people. During a wild night of orgy, María Cristina is killed. Dionisio too is becoming involved with a variety of highly questionable characters who turn him more and more toward the underworld. There seems to be an upturn in his fortunes when he lays hands on the hoard left by José María and opens a store, but again he fails. He invests heavily in a cheap tavern called La Noche Buena as a partner of la Generala, an overpowering sort of woman.

While this venture makes money, it also contributes to Dionisio's degeneracy, for he is soon a confirmed alcoholic and marijuana addict. At this point Sebastián, one of the children, becomes seriously ill, Conchita is distraught, but Dionisio is too wrapped up in La Noche Buena and too far down the ladder to be concerned. When the boy dies, Conchita, driven beyond the point of endurance, makes good her threat to take the remaining two children back to Cieneguilla.

The story now swings to her life in the provincial town, where her integrity, dignity, and self-sufficiency win the respect of all. One day the message reaches her that Dionisio (now fallen to depths not known before), has been stabbed and is near death. To the dismay of the townspeople, Conchita sells her things to buy tickets back to Mexico City ("I'm fulfilling my duty"). She and the children reach the hospital as Dionisio is being released. On seeing them, he smiles "without surprise, without emotion, without expression," and the story ends as he says "I had a hunch you would have to come back."

The message of *La luciérnaga* has already been revealed in these lines referring to Conchita: "She is not just a mother; a mother can be a she-wolf, a hyena, a snake. She is the Christian wife who follows her companion, even if he is beset by sickness, by misery, by vice, or by crime itself. If the mission of the firefly is to make the night blacker with its tiny light, the firefly, by twinkling, fulfills its mission."

La luciérnaga brings to a peak the obscure, hermetic style first attempted by Azuela in *La Malhora*. Here he has refined it and has it better under control. Actually, the probing of the subconscious and the use of interior monologue play a much larger role in this work than in *La Malhora*, further confirming Azuela as a precursor of Yáñez and the many who followed him. While Azuela later belittled his three experimental novels, the critics now are largely agreed that in writing them he achieved more than he realized. (pp. 24–30)

Perhaps Azuela's outstanding trait as a novelist is his unswerving support of the little man, the common person, the underdog whereever found, and his unceasing and scornful attack on venality, corruption, opportunism, and misused bureaucracy. His heroes practically without exception are the uprooted, the downtrodden, the maladjusted, the exploited, the well-intentioned turned sour or evil by environment. The fact that hardly any of these protagonists wind up on top was undoubtedly intended by Azuela as a searing indictment of the morals, motives, values, and practices of those who had benefited by the Revolution and, like a tossed kitten, knew how to land on their feet in any situation, however ruthless their means.

From the publication of *Andrés Pérez, maderista* onward, Azuela carried on an implacable and running battle against the nonrevolutionaries and the counterrevolutionaries who infiltrated the Revolution and emasculated its principles and ideals. As the years rolled on, his contempt for these *sinvergüenzas* (shameless ones) grew and his assaults acquired a tone of bitterness which stained somewhat the superb satire and sarcasm he heaped upon these enemies of society almost from his earliest works. Azuela may have wearied of the battle but he never called a truce.

While it may be proper to contend that Mexico has seen better novelists (technically and stylistically, for example) in recent decades, it would seem that only Agustín Yáñez is in a position to challenge Azuela in terms of his influence in shaping the course of the Mexican novel. Both literally and figuratively Mariano Azuela brought the Mexican novel into the twentieth century. He gave it a new direction, new characteristics, a new life. The road he opened is traveled by so many followers that the old one is abandoned forever. It is probably true that if some of Azuela's best works were published today for the first time they would not create too much of a stir. He would be outflanked by the army of young writers who are devotees of the new type of novel featuring a variety of techniques and experimentation. But any writer must be judged by the circumstances of his times and by the impact he exerts upon his contemporaries. By this yardstick Mariano Azuela remains one of the few and true beacons of Mexican literature. (pp. 32–3)

Walter M. Langford, "Mariano Azuela: A Break with the Past," in his *The Mexican Novel Comes of Age*, University of Notre Dame Press, 1971, pp. 14–35.

D. BRADLEY

(essay date 1980)

[In the following essay, Bradley explores the mythological theme of the "sacrificial warrior-victim" in *Los de abajo* and how it influences the novel's structure.]

Despite the numerous works of later writers dealing with the same troubled period, Mariano Azuela's novel, *Los de abajo*, first published in 1915, remains the outstanding novel of the Mexican Revolution; in its brief pages, through the realistic portrayal of the experiences of a band of rebel *guerrilleros*—minor characters in the national drama—Azuela presents and assesses in authentic detail and with the authority of experience the moral course of the Revolution and its effects on Mexican society. For, although the immediate theme of the novel is the activities of a minor band of rebels, crucial developments at national level, such as the murder of President Madero, the rise and fall of Pancho Villa, the convention of Aguascalientes, influence the action and are in turn evaluated explicitly and by implication in the course of the narrative.

For this reason alone *Los de abajo* would have to be seen as more important than the other works of Azuela set in the period of the Revolution. In addition, however, the novel subtly enfolds the tragic fate of Demetrio Macías, the central character of *Los de abajo*, who is trapped and led to his doom by circumstances he can neither control nor comprehend. Despite the degree of unity in the novel implied by the presence of the two elements just mentioned, a recurring theme in critical commentaries on *Los de abajo* is that it lacks unity, a view firmly upheld in Rutherford's conclusions on the structure of the work [in his *Mexican Society during the Revolution*, 1971] which may usefully be quoted to illustrate the tradition: 'The style and structure of Azuela's novels of the Revolution are essentially fragmentary. . . . Each one is a series of loosely-linked "tableaux and scenes". . . . The Revolution is presented as a collection of rather meaningless, even sordid, little occurrences with only the inexorable guiding hand of destiny behind them.'

Others, while admitting the presence of structural flaws, have attempted to interpret them positively, suggesting that they represent a conscious artistic reflection of the fragmentary nature of the Revolution. Seymour Menton broke new ground [in 'La estructura épica de *Los de abajo* y un prólogo especulativo,' *Hispania* 50 (1967)] in arguing that to a noticeable extent the work was shaped by epic themes; he also pointed to the unifying function of stylistic motifs such as parallels between scenes and character and the prevalence of triadic patterns in events and lexis. Although briefly noting, in this context, the religious elements in the work, he clearly found it hard to ascribe any major importance to them, noting that they seemed at variance with what might be expected in a novel written by 'un médico que se inició en las letras bajo la influencia del naturalismo'. The religious motif, however, is more important than he realized and, as I hope to show, is related in the novel to the mythological theme of the sacrificial warrior-victim whose mission, death, and regeneration extensively shape the novel and provide its thematic unity.

Mythic motifs may be employed in a novel primarily with two objectives in view. First, they may serve as a shaping principle in the structure of the narrative, guiding the novelist in his 'groping for intelligible form in the chaos of the empirical world', by providing a 'scheme of the imagination capable of organizing our view of the world' [W. Righter, *Myth and Literature*, 1975]. Secondly, they may enrich the meaning of the text with resonances of related patterns or analogies already familiar to the reader. Myth is effectively introduced only 'if it backs up the realistic theme by making the reader feel the chosen analogy has enriched the primary material' [J.J.White, *Mythology in the Modern Novel*, 1971]. The present study attempts to identify the most important mythic elements in *Los de abajo* and to evaluate their structural and thematic significance.

Azuela explains how his characters are created:

Just like a baby who begins to walk, I take the characters by the hand and help them along, but only as far as to place them securely in the direction that they themselves want to take. I do not force them. I only help them avoid the first stumbling blocks they may find in their way, and prevent them from leaving the tracks. Soon they do not need me and from that moment on my mission is pleasantly reduced to that of a simple stenographer: they speak and I write what they say. I let them do whatever they want and only try to have them express themselves with clarity.

Azuela, quoted by Luis Leal in his *Mariano Azuela*, 1971.

It may be objected at this point that a realistic novel like *Los de abajo* deals not with symbolic or mythical characters but, in the words of J. P. Stern [*On Realism*, 1973] 'finds its proper point of perspective in the most familiar thing in all literature. . . the fictional creation of people, of individual characters and lives, [for] it is with individuals that the social truth of realism is concerned'. It is, in fact, Azuela's achievement that he succeeds in creating characters and plot that are so convincingly true to life that *Los de abajo* has been described as a work of photographic realism, while at the same time imbuing the work with resonances whose secret powers even his severest critics have felt themselves impelled to admire. It will be suggested that such powers may be partially traceable to the configuring force of the archetype of warrior function and in part to the presence of a related one, that of sacrificial death and regeneration, which colour *Los de abajo* with the accumulated suggestive power of myth.

Of the many and varied definitions which attempt to express the essence of myth, that offered by Dumézil in his study of Indo-European warrior mythology [*The Destiny of the Warrior*, 1970] seems particularly pertinent to a study of *Los de abajo*. He postulates that the original purpose of such tales was to enshrine for society 'the values it recognises. . . , but above all to express its very being and structure, the elements the connections, the balances, the tensions that constitute it', the whole system being centred on the archaic perception that 'the world and society can live only through the harmonious collaboration of the three stratified functions of sovereignty, force and fecundity'. Azuela does not directly rework any of the associated myths, but a number of the archetypal themes identified by Dumézil are clearly reflected in aspects of, and occur at significant points in, the development of the novel; more significantly, the way in which they are employed in the novel recreates the ideological values expressed through the myths.

Demetrio Macías clearly reflects the third function, that of fertility; not only is he initially depicted as the husbandman, surrounded by his family and agricultural implements, but later, when he is a successful warrior, he recalls his primary identity, noting that 'si no hubiera sido por el cacique Don Mónico . . . andaría a estas horas con mucha prisa preparando la yunta para las siembras'. His closest companion, Anastasio Montañés, who embodies further aspects of the same function, in accordance with the technique of fragmentation, similarly draws attention to his unnatural role, remarking so frequently it becomes a source of amusement to the others that 'no soy lo que parezco. . . yo no tengo necesidad;. . . tengo mis diez fanegas de siembra'. The vacuum created in the sphere of sovereignty by Madero's overthrow was filled by the spurious objectives proposed by charlatan guides. In the resulting confusion, Demetrio tries in vain to protect his band from falsehood, through the ritual of confession to which magical powers are clearly attributed. Traditional folk values, the wisdom of the common people, also fail; the three old peasant women, who recall the beneficent figures, sometimes spirits of nature, that invariably offer assistance to the mythic hero, sacrifice in vain their precious dove (*palomo*) in an effort to alleviate Demetrio's fever, to exorcize the devil that possesses him. Whereas Demetrio had been successfully protected by his dog, *El Palomo*, from the threat to his life posed by Federal troops, an action in which his dog sacrificed its life, he is now in the clutches of a greater danger which the new sacrifice cannot counteract. His illness is cured only by applying what is a pale reflection of the 'creative and terrible power' which was one attribute of sovereignty [Dumézil]. Employing his cunning and the limited knowledge derived from an incomplete medical course, Cervantes can heal Demetrio's body, but at the expense of infecting his mind, a perversion of the other attribute of sovereignty, 'its organizing and benevolent authority. This is also usurped by the illusory charisma of leaders like Villa, 'nuestro gran Napoleón', as he is called, not without ambiguity. He proves a monstrous growth, 'el guerrero invicto que ejerce ya a distancia su gran fascionación de boa', but on closer examination shrinks to insignificance.

In the sphere of power, however, there are genuine warriors like Natera whose advice Demetrio, observing the hierarchy of functions, seeks, and whom he acknowledges as his true superior: 'La aguilita que traigo en el sombrero usté me la dio. . . Bueno, pos ya sabe que no más me dice: "Demetrio, haces esto y esto"; y se acabó el cuento'. Natera, however, reflects the helplessness of such men of action in the absence of authentic sovereignty; instead of issuing instructions to Demetrio, he can only ask questions that reveal his own uncertainty. Later, when orders arrive for Demetrio, they prove contradictory and finally lead him to his death.

Demetrio was forced to become a rebel because of the threat posed by the very 'warriors' who should truly represent the power and justice of sovereignty. But as the function of sovereignty had been betrayed, both locally

(by Don Mónico seeking private revenge) and nationally (by the treachery of Madero's killers, it is only appropriate that the federal officers who raid Demetrio's house should claim by way of exculpation that their brutality and repaciousness spring from their falsified role: 'Aqui tiene la mano de un amigo. . . .Está bueno, Demetrio Macías, usted me desaira. . . .Es porque no me conoce, es porque me ve en este perro y maldito oficio'. Thus, the frequently-recurring theme of false and unnatural appearances is linked directly to the central and related theme of violence and social disorder which generates the apprehension and uncertainty so strikingly introduced in the novel's opening exchange between the nameless—universal—man and woman: '—Te digo que no es un animal. . . Oye como ladra el *Palomo*. . . . Debe ser algún cristiano. . . —¿y que fueran siendo federales?'

The dehumanizing effect of violence is not confined to the Federal forces; a number of parallels show how the revolutionaries, opposed to social disorder, are similarly affected. The pitiless discipline that decrees the shooting of deserters under fire, first applied by Federal officers, is later furiously invoked by Macías against his now reluctant followers. The non-combatant population at first eagerly identify themselves with the rebels, for, like them, they are 'perseguidos por estos condenados del gobierno que nos roban. . . hasta el maicito que tenemos que comer . . . y donde dan con uno, allí lo acaban como si fuera perro del mal'. But they later develop the same fear and hatred of Demetrio's forces, for the revolutionaries too take their corn from the poor and boast of their innumerable killings. Not only does war turn *cristianos* into *federales*, it also converts them into *animales*—a transformation that may impress as when, in Demetrio's decisive charge in the battle for La Bufa, his men follow him 'como venados sobre las rocas, hombres y bestias hechos uno'. At close range, however, the change induced by blood-lust reveals more sinister aspects: despite the childlike innocence of Anastasio's face it gleams in battle with 'la amoralidad del chacal'. Here, too, Azuela echoes a recurring theme in the warrior myths in which 'due either to a gift of metamorphosis or to a monstrous heredity, the eminent warrior possesses a veritable animal nature . . . the connection Othinn's *berserkir* had with wolves, bears, etc., was not only a resemblance in matters of force and ferocity; in a certain sense they were these animals themselves' [Dumézil]. Aspects of the myths reflect the precautions that are required to ensure that the warrior's fury is directed only against outsiders; in a civil war these barriers are swept aside and animality threatens to overwhelm humanity, as the novel illustrates. Even the most natural acts are affected; an angry encounter can be described in the following terms: 'Pancracio enfrentaba su rostro de piedra ante el del Manteca que lo veía con ojos de culebra', but even when people meet for the first time they watch each other like 'perros desconocidos que se olfatean con desconfianza'. Not surprisingly, the enemy are constantly seen as animals, 'ratas aturdidas', 'gallinas asustadas', who offer little satisfaction in battle, for killing them is like killing 'liebres y guajalotes'; the revolutionaries, however, also prove less than human: El Manteca is described as 'una piltrafa humana', Pancracio has 'todo un aspecto bestial.' Women, too are affected, the campfollowers moving among the troops like 'perros callejeros', or scavenging on the fresh battlefields like 'famélicos coyotes'; the metamorphosis finally affects the whole community.

In such circumstances it is difficult for Demetrio to escape guilt; moreover, like his Indo-European predecessors, whether heroes or gods, he is, although unlike them a reluctant warrior, inescapably exposed by his role to wrongdoing. For, if he is effectively to defeat his enemies, he must display qualities 'which bear a strong resemblance to the blemishes of his adversaries, and respond to boldness, surprise, pretence and treachery with operations of the same style, only more effective. . . '[Dumézil]. He thereby incurs, as the traditions surrounding Horatius and Mitra make clear, the guilt of a necessary but blameworthy deed which requires a purification of the warrior function and of the 'society he represents so that he finds himself to be the specialist, the agent and the instrument of this purification, a sort of scapegoat after having been a champion'. In pursuing this destiny, he follows the standard path of the mythological adventure of the hero in a magnification of the formula represented in the rites of passage: 'separation—initiation—return'.

At first sight, Demetrio may seem an improbable sacrificial victim, especially to those who agree with Rutherford's view that Macías shares with the other peasants 'the basic traits Azuela evidently thinks are normal and definitive peasant characteristics—stupidity, slowness, feeblemindedness and gullibility, compensated for only by a certain animal courage and cunning'. Azuela's own assessment of Demetrio was rather different, for his conception of him was such that, as he wrote, 'si yo me hubiera encontrado entre los revolucionarios un tipo de la talla de Demetrio Macías lo habría seguido hasta la muerte'; he is, significantly, a *ranchero*, one of that group which Azuela saw as the 'producto legítimo de la guerra de Independencia. El ranchero que desde entonces ha sido factor de primerísimo orden en las sucesivas revoluciones de México y a cuya sangre se deben los cambios verificados en nuestra estructura social'; he is also unmistakably Indian and is deliberately contrasted with Cervantes, whose fair skin and name must inevitably recall the Spanish tradition and who represents the minority ruling élite of European origin. Finally, it is important to note that his persecution by Don Mónico is associated indirectly with the assassination of Madero, and that he is accused of being a *maderista*. These features indicate that he is clearly to be identified with those qualities and attitudes that for Azuela exemplify what is authentically Mexican.

Demetrio is, therefore, truly representative of his community; he is also the epic figure described by Menton; in addition, however, he is clearly related to nature and, as his name suggests, may be regarded as a Demeter-figure, embodying some aspects of the goddess's essence. Clearly a deity of the third function, Demeter, the 'grain-mother' or 'earth-mother', was a Corn-goddess associated with the ploughed field, as is Demetrio who remarks: 'Antes de la revolución tenía yo hasta mi tierra volcada para sembrar'. Demeter was the general title for the goddess in triad, composed of Core, Persephone, and Hecate, the first two being frequentiy identified with each other. Demetrio's relations with the triad formed by his wife, Camila, and La Pintada reflect significant parallels with the mythological one.

Camila, 'the servant of the deity', nymph and goddess of the ripening grain, for whom Demetrio pines as Demeter did for Persephone, is the voice of goodness, heard but unheeded by Demetrio in his warrior role. It is significant that her first service for Demetrio is to give him the drink he pleads for as he lies ill from his wound, for she is thereby associated with water which constitutes a central motif in the novel, in which its function, at one level, corresponds with the Indo-European apportionment of elements whereby 'the waters—fertilizing, nourishing, healing, cleansing—belong as fundamentally as does the earth to the third function' [Dumézil].

The motif is also, not unexpectedly, associated directly with Demetrio, who, when threatened in the opening scene of the novel by unknown dangers, 'bebió agua a borbotones', before dealing with the threat. Later, he sleeps in total harmony with nature on the banks of a river 'que se arrastraba cantando en diminutas cascadas.' His home stands near the river which he crosses as he begins his wandering. Camila's village, it should be noted, also stands on a riverbank; the parallel is not fortuitous, for the water motif serves to link both to the theme of the sacrificial victim on their visit to Tepatitlán, where at a farmhouse, 'a orillas de un arroyuelo' and surrounded by a vast and empty expanse of 'dorados barbechos', they are welcomed by the nameless owner who, to provide them with a place to sleep, 'corrió por un apaste de agua y una escoba, pronto a barrer y regar el mejor rincón de la troje para alojar decentemente a tan honorables huéspedes'. The pattern of triads—houses, trees, and animals—the servant's name (Pifanio: Epiphany), and his misshapen leg, 'seca y retorcida, que remataba en algo como pesuña de chivo', hint that the scene is of particular significance. Indeed the fallow plain, the granary, the ritual sprinkling and brushing recall the fertility rites with which Demeter was associated and which Demetrio and Camila re-enact. Demetrio, who complains that the place makes him feel inexplicably sad, has a premonition of doom the following morning; his sense of malaise is echoed by Anastasio, who complains of 'una tristeza y una murria,' caused, in his view, by the plain. Only much later does Demetrio realize the true source of his dread: in Pifanio he had

Azuela receiving the 1949 National Prize for Literature in Mexico.

mysteriously glimpsed his fate, that of being compelled to endure a destiny which had inexplicably decreed his being trapped, without hope of escape, by the war, 'a reniega y reniega, a mátenos y mátenos'.

The third character forming the Demeter triad is La Pintada. At one level, Margarito's jeering reference to her on her first appearance in the novel—'¡Diablo de Pintada tan lista!'—is no more than a jibe at her opportunistic overtures to Demetrio; at another level, however, it hints at her identification with Hecate, the goddess of the underworld, the real ruler of Tartarus. In an action which recalls Hecate's ancient power of granting all gifts to men, La Pintada leads the rebels in their looting, urging them to see the Revolution as an opportunity to seize all: 'Llega uno a cualquier parte y no tiene más que escoger la casa que le cuadre y ésa agarra sin pedirle licencia a naiden'. But La Pintada also celebrates Margarito's ill-treatment of the father who seeks for his family's sake the return of ten measures of maize stolen by the troops, for, like Hecate, she also delights in withholding goods and even in destruction. The parallel is clearer in her treatment of Camila, whom she persecutes and finally deprives of life and, in so doing, also deprives Demetrio of his loved companion. She is, of course, Camila's rival for his attentions, having already led the drunken Demetrio through the saturnalia

that are the rebels' premature victory celebrations in a parody of the sacred union he was later to enact with Camila. It must also be noted, however, that Hecate was the goddess of death and that La Pintada's association with death is closely established in the chapter in which she first appears, through which there runs insistently the refrain 'yo maté. . . .' That aspect of La Pintada suggests one reason why Demetrio finds he cannot kill her when he attempts to avenge Camila's murder; as he prepares to stab her in response to her challenge, 'mátame tú, Demetrio', 'sus ojos se nublaron, vaciló y dio un paso atrás'.

La Pintada is sent away, but the murder and its aftermath remain to provide for Demetrio a second glimpse of his fate, a second 'epiphany of law, of that which is and must be' [N. Frye, *The Anatomy of Criticism*, 1957]. His premonition of doom, expressed in a ballad he hums obsessively, acquires a clearer but not yet explicit shape in the veiled words of the song: 'En la medianía del cuerpo/una daga me metió/sin saber por qué/ni por qué sé yo. . . /él sí lo sabía,/pero yo no'.

His nameless wife is the centre to which his thoughts return in times of trial, seeing her as the archetypal mother, 'una mujer con su hijo en los brazos', and to whom, completing the circle of his travels, he returns as his impending fate grows clearer. Significantly, it is his wife who voices the third premonition just before the final battle; in her words, the warning acquires certainty and immediacy. It is significant, too, that in the pages leading up to Demetrio's death one should find once again references to sexual union, here in the prominently-placed references to marriage, one ('Fue una verdadera mañana de nupcias') opening the final chapter and another describing the *sierra* as he dies, which appropriately combines marriage and death: '[Sobre la sierra] cae la neblina albísima como un crespón de nieve sobre la cabeza de una novia'.

Demetrio's son, hidden in the folds of his mother's clothing, resembles but does not recognize his father, and foreshadows the continuity of generation as Demetrio leaves to share the fate of his men, who under the hail of enemy fire 'caen como *espigas cortadas por la hoz*' (emphasis added).

Although further details and incidents could be cited, sufficient evidence has been adduced to establish that, in his relationships with the three women and their consequences, clear parallels emerge between Demetrio and the archetypal mythic hero, the victim-king. What must now be established is the nature of Demetrio's guilt and whether, following the historical evolution of myth into drama, one can see him as a tragic figure. Here the water motif once more proves important, for in addition to linking closely Demetrio and Camila, it also serves to elucidate their separate functions in the work. El güero Margarito, who represents the principle of undisciplined force, assaults a waiter who cannot provide iced-water; such is the behaviour of disorderly and ultimately self-destructive violence, as his shooting at his image in the bar-room mirror suggests and his later suicide makes clear. Macías, in contrast, is most grateful for ordinary water but even a disinterested and reluctant warrior like Demetrio is, *qua* warrior, 'constrained to commit sinful acts . . . and sins against the ideals of each of the three functions, including his own' [Dumézil]. The last point may be illustrated by a detail from the description of Demetrio's initial ambush of the Federal forces which also epitomizes the skilful economy with which Azuela conveys meaning through action throughout the novel: '—¡A los de abajo!—exclamó Demetrio, tendiendo su treinta-treinta hacia el hilo cristalino del río. Un federal cayó *en las mismas aguas*. . . Pero *él sólo tiraba hacia el río*' (emphasis added).

Cervantes, too, destroys life in the vivifying element of water, as he explains to the incredulous Camila, who at that time still admires him. His sterilizing method, indeed, proves effective, healing his injured leg and, subsequently, that of Macías. Later, however, when Camila is injured on being dragged from her horse, she refuses the assistance he offers with the pointed words: '¿Ayuda de usted? ¡Ni agua!' She has learnt to distinguish between

good and evil and their appearances, having discerned beneath the iridescent surface of the stream a world that is 'mitad luz y mitad sombra'. Her discovery leads ultimately to her acceptance of Demetrio, her expectation that he should mete out justice, and, finally, to her death. Thereafter, water is associated only with desolation—as when the revolutionaries, on their last weary journey to the hills, come upon yet another set of 'tres casuchas regadas sobre los márgenes de un río', only to find them empty and abandoned—or with the theme of the sacrificial victim, present in the final thunderstorm and downpour, which recall the story of Dionysus, Demeter's son, who began as a type of sacred king ritually killed with a thunderbolt.

The water motif, then, expresses both Demetrio's guilt and destiny. It also recalls the necessity of purification for warriors 'who undertake the task which involves and occasions a stain and who then, passively or actively, have the task of cleansing eternally all such stains as are like their own' [Dumézil]. A clear echo of this requirement can be heard in the words describing the effects of the storm-waters with their emphasis on total purification: 'todo aparece acabado de lavar. . . Las rocas. . . vierten gruesas gotas de agua transparente'; the rebels too are restored to primaeval innocence, 'contagiados de la alegría de la mañana. . . En su alma rebulle el alma de las viejas tribus nómadas'. As the storm-gods and warrior-gods were frequently interchangeable, the purification may be seen as the work of the latter in anticipation of Demetrio's translation to their ranks in the closing lines of the novel, his final adventure as victim-king.

The exemplary function of Demetrio's purification and apotheosis will be discussed later; his guilt may suitably be considered here, for it springs directly from his activities as a warrior. Dumézil writes that in the archaic myths the main sources of guilt are identified in terms of: (i) the freedom which warriors have always prized but which the myths emphasize is also 'weighed with temptations and risks for the one who possesses it and is disturbing as well for the social order. . . '; (ii) the fact that even when fighting to sustain or restore order, warriors must, in order to be successful, outdo their enemies in battle 'in boldness, surprise, pretence and treachery. . . ; And above all dedicated to Force, they are the triumphant victims of the internal logic of Force, which proves itself only by surpassing boundaries—even its own boundaries and those of its *raison d'être*'.

Los de abajo also offers an example of both of these themes. On the one hand, freedom is vividly presented as exhilarating liberation from the miseries of ordinary life or as lyrical communion with nature; on the other hand, it is shown as degenerating at individual level into the sadism of El güero Margarito, and in the case of society, into the violent anarchy that grips Zacatecas after the battle of La Bufa. It is difficult to pinpoint Demetrio's fault in this sphere. It is true that he regularly drinks to excess but in the myths that is seen as a permissible way to relieve the nervous tension of battle. Unlike most of the combatants, he is not given to looting or to gratuitous killing. His loyalty to General Natera is unquestioning. It is from the abuse of force that his guilt derives. Demetrio, initially a fugitive from the abuse of authority and then a reluctant rebel, gradually succumbs unwittingly and inexorably to the temptations of force. His degree of surrender may be gauged by reference to his growing belief in the exaggerated accounts of his exploits that are created by sycophants and even by his disinterested admirers like Solís. It is paralleled by a growing callousness: once he had shared all his drink and salt with his comrades, now his dead followers are referred to with a dismissive shrug and comment ¡'Psch!...Pos que los entierren'; the man who once spared those who had attempted to rape his wife now ignores the desperate '¡No me mates, padrecito!' of a defeated old soldier. The alienation grows until Demetrio discovers on his final return to his native hills that his own people flee from him as they formerly fled from the Federal troops. Once his calloused peasant hands had meant automatic acceptance there; now Demetrio admits 'ya no nos quieren'. Seeking to mitigate Demetrio's draconian measures against them, Valderrama feels it necessary to remind him that 'los serranos son carne de nuestra carne. . . están hechos de nuestra madera. . . . De esta madera firme con la que se fabrican los héroes,' for Macías has suffered the fate of the mythic heroes who, in the grip of force, 'are transfigured, made strangers in the society they protect' [Dumézil].

It is, however, in his estrangement from the Church that Macías most noticeably transgresses the boundaries of force. To understand the particular significance of this transgression, one must consider the concept of sovereignty developed in the archaic myths, in which it was seen as having two aspects—power and law. In the world of *Los de abajo* the former has collapsed, leaving law to be symbolized by the remaining national institution, the Church. It has been pointed out that the second part of the novel, in its depiction of anticlerical activities, faithfully reflects developments among the revolutionaries in 1914 and 1915; Azuela's skill in incorporating them into the mythic structure of the novel also deserves attention. He uses them to show in a few brief scenes how Demetrio succumbs to 'the internal logic of Force' and betrays his pre-Revolutionary code of conduct. Whereas in peacetime Macías had been a practising Catholic, in the course of the war he is led to desecrate a church by using it as a platform from which to ambush and kill the enemy. He blasphemously excuses the sacrilege:'"obra de Dios", pensó Demetrio.' The falsity of his interpretation is revealed in the subsequent merciless slaughter of the other side and the clear desecration of the building implicit in Pancracio's killing of the garrison commander by throwing him 'como un saco de piedras que cae de veinte metros de altura sobre el atrio de la iglesia.' Much later Demetrio's forces attack a procession marching behind a banner inscribed 'Religión y Fueros', killing the marchers, looting the church, and hanging the priest. While Camila is shocked by the incident, Demetrio is merely 'malhumorado por lo insulso de la hazana,' having by now clearly become insensible to moral values and human worth. Some pages later, a succinct paragraph offers an eloquent symbol of the completion of Demetrio's fated trajectory, by which time force has completely supplanted law: 'Las escuelas quedaron convertidas en cuarteles. Demetrio se alojó en la sacristía de una capilla abandonada'.

In addition to combining mythemes identifiable with the archaic warrior myths and those drawn from the cluster of myths revolving around Demeter, *Los de abajo* also incorporates elements more widely diffused in mythic literature. One such is the theme of reconciliation with a father-figure, which underlies Demetrio's encounter with Don Mónico and which corresponds with the hero's testing and triumph. The meeting is described in markedly ritualistic terms. Demetrio anticipates it ironically in terms of an *agape*: 'vamos a almorzar con Don Mónico, un amigo que me quiere mucho', but *amigo*, used three times in the passage, becomes a keyword in the action. On Demetrio's instructions Pancracio twice knocks three times on the locked door before he is allowed to break the lock. On entering, Demetrio seats his men at table and makes three requests (for wine, weapons, and money) before giving his men permission to ransack the house. When Don Mónico appears he twice appeals to their friendship in pleading for his life. Macías is prevented by the memory of his wife and child from using his gun, whereupon 'Don Mónico y las señoras le besan las manos'. Having thus been recognized as an equal in power by Don Mónico, Demetrio confirms the fact by burning the house, recalling the manner in which his own home had been destroyed. The act acquires resonances of ancient ritual in the killing of the youth who attempts to enter the condemned house, for his death recalls the human sacrifice that in primitive societies often attended important events. This too is an important event, as is suggested by the fact that Cervantes personally supervises the burning 'con rara solicitud' and by the aura of mystery surrounding it, for 'nadie comprendió el extraño proceder del general'.

This encounter marks the successful completion of Demetrio's personal cycle, showing, as it were, that man to man he is Don Mónico's equal. Personal destiny is, however, no longer controlled by *hombría* or decided at local level but shaped by the imperatives of the war. The scene in Don Mónico's house contains a reference to another archetypal story that points to such wider perspectives. The women of Don Mónico's household are terrified when they see Pancracio, for 'han visto al sayón que está crucificando a Nuestro Señor en el vía crucis de la parroquia!' Like Anastasio, Pancracio has accompanied

Demetrio from the beginning; but while Anastasio is religious and 'de mirada dulzona', Pancracio's appearance—'todo un aspecto bestial'—with his 'rostro de piedra' and 'duro perfil de prognato', reflects in yet another way the uncontrolled violence unleashed by the war which in its irrational way threatens to destroy even the best in the nation. Pancracio's identification with Christ's executioners clarifies a pattern created by his desecration of the church and his murder of a sacristan. The full significance of the pattern is revealed in Valderrama's ecstatic declamation, recalling the poet's primitive role as *vates*, of the words spoken by Peter at Christ's transfiguration (Matthew 17. 4; Luke 9. 33): 'Señor, Señor, bueno es que nos estemos aquí. Levantaré tres tiendas, una para ti, otra para Moisés y otra para Elías'. Both evangelists place the event between two of Christ's prophecies of his approaching Passion. Valderrama's words are similarly preceded and followed by Demetrio's request that he should sing a ballad whose title, *El enterrador*, points again to his sense of approaching death. The parallels with the New Testament clearly relate Demetrio's fate to that of Christ; his *via crucis*, a journey of 'tres jornadas muy bien hechas,' the period associated in various myths with the death of the victim-god, reaches from the isolated farm where he first experienced epiphany, which, as Northrop Frye notes, marks in the hero's course 'the top of the wheel of fortune, the point from which the tragic hero falls' to his death in the longed-for *sierra*.

Other uses of myth as a structural principle could easily be identify in *Los de abajo*. The present study, however, has had the limited aim of tracing the main structures of mythic prefiguration, patterned predominantly on those of Demeter and the victum-kings, as the very title of the novel obliquely suggests. What remains is to assess how effectively the mythological parallels have enriched the significance of the primary material. It should be mentioned, in the first place, that the parallels reinforce Azuela's realistic analysis of the Revolution. As a result, Demetrio, the exemplary representative of the nation, emerges more clearly as the propitiatory victim betrayed and sacrificed by inadequate leaders, civil, military, and intellectual. The mythic element also gives an added perspective to Azuela's concern with the moral dilemma which violence poses for the peaceful citizen and its effect on his community. In the second place, however, the mythological analogies imbue Demetrio's struggle against fate with tragic dimensions, thereby giving *Los de abajo* a universality transcending the historical circumstances it ostensibly depicts. Demetrio conforms to the classical pattern of the tragic hero in his incapacity to decipher the inscrutable clues which hint at but conceal his destiny and in his fateful flaw or *hamartia*, that in his case comes from over-reliance on the imagined invincibility of his military prowess. While the gods may prophesy, man must await *anagnorisis*, the enlightenment which invariably comes too late, as is implicit in the incident of the

falling stone which Demetrio offers to his wife as a symbolic representation of his belated realization of his fate: 'mira esa piedra como ya no se para'.

A consideration of the mythic pattern evident in the novel suggests that it is mistaken to interpret Demetrio's fate in terms of pessimistic fatalism or nihilism. This is a view expressed by several critics including, for example, W. A. R. Richardson, who writes [in his edition *M. Azuela, Los de abajo*, 1973]: 'Demetrio dies, having achieved nothing, precisely in the Juchipila canyon where he sets out, thus symbolizing the futility of the birth, life, death cycle of human existence on a personal level. The victim-king motif, culminating in the references to Christ, suggests rather that Azuela had in mind what he was later to describe as 'la secular idea . . . de que el hombre que quiera ganarse ha de perderse . . . , que el hombre que sabe que se frustra en el frustrarse lee la cifra de su ser (que es) *doctrina que siempre me ha seducido*' (emphasis added). (pp. 94–104)

D. Bradley, "Patterns of Myth in 'Los de abajo'," in *The Modern Language Review*, Vol. 75, No. 1, January, 1980, pp. 94–104.

CLIVE GRIFFIN
(essay date 1981)

[In the following essay, Griffin closely examines the structure of *Los de abajo*, asserting that it reflects Azuela's pessimistic view of the failed ideals of the Mexican Revolution.]

Most critics who discuss the structure of Mariano Azuela's novel, *Los de abajo*, refer, on the one hand, to his own statement that the novel is "una serie de cuadros y escenas de la revolución constitucionalista, débilmente atados por un hilo novelesco" and, on the other, to the novel's obviously circular pattern. There is, however, a discrepancy between the assertion that *Los de abajo* has an arbitrary and episodic structure, and the novel's circularity which necessarily supposes a predetermined plan. This discrepancy has given rise to considerable debate. One source of confusion is Azuela's own writing about his fiction; he commented extensively upon his own novels, particularly upon his method of working, yet his overt statements often served to cloud, rather than to illuminate the problem of the structure of *Los de abajo*. Azuela, for instance, appears to have been particularly resentful of criticism, and his defences against his critics are liable to take contradictory forms. Replying, on the one hand, to those who claimed that he had distorted the truth of

Leal on Azuela's view of the value of pain and suffering:

His primary theme, he wrote, is as old as time but in-exhaustible: that pain and suffering are the most fruitful source of noble deeds. Though many of the formerly favored class failed to meet the test imposed by the events of the Revolution, many found in it their "structure as men." Many enriched in the days of Porfirio Díaz, now ruined, regenerated themselves by undertaking humble tasks, ultimately achieving respectable positions gained by their own efforts. Such men were, he stated, in striking contrast to the crowd of grasping self-seekers suddenly in possession of power and riches "whose faces revealed their insatiable voracity."

Luis Leal in his *Mariano Azuela*, 1971.

the Mexican Revolution and had written profoundly anti-revolutionary works, he claimed that *Los de abajo* was a faithful reproduction of his own experiences of the Revolution and that many of the events and characters were only lightly transmuted reality. On the other hand, replying to those who accused him of being nothing more than a reporter of the events he witnessed during his participation in the Revolution, he asserted that a writer, if he is to make his work aesthetically satisfying, must organise his material and give it a coherent structure. Similarly, on some occasions Azuela claimed to have no thesis to expound in his fiction and to have been an "objective" and "dispassionate" observer of the Revolution (not perhaps, a surprising claim for a declared admirer of Zola and the brothers Goncourt). At other times, he maintained that in his novels he could not but be a partial and passionate witness of events. It is, therefore, prudent not to attribute too much value to Azuela's own statements about his work; they are often either perfunctory or misleading. If we want to examine the structure and its implications in *Los de abajo* we would be well-advised to turn to the text itself.

Two critics in particular, Seymour Menton [in his "La estructura épica de *Los de abajo* y un prólogo especulativo" *Hispania* (1967)] and Richard Young [in his "Narrative Structure in Two Novels by Mariano Azuela: *Los caciques* and *Los de abajo*," *Revista canadiense de estudios hispánicos* 2 (1978)] have concentrated upon the structure of *Los de abajo*. Menton attacks those who find the novel episodic and fragmentary, alleging that it is carefully structured and that we become clearly aware of this if we consider the work to be an epic. More recently, Young has echoed Menton's belief in an ordered structure, and has compared it in this respect to Azuela's earlier novel, *Los caciques*. His major contention is that "it is important to acknowledge the quality of Azuela's episodic narrative

and to understand that he exploited it deliberately as an appropriate structure within which to encompass a view of the significant 'episodes' of the Revolution as well as of the Revolution as a whole, a view, therefore, that is both fragmented and integrated." Other writers, particularly Marxist critics such as Adalbert Dessau [in his *La novela de la Revolución Mexicana*, 1972], have claimed that, while Part I of the novel is ordered, there is increasing incoherence in Part II. They attribute this development to Azuela's bourgeois disillusion at the way the Revolution developed after the battle of Zacatecas when the peasantry went beyond the original liberal *maderista* aim of bringing to an end the rule of Porfirio Díaz. They contend that Azuela failed to understand fully the revolutionary process and was therefore incapable of giving anything more than an incoherent and fragmented structure to his work after the capture of Zacatecas, an event which takes place at the end of Part I of the novel.

I agree with Menton and Young that the novel is not incoherent and that, despite its evident shortcomings, a certain structure can be discerned. However, I find Menton's major contention that the structure is "epic" improbable, for it is difficult to make Demetrio Macías in any meaningful sense into an epic hero and the events recounted in the novel are scarcely either epic or heroic. Young's observations are illuminating, but he appears to draw no overall conclusions from them for *Los de abajo*. I hope to show that Dessau's comments concerning the lack of organisation in Part II of the novel are based upon a particular interpretation of the history of the Revolution and that different conclusions about this Part can be reached if another interpretation of the historical events is adopted.

While not claiming that Azuela maintained a rigorous control over his narrative structure throughout *Los de abajo*, I wish in this article to draw the reader's attention to some details of patterning and development which have previously been overlooked and to make some general observations based upon them. By the term "structure" I refer here both to the creation of some measure of unity between and within the three Parts and to the ordering of events in the novel. As structure is not an empty vessel into which content is poured, but plays an active part in carrying the message of a work, some general conclusions about the implications of *Los de abajo* may legitimately be drawn from an examination of this ordering.

Let us return to the circular nature of the structure. The novel ends where it began, in the canyon of Juchipila, where Demetrio Macías and his band are ambushed and killed by *carrancista* troops at the very same place in which they set their first ambush for the *federales*. The irony of this *dénouement* is obvious enough and it can be interpreted as a comment upon the futility of the Revolution, a point which Azuela stresses throughout the novel, While pointing out this circularity, critics have been reluctant to draw wider conclusions for the rest of the novel, but this cyclical structure which implies a particular thesis should lead us to examine the whole of the novel's structure as a possible reflection of the author's didactic views on the Revolution. I shall examine the organisation of Part II in this light and then, in less detail, that of the whole novel.

In the final chapter of Part I, Azuela makes Solís pronounce a pessimistic, aphoristic judgment upon the genetic deficiencies of the Mexican "race," and here Azuela reflects some of the positivist racial ideas of Mexican predecessors and of his favourite French authors. Solís comments, "la psicología de nuestra raza, condensada en dos palabras: ¡robar, matar!" Didactic works frequently employ the structural technique of introducing an aphorism and then illustrating it to "prove" the validity of the initial generalized comment by the use of particular pieces of evidence. In the case of **Los de abajo**, Azuela's statement, placed in the mouth of Solís, is illustrated in Part II, and the structure of this section of the novel is determined to some extent by the aphorism. Chapter I is set in Zacatecas during the looting of that city by the revolutionaries who include Macías's band. One group sits drinking in a restaurant and the conversation soon turns to the subject of killing:

– Yo, maté dos coroneles–clama con voz ríspida y gutural un sujeto pequeño y gordo [. . .]
– Yo, en Torreón, maté a una vieja que no quiso venderme un plato de enchiladas. [. . .]
– Yo maté a un tendajonero en el Parral porque me metió en un cambio dos billetes de Huerta [. . .]
– Yo, en Chihuahua, maté un tío porque me lo topaba siempre en la mesma mesa y a la mesma hora, cuando yo iba a almorzar [. . .]
– ¡Hum!. . . Yo maté. . . [. . .].

The narrator then interrupts sententiously to add the statement, "El tema es inagotable." Predictably enough the last chapter of Part II illustrates the other defect of the Mexican "race" mentioned by Solís: the love of robbery. Macías's band is travelling by train to the Aguascalientes Conference when an old woman appeals to them for alms because she has been robbed of her life savings. The conversation then turns to the subject of theft:

– [. . .] La purita verdá es que yo he robao [. . .]
– Hum, pa las máquinas de coser que yo me robé en Mexico! [. . .]
– Yo me robé en Zacatecas unos caballos tan finos [. . .]. Lo malo fue que mis caballos le cuadraron a mi general Limón y él me los robó a mí [. . .]
– [. . .] Yo también he robado [. . .]

The narrator again steps in with,"El tema del "yo robé," aunque parece inagotable, se va extinguiendo cuando en cada banca aparecen tendidos de naipes." The similarity of these two passages which are to be found at the beginning and end of Part II of the novel, enables us to see this Part—which does, after all, deal in the main with looting and killing—as an illustration of Solís's, or Azuela's judgement upon the Mexican "race." Far from being incoherent, as Dessau claims, this Part is rounded, as are some of its constituent chapters.

This conscious patterning is not seen only in the illustration of Solís's aphorism in the first and last chapters of Part II. There is a similar balance in the second and penultimate chapters where the revolutionary band is described in the most unfavourable of lights as threatening normal, civilized life. In chapter 2, La Pintada, who has only recently joined the group, leads the search for booty in a wealthy mansion. Indeed, so soon after her appearance she is already the dominant force, even giving orders to the men. Azuela concentrates upon the gratuitous destruction of beautiful objects which culminates in the abuse of culture represented in the ripping apart by a young, syphilitic prostitute of a copy of Dante's *Divine Comedy*. It is no coincidence that, in the balancing penultimate chapter, it is La Pintada's companion, el Güero Margarito, who has now become the dominant force in the group. He shoots up a restaurant in Lagos and later endangers the life of an innocent shopkeeper who is going about his own business. The scenes of anarchy led by these two characters are carefully counterposed.

Nevertheless, it would be wrong to claim that Azuela neatly balances chapter against chapter throughout Part II; his structure is not this systematic or obvious. But a progression can be identified which tends again to argue against the claim that the Part is composed merely by stringing together unconnected episodes. This Part parallels Part I by setting the limited and private concerns of Macías and his band against the important historical events of the Revolution. In Part I the band is formed for parochial reasons (the persecution of Macías by Don Mónico and the *federales* etc.), yet it is sucked into major events at Zacatecas due to Cervantes' advice. In Part II there is a similar progression: the major event of the Part is the band's parochial concern to return to Moyahua in order to wreak revenge upon Don Mónico, but Macías is again drawn into the main events of the Revolution by being ordered to attend the Aguascalientes Conference. However, Part II is based not only upon the alternation of the parochial and the national, but also upon the alternation of aimless and purposeful activities. Thus, the aimless looting of Zacatecas (chapters 1–4) is followed by the purposeful return to Moyahua (chapters 5–7); the aimless wandering in a vain attempt to locate *orozquistas* (Chapters 8–11) is followed by the purposeful journey to Aguascalientes (Chapters 12–14). The burning of Don Mónico's house closes the cycle of parochial events opened at the very beginning of the novel. This is the only cycle of events which Macías is capable of understanding and it is therefore natural that he should be confused by all that follows and that the structure of the novel should reflect this confusion. This is made clear by the orgainsa-tion of Part II after the scene of Macías's revenge on Don

Mónico, for this part does appear to become particularly fragmentary as the band wanders hither and thither looting and killing for no reason. It is not Azuela who fails to understand the Revolution; rather, he is making the point that the revolutionaries were incapable of understanding it. This is made even more explicit by the final paragraph of Part II.

In a similar way, Part II chronicles a gradual process of degeneration; there is here a definite development rather than a simple accumulation of unrelated episodes. This part witnesses the growing dominance over the band of the values of La Pintada and el Güero Margarito, two characters who appear in the first chapter of the Part and have disappeared by the beginning of Part III. The most graphic illustration of the group's degeneration is the death of Camila. Camila is the only character to plead for an end to merely gratuitous cruelty and she is killed by the evil La Pintada. So powerful is the influence of La Pintada, however, that Macías is unable to kill her as a punishment for the murder and she goes free. Similarly, in Part II, Macías's previous reluctance to take advantage of the weak peasants in the villages they encounter and his opposition to looting in his own region disappear and he will eventually approve the theft of the only sustenance of the family of a poor widower. It is el Güero Margarito who is a prime mover of this cruelty shown to the poor by Macías's band. The degeneration which is depicted in this Part is emphasized by Cervantes's open declaration to Macías that their aim should be to make a quick profit from the Revolution and then leave Mexico; he ceases even to pretend that they are fighting for any ideals.

Part II, then, is increasingly pessimistic, and the gradual process of degeneration which it portrays serves again to convey Azuela's thesis that the revolution has been betrayed.

These examples may be sufficient to indicate that this Part of the novel has a certain unity and is structured to a particular end. However, it is true that Part II does *appear*, on a first reading, to be unstructured and fragmentary. Indeed, the whole book is built on a series of minor climaxes which occur at the end of many chapters and tend to make the novel seem disjointed. Nevertheless, I do not agree with Dessau's view that this superficial impression of incoherence and fragmentation is necessarily the result of Azuela's ceasing to understand the Revolution at the point described at the beginning of Part II; indeed, if the historical events are interpreted in another way, it can be argued that this structure accurately reflects the course taken by the Revolution. Part I deals with the linear development of Macías's "revolutionary" activities as his band haphazardly fights its first skirmishes and is then drawn into the mainstream of the Revolution. This situation parallels the unfolding of the Mexican Revolution before the capture of Zacatecas in June 1914. The capture of that city is considered by some historians to

be the climax of the Revolution as it was the result of the struggle of the combined revolutionary forces against Huerta and the *federales* who represented Porfirian Mexico. Therefore Azuela's placing of the battle of Zacatecas at the mid–point of the novel is not fortuitous. But, after the capture of Zacatecas, the revolutionaries fell out among themselves and polarised around the figures of Villa and Carranza respectively. This disintegration of the Revolution, due to some extent to the lack of any leadership from the middle-class intellectuals, is faithfully reflected by the structure of Part II of *Los de abajo*, for it is at least apparently, chaotic. Again Azuela is employing structure to reflect his view about the distortion and loss of the sort of ideals of which he, as a *maderista*, approved in the early stages of the Revolution, but which he thought were betrayed by squabbling opportunists after the battle of Zacatecas.

Therefore, Part II of *Los de abajo* is not simply a series of loosely-linked episodes; rather it can be seen on close scrutiny to possess a certain roundness, balance and development which are both aesthetically satisfying and pass a judgement on the Revolution. Nevertheless, it is superficially chaotic and this superficial chaos implies a particular interpretation of the Revolution.

Many of the features which I have identified in the structure of Part II have their parallels in the organisation of the whole novel. I shall elucidate two aspects of the overall structure much as I have done in my brief analysis of Part II: first I shall give some selected examples of the aesthetically satisfying, if somewhat elusive, balance and unity in the novel; secondly, I shall examine how Azuela's pessimistic thesis is expounded in the development of the work.

Among the techniques employed to give the whole novel some measure of unity is the use of parallelism between and within the various Parts in the pattern of events, characters, repeated phrases, leitmotifs, themes and descriptions. Let us take a few examples to illustrate these various types of parallelism. Part I and Part II follow a similar pattern of events. Each contains an extensive sequence during which Macías's band is static—in Camila's village in Part I and in the looted Zacatecas in Part II. This static sequence then gives way to movement in both Parts. Into village and town alike come characters from the outside who disrupt and corrupt: in Part I the outsider is Luis Cervantes; in Part II the outsiders are el Güero Margarito and La Pintada who represent the worst aspects of this Revolution. In the first chapter of Part I, Macías's domestic peace is shattered by a Federal soldier who claims to have known him in the Penetenciaría de Escobedo; in the first chapter of Part II, Macías's band is similarly disrupted by the introduction of el Güero Margarito who had known Anastasio Montañés in that same prison. At the beginning of Part I, the band sets out from its native region; in Part II it goes back there, only to leave again; in Part III it returns home definitively. There are three significant deaths and three survivals , one in each Part: at the end of Part I, Solís, the disillusioned idealist, is killed but Cervantes, who was inadvertently the cause of his death, survives. Near the end of Part II, Camila, the one kind and warmhearted character in the novel, is killed, yet the bestial whore, La Pintada, survives although she is Camila's murderess. At the end of Part III, Macías himself is killed, but the survival of Cervantes is ironically emphasized in the first chapter of that Part. In a similar way, Pancracio, a sadistic member of Macías's band, is associated with sordid killing in each Part. In Part I he kills the brother of a villager who helped Macías to defeat an enemy garrison; in Part II Pancracio gratuitously murders a sacristan; in Part III he kills a companion, and is killed himself, in a brawl. In Part I Macías's house is burnt down; in Part II he burns down that of Don Mónico. In Part I the *federales* are accused of a series of crimes; in Part II these same crimes are committed by Macías's band. The ambush of the *federales* by Macías in Part I is paralleled by that of Macías himself in Part III; not only do both actions take place in the same canyon, but they also have in common many similar descriptive details. There are, therefore, many examples of events which unify the various Parts, and the whole, of the novel.

When we turn to an examination of Azuela's treatment of characters we again find him employing parallelism. In Part I Camila falls in love with Cervantes but he later introduces her into the band to be seduced by Macías; in Part II Cervantes introduces a second girl, an unnamed and terrified fourteen-year-old, who will be seduced by el Güero Margarito. In Part I the dark and ugly Camila is used rather unsubtly to represent the goodness and innocence of the simple Mexican peasant woman. In Part II the blonde girl represents the innocence of the white city-dwelling middle-classes. Her purity is carefully stressed by the author, "su piel era fresca y suave como un pétalo de rosa; sus cabellos rubios";"la chiquilla de grandes ojos azules y semblante de virgen." A filthy rag is symbolically thrown over her shoulders after she has been raped by el Güero Margarito; after, that is, she has had contact with the revolutionaries who destroy her idealised beauty just as the middle-class ideals of the *maderistas* have been defiled by the Revolution. Cervantes is always the passive intermediary who interprets and yet avoids all direct involvement; in sexual relations he plays the role of conscious or unwitting pander. It is not insignificant that it is he who is the cause of the abasement of both girls: the intellectual is instrumental in the betrayal of both the peasantry and the middle-classes.

Leitmotifs, such as that of Macías remembering his wife or Camila at moments of disillusion, and even entire phrases echo each other from Part to Part and thus endow the novel with a certain unity.

Certain themes are also constantly echoed through-

out the novel. In all three Parts the Revolution gathers its own irresistible momentum; in each there is a statement which indicates both this and the fact that, despite the enormous amount of energy expended, the hectic action of revolution will lead nowhere. Near the end of Part I Solís points to this futile momentum, "La revolución es el huracán, y el hombre que se entrega a ella no es ya el hombre, es la miserable hoja seca arrebatada por el vendaval. . . ."

This image of the leaf at the mercy of an uncontrollable wind, a pessimistic and positivistic comparison, is one which recalls an earlier passage in the novel where such a leaf falls at the feet of Camila who will herself be swept up and destroyed by the violence of the Revolution. At the end of Part II, we again witness this irresistible momentum taken on by the Revolution when Natera cheerfully informs the bewildered Macías,"¡Cierto como hay Dios, compañero; sigue la bola!"and, at the end of Part III there is the oft-quoted statement made by Macías when he is attempting to explain to his wife why he has to continue to fight: he throws a stone into a canyon and remarks, "Mira esa piedra cómo ya no se para . . . ."

Other simple, recurrent elements which endow the three Parts with a certain unity range from the evident idea of the futility of the Revolution to more complex ones such as the beauty of violence which is seen in both the first and last Parts and which might reflect the ambiguity of Azuela's view of the Revolution. This ambiguity seems to coexist with his predominantly didactic stance towards the Revolution which we have already seen. For Azuela, the Revolution meant freedom for the poor and oppressed with whom he sympathised, but it also unleashed a huge wave of ignorant and powerful peasants whose violence he found fascinating yet terrible. In the first Part it is Solís again who cries in the thick of battle, "¡ Qué hermosa es la Revolución, aun en su misma barbarie!" In Part III, it is Solís's counterpart, Valderrama, who repeats the theme "¡ Amo la Revolución como amo al volcán que irrumpe! ¡Al volcán porque es volcán; a la Revolución porque es Revolución!" As so often in *Los de abajo*, violence exercises a strange attraction. Even more striking is the scene to be found in the last chapter of the book when Macías and all his men are mown down by machine guns. Here the violence is interwoven with a beautiful description of nature in its gayest of moods, and Azuela employs a sustained and incongruous image of the dazzling whiteness of a wedding day, "Fue una verdadera mañana de nupcias", "La sierra está de gala; sobre suscúspides inaccesibles cae la niebla albísima como un crespón de nieve sobre la cabeza de una novia." In Part III of the novel a cockfight is arranged by some of the soldiers. The description of it begins with a much-quoted phrase which ironically likens the fight to that between humans during the Revolution, but what is often overlooked is the fact that the description of the cocks tearing each other to pieces is a carefully wrought piece of artistic prose in which Azuela employs recherché vocabulary, internal rhythms and alliteration:

> Sus cuellos crespos y encorvados, los ojos como corales, erectas las crestas, crispadas las patas, un instante se mantuvieron sin tocar el suelo siquiera, confundidos sus plumajes, picos y garras en uno solo. [. . .] Sus ojos de cinabrio se apagaron, cerráronse lentamente sus párpados coriáceos, y sus plumas esponjadas se estremecieron convuleas en un charco de sangre.

These descriptions emphasising the beauty of violence act like a leitmotif throughout the novel, again providing it with a sense of overall coherence. But other descriptive passages also fulfil this function. This is particularly true of the end of the novel where Azuela, by the use of such description, manages to build up an impression of inevitable doom which fits in well with his pessimistic and deterministic view of the Revolution. As the band arrives back in Juchipila, near which they will meet their end, Azuela inserts a very brief picture of a church: "Desembocaban en una plaza, frente a la iglesia octagonal, burda y maciza, reminiscencia de tiempos coloniales." This brings to mind another description of a church in the novel, that of the town in which they were ambushed by the *federales* in Part I: "Dominando el caserío se alzaba la ancha cúpula cuadrangular de la iglesia. —Miren, siñores, al frente de la iglesia está la plaza.[. . .] De pronto desembocaron en una plazoleta." Similarly, as the band sets out optimistically for the Juchipila canyon, Azuela's description of their feeling of freedom recalls a similar passage dealing with their departure for that same town in which they were almost to fall into the trap set by the *federales*. These reminders of the occasion, in Part I, when the band almost met its doom in an enemy trap, serve to prepare the reader for the ambush which will bring the novel to a close. Not only does this reinforce Azuela's determinism in *Los de abajo*, but it also provides an aesthetically pleasing sense of roundness to the work, despite the fact that this patterning may not be obvious on a first reading.

These few examples indicate that the whole book possesses a certain unity, but what of its overall development and the implication of this development? The work is certainly episodic; it is based upon a series of journeys and this tends to produce an apparently loose structure where a cumulative effect can be achieved by the linking together in a linear manner of various adventures. However, although apparently loosely connected, they do follow a general development which reflects the author's thesis about the lack of ideals among those fighting in the Revolution: the gradual degeneration of some of the fighters and the opportunism of others. This process of degeneration has already been identified as a key element of the structure of Part II. But now let us examine some examples of this process throughout the whole novel.

Macías's gradual loss of scruple about robbery from

the poor—a point which I referred to as a feature of Part II—is carefully developed in all three Parts. In Part I he promises the inhabitants of Camila's village that after the Revolution he will remember their kindness; he is also anxious to avoid alienating them as the *federales* had done by their theft and abduction of a young girl. However, when his men join the main revolutionary forces for the attack on Zacatecas, they witness the indiscriminate sacking of even the poorest dwellings by these forces. In Part II after the burning of Don Mónico's house, Macías is anxious, at least in his native region, not to give the impression that profit is his motive for fighting although he is not averse to allowing his troops to rob the poor in other regions. In Part III Azuela again returns to this theme and depicts the band now attempting to loot the villages of their own region. This degeneration is paralleled by the reception given to the revolutionaries in the villages through which they pass. In Part I they are well fed and cared for by the poor, and, when they are ambushed by a *federal* garrison, one villager volunteers to help them although the more prosperous inhabitants support the garrison. In Part II, when the band arrives in Moyahua, the poor now remain hidden in terror, but are not unwilling to profit from the presence of Macías's men in order to loot the homes of the rich. In Part III Macías's men encounter only hostility from the poor who give them no food and mock their humiliation. This process of the loss of the support of the poor due to the soldiers' excesses is pointed up sharply by Anastasio Montañés's nostalgic thoughts near the end of the novel:

> Se me figura, compadre, que estamos allá en aquellos tiempos cuando apenas iba comenzando la revolución, cuando llegábamos a un pureblito y nos repicaban mucho, y salía la gente a encontrarnos con músicas, con banderas, y nos echaban muchos vivas y hasta cohetes nos tiraban.

A similar development is seen in the growth of Macías's band. As it increases its numbers it takes in members from outside the Juchipila region who introduce dissension and usurp power from Macías for their own ends. Cervantes does this in Part I where he begins to influence Macías's decisions while being resented by some of the men. In Part II the influence is more brutal when, as I have shown, La Pintada and el Güero Margarito become the dominant forces and threaten the group's unity by internal strife and indiscipline. In Part III ex-*federales* have become officers and even conceal information from Macías and some of the veteran members of the group.

Just as the wandering of the group is increasingly purposeless, so does the group itself begin to disintegrate; both Cervantes and Valderrama desert and, in Part III, even the faithful Anastasio Montañés momentarily becomes critical of Macías's leadership. Solís's prophecy of Part I Chapter 18 is fulfilled: the Revolution is betrayed and the only future for the revolutionaries is to degenerate into simple banditry, as do Macías's men, or to desert, as do Cervantes and Valderrama.

A final example of such progressive loss of purpose can be seen in the band's growing aimlessness. I have already discussed this with regard to Parts I and II, but it is in Part III that Azuela now drives home his point. The troops range wide—we hear at one stage that they have been as far as Tepic in the province of Nayarit—and, until they return to Juchipila, the location of the action remains very vague. The narrator stresses the lack of purpose of their wandering: "Su marcha por los cañones era ahora la marcha de un ciego sin lazarillo; se sentía ya la amargura del éxodo." This deterioration where movement becomes an end in itself, just as fighting has become for Macías's men, clearly illustrates Azuela's thesis that the guiding ideals of the Revolution have been lost. As if this were not clear enough already, Azuela makes sure that the reader does not miss the message; when the ragged and demoralised revolutionaries return to Juchipila, Valderrama apostrophizes the town, praising it as the cradle of the Revolution, but his rhetoric is cynically deflated by an ex-*federal* officer and Valderrama leaves his lament in order to beg a drink of tequila.

We have thus seen that the novel possesses a certain overall unity created through the use of balance, the fulfilment of prophecy, constant thematic concerns and repeated echoes of actions, characterisation, and description. Also while its structure is clearly episodic, the novel is not arbitrarily ordered, but rather, progressively develops a thesis: that the Revolution lost its ideals and gradually degenerated into gratuitous violence.

This didactic purpose now explains the way in which events such as the battle of Zacatecas, the Aguascalientes Conference and Villa's defeat at Celaya are portrayed. These three events, one seen in each part of the novel, are said by some historians to be the three most crucial events of the armed period of the Mexican Revolution referred to in *Los de abajo*. (The American occupation of Veracruz, which was also politically extremely important and took place during the period covered by the novel, is not even mentioned.) Yet the early stages of the battle of Zacatecas are seen only very remotely in the final chapter of Part I. We have no depiction of the victory itself in this Part—even if the account of Macías's bravery suggests that the attack has been successful—and the first chapter of Part II is set after the victory has been won. In a similar manner, the final chapter of Part II does not portray the Aguascalientes Conference itself or its major historical protagonists, while, as Young points out the first chapter of Part III deals with events taking place some six months after the conclusion of the Conference. The battle of Celaya is narrated some weeks after it has taken place and then only by some deserters from Villa's defeated army whom Macías meets by chance. It comes as some surprise to us initially to find that Azuela places the climaxes of two major historical events in the gaps between the Parts of his novel and only alludes to a third in passing, yet this fits in well with his generally pessimistic view of the Revolution, a view which dwells upon sordid skirmishes, scarcely mentioning the major historical protagonists and events which have passed into modern Mexican folklore. His particularly limited perspective of a single unimportant group of fighters who are merely on the fringe of only some of the major historical events allows us to relate the fictional action to its historical background but, at the same time, gives us a far more "typical" account of the Revolution than would a narrative which dwelt upon the historical climaxes, for these are, by definition, untypical. More importantly, Azuela never allows any optimism to creep in, for the victory at Zacatecas is juxtaposed with the death of Solís and the sordid looting of the town. This juxtaposition reflects the pessimistic thesis which is present throughout the novel.

I would conclude, therefore, that not only Part II, but also the other Parts possess an aesthetically pleasing, if somewhat elusive, unity, and that the structure conveys a message. If these conclusions are correct, we are obliged to offer some explanation why Azuela organises his novel with evident care and yet still manages to give the reader the initial impression that the work is somewhat disjointed, thus paralleling his own ambiguous comments about a writer's ordering of his material to which I made reference at the beginning of this article. A simple external reason for this structure could be that the author realised that *Los de abajo* might not be offered to the public only in the form of a novel, but might be serialised in a newspaper. The results of this awareness might will have been that, with serialisation in mind, he wrote a number of episodes of approximately equal length which would maintain the interest of a popular readership from edition to edition of a newspaper. This might go some way to explain the way in which each episode would end on a climax and be virtually self-contained. However, there might be more subtle explanations for this ambiguous structure. One such explanation could be that he believed that a situation such as that of the Mexican Revolution, was best depicted in a particular type of episodic narrative. A result of this belief, and of a desire for concision, might be that he wrote a series of representative cameos which would be seen to be linked only on careful examination and the effect of which would be cumulative. An episodic structure would have the virtue of presenting an impressionistic picture of the Revolution; this picture would persuade the reader by means other than argument to reach the same pessimistic conclusions about the Revolution and the Mexican "race" as did Solís, and it would do so by an identical process: that of providing apparently unconnected pieces of evidence which eventually present the reader with an inescapable conclusion. This process is described by Solís in Part I, chapter 18:

—¿Hechos?.... Insignificancias, naderías: gestos inadvertidos para los más; la vida instantánea de una línea que se contrae, de unos ojos que brillan, de unos labios que se pliegan; el significado fugaz de una frase que se pierde. Pero hechos, gestos y expresiones que, agrupados en su lógica y natural expresión, constituyen e integran una mueca pavorosa y grotesca a la vez de una raza . . . ¡De una raza irredenta!

Another explanation for the structure of *Los de abajo* is that Azuela possibly wanted to give the common revolutionary's view of events of a chaotic war. This results in the use of a structure which reflects the confusion which an isolated band of guerrillas must feel in any war and especially in a war as complex and fragmentary as the Mexican Revolution. Furthermore, the structure might well be Azuela's solution to the problem of presenting how the Revolution was seen by men who did not relate one experience to another discursively. Macías's band is composed of men of action, but of few words; in this they are constantly contrasted with Cervantes's verbal fluency. The apparent fragmentation of the structure is thus a reflection of the peasants' lack of coherent appreciation, and, especially, verbalisation of their experience. However, more enlightening as a source of explanation for Azuela's choice of structure is a passage which is again to be found in Part I, chapter 18. Macías and his band have reached Fresnillo just before the attack on Zacatecas and here they have met Solís proceeds to tell Macías the story of the latter's own heroic military exploits:

Alberto Solís, con fácil palabra y acento de sinceridad profunda, lo felicitó efusivamente por sus hechos de armas, por sus aventuras, que lo habían hecho famoso, siendo conocidas hasta por los mismos hombres de la poderosa División del Norte.

Y Demetrio, encantado, oía el relato de sus hazañas, compuestas y aderezadas de tal suerte, que él mismo no las conociera. Por lo demás, aquello tan bien sonaba a sus oídos, que acabó por contarlas más tarde en el mismo tono y aun por creer que así habíanse realizado.

As Bradley intimates [in his "Aspects of Realism in Azuela's *Los de abajo*," Ibero–Amerikanisches Archiv 4 (1978)], Azuela may here be making an important comment on the process of narration. The writer, or story-teller, interprets events and distorts them beyond all recognition even for those who have been their protagonists. Yet, ironically, this mendacious version of events is the one which the listener wants to hear far more than he wants the truth (and Azuela's ironic style at this point clearly indicates his opinion of the sham with which Macías is being regaled). Both in *Los de abajo* and in some of his other fictional works Azuela describes how opportunists jump on to the bandwagon of the Revolution. In a similar way, he seems here to be prophesying how the official Mexican historians would, like Solís, order and embellish the events of the Revolution and, in so doing, would distort them into myths. If this is the case, he is telling his readers that in *his* narrative he cannot be accused of giving a neatly organised but false version of the Revolution. Accordingly, he preserves the *illusion* of the disordered, fragmentary, and therefore "truthful" and unembellished "slice of life", yet, in order to convey a coherent message in an aesthetically satisfying work, he is obliged to order and structure the novel—albeit surreptitiously—in the ways I have suggested.

Los de abajo would thus appear to be a novel which is consciously if covertly structured by its author. Far from being his "serie de cuadros y escenas de la revolución constitucionalista, débilmente atados por un hilo novelesco," or the "Cuadros y escenas de la Revolución Mexicana" of his original subtitle, it is ordered and directed towards a particular goal, that of communicating Azuela's thesis about the corruption and failure of the Revolution, and of doing so in a form which is both persuasive and palatable. (pp. 25–39)

Clive Griffin, "The Structure of 'Los de abajo'," in *Revista Canadiense de Estudios Hispánicos,* Vol. VI, No. 1, Autumn, 1981, pp. 25–41.

SOURCES FOR FURTHER STUDY

Bradley, D. "The Thematic Import of Azuela's *Los de abajo*: A Defence." *Forum for Modern Language Studies* XV, No. 1 (January 1979): 14–25.

Explores how Azuela incorporated his personal revolutionary experiences into *Los de abajo* and the author's disillusionment over the failure to implement the revolution's ideals into the country's postwar regime.

Brushwood, John S. In his *Mexico in Its Novel: A Nation's Search for Identity*. Austin: University of Texas Press, 1966, 292 p.

Includes discussion of Azuela's major works, generally focusing on the author's treatment of the Mexican Revolution and its aftermath.

Englekirk, John E. "The 'Discovery' of *Los de abajo*." *Hispania* XVIII, No. 1 (February 1935): 53–62.

Comments on the Mexican literati's rediscovery of *Los de abajo* and the controversy surrounding its eventual recognition as a vibrant, artistic potrayal of the Mexican Revolution.

———. "Mariano Azuela: A Summing Up (1873–1952)." In *South Atlantic Studies for Sturgis E. Leavitt*, edited by Thomas B. Stroup and Sterling A. Stoudemire, pp. 127–35. Washington, D.C.: The Scarecrow Press, 1953.

Discusses Azuela's changing artistic expression by contrasting the style of his early revolutionary novels with that of his experimental novels in the postrevolutionary period.

Leal, Luis. *Mariano Azuela*. New York: Twayne Publishers, Inc., 1971, 145 p.

Presents a comprehensive overview of Azuela's life and major works.

Levy, Kurt L. "*La luciérnaga*: Title, Leitmotif and Structural Unity". *Philological Quarterly* 51, No. 1 (January 1972): 321–28.

Examines the structure of Azuela's *La luciérnaga*, asserting that "[if] in *Los de abajo*, one human being holds the novel together and three distinct leitmotif moods reflect its architectural pattern, the process is reversed in *La luciérnaga* where one single leitmotif is scrutinized in three human beings."

Martínez, Eliud. "Point of View in Mariano Azuela's *El desquite*." *Hispanofila* 24, No. 72 (May 1981): 51–67.

Maintains that Azuela's skillful rendering of the narrative point of view and several leitmotifs help to unify the various disparate elements of *El desquite*.

Murad, Timothy. "Animal Imagery and Structural Unity in Mariano Azuela's *Los de abajo*." *Journal of Spanish Studies: Twentieth Century* 7, No. 2 (Fall 1979): 207–22.

Explores the animal imagery in *Los de abajo*, arguing that Azuela used it to underscore the meaning and emotional intensity of many of the novel's scenes.

Robe, Stanley L. *Azuela and the Mexican Underdogs*. Berkeley: University of California Press, 1979, 233 p.

Presents selections from Azuela's notebook, which chronicles his years with Pancho Villa, as well as a Spanish copy and an English translation of *Los de abajo*, and some general reflections designed to give the reader a broad view of Azuela's life and career.

Spell, Jefferson Rea. "Mariano Azuela, Portrayer of the Mexican Revolution." In his *Contemporary Spanish–American Fiction*, pp. 64–100. Chapel Hill: The University of North Carolina Press, 1944.

Analyzes Azuela's pessimistic treatment of the Mexican Revolution and its aftermath in his novels.

Additional coverage of Azuela's life and career is contained in the following sources published by Gale Research: *Contemporary Authors*, Vols. 104, 131; *Twentieth Century Literary Criticism* Vol. 3; *Hispanic Writers; Major Twentieth Century Writers*.

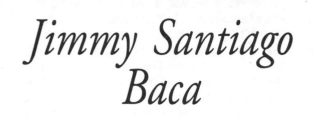

Jimmy Santiago Baca

1952–

(Born José Santiago Baca) Mestizo poet.

INTRODUCTION

*B*aca is recognized as a leading figure in contemporary Hispanic literature and has been praised for the rich imagery and lyricism of his poetry. An ex-convict who taught himself to read while in prison, he writes of spiritual rebirth and triumph over tragedy—unlike many "prison writers" whose works teem with rage and desolation. "You really don't have time to be angry," Baca has asserted. "If you compare a life to daytime photography, my life has been more like nighttime photography. My life as a background has had darkness; the only way to survive the darkness is to have my soul flash." Baca's poetry has also garnered praise for the insight it offers into the experience of Hispanic and Amerindian peoples.

A Mestizo of Chicano and Apache descent, Baca was abandoned by his parents at the age of two and, after a brief stay with a grandparent, was placed in a New Mexico orphanage. He fled at age eleven, spending most of his teen years on the streets of Albuquerque. In 1972, Baca was convicted on a narcotics charge and sentenced to five years in an Arizona maximum security prison. Recalcitrant behavior earned him additional time on his sentence, as well as electric shock treatments and nearly four years in solitary confinement. Baca took advantage of his incarceration, however, teaching himself to read and write. He has explained: "[In prison], I saw all these Chicanos going out to the fields and being treated like animals. I was tired of being treated like an animal. I wanted to learn how to read and to write and to understand. . . . The only way of transcending was through language and understanding." Baca began writing poetry and, encouraged by a fellow inmate, sent a sample of his work to *Mother Jones* magazine. Not only were these poems accepted for publication, but the journal's poetry editor, Denise Levertov, assisted Baca in finding a publisher for his first collection of poetry, *Immigrants in Our Own Land* (1979). *Immigrants* was followed by two more collections, *Swords of Darkness* (1981) and *What's Happening* (1982). Baca's fourth book, *Martín and Meditations on the South Valley* (1987), a semi-autobiographical work that critics termed a novel in verse, won the prestigious American Book Award from the Before Columbus Foundation in 1988. The following year he published *Black Mesa Poems*, for which he earned the Wallace Stevens Poetry Award and the National Hispanic Heritage Award. He has also published a collection of autobiographical essays entitled *Working in the Dark: Reflections of a Poet in the Barrio* (1992). Baca has been poet in residence at both Yale University and the University of California at Berkeley, but has rejected many further offers to lecture and teach, remaining primarily on his farm in Albuquerque with his wife and children.

While Baca's poetry expresses much concerning the Chicano-Mestizo experience in the American southwest, it also explores the more universal theme of an individual's painful search for identity and meaning. The bold poetic images for which he is noted are not the collected perceptions of a large ethnic group, but the sharp vision of a single Mestizo struggling to find himself. Scott Slovic has written, "to read Jimmy Santiago Baca's poetry is to tramp across the uneven terrain of human experience, sometimes lulled by the everydayness of work or relationships, and then dazzled by a flood of emotion or vibrant observation." In *Immigrants*, Baca vividly conveys the physical and mental barriers of prison life; in the poems comprising *What's Happening*, he relates his struggle to re-enter a world and culture which has brought him much pain and suffering. Within these accounts, however, there resonate the broader elements of Baca's Mestizo heritage. *Martín and Meditations* explicitly links the success of the hero's self-exploration with the discovery of his ancestry. "I wanted Martín to be a real human being and let him live in this world and have a mythology that was his as well as the people's," Baca has written. "I was trying to take images and, without compromising their mythology, bring them into contemporaneity."

Critics have repeatedly applauded Baca's forthright style and the passion he generates in his poetry. Denise Levertov, in her introduction to *Martín and Meditations*, has stated: "[Baca] writes with unconcealed passion: detachment is not a quality he cultivates." His work has been likened to both that of Alan Ginsberg, whose poems were among the first he read in prison, and of Walt Whitman. But beyond his direct approach, it is the lyric quality of his verse that has received the most praise. Marion Taylor called the poems in Baca's first collection "astonishingly beautiful," and Levertov added, "his work is rich in image and music, full of abundant energy and love of life even when describing the brutal and tragic." Renowned Hispanic novelist Ron Arias has also expressed admiration for Baca's impassioned writings, commenting: "Baca reminds me of a jazz musician searching for a melody, and when he finds it he takes it wherever it may lead him. Whether or not the melody or train of images works as a unified piece with a clear theme is of secondary importance to the journey itself, a journey of discovery unbound by prison walls and fences."

CRITICAL COMMENTARY

MARION TAYLOR
(review date 1980)

[In the following favorable review of *Immigrants in Our Own Land,* Taylor comments on the lyricism of Baca's poetry, calling it "astonishingly beautiful."]

Immigrants in Our Own Land is a very disturbing book of poems because it's so astonishingly beautiful, one does not expect such to come from the pen of a man serving a long prison sentence, as is the case with this poet. These poems go against the current trend of so-called "prison poetry." While these poems do not neglect the bleak realities of prison life what is absent entirely is the strident voice and the ascerbic vision. What these poems discover is a center of freedom and humaneness beyond the bleak realities; they are in their way a hymn and a celebration of the human spirit in extreme situations.

In a world which offers virtually no concrete means of rebuilding a broken life, these poems propose just such a means. By defining the prison experience as primarily

---

Principal Works

Immigrants in Our Own Land (poetry) 1979

Swords of Darkness (poetry) 1981

What's Happening (poetry) 1982

Martín and Meditations on the South Valley (poetry) 1987

Black Mesa Poems (poetry) 1989

Working in the Dark: Reflections of a Poet in the Barrio (reminiscences) 1992

---

one of learning how to endure, the mastery of which can be a genuinely liberating experience, the poet suggests not only that poetry can be restorative, but also that human life if given a chance is resilient.

In **"It Started"** Baca describes his first encounter with the state-funded poetry workshop and the timid, suspicious first days that finally gave way to communication and friendship. He writes:

. . . But you didn't treat me like a wild ape
or an elephant. You treated me like Jimmy.
And who was Jimmy?
A mass of molten fury in this furnace of steel,
and yet, my thoughts became ladles, sifting carefully
through my life, the pain and endurance,
to the essence of my being. . .

But beyond the human qualities abundantly present, the real strength of these poems derive from the fact that Baca writes so well. He has a fine, superb, lyrical gift and a firm command of the resources of language. There are no rough edges and the poems move forward with utmost economy. This is a book determined to bear witness to the truths of the human heart in adversity and it does it with wisdom, courage, beauty and above all, hope.

Marion Taylor, in a review of *Immigrants in Our Own Land,* in *Kliatt Young Adult Paperback Book Guide,* Vol. 14, Spring, 1980, p. 20.

RON ARIAS

(review date 1982)

[Chicano journalist and author Arias is best known for his 1975 novel *The Road to Tamazunchale,* a work of "magic realism" in the style of Gabriel García Márquez that was nominated for the National Book Award. In this review, Arias distinguishes a variety of moods and styles in the poems comprising *Immigrants in Our Own Land.*]

A poet named Jimmy Santiago Baca is running around a prison track field when he stops to look at a chain gang pulling weeds by the prison preacher's house. It's hot and in the distance away from the prison is a nearby town courthouse. In the shade, a hard-eyed preacher, sipping tea, watches the men work.

Suddenly Baca's thoughts explode. Why don't the men tear down the courthouse? Why don't they burn the preacher's house? Why don't they eliminate him, that "lazy glob of pulpish meat"?

Of course, nothing happens, Baca's eyes and thoughts clear, and he ends his poem—**"On a September Day"**—by running another lap, his fist clenched, "trying to run the ache out of my heart."

Typical jailhouse rage and frustration, you might say. However, for Baca such an obvious peek into the furnace of his anger is quite rare. Most of the 37 poems in *Immigrants In Our Own Land,* his first published collection, focus on other emotions, other visions. The comfort of a routine workday, for example, leads Baca to list all the image details of a road gang's chores except memories and "things we never talk about."

Or in the poem **"In My Land,"** which is a portrait of his rural New Mexican origins, Baca speaks of age, of howls, of wind, of time lost, of solitude, and of ignorance and the city-bound. But most of all he speaks of rebirth amid the "courage of love."

Or in another poem, **"Unity of Hearts,"** Baca reveals a deep sympathy for workers of the fields. It is a sympathy that evokes these bitter yet tender lines:

In your old shoes and hats and clothes,
             durable and desertlike,
cactus-spun lizard-fingered wing-souls,
your sighs like feathers dropping lightly,

For a man who spent ten years in prison, such sentiments and their delicate expression may seem too mild, too tame, for the subject at hand. Yet Baca frequently transcends the obvious. Even his style surprises. At times he can be terse, narrowly focused, directly to the point, as in **"Stony, Fifteen Years in the Joint,"** a short-lined profile of a tough, veteran con. Other times he can resemble an exuberant Walt Whitman in the long-line rhythm and sweep of his emotions— expansive, wordy, even conversational.

Whatever his approach, however, my favorite moments occur when Baca springs into a dream or remembered scene. In **"I'm Sure of It,"** he looks down from his cell window and sees some convicts in the prison yard. Then he gazes at trees beyond the outer fence. Eventually, as night comes, his mind settles on distant headlights, car sounds, freeways, people:

construction workers coming and going

into homey bars,
greasy caps cocked to one side, smoking
                              cigarettes,
stroking pool cues through gritty thick
                                    fingers,
suck their unbrushed teeth watching
                              intently,
as Tammy Wynette wails out her country
                              hits
to dimes and quarters plunked in the
                              jukebox,
among the bearish beer-drinking, smoke-
                              swirling workers,
coughing and cursing and smiling,
while their fathers push on screen doors,
enter yellowed kitchens and drink coffee
                              with married daughters,
as night darkens over the city
and porch lights collect bugs in their
                              nets. . . .

Baca reminds me of a jazz musician searching for a melody, and when he finds it he takes it wherever it may lead him. Whether or not the melody or train of images works as a unified piece with a clear theme is of secondary importance to the journey itself, a journey of discovery unbound by prison walls and fences.

Aside from these moments of discovery, Baca continually surprises by squeezing meaning out of ordinary sights, such as in this inventive description of the prison entrance.

The sun on those green palm trees, lining the entry road to prison. Stiff rows of husky-scaled bark, with a tuft of green looping blades on top, sword twirling in wind, always erect and disciplined, legallike.

For my taste, the weakest poems are the several "essay" pieces in the collection. These state, in obvious, flat language, the poet's position toward a person or a situation. The most message-laden pieces—and there are very few—are **"So Mexicans Are Taking Jobs from Americans"** and **"The New Warden."** But even in these poems of some protest, what is said needs to be said. Fine, and we read on for more of those surprises, those chances taken, in the more lyrical pieces.

Baca, who is now out of prison and lives in North Carolina, can be tight-lined, expansive, gentle, quick-paced or unrushed, quite sober or quite funny. He is a freshly aggressive poet of many abilities, and he tries them all. His is a gifted, young vision, and judging from this collection, I get the feeling he is just warming up. I look forward to more. (pp. 11–12)

Ron Arias, in a review of *Immigrants in Our Own Land*, in *The American Book Review*, Vol. 4, No. 2, January–February, 1982, pp. 11–12.

JOHN ADDIEGO
(review date 1983)

[In the following excerpt, Addiego reviews *Immigrants in Our Own Land*, praising Baca's style and comparing him favorably to Walt Whitman.]

[Jimmy Santiago Baca's] *Immigrants in Our Own Land* is a howl, a growling wail, a "trip through the mind jail" (as Raul Salinas' poem by that title described the agonizing process of remembering from inside the confines of oppression 15 years ago). This is the jail for real: most of Baca's poetry was written while he was in prison, and I think it's valuable for two reasons: because it addresses a constituency in desperate need of articulate voices (a 1979 study [for Ricardo Chavira's "West Coast Story," *Nuestro*, May, 1980] showed a rising death rate of over 250 Latino gang members per year in the Los Angeles area alone), and because Baca's uneven, unschooled style achieves some exceptionally exciting moments in these poems.

Concerned with his Chicano heritage (the book's title is a reference to the recent acquisition of that part of northern Mexico, or Aztlan, by the U.S., and the creation of a second–class citizenry supposedly protected by the unrecognized Treaty of Hidalgo) and wrestling with imprisonment and poverty, Baca's howl has a slight flavor of Ginsberg, and much more of Ginsberg's spiritual mentor, Whitman. His self-explorations are at times so heartbreakingly honest that the reader cannot help but be disturbed. At other times his singing and cataloguing have such visual power that the reader is taken back to Whitman's spear of grass (with the succinct impression that, in our times, the police are likely to arrest for vagrancy somebody lying on the grass):

Ah, how lovely, how happy I am just to be me.
I raise my pink gums like a wild chimpanzee, tilt my
    head back,
chortling white-toothed, at this amazing zoo and its
    visitors,
pockets filled with popcorn, and crunching candy
    apples.

and later, in the same poem,

I see it all; the glare of chrome and glaze of windows, the suspense and ambition of young boys playing baseball in parks, and sidewalks splattered with the night's blood, and the policeman sleeping with his wife and farting in the bathroom, and then after, so groomed and polished, passing shops along the street, hello he says to one, hello to another. I sleep in the grass thinking of this, and can be arrested for sleeping on the

grass, and I laugh looking at the sky, filling the sky
with my laughter. (pp. 154–55)

John Addiego, in a review of *Immigrants in Our Own Land,*
in *Northwest Review,* Vol. XXI, No. 1, 1983, pp. 154–55.

MICHAEL HOGAN

(review date 1983)

[American poet and critic Hogan, like Baca, began
his career as a writer while still in prison. In the following review of *What's Happening,* Hogan identifies
Baca as a writer with "superb natural gifts," but contends that the collection is of a lesser quality than his
earlier work.]

Jimmy Santiago Baca first sent poems to me when I was
working as an editor of an anthology of prison poetry
in 1974. I noticed then two strengths which contained
within them a strong potential for weakness if his craft
were not carefully controlled or if he became too impressed by academia's wooing of the imprisoned or alienated minorities. The first strength was that he wrote primarily from an emotional rather than a rational language.
This, while offering a passion and a color to his language,
offered as well the possibility that his work could become
didactic or self-indulgent.

His second strength was that, while his poems were
unruly and moved more rapidly by an appeal to the senses
than by lucid exposition, they were powerfully evocative
when not overwritten. Hence the need for a good editor.
William Stafford once said that he had been "saved" by
his editors. Unfortunately, Baca has not been so lucky in
this volume.

He is, without a doubt, a writer with superb natural gifts. His first volume *Immigrants in Our Own
Land* (Louisiana State University Press, 1979) was well-
received by critics and contained within its narrow limits
the voice of a young Neruda without any debt to the
South American poet's style. His poems were rich with
imagery and passionate, although showing a tendency toward looseness and the prosaic which, unfortunately, finds
its bottom in this recent collection.

While his subject matter is powerful: the oppression
of a race by a dominant culture, the exploitation of casual
or transient labor, the atrocities in state prisons, there
is entirely too much telling and too little showing. For
example in the poem **"Overcrowding"**:

Prison is a dead man's zone.
Look into the eyes of men here,
There is something more
than cautiousness,

A sense of complete,
cold barren knowledge,
Of being abused too long and too far,
Coerced into indignities that
pile up on them,
In conditions that make them reckless and savage. . .

Baca would have done better in poems such as this
one to have given us the narrative account of one man, or
let us into *his* emotional state, or distanced, and thus given
his observation the force of understatement. It is unfortunate that no editor made these or similar suggestions
because the subject matter of the poems in this collection
is powerful, the writing passionate (if uncontrolled), and
the sense of poetic commitment strong.

Poetry, whether written out of a prison experience,
a war, a personal tragedy, does not become poetry simply
because it is a description of injustice, random terror, personal loss or abandonment. It becomes poetry, William
Wantling once said, if it can speak of these things with
"style, concrete, sensory detail, stark outlines of emotionally charged events, extreme economy. . . " Unfortunately, these qualities are largely lacking in Baca's new
collection.

That said, there is still praise due some of the pieces
in this small volume. Baca has a natural gift for the dramatic monologue. The voice is usually that of a street-wise
chicano who is trying just for his own personal satisfaction to figure out who gives the police their orders, who
runs the "whole bunch of things in the world/like boat
companies and oil companies and things like that." And
the man with the computer, "Now where'd he get them
numbers?" (**"There's Me"**).

There is a wry humor in poems like this and a disarming ingenuousness which makes the *persona* of the
young, alienated chicano attractive. He is not telling us
anything directly, merely trying to find out for himself.
And this device of the naive narrator, this distancing from
the poet's natural inclination to preach at us, is precisely
why this poem and one or two others succeed while the
remainder fall flat.

One is tempted to compare this volume to his first
book and wonder if—in his haste to have a new volume
out since his release from prison—he merely went back to
old manuscript material rejected in the first look. There
is that feel about the poems. There is also no sense of
progression from the first volume of poems and this one;
no sense, either, of development and growth.

Baca is a gifted poet and has a natural lyricism in
the best of his work. This small slip should not affect
that reputation; other poets have made such slips without
disastrous consequences. One hopes to see his new work
in magazines, testing the limits of his art. One hopes to see
the promise of his first book realized (after that testing)

in a future, better crafted volume. (pp. 19–20)

Michael Hogan, in a review of *What's Happening*, in *The American Book Review*, Vol. 6, No. 1, November–December, 1983, pp. 19–20.

DENISE LEVERTOV
(essay date 1987)

[An English-born American, Levertov is a renowned poet, essayist, translator, and editor. She was acting poetry editor at *Mother Jones* when Baca submitted his first work to that journal for publication, and she also found a publisher for his first collection of poems. Here, Levertov introduces *Martín and Meditations on the South Valley*.]

Novels in verse, poetic autobiographies, epics—none of these genres is encountered very frequently, though perhaps each generation produces a few examples of the first two (the genuine epic is obviously far rarer) and there has been a distinct interest in narrative poetry in general in the last few years. Notable examples of the novel in verse to appear in recent years have been Vikram Seth's witty (and often moving) *The Golden Gate*, modeled on Pushkin's *Eugene Onegin*, and the English translation (by Randy Blasing and Mutlu Konuk) of Nazim Hikmet's *Human Landscapes*, that amazing work which borders on epic, and is more closely related to Kazantzakis's continuation of The Odyssey (and to its inspiration) than to Pushkin or, let's say, Crabbe. Jimmy Santiago Baca, in **"Martín"** and its sequel, **"Meditations on the South Valley,"** clearly has more affinity with Hikmet than with Seth's "new formalism." He draws directly upon personal and documentary material rather than on more distanced fictive constructions; and he writes with unconcealed passion: detachment is not a quality he cultivates. But he is far from being a naïve realist; what makes his work so exciting to me is the way in which it manifests both an intense lyricism and that transformative vision which perceives the mythic and archetypal significance of life-events.

The story told in **"Martín"** draws upon elements of Baca's own history, but does not duplicate them. Fictive names are employed, events telescoped, and whole epochs of experience eliminated, so that the core significance not be obscured or cluttered. The tale may be outlined: A boy abandoned by his parents lives first with a grandmother, then is placed in an orphanage. Relatives from both sides—the rural poor ones and the town bourgeois—take him out to visit occasionally. At ten he runs away. He lives from hand to mouth and becomes, outwardly, just another example of that familiar figure, a young man with "nothing to do, nowhere to go," hanging out on the corner of any Main Street—often a Black, Native American or Hispanic, and in this case a mestizo, Mejicano, "detribalized Apache." But Martín has the mind of a poet (and the reader—though not deliberately—is challenged: next time you see such a figure, remember that though his head *may* be filled only with quotidian banalities and with crude and trivial wishes, it is also very possible that he is living an inner life at least as vivid as your own). His imagination is engaged; in poverty, and witness to much brutality and degradation, he retains an innocent eye—a wild creature's eye—and a deep and loving respect for the earth. As a child he had dreamed an Indian spirit-dream, and sung "all earth is holy" over and over to his heart's drum beat. The street-wise youth holds secretly to that wisdom.

After some personal disasters he takes to the road and for some years wanders from state to state. While he is far from home the need to seek out his origins, to know his parents' stories, becomes strong in him. He calls to mind those who had known them, is haunted by their voices telling him of the tragic lives from which he sprang. He returns, and explores those lives, and experiences their bitter deaths.

Then Martín again goes wandering, from state to state, city to city: searching now for a point of rest, dreaming of a bit of land, and a house, and a woman who will be his wife. He searches, searches, in and out of trouble, discontented, broke, "thin with addiction," drifting. At last he is drawn back once more to "Burque," to his own New Mexican reality, and at last finds the woman he has dreamed of.

To make a home for her and himself and their coming child he guts and rebuilds an old shack and clears decades of scrap from the half-acre of land behind it. At the poem's end he has received the newborn into his own hands and sworn to his son that he will never abandon him.

Reduced to outline, it is a simple story, with barely a "plot." But in its poetic richness it is so much more—a Hero Tale, an archetypal journey, not only through a personal desolation but into, and out of, the desolated, benighted lives of his parents. Passing through the desert he emerges into a green and fertile valley of love and birth, but he has learned that the valley will be his to keep only if he cherishes it. The vow never to abandon his child as he had been abandoned (and as his father had abandoned *himself*—to drink; or as his mother had been essentially abandoned by *her* father, who exchanged responsible fatherhood for incestuous rape) extends beyond the child to "all living things." And this of necessity includes Martín's self; the vow implies that he will respect the holiness of his own life too, henceforth. Thus the poem is essentially a myth of redemption.

The second half of this volume, **"Meditations on the South Valley,"** can be recognized a sequel to

"**Martín**" even though it is told in the first, not the third, person; but it is also an autonomous self-contained work. And within its totality, which forms a narrative, its parts can each be read as discrete entities, some of them meditative lyrics such as XVII or XIII for example, some of them stories within the framing story.

The *myth recognized in reality* in this poem is parallel to that told in "**Martín.**" "**Meditations**" opens with the destruction by fire of the hard-won house, the secure locus, the nest whose construction, along with the birth of a child, brought "**Martín**" to completion. The fire necessitates a period of residence in a neighborhood whose alien character, combined with the shock of that disaster, impels the writer to take stock of all that his own South Valley signifies to him: the warmth, passion, tragedy, *reality* of the barrio thrown into sharp relief by the suburban blandness of "the Heights." The resulting poems portray and evoke the values embodied in the barrio, despite—and in certain ways even because of—all its poverty and racial oppression. Cherished *old* things mended to serve anew are perceived in their beauty, compared to the glare and glitz of things shiny with newness.

> Ah, those lovely bricks
> and sticks I found in fields
> and took home with me
> to make flower boxes!
> The old cars I've worked on
> endlessly giving them tune-ups,
> changing tires, tracing
> electrical shorts. . .
> . . . the process of making-do,
> of the life I've lived between
> breakdowns and break-ups. . .
> I could not bear a life
> with everything perfect.

In contrast, the rented "**Heights**" apartment "reflects a faceless person . . . an emptiness" with its "white walls/thin orange carpet" all "strangely clean and new" where there are no homely chores for him to do. On the groomed suburban street people with "ceramic faces" are walking their elegant clipped poodles, and "the air is blistered with glaze/of new cars and new homes." As he longs for the barrio, an organic *neighborhood*, he tells stories of its people, stories at once typical and unique: "bad little Eddie," who cried out against injustice, cared for his old grandmother, was illiterate, generous, a delinquent piece of rubbish in the eyes of society, and died playing "chicken"; Pablo the powerful gang-leader, now a janitor, "still proud," still "cool to the bone," who leads "a new gang of neighborhood parents" to fight against water pollution; Feliz the *curandera*, who bewitches Caspar the Ghost, who used to pick fights all the time and now stands on the Río Grande bridge each day muttering religious curses, his shack papered with images of the Sacred Heart; Maria the young witch; Pancho "the barrio idiot," who identifies with the animals and lives his harmless life, rich with fantasies, unmolested; Benny whom the Rio Grande

takes to itself. . . . All these are seen within the society of which they are a part, and thus the autonomy of each story, each poem within the poem (including those which are most lyrical and personal) is never detached from that wholeness of view which results from an artist's dedicated engagement with experience.

Social criticism is implicit, not abstracted, throughout Baca's work—most obviously in the prison poems of an earlier volume, *Immigrants in Our Own Land*, though even there not divorced from a prevailing lyricism. In the present book it is felt as the underlying theme: the tragedy of waste, deprivation, disinheritance. The illiterate youths "lean[ing] on haunches in the sun/back[s] against a wall," "entangled in the rusty barbed wire of a society [they] do not understand" are brothers and comrades of Martín/Baca. He is aware, with Blakean vision, studying "the faces of boys/playing in dirt yards," of Cuauhtémoc; in men who, "eyes sleek with dreams,/lounge on porches/reading the flight of geese/above the Río Grande," he perceives Netzahualcoyotl. But all of this could not engage one, the reader could not really hear and feel it, if Baca's language itself did not engage the ear. It is not only his responsive sensibility that, at the very opening of "**Martín**" enters presences that linger in the air of an abandoned pueblo like the former presence of a picture on a wall; it is the donative articulation with which he can transmit experience. How rich the spare, mostly monosyllabic cadences can be! He evokes his childhood:

> On *that* field
> I hand swept smooth
> top crust dirt and duned a fort.
> Idling sounds of Villa's horse
> I reared my body and neighed at weeds.

Or the childhood of his mother, after the school bus has dropped her off at the edge of the field track she must follow home:

> The lonely afternoon in the vast expanse of llano
> was a blue knife
> sharpening its hot, silver edge on the distant
> horizon of mountains, the wind blew over
> chipping red grit, carving a prehistoric scar-scaled
> winged reptile of the mountain. . . .

His imagery often has the Gongoresque character (which in Neruda is called "surreal" but has little to do with cerebral French-style surrealism) common to much Hispanic writing (traceable, perhaps, to Arabic influences in Spain, and to Native American influences in the New World?). Such images surprise, but are rooted in actual observation. "Laughter rough as brocaded cloth . . . teeth brilliant as church tiles"—the comparisons are fresh and real, and give a kind of beauty to the roughness, a dignity to the sensual gleam of teeth.

The young, homeless Martín makes friends with old women who hang out by the bars, "blue teardrops tattooed on their cheeks,/initials of ex-lovers on their hands." They are perceived as

drawn out from the dark piss-stinking rooms
they lived in,
by the powerful force of the moon,
whose yellow teeth tore the alfalfa out of their hearts
and left them stubbled,
parched grounds old goats of Tecatos and winos
nibbled

—a metaphor that beautifully balances both its terms; they have equal, virtually interchangeable validity.

By the time we return, in the **"Meditations,"** to the narrator's own story, the containing frame, we can perceive that what makes it so imperative to rebuild the burned house is not only the obvious practical and psychological need anyone, anywhere, might have after a fire, but the need once more to reenter the history and struggle of his own people.

The actual reconstruction (aided by friends whose character, once again, might seem highly dubious to the world at large, but who, in solidarity, rise to the occasion with honor) is a miniature epic, Homeric in its condensed enumeration of the details the herculean labor involved.

The felling of an ancient elm which precedes the clearing of the house-site before the building begins is a particularly powerful passage, which once more demonstrates Baca's unforced feeling for symbolic significance. The death of the great elephantine tree is a necessary ritual of mythic character; the author, although now "where the tree had stood/a silver waterfall of sky poured down," feels as if he had "just killed an old man." But myth is entered through the graphic, sonic, and kinesthetic evocation of an actual, strenuous event, in which human effort and the last "leaf-heave" breath of a shuddering, cracking, down-crashing tree become part of the reader's own experience.

At last the work of construction is done, and a new house much better than the first has come into being. It is a birth, to parallel the birth of the little son in **"Martín."** Ten years of poems had been burned in the fire—new ones are born in meditation and action. Not the house nor the poems only, and not even the return to the South Valley and what is symbolizes, but—parallel to the vow of commitment at the end of **"Martín"**— new levels of awareness, dedication, purpose, and personal freedom, emerge as phoenix from these ashes. (pp. xiii-xviii)

Denise Levertov, in an introduction to *Martín and Meditations on the South Valley* by Jimmy Santiago Baca, New Directions, 1987, pp. xiii–xviii.

LIAM RECTOR
(essay date 1988)

[In the following excerpt, Rector comments on the loss of innocence and coming of age of the protagonist in *Martín and Meditations on the South Valley.*]

[*Martín and Meditations on the South Valley* is] a powerful orchestration and revision of a narrative and lyrical admixture—both constructivist and expressionist in its execution—with an utterly compelling dramatic form fueling the entire vivisection and the pilgrim's progress which makes it so much more than another "collection" of poems.

Baca's book is a page-turner, almost a novel in verse, though its narrative is primarily elliptical (prodded structurally forth by the sectioning, the juxtaposition of poems, and the jump-cuts of time both presuppose). Its basic unit of construction is the sequence, poem by poem. I don't want to rehearse here the entire story and ruin its unfolding for the reader, but suffice to say that it is the story's masterful arc of dramatic form that commands both our emotional and our formal attentions. Martín, the orphaned protagonist, sets off on a journey that is studded with the particulars of his mestizo or "detribalized Apache" background, one which finally enacts a mythical rite which speaks to us all.

For many of the poets now in their thirties the word *memory* has become a kind of poetic buzzword, and memory is often the route travelled, the road deified, in their voyage towards meaning in poems. A romantic nostalgia (forever pumping the fog machine) weakens the decorative, essentially descriptive poems of many in this generation, where memory is no more than a whining, not a keening, about the passage into adulthood, the passage into complicity. But in poems such as Baca's. . . the loss of innocence is made specific, personal, grounded in tribe, class, and finally myth—*made* into a kind of depersonalized self-dramatization which, if it is romantic and betrays deep sentiment, is also very hard-boiled and without any *poseur* sentimentality. One innocence often remembered by this generation is the political/social innocence of coming to age amidst the Vietnam War and all it embodied of a civil war wherein family member was pitted against family member. Another most remembered (or most longed for) is characteristically the existence of the family itself, the mother and the father of it, before the "broken home" of the fifties became the "single-parent dwelling" of the eighties or no home, no family at all.

Your departure uprooted me mother,
hallowed core of a child

An excerpt from *Working in the Dark*

With a stub pencil I whittled sharp with my teeth, I propped a Red Chief notebook on my knees and wrote my first words. From that moment, a hunger for poetry possessed me.

Until then, I had felt as if I had been born into a raging ocean where I swam relentlessly, flailing my arms in hope of rescue, of reaching a shoreline I never sighted. Never solid ground beneath me, never a resting place. I had lived with only the desperate hope to stay afloat; that and nothing more.

But when at least I wrote my first words on the page, I felt an island rising beneath my feet like the back of a whale. As more and more words emerged, I could finally rest: I had a place to stand for the first time in my life. The island grew, with each page, into a continent inhabited by people I knew and mapped with the life I lived.

I wrote about it all—about people I had loved or hated, about the brutalities and ecstasies of my life. And, for the first time, the child in me who had witnessed and endured unspeakable terrors cried out not just in impotent despair, but with the power of language. Suddenly, through language, through writing, my grief and my joy could be shared with anyone who would listen. And I could do this all alone; I could do it anywhere. I was no longer a captive of demons eating away at me, no longer a victim of other people's mockery and loathing, that had made me clench my fist white with rage and grit my teeth to silence. Words now pleaded back with the bleak lucidity of hurt. They were wrong, those others, and now I could say it.

Through language I was free. I could respond, escape, indulge; embrace or reject earth or the cosmos. I was launched on an endless journey without boundaries or rules, in which I could salvage the floating fragments of my past, or be born anew in the spontaneous ignition of understanding some heretofore concealed aspect of myself. Each word steamed with the hot lava juices of my primordial making, and I crawled out of stanzas dripping with birth-blood, reborn and freed from the chaos of my life. The child in the dark room of my heart, that had never been albe to find or reach the light switch, flicked it on now; and I found in the room a stranger, myself, who had waited so many years to speak again. My words struck in me lightning crackles of elation and thunderhead storms of grief.

Jimmy Santiago Baca, in his *Working in the Dark: Reflections of a Poet of the Barrio*, Red Crane Books, 1992.

---

your absence whittled down
to a broken doll
in a barn loft. The small burned area of memory,
where your face is supposed to be,
moons' rings pass through
in broken chain of events
in my dreams.

   Martin's loss is an extreme one, and he travels to seek out friends of his parents to tell him who and how his parents were. In Martín's sojourn across the country we're made to feel that even within the genocidal colonization that established America it is now an America of emigres who have all in effect orphaned themselves, moving in radical disjunction away from their parent/precursors. Martín's own history is poised within the roughage, the barely digestible:

I was caught in the middle—
between white skinned, English speaking altar boy
at the communion railing,
and brown skinned, Spanish speaking plains nomadic
   child
with buffalo heart groaning underworld earth powers,
between Sunday brunch at a restaurant
and burritos eaten in a tin-roofed barn,
between John Wayne on the afternoon movie
rifle butting young Braves,
and the Apache whose red dripping arrow
was the altar candle in praise of the buck
just killed.

   Out of the collisions of these histories and absences Baca fashions the first movement of the book, **"Martín,"** where a child passes from "field prey" to form eventually his own family and house, persons and a place he promises never to abandon.

   "Meditations on the South Valley," the second movement in the book, is a further tale of breakdown and rebuilding, one in which Baca draws portraits of barrio life with great telescopic accuracy and poignance. This section meanders a bit and loses some of the compression that drove so convincingly the arc of the first section, but if there is a loss of through-line tension it is also an interlude before the books' triumphant climax. This is a book of abandonment and what people abandon themselves to—drink, the irresponsibility of incest, their own youths, and passivity—and it is also a book of great complicity, maturity, and finally responsibility. As Levertov says, it is a contemporary hero tale . . . . The skills brought to the writing are likewise heroic, combining as they do both narrative and startling lyric talents, forging a form which supersedes any discussion of the craft brought to bear. (pp. 394–96)

Liam Rector, "The Documentary of What Is," in *The Hudson Review*, Vol. XLI, No. 2, Summer, 1988, pp. 393–400.

BRUCE-NOVOA

(essay date 1989)

[Bruce-Novoa is a Costa Rican born American poet

and critic who has written extensively on Chicano literature. In the following excerpt, he examines the style and content of Baca's poetry, concluding that it "remains essentially self-centered, personal in an egotistical way."]

[Both Baca and Leo Romero (with his *Celso,* 1985)] begin in a personal search that channels itself into a character, in Baca's case Martín. The significance of that evolution is, nevertheless, different. Whereas Romero relinquishes the personal voice to a folkloric character, the pícaro outsider, Baca's personal *I* coincides with the figure of the outlaw and he moves away from it in his search for deeper personal understanding. Ironically, to do so he seems compelled to open a distance between himself and his persona by creating a character, Martín, who will take on an epic quality of historical searcher, although restricting himself to the immediate family. Martín recuperates, as Baca recreates, a reason for his situation, and then transcends it by finding a new common spirit and purpose. The poems of the second book **"Meditations on the South Valley"** are the record of his pilgrimage.

Immigrants in Our Own Land contains prison poems with almost no references to Baca's ethnicity. Clues can be found, but they are so subtle as to be more the reader's invention than the author's intention. The mention of "piñon trees" stands out in its uniqueness among the many images that bear no ethnic specificity. The few references to Chicanos are not tied to the persona's identity, and in **"So Mexicans are Taking Jobs from Americans,"** a pro-Mexican poem, the persona does not assume the identity of the accused, preferring to remain an ambiguous defender. Even the title poem, which one might expect to allude to Chicanos, is actually about how prisoners are treated. The essence of the collection lies not in ethnicity, but in individual self-knowledge and affirmation. **"I Will Remain"** offers the key.

I am after a path you cannot find by looking at green
  fields,
        smelling high mountain air that is clear and
  sweetly
Odorous as when you fall in love again and again and
  again.
I am looking for a path that weaves through rock
        and swims through despair with fins of
  wisdom.
A wisdom to see me through this nightmare,
        . . . .
I will take the strength I need from me,
        not from field or new friends. With my old
  friends fighting!
Bleeding! Calling me crazy! And never getting the
  respect I desire
        . . . .
I stay because I believe I will find something,
        . . . .
Here on this island of death and violence,

I must find peace and love in myself, eventually
  freedom
And if I am blessed, then perhaps a little wisdom.

Prison here fits into the ancient motif of the voyage into the wilderness, the descent into hell, from which the pilgrim emerges illuminated with truth. But it is not a voyage into a community, rather into the self. The book ends with no sign of the freedom he seeks and not much of the wisdom either.

While *Swords of Darkness* was published after *Immigrants*, the poems are dated two years earlier and are stylistically similar. Long verses dangerously close to prose, express the outsider's perspective, the prisoner's isolation from society. The last poem, **"Walking Down to Town and Back,"** contains, however, childhood memories among which appear typical New Mexican motifs, to say nothing of specific place names like Belén and Sandía mountains. A horse-riding father takes the son to see a woman "who had seen our Virgin Mary." Suddenly the poem turns into a new Mexican folktale, with death, strange events involving malicious animals, the spirit of the deceased attempting to kill the spouse and causing a fire (a similar story appears in Romero's "His Sister" *Agua Negra*), and salvation coming in the form of divine intervention. The persona then claims to have also seen the Virgin and is marked for life by the apparition. The community treats him like a crazy drunk, resembling the pícaro. The poem is an origin myth of the outsider figure, an explanation of the category in which Baca finds himself in **"Immigrants."** And that situation is attributed to his father's intervention—in traditional guise of horse rider—-a version of the cycle-of-history motif in which one generation inherits its destiny from the elders. Somehow that destiny is to speak of the dark unknown side of existence, to be the voice of "rude life" as the last poem states. In this context, *Immigrants* becomes a voyage into a wilderness to garner the wisdom necessary to live up to the destiny with which the young persona was marked.

Baca's recent book *Martín and Meditations on the South Valley* is a personal voyage into a dark personal past. Martín, the central character, orphaned—actually abandoned by his parents—in early childhood like a classic pícaro, goes in search of his parents' history. He begins with his memories—"My mind circles warm ashes of memories,/the dark edged images of my history," adds what he can learn from others—"For some years I wandered cross country,/and those who had known my parents / came back to me again," which in turn further provokes his own. He manages to reconstruct his parents' unhappy life and pathetic death. His arrival at the conclusion of their story releases him to begin his own search for a future, one with set goals that contrast sharply with his parents' experience: "I left Burque [Alburquerque] again, to buy a house,/a small piece of land, and marry a woman." His mistake, however, is that he actually is repeating his parents' pattern of running away from a difficult home situation, and the result is equally unsettling: "Each city was filled/with children/like the child I had once been." This encounter with his own past image sends him back to his origins where he discovers an identity even more basic than family ties: he is the "grit and sediment. . . mineral de Nuevo Mexico," and specifically of the rural Manzano Mountain area. From this self-knowledge he draws strength and direction. Utilizing his mestizo heritage—"Apache words" plus "Spanish names of things"— he will work a plan that sounds simple.

> I am ready to work
> all I ask is that I don't starve,
> that I don't fail at being a good man,
> that things go good for me,
> that I meet a woman who will love me deeply,
> that I meet strong spiritual brothers and sisters,
> and that I have healthy children.

This commitment to region and basic values culminates in the rewards of revelation in the form of a vision of belonging, significantly stated in terms of New Mexican imagery: mountains, rocks, arrowheads, piñon nuts, pine cones, a red sun, and the brightly illuminated ruins of the Quaraí mission. Against this typical landscape, the poet projects archetypal images of a traditional mestizo family heritage:

> I thought I saw the dark skinned ghost
> of my grandfather, on his horse, with sombrero
> waving to me from QUARAI,
> and the gray haired ghost of my grandmother,
> carding sheep fur
> beneath the green teepee of a pine tree,
> by the arroyo.

Hispano male and Indian female set in a traditional ranching scene seen against the backdrop of the mission in the midst of nature; this is Baca's most nostalgic and idealistic moment.

The first half of the book culminates in an affirmation of success. Martín finds a mate, buys land, remodels a house, and has a child. Within this model of the nuclear family, the last poem ends on an apparently positive note.

> I went inside ,
> took Pablito from Gabriela
> to let her sleep and rest,
> then circled my arm around your body Pablo,
> as we slept in the bed next to mama,
> I promised you and all living things,
> I would never abandon you.

Martín declares a new life diametrically opposed to his experience of having been abandoned, left to live without home or parents.

In that context of fulfillment, the second half is remarkable. It opens with the burning of the house and with it, ten years worth of poems. Martín will eventually build another house on the same spot, thus transcending his set-back, but the ending, quite expected and anticli-

mactic, is less significant than the transformation Martín undergoes in the process.

The poems now become echoes of Chicano literature through the New Mexican motifs seen above. First, we have the threat of disappearance in the house burning, given particular significance of personal death of a sort by the loss of the poems. The wife then extends the circle of destruction to the family by stating, "'Oh, Martín, it's all gone.'" Then Martín goes into a form of exile, a stranger in a middle-class neighborhood, appropriately called the Heights to contrast with the South Valley where he lived before. The symbolic division of society into upper and lower, alienated and those still in touch with real life, is clichéd, but it is also Baca's entré into Chicano literature's superficial code. In this situation of impending loss of meaning, Martín begins recuperating the images of his source of orientation in the world. From his exile he recalls the barrio in which he has lived for an unspecified number of years—the ten years of writing is one hint, while later he mentions another son, now old enough to play on his own—and where he had become one of the people.

The poems enumerate characters, environments, and events, filling in that gap of years, bridging it as well as the new distance of exile. These memories are simultaneously an enumeration of New Mexican characters and motifs. Characters include outsider figures—drunks, lowriders, gang members, the barrio fool—the *curandera*, the witch, the elders, the veteran, and two figures evoked through allusion: Doña Sebastíana, death in the form of a woman, and the *santero* statue carver. The dominant motif is the closeness to the natural order in which trees are personified. Yet there is also a Chicano updating here noticeable in the inclusion of lowriders and gang members among the outsiders. In a distancing move, reminiscent of Montoya's breaking off of his nostalic memory with a *Chale* from the contemporary barrio idiom, Baca turns back to his own romantic image of the grandfather and rejects it in the form of a scene from a Western movie. Apparently he recognizes that his nostalgic ideals are no longer fit for the present. "My heart is an old post / dreams I tied to it years ago / yank against / to get free." Martín turns off the television and immediately a contemporary form of the image appears to replace the old one: "A chavalo riding his bicycle / at dawn down Barcelona road, / clenching roses in his teeth, / in the handlebar basket / are apples he took from random trees on the road." Note that the boy is a picaresque character involved in petty theft, but with a flare for the beauty of nature, a worthy successor of Romero's Celso, but urbanized.

It is this urbanizing up-dating Baca undertakes in the poems that follow, beginning with a parody of Montoya's famous elegy to a dead pachuco, "El Louie." The elegy to Eddie allows Baca to evoke common Chicano motifs of police oppression, gang graffiti as alternative to illiteracy, barrio slang, and the bitter cry of "stop it," all of which culminates in a typical plea for a place in the communal memory. "Your voiced whispered/in the dust and weeds,/a terrible silence/not to forget your death." Martín's renewed pilgrimage takes him not back to the family past, a question he resolved in the first section of the book, but into the community. Perhaps more significantly, it takes him, for the first time, into an open intertextual dialogue with the specific code of contemporary Chicano literature. The second poem shifts focus, but continues this endeavor by first repeating the cycles-of-history motif, and then using another stock Chicano strategy: overlaying pre-Columbian figures onto contemporary barrio people, ending in an evocation of Alurista through citation when he calls a Chicano "a distant relative/of Aztec warriors." His wind-through-the-barrio poem also reminds one of Alurista. His bad-dude-turned-political-activist rings with an echo of Ricardo Sánchez, while another set of verses contain so many key references to Gary Soto that it is difficult not to read them as a tribute. The specifics of the intertextualities, however interesting, are less important than the general effect of weaving this poetry into the fabric of established Chicano literature that readers knowledgeable in that canon will recognize or at least sense.

Within this context Martín builds his new house, which we cannot avoid reading as a more authentic expression of his soul and art than the first. It is through this last image that we must reread the first section's culminating images to understand the meaning of the book. Martín portrays the new house as his child, and inversely, he is born from it. The symbol is of a self-generating circular flow of energy. Compared to the image of shared childbirth in section one, Baca here offers a disturbingly self-centered and even egotistical birthing, to say nothing of it being strictly male. When we recall that Pablo's birth, at which Martín was present as an assistant, was called a "Fertility dance of women," we can read the building of the house as the fertility dance of men. What is disturbing . . . is that when Baca describes the ultimate act of creating origins—as opposed to tracing biological roots—women are conspicuously absent. If we extend the circle of that act, we find Martín in the company of men, who, in turn, are characterized as social loners and outsiders united in their willingness to help Martín. They are, in fact, representatives of the community that Martín had been recalling during his exile in the Heights, as if once beckoned from silence, the barrio community reciprocates by coming to Martín's rescue. At no point after the fire, however, does the wife or the first son reappear. Martín ventured into this new life alone and remains essentially solitary at the end, even among his peers.

Perhaps history is a cycle of repetitions in which fathers seal their son's fate. While Martín seems quite different from his self-destructive, alcoholic father, in the end he also has abandoned his family, preferring to live among men in a loose community of mavericks. His first son has been erased from his father's contexts, and another, Anto-

nio, is recalled to allow Martín to fix him into a repetition of the motif of the macho horse rider escaping into the distance. Gone is the tight heterosexual intimacy of the closing of the first section. Gabriela, named repeatedly in the verses where she appears to love and reproduce for Martín, becomes the nameless "wife" in section two. The idyllic passion of first love has faded, replaced by the comradery of the all-male work crew. This should not be seen as progress, however, because Baca has Martín define his state before meeting Gabriela as "drifting" and then has him return to it after the burning of the house and the last appearance of his wife. Her role, that of companion and collaborator in the project of home creation, is assumed by men friends. It is as though Martín, or Baca, has replanted a parody of the prison experience in the middle of his self-created utopia, an all-male bastion, but free of society's dictates. Perhaps we are to interpret this to mean that marriage and family are too restrictive. Tied as they are to the image of the first house, we could see them as a forced fitting of Martín's will to live outside the norms into an old mold. Despite the remolding, the shell still imposed conformity, as wife, marriage, and child apparently did also. He breaks with them to free himself from preestablished norms of living, just as he throws away the building plans and improvises the new house with the help of his friends. At the end we are expected to read this as an improvement: "create a better world, a better me,/ out of love. I became a child of the house,/ and it showed me/ the freedom of a new beginning."

The pattern is so traditional as to be archetypal: after the initial euphoria of love, come children, and the lover becomes just mother and wife. Nothing new here, just an old story in populist macho rhetoric. Even Baca's affirmation of freedom from social norms in the self-creating act among buddies is actually another, more insidious norm, that of the macho loner fleeing into his own world. In the end, Baca has replaced the grandfather's horse with Martín's lowrider, the mountain background with the vaulted livingroom, the great expanse of nature with his backyard: a Chicano version of the sublimated American Dream. Updated of course, because, although relegated to a static position, the grandmother was at least remembered.

In the end, Baca's poetry, while seeming to merge with the concerns of the groups discussed above, remains essentially self-centered, personal in an egotistical way. The community, women included, is there for his gratification, as almost everything else in the poetry we have reviewed here. The poetry is personal in that he focuses clearly on his intimate self, caring truly for almost no one else. (pp. 280–86)

Bruce-Novoa, "New Mexican Chicano Poetry: The Contemporary Tradition," in *Pasó por Aquí: Critical Essays on the New Mexican Literary Tradition, 1542–1988*, edited by Erlinda Gonzales–Berry, University of New Mexico Press, 1989, pp. 267–96.

CORDELIA CANDELARIA

(review date 1990)

[In the following excerpt, Chicana essayist and poet Candelaria discusses the presentation of Hispanic culture as well as the treatment of gender in *Martín and Meditations on the South Valley*.]

[*Martín & Meditations* is] strikingly like other Chicano works in concept, theme, and motivation. Like them, it configures America in thoroughly Chicano/a (Latino/a) terms to reach, in this case, a poetic subjectivity that can only, ultimately, be private and self-revealing. *In being so,* however, it makes itself accessible to the reader outside. Just as we encounter, say, Ginsberg or Plath through the stark subjectivity of their words, so too do we apprehend Baca through the directness of his persona, raw, inside his culture.

> Each night I could hear the silver whittling blade
> of La Llorona,
> carving a small child on the muddy river
> bottom. . .
> A voice in me soft as linen
> unfolded on midnight air
> to wipe my loneliness away—the voice blew open
> like a white handkerchief in the night
> embroidered with red roses. . .

The overt reference to the Weeping Woman of Mexican folklore and the embedded allusion to the Virgen de Guadalupe with her mantle of roses—both aching with a child's hurt—locate Martín's self, rebuilding after parental abandonment, within the solid "adobe" reality of "Burque barrios" and the "rock-pit" truth of Quarai, the seventeenth-century mission church ruins now an official state monument of New Mexico. Like the anthology, the poems express their ideas and themes without a concern to translate or dilute them for dominant-culture consumption.

Baca refuses to treat gender thoughtlessly as a category of received meanings and known terms. Intelligent in his approach, he understands gender as a condition that requires fresh contemplation and painstaking treatment if its rendering of men and women is to be as authentic and full as possible. He tries to comprehend the "misery" that made his parents abandon him, leaving him vulnerable as "field prey," and he succeeds in capturing the abject pathos of their self-destructions. In imagining experience from inside their skins and inside those of Caspar the Ghost, *la curandera Feliz,* Grandma Lucero, the *cholos* and *vatos locos* who are his peers, and all the other "real lives in the South Valley," Baca seeks a compelling hon-

esty that means he cannot rely on conventional norms of sex and gender for his language and metaphor. He mostly succeeds, and often brilliantly. Where he doesn't, it is usually in a momentary lapse of diction, not at the profounder level of conceptualization. For example, the word "afterglow" is absolutely wrong to use in description of a girl's sexual molestation, and in the crucial "Quarai" epiphany scene, it struck me as incomplete for Martín not to explicitly express his desire to love others, only his need to be loved, although his desire is implicit in the scene.

All in all, *Martín & Meditations* works superbly:

> I wished I had had a chance to be a little boy. . .
> and wished I had had a family—but these
> were silver inlaid pieces of another man's life
> whose destiny fountained over stones and ivy. . .

> Eddie blew his head off
> playing chicken
> with his brother. Para proof
> he was man. . .
> Don't toll the bell brother,
> 'cus he was not religious. . .
> [but] he saw injustice hanging out en las calles
> sunrise 'til sunset with the bros and sisters.
> [until] you picked up God's blue metal face
> and scattered the seed of your heart
> across the afternoon air. . .

Lines like these etch indelibly in the mind because they have first struck the nerve of feeling. And, like the ruins of Quarai—emblem of Martín's shattered boyhood and, later, of the fire-destroyed house he lovingly rebuilt with his friends—the poems promise to "linger in the air/like a picture/removed/leaves its former presence on the wall," to live in the "warm ashes of memories." (p. 15)

Cordelia Candelaria, "Nerve of Feeling," in *The American Book Review*, Vol. 11, January, 1990, pp. 1, 13, 15.

SESSHU FOSTER

(review date 1990)

[Here, Foster praises Baca for his "heart-rending narrative" of the hero's maturation in *Martín*.]

Martín & Meditations on the South Valley is a solid achievement, a Chicano landmark on the North American literary landscape. Justifiably, this book has been widely praised and its author has received a warm response from readers, audiences and critics alike. Baca was previously known in certain circles as a strong, passionate poet, and this work delivers his tales before even wider audiences. It's about time that a respected literary press such as New

Directions picks up and promotes one of the multitude of fine Latino poets in the U.S., many of whom are currently ignored, unpublished or unpaid because they are not as exotic or famous as Latin American writers who rode the Boom into the offices of corporate publishing in NYC.

Baca himself could have sat on his "laurels" and been satisfied to be known as a contender for the popular and critical admiration which follows, however distantly or detached, poets such as Luis Omar Salinas. But this book shows that Baca is willing to go an extra length, willing to press all his strengths to their limit, willing to risk aesthetic failure and leave the safety of poems that he has already proven that he can write.

Baca could have followed up his *Immigrants in Our Own Land* or *What's Happening* with a similar book of shorter poems, but instead, prompted by an ambitious feeling "that the entire Southwest needed a long poem that could describe what was happening here in the last twenty years," Baca attempted the two epic poems here in this book. With ample space to fail, Baca is actually largely successful in the undertaking; he gives us a full Whitmanesque "democratic vista" of this human landscape. These extended treatments of Baca's themes of oppression and struggle show qualitative advancement, bravely confirming Baca's potent poetics.

"Martín" is a fictionalized autobiography along the lines of Woody Guthrie's *Bound For Glory*. It recounts a hard-won coming of age, human survival against long odds, arriving at a new consciousness. Martín is a "de-tribalized Apache" with a mestizo background, left to raise himself (into/out of) the barrios of New Mexico. Glossaries in the back of the book provide translations of New Mexican caló woven organically throughout the text. Linguistically, then, Martín's environment is brought home in direct and concrete colloquialisms of his people:

> The religious voice of blind Estela Gomez
> Blackened the air one day.
> "92 years mijito. ¿Qué pasó? There were no more
> beans to pick, no crops to load on trains.
> Pinos Wells dried up, como mis manos.
> Everyone moved away to work. I went to Estancia,
> con mi hijo Reynaldo.
> Gavachos de Tejas, we worked for them. Loading
> alfalfa, picking cotton for fifty cents a row.
> yDanny? La borrachera. Y Sheria? La envidia.
> That's what happened, Martín, to your familia."

Martín's father dies like Ira Hayes, frozen stiff in a drunken ditch. Later, Martín is the one who sits at his mother's hospital deathbed, her lifelong absence terminated only by her murder. The account is not merely a superb depiction of life on the New Mexican land, but a vibrant, complete synthesis of popular voices from his past, descriptions of the poor side of the tracks, as well as Martín's inner world. A child, orphaned in real hard times, he serves as allegorical symbol for all those shattered peo-ples who are aliens in their own land. His recollections and deliverance from his past is at once a discovery of his own identity and an identification with his own people.

> de-tribalized Apache
> entangled in the barbwire of a society I do not
>   understand,
> Mejicano blood in me splattering like runoff water
> from a roof canal, glistening over the lives
> who lived before me, like the rain over mounds of
>   broken pottery,
> each day backfills with the brown dirt of my dreams.
> I lived in the streets,
> slept at friends' houses, spooned
> pozole and wiped up the last frijoles with tortilla
> from my plate. Each day
> my hands hurt for something to have,
> and a voice in me yearned to sing,
> and my body wanted to shed the gray skin of streets,
> like a snake that grew wings. . .
> I wished I had a chance to be a little boy,
> and wished a girl loved me,
> and wished I had a family—but these
> were silver inlaid pieces of another man's life. . .

And in similar lines that deliver moving detail after detail, a heart-rending narrative for anyone with the least sense of what it's like for broken families strung out across America's migrant highways since long before *The Grapes of Wrath*, Martín achieves his self-understanding by embracing the experience of his people as a class:

> There were children like me
> all across the world. In the yellowed pages
> of afternoons, while back-yard trash smoldered in
>   barrels,
> and greasy motors hanging on welded tripod pipes
> dripped oil and penned black letters
> on driveway cement,
>   about Johny who married
>   Lorenzo killed in Nam,
>   Eddie in la Pinta,
>   Roman who OD'd in Califas,
> these children once with a dream,
> now grown into adults, let their dream
> dull against the iron hour-files
> of minimum wage jobs,
> emptied their dream
> with each bottle of Tequila drained,
> 'til eventually it lost its cosmic luster.

The triumph of Martín the character as well as "Martín" as a poem is that Baca is able to produce from his own experience of deprivation, imprisonment and oppression, both a true and faithful evocation of the world which shatters the dreams of such young people, as well as a recreation of the rough road and hard struggle taken by someone from that world who never surrenders his dreams, and who in the struggle is able to build himself a life.

"Meditations on the South Valley" pales somewhat in comparison. It is more fragmentary, its poems forming a cycle of briefer duration, and it lacks the intense agony of Martín's childhood. Each of the sections is less integrated in a linear narrative than the sections which make up **"Martín."** Rather than dealing with life or death questions, the balance of moment-by-moment survival and the arrival at a decisive understanding of one's world, **"Meditations on the South Valley"** deals more with the also substantial achievement of learning to live in and love such world. The chracter has come to terms with himself and in **"Meditations on the South Valley"** is building a life with a wife and child, even as (in the first stanzas of the poem) he copes with his home burning down, destroying "10 years of poems/cocooned in pages/unfolding their flaming wings/ in silky smoke/ and fluttered past blackened rafters." While lacking the raw power of the preceding work, **"Meditations on the South Valley"** retains its confirmed evocation of important beginnings. (pp. 114–16)

Sesshu Foster, in a review of *Martín & Meditations on the South Valley*, in *The Americas Review*, Vol. 18, No. 2, Summer, 1990, pp. 114–16.

JIMMY BACA WITH JOHN CRAWFORD AND ANNIE O. EYSTUROY

(interview date 1990)

[Here, Baca discusses his approach to writing and comments on Chicano culture and his experiences as a Mestizo.]

[Crawford]: *How do you feel about the Southwest?*

[Baca]: Our history was so fragmented by colonialism that I have felt mythology was needed, a putting together of everything in a modern sense. If you have a mythology then you have a place; if you don't have a mythology, you ain't got nothing. When I came back from prison, I decided to start writing about things I thought were as old as the earth; and so I started writing **"Martín"** keeping in mind that I wanted to describe my existence in New Mexico. Whether those things are "true" or not is another question. A lot of them are not, but they are true in the sense that I needed something to explain my existence, and I did it best by going through the land and asking it its secrets.

[J.C.]: *At that time in your work it was important?*

It was important because my values are not money or strength; I am not trying to be the strongest person around. My values are pretty much trying to find meaning, why I do something and why I am here. So I started looking into the land and the experience of the people, and trying to write in such a way that it didn't deny the

humanity of Martín. I wanted Martín to be a real human being and let him live in this world and have a mythology that was his as well as the people's. I was trying to take images and, without compromising their mythology, bring them into contemporaneity.

[J.C.]: *But it seems to me you never lost contact with your own origins. They are still here, and you are still here.*

I believe there was a violent, violent attempt by the authorities to bleed the Chicanos and the Indios and the Mestizos of any identity, any cultural remnants. There was a really strong effort at that, a most sophisticated effort. It was not outright "Let's go out and shoot them"; it was, "Let's do it through education, let's do it through religion, let's bleed these people so they haven't got nothing left, so their only alternative is to become who we want them to become," right? And they accomplished that to a certain degree.

[J.C.]: *Did you have this in mind when you started to write about Martín?*

I didn't know anything about Martín at all. I didn't have any premeditated thinking about how it was all to come out, or what the metaphors meant, even really simple metaphors like bell-ropes, for example.

As a child one of the big images you got was bell-ropes swinging all the time in the wind; the pueblos were so lonely that growing up you noticed bell-ropes swinging by themselves. Now, thirty-some years old, I write something and the image comes of the bell-rope swinging in the wind searching for a hand, and it is the searching for a hand that brings the whole mythology together. I find out later that the Pueblo Indians used to have games where they would swing ropes, and it would constitute the image of a song, and whoever grabbed the rope had to sing the song. I learned that only after I had written all this out.

These things are buried in the subconscious; as I was writing a book about a place, I realized that the more you go into your subconscious, the more these things are alive, and all you have to do is bring them forward and have the faith that what you are saying makes sense. My self is a recipient of the Mestizo culture, and that culture is so much embedded in the earth, and the earth is so much embedded in the subconscious, that you can't pull them apart; we are part of the earth, it is part of us.

[Eysturoy]: *So you see the physical landscape and the mythology as very closely connected in the subconscious?*

I think there is an intermarriage such that if it is ever broken then you will be broken. You can have all the mythology you want to learn in your English classes and not have the earth. You have got to find the beating heart of that which is you, and if you are able to find that then you are in business.

[A.E]: *What has sustained the people of the Southwest, do you think?*

Visions. . . I think that Chicano or Mestizo literature from the Southwest is going to become very powerful in the next decade, and it is because there are certain Chicanos and Chicanas who are going through the dark area where those things have been lost; and they ask, "What is Chicano culture?" because they don't know. The challenge is that they have to jump into the abyss, and once they jump, then they become the creators, they become the people who receive what has always been there, what has been lost.

It is not a static thing; you cannot lose something so that it is gone forever. It comes to you in dreams, and that's why I say visions. Visions are probably the biggest impetus toward leaping into the darkness to retrieve the mythology that has been buried by violence and injustice.

[J.C.]: *Has everything been damaged by this other culture that has come in?*

Yes. You know, when universities and foundations fund organizations to go out and accumulate sayings and folklore, you have a folklore that is really superficial and thin. You have fairytales, and if you ask the old people, the majority will say that there is nothing to tell other than "I came from there and nothing was happening." In fact, the destruction was right before their eyes, but they weren't able to see it as destruction. All they were concerned about was having their sons speak English, so they could go to the city and go to school.

Now with this generation, we see a huge empty space that has got to have something in it. It is those people who go into that massive empty space that come back with something. Each writer is doing that in his or her own way, putting the whole thing together and making a literature immensely strong and important for the kids of tomorrow. That is the most essential thing, that the kids are able to read something and say in their blood, "Ah, this is me!"

It is like an epiphany. As a young child, you have a really beautiful experience reading something that you are familiar with, you know. Reading a story about your father and making your father into a figure, a very big figure, as opposed to a sleepy Mexican, the whole thing changes, all the rules change and the authoritarian, colonial way of thinking becomes rubbish, and you become a human being full of pride and integrity.

Visions are very important. I am not talking about visions in a prophetical sense. I am talking about having a beautiful relationship with hummingbirds as a child, you know, and studying them and putting enough faith into that experience to pursue it.

What has been really hard and destructive is that we haven't taken ourselves seriously. We grew up thinking of ourselves as wards. If you are in a mental institution, people put their hands up for pills. You know what I am saying? If you grow up thinking that you are very important, then everything changes.

[J.C.]: *You mentioned the educational system, and one thing I see as a college teacher is that students come into it with a pretty good feeling about themselves, but it is stripped from them in a couple of years unless they are very careful. The institution keeps telling them they are not competent according to its rules. How would you deal with the education of somebody who is in their teens, and not do that to them?*

I think you have to take the person's experience seriously. You have a big responsibility to be open enough to encourage the students first of all—if they are in an English class—to use the language that best describes their experience, and not the experiences of Wordsworth in England; and to have each student reciprocate by giving as much effort as he or she can give to it.

[J.C.]: Then *the problem is going to be that you are going to "marginalize" kids and they are going to stay out of the mainstream culture. It becomes a question of economics, more than anything else.*

It all comes down to the bucks, that's right. I don't give a damn how good you write; if you are starving you are not going to write. So if someone is writing good stuff, the best thing you can do to help them is to find them some money.

[J.C.]: *But if you take them out of the community and stick them in a research place somewhere, you have made them into institutional wards again. You have to enable them to do what they want to do where they are.*

Exactly; you have to "give" them their own environment. But that's a problem not only with Chicanos, but whites and blacks as well. Unfortunately the more you lose yourself, the more accessible you are to the people with the bucks, and the more you are able to compromise, the more they are willing to set you up and give you loads of distinctions. The more you remain who you are, the deeper you stay in your work and your writing, the more they are inclined to ostracize you from their little funds and foundations.

[A.E.]: *Has that been a big problem for you? You have a lot of poems about the economics of writing.*

My experience is that the most essential and important thing in my life is writing, but while I am writing I have to work at different jobs, right? And all these other people are writing, not working, but what they write, in my opinion, is not going to stand up to the sun. It is a speck and it glows for a second and goes out, but they are getting all this money, and I wonder how they do it.

A couple of years ago I found this book on funding, and realized that these people had been spending 95 percent of their time sending off for money while I have been working on poems. So it comes down to access to information. A lot of writers spend their time in libraries getting access to information that will enable them to survive, and that hurts their writing.

[A.E.]: *Where I come from the fisherman is a poet, or the poet is a fisherman. Don't you think it is a fruitful combination to be a worker and a poet?*

I think that's beautiful and extremely important. A lot of writers today have to ask themselves, "How much time am I going to give to writing and how much to living with people or to the antinuclear movement, for example, and how much am I going to subject myself to what's happening in the world?" You can't have your ivory tower and be a good writer; you have got to have your writing hours and your struggle hours. If you begin to sacrifice one or the other, then you're going to really suffer.

I wouldn't be worth a piss if I let my family starve and they suffered because of my writing too much. I have to write, I have to close the door and go out and work, and then come home and be a father and love them and kiss them. You have got to put all that into one day, which makes it really hard.

[A.E.]: *But you also participate in a reality that other people can relate to and are able to put that into your creativity.*

It is very hard, you know. What makes it so difficult is that you go out, like I have done the last couple of days,

spend a good many hours planting trees, and then write a tree-planting poem. That's okay, but the experience of actually sweating and straining and having your back hurt and feeling the earth and watering it and looking at the leaves, that's really life, as the Beatles were saying in that song; life is what you live while you are thinking about what life is.

The thing is not *just* to write a poem, you know. I call it commercial thinking; our minds are accustomed to commercials. We see something for seven minutes, then a commercial comes on; we write a poem for seven minutes and then we stop. A lot of poets and novelists and writers are doing it; their thinking is sequenced to commercials. So I have to go in and write the poem down and then I have to give that poem a day or two or a week, to really get the same heavy experience I got out of actually digging the hole and planting the tree. I want the same sort of depth and breadth in that poem as when I planted the tree. That's what is hard, to slow yourself down. . .

When you begin to deal with language you have to be loyal to the language that speaks for the "we" of the people. I say "we," because I don't take all the credit for it; I simply bring in the information; I bring it all together like a big puzzle, and there it is.

[J.C.]: *It has always struck me in your written work and when you talk that for someone who has been through such hardships you are very optimistic. Not that you don't know there are bad things out there, but the way you deal with it is always at the level of opportunity.*

Let me tell you something about that: I once came out of my cell in the dungeon; I was teaching these guys how to write, and they happened to be "soldiers" of this particular gang. The leaders came down and said that they were going to kill me if I didn't stop teaching their people how to read and write, and I said, "Well, what the heck. . . " So I come up from my shower and there are these two guys walking towards me and both of them have knives. Speaking of being opportunistic, having a bright outlook on life? . . . I look at these two guys and I think, "Holy shit, these two guys are going to kill me," right? So what am I going to do? I look around and there is a wash bucket and I pick it up and run at them with a wash bucket, just like the Apaches would do, my ancestors. I went "Wha. . . " and they took off running. It was not that I was courageous or brave, it was just that you cannot just sit there and let it happen. I was lucky in so many instances, but that's the way I approach life, you know; you do what you do and hope for the best.

But I have fallen through some deep holes, and I am not as disciplined as I should be. What you do is that you try to submit yourself, your humanity, to the very, very edge of the cliff where you think you may be able to fly, but you don't actually jump. And you kind of go there and put yourself there; it is that instinct of wanting to do it and not doing it, purposely reversing it—that is where your humanity is able to be creative. You begin to write knowing that you would love to pick up a gun and go down to the police department and blow some of them executioners away, right? And you carry that with you when you write creatively about peace and love and so forth; you have that in you.

[J.C.]: *I see how "Martín" as a poem fills up creative space for you. What about some of the other work you have been doing in the last few years? How does it satisfy you creatively?*

I don't know. I am not being facetious here or humble, but honestly I don't think I will know how to write until I am forty-five. *Immigrants in Our Own Land* was a passionate try to bring life into a really barren, dead place. It was a weapon against sterility, mental and spiritual and emotional sterility. In some of the other things I write, I run the spectrum of the emotions. *Poems Taken From My Yard* was written in a week; I just sat down because I was tired, I sat down in the kitchen and wrote all these poems out. And it was fun, I enjoyed it, and people enjoy them. "**Martín**" was different. One of the big issues there was that the Chicano experience has been described so much in rural terms. I grew up in a city, a hot, slick kid, and there were millions of people like me who did not have anything to refer to that reflected their experience. So I wanted to write a book that was partly rural, but for the most part incorporated the city experiences, and gave them an element of dignity. You're hanging out by the railroad tracks, but you can have the same dignity as if you were hanging out by the ruins. I wanted to give that dignity back to the people. That is how I approached that.

[A.E.]: *You say somewhere that you write to lure yourself to your inner self, "to the very edge of my eye." Is that still so?*

You know what I do as a habit? I go to my office, I turn on the typewriter, and before I start working on this book I am writing, *The Three Sons of Julia*, I will type five or six poems as a warm-up, pretty much like you warm up your engine. I will look out the window and just start. I can see a leaf and start writing about it; then I'll put it away and start writing about my son's expression last night; and I'll put that away and write about fish. And when I think I am sufficiently past the stage of being *crudo* from sleep, I drop all these poems into a big hole in my desk, and then I start on my *Three Sons of Julia*. It would be interesting if I were to show all these warm-up poems to somebody what they would think of them.

[A.E.]: *When you started writing, was there more a search for yourself, while now you have moved into a different stage?*

Yes, I have found that I work best in book-length poems, as opposed to a single page poem. I don't think you can imagine Whitman working best in a sonnet. A single poem does not fully describe your poetic temperament as opposed to a book. The book may actually be one poem, but you're like a wild pony and need that much space to say it. And it is those poets out in the wilderness, who have to work and who know a woman's cry of birth and so forth, who know that you have to have a lot of space to write a real poem if you want it to reflect who you are or what you are writing about. So it is really difficult to write those small poems.

It all goes back to what your vision is. If your vision is a very small one of making thirty-five thousand a year, teaching three classes a semester, and having enough time to go to the Caribbean, then your writing is going to reflect that; and if your vision is to reach all these people and have them read your book, crying and weeping, then your vision is going to reflect a much deeper, broader sort of book. So it is who you are. And we are in an age where single poems win ten-thousand-dollar awards.

[A.E.]: *Maybe a reflection of the fragmentation of reality that we see in all areas of life?*

I think so. . . . I was in Mexico a couple of weeks ago and I was sitting next to this novelist and he tells me, "I have fifty-two books." And I look at him wondering what I should say, and realize that nothing I have been taught or have experienced has enabled me to answer someone who tells me that he has written fifty-two books. Somehow I cannot see how those people can take their lives seriously; there has to be something missing. They fall into a syndrome where they produce a book a year. It is really destructive, too, because your words become ticker tapes and your mind a computer, and all emotions become ideology; you just send it through the computer and it puts it out on the page.

[J.C.]: *You are very prolific, but you are not thinking in terms of product.*

Yes, I am extremely prolific. Everything I do seems like a rockchip in an Indian ruin, with a question of where it belongs. There is a bigger figure to this; something big is looming in the darkness and these are all the clues. So if I can put all these together, I'll find the great God and He'll show me all the secrets.

[A.E.]: *In your most recent collection of poems, you end by saying that you use every poem to break the shackles on your legs. What are your shackles now?*

What I meant by shackles are those things that hinder creativity, and there are so many things that hinder my creativity it is incredible. I love drinking whiskey with friends until all hours of the night. I love it, you know, and I should be writing, but I am not. I sometimes find that life is too good to write. I mean, why sit around writing? It is the worst thing anybody could do while you are on earth; there are so many other things to do, you can sing, dance, fight. . .

[A.E.]: *But without one you cannot do the other. . .*

That's why writing for me has become a really lonely type of occupation now. It wasn't like that before.

[J.C.]: *When you were in prison, writing would be a way of saving yourself, defining a new identity?*

If I hadn't written in prison, I would still be in prison. . . I had to go back to my tablet and write in order to find a deeper understanding than the immediate satisfaction or gratification.

[A.E.]: *Would you have become a writer if you hadn't gone to prison? Was that experience the catalyst for your creativity?*

Probably.

[J.C.]: *There is also this sense of growth, that this is a new page—I am starting afresh, and I can do what I want.*

You know what I have been experiencing in the last eight, nine years? Learning. I have learned that I didn't know how to be a loving person. I am learning how to get up in the morning and listen to my son. It becomes really sweet when you realize that you have learned what you didn't know. So the process, even as a man, is one of continuous learning.

That's why I have survived, and why the Native Americans and the Chicanos have survived, because we have learned, we haven't stopped learning; even when we don't want to, we learn.

[J.C.]: *You taught yourself a lot about poetry and writing, right?*

Yes, I taught myself everything in writing, and I don't say that arrogantly. Nobody is going to teach you how to write what you see, you know; the only way to learn is to write and write until you are able to come really close to the way you see life.

[J.C.]: *You have a way of saying "seeing" that is unlike ours.*

The way the Indians say "seeing" is how close you can come to the way things really are, the way a deer sees a rock, or the way a frog sees water; we call that "seeing." Every human being has that seeing in them, and someone who gets up and writes every day, all he or she is trying to do is to get close to his or her seeing capabilities; that's where the good poems come, when you are able to see. No class is going to teach you that. Lucy Tapahonso is a good example. Her poetry could not have been written by anyone but her. She sees things and she has to use her Navajo culture and this other culture and the English language. She has to put them together in such a way that is Lucy Tapahonso and only her. She can of course read all the books she likes to, but nothing is going to teach her her own voice.

[J.C.]: *I sometimes think that the best a writing teacher can do is to give you some space and encouragement.*

Encouragement is important, but not *that* important. It's a funny thing, and I have to live with it, but I don't encourage anybody. I say that is good, yes, but I'll say that it is good to a lot of people. But if it is someone I think is really born to be a writer, I won't tell that person whether it is good or bad; I won't say anything to that person, because I think the most valuable experience comes from when the person is left in doubt all the time about his or her work and has to struggle that much harder to prove that what he or she is writing says something.

The minute you tell someone that it is good or bad, it is no good. It's like when you go out there and fast for three days, and whatever you find is yours, and that's real. The same rule should be applied to a writer: go out there and find what you are going to find and then develop it.

What it all boils down to is that anybody can write. You can pick up any magazine in the country and find that the writing is very bland. Everything falls into the same pool. It is like the forest rangers who breed fish to stock the streams. The schools do the same thing; they stock the streams of the literary magazines around the country, you know.

As a reader, almost anything I catch is going to be a simple trout. It is not going to be the beautiful experience of seeing the golden carp flash by your eyes. But that's what a poet wants to see. And when you see that in a poem, then you know that all the effort you put into a poem is worth it. As long as from the unconscious will come that beautiful surge of golden liquid that will make a good poem glow, that's what you want.

The grading system fosters the other kind of fish. All those poems about eight inches, right? They all have certain words like *brown*; and you get really tired of catching eight-inch trout. Creative writing programs are fish hatcheries.

[J.C.]: *You have mentioned the Mestizo a couple of time. How would you define Mestizo culture?*

Half of my family are Apaches, on my father's side; and on my mother's side everybody is Hispanic, European. I haven't read much, but I have heard from friends as I was growing up that a large number of the Mexicans that were living here, or Hispanics—whatever you wish to call them—*really* intermingled with the Indians to a great degree. In the dances they played all their music. The Indians would have their corn dances and it would be the Mexicans playing their accordions and their trumpets. That's the way it was. You couldn't have an event without having both people coming together, and that's who I am.

But if you listen to the historians, you get the idea that these two people really never intermingled. I know for a fact that there are pictures of Mexicans carrying La Virgen of Guadalupe through Indian pueblos, and all the Indians are behind her, and they all go around the pueblo blessing the homes. But they are not willing to accept the fact that we came extremely close to being one people. They do studies to set us really far apart, when all I have heard, and my own memory and so forth, tells me that we really were together.

When the Indians ran from another Apache tribe, they would run to a village that was all Mexicanos, and then when those Apaches came, the Mexicanos and the Indians both ran to another village. Everybody was marrying everybody, and the Indians hate the Mexicans more than they do the whites because we were sleeping in their beds, and they were sleeping in our beds; hatred runs highest in the family, you know. So I think that Mestizo means that we are *deeply* mixed bloods.

[A.E.]: *And you identify with both groups, not saying that you are Chicano or Indian, but both?*

Yes, I am Mestizo. I go up there to the Black Mesa behind us; the Indians go up there, that's their holy mountain—the Isletas—and I go up there with the Isletas; we sit up there and we talk. They tell me what they think of the yucca blossom—there are a lot of yucca blossoms up there—and I tell them what I think about it, and we find out that we both talk about it in the same way, we both see it in the same way. And it comes from that, you know, that we are really close to each other. That is not to say that we are more spiritual than any other ethnic group; that is just to say that that is the way things are.

[J.C.]: *But a lot of your creative work comes out of the ways those cultures are intermingling.*

Very difficult, John, because I cannot ignore the city experience and I can't ignore my Indian ancestry; somehow I have to pull it all together, the ruins and the holy Red Rock there together with the hamburger stand in the barrio.

The English have a way of saying, "Find your voice," and that represents the egotistical sense of the English people. The Native American way is "to see." It does not entail a voice; someone like Black Elk, his seeing was very strong, nothing could boggle it. But the Anglo people always have this aggressive voice thing—"Your voice is very strong in this piece," right?—while the Indians say, "Your seeing is very strong in this piece."

So, right away, if you send an Indian piece to Harper and Row, they are going to say that his voice is not that good, and that's because it is his seeing that's strong and not his voice. How many times have you heard an Indian scream, except on the warpath? They do a lot of their anger through seeing. They look at you, and you know that you'd better get out of here. It's funny. I think that the seeing is a lot stronger than the voice. I know that when my brother got mad at me, I would look at his eyes, and his voice could have been Mary Poppins', but those eyes. . . ! I'd better get out of that room fast. . .

[A.E.]: *So you see your creative process as incorporating all these different aspects of your background, all the* ways of seeing that you do—Chicano, Indian, urban—in your search for your own identity.

Yes. But you know, I think I lost it sometime when I was around eighteen years old. (Laughs) I don't have one personality; I depend so much on writing that whatever I am writing, I go into that personality and I adopt it as my personality. Now I am writing about Julia and I have a lot of feminine thoughts in me now, you know, so that's really who I am.

I know that if I always acted like a father around my kids, my kids would grow up to be monsters. I have to be a kid with them, and sometimes I have to be wrong, and sometimes I have to be stupid. If I was always *the* father, father knows best, I would be crazy and they would be crazy. And my writing is like that. I don't see how I can approach my writing with really hard-core laws; it doesn't work.

[A.E.]: *But that also brings a vitality to your writing in that you are searching all the time. . .*

Yes. If there is anything true, Annie, about me, it is that I am always searching, and that is from a really deepseated insecurity. I am always searching.

It was a survival mechanism for years and years, and a very deep one, too. I knew that without my writing I would not survive. I will never forget when I was in prison, there was a workshop conducted by Richard Shelton and Michael Hogan, who was the poet laureate of all prisoners in America, right? I remember the writing that came out of their workshop was really structured. They were pursuing poetical craft while I in my cell was pursuing survival. And I will never forget when they got hold of one of my poems I had sent to my friend within the prison population who went to the workshop. When it got back to me, the criticism was that it was too romantic, too farfetched, too dreamy. And, really, that's the only thing you have to survive with when you are put in the dungeon, to dream. But I stuck with it and said dreams *do* mean something, and to be romantic and think that you can go across the sea on a canoe does mean something. It says something about the human spirit, that without it is devastating.

[A.E.]: *What do you think you are searching for in* The Three Sons of Julia?

Well, I have an idea that violence and drug addiction is wrong, and I am finding out that these old pieces I wrote fit together really well, but that I need to add a piece about someone who overcomes violence and drug addiction. That is not a search, that's more the *benefit* of searching; you learn how to put things *together* when you are searching for something. I think my searching has taught me to recognize things in their order.

Every barrio, every neighborhood and village has a family of sons. Every neighborhood has a mother without a man who has these three or four sons to nurture, and those sons acquire a reputation of mythological status. "Flaco shot the cops last night," you know, and don't mess with *him*, because Benito below him is another bad dude. It's the Domingo family, or the Redfeather family, or whatever, right? So you have this family, headed by a woman with all these strong kids; and I realize that these pieces that I had written ten years ago, and one that I wrote five years ago, and one I am writing now, all fit together as *The Three Sons of Julia.*

One goes to prison and stays in prison forever; one becomes a drug addict and roams on his motorcycle across the country; and the other one goes to the university, graduates, and becomes a writer. He breaks the violence and the drug addiction, and he does it with integrity and love. And you see, when it is published and goes back to the children and they read it, they don't have to say, "Hey, well, I'm gonna go to prison, you know, like Octavio went to prison," they'll say, "No, Esteban over here, look at what Esteban did, he broke the cycle." So you give them something.

[J.C.]: *This is a book that has had a long gestation, about thirteen years.*

Yes, and I have never been more uncertain about any book in my life than I am about this one. It is very strange after *Martín* going on to get some acclaim, right, that I would try another book and feel so frail in its presence, not knowing what it is. I had thought I would have more confidence . . . but that's how life works.

[J.C.]: *Is there anything else you can think of?*

I'd just say, take the leap into the abyss and uncover some of the mythological artifacts that float around in the mind. The more you fall into that abyss, whether you are a painter or writer or whatever, and the more you are able to come back like a messenger from the land of death, the more you are able to come back with *something*, the more it helps writers like myself to say, "Wow, yeah," and it pushes me forward. (pp. 183–93)

Jimmy Baca, John Crawford, and Annie O. Eysturoy, in an interview in *This Is About Vision: Interviews with Southwestern Writers,* William Balassi, John F. Crawford, Annie O. Eysturoy, eds., University of New Mexico Press, 1990, pp. 181–93.

SCOTT SLOVIC
(review date 1991)

[In the following favorable review of *Black Mesa Poems,* Slovic praises Baca's style, commenting that reading the collection "is an experience at once stirring and soothing."]

Black Mesa Poems is an impressive achievement, at once universal and thoroughly regional, even private. To read Jimmy Santiago Baca's poetry is to tramp across the uneven terrain of human experience, sometimes lulled by the everydayness of work or relationships, and then dazzled by a flood of emotion or vibrant observation.

Baca has a compelling fondness for contrasts. The moods and imagery of entire poems resonate against each other, like a medley of voices echoing in a canyon. One of my favorite pieces in this book is the brief, melancholy sketch called **"Hitchhiker."** Other poems, however, consider life with a mixture of humor and tenderness. **"Since You've Come,"** which was selected for the *Pushcart Prize: Best of the Small Presses 1989,* opens with the exaggerated complaint of an unappreciated parent. But the final couplet, sixteen lines later, expresses the inevitable truth: "We have never loved anyone more than you/ my child."

Poems about friends and family abound in this collection. But the presence of the landscape of Northern New Mexico is equally strong. Details of the natural world are, for the poet, either invigorating or stabilizing, sometimes both. In the poem **"Spring"** he recalls watching new life "swell" above and beside a community irrigation ditch; in **"Picking Piñons"** he receives "murmur[s]" of a "stable world" from a tree. Many of the pieces in *Black Mesa Poems* suggest a fine line between dream and reality; in **"What's Real and What's Not,"** Baca regains contact with the elemental landscape during a two-day camping trip with an "ex-vet Nam grunt": "My singleness glimmers bright,/and my first time from home in months/makes the land glow, the sky bluer,/and the asphalt road/winding to the foothills ignites each nerve into a sacred torch."

"Black Mesa," the penultimate poem of the book, ties together many of the collection's prominent motifs, tracing the congruence between the "northern most U-tip/of Chihuahua desert" and the poet's mind. Baca's poetry itself, like the land which inspires it, is life-sustaining, life-vivifying—it makes life seem "real." Reading *Black Mesa Poems* is an experience at once stirring and soothing. (pp. 180–81)

Scott Slovic, in a review of *Black Mesa Poems,* in *Western American Literature,* Vol. XXVI, No. 2, August, 1991, pp. 180–81.

SOURCES FOR FURTHER STUDY

Krier, Beth Ann. "Baca: A Poet Emerges from Prison of His Past." *The Los Angeles Times* (15 February 1989): Part V, pp. 1, 6–7.

> Presents a sketch of Baca's life and an introduction to his poetry.

Olivares, Julián. "Two Contemporary Chicano Verse Chronicles." *The Americas Review* 16, Nos. 3–4 (Fall-Winter 1988): 214–31.

> Argues that *Martín and Meditations* does not succeed in its goal of describing "what has happened [in the Southwest] in the last twenty years," asserting that it describes instead what happened to Baca himself.

Additional coverage of Baca's life and career is contained in the following sources published by Gale Research: *Contemporary Authors*, Vol. 131; *Dictionary of Literary Biography*, Vol. 122; and *Hispanic Writers*.

Pío Baroja

1872–1956

(Born Pío Baroja y Nessi) Spanish novelist, poet, essayist, and short story writer.

INTRODUCTION

A prolific and imaginative author, Baroja is heralded as modern Spain's leading novelist. While critics generally place him among the "Generation of '98," a group of writers concerned with the social problems of the early twentieth century, Baroja himself disclaimed inclusion in this group. Nevertheless, his novels—*Camino de perfección* (1904), *Zalacaín el aventurero* (1909), *El árbol de la ciencia* (1911; *The Tree of Knowledge*), and others—characteristically discuss the plight of working-class people and expose the injustice, poverty, and hypocrisy that haunts them. Composing in a simple style and employing idiomatic, everyday language, Baroja adopted a cynical and critical view of life in his works, finding little hope for improvement in the future. As Sherman H. Eoff has written, Baroja "is a spokesman of his age and as such a very subjective writer who reveals his intense loneliness. . . . The novelist's outlook, in fact, appears to be an all-inclusive pessimism impregnated with a paralyzing doubt growing out of the scientific and philosophical literature of the nineteenth century."

Born in the Basque coastal city of San Sebastián, Baroja was reared in a family that valued education; his father, a prosperous mining engineer, had an extensive library and introduced his son to such romantic and adventure novelists as Victor Hugo, Honoré de Balzac, and Jules Verne. After moving to Spain's capital, Baroja entered medical school at the University of Madrid in 1887, completing his studies in Valencia four years later. During his medical practice as a village doctor, he began to write short stories set in the Basque provinces. Dissatisfied with medicine, Baroja eventually left the profession to become the administrator of his aunt's bakery in Madrid, where he discovered a stimulating cultural and intellectual atmosphere. Baroja visited Paris in 1898 and there became acquainted with the nagativist philosophy of Friedrich Wilhelm Nietzsche and Arthur Schopenhaur. Having decided to devote himself solely to a literary career, he returned to Madrid and published his short stories as *Vidas sombrías* (1900). They were favorably received by Miguel de Unamuno, Benito Pérez Galdós, and José Azorín—the senior members of the Generation of '98. With their support, Baroja composed his first novel, *La casa de Aizgorri* (1900; *The House of the Aizgorri),* the story of society's purging of a decadent family whose distillery is ravaged by fire. Over the next twelve years Baroja produced several more novels that most critics consider his finest work. Included among these are *Aventuras, inventos y mixtificaciones de Silvestre Paradox* (1901), *La busca* (1904; *The Quest*), *Paradox, rey* (1906; *Paradox, King*), *César o nada* (1910; *Caesar or Nothing*), and *El mundo es ansí* (1912). After 1912 Baroja's novelistic production became more diverse and included autobiographical fiction, historical novels, escapist adventure fiction, as well as several other types. From 1913 to 1935 he devoted his energies to the twenty-two volume *Las memorias de un hombre de acción*, an historical novel about a nineteenth-century romantic involved in Spain's War of Independence against France (1814). In his later years, Baroja became increasingly critical of the warring leftist syndicalists as well as the rightist bureaucratic establishment, often incorporating negative references to both factions in his novels. When agents of the extreme right arrested him during the Spanish Civil War (1936–39), Baroja went into self-imposed exile in France, remaining there until the end of the war. He returned to Madrid in 1940 and spent his final years writing his memories and a collection of poetry entitled *Canciones del suburbio* (1944). Baroja died in Madrid in 1956.

Although Baroja composed in a variety of genres, he favored fiction is which he explored lowlife degradation, social and moral injustice, and hypocrisy. Most of his novels were published as trilogies that expansively convey Baroja's observations of life. His first work, *The House of the Aizgorri*, is part of the trilogy *Tierra vasca,* which surveys Basque culture as it succumbs to vice and industrialization. Also included in the trilogy is *Zalacaín el aventurero,* a narrative that traces the decaying atmosphere of a Basque village in the picaresque style of Golden Age Spain. Among the novels in his trilogy *La vida fantastica, Camino de perfección* features a wandering neurasthenic outcast who discovers that there are no lasting ideals. In *Aurora roja* (1904; *Red Dawn*)— from the trilogy *La lucha por la vida*—Baroja again exposes the hopelessness of idealism and the moral impotence of intellectuals. Likewise, the works of the trilogy *Las ciudades* elucidate Spain's willingness to cooperate with the hypocrisy of the modern world; representative is the novel *El mayorazgo de Labraz* (1903; *The Mayor of Labraz*), which serves as an outstanding example of Baroja's power to depict society's passivity in the face of evil and poverty. Generally regarded as Baroja's greatest novel, *The Tree of Knowledge* is a carefully structured narrative that contemplates life's carnal aspects. The book relates the life of Andrés Hurtado, a physician in search of an ethical system that explains the world's manifold injustices. Unable to achieve sexual satisfaction and an integrated life, he withdraws to a rural community and eventually kills himself. As Beatrice P. Patt has explained, Hurtado's "decision to be conquered by death rather than to be the conqueror is indicative of Baroja's virtually obsessive need to flee rather than to confront, to terminate an unbearable reality by ultimately refusing to deal with it in positive terms."

Critics have described Baroja's novelistic technique as highly personal and individualistic. More concerned with content than form, he eschewed the rhetoric and figures of speech traditionally associated with nineteenth-century Spanish literature, preferring the graphic language of the street. Writing spontaneously and seldom revising his work, Baroja tended towards short, brisk sentences and to the pregnant, precise word. As scholars have observed, Baroja's prose is flat—yet forceful—and lacking a balanced, rhythmical flow. Leo L. Burrow has stated that "the sound of words or their musicality is of no importance to Baroja." Although some have denounced his narratives' rapidity, restlessness, and uneven cadence, others have found these same features their most salient qualities.

Baroja's oeuvre has engendered substantial critical discussion covering a wide range of topics and opinions. Many commentators, such as Salvador de Madariaga, have pointed out that Baroja's novels are episodic and loosely structured, revealing a lack of discipline and disdain for artistry; for some, like Ernest Hemingway, this seeming carelessness is a positive attribute indicating an imaginative and vital temperament. Another major critical concern is Baroja's negativism, particularly in regard to characterization. Scholars have noted that his novels' leading male protagonists— Hurtado, César Moncada, and Silvestre Paradox, for example—are usually depicted as failures or disenchanted outcasts, leading some critics to challenge Baroja's reputation as a keen observer of human nature. Others, however, have praised his insight, acknowledging his characterizations as some of the richest in Spanish literature. Recent Barojan scholarship has focused on a variety of issues, including the novelist's treatment of women, his contempt for social institutions, and his commitment to political change. Commentators today, for the most part, contend that Baroja has been misunderstood as an artist and that his works cannot be easily dismissed as disordered or purposeless. On the contrary, critics applaud his craftsmanship, commending his ability to weave seemingly disparate elements into a cohesive narrative that reveals, in the words of Kenneth G. Eller, Baroja's "philosophy about the nature of existence and about the novel as an art form."

CRITICAL COMMENTARY

SALVADOR DE MADARIAGA
(essay date 1923)

[Madariaga is widely considered Spain's outstanding intellectual figure of the twentieth century and was a prominent diplomat in pre-revolutionary Spain, holding several posts, including that of ambassador to the United States. Trilingual, he wrote plays in Spanish, French, and English, all of which have been praised for their clarity and elegance of style. In the following excerpt, Madariaga evaluates Baroja's realistic approach to the human condition and criticizes his "loose and distracted" novelistic technique.]

[With] the same singlemindedness, the same courage, and the same uncompromising fierceness with which Loyola fought for Christ in the sixteenth century, Pío Baroja, born in the nineteenth century, battles for Truth.

The arms of the Knight of Christ could be either prayer or the sword. The arm of the Knight of Truth is his pen. And the first care of Pío Baroja is to purify his pen from all worldly ambitions. What more worldly than Rhetoric? Baroja fears Rhetoric almost as much as Loyola the Devil. And he takes of the one no less strict a view than Loyola did of the other. He never condescends to please. Not only does he banish from his style all adventitious ornament, but he even refrains from yielding to the slightest of those waverings with which the natural instinct for rhythm and expression tends to animate the curve of form. Not content thus to deprive his works of both painted and natural flowers, he seems almost deliberately to cultivate a graceless delivery, even to the point of ungrammatical slovenliness. He has been accused by unkind, though superficial, critics of ignorance of Spanish. The reasons which explain his careless and formless style are more numerous and deeper. They must be sought in his race, his character, and his absolute, nay, his fanatical devotion to Truth. As a true Basque, Baroja has a peasant nature and finds himself most at home in simple surroundings. He has expressed the attractiveness of refined society in words full of that almost naïve sincerity which is perhaps his main literary asset. . . . [For] Baroja, refinement is on a higher plan than nature, difficult to attain, still more to keep. And thus the carelessness and primitiveness of his style appear at first as the easiest path for a nature poorly gifted with the sense of refinement. This racial characteristic takes in Baroja a certain boorish aspect which is peculiar to his own individual nature. Baroja is a solitary man, and, like most solitary men, he tends to divide the world into two parts: himself, and the rest. Hence an exaggerated, if perhaps unconscious, sense of the importance of his ways and a tendency to strike the world by saying unusually hard things in an unusually hard way. Since the general trend of the Southern mind, which tends to overrule Spanish literature, is towards splendour of form, Baroja will be dry. And since most of us are weak enough to enjoy the implicit flattery which we detect in an author's efforts to please, Baroja will be terribly independent and refuse to smile. Thus, his style is as uncompromising as his matter, and words and sentences are served raw, with a 'take it or leave it' gesture full of an independence bordering on ill temper which is, on the whole, amusing and does no harm to his books. Nor is it possible to pass by this feature of Baroja's work without connecting his contempt for form with that monkish contempt for the world which is so deeply ingrained in the Basque mind. Thus Baroja's style is but the twentieth-century manifestation of a tendency which, in the sixteenth century, would have made his wear a hair shirt and eat stale bread and spinach boiled in water without salt.

Were there none but negative features in his style no one would read him. Yet Baroja is widely read and daily gains ground. This, in so far as style is concerned, is due to the fact that in renouncing most of the attractive methods of the literary art, he has gained a freer scope for the intensity and power of his vision. The result is a writing which for directness and simplicity has no rival in

Principal Works

La casa de Aizgorri (novel) 1900
  [*The House of the Aizgorri*, 1958]

Vidas sombrías (short stories) 1900

Aventuras, inventos y mixtificaciones de Silvestre Paradox (novel) 1901

Camino de perfección (novel) 1902

El mayorazgo de Labraz (novel) 1903
  [*The Lord of Labraz*, 1926]

Aurora roja (novel) 1904
  [*Red Dawn*, 1924]

La busca (novel) 1904
  [*The Quest*, 1922]

Mala hierba (novel) 1904
  [*Weeds*, 1923]

El tablado de Arlequín (essays) 1904

La feria de los discretos (novel) 1905
  [*The City of the Discreet*, 1917]

Paradox, rey (novel) 1906
  [*Paradox, King*, 1931]

Los últimos románticos (novel) 1906

Las tragedias grotescas (novel) 1907

La dama errante (novel) 1908

La ciudad de la niebla (novel) 1909

Zalacaín el aventurero (novel) 1909

César o nada (novel) 1910
  [*Caesar or Nothing*, 1919]

El árbol de la ciencia (novel) 1911
  [*The Tree of Knowledge*, 1928]

Las inquietudes de Shanti Andía (novel) 1911
  [*The Restlessness of Shanti Andía* published in *The Restlessness of Shanti Andía, and Other Writings*, 1959]

El mundo es ansí (novel) 1912

Las memorias de un hombre de acción. 22 vols. (novels) 1913–35

Juventud, egolatría (essays) 1917
  [*Youth and Egolatry*, 1920]

Nuevo tablado de Arléquín (essays) 1917

La sensualidad pervetida (novel) 1920

La leyenda de Juan de Alzate (novel) 1922

El laberinto de las sirenas (novel) 1923

El gran torbellino del mundo (novel) 1926

Las veleidadas de la fortuna (novel) 1926

Los amores tardíos (novel) 1927

Los pilotos de altura (novel) 1929

La estrella del captain Chimista (novel) 1930

Canciones del suburbio (poetry) 1944

Memorias. 6 vols. (autobiography) 1944–49

Obras Completas. 8 vols. (novels, short stories, poetry, and essays) 1946–51

Spain. Baroja merely states. There are whole pages in his novels which are but a succession of facts, noted in short sentences which sound like the steady fall of packets that are being unloaded in a factory. Not the slightest attempt at explaining them, relating them, exploiting them for emotional, critical, or historical purposes within the novel. Things seen and done pass unconnectedly before the eyes of the reader and the tone of the narrator never wavers, never warms up. There is no doubt in all this a scruple for truthfulness. Baroja, the Knight of Truth, fears lest any development of the fact for the sake of aesthetical construction might ultimately destroy the freshness of the first impression. But it must be owned that in this restraint from all further manipulation of the vital fact, there is also a Basque incapacity for following up the promptings of the soul touched by reality, and for grouping them into a system, whether aesthetical or philosophical. Baroja instinctively feels that the Basque soul is at its highest when reacting on an impact from the world. He therefore gives us a quick succession of first impressions and does not allow himself to dwell on any point of reality one second longer than the indispensable minimum to see, feel, and note down. He himself has commented in this incapacity for literary development in a passage typical both for its penetration of the bare fact and for the critical inability of his mind to receive and express it.

> When my critical sense heightens I often think: if I had now to write those books, now that I see their defects, I would not write them. And yet, I go on writing new ones with the same old faults. Shall I ever attain that spiritual ripeness in which the intensity of the impression endures, and yet one can render the expression more perfect? I believe not. Probably, when I arrive at wanting to subtilize (*alambicar*) my expression I shall have nothing to say and I shall keep silent [*Juventud, egolatría*, 1917].

(pp. 112–16)

Realism is generally the healthy reaction of a community against its own tendency to hide away its more unpleasant aspects. It is therefore but natural that eagerness for truth in a novelist should manifest itself in the emphasizing of the sordid side of reality. The picaresque novels and Baroja have this feature in common. Baroja seems to prefer for his subjects the evils which seethe in an atmosphere of destitution. No other Spanish author has dwelt more frequently and insistently on the peculiar aspect which human nature take under the grey twilight ever hovering over the borders of hunger. Hunger and poverty were also familiar subjects with the picaresque authors, but how differently treated! For, though picaresque in many of his subjects, Baroja can hardly be described as such if the mood be considered in which he approaches them. The picaresque authors were wholly indifferent to the ethical aspects of the life they depicted. True, they often overburdened their narrative with sermons suggesting that their only concern in writing of evil things was to show how abhorrent vice really is; but it is doubtful whether these sermons were ever taken at their face value even by the inquisition officials to whose wary eyes they were really directed, and the sermon once over, the story went on gaily and remorselessly. Baroja, on the other hand, is deeply concerned with the ethical monstrosity of the horrors which he illustrates. Nor is his concern due to any hard and fast theory of conduct. On ethics his ideas seem to be as fluid, nay, as confused, as in all other realms of human thought. What troubles him is not sin but suffering. It is the sight of humanity dishonoured by disease, divided by crime and brute authority, left to her weakness, tricked by nature, exposed to the animal shame of hunger.

This aspect of the ugly side of nature seems to haunt Baroja. He sees it with an acuity in which the pitiless genius for observation of the Spanish race is mingled with the professional training of the doctor of medicine. In him, the medical man is ever in company with the novelist. Few men start life with the settled intention of becoming artists, and therefore the number of artists who are trained for a profession is relatively high. The influence of professional training over artists is one of those by-questions of criticism which would repay study. There is little doubt that doctors are handicapped in their artistic development by a scientific training which plunges them so deep in the most material recesses of human nature. The sciences of the body which constitute of ground of all medical education study the physical terminal of human nature, just as the sciences of the spirit—theology, metaphysics, poetry—deal with its spiritual terminals. It is small wonder that doctors should evince a tendency to interpret everything human in terms of bodily phenomena, and when literary men, that they should use their pen as a dissecting knife. One thing doctors cannot do, that is obtain a living synthesis. Thus, a purely professional handicap is added to that natural incapacity for organic work which we have observed in Baroja, while the habit of looking at human miseries with the cool eye of the doctor adds a touch of the hospital clinic to his realism.

This is not, however, a reflection on Baroja's sensibility. Far from being an insensitive man, he is rather a repressed sentimentalist, who refuses to show his feeling, partly from pride, partly from timidity, partly from a self-conscious fear of the ridicule attached to sentiment in a country in which fire is more prized than water. But though not expressed nor even admitted, feeling is there as it were in an undercurrent, or rather in a parallel current. Baroja tells things plainly and coldly, but in a tone which unmistakably comments: 'Now, if you don't think that horrible you are a brute.' Like all men whose feelings are restrained by the fear of losing their liberty in reciprocity—a usual enough situation with ultra-individualists—Baroja bestows the best of his tenderness on such creatures as cannot reciprocate in terms of equality. Hence his love of animals and children. Throughout his work, harm done to children or animals is sharply brought into relief in all its naked repulsiveness with an intensity due to true feeling. But this feature of Baroja's sensibility is linked up with his general attitude towards the world and its evil.

There is in Baroja's latent protest against the sufferings of children and animals a touch of irritation at the irrationality of a world in which such things can happen. It is a mere heightening of his general attitude to all evil, due partly to a sentimental cause—his special solicitude of the victims—partly also to a logical cause—that, in the case of defenceless and innocent victims, the monstrosity and uncalled-for character of evil is most repellent. Here, therefore, we find the earnestness of the Basque mind. In his critical attitude towards the world Baroja is closely akin to Dostoievsky, who seems to have exerted a strong if limited influence over him. This earnestness of his outlook, and the uncompromising way in which he keeps to his level and refuses to waste time on minor matters, constitute the positive element of his art. We go to Baroja knowing that his novels deal with acts and motives that matter. We go to him knowing that, right or wrong, he is sincere, and that no tradition, no prejudice, no social respect will prevail upon his sense of truth.

And yet, having read him with more respect than real pleasure, we come to the conclusion that there is something unsatisfactory about his work. Our first objection may be summed up in one word: disorder. This style, the directness of which we duly value, strikes us as more than merely careless. It is unequal. Here and there tense and fitting closely to the matter, it becomes now and then loose and distracted, vague and uncontrolled by thought. At moments we guess the meaning by the general direction of thought as we guess the aim of a bad hitter by the direction of his eyes. But the words are wide of the mark. Improvisation, a Spanish habit which explains much that is bad and even a little of the good in Spanish literature, is frequently the cause of these lapses of Baroja's style. More often than not his books flow from him 'al correr de la pluma', as the saying goes. But there is in the unevenness of his style something more than mere carelessness and improvisation. It is unequal not only in that it evinces differences of level within the same quality, but in that it results from a mixture of qualities. His general tendency is towards bareness and simplicity. Often, both in his critical works and in the explanatory pages on style and composition which he is wont to insert in the midst of his narratives, he pours contempt on 'rhetoric', by which he means, amongst other really contemptible things, all attempts at raising expression above a mere statement of fact. But he nevertheless allows himself full freedom to forget his theories and so breaks out unexpectedly into such 'rhetorical' pranks as elaborate descriptions of landscape and even pseudo-lyrical flights which he naïvely recommends to the attention of the reader by the simple device of adding a few dots to the paragraph . . . . And thus the mere examination of his style brings us to the conclusion that it is the expression of a mind which has little natural clearness and little also of that acquired clearness which is at bottom that we understand by 'culture'.

Baroja usually speaks of culture in terms of almost awestruck respect which come as a surprise from the pen of so ill-tempered an iconoclast. 'I look upon Ortega y Gasset as the wayfarer who has travelled into the lands of culture. It is a higher step which is difficult to attain and still more difficult to establish oneself on' [*Juventud, egolatría*]. This sentence may be put alongside of the one already quoted, in which he expresses his pleasure in refined society. Needless to say, Baroja is far from being an ignorant man. Not only does he possess the professional knowledge of a doctor of medicine, but he has read widely, scientific as well as philosophic and literary books, both old and new. Yet, despite all this reading, he can hardly be described as a cultured man. There is something in his nature which seems to be as rebellious to culture as it is to refinement. It is probably that same incapacity for following up first inspirations, impressions, thoughts, and weaving them into a complex unity.

A curious feature of his character renders relatively easy the search for lacunae in his powers. There is a pride in him which leads him to minimize or ridicule, or both, whatever force he feels he does not posses. And in his curious antagonism towards France we may perhaps find the root of his refractoriness to culture. France is one of the favourite objects of his scorn. . . . In France, by the action of centuries of refinement, the world is naturally seen in an intellectual order which gives a majesty and a harmony to what otherwise would be a chaos as formless, if as lively, as one of Baroja's novels. This capacity for intellectual vision has been denied Baroja, and the lack of it is apparent not only in the loose texture of his style and in his utter lack of all sense of composition, but also in a certain feeling of helplessness which is never absent from the intellect that has not found its bearings as from the heart that has not found its faith.

For, gallant as are his efforts to impress his read-

ers with the courage of a modern *esprit fort* who dares proclaim his atheism without lifting his arm lest Heaven should fall on his head, Baroja is nevertheless a child, and we can hear his voice tremble whenever he shouts towards the void. His hatred for priests and all kinds of religion can only be compared superficially with that shallow rationalism which the indiscriminate spread of so-called education tends to foster in Spain as elsewhere. It is a hatred with a personal touch in it, a hatred which can be best explained by Unamuno's penetrating remark [in his *El sentimento trágico de la vida;* 1913] that most rationalists, 'possessed by the rage of being unable to believe, fall into the irritation of an *odium antitheologicum*'. Now, this irritation itself belongs to the religious, not to the 'cultural' or scientific order, which of itself is dispassionate and calm. Hence an amusing discord within Baroja's attitude towards religion and its ministers. For while he dismisses the one and the other as vestiges of error and superstition, he does so in a manner which strangely resembles that which it means to disown. But of these contradictions between manner and substance, between thought and the vital texture of thought, the Basque race in general and Baroja in particular, present abundant examples.

Deprived of a religious explanation of the world, Baroja turns to science. He is too intelligent to expect from science an answer to the riddle of the world, but he comes to science because it is made of the very stuff of truth and also because he is proud and feels that in science man is grown up and looks straight in front of him, not upwards, as in religion. There is a book of his— *Paradox, King*—in which he has tried to express in a humorous form this belief in science as the organizing element of the world. Silvestre Paradox, a hero borrowed from one of his earlier novels, is but a transfiguration of Pío Baroja himself. It is, therefore, worth while observing the name chosen by Baroja for his literary double: boorishness is expressed in the Christian name—Silvestre; self-imagined originality in face of a gaping world, in the name—Paradox. Silvestre Paradox, however, deserves his Christian name better than his patronymic, for his ideas could hardly sound paradoxical outside the *Casino Tradicionalista* of Itzea, the village in which Baroja himself, as a terrible atheist, is known by the name of 'The Bad Man'. He is a simple, kindly, boorish, and solitary man, fond of animals and children, who hates all cant and hypocrisy, and believes that is is easier to conquer negroes by showing them the advantages of civilization than by shooting them down under martial law. There is an undercurrent of political criticism, though discreet, irrelevant, in this tale of an expedition to Africa in the course of which a group of Spanish, French, and English adventurers fall into the hands of a cannibal tribe and pass from the chief's larder to high positions of power and authority through sheer superiority of mind and will. This idea of reason as the guiding light of the world of men is expanded by Baroja to embrace all nature, and results in a picture in which every stone, tree, animal, star, man, voices his own point of view. Yet here, in his scientific mood, no less than in his creative capacity, Baroja fails to unite, to make a whole out of his cacophony of separate voices. As a thinker no less than as an artist he remains in the first stage of perception, a recorder of disconnected facts.

On the intellectual side, this feature is due to a lack of what the French call *esprit de suite*. On the creative side, it results from that all-important deficiency in Baroja's character as an artist: his utter lack of lyrical power. Here again, were we not made aware of it on every page by the loveless tone of his writings, Baroja would of himself draw our attention to the week spot by his constant scornful remarks on poetry [in *La busca*, 1904]:

It was. . . the hour in which the poet thinks on immortality, rhyming *wind* with *unkind* and *love* with *dove*.

Such sentences reveal in Baroja an underworld of antipoetical feeling similar to his feelings against religion and against France—three revelations respectively of his lack of poetry, of religion, and of refinement. No Spaniard ever lived farther away from the hearth whereon the fire which gives warmth and glow to all the arts burns in generous flames of love—for love is after all the spirit of poetry and poetry the spirit of all art. Baroja is an excellent illustration of this truth, so often forgotten in criticism, that sensitiveness is not necessarily love. He is genuinely sensitive, not merely aesthetically, but humanly and ethically so. He is, indeed, far more sensitive as a man than as an artist. Yet, he is loveless. His sensitiveness is purely receptive and never results in an outgoing flow of feeling. It adds to his burden of pain—a pain in which the physical and the mental elements predominate over the emotional; but it never brings him any pleasure. His reaction to nature's sights and doings, particularly to those of human nature, is we feel, a kind of shrinking, as of a nerve that is being irritated by an experimenter; never of that expanding quality which is the privilege of great, all-embracing hearts. He carries into his views of love that unfortunate absorption by the physical which is the hallmark of his medical studies and tends to degrade all affection to the level of disease or of vice. His attitude towards women is free and masterful enough when he deals with the lowest types of feminine degradation. But when he attempts to rise higher in the spiritual scale he is awkward, distant, and scornful, with an undercurrent of repressed irritation always ready to burst out into the open. True to his physiological interpretation of man-and-woman love, he seems to incline towards that type of masculine, head-strong woman with which Mr. Bernard Shaw has peopled the contemporary English stage and Tirso before him the stage of the Spanish Golden Century. It is a type which only hopeless sentimentalists can overlook in life, and with which only hopeless sentimentalists can be fascinated to the point of overlooking all others. For it requires all the sentimentalist's secret hatred of love—living love, with its

wars and its peaces, its prides and its humilities—to reduce all love to the level of a Darwinian low. It is this absence of all sense of love, whether human or divine, which dries up the springs of poetry in Baroja. Feeling is there and moves darkly in the recesses of his being. But he will not let go. He is a grown-up man, an Arch-European, believing in reason and no sentiment. And as he thinks more of what he is than of what he would fain feel if only he dared, poetry in him is stillborn.

A curious trilogy of paradoxes, this author of trilogies, this creator of Silvestre Paradox. He is a sentimentalist without love; an 'Arch-European' without culture; a rationalist with a true religious hatred of priests. He gave himself as his high aim a fearless devotion to Truth. Yet, lacking in refinement, in philosophical *esprit de suite*, and in poetical feeling, which are the social, the mental, and the aesthetic avenues towards a synthetic view of life, our uncompromising Knight of Truth is denied the full sight of his Lady's face, and he must remain content to catch whatever glimpses of her he can espy in the by-streets of the world.

Baroja is eminently a *modern* novelist. There was a time when men delighted in works of art and sought in them either the exhilaration of life re-felt and recreated by the power of an emotional spirit or the quiet enjoyment of a harmonious grouping of natural elements selected by a serenely creative mind. Nowadays, art ministers to wholly different wants. We are neither Dionysian nor Apollinian. We are devotees of Minerva. We do not want to feel, we do not want to enjoy. We want to know. We suspect the artist because we feel, and rightly, that he may twist reality to his own ends. Yet we are aware that there is such a thing as aesthetic knowledge, and even that it is probably the most satisfactory of all the ways of knowing. Our ideal approach to reality through our aesthetic sense is therefore by means of a sensitive author lacking constructional power and all sense of development. Such an author is like a physical instrument which we plunge into the depths of human nature, knowing that it will report true. Baroja answers almost perfectly to these requirements. His love of truth thus appears as the functional instinct of a human instrument for measuring life by means of a living sensibility. Baroja is, in fine, a living *biometer*. Such a view of his utility and function as an author ought to commend itself to his love of science. It is at any rate truly Arch-European. (pp. 117–27)

Salvador de Madariaga, "Pío Baroja," in his *The Genius of Spain and Other Essays on Spanish Contemporary Literature*, Oxford at the Clarendon Press, 1923, pp. 111–27.

PÍO BAROJA

(essay date 1925)

[In the essay below, Baroja discusses the modern novel's purpose and the technique of novel writing.]

It is always pleasanter to converse with a woman alone. Although there may not be the slightest suspicion of romance in the conversation, a third person makes a crowd. On the other hand, it is pleasanter to converse with two men than with one. When three men are talking and disputing they supplement each other. Two are not enough to cover a theme comfortably and pleasantly; four are too many. So I always prefer three—what might be called a triangle of friendship.

We three friends had left Madrid in December, and were waiting at a town on the coast of Malaga for some repairs to be made on our motor-car. All three of us were writers, chronic controversialists who loved to debate all kinds of questions. To a person who did not know us we must have seemed very silly people. A person who was familiar with some of our works and had us already catalogued as makers of vain and useless things would have remarked nothing to surprise him in our conversation. Of the three in our party, one was chiefly a writer of philosophical essays, the second a specialist in pedagogical questions, and I almost exclusively a novelist—with or without preludes.

After eating luncheon at an inn we took a stroll along the sea. Our walk led us to a point overlooking the harbor. Below us several little boats were drawn up on the beach. Two or three larger ones with patched sails were moored near the shore. Near by were several yoke of oxen. Sun-bronzed fishermen were going and coming and mending their nets, their yellow and red shirts giving a note of color to the picture.

At the farther end of the harbor, in a little corner between two houses, a group of men and boys was engaged in a favorite local sport, which consists in throwing a stalk of sugar cane into the air and cutting it in two with a knife as it descends.

We should have been highly gratified to be able to make certain observations, and perhaps to compose a few metaphors, on the beauty of the Mediterranean and the mildness of the climate; but as a matter of fact the 'sunny Latin sea' was gray and gloomy—the color of mica under a cloudy sky. It was not a good day for metaphors, and for lack of something better upon which to exercise our wits we returned to the theme that had served us as material for a conversation during the whole trip: What ought a novel to be, and how far is it possible to have a clear, precise, concrete technique for this form of literature?

Whenever we had nothing better to talk about, when we were not arguing over what road to take or whether to stop at the upper or the lower inn, and when we were not busy writing more or less eloquent messages to our friends on picture postal cards, we always reverted to this subject.

For some time I had been mentally preoccupied with the question, not exactly in its general application, but as it applied to my personal work. Unquestionably such a technique is possible in theory, but I do not see that it is equally applicable in practice; or, better said, I do not see its usefulness, for as soon as I try to formulate my ideas on the technique of novel-writing I find they are so few, and so much like trusting to instinct, that they seem disappointingly mearge.

All this did not prevent my two companions and myself from arguing the matter interminably, each insisting on his personal view. Later, when I had leisure to think the matter over alone, I tried to discover if I had learned anything from the conversation that I could apply in a new book I had in mind, and which I planned to call *La nave de los locos*. Although some of my friends will not believe it, I am not set in my ideas. The thought of changing them does not trouble me in the least; quite the reverse, it intrigues me. I have tried every literary device I ever heard of. I have avoided being dogmatic. I have finally come to the conclusion of the pragmatists—that a theory in most cases is valuable more for its results and its future promise than for its possible approximation to truth. I have also regarded literature as a sport, in the sense that it should be disinterested. I have not viewed it in general or in my particular works, from the exclusively personal stand-point. I am always glad to hear criticisms of my books, and only regret that they are not more concrete and detailed. An acute and penetrating critic who will take your book dissect it, point out its defects, and say, 'You have tried to do this, but you did not "put it over," for such and such a reason,' would be one of the greatest helps a writer could have.

To be sure, it is very possible that most of an author's fundamental defects are incorrigible and cannot be cured; but surely there are some that might be remedied. With all our psychological limitations, it ought to give us great pleasure consciously to perfect the children of our brain as much as lies in our power. I have always clung to this illusion, although I have not been able to put the idea into practice.

If I could refine and perfect the work of my pen I should do so, partly perhaps for the sake of the public, but principally for my own sake. I love things in themselves more than for the rewards they bring in money and reputation; and even if a pessimist were able to persuade me that I could be more successful writing poorer books, I should nevertheless make them as good as I was able. I think I should do the same in case of anything that I really loved.

Is there a distinct novel type? That question kept recurring to me whenever, in the course of our discussions, the essayist spoke of the novel as a concrete and well-defined form of literature. I do not think it is. The novel as it exists to-day is multiform, protean, in formation, in fermentation. It tries everything. It may be philosophical or psychological; it may deal with adventure, Utopia, an epic theme—anything whatever. To imagine that there can be a single mould for such an immense variety of things seems to me to show doctrinarism and dogmatism. If the novel were a well-defined class of literature, like the sonnet, it might also have a well-defined technique.

But the novel embraces a great variety of species. The critic who analyzes and understands them never thinks of judging one species by the criteria of another. That would be like judging a Gothic cathedral by the formulas of Greek art. For there are novels that might be compared with melody—many of those of Mérimée, of Turgenev, of Stendhal. There are novels that suggest harmony, like those of Zola, Dostoevskii, and above all Tolstoi. And there is. . . an infinite number of other kinds of novels. If such a thing as a true technique of novel-writing existed, the novel is so multiform that it would necessarily be a multiform technique—there would be as many kinds of technique as there are kinds of novels.

It is conceivably possible to write a clear, limpid, serene, perfectly symmetrical, artistic novel without philosophical disquisitions, dissertations, or psychological analyses, like a Mozart sonata. But it is possible and nothing more, inasmuch as we do not know of any actual novel that approaches this ideal.

I have read somewhere that when everyone was admiring Mozart's *Don Juan* the King or some high personage at the Court said to the musician: 'Your opera is excellent, but there are too many notes in it.' To which the composer replied simply: 'No more than necessary.'

Who could say that of literature? Who could honestly declare that he had said no more or less than was necessary? No one. Neither Homer, not Vergil, nor Shakespeare, nor Cervantes could say that of his writings.

Undoubtedly it is theoretically possible to have this clear, limpid, serene, smiling novel, without the slightest discord or departure from perfect symmetry; but so far we see only its possibility and not the way to realize it.

Although we were to see both the possibility and the way to its attainment, it would not be easy for us writers who began our careers when the apostles of social literature—Tolstoi, Zola, Ibsen, Dostoevskii, and

Nietzsche—were at the apogee of their fame to write clear, limpid, serene, purely artistic works.

Let us assume that there is a free novel something like free verse, and a novel confined within classical canons like verse strictly subservient to the laws of meter and poetic construction. A scoffer would say that the free novel is for rainy days and the other for bright days, but I overlook this facile and frivolous irony. The advantage of the free novel, in dealing with the actual realities of life, is that it saves us from the danger of arteriosclerosis, ossification, and death. It resembles a flowerpot. A porous flowerpot is permeable to all the natural influences that surround it. Its surface becomes covered with moss and lichens. The soil inside it and whatever it planted in it draws vigor and vitality from all the world around it. On the other hand, a glazed jar or vase isolates the plant and its soil from the rest of nature. There is no give and take between what is inside and outside—no endosmosis and exosmosis. Consequently the plant is left a sort of cosmic pauper—to die a victim of rachitis and malnutrition.

Something similar happens in case of the classical and the romantic garden. The classical gardener may exaggerate symmetry and unity, until he produces a garden of stones, vases, and statues, where Nature is scarcely visible except in a timid, emasculate form. One the other hand, if the romantic gardener overdoes naturalness his garden ceases to be a garden and becomes merely a bit of jungle. Limitation is all right as long as it does not produce the impression of something artificial and inexorable. As soon as that point is reached it becomes a tragedy, and in our age an impertinent and grotesque tragedy.

It is natural enough that a young man of the best family in Santander should meet social obstacle to marrying a fisherman's daughter. But it is a little absurd to make these impediments as terrible as they are in one of Pereda's novels, so that they defeat the course of true love and utterly ruin the happiness of two human beings. For after all the world is a little bigger than Santander and its social distinctions, and I imagine that Pereda's young man, no matter how devoted he were to his native town, might prefer to live with the woman of his heart in León, Oviedo, or Ribadeo in preference to marrying a woman he did not love and remaining in Santander. Limitation seems all right to me until it shortens our range of vision to that of a mole; and it should never make it impossible for us to enjoy sometimes the vision of the eagle.

Some time ago a Madrid carpenter named Joaquín, who lived in the street of Magallanes near the deserted cemeteries next to Dehesa de la Villa, was working at my house. This carpenter possesses a professional vocabulary relating to his trade and other trades with which he came in contact that fills me with admiration. If I were a person in authority I should send him to the Spanish Academy to help them on their dictionary. One day Joaquín, while at work, got into an argument with some pastry-cooks, confectioners, and kitchen boys as to the relative advantages of different trades. Finally he dismissed the subject with the heated remark: 'To my mind, a trade where you don't use a rule and measure ain't no trade at all.'

That remark struck me forcibly, and I said to myself: 'Joaquín is right. A trade that does not use a rule and measure is not an exact and proper trade!' Now we must admit that the novelist's trade does not use the rule and measure. In that respect we are on the same level with cooks, pastry-cooks, sausage-makers, and the like, and cannot claim equality with watchmakers, surveyors, mechanics, or even with poets, who have their own meter, although it is not equal to the ten millionth part of the quadrant of the terrestrial meridian. So we are bereft of rule and measure, and probably shall be so throughout eternity. All we can say about our trade is that in order to write novels one must be a novelist—and that is not always enough.

In discussing the technique of the French type of novel Flaubert laid it down as a dogma that the author must be unmoved and impassive, that he must not sympathize with his characters. Is this impartiality and impassivity real? I do not think so. It seems to me very difficult to avoid liking and disliking creatures of your imagination. We can affect indifference, but that is all. One curious trait of Dostoevskii—which, however, I do not attribute especially to his method —is the inconsistency he shows in his liking and disliking of his characters. All of a sudden one of them will seem to have won his affection or to have incurred his disgust. This gives the impression that the author is entirely disconnected with his creations, that they evolved independently of him. That effect, which is ultimately of great artistic value, was not, I imagine, produced by deliberate design, but was a consequence partly of a certain double personality of Dostoevskii himself and partly of the haste with which he wrote.

They also say that an author never ought to speak in his own voice, but only through the mouths of his characters. This is assumed as indisputable. But do not Cervantes, Fielding, Dickens, and Dostoevskii speak in their own voice, interrupting their stories to do so? Does not Carlyle break into his histories with his magnificent sermons? Why may there not be a type of novel in which the author speaks directly so his public, just as the barker speaks for the wax figures inside his show? Some imagine that it is no longer permissible to do this, because the art of novel-writing has been perfected since these men wrote. What simplicity!

A writer, and above all a novelist, possesses a definite stock of sentiment and emotion, which forms his personal capital. We may use the word emotional or sentimental with a derogatory meaning of affectation, of hypersensitiveness. I do not use it here in that sense. This emotional stock-in-trade includes the writer's matured and clarified good and evil instincts, his memories, his successes, his

failures. He lives upon this capital. There comes a time in which it shows signs of exhaustion—whereupon the writer becomes a photographer and a tourist. He sets forth into the world to find something to tell about, simply because he has made telling tales his trade. But henceforth he has no original personal capital to use; he must find his capital outside. Some writers have had a very large emotional stock-in-trade—for instance, Dickens and Dostoevskii. Others were meagrely endowed with it from the first, like Flaubert, Galdós, and even Anatole France. A few—Zola, for instance—were photographers from the beginning, world tourists, but masters in that line. Every novelist, even the most humble, has some personal stock-in-trade of the kind I mention. It is like the mud from which children fashion mud dolls, or like the cloth from which they make the scenery for their puppet shows. Taking myself, I have observed that my stock of sentiment was accumulated during a relatively short period in my childhood and youth—roughly, between my tenth or twelfth and my twenty-second or twenty-third year. At that age everything was transcendental for me. Persons, ideas, things, moody caprices—they all remained indelibly engraved on my character. But as I became older this sensitive receptivity for experiences grew duller and promptly disappeared. My emotions acquired the character of mere passing and more or less agreeable sensations—those of a tourist in life. Now, with my youth thirty years behind me, if I want to revive any profound emotion, I have to go back and try to reconstruct one from the memories of that distant and turbulent epoch. My experiences have for many years arranged themselves in my mind like a collection of photographs—dry prints of a more or less picturesque or humorous kind. That is a symptom of exhaustion, of decadence. I believe that an author's emotional stock-in-trade—associated in case of one with his childhood and youth, in case of another with his native land, in case of another with his love affairs, his studies, or the dangers he has encountered in some great crisis—are what give character to the novelists, are what make him what he is.

What influence would a technique of novel-writing, half-comprehended, vague, largely useless in practice, have upon this emotional capital derived from a thousand obscure experiences, most of them unconscious, in one's past life? I think, little or none.

Accent is everything in a writer, and this accent springs from the depth of his personality. Limpid water will never flow from a muddy pond, or pure breezes come from a fetid marsh. Yet the air that is wafted to us from a meadow of fragrant flowers will be sweeter-scented than all the spices of the Orient.

Someone will say: 'That may all be true. Novelists may employ different materials, but there are definite rules of architecture, for brick, for stone, for adobe.'

One can hardly speak of rules of architecture for a

novel. Every other form of literature, from a sonnet to an oration, has its rules. We cannot conceive a drama without construction, without an argument. We cannot conceive a short story without a plot. But a novel is possible without an argument, without construction, and without a plot. I do not mean to say that there are not novels that can be described as Parnassian. They don't interest me much, but they exist. Each form of novel has its own type of skeleton, and some are characterized precisely by not having any. Biologically they are not vertebrate but invertebrate. The novel in general is like the course of history: it has no beginning and no end; it starts and it stops wherever one wishes. Something like that applies to an epic poem. The authors of *Don Quixote*, the *Odyssey*, the *Romance of the Cid*, or *Pickwick Papers* might add or take away chapters without materially affecting the character of the work itself. To be sure, there are skillful people who know how to impound the current of history and imprison it in great reservoirs. Certain people like that sort of things, while it tires and disgusts others of us.

How can we reconcile the Parnassians and the non-Parnassians—the partisans of classical meter and free-verse enthusiasts? Our natural instincts drive some of us to one extreme and others to the opposite extreme. I do not deny that it is possible to cut a novel to exact pattern like a fashionable dress-coat. . . . But the first thing that troubles me when I contemplate that procedure is the necessity of reducing the number of characters in my book, of picking out certain specific creations of my imagination and excluding all who do not come up to a certain standard. It reminds me of the notices they used to post up at certain dances in Valencia: 'Gentlemen in ponchos not admitted.' I am not fitted by nature to be a floor-master at a dance. To my mind all of my characters, irregular and 'bar-roomy,'—that term was applied to them by a certain reverend Jesuit father,—seem to have their place in my picture. What am I to do? Among my many faults, according to a friend, is that of being an anarchist and an equalitarian, with no eye for social distinctions.

When my travelling companions and I resumed our motor journey I fancied to myself that all my characters, half envisioned, half imagined, were watching my mental vacillation with somewhat anxious faces. In order to reassure them I whispered to myself, while the landscape and the somber sea rolled past my eyes:

> Dear children of my mind, you will all enter, if not into the kingdom of Heaven, at least into my little barque. You will all come aboard, good and bad, those in the poncho and those in the swallowtail, the straight and the crooked alike. The humblest among you shall sit on the right hand of the proudest. We shall laugh to scorn the rhetoricians and the gentry of fashion, the aristocrats and the democrats, the exquisites and the Parnassians, the young sociologists and the whole tribe of literary calligraphers. We shall defy all three of the classical unities. The author will take the floor when-

ever he wants to, whether the occasion seems to demand it or not. Sometimes we shall chant piously the *Tantum ergo,* and at other times we shall roar truculently the *Ça ira.* We shall do whatever the spirit of the moment bids. (pp. 419–24)

Pío Baroja, "On the Making of Novels," in *The Living Age*, Vol. CCCXXV, No. 4220, May 23, 1925, pp. 419–24.

DANIEL M. FRIEDENBERG
(essay date 1956)

[Here, Friedenberg examines Baroja's life and career, describing his novels as both provincial and universal and his writing as "inverted irony, a spiritual isolation, a mocking not at the universe but at man's inability to find complete satisfaction in his own limited goals."]

On October 30 of this year, Pío Baroja, one of the great figures in all Spanish literature, died at the age of 83 in Madrid. The world press obediently devoted its usual half column obituary for the obscurely famous of other lands. In several papers, an earlier judgment was piously quoted: "the best known, the most translated and the least read novelist of contemporary Spain." The readers then turned back to accounts of murder, rapine, hydrogen explosions and mass brutality, subjects of more pressing interest in the 20th Century.

For some of us, however, the death of Pío Baroja y Nessi was both a personal of world tragedy. Baroja, with the exception of "Azorin", was the last great figure of the, 98ers, the tremendously creative generation of Spanish writers born out of the ashes of the collapse of Spanish empire in 1898, the generation which had sworn to redeem Spain and make it a proud member of European society. Benavente, Valle-Inclán, Unamuno, Ortega y Gasset, one by one the patricians of the intellect had died, and only the fossil of former and better times had brooded in Spain, tolerated though disapproved by the present regime. Now he too is dead and, symbolically, the government of Franco has at last completely won.

Pío Baroja was born in 1872 at San Sebastian, the son of a well-to-do Basque engineer. Sent to study medicine, he was suspended three times but finally received his medical degree. Establishing himself as municipal physician in Cestona, a small Basque town where "to occupy the too slow and tedious hours," as he openly admitted later, he began to write short stories. The medical profession was not congenial to his temperament and, after less than two years, he abandoned his position to join a brother as a baker in Madrid.

Anthony Kerrigan on Baroja's literary style:

It is with the element of style with is selectivity that Baroja is most sensitive and most decisive. His dramatic end he achieves by understatement. What he chooses to say is a résumé of the unsaid, and his characters are sketched with the rapidity of a sharp-eyed master draftsman. His visual approach is that of an artist filling his sketchbook. The Madrid books are triumphs of a black and white technique; the Basque books have pages of subtle water color and occasionally the larger composition of a colorist working in oils.

The poetry of his prose is quickened by his pantheistic feeling for nature; there is a Celtic peopling of the forests and water-courses, a druidical awe before trees and rocks. In *Shanti Andía* the Basque coast is alive with titanic struggle and microcosmic forces, and natural description tends toward verse: "The brackish seaweed forms into skeins like long leashes, and bladderwrack and jellyfish shimmer in the sand." Luis Navascués puts into English a line from *Camino de perfección* which typifies Baroja's naturalism: "What a beautiful poem the bishop's body in a peaceful field!"

Anthony Kerrigan, in his "The world of Pío Baroja,"in *The Restlessness of Shanti Andía and Other Writings* by Pío Baroja, University of Michigan Press, 1959.

Shortly thereupon he published at his own expense a group of short stories, in 500 copies, which was received so dismally he took back the unsold volumes and burned them. The seed, however, had taken root. A young fellow-Basque, Miguel de Unamuno, wrote a fine review comparing the work to Poe and Dostoevsky. And, most important, the stories came to the attention of another young man, Martinez Ruiz, later known by the *nom de plume* of Azorin, and the two became fast friends and center of a group of literary rebels. Novels began to pour forth from the pen of Pío Baroja with incredible speed, and in short years his name was celebrated not only in Spain but throughout the world. Yet, driven by inner complusions, constantly writing, always writing—like Dumas, *pére*, he could toss off a novel in a matter of days—he moved in unquiet contemplation, an Iberian vagrant, through the villages and towns of Spain and the cities of Europe.

Free of all money difficulties, contemptuous of the laurels attendant on fame, skeptical of political panaceas, Baroja tried to realize in his own life the ideal of anarchism, perfect individual liberty. But even the most ironic detachment was of no avail in the 20th Century. With the coming of the Spanish Civil War, although not a Republican and outspokenly anti-Communist, he joined the Loyalist cause and almost shared the fate of F. García Lorca. About to be executed after being captured by the Franco forces near Pamplona, he was released at the last moment and escaped across the French border. When the Germans invaded France, he returned voluntarily to Spain, where he lived with a nephew in Madrid until his passing.

The writing of Pío Baroja falls into two periods. Suffering from extreme depression because of the death of a beloved brother from tuberculosis at the age of 23, his first printed matter was his doctoral thesis on "Pain." Life seemed to him meaningless, "man the most disgusting thing on the planet." About this time the collapse of the rotting Spanish empire added an outer object of melancholia to his own native dejection. His earliest novels, perhaps best typified by *Vida sombrías* dealt with outcasts—gamblers, vagrants, suicides—those who couldn't put up with the sterile pattern of small town society. As his natural anarchism hardened through closer contact with the hopeless misery of the Madrid slums, he was drawn to write what many consider his finest work, the trilogy called *La lucha por la vida*, a deeply sympathetic study of the life of the poor, a precursor of the proletarian novel with, however, a pessimistic view and tendency toward exclusive polemic which showed the influence of Zoal. This first period, devoted to the study of vagabonds, broken human beings and outcasts, lasted from approximately 1900 to 1909.

What induced Baroja to abandon the theme of the outcast was his discovery of the personality of his uncle Eugenio Aviraneta, one of those amazing figures thrown up by the turmoil of the early 19th Century. Eugenio Aviraneta had begun as a boy fighting the Napoleonic invaders in 1809. Later he became a Liberal, a Mason and Nationalist, and fought against the Basque traditionalists of his own native province. He went to Greece with Byron and then volunteered for the Mexican wars. Out of nowhere he appeared in Paris at the time of the Revolution of 1830, enthusiastically supporting the Republicans. When civil war broke out in Spain shortly thereafter between the Carlists and the followers of the infant Queen Isabel II, he returned to his native land and was a center of intrigue for the liberals against the Carlist element.

The extraordinary life of this picaresque man, so universally adventurous and yet typically Spanish, acted as a catharsis on Baroja. The dynamism, the life force, which Baroja preached, was more sympathetic to the adventurer than the vagabond; although both were on the margin of society, although both had contempt for the ordinary "moral" man (defined by Baroja as a farce, since either he didn't feel and believe anything or felt and believed insufficiently to act), the adventurer lived for action and thus at least gave his whole being to a vital passion. Baroja devoted a long series of books to his uncle, disguised autobiography more than 'biography' strictly speaking, under the collective title *Memorias de un hombre de acción*. Probably the best known of his picaresque stories in this theme, however, are *Zalacaín el aventurero* and *Las inquietudes de Shanti Andía*.

What is it that distinguishes the novels of Pío Baroja from the many other writers of our century? Why is it that Ortega y Gasset, perhaps the greatest critic of modern times and one given to few compliments, called Baroja "a free and pure man"and claimed he would be read 75 years hence in order to understand Spanish society?

One important reason is the relation of Baroja to his native land. In Spain, a society of primitive economic structure, the available professions are few and hieratic, and the man suffering from imagination and spiritual tension has fewer outlets for his innate talent than in any other Western county. This partly accounts for the explosive and extremist character of Spanish political life. Baroja acutely felt these tensions, the rage and frustration induced by such an anachronistic social system, and sought to picture its life-denying effect. In one sense, Baroja's books might be described as a continual flagellation of Spanish culture, one which forced him to turn to the vagabond and adventurer, the only men who break their bonds in order to find freedom.

But in the largest sense, Baroja, though typically Spanish, is yet universal. His emphasis on action in the development of plot and his distaste with flowery word forms explain the affinity of Baroja with Hemingway, who considered him the greatest modern Spanish writer. What most of all distinguishes Baroja's writing is an inverted irony, a spiritual isolation, a mocking not at the universe but at man's inability to find complete satisfaction in his own limited goals. A certain distance is always perceived between man and his aim; and we are conscious that the personality of the author stands between us and complete absorption in the plot; an ironic and hard type of sentiment which makes us question ourselves and the meaning of our own objectives. The world is in flux, always moving, moving, like the Heraclitean image of fresh waters ever flowing in upon us, and poor little man gropes for a foothold on a river bed forever changing. The same giddiness, a cinematograph of meaningless events tripping one after the other, the essential nihilism to which Nietzsche reacted and which one feels both in Hemingway and Malraux, is seen in a more primitive form in Baroja: only irony prevents it from being channelized into the harbor waters of doctrine. There is no intellectual vision or world purpose; as though man were clipped of his frontal lobes at birth, he wanders through successive unco-ordinated incidents.

Ortega y Gasset claimed that Baroja failed to be a supreme artist by an excessive dispersion of plot and lack of internal unity, and this is true as a classical criticism. Yet, because of this, Baroja's novels are more like life than art. In life we proceed from event to event, meeting and then losing lovers and friends, imagining aims and then discarding them because of timidity or disinterest. Art pretends life is more concentrated, richer, has deeper unity. Baroja prefers to make art life; in this, though he may fail

to be a titanic master, he sees life more truly. It is not out of place to comment that Camilo José Cela, the foremost Spanish writer living in Spain today, uses Baroja's technique. And it is curious to note that the terminal works of Stendhal and Mann, *The Charterhouse of Parma* and *The Confessions of Felix Krull* respectively, approach the world view of Baroja: the gifted charlatan, the adventurer who plays his tricks on the stage of life, posturing ironically in the mirror yet finding enormous pleasure in the mere fact of being alive.

Pío Baroja becomes more and more a paradox as we dip into his personality. His novels preached the life-force, action and human struggle against the sterility of equating value alone with social utility, while the man himself was passive and inclined toward extreme melancholia. His main fictional characters are distinctly anti-intellectual while Baroja in real life liked nothing better than to explore the most abstruse theoretical matter. When I had the good fortune to spend an afternoon with him in Madrid several years ago, he showed me an inscribed photograph of Einstein and told me with great pride of their friendship. There were undoubtedly several Barojas uneasily residing in the same mortal frame, as there were several Einsteins, and one facet of each came together when Einstean made the illuminating Barojian remark at the end of his life that he would have preferred to be a plumber. (pp. 18–20)

Daniel M. Friedenberg, "The Death of a Symbol," in *The New Republic*, Vol.135, No. 23, December 3, 1956, pp.18–20.

BEATRICE P. PATT

(essay date 1971)

[In the following excerpt, Patt surveys Baroja's major works, finding his prolific production "an outstanding example of literary overkill."]

Baroja's first collection of short stories was published in 1900 under the general title of *Vidas sombrías* ("Somber Lives"). (p. 78)

As the title suggests, *Somber Lives* is a melancholy book, full of delicate feeling poetically expressed. The concern of the Generation of 1898 for everyday life, for the enduring traditions of the humble people, in short, for "infrahistory," is particularly apparent in this collection. The vein of tenderness in Baroja, which diminished with the passage of time and with the concomitant acquisition of many opinions, is at its freshest and most poignant in this youthful work.

La casa de Aizgorri (*The House of Aizgorri*), published in the same year as *Somber Lives*, stands somewhat apart from the mainstream of the author's production in both form and content. At first conceived as a play, it is in effect a novel in dialogue form. (pp. 80–1)

It is the derivative nature of the work that both sets it apart from the bulk of Baroja's production and links it with some of the pieces in *Somber Lives*. The idea of the hereditary taint owes much to Ibsen and [the author of *Degeneration*, Max] Nordau and the sharp line of demarcation between the symbols of good and evil recall the stylized, rhetorical dramas of the nineteenth century. Everything is clear in *The House of Aizgorri*, there are no ambiguities, there is no greyness. (p. 81)

Similar in ethical intent is *El mayorazgo de Labraz* (*The Lord of Labraz*), published three years later. *The Lord of Labraz* is a somber novel, medieval in atmosphere, and romantic is spirit. Baroja had gone to Labraz, a decrepit and moribund *pueblo terrible* because its lugubrious atmosphere was in keeping with his anguished spirit, deeply saddened by "the destruction of [my] romantic illusions." Availing himself of an old and respectable fictional device, Baroja states that his novel is merely a transcription of a fantasy imagined by the Englishman Mister Samuel Bothwell Crawford. Mister Bothwell, as he is usually designated in the novel, therefore plays the dual role of playwright and actor, mirroring the double role often played by Baroja. When Bothwell begins to express the author's opinions, the reader is introduced into a hall of mirrors. (pp. 81–2)

It is evident that Baroja's view of mankind made it relatively easy for him to depict collective evil and vice, but what he fails to do in this novel is to portray evil successfully in an individualized fashion. . . . The evil that the author sees is a characteristic of the generic *homo sapiens*, for nowhere are there concrete, full-scale villains, capable of overflowing a page and filling a book. (p. 83)

The romantic nature of *The Lord of Labraz* places the work at the head of a long line of rather melodramatic novels of fantasy produced by Baroja over his long life-span. In works of this type of critical note becomes attenuated over the years while the melodrama is noticeably accentuated. . . .

Between *The House of Aizgorri* and *The Lord of Labraz*, neither of which is distinguished for its originality, Baroja wrote *Aventuras, inventos y mixtificaciones de Silvestre Paradox* (*Adventures, Inventions and Hoaxes of Silvestre Paradox*), the first novel that can be labelled, *a posteriori*, genuinely Barojian. In the *Adventures*. . . , published in 1901, Baroja finds his authentic style, and the texture and tone are as unmistakably his in this early work as they are in [*El árbol de la ciencia* (*The Tree of Knowledge*)] or [*La sensualidad pervertida* (*Sublimated Sensuality*)]. (p. 84)

With the publication of [*Camino de perfección* (*The Way to Perfection*)] in 1902, Baroja emerges as a serious novelist-critic, joining Azorín as spokesman for the Generation of 1898. The vitriolic tone is an augury of the sharply critical novels and essays yet to come, and the central themes reflect the readings and synthesize the preoccupations of his cogenerationists. (p. 88)

The style of the novel is alternately lyrical and strident; while the landscapes of Spain, sometimes radiant, sometimes grim, are painted with the delicate brush of the impressionist, the institutions of Spain are probed with a merciless scalpel. With its harsh social criticism and its portrayal of a fundamentally flawed protagonist, *The Way to Perfection* takes its place next to Azoríns *La Voluntad* as one of the earliest authentic literary manifestations of the temper of the Generation of 1898, but does not fully indicate the path that Baroja was later to follow with such consistency in his major works. The progression from the representation of a partial alter ego, as exemplified by Silvestre Paradox and Dr. Labarta in 1901, is irregular and full of gaps; the free utilization by the author of Nordau and Nietzsche in the delineation of Ossorio's personality indicates strongly that the latter is not a link in the progression.

La lucha por la vida (*The Struggle for Life*) is the trilogy published in 1904 which earned for its author the Orteguian designation *el Homero de la canalla* ("the Homer of the rabble"). In [*La busca* (*The Quest*) and *Mala hierba* (*Weeds*)], the first two novels of the series, the writer becomes the photographer and poet of the slums of Madrid; thieves and prostitutes, murderers and Don Juans, confidence men and degenerates, the hungry and the needy, crowd the pages of a work dedicated to the exploration of all the manifestations of abject misery that an urban center can produce. The wind and the cold, the rain and the snow are chronicled with the precision of a meteorological report, and the teeming sublife of Madrid at night and by day is observed and catalogued with the zeal of a scientist. Baroja has called both novels a copy from nature, with antecedents in the Spanish picaresque novel, in Dickens, the Russians, and in French serial literature of the *bas fonds* (lower depth). (pp. 93–4)

The whole of *The Struggle for Life* is in fact an illustration of Goethe's statement that reality has more genius than invention. Baroja paints observed details and creates multitudes of rapid vignettes; the total number of figures in the three novels is enormous and the variety of episodes and subplots makes a detailed summary extremely lengthy. If the vision of *The Struggle for Life* is Goyesque, the execution is by Breughel. (p. 96)

Baroja's view throughout the work is compassionate and humane, yet at the same time puritanical in its insistence on morality, work, and steadfastness. For all its crude realism, the note of sentimentality is not absent. . . . Baroja is not yet ready to follow his own thinking to its logical conclusion but seeks, however artificially, to mitigate the consequences of his apparent nihilism. . . .

One year after the publication of *The Struggle for Life*, the puritanical collector of specimens from the lower depths again takes up the cudgels in defense of morality and decency. In [*La feria de los discretos* (*The School for Rogues*)] what has been implicit all along is now explicit: paradise is reserved for the pure in heart. (pp. 96–7)

The mystery surrounding the hero's origin as well as the proliferation of subplots and episodes involving gambling, kidnapping, the robbery, *inter alia*, make the association with serialized novels inevitable and give the reader the uneasy feeling that he has inadvertently stumbled into a theater specializing in plays of the Romantic era. (p. 98)

Paradox, Rey (*Paradox, King*), which followed the *Adventures*. . . after a period of five years, is a sequel only in the sense that Silvestre Paradox and Don Avelino again figure prominently in the plot. *Paradox, King* like *The House of Aizgorri*, is a dialogued novel, a form Baroja used infrequently but with considerable skill. (pp. 98–9)

Baroja classifies *Paradox, King* as half-fantasy, half-satirical poem and it is in this work, particularly, that his formidable comic talents are most apparent. The arthritic, the author informs his readers, is timid and melancholy, ill-tempered and hypochondriacal, but ". . . comedy often emerges in the midst of ill temper." The misanthropy in *Paradox, King* is obviously of the jovial type described by Escobedo in *The School for Rogues*. The opportunity to feel *robinsoniano* (like Robinson Crusoe) fills Baroja with youthful cheer and vitality, and it is this vigor that gives to the work its bright ebullience.

Los últimos románticos (*The Last Romantics*) and *Las tragedias grotescas* (*Grotesque Tragedies*), published in 1906 and 1907 respectively, reveal in a more convincing manner than *The School for Rogues* the author's consuming interest in nineteenth-century history. . . . In accordance with his belief that only relatively recent history can be recreated with any sense of reality and vividness, Baroja sets both novels in Paris in the last years of the Second Empire. The materialism, vanity, and corruption as well as the revolutionary fervor of the era are conveyed through the descriptions of the amatory escapades and the political involvements of a group of French aristocrats, Spanish émigrés, and miscellaneous adventurers and idealists. (pp. 100–01)

Some of the non-historical aspects of the two novels again reveal Baroja's love for romantic fiction: a letter, a picture, blackmail, discoveries of hidden identities, the claiming of a fortune, still mar the author's plots. The valuable aspects of the work lie in the sensitive descriptions of the old and picturesque Paris and in the evocations of the Spanish émigrés living in that city in the 1860's. (pp. 101–02)

The recent past rather than the nineteenth century supplies the material for *La dama errante* (*The Wandering Lady*) and *La ciudad de la niebla* (*The City of Fog*), published in 1908 and 1909 subsequent to a visit to London. . . .

[*The Wandering Lady*] is in many respects a travel book of the variety cultivated first by Azorín and Unamuno and later by Ortega and Cela, the plot merely serving as a pretext for the evocation of landscape and incident. (p. 103)

The City of Fog is the London novel for which *The Wandering Lady* was the preparation. . . .

The discursive tone that is usually associated with the Barojian novel is more in evidence in these two novels than in the previous works. (p. 104)

The Paris novels and *The City of Fog*, in particular, are of greater interest for their atmosphere than for their ideological content, and the poet is for more persuasive than the social critic. The Madrid, Paris, and London novels are antivalentines, loving evocations of the abject and dismal as well as of the romantic and the picturesque; the authentic valentine can be addressed only to the Basque countryside and to its heroes. . . . [*Zalacaín el aventurero* (*Zalacaín the Adventurer*)] found great favor both in Spain and abroad, and was considered by Baroja to be one of his best novels. The popularity of *Zalacaín* may have done much to bring the name of the author to the public, but its merit lies less in its intrinsic excellence than in its interest as a rehearsal for the Aviraneta series. (p. 105)

Zalacaín is the most objective of Baroja's early novels and it is his only extended work that is truly redolent of youth. Basque songs are interpolated into the text, and Baroja's almost Cervantine custom of including independent narrative sometimes yields surprisingly happy results. (p. 106)

Baroja decided to compose a work with a modern setting, but with reminiscences of the Borgia type; [*César o nada* (*Caesar or Nothing*)], which was published in 1910 after having appeared serially in *El Radical*, was the result. Aside from its function as a surrogate historical novel, *Caesar or Nothing* is also the reflection of the author's first serious brush with politics, for it was in 1909 that Baroja ran unsuccessfully for municipal councilman. . . . (p. 107)

Baroja's ambiguous portrayal of Moncada has given rise to contradictory interpretations. Gonzalo Sobejano considers Moncada *el hombre de acción que más cerca está de la Voluntad nietzscheana*. . . ("the man of action who comes closest to the Nietzschean Will. . .") while Sherman Eoff considers *Caesar or Nothing* to go counter to Nietzsche's aggressive egoism, for César ". . . attempts self-glorification in a Machiavellian way and is made to know. . . the futility of his ego." Moncada's dual nature. . . accommodates either interpretation.

The *Adventures, The Way to Perfection,* and *Caesar or Nothing* can be regarded as Baroja's modern reworking of the medieval debate between water and wine, between carnality and self-denial. The elements of the modern debate have been transformed and the new struggle is acted out between affirmation and negation, between vitality and passivity, between life-giving and life-destroying tendencies. To the so-far uncommitted author, neither side appears to win and the contest ends in a draw. . . .

Las inquietudes de Shanti Andía (*The Restlessness of Shanti Andía*) made its appearance one year after publication of *Caesar or Nothing,* and on the surface at least, it is difficult to conceive of two more widely differing novels. (p. 110)

Baroja could have said with Faust *zwei Seelen wohnen, ach! in meiner Brust* "two souls are housed, alas, in my breast"). One of Baroja's tendencies is dynamic and restless, craving constant movement; the innumerable adventures in *Zalacaín* and *The Restlessness of Shanti Andía* and the veritable shower of episodes in *The Struggle for Life* fulfill this need. The other tendency, contemplative and philosophical, lies just below the surface, a variety of figured bass. All is vanity, the author whispers, all effort and life itself are futile. In *The Restlessness of Shanti Andía* the novelist seeks once again to mitigate the consequences of his lucid pessimism. . . . The conflict between affirmation and negation remains unresolved.

The closing lines of the novel, "But there was something of the precursor in him" although far from explicit, have the effect of mitigating the tragedy of Hurtado's death. The latter can be considered a precursor to the extent that he prefigures the new man who will be capable of both contemplation and action, who will be able to sustain his vitality and exercise his will despite his knowledge, despite his awareness of the precarious nature of existence. In a reminiscence of Zarathustra, Baroja implies that what is not fulfilled in the present will be fulfilled in the future: the new man will affirm life in the face of death. He will be, in short, the existentialist hero. (p. 116)

The Tree of Knowledge is Baroja's most authentic novel because it is his least contrived; invention is subordinated to reality with respect to atmosphere, incident, and character. Nothing was ever to be more vivid to the author than the year of his youth, and the inclusion in the novel of many real characters recollected from his student days is indicative of Baroja's reluctance, not to say refusal, to sever the link with his earlier self. (p. 117)

The purely autobiographical character of many aspects of the novel accounts for its dense atmosphere of emotion recollected and incident relived, but it is the principal character who gives *The Tree of Knowledge* its never-to-be-repeated vitality. Andrés Hurtado is perhaps

Baroja's only fully realized fictional protagonist; he lives, he suffers, and he changes, responding to his environment with the sensitivity of a finely-tuned instrument. Paradoxically, it is his role as Baroja's mirror that gives him his authenticity and freedom. As the author unwinds the film of his earlier life, Andrés is on each successive frame, appearing to have no prior identity, but observed in the process of becoming. It is this becoming that gives to Hurtado his particular flesh-and-blood quality, a quality noticeably absent from most of the novelist's main characters. Hurtado has what Ortega called a *quehacer vital* (a vital task), and the content of his life is the attempted fulfillment of this *quehacer.* The fact that the task itself is more of a beginning than an end does not diminish its value: the search for an acceptable method of confronting the world is the proper occupation of the philosopher. Where Hurtado failed, others would succeed. (p. 120)

The episodes included in [*El mundo es ansí* (*The Way of the World*)] belong to a somewhat older Baroja, the man in his thirties who was less affected by what he saw and what he did. . . .

If this particular novel does not appear to have fully engaged either Baroja's mind or sentiments, a further cause may be sought in his involvement with the figure of Aviraneta. It was in 1911 that the novelist became interested in the somewhat shadowy figure of this distant relative and began to do some research with a view of devoting a chapter to him. This short piece ultimately expanded into the twenty-two volumes that make up the Aviraneta series [*Las memorias de un hombre de acción* (*Memoirs of a Man of Action*)]. (p. 125)

The ubiquitous Aviraneta, by virtue of a long life that stretched from the War of Independence to within a year of the establishment of the First Republic, and by virtue of his blood relationship to Baroja, was admirably suited to the author's needs. . . .

Baroja's novels in the Aviraneta series constitute "imaginary reportage" rather than completely accurate history, hence the freedom of the novelist to invent and reinvent. Baroja's insistence on the rôle of the imagination should not, however, lead the reader to false conclusions. He consulted whatever historical documents were available to him as is evident from his accounts in the prologue to *Aviraneta, o la vida de un conspirador* (*Aviraneta, or the Life of a Conspirator*) and in the *Memoirs.* (p. 126)

In Aviraneta there is more restlessness than striving, less will to power than indiscriminate political dabbling. Aviraneta, like his presumed opposite José Larrañaga, goes out with more of a whimper than a bang. Maravall has called Baroja a novelist of the *élan vital,* but this élan belongs to virtually every aspect of the *Memoirs of a Man of Action* with the exception of Aviraneta. The interference of the author's temperament and, to a lesser degree, his experiences, makes of the archadventurer a figure smaller than life. (p. 128)

Aviraneta weaves in an out of the novels in his long series, sometimes all but forgotten in the mass of details on battles, conspiracies, Freemasonry, and royal scandals. Secondary plots abound, and hundreds of characters sail briefly into the reader's field of vision, soon to disappear without a trace. At the end of the last volume, *Desde el principio hasta el fin* (*From the Beginning to the End*), Baroja take leave of Aviraneta as his fellow countryman and "coreligionist in liberalism, individualism, and in a somewhat unfortunate life." The violence that underlies the series proceeds from the events themselves and the collision of opposing forces, with Aviraneta's voice often drowned by the clashing cymbals and thounderous drum rolls of his heroic symphony. (p. 134)

Between 1917, by which time six volumes of the Aviraneta series had appeared, and 1919, when three more had been written, Baroja published several collections of essays: *Juventud, egolatría* (*Youth, Egolatry*) and *Nuevo tablado de Arlequín* (*New Harlequinade*), . . . *Las horas solitarias* (*Solitary Hours*). . . , and *Momentum catastrophicum* (*Time of Crisis*) and *La caverna del humorismo* (*The Grotto of Humor*). . . . The shift from the personal narrative to the form of the essay is, in reality, scarcely perceptible. Baroja's fictions often resemble essays and vice versa. . . . (pp. 134–35)

The Tree of Knowledge and *Sublimated Sensuality* together provide Baroja's intellectual and sentimental biography up to 1920. That Baroja had finally reached a *modus vivendi* with himself is evident in the shift from Hurtado's anguished rejection of life to Murguía's half-willing acceptance. He lacks, to use Machado's phrase, "physiological joy," but his self-characterization as "a rotted fruit on the tree of life" is too highly colored. Murguía is not a brilliant social success, surely, yet he is less a failure than he would like to believe. There is a disparity between Murguía's behavior, which is not particularly striking for its outlandishness, and his theorizing about himself. He is not quite the misfit he declares he is. In comparison with Andrés Hurtado, he is almost a social butterfly and Hurtado did not become a semi-hermit until the latter part of his life. Baroja surrounds Murguía with his now-familiar philosophical ideas, but this protagonist is not easily drowned in literature. The faun, the satyr, still peers out from the side of the vase. (p. 143)

[*El laberinto de las sirenas* (*The Labyrinth of the Sirens*)] is a purely visual book, a work of the imagination rather than of the intellect. The sea, the weather, the changing light are painted with the delicacy of the artist's brush, and the author's facility for detailed description is given the freest possible rein. Baroja's artistic sensibility, often submerged under a wealth of ideological digressions in so many of the other works, here holds sway, and is perhaps the only *raison d'être* of the novel.

The Labyrinth of the Sirens apparently did not displease Baroja entirely, for in **"Ciudades de Italia"** (**"Cities of Italy"**) he diffidently suggests that some aspects of the novel may not be "entirely bad." It seems ungrateful to disagree with so modest a judgement. (pp. 144–45)

The nostalgia for a world where adventure replaces ratiocination and where unreality can be lavishly embroidered with rich detail holds Baroja in its iron grasp even during the years of the Spanish Civil War and the ensuing World War, as evidenced by a collection of four stories written between 1928 and 1941 and published under the general title of *Los impostores joviales* (*The Jovial Imposters*). (p. 146)

[*El cura de Monleón* (*The Curate of Monleón*)] is both the story of the priest Javier Olarán and an historical survey of Christianity. . . . The loss of faith or the struggle to believe achieves the dimensions of tragedy in the hands of Unamuno, but when Baroja takes up the theme he is floundering in uncharted waters. The failure to give solidity to . . . Javier is the measure of Baroja's radical incapacity to so much as imagine the agonies that doubt and incredulity inflict on the truly religious; the dark night of the soul is as alien to the author as a sustained period of exhilarating exuberance. (pp. 152–53)

[*Intermedios* (*Intermezzi*)] provides excellent illustrations of the short sketch that was Baroja's specialty; bohemians, eccentrics, imposters, anarchists, and mystics pass in rapid succession, some receiving the benefit of only a short but vivid paragraph. Reminiscences, anecdotes, observations on literary topics, even playlets, round out the exceedingly heterogeneous collection. (p. 157)

[The *Vitrina pintoresca* (*Picturesque Showcase*)] touches on a variety of topics including hangmen, beggars, Jesuits, Freemasons, and Jews; an essay on the rivers of Spain is followed by a "travellers' bestiary" as the concrete and the abstract, the past and the present, history and folklore occupy the author's restless attention. One essay, entitled **"Epigrafía callejera"** (**"Street Signs"**), represents Baroja at his humorous best, while the pieces on carnivals, fairs, and the old streets of Madrid once again reveal Baroja's love for the outlandish and the mysterious.

The essay **"Nuestra juventud"** (**"Our Youth"**) is a self-interview which casts an interesting light on the nature of the author's true tastes. . . .

Juan Uribe Echevarría uses the apt designation of *microensayismo* ("microessayism") to describe the special nature of the Barojian essay. This "microessay", with its opportunities for the quick rendition of impression or the synthetic imparting of information, is Baroja's most authentic genre. What is chaos in a novel is diversity in the essay, and the movement and change that are so often unmotivated in the works of fiction are fully justified in collections that do not pretend to unity or harmony. (p. 158)

[*Susana*] exemplifies what must finally be called the impermeability of the author, the radical inability to reflect the outer world without at the same time casting his own shadow. The badly articulated plot of *Susana* purportedly concerns the ill-fated love of Miguel Salazar for the Susana of the title, and the details need not detain the serious reader. (pp. 158–59)

[It] might be more accurate to consider *Susana* less of a joke than the visible and concrete evidence of failing powers and flagging resources. (p. 159)

The complete works of Baroja are a chronicle of the author's times, the concrete evidence of a talent that is primarily reportorial. That the sum is greater than the parts is beyond question, although the difficulty of reading the collected works is not to be underestimated. The sensation of *déjà vu* is at times overpowering, for the totality of Baroja's production is an outstanding example of literary overkill.

Camilo José Cela, one of Spain's most prominent contemporary literary figures, has affirmed that Baroja opened the doors to *una España novelesca*, revealing the infinite possibilities of the novelistic art: . . . *de Baroja sale toda la novela española a él posterior* ("the entire Spanish novel after Baroja stems from him"). (p. 171)

Beatrice P. Patt, in her *Pío Baroja*, Twayne, 1971, 208 p.

KENNETH G. ELLER

(essay date 1984)

[In the excerpt below, Eller refutes the charge that Baroja was a misogynist by examining the author's propitious depiction of women in several novels.]

Most analytical studies of people in Baroja's novels have focused principally on his male characters. Relatively little attention has been paid to women, even though women do play a major role in many of his works. In fact, a woman is the protagonist of each of the following novels: *El mundo es ansí* ("Sacha Savarof"), *La dama errante* and *La ciudad de la niebla* ("María Aracil"), *Los últimos romanticos* (Blanca de Montville), and *Laura o la soledad sin remedio* (Laura Golowin). Many critics, noting that Baroja never married, included few romances in his novels, and made some of his women characters evil and villainous, believe that the author disliked the opposite sex and was probably even a misogynist.

Only a few scholars have felt that Baroja regarded women as positive factors in his life and works. But a close look at the principal female characters in his novels will reveal that women are for the most part treated favorably

and that, based on his treatment of them in his novels, there is little evidence to justify the frequent assertion that Baroja was in fact a misogynist. As the topic of women as a positive aspect in Baroja's novels has largely been ignored, I will in this study identify numerous principal women characters and attempt to show how and why they are treated favorably and how they are different or similar to some of his well-known male characters. The study will give—it is hoped—some additional perspectives on Baroja's views on women and his use of them in his creative process.

Of the major female characters in Baroja's novels none is treated more favorably than María Aracil, the main character of *La dama errante* and *La ciudad de la niebla*. Baroja begins *La dama errante* with an essay in which he explains explicitly how María's basic character has been formed and at the same time expresses his opinions about the educational system of Spain and Spanish society and its rôle in the development of a woman's personality. In Spain, he claims, children are not allowed to act like children. Social pressures applied by parents, servants, teachers, and the government all require them to behave like adults. Consequently, their spirit, their enthusiasm for life, and their natural instinctive impulses are suppressed and they become insincere, hypocritical, perverted, and warped.

He is particularly critical of schools because girls are not permitted to have physical exercise and are forced to learn "stupid abstractions", which makes them "hysterical", "mystical", and "disoriented". But María Aracil is educated by her grandmother and is not burdened with abstract studies at an early age. She is therefore able to think and act like a child and remains simple and uncomplicated. Her natural enthusiasm and imagination have not been dulled. Furthermore, the fact that she has had a home but not a family has allowed her to develop a strong will and think independently. The basic social unit, the family, according to the author, only makes the individual dependent on others for thought and guidance, a situation which has had a debilitating effect on the majority of Baroja's countrymen, particularly women.

In addition to not having had a formal education, María has never been taught anything about religion. Typically educated Spanish girls have been instructed in religious dogma which includes the concept that sex is evil, a sinful act, if not performed within the bounds of matrimony. Baroja calls the concept of sin a stimulant in itself, an invitation to engage in illicit sex.

Catholic theology has no influence on her thinking, but María Aracil has her own profound sense of right and wrong, especially with respect to sex which she totally avoids. She is even repelled by reading materials which have any erotic or sexual content. A comparison is made between her and her cousins who have had a conventional upbringing. They spend all their time hunting for a husband and thinking up ways of sexually attracting men, without ever considering that they could have their own life, independent of them.

Recognizing María's superiority, her cousins become resentful of her and try to exclude her from their social circles. But she proves to be more popular socially and can attract all the men she wants. María, however, dislikes the insincerity and superficiality of the mating game and prefers to be alone where she can think honestly and seriously. Baroja constantly defends his heroine, saying with typical sarcasm that she is not a snob and does not consider herself to be superior.

In many respects María Aracil is like one of Baroja's ideal male characters, Martín Zalacaín of *Zalacaín el aventurero*. Both have similar social backgrounds. Neither has been formally educated not been given any religious training. Each one has been taught by an astute member of the family. Both pay little attention to class distinctions and social conventions; and they scorn hypocrites and aristrocrats. Both attempt to live an independent, dynamic life free from intellectual preoccupations.

Later in *La dama errante* María's good qualities are further highlighted and are placed in direct contrast to her weak father. When he is forced to flee from the police as a result of his relationships with a group of violent anarchists, he becomes extremely nervous, indecisive, and confused. María, not wanted by the authorities, does not have to go along with him but does so out of a deep sense of respect and loyalty. Without complaining, she suffers great physical exhaustion and eventually becomes very ill after days of traveling through rough, wild terrain. But she remains gracious. During her convalescence, Baroja describes her as "encantadora, perezosa, sonriente lánguida como una niña."

When María and her father finally arrive in London, "La ciudad de niebla", María immediately strives to adjust to here new life by learning English and seeking employment, while here father can only complain about the things he dislikes in England. He soon marries a rich widow and departs for Argentina. María refuses to accompany the newlyweds, preferring to work and live independently, and not owe her existence to the charity of her father's new wife. Living alone in England, María has to overcome one obstacle after another. She is denied employment time and again, not as a result of her lack of acceptable qualifications, but because she does not nave the same moral values as other women.

In one case, she is rejected because she is not religious; in another, an aristocratic writer denies her a job because she does not have any lovers. As a poor foreigner she is given little or no consideration by the working classes, and, when she does find work in a library, she only sees repulsive, depraved and vile people. She finds most men insincere and lascivious. Although she is greatly saddened and discouraged, she triumphs in her continuous struggle to remain chaste and maintain her sense of dignity.

Baroja's praise of María now reaches its high point as we see in the following artistic, lyrical passage:

> Hay arbustos que han nacido al borde del torrente; las aguas tumultuosas los atacan, descarnan sus raíces, pero ellos se agarran con firmeza a la tierra, y en la primavera tienen el supremo lujo de echar florecillas. Así esta mujer abeja, en medio del fango de la gran ciudad, trabaja todo el día y desafía las aquas turbias del torrente, como esos arbolillos heroicos.

Such praise of anyone, man or woman, is indeed rare in Baroja works.

But María is not totally idealized. She finally does succumb to the pressures of London society and can't stand to work there any longer. Like so many of Baroja's male characters, she believes she is a failure and that all of her efforts have been futile. Baroja does not blame her and states that she is simply a victim of the unhappy state of affairs for Spanish women. According to the eccentric philosopher, Dr. Iturrioz, one of Baroja's spokesmen in this novel, women have to depend on men for survival and cannot be financially secure or live a prosperous life without them. Spanish women form part of an exhausted, weak race and just do not have the strength to go it alone. Baroja's attitude is really one of pity and sympathy.

Baroja ends *La ciudad de la niebla* with a short one-page epilogue in which he explains that María Aracil has returned to Madrid, married, and apparently is happy. Baroja himself never married and seldom wrote at length about married couples. Most of his main characters are single individuals who reflect his personal views and attitudes. María Aracil is no exception. Through her, he expresses his own opinions with regard to the Catholic Church, education, the family, and conventional morality, all factors which have a negative effect on the formation of a woman's character. María is a good person, not so much because of her favorable experiences, but rather because she has been fortunate enough not to have had a conventional childhood. Even her attitude towards many people is reminiscent of Baroja's own harsh view, a feature of her personality which detracts from her femininity. In describing her critical opinion of a violent, egotistical anarchist she despises, Baroja, for instance, uses the same rough, disrespectful words he has used many times before in his other novels and auto-critical essays: "farsante peligroso", "majadero" and "malintencionado" (*La dama errante*). No wonder María Aracil is treated favorably; her outlook virtually matches that of her creator.

Laura of *Laura o la soledad sin remedio* also reveals many of her creator's ideas and concerns and is, in many respects, similar to a number of Baroja's male characters. Like Andrés Hurtado (*El árbol de la ciencia*), Fernando Ossorio (*Camino de perfección*), Luis Murguía (*La sensualidad pervertida*), Miguel Salazar (*Susana y los cazadores de moscas*), and Baroja himself, Laura is a hypersensitive, introspective intellectual with a scientific, medical background. Her knowledge of human biological functions has left her cold and aloof. She senses that life itself and people as well are repugnant and pathetic. Excessively pessimistic and too intellectual to enjoy any intimate, instinctive pleasure with men, she suffers a constant feeling of loneliness. Like Laura, Baroja was an intellectual and usually viewed life scientifically. But science left him cynical and warped his instinctive inclinations to be sociable. Laura is in large part a projection of Baroja's own temperament and, because he is always justifying, rationalizing and identifying with her sadness and anguish, the reader tends to feel sorry for her.

Baroja's view that marriage is futile is also reflected in her empty marriage. She marries a wealthy physician, seeking a peaceful, simple way of life and looks forward to doing such basic domestic chores as sewing, cleaning and cooking. But she soon discovers that life as a housewife is monotonous and boring. Constantly analyzing herself

and her life, as did the author, she philosophizes that man is always searching for inner peace, but when he finds himself in a secure, tranquil situation—one which he thought would bring him happiness—he becomes restless and feels unfulfilled. Many of Baroja's principal male characters feel the same way. In *Paradox, rey*, Silvestre Paradox, who tires of the very utopian civilization which he has created, soon comes to realize that people are always dissatisfied with life and are constantly looking for something new and better. Once one has reached his goal, he discovers that it no longer means anything to him; it had only been an illusion.

Most of Baroja's other major women characters are much less pessimistic than Laura. Dolores of *Camino de perfección* actually brings a note of optimism. A relatively unpretentious, simple woman, she lives a dynamic, spontaneous existence close to nature. Unlike Laura, she is never given to introspection and is content to stay at home and do housework. Dolores plays a major role in the development of the personality of the main character and in the philosophical point of this work. Greatly influenced by the ideas of the German philosopher Friedrich Nietzsche (1844–1900), Baroja demonstrates in *Camino de perfección* that existence, as Nietzsche suggests, can be more rewarding and meaningful if one lives instinctively and willfully, close to nature, without respecting or regarding social conventions—things which only weaken and inhibit individuals. The protagonist, Fernando Ossorio, mostly because of his religious training and his medical background, has become a hypersensitive, introspective, perverted *abúlico* who finds little purpose and happiness in life. When he meets Dolores he begins to lead a dynamically active life and regains his lost will. After he marries Dolores, his internal strife and self-analytical anxieties dwindle away. He becomes a new man and compares his wife to a wide, peaceful river full of love into which he flows. His previous experiences with women—particularly with the sexually devious ex-nun, Laura—had been unfortunate. But now, with Dolores as his companion, he has a feeling of affection and tenderness, and senses the "immense grandeur" of women whom he begins to consider as a "sacred mystery".

Their marriage is one of the few successful ones in Baroja, but, as usual, the author occupies very few pages characterizing their relationship. The reality of Dolores a woman is less than convincing. She is almost always portrayed indirectly through the eyes of Fernando Ossorio who idealizes her and admits that he has made no attempt to know or understand her fully. To do so, Baroja adds, would only destroy the feelings Fernando has for her. She is a symbol, a device used to attract Fernando back to nature.

Dolores appears to be the exact opposite of Lulú, the wife of Andrés Hurtado of *El árbol de la ciencia*. If Dolores represents the natural, instinctive woman, Lulú, as seen by her husband, is "una mujer cerebral, sin fuerza orgánica y sin sensualidad, para quien todas las impresiones son puramente intelectuales". Baroja modelled the character of Lulú on a young girl, also named Lulú, whom he knew during his student days. Lulú is not at all physically attractive and actually looks abnormal and unhealthy. The distance between her nose and mouth and her mouth and chin is too great, giving her the appearance of a monkey. She also has dark circles under her eyes and her face is excessively pale. Andrés Hurtado thinks she is lacking in ingenuity, freshness and liveliness—features he believes are supposed to make females attractive—but marries her anyway.

Andrés, who has found most women to be flirtatious, hypocritical, egotistical, deceitful and devious, sees Lulú as a wholly sincere, honest, and candid individual in whom he can confide. Honesty, sensitivity, and a heartfelt sense of right and wrong are common to both Andrés and Lulú. They are truly noble characters in this novel. Lulú is in many respects the feminine counterpart of Andrés Hurtado who is in turn the character most like the author by his own admission. But both Andrés and Lulú are made subservient to the central point of this novel which is to show that intellectualism is sterile and that it will eventually bring about man's self-destruction. This is exemplified at the end of the novel when the couple fail to reproduce. About the only "natural", non-intellectual event in their marriage is Lulú's pregnancy. During this time Lulú's health deteriorates and Andrés becomes nervous and fidgety about the whole situation. What was once a happy arrangement starts to turn sour. At childbirth both Lulú and her child die and shortly afterwards Andrés commits suicide with a powerful modern drug. Both have been victims of modern civilization, science and intellect. Dr. Iturrioz, also spokesman for Baroja in *La ciudad de la niebla*, says that both would probably have survived and lived instinctively in the country without any help from doctors and without any philosophical or intellectual concerns whatsoever.

Many of the secondary female characters are treated favorably or unfavorably depending on their treatment of a principal male character with whom the author sympathizes. In *Zalacaín el aventurero* Martín Zalacaín is portrayed as a hero, victorious and successful in just about everything he attempts. He has been categorized as one of Baroja's "personajes nietzscheanos"—an impulsive, impetuous and anarchistic Übermensch who lives on the fringes of society and is considered a criminal by most people. Zalacaín in strongly attracted to the cute, rosy-cheeked Catalina, an intelligent, lively, happy, smiling blonde, whose attractive physical features and charming personality appeal to men and women alike. Despite the fact that she comes from a wealthy aristocratic family, she is not at all snobbish or arrogant and treats rich and poor with equal respect. She admires the strong, superior qualities of Zalacaín, becomes romantically involved with

him, and they eventually get married. But her despicable brother, Carlos, a strong believer in social order, category and class discrimination, believing that his sister has dishonored the family, has Zalacaín murdered. Catalina is one of the few good aristocrats in Baroja's novels. The author almost always shows his contempt for aristocrats and satirizes them mercilessly, as he does Carlos in this work.

In *El mayorazgo de Labraz* Marina and Rosarito are positive factors in the life of Juan, the blind main character who is exploited by the local townspeople. Juan feels there is nothing left in his life of any value except his little niece, Rosarito, whom he treats as a daughter. When Rosarito becomes seriously ill, Juan is about ready to give up any hope and practically loses his will to live. Another woman, Marina, helps him care for Rosarito and spends many hours at his house. Marina, the daughter of an innkeeper, is regarded by the "respected" social class of Labraz as a woman of questionable moral character. She becomes the object of public gossip and further scorn when she is observed frequenting Juan's house on a regular basis. But Marina is just about the only person in Labraz who has any real, sincere, unselfish interest in other people. Marina bases her actions on genuine feelings and has enough strength and stamina to follow through with her convictions. Seeing her courage and determination, Juan regains his willpower and rebels against the depressing social conditions of Labraz which have practically destroyed him.

Marina has many positive features in common with the other female characters considered in this study. Strong-willed, independent and individualistic, these female characters have their own sense of right and wrong. They dislike social classes and distinctions and, in their place, value personal honesty, sincerity, candor and dignity. They are chaste but not at all religious in the traditional Catholic sense. They remain loyal to their family and friends, and are willing to make personal sacrifices for them. Most of the major female characters are the opposite of the pretentious, snobbish, aristocratic pseudo-intellectual types—usually of secondary importance—which Baroja so frequently satirizes. It is noteworthy that in one of his critical essays ("**La hipocresía de las mujeres**") he actually sympathizes with women in general, claiming that, if they are hypocritical and insincere, they are not that way by nature. He blames society, the Catholic Church, and men for oppressing women and causing them to defend themselves through deception and pretense.

Many of the major female characters, particularly María Aracil, Laura, and Lulú. . . are projections of the author's own philosophical points of view, his prejudices and his personal preferences. They even express themselves in the same direct, blunt, and harsh manner as he does. They are never criticized, as are almost all of Baroja's secondary characters, but rather are seen as victims of society and their own intellect and hypersensitivity. They generally feel incomplete, inadequate, and frustrated. These characteristics are also typical of Baroja's principal male characters. With a few exceptions, both male and female characters who are treated in length are extentions of his own personality.

Commenting on the development and presentation of his female characters, Baroja declares that he only treats them superficially, making no attempt to understand them. . . .

Despite this statement, he does view women from within, but when he does so, he essentially draws a psychological portrait of himself. Among the women considered in this study, only Dolores of *Camino de perfección* and several of the relatively minor ones, such as Catalina (*Zalacaín el aventurero*) and Marina (*El mayorazgo de Labraz*) are viewed from without. Baroja is chiefly concerned with explaining a woman's personality and character and does not focus much on her outward appearance.

Baroja's portrayal of his principal female characters exemplifies the existentialistic nature of his novels. Virtually all of his female characters fail to communicate intimately for any length of time with other human beings. Baroja's male characters have the same problem. Rather than be considered as a misogynist, Baroja ought to be considered as an existentialist who felt—in all probability—that his individualistic, negative and pessimistic outlook drew a picture of reality which would be more accurate and true to life than the traditional "realistic" works which immediately preceded him. (pp. 17–20)

Kenneth G. Eller, "Favorable Portrayals of Women in Pío Baroja's Novels," in *The University of South Florida Language Quarterly*, Vol. XXIII, Nos. 1–2, Fall-Winter, 1984, pp. 17–21.

KENNETH G. ELLER

(essay date 1987)

[Here, Eller analyzes the various elements of Baroja's novelistic technique, asserting that features that seem disordered and purposeless, actually reveal the author's "philosophy about the nature of existence and about the novel as an art form."]

Baroja fills his novels with many diverse elements, developing his stories loosely and unevenly on purpose. Some critics believe these features make his novels appear to be disorganized and lacking in unity. However, it can be shown that many of the aspects of Baroja's novels, which may appear to be superfluous, really do have a purpose.

Rather than detract from the central theme of a given novel, they enhance it. In fact, there is generally an accord between the form of a novel and its content. This is particularly true of his well-known early novels, such as *Camino de perfección* (1902), *El árbol de la ciencia* (1911), and *Paradox, rey* (1906).

Well aware of criticisms of his technique, Baroja would often explain and defend the form of his novels in his numerous auto-biographical and auto-critical essays. He thought the most important years of a person's life occurred during adolescence and early manhood, from about age twelve to twenty-four. He therefore emphasizes the life of people, mostly single males, in their late teens and early twenties, the period when his own personality was definitely shaped. The main characters of many of his novels are active, young adults, including Martín Zalacaín of *Zalacaín el aventurero*, Fernando Ossorio of *Camino de perfección*, Andrés Hurtado of *El árbol de la ciencia*, María Aracil of *La dama errante* and *La cuidad de la niebla*, Sacha Savarof of *El mundo es ansí*, Luis Murguía of *La sensualidad pervertida*, and Martín, the protagonist of the trilogy *La lucha por la vida*. These characters are constantly on the move. As they travel about, the author presents a rapid succession of scenes, episodes, incidents, and descriptions of people and of landscapes, producing an uneven, coarse effect. But there is usually a certain cohesiveness, since practically all of the action revolves around the protagonist, and the secondary figures are presented in contact with him.

Unconcerned with unity in a strict sense, Baroja defends the rambling form of his novels. . . . He also believes a novel should be read a little at a time. This is why he divides a work into many short chapters. For example, his most famous novel, *El árbol de la ciencia,* is divided into seven parts of unequal length, and each of these sections contains numerous chapters. Altogether there are fifty-two short chapters in the novel, each one with its title. Baroja also defends the staccato pace of his novels.

The frequent changes in focus draw attention to the impulsive, restless disposition of many of his principal characters. One such character, Fernando Ossorio of *Camino de perfección*, constantly roams about Spain searching for peace of mind and happiness. He react strongly and sensitively to everything and everyone he sees. In his narration of Fernando's travels, Baroja bounces from one thing to another, making many abrupt transitions:

El día era domingo. A la caída de la tarde, entre dos luces, llegaron a la Puerta de Hierro. Hacía un calor sofocante.

En el cielo, hacía el Prado, se veía una faja rojiza de color de cobre.

En la Casa de Campo, por encima de la tapia blanca, aparecían masas de follaje, que en sus bordes se destacaban sobre el cielo con las ramitas de los árboles como las filigranas esculpidas en las piedras de una catedral.

En el río sin agua, con dos o tres hilillos negruzcos, se veían casetas hechas de esparto y se levantaba de allí una peste del cieno imposible de aguantar.

En los merenderos de la Bombilla se notaba un movimiento y una algarabía grandes.

El camino estaba lleno de polvo. Cuando llegaron en el carro, cerca de la Estación del Norte, había anochecido.

In this excerpt, Fernando is going into Madrid in a cart. In only a few lines, Baroja has mentioned the sky, the "Casa de Campo," the Manzanares River, the refreshment stands, and the road. He has presented them rapidly, one after another, showing Fernando's spontaneous impressions of the city as he travels toward it. This rambling technique matches the Main subject matter of the novel which concerns the neurotic, hyper-active Fernando Ossorio who has no clearly defined goals for his life. The technique also reminds us of Baroja's own anxieties and impulsiveness as a writer. When he presents many scenes and episodes, he is often reproducing the impressions he received as he walked through the streets of Madrid. He would write about these experiences in the same spontaneous way they had really occurred. Baroja writes his novels without a definite plan, claiming that if he had had a plan, he would never have been able to complete a novel. . . . By not having a highly structured plan, he felt that he could tell his stories more realistically and accurately, giving an impression of spontaneity, vitality, and originality. A highly structured plan, he claims, would hamper his efforts to achieve these effects.

The inclusion of a large number of secondary characters may on the surface appear to detract from the main plot or intention of Baroja's novels. In *El árbol de la ciencia* more than thirty-five minor characters are presented. But through them the reader is given a partial explanation of why the main character, Andrés Hurtado, is so cynical, aloof, melancholy, pessimistic, and bitter. Andrés comes into brief contact with many deceptive, dishonest and scandalous people from virtually all walks of life. From the prominent classes of society there are priests, doctors, and professors. One priest is irreverent and blasphemous; several of the doctors are indifferent and at times mean to their patients. And the elderly, practically senile university professor who appears at the beginning of the novel is wholly incompetent and behaves like a ham actor in front of an audience. Many people of the lower classes are scoundrels with no sense of morality who take advantage of others. A loan shark, *Tío Miserias,* takes the last cent from his poor clients; a poor woman, *Tía Negra,* is always intoxicated; and another, Doña Pitusa, is a beggar and compulsive liar. All of these characters are judged and criticized by Andrés Hurtado.

This same technique is used in almost all of his other novels. The greatest and most diverse number of secondary characters appears in *Mala hierba* the second novel of his trilogy *La lucha por la vida*. The title *Mala hierba* (weeds), refers to the many vile characters throughout the work. Like weeds, they corrupt and contaminate and are useless and unwanted. These characters paint a cruel picture of reality which horrifies and shocks Manuel, the main character of this trilogy. Furthermore, the narration of Manuel's sense of frustration and lack of purpose in life is enhanced by the technique Baroja uses in the first two novels of the trilogy, *La busca* and *Mala hierba*. There is no ending to either—just a rapid succession of secondary characters and occurrences abruptly terminated in *La busca,* and then continued in *Mala hierba,* to be again stopped all of a sudden, then started again in *Aurora roja.*

Baroja bases many of his secondary characters on the numerous bohemians, radicals, and misfits he knew or saw in Madrid. He uses some of these characters to express an unconventional, non-traditional point of view or a philosophy or ideology which can be directly related to the central topic of a novel. The philosophical point and the title of *El árbol de la ciencia* is explained by the eccentric, nihilistic Dr. Iturrioz. During one of his long, intellectual discussions with Andrés Hurtado, he gives his own warped interpretation of the downfall of Adam. According to him, God placed two trees in the center of the Garden of Eden: one, the tree of knowledge of good and evil; the other, the tree of life. God told Adam not to eat the fruit of the free of knowledge ("el árbol de la ciencia") because it would be sinful and would eventually lead to his self-destruction. . . Iturrioz claims that eating the fruit of *either* tree would produce unhappy results. If man ate the fruit of the tree of knowledge, he would destroy himself. If, on the other hand, man ate the fruit of the tree of life, he would lose his dignity and integrity and become ignoble, egotistical, and hypocritical. Through the presentation of many secondary characters, Baroja demonstrates that most people act as if they had eaten the fruit of the tree of life. Later in the work he also illustrates, as Iturrioz has observed, that it is futile to attempt to change one's existence for the better. Andrés and his wife both act as if they had eaten the fruit of the tree of knowledge, for they try to make their lives more noble and dignified, but they die tragically.

There are eccentric philosophers in other novels whose point of view, usually expressed in long, philosophical discussions with the principal character, has an impact on the development of the story. In *Camino de perfección*, Max Schultze, a disciple of the German anarchist, Nietzsche, tells the main character, Fernando Ossorio, to disregard all religious and metaphysical concepts and get plenty of physical exercise. Fernando takes his advice and regains his *voluntad* and emotional stability by roaming the countryside. In *El mayorazgo de Labraz* the blind main character, Juan, also regains his lot will after he is advised by the radical, Mr. Bothwell, to rebel against society which is represented by the small, backward town of Labraz.

In addition to the many secondary characters in Baroja's novels there are large numbers of scenes and descriptions of rural and urban areas, all presented at a staccato pace. These descriptions help form a more complete background while adding color and variety. In many cases they are not a superfluous element in the formation of the central thread of a story. *Camino de perfección,* for instance, is full of descriptions of the environment. Most of them are made to mirror the state of mind of Fernando Ossorio. At the beginning of the novel, Baroja emphasizes the fact that Fernando is apathetic, dejected, and disoriented. These characteristics are reflected in the description of his room. . . . The descriptions are similar to either impressionistic or expressionistic paintings, although expressionistic techniques were not widely used until after 1910. . . . In *Camino de perfección,* some of the same scenes of the Guadarrama are described several times to show how everything seems to change its form and color as the amount of sunlight or moonlight varies. As Fernando looks down the mountains in the middle of the night, the countryside in the starlight appears to be "cósmico, algo como un lugar de planeta inhabitado, de la Tierra en las edades geológicas de icthiosauros y plesiosauros." But later, at sunset, everything turns red; nature now becomes a dream-like vision and is "algo apocalíptico." These multiple perspectives are highly characteristic of impressionistic works of art. Fernando is an impressionistic painter, himself. The description highlights his artistic sensitivity. The subsequent descriptions of Toledo emphasize his increasing preoccupation with the metaphysical and reveal that he believes there is some religious meaning in everything he perceives (the sub-title of *Camino de perfección* is *pasión mística*). . . . Later descriptions of Valencia call attention to changes in Fernando's mental outlook and state of health. Having regained his energy and emotional balance, he views the landscape as something beautiful and voluptuous, teeming with dynamic wildlife. Fernando's inner feelings of joy and happiness are being projected onto the landscape.

There are also impressionistic and expressionistic descriptions in some of Baroja's other novels, but not nearly as many as in *Camino de perfección.* In *El mundo es ansí,* the city of Florence, which is characterized as gloomy, overcast, and damp, seems to reflect Sacha Savarof's sadness and depression.

Other less subjective descriptions can be found in the trilogy *La lucha por la vida,* where Baroja focuses on the sordid and dismal slums of Madrid. These descriptions, illustrating depravity and great poverty, allow the author to sympathize with the downtrodden who live in these oppressive environments and leaves no doubt as to why his main character has such a bleak outlook on life.

Another aspect of Baroja's technique that matches the varied content of his novels is his style, or use of language. His manner of expression is generally direct, simple, and unpoetic—a contrast with the declamatory style of most nineteenth century writers. He felt that eloquent, rhetorical and excessively formal language was used to conceal some weakness or obfuscate an issue and thereby deceive others. Those few characters who speak this way in his novels are despised and consequently belittled. The know-nothing chemistry professor who appears at the beginning of *El árbol de la ciencia* talks with dramatic grandiloquence. The students ridicule him by applauding him. The French Minister of Defense of *Paradox, rey* gives a formal speech which might lead one to believe that he is kind, sophisticated, courteous, and well-educated. But he is an unjustifiably brutal and cruel man who is delighted that his army—just to prove that it still is a viable force—has mercilessly annihilated a defenseless, peaceful society.

Most of Baroja's main characters, disenchanted with society and the human race, complain about their environment and freely express their harsh opinion of others. It is not surprising then that they express themselves in a direct, abrupt, and clipped manner which makes Baroja's novels all the more sarcastic and disrespectful in tone. Strong and derogatory words and phrases are used copiously. Silvestre Paradox, the main character of *Aventuras, inventos y mixtificaciones de Silvestre Paradox* and *Paradox, rey* condemns artists, teachers, and scientists in general. Then he goes on to say: "Hay nada más repulsivo, más mezquino, más necio, más francamente abominable que un hombrecillo de esos con los nervios descompuestos que se pasa la vida rimando palabras o tocando el violín?" The diminutive "hombrecillo" and "de esos" and the words "repulsivo," "mezquino," "necio" and "abominable" make Paradox's criticism particularly sour and unrelenting. It is not unusual for characters to show their disrespect for others by calling them names. In *Paradox, rey,* Paradox refers to his former secretary, Don Pelayo, as "aquel bandolero que me engañó como a un chino." One of the men alludes to the feminist Miss Pich as "esa vieja loca," and Sipsom calls the captain of their ship an imbecile. Such rough language give Baroja's novels a stong, masculine, "macho" quality. But even the principal women characters, such as Lulú of *El árbol de la ciencia* and María Aracil of *La dama errante* and *La ciudad de la niebla* talk this way.

But not all of the dialogue is short, gruff, and rude. In the following passage, [from *El árbol de la ciencia*] there are a series of long, rather simple constructions, sometimes parallel, which are connected by commas or by such conjunctions as "y" and "pero"; or they may be divided by semi-colons rather than periods:

No; no sólo es absurdo, sino que es práctico. Antes para mí era una gran pena considerar el infinito del espacio; creer el mundo inacabable me producía una gran impresión; pensar que al día siguiente de mi muerte el espacio y el tiempo seguirían existiendo, me entristecía, y eso que consideraba que mi vida no es una cosa envidiable; pero cuando llegué a comprender que la idea del espacio y del tiempo son necesidades de nuestro espíritu, pero no tienen realidad; cuando me convencí por Kant que el espacio y el tiempo no significan nada; Por lo manos que la idea que tenemos de ellos puede no existir fuera de nosotros, me tranquilicé.

Baroja uses this style in serious, lengthy conversations having to do with political, social, moral, or philosophical problems—topics appropriate for an essay. The manner of expression is not unlike that an essayist might use.

A further variation of style can be found in his impressionistic descriptions which are full of poetic devices. In *Camino de perfección,* he animates nature, comparing animals to animate or inanimate objects and vice-versa. His images, which are largely based on the senses, sometimes indicate that one type of stimulus produces a secondary, subjective sensation. For example, flowers produce an aroma of desire. This poetic device, synesthesia, was employed by Baroja's compatriot and contemporary, Valle-Inclán, by the French Symbolists, and the Spanish American Modernists. Like them, he attributes unusual qualities to objects: "Viciosas hierbas," "penumbra luminosa," "puertas hurañas," and "casas amarillentas ictéricas." These unusual images illustrate the main character's fertile artistic sensitivity as well as his warped view of the world. Baroja also stress his main character's reaction to his environment by placing adjectives before, rather than after, the nouns they modify.

The author generally alters his style from work to work in an attempt to make a closer relationship between the manner of expression and the topic under consideration. In *El árbol de la ciencia,* Andrés Hurtado is a general parctitioner and his friend, Dr. Iturrioz, is a retired army doctor. Both view the world from a cynical, scientific, medical point of view.

Consequently, they use unusual scientific and medical terms in their discussions. Iturrioz thinks that life is a constant and merciless struggle where everything has a parasitic existence and only the fittest survive. When describing people he despises, he does not hesitate to use bacteriological and entomological words, such as: "acinéticos," "ichneumon," "sustancia protoplasmática," "infusorios," "cloroformo."

The novel *Paradox, rey* is probably Baroja's most unusual from the standpoint of both the content and the style. The action takes place in a remote part of Africa and practically all the characters are eccentric and bizarre. There are unusual metaphors, similes, and personifications as well as alliterations and onomatopoeia. Two completely lyrical chapters are called, respectively "Elogio sentimental del acordeón" and "Elogio metafisico de la destrucción." The spelling, the sound, or the meaning of many of the characters' names is funny or strange. There are puns; some of the African characters use the infinitive form exclusively when they talk; and images based on exotic widelife are used to describe some of the characters. Even animals and some of the elements of nature talk. All these devices contribute to the fantastic, exotic quality of the novel. Some of these same stylistic devices are used in *La leyenda de Juan de Alzate,* another unrealistic, humorous novel.

These and the various other diverse elements of Baroja's novelistic technique which I have discussed all serve a purpose and *do* contribute to the development of the main subject matter of his novels. Rather than write a closely-knit *story* where what happens was of paramount importance, Baroja usually wanted to focus on the individual and explain his reaction to his surroundings in a spontaneous, original manner. There is unity because most of the different episodes, scenes, descriptions, and secondary characters form an environment into which his main characters are placed. There is also unity in the sense that virtually everything Baroja includes in his works and the way he presents it is a reflection of his own philosophy about the nature of existence and about the novel as an art form. (pp. 72–8)

Kenneth G. Eller, "Form and Content of Baroja's Novels: Harmony or Chaos?" in *Neophilologus*, Vol. LXXI, No. 1, January, 1987, pp. 72–80.

SOURCES FOR FURTHER STUDY

Barrow, Leo L. *Negation in Baroja: A Key to His Novelistic Creation.* Tucson: The University of Arizona Press, 1971, 238 p.

Elucidates Baroja's use of negation, its relation to his theory of the novel, and its importance to the totality of his production.

Brown, James Franklin. "Structure and Theme in *Cesar o nada.*" *Hispaonofila* 30, No. 90 (May 1987): 39–46.

Analyzes the novel's bipartite organization, finding that its two sections are connected in several ways: the ambiance of negation found in both, the *ambulia-voluntad* scheme, and Cesare Borgia's life, which centers around Rome and then Spain.

Eller, Kenneth G. "The Thematic and Artistic Unity of Baroja's *El árbol de la ciencia.*" *Modern Language Studies* XVII, No. 4 (Fall 1987): 23–32.

Responds to the charge that Baroja's works are disjointed and loosely structured by demonstrating how in *El árbol de la ciencia* disparate elements are woven together to create a cohesive novel.

Ginsberg, Judith. "In Search of a Voice: Baroja's Early Writings and Political Career." *Revista de Estudios Hispanicos* XV, No. 2 (May 1981): 221–32.

Examines Baroja's early journalistic writings, finding that they "reveal a vehement, youthful commitment to political change that . . . propelled him to the front lines of radical political activity in Restoration Spain."

Macklin, J.J. "The Modernist Mind: Identity and Integration in Pío Baroja's *Camino de perfección.*" *Neophilologus* LXVII, No. 4 (October 1983): 540–55.

Considers the novel's modernity by examining the psychology of its leading protagonist, Fernando Ossorio.

Owen, Arthur L. "Concerning the Ideology of Pío Baroja." *Hispania* XV, No. 1 (February 1932): 15–24.

Presents Baroja's perspective on a variety of subjects, including the human condition, the relation of political power to morality, the Catholic religion, and society.

Shaw, Donald L. "Baroja: Anguish, Action, and *At Araxia.*" In his *The Generation of 1898 in Spain,* pp. 95–126. New York: Barnes & Noble, 1975.

Overview of the novelist's life and career.

————. "Classifying *Camino de perfección.*" *Romance Quarterly.* 36, No. 3 (August 1989): 353–59.

Addresses "whether Baroja's *Camino de perfección* contains enough decandentist or *modernista* elements to justify regarding it as in a different category from later Barojan novels from which, by and large, these elements are absent."

Smith, Gilbert. "Feminism and Decadence in Baroja's *El mundo es ansí.*" *Romance Quarterly* 36, No. 3 (August 1989): 361–68.

Investigates the gender identification of the various narrative voices, the text's artifice, and the philosophical questions posed by the character Sacha, concluding that *El mundo es ansí* is directly concerned with feminist issues and "the phenomenon of decadence as a literary movement and as a worldview."

Additional coverage of Baroja's life and career is contained in the following sources published by Gale Research: *Contemporary Authors,* Vol. 104; and *Twentieth-Century Literary Criticism,* Vol. 8.

Adolfo Bioy Casares

1914–

(Also wrote under the pseudonyms Martin Sacastru and Javier Miranda, and with Jorge Luis Borges under the joint pseudonyms Honorio Bustos Domecq, B. Lynch Davis, and B. Suarez Lynch) Argentine novelist, short story writer, screen writer, and essayist.

INTRODUCTION

An Argentine author of fantastic literature, Bioy Casares is best known for his imaginative and complex narratives ridiculing societal values and institutions. Not bound by space and time, his inventive works have been considered "comic masterpieces" offering thought-provoking insight into the human condition. Critics note that Bioy Casares's adept use of irony allows him to treat in original ways such universal themes as love, old age, and evil and suffering. Although some commentators have pointed out that Bioy Casares's characters lack depth, most focus instead on the humor, intricate plotting, and poignant social commentary in his work.

Bioy Casares was born in Buenos Aires. Growing up in a wealthy, attentive family, he was afforded many educational opportunities which he ultimately rejected when he dropped out of the University of Buenos Aires in 1935 to pursue a writing career. His interest in western literature and philosophy provided the stimulus for much of his writing, which first received critical acclaim with the publication of his novel *La invención de Morel* (*The Invention of Morel*) in 1940. That same year he married the poet and short story writer Silvina Ocampo, with whom he later collaborated on a detective novel entitled *Los que aman, odian* (1946). Bioy Casares also collaborated with his close friend Jorge Luis Borges on several popular works, including the farcical *Crónicas de Bustos Domecq* (1967; *Chronicles of Bustos Domecq*). This book—one of many writings the two penned under the pseudonym Bustos Domecq—has been described as "fictional criticism," for it makes fun of itself while mocking a variety of recognizable subjects, from locally known Argentine artists and writers to such great modernist icons as Pablo Picasso, Charles-Edouard Le Corbusier, and James Joyce (to whom the book is jocularly dedicated). Bioy Casares has received numerous honors for his writings, including the Premio Municipal de la Ciudad de Buenos Aires, 1940, for *The Invention of Morel*; the Premio Mondello,1984, for *Historias fantásticas* (1972); and the Premio Internacional Literario IILA (Rome), 1986, for *Historias fantasticas* and *Historias de amor* (1972).

Humor and irony are in all of Bioy Casares's writings, and critics note that he uses these devices to couch his often serious commentary on aging, death, love, and artistic expression. His widely acclaimed *Invention of Morel* satirically examines the nature of love and human relationships and the role of the artist in contemporary society. The story depicts a fugitive from Venezuela who hides on an island, where he falls in love with what turns out to be the hologram of a beautiful girl whose image has been captured and preserved by a projector. Learning to operate the machine, he relinquishes his life in an attempt to join her, but to his horror discovers that they will never meet because each lives in separate projections. In search of allegorical interpretations for the work, some critics have suggested that *The Invention of Morel* comments ironically on the relationship between the reader/spectator (the fugitive) and the text/art (the scientist's machine). Another highly praised novel, *Plan de evasión* (1945; *A Plan for Escape*), also takes place on an island—a recurring motif in Bioy Casares's stories, suggesting isolation and estrangement. Here the protagonist finds prisoners undergoing a surgical procedure which completely reverses their perceptions of reality. In effect, the protagonist becomes the prisoner of a fantasy world and struggles to escape to reality. In *La aventura de un fotógrafo en La Plata* (1985; *The Adventures of a Photographer in La Plata*), relationships, love, and alienation are again principal themes. The story concerns a young suitor who falls in love with the daughter of an elderly man. Through magic, the girl's father enters the body of the young photographer to woo his own daughter. The photographer eventually leaves town, and all three remain alone in their solitude without the love each sought. A tragicomedy typical of the stories comprising Bioy Casares's oeuvre, *The Adventures of a Photographer in La Plata* features the "fundamental joke" that according to D. P. Gallagher lies at the heart of Bioy Casares's comedy: "the gap that separates what his characters know from what is going on."

There is some disagreement in the critical estimate of Bioy Casares's writings. Several commentators have noted that his works lack originality, often drawing their adventure plots from the works of H. G. Wells, Edgar Allan Poe, and Robert Louis Stevenson, as well as from detective and science fiction stories. Other scholars, however, have maintained that Bioy Casares's creative reworking of the elements of linear time and space imbues his works with a surrealistic quality that distinguishes them from the fiction of his predecessors. Similarly, while some commentators have observed that his characters are frequently dull and flat, many more have insisted that Bioy Casares deliberately suppresses their development in order to emphasize the action of the story, through which his themes are more directly conveyed. Bioy Casares's intricate plotlines have also generated much commentary; although many critics have found his stories convoluted and confusing, others have praised them as inventive and engaging. Many agree, however, that Bioy Casares's ironic humor makes his writings both appealing and memorable.

CRITICAL COMMENTARY

D. P. GALLAGHER

(essay date 1975)

[Below, Gallagher contends that *Invention of Morel* and *A Plan for Escape* are humorous stories expressing Bioy Casares's view of the insular nature of human perception.]

Bioy Casares's novels and short stories are comic masterpieces whose fundamental joke is the gap that separates what his characters know from what is going on. The most notorious victim of that gap is the narrator of *La invención de Morel*, who frequently attempts to declare his love for one Faustine without realizing that she is a sort of holographic image who cannot therefore perceive his presence. Yet even the most trite situations that occur in Bioy's work contain the same fundamental dilemma. Thus his sex comedies in ***Guirnalda con amores*** or ***El***

Principal Works

La invención de Morel (novel) 1940
[*The Invention of Morel* published in *The Invention of Morel and Other Stories from "La trama celeste,"* 1964]

Seis problemas para don Isidro Parodi [with Jorge Luis Borges under the joint pseudonym H. Bustos Domecq] (short stories) 1942
[*Six Problems for Don Isidro Parodi*, 1981]

Plan de evasión (novel) 1945
[*A Plan for Escape*, 1975]

Los que aman, odian [with Silvina Ocampo] (novel) 1946

La trama celeste (short stories) 1948

El sueño de los héroes (novel) 1954
[*The Dream of Heroes*, 1987]

Crónicas de Bustos Domecq [with Jorge Luis Borges under the joint pseudonym H. Bustos Domecq] (short stores) 1967
[*Chronicles of Bustos Domecq*, 1976]

Diario de la guerra del cerdo (novel) 1969
[*Diary of the War of the Pig*, 1972]

Historias de amor (short stories) 1972

Historias fantásticas (short stories) 1972

Dormir al sol (novel) 1973
[*Asleep in the Sun*, 1978]

La aventura de un fotógrafo en La Plata (novel) 1985
[*The Adventures of a Photographer in La Plata*, 1989]

Una muñeca rusa (novel) 1991
[*Russian Doll* published in *Russian Doll and Other Stories*, 1992]

---

gran serafín depict situations in which a man is convinced he has achieved a spectacular success only to discover that the girl's motives were notoriously less flattering than he imagined them to be. For not only the universe but every individual person is an enigma, and when one man confronts another, he can only work on the evidence the other chooses to project, and if the other is a woman his perception of that limited evidence will most likely be coloured anyway by his longing for her.

Bioy's little men are safe if they stick to their dingy rooms, or to their club or local café playing dominoes or talking horse-racing. They are in danger when they move out into the street—'Por no quedarse en su cuarto los hombres tropiezan con las desgracias' (*Diario*)—or, more seriously, when they travel. In other words disaster strikes when they move 'out of their element' into an area where their stock responses can no longer be applied, and it is there that the gap that separates what they know from

what is going on begins to manifest itself. Sometimes, the adventure is voluntary. Other times it is forced upon the characters by unforeseen circumstances: the presence of 'holographic images' indistinguishable from real people (*La invención de Morel*), the end of the world ('*El gran serafín*'), an unannounced yet speedily enacted decision to eliminate old men (*Diario*). In the latter cases *fantasy* is called upon to emphasize the perplexity in face of the unexpected of people who are unprepared for any but the most hackneyed conditions. In general, Bioy Casares imposes upon his characters an *adventure*, whether plausible or fantastic, in order to reveal their comic puniness.

Traditional adventure stories (those of say Stevenson, Defoe, Wells or Verne) have long been dear to Bioy as they have to Borges. Now what really are *Treasure Island*, *Robinson Crusoe* or *The Island of Dr Moreau* for instance but books in which a character has by choice or by necessity taken the inscrutable universe by the horns as it were, has left the bedsitter and risked going to find out what there is *over there*? Bioy Casares's novels, and in particular *La invención de Morel* and *Plan de evasión* (1945), are to a large extent *readings* of earlier, less sophisticated adventure stories. They are novels which reveal the extent to which the adventure story furnishes a dynamic dramatic form to express the gap that separates what a man knows from what there is. Of course Hawkins discovers what Long John Silver was up to and beats the pirates; Edward Prendick finds out all there is to know about Dr. Moreau's menacing monsters and escapes them and Robinson Crusoe gets back to England. Yet what if the 'happy endings' were removed? What if the enigma remained an enigma?

In many adventure stories the cornerstone is often the hero's decision to enter a mysterious house, preferably on a windswept hill or in a dark forest. The rusty wrought iron gate creaks, there's a rustling noise (wind? a ghost? a hidden assassin crouching in wait?), he stumbles, there's a distant laugh: in short, a terrible suspense is created which reveals the hero's ignorance and fragility, even if in the end he solves everything. But what if he didn't? What if he were killed, like Borges's Lönnrot in the house through whose creaking gate he enters at Triste-le-Roy? What if he discovers that the house is controlled by omnipotent seals who will never again allow him to leave it, as occurs in Bioy Casares's '**De los reyes futuros**'? What if he discovers, like Joseph K, that he will somehow never *reach* the house, or castle, at all? Then we will have a story that devastatingly dramatizes the puniness of man. Or alternatively, is not the *end* of the conventional adventure story an exercise in wish-fulfilment, a fictive assertion (and in fiction there is no imaginable thing that cannot be asserted) that man can triumph over impossible odds and decipher enigmas? Bioy's adventure stories emphasize the suspense and mystery of the adventures without in the end resolving them. Sometimes, the *appear* to be resolved; the concluding 'explanation' seems to fit exactly. But usually the attentive reader will find that an alternative explanation fits equally well. Some, such as in *La invención de Morel*, are written in diary form: the man writing doesn't know, at the time of writing, what the next stage of the adventure has in store for him, so that we are immersed much more forcefully in the unpredictable contingencies of the present moment. Not only does he not know what is written on the last page: he will never reach it, and if he does, it will only be to write a final hurried note before the ultimate disaster. Others, such as *Plan de evasión*, are written in letter form: again, the present is immediate, the future unknown, the end an enigma to be conjectured by the reader after the narrator's correspondence briskly ceases. Always the effect is one of bringing to bear on the conventional adventure story a new perspective, a new reading, one in which we visualize what is implied, what is at stake in stories which we traditionally hurried through as a 'good read', unaware, perhaps, of how much our breathless longing to reach the explanatory end was telling us about our fundamental ignorance.

Now in two of Bioy's novels, in *La invención de Morel* and *Plan de evasión*, the adventure takes place on an island. The island is, I think, as important for Bioy as the labyrinth is for Borges. No doubt Bioy sees the universe as a labyrinth just as Borges does, but the island would seem to be significant for him because it is a *shut-off* and *isolated* component of the universe-labyrinth. For Bioy every human being would seem to be an island, the gulf between one human being and another being as relentless as the sea that separates two islands. Local groups—*porteño* club-members, horse-racing enthusiasts, domino-players, football fans, patriots—also constitute islands, attempts to be shut off from the labyrinth or to settle for a convenient niche in it. And to leave the island is as dangerous as to embark on a stormy sea voyage.

The novel in which islands are most prominently significant is *Plan de evasión*. Enrique Nevers, after a family disgrace, is despatched from France on a mission to French Guiana. He discovers that the Governor, Castel, whom he must contact, is living on Devil's Island, and that for some reason access to Devil's Island has been prohibited by him. So he decides to instal himself on another island facing Devil's Island in order to discover what Castel, about whom the most peculiar rumours are circulating, is up to. For one, Devil's Island appears to be 'camouflaged', its buildings made almost indistinguishable from the vegetation. Is Castel mad? Has war been declared, the camouflage being designed to avert bombers? How much does Dreyfus (*sic*), the man who has been assigned to attend Nevers, know? Perhaps Castel's entire performance is 'una broma inescrutable, para confundirlo o distraerlo, con designios perversos?' At once, the gap that separates what Nevers knows from what is going on is established, and almost the entire novel consists of the 'furor conjectural' Nevers mush bring to bear on the elusive and fragmented evidence at his disposal. On Devil's Island he can glimpse signs, goings on, yet all the time new evidence presents itself that forces him to discard a previous interpretation. All the time his central problem is that he cannot perceive the *design* behind what present themselves as purely gratuitous manifestations. In the end, he is forced to cross the channel and go and find out, risk the danger of *disembarking* on the prohibited island. When he does, he discovers a great deal, but he dies.

The island structure serves to dramatize the fact that man's perception of what there is is circumscribed by an *insular* perspective. That is to say, when examining the evidence of another island, he is fated to view it from the perspective of his own island. What he notices depends not only on what there is but also on what from his insular perspective he *expects* to find or is able to see, and his interpretation of what he happens to find depends not only on how it is but also on how he expects it to be, because he is fated to view it with *a priori* assumptions, because he examines it not on its merits, but in terms of whether or not it confirms an already adopted hypothesis. Finally, there is a *third* island, that which the reader inhabits, because the reader too in attempting to decipher the book is also in the dark. He in turn must deploy a whole series of conjectures of his own: for instance, Nevers, in view of his somewhat frantic and disjointed prose style, may well be mad. He is certainly a most unreliable witness. May *he* not have an ulterior motive—'un designio perverso'— that he has not revealed? Is the reader too not a victim of 'una broma inescrutable'? How do we know that Castel's peculiar behaviour is not a figment of Nevers's imagination, or a lie of Nevers's obeying some arcane purpose? And like Nevers are we not too, as readers, doomed to an insular perspective? How much of the evidence are we missing, how subjective and partial is our interpretation of it? And finally how much of the evidence is withheld, how much of it is outside the field of vision open to us from our own island? Bioy Casares delights in his novels in playing with the impression that important evidence is missing (he is frequently cutting off conversations in mid-sentence or offering us *fragments* of revelatory letters), and that there is a great deal *he* knows which isn't in the text: for all we know there is an entire continent behind the island *we* perceive.

Now if islands are traps, prisons (Devil's Island doubly so, of course) the novel, as the title suggests, contains a *plan of escape*. This plan is Castel's mysterious design. Like Morel, Castel is prodigious inventor, and he has devised a method of altering by surgery the sensory nerves so that there may occur a change in the interpretation of the stimuli they receive. 'Un cambio en el ajuste de mis sentidos haría, quizá, de los cuatro muros de esta celda la sombra del manzano del primer huerto.' Castel points out that our perception of the world depends on our sensory faculties. We can only perceive what they permit us to perceive. Change those faculties, and who knows what we would perceive?

Admitimos el mundo como lo revelan nuestros sentidos. . . .Si hubiéramos nacido ciegos ignoraríamos los
colores. Hay colores ultravioletas que no percibimos.
Hay silbatos que oyen los perros, inaudibles pare el
hombre. Si los perros hablaran, su idioma sería tal vez
pobre en indicaciones visuales, pero tendría términos
para denotar matices de olores, que ignoramos. Un
sentido especial advierte a los peces el cambio de las
presiones del agua y la presencia de rocas u otros
obstáculos profundos, cuando nadan en la noche. . . .

Todas las especies animales que aloja el mundo
viven en mundos distintos. . . . Nuestro mundo es una
síntesis que dan los sentidos, el microscopio da otra.
Si cambiaran los sentidos cambiaría la imagen. Pode-
mos describir el mundo como un conjunto de símbolos
capaces de expresar cualquier cosa; con solo alterar la
graduación de nuestros sentidos, leeremos otra palabra
en ese alfabeto natural.

One need not stress how relevant these observations are
to the fact of our insular perspective. To be a man is to
be an island as much as to be a *Nevers* or a football fan
is to be one, for we are shut off from a whole series of
unsuspected phenomena not only by our situation in life
but also by the limitations of our senses themselves.

Now it is not accidental that Devil's Island is, indeed, a prison settlement, and Castel's *plan de evasión*
consists of an attempt to alter the sensory nerves of three
chosen prisoners in such a way that when locked in a cell
they will interpret colour stimuli which he paints on its
walls as the components of an altogether more liberating
landscape. But what is this landscape to be? An island!

Pensé: para los pacientes, las celdas deben parecer lu-
gares bellos y deseables. No pueden ser las casas na-
tales, porque mis hombres no verán la infinidad de
objetos que había en ellas; por la misma razón, no
pueden ser una gran ciudad. Pueden ser una isla. La
fábula de Robinson es una de las primeras costumbres
de la ilusión humana. . . .

Luego, mis problemas fueron: preparar las celdas
de modo que los pacientes las percibieran y las vivieran
como islas; preparar a los pacientes de modo que ex-
humaran una isla del tumultuoso conjunto de colores,
de formas y de perspectivas, que serían, para ellos, las
celdas.

In other words, by altering their sensory faculties he is
able to liberate them from one island of limitations—their
cell—in order to transport them to yet another *island*, less
limited and more idyllic but nevertheless an island, limited by definition. Whatever combination of their sensory
nerves he devises for them it will still be a combination,
only one of a vast quantity of possible ones.

In *Plan de evasión* the island symbol is more explicit than in Bioy Casares's other books because the novel
presents us so conspicuously with two main characters
confronting each other from two respective islands. In
La invención de Morel all the characters (insofar as there

is more than one, since Morel and his friends turn out to
be three-dimensional images of their deceased selves) are
grouped together on one sole island. Yet *La invención de
Morel* offers a formula that is not all that different from
that of *Plan de evasión*. (pp. 247–52)

In the manner of Wells, Bioy Casares has devised a
splendid plot in *La invención de Morel* but, unlike Wells,
he has furnished it with almost inexhaustible implications.
Let us look at some of them.

In the first place the plot functions as a symbol of
man's confrontation with an enigmatic universe, or with
any more specific enigma. Needless to say Faustine, the
member of Morel's party with whom the narrator falls
in love, is one for the narrator. For the fact that Faustine is a sort of perfected holographic image means that
though she has all the appearance of being a human being like any other, she cannot of course hear or see the
narrator, because she can only perceive what she actually
perceived when being filmed. Yet does any person really
hear what another says to him? Are we not all living on
different planes? Are we not all inscrutable *islands*, like
the narrator and Faustine? The comedy rests of course
on the gap that separates what the narrator knows about
Faustine and the fact of what she is. The gap is a very
spectacular one because Faustine is only an image, but
it is merely a hyperbole of a gap that always separates
Bioy Casares's characters when they confront each other.
The enigmas that the narrator strains to solve are extreme
versions of the enigmas that all Bioy Casares's lovers are
faced with: like the lovers of '**Encrucijada**', '**Confesiones
de un lobo**' or '**Ad porcos**' he must resign himself to *interpret* the girl's *behaviour*, without ever being sure of its
motives or causes.

Men are islands, a man's decision to make advances
at a woman is comparable to an adventurer's decision
to embark on a mysterious island. The advance is always
comically magnified to almost epic proportions. Take this
description of the narrator's attempts to make advances
at Faustine:

Verla: como posando para un fotógrafo invisible, tenía
la calma de la tarde, pero más inmensa. Yo iba a inter-
rumpirla.

Decir algo era una *expedición* alarmante. Ignor-
aba si tenía voz. La miré, *escondido*. Temí que me sor-
prendiera *espiándola*; aparecí, talvez demasiado bruscamente, a su mirada; sin embargo, la paz de su pecho
no se interrumpió; la mirada prescindía de mí, como
si yo fuera invisible.

No me detuve.

—Señorita, quiero que me oiga—dije con la esperanza que no accediera a mi ruego, porque estaba
tan emocionado que había olvidado lo que tenía que
decirle. Me pareció que la palabra *señorita* sonaba
ridículamente en la isla. Además la frase era demasiado
imperativa (comparada con la aparición repentina, la
hora, la soledad).

Insistí:

—Comprendo que no se digne. . .

No puedo recordar, con exactitud, lo que dije. Estaba *casi inconsciente*. Le hablé con una voz mesurada y baja, con una compostura que sugería obscenidades. Caí, de nuevo en *señorita*.

And so it goes on. The most normal activity—talking to a woman—is transformed into an epic *expedition*, full of the trappings of an adventure story: hiding in wait, spying before acting, putting a foot wrong (*señorita*: the atmosphere is that of a man scaling a mountain), losing consciousness, etc. (pp. 253–54)

At the end of *La invención de Morel*, the narrator decides to incorporate himself into the three-dimensional film of which Faustine is a part. After studying Faustine's gestures over the week that the film lasts, he deploys Morel's cameras and films himself next to Faustine, makes her words (which are generally spoken to Morel) sound as though they were replies to *his* questions, and in short creates scenes that, to a potential outside observer, might suggest that Faustine was in love with him. Now *La invención de Morel* is said to have influenced the film *L'année dernière à Marienbad*, and certainly Robbe-Grillet [in *Cáhiers du Cinema*, 1961] has acknowledged a similarity between the two works. And there would indeed seem to be one thing that they have in common: the suggestion that when people (even lovers) talk to each other they don't really communicate. Someone's words may appear to be an answer to another's question, but are they really? Are we not all living (if one may borrow a perceptive expression that would have been relished by Castel) 'worlds (or islands!) apart' from each other?

There are further implications in Morel's invention. One could, for instance, read the narrator's dilemma as the dilemma of the ignorant layman with regard to the omnipotent, enigmatic and designing scientist. The layman can only witness the *behaviour* of a scientist's inventions; the causes of that behaviour are an enigma to him. And the scientist is moreover always many steps ahead of the layman. We noted that Bioy's characters frequently have an intimidated sense that 'others' are in control of things, and with respect to scientists perhaps we all do. The narrator's dilemma could also be that of the inhabitant of an under-developed country with respect to the developed world, where all the technology is and where the decisions are made. The narrator is deliberately set up as a somewhat absurd Venezuelan sage, humiliatingly aware that Morel might well be famous, but that he probably wouldn't have heard of him in Caracas. Finally, the narrator (and the reader) can be seen as a perplexed man witnessing the inscrutable machinations of God, or as a perplexed critic attempting to decipher a book. But whatever its specific detail, the pattern of confrontation is always the same one: that of a limited perspective brought to bear on a situation too vast for it to cope with. (p. 255)

D. P. Gallagher, "The Novels and Short Stories of Adolfo Bioy Casares," in *Bulletin of Hispanic Studies*, Vol. LII, No. 3, July, 1975, pp. 247–66.

DEBORAH WEINBERGER
(essay date 1975)

[In the following essay, Weinberger analyzes *A Plan for Escape*, maintaining that Bioy Casares's characters demonstrate the inadequacy of "sensory and mental" perceptions.]

[The] world of Bioy Casares is endless: a world of unlimited possibilities for new worlds which then will form part of it. Everything Bioy Casares writes offers a world or postulates the possibility of worlds different from the one we inhabit, or think we inhabit. Sometimes a character may be a world apart from others and from his surroundings. Frequently the worlds we discover in the works of Bioy Casares are fantastic, and consist of rearrangements of the elements of our own "real" world. Because of their departure from a natural order, these new worlds are at first not understood by those who stumble into them. Unaware that they have discovered new worlds, they only understand that they are faced with something strange and puzzling. Thus, Bioy Casares' fiction frequently involves a character's confrontation with an enigma.

Access to these enigmatic worlds is through perception and the character must consider his mental perception of his sensory perceptions. In his attempt to decipher the unknown then, the character is limited in two ways: he can only perceive what his senses permit him to perceive; he can only interpret his sensory data according to his ability to use his imagination. Accordingly, Bioy Casares demonstrates through the characters' reactions to these enigmatic worlds the inadequacy of perception, both sensory and mental.

A Plan for Escape is based on a theory of perception, although this theory and the importance of sensory perception and possible variants on it, are concealed throughout most of the novel, which is taken up with Henri Nevers' perception of the mystery and the evidence which might explain it. Nevers realizes that there is something odd happening on Devil's Island but since he is forbidden entry, he tries to explain the oddness by the evidence he gathers from observation, from what others tell him and from his own imagination. (p. 45)

Nevers is not an objective observer who can collect evidence without preconceived notions as to what the explanation may be. Because he wants to avoid any serious complications, he would rather see the mystery of Devil's Island explained by something quite innocent; Nevers often deliberately chooses what he will see with that end in mind. As a result of his physical state, his perspective, his emotional condition, his lack of objectivity, Nevers' perception—even the information on which he must base his conclusions—may not be accurate. His perceptions may be flawed, as may be his reasoning.

Throughout the novel, the reader follows Nevers' observations and conclusions, watching them change as Nevers obtains evidence to support or destroy his latest theory. (p. 46)

[When] he has discovered the true explanation, Henri rejects it because it is too fantastic to be acceptable. . . . He will not doubt that he sees what he sees, but since he cannot believe it, he must find an explanation which will not contradict what he can accept: he concludes that they must be mad, because four men slowly rotating in outrageously painted cells cannot be fit into a sane scheme. Hence, Castel is mad. (Ironically, Henri's conclusion is similar to Castel's plan for curing mental illness by changing the patient's sensory perception of the world to conform with the patient's mental view of it.)

In Nevers' rejection of a fantastic explanation there is another example of the inadequacy of perception. It is not sensory perception which is the problem here, but the mental perception: Nevers rejects what he considers an impossible explanation for the apparently inexplicable behavior of Castel because it does not conform to what one may normally expect. His lack of imagination, his thinking only in set patterns which allow him to accept only what he already knows, are further limitations on sensory perception. The perceptions themselves—no matter how accurate—are useless, except as an aid to gaining understanding or knowledge. Nevers neither perceives entirely accurately nor makes the most of his perceptions. (p. 48)

It is not necessary for there to be a change in the senses for the image to change: it is enough that the interpretation of the sensory perceptions change; in other words, that the mental perception or understanding of the information provided by the senses be different. For example, Nevers and Bernheim see the same thing but interpret it differently; Castel and Nevers make the same observations about the nature of things, but their mental perception of such ideas differs.

Of course Nevers is correct in maintaining that symbols are the only way man has for dealing with reality, but he does not realize the significance of his idea. For him, an object *is* that object, not a symbol of an object. In Castel's newly created world, there are no objects as we perceive them, merely symbols which are interpreted as objects because of the alteration in the prisoners' sensory perception. Thus, a yellow sheet of paper is a symbol of a lance, because with the altered perception, yellow is perceived as length. Thus, a cell, rather than imprisoning,

is experienced as liberating because it is perceived as an island paradise. . . .

Through Castel with his experiments in perception, and Nevers with his problems in perception, Bioy Casares suggests that perception, both mental and sensory, is generally inadequate. The world is as we see (and hear and taste and smell and feel) it. Beyond that knowledge is impossible. Even within this world, though, our senses and perceptions are inadequate, and because they are, so is our imagination. Bioy Casares therefore calls some of the unknown worlds to our attention. Perhaps he considers us incapable of perceiving them on our own. (p. 49)

Deborah Weinberger, "Problems in Perception," in *Review: Latin American Literature and Arts*, Fall, 1975, pp. 45–9.

ALFRED J. MAC ADAM

(essay date 1977)

[In the following excerpt, Mac Adam asserts that Bioy Casares's *The Invention of Morel* is metaphorical in its presentation of reality and in the "distinction between the artist as man and man as artist."]

Bioy Casares in *Morel* creates a series of linked metaphors to describe the transformation of a man into an artist and, finally, the artist into art. Like Machado, Bioy uses the first-person narrator, but unlike the Brazilian, he delineates more sharply the "textual" nature of his work by defining it as a diary. What we are reading is a remainder, a leftover, and by emphasizing this dead or inert side of any work of art, its existence as the object of attention, Bioy declares its alien nature. The reader can never have direct contact with the narrator: he is not speaking to us or confessing his sins to God in our presence. Like Sartre's *La Nausée*, *Morel* is itself a kind of cadaver. The "new" Roquentin exists beyond the text (and the life) he has left behind, and, in the same way, we are encouraged to follow his example. Bioy has no overt ideological message in his text; there is no hortatory aspect to his satire; and yet, it is clear that he is making an esthetic statement. He is interested in expressing what it is that the artist becomes when he commits himself to his work.

To demonstrate his point, Bioy revitalizes the story of the man who goes to a desert island. Borges himself notes that H. G. Wells's *The Island of Dr. Moreau* is alluded to in Bioy's title; we might add that such a reference would automatically conjure up Swift, Defoe, Stevenson (also mentioned by Borges), Verne, Dante, and a host of others. One island text suggests another because they all deal with extraordinary circumstances, a hiatus in "normal" affairs. Even true stories about island visits contain the element of adventure that stimulates our appetite for the exotic, which, even when real, is somehow beyond literary realism. No matter what the text is, the sea we cross divides us from the world of our dreams. The sea may be real, but it is also our subconscious; and for that reason, no voyage to an island can be absolutely free from symbolic or metaphoric traits. Ordinary tourist advertising realized this long ago and continues to play on our desire for adventure.

Bioy's story is simple. A man fleeing from political persecution seeks refuge on an island supposed to be the epicenter of a fatal disease. Once on the island he begins to notice strange things: the seasons seem to accelerate, and then, with no warning, people appear out of nowhere. He writes to leave testimony about the climatic change, but his diary changes as he grows increasingly interested in the strange visitors. This interest becomes critical when he falls in love with Faustine, one of the women in the company. He learns that to them he is invisible, although he only learns why when he discovers that they are not really people but images projected by cameras operated by the tides. They have bulk, need no screen, and will last as long as the machines function. Desperate, the unnamed diarist decides to interpolate himself into the film (an act which kills all who are photographed) so that anyone who comes to the island will think he is part of the original.

The protagonist's life consists of a series of spatial reductions. First he shares a political and social life with others, then he becomes a fugitive, constantly in motion. On the island his possibilities for movement are limited. He has fled society and history; all he has left is his own mind, the island, and the various texts he projects and the diary he writes. The withdrawal from the world (for no matter what reason) is a metaphor for the writer who withdraws from the world to compose his text. The voyage to the island is that withdrawal, just as the blank page is the island which will be "populated" by words.

The reader, again the writer's mirror twin, recapitulates the writer's self-exile when he withdraws from the world to read the text, which is his island. The portrait of Saint Ambrose that Augustine gives in the *Confessions* (book 6, chapter 3) constitutes a perfect image of this act: Augustine describes the saint reading silently, so absorbed in his reading that he does not notice the presence of other people in the room. The reader, like the narrator, is alone on an island filled with people.

Our relationship with the text is as complex as that of the narrator with the images he finds on the island. He cannot reconcile himself to the idea that they are not real (his last words are a plea for someone to make Faustine truly aware of his existence) just as we might be tempted to affix a personality and a psychology to the narrator himself. We must realize that such an act would betray both the text and our roles as readers. The lesson Bioy implants in his text is the concept of art as suicide, an act mirrored in the suicide the unwitting reader commits when he takes fictions for realities: to create a text means

to create an artist, and to do that it is necessary to "kill" a man. *Morel* is elegiac in that it celebrates the death of a man who has achieved immortality, the ironic immortality of art which requires the death of a man. Like '**Borges and I**,' although less ironic because it is not toying with the idea of autobiography, the mode whereby the self is immortalized by being transformed into a fiction, *Morel* is concerned with the distinctions between the artist as man and man as artist. It is no less involved with our identities as individuals and our identities as readers. We must also give up something, "die" a bit, before we are reborn in the act of interpretation, the act by which we liberate ourselves from the text, deforming it into our own image. A failure to interpret is the situation described in Borges's "Tlön, Uqbar, Orbis Tertius," where all fictions are subsumed into the insidious and false encyclopedia because no one treats the fiction as a fiction.

Both Machado's and Bioy's texts invite interpretation, but they also demand one sort of interpretation instead of another. The fact that the "real" narrator is always separated from us by a linguistic void is never attenuated in these books by the creation of sentimental links between us and him. We are made to realize that what is speaking to us is a text and not a person, that if there ever was a person behind these words he is irretrievably lost. The narratives themselves are metaphors for communication, since they are composed without the presence of any known listeners, again in direct contrast to Augustine's ideal listener or the gentleman who asked Lazarillo to write his autobiography. It is the nature of first person narratives always to be "about" something, even if that subject is forever absent, replaced by words, that is, by metaphors. This is less explicit, perhaps, in Machado than in Bioy, who resuscitates the Renaissance found-and-edited manuscript to underline further his speaker's purely verbal identity.

In *Morel,* the verbal artifact is ironically juxtaposed to another absence, Morel's film. The film literally swallows up the narrator, who can look at himself in it in the same way someone who has written his autobiography can read about himself. There is of course a difference: the narrator has deliberately inserted himself in someone else's creation, hoping that his intrusion will pass unnoticed by newcomers. In any case, the elegiac note is again sounded, and the dying man sees himself transformed into a work of art, although that work of art is itself bizarre. Morel, not an artist but a sentimental scientist, creates a *tranche de vie*, a direct copy of life. In explaining to his friends what he has done, he states: "My abuse consists in having photographed you without permission. Of course mine is not a common photographic method; it is my latest invention. We shall live in that photograph forever. Imagine a stage on which our life during these last seven days will be acted out completely." The machine neither edits nor selects; it simply captures whatever images it can. It is the narrator who imposes his will on the film when he creates a new reality by interpolating himself. He does what the reader should not: he enters a world with which he can have no real contact.

Paradoxically, however, the text, like the film, requires the reader to "make something" of it. Why should this invitation to interpret be part of the text instead of part of the reader? How do we know *Morel* is a metaphorical text? There is no answer except to point out the elements of the text itself: the island voyage, the decision to write, the relationship between the narrator and the woman in the film (a variation of the Romantic *belle dame sans merci* theme, where she comes to stand for the text itself in its complete otherness), and, of course, Borges's preface, which prejudices the reader. These same elements may nevertheless remain insignificant to another reader. Unlike Renaissance literature, where mythology, symbolic names, and rhyme signalled to the reader what sort of reading he was to do, these texts leave everything to the reader's instincts. (pp. 32–6)

Alfred J. Mac Adam, "Adolfo Bioy Casares: Satire and Self-Portrait," in his *Modern Latin American Narratives: The Dreams of Reason*, The University of Chicago Press, 1977, pp. 29–36.

JOHN UPDIKE

(essay date 1990)

[Updike is considered one of America's most distinguished writers and is best known for such novels as *Rabbit Run* (1960) and *Rabbit Redux* (1971), as well as his writings on Søren Kierkegaard and Karl Barth. In the following excerpt from an essay first published in *The New Yorker* magazine in 1990, Updike contends that Bioy Casares's *Adventures of a Photographer in La Plata* is a parody of "traditional novels" and their "psychological, erotic, perilous relational currents among 'nervous complicated people'."]

The reputation of the Argentine writer Adolfo Bioy Casares is still associated, in the United States, with that of his friend and sometime collaborator Jorge Luis Borges. They wrote spoofs and parodies together, and worked on film scripts, anthologies, and translations; it might be said that Bioy Casares, though a generation younger, called the older man out of his shell, and inspired Borges's first and most mind-blowing book of prose, the collection *Ficciones*. Bioy Casares is known, on his own, as the author of the betranced science-fiction novella *The Invention of Morel*, and of number of novels few non-Latin Americans have read. His latest novel to be published here, *The Adventures of a Photographer in La Plata*, is

a slight and sly tale not apt to widen his local audience greatly, yet it has a charm and a sinister wit and a sudden sadness only an assured literary performer could deliver. It tells, in a terse and flat but not unfriendly style, of a young small-town photographer, Nicolasito Almanza, who arrives with his equipment in the city of La Plata, the capital of Buenos Aires Province. No sooner has Almanza emerged into the city from his all-night bus ride than he is hailed by a stranger—a tall, rosy-faced "older gentleman" who is leading an entourage consisting of two attractive young women, an infant in arms, and a little girl. These, it develops, are the Lombardos, also newly arrived in the capital, from the district of Magdalena. Before the novel is over, our hero will give blood to save the father, Don Juan, from dying, and will sleep with both of Don Juan's daughters—Griselda, the mother of the children, and Julia, who assists Almanza with his photography. The photographer is amply warned to disentangle himself from this family, who have evidently fled their native soil in some financial embarrassment, and whose patriarch is rumored to be none other than Satan, but a certain modernist glue prolongs entanglements, delays deliveries, and complicates arrangements in this plot, and Almanza extracts himself only when he moves on to photograph the sights of another city, Tandil. In fact no harm befalls him, except the loss of Julia, with whom he has, without the reader's much noticing it, fallen in love.

The pleasure and the discomfort the book affords derive from what we might call the comedy of daily intercourse—the great amounts of time (the characters') and words (the author's) expended in going back and forth among boarding houses and restaurants, explaining and fulfilling or missing appointments, chasing disappearing suitcases and delayed remittances, observing obscurely motivated conversational courtesies. Hastening from place to place, "Almanza remembered a dream situation: being in a hurry and walking slowly with tired legs that weigh him down. The truth was that everything that day was taking too much time." The grid of numbered streets whereon the characters pursue one another is indicated with a mathematical precision; upon the grid, however, human conduct oscillates unpredictably. Almanza and Griselda rent a hotel room for two hours for a tryst, but the electricity between them shorts out:

Again she held him close. How strange, he thought, so slender and so strong. She looked beautiful but attracted him less than before, and at moments she irritated him a little. Perhaps because she had lied to him (not meaning any wrong, one must admit) and also, incredible as it seemed, because she had confessed her lie. He had discovered that he didn't feel at ease with nervous, complicated people. While he was thinking this, a hard arm held him by the neck. He felt some pain and couldn't move; meanwhile Griselda was rubbing against him. Suddenly, with noticeable force, she pushed him away. Almanza wanted to wipe his forehead with his handkerchief. He was still looking for it in his pant pockets and jacket, when he saw her fall as if she had fainted with her head hanging off the edge of the bed, looking up wildly, her mouth half-open and her breast bare. One is always being manipulated, he thought and got angry again. He reconsidered: It's not that bad.

The encounter ends oddly; Almanza obeys "an impluse that was familiar to him" and takes out his camera and photographs Griselda, no fewer than twenty times. "She looked up coyly and shook her hair. He photographed her again." The one thing that proceeds smoothly for him in La Plata is his photography of the city's buildings and monuments; his lens cuts through the maze, as art saves us from life.

Bioy Casares is a deadpan parodist, and what is parodied here seems to be the traditional novel itself—its solemn tracing of the psychological, erotic, perilous relational currents among "nervous, complicated people." No wonder that Almanza, caught in the web of the Lombardos' seductions, and beset by gossip from all sides, takes an interest, while in Griselda's bedroom, in a magazine article that tells "how the great powers and even your country were only a smoke screen and how everything that happens on God's earth—even what happens to you and me—depends on the decisions of a handful of men in dark suits sitting around a table." In our hunger for a pattern behind things we entertain fantasies of conspiracy. At several points in the book, Almanza senses an echoing: "Everything happens to me in pairs." When he and Julia part, she gives him a kaleidoscope, a toy that fetches symmetry out of accidental arrangements.

The novels's mood, laconic style, and mechanisms—the careful notation of happenstance, the plurality of ominous characters—are those of a mystery novel, but one whose minor mysteries (What do the Lombardos want? Is Don Juan the Devil or a garrulous old con man with two daughters at loose ends?) and major mystery (What do the photographer's seemingly aimless adventures add up to?) are left unresolved. The novel arrests our attention and wins our respect by the things it disdains to do: it does not overdramatize or moralize, it denies events a deeper meaning. A clean if desolate flatness results—the spookiness of the minimal, haunted by the absence of ghosts. Whodunit? Nobodaddy. In using the mystery-novel format to tease forth nihilist sensations, *The Adventures of a Photographer in La Plata* resembles, among many other modernist works, Robbe-Grillet's *Les Gommes*, Raymond Queneau's *We Always Treat Women Too Well*, Borges's story "The Garden of Forking Paths," and that surprising best-seller, Umberto Eco's *The Name of the Rose*. (pp. 685–88)

John Updike, "Hyperreality: 'In Borges's Wake'," in his *Odd Jobs: Essays and Criticism*, Alfred A. Knopf, 1991, pp. 685–93.

DANIEL BALDERSTON
(essay date 1992)

[In the following excerpt, Balderston reviews Bioy Casares's *Russian Doll and Other Stories*, focusing on "his quest to present a contemporary reality distorted by elements of the fantastic and the grotesque."]

In "Tlön, Uqbar, Orbis Tertius," Jorge Luis Borges's great story of the creation of an encyclopedia about an imaginary planet, everything begins with a conversation between Borges and Adolfo Bioy Casares about the possibility of a work of fiction in which the presence of minute contradictions would permit a few readers to discover a disquieting plot quite different from the apparent one. The story was published in 1940, the year in which Mr. Bioy Casares published his first major novel, *The Invention of Morel* with a plot pronounced "perfect" by Borges in his review of it, and also the year that Borges and Mr. Bioy Casares—together with Silvina Ocampo, Mr. Bioy Casares's wife and herself a major writer—published an anthology of fantastic literature (recently issued in English as "A Book of Fantasy") that changed the course of Latin American literature.

A half century later, *The Invention of Morel* has inspired a disquieting parable of totalitarian power, Eliseo Subiela's film "Man Facing Southeast." Mr. Bioy Casares, by now the author of a number of other significant books including *A Plan for Escape, The Dream of Heroes* and *The Diary of the Year of the Pig,* has stayed faithful to the task of unsettling the reader with understated works of fiction in which some details don't quite fit, in which something is not quite right. His latest book *A Russian Doll: And Other Stories*, continues his quest to present a contemporary reality distorted by elements of the fantastic and the grotesque.

Two stories in the collection, **"A Russian Doll"** and **"Underwater,"** invite the reader to take a look at what the interventions of modern science have done to life underwater. In one, an Argentine visitor to Aix-les-Bains in France encounters an old acquaintance, Maceira, who (inspired by the movies) has come to the spa to look for an heiress to marry; the ensuing complications turn out to be more than the gold digger bargained for. The story resembles one of Kafka's in that the extraordinary happenings disrupt a dull and rather dreary reality; the fantastic events, however, grow out of an apocalyptic series of ecological catastrophes.

This contemporary flavor also informs **"Underwater,"** in which a story of unrequited love turns into a tale of horror, again because of scientific meddling with the natural environment.

One of the most impressive stories, **"The Navigator Returns to His Country,"** is also the briefest in the collection, and the least like Mr. Bioy Casares's other work. Here an employee at a South American embassy in Paris discovers an unexpected likeness between himself and a disheveled Cambodian student on the subway. The dream sequence in the story is brief and beautifully understated, serving to underscore the pain of both foreigners' waking reality.

This collection also contains some understated homages to two of the closest associates of Mr. Bioy Casares. **"A Meeting in Rauch"** is strongly reminiscent of the stories in Borges's 1975 collection, *The Book of Sand*, down to the bookish reference to Swedenborg's "Heaven and Hell," a treatise on the world of spirits, that provides the idea for the metaphysical conceit in the story and even the name of the protagonist (Swerberg). More surprising, given the extreme differences in tone between their earlier writings, are Mr. Bioy Casares's quiet homages to Silvina Ocampo. **"Our Trip (A Diary)"** and the final **"Three Fantasies in Minor Key"** sound and feel like Ms. Ocampo, though perhaps the black humor and the vio-

lence are not so intense as in her own writing (a selection of her stories, *Leopoldina's Dream*, is available in English).

It is surprising to see Mr. Bioy Casares imitating Borges and Ms. Ocampo so late in his career. No doubt Mr. Bioy Casares began his career as a writer imitating Borges, but the imitation of Ms. Ocampo (considered by many a stronger writer than her husband) is new and unexpected. . .

In the last two or three years Adolfo Bioy Casares has won a number of important awards, including Spain's coveted Cervantes Prize and his work has been discovered by a new generation of readers across the Spanish-speaking world. His writing is not marked by the excess that many North American readers associate with Latin American writing; his brand of the fantastic is never disconnected from reality, and he is always attentive to the cadences—and the commonplaces—of everyday speech. One can only hope that the charms of this little collection will entice readers to discover—or rediscover—his earlier work, particularly *The Invention of Morel* and *The Dream of Heroes*.

Daniel Balderston, "Fantastic Voyages," in *The New York Times Book Review*, November 29, 1992, p. 15.

SOURCES FOR FURTHER STUDY

Frankel, Haskel. "Stories from Three." *New York Times Book Review* (15 November 1964): 62–3.
>   Contends that Bioy Casares combines the format of an adventure story with science fiction to create a "cerebral adventure" in *The Invention of Morel*.

Levine, Suzanne Jill. "Parody Island: Two Novels by Bioy Casares." *Hispanic Journal* 4, No. 2 (Spring 1983): 43–9.
>   Demonstrates Bioy Casares's use of parody in *The Invention of Morel* and *A Plan for Escape*.

Mac Adam, Alfred J. "The Mirror and the Lie: Two Stories by Jorge Luis Borges and Adolfo Bioy Casares." *Modern Fiction Studies* 19, No. 3 (Autumn 1973): 353–62.
>   Explores the symbolic use of language in two stories

by Borges and Bioy Casares: "El hijo de su amigo" and "La fiesta del Monstruo."

Snook, Margaret. "The Narrator as Creator and Critic in *The Invention of Morel*." *Latin American Literary Review* VII, No. 14 (Spring/Summer 1979): 45–51.
>   Contends that *Morel* explores "questions of literary criticism and issues related to fantastic prose" while challenging the concept of realistic prose fiction.

Updike, John. "The Great Paraguayan Novel and Other Hardships." *New Yorker* LXII, No. 31 (22 September 1986): 104–16
>   Discusses Bioy Casares's reliance on the works of H. G. Wells and Edgar Allan Poe as plot material for *The Invention of Morel*.

Additional coverage of Bioy Casares's life and career is contained in the following sources published by Gale Research: *Contemporary Authors*, Vols. 29–32; *Contemporary Authors New Revision Series*, Vol. 19; *Contemporary Literary Criticism*, Vols. 4, 8, 13; *Dictionary of Literary Biography*, Vol. 113; *Hispanic Writers*; *Major Twentieth Century Writers*.

Leonardo Boff

1938–

Brazilian theologian.

INTRODUCTION

*B*off is generally regarded as one of the most controversial Roman Catholic religious thinkers of the post-Vatican II era. A distinguished scholar noted for explicating fundamental Christian doctrines in the light of contemporary experience, Boff is best known as a leader in the development of liberation theology, a twentieth-century school of Christian thought that provides believers with a theoretical basis for changing economic and political institutions that perpetuate social injustice. His works, notably *Jesus Cristo libertador; ensaio de cristologia crítica para o nosso tempo* (1972; *Jesus Christ Liberator: A Critical Christology for Our Time*) and *Ingreja, carisma e poder: ensaios de eclesiologia militante* (1981; *Church: Charism and Power; Liberation Theology and the Institutional Church*), expound a Latin American theology intended to make religion responsive to the needs of economically and politically marginalized people.

Born in Concordia, Brazil, Boff entered the Franciscan order as a young man and was ordained to the priesthood in 1964, the same year that a military coup ushered in twenty-one years of dictatorial rule and flagrant abuses of human rights in Brazil. Following his ordination, he took advanced courses in theology at various prominent European universities, including the University of Munich, where he studied under the eminent Catholic theologian, Karl Rahner. Boff received his doctorate in theology in 1972, writing his dissertation on the Second Vatican Council documents which summoned the faithful to work for justice and world peace. After completing his studies, Boff returned to Brazil and joined the seminary faculty at Petrópolis. During the 1970s and 1980s Boff traveled throughout Brazil and other Latin American countries, visiting grassroots "ecclesiastical base communities"—Christian groups committed to deepening the Catholic faith and affirming economic and social justice. Profoundly influenced by his contact with these assemblies, Boff began to develop his liberation theology. Popular among oppressed Third World and Latin American countries, Boff's ideas were initially well-received by the Church for his condemnation of capitalistic abuses; however, when Boff began to apply the premises of liberation theology to the Church itself, criticizing human rights violations and calling for a more democratic ecclesiastical structure within the institution, he met with increasing opposition form Church authorities. In 1985 these events culminated in the Vatican citing liberation theology's doctrinal errors and affinity with Marxism and imposing a year-long enforced penitential silence on Boff—forbidding him to write, teach, or preach—but lifting the ban eleven months later. The Vatican's censure, however, served only to heighten media interest in Boff and his writings. Although Church authorities have generally been less critical of Boff and liberation theology since that time, Boff voluntarily resigned from the Franciscan Order in 1992. Regarding his choice to leave the religious life, he wrote: "Before I become bitter, before I see the human bases of Christian faith and hope destroyed in me, before I see the evangelical image of God-the-communion-of-persons shaken, I prefer to change course. Not direction. . . . I will not cease to love the mysterious and sacramental character of the church and to understand its historical limitations with lucidity and the necessary tolerance."

Commentators have pointed out that Boff's writings must be understood against the background of economic exploitation and political oppression in Brazil. Since the late 1960s, the Brazilian bishops had become the chief critics of Brazil's military regime, decrying the economic disparity between the wealthy and the poor. In 1968 the Latin American bishops met in Colombia and together raised their voices against economic dictatorship and liberal capitalism, encouraging the formation of ecclesial organizations devoted to improving the lot of the poor. In his first work, *Jesus Christ Liberator*, Boff echoed the bishops' sentiments by representing Jesus as a militant preacher whose call for an egalitarian restructuring of society was met with hostility from the religious and political establishment of his day. The same theme pervades *São Francisco de Assis, ternure e vigor* (1981; *Saint Francis: A Model for Human Liberation*), which explores the tension between the saint's commitment to the poor and his allegiance to ecclesiastical authorities indifferent to their plight. Two of Boff's works, *Via sacra de justiça* (1978; *Way of the Cross—Way of Justice*) and *O Pai-noss: a oração de libertação integral* (1979; *The Lord's Prayer: The Prayer of Integral Liberation*), reinterpret traditional prayers and Catholic devotions, relating them to the Latin American struggle against oppression. Beginning in 1979, Boff began to examine the Church's organiza-

tion in terms of liberation theology. In *Eclesiogênese: as comunidades eclesiais de base reinventam a Ingreja* (1977; *Ecclesiogenesis: The Base Communities Reinvent the Church*) he described the assemblies he visited during the 1970s as democratic, alternative local churches dedicated to social justice, advocating the ordination of woman to the priesthood and the celebration of the Eucharist by lay designates. In *Church: Charism and Power* Boff attacked the Church's authority structure, applying the methodology of a Marxist critique of capitalism: he charged that the ecclesiastical hierarchy dispenses the sacraments just as capitalist lords sell consumer goods, thereby depriving the faithful of the grace that is freely theirs by virtue of baptism. Calling for a democratization of the entire system, Boff asserted that the Church's authority must rest on orthopraxis (correct action) rather than orthodoxy (correct belief).

While some critics, like Robert McAfee Brown, praised *Church: Charism and Power* as a "powerful and clearly written book," others, such as Peter Hebblethwaite, dismissed it as a "useful but unremarkable contribution to post-conciliar ecclesiology." Church authorities responded to Boff's work by summoning him to Rome for a colloquy, or a formal discussion of the controversial nature of his writings. Four days prior to the September 1984 colloquy, the Sacred Congregation for the Doctrine of the Faith—the Vatican office charged with overseeing Church teaching—published an "Instruction on Certain Aspects of the 'Theology of Liberation'," which highlighted several of the ideology's doctrinal errors, namely, the unorthodox reading of fundamental religious concepts against the background of Marxist hermeneutics. According to the document, theologies of liberation confuse "the *poor* of the Scripture and the *proletariat* of Marx. In this way they pervert the Christian meaning of the poor, and they transform the fight for the rights of the poor into a class fight within the ideological perspective of the class struggle." Boff made an impassioned public reply to the Vatican in his *Teologia de libertação no debate atual* (1985; *Liberation Theology: From Dialogue to Confrontation*), written with his brother, Clodovis. Reaffirming his belief that liberation is an action, not an academic "aspiration," Boff criticized the Church hierarchy for failing to analyze the social structures that create and perpetuate poverty. Upon publication of the book, the Sacred Congregation notified Boff that it considered certain aspects of his writings dangerous to the faith and to the acceptance of hierarchical authority. Although Boff accepted their rebuke, he also indicated that he would continue his theological work. In 1986 the Sacred Congregation issued a second document on liberation theology, "Instruction on Christian Freedom and Liberation." More conciliatory in tone, it reiterates that the Church's mission is not the political and economic reordering of society, but underscores liberation theology's contribution to the cause of social justice.

Although Boff's writings have been attacked as unorthodox by church authorities and theologians alike, most reviewers have commended his works for their clarity, systematic organization, and effort to integrate Christian praxis with theological reflection. Boff, no longer active in the religious life, continues to write with a view to make faith encompass more than personal belief or strict adherence to doctrine. He continues, in his words, to be inspired by "the fight for the kingdom which begins with the poor; the passion for the gospel; compassion for the suffering; commitment to the liberation of the oppressed."

CRITICAL COMMENTARY

RICHARD QUEBEDEAUX
(essay date 1978)

[In the essay below, Quebedeaux offers a positive assessment of *Jesus Christ Liberator*, commending the book as an outstanding introduction to liberation Christology and thought.]

During the 1970s, "liberation theology" has emerged out of the concrete experience of political and social oppression suffered by the majority of Latin Americans—Catholic, Protestant and non-Christian alike. In the opinion of the liberation theologians, theology itself is "critical reflection on praxis"—that is, reflection within and upon the process of actual *engagement* in the struggle for liberation from that oppression. These religious thinkers therefore utilize sociopolitical analysis—generally Marxist in character—in their theology and Christian practice, to secure and concretize engagement in the process. They believe, moreover that theology must *emphasize* the intrinsic relationship between sin, salvation and the Kingdom of God on the one hand, and the historical Process and struggle for sociopolitical liberation on the other.

Leonardo Boff, a Franciscan, is professor of theology in Petropolis, Brazil, and an adviser to the Brazilian Conference of Bishops and the Latin American Conference of Religious. *Jesus Christ Liberator* was first published in Brazil in 1972, and now appears in English with a new epilogue by the author. Here Boff attempts to look at Jesus—his message, life and work—in the context of the current oppression dominant in Latin American society.

To begin, Boff critically evaluates the different views of Jesus inherent in the "historical Jesus"/"Christ of faith" debate, in "death of God" thought, in philosophical-transcendental Christology, in cosmic-evolutionist Christology, in depth psychology, in secular, sociocritical analysis, and in the "experience of Christ" among modern youth. He then goes on to assess the "hermeneutical problem"—the major divergent christological findings of the various schools of biblical hermeneutics, including the hermeneutics of historical criticism (form, tradition, redaction criticism), existential hermeneutics, and hermeneutics of "salvation history."

Informed by all of these, Boff articulates his own Latin American Christology "for our time" with its primacy of a "social over personal" understanding of Jesus, and its focus on "orthopraxis over orthodoxy." Jesus "did not come to alienate human beings and carry them off to another world. He came to confirm the good news: This sinister world has a final destiny that is good, human, and divine"—the Kingdom of God, the central tenet of Jesus' life and message. Indeed, the author insists in his creative and forceful biblical exegesis that the "preaching of Jesus about the Kingdom of God concerns not only persons, demanding conversion of them. It also affects the world of persons in terms of a liberation from legalism, from conventions without foundation, from authoritarianism and the forces and powers that subject people."

In a felicitous, easily understood and generally non-sexist style, Boff puts forward an activist Jesus who calls his followers—and human society as a whole—to the Kingdom,

a fully reconciled world, a utopia that is prepared and begun here and now in history through the committed action of people of good will. . . . Wherever people seek the good, justice, humanitarian love, solidarity, communion, and understanding between people, wherever they dedicate themselves to overcoming their own egoism, making this world more human and fraternal, and opening themselves to the normative Tran-

Principal Works

Jesus Cristo libertador; ensaio de cristologia crítica para o nosso tempo (essays) 1972
[*Jesus Christ Liberator: A Critical Christology for Our Time*, 1978]

Die Kirche als Sakrament im Horizont der Welterfahrung; Versuch einer Legitimation und einer struktur—funktionalistischen Grundlegung der Kirche im Anschluss an das II. Vatikanische Konzil (essay) 1972

A graça libertadora no mundo (essays) 1976
[*Liberating Grace*, 1979]

Eclesiogênese: as comunidades eclesiais de base reinventam a Ingreja (essays) 1977
[*Ecclesiogenesis: The Base Communities Reinvent the Church*, 1986]

Paixão de Cristo, paixão do mundo (essays) 1977
[*Passion of Christ, Passion of the World: The Facts, Their Interpretation, and Their Meaning Yesterday and Today*, 1987]

Fé na periferia do mundo (essays) 1978

Via sacra de justiça (poetry) 1978
[*Way of the Cross—Way of Justice*, 1980]

Da libertação [with Clodovis Boff] (essays) 1979
[*Salvation and Liberation: In Search of a Balance between Faith and Politics*, 1984]

O Pai-nosso: a oração de libertação integral (essays) 1979
[*The Lord's Prayer: The Prayer of Integral Liberation*, 1983]

Orosto materno de Deus (essays) 1979
[*The Maternal Face of God: The Feminine and Its Religious Expression*, 1987]

O caminhar de Igreja com os oprimidos (essays) 1980

Ingreja, carisma e poder: ensaios de eclesiologia militante (essays) 1981
[*Church: Charism and Power; Liberation Theology and the Institutional Church*, 1985]

São Francisco de Assis, ternure e vigor (essays) 1981
[*Saint Francis: A Model for Human Liberation*, 1982]

Do lugar do pobre (essays) 1984
[*When Theology Listens to the Poor*, 1989]

Teologia da libertação no debate atual [with Clodovis Boff] (essays) 1985
[*Liberation Theology: From Dialogue to Confrontation*, 1986]

A Trinidade, a sociedade e a libertação (essays) 1986
[*Trinity and Society*, 1988]

Como fazer teologia de libertação [with Clodovis Boff] (essays) 1986
[*Introducing Liberation Theology*, 1987]

*Faith on the Edge: Religion and Marginalized Existence (essays) 1989

Nova evangelização (essays) 1990
[*The New Evangelization and the Perspective of the Oppressed*, 1990]

Ecology and Spirituality (essays) 1991

*The first four chapters of this work are taken from *O caminhar de Igreja com os oprimidos* and the last six chapters from *Fé na periferia do mundo*.

scendent for their lives, there we can say, with all certainty, that the resurrected one is present.

Boff does not link his activist Jesus unequivocally with Marxist programs for social reconstruction in the manner of some liberation theologians. Also, despite the fact that the humanity of Jesus is stressed, his divinity—deity, really—is affirmed too.

This book will offer little that is new to those who are well versed in social-action Christianity in general and liberation theology in particular; but for those who aren't, it provides an excellent introduction to the basics of contemporary, liberation Christology and thought, written from a position of deep faith. Socially concerned evangelicals, with ministers and laypeople, will be certain to find this study particulary helpful in its biblically faithful assessment of the politics of Jesus (pp. 1051–52)

Richard Quebedeaux, "An Activist Jesus," in *The Christian Century*, Vol. XCV, No. 35, November 1, 1978, pp. 1051–52.

LEONARDO BOFF

(essay date 1978)

[In the following excerpt from the epilogue to the 1978 edition of his *Jesus Christ Liberator* (1972), Boff explicates the connection between theology and social action, stating that "a Christology that proclaims Jesus Christ as the Liberator seeks to be committed to the economic, social, and political liberation of those groups that are oppressed and dominated."]

When we talk about Jesus Christ the Liberator, we are presupposing certain preliminaries that must be noted. Liberation is the opposite correlate of domination. To worship and proclaim Jesus Christ as the Liberator is to ponder and live out our christological faith within a socio-historical context marked by domination and oppression. This faith seeks to grasp the relevance of themes that will entail structural changes in a given socio-historical situation. It explores this relevance analytically and produces a Christology centered around the theme of Jesus Christ the Liberator. Such a Christology entails a specific socio-political commitment to break with the situation of oppression.

To properly understand the articulation of such a Christology, we must first consider two preliminary data: (1) the relevance of socio-political liberation for Christology; (2) the social setting that is the point of departure for this christological reflection.

By "relevance" here I am referring to the importance that a particular set of historical circumstances has for reflection on our faith in Jesus Christ. Those circumstances pose numerous basic questions to us: e.g., in the face of a given situation and its exigencies, how are we to ponder, preach, and live Jesus Christ in such a way that he appears as the Savior, as that which our faith proclaims him to be? Looking at it from the other side, we can say that the relevance has to do with the connection between a particular theological theme and a particular set of historical circumstances. That is to say, in what way does the former help to explain, maintain, or transform the latter? For whom is a particular image of Christ relevant? Who is helped by a particular theme or a particular type of Christology? What interests does it represent and what concrete projects does it support?

These questions make it clear that any such relevance is always quite ambiguous. It always brings us back to a deeper underlying issue: i.e., the social setting or context (concrete practices, commitments, and stances) in which our faith in Jesus Christ is elaborated.

Theologians do not live in the clouds. They are social actors with a particular place in society. They produce knowledge, data and meanings by using instruments that the situation offers them and permits them to utilize. Their findings are also addressed to a particular audience. Thus theologians are framed within the overall social context. The themes and emphases of a given Christology flow from what seems relevant to the theologian on the basis of his of her social standpoint. In that sense we must maintain that no Christology is or can be neutral. Every Christology is partisan and committed. Willingly or unwillingly christological discourse is voiced in a given social setting with all the conflicting interests that pervade

it. That holds true as well for theological discoures that claims to be "purely" theological, historical, traditional, ecclesial, and apolitical. Normally such discourse adopts the position of those who hold power in the existing system. If a different kind of Christology with its own commitments appears on the scene and confronts the older "apolitical" Christology, the latter will soon discover its social locale, forget its "apolitical" nature, and reveal itself as a religious reinforcement of the existing status quo.

Every given type of Christology is relevant in its own way, depending on its functional relationship to the socio-historical situation; in that sense it is a committed Christology. So let us set down this basic affirmation: As an ordered and elaborated knowledge of the faith, Christology takes shape within the context of a particular moment in history; it is produced under certain specific modes of material, ideal, cultural, and ecclesial production, and it is articulated in terms of certain concrete interests that are not always consciously adverted to. Hence the real question is who or what cause is served by a given Christology.

A Christology that proclaims Jesus Christ as the Liberator seeks to be committed to the economic, social, and political liberation of those groups that are oppressed and dominated. It purports to see the theological relevance of the historic liberation of the vast majority of people on our continent. Such a Christology believes that its thinking and practice should be centered on such liberation. It seeks to create a style and to develop the content of Christology in such a way that it can bring out the liberative dimensions present in Jesus' historical course.

In other words, it is the overall context of dependence and oppression at every level of life that prompts Christology in Latin America to ponder and love Jesus Christ as Liberator. The theme was not willed into being by a few theologians trying to find interesting topics for discussion. It arose as a concrete demand of faith for christians who felt summoned by their consciences to help wipe out the humiliating condition imposed on their fellow human beings. In Jesus Christ they found motives and stimuli for the cause of liberation.

This brand of Christology presupposes and depends on a specific social practice designed to break with the existing context of domination. The social setting of this Christology is the setting of those social groups for whom a qualitative change of the social structure would represent an opportunity to liberate themselves from existing forms of domination. Taking a clear social stand in favor of the oppressed has entailed a real hermeneutic conversion for many. They have turned to the new questions now posed to them for reflection and they have been forced to consider what sort of style is needed to serve as a vehicle for them.

It should be realized, of course, that this commitment does not guarantee the intrinsic quality of any Christology. Considerations of relevance and social setting seek to point up the inevitable link between practice and theory, politics and Christology; they shed light on the basic underlying conditions that enable a Christology to define its thematic object and its mode of treatment.

Here we must carefully distinguish between the area of autonomy and the area of dependence in any Christology or theology. The former has to do with epistemology (the epistemic setting); the latter has to do with the sociology of knowledge (the social setting). Christology enjoys autonomy in elaborating its discourse in line with its own methodology. It has its own mode of theoretical praxis, and it does not have to justify itself before some outside tribunal. It possesses its own inner laws and the criteria to determine its own internal truth.

In this epistemological realm it makes no sense to talk about a "Latin American" as opposed to a "North Atlantic" Christology, or about a Christology of the oppressed as opposed to a Christology of the oppressors. In its internal regimen such designation are not theoretical tools enabling us to pass judgment on the value of a given christological production. A Christology is not better or worse epistemologically because it was produced in the metropolitan centre of power or in the dominated periphery. The same holds true when a Christology is designated as "traditionalist" or "progressivist" or "liberation-oriented." None of these adjectives can determine the correctness or "truth" of a Christology. They point outward to the social reference of a given Christological production. They help us to realize that a given Christology entails a given social commitment and can reinforce one or another group in society.

On the other hand Christology (and all theology) is subject to external dependence as well. Its selection of topics and its emphases are dependent on the social position of the theological actors and what they see as the relevance of christological reflection vis-à-vis the social, historical, and religious context. (pp. 264–68)

Leonardo Boff, "Epilogue: A Christological View from the Periphery," in his *Jesus Christ Liberator: A Critical Christology for Our Time*, translated by Patrick Hughes, Orbis Books, 1978, pp. 264–95.

BRIAN O. MCDERMOTT
(essay date 1980)

[In the excerpt below, McDermott negatively assesses *Jesus Christ Liberator* for its failure to contribute any new ideas regarding Jesus Christ that will motivate Christian believers to take seriously their responsibility to transform the world's unjust political and social structures.]

In the epilogue to his book [*Jesus Christ Liberator: A Critical Christology for Our Time*], Leonardo Boff makes it clear that this is not the Christology he wanted to write. Rather, it is an expression of Christian reflection in the midst of severe political repression with the guardedness that such difficult circumstances can demand.

Nonetheless, Boff has developed a Christology that is the fruit of serious dialogue with European scholarship with accent given to the political and structural dimensions of the Gospel. For students of recent Roman Catholic Christology, there is little that is new in Boff's treatment. Boff is trying to clear the ground, to lead the reader into relativizing hardened images and titles of Jesus Christ so that the fruits of recent scholarship can lead Christians to accept responsibility for their world as they allow the living Christ to empower them.

The interesting aspect of Boff's book is precisely the juxtaposition of main text and epilogue. The tone in the latter is urgent, critical and partisan. Liberation Christology is of two kinds: Either it is written out of concern to summon people to engage in change of social structures ("ethical indignation is transformed into an appeal for changes"), or it is written out of concern which engages in a social analysis that "stresses the notion of struggle and conflict and sees society fraught with contradictions." It is clear that Boff opts for the latter approach as the only really helpful one, but that is not the book he himself wrote.

Several puzzling aspects of Boff's book appear when he discusses the Chalcedonian formula. He identifies the one hypostasis of the council statement with the divine Logos that is actually an identification appearing only after Chalcedon. Furthermore, he speaks of two abstract natures concretely united by the Logos, which is problematic indeed. Finally, Boff seems to have little problem with the anhypostasis of Jesus' human nature, that is, the view that Jesus did not exist in a human personal mode of being. Current Roman Catholic Christology as represented by Schoonenberg and Schillebeeckx seems much more alive to the problems involved here than is this author.

In brief, this book, respectable on many counts, does not break new ground either as a work wrestling with traditional questions or as a liberation Christology in the social-analytical sense the author gives that phrase. (pp. 174–75)

Brian O. McDermott, in a review of "Christ the Liberator: A Critical Christology for Our Time," in *America*, Vol. 142, No. 8, March 1, 1980 pp. 174–75.

ROBERT P. IMBELLI
(essay date 1980)

[Below, Imbelli presents a mixed review of *Liberating Grace*. Although he finds the book's major themes fragmented, he nevertheless commends the work for its clarity, systematic organization, and effort to integrate Christian praxis with theological reflection.]

Of all the worn and misleading dichotomies, none seems more so than that which pits theological "progressives" against theological "traditionalists". For how can one be seriously theological without being deeply rooted in one's tradition, or truly traditional without advancing that tradition to meet contemporary questions and concerns? Leonardo Boff's *Liberating Grace* transcends such dichotomous thinking as it creatively unites Dionysius and Rahner, Chrysostom and Gutierrez. For Boff the mystical and the politcal (to mention one last contrast) cannot ultimately be sundered, for the integrity of each demands that they be suffused with grace.

The perennial difficulty with books about "grace" is that, being the most universal of theological themes, it is notoriously all-inclusive. In effect, if "all is grace," then nothing can be omitted. This easily leads the reader beyond delight to indigestion. Two features of Boff's work permit the delight to be paramount. Firstly, it is clearly and straightforwardly written (and the translator seems to have served the author extremely well). Secondly, it is *systematically* organized, so that the reader is not subjected to stream of consciousness musings but well-ordered observations, coherently linked.

Boff divides his work into four major sections. In Part One he places the theology of grace into its concrete historical and cultural context, showing the multi-faceted interplay between theological reflection and social reality. Part Two examines the experiences which underlie and animate theological constructions and explores the challenges emanating today from a scientific world view and from the specific socio-political situation of Latin America. Part Three then initiates Boff's own systematic proposal by presenting a theological anthroplogy whose key category is "historical project". Finally, Part Four sketches a doctrine of God as trinity, upholding and favoring humanity's liberation in history.

At a time when much theological writing sounds a reductionist key, Boff's work recommends itself as an exercise in a truly catholic vision. He rightly insists on the primacy of praxis in Christian living, yet never construes that praxis one-dimensionally. He is sensitive to the urgent need for committed action in the public domain, yet does not neglect the place of prayer and suffering in Gospel-inspired transformation. He seeks to recover the engendering experience at the origin of doctrinal formulations, yet does not deprecate analysis (even of the ontological variety). Finally, he recognizes that the Gospel call to conversion, though its implications are multiform, addresses all, and not merely one social class or power bloc.

If there is an area of weakness in Boff's work, it lies, I think, in Part Four, where he reflects theologically upon the God who sustains the movement of liberating grace. Boff is quite insightful in suggesting that only the living, triune God (whose mystery the theological and spiritual tradition has symbolized in terms of trinitarian processions) can originate and sustain the process of history and humanization. But, having so affirmed, Boff's discussion grows curiously less bold. Thus he entitles chapter eighteen, "The Holy Spirit: One Person in Many Persons." [and the] subsection of the chapter is headed, "The Era of the Holy Spirit"; yet the chapter disappoints on the whole, and its promise goes unfulfilled. Not that one disagrees with what is said; rather, one's expectation that the vision which structures and supports the praxis will here find a theoretical foundation is not met. The failure is all the more regrettable in that Boff repeatedly shows himself sensitive to the function and importance of thematization in clarifying and empowering experience. What results from this is that the great themes of the book—grace in its individual and communal manifestations, its mystical and political shapes—seem suggestively juxtaposed, rather than satisfactorily integrated.

This task of integration remains, undoubtedly, the central theological challenge posed by post-Vatican II reflection and praxis. Boff's work significantly confronts the challenge and provides important markings for the journey. It is no small achievement to have accomplished so much. Even more impressive is that he has done so in the very spirit he himself counsels for the meditation upon "holy things": "the spirit of delicacy, cordiality, and courtesy." (pp. 137–38)

Robert P. Imbelli, in a review of "Liberating Grace," in *New Catholic World*, Vol. 223, No. 1335, May–June, 1980, pp. 137–38.

GERALD TWOMEY
(essay date 1981)

[In the following essay, Twomey discusses *Way of the Cross—Way of Justice*, finding it a systematic and prophetic reflection on social inequities in light of Jesus Christ's passion, death, and resurrection.]

In introducing [*Way of the Cross—Way of Justice*], Brazilian theologian Leonardo Boff comments that theology "is born of the concrete experience of faith, and it should nurture that faith. The ultimate criterion of any and all theology is whether it produces a life of faith, hope and charity. Theology is true insofar as it is translated into meditation, prayer, the following of Christ and commitment to our fellow human beings."

Boff ranks among the premier Latin American liberation theologians, and for years he has directed the focus of his theological inquiry toward the mystery of Christ. His efforts have born fruit in five books over the past decade, among them the highly acclaimed *Jesus Christ Liberator*. He offers this *Way of the Cross* as a "prayerful theology or a theological prayer." Father Boff's extensive systematic and pastoral reflection and hunger for justice and for the assurance of human rights gave rise to this collecion of prose-poems centering upon the traditional Stations of the Cross. The book is handsomely laid out and designed, and contemporary photos complement the text.

Boff uses "both eyes of theology" in looking back to the past, where salvation broke in through the cross and Resurrection of Jesus the Christ, and in focusing in on the continued passion of Christ today in the pain and suffering of our own contemporaries. He reminds his readers that Jesus' Resurrection is not complete while his passion still goes on in the passion of his sisters and brothers, yet he sees salvation taking place "when we make the leap from theory to real, authentic practice." He perceives Jesus' Resurrection as the final triumph of justice, and also as a process which will continue until it embraces all of creation. This is truly a work of liberating theology that promises to be of interest to a broad range of Christian readers.

While Christological reflection takes the fore in this work, Boff has produced some fine contemporary Mariology in the chapter entitled, "Jesus meets his afflicted mother." He demonstrates a consistent ability to stress the truth of Christian theology, and to translate it into meditation, prayer, commitment to Christ and commitment to other persons.

Occasionally the work shows an undercurrent of harshness, conditioned in large measure by the experience of violence and repression which frames the author's third world field of vision. For instance, he writes: "Those who violated life, deprived others of life, and crucified the living will ever remain seeds that failed to take root, buds that failed to open, and cocoons that were forever closed in upon themselves. Their fate is absolute and total frustration." While this tendency may generate some discomfort, it is in line with the cutting edge of the Gospel's

prophetic message, and well founded in the Christian tradition. Dante could not have said it better. (pp. 107–08)

Gerald Twomey, in a review of "Way of the Cross—Way of Justice," in *America*, Vol. 144, No. 5, February 7, 1981, pp. 107–08.

JOSEPH D. AYD

(essay date 1983)

[Here, Ayd briefly reviews *Saint Francis: A Model for Human Liberation*, finding that the work's technical vocabulary detracts from an otherwise penetrating and moving study of liberation theology.]

In 1924 G. K. Chesterton wrote a popular little book about St. Francis of Assisi. Still in print, that small masterpiece remains the best thing I have read on *il Poverello*. Summing up the saint, whom he thought of as a troubador, Chesterton said, "He was a lover. He was a lover of God and he was really and truly a lover of men; possibly a much rarer mystical vocation."

Father Boff, who teaches theology in the major seminary of Petroplis in Brazil, has captured much of Francis' spirit in the pages of his book, but he has gone beyond his saintly subject to reflect on: an oppressive consumer-oriented society, the spiritual and economic walls between rich and poor, a freedom achieved not by violence but by inner strength, the new Church reflecting and ministering to existing realities, and the integration of the negative into everyday life.

Saint Francis is an interesting and moving book but, being the work of a theologian, it is laden with the freight of words like *Logos, Eros, Pathos*, and *Techne*, as well as phrases like "Confraternization with Nature: The Cosmic Democracy," "The Synthesis of Interior Archaeology and Exterior Ecology," and "Radical 'Disappropriation' and Total Rejection of 'Appropriation'." Such terms are hardly inviting to the general public. While professionals might have preferrd either a treatise on liberation theology or a more complete biography of Francis of Assisi, Boff has attempted to integrate the two with some success, but the writing—perhaps his prose is translated—is not the kind that will provide pleasure.

If a reader wants to delight in style, he would be better advised to turn to Chesterton in whose pages he will find a remarkable number of the same insights that Boff exposes in the book at hand. But if he wants a rather restrained view of the Little Poor Man as a model for human liberation in the modern world, he will find much to admire in Boff's volume. Neither Chesterton nor Boff has produced a thorough-going, chronological biography of St. Francis. For that, I have no suggestions to offer.

Joseph D. Ayd, in a review of "Saint Francis: A Model for Human Liberation," in *Best Sellers*, Vol. 43, No. 1, April, 1983, p. 26.

SACRED CONGREGATION FOR THE DOCTRINE OF THE FAITH

(essay date 1984)

[The Sacred Congregation published the document from which this excerpt is drawn four days prior to its September 1984 colloquy with Boff. It outlines several of liberation theology's doctrinal errors, focusing particulary on the partisan reading of fundamental religious concepts against the background of Marxist hermeneutics.]

The Gospel of Jesus Christ is a message of freedom and a force for liberation. In recent years, this essential truth has become the object of reflection for theologians, with a new kind of attention which is itself full of promise.

Liberation is first and foremost liberation from the radical slavery of sin. Its end and its goal is the freedom of the children of God, which is the gift of grace. As a logical consequence, it calls for freedom from many different kinds of slavery in the cultural, economic, social and political spheres, all of which derive ultimately from sin, and so often prevent people from living in a manner befitting their dignity. To discern clearly what is fundamental to this issue and what is a by-product of it, is an indispensable condition for any theological reflection on liberation.

Faced with the urgency of certain problems, some are tempted to emphasize, unilaterally, the liberation from servitude of an earthly and temporal kind. They do so in such a way that they seem to put liberation from sin in second place, and so fail to give it the primary importance it is due. Thus, their very presentation of the problems is confused and ambiguous. Others, in an effort to learn more precisely what are the causes of the slavery which they want to end, make use of different concepts without sufficient critical caution. It is difficult, and perhaps impossible, to purify these borrowed concepts of an ideological inspiration which is incompatible with Christian faith and the ethical requirements which flow from it. (pp. 3–4)

The present Instruction has a . . . limited and precise purpose: to draw the attention of pastors, theologians, and all the faithful to the deviations, and risks of deviation, damaging to the faith and to Christian living,

---

An Excerpt from *Church: Charism and Power*:

The specific function of the hierarchy (those who are in leadership roles) is not accumulation but integration, making way for unity and harmony among the various services so that any single one does not trip up, drown out, or downplay another. From this comes the immediate subordination of the members to those in the hierarchy. However, the hierarchy does not exist to subordinate but rather to nourish the spirit of fraternity and unity. This charism of unity implies all other charisms, such as dialogue, patience, listening, serenity, knowledge of the human heart with its desire for power and self-affirmation. This hierarchical function is carried out by the coordinator of a local ecclesial community, by the bishop in his diocese, and by the Pope in the universal Church.

Due to the charism of unity, there are those who preside at the celebrations of the community, those who are primarily responsible for orthodox doctrine, and for the order of charity. It is particularly necessary for these persons to discern the spirit of the community and to watch that all charisms retain their nature as charism, in service for the good of the community.

This model of organization may shape the living of the Gospel in small groups, building more and more of a netwerk of communities that embrace Christians, religious, priests and bishops. It provides the opportunity for the Church, born from the faith of the people through the Spirit of God, to make this organization, envisioned by Paul, real and viable. At the very least, it will foster a spirit which, in the strength of the Holy Spirit, will revitalize the traditional and hierarchical institutions of the Chruch. And, the history of salvation tells us that where the Spirit is active, we can count on the unexpected, the new that has not yet been seen.

Leonardo Boff, in his *Church: Charism and Power: Liberation Theology and the Institutional Church*, translated by John W. Diercksmeier, Crossroad, 1985.

---

that are brought about by certain forms of liberation theology which use, in an insufficiently critical manner, concepts borrowed from various currents of marxist thought.

This warning should in no way be interpreted as a disavowal of all those who want to respond generously and with an authentic evangelical spirit to the "preferential option for the poor". It should not at all serve as an excuse for those who maintain an attitude of neutrality and indifference in the face of the tragic and pressing problems of human misery and injustice. It is, on the contrary, dictated by the certitude that the serious ideological deviations which it points out tend inevitably to betray the cause of the poor. More than ever, it is important that numerous Christians, whose faith is clear and who are committed to live the Christian life in its fullness, become involved in the struggle for justice, freedom and human dignity because of their love for their disinherited, oppressed and persecuted brothers and sisters. More than ever, the Church intends to condemn abuses, injustices and attacks against freedom, wherever they occur and whoever commits them. She intends to struggle, by her own means, for the defense and advancement of the rights of mankind, especially of the poor. (pp. 4–5)

MARXIST ANALYSIS

1. Impatience and a desire for results has led certain Christians, despairing of every other method, to turn to what they call "marxist analysis".

2. Their reasoning is this: an intolerable and explosive situation requires *effective action* which cannot be put off. Effective action presupposes a *scientific analysis* of the structural causes of poverty. Marxism now provides us with the means to make such an analysis, they say. Then one simply has to apply the analysis to the third-world situation, especially in Latin America.

3. It is clear that scientific knowledge of the situation and of the possible strategies for the transformation of society is a presupposition for any plan capable of attaining the ends proposed. It is also a proof of the seriousness of the effort.

4. But the term "scientific" exerts an almost mythical fascination even though everything called "scientific" is not necessarily scientific at all. That is why the borrowing of a method of approach to reality should be preceded by a careful epistemological critique. This preliminary critical study is missing from more than one "theology of liberation".

5. In the human and social sciences it is well to be aware above all of the plurality of methods and viewpoints, each of which reveals only one aspect of reality which is so complex that it defies simple and univocal explanation.

6. In the case of marxism, in the particular sense given to it in in this context, a preliminary critique is all the more necessary since the thought of Marx is such a global vision of reality that all data received from observation and analysis are brought together in a philosophical and ideological structure, which predetermines the significance and importance to be attached to them.

The ideological principles come prior to the study of the social reality and are presupposed in it. Thus no separation of the parts of this epistemologically unique complex is possible. If one tries to take only one part, say, the analysis, one ends up having to accept the entire ideology. That is why it is not uncommon for the ideological aspects to be predominant among the things which the "theologians of liberation" borrow from marxist authors.

7. The warning of Paul VI [in *Octogesima Adveniens*, 1971] remains fully valid today: marxism as it is actually lived out poses many distinct aspects and questions for Christians to reflect upon and act on. However, it would be "illusory and dangerous to ignore the intimate bond which radically unites them, and to accept elements of the marxist analysis without recognizing its connections with the ideology, or to enter into the practice of class-struggle and of its marxist interpretation while failing to see the kind of totalitarian society to which this process slowly leads."

8. It is true that marxist thought ever since its origins, and even more so lately, has become divided and has given birth to various currents which diverge significantly from one another. To the extent that they remain fully marxist, theses currents continue to be based on certain fundamental tenets which are not compatible with the Christian conception of humanity and society. In this context, certian formulas are not neutral, but keep the meaning they had in the original marxist doctrine. This is the case with the "class-struggle". This expression remains pregnant with the interpretation that Marx gave it, so it cannot be taken as the equivalent of "severe social conflict", in an empirical sense. Those who use similar formulas, while claiming to keep only certain elements of the marxist analysis and yet to reject this analysis taken as whole, maintain at the very least a serious confusion in the minds of their readers.

9. Let us recall the fact that atheism and the denial of the human person, his liberty and his rights are at the core of the marxist theory. This theory, then, contains errors which directly threaten the truths of the faith regarding the eternal destiny of individual persons. Moreover, to attempt to integrate into theology an analysis whose criterion of interpretation depends on this atheistic conception is to involve oneself in terrible contradictions. What is more, this misunderstanding of the spiritual nature of the person leads to a total subordination of the person to the collectivity, and thus to the denial of the principles of a social and political life which is in keeping with human dignity.

10. A critical examination of the analytical methods borrowed from other disciplines must be carried out in a special way by theologians. It is the light of faith which provides theology with its principles. That is why the use of philosophical positions or of human sciences by the theologian has a value which might be called instrumental, but yet must undergo a critical study from a theological perspective. In other words, the ultimate and decisive criterion for truth can only be a criterion which is itself theological. It is only in the light of faith, and what faith teaches us about the truth of man and the ultimate meaning of his destiny, that one can judge the validity or degree of validity of what other disciplines propose, often rather conjecturally, as being the truth about man, his history and his destiny.

11. When modes of interpretation are applied to the economic, social and political reality of today, which are themselves borrowed from marxist thought, they can give the initial impression of a certain plausibility, to the degree that the present-day situation in certain countries is similar

to what Marx described and interpreted in the middle of the last century. On the basis of these similarities, certain simplifications are made which, abstracting from specific essential factors, prevent any really rigorous examination of the causes of poverty and prolong the confusion.

12. In certain parts of Latin America, the seizure of the vast majority of the wealth by an oligarchy of owners bereft of social consciousness, the practical absence or the shortcomings of a rule of law, military dictators making a mockery of elementary human rights, the corruption of certain powerful officials, the savage practices of some foreign capital interests constitute factors which nourish a passion for revolt among those who thus consider themselves the powerless victims of a new colonialism in the technological, financial, monetary or economic order. The recognition of injustice is accompanied by a *pathos* which borrows its language from marxism, wrongly presented as though it were scientific language.

13. The first condition for any analysis is a total openness to the reality to be described. That is why a critical consciousness has to accompany the use of any working hypotheses that are being adopted. One has to realize that these hypotheses correspond to a particular viewpoint which will inevitably highlight certain aspects of the reality while leaving others in the shade. This limitation which derives from the nature of human science is ignored by those who, under the guise of hypotheses recognized as such, have recourse to such an all-embracing conception of reality as the thought or Karl Marx.

SUBVERSION OF THE MEANING OF TRUTH AND VIOLENCE

1. This all-embracing conception thus imposes its logic and leads the "theologies of liberation" to accept a series of positions which are incompatible with the Christian vision of humanity. In fact, the ideological core borrowed from marxism, which we are referring to, exercises the function of a *determining principle*. It has this role in virtue of its being described as "scientific", that is to say, true of necessity.

In this core, we can distinguish several components.

2. According to the logic of marxist thought, the "analysis" is inseparable from the *praxis*, and from the conception of history to which this *praxis* is linked. The analysis is for the marxist an instrument of criticism, and criticism is only one stage in the revolutionary struggle. This struggle is that of the proletarian class, invested with its mission in history.

3. Consequently, for the marxist, only those who engage in the struggle can work out the analysis correctly.

4. The only true consciousness, then, is the *partisan* consciousness.

It is clear that the concept of *truth* itself is in question here, and it is totally subverted: there is no truth, they pretend, except in and through the partisan praxis.

5. For the marxist, the *praxis*, and the truth that comes from it, are partisan *praxis* and truth because the fundamental structure of history is characterized by *class-struggle*. There follows, then, the objective neccessity to enter into the class struggle, which is the dialectical opposite of the relationship of exploitation, which is being condemned. For the marxist, the truth is a truth of class: there is no truth but the truth in the struggle of the revolutionary class.

6. The fundamental law of history, which is the law of the class struggle, implies that society is founded on violence. To the violence which constitutes the relationship of the domination of the rich over the poor, there corresponds the counter-violence of the revolution, by means of which this domination will be reversed.

7. The class struggle is presented as an objective, necessary law. Upon entering this process on behalf of the oppressed, one "makes" truth, one acts "scientifically". Consequently, the conception of the truth goes hand in hand with the affirmation of necessary violence, and so, of a political amorality. Within this perspective, any reference to ethical requirements calling for courageous and radical institutional and structural reforms makes no sense.

8. The fundamental law of class struggle has a global and universal character. It is reflected in all the spheres of existence: religious, ethical, cultural and institutional. As far as this law is concerned, none of these spheres is autonomous. In each of them this law constitutes the determining element.

9. In particular, the very nature of ethics is radically called into question because of the borrowing of these from marxism. In fact, it is the transcendent character of the distinction between good and evil, the principle of morality, which is implicitly denied in the perspective of the class struggle.

THE THEOLOGICAL APPLICATION OF THIS CORE

1. The positions here in question are often brought out explicitly in certain of the writings of "theologians of liberation". In others, they follow logically form their premises. In addition, they are presupposed in certain liturgical practices, as for example a "Eucharist" transformed into a celebration of the people in struggle, even though the persons who participate in these practices may not be fully conscious of it. We are facing, therefore, a real system, even if some hesitate to follow logic to its conclusion. As such, this system is a perversion of the Christian message as God entrusted it to His Church. This message in its entirety finds itself then called into question by the "theologies of liberation".

2. It is not the *fact* of social stratification with all its inequity and injustice, but the *theory* of class struggle as the fundamental law of history which has been accepted by these "theologies of liberation" as a principle. The conclusion is drawn that the class struggle thus understood

divides the Church herself, and that in light of this struggle even ecclesial realities must be judged.

The claim is even made that it would [be] maintaining an illusion with bad faith to propose that love in its universality can conquer what is the primary structural law of capitalism.

3. According to this conception, the class struggle is the driving force of history. History thus becomes a central notion. It will be affirmed that God Himself makes history. It will be added that there is only one history, one in which the distinction between the history of salvation and profane history is no longer necessary. To maintain the distinction would be to fall into "dualism". Affirmations such as these reflect historicist immanentism. Thus there is a tendency to identify the kingdom of God and its growth with the human liberation movement, and to make history itself the subject of its own development, as a process of the self-redemption of man by means of the class struggle.

This identification is in opposition to the faith of the Church as it has been reaffirmed by the Second Vatican Council [in *Lumen Gentium*].

4. Along these lines, some go so far as to identify God Himself with history and to define faith as "fidelity to history" which means adhering to a political policy which is suited to the growth of humanity, conceived of as a purely temporal messianism.

5. As a consequence, faith, hope and charity are given a new content: they become "fidelity to history", "confidence in the future", and "option for the poor". This is tantamount to saying they have been emptied of their theological reality.

6. A radical politicization of faith's affirmations and of theological judgments follows inevitably from this new conception. The question no longer has to do with simply drawing attention to the consequences and political implications of the truths of faith, which are respected beforehand for their transcendant value. In this new system, every affirmation of faith or of theology is subordinated to a political criterion, which in turn depends on the class struggle, the driving force of history.

7. As a result, participation in the class struggle is presented as a requirement of charity itself. The desire to love everyone here and now, despite his class, and to go out to meet him with the non-violent means of dialogue and persuasion, is denounced as counterproductive and opposed to love.

If one holds that a person should not be the objcet of hate, it is claimed nevertheless that, if he belongs to the objective class of the rich, he is *primarily* a class enemy to be fought. Thus the universality of love of neighbour and brotherhood become an eschatological principle, which will only have meaning for the "new man" who arises out of the victorious revolution.

8. As far as the Church is concerned, this system would see her *only* as a reality interior to history, herself subject to those laws which are supposed to govern the development of history in its immanence. The Church, the gift of God and mystery of faith, is emptied of any specific reality by this reductionism. At the same time, it is disputed that the participation of Christians who belong to opposing classes at the same Eucharistic Table still makes any sense.

9. In its positive meaning the *Church of the poor* signifies the preference given to the poor, without exclusion, whatever the form of their poverty, because they are preferred by God. The expression also refers to the Church of our time, as communion and institution and on the part of her members, becoming more fully conscious of the requirement of evangelical poverty.

10. But the "theologies of liberation", which reserve credit for restoring to a place of honor the great texts of the prophets and of the Gospel in defense of the poor, go on to a disastrous confusion between the *poor* of the Scripture and the *proletariat* of Marx. In this way they pervert the Christian meaning of the poor, and they transform the fight for the rights of the poor into a class fight within the ideological perspective of the class struggle. For them, the *Church of the poor* signifies the Church of the class which has become aware of the requirements of the revolutionary struggle as a step toward liberation and which celebrates this liberation in its liturgy.

11. A further remark regarding the expression, *Church of the People*, will not be out of place here. From the pastoral point of view, this expression might mean the favored recipients of evangelization to whom, because of their condition, the Church extends her pastoral love first of all. One might also refer to the Church as people of God, that is, people of the New Covenant established in Christ.

12. But the "theologies of liberation" of which we are speaking mean by *Church of the People* a Church of the class, a Church of the oppressed people whom it is necessary to "conscientize" in the light of the organized struggle for freedom. For some, the people, thus understood, even become the object of faith.

13. Building on such a conception of the Church of the People, a critique of the very structures of the Church is developed. It is not simply the case of fraternal correction of pastors of the Church whose behavior does not reflect the evangelical spirit of service and is linked to old-fashioned signs of authority which scandalize the poor. It has to do with a challenge to the *sacramental and hierarchical structure* of the Church, which was willed by the Lord Himself. There is a denunciation of members of the hierarchy and the magisterium as objective representatives of the ruling class which has to be opposed. Theologically, this position means that ministers take their origin from the people who therefore designate ministers of their own

choice in accord with the needs of their historic revolutionary mission.

A NEW HERMENEUTIC

1. The partisan conception of truth, which can be seen in the revolutionary *praxis* of the class, corroborates this position. Theologians who do not share the theses of the "theology of liberation", the hierarchy, and especially the Roman Magisterium are thus discredited *in advance* as belonging to the class of the oppressors. Their theology is a theology of class. Arguments and teachings thus do not have to be examined in themselves since they are only reflections of class interests. Thus, the instruction of others is decreed to be, in principle, false.

2. Here is where the global and all-embracing character of the theology of liberation appears. As a result, it must be criticized not just on the basis of this or that affirmation, but on the basis of its classist viewpoint, which it has adopted *a priori*, and which has come to function in it as a determining principle.

3. Because of this classist presupposition, it becomes very difficult, not to say impossible to enagage in a real dialogue with some "theologians of liberation" in such a way that the other participant is listened to, and his arguments are discussed with objectivity and attention. For these theologians start out with the idea, more or less consciously, that the viewpoint of the oppressed and revolutionary class, which is their own, is the single true point of view. Theological criteria for truth are thus relativized and subordinated to the imperatives of the class struggle. In this perspective, *orthodoxy* or the right rule of faith, is substituted by the notion of *orthopraxy* as the criterion of the truth. In this connection it is important not to confuse practical orientation, which is proper to traditional theology in the same way that speculative orientation is, with the recognized and privileged priority given to a certain type of *praxis*. For them, this praxis is the revolutionary *praxis*, which thus becomes the supreme criterion for theological truth. A healthy theological method no doubt will always take the *praxis* of the Church into account and will find there one of its foundations, but that is because that praxis comes from the faith and is a lived expression of it.

4. For the "theologies of liberation" however, the social doctrine of the Church is rejected with disdain. It is said that it comes from the illusion of a possible compromise, typical of the middle class which has no historic destiny.

5. The new *hermeneutic* inherent in the "theologies of liberation" leads to an essentially *political* re-reading of the Scriptures. Thus, a major importance is given to the *Exodus* event inasmuch as it is a liberation from political servitude. Likewise, a political reading of the *Magnificat* is proposed. The mistake here is not in bringing attention to a political dimension of the readings of Scripture, but in making of this one dimension the principal or exclusive component. This leads to a reductionist reading of the Bible.

6. Likewise, one places oneself within the perspective of a temporal messianism, which is one of the most radical of the expressions of secularization of the Kingdom of God and of its absorption into the immanence of human history.

7. In giving such priority to the political dimension, one is led to deny the *radical newness* of the New Testament and above all to misunderstand the person of Our Lord Jesus Christ, true God and true man, and thus the specific character of the salvation he gave us, that is above all liberation from sin, which is the source of all evils.

8. Moreover in setting aside the authoritative interpretation of the Church, denounced as classist, one is at the same time departing from tradition. In that way, one is robbed of an essential theological criterion of interpretation and, in the vacuum thus created, one welcomes the most radical theses of rationalist exegesis. Without a critical eye, one returns to the opposition of the *"Jesus of history"* versus the *"Jesus of faith"*.

9. Of course the creeds of the faith are literally preserved, especially the Chalcedonian creed, but a new meaning is given to them which is a negation of the faith of the Church. On one hand, the Christological doctrine of Tradition is rejected in the name of class; on the other hand, one claims to meet again the "Jesus of history" coming from the revolutionary experience of the struggle of the poor for their liberation.

10. One claims to be reliving an experience similar to that of Jesus. The experience of the poor struggling for their liberation, which was Jesus' experience, would thus reveal, and it alone, the knowledge of the true God and of the Kingdom.

11. Faith in the Incarnate Word, dead and risen for all men, and whom "God made Lord and Christ" [Acts 2:36] is denied. In its place is substituted a figure of Jesus who is a kind of symbol who sums up in Himself the requirements of the struggle of the oppressed.

12. An exclusively political interpretation is thus given to the death of Christ. In this way, its value for salvation and the whole economy of redemption is denied.

13. This new interpretation thus touches the whole of the Christian mystery.

14. In a general way, this brings about what can be called an inversion of symbols. Thus, instead of seeing, with St. Paul a figure of Baptism in the Exodus [I Corinthians 10: 1-2], some end up making of it a symbol of the political liberation of the people.

15. When the same hermeneutical criterion is applied to the life and to the hierarchical constitution of the Church, the relationship between the hierarchy and the "base" becomes the relationship of obedient domination

to the law of the struggle of the classes. Sacramentality, which is at the root of the ecclesial ministries and which makes of the Church a spiritual reality which cannot be reduced to a purely sociological analysis, is quite simply ignored.

16. This inversion of symbols is likewise verified in the area of the *sacraments*. The Eucharist is no longer to be understood as the real sacramental presence of the reconciling sacrifice, and as the gift of the Body and Blood of Christ. It becomes a celebration of the people in their struggle. As a consequence the unity of the Church is radically denied. Unity, reconciliation and communion in love are no longer seen as a gift we receive from Christ. It is the historical class of the poor who by means of their struggle will build unity. For them, the struggle of the classes is the way to unity. The Eucharist thus becomes the Eucharist of the class. At the same time, they deny the triumphant force of the love of God which has been given to us.

ORIENTATIONS

1. The warning against the serous deviations of some "theologies of liberation" must not at all be taken as some kind of approval, even indirect, of those who keep the poor in misery, who profit from that misery, who notice it while doing nothing about it, or who remain indifferent to it. The Church, guided by the Gospel of mercy and by the love for mankind, hears the cry for justice and intends to respond to it with all her might.

2. Thus a great call goes out to all the Church: with boldness and courage, with farsightedness and prudence, with zeal and strength of spirit, with a love for the poor which demands sacrifice, pastors will consider the response to this call a matter of the highest priority, as many already do.

3. All priests, religious and laypeople who hear this call for justice and who want to work for evangelization and the advancement of mankind, will do so in communion with their bishop and with the Church, each in accord with his or her own specific ecclesial vocation.

4. Aware of the ecclesial character of their vocation, theologians will collaborate loyally and with a spirit of dialogue with the Magisterium of the Church. They will be able to recognize in the Magisterium a gift of Christ to His Church and will welcome its word and its directives with filial respect.

5. It is only when one begins with the task of evangelization understood in its entirety that the authentic requirements of human progress and liberation are appreciated. This liberation has as its indispensable pillars: *the truth about Jesus the Savior, the truth about the Church,* and *the truth about man and his dignity.*

It is in light of the Beatitudes, and especially the Beatitude of the poor of heart that the Church, which wants to be the Church of the poor throughout the world, intends to come to the aid of the noble struggle for truth and justice. She addresses each person, and for that reason, every person. She is the "universal Church. The Church of the Incarnation. She is not the Church of one class or another. And she speaks in the name of truth itself. This truth is realistic". It leads to a recognition "of every human reality, every injustice, every tension and every struggle" [John Paul II, "Address to the Farela 'Vidigal' at Rio de Janeiro," 2 July 1980].

6. An effective defense of justice needs to be based on the truth of mankind, created in the image of God and called to the grace opf divine sonship. The recognition of the true relationship of human beings to God constitutes the foundation of justice to the extent that it rules the relationship between people. That is why the fight for the rights of man, which the Church does not cease to reaffirm, constitutes the authentic fight for justice.

7. The truth of mankind requires that this battle be fought in ways consistent with human dignity. That is why the systematic and deliberate recourse to blind violence, no matter from which side it comes, must be condemned. To put one's trust in violent means in the hope of restoring more justice is to become the victim of a fatal illusion: violence begets violence and degrades man. It mocks the dignity of man in the person of the victims and it debases that same dignity among those who practice it.

8. The acute need for radical reforms of the structures which conceal poverty and which are themselves forms of violence, should not let us lose sight of the fact that the source of injustice is in the hearts of men. Therefore it is only by making an appeal to the *moral potential* of the person and to the constant need for interior conversion, that social change will be brought about which will truly be in the service of man. For it will only be in the measure that they collaborate freely in these necessary changes through their own initiative and in solidarity, that people, awakened to a sense of their responsibility, will grow in humanity.

The inversion of morality and structures is steeped in a materialist anthropology which is incompatible with the dignity of mankind.

9. It is therefore an equally fatal illusion to believe that these new structures will of themselves give birth to a "new man" in the sense of the truth of man. The Christian cannot forget that it is only the Holy Spirit who has been given to us Who is the source of every true renewal and that God is the Lord of History.

10. By the same token, the overthrow by means of revolutionary violence of structures which generate violence is not *ipso facto* the beginning of a just regime. A major fact of our time ought to evoke the reflection of all those who would sincerely work for the true liberation of their brothers: millions of our own contemporaries legitimately yearn to recover those basic freedoms of which they were deprived by totalitarian and atheistic regimes which came to power by violent and revolutionary means,

precisely in the name of the liberation of the people. This shame of our time cannot be ignored: while claiming to bring them freedom, these regimes keep whole nations in conditions of servitude which are unworthy of mankind. Those who, perhaps inadvertently, make themselves accomplices of similar enslavements betray the very poor they mean to help.

11. The class struggle as a road toward a classless society is a myth which slows reform and aggravates poverty and injustice. Those who allow themselves to be caught up in fascination with this myth should reflect on the bitter examples history has to offer about where it leads. They would then understand that we are not talking here about abandoning an effective means of struggle on behalf of the poor for an ideal which has no practical effects. On the contrary, we are talking about freeing oneself from a delusion in order to base oneself squarely on the Gospel and its power of realization.

12. One of the conditions for necessary theological correction is giving proper value to the *social teaching of the Church*. This teaching is by no means closed. It is, on the contrary, open to all the new questions which are so numerous today. In this perspective, the contribution of theologians and other thinkers in all parts of the world to the reflection of the Church is indispensable today.

13. Likewise the experience of those who work directly for evangelization and for the advancement of the poor and the oppressed is necessary for the doctrinal and pastoral reflection of the Church. In this sense, it is necessary to affirm that one becomes more aware of certain aspects of truth by starting with *praxis*, if by that one means pastoral *praxis* and social work which keeps its evangelical inspiration.

14. The teaching of the Church on social issues indicates the main lines of ethical orientation. But in order that it be able to guide action directly, the Church needs competent people from a scientific and technological viewpoint, as well as in the human and political sciences. Pastors should be attentive to the formation of persons of such capability who live the Gospel deeply. Laypersons, whose proper mission is to build society, are involved here to the highest degree.

15. The theses of the "theologies of liberation" are widely popularized under a simplified form, in formation sessions or in what are called "base groups" which lack the necessary catechetical and theological preparation as well as the capacity for discernment. Thus these theses are accepted by generous men and women without any critical judgment being made.

16. That is why pastors must look after the quality and the content of catechesis and formation which should always present the *whole message of salvation* and the imperatives of true liberation within the framework of this whole message.

17. In this full presentation of Christianity, it is proper to emphasize those essential aspects which the "theologies of liberation" especially tend to misunderstand or to eliminate, namely: the transcendance and gratuity of liberation in Jesus Christ, true God and true man; the sovereigny of grace; and the true nature of the means of salvation, especially of the Church and the sacraments. One should also keep in mind the true meaning of ethics in which the distinction between good and evil is not relativized, the real meaning of sin, the necessity for conversion, and the universality of the law of fraternal love.

One needs to be on guard against the politicization of existence which, misunderstanding the entire meaning of the Kingdom of God and the transcendence of the person, begins to sacralize politics and betray the religion of the people in favor of the projects of the revolution.

18. The defenders of orthodoxy are sometimes accused of passivity, indulgence or culpable complicity regarding the intolerable situations of injustice and the political regimes which prolong them. Spiritual conversion, the intensity of the love of God and neighbour, zeal for justice and peace, the Gospel meaning of the poor and of poverty, are required of everyone, and especially of pastors and those in positions of responsibility. The concern for the purity of the faith demands giving the answer of effective witness in the service of one's neighbour, the poor and the oppressed in particular, in an integral theological fashion. By the witness of their dynamic and constructive power to love, Christians will thus lay the foundations of this "civilization of love" of which the Conference of Puebla spoke, following Paul VI. Moreover there are already many priests, religious and laypeople who are consecrated in a truly evangelical way for the creation of a just society.

CONCLUSION

The words of Paul VI in his *Profession of Faith* [30 June 1968], express with full clarity the faith of the Church, from which one cannot deviate without provoking, besides spiritual disaster, new miseries and new types of slavery.

"We profess our faith that the kingdom of God, begun here below in the Church of Christ, is not of this world, whose form is passing away, and that its own growth cannot be confused with the progress of civilization, of science or of human technology, but that it consists in knowing ever more deeply the unfathomable riches of Christ, to hope ever more strongly in things eternal, to respond ever more ardently to the love of God, to spread ever more widely grace and holiness among men. But it is this very same love which makes the Church constantly concerned for the true temporal good of mankind as well. Never ceasing to recall to her children that they have no lasting dwelling here on earth, she urges them also to contribute, each according to his own vocation and means, to the welfare of their earthly city, to promote justice, peace and brotherhood among men, to lavish their assistance on their brothers, especially on the poor and the most dispirited. The intense concern of the Church, the bride of Christ, for the needs of mankind, their joys and their hopes, their pains and their struggles, is nothing other than the great desire to be present to them in order to enlighten them with the light of Christ, and join them all to Him, their only Savior. It can never mean that the Church is conforming to the things of this world, nor that she is lessening the earnestness with which she awaits her Lord and the eternal Kingdom". (pp. 17–35)

Sacred Congregation for the Doctrine of the Faith, in *Instruction on Certain Aspects of the "Theology of Liberation,"* United States Catholic Conference, 1984, 35 p.

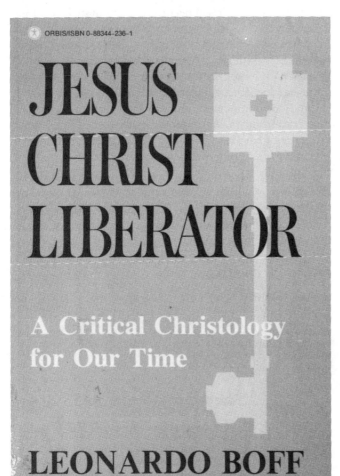

ORBIS/ISBN 0-88344-236-1

JESUS CHRIST LIBERATOR

A Critical Christology for Our Time

LEONARDO BOFF

Dust jacket of Boff's first work on liberation theology in which he stressed a "social over personal" understanding of Jesus Christ.

FRANCIS SCHÜSSLER FIORENZA
(essay date 1985)

[Here, Fiorenza offers an overview of Boff's principal works, namely, *Church: Charism and Power*, *Salvation and Liberation*, and *The Lord's Prayer*. He also elucidates the controversial nature of Boff's writings, particularly his call for a democratization of the institutional church.]

Leonardo Boff has had the reputation of being the most productive and scholarly of the liberation theologians. The publicity surrounding the Holy Office's interrogation of his orthodoxy has now made him one of the most controversial. Of the three volumes [reviewed here] *Church: Charism and Power* is by far the most significant and breaks new ground, whereas the first two volumes develop familiar themes.

Salvation and Liberation provides in three short essays a brief but one of the best introductions to liberation theology. The first essay outlines the basics of liberation theology, its starting-point and method. The second sketches the relationship between integral liberation and partial liberations by outlining four models of the relation between salvation in Jesus and historical, social, and political liberations: Chalcedonian, sacramental agapic, and anthropological. Each of these models demonstrates an "*identification* without total identity." The concluding essay by Clovis Boff, Leonardo's brother, written in the form of a dialogue between a priest, a theologian, and an activist clarifies issues of liberation theology. Whereas Leonardo emphasizes that the integration between salvation and liberation does not entail a simple identity, Clovis criticizes previous liberation theologians for distinguishing the various levels that distort the total integration between liberation and salvation.

In *The Lord's Prayer* Boff offers a verse by verse commentary that illustrates the contrast between Christian spirituality and any combination of reductive Marxist and psychoanalytic analyses. The Fatherhood of God is not a projection compensating for infantile helplessness. The sanctification of God's name implies the irreducibility of the human person. Christian spirituality with its belief in God's righteousness and kingdom does not withdraw from social responsibility but makes ethical and social behavior a criterion of Christian existence. Boff interprets eschatology as an "inaugural eschatology" and there by undercuts the previous interpretations of *The Lord's Prayer* as simply an apocalyptic expectation of the end-time. He stresses that God's reign has begun in Christ, awaits an eschatological completion, but its presence entails a commitment to justice for the poor.

Church: Charism and Power develops as its central thesis that the liberation of the world cannot take place without a prior liberation of the church. The struggle for justice and rights in the world is intertwined with the struggle for justice and rights in the church. North American theologians, especially Richard McBrien, have often objected that liberation theology in its commitment to justice in the world overlooks the need for justice within the church. Taking up this challenge, Boff argues that liberation theology entails the formation of the church in base communities, not simply as a pastoral activity, but as the very function of theology and the center of Christian and Catholic identity. He offers a vision of liberation theology that is at the same time a new vision of the Catholic church.

The preferential option for the poor demands certain shifts within Roman Catholicism. It entails a shift from theology as an exposition of the deposit of the faith to theology as the discernment of the signs of the times, especially the need for justice and the presence of God's Spirit in the church's concern for liberation. It requires a conversion of the institutional church from a reliance on power and coercion to deal with dissent to an openness for free speech. It challenges the church to shake off its characteristics as an upper-and middle-class church and to acquire those characteristics attuned to the poor. It presupposes an equality of persons that does not exclude women from ordination. And it demands an alternative model and structure of the church that overcomes the split between a teaching church and a discerning church. For Boff this alternative model is the church as the sacrament of the Spirit with charisms as its organizing principle.

Throughout *Church: Charism and Power* Boff argues that liberation theology is as much a vision of the church and Catholicism as it is a vision of a new politics. From the perspective of North America and the pluralisitic situation in the United States, liberation theology does not reflect sufficiently on the pluralism of the political programs and the option for the poor, and on the need for a political ethics to mediate between Christian faith and political praxis. If one reads Boff for answers to some of these problems, one will be disappointed, for he does not focus upon his choice of political options, but rather upon the necessary changes within the church.

Boff's strength lies in his analysis of traditional theology, especially the origin and nature of the church. His German doctoral dissertation has long been the classic study on the nature of the church as a sacrament. He now devolops his ecclesiology from an emphasis on the church as the sacrament of Christ to an emphasis on the church as the sacrament of the Spirit. He builds on the historical consensus worked out by Cardinal Ratzinger and others in regard to the foundation of the church. Since Jesus' mission was primarily to Israel, the foundation of the church takes place only after his death and resurrection. The church is a post-Easter creation of the Spirit.

Boff draws out the systematic and practical implications of this position for the nature, formation, and structure of the church. In the contemporary situation the base communities exemplify within the present that structure of the formation of the church under the influence of God's Spirit. Such a vision of the church leads to the present theological controversy surrounding Boff's work. Referring to the "good example that base communities give," Cardinal Ratzinger had previously written that "in the present situation it is necessary to form living cells, that consciously step out of the compulsion of the modern milieu and live with one another the alternative of the Gospel." (*Theologische Prinzipienlehre*, 1982). He had suggested that it will become evident in such communities that the "Catholic principle does not produce only the hardenedness and anonymity of large organizations, but rather is vivifying." A similar vision of the "Catholic" priniciple underlies Boff's book. It combines the struggle for justice and liberation with the formation of the church through the democratic freedom and charismatic spirit of base communities. A point of controversy! For despite his praise of base communities, Ratzinger warned in that very same essay against bringing into such communities the culturally conditioned ideas of modern democracy.

Boff's *Church: Charism and Power* is a powerful defense of liberation theology. He admirably demonstrates that the issues of liberation theology are at the centre of the church's self-understanding. The controversy is not about one movement within theology but about one's vision of Catholicism. (pp. 79, 81–2)

Francis Schüssler Fiorenza, "Reenvisioning Church," in *Commonweal*, Vol. CXII, No.3, February 8, 1985, pp. 79, 81–2.

PETER HEBBLETHWAITE

(essay date 1985)

[In the following essay, Waite reviews *Church: Charism and Power: Liberation Theology and the Institutional Church*, finding it "a useful but unremarkble contribution to post-conciliar ecclesiology." He also comments on the controversial nature of Boff's writings and the potential threat that liberation theology poses to the institutional church.]

The cover of this translation of Leonardo Boff's book shows him in his Franciscan habit speaking to the crowd of journalists who surrounded him after his "colloquy" with Cardinal Joseph Ratzinger on September 7, 1984. Microphones and cassette recorders are pointed at him.

He looks (and was) confident and relaxed. He had been vigorously defended by his own Brazilian bishops. Yet by March 11, 1985, Cardinal Ratzinger wrote a letter saying that "some of Boff's options were such as to endanger the sound doctrine of the faith" which the cardinal's office (the Congregation for the Doctrine of Faith, formerly the Holy Office) has to uphold. That didn't sound like a hanging matter. But within the month, it was revealed that Fr Boff had been relieved of the editorship of Brazil's leading theological journal, forbidden to write or lecture or give retreats or preach and—above all—forbidden to give interviews to the press. Boff, in short, has been silenced.

It is difficult for a reviewer to ignore these facts and to treat *Church: Charism and Power: Liberation Theology and the Institutional Church* as what it really is: a useful but unremarkable contribution to post-conciliar ecclesiology, based on European and in particular German thinking but delivered in a Latin-Amercian accent. Ironies abound. Boff's preface begins: "We are living in privileged times. There is an upsurge of life in the Church that is revitalizing the whole body from head to toe." The only reason for quarrelling with that judgment would be that it is over-optimistic. But Boff goes on, already causing a twitch of the inquisitorial eyebrow: "The Church has been placed on the road to renewal, which will surely result in a new manifestation of the Church as institution." It is precisely "new manifestations of the Church as institution" that the Vatican finds threatening. They arise, unpredictably, uncontrollably from below.

The whole of Boff's book, a collection of previously published articles, illustrates this proposition. There is a new model of the Church derived from what the translator calls "the base ecclesial community". It is in effect a small neighbourhood group which works—rather like the Liberals—at the local community level, but with the difference that it starts from the Gospels. These communities are poor. They realize that preferential "option for the poor" which is the chosen policy of the Brazilian bishops.

Boff's book can best be understood as a reflection on the significance of basic communities. He sketches their history and proclaims their potentiality. The sub-headings of Chapter Nine give the outline of the story: "An oppressed yet believing people", "Born from the Word of God", "A new way of being Church", "Sign and instrument of liberation", "A celebration of faith and life". From that it is only a step towards declaring as he does in Chapter Eleven (previously an article in *Concilium*) that the distinction between *ecclesia docens* (the teaching Church) and the *ecclesia discens* (the Church that is taught) has already broken down.

Frankly, I do not see any reason to be alarmed by that suggestion, but it seems to be the grounds for Cardinal Ratzinger's concern; especially since it combines with another theme that Boff learned about—another irony—

in Germany, where he studied in the early 1970s. It was part of long-running debate about the relation between "Catholicism" and "Christianity". The "pure" Protestant position, now abandoned, held that Catholicism was simply the corruption of Christianity. Catholics replied that Catholocism is an embodiment of the Gospel—and one that was necessary if the Gospel were ever to be capable of shaping an entire society. That is the difference between a private hole-in-the-corner sect and a Church socially engaged in the world. Boff repeats this apologia for Catholicism. It is not some falling away from a primitive ideal. It was the only way the Gospel could be made effective.

But—again the inquisitorial eyebrows twitch, more nervously this time—Boff concedes to the "Protestant" view, that Catholicism runs the risk of taking aboard some of the characteristics of the society that it wishes to convert. It will be feudal in a feudal society, autocratic in an autocratic society. Boff calls this the "pathology of Catholicism" and provides a searing diagnostic of how this admirable thing can go utterly wrong. Thus he writes about an unspecified historical period (it sounds like the Counter-Reformation, but it could be now):

> All decisions were centralized in a small hierachical elite through the absolutizing of doctrine, cultural forms and the distribution of power within the community. The absolutizing of a form of the Church's presence in society led to the oppression of the faithful. Institutional arthritis led to the lack of imagination, of the critical spirit, of creativity. Anything new was immediately under suspicion. . . . The drive for security was much stronger than that for truth and authenticity. Tensions were, and often are, frequently suffocated through a repression that often violates the basic human rights that are manifested even by officially atheistic societies.

More ironies here. In the act of silencing Boff, indefinitely, the Vatican proves him right. It also makes legitimate objections to the incoherence of some of his theological positions more difficult to state: he has been removed from the ordinary theological rough-and-tumble. Final irony: liberation theology habitually presented itself as "the voice of those who have no voice". But now "the voice of those who have no voice" has no voice. That hardly confirms Boff's optimism about the "upsurge of life in the Church that is revitalizing the whole body".

Peter Hebblethwaite, "Learning from the Voiceless, " in *The Times Literary Supplement*, No. 4301, September 6, 1985, p. 986.

force readings of Scripture and Councils.

Frederick A. Homann, in a review of "Ecclesiogenesis," in *Best Sellers*, Vol. 45, No. 12, March, 1986, p. 470.

FREDERICK A. HOMANN
(essay date 1986)

[Below, Homann briefly analyzes Boff's theory of the church's origin and related disputations in *Ecclesiogenesis*.]

Franciscan Leonardo Boff is known today in more than theological circles after his Roman encounter with Cardinal Ratzinger and the Congregation for the Doctrine of the Faith. With Gustavo Gutierrez and Juan Luis Segundo he leads the Latin American school of liberation theology. [*Ecclesiogenesis*] first appeared in Portuguese in parts in 1977 and 1981; it has a stapled-together quality in its organization. Boff tackles elusive problems, notably that of a viable ecclesiology that allows both authority and the *sensus fidelium* to function with vigor. His experience with Brazilian base communities moves him to sketch a theory (Roman authorities view it with skepticism) of churches arising from groups of the faithful hearing God's Word and being energized by the Spirit to work for liberation. In this matrix authority emerges with an essential role to play. This is ecclesiogenesis. Base communities "reinvent" the church. An older approach says rather God's Word is proclaimed with authority by duly chosen apostles, and the effect is Christian community and church of those who believe.

It is good to learn the lines of Boff's new ecclesiology (which, he insists, meets the real here and now needs of his Latin American people), and see how he grounds and harmonizes it with Scripture and church practice. Innovative as they are, his ideas merit careful response from pastors and theologians.

Three *Quaestiones Disputatae* treat related problems. Did the historical Jesus will only one institutional form for the Church? Boff: Jesus willed that form which the apostolic community, enlightened by the Holy Spirit and confronted with the urgencies of its particular (and mutable) situation, decided and in all responsibility assumed. Why cannot lay coordinators consecrate the Eucharist and absolve, now that they perform all the ecclesial tasks an ordained minister performs? Boff: Christ, present but invisible in the community without priest, would through the person of the nonordained coordinator be made sacramentally visible in the celebration of the Lord's Supper in an extraordinary way, but not one opposed to the mind of the Church. May women be ordained to the priesthood? Boff: There is neither Scriptural argument or theologically grounded tradition to justify the concentration of the priesthood today in the hands of men exclusively. Boff is succinct; he seems at times to

ROBERT MCAFEE BROWN
(essay date 1986)

[In the following excerpt, Brown reviews several of Boff's most prominent writings, identifying controversial aspects that led to his censure by the Vatican.]

The Vatican's recent lifting of the "silencing" of Brazilian Franciscan theologian Leonardo Boff for writings deemed injurious to the faith means that his voice and pen once more have their full power. This happy outcome provides an occasion to examine the broad sweep of Boff's writings —not only those that got him in trouble. Whatever Boff's ongoing difficulties with Rome may be, he is an important theologian for all Christians, both Protestants and Catholics.

A review of Boff's writings does not make him seem like a "dangerous" theologian. Christology . . . grace . . . stations of the cross . . . the Lord's Prayer . . . St. Francis—what could be more appropriate subjects for a Catholic theologian? But Boff's unyielding insistence on a theology with two eyes—relating the gospel to the contemporary scene—finally overstepped the presumably appropriate boundaries.

In 1981, not caring to quit while he was ahead, Boff published a collection of essays, **Church: Charism and Power** which, in the original Portuguese, carried the exquisitely descriptive subtitle, *Essays in Militant Ecclesiology*. There is a message here for theologians who want to stay out of trouble: if you must write, don't write about ecclesiology; and if you must write about ecclesiology, don't write militantly. Boff did. And he got into trouble.

Boff's troubles actually have their roots in his doctoral dissertation, which he wrote in Germany under a fellow Franciscan, Bonaventura Kloppenburg. Interestingly enough, his other *Doktorvater* was Joseph Ratzinger, present prefect of the Sacred Congregation for the Doctrine of the Faith. When a summary of Boff's dissertation appeared some years later as a chapter in **Church: Charism and Power**, Kloppenburg—who, in the interval, had become an ardent foe of liberation theology—wrote a long review charging Boff with heresy.

Understandably startled by this about-face on the part of his former teacher, Boff sent a copy of the review and the book to Ratzinger—his other former teacher—asking for advice. Ratzinger suggested that he reply to Kloppenburg's charges, which Boff did.

That, one might have presumed, would have been the end of the matter—save, perhaps, a series of exchanges in some learned theological journal. It wasn't.

In May 1984, Boff received at six-page letter from Ratzinger, detailing charges against him and summoning him to Rome for an accounting. Ratzinger charged Boff with distorting old doctrines by reinterpreting them in new contexts. Boff's language lacked "serenity" and "moderation," and, more substantively, he employed "ideological" perspectives from history, philosophy, sociology and politics that were not fully enough informed by theology. Thus, Ratzinger asked, is Boff guided by faith or by "principles of an ideological nature"?

Ratzinger was deeply disturbed by three areas of Boff's book. He first accused Boff of suggesting that Jesus did not determine the *specific* form and structure of the church, thus implying that other models besides the Roman Catholic one might be consistent with the gospel. A second charge was that he is cavalier about dogma and revelation. Boff responded by acknowledging that dogma is needed to protect against heresy, but not in the same way in all times and places. It is ultimately the life of the Spirit in the church that protects faith against encrustation in "timeless truths" that can only negate spiritual progress. Ratzinger feared that such a doctrine of the Spirit would legitimate the theological whim of the moment.

Finally, Boff is charged with being unnecessarily polemical and disrespectful in his comments on the church's use and abuse of power. Boff certainly does not mince words, and in one place even offers a kind of Marxist analysis of institutional church life, citing "the expropriation of the religious means of production" (forgiveness, sacraments and so forth) as means by which the clergy deny power to the people. Such excessive concentration of power, Boff believes, leads to domination, centralization, marginalization of the faithful, triumphalism and institutional *hubris*—an extensive laundry list of aberrations from which not even the Sacred Congregation itself is exempted. In the notorious Chapter 12—the precis of his dissertation—Boff offers an alternate model of power for the church—a model based on the "service" of a living, changing church in which theological privileges are not concentrated in the few, but shared among the many.

It is clear that the congregation's main fear with Boff is not Marxism (as it is with many other liberation theologians) but his central emphasis on the Holy Spirit, which could challenge the validity of present ecclesial structures. (One is reminded of a comment by Cardinal Ernesto Ruffini during a debate at Vatican II, when, after a number of speeches about the Holy Spirit, he responded, "We don't need the guardianship of the Holy Spirit; we have the hierarchy.")

Boff met with the Sacred Congregation in Rome in September 1984. Though the curtain of secrecy is drawn over such meetings (one of the abuses that Boff had criticized in his writings), Boff emerged from the encounter smiling, believing that he had made the point that, when dealing with liberation theology, the church ought to consult people directly involved in the struggle, rather than relying solely on European theologians who, as he told reporters, "look on poverty from the outside, from a position of security, in a paternalistic way."

One reason that Boff may have escaped censure on this occasion is that (in a move indicating that Franciscans know how to combine the wisdom of the serpent with the gentleness of the dove) he had chosen as the theologian to defend him at the closed-door proceedings His Eminence Cardinal Alois Lorscheider, head of the Brazilian hierarchy—neither a person nor an office that the Sacred Congregation would instinctively care to challenge.

Boff seemed to be home free. He wasn't. Some months later the unexpected order came, consigning him to "silence" for "an opportune period."

It is important to correct any misapprehension that *Church: Charism and Power* is only a polemical tract of interest to those who follow intramural Catholic power struggles—though it is, indeed, eminently illustrative on that level. It is also an example of fresh creativity in Roman Catholic ecclesiology, quite apart form the controversy it has engendered. More important still, it can serve as a vehicle for re-examining the meaning of the church in the lives of all Christians, as we both challenge ossified church structures and engage in rebuilding after some necessary demolition. Boff's own intention is clear:

> Through this analysis we hope to nourish faith in the strength of the Spirit that is capable of awakening the dormant heart of the institutional Church, encouraging the living presence and the dangerous yet powerful memory of the life, death, and resurrection of Jesus Christ.

It would be difficult to overstress the richness of this powerful and clearly written book. Even a look at the table of contents will make the point. The initial essays (1–3) are clear, positive statements about pastoral practices in the church. The next three (4–6) are critiques of current Roman Catholic institutional practices, which with the change of a word here and there, describe Protestant ecclesiastical sins with devastating accuracy. After a transitional essay "In Favor of Syncretism" (7), there are three informative and challenging essays on the "base communities" (8–10), and then three concluding essays (11–13) that profoundly explore an alternative way to view the church as "A Sacrament of the Holy Spirit" with "Charism as the Organizing Principle."

Church: Charism and Power is only the most recent of many books. For more than 15 years, Boff has been among the most important—and prolific—contributors to the developing theology of liberation in Latin America.

In 1972 he provided the first substantial Christology from the new perspective, *Jesus Christ Liberator* just one year after Gustavo Gutiérrez's *A Theology of Liberation* brought Third World theology to the attention of the rest of the world. That year was a bad one for freedom of expression in Brazil, and Boff worked with certain external constraints in saying what he wanted to say about the liberating work of Christ. This caution was overcome in an epilogue, added to English translation in 1978 when the Brazilian political climate had become less repressive. This exciting 31- page essay situates the mission and message of Jesus in a socio-economic setting that illumines the earlier pages.

Another large book, *Liberating Grace*, appeared in 1976, exploring many facets of the traditional doctrine of grace in both social and individual terms. Boff sees grace at work in the midst of a situation of dependency and exploitation, and his whole approach gives special meaning to first word of the title, "liberating." (The combination of "liberation" and "grace" is considered to be so dangerous that one North American writer subsequently cited the book as "among the most significant Socialist or Marxist titles" to come out of Latin America.)

One of Boff's most powerful books is *Way of the Cross—Way of Justice*. Written in blank verse, it is a series of meditations on the stations of the cross, a traditional exercise of individualistic Catholic piety that Boff transforms into a communal exercise as well. He effects this transformation by offering meditations on each of the "stations" of Jesus' original journey along the Via Dolorosa, all of which are followed by second meditations reflecting on the meaning of the station for Jesus' followers in today's world. The practice exemplifies Boff's conviction that theology must have "two eyes, " one looking to the past "where salvation broke in" and the other looking toward the present "where salvation becomes a reality here and now." The "way of the cross" focuses on the historical Jesus, but the "way of justice" focuses "on the Christ of faith who continues his passion today in his brothers and sisters who are being condemned, tortured and killed for the cause of justice. The parallels between what Jesus suffered then and what his followers suffer today are acute and heartrending. The book has intense power, and will surely become one of the spiritual classics of our time.

Another book dramatizing Boff's contention that "devotional" literature and the world of the nitty-gritty cannot be separated, is *The Lord's Prayer: The Prayer of Integral Liberation*. The word "Integral" is the key. "Integral" means "whole, " "entire, " "complete," and Boff insists that the Lord's Prayer gives no support to a merely "spiritual" liberation divorced from the world of poverty and hunger. The book attacks "reductionism, " whether as "theologism" or "secularism." Praying must be done in context: "Prayer is not first thing a person does. Before praying, one experiences an existential shock." Each phrase of the Lord's Prayer is then examined in terms of theology's two eyes. Prayer is always "toward God" and "toward us"; we are not allowed the luxury of separating them.

Boff has also written an engaging and challenging book about the founder of his religious order, *Saint Francis: A Model for Human Liberation*. He is not so naive as to suggest that we can transplant Francis—in all of his breathtaking simplicity—to the complications of the 20th century. But he does believe that important connections can be made. The methodology in each chapter is a clue: after a brief vignette from Francis's life, Boff carefully analyzes some characteristic of our modern world, and then suggests how St. Francis's perspective might illuminate that situation. After describing St. Francis as "a model of gentleness and care" (qualities desperately lacking in our culture), Boff jumps into the fray by dealing with the contribution St. Francis could make to our understanding of "the preferential option for the poor." Another chapter, "Creation of a Popular and Poor Church," indicates what St. Francis could offer to the formation of contemporary "base communities." Throughout, St. Fancis contributes to an "integral liberation"—liberation that is not exclusively "spiritual" or "economic, " but both tied together.

The original terms of Boff's "silencing" were subsequently modified. Although he was still forbidden to publish or give public lectures, he was permitted to teach his seminary classes and, curiously, to preach (a decision that suggests that the Vatican has yet to come to terms with the power of the sermon). At all events, the decision enabled the camel's nose of proclamation to enter the tent of curial repression, for Boff, who is very popular in Brazil, was soon receiving countless invitations to offer "homilies" at Catholic liturgical gatherings.

The recent lifting of the ban (a month ahead of schedule) may be an olive branch from the Curia, and its timing, coincident with the release of Cardinal Ratzinger's temperate second "Instruction" on liberation theology, . . . suggests that the aggressive warlock-hunt (as we must call it in this case) against liberation theologians is being placed on a Vatican back burner, if not on hold. There is no doubt that the Vatican's image suffered as a consequence of a punitive action, suited (if at all) to other centuries than our own, while Boff became an instant folk hero throughout the Third World.

We can be sure, furthermore, that during the time he was forbidden to publish, it crossed his mind that he had not been forbidden to write. The curtailment of outside speaking engagements may even have provided more time than usual to put pen to paper. (When this possibility was mentioned to Gustavo Gutiérrez, one of Boff's *compañeros* in the liberation struggle, he replied, "Yes! After one year, four books!")

Even if that estimate should prove excessive (and

it may not), we can now look forward to more writings by Boff than might have resulted if Rome had left him alone. For this, at least, we can render oblique thanks to the Sacred Congregation of the Doctrine of the Faith. (pp. 615–17)

Robert McAfee Brown, "Leonardo Boff: Theologian for All Christians," in *The Christian Century,* Vol. 103, No. 21, July 2–9, 1986, pp. 615–17.

ANN E. CARR

(essay date 1987)

[In the excerpt below, Carr negatively evaluates *The Maternal Face of God,* faulting Boff's neglect "of recent feminist theology and the ecumenical work on the scriptural data about Mary."]

Leonardo Boff is the Brazilian liberation theologian who received wide publicity . . . when he was silenced by Rome for his pointedly critical analysis of the institutional elements of the Roman Catholic Church in his 1985 *Church: Charism and Power*. His new book on Mariology [*The Maternal Face of God: The Feminine and Its Religious Expressions*], a translation of a 1979 Portuguese publication, is radically novel, yet at the same time clearly in the "maximalist" tradition of Marian thought that was tempered by the decision of the Second Vatican Council (*Lumen Gentium*) to place discussion of Mary in the context of the church. For Boff argues that the Virgin Mary "is to be regarded as hypostatically united to the Third Person of the Blessed Trinity."

To support this thesis, the author offers a series of anthropological, philosophical and theological meditations in which he adopts Jungian categories to describe "the feminine" as the pole of "darkness, mystery, depth, night, death, interiority, feeling, receptivity" in contrast to "the masculine" as "power, order, exteriority, objectivity, reason, . . . aggressiveness transcendence."

These ontological qualities, he asserts, are present in both sexes and in culture itself, and need to be integrated into individual and social life. In Boff's view, the current feminist movement witnesses to the need for the feminine in an overly masculinized, patriarchal society. And a central resource in this task is the Catholic tradition's teaching on Mary, the mother of Jesus, which may be reenvisioned by understanding the feminine as the basic mariological principle.

In Mary's virginial motherhood, Boff writes, the feminine has been subsumed into the divine. Thus it is as correct—within a trinitarian framework—to speak of God the mother as it is of God the father. Just as the

masculine side of humanity has been divinized and eternalized through the male Jesus, Boff speculates, it is the Holy Spirit who will divinize the feminine at the end of history. And he believes that an eschatological anticipation of "this infinitely sweet event" has been given in the mystery of Mary. In addition to the biblical evidence and a questionable suggestion that it is not Christian but Hebrew thought that is patriarchal, Boff uses the titles of co-redemptrix and co-mediatrix, and the patristic symbolism of Eve-Mary as the correlate of Adam-Christ, to claim that Mary is the feminine parallel of Jesus. "Together they translate absolutely what it means to say that the human being is the image of God." Boff finds hints of this "theologoumenon" in various thinkers from both the Eastern and Western Christian traditions.

Boff's work would have benefited from a closer study of recent femininst theology and the ecumenical work on the scriptural data about Mary. The former has pointed to the negative uses and effects which the mariological tradition has had for women; the Eve-Mary symbolism; and the dangers of blaming Israel for patriarchy—as well as to the androcentrism and possible stereotypes of Jungian thought (though the latter is more nuanced than is Boff about the biblical data on Mary). Both Protestants and Catholics may have difficulty with the theological views expressed in this work.

Anne E. Carr, in a review of "The Maternal Face of God: The Feminine and Its Religious Expressions, " in *The Christian Century,* Vol. 104, No. 19, June 17–24, 1987, p. 560.

VIRGINIA SLOYAN

(essay date 1989)

[In the following essay, Sloyan examines *When Theology Listens to the Poor,* praising Boff's attempt to reconcile the liturgical celebration of the Eucharist with conditions of injustice.]

How can we celebrate the Eucharist worthily, in a manner that harmonizes with the character of Jesus' own Eucharist, in a world of injustice and disregard for human rights? Leonardo Boff, in his *When Theology Listens to the Poor* asks that question in as many ways as there are kinds of deprivation in the world and respects his readers by not always coming up with answers.

I would venture that Sunday assemblies across the land include countless worshipers whose concern for social justice is intense, matched only by frustration at their own powerlessness to take effective action. These same persons have figured out that eucharistic worship and a more just communion of sisters and brothers are intimately related, but too often their worship experience weakens the connection and sometimes belies it.

Only when the church—Boff transforms the word into "we" in a way few are able to achieve—sees reality from the eyes of the poor can the crucial connection between celebration and conflict be made. "What is being celebrated is the obliteration of the conflict, " Boff says. "When we view reality from the perspective of the poor, that reality simply must be transformed."

While that summarizes much of the book's intent, it doesn't do justice to Boff's connections and the distinctions. Readers, not skimmers, have a treat in store—but it's the kind of visual treat that opens our eyes wider than many of us had bargained for. (p. 148)

Virginia Sloyan, "Critics' Choices," in *Commonweal*, Vol. CXVI, No. 5, March 10, 1989, pp. 148–49.

SHIRLEY C. GUTHRIE

(essay date 1989)

[In the essay below, Guthrie comments on Boff's innovative and complex interpretation of the doctrine of the Trinity in *Trinity and Society*, particularly citing the theologian's practical application of the teaching to society and the church.]

The doctrine of the Trinity is one of those articles of faith all Christians are "supposed" to accept, though many agree with Kant that it "provides nothing, absolutely nothing, of practical value." In [*Trinity and Society*], Brazilian Leonardo Boff, Franciscan priest and professor of theology, joins other contemporary theologians in defending both the truth and the practical value of this doctrine. For Boff, the community of Father, Son, and Holy Spirit is not only the truth about God; it is also the "prototype of human community dreamed of by those who wish to improve society, " the "model for any just, egalitarian (while respecting differences) social organization."

Frequently expressing agreement with Moltmann's *The Trinity and the Kingdom*, Boff argues that true and relevant trinitarian faith must begin not with the oneness, but with the threeness of God; not with theistic speculation about God as the solitary One, but with openness to the self-revelation of God as a community or society of divine persons, who are what they are in their co-existence, co-relatedness, and self-surrender to each other. More technically expressed, Boff argues that we must not begin with the classical Eastern emphasis on the divine monarchy of God or with the classical Western emphasis on the

one substance shared by the three persons, but with the sixth-century doctrine of *perichoresis*, the interpretation, begin, and indwelling of each of the three in the others.

Beginning with a theistic (monotheistic) understanding of God inevitably leads to a doctrine of the Trinity tinged either by subordinationism (the heresy of the East) or modalism (the heresy of the West). Moreover, it justifies every form of authoritarianism, paternalism, tyranny, or autonomous individualism in political, economic, ecclesiastical, sexual, and familial realationships.

If we begin with the self-revelation of God as Father, Son and Holy Spirit, we come to know the true God whose inner being (immanent trinity) as well as outward activity (economic Trinity) is the unity of communion. This understanding of God leads to a vision of human society in the image of God that on every level is marked by unity in diversity, individuality realized in relatedness, community that includes rather than excludes, mutual giving and receiving that rejects all domination and control, dependency and inferiority.

The book is a careful and clear history and interpretation of the orthodox doctrine of the Trinity. It also contains some provocative suggestions for breaking out of some old impasses—for instance the *filioque* controversy that still separates churches in the East from churches in the West. But Boff becomes most passionate and most interesting when he suggests how a social doctrine of the Trinity enables us to overcome the conflict between individualistic capitalism and collectivistic socialism, oppressor and oppressed, male and female, church authorities (hierarchy) and church members.

Some Roman Catholics as well as Protestants will be troubled by Boff's argument that Mary and indeed all creation are "divinized" by the presence of the Holy Spirit. Even sympathetic readers may question the success of his valiant attempt to achieve a non-sexist understanding of "father, " "son" and "spirit." Others may suspect that however carefully Boff tries to avoid it, his beginning with three instead of one inescapably implies a plurality of deities. But whatever its weaknesses, this is a fine book. In my opinion, Boff does an even better job than Moltmann of developing a trinitarian theology centered in the doctrine of *perichoresis* that is not vulnerable to the charge of tritheism. He also does better than some liberation theologians in providing theological criteria for criticizing *all* ideologies and is thus less vulnerable to the criticism that liberation theology is only the attempt to use God to justify a particular ideology. (pp. 205–06)

Shirley C. Guthrie, in a review of "Trinity and Society," in *Theology Today*, Vol. XLVI, No. 2, July, 1989, pp. 205–06.

JOSEPH P. FITZPATRICK

(essay date 1990)

[In the following essay, Fitzpatrick discusses *Faith on the Edge*, maintaining that the work is a useful introduction to and an outstanding synthesis of Boff's liberation theology. He also praises Boff's effort to relate liberation theology to Marxism, Catholic spirituality, and other movements in the Church's life.]

Leonardo Boff, O.F.M., one of the outstanding representatives of liberation theology, enjoys the notoriety of having been silenced for a year by Vatican officials. *Faith on the Edge* is an English translation of selections from two of his books in Portúguese. The first four chapters are taken from *O Caminhar da lgreja com os Oprimidos* (1980); the last six chapters from *Fé na Perijeria do Mundo* (1978). Many of the chapters overlap, but taken together, they present an excellent brief compendium of Father Boff's concept of liberation theology. To readers familiar with liberation theology, the book offers a well-organized review with some clarifying statements about criticisms of liberation theology; for newcomers to the field, the book serves as a brief, readable and inspiring introduction. It is well translated and easily read.

One great value of the book is the way Boff relates liberation theology to other theological orientations, to major developments in the life of the church, to Marxism and especially to genuinely Catholic spirituality. In these perspectives, liberation theology is seen, not as some unanticipated sport, but as an understandable manifestation of the faith in the presence of oppression with its roots in Catholic traditions.

> Liberation theology represents the first theological current born on the periphery of the metropolitan centres of culture and theological production that has had a repercussion on the entire Church . . . liberation is the comprehensive backdrop against which theologians reflect on the entire content of their faith.

Boff's skillful use of the sociology of knowledge enables him to explain why theologians of other ages interpreted the faith within the total social, cultural, political and economic realities of their day. It also prompts him to declare why the perspective of liberation theology is the only authentic interpretation of the faith in the presence of the massive inhumanity, oppression and injustice of our day. It is the only "responsible theology." Typical of the liberation theologians, and of many other social critics, Boff finds a major cause of this inhuman situation in the functioning of international capitalism. "Underde-

velopment is the direct consequence of developement." But he is careful not to identify "liberation" with any one particular ideology or political theory.

Boff sees three signifcant moments in the unfolding of the life of Jesus in the church: 1) The period of the church "outside the world, " when the church was seen as the sole vehicle of salvation inspired by Jesus' command to bring salvation to all the world. ldentity and homogeneity were the watchwords. One unfortunate consequence of this was a kind of religious colonialism, imposing its uniformity on the converted; 2) The period of the church in the world, the period exemplified in *Gaudium et Spes*, the remarkable "Dogmatic Constitution on the Church in the Modern World" of Vatican II. The church recognizes the great values in world developments, in diverse cultures, in the benefits of modern science and technology and seeks to find an expression of the life and teaching of Jesus within this framework. This orientation is directed more to a sophisticated intellectual elite; (3) The church in the subworld, the church proclaimed at Medellín, the commitment of the church to identify with the poor, the oppressed, the victims of injustice. The church proclaimed that "this destitution as a collective fact, is an injustice that cries to heaven." This is a call to the third world, to the poor and oppressed.

Boff makes it clear that this does not fragment the universality of the church by identifying it with one class against another. It commits the church to bringing the life of Christ, with its human dignity and fulfillment, to all persons, particularly in this case to the downtrodden who have never enjoyed it before. Thus the pastoral consequences of liberation theology and the basic Christian communities enable the church to fulfill its universality in the modern world. On the level of the institutional church, the universality is expressed in the prophetic condemnations of oppression and violence, which have become characteristic of the official church in our day and which legitimizes many of the liberation movements.

The long discussion of Marxism in Chapter Four is excellent and provides a clear rejection of aspects of Marxism than are incompatible with the Catholic faith and a clarification of the use of a method of sociohistorical analysis. In his discussion of spirituality in this chapter and in Chapter Ten, Boff's deep involvement in the life and spirit of the church shines forth. "Here God is seen not as a closely defined, limited category in a religious framework but as an event of meaning, of absolute future for men and women in their history. This experience breeds a peculiar, typical experience of the mystery of God. His concept of *contemplativus in liberatione* is an interesting application of the *in actione contemplativus* of Saint Ignatius.

Joseph P. Fitzpatrick, "'Underdevelopment Is the Direct Consequence of Development'—Leonardo Boff, O. F. M," in *America*, Vol. 163, No. 7, September 22, 1990, p. 164.

SOURCES FOR FURTHER STUDY

Amorós, José Alejandro. Review of *Liberation Theology: From Confrontation to Dialogue. Religious Studies Review* 13, No. 4 (October 1987): 330–31.

> Finds the work a useful summary of liberation theology and applauds Boff's application of the ideology to the problem of Soviet imperialism.

Apel, W. D. Review of *Salvation and Liberation: In Search of a Balance between Faith and Politics. Choice* 22, No. 5 (January 1985): 698.

> Deems the work an effectual introduction to liberation theology that is simultaneously "self-critical and adopting a needed historical perspective."

Cox, Harvey. *The Silencing of Leonardo Boff: The Vatican and the Future of World Christianity.* Oak Park, Ill.: Meyer-Stone Books, 1988, 208 p.

> Analyzes Boff's controversy with the Vatican and its implications for the Church's future.

Furlong, Monica. "In the Wreck of Patriarchy." *The Times Literary Supplement*, No. 4414 (November 6–12, 1987): 1232.

> Mixed assessment of *The Maternal Face of God*, commending Boff's insistence on including the feminine aspect in regard to God and the church, while censuring his limited application of Carl Jung's concept of *anima*.

Keylock, Leslie R. "The Vatican Tries to Rein in a Leading Proponent of Liberation Theology." *Christianity Today* 28, No. 15 (19 October 1984): 46–7.

> Documents the Vatican's objections to aspects of liberation theology with particular attention to the controversial nature of Boff's writings.

Mainwaring, Scott. *The Catholic Church and Politics in Brazil,* 1916-1985. Stanford, Calif.: Stanford University Press, 1986, 328 p.

> Focuses on the origins, development, and dilemmas of the "popular" Church, that includes, in Mainwaring's words, "those sectors that have a progressive political vision of the Church's mission." The author also examines various theological conceptions that support a radical social transformation of Brazil and Latin America.

Novak, Michael. "The Case against Liberation Theology." *The New York Times Magazine* (21 October 1984): 51, 82–7, 93–5.

> Elucidates the reasons for the Vatican's opposition to liberation theology, citing the ideology's affinity with Marxism. As Novak states: "Critics of liberation theology argue that it is fundamentally naïve and may deliver South America into the hands of Communism."

Ostling, Richard N. "Deliberation at the Vatican." *Time* 124, No. 10 (3 September 1984): 86.

> Briefly summarizes Boff's conflict with the Vatican over aspects of liberation theology.

Planas, Ricardo. *Liberation Theology: The Political Expression of Religion.* Kansas City, Mo.: Sheed & Ward, 1986, 289 p.

> Examines liberation theology in its political aspects, particularly citing the ideology's concern "with the most troubling issues of the contemporary world."

Salholz, Eloise, Nagorski, Andrew, and Margolis, Mac. "Liberation Theology on Trial." *Newsweek* CIV, No. 12 (17 September 1984): 83, 85.

> Outlines the controversial dimensions of Boff's liberation theology that led to his eventual censure by the Vatican.

Jorge Luis Borges

1899–1986

(Also wrote in collaboration with Adolfo Bioy Casares under the joint pseudonyms Honorio Bustos Domecq, B. Lynch Davis, and B. Juarez Lynch) Argentine short story writer, essayist, poet, translator, critic, biographer, travel writer, novelist, and scriptwriter.

INTRODUCTION

*A*mong the foremost literary figures to have written in Spanish, Borges is best known for his erudite short stories in which he blended fantasy and realism to address complex philosophical problems. Involving such thematic motifs as time, infinity, identity, and memory, Borges's stories combine elements of fiction and the personal essay in forms that resist classification. His prose works were commended by André Maurois for "their wonderful intelligence, their wealth of invention, and their tight, almost mathematical, style." Making minimal use of plot and characterization, Borges employed paradox and oxymoron to combine such seemingly contradictory concepts as universality and particularity, illusion and reality. Occasionally faulted by critics for his refusal to address social and political issues, Borges maintained: "I have no message. I am neither a thinker nor a moralist, but simply a man of letters who turns his own perplexities and that respected system of perplexities we call philosophy into the forms of literature."

Borges was born in Buenos Aires, where he lived for most of his childhood. His father, Jorge Guillermo Borges, was a respected lawyer, author, and educator. Borges once commented: "If I were asked to name the chief event in my life, I should say my father's library." He learned to read English before Spanish due to the influence of his English grandmother, and when he was seven years old he translated Oscar Wilde's short story "The Happy Prince." Borges's first original story, "El rey de la selva," was published when he was thirteen. While his family was stranded in Switzerland following the outbreak of World War I, Borges enrolled at the Collége de Génève, where he studied French and German and familiarized himself with such European philosophers as Arthur Schopenhauer and George Berkeley. Upon graduating in 1918, Borges traveled to Spain. There he published reviews, essays, and poetry and associated with the Ultraístas, an avant-garde literary group whose fiction combined elements of Dadaism, Imagism, and German Expressionism. Striving in their poetry to transcend boundaries of time and space, the Ultraístas championed metaphor as the ultimate form of expression; their influence permeates much of Borges's early work, particularly *Fervor de Buenos Aires* (1923), his first poetry collection.

Borges returned to Buenos Aires in 1921. He helped develop several small Argentinian publications, including the literary magazine *Prisma* and the journal *Proa*, and became reacquainted with Macedonio Fernandez, a writer and colleague of his father. Encouraged by Fernandez to develop his interest in metaphysics and the complexities of language, Borges began publishing essays on these topics. In 1938 he developed septicemia, a form of blood poisoning, from a head wound he suffered in a fall down a staircase. Concerned that the condition had impaired his writing ability, Borges published a short story as his first work after the accident, intending to attribute its possible failure to inexperience in the genre rather than a loss of literary skill. The tale, "Pierre Menard, autor del *Quijote*" ("Pierre Menard, Author of the *Quixote*"), unexpectedly garnered positive reactions, and Borges's ensuing short fiction earned increasingly widespread critical recognition in Argentina.

In 1943, after signing a manifesto denouncing Argentinian military dictator Juan Perón, Borges was demoted from his government post as an assistant librarian to poultry inspector, a position he refused, however, in favor of becoming an itinerant lecturer and teacher. During this time, he published his collection of short fiction entitled *Ficciones* (1944), which helped establish his reputation throughout the world. Following the ouster of Perón in 1955, Borges was named director of the prestigious National Library of Argentina and later awarded the Premio Nacional de Literatura, the country's highest literary honor. In 1961 Borges and Irish dramatist Samuel Beckett shared the Prix Formentor, an international prize established in 1960 by six avant-garde publishers to recognize authors whose work they deemed would "have a lasting influence on the development of modern literature." Beginning in the late 1950s, Borges's eyesight started to fail; although his increasing blindness slowed his literary output, he continued to publish volumes of stories, poetry, and essays. During this period, Borges's mother increased her role as his secretary, a position she had occupied throughout his career, taking dictation of his work and reading to him in Spanish, English, and French. In 1985 Borges was diagnosed with liver cancer, and he left Buenos Aires for Geneva, Switzerland where he married his companion and former student, María Kodama. Three weeks later, at age eighty-seven, Borges died.

Although he became best known for his imaginative short fiction, in the early years of his career Borges wrote poetry and criticism almost exclusively. In his first collection of poetry, *Fervor de Buenos Aires* (1923; revised 1969), Borges utilized Ultraíst concepts to portray colorful individuals and events in Buenos Aires. His next volume, *Luna de enfrente* (1925), contains confessional and love poetry as well as pieces that anticipate his later concern with such topics as time and memory. *Cuaderno San Martín* (1929) consists chiefly of tributes to deceased poets, among them Francisco López Merino, Borges's friend and associate, who committed suicide. Borges's best-regarded volumes of early essays include *Inquisiciones* (1925), *El tamaño de mi esperanza* (1927), and *El idioma de los argentinos* (1928). Borges won praise for "The Language of the Argentines," the title essay of the third collection, in which he urged writers to reject the artificial stylization common to Latin American letters at the turn of the century. *Discusión* (1932), a collection of film reviews and articles on metaphysical and aesthetic topics, includes the noted essay "Narrative Art and Magic," in which Borges defended the capacity of fantasy literature to address realistic concerns. *Historia de la eternidad* (1936), a volume exploring humanity's concepts of eternity from ancient times to the present, includes "The Approach to al-Mu'tasim," Borges's review of an imaginary detective novel. By critiquing a nonexistent work, Borges proposed that content exists in the reader's imagination and, according to John Sturrock, "that the 'real' aspect of books, their physical presence, does not matter."

Borges's early short stories derive in style and subject from his essays and are often interpreted as parables illustrating the potentialities and limitations of creative art. "Pierre Menard, Author of the *Quixote*" depicts a modern writer who independently composes portions of a text corresponding precisely to Miguel de Cervantes's *Don Quixote*. According to Katherine Singer Kovács, Menard creates "a new and more profound work, one of particular relevance to his own historical period and life." Borges's first short story collection, *Historia universal de la infamia* (1935; *A Universal History of Infamy*), purports to present a fictional felon's encyclopedia of criminals drawn from history. The translated edition includes "The South," a semiautobiographical story in which a troubled librarian, desiring the chivalric life of the Argentinian gaucho, becomes involved in a fatal knife fight that may exist only in his imagination. The title piece of *El jardín de senderos que se bifurcan* (1941), which Borges described as "a detective story," links two apparently unrelated crimes, one committed in the present, the other in the past. Max Byrd has observed that "both crimes blend in a single moment; the solution of one simultaneously resolves the other." This collection also includes Borges's acclaimed story "The Library of Babel," in which a symmetrically arranged library, representing humanity's rational view of the universe, is revealed to contain illegible books.

Ficciones (1944) is generally regarded as Borges's most significant work. In this story collection, which is primarily concerned with conflicts between reality and imagination, Borges utilized what he considered to be the four fundamental aspects of fantasy. James E. Irby described these aspects in his introduction to Borges's 1962 collection *Labyrinths:* "the work within the work, the contamination of reality by dream, the voyage in time, and the double." In "Tlön, Uqbar, Orbis Tertius," one of his most frequently analyzed stories, Borges combined fiction with such elements of the essay as footnotes and a postscript to describe the attempts of a secret philosophical society to create an invented world free of linear space and time. As their ideas cohere, objects from their imagined realm surface in reality. Frances Wyers Weber has commented: "The story develops the contrasts not only between the cohesiveness of Tlön and the incomprehensible, unstable realities of the experienced world, but also the inevitable mutilation that order imposes. The utopian world of unlimited capricious speculation becomes a carefully wrought complex that eliminates all alternatives and bewitches humanity with its utter intelligibility."

The enlarged English edition of El Aleph (1949), entitled *The Aleph and Other Stories, 1933–1969* (1970), consists of stories and essays from various periods in Borges's career. This work is the first of several acclaimed collaborations between Borges and translator Norman Thomas di Giovanni, aimed at producing creative translations that read as though the original pieces were written in English. The "aleph" of the title story is a stone representing the equivalent of all visual images of the universe, containing all points of space, and indicative of humanity's limitless but not entirely lucid perspectives and possibilities. The aleph's opposite, described in "The Zahir," is a magical coin universally representative of every particular coin, real or imagined. According to Diana Armas Wilson, the zahir differs from the universal aleph in that it signifies "a local and particular perspective that a man uses to order reality—any belief, scheme, or dogma that saves him from chaos."

For several years after his vision began to fail, Borges limited his literary work to lectures, translations, and poetry. Keith Botsford has deemed these later poems "among the most skillful and immaculate in Spanish. Strict in their rules and sober in their imagery, gentle in tone, recollected in tranquility, they are elegiac, formal, symmetrical." *El hacedor* (1961; *Dreamtigers*), a collection of brief poems, quotations, and parables, uses the tiger as an ambivalent symbol of unnatural evil and natural change. In the title poem of *Elogio de la sombra* (1969; *In Praise of Darkness*), Borges proposed the paradoxical notion that old age and blindness may signify deep happiness because of the imminence of death. Dualities involving physical blindness and spiritual sight also pervade *El oro de los tigres* (1972; *The Gold of the Tigers: Selected Later Poems*).

Borges returned to writing fiction in the 1970s, preferring a straightforward, realistic approach to the elaborate fantasies and literary games of his earliest work. Edward G. Warner described the stories in *El informe de Brodie* (1970; *Doctor Brodie's Report*) as "mostly plain, unadorned tales—some harsh, some tender—of love, hate, and the inevitability of death." *El libro de arena* (1975; *The Book of Sand*), although similar in style, returns to the fantastical themes of Borges's early fiction. This volume includes "The Congress," a long story in which a world congress attempts to incorporate all humanity's views and ideologies by securing thousands of books. Realizing the arbitrary and conjectural nature of their task, the congress eventually recognizes the need to reject limited, predominating worldviews and destroys the books, concluding that "every few centuries, the library of Alexandria must be burned down."

Although critics have praised the formal precision and mellifluous tone of Borges's poetry and the stylistic originality of his essays, it is for his short fiction that Borges is recognized as one of the most influential and innovative Latin American authors of the twentieth century. His experiments with the intermingling of fantasy and realistic detail presaged the magical realist style of writing practiced by such major Latin American authors as Gabriel García Marquez and Julio Cortázar; the latter writer has referred to Borges as "the leading figure of our fantastic literature." His insights into the nature of learning, literature, and the fictive process, exemplified in such works as "The Circular Ruins," have established him as one of modern literature's most philosophically accomplished authors. While some critics have charged that Borges's writings are esoteric, intellectually rarified games, most consider the author's work particularly relevant to his time, when, as Borges himself remarked in an essay, traditional fictional treatments of character and emotion were too greatly exhausted to illuminate further the human condition. By exploring intellectual and philological issues, they contend, Borges also addressed humankind's deepest concerns about the nature of mind and existence. As critic Carter Wheelock has commented: "[Borges] plays only one instrument—the intellectual, the epistemological—but the strumming of his cerebral guitar sets into vibration all the strings of emotion, intuition, and esthetic longing that are common to sentient humanity."

CRITICAL COMMENTARY

PAUL DE MAN
(essay date 1964)

[De Man was a Belgian-born American critic and educator whose collection of essays *Blindness and Insight* (1971) is regarded as a seminal reevaluation of the status and function of language. In the following essay, he discusses the presence of mirrors in Borges's *Dreamtigers* and *Labyrinths*.]

Although he has been writing poems, stories, and critical essays of the highest quality since 1923, the Argentinian writer Jorge Luis Borges is still much better known in Latin America than in the U. S. For the translator of John Peale Bishop, Hart Crane, E. E. Cummings, William Faulkner, Edgar Lee Masters, Robert Penn Warren, and Wallace Stevens, this neglect is somewhat unfair. There are signs however, that he is being discovered in this country with some of the same enthusiasm that greeted him in France, where he received major critical attention, and has been very well translated. Several volumes of translations in English have recently appeared, including a fine edition of his most recent book *El hacedor (Dreamtigers)* and a new edition of *Labyrinths*, which first appeared in 1962. American and English critics have called him one of the greatest writers alive today, but have not as yet (so far as I know) made substantial contributions to the interpretation of his work. There are good reasons for this delay. Borges is a complex writer, particularly difficult to place. Commentators cast around in vain for suitable points of comparison and his own avowed literary admirations add to the confusion. Like Kafka and contemporary French existential writers, he is often seen as a moralist, in rebellion against the times. But such an approach is misleading.

It is true that, especially in his earlier works, Borges writes about villains: The collection *History of Infamy (Historia universal de la infamia,* 1935) contains an engaging gallery of scoundrels. But Borges does not consider infamy primarily as a moral theme; the stories in no way suggest an indictment of society or of human nature or of destiny. Nor do they suggest the lighthearted view of Gide's Nietzschean hero Lafcadio. Instead, infamy functions here as an aesthetic, formal principle. The fictions literally could not have taken shape but for the presence of villainy at their very heart. Many different worlds are conjured up—cotton plantations along the Mississippi, pirate-infested South seas, the Wild West, the slums of New York, Japanese courts, the Arabian desert, etc.—all of which would be shapeless without the ordering presence of a villain at the center.

A good illustration can be taken from the imaginary essays on literary subjects that Borges was writing at the same time as the *History of Infamy.* Borrowing the stylistic conventions of scholarly critical writing, the essays read like a combination of Empson, Paulhan, and *PMLA,* except that they are a great deal more succinct and devious. In an essay on the translations of *The Thousand and One Nights,* Borges quotes an impressive list of examples showing how translator after translator mercilessly cut, expanded, distorted, and falsified the original in order to make it conform to his own and his audience's artistic and moral standards. The list, which amounts in fact to a full catalogue of human sins, culminates in the sterling character of Enna Littmann, whose 1923–1928 edition is scrupulously exact: "Incapable, like George Washington, of telling a lie, his work reveals nothing but German candor." This translation is vastly inferior, in Borges's eyes, to all others. It lacks the wealth of literary associations that allows the other, villainous translators to give their language depth, suggestiveness, ambiguity—in a word, style. The artist has to wear the mask of the villain or order to create a style.

So far, so good. All of us know that the poet is of the devil's party and that sin makes for better stories than virtue. It takes some effort to prefer *La nouvelle Héloïse* to *Les liaisons dangereuses* or, for that matter, to prefer the second part of the *Nouvelle Héloïse* to the first. Borges's theme of infamy could be just another form of *fin-de-siècle* aestheticism, a late gasp of romantic agony. Or, perhaps worse, he might be writing out of moral despair as an escape from the trappings of style. But such assumptions go against the grain of a writer whose commitment to style remains unshakable; whatever Borges's existential anxieties may be, they have little in common with Sartre's robustly prosaic view of literature, with the earnestness of Camus's moralism, or with the weighty profundity of German existential thought. Rather, they are the consistent expansion of a purely poetic consciousness to its furthest limits.

The stories that make up the bulk of Borges's literary work are not moral fables or parables like Kafka's, to which they are often misleadingly compared, even less attempts at psychological analysis. The least inadequate literary analogy would be with the eighteenth-century

Principal Works

Fervor de Buenos Aires (poetry) 1923; revised edition, 1969

Inquisiciones (essays) 1925

Luna de enfrente (poetry) 1925

El tamaño de mi esperanza (essays) 1927

El idioma de los argentinos (essays) 1928

Cuaderno San Martín (poetry) 1929

Evaristo Carriego (biography) 1930
   [*Evaristo Carriego: A Book about Old Time Buenos Aires*, 1984]

Discusión (essays and criticism) 1932

Historia universal de la infamia (short stories) 1935
   [*A Universal History of Infamy*, 1972]

Historia de la eternidad (essays) 1936

El jardín de senderos que se bifurcan (short stories) 1941

Poemas, 1922–1943 (poetry) 1943

Ficciones, 1935–1944 (short stories) 1944
   [*Ficciones*, 1962; also published as *Fictions*, 1965]

El Aleph (short stories) 1949
   [*The Aleph and Other Stories, 1933–1969* (revised edition), 1970]

Otras inquisiciónes, 1937–1952 (essays) 1952
   [*Other Inquisitions, 1937–1952*, 1964]

Obras completas. 10 vols. (essays, short stories, and poetry) 1953–67

Manual de zoología fantástica [with Margarita Guerrero] (essays) 1957; also published as *El libro de los seres imaginarios* (revised edition), 1967
   [*The Imaginary Zoo*, 1969; also published as *The Book of Imaginary Beings* (revised edition), 1969]

Poemas, 1923–1958 (poetry) 1958

Antología personal (poetry and prose) 1961
   [*A Personal Anthology*, 1967]

El hacedor (prose and poetry) 1961
   [*Dreamtigers*, 1964]

Labyrinths: Selected Stories and Other Writings (short stories and essays) 1962

Obra poética, 1923–1967 (poetry) 1967
   [*Selected Poems, 1923–1967*, 1972]

Elogio de la sombra (poetry and prose) 1969
   [*In Praise of Darkness*, 1974]

Nueva antología personal (poetry and prose) 1969

El informe de Brodie (short stories) 1970
   [*Doctor Brodie's Report*, 1972]

*El oro de los tigres (poetry) 1972

Borges on Writing (lectures) 1973

El libro de arena (short stories) 1975
   [*The Book of Sand*, 1977]

*La rosa profunda (poetry) 1975

Historia de la noche (poetry) 1977

Obras completas (poetry and prose) 1977

Obras completas en colaboración [with Adolfo Bioy Casares, Betina Edelberg, Margarita Guerrero, Alicia Jurado, Maria Kodama, Maria Esther Vazquez] (short stories, essays and criticism) 1979

Prosa completa. 2 vols. (prose) 1980

Siete noches (lectures) 1980
   [*Seven Nights*, 1984]

Antología poética, 1923–1977 (poetry) 1981

Atlas [with María Kodama] (prose and poetry) 1984
   [*Atlas*, 1985]

*These works were translated and published as *The Gold of the Tigers: Selected Later Poems* in 1977.

---

conte philosophique: their world is the representation, not of an actual experience, but of an intellectual proposition. One does not expect the same kind of psychological insight or the same immediacy of personal experience from *Candide* as from *Madame Bovary*, and Borges should be read with expectations closer to those one brings to Voltaire's tale than to a nineteenth-century novel. He differs, however, from his eighteenth-century antecedents in that the subject of the stories is the creation of style itself; in this Borges is very definitely post-romantic and even post-symbolist. His main characters are prototypes for the writer, and his worlds are prototypes for a highly stylized kind of poetry or fiction. For all their variety of tone and setting, the different stories all have a similar

point of departure, a similar structure, a similar climax and a similar outcome; the inner cogency that links these four moments together constitutes Borges's distinctive style, as well as his comment upon this style. His stories are about the style in which they are written.

At their center, as I have said, always stands an act of infamy. The first story in **Labyrinths**, "**Tlön, Uqbar, Orbis Tertius,**" describes the totally imaginary world of a fictitious planet; this world is first glimpsed in an encyclopedia which is itself a delinquent reprint of the *Britannica*. In "**The Shape of the Sword,**" an ignominious Irishman who, as it turns out, betrayed the man who saved his life, passes himself off for his own victim in order to tell his story in a more interesting way. In "**The Garden** of the Forking Paths" the hero is a Chinese who, during World War I, spies on the British mostly for the satisfaction of refined labyrinthine dissimulation. All these crimes are misdeeds like plagiarism, impersonation, espionage, in which someone pretends to be what he is not, substitutes a misleading appearance for his actual being. One of the best of his early stories describes the exploits of the religious impostor Hakim, who hides his face behind a mask of gold. Here the symbolic function of the villainous acts stands out very clearly: Hakim was at first a dyer, that is, someone who presents in bright and beautiful colors what was originally drab and gray. In this, he resembles the artist who confers irresistably attractive qualities upon something that does not necessarily possess them.

The creation of beauty thus begins as an act of duplicity. The writer engenders another self that is his mirror-like reversal. In this anti-self, the virtues and the vices of the original are curiously distorted and reversed. Borges describes the process poignantly in a later text called **"Borges and I"** (it appears in *Labyrinths* and also, in a somewhat better translation, in *Dreamtigers*). Although he is aware of the other Borges's "perverse habit of falsifying and exaggerating," he yields more and more to this poetic mask "who shares [his] preferences, but in a vain way that converts them into the attributes of an actor." This act, by which a man loses himself in the image he has created, is to Borges inseparable from poetic greatness. Cervantes achieved it when he invented and became Don Quixote; Valéry achieved it when he conceived and became Monsieur Teste. The duplicity of the artist, the grandeur as well as the misery of his calling, is a recurrent theme closely linked with the theme of infamy. Perhaps its fullest treatment appears in the story **"Pierre Ménard, Author of the Quixote"** in *Labyrinths*. The work and life of an imaginary writer is described by a devoted biographer. As the story unfolds, some of the details begin to have a familiar ring: even the phony, mercantile, snobbish Mediterranean atmosphere seems to recall to us an actual person, and when we are told that Ménard published an early sonnet in a magazine called *La conque*, a reader of Valéry will identify the model without fail. (Several of Valéry's early poems in fact appeared in *La conque*, which was edited by Pierre Louys, though at a somewhat earlier date than the one given by Borges for Ménard's first publication.) When, a little later, we find out that Ménard is the author of an invective against Paul Valéry, as well as the perpetrator of the shocking stylistic crime of transposing "*Le cimetière marin*" into alexandrines (Valéry has always insisted that the very essence of this famous poem resides in the decasyllabic meter), we can no longer doubt that we are dealing with Valéry's anti-self, in other words, Monsieur Teste. Things get a lot more complicated a few paragraphs later, when Ménard embarks on the curious project of re-inventing Don Quixote word for word, and by the time Borges treats us to a "close reading" of two identical passages from Don Quixote, one written by Cer-

vantes, the other by Pierre Ménard (who is also Monsieur Teste, who is also Valéry) such a complex set of ironies, parodies, reflections, and issues are at play that no brief commentary can begin to do them justice.

Poetic invention begins in duplicity, but it does not stop there. For the writer's particular duplicity (the dyer's image in **"Hakim"**) stems from the fact that he presents the invented form as if it possessed the attributes of reality, thus allowing it to be mimetically reproduced, in its turn, in another mirror-image that takes the preceding pseudo-reality for *its* starting-point. He is prompted "by the blasphemous intention of attributing the divine category of *being* to some mere [entities]". Consequently, the duplication grows into a proliferation of successive mirror-images. In **"Tlön, Uqbar Orbis Tertius,"** for example, the plagiarized encyclopedia is itself falsified by someone who adds an entry on the imaginary region Uqbar, presenting it as if it were part of an imaginary country as *his* starting point, another falsifier (who, by the way, is a Southern segregationist millionaire) conjures up, with the assistance of a team of shady experts, a complete encyclopedia of a fictional planet called Tlön—a pseudo-reality equal in size to our own real world. This edition will be followed in turn by a revised and even more detailed edition written not in English but in one of the languages of Tlön and entitled *Orbis Tertius*.

All the stories have a similar mirror-like structure, although the devices vary with diabolical ingenuity. Sometimes, there is only one mirror-effect, as when at the end of **"The Shape of the Sword"** Vincent Moon reveals his true identity as the villain, not the hero, of his own story. But in most of Borges's stories, there are several layers of reflection. In **"Theme of the Traitor and the Hero"** from *Labyrinths* we have: (1) an actual historic event—a revolutionary leader betrays his confederates and has to be executed; (2) a fictional story about such an occurrence (though in reversed form)—Shakespeare's *Julius Caesar;* (3) an actual historic event which copies the fiction: the execution is carried out according to Shakespeare's plot, to make sure that it will be a good show; (4) the puzzled historian reflecting on the odd alternation of identical fictional and historical events, and deriving a false theory of historical archetypes from them; (5) the smarter historian Borges (or, rather, his duplicitous anti-self) reflecting on the credulous historian and reconstructing the true course of events. In other stories from *Labyrinths*, **The Immortal, "The Zahir,"** or **"Death and the Compass,"** the complication is pushed so far that it is virtually impossible to describe.

This mirror-like proliferation constitutes, for Borges, an indication of poetic success. The works of literature he most admires contain this element; he is fascinated by such mirror-effects in literature as the Elizabethan play within the play, the character Don Quixote reading *Don Quixote*, Scheherazade beginning one night to retell *verbatim* the story of *The Thousand and One Nights*. For each mirrored image is stylistically superior to the preceding one, as the dyed cloth is more beautiful than the plain, the distorted translation richer than the original, Ménard's Quixote aesthetically more complex than Cervantes's. By carrying this process to its limits, the poet can achieve ultimate success—an ordered picture of reality that contains the totality of all things, subtly transformed and enriched by the imaginative process that engendered them. The imaginary world of Tlön is only one example of this poetic achievement; it recurs throughout Borges's work and constitutes, in fact, the central, climactic image around which each of the stories is organized. It can be the philosophically coherent set of laws that makes up the mental universe of Tlön, or it can be the fantastic world of a man blessed (as well as doomed) with the frightening gift of total recall, a man "who knows by heart the forms of the southern clouds at dawn on the 30th of April 1882" as well as "the stormy mane of a pony, the changing fire and its innumerable ashes" (**"Funes the Memorious,"** in *Labyrinths*), It can be vastly expanded, like the infinitely complex labyrinth that is also an endless book in **"The Garden of the Forking Paths,"** or highly compressed, like a certain spot in a certain house from which one can observe the entire universe (**"The Aleph"**), or a single coin which, however insignificant by itself, contains "universal history and the infinite concatenation of cause and effect **"(The Zahir")**. All these points or domains of total vision symbolize the entirely successful and deceiving outcome of the poets irrepressible urge for order.

The success of these poetic worlds is expressed by their all-inclusive and ordered wholeness. Their deceitful nature is harder to define, but essential to an understanding of Borges. Mirror images are indeed duplications of reality, but they change the temporal nature of this reality in an insidious fashion, even—one might say especially—when the imitation is altogether successful (as in Ménard's Quixote). In actual experience, time appears to us as continuous but infinite; this continuity may seem reassuring, since it gives us some feeling of identity, but it is also terrifying, since it drags us irrevocably towards an unknowable future. Our "real" universe is like space: stable but chaotic. If, by an act of the mind comparable to Borges's will to style, we order this chaos, we may well succeed in achieving an order of sorts, but we dissolve the binding, spatial substance that held our chaotic universe together. Instead of an infinite mass of substance, we have a finite number of isolated events incapable of establishing relations among one another. The inhabitants of Borges's totally poetic world of Uqbar "do not conceive that the spatial persists in time. The perception of a cloud of smoke on the horizon and then of the burning field and then of the half-extinguished cigarette that produced the blaze is considered an example of association of ideas." This style in Borges becomes the ordering but dissolving act that transforms the unity of experience into the enumeration of its discontinuous parts. Hence his rejection of *style lié*

and his preference for what grammarians call parataxis, the mere placing of events side by side, without conjunctions; hence also his definition of his own style as baroque, "the style that deliberately exhausts (or tries to exhaust) all its possibilities." The style is a mirror, but unlike the mirror of the realists that never lets us forget for a moment [that it creates] what it mimics.

Probably because Borges is such a brilliant writer, his mirror-world is also profoundly, though always ironically, sinister. The shades of terror vary from the criminal gusto of the *History of Infamy* to the darker and shabbier world of the later *Ficciones*, and in *Dreamtigers* the violence is even starker and more somber, closer, I suppose, to the atmosphere of Borges's native Argentina. In the 1935 story, Hakim the impostor proclaimed: "The earth we live on is a mistake, a parody devoid of authority. Mirrors and paternity are abominable things, for they multiply this earth." This statement keeps recurring throughout the later work, but it becomes much more comprehensible there. Without ceasing to be the main metaphor for style, the mirror acquires deadly powers— a motif that runs throughout Western literature but of which Borges's version is particularly rich and complex. In his early work, the mirror of art represented the intention to keep the flow of time from losing itself forever in the shapeless void of infinity. Like the speculations of philosophers, style is an attempt at immortality. But this attempt is bound to fail. To quote one of Borges's favorite books, Sir Thomas Browne's *Hydrothapia, Urne-Buriall* (1658): "There is no antidote against the *Opium* of time, which temporally considereth all things . . . " This is not, as has been said, because Borges's God plays the same trick on the poet that the poet plays on reality; God does not turn out to be the arch-villain set to deceive man into an illusion of eternity. The poetic impulse in all its perverse duplicity, belongs to man alone, marks him as essentially human. But God appears on the scene as the power of reality itself, in the form of a death that demonstrates the failure of poetry. This is the deeper reason for the violence that pervades all Borges's stories. God is on the side of chaotic reality and style is powerless to conquer him. His appearance is like the hideous face of Hakim when he loses the shining mask he has been wearing and reveals a face worn away by leprosy. The proliferation of mirrors is all the more terrifying because each new image brings us a step closer to this face.

As Borges grows older and his eyesight gets steadily weaker, this final confrontation throws its darkening shadow over his entire work, without however extinguishing the lucidity of his language. For although the last reflection may be the face of God himself, with his appearance the life of poetry comes to an end. The situation is very similar to that of Kierkegaard's aesthetic man, with the difference that Borges refuses to give up his poetic predicament for a leap into faith. This confers a somber glory on the pages of *Dreamtigers*, so different from the shining brilliance of the stories in *Labyrinths*. To understand the full complexity of this later mood, one must have followed Borges's enterprise from the start and see it as the unfolding of a poetic destiny. This would not only require the translation into English of Borges's earlier work, but also serious critical studies worthy of this great writer. (pp 8–10)

Paul de Man, "A Modern Master," in *The New York Review of Books*, Vol. III, No. 7, November 19, 1964, pp. 8–10.

GEORGE STEINER

(essay date 1970)

[Steiner is a French-born American critic, poet, and fiction writer. A central concern of his critical thought is whether or not literature can survive the barbarism of the modern world. Though some commentators have found fault with his sometimes exuberant prose style, Steiner is generally regarded as a perceptive and erudite critic. In the following essay, which first appeared in *The New Yorker* in 1970, he examines philosophical themes present in Borges's fiction and poetry, maintaining that although Borges is a major artist, the fabric of his art "has severe gaps."]

Inevitably, the current world fame of Jorge Luis Borges entails a sense of private loss. As when a view long treasured—the shadow-mass of Arthur's Seat in Edinburgh seen, uniquely, from the back of number sixty The Pleasance, of Fifty-first Street in Manhattan angled to a bronze and racing canyon through a trick of elevation and light in my dentist's window—a collector's item of and for the inner eye, becomes a panoptic spectacle for the tourist horde. For a long time, the splendor of Borges was clandestine, signaled to the happy few, bartered in undertones and mutual recognitions. How many knew of his first work, a summary of Greek myths, written in English in Buenos Aires, the author aged seven? Or of opus two, dated 1907 and distinctly permonitory, a translation into Spanish of Oscar Wilde's *The Happy Prince*? To affirm today that **"Pierre Menard, Author of the Quixote"** is one of the sheer wonders of human contrivance, that the several facets of Borges' shy genius are almost wholly gathered in that spare fable, is a platitude. But how many own the *editio princeps* of *El jardin de senderos que se bifurcan* (Sur, Buenos Aires, 1941) in which the tale first appeared? Only ten years ago, it was a mark of arcane erudition and a wink to the initiate to realize that H. Bustos Domecq was the joint pseudonym of Borges and his close collaborator, Adolfo Bioy Casares, or that the Borges who, with Delia Ingenieros, published

---

Borges on the man of letters:

In many of my stories and poems the central character is a literary man. Well, this means to say that I think that literature has not only enriched the world by giving it books but also by evolving a new type of man, the man of letters. For example, you might not care for the works of Coleridge, you might think that outside of three or four poems, "The Ancient Mariner," "Christabel," "Kubla Khan," maybe "Time, River, and Imaging," what he wrote is not very interesting, it's very wordy, and very perplexed and perplexing stuff, confused and confusing stuff and yet I'm sure that you think of Coleridge as you might think of somebody you had known, no? I mean, that though his writing is sometimes rather unreal, yet you think of him as being a real man — perhaps because of his unreality also, and because he lived in a kind of haze world or dream world, no? So that I think literature has enriched the world, not only through books, but through a new type of man, the man of letters.

Jorge Luis Borges, in *Conversations With Jorge Luis Borges*, by Richard Burgin, 1968.

---

a learned monograph on ancient Germanic and Anglo-Saxon literatures (Mexico, 1951) was indeed the Master. Such information was close-guarded, parsimoniously dispensed, often nearly impossible to come by, as were Borges' poems, stories, essays themselves, scattered, out of print, pseudonymous. I recall an early connoisseur, in the cavernous rear of the bookstore in Lisbon showing me—this, remember, was in the early 1950's—Borges' translation of Virginia Woolf's *Orlando*, his preface to Buenos Aires edition of Kafka's *Metamorphosis*, his key essay on the artificial language devised by Bishop John Wilkins, published in *La Nación* on February 8, 1942, and, rarest of rare items, *Dimensions of My Hope*, a collection of short essays issued in 1926 but, by Borges' own wish, not reprinted since. These slim objects were displayed to me with an air of fastidious condescension. And rightly so. I had arrived late at the secret place.

The turning point came in 1961. Together with Beckett, Borges was awarded the Formentor Prize. A year later, *Labyrinths* and *Fictions* appeared in English. Honors rained. The Italian government made Borges *Commendatore*. At the suggestion of M. Malraux, President de Gaulle conferred on his illustrious fellow writer and master of myths the title of Commander of the *Ordre des Lettres et des Arts*. The sudden lion found himself lecturing in Madrid, Paris, Geneva, London, Oxford, Edinburgh, Havard, Texas. "At a ripe old age," muses Borges, "I began to find that many people were interested in my work all over the world. It seems strange: many of my writings have been done into English, into Swedish, into French, into Italian, into German, into Portuguese, into some of the Slav languages, into Danish. And always this comes as a great surprise to me, because I remember I published a book—that must have been way back in 1932, I think—and at the end of the year I found out that no less than thirty-seven copies had been sold!" A leanness that had its compensations: "Those people are real, I mean every one of them has a face of his own, a family, he lives in his own particular street. Why, if you sell, say, two thousand copies, it is the same thing as if you has sold nothing at all, because two thousand is too vast, I mean for the imagination to grasp. . . perhaps seventeen would have been better or even seven." Cognoscenti will spot the symbolic role of each of these, numbers, and of the kabbalistic diminishing series, in Borges' fables.

Today, the secret thirty-seven have become an industry. Critical commentaries on Borges, interviews with, memoirs about, special issues of quarterlies devoted to, editions of, pullulate. Already to 520-page exegetic, biographical, and bibliographical Borges compendium issued in Paris, by *L'Herne*, in 1964, is out of date. The air is gray with theses: on "Borges and Beowulf," on "The Influence of the Western on the Narrative Pace of the Later Borges," on "Borges' Enigmatic Concern with *West Side Story*" ("I have seen it many times"), on "The Real Origins of the Words *Tlön* and *Uqbar* in Borges' Stories," on "Borges and the Zohar." There have been Borges weekends at Austin, seminars at Harvard, a large-scale symposium at the University of Oklahoma—a festivity perhaps previewd in Kafka's *Amerika*. Borges himself was present, watching the learned sanctification of his other self, or, as he calls it, *Borges y yo*. A journal of Borgesian studies is being founded. Its first issue will deal with the function of the mirror and the labyrinth in Borges' art, and with the dreamtigers that wait behind the mirror or, rather, in its silent crystal maze.

With the academic circus have come the mimes. Borges' manner is being widely aped. There are magic turns which many writers, and even undergraduates gifted with a knowing ear, can simulate: the self-deprecatory deflection of Borges' tone, the occult fantastications of literary, historical reference which pepper his narrative, the alternance of direct, bone-spare statement with sinuous evasion. The key images and heraldic markers of the Borges world have passed into literary currency. "I've grown weary of labyrinths and mirrors and of tigers and of all that sort of thing. Especially when others are using them. . . . That's the advantage of imitators. They cure one of one's literary ills. Because one thinks: there are so many people doing that sort of thing now, there's no need for one to do it any more. Now let the others do it, and good riddance." But it is not pseudo-Borges that matters.

The enigma is this: that tactics of feeling so specialized, so intricately enmeshed with a sensibility that is private in the extreme, should have so wide, so natural, an echo. Like Lewis Carroll, Borges has made of his autistic dreams discreet but exacting summons which readers the world over are responding to with a sense of recognition. Our streets and gardens, the arrowing of a lizard across the warm light, our libraries and circular staircases are beginning to look precisely as Borges dreamed them, though the sources of his vision remain irreducibly singular, hermetic, at moments almost moon-mad.

The process whereby a fantastically private picture of the world leaps beyond the wall of mirrors behind which it was created, and reaches out to change the general landscape of awareness, is manifest but exceedingly diffcult to talk about (how much of the vast critical literature on Kafka is baffled verbiage). That Borges' entrance on the larger scene of the imagination was preceded by a local genius of extreme rigor and linguistic *métier* is certain. But that will not get us very far. The fact is that even lame translations communicate much of his spell. The message, set in kabbalistic code, written, as it were, in invisible ink, thrust, with the proud casualness of deep modesty, into the most fragile of bottles, has crossed the seven seas (there are, of course, many more in the Borges atlas, but they are always multiples of seven), to reach every kind of shore. Even to those who know nothing of his masters and early companions—Lugones, Macedonio Fernandez, Evaristo Carriego—or to whom the Palermo district of Buenos Aires and the tradition of gaucho ballads are little more than names, have found access to Borges' *Fictions*. There is a sense in which the Director of the Biblioteca Nacional of Argentina is now the most original of Anglo-American writers. This extraterritoriality may be a clue.

Borges is a universalist. In part, this is a question of upbringing, of the years from 1914 to 1921, which he spent in Switzerland, Italy, Spain. And it arises from Borges' prodigious talents as a linguist. He is at home in English, French, German, Italian, Portuguese, Anglo-Saxon, and Old Norse, as well as in a Spanish that is constantly shot through with Argentine elements. Like other writers whose sight has failed, Borges moves with a cat's assurance through the sound-world of many tongues. He tells memorably of **"Beginning the Study of Anglo-Saxon Grammar"**:

At fifty generations' end
(And such abysses time affords us all)
I returned to the further shore of a great river
That the vikings' dragons did not reach,
To the harsh and arduous words
That, with a mouth now turned to dust,
I used in my Northumbrian, Mercian days
Before I became a Haslam or a Borges . . . .
Praised be the infinite
Mesh of effect and causes
Which, before it shews me the mirror
In which I shall see no one or I shall see another,
Grants me now this contemplation pure
Of a language of the dawn.

"Before I became a Borges." There is in Borges' penetration of different cultures a secret of literal metamorphosis. In **"Deutsches Requiem,"** the narrator becomes, *is*, Otto Dietrich zu Linde, condemned Nazi war criminal. Vincent Moon's confession, **"The Shape of the Sword,"** is a classic in the ample literature of the Irish troubles. Elsewhere, Borges assumes the mask of Dr. Yu Tsun, former professor of English at the *Hochschule* at Tsingtao, or of Averroes, the great Islamic commentator on Aristotle. Each quick-change brings with it its own persuasive aura, yet all are Borges. He delights in extending this sense of the unhoused, of the mysteriously conglomerate, to his own past: "I may have Jewish ancestors, but I can't tell. My mother's name is Acevedo: Acevedo may be a name for a Portuguese Jew, but again it may not. . . . The word *acevedo*, of course, means a kind of tree; the word is not especially Jewish, though many Jews are called Acevedo. I can't tell." As Borges sees it, other masters may derive their strength from a similar stance of strangeness: "I don't know why, but I always feel something Italian, something Jewish about Shakespeare, and perhaps Englishmen admire him because of that, because it's so unlike them." It is not the specific doubt or fantastication that counts. It is the central notion of the writer as a guest, as a human being whose job it is to stay vulnerable to manifold strange presences, who must keep the doors of his momentary lodging open to all winds:

I know little—or nothing—of my own forebears;
The Borges back in Portugal; vague folk
That in my flesh, obscurely, still evoke
Their customs, and their firmnesses and fears.
As slight as if they'd never lived in the sun
And free from any trafficking with art,
They form an indecipherable part
Of time, of earth, and of oblivion.

This universality and disdain of anchor is directly reflected in Borges' fabled erudition. Whether or not it is "merely put there as a kind of private joke," the fabric of bibliographical allusions, philosophic tags, literary citations, kabbalistic references, mathematical and philological acrostics which crowd Borges' stories and poems is, obviously, crucial to the way he experiences reality. A perceptive French critic has argued that in an age of deepening illiteracy, when even the educated have only a smattering of classical or theological knowledge, erudition is of itself a kind of fantasy, a surrealistic construct. Moving, with muted omniscience, from eleventh-century heretical fragments to baroque algebra and multi-tomed Victorian *oeuvres* on the fauna of the Aral Sea, Borges builds an anti-world, a perfectly coherent space in which his mind can conjure at will. The fact that a good deal of the alleged source material and mosaic of allusion is a pure fabrication—a device which Borges shares with Nabokov and for which both may be indebted to Flaubert's *Bouvard et Pécuchet*—paradoxically strengthens the impression of solidity. Pierre Menard stands before us, instantaneously substantial and implausible, through the invented catalogue of his "visible works"; in turn, each arcane item

in the catalogue points to the meaning of the parable. And who would doubt the veracity of the **"Three Versions of Judas"** once Borges has assured us that Nils Runeberg—note the runes in the name—published *Den hemlige Frälsaren* in 1909 but did not know a book by Euclides da Cunha (*Revolt in the Backlands*, exclaims the reader) in which it is affirmed that for the "heresiarch of Canudos, Antonio Conselheiro, virtue 'was almost an impiety'"?

Unquestionably, there is humor in this polymath montage. And there is, as in Pound, a deliberate enterprise of total recall, a graphic inventory of classical and Western civilization in a time in which much of the latter is forgot or vulgarized. Borges is a curator at heart, a treasurer of unconsidered trifles, an indexer of the antique truths and waste conjectures which throng the attic of history. All this arch learning has its comical and gently histrionic sides. But a much deeper meaning as well.

Borges holds, or, rather, makes precise imaginative use of, a kabbalistic image of the world, a master metaphor of existence, which he may have become familiar with as early as 1914, in Geneva, when reading Gustav Meyrink's novel *The Golem*, and when in close contact with the scholar Maurice Abramowicz. The metaphor goes something like this: the Universe is a great Book; each material and mental phenomenon in it carries meaning. The world is an immense alphabet. Physical reality, the facts of history, whatever men have created, are, as it were, syllables of a perpetual message. We are surrounded by a limitless network of significance, whose every thread carries a pulse of being and connects, ultimately, to what Borges, in an enigmatic tale of great power, calls the Aleph. The narrator sees this inexpressible pivot of the cosmos in the dusty corner of the cellar of the house of Carlos Argentino in Garay Street on an October afternoon. It is the space of all spaces, the kabbalistic sphere whose center is everywhere and whose circumference is nowhere, it is the wheel of Ezekiel's vision but also the quiet small bird of Sufi mysticism, which, in some manner, contains all birds: "I was dizzy and I wept, for mine eyes had beheld this secret and conjectural object, whose name is usurped by men, but which no man has looked upon: the inconceivable universe."

From the point of view of the writer, "the universe, which others call the Library," has several notable features. It embraces *all books*, not only those that have already been written, but every page of every tome that will be written in the future and, which matters more, that could conceivably be written. Re-grouped, the letters of all known or lost scripts and alphabets, as they have been set down in extant volumes, can produce every imaginable human thought, every line of verse or prose paragraph to the limits of time. The Library also contains all extant languages and those languages that either have perished or are yet to come. Plainly, Borges is fascinated by the notion, so prominent in the linguistic speculations of the Kabbala and of Jacob Boehme, that a secret primal speech, an *Ur-sprache* from before Babel, underlies the multitude of human tongues. If, as blind poets can, we pass our fingers along the living edge of words—Spanish words, Russian words, Aramaic words, the syllables of a singer in Cathay—we shall fell in them the subtle beat of a great current, pulsing from a common center, the final word made up of all letters and combinations of letters in all tongues that is the name of God.

Thus, Borges' universalism is a deeply felt imaginative strategy, a maneuver to be in touch with the great winds that blow from the heart of things. When he invents fictitious titles, imaginary cross-references, folios and writers that have never existed, Borges is simply regrouping counters of reality into the shape of other possible worlds. When he moves, by word-play and echo, from language to language, he is turning the kaleidoscope, throwing the light on another patch of the wall. Like Emerson, whom he cites indefatigably, Borges is confident that this vision of a totally meshed, symbolic universe is a jubilation: "From the tireless labyrinth of dreams I returned as if to my home to the harsh prison. I blessed its dampness, I blessed its tiger, I blessed the crevice of light, I blessed my old, suffering body, I blessed the darkness and the stone." To Borges, as to the transcendentalists, no living thing or sound but contains a cipher of all.

This dream-logic—Borges often asks whether we ourselves, our dreams included, are not being dreamed from without—has generated some of the most witty, original short fiction in Western literature. "Pierre Menard," "The Library of Babel," "The Circular Ruins," "The Aleph," "Tlön, Uqbar, Orbis Tertius," "Averroes' Search" are laconic masterpieces. Their concise perfection, as that of a great poem, builds a world that is closed, with the reader inescapably inside it, yet open to the widest resonance. Some of the parables, scarcely a page long, such as "Ragnarök," "Everything and Nothing" or "Borges and I," stand beside Kafka's as the only successes in that notoriously labile form. Had he produced no more than the *Fictions* (1956), Borges would rank among the very few fresh dreamers since Poe and Baudelaire. He has, that being the mark of a truly major artist, deepened the landscape of our memories.

Nonetheless, despite its formal universality and the vertigo breadths of his allusive range, the fabric of Borges' art has severe gaps. Only once, in a story called "Emma Zunz," has Borges realized a credible woman. Throughout the rest of his work, women are the blurred objects of men's fantasies or recollections. Even among men, the lines of imaginative force in a Borges fiction are stringently simplified. The fundamental equation is that of a duel. Pacific encounters are cast in the mode of a collision between the "I" of the narrator and the more or less obtrusive shadow of "the other one." Where a third person turns up, his will be, almost invariably, a pres-

ence alluded to or remembered or perceived, unsteadily, at the very edge of the retina. The space of action in which a Borges figure moves is mythical but never social. Where a setting of locale or historical circumstance intrudes, it does so in free-floating bits, exactly as in a dream. Hence the weird, cool emptiness which breathes from many Borges texts as from a sudden window on the night. It is these lacunae, these intense specializations of awareness, which account, I think, for Borges' suspicions of the novel. He reverts frequently to the question. He says that a writer whom dimmed eyesight forces to compose mentally, and, as it were, at one go, must stick to very short narratives. And it is instructive that the first important fictions follow immediately on the grave accident which Borges suffered in December, 1938. He feels also that the novel, like the verse epic before it, is a transitory form: "the novel is a form that may pass, doubtless will pass; but I don't think the story will. . . . It's so much older." It is the teller of tales on the highroad, the *skald*, the raconteur of the pampas, men whose blindness is often a statement of the brightness and crowding of life they have experienced, who incarnate Borges' notion of the writer. Homer is often invoked as a talisman. Granted. But it is as likely that the novel represents precisely the main dimensions lacking in Borges. The rounded presence of women, their relations to men, are of the essence of full-scale fiction. As is a matrix of society. Number theory and mathematical logic charm Borges (see his "Avatars of the Tortoise"). There has to be a good deal of engineering, of applied mathematics, in a novel.

The concentrated strangeness of Borges' repertoire makes for a certain preciousness, a rococo elaboration that can be spellbinding but also airless. More than once, the pale lights and ivory forms of his invention move away from the active disarray of life. Borges has declared that he regards English literature, including American, as "by far the richest in the world." He is admirably at home in it. But his personal anthology of English writers is a curious one. The figures who signify most to him, who serve very nearly as alternate masks to his own person, are De Quincey, Robert Louis Stevenson, G. K. Chesterton, and Rudyard Kipling. Undoubtedly, these are masters, but of a tangential kind. Borges is perfectly right to remind us of De Quincey's organ-pealing prose, and of the sheer control and economy of recital in Stevenson and Kipling. Chesterton is a very odd choice, though again one can make out what *The Man Who Was Thursday* has contributed to Borges' love of charade and high intellectual slapstick. But not one of these writers is among the natural springs of energy in the language or in the history of feeling. And when Borges affirms, teasingly perhaps, that Samuel Johnson "was a far more English writer than Shakespeare," one's sense of the willfully bizarre sharpens. Holding himself beautifully aloof from the bombast, the bullying, the strident ideological pretensions that characterize so much of current letters, Borges has built for himself a center that is, as in the mystical sphere of the Zohar, also a far-out place.

He himself seems conscious of the drawbacks. He has said, in more than one recent interview, that he is now aiming at extreme simplicity, at composing short tales of a flat, sinewy directness. The spare encounter of knife against knife has always fascinated Borges. Some of his earliest and best work derives from the legends of knifings in the Palermo quarter of Buenos Aires, and from the heroic razzias of gauchos and frontier soldiers. He takes eloquent pride in his warring forebears: in his grandfather, Colonel Borges, who fought the Indians and died in a revolution; in Colonel Suarez, his great-grandfather, who led a Peruvian cavalry charge in one of the last great battles against the Spaniards; in a great-uncle who commanded the vanguard of San Martín's army:

> My feet tread the shadows of the lances that spar for the kill. The taunts of my death, the horses, the horse-men, the horses' manes, tighten the ring around me.... Now the first blow, the lance's hard steel ripping my chest, and across my throat the intimate knife.

"The Intruder," a very short story, illustrates Borges' present ideal. Two brothers share a young woman. One of them kills her so that their fraternity may again be whole. They now enjoy a new bond: "the obligation to forget her." Borges himself compares this vignette to Kipling's first tales. "The Intruder" is a slight thing, but flawless and strangely moving. It is as if Borges, after his rare voyage through languages, cultures, mythologies, had come home, and found the Aleph in the next patio.

In a wonderful poem, **"In Praise of Darkness,"** which equivocates with amused irony on the fitness of a man nearly blind to know all books but to forget whichever he chooses, Borges numbers the roads that have led him to his secret center:

> These roads were footsteps and echoes,
> women, men, agonies, rebirths,
> days and nights,
> falling asleep and dreams,
> each single moment of my yesterdays,
> and of the world's yesterdays,
> the firm sword of the Dane and the moon of the
>   Persians,
> the deeds of the dead,
> shared love, words,
> Emerson, and snow, and so many things.
> Now I can forget them. I reach my center,
> my mirror.
> Soon I shall know who I am.

It would be foolish to offer a simple paraphrase for that final core of meaning, for the encounter of perfect identity which takes place at the heart of the mirror. But it is related, vitally, to freedom. In an arch note, Borges has come out in defense of censorship. The true writer uses allusions and metaphors. Censorship compels him to

sharpen, to handle more expertly the prime instruments of his trade. There is, implies Borges, no real freedom in the loud graffiti of erotic and political emancipation that currently pass for fiction and poetry. The liberating function of art lies in its singular capacity to "dream against the world," to structure worlds that are *otherwise*. The great writer is both anarchist and architect, his dreams sap and rebuild the botched, provisional landscape of reality. In 1940, Borges called on the "certain ghost" of De Quincey to "Weave nightmare nets / as a bulwark for your island." His own work has woven nightmares in many tongues, but far more often dreams of wit and elegance. All these dreams are, inalienably, Borges'. But it is we who wake from them, increased. (pp. 22–34)

George Steiner, "Tigers in the Mirror," in his *Extraterritorial: Papers on Literature and the Language Revolution*, Atheneum, 1971, pp. 22–34.

Borges (right front) with his sister Norah (left, rear) at their family home in Geneva, 1916.

V. S. NAIPAUL

(essay date 1972)

[Naipaul is a Trinidadian-born English writer whose novels focusing on life in the Third World, especially *A House for Mr. Biswas* (1961), have been highly acclaimed. In the following essay, Naipaul provides a survey of Borges's life and career, stating that the Argentine author's themes have remained unchanged since his first book of poetry, *Fervor de Buenos Aires,* was published in 1923.]

Borges, speaking of the fame of writers, said: "The important thing is the image you create of yourself in other people's minds. Many people think of Burns as a mediocre poet. But he stands for many things, and people like him. That image—as with Byron—may in the end be more important than the work."

Borges is a great writer, a sweet and melancholy poet; and people who know Spanish well revere him as a writer of a direct, unrhetorical prose. But his Anglo-American reputation as a blind and elderly Argentine, the writer of a very few, very short, and very mysterious stories, is so inflated and bogus that it obscures his greatness. It has possibly cost him the Nobel Prize; and it may well happen that when the bogus reputation declines, as it must, the good work may also disappear.

The irony is that Borges, at his best is neither mysterious nor difficult. His poetry is accessible; much of it is even romantic. His themes have remained constant for the last fifty years: his military ancestors, their deaths in battle, death itself, time, and old Buenos Aires. And there are about a dozen successful stories. Two or three are straightforward, even old-fashioned, detective stories (one was published in *Ellery Queen's Mystery Magazine*). Some deal, quite cinematically, with Buenos Aires low life at the turn of the century. Gangsters are given epic stature; they rise, they are challenged, and sometimes they run away.

The other stories—the ones which have driven the critics crazy—are in the nature of intellectual jokes. Borges takes a word like "immortal" and plays with it. Suppose, he says, men were really immortal. Not just men who had grown old and wouldn't die, but indestructible vigorous men, surviving for eternity. What would be the result? His answer—which is his story—is that every conceivable experience would at some time befall every man, that every man would at some time assume every conceivable character, and that Homer (the disguised hero of this particular story) might in the eighteenth century even forget he had written the *Odyssey*. Or take the word "un-

forgettable." Suppose something was truly unforgettable, and couldn't be forgotten for a single second; suppose this thing came, like a coin, into your possession. Extend that idea. Suppose there was a man—but no, he has to be a boy—who could forget nothing, whose memory therefore ballooned and ballooned with all the unforgettable details of every minute of his life.

These are some of Borges's intellectual games. And perhaps his most successful piece of prose writing, which is also his shortest, is a pure joke. It is called **"Of Exactitude in Science"** and is meant to be an extract from a seventeenth-century book of travel:

> In that Empire, the craft of Cartography attained such Perfection that the Map of a Single province covered the space of an entire City, and the Map of the Empire itself an entire Province. In the course of Time, these Extensive maps were found somehow wanting, and so the College of Cartographers evolved a Map of the Empire that was of the same Scale as the Empire and coincided with it point for point. Less attentive to the Study of Cartography, succeeding Generations came to judge a map of such Magnitude cumbersome and, not without Irreverence, abandoned it to the Rigours of sun and Rain. In the western Deserts, tattered Fragments of the Map are still to be found, Sheltering an occasional Beast or beggar; in the whole Nation no other relic is left of the Discipline of Geography.

This is absurd and perfect: the accurate parody, the grotesque idea. Borges's puzzles and jokes can be addicting. But they have to be recognized for what they are; they cannot always support the metaphysical interpretations they receive. There is, though, much to attract the academic critic. Some of Borges's hoaxes require— and sometimes disappear below—an extravagant display of curious learning. And there is the occasional baroque language of the early stories.

"The Circular Ruins"—an elaborate, almost science-fiction story about a dreamer discovering that he himself exists only in somebody else's dream—begins: *"Nadie lo vio desembarcar en la unánime noche."* Literally, "Nobody saw him disembark in the unanimous night." Norman Thomas di Giovanni, who has been translating Borges full time for the last four years, and has done more than anyone else to push Borges's work in the English-speaking world, says,

> You can imagine how much has been written about that "unanimous." I went to Borges with two translations, "surrounding" and "encompassing." And I said, "Borges, what did you really mean by the unanimous night? That doesn't mean anything. If the unanimous night, why not the tea-drinking night or the card-playing night?" And I was astonished by his answer. He said, "Di Giovanni, that's just one example of the irresponsible way I used to write." We used "encompassing" in the translation. But a lot of the professors didn't like losing their unanimous night. . . .

There was this woman. She wrote an essay on Borges for a book. She didn't know any Spanish and was basing her essay on two rather mediocre English translations. A long essay, about forty pages. And one of the *crucial* points was that Borges wrote a very Latinate prose. I had to point out to her that Borges could not help but write a Latinate prose, because he wrote in Spanish, and Spanish is a dialect of Latin. She didn't consult anybody when she was laying the foundation. At the end she calls out "Help!" and you run up and see this enormous skyscraper sinking in quicksand.

Di Giovanni went with Borges on a lecture tour of the United States in 1969:

Borges is a gentleman. When people come up and tell him what his stories really mean—after all, he only wrote them—he has the most wonderful line you've ever heard.

"Ah, thank you! You've enriched my story. You've made me a great gift. I've come all the way from Buenos Aires to X—say Lubbock, Texas—to find out this truth about myself and my story."

Borges has for years enjoyed a considerable reputation in the Spanish-speaking world. But in **"An Autobiographical Essay,"** which was published as a "Profile" in *The New Yorker* in 1970, he says that until he won the Formentor Prize in 1961—he was sixty-two then—he was "practically invisible—not only abroad but at home in Buenos Aires." This is the kind of exaggeration that dismays some of his early Argentine supporters; and there are those who would say that his "irresponsibility" has grown with his fame. But Borges has always been irresponsible. Buenos Aires is a small town; and what perhaps was inoffensive when Borges belonged only to this small town becomes less so when foreigners queue up for interviews. Once, no doubt, Borges's celebration of his military ancestors and their deaths in battle flattered the whole society, giving it a sense of the past and of completeness. Now it appears to exclude, to proclaim a private grandeur; and to many it is only egotistical and presumptuous. It is not easy to be famous in a small town.

Borges gives many interviews. And every interview seems to be like every other interview. He seems to make questions irrelevant; he plays, as one Argentine lady said, his *discos*, his records; he performs. He says that the Spanish language is his "doom." He criticizes Spain and the Spaniards: he still fights that colonial war, in which, however, the old issues have become confused with a simpler Argentine prejudice against the poor and backward immigrants from Northern Spain. He makes his tasteless, and expected, jokes about the pampa Indians. Tasteless, because just twenty years before he was born these Indians were systematically exterminated; and yet expected, because slaughter on this scale becomes acceptable only if the victims are made ridiculous. He talks about Chesterton, Stevenson, and Kipling. He talks about Old English

with all the enthusiasm of a man who has picked up a subject by himself. He talks about his English ancestors.

It is a curiously colonial performance. His Argentine past is part of his distinction; he offers it as such; and he is after all a patriot. He honors the flag, an example of which flies from the balcony of his office in the National Library (he is the director). And he is moved by the anthem. But at the same time he seems anxious to proclaim his separateness from Argentina. The performance might seem aimed at Borges's new Anglo-American campus audience, whom in so many ways it flatters. But the attitudes are old.

In Buenos Aires it is still remembered that in 1955, just a few days after Perón was overthrown and that nine-year dictatorship was over, Borges gave a lecture on—of all subjects—Coleridge to the ladies of the Association for English Culture. Some of Coleridge's lines, Borges said, were among the best in English poetry, "es decir la poesía, that is to say poetry." And those four words, at a time of national rejoicing, were like a gratuitous assault on the Argentine soul.

Norman di Giovanni tells a balancing story. "In December, 1969, we were at Georgetown University in Washington, D. C. The man doing the introduction was an Argentine from Tucumán and he took advantage of the occasion to point out to the audience that the military repression had closed the university in Tucumán. Borges was totally oblivious of what the man had said until we were on our way to the airport. Then someone began to talk about it and Borges was suddenly very angry. 'Did you hear what that man said? That they'd closed the university in Tucumán.' I questioned him about his rage, and he said, 'That man was attacking my country. They can't talk that way about my country.' I said, 'Borges, what do you mean, "that man"? That man is an Argentine. And he comes from Tucumán. And what he says is true. The military *have* closed the university.'"

Borges is of medium height. His nearly sightless eyes and his stick add to the distinction of his appearance. He dresses carefully. He says he is a middle-class writer; and a middle- class writer shouldn't be either a dandy or too affectedly casual. He is courtly: he thinks, with Sir Thomas Browne, that a gentleman is someone who tries to give the least amount of trouble. "But you should look that up in *Religio Medici*." It might seem then that in his accessibility, his willingness to give lengthy interviews which repeat the other interviews he has given, Borges combines the middle-class ideal of self-effacement and the gentleman's manners with the writer's privacy, the writer's need to save himself for his work.

There are hints of this privacy (in accessibility) in the way he likes to be addressed. Perhaps no more than half a dozen people have the privilege of calling him by his first name, Jorge, which they turn into "Georgie." To everyone else he likes to be just "Borges," without the *señor*, which he considers Spanish and pompous. "Borges" is, of course, distancing.

And even the fifty-page **"Autobiographical Essay"** doesn't violate his privacy. It is like another interview. It says little that is new. His birth in Buenos Aires in 1899, the son of a lawyer; his military ancestors; the family's seven-year sojourn in Europe from 1914 to 1921 (when the peso was valuable, and Europe was cheaper than Buenos Aires): all this is told again in outline, as in an interview. And the essay quickly becomes no more than a writer's account of his writing life, of the books he read and the books he wrote, the literary groups he joined and the magazines he founded. The life is missing. There is a barest sketch of the crisis he must have gone through in his late thirties and early forties, when—the family money lost—he was doing all kinds of journalism; when his father died, and he himself fell seriously ill and "feared for [his] mental integrity"; when he worked as an assistant in a municipal library, well-known as a writer outside the library, unknown inside it, "I remember a fellow employee's once noting in an encyclopedia the name of a certain Jorge Luis Borges—a fact that set him wondering at the coincidence of our identical names and birth dates."

"Nine years of solid unhappiness," he says; but he gives the period only four pages. The privacy of Borges begins to appear a forbidding thing.

> Un dios me ha concedido
> Lo que es dado saber a los
>   mortales.
> Por todo el continente anda mi
>   nombre;
> No he vivido. Quisiera ser otro
>   hombre.

Mark Strand translates:

> I have been allowed
> That which is given mortal man to
>   know.
> The whole continent knows my
>   name.
> I have not lived. I want to be
>   someone else.

This is Borges on Emerson; but it might be Borges on Borges. Life, in the **"Autobiographical Essay,"** is indeed missing. So that all that is important in the man has to be found in the work, which with Borges is essentially the poetry. And all the themes he has explored over a long life are contained, as he himself says, in his very first book of poems, published in 1923, a book printed in five days, 300 copies, given away free.

Here is the military ancestor dying in battle. Here, already, at the age of twenty-four, the contemplation of glory turns into a meditation on death and time and the "glass jewels" of the individual life:

> . . . cuando tú mismo eres la continuación realizada
> de quienes no alcanzaron tu tiempo

> y otros serán (y son) tu inmortalidad en la tierra.

In W. S. Merwin's translation:

> . . . when you yourself are the
> embodied continuance
> of those who did not live into
> your time
> and others will be (and are) your
> immortality on earth.

Somewhere around that time life stopped; and all that has followed has been literature: a concern with words, an unending attempt to stay with, and not to betray, the emotions of that so particular past.

> I am myself and I am him today,
> The man who died, the man
>   whose blood and name
> Are mine.

This is Norman di Giovanni's translation of a poem written forty-three years after that first book:

> Soy, pero soy también el otro, el
>   muerto,
> El otro de mi sangre y de mi
>   nombre

Since the writing of that first book nothing, except perhaps his discovery of Old English poetry, has provided Borges with matter for such intense meditation. Not even the bitter Perón years, when he was " 'promoted' out of the library to the inspectorship of poultry and rabbits in the public markets," and resigned. Nor his brief, unhappy marriage late in life, once the subject of magazine articles, and still a subject of gossip in Buenos Aires. Nor his continuing companionship with his mother, now aged ninety-six.

"In 1910, the centenary of the Argentine Republic, we thought of Argentina as an honorable country and we had no doubt that the nations would come flocking in. Now the country is in a bad way. We are being threatened by the return of the horrible man." This is how Borges speaks of Perón: he prefers not to use the name.

> I get any number of personal threats. Even my mother. They rang her up in the small hours—two or three in the morning—and somebody said to her in a very gruff kind of voice, the voice you associate with a *Peronista*, "I've got to kill you and your son." My mother said, "Why?" "Because I am a *Peronista*." My mother said, "As far as my son is concerned, he is over seventy and practically blind. But in my case I should advise you to waste no time because I am ninety-five and may die on your hands before you can kill me." Next morning I told my mother I thought I had heard the telephone ringing in the night. "Did I dream that?" She said, "Just some fool." She's not only witty. But courageous. . . . I don't see what I can do about it— the political situation. But I think I should do what I can, having military men in my family.

Borges's first book of poems was called *Fervour of Buenos Aires*. In it, he said in his preface, he was attempting to celebrate the new and expanding city in a special way. "Akin to the Romans, who would murmur the words *'numen inest'* on passing through a wood, 'Here dwells a god,' my verses declare, stating the wonder of the streets. . . . Everyday places become, little by little, holy."

But Borges has not hallowed Buenos Aires. The city the visitor sees is not the city of the poems, the way Simla (as new and as artificial as Buenos Aires) remains, after all these years, the city of Kipling's stories. Kipling looked hard at a real town. Borges's Buenos Aires is private, a city of the imagination. And now the city itself is in decay. In Borges's own Southside some old buildings survive, with their mighty front doors and their receding patios, each patio differently tiled. But more often the inner patios have been blocked up; and many of the old buildings have been pulled down. Elegance, if in this plebeian immigrant city elegance really ever existed outside the vision of expatriate architects, has vanished; there is now only disorder.

The white and pale blue Argentine flag that hangs out into Mexico Street from the balcony of Borges's office in the National Library is dingy with dirt and fumes. And consider this building, perhaps the finest in the area, which was used as a hospital and a jail in the time of the gangster-dictator Rosas more than 120 years ago. There is beauty still in the spiked wall, the tall iron gates, the huge wooden doors. But inside the walls peel; the windows in the central patio are broken; further in, courtyard opening into courtyard, washing hangs in a corridor, steps are broken, and a metal spiral staircase is blocked with junk. This is a government office, a department of the Ministry of Labor: it speaks of an administration that has seized up, a city that is dying, a country that hasn't really worked.

Walls everywhere are scrawled with violent slogans; guerrillas operate in the streets; the peso falls; the city is full of hate. The bloody-minded slogan repeats: *Rosas vuelve*, Rosas is coming back. The country awaits a new terror.

Numen inest, here dwells the god: the poet's incantation hasn't worked. The military ancestors died in battle, but those petty battles and wasteful deaths have led to nothing. Only in Borges's poetry do those heroes inhabit "an epic universe, sitting tall in the saddle," *"alto. . . en su épico universo."* And this is his great creation: Argentina as a simple mythical land, a complete epic world, of "republics, cavalry, and mornings," "las repúblicas, los caballos y las mañanas," of battles fought, the fatherland established, the great city created, and the "streets with names recurring from the past in my blood."

That is the vision of art. And yet, out of this mythical Argentina of his creation, Borges reaches out, through his English grandmother, to his English ancestors and, through them, to their language, "at its dawn." "People tell me I look English now. When I was younger I didn't look English. I was darker. I didn't feel English. Not at all.

Maybe feeling English came to me through reading." And though Borges doesn't acknowledge it, a recurring theme in the later stories is of Nordics growing degenerate in a desolate Argentine landscape. Scottish Guthries become *mestizo* Gutres and no longer even know the Bible; an English girl becomes an Indian savage; men called Nilsen forget their origins and live like animals with the bestial sex code of the *macho* whoremonger.

Borges said at our first meeting, "I don't write about degenerates." But another time he said, "The country was enriched by men thinking essentially of Europe and the United States. Only the civilized people. The gauchos were very simple-minded. Barbarians." When we talked of Argentine history he said, "There is a pattern. Not an obvious pattern. I myself can't see the wood for the trees." And later he added, "Those civil wars are now meaningless."

Perhaps, then, parallel with the vision of art, there has developed, in Borges, a subsidiary vision, however unacknowledged, of reality. And now, at any rate, the real world can no longer be denied.

In the middle of May Borges went for a few days to Montevideo in Uruguay. Montevideo was one of the cities of his childhood, a city of "long, lazy holidays." But now Uruguay, the most educated country in South America, was, in the words of an Argentine, "a caricature of a country," bankrupt, like Argentina, after wartime wealth, and tearing itself to pieces. Montevideo was a city at war; guerrillas and soldiers fought in the streets. One day, while Borges was there, four soldiers were shot and killed.

I saw Borges when he came back. A pretty girl helped him down the steps at the Catholic University. He looked more frail; his hands shook more easily. He had shed his sprightly interview manner. He was full of the disaster of Montevideo; he was distressed. Montevideo was something else he had lost. In one poem, "mornings in Montevideo" are among the things for which he thanks "the divine labyrinth of causes and effects." Now Montevideo, like Buenos Aires, like Argentina, was gracious only in his memory, and in his art. (pp. 3–4,6)

V. S. Naipaul, "Comprehending Borges," in *The New York Review of Books*, Vol. XIX, No. 6, October 19, 1972, pp. 3–4, 6.

V. S. PRITCHETT

(essay date 1979)

[Pritchett is a highly esteemed English novelist, short story writer, and critic. Considered on of the modern masters of the short story, he is also one of the world's most respected literary critics. Pritchett

Borges on death:

Death means you stop being, you cease from thinking, or feeling, or wondering, and at least you're lucky in that you don't have to worry. You might as well worry, as the Latin poet said, about the ages and ages that preceded you when you did not exist. You might as well worry about the endless past as the endless future uninhabited by you . . . . Infinity, yes, that's a problem, but death isn't a problem in that sense. There's no difficulty whatever in imagining that even as I go to sleep every night, I may have a long sleep at the end. I mean it's not an intellectual problem. I don't understand Unamuno, because Unamuno wrote that God, for him, was the provider of immortality, that he couldn't believe in a God who didn't believe in immortality. I don't see that. There might be a God who might not want me to go on living, or who might think that the universe does not need me. After all, it did not need me until 1899, when I was born. I was left out until it did.

Jorge Luis Borges, in *Conversations With Jorge Luis Borges*, by Richard Burgin, 1968.

writes in the conversational tone of the familiar essay, approaching literature from the viewpoint of a lettered but not excessively scholarly reader. In his criticism, Pritchett stresses his own experience, judgment, and sense of literary art, rather than following a codified critical doctrine derived form a school of psychological or philosophical speculation. In the following essay, Pritchett examines Borges's short stories as meditations on the theme of "the timelessness of a precise human experience."]

In one of his terse utterances about himself as an artist, Jorge Luis Borges says, 'I have always come to life after coming to books.' In a general sense this could be said by most storytellers and poets, but in Borges the words have a peculiar overtone. He appears to speak of something anomalous with the dignity of one who has been marked by an honourable wound received in an ambush between literature and life. Like Cervantes, he would have preferred to be a soldier who had pride in his wounded arm and had been forced by singularity into turning to the conceits of the *Exemplary Novels* and the *Romances* out of which he made *Don Quixote*.

Among South American writers Borges is a collection of anomalies, exceptional in the first place in having been brought up on English rather than French models; towards the Spaniards outside of *Don Quixote* (English translation preferred) and Quevedo, he is condescending. He had an English grandmother and an Anglophile father who was himself a writer and who brought up his son on *Tom Brown's Schooldays*, Kipling, Wells, Stevenson, Chesterton and Emerson. The poetry of Swinburne, Tennyson and Browning was important in the Argentine

family who, on the Spanish side, had been violently concerned in earlier generations in the savage South American civil wars. The boy was frail and too near-sighted to follow a military career. Father and son, both slowly going blind, went to Europe for cure and education, mainly in Geneva, Germany and Spain. They detested Paris and thought Madrid trivial. One would guess that the erudition of Browning and the abrupt images of his dramatic narratives, made the deepest impression, though one sees no trace of this in Borges's own poetry. Returning to Buenos Aires where at first he could hardly leave his house, he eventually became a librarian in a small municipal library (from which he was dismissed for political reasons at the time of Perón), and later the Director of the National Library itself.

Borges has also spoken of how, after the age of thirty, when he began to go blind, he has lived physically in a growing twilight in which the distinctions between visible reality, conjecture and an immense reading are blurred. He had to remember, and a memory, in which he is rarely at a loss for the exact words of a long poem, has become literary, and the library a printed yet metaphysical domain. It is not surprising that Berkeley and Schopenhauer are his philosophers, and no more than natural, to one so attached to English literature, that he should have read William Morris and De Quincey. In conversation with Borges one hears life emerging out of phrases and scenes from literature and this, one understands at once from his writing, is not a merely browsing habit of mind. The emergence is dramatic, a creative act, as new landscapes are imagined and populated.

Such a reader is a full man, too full for the novelist. He has said:

I have read but few novels and, in most cases, only a sense of duty has enabled me to find me way to the last page. At the same time, I have always been a reader and re-reader of short stories—Stevenson, Kipling, Henry James, Conrad, Poe, Chesterton, the tales in Lane's translation of *The Arabian Nights*, and certain stories of Hawthorne have been a habit of mine since I can remember. The feeling that the great novels like *Don Quixote* and *Huckleberry Finn* are virtually shapeless, reinforced my taste for the short story form whose indispensable elements are economy and a clearly stated beginning, middle and end.

This sounds conventional enough. But in the writer of short stories as in the poet, a distinctive voice, unlike all others, must arrest us; in Borges the voice is laconic, precise yet rapt and unnerving; it is relieved by the speculations of the essayist and the disconnecting currents of memory. Even in a banal paragraph each word will create the sudden suspense made by a small move in chess. In the story of "**Emma Zunz**," a woman is shown getting a letter which tells here that her father, whom she has not seen for years, has committed suicide: I give the English translation in which the dry exactitude of the Spanish is weakened—but still it catches the effect he desires:

> Her first impression was of a weak feeling in her stomach and in her knees: then of blind guilt, of unreality, of coldness, of fear; then she wished that it were already the *next* day. Immediately afterwards she realised that the wish was futile because the death of her father was the only that had happened in the world and it would go on happening endlessly.

Why did 'she wish it were the next day'? Why would the death 'go on happening endlessly' in real life? Because she is intent on revenge. These phrases ring in the imagination like an alarm bell, and this alarm is at the heart of all Borges's writing. The endlessness, the timelessness of a precise human experience, is his constant subject. How to convey the sense of endlessness curtly—with a vividness that is, on the face of it, perfunctory—will again and again be his dramatic task.

Nearly all the stories of Borges, except the earliest ones, are either constructed conundrums or propositions. The early ones are trial glosses on the American gangster tale transferred to the low life of Buenos Aires. He moved on to the stories of the gaucho: he heard many of these from his grandmother. They begin deceptively as short, historical reminiscences and then, at the crisis, they burst into actuality out of the past; he is recovering a moment:

> Any life, no matter how long and complex it may be, is made up of a *single moment*—the moment in which a man finds out, once and for all, who he is.

In his stories of the gauchos, their violence will strike us as meaningless until Borges says:

> the gauchos, without realising it, forged a religion— the hard and blind religion of courage—and this faith (like all others) has its ethic, its mythology and its martyrs. . . they discovered in their own way the age-old cult of the gods of iron—no mere form of vanity, but an awareness that God may be found in any man.

The task of the writer in each story—it is usually a fight—is to find the testing crisis of *machismo*, as if he were chiselling it all out in hard, unfeeling stone. He is very careful to keep the tone of landscape or street low— he even refers to 'insipid streets'—in order to heighten the violence. The test may not be heroic, but will contain a dismissive irony. In **"The Dead Man"** a swaggering tough has been boasting to an able but ageing gangleader. The gangs are expert cattle stealers. To the young man's surprise the old leader of the gang lets him get the better of him and even sends him up-country in charge of the next job. The gang obey the new young leader admiringly: the young man has even had the impudence to take the old leader's girl. They obey and love the young man. Why? Because he is the supplanter and winner? Because they are naturally treacherous time-serving cowards? Or simply recklessly indifferent? None of these thing. An ancient knowledge comes to them. They *love* the young man because he is virtually dead already. He must be loved for his moment. They are really waiting, with interest, for the time when the old leader will come up-country, take his rightful revenge and kill him.

Or again, in a superb tale **"The Intruder"**, there are two brothers. A girl servant looks after them. She becomes the mistress of one brother, but when he goes off on his work the other brother sleeps with her. Both brothers fear their jealousy, so in the end they put the girl in a brothel. This does not solve their problem, for both secretly visit her. What is to be done? The test of their love for each other has arrived. They take her off at night and kill her. Lust is dead and now their love for each other is secure. Or there is the tale of Cruz, a soldier with a savage career behind him, who has been sent off to capture an outlawed murderer. The outlaw is cornered by Cruz and his soldiers and fights back desperately. Borges writes:

> Cruz while he fought in the dark (while his body fought) began to understand. He understood that one destiny is no better than another, but that every man must obey what is within him. He understood that his shoulder braid and his uniform were now in his way. He understood that his real destiny was as a lone wolf, not a gregarious dog. He understood the other man was himself.

So he turns against his own men and fights beside the outlaw. This is the story of the semi-mythical hero of the gauchos, Martin Fierro.

Because of the influence of the cinema, most reports of stories of violence are so pictorial that they lack content or meaning. The camera brings them to our eyes, but does not settle them in our minds, nor in time. Borges avoided this trap by stratifying his tales in subtle layers of flat history, hearsay and metaphysical speculation : he is not afraid of trailing off into a short essay, ending with an appendix, for the more settled a violent subject looks, the more we can be misled, the more frightening the drama. It will not only be seen to be true, but will have the sadness and dignity of a truth that our memories have trodden away. History, in Borges, is never picturesque or romantic. It is the past event coming back like a blow in the face.

When we turn to the fantasies of the poet in Borges we find him first of all at play with spoof learning. In one of his best known works with the extraordinary title of **"Tlön, Uqbar, Orbis Tertius,"** the librarian puts on a learned, dry-as-dust air of research and slyly reveals how for generations a secret society of pedestrian scholars have slowly invented an imaginary planet, complete with civilization and language derived from a faked edition of the Encyclopaedia Britannica, so that the non-existent has become established. Or in another tale he pretends to have discovered how the Idea of lunch gradually became rooted in the thought of a Companía—a religious Order—who since ancient times have been inventing luck, little by little, by trial and error, until it pervades life and may be life itself. What they were really documenting was the monotony of life.

A more serious preoccupation comes close to nightmare. Our imaginations may be housed in intellectual constructions. The labyrinth is one. Or we may be enacting feelings, scenes or events that simply belong to 'an endless series'—a favourite phrase—over which we have no control. A fatalistic symbol of time or memory is a corridor with two mirrors facing each other: the infinitely repeated reflections are symbols of our consciousness of people, sensations and even things. Indeed things—a knife, a room, for example, and fact of landscape, having a threatening existence of their own and the dead force of inventory. In the story called **"The Aleph"** which contains his characteristic changes of voice, the narrator talks flatly of the death of a shallow society woman whom he had vainly loved:

> On the burning February morning Beatriz Viterbo died after an agony that never for one single moment gave way to self-pity or fear, I noticed that the billboards on the sidewalk round Constitution Plaza were advertising some new brand of American cigarette. The fact pained me for I realised that the wide, ceaseless universe was already slipping away from her and that this slight change was the first of an endless series.

The narrator who is a poet heightens his pain by going to visit another poet, a boring man called Carlos Argentino Daneri who was a cousin of Beatriz and probably her lover. Daneri is

> authoritarian and unimpressive. His mental activity was continuous, deeply felt, far-ranging and—all in all—meaningless.

Daneri is writing an enormous poem which will conscientiously describe 'modern man' and everything on modern man's earth. The attack on realism and fact fetishism is obvious:

> Daneri had in mind to set to verse the entire face of the planet, and by 1941, had already despatched a number of acres of the State Queensland, nearly a mile of the course run by the River Ob, a gasworks to the north of Vera Cruz, the leading shops in the Conception quarter of Buenos Aires, the villa of Mariana Cambaceres de Alvear in the Belgrano section of the Argentine capital, and a Turkish baths establishment not far from the well known Brighton Aquarium.

In this curtly sarcastic comedy of jealousy over the grave of Beatriz Viterbo, Borges is leading us by the nose. He is preparing us for one of his eloquent imaginative leaps out of the dead world of things into a rhapsody on the tragedy of human loss. Daneri is annoyed that the narrator does not praise his poem and, knowing his man, says that embedded in the staris of his cellar he possesses a great

wonder which has inspired him and which will vanish tomorrow because the house is going to be pulled down. The wonder is a magic stone called the Aleph. The Aleph is a microcosm of the alchemists and Kabbalists, 'our true proverbial friend' (he calls it) 'the multum in parvo':

> Go down into the cellar, you can babble with all Beatriz Viterbo's images.

The narrator is locked in the cellar. He sees the stone which is only an inch wide:

> In that single gigantic instance I saw millions of acts both delightful and awful; not one of them amazed me more than the fact that all of them occupied the same point in space, without overlapping or transparency. . . I saw, close up, unending eyes watching themselves in me as in a mirror; I saw all the mirrors on earth and none of them reflected me; I saw in a back-yard of Soler Street the same titles that thirty years before I'd seen in the entrance of a house in Fray Bentos; I saw bunches of grapes, snow, tobacco, lodes of metal, steam; I saw convex equatorial deserts and each one of their grains of sand; I saw a woman in Inverness whom I shall never forget; I saw her tangled hair, her tall figure; I saw the cancer in her breast; I saw a ring of baked mud in a sidewalk, where before there had been a tree. . . . I saw in a closet in Alkmaar a terrestrial globe between two mirrors that multiplied it endlessly. . . . I saw in the drawer of a writing table (and the handwriting made me tremble) unbelievable, obscene, detailed letters, which Beatriz had written to Carlos Argentino; I saw the circulation of my own dark blood; I saw the coupling of love and the modification of death. . . .

The story ends in what is a typical Borges manner. There is a short discussion of the metaphysical theories about the Aleph which contains the malicious phrase 'Incredible as it may seem, I believe that the Aleph of Garay Street was a false Aleph':

> Our minds are porous and forgetfulness seaps in. I myself am distorting and losing, under the wearing away of the years, the face of Beatriz Viterbo.

In the story of shock of jealousy, grief and loss is transposed into a reel of mechanical effects.

In the elaborate fable of **"The Circular Ruins,"** a grey and silent teacher takes refuge in a ruined temple. 'His guiding purpose, though it was supernatural, was not impossible. He wanted to dream a man; he wanted to dream him down to the last detail and project him into the world of reality.' He 'creates' this phantom, thinks of him as his son; and then remembers that Fire is the only creature in the world who would know he was a phantom. In the end Fire destroys the dreamer. What is the meaning of the fable? Is it a fable of the act of creation in art? A solipsist conceit? A missing chapter from the Book of

Genesis? An experience of panic caused by insomnia or reading Berkeley? Borges says,

> With relief, with humiliation, with terror, he understood that he too was a mere appearance dreamt by another.

One can argue that the later Borges is a learned pillager of metaphysical arguments: one who has made Chesterton rhapsodic, put blood into the diagrams of Euclid, or a knife into the hands of Schopenhauer, but the test of the artist is—Can he make his idea walk, can he place it in a street, a room, can he 'plant' the aftermath of the 'moment of truth'? Borges *does* pass this test. The poet is a master of the quotidian, of conveying a whole history in two or three lines that point to an exact past drama and intensify a future one.

To go back to the tale of Emma Zung. We see her preparing to avenge her father's death. To kill is a degrading act; first of all, therefore, she has to initiate herself into degradation by posing as a prostitute and sleeping with a sailor. She tears up the money he leaves her because to destroy money is impiety.

> Emma was able to leave without anyone seeing her; at the corner she got on a Lacroze streetcar heading west. She selected, in keeping with her plan, the seat farthest toward the front so that her face would not be seen. Perhaps it comforted her to verify in the insipid movement along the streets that what had happened had not contaminated things.

A small fact creates the impression of a link with some powerful surrounding emotion or some message from the imagination or myth. The very casualness of the sudden observation suggests the uncertainty by which our passions are surrounded.

Borges loves to borrow from other writers, either good or second-rate. He admires Poe who defined for all time what a short story intrinsically is. He certainly has been influenced by Kafka—he translated *The Castle* into Spanish—although he is far from being a social moralist. On the face of it he looks like one of the European cosmopolitans of the first thirty years of this century and, like them, very much a formalist. But on second thoughts one sees that his mind is not in the least European. The preoccupation with isolation, instant violence and the metaphysical journey of discovery or the quest for imagined treasure, marks him as belonging to the American continents. His sadness is the colonial sadness, not the European.

A bookish comment occurs to me. A few years ago when I was reading Borges for the first time I read two of the very late stories of Prosper Mérimée: "Lokis" and "La Vénus d' Ille." There is a vast difference between the French Romantic and Borges, but they have one or two singular things in common. A short story writer cannot help being struck by the similarities that, in the course of

more than 100 years, have diverged. Both writers have the English coolness and *humeur*, the background of the linguistic, historical, archaeological and mystical erudition. Mérimée was very much the wounded man, cold and detached, conservative and rational, but he had the civilized Romantic's fascination with the primitive and the unbelievable. In these two late stories—possibly because of a personal crisis—he is suddenly concerned with dream and the unconscious. It is true that the polished and formal Mérimée plays with his metaphysical anxieties, and has no interest in the self-creating man or woman, but he shares with Borges a love of hoaxing pedantry and the common approach of the misleading essay. The terrible story "Lokis" affects to arise in the course of a serious study of the Lithuanian language. (Mérimée was a philologist, so is Borges.) Mérimée uses his learning to play down his subject for it will suddenly become a fantastic dream of the unconscious turned into gruesome reality. The same may be said of Mérimée's tale of Corsican vendetta and in the ghost story of "La Vénus d' Ille."

A hundred and thirty years separate Mérimée and Borges. Where Mérimée documentation is a closed study of folklore or custom, Borges takes a leap into space, into the uncertain, the mysterious and the cunning. The record has become memory feeding on memory, myth feeding on myth. Where Mérimée is the master of anecdote in which lives end when the artist decides, Borges has the poet's power to burst the anecdote open. He seems to say that the story must be open, because I, too, am like my characters, part of an endless series or repetitions of the same happenings. The risk is—and there are some signs of this already—that criticism of Borges will become an accretion that will force us to see his stories as conceits alone. (pp. 174–84)

V.S. Pritchett, "Jorge Luis Borges: 'Medallions'," in his *The Myth Makers: Literary Essays*, Random House, 1979, pp. 174–84.

Borges (right) with his collaborator and close friend Adolfo Bioy Casares.

JAIME ALAZRAKI

(essay date 1981)

[Alazraki is an Argentine-born American educator and critic who has written and edited several scholarly studies on Latin American authors, including Borges, Julio Cortázar, and Pablo Neruda. In the following essay, he provides an overview of Borges's development as a poet, focusing in particular on *Historia de la noche*.]

From his early poems of the Twenties to his most recent collection *Historia de la noche* (*A History of the Night,* 1977), Borges' poetry has travelled a long way. It first moved from a nostalgic rediscovery of his birthplace, Buenos Aires, to a cult of his ancestors and an intimate history of his country: heroes, anti-heroes, counterheroes. He then found that metaphysical subjects, literary artifacts, and religious myths were not unworthy material for poetry: **"The Cyclical Night," "Poem Written in a Copy of Beowulf,"** and **"The Golem"** are samples which illustrate this later period. His perception of poetry in those years could be defined, in T.S. Eliot's dictum, "not as a turning loose of emotions, but as an escape from emotion; not as the expression of personality, but as an escape from personality." A reflective and ruminative poetry. His rumination were not about the fortunes or misfortunesof the heart, or existential angst, or the conundrum of life but about the monuments of the imagination, and particularly those of literature: intellect as passion, culture as the true adventure, knowledge as invention. A rather selfless poetry, a poetry in which the most powerful presence of the self is in its absence.

A grandson and great-grandson of military heroes, Borges turned his poetry into an epic exploration by evoking everything poetry can possibly evoke other than his own personal drama. In his more recent poetry this drama is defined as a lack of personal drama. Borges muses relentlessly and painfully about his life devoid of heroic violence: "Soy. . . el que no fue una espada en la guerra" (I am that who did not wield a sword in battle); "Yo, que padeci la vergüenza de no haber sido aquel Francisco Borges que murió en 1874" (I, who suffered the shame/of not having been that Francisco Borges who died in 1874) :

Estoy ciego. He cumplido los setenta;
No soy el oriental Francisco Borges
Que murió con dos balas en el pecho,
Entre las agonías de los hombres,
En el hedor de un hospital de sangre. . .

I am blind, and I have lived out seventy years.
I am not Francisco Borges the Uruguayan

who died with a brace of bullets in his breast
among the final agonies of men
in the death-stench of a hospital of blood. . .

Soy también la memoria de una espada

I am also the memory of a sword

Since he is denied a sword, he turns poetry into a sword; since epic action has been ruled out of his life, he converts poetry into an epic exercise.

Dejame, espada, usar contigo el arte;
Yo, que no he merecido manejarte.

Let me, sword, render you in art;
I, who did not deserve to wield you.

How did he accomplish this? By effacing himself from his own poetry, by speaking of everybody but forgetting about himself. Borges has said of Bernard Shaw that "he is the only writer of our time who has imagined and presented heroes to his readers," and he explains further:

On the whole, modern writers tend to reveal men's weaknesses and seem to delight in their unhappiness; in Shaw's case, however, we have characters who are heroic and whom one can admire. Contemporary literature since Dostoevsky—and even earlier—since Byron—seems to delight in man's guilt and weaknesses. In Shaw's work the greatest human virtues are extolled. For example, that a man can forget his own fate, that a man may not value his own happiness, that he may say like our Almafuerte: 'I am not interested in my own life,' because he is interested in somthing beyond personal circumstances.

Here we find a first explanation of the seemingly impersonal quality of his poetry; yet what Borges defends is not impersonality but an epic sense of life. The poet disregrads his own tribulations to become the singer of virtues, values, people, and literary works dear to him. Haunted by the memories of his ancestors' "romantic death," Borges celebrates the courage of heroes and knife-fighters ready to die in defense of a cause or belief more precious than their own life. Since he is denied an epic destiny on the battlefield, he'll turn literature into his own battlefield by refusing to speak about himself, by lending his voice to others. This epic attitude has been deliberate, and it stems from his family background as well as from the fact that, as he put it, "my father's library has been the capital event in my life": books as events, intellection as life, past as present, literature as passion.

Until 1964. That year Borges published a sonnet entitled "1964" with which he inaugurates a new theme in his poetry. To what he has called his "habits"—"Buenos Aires, the cult of my ancestors, the study of old Germanic languages, the contradiction of time"—he now adds his broodings over what can be called a vocation of unhappiness. The sonnet opens with the line "Ya no seré felix. Tal vex no importa" (I shall no longer be happy. Perhaps it doesn't matter) a motif that appears and reappears in his last four collections between 1969 and 1976, and culminates in the 1976 sonnet **"Remordimiento"** (Remorse), included in *La moneda de hierro* (The Iron Coin):

> He cometido el peor de los pecados
> Que un hombre puede cometer. No he sido
> Feliz. Que los glaciares del olvido
> Me arrastren y me pierdan, despiadados.
> Mis padres me engendraron para el juego
> Arriesgado y hermoso de la vida,
> Para la tierra, el agua, el aire, el fuego.
> Los defraudé. No fui feliz. Cumplida
> No fue su joven voluntad. Mi mente
> Se aplicó a las simétricas porfías
> Del arte, que entreteje naderías.
> Me legaron su valor. No fui valiente.
> No me abandona. Siempre está a mi lado
> La sombra de haber sido un desdichado,

> I have committed the worst sin of all
> That a man can commit. I have not been
> Happy. Let the glaciers of oblivion
> Drag me and mercilessly let me fall
> My parents bred and bore me for a higher
> Faith in the human game of nights and days;
> For earth, for air, for water, and for fire.
> I let them down. I wasn't happy. My ways
> Have not fulfilled their youthful hope. I gave
> My mind to the symmetric stubbornness
> Of art, and all its webs of pettiness.
> They willed me bravery. I wasn't brave.
> It never leaves my side, since I began:
> This shadow of having been a brooding man.

I have dealt with and elaborated on this subject, and I won't repeat myself. It will suffice to say that Borges' treatment of this intimate side of his life has little to do with romantic confessionalism, or with yielding to the same weakness he earlier condemned in modern literature. If he now breaks the silence about himself and tells us about his unhappiness, he does so without self-pity, without tears or pathos, simply by acknowledging it as a fact, or rather, as a sin. The poem represents the acceptance of that sin as guilt, and throughout the poem he assumes this sin of unhappiness with the same poise and endurance with which epic heroes accept defeat. He breaks the diffidence of his previous poetry without outcries, almost restating his early selflessness, since his misfortune, his having been unhappy, is not a torment one mourns over but a sin one must accept quietly or even expiate, or perhaps sublimate in the silence of a verse. "One destiny," he wrote in **"The Life of Tadeo Isidoro Cruz,"** "is no better than another, but every man must obey the one he carries within him." Such is the spirit of his own acceptance: a heroic stamina that welcomes triumph and adversity with equal courage.

His latest collection of poems to date—*Historia de la noche*—adds yet new paths into the elusive territory of his intimacy. The accomplished writer, the celebrated poet, the man who welcomes love and death with equal resignation and joy, feels now that decorum could also be an expression of vanity, that modesty in the face of death is but another form of pettiness blocking total reconciliation. The circle of life closes in, unhappiness no longer matters, and a mundane virtue matters even less. Borges seeks oblivion, but since oblivion is a privilege denied to his memory, he backtracks through its meanders, paths, and deep chambers:

> A veces me da miedo la memoria.
> En sus cóncavas grutas y palacios
> (Dijo San Agustín) hay tantas cosas.
> El infierno y el cielo están en ellas

> Sometimes I fear memory.
> In its concave grottoes and palaces
> (Said Saint Augustine) there are so many things.
> Hell and Heaven lie there.

There is no way out of memory but death:

> Soy el que sabe que no es más que un eco,
> El que quiere morir enteramente.

> I am he who knows he is but an echo,
> The one who wants to die completely.

Two elements set *Historia de la noche* apart from his previous collections: a restrained celebration of love, and a serene acceptance of everything life brings, for better or for worse, including the imminence of death. Not that the old motifs or "habits" are missing here; they are present but in a different way. They are part of his indefatigable memory, and as such they inevitably reappear: tigers, mirrors, books, dreams, time, ancestors, friends, authors, knieves, cities, and countries. The manner in which these motifs enter into the poem has changed. **"El tigre"** (The Tiger), for example, is an evocation of the animal that fascinates Borges as an obsession of his childhood, for its beauty, and because it brings reverberations of Blake, Hugo, and Share Kahn. Yet the last line reads: "We thought it was bloody and beautiful. Norah, a girl, said: It is made for love." This last line makes the difference, and gives the poem an unexpected twist. The recalled anecdote—a visit to the Palermo Zoo—was an old strand in his memory, but only now has its true momentum been recaptured, only now does the tiger's face of love surface and overshadow all previous faces to mirror the author's own. In no other book of poems has Borges allowed himself to deal with love with such freedom and with a distance which ultimately is the condition of love's magic. **"Un escolio"** (A Scholium) offers a second example of this new theme. Borges returns to the world of Homer, and here too, as in previous poems, he chooses Ulysses' homecoming to Ithaca as one of the four stories that, he believes, comprise everything literature could ever tell. It appears in the brief prose piece **"Los Cuatro Ciclos"** (The Four Cycles) from *The Gold of the Tigers* where Borges comments: "Four are the stories. During the time left to us, we'll keep telling them, transformed." The story first appears in one of his most successful early poems, "**Ars Poetica,**" as a metaphor for art:

> They say that Ulysses, sated with marvels,
> Wept tears of love at the sight of his Ithaca,
> Green and humble. Art is that Ithaca
> Of green eternity, not of marvels.

Four years later, in the collection *El otro, el mismo* (*The Self and the Other,* 1964), Borges turned the episode into a sonnet, "**Odyssey, Book Twenty-Three,**" but the emphasis is now on the unpredictabiltiy of fate. In "**A Scholium,**" on the other hand, the story becomes a love poem. Borges chooses the moment when the queen "saw herself in his eyes when she felt in her love that she was met by Ulysses' love." In each of the four versions of the story, one witnesses a switch of emphasis and preference: in the first, the focus is on the notion that literature is "the history of the diverse intonations of a few metaphors;" in the second, Ulysses' return to Ithaca is seen as a metaphor for art; the third captures the idea that "any life, no matter how long or complex it may be, is made up essentially of a *single moment*—the moment in which a man finds out, once and for all, who he is;" and in the fourth, the accent is on love as an inviolable common secret. But the last version reveals also that the old metaphor has beome Borges' own metaphor, because what the last poem underlines is the nature of love as a secret bond, as an unwritten pact expressing itself through its own code: "Penelope does not dare to recognize him, and to test him he alludes to a secret they alone share: their common thalamus that no mortal can move, because the olive tree from which it was carved ties it down to earth." Borges chooses allusion as the language of love, but allusion also as the literary language he prefers. In the same prose poem, he adds: "Homer did not ignore that things should be said in an indirect manner. Neither did the Greeks, whose natural language was myth." What we have here, therefore, is a double metaphor: Penelope resorts to allusion to communicate with Ulysses; Borges, in turn, alludes to Homer's story to communicate his own perception of love. The thalamus as the metaphor for Penelope's love becomes the metaphor Borges conjures up to convey his own feelings about love. It is worth pausing on this aspect of his art. Not only because this example dramatizes an all too well known device of his writing—the Chinese box structure to which he subjects much of his fiction and poetry—but because this last volume of poems further refines that device to the point of perfection. In the epilogue to *Historia de la noche,* he offers a possible definition of this literary artifice:

> Any event—an observation, a farewell, an encounter, one of those curious arabesques in which chance delights—can stir esthetic emotions. The poet's task is to project that emotion, which was intimate, in a fable or in a cadence. The material at his disposal, language, is as Stevenson remarks, absurdly inadequate.

What can we do with worn out words—with Francis Bacon's *idola Fori*—,and with a few rhetorical artifices found in the manuals? On first sight, nothing or very little. And yet, a page by Stevenson himself or a line by Seneca is sufficient to prove that the undertaking is not always impossible.

Borges, who in his early writings held that "unreality is the necessary condition of art," knows only too well that literature, and art in general, as Paul Klee once said, "is different from external life, and it must be organized differently." What Borges restates in the epilogue is his old belief that "since Homer all valid metaphors have been written down," and the writer's task is not to write new ones but to rewrite the old ones, or rather to translate them into his own language, time, and circumstance, very much in the way the nineteenth-century symbolist writer, Pierre Menard, undertook the rewriting of the *Quijote.* The creative act lies, then, not so much in the invention of new fables as in their transformation into vehicles of new content, in the conversion of an old language into a new one. Borges retells Ulysses' story of his return to Ithaca, but in each of his four versions a new perception has been conveyed.

The same principle can be applied to his other "fables." He keeps repeating them, as he himself has acknowledged, but it is a repetition of the materials, not of their substance. There is no escape from that "absurdly inadequate" tool—language—yet with those same trite words the poet shapes the uniqueness of his emotion. "Gunnar Thorgilsson" offers a third example of this outlook on literature which sees in the new a derivation from the old: Iceland, which appears and reappears in Borges' poetry, is evoked once more, but now the focus is not on the ship or the sword of the sagas, but on the wake and the wound of love. The poem concludes simply: "I want to remember that kiss / You gave me in Iceland." "**El enamorado**" (**The Lover**) and "**La espera**" (**The Waiting**) are also love poems in which Borges tersely reviews some or his literary habits—moons, roses, numbers, seas, time, tigers, swords—but they are now shadows which vanish to uncover the only presence that truly counts:

> Debo fingir que hay otros. Es mentira.
> Sólo Tú eres. Tú, mi desventura
> Y mi ventura, inagotable y pura.

> I should feign that there are others. It's a lie.
> Only you exist, You, my misfortune
> And my fortune, inexhaustible and pure.

If literature is, as Borges once wrote, "essentially a syntactic event," it is clear that his latest volume of poetry should be assessed not for whatever is new at the level of theme (love being the thematic novelty), but by how he succeeds in bestowing on old subjects a new intensity and a rekindled poetic strength. The reader of his last collection can find here the vertex of his new achievement.

Those of us who have been closely following Borges'

poetry of the last ten years have witnessed several changes in his voice. His earliest poems strove to convey a conversationl tone. They were a dialogue with the familiar city, its myths and landscapes, sometimes bearing Whitmanesque overtones. To emphasize that intimate and nostalgic accent, he often used free verse, local words, and Argentine slang. Then when he "went from myths of the outlying slums of the city to games with time and infinity," he opted for more traditional meters and stanzaic forms. This alone conferred a certain stilted inflection on his poetic voice. Rhymes were strong and at times even a bit hammering (Scholem was made to rhyme with Golem). He brought the hendecasyllable and the sonnet to new heights, stimulated undoubtedly by his advanced blindness. In spite of this scluptural perfection, there was still a declamatory falsetto in his voice that was particularly apparent when he read (or rather recited) aloud his own poetry. It goes without saying that this stiffness, however slight, disappeared in his best poems. In 1969, five years after his previous collection *El otro, el mismo,* he published *In Praise of Darkness*. With this volume Borges freed his verse from any linguistic slag. The sonnet, the most frequent form he has been using since, bordered on perfection: these sonnet are masterfully craved, with chiseled smoothness and a quite flow that turns them into verbal music.

Poetry as music has always been to Borges a crystallizing point at which language succeeds in bringing forth its melodic core. This is not a music produced by sound; the poem turns words into a transparent surface which reveals a certain cadence, a harmony buried under the opacities of language, much in the same manner as music rescues a privileged order of sound and silience from a chaotic mass of sounds. In the prologue to the collection *El otro, el mismo,* he has explained this understanding of poetry:

> On occasion, I have been tempted into trying to adapt to Spanish the music of English or of German; had I been able to carry out that perhaps impossible adventure, I would be a great poet, like Garcilaso, who gave us the music of Italy, or like the anonymous Sevillian poet who gave us the music of Rome, or like Darío, who gave us that of Verlaine and Hugo. I never went beyond rough drafts, woven of words of few syllables, which very wisely I destroyed.

My contention is that Borges, whose "destiny"—as he put it—"is in the Spanish language," has found in his most recent poetry not the music of English or German or of any other poet, but his own voice, and through it a music the Spanish language did not know before him. Not that Spanish did not produce great poets. It certainly did, and each of them represents an effort to strike a different chord of that musical instrument language becomes at the best moments of its poetry. One has only to think of Jorge Guillén as a definite virtuoso of that instrument, as a poet whose voice has given to Spanish some of the most luminous and joyous movements of its hidden music. Like Borges, Jorge Guillén has sought through his work to touch that musical kernel contained in language very much the way brandy is contained in the residual marc. For Borges, as for Guillén, poetry is a form of linguistic distillation.

In *Historia de la noche,* there is hardly a subject or motif that has not been dealt with in his previous collections, love being the exception. "**Ni siquiera soy polvo**" (**I Am Not Even Dust**), which deals with the trinity Cervantes-Alonso-Don-Quijote as a dream-within-a-dream-within-a-dream, is a variation on a theme previously treated in "**Parable of Cervantes and Don Quijote**" (*Dreamtigers*) and in "**Alonso Quijano Dreams**" (*The Unending Rose*). "**The Mirror**" returns to his old obsession with mirrors first recorded in the short piece "**The Draped Mirrors**" (*Dreamtigers*), and then meticulously explored in the thirteen quatrains of "**The Mirrors**" (*El otro, el mismo*). The same could be said of "**Lions**" vis à vis "**The Other Tiger**," "**Dreamtigers**," and "**The Gold of the Tigers**," Or "**Iceland**" as a new avatar of "**To Iceland**" (*The Gold of the Tigers*). Or "**Milonga del forastero,**" which is a sort of Platonic summation of all his other *milongas*. But precisely because Borges returns to his old subjects (he once stated: "A poet does not write about what he wants but about what he can"), the subject matters less than the voice. Furthermore: the voice is the subject.

In this last collection Borges further refines a device first developed in "**Another Poem of Gifts**": the poem as a long list, listing as a poetic exercise. "**Metaphors of the Arabian Nights**," "**Lions**," "**Things That Might Have Been**," "**The Lover**," "**The Causes**" follow this pattern. The device accentuates the magic character of poetry as a voice speaking in the dark, words reaching out for meanings that are beyond words. What is left is a music that speaks from its innumerable variations, but the variations are not repetitions. They are, as in the art of the fugue, new versions of the same tune, and in each variation the theme is further explored, condensed, and simplified, until it becomes so transparent that one sees the bottom, the poet's deepest voice, a face free of masks, a certain essence that more than saying, sings. It is as if Borges had put behind him his old habits as themes to focus on the tones and inflections of his own voice; and what that voice expresses is a serenity, a calm not heard in the Spanish language since Juan de la Cruz or Luis de León. Borges must have felt that he was nearing that shore of harmony glimpsed by the mystical poets. In the last poem of the collection, "**A History of the Night**," he wrote referring to the night: "Luis de León saw it in the country/of his staggered soul." Yet the soul that surfaces from Borges' last poems is not one pierced by divine emotion, but a fulfilled and resigned soul that can see life as a river of "invulnerable water," an earthly soul anchored in life and yet unfearful of death, one that can look upon life from a timeless island against whose shores time breaks and recedes like sea waves:

"Adán es tu ceniza"
La espada morirá como el racimo.
El cristal no es más frágil que la roca.
Las cosas son su porvenir de polvo.
El hierro es el orín. La voz, el eco.
Adán, el joven padre, es tu ceniza.
EL último jardín será el primero.
El ruiseñor y Píndaro son voces.
La aurora es el reflejo del ocaso.
El micenio, la máscara del oro.
El alto muro, la ultrajada ruína.
Urquiza, lo que dejan los puñales.
El rostro que se mira en el espejo
No es el de ayer. La noche lo ha gastado.
El delicado tiempo nos modela.

Qué dicha ser el agua invulnerable
Que corre en la parábola de Heraclito
O el intrincado fuego, pero ahora,
En este largo día que no pasa,
Me siento duradero y desvalido.

"Adam is Your Ash"
The sword will die like the vine.
Crystal is no weaker than rock.
Things are their own future in dust.
Iron is rust, the voice an echo.
Adam, the young father, is your ash.
The last garden will be the first.
The nightingale and Pindar are voices.
Dawn is the reflection of sunset.
The Mycenaean is the gold mask.
The high wall, the plundered ruin.
Urquiza, what daggers leave behind.
The face looking at itself in the mirror
Is not yesterday's. Night has wasted it.
Delicate time is shaping us.

What joy to be the invulnerable water
Flowing in Heraclitus's parable
Or intricate fire, but now, midway
Through this long day that does not end,
I feel enduring and helpless.

(Trans. Willis Barnstone)

A restatement of his famous line "Time is the substance I am made of. It is a river that carries me away, but I am the river." Now, however, the same idea flows without the lapidary sententiousness of the essay; simply, with ease and resolution, unconcerned with rejections or acceptances, free of outcomes or outcries, a meditative voice reconciled with life, accepting its gifts and losses with the same acquiescent gesture.

In the poem **"The Causes,"** Borges goes through an inventory of mementoes from history, literature, and life. The list encompasses some of the most memorable moments of his own poetry and becomes a sort of miniature of his poetic *oeuvre*. The poem closes with two equally compressed lines: "All those things were needed/so that

our hands could meet," a masterful coda that renders his tight survey of motifs into a love poem. This is the surface however impeccable, of the text, its outer meaning. But what the text also says, between the lines, is that its laconic eloquence, terse to the point of diaphaneity, is sustained by sixty long years of poetic creation, the understated notion being: all those poems were needed so that this one could be written. The idea appears at the end of one of his most relaxed and subtly personal short stories, **"Averroes' Search"** (1974): "I felt, on the last page, that my narration was a symbol of the man I was as I wrote it and that, in order to compose that narration, I had to be that man and, in order to be that man, I had to compose that narration, and so on to infinity." Literature, as well as life, as an inexorable concatenation of causes and effects; each poem as a stepping stone toward the poem; the poem as a symbol of the poet: in order to write this poem I had to write all the others; in order to write this poem I had to be the man I was. But this last poem does not form a circle with the others, it is rather the answer to the others, a sort of prism that reintegrates the dispersed shades of his poetry into one text, and this text gleams like a single beam of white light with a radiant simplicity that none of the individual texts had. With *Historia de la noche* Borges' poetry has found an equilibrium that undoubtedly conveys his own inner serenity; but this serenity, being a linguistic externalization, is also a song through which the Spanish language voices a music unheard before: an austere, poised, dignified, and quiet music:

Soy el que no conoce otro consuelo
Que recordar el tiempo de la dicha.
Soy a veces la dicha inmerecida.
Soy el que sabe que no es más que un eco,
El que quiere morir enteramente.

I am one who knows no other consolation
Than remembering the time of joy,
I am at times unmerited joy,
I am one who knows he is only an echo,
One who wants to die totally.

(Trans. Willis Barnstone)

The young poet who once delighted in the exhilaration of his own performance has been left far behind. The voice we hear now is that of a consummate musician who has achieved total mastery over his medium. The music we hear now is that of the Spanish language attuned to its own registers, and that of a poet skillfully true to his own perceptions. (pp. 60–5)

Jaime Alazraki, "Borges Revisited : Language as a Musical Organism," in *Review*, No. 28, 1981, pp. 60–5.

Borges on the *Odyssey*:

I am very fond of going back to my boyhood. I seem to be doing that all the time. Now I will go back to a certain book I read in Buenos Aires. I must have been eleven or twelve years old at the time. That book happened to be the *Odyssey* done into English by Butcher and Lang. Although young, I read the book and I found to my pleasure and to my amazement that I fully enjoyed the reading. I had attempted it before in Pope's fine verse translation. Of course Pope was beyond me, beyond my years. Afterwards I went back to Pope and I found in him a very fine version also. I remember the many things that happened to me; for example, leaving the War of Troy, traveling through the Mediterranean with my friends, since I became Ulysses—the sort of man who, reading the *Odyssey*, becomes *Ulysses.* And then I came on a certain passage and I think that it ran somehow thus: "The gods send joys and sorrows to man in order that coming generations should have something to sing about." What I would like to insist on now is the fact that I found those words fine, but I did not find them surprising. I thought that is the way things went: things happen to us in order that coming generations of men should have some matter for their songs.

Jorge Luis Borges, in his "Simply a Man of Letters," printed in *Simply a Man of Letters: Panel Discussions and Papers from the Proceedings of a Symposium on Jorge Luis Borges Held at the University of Maine at Orono,* University of Maine at Orono Press, 1982.

SEYMOUR MENTON

(essay date 1982)

[In the following essay, Menton analyzes Borges's short stories as examples of magic realism.]

In the epilogue to the 1949 edition of *El Aleph,* Jorge Luis Borges states that with the exception of **"Emma Zunz"** and **"Historia del guerrero y de la cautiva,"** "las piezas de este libro corresponden al género fantástico." This statement by Borges confirms the axiom that an author's words about his own works may not always be taken at face value. Although some of the stories in the volume do fall into the category of the fantastic, it would be difficult to justify that label for **"Biografía de Tadeo Isidoro Cruz (1829–1874),"** **"La Otra muerte,"** or **"Deutsches Requiem."** However, in order to dispute Borges, statement, the term "género fantástico" must first be defined. Although Tzevetan Todorov's categories of the marvelous, the uncanny, and the fantastic [in his

Introduction á la littérature fantastique, 1970], are often cited it is my contention that by contrasting the fantastic with Magic Realism, both terms will become more clearly delineated, and this in turn will help us arrive at a clearer understanding and appreciation of Borges' short stories.

It should first of all be pointed out that the two terms are essentially dissimilar. Whereas "lo fantástico" is a genre, a type of literature that may be found in any chronological period, Magic Realism is an artistic movement or tendency that began in 1918 as a direct reflection of a series of historical and artistic factors and continued in varying degress of intensity until approximately 1970. Accrording to the Magic Realism *Weltanschauung,* the world and reality have a dream-like quality about them which is captured by the presentation of improbable juxtapositons in a style that is highly objective, precise, and deceptively simple. The Magic Realist painting or short story or novel is predominantly realistic and deals with the objects of our daily life, but contains an unexpected or improbable element that creates a strange effect leaving the viewer or reader somewhat bewildered or amazed.

By contrast, the literature of the fantastic seems to conform rather well to the dictionary definitions of fantasy: "an imaginative or fanciful work, especially one dealing with supernatural or unnatural events or characters;" or "fantasy fiction: imaginative fiction dependent for effect on strangeness of setting (as other worlds or times) and of characters (as supernatural or unnatural beings)." Magic Realism, involved as it is with the improbable rather than the impossible, never deals with the supernatural. Furthermore, some of the dictionary definitions of "fantastic" not only sharpen the contrast between the fantastic and Magic Realism but also associate the former with Expressionism, the artistic and literary movement against which Magic Realism rebelled; and Surrealism, which upstaged Magic Realism in the late 1920's and 1930's: "conceived or appearing as if conceived by an unrestrained imagination; grotesque; eccentric; odd. . . imaginary or groundless; not real or based on reality. . . extravagantly fanciful; irrational."

These plebeian dictionary definitions may well be more useful than all the aforenoted theoretical articles and books in sharpening our perception of Magic Realism. The two basic dictionary definitions of magic also reflect clearly the dichotomy between what Carpentier has called "lo real maravilloso" and Magic Realism. According to Carpentier (and Miguel Ángel Asturias), the Indian and African cultures have made Latin American a continent or world of magic in the dictionary sense of "the art of producing a desired effect or result through the use of various techniques as incantation, that presumably assure human control of super-natural agencies or the forces of nature." On the other hand, Magic Realists, like modern-day magicians, bewilder the spectators by making reality appear to be magic: "the art of causing illusions as entertainment by the use of sleight of hand, deceptive devices, etc." According to the dictionary, as is usually the case with Magic Realism, magic is "mysteriously enchanting" and "may have glamorous and attractive connotations."

Since Jorge Luis Borges is an Argentinean, and a very English-oriented one at that, it would be absurd to attribute his predilection for magic to an Indian or African cultural heritage. Borges' individual genius cannot be accounted for by generational circumstances, but it was in the early 1920's that he made his literary debut, the same early 1920's in which Magic Realism painting flourished in Germany and elsewhere, and the same 1920's in which the writings of Carl Jung became more influential. Whereas Surrealism is strongly based on each individual's Freudian sub-conscious dream-world, Magic realism adheres to the Jungian collective unconscious, to the idea that all mankind is compressed into one, that all time periods are compressed into the one moment of the present, and that reality itself is dream-like. From his own texts, it's obvious that Borges shares Jung's view of the world and rejects Freud's. Moreover, the following interview with Richard Burgin could not be more explicit:

BURGIN: I take it you don't think much of Freud, either.

BORGES: No, I always disliked him. But I've always been a great reader of Jung. I read Jung in the same way as, let's say, I might read Pliny or Frazer's *Golden Bough;* I read it as a king of mythology, or as a kind of mythology, or as a kind of museum or encyclopedia of curious lores.

BURGIN: When you say you dislike Freud, what do you mean?

BORGES: I think of him as a kind of madman, no? A man laboring over a sexual obsession. Well, perhaps he didn't take it to heart. Perhaps he was just doing it as a kind of game. I tried to read him, and I thought of him either as a charlatan or as a madman in a sense. After all the world is far too complex to be boiled down to that all-too-simple scheme. But in Jung, well, of course, Jung I have read far more widely than Freud, but in Jung you feel a wide and hospitable mind. In the case of Freud, it all boils down to a few rather unpleasant facts. But, of course, that's merely my ignorance or my bias.

Although Magic Realism is evident in Borges' first stories of *Historia universal de la infamia* written in the early 1930's, it was not until the 1940's that he wrote his most famous stories and it was not until the 1950's that his fame attained international proportions, coinciding with the Latin American rejection of *criollismo* and Social Realism and the reemergence of Magic Realism. It was also during this period that Borges wrote most of the essays published in *Otras inquisiciones* (1952), where both the world view and some of the specific stylistic traits of Magic Realism may be found. In **"Magias parciales del Quijote,"** Borges, while commenting on the particular

brand of realism in the *Quijote*, refers to Joseph Conrad's world view, which coincides with that of Borges and that of the Magic Realist painters and authors in general: "Joseph Conrad pudo escribir que excluía de su obra lo sobrenatural, porque admitirlo parecía negar que lo cotidiano fuera maravilloso." A similar attitude of amazement and optimism is ascribed by Borges to one of his most favorite authors: "Chesterton pensó como Whitman, que el mero hecho de ser es tan prodigioso que ninguna desventura debe eximirnos de una suerte de cómica gratitud." In praising Quevedo as the "primer artífice de las letras hispánicas," greater than Cervantes, Borges stresses the same extreme objectivity and ultraprecision employed by the Magic Realists to invest reality with a touch of magic. Borges attributes Quevedo's relative lack of international fame to the fact that "sus duras páginas no fomentan, ni siquiera toleran, el menor desahogo sentimental." Borges discusses various styles that Quevedo used in his different works but he singles out for special treatment that of the treatise *Marcus Brutus,* almost all of whose characteristics are typical of Borges' own Magic Realist style: "el ostentoso laconismo, el hipérbaton, el casi algebraico rigor, la oposición de términos, la aridez, la repetición de palabras, dan a ese texto una precisión ilusoria."

One of the most incontrovertible indications of Borges' identification with magic Realism is his constant use of oxymoron from his first stories of 1933 up through what is generally considered his best story **"El Sur"** (1952) and beyond. Regarding *Historia universal de la infamia,* the very title of the volume produces a bemused reaction on the part of the reader. A universal history of infamy is a rather unusual and improbable undertaking. Even more improbable is that the protagonists of the seven stories, with the exception of Billy the Kid, are not well-known historical figures. Oxymoron, strictly speaking, is a juxtaposition of apparently self-contradictory words such as "cruel kindness." Varying degrees of oxymoron are present in most of the titles of the volume's seven principal stories: **"El espantoso redentor Lazarus Morell," "El impostor inverosímil Tom Castro," "La viuda Ching, Pirata," "Ei asesino desinteresado Bill Harrigan," "Ei incivil maestro de ceremonias Kotsuké no Suké."** Although the title of the book announces the author's intent to be all-encompassing, the juxtaposition in the same volume of a nineteenth-century southern U.S. slave dealer and twentieth-century New York gangsters with an eighth-century Arab dyer, an early eighteenth-century Chinese widow pirate, and an eighteenth-century Japanese Samurai, is rather amazing.

One of the most successful stories of the volume is **"El imposter inverosímil Tom Castro,"** whose title reflects the oxymoron-like nature of the whole story. Whereas an impostor usually does his best to assume the physical appearance and general traits of the individual he is impersonating, Tom Castro is the "implausible impostor" because he does nothing of the kind. Incredible it may be, but there is nothing fantastic about the success of his impersonation. Lady Tichborne wanted to believe in the reappearance of her long-missing son; she was rather old; and "los ojos fatigados de Lady Tichborne estaban velados de llanto." Furthermore, in an oxymoron-like paradox, "la luz hizo de máscara." Light usually clarifies things, unmasks them, however in this case, the sudden opening of the window blinds caused Lady Tichborne to be blinded by the strong sunlight.

The Magic Realist world view is borne out by the characters and events of the story: reality is stranger than fiction; things occur unexpectedly; absolute truth or reality is impossible for mortal man to grasp, but there is nothing in the story that would warrant its being included in the realm of fantastic literature. The transformation of Arthur Orton into Tom Castro and then into Roger Charles Tichborne is highly improbable but not impossible or fantastic. The relationship between Tom Castro and his Negro servant Ebenezer Bogle is likewise improbable. Bogle had a terrible fear of crossing the street but after Tom Castro offered the Negro his arm one day in Sydney, Australia, "un protectorado se estableció: el del negro inseguro y monumental sobre el obeso tarambana de Wapping." Since the story is set in the nineteenth century when Great Britain was taking on itself the burden of "civilizing" a large part of the African continent, Bogle's protectorate over Tom Castro is obviously intended to amaze and amuse the reader. It is Bogle's "ocurrencia genial" which, according to the narrator, "determinados manuales de etnografía han negado a su raza," that is responsible for the unexpected turn of events in Tom Castro's life. In fact, Bogle has two sudden inspirations: the plan to have Tom Castro impersonate Roge Tichborne and the plan to marshal public opinion in England on the impersonator's side by publishing an apocryphal attack on him signed by a Jesuit. Paralleling the two inspirations, Tom's fortunes are adversely affected by two sudden deaths. Lady Tichborne dies only three years after accepting Tom as her son and thereupon her relatives bring suit against him for false impersonation. Tom would probably have been exonerated with the aid of still another Bogle inspiration but the latter, as had been anticipated, is unexpectedly killed while crossing the street. Tom is sentenced to fourteen years in prison, is released after only ten, and spends the rest of his life alternately pleading his innocence or his guilt "al servicio de las inclinaciones del público."

What makes the improbabilities of this story even more improbable is that its source is the 1911 edition of *The Encyclopedia Britannica*. Its authenticity is further substantiated by the narrator's giving the exact dates (day, month, and year) of Tom's birth, of his appearance before Lady Tichborne, of his sentencing and of his death. This chronological precision, the initial statement of what fate had in store for Bogle, as well as the implausible situations and unexpected events were to become trademarks

of several of Borges' more authentic short stories (the less essayistic ones) and of Magic Realism in general.

Although Borges' stories have usually been labeled fantastic, a more accurate approach would be to designate some of the more authentic ones as Magic Realist and some of the more essayistic ones as fantastic. Borges himself, in his 1941 prologue to *El jardín de senderos que se bifurcan,* calls the title story a detective story and "las otras [piezas] son fantásticas." While "El jardín de senderos que se bifurcan," like "El impostor inverosímil Tom Castro," is very clearly based on the typical constellation of Magic Realist traits, **"Tlön, Uqbar, Orbis Tertius," "El acercamiento a Almotásim," "Pierre Menard, autor del *Quijote*,"** and **"Examen de la obra de Herbert Quain"** are essayistic commentaries on imaginary, nonexistent countries, authors, or books and therefore more deserving of the fantastic lable. **"Las ruinas circulares,"** in which the protagonist succeeds in creating another man by dreaming him only to realize that he too may be a dream creature, is obviously fantastic.

Whereas only one of the eight pieces of *El jardín de senderos que se bifurcan* may be labeled Magic Realist, in *Artificios* (1944), the second part of *Ficciones,* six of the nine stories are Magic Realist. It is no accident that Borges himself recognized the superiority of the more authentic short stories of *Artificios.* He calls them "de ejecución menos torpe." Two of the stories are clearly essayistic, **"Tres versiones de Judas"** and **"La secta del Fénix,"** while **"Funes el memorioso,"** in addition to being somewhat essayistic, is too subjective to qualify for the Magic Realist label.

Although **"El jardín de senderos que se bifurcan"** has a relatively long labyrinthine philosophical discussion between Dr. Yu Tsun and Stephen Albert, the story may be better understood in terms of the world view and stylistic traits of Magic Realism. The ultraprecision and objectivity of the first paragraph not only represents a refreshing departure from the more typically Hispanic florid style but also parallels the sharp-focus, Magic Realist painting of the American Charles Sheeler (1883–1965), or the German Christian Schad (1894). Sheeler was praised by his friend, doctor-poet William Carlos Williams, for "the bewildering directness of his vision" while Schad is considered by Wieland Schmied "the coldest, sharpest, most precise" of all the Magic Realists. The Magic Realist concept of history's being stranger than fiction is borne out by the improbable fact that Stephen Albert, a name picked out of the telephone directory in order to identify the site of the new British artillery park in France, should turn out to be a sinologist. Equally improbable is that the German spy should be a former Chinese teacher of English at a German high school in Tsingtao. The air of Magic Realism that pervades the story is strengthened by other oxymoron-like phrases: "un joven que leía con fervor los *Anales* de Tácito" and "un soldado herido y feliz"—possible but not probable.

In keeping with Magic Realism's rejection of the subjectivity and emotionalism of Expressionism, Borges' characters are capable of acting without the slightest trace of emotion and Borges never arouses the reader's sympathy for his characters. In **"El jardín de senderos que se bifurcan,"** Yu Tsun kills Albert with painstaking precision reflected in the utmost simplicity of the following two sentences : "Yo había preparado el revólver. Disparé con sumo cuidado: Albert se desplomó sin una queja, inmediatamente." The reader feels absolutely no anger at the murder of this innocent man nor does he feel any compassion for Yu Tsun who feels no fear of his impending death: "ahora que mi garganta anhela la cuerda." Even in the heinous execution of Jaromir Hladík by the Nazis in **"El milagro secreto,"** Borges purposely prevents the reader from feeling any emotion—he is too involved in the intellectual process of finding his way out of the labyrinth. Also consistent with Magic Realism are Borges' Jungian ideas of the simultaneity of past, present, and future; of the relative insignificance of the individual human being; and of man's identity not only with his ancestors but with every man. Jung's and Borges' cyclical view of history is reinforced stylistically in **"El jardín de senderos que se bifurcan,"** by "la luna baja y circular," "el disco del gramófono," "un alto reloj circular," and "el vívido círculo de la lámpara."

Whereas **"El jardín de senderos que se bifurcan,"** as the title indicates, involves the reader in a labyrinthine experience, **"El fin"** reflects the relative simplicity of its title. Nonetheless, it too illustrates Borges' affiliation with magic Realism. The poetic tone which pervades the story is highly unusual for Borges and may be explained by his projecting himself into the world of *Martín Fierro.* However, José Hernández' long narrative poem does not have the same poetic and nostalgic tone as Borges' story. In **"El fin"** Borges creates the same poetic, tranquil, dream-like atmosphere that is found in the Munich Magic Realist painter Georg Schrimpf (1889–1938): "He also possessed a background in genuine naïveté rooted in a strongly-stamped feeling for the magical efficiency of the dreamy world of objects." Just as Schrimpf's women gaze impassively out at the world through a window, Recabarren observes the tragic knife duel between Martín Fierro and the Negro through a window as he lies on his cot. The effect of the action's being presented through an intermediary is to make it less vivid, less emotional, more static and more plastic—as in *Parson Weems' Fable* (1929) by Grant Wood (1892–1942), and in keeping with Brecht's theory of keeping an emotional distance between the action of the play and the audience.

The tone of the story is set in the first few lines which describe the paralyzed Recabarren's awaking from his noon-day nap: "recobró poco a poco la realidad, las cosas cotidianas que ya no cambiaría nunca por otras."

This view of reality after awaking from a sleep is tinged with the same magic captured by Joan Miró (1893) in his early Magic Realist phase. Although Borges compares reality to a dream, what Recabarren sees is not a dream; it is reality enveloped in a magic aura: "la llanura bajo el último sol, era casi abstracta, como vista en un sueño." The dream-like quality of the scene is maintained by the unemotional low-key, somewhat stoic and somewhat poetic dialogue between the two combattants. It's almost as if the two men realize that they are acting out their predetermined roles in a drama written by an unknown author. The belated identification of the stranger as Martín Fierro provides the unexpected ingredient typical of Magic Realism.

The same belated identification is also evident in the final sentence of **"Biografía de Tadeo Isidoro Cruz (1829–1874),"** which informs the reader that the protagonist was not a historical figure but Martín Fierro's companion. The fact that Borges in a matter-of-fact manner converts the literary figures of *Martín Fierro* into the reality of his stories is also typical of Magic Realism and may be likened to García Márquez' use of Victor Hugues, Artemio Cruz and Recamadour in *Cien años de soledad.*

Written in the same year of 1952 as **"El fin"** **"El Sur"** has a similar dream-like tone but is more complex, more transcendent, and is considered by Borges to be "acaso mi mejor cuento." What makes **"El Sur"** perhaps Borges' best story is its excellent application of Magic Realism to the portrayal of Argentina's national psyche. One of the reasons why **"El Sur"** is so appealing to the modern reader is that it is one of the very few of Borges' stories that allow for more than one interpretation. No matter how labyrinthine most of his stories may be, once they are solved, it becomes clear that there is only one solution. This is not the case in **"El Sur."** Borges himself suggests "que es posible leerlo como directa narración de hechos novelescos, y también de otro modo." Borges was even more explicit in an interview with James E. Irby:

> "Todo cuanto sucede después que Dahlmann sale del sanatorio puede interpretarse como una alucinación que él habría tenido en el momento de morir de septicemia, como una visión fantástica de la manera en que hubiera querido morir. Es por ello que existen correspondencias tenues entre las dos mitades del cuento.

Although the second half of the story may be interpreted as an hallucination as Allen W. Phillips has very carefully demonstrated, **"El Sur"** is a better story when read "como directa narración de hechos novelescos."

The key to an understanding of the literal interpretation lies in Borges' much greater affiliation with Magic Realism than with either Surrealism or the fantastic. As has already been shown in the comments on **"El impostor inverosímil Tom Castro"** and **"El fin,"** Borges has a Magic Realist world view. Truth is stranger than fiction and the most unexpected and amazing events may

take place. As the character Unwin in **"Abencaján el Bo-
jarí, muerto en su laberinto"** says, "no precisa erigir un
laberinto, cuando el universo ya lo es." The juxtaposition of self-contradictory words or pharases, oxymoron,
is not only Borges' favorite stylistic device, it is one of
the basic structures of many of his stories. Although critics have generally divided **"El Sur"** into two parts, before and after Juan Dahlmann's release from the hospital (literally or through hallucination), it is more significant to note the juxtaposition throughout the story of an
overly precise, objective, expository style and the transformation, without distortions, of reality into a dream
world. The story begins, as several of Borges' stories do,
with a kind of encyclopedia-style objective description of
Juan Dahlmann's family background: "El hombre que de-
sembarcó en Buenos Aires en 1871 se llamaba Johannes
Dahlmann y era pastor de la iglesia evangélica." This staccato factual style, however, is subverted by Borges' typical
use of the self-questioning "tel vez," within or without
parentheses: "Juan Dahlmann (tal vez a impulso de la sangre germánica) eligiól de ese antepasado." "Las tareas y
acaso la indolencia lo retenían en la ciudad." The parallelism established between "tareas" and "indolencia" is
still another example of a type of oxymoron. By the same
token, the initial description ends with a contrast between
the precision of the date and the absence of adjectives
on the one hand, and the vagueness of "algo": "En los
últimos días de febrero de 1939, algo le aconteció."

In the next two sentences the tone of the narrator
changes completely. He philosophizes about destiny and
tells us that Dahlmann "había conseguido, esa tarde, un
ejemplar descabalado de las *Mil y una noches* de Weil."
Although the rest of the action is developed in a dream-
like tone, certain phrases, clauses or sentences stand out
because of their brusque, every-day unrhetorical style:
"cuando el cirujano le dijo que había estado a punto de
morir de una septicemia;" "recordó bruscamente que en
un café de la Calle Brasil"; "de esa conjetura fantástica lo
distrajo el inspector."

Most of the story's Magic Realism is based on its
tone, created by the emphasis on the protagonist's remembering ("recordar") or vaguely recognizing ("creyó
reconocer"). It is symbolized by the emotionless, inscrutable, and improbably enormous cat living in the
present: "como una divinidad desdeñosa," "el mágico
animal." The same inscrutable and enormous cat also
appears as a symbol of the narrator in **"Deutsches Requiem"**: "símbolo de mi vano destino, dormía en el
reborde de la ventana un gato enorme y fofo." Although
the cat has not hitherto been recognized as symbolic
of Magic Realism in general, it appears significantly in
perhaps the very first examples of Magic Realist painting: Niklaus Stöcklin's 1917 *Rhein Lane* and in Georg
Schrimpf's *Still-Life*, which was included in Franz Roh's
1925 seminal book on Magic Realism.

The element of chance is also a basic characteristic

of the Magic Realist's view of the world. The protagonist
is injured because he had purchased *The Thousand and
One Nights* and he was so eager to read the book that he
didn't wait for the elevator. Instead he rushed up the stairs
and accidentally scratched his face on a splinter. That the
scratch should become infected and cause a serious fever is
still more implausible. The other "algo" that happened to
Juan Dahlmann is equally implausible. When the young
rowdies challenge Dahlmann to a knife fight, it is only
the unexpected coming to life of the old gaucho and his
tossing his naked dagger to Dahlmann that insures the
latter's probable death.

How did Dahlmann actually die? Was the fight
with the rowdies only an hallucination which permitted Dahlmann to die the hero's death that he would
have preferred? As I stated above, the Magic Realism
interpretation is more effective. Dahlmann, after almost
dying from septicemia, is released from the hospital one
morning. His rediscovery of the city at 7 A.M. parallels
statements by the early de Chirico regarding the way
he felt and painted reality: "I had just come out of a
long and painful illness, and I was in a nearly morbid
state of sensitivity . . . then I had the strange impression
that I was looking at all these things for the first time."
Dahlmann states categorically that the morning and his
being alive were greater marvels than the adventures of
The Thousand and One Nights. In **"El Zahir,"** the narrator tells us that "Según la doctrina idealista, los verbos
vivir y *soñar* son riguro samente sinónimos." Borges is
also quite fond of the phrase "como en un sueño" and
his story **"La espera"** begins with an apparently precise,
objective, unrhetorical sentence in which the house number is obviously intended to recall *The Thousand and One
Nights*: "el coche lo dejó en el cuatro mil cuatro de esa
calle del Noroeste." As the train carried Dahlmann south-
ward, he felt as though he were two men, the man riding
on the train and the man who had suffered so much in
the hospital. With his hospital experience so fresh in his
mind, it's only natural that Dahlmann compares people,
objects and events of the immediate present to those of
the immediate past.

Although, as Allen Phillips has pointed out, there
are many indication that Dahlmann's trip south is an hallucination, it is difficult to determine exactly where in the
story the hallucination or dream, begins. According to
Phillips, the hallucination starts precisely after the sentence, "Increíblemente," el día prometido llegó ." However, the word "Increíblemente," actually defines Borges'
view of reality: the most implausible, incredible, and unexpected things may happen. Furthermore, a Magic Realist interpretation would indicate that the narrator makes
reality seem dream-like not only at the moment when
Dahlmann leaves the hospital but also at the moment he
falls asleep after being injured—"Dahlmann logró dormir,
pero a la madrugada estaba despierto y desde aquella hora
el sabor de todas las cosas fue atroz" and at the moment

the anesthesiologist in the hospital sticks a needle into his arm—"se despertó con náuseas, vendado, en una celda que tenía algo de pozo."

Besides reflecting Borges' Magic Realist view of life and reality with a carefully structured set of parallelisms and symmetries, **"El Sur"** is unique among Borges' stories because it is a commentary on the basic oxymoron-like antithesis of civilization-barbarism that has prevented Argentineans from developing a true national consciousness. Juan Dahlmann is killed because he can not resist the call of his gaucho or barbarous past. Juan Dalhmann, a clerk in a municipal library of Buenos Aires, is undoubtedly killed by a drunken rowdy after picking up the dagger tossed at his feet by the ancient archetypal gaucho. If Argentina is to progress—**"El Sur"** tells us—the civilized elements of Buenos Aires must predominate over the barbarous rural tradition reincarnated in the military juntas led by Perón, or more recently by Onganía and Videla. If Argentine is to progress, Juan Dahlmann or Juan Argentino must accept the fusion of his oxymoron-like lineage and not choose the more "macho " one . . . only at the moment of his death. In this respect, Rómulo Gallegos' hero Santos Luzardo is able to triumph over the barbarous forces of the Venezuelan *llanos* because he is closer to his rural ancestry than Juan Dahlmann and still knows how to rope a steer and fire a gun. If Juan Dahlmann had visited his ranch more frequently, he would have been more adept at handling the knife and might have been able to defend himself against his barbaric compatriot. **"El Sur,"** with Juan Dahlmann as its protagonist, is obviously intended to be a metaphor of Argentine history. However Dahlmann's death is interpreted, it does represent the triumph of barbarism over civilization, the triumph of brute force over innocent ivory-tower intellectualism, the triumph of the Perón dictatorship over the Argentine intellectuals, paralleling the Rosas dictatorship's persecution of the Unitarian intellectuals in the 1830's.

The interpretation of **"El Sur"** and other stories by Borges in the light of Magic Realism will hopefully help convince scholars that Borges' stories do not all fit into the category of "lo fantástico." It should also clarify the distinction between Magic Realism, "lo fantástico," and "lo real maravilloso." Whether Borges consciously identified with the Magic Realist tendency in painting or not, some of his better stories share the same world view and stylistic traits indicated by Franz Roh and may therefore be better appreciated in this context. (pp. 411–26)

Seymour Menton, "Jorge Luis Borges, Magic Realist," in *Hispanic Review*, Vol. 50, No. 4, Autumn, 1982, pp. 411–26.

SOURCES FOR FURTHER STUDY

Agheana, Ion T. *The Prose of Jorge Luis Borges.* New York: Peter Lang Publishing, 1984, 320 p.

    Examination of existentialist elements in Borges's prose fiction.

Alazraki, Jaime. *Jorge Luis Borges.* New York: Columbia University Press, 1971, 48 p.

    Concise essay treating Borges's fictional world view and literary themes.

Bell-Villada, Gene H. *Borges and His Fiction: A Guide to His Mind and Art.* Chapel Hill: The University of North Carolina Press, 1981, 292 p.

    Chronological examination of Borges's works.

Cheselka, Paul. *The Poetry and Poetics of Jorge Luis Borges.* New York: Peter Lang Publishing, 1987, 197 p.

    Study of Borges's poetry from his first ultraist poems published in Spain to the publication of *Obra Poética 1923–1964.*

Christ, Ronald J. *The Narrow Act: Borges's Art of Allusion.* New York: New York University Press, 1969, 244 p.

    Analysis of the "esthetic origin, development, and masterful practice" of Borges's use of allusion.

McMurray, George R. *Jorge Luis Borges.* New York: Frederick Ungar Publishing, 1980, 255 p.

    Thematic study of Borges's prose fiction.

Monegal, Emir Rodriguez. *Jorge Luis Borges : A Literary Biography.* New York: E. P. Dutton, 1978, 502 p.

    Detailed study of Borges's life and career.

Stabb, Martin S. *Jorge Luis Borges.* Boston: Twayne Publishers 1970, 179 p.

    General survey of Borges's life, career, and critical reception.

Sturrock, John. *Paper Tigers: The Ideal Fictions of Jorge Luis Borges.* Oxford: Oxford University Press, 1977, 227 p.

    Examination of Borges's theory of fiction, maintaining that the Argentine author's stories are "formal to a degree that no writer of fiction, surely, has ever surpassed."

Additional coverage of Borges's life and career is contained in the following sources published by Gale Research : *Contemporary Authors*, Vols. 21–22; *Contemporary Authors New Revision Series*, Vol. 19; *Contemporary Literary Criticism*, Vols. 1, 2, 3, 4, 6, 8, 9, 10, 13, 19, 44, 48; *Dictionary of Literary Biography Yearbook*: 1986; *Hispanic Writers*; *Major 20th-Century Writers*; *Short Story Criticism*, Vol. 4; and *World Literature Criticism*.

Luis Buñuel

1900–1983

Spanish screenwriter, filmmaker, and autobiographer.

INTRODUCTION

The hallucinatory and imaginative qualities of Buñuel's films have earned him a reputation as Spain's greatest filmmaker and as one of the most significant director-writers in the history of the cinema. Though he acquired enduring fame as a result of his early surrealistic works, many of his most critically acclaimed films are more traditionally narrative in structure and contain graphic depictions of the ways in which the individual's impulses and desires are thwarted by social conventions. His work has often been considered obscure and difficult, an attitude stemming in the view of many critics from Buñuel's paradoxical nature: he was a religious man who thanked God that he was an atheist; a tender man who admired the Marquis de Sade; and a realist obsessed with fantasy.

Buñuel was born into a middle class family in the Spanish region of Aragón. During the years 1906 to 1915 he was educated at Jesuit schools in Zaragoza, where the prevailing atmosphere of repressiveness instilled in him a lifelong penchant for anti-clericalism and blasphemy. At the University of Madrid in the early 1920s, Buñuel studied engineering and entomology and became interested in the arts through personal contact with such figures as José Ortega y Gasset, Federico Garcia Lorca, and Salvador Dalí. Upon graduation he went to Paris, where he studied at the Academie du Cinéma and assisted the filmmaker Jean Epstein. At this time he frequently discussed aesthetic issues with members of the avant-garde artistic community, including André Breton, Pablo Picasso, Max Ernst, Giorgio de Chirico, and Joan Miró. In 1928 Buñuel collaborated with Dalí to produce his first film, *Un Chien andalou*. Owing to the film's disturbing assemblage of images, specifically intended to offend the bourgeoisie, Buñuel expected such a negative reaction from the audience that he went to the opening with his pockets filled with stones. Somewhat to his embarrassment, the film was enthusiastically received. Buñuel's next film, *L' Age d'or* (1930), contained a more overt denunciation of bourgeois values, with the result that its second showing prompted a fight in the audience and the crowd's destruction of paintings by Dalí, Ernst, and Miró in the theater's lobby.

While controversy raged over *L' Age d'or*, Buñuel studied American film sequences in Hollywood. He returned to Spain to film *Las Hurdes* (1932; *Land without Bread*), an eerie documentary exposing the poverty of rural Spain. After the Spanish Civil War, Buñuel returned to America, where he worked on several film projects that were eventually abandoned. In 1947 he moved to Mexico where he made commerical films and melodramas, as well as one of his most highly regarded works, *Los Olvidados* (filmed in 1951). Many of Buñuel's Mexican films, including *Ensayo de un Crimen* (1955; *The Criminal Life of Archibaldo de la Cruz*), feature a distinctive black humor and eroticism that helped earn the filmmaker an international reputation.

In the late 1950s and 1960s, Buñuel worked in both France and Spain. Many of his films from this period, especially *Viridiana* (1961) and *El ángel exterminador* (1962), display pessimism, social protest, and anti-Catholicism, and were occasionally censored by officials in Catholic countries. Although it won the Golden Palm award at the 1961 Cannes film festival in France, *Viridiana* was nevertheless banned in both France and Spain. In the late 1960s, Buñuel settled in France and embarked on a period of collaboration with producer Serge Silberman and screenwriter Jean-Claude Carrière. His last films, culminating in the critically acclaimed *Le Fantôme de la liberté* (1974; *The Phantom of Liberty*), reveal the same iconoclastic stance towards social conventions that characterizes his oeuvre as a whole. In 1982 he completed his memoirs, *Mon dernier soupir* (1983; *My Last Sigh*). One year later he died of cirrhosis of the liver in Mexico City.

Buñuel's first two films have often been viewed as cinematic representations of Surrealist ideas. In accordance with the tenets of Surrealism, Buñuel believed that the desire for continuity and coherence reflects humanity's attempt to civilize irrationality by imposing an arbitrary organization on nature. *Un Chien andalou* condemns this effort by presenting a series of fragmented and startling images, including a man slitting a woman's eyeball and a pair of breasts transforming into buttocks. The cumulative effect is one of dreamlike irreality present in these and most of Buñuel's later films, and mirrors his belief that sleep is the mind's most natural state. *L' Age d'or* differs from *Un Chien andalou* in eschewing random imagery in favor of a more straightforward narrative. The story concerns the struggle of two lovers to remain together despite efforts on the part of the bourgeoisie to separate them. The film ends with the lovers reunited and a sequence of Surreal images, including Christ leading a band of celebrants from an orgy at the Marquis de Sade's castle. After a hostile initial reception, *L' Age d'or* was virtually ignored until the 1960s. It is now considered a masterpiece, and Carlos Fuentes has described it as "the greatest of the surrealist films and one of the most personal and original works in the history of the cinema."

Buñuel's early Surrealist films explore themes which became central to his later works. Paramount among these are the themes of social injustice and hypocrisy. *Land without Bread*, for example, documents the primitive living conditions of villagers who have inbred for generations and lack the resources to improve their lot. One commentator notes that "the only luxurious buildings we came across were the churches." A similarly intense depiction of poverty is presented in *Los Olvidados*, a film portraying the lives of young criminals in the slums of Mexico City. Critics have noted that Buñuel refuses to sentimentalize the slum boys, while nevertheless offering implicit criticism of the social agencies which make only token gestures at ameliorating their condition.

The anti-bourgeois sentiment in Buñuel's films is complemented by attacks against the institutions and doctrines of Christianity. Considered one of his broadest treatments of religion, *Nazarin* (1958) focuses on a defrocked priest's struggle to emulate the life of Christ. In seeking to better the lives of his fellow men, he unwittingly causes catastrophe at every turn. At the film's conclusion, the priest is offered a pineapple by a kind stranger and is thereby led to replace his faith in Christ with faith in humanity. *Viridiana* presents the story of a young woman intent on becoming a nun, who inherits a country estate that she converts into a refuge for local beggars. The latter abuse Viridiana's charity by engaging in bacchic revelry, filmed by Buñuel in one of his most celebrated sequences as a grotesque parody of Leonardo da Vinci's *Last Supper*. The film ends with Viridiana playing cards with her friends while her religious possessions—including a cross, nails and a crown of thorns—are consumed in a bonfire.

Many of Buñuel's films additionally depict sexual repression resulting from bourgeois values and religiosity. *The Criminal Life of Archibaldo de la Cruz* features a protagonist who possesses a magic box that can cause the death of whomsoever its owner wishes and which is used to destroy the subjects of his sexual fantasies. *Belle de Jour* (produced in 1967) narrates the story of Séverine, a woman whose Catholic beliefs are so deeply ingrained that she is incapable of consummating her marriage. Instead, she resorts to erotic daydreams and eventually attempts to overcome her guilt and fears by working during the day as a prostitute.

During his long career, Buñuel modified his theory of the cinema. In 1960 he declared that "the screen is a dangerous and wonderful instrument, if a free spirit uses it." In 1974, however, with the release of *The Phantom of Liberty*, he acknowledged that "it is no longer possible to scandalize people as we did in 1930." His critics nevertheless maintain that by reveal-ing the emptiness of so many entrenched mores and by proclaiming the revolutionary freedom inherent in the imagination, Buñuel substantially realized his vision for the cinema as "a quest for pleasure and inquiry which isn't followed by the pounding hooves of guilt."

CRITICAL COMMENTARY

HENRY MILLER
(essay date 1938)

[An American novelist, essayist, and critic, Miller was one of the most controversial authors of the twenti-eth century. The ribaldry and eroticism of such works as *Tropic of Cancer* (1935) and *Tropic of Capricorn* (1939) made him perhaps the most censored major writer of all time. Many of Miller's best known works are autobiographical and describe the author's quest for truth and freedom as well as his rejection of mod-ern civilization. In the following excerpt, originally published in *Max and the White Phagocytes* in 1938, Miller offers a favorable response to Buñuel's *L' Age d'or*, describing it as "the only film I know of which reveals the possibilities of the cinema."]

In every art the ultimate is achieved only when the artist passes beyond the bounds of the art he employs. This is as true of Lewis Carroll's work as of Dante's *Divine Comedy*, as true of Laotse as of Buddha or Christ. The world must be turned upside down, ransacked, confounded in order that the miracle may be proclaimed. In *L'Age d'or* we stand again at a miraculous frontier which opens up be-fore us a dazzling new world which no one has explored. "Mon idée générale," wrote Salvador Dalí, "en écrivant avec Buñuel le scénario de *L'Age d'Or*, a été de présenter la ligne droite et pure de conduite d,un être qui poursuit l'amour á travers les ignorables idéaux humanitaires, pa-triotiques et autres misérables mécanismes de la réalité." I am not unaware of the part which Dalí played in the creation of this great film, and yet I cannot refrain from thinking of it as the peculiar product of his collaborator, the man who directed the film: Luis Buñuel.

Dalí's name is now familiar to the world, even to Americans and Englishmen, as the most successful of all the Surrealists to-day. He is enjoying a temporal vogue, largely because he is not understood, largely because his work is sensational. Buñuel's, on the other hand, appears to have dropped out of sight. Rumor has it that he is in Spain, that he is quietly amassing a collection of docu-mentary films on the revolution. What these will be, if Buñuel retains any of his old vigor, promises to be noth-ing short of staggering. For Buñuel, like the miners of the Asturias, is a man who flings dynamite. Buñuel is obsessed by the cruelty, ignorance and superstition which prevail among men. He realizes that there is no hope for man anywhere on this earth unless a clean slate be made of it. He appears on the scene at the moment when civilization is at its nadir.

There can be no doubt about it: the plight of civ-ilized man is a foul plight. He is singing his swan song without the joy of having been a swan. He has been sold out by his intellect, manacled, strangled and mangled by his own symbology. He is mired in his art, suffocated by his religions, paralyzed by his knowledge. That which he glorifies is not life, since he has lost the rhythm of life, but death. What he worships is decay and putrefaction. He is diseased and the whole organism of society is infected.

They have called Buñuel everything—traitor, anar-chist, pervert, defamer, iconoclast. But lunatic they dare not call him. True, it is lunacy he portrays in his film, but it is not of his making. This stinking chaos which for a brief hour or so is amalgamated under his magic wand, this is the lunacy of man's achievements after ten thou-sand years of civilization. Buñuel, to show his reverence and gratitude, puts a cow in the bed and drives a garbage truck through the salon. The film is composed of a succes-sion of images without sequence the significance of which must be sought for below the threshold of consciousness. Those who were deceived because they could not find or-der or meaning in it will find order and meaning nowhere except perhaps in the world of the bees or the ants.

I am reminded at this point of the charming little documentaire which preceded the Buñuel film the night it was shown at Studio 28. A charming little study of the abattoir it was, altogether fitting and significant for the weak-stomached sisters of culture who had come to hiss the big film. Here everything was familiar and com-

Principal Works

Un Chien andalou [with Salvador Dalí] (screenplay) 1928

L'Age d'or [with Salvador Dalí] (screenplay) 1930

Las Hurdes (screenplay) 1932
 *[Land without Bread]

Los Olvidados [with Luis Alcoriza] (screenplay) 1950

Las aventuras de Robinson Crusoe [with Hugo Butler] (screenplay) 1952
 *[The Adventures of Robinson Crusoe]

Ensayo de un crimen [with Eduardo Ugarte] (screenplay) 1955
 *[The Criminal Life of Archibaldo de la Cruz]

Nazarin [with Julio Alejandro] (screenplay) 1958

Viridiana [with Julio Alejandro] (screenplay) 1961

El ángel exterminador [with Julio Alejandro] (screenplay) 1962
 *[The Exterminating Angel]

Le Journal d'une femme de chambre [with Jean-Claude Carrière] (screenplay) 1963
 *[Diary of a Chambermaid]

Simon del desierto (screenplay) 1965
 *[Simon of the Desert]

Belle de jour [with Jean-Claude Carrière] (screenplay) 1966

La Voie lactée [with Jean-Claude Carrière] (screenplay) 1969
 *[The Milky Way]

Tristana [with Julio Alejandro] (screenplay) 1970

Le Charme discret de la bourgeoisie [with Jean-Claude Carrière] (screenplay) 1972
 *[The Discreet Charm of the Bourgeoisie]

Le Fantôme de la liberté [with Jean-Claude Carrière] (screenplay) 1974
 *[The Phantom of Liberty]

Cet obscur objet du désir [with Jean-Claude Carrière] (screenplay) 1977
 *[That Obscure Object of Desire]

Mon dernier soupir (memoirs) 1982
 [My Last Sigh, 1983]

*The translated titles are those under which the films were released in the United States.

succulent that the saliva flowed willy-nilly. (Not forgetting the shamrocks that were plugged up the ass-holes of each and every pig!) As I say, this was a perfectly comprehensible piece of butchery and indeed, so well was it performed, that from some of the more elegant spectators in the audience it brought forth a burst of applause.

It is five years or so ago since I saw the Buñuel film and therefore I cannot be absolutely sure, but I am almost certain that there were in this film no scenes of organized butchery between man and man, no wars, no revolutions, no inquisitions, no lynchings, no third degree scenes. There was, to be sure, a blind man who was mistreated, there was a dog which was kicked in the stomach, there was a boy who was wantonly shot by his father, there was an old dowager who was slapped in the face at a garden party and there were scorpions who fought to the death among the rocks near the sea. Isolated little cruelties which, because they were not woven into a comprehensible little pattern, seemed to shock the spectators even more than the sight of wholesale trench slaughter. There was something which shocked their delicate sensibilities even more and that was the effect of Wagner's *Tristan and Isolde* upon one of the protagonists. Was it possible that the divine music of Wagner could so arouse the sensual appetites of a man and woman as to make them roll in the gravelled path and bite and chew one another until the blood came? Was it possible that this music could so take possession of the young woman as to make her suck the toe of a statued foot with perverted lasciviousness? Does music bring on orgasms, does it entrain perverse acts, does it drive people truly mad? Does this great legendary theme which Wagner immortalized have to do with such a plain vulgar physiological fact as sexual love? The film seems to suggest that it does. It seems to suggest more, for through the ramifications of this Golden Age Buñuel, like an entomologist, has studied what we call love in order to expose beneath the ideology, the mythology, the platitudes and phraseologies the complete and bloody machinery of sex. He has distinguished for us the blind metabolisms, the secret poisons, the mechanistic reflexes, the distillations of the glands, the entire plexus of forces which unite love and death in life.

Is it necessary to add that there are scenes in this film which have never been dreamed of before? The scene in the water-closet, for example. I quote from the program notes:

"Il est inutile d'ajouter qu'un des points culminants de la pureté de ce film nous semble cristallisé dans la vision de l'héroïne dans les cabinets, où la puissance de l'esprit arrive à sublimer une situation généralement baroque en un élément poétique de la plus pure noblesse et solitude."

A situation usually baroque! Perhaps it is the baroque element in human life, or rather in the life of civilized man, which gives to Buñuel's works the aspect of cruelty and sadism. Isolated cruelty and sadism, for it is the great virtue of Buñuel that he refuses to be enmeshed in the

prehensible, though perhaps in bad taste. But there was order and meaning in it, as there is order and meaning in a cannibalistic rite. And finally there was even a touch of aestheticism, for when the slaughter was finished and the decapitated bodies had gone their separate ways each little pig's head was carefully blown up by compressed air until it looked so monstrously life-like and savoury and

glittering web of logic and idealism which seeks to mask from us the real nature of man. Perhaps, like [D.H.] Lawrence, Buñuel is only an inverted idealist. Perhaps it is his great tenderness, the great purity and poetry of his vision which forces him to reveal the abominable, the malicious, the ugly and the hypocritical falsities of man. Like his precursors he seems animated by a tremendous hatred for the lie. Being normal, instinctive, healthy, gay, unpretentious he finds himself alone in the crazy drift of social forces. Being thoroughly normal and honest he finds himself regarded as bizarre. Like Lawrence again his work divides the world into two opposite camps—those who are for him and those who are against him. There is no straddling the issue. Either you are crazy, like the rest of civilized humanity, or you are sane and healthy like Buñuel. And if you are sane and healthy you are an anarchist and you throw bombs. The great honor which was conferred upon Luis Buñuel at the showing of his film was that the citizens of France recognized him as a true anarchist. The theatre was taken by assault and the street was cleared by the police. The film has never been shown again, to my knowledge, except at private performances, and then but rarely. It was brought to America, shown to a special audience, and created no impression whatever, except perplexity. Meanwhile Salvador Dalí, Buñuel's collaborator, has been to America several times and created a furore there. Dalí, whose work is unhealthy, though highly spectacular, highly provocative, is acclaimed as a genius. Dalí makes the American public conscious of Surrealism, and creates a fad. Dalí returns with his pockets full of dough. Dalí is accepted—as another world freak. Freak for freak: there is a divine justice at work. The world which is crazy recognizes its master's voice. The yolk of the egg has split: Dalí takes America, Buñuel takes the leavings.

I want to repeat: *L'Age d'Or* is the only film I know of which reveals the possibilities of the cinema! It makes its appeal neither to the intellect nor to the heart: it strikes at the solar plexus. It is like kicking a mad dog in the guts. And though it was a valiant kick in the guts and well aimed it was not enough! There will have to be other films, films even more violent than Luis Buñuel's. For the world is in a coma and the cinema is still waving a peacock feathered plume before our eyes.

Wondering sometimes where he may be and what he may be doing, wondering what he could do if he were permitted, I get to thinking now and then of all that is left out of the films. Has anybody ever shown us the birth of a child, or even the birth of an animal? Insects yes, because the sexual element is weak, because there are no taboos. But even in the world of the insects have they shown us the praying Mantis, the love feast which is the acme of sexual voracity? Have they shown us how our heroes won the war—and died for us? Have they shown us the gaping wounds, have they shown us the faces that have been shot away? Are they showing us now what happens in Spain every day when the bombs rain down on Madrid? Almost every week there is another News Reel theatre opened up, but there is no news. Once a year we have a repertoire of the outstanding events of the world given us by the news getters. It is nothing but a series of catastrophes: railroad wrecks, explosions, floods, earthquakes, automobile accidents, aeroplane disasters, collisions of trains and ships, epidemics, lynchings, gangster killings, riots, strikes, incipient revolutions, putsches, assassinations. The world seems like a mad-house, and the world is a mad-house, but nobody dares dwell on it. When an appalling piece of insanity, already properly castrated, is about to be presented a warning is issued to the spectators not to indulge in demonstrations. Rest impartial! that is the edict. Don't budge from your sleep! We command you in the name of lunacy—*keep cool!* And for the most part the injunctions are heeded. They are heeded willy-nilly, for by the time the spectacle is concluded everybody has been bathed in the innocuous drama of a sentimental couple, plain honest folks like ourselves, who are doing exactly what we are doing, with the sole difference that they are being well paid for it. This nullity and vacuity is dished up to us as the main event of the evening. The hors d'œuvre is the news reel which is spiced with death and ignorance and superstition. Between these two phases of life there is absolutely no relation unless it be the link made by the animated cartoon. For the animated cartoon is the censor which permits us to dream the most horrible nightmares, to rape and kill and bugger and plunder, without waking up. Daily life is like we see it in the big film: the news reel is the eye of God; the animated cartoon is the soul tossing in its anguish. But none of these three is the reality which is common to all of us who think and feel. Somehow they have worked a camouflage on us, and though it is our own camouflage, we accept the illusion for reality. And the reason for it is that life as we know it to be has become absolutely unbearable. We flee from it in terror and disgust. The men who come after us will read the truth beneath the camouflage. May they pity us as we who are alive and real pity those about us.

Some people think of the Golden Age as a dream of the past; others think of it as the millennium to come. But the Golden Age is the immanent reality to which all of us, by our daily living, are either contributing or failing to contribute. The world is what we make it each day, or what we fail to make it. If it is lunacy that we have on our hands to-day then it is we who are the lunatics. If you accept the fact that it is a crazy world you may perhaps succeed in adapting yourself to it. But those who have a sense of creation are not keen about adapting themselves. We affect one another, whether we wish to or not. Even negatively we affect one another. In writing about Buñuel instead of writing about something else I am aware that I am going to create a certain effect—for most people an unpleasant one, I suspect. But I can no more refrain from writing this way about Buñuel than I can from washing my face to-morrow morning. My past experience of life leads up to this moment and rules it despotically. In asserting the value of Buñuel I am asserting my own values, my own faith in life. In singling out this one man I do what I am constantly doing in every realm of life—selecting and evaluating. To-morrow is no hazardous affair, a day like any other day: to-morrow is the result of many yesterdays and comes with a potent, cumulative effect. I am to-morrow what I chose to be yesterday and the day before. It is not possible that to-morrow I may negate and nullify everything that led me to this present moment.

In the same way I wish to point out that the film *L'Age d'Or* is no accident, nor is its dismissal from the screen an accident. The world has condemned Luis Buñuel and judged him as unfit. Not the whole world, because as I said before, the film is scarcely known outside of France, outside of Paris, in fact. Judging from the trend of affairs since this momentous event took place I cannot say that I am optimistic about the revival of this film to-day. Perhaps the next Buñuel film will be even more of a bomb-shell than was *L'Age d'Or*. I fervently hope so. But meanwhile—and here I must add that this is the first opportunity, apart from a little review which I wrote for *The New Review*, I have had to write about Buñuel publicly—meanwhile, I say, this belated tribute to Buñuel may serve to arouse the curiosity of those who have never heard the name before. Buñuel's name is not unknown to Hollywood that I know. Indeed, like many another man of genius whom the Americans have gotten wind of, Luis Buñuel was invited to come to Hollywood and give of his talent. In short, he was invited to do nothing and draw his breath. So much for Hollywood. . . .

No, it is not from that quarter that the wind will blow. But things are curiously arranged in this world. Men who have been dishonored and driven from their country sometimes return to be crowned as king. Some return as a scourge. Some leave only their name behind them, or the remembrance of their deeds, but in the name of this one and that whole epochs have been revitalized and recreated. I for one believe that, despite everything I have said against the cinema as we now know it, something wondrous and vital may yet come of it. Whether this happens or not depends entirely on us, on you who read this now. What I say is only a drop in the bucket, but it may have its consequences. The important thing is that the bucket should not have a hole in it. Well, I believe that such a bucket can be found. I believe that it is just as possible to rally men around a vital reality as it is around the false and the illusory. Luis Buñuel's effect upon me was not lost. And perhaps my words will not be lost either. (pp. 54–62)

Henry Miller, "The Golden Age," in his *The Cosmological Eye*, New Directions Publishing Corporation, 1939, pp. 47–62.

TONY RICHARDSON
(essay date 1954)

[In the following excerpt, Richardson examines several of Buñuel's films including *L'Age d'or, Land without Bread*, and *El*.]

By its first sequence, a brusque documentary account of scorpions, [*L'Age d'Or*] asks to be accepted as fact rather than as fiction. In style and subject this sequence symbolises the theme of the film. Among the rocks where the scorpions are found are a band of cut-throat beggars, hideous, blind and maimed, planning to attack the descent of civilisation on their territory in the form of robed and mitred bishops, consecrating the bitter crags. But weak and exhausted, they die before they can reach the priests; and civilisation, complete in top hats and frock coats, in cassocks and nuns' habits, has arrived to lay the foundation stone of a new city—imperial Rome. The mayor's official speech is interrupted by cries of violent lovemaking. Buñuel now introduces his main theme, the conflict of love with the moral and conventional pressures of society. The lovers are separated by force, but later meet at a fashionable music party where, after delay and subterfuge they again begin to make love, only to be interrupted when an imperturbable butler calls Modot, the hero, to the telephone. The girl is left alone to satisfy her desire on the big toe of a statue in the garden. On the telephone, the president of Modot's country (he is a diplomat) accuses him, by neglect of his duties, of starting a revolution. Clouded by guilt, he returns to the girl; but he attracts her no longer and she leaves him for the old, flabby, bearded conductor of the orchestra. At the same time, the survivors of the debauch at de Sade's Château de Selliny leave the castle. Symbol both of what love has become and by whom it has become what it is, the old, poxed gouty roués are led by Christ.

Surrealism is born out of despair; its only power is to hasten the general cataclysm by its own prophetic chaos. Max Ernst said of it, *"In turning topsy-turvy the appearances and relationships of reality, surrealism has been able, with a smile on its lips, to hasten the general crisis of consciousness which must perforce take place in our time."* No other work of the period expressed this so completely as *L'Age d'Or*. All civilisation is oppression, suffering, frustration; above, the cynical emptiness and callous show of the rich; below, the misery, hunger and incipient revolution of the poor; individuals are ridden with inhibition, anxiety and guilt; beauty is like Hans Schwitters' haphazard, delicate collages of tram tickets and paper money, the momentary chance of an afternoon's boredom—clouds pass in the mirror as the girl, restless and lonely, waits for Modot's arrival. Buñuel has taken a traditional romantic theme, love thwarted by circumstance and seen it with "un œil à l'état sauvage", stripped of any sentimental associations; love is a fierce lust with clumsy embraces and frustrated satisfaction. The honesty of his attitude is explosive and cauterising.

Yet it is not despair that finally pervades the film but a savage glee, almost optimistic in destruction. In a world where Marcel Schwob predicted "Le rire est probablement destiné à disparaître", surrealism answered disintegration with its own laughter. When Modot is deserted by the girl, he bundles out of a window, in fury, a burning plough, an enormous pine, a bishop, a toy giraffe. This same lusty and joyous iconoclasm gives unity to the film and binds the coda (which at first seems superfluous) to the main theme. It springs partly from a young man's desire to shock and outrage, partly from the ironic tradition of the picaresque; violence turned to joke. After a subtitle, "Parfois le dimanche", buildings explode and collapse; a tumbril is driven through a fashionable party; and a maid rushes in, faints, as flames leap out of a doorway behind her, while the guests unconcernedly chatter on. Surrealism gave Buñuel power to denounce but also, like Clair, freedom to romp.

But, though the props are still surrealist—the man with "patches" of living flies, the cow on the bed—and the general form loose and episodic, there are indications that Buñuel had exhausted the surrealist approach and had already begun to shape events into drama. Surrealism had become a techinque for exposing and analysing reality rather than a means of creating an independent world of fantasy. Its freedom had, too, as M. Kyrou points out, given him the means to introduce technical innovations, such as his use of the "monologue intérieure" and the brilliant sound montage, that were startling for his time. But he was to abandon surrealism completely in his next film, *Land Without Bread* (1932).

Land Without Bread is a documentary of the mountain district, Las Hurdes, in Northern Spain. Reality here surpasses the bitterest nightmares of surrealism. The land is barren and infertile; for two months the whole population live on nothing but unripe cherries; their bodies and necks are swollen with monstrous goitres; their crowded homes are bare, squalid, crumbling; children lie dead and abandoned in the gutters; there are idiots and morons everywhere; at night the crier tolls for those who have died of plague and typhus. Whatever slight alleviation there might be is destroyed by the peasants' ignorance and superstition. They are often bitten by vipers, whose bite is not mortal, but is made so by a herb they rub into the wound. Their miserable agriculture lacks tools and method, and effort is crippled by disease and apathy.

All this Buñuel records with a flatness and lack of comment that make it the more alarming. No moral is drawn, no response instructed, no easy attitude given. Buñuel is content, as was Goya in *Los Desastres de la Guerra*, to let the naked record speak for itself. In one sequence only, where bees attack a dying ass, is there any element of his old sensationalism. Though the material is organised with masterly skill, the very conception of "art" here seems irrelevant. It is the most profoundly disturbing film I have ever seen.

After *Land Without Bread*, Buñuel was brought to Hollywood at Chaplin's instigation, but none of the projects he worked on proved acceptable. He returned to Spain and produced a number of commercial films, and during the Civil War he was sent to the Republican Embassy in Paris. Afterwards, he went to America again, where he worked for some time at the Museum of Modern Art: he was asked to leave when it was discovered that he had made *L'Age d'Or*. Then he worked in Hollywood on the dubbing of Spanish films, until in 1947 he went to Mexico with a vague plan concerning a film version of Lorca's *La Casa de Bernarda Alba*. This fell through, but he made one commercial film before, in 1950, he directed what is perhaps his greatest work, *Los Olvidados*.

In *L'Age d'Or*, Buñuel had begun to create dramatic action; in *Land Without Bread* he had approached reality directly; *Los Olvidados* was the fulfilment of both these developments. This intense dramatic vision sees the story of a group of delinquent boys living on the outskirts of Mexico City in the terms of Blake's "Innocence and Experience." Everyone in the film, so concentrated in its logic, is set at some place in that scale. At the one end is the pathetic Indian boy, Ochitos; at the other, the brutal, lecherous blind beggar and the cruel, embittered Jaibo, leader of the gang, between them is Pedro, the Innocent twisted and brutalised by Experience.

As in all Buñuel's films, the treatment is conceptual. The characters are simplified to whatever aspect or passion Buñuel is creating, and all irrelevant traits are suppressed. The unique force of the film comes from the combination of austerity and strictness in conception with a startling, often ironic, poetry of expression, with its images of donkeys, black hens, doves that can cure fever, cripples, torn meat, pariah dogs, in an almost timeless setting of arid squalor. The images underscore the logic. Pedro at first guards tenderly his pet hen with its brood of chickens; later, he savagely beats a pullet to death. The prophecies and thunderings of *L'Age d'Or* have become fact, the horrors actual, the vision immensely darkened.

All the characters have to struggle to scrape a living from the misery and poverty of their surroundings; Jaibo's gang batter a boy to death, drag a legless man from his cart, bait and stone the blind musician, who, in turn, bullies the patient Ochitos and tries to rape the young girl, Meche. They live in hate and fear of each other, their only contact savage, brutish matings, out of which the unwanted Pedros are born, and the city has new dangers and vices. Perhaps only Goya has created horror so acute. Buñuel's vision is too uncompromising to permit any softening of its bestiality; but—and one cannot say this emphatically enough, in view of what many critics have written—he never uses horror inartistically. There is no sensationalism in the handling of violence in this film; terror is balanced by pity, hopelessness by humanity. And throughout there is a strong, warm delight in any momentary respite from suffering—the little girl entranced on the carousel, Meche pathetically bathing her face in milk to soften her skin—and a pity that can encompass not only the helpless Ochitos but Pedro's selfish, callous mother. Toughened and dulled by the appalling savagery of her existence, she neglects Pedro, is easily seduced by Jaibo, but, alone of Buñuel's characters, she is allowed a moment of consciousness. Compelled by the authorities, she goes to see Pedro in jail. He has become a vicious, desperate animal, love turned to resentment and hate. As she begins to reproach him, she understands suddenly her own responsibility for what he has become; impulsively she wants to comfort him, to ask forgiveness. Pedro shrinks from her. There is nothing to be done, nothing to be said. She turns and walks out of the room. If one defines tragedy as "the balance and reconciliation of discordant and opposite qualities," it is the word for *Los Olvidados*.

Those who can find only harshness and violence in Buñuel's work should see *Subida al Cielo* (1952), with which he followed two commercial films, *Susana* and *La Hija del Engano*. Written by the Spanish poet Manuel Altolaguirre, and set in an Indian village in the Mexican jungle, this is a feckless poetic comedy, whose mixture of folklore and fantasy is similar to Lorca's *Don Perlimperlin*. The plot is simple; Oliverio, about to be married, has to break off the ceremony as his mother is dying; to respect her wishes, he must get her will ratified by a lawyer, and it is the two-day bus journey that this entails, with its adventures and delays, that forms the substance of the film. The bus is stranded in a storm; it gets stuck in a river; a woman has a premature delivery; the party stop at the driver's home to celebrate his birthday; and besides these distractions, Oliverio is pursued by the local tart (splendidly incarnated by Lilia Prado). His mental conflicts are deliciously portrayed in a jaunty dream sequence in which, while his mother mounted on a pedestal unconcernedly knits, Oliverio dumps his wife in a river and is drawn along an immense umbilical cord to the tart, in a bus transformed to a lusciously romantic patch of jungle. Eventually, goaded as much by irritation as by desire, he sleeps with the girl, during a torrential storm, on the top of the mountain, Subida al Cielo. He returns to find his mother dead, but by pressing her thumbs on to the document he is able to secure the distribution of property she had wished.

In itself the idea for the film is contrived, and the characters—the chirpy cripple, the respectable, prim Spaniard, the opinionated politician—are stock types.

But Buñuel has given it a wonderfully poetic cast. From the first moment when the lovers, in a flower-wreathed canoe, embark for their honeymoon island, the film is impregnated with a rich sensuousness. The births, the loves, the deaths of the people underlie the farcical comedy, the journey mirroring the rhythm of life. Towards the end of the film, there is an exquisite change of key from the noisy gaiety of the beginning. When the bus half sinks in the river, all efforts to extricate it with oxen and tractor fail, and the tractor itself flounders. While the passengers try to rescue it the farmer's daughter, a wise, wide-eyed tot, casually leads the oxen and the bus out of the water. By the time the bus returns, she has died from a snakebite, and the whole party attend her funeral; this mood is sustained by the death of the mother; and Oliverio and his wife matured by their grief, stand hand in hand gazing out over the dark sea.

Yet, if these deeper complexities inform the film, the prevailing mood is one of happiness. Buñuel parodies himself in the dream sequence; the cripple jokes about his peg-leg; and the descent of the American Tourists, the Shriners' Convention, self-consciously speaking bad Spanish to each other and doggedly trying to buy an *old* sombrero, is satirised gently and without malice. Buñuel himself has praised *The Treasure of Sierra Madre* for putting Mexico so truly on the screen. This may be true of the deserts and the bitter traditions of the hacienda, but the other Mexico of the tropics, with its rich fruitfulness and lazy Indians, has never been so spontaneously and so poetically caught as in this enchanting film.

Two more commercial films, which I have not seen, followed: *Una Mujer Sin Amor* and *El Bruto*. Buñuel describes them as uninteresting, though the stills of the latter, with black cockerels and seduction among the carcasses hanging in a butcher's shop, look characteristic, and a poster has the intriguing description "fascinatingly bestial".

Buñuel's next film, *El* (1953), is a complete contrast in mood; uneasy, wintry, keen. The story of a paranoiac, it seems, in tone and in its upper middle-class setting, a return to *L'Age d'Or*. El (Arturo de Cordova) falls in love with his friend's fiancée (Delia Garces) and violently pursues her. Half-fascinated, half-repelled, she agrees to marry him; after the wedding, he becomes jealous to the point of insanity over every trifle. She confides in her mother, her priest, her ex-fiancée, but they discount her stories; these confidences enrage him even more, and he attempts to kill her. She leaves him and he, after complete breakdown, enters a monastery.

Relentlessly Buñuel watches, as if it were a snake, the paranoia unwind its fascinating coils; he gloats in the incidental comedy of its writhings (as when Cordova jabs a knitting-needle into a key-hole through which he imagines someone to be spying). Sometimes, though, one feels that Buñuel himself twists the tail of the snake to produce fascinating wriggles for their own sake. This is accentuated by the inadequacy of the players, neither of whose personalities are interesting enough to encompass the range and subtlety of characterisation demanded. But the failure lies deeper. The conventional, commonplace script has only been partly assimilated by Buñuel. The ruthlessness of his study of the paranoiac sits uneasily with the elements of comedy-of-situation in the script: it called, perhaps, for the hand of a Sturges. There are signs, too, of production difficulties and confusions in narration.

Buñuel's personality is most evident in the blasting anti-Catholicism of the film—a subject to which he always reacts in his grandest, most authoritative manner. The paranoiac is portrayed as deeply religious, and it is at a ceremony for the initiation of young priests, at which he is a lay official, that he first sees the girl. This magnificent sequence presents the heavy oppressively ornamented setting, the strain on the blanched faces of the boys, the weary ritual of the bishop, and Cordova's desperate attempt to keep his attention on the solemnity of the occasion while, despite himself, it wanders on to the legs of the spectators. The climax of the film provides a further opportunity. Cordova, desperate and exhausted, has gone into a church; in a rapidly mounting cross-cutting sequence all the congregation, the altar boy, the priest himself, seem to him to be cat-calling, pulling faces, thumbing noses. (pp. 125-29)

Tony Richardson, "The Films of Luis Buñuel," in *Sight and Sound—The Film Quarterly*, Vol. 23, No. 3, January–March, 1954, pp. 125–31.

LUIS BUÑUEL

(essay date 1960)

[Here Buñuel provides a brief statement on his conception of the cinema.]

1. In none of the traditional arts is there such a wide gap, between possibilities and facts as in the cinema. Motion pictures act directly upon the spectator; they offer him concrete persons and things; they isolate him, through silence and darkness, from the usual psychological atmosphere. Because of all this, the cinema is capable of stirring the spectator as perhaps no other art. But as no other art, it is also capable of stupefying him. Unfortunately, the great majority of today's films seem to have exactly that purpose; they glory in an intellectual and moral vacuum. In this vacuum, movies seem to prosper.

2. Mystery is a basic element of all works of art. It is generally lacking on the screen. Writers, directors

---

and producers take good care in avoiding anything that may upset us. They keep the marvelous window on the liberating world of poetry shut. They prefer stories which seem to continue our ordinary lives, which repeat for the umpteenth time the same drama, which help us forget the hard hours of our daily work. And all this, of course, carefully watched over by traditional morals, government and international censorship, religion, good taste, white humour and other flat dicteria of reality.

3. The screen is a dangerous and wonderful instrument, if a free spirit uses it. It is the superior way of expressing the world of dreams, emotions and instinct. The cinema seems to have been invented for the expression of the subconscious, so profoundly is it rooted in poetry. Nevertheless, it almost never pursues these ends.

4. We rarely see good cinema in the mammoth productions, or in the works that have received the praise of critics and audience. The particular story, the private drama of an individual, cannot interest — I believe — anyone worthy of living in our time. If a man in the audience shares the joys and sorrows of a character on the screen, it should be because that character reflects the joys and sorrows of all society and so the personal feelings of that man in the audience. Unemployment, insecurity, the fear of war, social injustice, etc., affect all men of our time, and thus, they also affect the individual spectator. But when the screen tells me that Mr. X is not happy at home and finds amusement with a girl-friend whom he finally abandons to reunite himself with his faithful wife, I find it all very moral and edifying but it leaves me completely indifferent.

5. Octavio Paz has said: "But that a man in chains should shut his eyes, the world would explode." And I could say: But that the white eye-lid of the screen reflect its proper light, the Universe would go up in flames. But for the moment we can sleep in peace: the light of the cinema is conveniently dosified and shackled. (pp. 41-2)

Luis Buñuel, "A Statement," in *Film Culture*, No. 21, Summer, 1960, pp. 41-2.

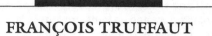

FRANÇOIS TRUFFAUT

(essay date 1971)

[Truffaut is a celebrated French screenwriter and
filmmaker. In the following excerpt, originally written
in 1971 and published in his *Les films de ma vie*
(1975), he examines Buñuel's film *The Criminal Life
of Archibaldo de la Cruz*.]

Luis Buñuel is, perhaps, somewhere between [film direc-
tors] Renoir and Bergman. One would gather that Buñuel
finds mankind imbecilic but life diverting. All this he tells
us very mildly, even a bit indirectly, but it's there in the
overall impression we get from his films. Even though he
has very little stomach for "messages," Buñuel did manage to make one of those rare, truly antiracist movies. *The
Young One* (1960), the only film he has shot in English.
It succeeded because of his masterful ability to intertwine
sympathetic and unsympathetic characters and to shuffle
the cards in his psychological game while he addresses us
in perfectly clear, logical language.

The antipsychological Buñuelian scenario functions
on the same principle as the hot-and-cold shower—
alternating favorable and unfavorable signs, positives and
negatives, reason and nonsense. He puts these elements
to work on both the action and the characters in his films.
Anti-bourgeois, anti-conformist, Buñuel is as sarcastic as
Stroheim but he has a lighter touch; his world view is
subversive, happily anarchist. (p. 261)

Buñuel is a cheerful pessimist, not given to despair,
but he has a skeptical mind. Notice, he never makes films
for, always *against*, and none of his characters ever appear
to be very practical. Buñuel's skepticism extends to all
those whom he finds playing too neat a social game, those
who live by accepted opinions. (pp. 261–62)

Too many commentators refer to Buñuel as a poet
of hallucination who follows the caprices of his fantastic imagination, while in reality he is a brilliant screenwriter very much concerned with dramatic construction.
(p. 263)

Let's look at how he constructed. . . *The Criminal
Life of Archibaldo de la Cruz* (*Archibald of the Cross*),
which he made in Mexico in 1955. He was not then universally recognized as a genius, and he was working in a
country in which the censors would have prohibited him
from showing a murderer who is not only likable but goes
unpunished into the bargain. (p. 264)

I'm not familiar with the literary sources of *Archibaldo de la Cruz*, but the cinematic inspirations are clear—
Hitchcock's *Shadow of a Doubt* (1948), which tells the

story of a man who murders widows. . . set against the
musical theme of *The Merry Widow*; a film by Preston
Sturges, *Unfaithfully Yours* (1948), in which an orchestra
conductor. . . imagines three different ways of killing his
wife as he conducts a symphony; and above all, Chaplin's
Monsieur Verdoux (1947). The distraught woman whose
path Archibaldo keeps crossing is obviously related to
the extraordinary Martha Raye (Captain Bonheur's wife)
whom Verdoux-Bonheur never quite succeeds in murdering.

But the true interest of *Archibaldo* lies elsewhere—
in the ingenuity of its construction, the audacious handling of time, the expertise of the cinematic narrative. If
you question the audience at the end of *Archibaldo*—
remember, its full title is, mischievously, *The Criminal
Life of Archibald of the Cross*—almost everybody will tell
you that they've just seen the story of a likable guy who
kills women. It is absolutely not true; Archibaldo has
killed no one. He's been satisfied simply to wish, after
the death of his governess when he was a little boy, for
the deaths of the nun who was a nurse in the hospital,
the beautiful disturbed woman, the sultry guide, and his
unfaithful fiancée. Four of the five women have died in
one way or another shortly after Archibaldo has expressed
his desire. We have anticipated these deaths as fantasies
(flashes forward), and then we've seen certain of them
really occur, but only as recounted by Archibaldo in flashback.

In the hands of most film writers, *Archibaldo* would
have become a series of sketches, but Buñuel and Eduardo
Ugarte were able to intertwine the individual episodes by
introducing us to all the female characters early in the
story, and then, in the second half of the film, gathering
them delicately for their ten-minute scenes to show them
as real women.

Archibaldo is one of those rare films so finely constructed, written with such a sense of how to put images
on a screen, that reading the screenplay gives only a weak
idea of the result, maybe even a completely inaccurate impression. . . . If one simply recounted its scenes literally,
it would seem ridiculous. Lubitsch and Buñuel are the
masters of the invisible flashback, the flashback that interrupts without breaking the story line and, on the contrary,
refreshes it when it threatens to flag. They are also masters at bringing us back to the present without startling
us. They both use a two-pronged hook with which they
jerk us backward and forward. The hook is almost always a gimmick—comic in Lubitsch's work, dramatic in
Buñuel's.

Too many screenplays are conceived for their literary
effect, and they end up as novels written in pictures. They
are pleasant to read, they make easy promises, and they
deliver on them, presuming the director and the actors
have as much talent as the writer. I am not out to criticize the straight story-line movies—of which *Bicycle Thief*
is one of the most beautiful examples—but to suggest

that the talents of the scenarists who wrote *The Big Sleep, North by Northwest, Heaven Can Wait,* or ***Archibaldo de la Cruz*** are far greater. The discipline of film has its own rules, which have not yet been fully explored, and it is only through works such as those of Buñuel and the other great director-writers that we will one day realize them fully. (pp. 267–68)

François Truffaut, "Buñuel the Builder," in his *The Films in My Life*, translated by Leonard Mayhew, Simon & Schuster, 1978, pp. 261–68.

A scene from *Nazarín.*

CARLOS FUENTES
(essay date 1973)

[Fuentes is a prolific, versatile Mexican writer noted for his innovations in language and narrative technique. His concern for affirming a viable Mexican identity is revealed in his allegorical and thematic use of his country's history and legends, from the myths of the Aztecs to the Mexican Revolution. In the following excerpt, Fuentes explores the various ways in which sight acts as a unifying factor in Buñuel's films.]

An obsessive artist, Buñuel cares about what he wants to say; or rather, what he wants to see. A really important director makes only one film; his work is a sum, a totality of perfectly related parts that illuminate each other. In Buñuel films, from ***An Andalusian Dog*** to ***The Discreet Charm of the Bourgeoisie***, the essential unifying factor is sight. His first image is that of a woman's eye slit by a

razor and throughout the body of his work there is this pervading sense of sight menaced, sight lost as virginity is lost; sight as a wound that will not heal, wounded sight as an interstice through which dreams and desires can flow. Catherine Deneuve's absent regard in ***Belle de Jour*** is calculated: She is constantly looking outside the confines of the screen, enlarging the space of the screen, looking at something beyond that isn't there, that probably connects the two halves of her life.

But Buñuel's violent aggressions against sight actually force us back to his particular way of seeing. His world is seen first as a grey, hazy, distant jumble of undetermined things; no other director shoots a scene from quite that neutral, passive distance. Then the eye of the camera suddenly picks out an object that has been there all the time, or a revealing gesture, zooms into them, makes them come violently alive before again retiring to the indifferent point of view.

This particular way of seeing, of making the opaque backdrop shine instantly by selecting an object or gesture, assures the freedom and fluid elegance of a Buñuel film. Sight determines montage; what is seen flows into what is unseen. . . .

Sight and survival, desires and dreams, seeing others in order to see oneself. This parabola of sight is essential to Buñuel's art. Nazarin will not see God unless he sees fellow men; Viridiana will not see herself unless she sees outside herself and accepts the world. The characters in ***The Discreet Charm*** can never see themselves or others. They may be funny, but they are already in hell. Elegant humor only cloaks despair.

So in Buñuel sight determines content or, rather, content is a way of looking, content is sight at all possible levels. And this multitude of levels—social, political, psychological, historical, esthetic, philosophic—is not predetermined, but flows from vision. His constant tension is between obsessive opposites: pilgrimage and confinement, solitude and fraternity, sight and blindness, social rules and personal cravings, rational conduct and oneiric behavior. His intimate legacies, often conflicting, are always there: Spain, Catholicism, surrealism, left anarchism. But, above all, what is always present is the liberating thrust that could, only come from such a blend of heritages. Certainly no other filmmaker could have so gracefully and violently humanized and brought into the fold of freedom, rebellion and understanding so many figures, so many passions, so many desires that the conventional code judges as monstrous, criminal and worthy of persecution and, even, extermination. . . . Buñuel incriminates all social orders while liberating our awareness of the outcast. . . .

[This] respect for freedom of his characters is translated into respect for the freedom of his audience. As they end, his films remain open, the spectator remains free. (p. 373)

Carlos Fuentes, "Spain, Catholicism, Surrealism, Anarchism: The Discreet Charm of Luis Buñuel," in *The New York Times Biographical Edition*, The New York Times Company, 1973, pp. 369–76.

LUIS BUÑUEL

(essay date 1982)

[In the following excerpt from Buñuel's autobiography, originally published as *Mon dernier soupir* (1982), the filmmaker discusses the making of his film *Un Chien andalou* and his early contact with the Surrealists.]

I went to Madrid to talk on avant–garde cinema. I brought along a few films to show—René Clair's *Entr'acte*, the dream sequence from Renoir's *La Fille de l'eau*, Cavalcanti's *Rien que les heures*. I also planned to explain the slow–motion sequence and to illustrate it with shots of a bullet slowly emerging from the barrel of a gun. The *tout*-Madrid turned out, and after the screenings Ortega y Gasset confessed to me that if he were younger, he'd love to try his hand at movies too. True to form, when I realized how aristocratic my audience was, I suggested to Pepín Bello that we announce a menstruation contest and award prizes after the lecture; but like so many other surrealist acts, this one never happened.

At the time, I was probably the only Spaniard among those who'd left Spain who had had any experience with the cinema. When the Goya Society of Saragossa asked me to make a film about the life of the painter to celebrate the one hundredth anniversay of his death, I wrote a complete script, with some technical advice from [French director Jean Epstein's] sister, Marie Epstein. Afterwards, however, when I went to see Valle Inclán at the Fine Arts Institute, I discovered that he too was making a movie about Goya. I was all ready to bow out gracefully before the master when he himself withdrew; but, in the end, the project was abandoned for lack of funds.

One of my favorite authors was Ramón Gómez de la Serna, whose short stories inspired my second screenplay. As a unifying device, I experimented with clips from a documentary showing the making of a newspaper. A man buys a paper from a kiosk and sits down on a nearby bench to read it; as he reads, Serna's stories appear on the screen, each preceded by a newspaper headline—a local crime, a football match, a political event. When the "stories" are over, the man gets to his feet, crumples up the paper, and throws it away.

A few months later, I made *Un Chien andalou*, which came from an encounter between two dreams. When I arrived to spend a few days at Dalí's house in Figueras, I told him about a dream I'd had in which a long, tapering cloud sliced the moon in half, like a razor blade slicing through an eye. Dalí immediately told me that he'd seen a hand crawling with ants in a dream he'd had the previous night.

"And what if we started right there and made a film?" he wondered aloud.

Despite my hesitation, we soon found ourselves hard at work, and in less than a week we had a script. Our only rule was very simple: No idea or image that might lend itself to a rational explanation of any kind would be accepted. We had to open all doors to the irrational and keep only those images that surprised us, without trying to explain why. The amazing thing was that we never had the slightest disagreement; we spent a week of total identification.

"A man fires a double bass," one of us would say.

"No," replied the other, and the one who'd proposed the idea accepted the veto and felt it justified. On the other hand, when the image proposed by one was accepted by the other, it immediately seemed luminously right and absolutely necessary to the scenario.

When the script was finished, I realized that we had such an original and provocative movie that no ordinary production company would touch it. So once again I found myself asking my mother for backing, which, thanks to our sympathetic attorney, she consented to provide. I wound up taking the money back to Paris and spending half of it in my usual nightclubs; ultimately, however, I settled down and contacted the actors Pierre Batcheff and Simone Mareuil, Duverger the cameraman, and made a deal to use the Billancourt studios.

The filming took two weeks; there were only five or six of us involved, and most of the time no one quite knew what he was doing.

"Stare out the window and look as if you're listening to Wagner," I remember telling Batcheff. "No, no—not like that. Sadder. Much sadder."

Batcheff never even knew what he was supposed to be looking at, but given the technical knowledge I'd managed to pick up, Duverger and I got along famously. Dalí arrived on the set a few days before the end and spent most of his time pouring wax into the eyes of stuffed donkeys. He played one of the two Marist brothers who in one scene are painfully dragged about by Batcheff. For some reason, we wound up cutting the scene. You can see Dalí in the distance, however, running with my fiancée, Jeanne, after the hero's fatal fall.

Once the film was edited, we had no idea what to do with it. I'd kept it fairly secret from the Montparnasse contingent, but one day at the Dôme, Thériade, from the

Cahiers d'Art, who'd heard rumors about it, introduced me to Man Ray. Ray had just finished shooting *Les Mystères du château de Dé*, a documentary on the de Noailles and their friends, and was looking for a second film to round out the program. Man Ray and I got together a few days later at La Coupole, where he introduced me to a fellow surrealist, Louis Aragon, who had the most elegant French manners I'd ever seen. When I told them that *Un Chien andalou* was in many ways a surrealist film, they agreed to go to a screening the following day at the Studio des Ursulines and to start planning the premiere.

More than anything else, surrealism was a kind of call heard by certain people everywhere—in the United States, in Germany, Spain, Yugoslavia—who, unknown to one another, were already practicing instinctive forms of irrational expression. Even the poems I'd published in Spain before I'd heard of the surrealist movement were responses to that call which eventually brought all of us together in Paris. While Dalí and I were making *Un Chien andalou* we used a kind of automatic writing. There was indeed something in the air, and my connection with the surrealists in many ways determined the course of my life.

My first meeting with the group took place at their regular café, the Cyrano, on the place Blanche, where I was introduced to Max Ernst, André Breton, Paul Eluard, Tristan Tzara, René Char, Pierre Unik, Yves Tanguy, Jean Arp, Maxime Alexandre, and Magritte—everyone, in other words, except Benjamin Péret, who was in Brazil. We all shook hands, and they bought me a drink, promising not to miss the premiere of the film that Aragon and Man Ray had already spoken of so highly.

The opening of *Un Chien andalou* took place at the Ursulines, and was attended by the *tout*-Paris—some aristocrats, a sprinkiling of well–established artists (among them Picasso, Le Corbusier, Cocteau, Christian Bérard, and the composer Georges Auric), and the surrealist group in toto. I was a nervous wreck. In fact, I hid behind the screen with the record player alternating Argentinian tangos with *Tristan und Isolde*. Before the show, I'd put some stones in my pocket to throw at the audience in case of disaster, remembering that a short time before, the surrealists had hissed Germaine Dulac's *La Coquille et le clergyman*, based on a script by Antonin Artaud, which I'd rather liked. I expected the worst; but, happily, the stones weren't necessary. After the film ended, I listened to the prolonged applause and dropped my projectiles discreetly, one by one, on the floor behind the screen.

My entry into the surrealist group took place very naturally. I was simply admitted to the daily meetings at the Cyrano or at André Breton's at 42, rue Fontaine. The Cyrano was an authentic Pigalle café, frequented by the working class, prostitutes, and pimps. People drank Pernod, or aperitifs like *picon*-beer with a hint of grenadine (Yves Tanguy's favorite; he'd swallow one, then a second, and by the third he had to hold his nose!)

The daily gathering was very much like a Spanish peña. We read and discussed certain articles, talked about the surrealist journal, debated any critical action we felt might be needed, letters to be written, demonstrations attended. When we discussed confidential issues, we met in Breton's studio, which was close by. I remember one amusing misunderstanding that arose because, since I was usually one of the last to arrive, I shook hands only with those people nearest me, then waved to Breton, who was always too far away to reach. "Does Buñuel have something against me?" he asked one day, very out of sorts. Finally, someone explained that I hated the French custom of shaking hands all around every time anyone went anywhere; it seemed so silly to me that I outlawed the custom on the set when we were filming *Cela s' appelle l'aurore*.

All of us were supporters of a certain concept of revolution, and although the surrealists didn't consider themselves terrorists, they were constantly fighting a society they despised. Their principal weapon wasn't guns, of course; it was scandal. Scandal was a potent agent of revelation, capable of exposing such social crimes as the exploitation of one man by another, colonialist imperialism, religious tyranny—in sum, all the secret and odious underpinnings of a system that had to be destroyed. The real purpose of surrealism was not to create a new literary, artistic, or even philosophical movement, but to explode the social order, to transform life itself. Soon after the founding of the movement, however, several members rejected this strategy and went into "legitimate" politics, especially the Communist party, which seemed to be the only organization worthy of the epithet "revolutionary."

Like the *señoritos* I knew in Madrid, most surrealists came from good families; as in my case, they were bourgeois revolting against the bourgeoisie. But we all felt a certain destructive impulse, a feeling that for me has been even stronger than the creative urge. The idea of burning down a museum, for instance, has always seemed more enticing than the opening of a cultural center or the inauguration of a new hospital.

What fascinated me most, however, in all our discussions at the Cyrano, was the moral aspect of the movement. For the first time in my life I'd come into contact with a coherent moral system that, as far as I could tell, had no flaws. It was an aggressive morality based on the complete rejection of all existing values. We had other criteria: we exalted passion, mystification, black humor, the insult, and the call of the abyss. Inside this new territory, all our thoughts and actions seemed justifiable; there was simply no room for doubt. Everything made sense. Our morality may have been more demanding and more dangerous than the prevailing order, but it was also stronger, richer, and more coherent. (pp. 102–07)

Luis Buñuel, in his *My Last Sigh*, translated by Abigail Israel, Alfred A. Knopf, 1983, 256 p.

An excerpt from *My Last Sigh*

Two years after *Exterminating Angel*, Alatriste suggested I make a film in Mexico on the strange character of Saint Simeon Stylites, the fourth–century hermit who spent forty years perched on top of a column in the Syrian desert. I'd been intrigued by this figure ever since Lorca introduced me to Jacobus de Voragine's *The Golden Legend* when we were both university students in Madrid. He used to laugh when he read how the hermit's excrement, which ran the length of the column, looked like the wax from a taper. (In reality, since all St. Simeon ate was lettuce leaves, it must have looked more like goat turds.)

Luis Buñuel in his *My Last Sigh*, translated by Abigail Israel, Alfred A. Knopf, 1983.

DAVID THOMSON
(review date 1983)

[In the following review of Buñuel's autobiography, Thomson offers a general assessment of his career, describing the filmmaker as "the proper human landmark for a moment when Europe met America and the schemes of religion, property, and progress were reassessed as dreams."]

Only days after receiving [*My Last Sigh: The Autobiography of Luis Buñuel*] to review there came news of Luis Buñuel's death. Gone in Mexico, before I had opened the book or given its sigh a chance. Some people are always drawing a razor across our path to remind us. So as I read this short, lovely, insolent variation on a life, I found a suitable postcard of Louise Brooks—all silk, leg and flagrant wish-you-were-here—to mark my palce and to furnish Buñuel with dreams. (Where is the harm? He is dead and she is utterly flat.)

Buñuel would appreciate those two intimations of the occult, coincidence and superstition. He might even have directed my attention to a further coincidence, that Miss Brooks, that raw blade of *femme fatale*, was another LB. "We should have worked together," he could have sighed. And in a sense they did. For anarchists, *amants fous*, and surrealists, all shining in hopelessness, inhale the same air and breathe it out with a blast of amused fatalism.

My last sigh, Buñuel promised, a little disgruntled because death was being tardy while he itched to get himself into that nothingness where ghosts, chance imagination, and immortality thrive. For fifteen years he had been announcing every film as his last—for he was going deaf, crotchety, and forgetful, riddled with small failings:

The diagnosis couldn't be simpler: I'm an old man, and that's all there is to it. I'm only happy at home following my daily routine: wake up, have a cup of coffee, exercise for half an hour, wash, have a second cup of coffee, eat something, walk around the block, wait until noon. My eyes are weak, and I need a magnifying glass and a special light in order to read. My deafness keeps me from listening to music, so I wait, I think, I remember, filled with a desperate impatience and constantly looking at my watch.

Boredom and impatience, sitting as close together as an endlessly green apple and a Magritte bowler-hat head—it is the perpetual surrealist juxtaposition of unconsciousness and the marvelous. It is the momentary twitch in so many of Buñuel's films, when we are not sure whether a character is daunted by a fly landing on his hand or by sin eclipsing mankind—or even whether the character is the insect. More than any other director, Buñuel let us see awful pregnancy in familiar objects and warped destiny in fatuous occasions. He combined the lucidity of an entomologist with the sleeplessness of a thundery siesta. So often regarded as intimidating (that razor was never forgotten—its threat lasted), he was also a maker of deadpan farce, the sort in which significance gives up the ghost; and so the ghost goes free.

It's no great wonder then that there isn't very much organized life in *My Last Sigh*. As Buñuel admits, he'd be content with twenty-two hours of dreaming in any day, and just two of gin and small talk. There's a plausible outline, the kind of dossier to impress Franco's secret police—born in Calanda, in Aragon, in 1900, raised in Sargossa, a student in Madrid, a layabout in Paris, then those bombs, *Un Chien Andalou* and *L'Age d'Or*, calls to murder, tangos of disappointment, the first films that consciously reached out for the unconscious rapture of dreams.

As if he guessed that those two were enough for most careers, Buñuel the drifter and idler stopped making films. You can't have that many dreams without great expanses of sleep. Between *Las Hurdes* (1932), a caustic documentary on the irredeemable plight of some Spanish peasants, and 1946, he did not direct a film. Take that, golden years of maturity! Instead, he lived in Spain and France, sat around in cafés with brilliant rascal friends, produced a few movies, and, after the Civil War, slipped off to America where he was briefly employed by the Museum of Modern Art, only to be bumped from that post on the word of onetime friend and collaborator, Salvador Dalí, that he was an atheist. He also supervised the dubbing into Spanish of Hollywood pictures, watching to see that the hidden Castilian fitted approximately with the fishy lisp of Peter Lorre. It sounds like a story of inspired waste and humiliation, placidly, even lovingly, accepted.

You can see Fernando Rey playing Buñuel, the distinguished outcast, perversely pursuing everthing except his art. It is like meals not eaten, and beauties not ravished; desire depends on its own frustration.

Buñuel appreciated America, like any connoisseur of the fantastic. He had come here first in 1930, just because his films had made a stir in Europe, no matter that no one in Hollywood had bothered to see them. He was taken on by MGM to learn the business: he went on Garbo's set and alarmed the lady with the passion of his scorched eyes. Thereafter he went to the studio once a week to collect his paycheck, and to marvel at the expense and obsession of the make-believe. Buñuel is sometimes enlisted, as a committed social critic. But the first surrealists recognized that daft Hollywood had made the most dreamy of films, the most thorough aspirations to disorder. As Buñuel wandered the MGM lot, he may have felt himself in the kingdom of the surrealist manifesto: "In these studios, everthing seemed possible; had they wanted to, they could have reconstructed the universe."

He hobnobbed with Josef von Sternberg and Chaplin. Charlie had him home several weekends, always insisting that the shocking *Chien Andalou* be run for guests already stunned by sun and glamor. (Years later, Buñuel learned that the apparently admiring Chaplin had also used the movie as an ogre-deterrent to the naughtiness of his daughter, Geraldine.) One day, Buñuel attended an MGM fete as Louis B. Mayer congratulated the entire staff on their spirit of cooperation. "I was beside myself," writes our LB, "the whole scene was beyond me." At last the studio realized he was doing nothing for them. He provoked the crisis with the zeal of all self-destructives. Asked to listen to Lily Damita speaking Spanish to discover whether she had an accent, he retorted, "I am not here as Spaniard. I'm here as a Frenchman. And what's more, you go tell Thalberg that I don't waste my time listening to women who sleep around!"

As he departed, and even afterwards, he treasured the dreamland: "When I remember that strange way of life, the Californian heat, the American naiveté, I still have the same good, warm feelings as I did then." That's not irony; it's rather more the pleasure of someone who has found an environment of madness, luck and sleepy enchantment. Buñuel seems never to have treated his own life as a bank balance or a locomotive: it neither grows nor gets anywhere. He gives himself up to whim, coincidence, and fate, living eventually in Mexico, despite his aversion to the heat, resuming his career as a director in the 1940s only because someone asked him, giving up imminent U.S. citizenship to make cheap quickies in Mexico, one of the least esteemed film industries in the world.

Yet Mexico allowed Buñuel to reenter the film community. All of a sudden, the dreamer reliant on his mother's money became a professional director, working on assignments, but knifing his own fun into the cracks between clichés. He seldom outraged the Mexican system; he merely showed how far all "sensible" or "businesslike" films partake of fantasy and long for obscure objects of desire. In middle age, he settled down, spacing out his favorite café-life with movies, shot in four weeks for a couple of hundred thousand dollars each—*Gran Casino, Los Olvidados, La Hija del Engano, Subida al Cielo, Robinson Crusoe, El,* a version of *Wuthering Heights, La Illusion Viaja en Tranvia, Ensayo de un Crimen, Nazarin,* and so on.

These are still his least-known works, handicapped by (yet indifferent to) poor acting, rough technique, and enforced economies. They also revealed Buñuel as an intense poet of the automatic, insensate inner life, so convinced of film's fantastic instinct that he hardly distinguished between the "social realism" of *Los Olvidados* (about slum kids) and the landscape of paranoia's certainty in *El.* He learned the importance of scripts, and the necessary rejection of the picturesque in filmmaking. Buñuel's camera never sucks up to us with beauty. His style is off-hand, obvious, efficient—a way of seeing the extraordinary. He is one of those directors who knows the medium is so marvelous that the visual does not have to be stressed with point of view. Just look, the cinema says, and see this lifelike lie. So fixed on the enigma of the medium's achievement, Buñuel transcended issues of style.

Film reclaimed him. *Los Olvidados* won the prize for direction at Cannes; several of the Mexican films were released abroad. And so, in 1960, Spain invited him home to make a film. *Viridiana* was his most pungent attack on established religion, one of his best practical jokes, and an embarrassment to Spain when it won critical acclaim and the Palme d'Or at Cannes. By now, Buñuel was set on a pattern of living in Mexico and going to Europe to make films. He had attractive stars and larger budgets. His plain mysteries took on luster and stealth. The ailing man complained and said he was worn out. Perhaps he could not make masterpieces without believing they were inflicted on him. But they came anyway, one after another, so famous that most have English titles—*The Exterminating Angel, Diary of a Chambermaid, Belle de Jour, The Milky Way, Tristana, The Discreet Charm of the Bourgeoisie, The Phantom of Liberty* (perhaps his favorite), and *That Obscure Object of Desire.*

Just as there was nothing boastful or ingratiating in the films, so the autobiography has no pressing wish to be liked. The writer assumes both that we have seen the films, and that we know he would not have made them if he could explain them. So faithful to chance, impulse, and the unexpected, Buñuel filmed our daydream of hope and anxiety. He knew that film had so much force and drive—an express train of verisimilitude in whose slipstream we are windblown and exhilarated—that narrative or causal connection was redundant. He never thought to grow rich as a filmmaker; he never took the task that seriously. It was something to do, pleasant enough and amusing sometimes, but finally no more or less worthy than a sigh or a dry martini.

The man never emerges fully, not from secrecy or reticence, but because of his mistrust of palpable or reliable personality and his preference for ghosts. Buñuel and Dalí always claimed that they had meant *Un Chien Andalou* to be beyond interpretation. And in his last film, *That Obscure Object of Desire*, there was a moment when Buñuel had Fernando Rey pick up a sack and walk off carrying it, without knowing or even wondering why. There was just a rightness in the look, a mystery, that said more than all the answers in all the thrillers.

The book is as cryptic and elusive as the films. It is idiosyncratic, but never intimate. Something harsh and haughty remains. It may be a Spanish trait, or a ghost's lack of belief in real people. But the reader cannot quite ignore the streaks of malice in Buñuel's jokes, his absentminded cruelty, the interest in guns, the neglect of family life, and the throwaway remarks about liquor, whores, and violent death. He does truly reckon on life as a kind of brutal illusion, not worthy of gravity or sincerity. But the scorn may be a defense, like the gloom of a god who has given up on his world. Despite his lifelong defiance of God, Buñuel's sensibility invokes some designer of the game who watches the fools we make of ourselves. This is a god somewhere between a gambler and a film director.

As befits a book by a god masquerading as an atheist, it is not simply honest and not quite all Buñuel. It includes a chapter of memoirs by a sister, Conchita, and the rest was put together by Buñuel (in French first, not Spanish) with his recent scenarist, Jean-Claude Carrière. One can imagine them sitting down on cool days, being bored by the blunt facts of the life and bending towards digression. So the chronology is made picaresque with chapters on love affairs, bars, dreams, and chance, with anecdotes about guns, and with an entire chapter, "Pro and Con," that is a list of Buñuel's heartfelt but arbitrary tastes—for de Sade, Wagner, Fritz Lang, the cold, the north, the rain; against the blind, Borges, the press, statistics, vivisection; for cream pies, marinated herring, Toledo, snakes and rats, firearms, and secret passageways; against politics and prophets; for dwarves, funerals, and all sorts of little tools.

It is the best part of the book, the one most like a film. But, without ever setting out to be this, *My Last Sigh* is as true an addition to Buñuel's work as *Fun in a Chinese Laundry* was the ghost of an extra film by von Sternberg. It is deceptively simple and candidly devious. It is as chilly as the climate Buñuel preferred, and as pitiless as chance. Whether written, dictated, or talked out, it is one of the best books ever offered by a moviemaker. Though that context is not demanding enough to give proper credit, *My Last Sigh* is a delight and a scourge, like all of its writer's films.

And so Buñuel is dead, along with so many of

that generation of directors born when the medium was young and all-important—Renoir, Hitchcock, René Clair, George Cukor, Vittorio De Sica, Sergei Eisenstein, John Ford, Howard Hawks, Leo McCarey, Kenji Mizoguchi, Max Ophuls, Yasujiro Ozu, Roberto Rossellini, Alf Sjoberg, Preston Sturges, Irving Thalberg, Dziga Vertov, King Vidor, Jean Vigo, Josef von Sternberg—all born between 1894 and 1905. It is an astounding generation, and no one aware of its films and of those made now can hope that we will see their like again. Luis Buñuel is the proper human landmark for a moment when Europe met America and the schemes of religion, property, and progress were reassessed as dreams.

Buñuel was not as impressed by the world as he was by the imagination. He foresaw an afterlife in which he is as ghostly as all the creatures in films:

> Frankly, despite my horror of the press, I'd love to rise from the grave every ten years or so and go buy a few newspapers. Ghostly pale, sliding silently along the walls, my papers under my arm, I'd return to the cemetery and read about all the disasters in the world before falling back to sleep, safe and secure in my tomb.

Luis Buñuel: vague man, wholly ghost. A man devoted to sword canes. He had six of them, and felt safer when walking to think of his secret blade. Against sombreros, for solitude. (pp. 26–30)

David Thomson, "A Genius and His Ghosts," in *The New Republic*, Vol. 189, No. 18, October 31, 1983, pp. 26–7, 29–30.

A scene from *L'Age d'Or.*

MICHAEL WOOD
(essay date 1983)

[Wood is an English scholar and critic who has written extensively on film and contemporary Hispanic literature. In the following excerpt he reviews Buñuel's autobiography, paying particular attention to the themes Buñuel perceived as recurrent in his own work.]

Until he was about seventy-five, old age was a joke or an abstraction for Luis Buñuel. He had been seriously deaf since his forties, and had carefully cultivated the role of the hermit: lively in his mind, but not living in the world. "Look," he would say when he caught sight of a decrepit ancient on the street, "Have you seen Buñuel? Only last year he was still going strong. What a collapse." On the other hand, as this gag itself indicates, he was always capable of boyish humor, the sort of thing that made him a heroic mischief-maker in Spain before he turned his hand to the mischief of the movies. There is a nice late example in *My Last Sigh*, slightly flubbed by the eager economy of the English version. When the question of an Oscar came up for *The Discreet Charm of the Bourgeoisie*, Buñuel, straight-faced, told a group of Mexican reporters that everything would be all right, he had paid the $25,000 he had been asked for. "Americans may have their faults," he said, "but they are men of their word." Banner headlines in Mexico, scandal in Los Angeles, floods of telexes. Buñuel explains that it was a joke, calm returns. Three weeks pass, and the film receives an Oscar. Buñuel remarks to his friends, "Americans may have their faults but they are men of their word." The translation drops this admirable punch line.

In his life as in his films, Buñuel managed to cheat time, reshuffling its cards, making it seem tame or trivial. Then, as he says, in the last five or six years, old age began in earnest, *la vraie vieillesse*. Weakness of legs, eyesight, prostate. Dizziness, lapses of memory, failures of coordianation. Hospitals. The diagnosis is easy, he would say. I'm old, that is my chief disease. This would be his answer when you asked him how he felt. You might add, "Well, apart from old, how do you feel?" Then he would grin and say, "Apart from that, I feel terrible." There is a funny scene in his last film but one, *The Phantom of Liberty*, which records a personal brush with medicine. A doctor called Pasolini says to his worried client, "I should like to make a small incision. Simple medical curiosity. Whenever you like. When you can find the time." A pause. "Will tomorrow suit you?"

In his last years, Buñuel was waiting for death with something like impatience—the sort of impatience you show to a child who is slow with his shoelaces. The jokes would still come, though, and he welcomed occasional visitors. "I like solitude," he wryly says in his book, "as long as a friend comes and discusses it with me now and then."

The last time I saw him he was toying, quite theoretically, with the idea of political preferment in Mexico, that land of rising and falling favor. "If I had the choice," he mused, "I think I should like to be made director of a Thanatological Institute. . . ."

The irony doesn't reach us as easily from the pages of *My Last Sigh*, which is offered as an autobiography. In fact, it is a version of Buñuel's conversation as reconstructed by his friend and scriptwriter Jean-Claude Carrière and published in French last year. It does tell the story of Buñuel's life, and includes meditative interludes on topics like drink, dreams, chance, memory, and love. The English text reads extremely well, although it is marred by innumerable elisions, additions, and errors. In this review I have quoted from the translation whenever it doesn't seem to miss or mislay the point. We shall not, in any case, catch Buñuel's voice in French or in English—either his actual voice or the voice we may want to imagine for the author of his films. This is another, for him minor, medium. He doesn't want us to confuse his life and his work, and he is, as he reminds us, not a writing man. The transcription of talk is already a translation, even when the language doesn't change; it must edge the speaker toward coherence and keep stopping in the face of silence. We do see quite often, though, in both versions, something of the movement of Buñuel's mind. We recognize him clearly in the reasons he gives for liking the actor Michel Piccoli ("his humor, his secret generosity, his touch of madness and the respect he never shows me") and in the following confession, which faintly mocks but does not deny an authentic anxiety:

> When people ask me why I don't travel more, I tell them: Because I'm afraid of death. Of course, they all hasten to assure me that there's no more chance of my dying abroad than at home, so I explain that it's not a fear of death in general. Dying itself doesn't matter to me, but not while I'm on the road. I don't want to die in a hotel room with my bags open and papers lying all over the place.

Luis Buñuel died in a hospital in Mexico city on July 29 of this year; of heart and kidney failure or, as he would have said, of terminal old age. He was eighty-three.

After Hitchcock, Renoir, Lang, and Ford, Buñuel was the last of the great directors who began in silent films. His longevity, like theirs, was exaggerated by the rapid changes in the cinema itself. They all seem to have started in prehistory and stayed with us. And yet Buñuel's career was different from any other. It opened and closed in France, although he was originally Spanish and became a Mexican citizen. It very nearly halted as soon as it was underway, thanks to Buñuel's initial unwillingness to direct commercial movies and to Franco's sudden intervention in the affairs of Spain. After making three highly personal films (*Un Chien andalou, L'Age d'or, Las Hurdes*), Buñuel produced some Spanish potboilers and worked in dubbing and documentaries in France and the US, but didn't direct a film for fifteen years. Given the striking signature of his completed works, the way they pursue their unmistakable preoccupations, this long interruption becomes a sizable mystery. We can see how it came about, but how did he survive it, keep his vocation afloat?

He says in his book that he was sure at one stage that he would not make movies again. He once told me that he almost got a job teaching history at Princeton— he had a degree from Madrid in the subject—but that the Spanish friend who could have arranged matters simply refused to, because he would rather see Buñuel starve than give up the cinema. Buñuel sees this response as an aspect of his luck, an interruption in one line that fed a continuity in another. I'm inclined to see it as a reflection of his own enduring, if subterranean, determination. Franco incidentally is said not to have disliked *Viridiana*, although the film was banned in Spain. Still, Buñuel murmurs with deceptive mildness, "given what he'd seen in his lifetime, it must have seemed incredibly innocent to him." (p. 6)

We can't psychoanalyze a man at this sort of distance and with this sort of material, and I couldn't do it anyway. But we can hardly miss the torment in these images, the layer upon layer of rage and the refusal of rage. "I've managed to live my life," Buñuel says in his book, "among multiple contradictions without ever trying to rationalize or resolve them"; but he overstates his equanimity. He did what I suppose many artists do, although I don't know another case as clear as his. He saved his nightmares for his work, cherished them by protecting them from all explication or cure, emptied them, more or less unexamined but craftily situated, into his haunted and haunting films.

He speaks in *My Last Sigh* of "the perfect innocence of the imagination," which he discovered, he says at the age of sixty or sixty-five—somewhere between *Viridiana* and *Belle de jour*, I would suggest. "Since then, I accept everything. I say, 'All right, I sleep with my mother, so what?' and *almost* immediately the images of crime and incest depart, driven off by my indifference." The *almost* is a very delicate touch. It is this feeling that accounts for what critics have called the serenity of Buñuel's last films. The element of untruth or impossibility in the feeling, the sense that the imagination, even if it is less guilty than we have always feared, can't be as innocent as all that, stains the serenity with unforgettable flecks of unease and disgust. A man who started in film by slashing an eye can't take it all back. It would be like another miracle at Lourdes, or the recantation of W. C. Fields.

In his personal life things must have been easier, resolved by Buñuel's permanent commitment to courtesy. It is possible, he would say, to have the whole story of Oedipus playing in your head and still behave properly at the table. By contrast, a surrealist insult, for Buñuel as for Breton, was an extravagant ethical gesture, and not at all to be confused with bad manners. At Chaplin's Hollywood home Buñuel and his friends once tried to tear down a Christmas tree (shouting, in one version of this exploit, "Down with symbols!"). They succeeded only in scraping their hands, and settled for jumping on the presents instead. "Luis," someone said, "that is genuine rudeness." "Not at all," Buñuel answered. "It is anything but rudeness. It is an act of vandalism and subversion." He was quick, later, to see the puerility of his behavior and his reply, but would, I think, have wished to maintain the distinction between discourtesy and deliberate provocation. It is one of the discreet arms of the bourgeoisie to pretend that all opposition is merely ill-bred or ignorant, cannot have serious motives.

Buñuel studied in Madrid, switching from agriculture and biology to history. He met Dalí and Lorca, and began to go to the movies, liking best of all the comedies of Ben Turpin, Harold Lloyd, and Buster Keaton, Buñuel was later to write that Keaton could give "lessons to reality," and the influence of these early films on his work is important. In Buñuel's world the arbitarary is always ready to pounce, to knock us off high ledges, or even, in *The Phantom of Liberty*, to strike us dead in the street. His art turns comedy toward panic; keeps the comedy but gives panic an unusual outing.

From Madrid, in 1925, Buñuel moved to Paris in order to change his scenery and pratice for a possible future in international affairs. He still had no thought of becoming a director, although he now saw as many as three films a day, until he came across Fritz Lang's *Destiny*, which, as he says, illuminated his life. He knew then "without the shadow of a doubt" that he wanted to make movies. He had directed an Amsterdam production of de Falla's *Retablo de Maese Pedro*, an opera for puppets, voices, and orchestra, and he now apprenticed himself for a while to the French film director Jean Epstein, with whom he soon fell out, Epstein telling him to beware of the surrealists. Then Buñuel and Dalí decided to pool their dreams ("I told him I had dreamed . . . of a thin cloud cutting the moon and of a razor blade slashing an eye . . . . He told me that he had seen in a dream. . . a hand full of ants") and wrote *Un Chien andalou*. The film was welcomed by the surrealists, after some hesitation on their part— it was not easy to join that chapel—and Buñuel's next film, *L'Age d'or*, to which Dalí's contribution was much slighter, was a full-blown surrealist event, complete with slogans and fighting and broken furniture and the banning of the work by the police.

Buñuel visited Hollywood at this time, and tells what I find the funniest story in his book about an encounter there. He had made up a synoptic chart of all the possible plot situations in the American movies of the day; setting (gangster, Western, tropical), period, main characters, the fate of the heroine were all foreseen, awaiting permutation. Buñuel's friend Ugarte was much amused by all this, and knew the system by heart. Returning from a sneak preview of Sternberg's *Dishonored* Buñuel is asked by the producer what he thinks. The film is fine, he says. The director is very good. And such an original story, the producer suggests. No, Buñuel has to disagree. The thing about Sternberg is that he takes banal stories and transforms them entirely. The producer is shocked. A banal story! When the star gets shot? Marlene Dietrich, no less. Buñuel politely says he knew in the first five minutes of the film that Dietrich would be shot at the end. The producer begins to get angry. Buñuel takes him home for a drink, and wakes up Ugarte—it is very late. "Listen," Buñuel says, "it's about a film." Ugarte nods, still half asleep. "Setting: Viennese. Period: the Great War. At the beginning of the film we see a whore. And we see clearly that she is a whore. She picks up an officer in the street, she. . . " "That's enough," Ugarte says, getting up, yawning, already on his way back to bed. "She gets shot at the end."

Buñuel returned to Spain to make one on the most remarkable of all his films, *Las Hurdes*, a documentary about a diseased and isolated community in the west of Spain, people, Buñuel says, who loved their lost country, "that hell which belonged to them." After this came the fifteen years' break I have mentioned. The freshest and least predictable part of Buñuel's book concerns his memories of the clashes and confusions of the civil war. He is sane without being pious. He was a theoretical anarchist, but bewildered by the actual anarchy on the streets, and his practical sympathies went to the organized communists—the syndicalists, he notes sadly, hated them even more than the fascists. With distressing frequency names come up in his book with the subsequent death of their owners tagging alone like a prophecy: these Dominicans were shot, this archbishop was killed, this boy was shot by the Republicans, this couple was executed by the fascists; these priests faced the firing squad. At times the book begins to sound like Charlus's roll-call of the dead in Proust's last volume. Buñuel thinks often of Lorca and how frightened he must have been that night in 1936 when he was taken to the olive grove to be murdered.

Buñuel worked in the embassy of the Spanish Republic in Paris, and then, when the civil war ended and the other war began, in the Museum of Modern Art in New York. He lost his job in an early witch hunt and a little later, in Hollywood, directed an eerie sequence, starring Peter Lorre and a severed hand, in Robert Florey's *Beast with Five Fingers*. Then he moved to Mexico, where he lived until his death, making what were for many years annual trips to Europe. He returned twice from the relative obscurity of his exile: with *Los Olvidados*, a grim portrait of destroyed childhood, a distant echo no doubt, buried

in the Mexican slums, of fights not fought in Calanda, Oedipus betrayed; and with *Viridiana*, a film famous for its blasphemous travesty of Leonardo's *Last Supper*, and notable because, among other things, it introduced into Buñuel's movies the actor Fernando Rey, who was to become in many ways the director's screen self, especially in *Tristana*. Buñuel's Mexican films are very patchy, some of them awful, others, like *El* and *The Criminal Life of Archibaldo de la Cruz*, triumphs over tiny budgets and insipid acting. After *Viridiana*, for which he went back, amid much outcry, to Franco's Spain, Buñuel made two fine films in Mexico, *The Exterminating Angel* and the short *Simon of the Desert*.

He shot *Tristana* in Spain, and parts of *That Obscure Object of Desire*; and meanwhile made *Diary of a Chambermaid*, *Belle de jour*, *The Milky Way*, *The Discreet Charm of the Bourgeoisie*, and *The Phantom of Liberty* in France. In his book he rememebers his life but gallops through his movies. When he reaches page 197 (out of 256), he is forty-six and has directed three films (out of thirty-two). He doesn't feel like talking about the rest of his work—that is not his job, he insists, sounding like the famous writer in James's "Figure in the Carpet," *ce n'est pas à moi de la faire*. He offers casual comments only, tells a few stories.

He was never in any case given to making critical remarks about his films ("all hopeless," was his favorite way of getting rid of the subject), but he does say two things of exceptional interest in this book. First, he observes that in life and in his films he has been fascinated by repetitions. A character in *The Exterminating Angel* raises his glass and proposes a toast. Everyone drinks. A few seconds later, as if nothing had happened, the man proposes exactly the same toast again. No one pays any attention to him, and he sits down, disconcerted. *My Last Sigh* opens with a similar scene, offered as an illustration of the eclipses of Buñuel's mother's memory in her later years.

I'd walk into her room, kiss her, sit with her awhile. Sometimes I'd leave, then turn around and walk back in again. She greeted me with the same smile and invited me to sit down—as if she were seeing me for the first time. She didn't remember my name.

What is striking here is not only the mother's separation from her son and her past, but the son's interest in provoking the repetition, like the little boy in *Beyond the Pleasure Principle* playing *fort* and *da*.

Second. Buñuel identifies as a recurring theme in his films the impossibility of satisfying a simple wish—like going home or having dinner with your friends—and still less, we may add, slightly more complicated ones, like making love or killing someone. Or like making a film during fifteen years of unwilling abstinence. Extraordinary obstacles fall across the paths of Buñuel's characters' plans: a phone call from a minister, a mysterious inability to leave a room, a corpse in a restaurant, the army on maneuvers dropping in for a meal. In *The Phantom of Liberty* stories are interrupted because the narrative forgets them, goes off somewhere else. In *The Criminal Life of Archibaldo de la Cruz* a man fails to murder a nun because she falls down an elevator shaft as he chases her, stranding him with the innocence he was trying to get rid of.

Repetitions, interruptions. They form an image of a life which moves in erratic circles, which will not go forward; which baffles linear time, as Buñuel's own life did until his last years. The price is that you yourself are baffled, desire becomes permanent and unappeasable, and lack is all you truly know. Buñuel's most frequent dream, he says, is that of the train—"I must have dreamed it hundreds of times." The train enters a station and stops. Buñuel would like to get out and stretch his legs, but is wary, because he knows this dream, the train will go without him if he does. He puts one foot on the platform, everything seems normal, other people are getting off. He decides to risk it, puts the other foot down, and the train departs like a cannon shot, whisking away all his luggage. He is alone on the platform and he wakes up. More speculatively he says, "It is not neccessary that we should be here living and dying." He is not discussing determinism and free will, he is describing the experience of contingency as a shudder, a form of vertigo. It is from this besetting, almost domesticated uncertainty, that Buñuel's irony springs, and his humanity too, which is a form of conquest, an assertion made not only against the odds but against his better judgment and knowledge. For many people the thought that we cannot have what we want is grounds for giving up wanting. For others, an occasion for bravura and stubbornness—the impossible will take a little while. For Buñuel it is simply a major fact about himself and the rest of us, and deserves all the patient scrutiny he can give it. He became an authority of what we miss.

The small voice of optimism may murmur that life is not all lack, that we sometimes get what we want, and Buñuel knows this too. There is a marvelous scene in *The Phantom of Liberty*, one of the most lyrical I can think of in the movies, where a young man, tortured by sexual desire for his aging aunt, has taken her to a hotel. There are quarrels, tears, delayed resistance on the aunt's part. Finally she gives in, asks him not to look, and undresses. The camera finds her naked in bed, but her body instead of the fading or crumpled carcass we expected, is that of a luminously healthy young girl. The boy can't believe his eyes, or his luck. There are further quarrels, even violence, but all ends in peace and connection. The imagination really does have its moments of innocence, even of grace.

"I'd love to rise from the grave," Buñuel says in the last lines of *My Last Sigh*, "every ten years or so and go buy a few newspapers. Ghostly pale, sliding silently along the walls, my papers under my arm, I'd return to the cemetery and read about all the disasters in the world before falling back to sleep, safe and secure in my tomb." We should not miss the mockery, of himself and of what we expect of him, in the faint enlargement of his appetite for disaster. Still, the newspapers will no doubt cater amply for appetites bigger than Buñuel's and he himself will manage something more substantial than these spectral decennial visits. From screens of all sizes, as long as there are screens and people to watch them, his films will seek us out, ruffling the most settled of feathers, and making us wonder how we can possibly keep mistaking the barely acceptable for the thoroughly inevitable, and how we can go on converting our haphazard moral and social constructions, the treacherous trains of our dreams, into prisons that cover the earth. (pp. 8, 10, 12)

Michael Wood, "Farewell Buñuel," in *The New York Review of Books*, Vol. XXX, No. 17, November 10, 1983, pp. 6, 8 10, 12.

SOURCES FOR FURTHER STUDY

Aranda, Francisco. *Luis Buñuel: A Critical Biography*. Translated and edited by David Robinson. London: Secker & Warburg, 1975, 327 p.
    Study of Buñuel's life and work that contains an anthology of his surrealist texts, film criticism, and scenarios.

Buache, Freddy. *The Cinema of Luis Buñuel*. Translated by Peter Graham. London: The Tantivy Press, 1973, 207 p.
    Critical exploration of sixteen films by Buñuel.

Doniol–Valcroze, Jacques and Bazin, André. "Conversation with Buñuel." *Sight and Sound* 24, No. 4 (Spring 1955): 181–85.
    Interview with Buñuel that focuses on his surrealist and Mexican films.

Durgnat, Raymond. *Luis Buñuel*. Berkeley: University of California Press, 1977, 176 p.
    General assessment of Buñuel's career that also discusses many of his films individually.

Higginbotham, Virginia. *Luis Buñuel*. Boston: Twayne Publishers, 1979, 222 p.
    Critical study that pays particular attention to Buñuel's later masterpieces.

Kyrou, Ado. *Luis Buñuel: An Introduction*. Translated by Adrienne Foulke. New York: Simon and Schuster, 1963, 208 p.
    Survey of Buñuel's life and career, containing excerpts

from his screenplays and criticism by such figures as Octavio Paz and Andre Breton.

Mellen, Joan, ed. *The World of Luis Buñuel: Essays in Criticism.* New York: Oxford University Press, 1978, 428 p.

Collection of biographical and critical essays on Buñuel.

Rubinstein, Elliot. "Buñuel's World, or the World and Buñuel." *Philosophy and Literature* 2, No. 2 (Fall 1978): 237–48.

Analysis of Buñuel's vision of humanity that maintains: "His particular achievement is the sheer variety of worlds he has discovered or reanimated."

Additional coverage of Buñuel's life and career is contained in the following sources published by Gale Research: *Contemporary Authors*, Vols. 101, 110; *Contemporary Authors New Revision Series*, Vol. 32; *Contemporary Literary Criticism*, Vol. 16; and *Hispanic Writers*.

Guillermo Cabrera Infante

1929–

(Has also written under the pseudonym G. Cain) Cuban-born novelist, short story writer, essayist, critic, scriptwriter, editor, journalist, nonfiction writer, translator, and poet.

INTRODUCTION

*C*abrera Infante is considered one of Latin America's most original and influential writers. Although he has lived in exile from Cuba since the mid-1960s, much of his fiction is set in Havana, where he was raised, and details the repressive and violent social and political climate during the Fulgencio Batista regime prior to the Cuban revolution (1959). Cabrera Infante relies heavily on playful use of language, and he has abandoned traditional literary forms, creating pieces that are loosely structured and nearly devoid of plot. His satiric, inventive prose has been compared to that of Lewis Carroll, James Joyce, Jonathan Swift, and Laurence Sterne.

Cabrera Infante was born in the Oriente province of Cuba. His mother, together with his father, a journalist and typographer, founded the local Communist party and suffered arrest and the confiscation of their property when Guillermo was seven years old. Following a brief period in prison, the parents moved their impoverished family to Havana. Cabrera Infante became interested in literature while attending the University of Havana, which he left in 1948 to pursue a literary career. He edited the journal *Bohemia* and founded the literary magazine *Nueva Generación*, and helped establish the Cinemateca de Cuba (Film Library of Cuba). In 1952 Cabrera Infante was jailed and fined for publishing a story in *Bohemia* that contained English-language obscenities. Two years later he became the film critic for *Carteles*, one of Cuba's most popular magazines, writing under the pseudonym G. Cain. Cabrera Infante's writing at this time was censored for its political content and reflects the author's clandestine activity against the Batista regime. When Fidel Castro seized power in 1959, Cabrera Infante became involved with the new government, serving on the Bureau of Cultural Affairs and later becoming cultural attache to Brussels. He also acted as the director of *Lunes de Revolución*, the literary supplement to the pro-Castro newspaper *Revolución*. In 1960 Cabrera Infante published his first fiction collection, *Así en la paz como en la guerra*. The following year Castro disbanded the *Lunes de Revolución* when its editors protested the censorship of a documentary film directed by Cabrera Infante's brother, Saba Cabrera Infante, which depicts Havana's nightlife during the height of Batista's rule. Leaving Cuba in 1965, Cabrera Infante eventually settled in London, where he currently resides. In 1967 his novel *Tres tristes tigres* (*Three Trapped Tigers*) was published, earning the author international recognition. For several years, however, his income was derived primarily from the writing of such screenplays as *Wonderwall* (1968), *Vanishing Point* (1970), and *Under the Volcano* (1972). Throughout the 1970s Cabrera Infante continued writing books in Spanish, including *Vista del amanecer en el trópico* (1974; *View of Dawn in the Tropics*), *Exorcismos de esti (l)o* (1976), and *La Habana para un Infante difunto* (1979; *Infante's Inferno*). In the 1980s he traveled and lectured throughout the United States and Latin America in addition to publishing his first book written in English, *Holy Smoke* (1985). Cabrera Infante continues to publish essays regularly in newspapers, popular magazines, and scholarly journals.

Cabrera Infante's fictional works typically deal with Cuba's political experience in the twentieth century. The short stories in *Así en la paz como en la guerra* are written in the mode of social realism and convey the author's contempt for the Batista dictatorship. Cabrera Infante later repudiated this work as being overly realistic at the expense of creativity. In *Three Trapped Tigers*, the novel which is generally regarded by critics as one of the most important contemporary works of fiction to emerge from Latin America, Cabrera Infante abandoned social realism in favor of a humorous narrative developed through a series of monologues. This work, which chronicles Havana nightlife on the eve of Batista's fall, abounds with puns, parodies, and wordplay. Written primarily in Cuban street vernacular and narrated by several characters, *Three Trapped Tigers* depicts a society devolving into physical and spiritual confusion. Within this society, language becomes grotesque and is reshaped by people struggling for new means of communication. In *View of Dawn in the Tropics* Cabrera Infante again explores pre-Castro Cuba. Similar in structure to *Así en la paz como en la guerra*, this book is a compendium of over one hundred vignettes tracing the entire history of Cuba. Comparing it to Cabrera Infante's earlier writings, however, commentators found *View of Dawn in the Tropics* austere and pessimistic. Jorge H. Valdes has contended that the collection depicts Cuban history "as a repetitive and often accidental course of events always leading to an unhappy ending." Set in Havana, Cabrera Infante's next book, *Infante's Inferno*, chronicles the sexual initiation of a youth who bears many of the author's biographical traits. Because of its abundant wordplay and satiric content, this work has been frequently compared to *Three Trapped Tigers*, but many critics have faulted the author's imaginative linguistics as overblown in the later work.

As with his novels and short stories, Cabrera Infante imbues his nonfictional works with verbal exuberance and rich evocations of Cuban society. He has published two collections of film criticism, *Un oficio del siglo XX* (1963 ; *A Twentieth-Century Job*) and *Arcadia todas las noches* (1978), which critics have praised for their judicious insights into the work of American and European filmmakers. John King has additionally noted that *A Twentieth-Century Job* provides "an engaging portrait of Cuban intellectual life in the 1950s." *Holy Smoke*, the first book Cabrera Infante wrote in English, is a factual account of the history of the cigar and contains an anthology of famous smoking scenes from literature and film. Like his previous work, *Holy Smoke* bristles with puns and parodistic wordplay. Of *Holy Smoke* John Gross has noted, "Conrad and Nabokov apart, no other writer for whom English is a second language can ever have used it with more virtuosity."

CRITICAL COMMENTARY

JOHN UPDIKE

(essay date 1972)

[Considered an extraordinary stylist, Updike is one of America's most distinguished men of letters. Best known for such novels as *Rabbit Run* (1960), *Rabbit Redux* (1971), *Rabbit is Rich* (1981), and *Rabbit at Rest* (1990), he is a chronicler of life in Protestant, middle-class America. Against this setting, and in concurrence with his interpretation of the thought of Søren Kierkegaard and of Karl Barth, Updike presents people searching for meaning in their lives while facing the painful awareness of their mortality and basic powerlessness. A contributor of literary reviews to various periodicals, he has frequently written the "Books" column in the *New Yorker* since 1955. In the following review, which originally appeared in the *New Yorker* in 1972, Updike maintains that while Cabrera Infante's *Three Trapped Tigers* contains verbal ingenuity, the novel is flawed by a lack of tension and economy and is derivative of James Joyce's *Ulysses*.]

Some things are more lost in translation than others; jokes and Racine, for instance, lose more than newspapers and de Maupassant. In its original Spanish, *Tres Tristes Tigres*, by G. Cabrera Infante, won the Biblioteca Breve and contended for the Formentor Prize; in French, it won the Prix du Meilleur Livre Etranger. In English, however, as *Three Trapped Tigers*, the novel comes over as a tedious, verbose, jejune, self-delighting mess, and unless the publisher decides to distribute good-sportsmanship awards to those few readers who preserve to the end it should generate no prizes. One can deduce that the life of *Three Trapped* (though "sad" is what they originally were) *Tigers* lay in its skin of Spanish, and that a creature so ectomorphic, so narrowly vital, was bound to perish away from the nurture of its native climate. Or one might, less kindly, conclude that the novel was derivative, that its excitement derived from the translation of the methods of *Ulysses* into Cuban idiom, and that, restored to Joyce's mother tongue, it shows up as a tired copy.

Three Trapped Tigers offers to do for the Havana of 1958 what *Ulysses* did for the Dublin of 1904: wandering itineraries are mapped street by street, minor characters reappear in a studied interweave, a variety of voices abruptly solioquize, a kind of "Oxen of the Sun" procession of literary parodies is worked on the theme of Trotsky's assassination, an endless "Nighttown" drunkenness episode picks up the deliberate hungover banality of the Eumaeus sequence, and a female interior monologue closes the book. Unlike Joyce, however, Cabrera Infante packs most of his pyrotechnics and montage into the novel's first half and winds down into a more natural narrative tone. And, instead of attentive, soft-spoken, gradually solidifying Bloom, *Three Trapped Tigers* has for its hero an insubstantial, logomaniacal trio of would-be writers—Arsenio Cué, Bustrófedon (who is dead), and the principal narrator, Silvestre. As these three compile reams of undergraduate gags ("*Crime and Puns*, by Bustrófedor Dostowhiskey," "*Under the Lorry*, by Malcolm Volcano," "*In Caldo Brodo*, by Truman Capone," "*The Company She Peeps*, by Merrimac Arty," etc., etc.) and tootle around Havana in a convertible (Bustrófedon is there in spirit, like the Paraclete, or—as Infante might say Parakeats), they make little significant contact with the nonverbal world around them. Havana of this era

was notoriously full of prostitution and pickups, but the only instance of achieved intercourse throughout four hundred and eighty-seven pages occurs in some *tableaux vivants* staged for tourists. There is a good deal of partial undressing, and the work of one long night of seduction does jimmy a girl loose from her underpants, "*but*, BUT, where old Hitch would have cut to insert and intercut of fireworks, I'll give it to you straight—I didn't get any further than that." Later, Silvestre and Cué pick up two street flowers and proceed to bore them silly with puns and nonsense. One of the girls at last cries out, "Youse weird. You say real strange things. Both of you say the same strange things. Youse like twins, youse somethin' else. Whew! And you talk and talk and talk. Whaddya talk so much for?" To which the reader says, "Amen," and to which the author says, "Could she be a literary critic in disguise?"

A fearful air of congestion, of unconsummation, hangs over this book. Which may be deliberate: Batista's Havana is about to go under to revolution. Cabrera Infante, we are told by the dust jacket, served Castro's government as head of the Council of Culture, as a director of the Film Institute, as editor of a weekly magazine called *Lunes de Revolución*, and as a staff member of the Cuban Embassy in Brussels; in 1965, after returning to Havana, he "decided to leave Cuba," and he now lives in London. So his involvement was not trivial, and his viewpoint cannot be simple. Yet the coming storm impinges on the action of *Three Trapped Tigers* only once, when Cué drunkenly announces his intention to "join Fffidel." Silvestre argues that he is crazy, it's like joining the Foreign Legion. "Nashional," Cué answers. "The National Leshion." The topic is then dropped, and the two spend another hundred pages driving and drinking and punning and remembering the palindromes of Bustrófedon. An American reader, especially now that Cuba is remoter than China, longs for a more anatomical portrait of this Havana that has vanished. In the first pages, such a portrait— a cross-section of corrupted and dissatisfied lives—seems to be promised. A sharp imitation of a night-club m.c.'s bilingual prattle lifts the curtain on some monologues by a kept woman, a movie-struck child, an underpaid printer. We read a letter written back to her village by a recent emigrant to the city; we eavesdrop on a psychiatric session that reappears throughout the book. Silvestre introduces himself:

I am a press photographer and my work at that time involved taking shots of singers and people of the *farándula*, which means not only show business but limelights and night life as well. So I spent all my time in cabarets, night clubs, strip joints, bars, *barras, boîtes*, dives, saloons, *cantinas, cuevas, caves* or caves. . . . Sometimes, when I had nothing to do after work at three or four in the morning I would make my way to El Sierra or Las Vegas or El Nacional, the night club I mean not the hotel, to talk to a friend

Principal Works

Así en la paz como en la guerra (short fiction) 1960

Un oficio del siglo XX [as G. Cain] (criticism) 1963
  [*A Twentieth-Century Job*, 1991]

Tres tristes tigres (novel) 1967
  [*Three Trapped Tigers*, 1971]

Wonderwall (screenplay) 1968

Vanishing Point (screenplay) 1970

Under the Volcano (screenplay) 1972

Vista del amanecer en el trópico (short fiction) 1974
  [*View of Dawn in the Tropics*, 1978]

O (essays) 1975

Exorcismos de esti(l)o (essays, poetry, and prose fragments) 1976

Arcadia todas las noches (lectures) 1978

La Habana para un Infante difunto (novel) 1979
  [*Infante's Inferno*, 1984]

Holy Smoke (nonfiction) 1985

who's the emcee there or look at the chorus flesh or listen to the singers, but also to poison my lungs with smoke and stale air and alcohol fumes and be blinded forever by the darkness. That's how I used to live and love that life and there was nobody or nothing that could change me.

O.K., fine; rather lengthily said, but we obediently settle down for a tour of tropical night life. We meet a bongo drummer; we don't quite catch his name, but it doesn't matter, since he talks in Silvestre's voice, though he seems to be hung up on a little gringo chick called Vivian Smith-Corona, whereas Silvestre is hung up on Cuba Venegas, a local singer who looks better than she sings. We go back to Silvestre, who is trying to tell us about a great Negro singer, La Estrella, but the story keeps unravelling on him—maybe because this is "an island of double and triple entendres told by a drunk idiot signifying everything." Our eyes begin to sting in the smoke and stale air. Now an American tourist, a writer called Campbell, writes a funny story about a walking stick he bought fresh off the ferry from Miami, and about taking another off an outraged native because he thinks it's his, and then his wife produces *her* version of what happened, and he rewrites it (or perhaps this is meant to be a translation by somebody called Rine), and the wife does a second version, and then we get pages of the anti-works of the late Bustrófedon, and the above-mentioned parodies of Cuban authors on Trotsky's assassination, which might be the best part of the book if you're Cuban (it seems funny even in English), but by now Arsenio Cué is revving up his convertible, and

we blearily realize that, whatever happened in Havana in 1958, this book isn't going to tell us. "Mare Metaphor is loosed upon the world. Rhetoric of the nation?" Cabrera Infante asks, as if hopeful that his stream of literary consciousness will somehow apply to Cuba. He applies it, but it doesn't stick. Though his translators work furiously to shore up the slippage, throwing in anachronisms like space-shot terminology, the slang word "gig," and "Agnewsticism," they can't keep the gobbets of "Esperanglish" and the limp avant gardisms and the liquorish 4 a.m. foolery from pulling loose from any reality we care to recognize or consent to care about.

The eclectic culture of Americanized Havana, Cabrera Infante seems to be saying, deserves an eclectic novel as its nostalgic monument. But eclecticism is itself a borrowed method by now. *Ulysses*, static and claustrophobic enough, is energized throughout by the tactful, evocative prose of a master short-story writer, and it draws for its allusions upon the immense perspective of European culture since Homer. Cabrera Infante writes run-on, like Faulkner but without Faulkner's intensity of self-hypnosis, and his perspective extends little farther than the mass culture of the giant nation to the north; the horizon of felt history for him appears to be Trotsky's murder in 1940. The book crucially lacks tact—the tension and economy that enforce themselves when method and material are in close touch. A mass of memories and a heap of verbal invention have been hopefully tossed toward one another, but confusion isn't fusion.

That Latin America can produce adventurously original novels has been shown many times over, from Machado de Assiz on. A recent striking instance, and an instructive contrast to *Three Trapped Tigers*, is Gabriel García Márquez's *One Hundred Years of Solitude*. Here an array of fantastic premises (substantial ghosts, everyday miracles, magic that works, a village so isolated only gypsies can find it, a man tattooed on every inch of his skin, a man who fathers seventeen sons by seventeen women, a family of repeating names and insatiable incest) is breezily set forth by topic sentences that seem jokes, and then maintained with an iron consistency and kept rolling until the amusing becomes the magnificent— a magnificent symbolic contraption expressing a family's fate, a continent's experience, and Time's impenetration of humanity. The novel's Olympian ease and its catholic acceptance of horror and splendor as they arise in this our "paradise of misery" could not have been achieved in the United States, and no European novel would contain its joyous emptiness, its awed memory of a world "so recent that many things lacked names, and in order to indicate them it was necessary to point." The book even has a texture all its own: a dense translucence, a flow of long paragraphs that yet do not linger, that feel laconic, like stories the teller and listener already obscurely share and that are being not so much invented as called from the shadows. Such a novel, unlike Infante's sophomoric farrago, has learned from other novels how to become itself. (pp. 365–69)

John Updike, "The Avant Garde," in his *Picked-Up Pieces*, Alfred A. Knopf, 1975, pp. 352–93.

MATEO PARDO

(essay date 1978)

[In the following review, Pardo faults Cabrera Infante's use of the prose vignette form in *View of Dawn in the Tropics*.]

Guillermo Cabrera Infante's new book, **View of Dawn in the Tropics**, is a curious example of what can happen when a writer returns to the scenes of his early successes. His admirers will look in vain for the freshness and charm of his first book of short stories or the wild and sometimes exciting verbal experimentation of his first novel. This collection of 101 historical vignettes, printed on 145 largely empty pages, is an attempt, Micheneresque in its audacity and Hemingwayesque in the laconism of its style, to tell the story of Cuba from its geological formation to the present day and for all eternity, but it succeeds only in making one wonder at the immensity of the author's hubris. What, one puzzles, was he thinking of?

The answer lies in Cabrera Infante's earlier work, to which **View of Dawn in the Tropics** is related by both title and narrative technique. The title was initially used for an earlier novel which won the Seix Barral prize in Barcelona in 1964. Banned by the Spanish censors because of its prorevolutionary passages, it was expurgated and rewritten by the author and resubmitted with a new title, **Three Trapped Tigers**. It was a great critical success and Cabrera Infante's name was associated by critics with those of Garcia Marquez and Vargas Llosa as another representative of the "boom" in the Latin American novel. The vignette form is also familiar to readers of Cabrera Infante: he used it in his first book, **Así en la Paz como en la Guerra**, published in 1960 and also widely acclaimed by critics.

The fifteen vignettes included in that work recounted some of the heinous crimes committed by the Batista regime against both revolutionaries and nonrevolutionaries. Each was followed by a short story which dealt with Cuban life during the 1950s. The impact of the whole was, at the time, quite powerful. Cabrera Infante was catapulted to fame along with an entire generation of Cuban writers who had turned 30 in 1959. The political and social revolution of the *barbudos* seemed to be bearing its literary fruits. The atmosphere of the period was, as the cliche goes, electric. Nothing seemed impossible because an impossible revolution had triumphed. Cabrera Infante, the editor of the island's newest and most avant-garde literary magazine, *Lunes de Revolución*, seemed to be securely placed in the very cockpit of history. But in 1961 the revolutionary government closed *Lunes* down, and Cabrera Infante went to Brussels as a member of the Cuban diplomatic mission. His first novel was not accepted for publication in Cuba and in 1965 he officially defected. He seemed to be exchanging the enviable role of revolutionary writer for the even more enviable one of writer as an anti-Communist exile. Famous and full of promise, he has spent the intervening years apparently producing a mammoth autobiographical novel, **Cuerpos Dirinos**, the prologue of which was published in 1968.

Only a writer of solid talents could have survived the sort of reputation that naturally grew out of such glamorous historical circumstances. Cabrera Infante has not proven to be such a writer. The passage of time has only served to bring out his weaknesses and sap his strengths. The appearance of **View of Dawn in the Tropics** in English confirms this. In **Three Trapped Tigers** Cabrera Infante had shown a marvelous ear for colloquial Cuban Spanish and a lively sense of humor that manifested itself in a seemingly unending flow of puns and absurd situations. He sustained a high degree of dramatic tension by the implied contrast between the corrupt night life of Havana and the struggle in the Sierra. But the years have taken their toll and when one reads **Three Trapped Tigers** today one realizes that this implied contrast was at least partially a product of the historical period in which it was first written and one is obliged to lament the amputation to which the work was subjected. Perhaps the passages dealing with the revolutionaries gave it the internally generated equilibrium it sorely lacks today.

Cabrera Infante's early book of short stories has suffered the same fate. The notoriety it gained him seems now to have been largely a product of those exciting early years of the revolution. The vignettes he wrote for it and which contributed so much to his fame seem more than ever to give themselves away for what they are, imitations of Hemingway. And his return to that genre in his new book is a mistake that can be explained only if we assume that he overestimated his own understanding of the vignette form.

Only two great books have been written exclusively in this form, La Bruyere's *Les Caracteres* and Baudelaire's *Le Spleen de Paris*. One is a work of moral and psychological insight while the other is a collection of prose poems. There is no question of linear progression or chronological development in either. Each is composed of parts which seem to bear no necessary relationship to the other. The genre simply doesn't give a writer room to develop any subject that requires characterization or plot. It is meant for quick soundings of the human condition.

Given the above, one can understand why Cabrera Infante was tempted to use this technique. After all, what he has attempted to demonstrate in *View of Dawn in the Tropics* is that history is a collection of accidental events, an idiot's tale, and that the true meaning of life lies in the manly stoic virtues that some men and women manifest in their confrontation with it. This is, of course, Papa Hemingway's lesson, and Cabrera Infante is so engrossed by it that he gives us 101 slightly differing versions of it. It is here that one becomes aware of how badly he has miscalculated the possibilities the prose vignette could offer him. He thought that the necessarily accidental relationship between the different vignettes would intensify his basic theme. He goes out of his way to accentuate this effect by eliminating names and dates. But the sequence of the vignettes is chronological. The resulting contradiction destroys the book. On the one hand the reader is expected to derive from a succession of accidentally juxtaposed events the impression that history is absurd while on the other hand he is asked to admire the *macho* and *hembra* heroics of a series of Hemingwayesque souls.

The true essence of man, the reader is asked to believe, is ahistorical. The rub is that in order to make the reader see this, Cabrera Infante has attempted to create the semblance of a historical progression. This false history must be there so that the reader can be led to see its lack of authenticity. The prose vignettes then, must appear to be related in a historical manner. Unfortunately the nature of the prose vignette works against even the appearance of a relationship so that the reader is not at all fooled. He has no need to read the whole book in order to understand what the writer is trying to say because the message is apparent from the first pages and it never changes.

But certainly the road to bad art is paved with good intentions, and one's heart does go out to all those tortured, maimed and killed Cubans who people Cabrera Infante's vignettes. They deserved a better fate in literature as well as in their own lives. They are all quite redundantly exemplary, from the immolated Indian chief who refuses conversion to Christianity because Spaniards can go to heaven, to the mother of the anti-Communist patriot who accuses the present regime of inhumanity and cowardice. They pass before our eyes like shadows in a series of fragmented historical events. Some of these are as well known to those familiar with Cuban history as the Boston Tea Party is to Americans. The burning of the Indian chieftain, or the death of Jose Marti are just two of the many that fall into this category. Even the less familiar events of the Batista period lack freshness here if only because they seem to be variations of those with which the author regaled us in his first book. And two decades of anti-Castro propaganda have familiarized us all with the plight of the Cuban refugee. Cabrera Infante has nothing new to say about their sufferings. What then is one to do with such wisdom as the author deigns to communicate in his final vignette, which I quote in entirety?

And it will always be there. As someone once said, that long, sad, unfortunate island will be there after the last Indian and after the last Spaniard and after the last of the Cubans, surviving all disasters, eternally washed over by the Gulf Stream: beautiful and green, undying, eternal.

Yes, one is tempted to add, it will even survive *View of Dawn in the Tropics.*

One parting comment should be made concerning Ms. Levine's translation. On the whole it is quite adequate. In spite of some stylistic awkwardness and a handful of mistranslations (*taller* is a shop and not a theatre, a *mariscal de campo* is a division general not a field marshal, *perseguidoras* are women persecutors not patrol cars and a *turba* is a crowd or rabble not a thug) it does the work no disservice. (pp. 477–78)

Mateo Pardo, "Bad Art and Good Intentions," in *The Nation*, New York, Vol. 227, No. 15, November 4, 1978, pp. 477–78.

GUILLERMO CABRERA INFANTE WITH REGINA M. JANES
(interview date 1979)

[In the following interview, conducted in London in August 1979, Cabrera Infante discusses the role of the writer and the state of contemporary writing in Latin America and the United States.]

[Janes] *Do you feel that there's any connection between being afraid of things and the kind of control you want to exert over language when you write?*

[Cabrera Infante]: Oh, no, no, no, no, not at all. It has nothing to do with it. I don't believe in writing's being organic at all. It is something you do with your hands. You make use of your mind, of course, but composition is digital. You can say I was a daring young man not on a flying typewriter, but a very slow-moving one. I type very slowly and very badly, two fingers, and I incorporate the mistakes in the text.

Many people seem to feel that if they tamper with their minds in any way, in particular by going through psychoanalysis, their creativity will vanish.

Those are people who think of themselves as precious. I don't see myself like that at all. Not as precious, not even as different, not even special. To think of oneself as special is a sort of aristocratic thinking, parallel to the English practice of speaking this language with certain intonations and pronunciations of particular words that they think are different and above the rest of their countrymen. All I am is an individual, and I left my country because they thought of me as just somebody not even in a group but in a conglomerate of other people. (pp. 48–9)

But you must regard yourself as in some way different since you know that you can do things other people can't.

I'm sure that that's of absolutely no consequence at all. I'm sure that if they put themselves to it, they would be able to do it.

You can't really believe that.

No, but I do, absolutely. It's only when physical prowess or powers are invoked that you can say 'you can do it,' or 'you can't,' in something difficult like ballet dancing or running, things like that. But writing is really so easy. There is nothing very special about writing, and writers are commonplace. At least I think I am. I don't believe I was elected by God to become a writer. (It so happens that I don't believe in God—how is He then going to believe in me?) I don't see myself as one of the many avatars of Homer, as Joyce so proudly did, as Borges so modestly does. (I suppose the fact that those contemporary writers are sightless makes it possible for them to become, respectively, a twosome with the Grand Old Blind Man.) I didn't feel myself destined, much less predestined, to become a writer. It happened through an unhappy combination of opportunism and chance. I came, I saw, and I became the sedulous ape. It was as easy as that. To be a writer is as easy as eating apple pie. Some writers should eat humble pie instead. Compare the writer to an architect or to an engineer, even more to a physicist or a physician. Those are really difficult things, but writing involves almost no effort. Of course, good writing is one thing, and great writing is another. The question of quality does bring in another problem. But for the most part, for what they do, I tend to think that writers are overpaid. In spite of their asking for praise all the time, they usually have more than they deserve.

Can there ever be too much praise for a writer?

From the point of view of the writer, of course not; but from the point of view of the reader, making too much fuss about a given writer or a given piece of writing can be rather silly. There are many, many instances of a writer's being praised incredibly; you examine the writing and you find that there's absolutely nothing to it. You had a writer in the States two or three years ago who was even called a feminine version of Chaucer.

Who was that?

You're sure I'm not going to be sued if I say? Erica Jong, for instance. I read her book and it was total crap. It was a version of Jacqueline Susann. You have a useful distinction in English between reviewers and critics, but sometimes critics can be taken by reviewers or they try to be as expedient and up-to-date as the reviewers are.

What do you think of current writing in the U.S.?

Well, I think in the States you have a problem with writing. Really bad writers are placed not only as good writers but as geniuses. Like Saul Bellow, for instance, who is an atrocious writer. There's something of a great desert in writing in the States now, and you find people like Donald Barthelme, who is incredibly good, who is a writer of fragments, and has the courage to say so, but who for the past four years has not been the writer he used to be. He isn't up to his standards anymore. (pp. 49–51)

Why should there be more of a problem with modern American fiction than with modern Latin American fiction?

Modern Latin American fiction is also in trouble, but I think that English has something to do with it. English is a beautiful, useful language, but it is also an over-written language. You can see the over-kill in English now even in reading *Time* magazine, as I do every week. But language is a great problem for writers. They have to compete with so many things anyway, that if they have to compete with an over-written language, they are in great trouble. You can't possibly do in English what Faulkner did—that prose taken from Joyce through other sources like the Bible and the southern religious tradition. You simply can't do it again, can't be in the same position with respect to his language that Faulkner was, who had a more or less plain language before he came, plain English struggling to become more and more plain in every book, as in, say, Sherwood Anderson. But he could do it, and he got away with so many things, with terrible problems of syntax, that no writer could do now without being panned and pummeled by the critics for writing bad syntax and imitating Faulkner.

But why do you think modern Latin American fiction is also in trouble?

Have you ever heard of a new, really young Latin American writer? I haven't. The last one I heard of was Reinaldo Arenas in Cuba, who was the only Cuban writer who developed within the revolution, though what he was writing wasn't revolutionary at all in the way that they think of 'revolutionary' in politically totalitarian countries. 'Revolutionary' is a dangerous word; even Goebbels called the Nazi movement and takeover of Germany 'our revolution.' But Arenas was the last to appear, and he hasn't written anything in many years. It's true he has had many problems because he is a homosexual. He was charged with assaulting a minor and sentenced to a four-year term in Cuba. He was released before his time was up, but I haven't heard from him since, and that was four years ago. In the other Latin American countries, there is nobody really. In Mexico there was Gustavo Sáinz, who was some kind of hope, but his last novel is not good at all. And I read recently a very good essay on the literary situation in Argentina in which the author said more or less that the situation was hopeless and talked about a new writer called Manuel Puig. Well, Manuel Puig is 48 years old, published his first book in 1967, and if you call that a new writer you must call José Hernández [1834–86] a recently born writer.

About three years ago, I thought the problem might have something to do with the effect of military dictatorships, since all of Latin America from Cuba to Argentina is an enormous army barracks. But there are other countries that are not military dictatorships, and you can't find writers in them either. There is Venezuela, which proves nothing since there have never been good writers in Venezuela, and I've lost hope that there is going to be one. There is Colombia, but you don't have anyone writing there now who is any good, and there is Costa Rica, but imagine Costa Rica. It's like a garden after six. And Mexico—it's a very, very awkward country to live in, not to say to write about or to think of writing about.

You must think that the way Cortázar and Fuentes and García Márquez console themselves for being novelists by calling all good art revolutionary is rather silly, though at worst a way of trying futilely to outflank attacks from the left for being novelists at all.

I would disengage Fuentes, ancien ecrivain engagé, from that triste trio, reducing it to a duo doloroso. Fuentes is too intelligent to admit, today, such a silly thing. But I can confide in you (I know your lips are sealed) and tell you that yet another Latin American writer said (and even wrote) that no good writer could ever be a reactionary. Why, it's almost Gramsci upside down! Good writing is always revolutionary. Which could mean that good is beautiful and all that Platonic jazz—a clash of symbols. Of course, I find all those statements stupid. Furthermore, they are not even false. At least lies can be amusing and what with fiction being the opposite of truth, all fiction is lying. The decay of lying is the decay of fiction, which has become poorer since the second coming of the Realists, now disguised as Socialist Realists. Fiction must cry out: Give me lies or let me lie dormant!

Do you think the attention writers get these days might be part of the problem?

Something perhaps can be attributed to an excessive amount of attention, which can paralyze anybody. Many of the writers most talked about were already adults, as persons and as writers, when all this thing about the Latin American novel came about, people like Cortázar who is now 68. When he published his most acclaimed novel, he was really a grown-up man. My own experience tells me that a writer is in his prime when he's in his 30s. It is then that he has either read or seen or lived long enough to be able to have anything to say and to have acquired sufficient skills to say it properly or to say it the best way he can. After 40, quite frankly, rigor mortis sets in. It is very difficult to find a writer who has done anything valid after 40. There are exceptions of course. In Latin America, you have Borges; Thomas Mann wrote *The Magic Mountain*

in his 40s, and it is probably his best book; Laurence Sterne had the wisdom to start late, at 46, and to die by 55.

Do you think that what enables a writer to keep writing is his relation to ideas, to some predominantly intellectual concerns? Sterne, after all, had both an epistemology and a genre that he wanted to make fun of.

Ideas are for essayists and short-story writers. An extremely intelligent person like Borges can be both those but cannot be a novelist. Novelists are actually dumb writers, who make mistakes and never notice them. They are capable of writing chapters and even whole books made of trash—which is something the essayist and the short-story writer can't afford to do. I know what you are thinking, about to mention Joyce and Proust, but *Ulysses* and *A la recherche* cannot be considered true novels, and Kafka never wrote a novel but parables and fables of a given length. Only in Faulkner do you have a pure specimen of the novelist in the twentieth century, a dumb ox tracing the boustrophedon of the family tree's shade. The other writer you can call intelligent, Nabokov, wrote only puzzles and riddles and chess problems.

After that, I'm not going to ask if you're a novelist. But why should there suddenly develop a deficiency of dumb oxen after such a spate of them?

I suspect there are probably too many compensations, too many easy gratifications for younger writers, since the one common pattern among the writers all the fuss was made about is exile. Exile was very good for me, even the revolution with everything it brought to so many people in Cuba, including myself. If Fidel Castro hadn't won in 1959 and everything had gone on as before, by now I would be the editor of *Carteles*, the magazine of which I was managing editor in 1959, and I would be locally a very important person, which is something that can always kill a writer. At the time, my situation with Miriam Gómez was not stabilized enough; I would have continued my adolescent practice of going to bed with as many women as possible, and the rest of the time I would have been terribly busy doing the magazine. So I would never have written anything except the film criticism I wrote before 1959 and that crappy book of short stories I published in 1960. So that's my case, which is the case I know most about. Other writers who were more or less in exile, like Carlos Fuentes, saw not the reality, because I don't think for a writer there is such a thing as reality, but their material, their possible or feasible material, and were able to write the way they did in Paris or wherever they were living at the time. The same applied to Cortázar, to García Márquez. Again, the only real exception is Borges.

He is incomparable, isn't he? I think of that line Pope made such mock of in Peri Bathous: *'None but himself can be his parallel.'*

Cabrera Infante on inspiration:

Let's call it *embullo*, a Cuban word that means easy eagerness, a particularly gracious way of climbing on the bandwagons of the mind. I write every time the Holy Ghost whispers some sweet something in my ear. Of course I also write to meet deadlines, but that's not really writing. Sometimes it comes just because I sit down at the typewriter.

Cabrera Infante in his "The Invisible Exile," in *Literature in Exile*, edited by John Glad, 1990.

Cabrera Infante in Havana in 1952.

But he is the same case as Lezama Lima; the pattern is uncanny, except for Lezama's spoiling the symmetry by dying in 1976. . . . An extraordinary man, he was the only writer I've known who actually spoke as he wrote. He was asthmatic, and he made the same pauses in talking as he made in writing.

Look, if you think Lezama is special, you must think writers are special, and that not just anybody can do it if he sits down and begins to pound at the typewriter. It's very Johnsonian to think that anyone can do anything if he simply sets himself doggedly to it, but is it true?

That's the way I started writing, and that's the way I've been writing ever since. I started writing because I saw somebody who was writing something that was considered valuable, and I knew it was feasible for me, and I did it. It was a parody, of course; it was words. But it was something I could do and something that somebody else was doing and was being paid for and was being praised for. I never thought I was going to be a writer, I never said to myself, I want to be a writer when I grow up. As a matter of fact, what I wanted to be was a major-league baseball player. Looking at my height, my build, my sense of coordination, you can see how ludicrous it was, but that's what I thought at the time. And I can still tell you the roster of the St. Louis Cardinals in 1946 and of the Cuban leagues of the time.

Do you reject another Johnsonian dictum, then, that no one but a fool ever wrote except for money?

I think Gertrude Stein was right when she said that a writer needs only three things: praise, praise, and praise. But isn't that what most human beings need? If I were to tell you that you have good legs. (pp. 55–6)

Guillermo Cabrera Infante and Regina M. Janes, in an interview in *Salmagundi*, Nos. 52–3, Spring–Summer, 1981, pp. 30–56.

MICHAEL WOOD
(essay date 1984)

[Wood is an English scholar and critic who has written extensively on Hispanic literature. In the following essay, he examines Cabrera Infante's conception of the past and his use of language in *Three Trapped Tigers* and *Infante's Inferno*.]

"Any resemblance between literature and history," Guillermo Cabrera Infante wrote some years ago, "is accidental." He meant, of course, to offer the familiar disclaimer of fiction, particularly since his novel *Three Trapped Tigers* (1967), the work to which the remark was attached, mixed the names of living persons with those of transposed or invented characters: a Havana hodgepodge. But he also meant to offer a provocation, a sly and long-armed distinction. History for Cabrera is the domain of power and preening ambition, a nightmare into which countless people can't wait to hurl themselves, and from which many will escape only into death. Is there such a thing, he wondered in an article published last year in the Mexican magazine *Vuelta*, as "the tedium of power," a weariness of history's heights? The question was rhetorical since he was suggesting that suicide has become a political ideology in Cuba, the result of a combination of hubris and disappointment. "Absolute power disillusions absolutely."

Literature on the other hand is a form of freedom, not because it deals with the imaginary, but because it reconstructs the real in the mind, which is a protectable playground, a place that can be whisked, if necessary, out of the clutches of political practice. "Do you believe in writing or in scripture," a character asks in *Three Trapped Tigers*, "en la escritura o en las escrituras?" I "believe," his writer friend answers, "in writers," "en los escritores." He believes, as Cabrera himself says, in *Infante's Inferno*, in "the flesh made Word." But then this makes the writer a very curious creature, a voluntary inhabitant not of Dante's hell but of Derrida's limbo, a paltry, scribbling Plato to a host of rambling tropical versions of Socrates. He is important not because he can write, but because he can listen, and his job, Cabrera says, is "to catch the human voice in flight." The epigraph to *Three Trapped Tigers* comes from *Alice in Wonderland*: "And she tried to fancy what the flame of a candle is like after it is blown out. . . ."

There is pathos in this project, as Cabrera well knows, since the human voice cannot be caught in the crowded silence of a page, and two extinguished voices, that of a manic, memorable joker and that of a great black singer whose only record provides no trace of her gift, dominate *Three Trapped Tigers*. They are ghosts, whose thin, second, textual life is plainly a shadow of their garrulous first existence. They are doubly dead, since they die in the story, and in any case could only be whispers in a book, the flesh made alphabet. Yet this same sad tale, of course, may be a triumph of memory and continuing affection, the only life that is left, and a means of preserving treasures where history sees only trash. It is very much in this spirit that Cabrera Infante, in exile first in Brussels and now in London, reinvents his Cuba, which is mainly Havana, an excited, talkative, many-layered city, a scene of mauve and yellow light, of trolley cars and the gleaming sea, of rainstorms and stopped traffic and palm trees and a seemingly endless supply of stunning girls. As early as 1894, I learn from an old and rather prim *Encyclopaedia Britannica*, the city was famous for its hectic pursuit of pleasure:

> Cafes, restaurants, clubs, and casinos are both exceedingly numerous and largely frequented, forming a good indication of that general absence of domestic life. . . which surprises the European visitant.

The sentence might be an epigraph to *Three Trapped Tigers*, a celebration of Havana's interminable nights on the town. In *Infante's Inferno*, we do see something of Cuban domesticity, the other side of a busy coin, and spend a lot of time in the city's myriad movie houses.

Cabrera Infante was born in 1929, in Oriente province, which also nurtured Batista and Castro. His parents were committed communists, and he himself was active in the early days of Castro's revolution. He had already by that time become a film critic and founded the Cuban cinematheque—later he wrote the script for a very good American film, *Vanishing Point*. From 1959 to 1961 he edited a magazine called *Lunes de Revolución*, and a volume of stories called *In Peace as in War (Así en la Paz como en la Guerra)* brought him a substantial Cuban and European reputation. With *Three Trapped Tigers* he won a major Spanish prize, and entered the front rank of Latin American novelists. The book belongs with Cortázar's *Hopscotch*, García Márquez's *One Hundred Years of Solitude*, and Donoso's *The Obscene Bird of Night*, works that opened up a whole culture both to us and to its isolated or unwitting possessors, and made the later modernist offerings of most of the rest of the world look rather skimpy. Cabrerra Infante had meanwhile fallen foul of the censorship in Castro's Cuba, and been sent out of harm's way to be cultural attache in Brussels. Later he severed all connection with the Cuban government, and became a British citizen, or subject, as we still quaintly put it.

He likes, he told Rita Guibert in *Seven Voices*, Bogart's trembling hands in *The Maltese Falcon*, Henry Fonda in *My Darling Clementine*, Marlene Dietrich as Catherine the Great, "Conrad's rancid prose," "Carroll's dreamlanguage," "the radiance of the city in some pages of Fitzgerald," the music of Bach, Vivaldi, Wagner, Mozart, "the exact moment when Charlie Parker begins to play a solo," and "above all, the privilege of memory, without which none of the things mentioned above would have any meaning. . . ." I am selecting what I hope are representative items from a much longer and very lively list. Characteristically, one of Cabrera's complaints against Castro is that he has forced a loquacious people to become laconic.

"He didn't understand," the writer in *Three Trapped Tigers* says of a friend's response to a story. "He didn't understand that it was not an ethical fable, that I told it for the sake of telling it, in order to pass on a luminous memory, that it was an exercise in nostalgia. Without rancor towards the past." Cabrera uses the last phrase earlier in the book, and it is a clue both to the particular qualities of his longer works of fiction (*Three Trapped Tigers* and *Infante's Inferno*) and to the pleasure that reading them provides. Both seem aimless and unstructured, the second even more so than the first, but they don't produce the irritation or boredom such appearances often promise. This is partly a matter of the frantically active language, to which I shall return in a moment, but it is also a matter of the tone of remembrance, the way in which the imagination is used to animate old places and distant people.

Rancor toward the past is very common, and if we feel it we either can't talk about the past or can't look at it straight, can't stop rewriting it. Sometimes we are in love with the past, as Proust was, but then we almost need to be Proust in order to prevent it from slipping through our over-eager fingers. Cabrera is not anxious about his past, and he has nothing against it. His impulse is not exactly nostalgia, even though that is what his character in *Three Trapped Tigers* claims. His attention to the past is brighter and more energetic than nostalgia usually manages to be. He treats the past simply as if it were the present, as if it had never been away, as if all those now demolished movie houses and now dispersed friends, and if Havana itself had found a permanent home in his prodigious memory. His master is surely not Proust but Nabokov—"odor or ardor," Cabrera wisecracks at one moment on the subject of his difficulties with loved women who give off too high a smell—for whom the past came when it was called, obedient, more than presentable, all its magical details intact. "The Past," Van Veen writes in *Odor*, or *Ada*, "is a constant accumulation of images. It can be easily contemplated and listened to, tested and tasted at random. . . ." And without rancor.

This kind of tender, circumstantial recreation is even more a feature of *Infante's Inferno* than of *Three Trapped Tigers*. "She flew away," Cabrera writes of one girl, "and into my memory "; and of another he says, "It wasn't the last time I saw her—it's never the last time one sees anybody." The book begins,

> It was the first time I climbed a staircase. Few houses in our town had more than one floor, and those that did were inaccessible. This is my inaugural memory of Havana: climbing marble steps. . . . A breeze moved the colored curtains that hid the various households: even though it was midsummer, it was cool in the early morning and drafts came from within the rooms. Time stopped at that vision. . . . I had stepped from childhood into adolescence on a staircase.

We know quite a number of things about the book without going any further. It is very well written, the work of a stylist; we may get a faint whiff of rancid Conrad in the prose ("Only the young have such moments," he says in *The Shadow Line*). It is well translated—by Suzanne Jill Levine in collaboration with Cabrera, who has cut out large chunks of the Spanish text, and embroidered all kinds of additions, mainly jokes but sometimes afterthoughts, on the English. When Rita Guibert asked him if he corrected much, he said, "eternally." Its focus is a personal past, historical in the widest sense, but likely to bear only tangential, or accidental, resemblances to what we usually call history. Carlos Franqui appears frequently, for example, as an old friend of Cabrera's and a great mover in his Havana circle, but the overlap be-

tween this character and the political activist is very slim. The book's main character is a boy from the provinces, dazzled by the big city, and we learn before long that he will always be dazzled by it, is dazzled even now as he writes, and that if the city is no longer the heroine, as it is in the *Three Trapped Tigers*, it is still a major character. "The city spoke another language," the boy thinks. "The streetlamps were so poor back home that they couldn't even afford moths."

Infante's Inferno—the title is a new gag to replace the untranslatable *La Habana para un Infante Difunto*, which relies not only on Ravel but on the similarity between *pavane* and Havana, and the fact that the French for *infanta* is *infante*—presents the discursive erotic memoirs of a character much like Cabrera himself, a Cuban Casanova, at least in longing and memory, and occasionally, it seems, in practice. This resemblance, Cabrera would no doubt say, is not accidental, but it is not crucial either. He is remembering and inventing, not confessing. He is twelve when he arrives in the tenement with the imposing staircase, in his twenties and married by the end of the book. Cuba still belongs to Batista. Cabrera encounters girls and women among his neighbors, discovers surprising homosexual inclinations in a respectable man, glimpses sexual paradise in a window across a passage, thereby anticipating a later career as a (near-sighted) voyeur. He writes lyrically of masturbation, comically of his first fiasco in a brothel, associates Debussy with various dreams of seduction, describes in baroque and at times moving detail his pursuit of women in cinemas, his high hopes of clutches and nudges in the conspiratorial dark.

> My finger brushed the back of her seat, a few centimeters—less, millimeters—beneath the girl's bare back. . . . I again passed my finger from left to right along the surf of her skin, going a little higher but not enough for her to feel the shadow of my hand. I don't remember her hair nor can I say why I didn't stay until she got up. . . but this back that night in the Alkazar pleasure palace presents itself as a unique vision. Surely life has mistreated her, time soiling, spoiling her splendor, the years disfiguring her face, but they can't age the memory: that back will always be on my mind. . . .

He wasn't always as discreet as this at the movies, and the book ends with a brilliant fantasy on the subject, a mixture of Rabelais, Jules Verne, and a schoolboy joke. Groping in the lower depths of a woman in the appropriately named Fausto Theater—a free-ranging exploration, unlike many other "sour gropes," as Cabrera calls them— he loses, first his wedding ring, then his watch, then his cuff links. They have fallen into the well of loneliness, and Cabrera, flashlight in hand, goes in after them, Gulliver in another country, a journey to the center of the birth, and wakes from his dream, if it is a dream, with that old moviegoer's cry: "Here's where I came in."

Cabrera and his Havana friends, once out of adolescence, were "crazy for culture," he says, and always making puns, "suffering insufferably from paronomasia as not only an incurable but contagious disease. . . mad echolalia." The disease is clearly permanent with him, and he unrepentantly mangles language and hops from one tongue to another like a frog released from the throat. Some of these jokes are so terrible that they seem heroic, make S.J. Perelman a sedate defender of the dictionary. "There was an old saw back home that said, 'The grass is where it's green.' It must be a rusty saw by now because I haven't heard it in ages (perhaps because I haven't been home in a coon's age). . . ": Groucho Cabrera Infante. "Whatever Zola wants, Zola gets," "lecher *de main*," "Daguerre c'est Daguerre." Others are so cumbersome, so fiendishly worked for, that the noise of grinding machinery deafens all chance of laughter. He admires Alida Valli, and finds a young girl who resembles her. This permits him to say "How green was my Valli." He likes the proximity of *glance* and *glans* so much that he mentions it twice. The "aisle of Rite" will perhaps be intelligible to people who have looked at maps of the south coast of England recently, and "*a coup de data* to abolish chaff*" depends on Mallarmé's "*Un coup de dés jamais n'abolira le hasard*" turning into English (abolish chance) halfway through.

Still other gags seem wildly compulsive, a form of fiddling with the text, a buzzing that can't let things be, and they are a genuine distraction then. Why would we want to think of a "baptism of pale fire," or associate vacillation with Vaseline? At other times the gags make wonderful, surprising sense, and whole worlds come tumbling down on top of each other, as they always do in the best of puns: "pathetic fallacy," "a fugitive from the gym gang." It is as if Humbert Humbert had got hold of all Nabokov's prose and wouldn't let go. This means that Cabrera Infante can't achieve Nabokov's irony—"you can always count on a murderer for a fancy prose style"—and must at times seem like a *précieux ridicule* rather than a ridiculer of preciosity. The trouble with dropping names, however frivolously, is that you have to pick them up in the first place.

But the book is a mixture of passionate memory and reckless spinning in the echo chamber of language, time regained in an avalanche of associations. "Our works," Carlos Fuentes wrote, thinking of Cabrera Infante and one or two contemporaries, "must be works of disorder: that is, works of a possible order, contrary to the present one." Cabrera Infante's disorder is that of the intelligence overwhelmed by gags that go to the head like drink; his possible order is that of the evoked past, a period that comes so thoroughly alive that its squandering by the present is itself a judgment on the reigning power, the reproach, without rancor, that literature makes to history.

Michael Wood, "Odor and Ardor," in *The New York Review of Books*, Vol. XXXI, No. 11, June 28, 1984, pp. 21–2.

Cabrera Infante on exile:

*I was born in Cuba, and I
hope to die in England.*

I live now in exiledom by the sea. Here I work and play, and even watch other people work and play from the cozy vantage point of my bay windows, which look out onto the bay. Here I read a romance that is the story of my life. (A historian is only a writer with hindsight.) Ensconced in a comfortable chair by the fire, while, outside, squalls made the street squalid, I began to read. "How horrible," said a voice. "But what deviltry must happen to make a man invisible?" "It's not deviltry," another voice responded. "It's a process." That's what it is : a process, and it began some years ago. Now I too am invisible. Not invincible, but the opposite. To be invisible means to be as vulnerable as the unseen. You are less a person than a nonperson. You are pure spirit and you can be blown out like a candle in the wind—and who's going to remember what kind of flame you were before the candle was blown out? It is a metaphysical problem.

Cabrera Infante in his "On Inspiration," *The Paris Review*,
Summer 1988.

JOHN BUTT
(essay date 1986)

[In the following essay, Butt praises Cabrera Infante's virtuoso handling of the English language in *Holy Smoke*.]

Latin America has given us many things which have revolutionized our lives—potatoes, syphilis (disputed), cocaine, tomatoes and, not least, tobacco. This last mixed blessing is the theme of the prolific ex-Cuban writer G. Cabrera Infante, who is now a naturalized Briton and effectively an English writer in all but his exotic name. With *Holy Smoke* he has turned his back not only on fiction, but also on the Spanish language: this book was written directly in English, and the author has thereby fulfilled a dream which has tormented several reputable Hispanic authors (Borges, Cernuda): that of being able to throw off sonorous Castilian for more laconic and less oratorical language.

But Cabrera Infante has done more than follow the same difficult path as Conrad and Koestler. They both played by the rules of the club which had lately admitted them, but Cabrera has decided to do to the language of Shakespeare what he previously did to that of

Cervantes: improve it. This, to put it mildly, is a daring liberty which sometimes pays off in coinages like "futility rites", "ruminiscences", "alliterate" (someone, like Cabrera, given to alliteration), and sometimes not, as in "Columbus. . . is our omnibus", "a tortoiseology", *"l'embarras du Joyce. . . "*. But the author seems to have curbed his promiscuous punning, and it must be said that this is a marvellous book which exploits the English language in an amazing way for someone who is also a virtuoso Spanish stylist, and it is full of witty details about a subject one might have thought unpromising for a full-length book. . . .

Recent history has all but stubbed out the cigar, which, unlike the cigarette, never spread to Asia or Africa. First the Cuban blockade, then the anti-smoking campaign have meant that few in the West now know the difference between a Lonsdale, a Perfecto, a Panatella, a Demitasse and a Margarita, and for most of us a cigar is one of those ignoble, machine-rolled, dried-out stinkers wrapped in plastic (for Cabrera the invention of cellophane was a turning-point in Western history) which we will only smoke under the inducement of television campaigns of painful ingenuity. And who now knows what a Vitola really is (even Spaniards have got it wrong) or dare pronounce on the right moment to remove the band, on whether ash should be docked or left to grow, or on the rights or wrongs of poking sharpened match-sticks in the butt? All this and more is illuminated by Cabrera, part of whose exhaustive research has consisted of scrutinizing virtually every book or film ever produced which features the lighting, passing or holding of cigars: if there can be feminist, black and gay criticism, then why not one for tobacco addicts, an increasingly terrified minority?

Saki's last recorded words, so Cabrera says, were "put that bloody cigarette out". Even Columbus, he surmises, turned down the second offer of a cigar from an Amerindian, thereby becoming the West's first ex-smoker. Cabrera is a stout lover of lost causes—punning, pre-revolutionary Cuba and tobacco—and he knows that his forces are on the run, which is why he cites Saki and even the London tobacconist who would not allow smoking in his shop. This is a rich book written by an extraordinary linguist, and anti-tobacco puritans might well retreat before such a brilliant counter-stroke, were it not for the fact that decent smokes, for example, Selectos Flor de Cano, retail at £51.70 a box of twenty-five, a fact no one present would even know if you tried to impress them by lighting one up.

John Butt, "Punning and Puffing," in *The Times Literary Supplement*, No. 4352, August 29, 1986, p. 946.

NICHOLAS RANKIN
(essay date 1989)

[In the following review, Rankin maintains that Cabrera Infante's *View of Dawn in the Tropics* fuses myth and history and is informed by "an exile's perspective."]

View of Dawn in the Tropics is a brief and poignant history of Cuba, related in 117 sections. These vignettes, fables and snapshot descriptions vary in length from a paragraph to four pages, and their first lines are logged in the index as if they were prose poems. This post-modern technique of making a history from a mosaic of fragments has been employed by the Uruguayan Eduardo Galeano in his epic trilogy *Memory of Fire*, but in G. Cabrera Infante's hands the method is also reminiscent of the *Extraordinary Tales* collated by the Argentines, Borges and Bioy Casares. Here factual history is worn down into fictive myth: the clutter of names and dates and elaborate particularity have been polished away to leave emblematic figures such as "the black general", "the old soldier" and "the comandante", whose violent fates are laconically described.

Key to the book is the first word of the title. As one would expect from this pun-loving writer, "view" has several meanings. In the sense of "opinion", the exiled Cabrera Infante's view of his native land since Fidel Castro took power thirty years ago is clear: Cuba is a tyrannical dictatorship, a black joke far from any "dawn" of progressive enlightenment. Many of the vignettes are distanced by a cool style ("the senator was eating bread when they killed him, and his white linen suit was stained with blood and spilled coffee") which pretends to objectivity. Other sketches are already at one remove, being verbal descriptions of scenes depicted in other media: engravings, a map, photographs, a film. It is an exile's perspective, contemplating the leaves of a scrap book of oppression and failed revolutions. And in the long view of Cuba's dire history—colonization by great powers, massacre of Indians, enslaving of blacks—the latest régime, with its persecution of dissidents and homosexuals, is regarded as quite consonant with what has gone on before.

The tone of the book does change, however, as chronology brings us up to date. The dead bodies and the gaol-bars become more bitterly personal than ironically picturesque. Three of the last nine vignettes have first-person narrators: a fugitive on a plank-and-tyre raft; a hungry convict in a labour camp; and a "disappeared" prisoner's mother raging with grief. The book is dedicated to one man who was shot by a firing squad and to another who shot himself.

Guillermo Cabrera Infante is perhaps the only naturalized British author who writes in Spanish. *Vista del amanecer en el tropico,* originally published in 1974, is here translated by Suzanne Jill Levine, but has been revised by the author. His hand is apparent in the English puns ("a joke is closer to a yoke than you think"), but they are fewer and less laboured than usual; appropriate to a book about a land which appears more sombre than sunny:

AND IT WILL ALWAYS BE THERE. As someone once said, that long, sad, unfortunate island will be there after the last Indian and after the last Spaniard and after the last African and after the last American and after the last Russian and after the last of the Cubans, surviving all disasters, eternally washed over by the Gulf Stream: beautiful and green, undying, eternal.

Nicholas Rankin, "A Scrapbook of Oppression," in *The Times Literary Supplement*, No. 4477, January 20–26, 1989, p. 58.

SOURCES FOR FURTHER STUDY

Foster, David William. "Guillermo Cabrera Infante's *Vista del amanecer en el trópico* and the Generic Ambiguity of Narrative." In his *Studies in the Contemporary Spanish-American Short Story,* pp. 110–20. Columbia: University of Missouri Press, 1979.

> Exploration of Cabrera Infante's narrative techniques in *View of Dawn in the Tropics.*

Janes, Regina. "Ta(l)king Liberties: On Guillermo Cabrera Infante." *Salmagundi,* Nos. 82–3 (Spring/Summer 1989): 222–37.

> Lecture originally delivered in 1986 that provides an overview of Cabrera Infante's life and career.

King, John. "Havana Buffs." *The Times Literary Supplement,* No. 4640 (March 6, 1992): 17.

> Praises Cabrera Infante's critical perspective and portrayal of Cuban intellectual life in the collection of film criticism *A Twentieth-Century Job.*

Lezra, Jacques. "Squared Circles, Encircling Bowls: Reading Figures in *Tres tristes tigers.*" *Latin American Literary Review* XVI, No. 3 (January–June 1988): 6–23.

> Discussion of Cabrera Infante's narrative strategy in *Three Trapped Tigers.*

MacAdam, Alfred J. "Guillermo Cabrera Infante: The Vast Fragment." In his *Modern Latin American Narratives,* pp. 61–

8. Chicago: University of Chicago Press, 1977.

> Discussion of satire in *Three Trapped Tigers.*

Ortega, Julio. "Three Trapped Tigers." In his *Poetics of Change: The New Spanish-American Narrative,* translated by Galen D. Greaser, pp. 160–72. Austin: University of Texas Press, 1984.

> Essay maintaining that the "*Three Trapped Tigers* poses literature as a game, and within this context the game has a more decisive role than literature because for Guillermo Cabrera Infante the infinite possibilities of the game compromise in a fundamental way the shaping of reality."

Schwartz, Ronald. "Cabrera Infante: Cuban Lyricism." In his *Nomads, Exiles, and Emigres: The Rebirth of Latin American Narrative, 1960–80,* pp. 60–9. Metuchen, N.J.: The Scarecrow Press, 1980.

> Critical overview of Cabrera Infante's career.

Siemens, William L. "Heilsgeschichte and the Structure of *Tres tristes tigers.*" *Kentucky Romance Quarterly* XXII, No. 1 (1975): 77–90.

> Argues that the structure of *Three Trapped Tigers* reveals the novel to be "an elevated vision of the historical reality of an elect people as expressed in the Scriptures."

Additional coverage of Cabrera Infante's life and career is contained in the following sources published by Gale Research: *Contemporary Authors,* Vols. 85–88; *Contemporary Authors New Revision Series,* Vol. 29; *Contemporary Literary Criticism,* Vols. 5, 25, 45; *Dictionary of Literary Biography,* Vol.113; *Hispanic Writers,* and *Major 20th-Century Writers.*

Ernesto Cardenal

1925–

Nicaraguan poet, translator, and nonfiction writer.

INTRODUCTION

A poet and Roman Catholic clergyman, Cardenal is a leading figure in the revolutionary literature of Latin America. Frequently compared to such distinguished authors as Ezra Pound and Pablo Neruda, Cardenal composes most of his poetry in a montage style that unites political ideology with theological reflection. His signature works—*Hora 0* (1960; *Zero Hour and other Documentary Poems*), *Oración por Marilyn Monroe y otros poemas* (1965; *Prayer for Marilyn Monroe and Other Poems*), *Homenaje a los indios americanos* (1969; *Homage to the American Indians*), among others—critique the values and ideology of modern capitalism in an effort to initiate societal change. Cardenal's technical skills and the sociopolitical relevance of his oeuvre have led renowned Catholic scholar and poet Thomas Merton to praise him "as one of the most significant of the newly mature generation of Latin-American poets."

Born in Granada, Nicaragua, Cardenal studied philosophy and letters at Mexico's National University and later attended Columbia University in New York City. During his college years, Cardenal composed love poems wherein he frequently incorporated news clippings or historical documents. He returned to his native country in the early 1950s and became involved in subversive activities directed against the regime of President Anastazio Somoza. When a 1954 assault on the dictator's life failed, Cardenal was forced to go underground; while in hiding he wrote his most famous poem, *Zero Hour*, a patriotic epic that recounts the assassination of a Nicaraguan revolutionary leader. After Samoza's murder in 1956, Cardenal, deeply shaken by the event, experienced a spiritual conversion and entered the Trappist Monastery of Gethsemani, in Kentucky. While there, he came under the guidance of Merton, whose commitment to non-violence influenced

Cardenal to denounce all forms of social injustice. Illness forced Cardenal to leave the monastery in 1957; two years later, he entered the Benedictine community at Guernavaca, Mexico, and composed *Gethsemani, Ky.* (1960), a book of short poems based on a journal he kept there. During this time Cardenal also began writing several works concerned with the history of Central America–*El estrecho dudoso* (1966) and *Homage to the American Indians*–as well as meditations on the commercialization of modern life; the most popular of these latter poems is "Prayer for Marilyn Monroe." In the early 1960s Cardenal resided in Colombia and traveled the upper Amazon, examining both past and contemporary native Indian cultures. A year after his ordination to the priesthood in 1965, Cardenal founded Solentiname, a Christian commune devoted to a life of manual labor, prayer, and scholarship. Cardenal visited Cuba in 1970 and later published *En Cuba* (1972; *In Cuba*), a nonfiction work which praises that country's social reforms while lamenting the absence of Christian beliefs there. Calling his Cuban sojourn a "second conversion," he returned to Solentiname convinced that Nicaraguan society could only be restructured through violence. In 1977, responding to the revolutionary activities of Cardenal and members of his community, the Nicaraguan government destroyed Solentiname, forcing Cardenal into exile in Costa Rica. When the Marxist Sandanistas seized control of Nicaragua in 1979, Cardenal was appointed Minister of Culture; however, Sandanistan human rights atrocities and ecclesiastical disapproval eventually forced him to resign. Presently, Cardenal conducts literacy workshops and continues to compose verse, viewing his poetry as a stern warning to political tyrants not to abuse their power at the expense of the poor and disenfranchised.

Cardenal's verse characteristically explores themes such as spiritual love and the quest for the transcendental life. *Gethsemani, Ky.*, for example, espouses a lyrical interpretation of the universe as having been formed by the outpouring of God's mercy. Likewise, *El estrecho dudoso* combines biblical rhetoric with prosody to show readers that history has an anagogical dimension. Echoing the form and content of the Old Testament psalms, the poems in *Salmos* (1967; *The Psalms of Struggle and Liberation*) frequently relate humanity's joy in beholding creation. In addition to religious motifs, Cardenal's poetry also manifests strong social and political concerns. Many of his works, such as the poems collected in *With Walker in Nicaragua and Other Early Poems, 1949–1954* (1985), examine Nicaragua's history, elucidating the roots of conflict in Central America. Critics have found that Cardenal's later verse is markedly more explicit regarding the author's political sympathies. The poems in *Zero Hour*, for instance, denounce gringoism, mixing archaic biblical prophetic teaching with contemporary Marxist ideol-

ogy. The dialectic between the past and the present is similarly explored in *Homage to the American Indians*: recapturing the quality of pre-Columbian life, Cardenal's descriptions of the psychic wholeness of extinct Mayan, Incan, and Nahuatl civilizations are contrasted with the superficiality of modern imperialism. F. Whitney Jones has stated that in *Homage to the American Indians*, Cardenal esteems "a way of life which celebrates peace above war and spiritual strength above personal wealth."

Commentators have pointed out that Cardenal's poetry bears many similarities to Pound's. Like Pound, Cardenal borrowed the short, epigrammatic form from Catullus and Martial, masters of Latin poetry, whose works Cardenal has translated. Cardenal also appropriated Pound's canto form—dividing poems into several sections to depict a cultural and political odyssey through time. Some reviewers, like Isabel Fraire, have asserted that Cardenal's use of the canto form "is much more *cantabile*" than Pound's, adding that in Cardenal's verse "we get passages of a sustained, descriptive lyricism . . . where the intense beauty and harmony of nature or of a certain social order or life style are presented." Although Cardenal and Pound both treat themes like greed, dishonesty, and the corruption of human values, Cardenal's work, unlike Pound's, has a broader social perspective. As Fraire has observed, "where Pound seems to spring up disconnected from his contemporary cultural scene and to be working against it, Cardenal is born into a ready-made cultural context and shared political conscience. Cardenal's past is common to all Latin Americans. His present is likewise common to all Latin Americans. He speaks to those who are ready and willing to hear him and are likely to agree on a great many points." Critics have also maintained that in his use of factual information, crosscutting, and contrast, Cardenal's poetic technique resembles that of documentary filmmakers. His multileveled narrative *El estrecho dudoso*, for example, relates the history of destruction in Central America; through comparison and juxtaposed images, however, the poem becomes a commentary on contemporary political and cultural exploitation.

Critical reaction to Cardenal's oeuvre has been mixed. Some reviewers have denounced his poetry as didactic and propagandistic; many have found his Marxist treatises incompatible with his Catholic beliefs, yet others have praised his writings' prophetic insight. However, most scholars have agreed that Cardenal avoids mere agitprop through his commanding verse style and his controlled approach to potentially melodramatic situations. As Gordon Brotherston has stated, "Among his contemporaries Cardenal is exceptional not just for having a faith of such intensity but for expressing it in terms that are politically so exuberant and accessible."

CRITICAL COMMENTARY

THOMAS MERTON

(essay date 1961)

[An American Catholic clergyman, poet, and essayist, Merton is generally regarded as one of the most widely read Catholic authors of the twentieth-century. His works—*The Seven Storey Mountain* (1948), *The Living Bread* (1956), *Mystics and Zen Masters* (1967), among others—have been acclaimed for their insight, religious fervor, and intellectual breadth. In the following excerpt, orginally published in 1961, Merton briefly comments on Cardenal's spirituality and its relation to his poetry.]

Born in 1925 in Granada, Nicaragua, Ernesto Cardenal is one of a number of significant young poets who have reached maturity in the poetic movement begun, in that country, by José Coronel Urtecho and Pablo Antonio Cuadra. Educated at the University of Mexico and Columbia University, Cardenal was involved in a political resistance movement under the dictatorship of the elder Somoza and this experience is reflected in a volume of *Epigrams* written before he entered Gethsemani, and published in Mexico, as well as in a long political poem, *La Hora O*.

Cardenal applied for admission to Gethsemani and we received him into the noviciate in 1957. He had just exhibited some very interesting ceramics at the Pan American Union in Washington, and during his noviciate he continued modeling in clay. He was one of the rare vocations we have had here who certainly and manifestly combined the gifts of a contemplative with those of an artist. However his poetic work was, by deliberate design, somewhat restricted in the noviciate. He set down the simplest and most prosaic notes of his experiences, and did not develop them into conscious "poems." The result was a series of utterly simple poetic sketches with all the purity and sophistication that we find in the Chinese masters of the Tang dynasty. Never has the experience of noviciate life in a Cistercian monastery been rendered with such fidelity, and yet with such reserve. He is silent, as is right, about the inner and most personal aspects of his contemplative experience, and yet it shows itself more clearly in the complete simplicity and objectivity with which he notes down the exterior and ordinary features of this life. No amount of mystical rhetoric could ever achieve so just an appreciation of the unpretentious spirituality of this very plain monastic existence. Yet the poet remains conscious of his relation to the world he has left and thinks a great deal about it, with the result that one recognizes how the purifying isolation of the monastery encourages a profound renewal and change of perspective in which "the world" is not forgotten, but seen in a clearer and less delusive light.

I do not know how much the selections from *Gethsemani, Ky.* will mean to someone who has never listened to the silence of the Kentucky night around the walls of this monastery. But Cardenal has, with perfect truthfulness, evoked the sounds of rare cars and trains that accentuate the silence and loneliness by their passage through it.

He was not destined to remain for life in this particular solitude. His health was not sufficiently strong and indications were that he should go elsewhere. He is still pursuing in Central America his vocation as priest, contemplative and poet. He is much published in Mexico and Colombia where he is rightly recognized as one of the most significant of the newly mature generation of Latin American poets. (pp. 114–16)

Thomas Merton, "Ernesto Cardenal," in his *Emblems of a Season of Fury*, New Directions, 1963, pp. 114–24.

ERNESTO CARDENAL WITH RONALD CHRIST

(interview date 1974)

[A distinguished American educator, editor, and translator, Christ has written extensively on contemporary Latin-American literature. In the following in-

Principal Works

Ansias lengua de la poesía nueva nicaragüense (poetry) 1948

Gethsemani, Ky. (poetry) 1960

Hora 0 (poetry) 1960
[published in *Zero Hour and Other Documentary Poems*, 1980]

Epigramas: Poemas (poetry) 1961

Oración por Marilyn Monroe y otros poemas (poetry) 1965
[*Prayer for Marilyn Monroe and Other Poems*, 1975]

El estrecho dudoso (poetry) 1966

Antología de Ernesto Cardenal (poetry) 1967

Salmos (poetry) 1967
[*The Psalms of Struggle and Liberation*, 1971]

Homenaje a los indios americanos (poetry) 1969
[*Homage to the American Indians*, 1974]

Vida en el amor (meditations) 1970
[*To Live is to Love*, 1972]

En Cuba (nonfiction) 1972
[*In Cuba*, 1974]

El Evangelio en Solentiname (dialogues) 1975
[*The Gospel in Solentiname*, 1976]

Poesía escogida (poetry) 1975

Apocalypse, and Other Poems (poetry) 1977

La paz mundial y la Revolución de Nicaragua (nonfiction) 1981

Tocar el cielo: poesias (poetry) 1981

Antología: Ernesto Cardenal (poetry) 1983

With Walker in Nicaragua and Other Early Poems, 1949–1954 (poetry) 1985

From Nicaragua with Love: Poems 1979–1986 (poetry) 1986

Golden UFOs: The Indian Poems; Los ovnis de oro: Poemas indios (poetry) 1992

terview, he asks Cardenal about his poetic vocation, his literary influences, and his various compositions.]

[Christ]: *Your best known poem [in the United States] is probably "Prayer for Marilyn Monroe." How did you come to write it?*

[Cardenal]: I was in the seminary, studying to be a priest in Colombia when one of the teachers gave us the news of Marilyn Monroe's death. I also read a story in *Time* magazine about her and that inspired the poem. At the same time, it was the date in the liturgy when we have the gospel about the expulsion of the money-lenders from the temple and that too gave me inspiration to write the poem.

Do you think most readers in the United States are missing the full scope of your work by knowing just that one poem?

Well, yes. My poetry is less known here than in other countries, and it is better known in Germany, for example, and in Europe in general. But now Johns Hopkins Press is bringing out a book of mine called **Homage to the American Indians**, which is a collection of poems on the theme of the indigenous cultures of America—North America, South America and Central America. It's about the wisdom, the mysticism and the spirituality of the indigenous tribes. That is one of the themes I've cultivated in my poetry: the theme of the indigenous.

How did you come to write poetry in the first place?

Well, I began to write poetry when I was about four years old. In other words, I've always been writing poetry.

Who are the poets you most read and admire?

The principal influence on me, and one could say this of almost all the Nicaraguan literature of today, is the North American influence, from Whitman to the contemporary writers, the very newest. Ezra Pound has had a special influence on me. The technique of Pound has been the greatest lesson for me. *The Cantos*, yes, *The Cantos*, not the earlier poems. Almost all South American poetry has been influenced by Europe and especially by France, but Nicaragua has been influenced by North American poetry and now the influence of Nicaragua has extended to other countries, most notably to Cuba. Current revolutionary poetry from Cuba has been greatly influenced by Nicaraguan and North American poetry.

But unlike The Cantos, *your poems are easy to read. They're straightforward and simple in their diction.*

I have tried not to be difficult as Pound is, I have tried to use technique but in a way that can be understood by the people. Pound was not interested in being understood by them, so yes, there is that difference between his poetry and mine.

But you haven't tried to write in a specifically revolutionary diction, have you?

Well, Pound wrote much economic, social and political poetry—principally economic—and I also have written quite a bit of economic poetry and some of those indigenous poems also have these themes. I have a poem about the Inca culture which is principally an economic poem about the socialism of the Incas. The poem is called **"The Economy of Tahuantinsuyo."** Tahuantinsuyo is the Quecha name of the Inca Emperor. I also have other poems about the Mayas and they too touch greatly on the economic, political and social themes.

But not from such a fixed point of view as Pound's?

I think that Pound's principal point, and this is very important for everyone to see today, is that the present capitalistic economy is an oppression of culture, of all aspects of man's life and we ought to liberate ourselves from this oppression. He called it usury, the oppression of money, of the power of money, and I try also to treat this theme in historical poems of indigenous cultures as well as in some poems touching upon the theme of imperialism. In these poems I'm working with a preoccupation with the religious and mystical aspect of man's life and not just the economic. Speaking of the Incas, I say that their socialistic economy was an economy with religion. I am not interested in an economic liberation of man without the liberation of the *whole* man.

Some people have compared your work to the anti-poetry of Nicanor Parra. How do you feel about that comparison?

I think there is something in common between his poetry and mine, something that consists in our trying to write realistic poetry; that is, poetry with images drawn from our present, real world. But I myself have never called what I write anti-poetry. I also think that my poetry should not be only known as the poetry of Ernesto Cardenal but rather as Nicaraguan poetry.

What about graffiti and slogans such as you find in Parra's work?

No, I'm not interested in those, because they are not poetry. Well, some anti-poets say they are. Slogan-making is *not* poetry.

Do you have a guiding esthetic for your own work?

A friend of mine from Nicaragua, José Coronel Urtecho, told me that for Pound poetry was "poetry containing history;" and he told me that my poetry was "poetry containing history *and* wisdom." In reality, what I would have wanted to say is that my preoccupation—and that, also, of José Coronel Urtecho—is that of writing a poetry which serves others in communicating its meaning. It was in this sense that he understood the word "wisdom"—in the Biblical sense of wisdom, in the sense the prophets gave to the word. For me, poetry is above all prophecy in the Biblical sense of guidance.

How about your epigrams? They are neither about revolution nor economics.

Well, there is more to life than revolution. There is also love. My epigrams were written when I was young and they are a poetry of love and hate, some of both love and hate at the same time, because while they are political poems they are also love poems. It was much later that I developed a different kind of poetry—social, political and prophetic. I would call it—in trying to find the solution for our problems, a poetry that serves for something in the construction of a new society, poetry that would be useful and poetry that might be more than just a vehicle for communicating something. I am not interested in poetry for poetry's sake. My poetry is not lyric. The epigrams are lyric because they come from my

youthful period of lyricism, but my other poetry is not lyric.

In what sense is the Marilyn Monroe poem not lyric?

I was actually referring to the poetry that I'm writing right now, poetry with a revolutionary theme, for example. You could say that **"Prayer for Marilyn Monroe"** is a lyric poem, but it is not properly a poem about an individual since there was no individual relation between her and me. Rather, with her as my subject, I speak of the current civilization and I consider her not as a symbol but as victim—victim, really, of the commercialization, of the falsification of this real world. That is my theme. (pp. 189–91)

Ernesto Cardenal and Ronald Christ, in an interview in *Commonweal*, Vol. C, No. 8, April 26, 1974, pp. 189–91.

ISABEL FRAIRE
(essay date 1976)

[In the following excerpt, Fraire compares Cardenal's verse to Pound's, finding that although both poets employ the canto form and share similar thematic concerns, Cardenal's work exhibits "a wider cultural conscience."]

Upon reading [Ernesto Cardenal's poetry] and being hit on the head by the striking and continuous similarities to Pound's poetry in so much of Cardenal's work, you do not get the impression that he is a young poet feeling his way, learning through imitation; these are not the first, promising efforts of a budding genius. You do not get the impression that he is going on to something else, to "find his own voice," etc. No. This is it. This *is* his own voice, and these poems are no fumbling, no lucky, naïve, "early work." They are memorable poems; rounded, masterful, mature work. This is it, all right. This is Ernesto Cardenal.

There seems to be a problem here.

Ernesto Cardenal copies Pound. Well, he does. Anybody can see that. In that case, why have Cardenal at all? Why not eliminate him and stick to Pound? (pp. 36–7)

Cardenal has something to offer us that Pound does not offer, and it is not just a matter of language. Even a good translation of all of Pound into Spanish could not possibly replace Cardenal's poetry. So something has changed, something has been added, making Cardenal's poetry worthwhile to readers of Spanish and even justifying the translation of his poetry into English. There we have it; there is a similarity, a remarkable similarity, which is the main subject of this article. And there is a difference. The result is poetry worth reading and translating, poetry which moves, which sticks in the mind and even, I

An excerpt from *Marilyn Monroe and Other Poems*

> Blessed is the man that heeds not the dictates of
> , the Party,
> nor attends any of its meetings;
> nor sits down at table with the gangsters
> nor yet with Generals in courts-martial.
> Blessed is the man that spies not on his brother
> nor betrays him with whom he went to school.
> Blessed is the man that reads not advertisements,
> nor pays heed unto broadcasts,
> nor yet gives credence unto slogans.
>
> > For he shall be like a tree, planted by the rivers
> > of water.

Ernesto Cardenal, "Blessed is the Man," in his *Marilyn Monroe and Other Poems*, translated by Robert Pring-Mill, Search Press, 1975.

would venture to say, is likely to influence some people's view of the world. Ernesto Cardenal *is* a great poet *despite* the fact that he obviously copies Pound. . . .

Cardenal is a great poet, but not an inventor of forms. After all, how many poets are? And . . . he merely took a form, a structure, a pattern which Pound had invented, and used it for his own purposes, filled it with his own content. A Latin American content. (p. 37)

As I see it Cardenal's poetry falls roughly into three batches:

(a) The short, epigrammatic poems. No need to overstress Pound's influence here since, guided or not by Pound, Cardenal had recourse to Pound's Latin models, and it is to them that final reference should be made. (pp. 37–8)

Incidentally, these short poems of Cardenal seem to have sparked or, perhaps, reinforced, a whole new trend among some of the younger Latin American poets.

(b) The longer, canto-like poems where Pound's influence is unquestionable and unquestioned. Cardenal himself willingly admits it.

(c) The rest of Cardenal's poems stemming from various other sources, although nearly always playing very closely on the original models, in a way reminiscent of Pound's personae. In ***Cantares Mexicanos I*** and ***II*** and ***Netzahualcóyotl*** we get a blend of *b* and *c* where, using the basic canto form, he sticks so steadily to the style of the Náhuatl originals, or rather to the Spanish versions of them, that the effect is quite different from either the canto or the Náhuatl poems.

Of these three categories the only one that concerns me here is *b*, since though Pound can hardly be said to

have invented the epigram, although he may have reactivated it, we can safely say that Pound invented the Canto. (p. 38)

In the first place, of course, the idea itself; history into poetry, but direct from the *sources* as often as possible and convenient. Since this history can be from any period, including the contemporary, the sources are of all kinds; histories, documents, letters, newspapers, books, anecdotes, personal recollections, etc. Either the exact words, or the style of the original are kept. Where the poet substitutes his own voice for the sources, he usually either imitates them or keeps to a terse, matter-of-fact retelling. This characteristic shows up very clearly on comparing Cardenal's poetry to Neruda's *Canto General*. Setting aside the metrical differences that are immediately obvious, you see an entirely different emotional approach to the matter at hand. Neruda is always exhorting or declaiming or dramatically questioning the reader. He is always present as first-person in the poem. This Whitmanesque attitude is radically different from the "reportage" attitude of Pound and Cardenal, which is strongly reminiscent of Brecht's approach: don't get the spectator emotionally involved, present the material and let him think for himself—but of course they do get the reader emotionally involved, they just go about it differently. This difference is quite enough to explain why, even though the subject matter of Neruda and Cardenal is more than similar—it is, in fact, nearly identical—the poetry is so different.

The dominant tone is usually one of plain statement or quotation: however, at times, it is much more *cantabile*. We get passages of a sustained, descriptive lyricism (or what I would call lyricism) where the intense beauty and harmony of nature or of a certain social order or life style are presented. This is more frequent in Cardenal, perhaps, than in Pound, and in these passages Cardenal indulges in a greater fluidity, linking each line to the next to make the general effect more singing and harmonious and carry the reader forward constantly. In the *reportage* passages the lines coincide more frequently with complete statements, stopping short at the end, achieving in this way a certain finality, and reinforcing the non-subjective attitude. I suppose one could say that Pound is more frequently choppy and Cardenal more frequently fluid.

The presentation is fundamentally that of the *collage,* the juxtaposition of fragmented material producing frequent and ever richer cross–references and slowly building up several levels of meaning.

The number of lines per canto and the length of the lines follow no set rule.

There are no rhymes at the end of the lines linking them in a set pattern; however, rhymes do occur quite often by repetition of words, or stems of words, or whole phrases, either at the end of lines or at the end of one line and in the middle or even at the beginning of another, or after intervening lines. Where they do occur, these rhymes serve a purpose related to the content.

You sometimes get whole chunks of poetry which seem to follow a rhythmical pattern clearly recognizable to the ear and the emotional response, but difficult or impossible to reduce to metrical rules. . . . [In] reading Cardenal I very often came across lines or sets of lines strongly reminiscent of Pound's from a rhythmical, aural point of view. So close as to be echoes, and often of a very poignant beauty.

Part of the reason for the Poundian ring to many of Cardenal's lines, and probably linked to the rhythm, is the syntactical peculiarity which distinguishes so many of them: inversion of the usual word order, elimination of, say, verbs, or of conjunctions or prepositions, use of nouns or participles instead of verbs, etc. (pp. 38–9)

There is also what I would call Pound's bag of tricks or rhetorical devices:

a) Repetition at long intervals of a single line (or word or phrase) with slight variations, tying the whole poem or series of poems together and giving a sub-theme or meaning. . . .

b) The use of words, phrases or sentences in parentheses as commentaries or reminders.

c) The capitalization of words and sentences either as a kind of visual shouting (Pound either realized or fancied that most people are deaf) or because these words or sentences are brand names or advertisements usually seen capitalized in print or signs.

d) The use of numbers, as a non-poetic intrusion into the poem and as a reference (sometimes ironic) to our number-ridden society, or to stress that what he is telling about actually happened.

e) The use of concrete, factual detail, here again to impress on the reader that what he is telling about actually happened.

f) The insertion of a single emotionally charged line in the middle of matter treated in a different, more prosaic way. . . .

g) The use of names and surnames of individuals, sometimes principal, sometimes very secondary characters.

h) The use of quotations in quotation marks.

i) The way of cutting into quotations, beginning them in midsentence, or breaking them off, thus heightening the dramatic effect and sometimes giving depth by oblique reference to the unquoted part.

j) The use of fragmentation or interruption, applied not only to quotations but to sentences or trains of thought, sometimes for economy, sometimes for drama, sometimes for both.

k) The use of words and sentences in foreign languages.

l) The explanation of same in parentheses next to the original word or sentence.

m) The use of repetition, not as in a) but in immediate or nearly immediate lines, in order to rub something in or explore different variations of meaning. . . .

n) The use of anecdotes as illustrations of meaning or as part of the story.

And, of course, although this has to do with content and not with form, one shouldn't forget the presence in Cardenal of certain recurring themes which form part of the basic conceptual network of his poetry, as of Pound's. These themes are the corrupting effect of moneymaking as the overriding value in a society; the importance of precision and truthfulness in language; the degradation of human values in the world which surrounds us; the search through the past (or, in Cardenal's poetry, in more "primitive" societies, a kind of contemporary past) for better world-models. (p. 40)

It might be pertinent here to indicate the similarity of the uses to which the Canto has been put, first by Pound and then by Cardenal: recreation of historical periods, both ancient and contemporary; biography; catchall for scraps of political, economic, philosophical theorizing, recreation of literary precedents and myths. It might justifiably be argued that Cardenal has used the Canto for all of them, but especially for the first two, in his recreation of the Spanish conquests, the pre-Columbian theocracies, the Somoza dictatorship and contemporary political scene in Central America, and the biographies of tyrants and indigenous leaders. When he uses it to sing the exploits of sixteenth-century conquerors or twentieth-century guerrillas, it becomes, even more than in Pound's hands, a *canción de gesta*, a song of action, and Cardenal rightly steps up the tempo, drops distracting elements, and gets closer to a good cowboy movie than to a Pound Canto in his effects. (p. 41)

And now, perhaps, it is time to point out the differences between Cardenal's cantos and Pound's. These differences can be boiled down to a more *classical* approach, a sparer and more economical and functional use of the resources discovered by Pound. A greater consideration for the reader, and a willingness to seduce him instead of making demands on him.

Where Cardenal uses Pound's break-off, juxtapositions, contrasts, and similar, effective but potentially confusing techniques, he does so more sparingly, leaving the structure much more visible to the naked eye than does Pound, easier to grasp and appreciate esthetically, less cluttered or hazy, and demanding less concentration and effort on the part of the reader.

On occasion, as I mentioned before, Cardenal presents his material in a highly dramatic way, creating a mounting suspense reminiscent of a good adventure movie that completely overwhelms the reader—*any* reader—and makes it impossible for him to put the book down until he finishes the poem. . . .

Cardenal makes few if any demands on the reader's previous education. This does not mean that there are not abundant literary and historical references in his work. (There are, and it is significant that the ordinary Latin American with a middling traditional education spots them easily.) Rather, I mean that Cardenal has realized Pound's fond hope that the reader would not need anything but the poems themselves in order to understand everything in them. I am afraid Pound was mistaken in this illusion in regard to his own Cantos, but Cardenal seems to me to have succeeded where Pound failed. I think any Spanish or Latin-American reader with a secondary or even a good grade-school education—which would ordinarily include a sketchy working knowledge of the Spanish conquest, of the great pre-Columbian civilizations and of the contemporary political scene—needs no reference books for a satisfactory reading of Cardenal's Cantos.

Perhaps another and deeper difference is that Cardenal is rooted in a wider cultural conscience. Where Pound seems to spring up disconnected from his own contemporary cultural scene and to be working against it, putting his roots through books into the past, Cardenal is born into a ready-made cultural context and shared political conscience. Cardenal's past is common to all Latin Americans. His present is likewise common to all Latin Americans. He speaks to those who are ready and willing to hear him and are likely to agree on a great many points. (p. 42).

Isabel Fraire, "Pound and Cardenal," in *Review*, No. 18, Fall, 1976, pp. 36–42.

ROBERT PRING-MILL
(essay date 1980)

[In the following excerpt, Pring-Mill identifies the ethical principles underlying Cardenal's poetry that reveal the author's commitment to societal change.]

All Cardenal's poetry "debunks," "corroborates," and "mediates" reality. His esthetic principles are clearly ethical, and most of his poems are more than just "vaguely" religious. (p. ix)

[All] eight texts of *Zero Hour and Other Documentary Poems* set out to "document" reality (and so redeem it) in a . . . dialectically visual way; picturing things, peoples, and events in the light of a clear-cut sociopolitical commitment; selecting, shaping, and imposing interpretative patterns on the world, with liberal use of such filmic "editing" techniques as crosscutting, accelerated montage, or flash frames; and pursuing "the redemption of physical reality" by bringing us "back into communication" with its harshness and its beauty. Poets and cameras can both affect what they record, but whereas a documentary camera's presence conditions the "on-going situations," Cardenal's recording of the present or the past is aimed at helping to shape the future—involving the reader in the poetic process in order to provoke him into full political commitment, thus fostering the translation of the poet's more prophetic visions into sociopolitical fact. (pp. ix–x)

None of the longer poems is simple, though they all aim at surface clarity, being meant for a wide public. They are strictly "factual," but facts can be double-edged, and their juxtapositions can also set up further meanings. Cardenal's reader cannot just sit back and "listen" to the words and rhythm: he has to visualize sequences of disparate images (each one a snatched glimpse of reality), noting their pairings and progressions, matching them both with each other and with what is left unsaid—and thereby sharing in the extraction of their fuller "meaning." These poems demand more than just an alert response, because the poet wishes to prod us beyond thought and into action: his texts are never just concerned to document and understand reality, but also to help change it—which is why they have been called "The Poetry of Useful Prophecy." But the data have to be recorded before reality can be reshaped, and the reshaping lies beyond the poems themselves: the changes for which the poet yearns lie in the future. (p. x).

[The environment in **"Trip to New York"** is familiar] and this account of a rushed six-day trip is the closest thing in any of the longer poems to the direct reporting of immediate experience, as in a personal diary. It ought to be read, however, as a deliberately "public" diary, and also *strictly as poetry*: its appearance of uncommitted objectivity is a studied one, achieving its effects (as almost always in his better poems) obliquely, by poetic means—although its "images" *are* real, not metaphorical. They may seem as clear and as immediately revealed as snapshots taken with a Polaroid camera—photos which materialize "before one's very eyes," often still in the presence of the objects photographed (in "real life") against which one is able to control the degree of "likeness" which the camera has captured. But readers cannot match these shots against what they depict, and they have all been carefully selected and assembled. . . . The process is less intellectual than intuitive; when pressed to say *how* he selects which details of "reality" to represent, Cardenal can never rationalize his procedure, saying no more than that he "knows" which details will turn out to be "poetic" in a given context. The shots he uses are, naturally, "angled" (so are a camera's): taken from the poet's individual viewpoint, which always has inherent ethical and moral preoccupations. They have been chosen and grouped (however intuitively) with a sure sense for thematic links and quiet ironies—some of which the poet makes explicit, but not all. Thus it would be rather naïve to take **"Trip to New York"** as no more than a simple diary, or a piece of instant reportage couched in free verse.

Readers would do well to examine Cardenal's methods in the familiar context of that known environment before they move into the half-alien Latin American world of the remaining poems, the first of which—**"Zero Hour"** (**"Hora 0"** or **"La hora cero"**)—is certainly the best-known of all his longer poems. As it is also the one which displays many of his favorite techniques in their most graspable form, it merits examination at somewhat greater length by way of introduction to the much later series of post-Cuban documentary poems. **"Zero Hour"** is in four parts; a brief opening section, in the nature of an introit, establishing the mood of Central American life under dictatorships, followed by three separate episodes. The first one concerns the economic factors underlying the politics of "banana republics"; the second is about Sandino, culminating in his treacherous execution (along with his brother Sócrates and two of his own commanders) on Tacho's orders, within three weeks of peace having been signed; while the third concerns the Conspiración de Abril, an anti-Somozan plot which misfired (in April 1954), in which Cardenal himself took part. (pp. xvi–xvii)

The whole introit depends on swiftly effective contrasts, whose "meaning" is not spoilt by being spelled out: the Guatemalan dictator with "a head cold," while his people are dispersed with phosphorous bombs; a single window of the Honduran dictator's office smashed, provoking an inappropriately violent response from armed police. Such introductory "shots" build up the setting and its atmosphere in the same terms and ways as does the opening sequence of almost any film. Other techniques which will recur appear in the three episodes. Thus the collage of documentary sources in the "economic" sequence, with its oppressive and depersonalizing lists of company names and alienating juxtapositions of contrastive factual details, will become a characteristically Cardenalian technique (one learned from Pound, and which has influenced many younger Spanish American poets through its use by Cardenal). Equally characteristic are the shafts of irony, often dependent on the reversal of an expected phrase—like "Carías is the dictator/who didn't build the greatest number of miles of railroad" (in Honduras).

The Sandino episode brings in many favorite themes; heroic self-abnegation, the purity of motives, and the egalitarian virtues of a guerrilla force "more like a community than like an army/and more united by love than by military discipline"—features he will all use much later as heroic precedents, when depicting the Sandinista *guerrilleros* of the following generation. At one stage, he punctuates the action with repeated snatches of "Adelita"

(perhaps the favorite song of the 1910 Mexican Revolution), intensifying the vision of Sandino's forces as a "happy army" since "A love song was its battle hymn." That is a typically filmic use of song. Filmic, too, is the accelerated montage of the death sequence, with its visual and aural crosscutting between parallel actions: the exchanges between Somoza and the American minister (and later between the American minister and Moncada) punctuated by the digging of a grave, a glimpse of prisoners, and the halting of Sandino's car, whose unnamed passengers are hustled off to face the firing squad.

Similar devices are used in the third episode. Cardenal's own entry on the scene intensifies the mood ("I was with them in the April rebellion/and I learned how to handle a Rising machine gun"). Its effect is—characteristically—heightened by the lack of further elaboration, as the "I-was-there" device gives way to the stark understatement of the hunting down and slaughter of Adolfo Báez Bone, whose identification with the land in which his body lies ensures his resurrection in the collective body of his people (a theme which becomes a leitmotif in later poems). The lyrical use of landscape and the seasons to echo or contrast with man's affairs—a striking feature of both the second and the third episodes—is a device which will achieve even greater prominence in **"Nicaraguan Canto,"** the **"Oracle,"** and both **"Epistles."**

An understanding of how **"Zero Hour"** establishes its points helps greatly with later poems, where the chronological sequence of events is deliberately dislocated by abrupt (but often unspecified) temporal intercutting, while the poetic texture is complicated by far greater use of understated or oblique "symbolic images"—or brief references whose wider connotations only emerge with hindsight, like the thrush which "sings / in freedom, in the North" (in the first few lines of **"Nicaraguan Canto"**): an unstated echo of Sandino, later to be revealed as the first hint of the presence of contemporary Sandinista freedom fighters in the same Northern hills. **"Nicaraguan Canto"** (whose Spanish title—**"Canto Nacional"**—is as much a Nerudian as a Poundian echo) culminates in one of Cardenal's most startling *tours de force;* its last nine lines consist entirely of birdsong—not a device which any translator could hope to reproduce with much success.

After the **"Canto,"** **"Mosquito Kingdom,"** (**"Reino mosco"**) provides easier reading, starting with the factual parody of Western pomp at the drunken coronation of a black British-sponsored puppet king as nominal ruler of the scattered nineteenth-century British settlements along the Mosquito Coast (all the way from Belize to Costa Rica), peopled by English-speaking former slaves from the West Indies, the Miskito Indians themselves, and the mixed race born of their intermarriage. The poem jumps forward in time to the pompous ostentation of Cornelius Vanderbilt's huge private yacht *North*

Star and Vanderbilt's involvement in the attempted exploitation of that Caribbean coast, and then cuts to a series of sordid and ill-fated dealings among its actual or would-be exploiters. Although the obscurity of this facet of nineteenth-century Nicaraguan local history may puzzle foreign readers, there is no missing the point of Cardenal's satirical devices.

"Oracle over Managua," (**"Oráculo sobre Managua"**) is a more somber and a far more complex poem. The earthquake which destroyed the city in 1972 is merely the latest stage of a long geological process, and the poem harks back to the long-past eruption which recorded the feet of fleeing prehistoric men and beasts in a layer of volcanic mud which later turned to stone, out at Acahualinca: the site of one of the worst of the shanty-towns which fringe Managua, to which the tourists and the seminarians used to go (their eyes averted from the slums) to view the Footprints. One of these seminarians, the poet Leonel Rugama, became a Sandinista, and in the sections of the poem which are addressed to him Cardenal expresses their shared view of "Revolution" as the natural next stage of "Evolution"—a process started in the stars, millions of years ago, and which will require social metamorphoses as startling as those from caterpillar into chrysalis or chrysalis to butterfly. Rugama was cornered in a house in Managua by the National Guard on January 15, 1970, along with two other young urban guerrillas, and the seige of the house where they holed up was watched by thousands of Managuans—as helicopters, planes, and even tanks were brought in to eliminate them. This small but epic incident in the Sandinista saga is made to interact, at numerous levels and in various complex ways, with the far greater catastrophe of the earthquake, in a highly intricate poetic structure.

After **"Oracle over Managua,"** the **"Trip to New York"** (**"Viaje a Nueva York"**) seems easy, and neither **"Epistle"** poses such problems of interpretation as the earlier poems because Cardenal's attitudes are stated more explicitly, for patently didactic purposes, while **"Lights"** (**"Luces"**) is equally accessible. The visual and associative material used to frame the ideas in these four poems is, however, handled with Cardenal's accustomed skill: shifts of focus or of angle; cuts from close up or detail shots right through to extreme long; jump-cuts for the sake of concision and abruptness; the poetic equivalent of pans and zooms; deft insert shots (to give additional data); the use of flashbacks (and flash-forwards), or of bridging shots (like those of railway wheels or newspapers in films); foreshortening and forelengthening, applied both to space and to time (where films would use the time lapse camera or slow motion); studied relational editing; match-cuts which link two disparate scenes by the repetition of an action or a shape (or a sound)—but most of all the dialectical process of "collisional" montage, which generates fresh meaning out of the meanings of adjacent shots. Cardenal's highly visual poetry displays the verbal

equivalent of each of those effects, and many of his most vivid sequences could almost serve as detailed shooting scripts.

All these devices, together with Poundian textual collage and the full range of more traditional poetic or rhetorical effects, are used in the course of Cardenal's documentary "redemption of reality," which successively "corroborates," "debunks," or "mediates" things, people, and events in a validation process designed to govern what we are to consider "true" and "real" and "meritorious" (or "false"—"illusory"—"contemptible") when viewed from the standpoint of his brave new revolutionary world. (pp. xxviii–xxi)

Robert Pring-Mill, "The Redemption of Reality through Documentary Poetry," in *Zero Hour and Other Documentary Poems* by Ernesto Cardenal, edited by Donald D. Walsh, translated by Paul W. Borgeson, Jr. & others, New Directions, 1980, pp. ix–xxii.

ERNESTO CARDENAL
(speech date 1981)

[Cardenal delivered the following address in Nicaragua at the Meeting of Intellectuals for the Sovereignty of the Peoples of America in 1981. Here, he discusses the scholar's prophetic role in the restructuring of Latin-American society.]

It's difficult to be the last to speak at an event where so much has been said by such important personalities, beginning with the inaugural speech by Comrade Minister Hart. At an event where not only so much has been said, but—I would say—everything has been said. Comrade Minister Hart has entrusted me with the closing words, but I suppose that he doesn't expect of me—nor would any of you—new words after all that's been said here. There's nothing I can do but repeat, but that's what we all must do when we leave here, repeat and repeat.

In the first place, it's my responsibility to repeat once again the importance of this event. Its importance, first of all, for being in Cuba. Everything in Cuba is of importance to Latin America and the world. The single word "Cuba" says everything. It was the first country in the New World that truly became independent. The one that has unleashed movements of absolute independence on the Continent. It began with twelve men in the Sierra Maestra, who changed the destiny of Cuba and Latin America and who changed history.

This event is also important because of the ominous international circumstance, rather the preapocalyptic circumstance we live in. It's a movie in which the cowboy

Robert Pring-Mill on the value of Cardenal's poetry:

[Cardenal's] poems deserve attention both for the ideas expressed (whether one agrees with these or not) and for their intrinsic poetic merit. The ideas themselves are generally simple, but the poetic artifact is often complex: deft in its manipulation of techniques, and many-layered in meaning. The obvious layer is immediately clear, conveyed with singular economy of means in a language lean and spare yet sonorous, and handled with meticulous precision. If asked to classify him (always a dangerous thing) one would have to label Cardenal a "protest poet." . . . [The] tag suits his purpose, and it situates him in a living Latin-American tradition, which relates to recurring situations in time-honored ways.

Cardenal's socioreligious thinking has a great appeal in Latin America, and its increasing militancy is symptomatic of much that is happening there among practising Christians. It demands our attention (whatever our own views may be) because it is becoming an important factor in both the spiritual and the political life of the Americas—perhaps even in the broader web of changing relationships between the peoples of the Third World and the First. Cardenal's poems help bridge the gap, mediating between peoples and giving us the "feel" of his situation. Poetry can offer insights of a special kind: experiential rather than discursive. Paradoxically, its "modes of indirection" enable it to strike the more directly home.

Robert Pring-Mill, in his introduction to Ernesto Cardenal's *Apocalypse and Other Poems*, edited and translated by Robert Pring-Mill and others, New Directions Books, 1977.

aims at the Indian with his pistol, but it's a movie that's reality.

To refer just to the case of we the Nicaraguan people, we're threatened in every way: with economic strangulation, with blockade, we're denied loans, we were denied wheat, Somoza's ex-guards are being trained in Miami and in many other places in the United States.

I've come from a trip to Libya where I went as part of a delegation headed by Commander Daniel Ortega, Coordinator of the Governing Junta of Nicaragua, for the twelfth anniversay celebration of the triumph of the Libyan Revolution. Shortly before leaving, the Governing Junta of Nicaragua received a message from Washington saying that it would be looked upon with disapproval if Commander Daniel Ortega traveled to Libya, and that if he went, to expect the consequences. Commander Daniel Ortega went to Libya and, furthermore, he related Washington's message in a public speech, which demonstrates our determination to be independent, whatever the consequences, and to struggle in defense of this independence to the very end.

And this event is also important because of the importance of so many intellectuals gathered here. It's something that has never occurred in the history of Latin America.

Roberto Fernández Retamar once said that in Cuba the intellectual avant-garde wasn't on a par with the political avant-garde, it had lagged behind. However, I think that now, in Latin America, intellectuals are also avant-garde on a par with the political avant-garde, and the proof is in this meeting.

This demands sacrifices from us—some may perhaps have to stop writing—which isn't the best, but to die isn't the best either and we may also have to die for liberation.

Comrade Armando Hart evoked the large number of intellectual martyrs incorporated into the enormous legion of martyrs from Latin America and those who suffer or have suffered in prison and those who are in exile. No one has ever seen such political commitment in writers and artists in our America. And this is characteristic of Latin America, because Europe, in general, continues with art for art's sake.

In the United States there's also an important current of socially and politically committed intellectuals, and they're our allies. I'm going to plagiarize here a North American writer, Richard Peck. One could say quote him, but I think that intellectual borrowing is as legitimate as borrowing from banks. What I've borrowed from him is the following:

In a prologue to an anthology in which he presents some interesting protest poetry, he says that poetry previously had very narrow limits—for example, on gravestones or in a love letter—but that now there aren't any limits to themes in poetry. The subject of an eight-column cover story in a newspaper can inspire a poem, moreover, the poem can be more real than a newspaper cover story. This is a new development in contemporary poetry, which deals with contemporary themes, the same themes as in newspapers. And it wasn't so before. It wasn't so in China, it wasn't so in Europe during the Middle Ages, partly because there weren't any newspapers. But poetry wasn't supposed to deal with social and economic problems; with the exception of some like Dante. And this can be said also of all contemporary literature and the arts. And it can be said also of theologians. It's interesting that theologians were invited here to this meeting.

I think it's very clear that the participation of Christians in the Revolution is of great importance, but it goes beyond that. In Latin America we have numerous Christians integrated into Marxism, but there's also going to be a union of revolutionary Christians and revolutionary Moslems, which will constitute a union of the Arab and the Latin American worlds as well. Christianity and Islam, which for centuries fought against one another in holy wars, will unite revolutionary Christians and revolutionary Moslems for a holy war against imperialism. The same can be said of Buddhism. And that union will be of Christians, Moslems, and Buddhists with Marxism.

This is in order to defend the world. Those of us who have met here are all the heirs of visionaries, philosophers, mystics, poets, and sages who throughout the centuries have wanted to change the world. We're the builders of the future, with a nostalgia for the future, a nostalgia for paradise, which isn't in the past but in the future. We're the realizers of dreams, and we shoud defend this dream-come-true in Cuba and Nicaragua, and the dream which is being fought for in El Salvador and Guatemala, the dreams of the southern cone, now in the darkness, and of all the liberation movements in Latin America. It's the defense of culture, which is the same as saying the defense of sovereignty. There's no complete culture without complete sovereignty.

In Nicaragua, with triumph of the Revolution, we've experienced an enormous cultural renaissance. Now laborers, artisans, members of the armed forces, the army and the police, write poetry—very good, modern poetry. We have many peasant and worker theater groups, and this began even before the triumph of the Revolution; it began with the insurrection in the barricades: many times the hand that brandished a gun was also the hand that strummed a guitar. And now in El Salvador many songs are being heard which are a prelude to victory. It's like hearing roosters sing in the darkness. But they're killing the young people there—simply for being young—as used to happen in Nicaragua; and the bodies appear with the eyes pulled out, the tongue cut out, the genitals torn off, as used to happen in Nicaragua; and the peasants, too, killed simply for being peasants. And Guatemala under the rule of death squads. And all of this being done by imperialism so that El Salvador and Guatemala won't become like Nicaragua is now. But there's something worse: imperialism is doing this against Nicaragua, too, because imperialists want again what once existed in Nicaragua and now exists in El Salvador and Guatemala. Another crime of imperialism is that we're being divided in Central America, the small brother countries. And speaking of crime, the death of that great statesman and revolutionary—and also an intellectual and, for me, a poet—Omar Torrijos, is clearly a crime, yes a crime, and he's one more martyr in the liberation of Latin America.

In Nicaragua we know very well that we're simply a re-won trench, a liberated territory. But there is only one Revolution and we're only one people in all Latin America, with more unity than in the Arab world—and we also include the Latin America inside the United States, as our Chicano brothers and sisters have shown us here.

The Indians gathered around the fire at night say in a poem: "What shall we do with these thoughts?" That's what we should say here: "What shall we do with these thoughts?"

Concretize ideas, go from words to action. What has happened here is something that has scarcely begun and that from now on will continue. The Second Meeting of Intellectuals for the Sovereignty of the Peoples of Our America may take place in Nicaragua.

All of this began, I say, with twelve men who, after being defeated, entered the Sierra Maestra. They say that Fidel said there: "Batista has been screwed." And not only Batista, but imperialism.

We now have Roque Dalton's tiny country, which is an example of how the smallest countries can confront the most armed one on earth. Grenada is a small island, with some two hundred thousand inhabitants, almost the size of an island in Lake Nicaragua, a small island, alone, in the middle of the ocean, defying the power of the United States.

And we have all of the Third World. We must populate the world—as Vallejo would say—with powerful, weak people. Revolutions are breaking out everywhere. In Libya, where I've just been, Khadafy threatened to bomb any ship loaded with nuclear weapons that approached the coasts of Libya and to burn the petroleum in Saudi Arabia and then Libya itself, and he declared that Libya would be the center of operations against imperialism being carried out throughout the world.

The struggle, then, is more than regional, it's worldwide. The Ayatollah Khomeini told me that all revolutions are only one and that when the whole world was liberated, then all men, women, and children of the world would march hand in hand.

We know very little about the atom and even less about stars, but between microcosm and macrocosm we have a role to fulfill. We have a role in the cosmos. The Bible as well as Marxism give us the reassurance that we're headed toward a perfect universe; if not, the universe wouldn't make any sense; if not, the Cuban Revolution wouldn't make any sense, and we well know that it does. Although to completely achieve what Marx called the attack on the sky, I'd say that we may perhaps need as much time as has passed from the *Homo abilis* to us.

But we intellectuals must work as hard as the most spirited of the *Homo abilis*. It's a matter of defending Latin America and it's also a matter of defending the human species; it's matter of defending all the species of living beings on the planet, of defending the planet itself. Defense is peace. (pp. 207–11)

Ernesto Cardenal, "Closing Address" translated by Cynthia Ventura, in *Lives on the Line: The Testimony of Contemporary Latin American Authors*, edited by Doris Mayer, University of California Press, 1988, pp. 206–11.

RICHARD ELMAN

(essay date 1985)

[A prominent American journalist, novelist, and short story writer who has traveled widely in Central America, Elman is best known for his trilogy—*The 28th Day of Elul, Lilo's Diary,* and *The Reckoning*—dealing with the Holocaust. In the following review of *With Walker in Nicaragua*, he examines Cardenal's early verse, praising it as "some of the best poetry of a modern master."]

[The] Cardenal of most interest to me is the poet of the late 1950s and early 1960s, whose work is represented in *With Walker in Nicaragua*, translated with great accuracy, simplicity and beauty by Jonathan Cohen. Cardenal's poetry of this period is exteriorist (documentary) and not so oracular as his Indian poems or his poems about Managua's earthquake. These early works are more available to us because of their subject: the penetration of the isthmus of Nicaragua by a succession of barely well-meaning and not-so-well meaning imperialists from the United States, chiefly during the nineteenth century. The subject was a natural for Cardenal. When young, he studied at Columbia University, was close to New York City's Upper West Side intelligentsia and, later, coming under the influence of Thomas Merton, resided in the Trappist monastery at Gethsemani. Cardenal was deeply influenced by Pound, Williams, Whitman, Marianne Moore and Muriel Rukeyser, whose free-verse styles he used to alter the more arty approach to exteriorism characteristic of Urtecho. His interest in the theme of the gringo in a strange land may also have been occasioned by more immediate identifications. During the nineteenth century, Cardenal's family had assimilated some European immigrants, including, legend has it, a defector from the William Walker expedition which sought to make Nicaragua a vassal state of the slave-holding Southern Confederacy. In choosing to write intimate accounts of these filibusters and verify passages from Ephraim George Squier's nineteenth-century treatise on Nicaragua, Cardenal—like Quentin Compson in *Absalom, Absalom*—was coming to terms with his own history:

> The ones who were hanged from trees
>   and left swinging
> beneath the stinking black vultures
>   and the moon
> or sprawled on the plain with a lone
>   coyote and the moon,
> their rifle beside them;
> or in the hot, cobbled streets filled

> with shouts,
> or white like shells on the seashore
> where the tides are always covering
>   and uncovering them.
> The ones who survived all those
>   dangers and are even still alive.
> The ones who stayed there afterwards
>   to get married
> and to live in peace in that land.
>   ("With Walker in Nicaragua")

"With Walker in Nicaragua" is narrated by a survivor, in a voice still awed by the jungle, the deaths, the tropics, the wonder of a land, a people. It is a report on a time when the land was unsullied, the air clear and the imperialists either bloody-minded or awestruck. The poem is tender toward the invaders without being sentimental. It presents us with their terror, their pain, their ordeal. It is these filibusters who were culturally deprived until they came to Nicaragua, where they were astonished by relatively simple beauties:

> And in León the nights were cool
> with distant guitars below wrought-
>   iron balconies
> and the wind swinging the golden
>   lamps in front of the houses.

When Cardenal's early poems are not about the contact between gringos and indigenous Nicaraguans, they are amatory and sometimes political. They were often printed anonymously, like certain poems composed for underground revolutionary handbooks. His single greatest historical poem about gringoism, a patriotic epic of sorts, is **"Zero Hour,"** which treats of the assassination of Sandino. It's a poem of heroic evocation in which the death of a hero is also seen as the rebirth of nationhood: when the hero dies, green herbs rise where he has fallen. It makes innovative use of English and Spanglais and is therefore hard to translate, but from its opening lines about "*noches tropicales*" through to its conclusion, it is very much a work of national consciousness and a unique poetic expression.

There are hardly any poems in this collection about Nicaraguan poverty; both Cardenal's middle-class origin and his historical perspective permit him to avoid describing the squalid cardboard shacks and 6-year-old laborers in the Tipitapa cotton fields of Abram Gorn, Somoza's crony. Cardenal's religious community on the island of Solentiname in Lake Nicaragua existed within peasant society and had peasants among its artists and contemplatives, but there is nothing in Cardenal's work that resembles the moving social realism of the Honduran poet Roberto Sosa, a great and original artist, who sees the children of the poor as having the "faces of indignant gods."

After **"Zero Hour,"** Cardenal's poetry became increasingly pious, almost doctrinaire, but very often effective as such. He is now so closely identified with the interests of the Sandinistas that he has been willing to allow the party to instruct him in his duties, and he complains often about his lack of time for poetry. His service as a kind of international ambassador does not always show him at his best. After chatting up the Ayatollah Khomeini, for example, he wrote enthusiastic nonsense in **Barricada** about ecclesiastics and politics, at a time when the Imam was sending prostitutes to the firing squad.

To put the matter only this way, though, is not to allow Cardenal's fine work to speak to us as it can and should. Publication of **With Walker in Nicaragua** in English provides us with examples of some of the best poetry of a modern master:

> The green, moss-covered sloth
> little by little climbing from branch to
> branch, with its eyes closed as if
> asleep but eating
> a leaf, stretching out one front claw
> followed by the other,
> not bothered at all by the ants biting
>   it,
> slowly turning its round funny-
>   looking
> face, first to one side
> and then the other,
> finally wrapping its tail around a
>   branch
> and hanging down heavily like
> a ball of lead.

"Squier in Nicaragua"

Cardenal imitates the sounds of birds and evokes the growth of erotic feeling in the gringo traveler. He can be such a superb poet that his occasional wordiness and heavy-handedness is all the more unforgivable, and Cohen's translations are so close that they make you aware of the poet's occasional faults as well as his virtues.

A considerable rivalry has always existed among the established poets of Nicaragua, whether they were courting the favor of some wealthy patron or the Sandinista state. Poets who have not joined the Sandinista movement are summarily dismissed as "old–fashioned" by those in favor. In response, the poetry of the President's wife and head of the cultural workers' unions, Rosario Murillo, was described for me by one of her poetic rivals as being hard to digest, like a *carne asado* [pot roast]." The greatest envy is directed against the international reputation of Cardenal, of whom it is now sometimes said: "What a pity. He publishes so much he doesn't even have the time to write." (pp. 374–75)

Richard Elman, "Fighting the Darkness," in *The Nation*, New York, Vol. 240, No. 12, March 30, 1985, pp. 372–75.

TAMARA R. WILLIAMS
(essay date 1990)

[In the excerpt below, Williams analyzes the epic structure and subject matter of *El estrecho dudoso*, maintaining that the poem is both secular and religious.]

Ernesto Cardenal's *El estrecho dudoso* (1966) is a book-length poem of over 3,000 lines. Divided into twenty-five cantos, the text's primary focus is on the historical events linked to the area now generally referred to as Mesoamérica, with a specific (but not exclusive) interest in Nicaragua. The poem concentrates on the first one hundred years of activity following the arrival of the Spanish on the American continent. It opens with Columbus' fourth voyage and his discovery of Terra Firma near the present Cape of Honduras in 1502, and concludes with a cataclysmic finale which narrates the destruction of the City of León, Nicaragua, by the volcano Momotombo in 1603.

The most remarkable feature of *El estrecho dudoso* is that it is constructed almost entirely from fragments of texts gleaned from an array of historical documents dating from the period in which the story takes place (1500–1650). The poet's use of history is not gratuitous; it serves the purpose of constructing a discourse which appeals to the reader as "authoritative" and evokes the illusion of truthfulness, objectivity, and adherence to fact rather than fancy and invention.

The concern for a narrative that is an accurate and truthful representation of the selected sequence of events is stated metapoetically. In Canto XXI, this concern is mediated through the quotation of metahistorical statements made by Bernal Díaz del Castillo in his *Historia verdadera de la conquista de la Nueva España*. Citing the *Verdadera Historia*, *El estrecho* outlines Bernal Díaz's reasons for writing his "verdadera historia." He wishes to tell the story of all those explorers and discoverers, conquerors and colonizers whose names were ignored and omitted in the chronicles of the period. Berating the inaccuracies of Francisco López de Gómara's *Historia de las Indias y conquista de México,* and advancing the need for a rewriting of history, Castillo initially expresses his insecurity about his abilities to write, actually abandoning the project for a time. Finally, motivated by the falsities and omissions of the chronicles and histories that precede his, he takes up the task of re-writing the "true" history of the conquest. These metahistorical statements establish "truth" as the basic criterion for the writing of history. They advance the need to rewrite history, if necessary, to attain the most accurate account and explanation of the historical sequence selected for narration. . . .

El estrecho dudoso, in constructing a historical account through a careful re-reading, selection and recombination of events recorded in "esas crónicas," embodies this same critical, corrective approach to the making of history. Like the old "regidor" from Medina del Campo, the poet in *El estrecho* scans the "viejas crónicas" like a pilot readjusting his compass and his direction, mapping out alternative coasts, new horizons, new contours of truth, and, ultimately, new meaning.

More specifically, the historical account presented to us in *El estrecho dudoso* is one that the author has deciphered and interpreted according to a particular set of religious beliefs. It is an account ordered into a relatively finite context in the sense that all historical activity is mediated within a specific ethical/theological imperative, which in turn, is informed by the author's vital commitment to Liberation Theology. In this account, Cardenal emplots historical events into an eschatological framework, rendering a story that is apocalyptic in structure and in tone, embracing the past and, in that past, looking forward to the future. Moreover, this eschatological framework, by invoking a specific theological imperative, creates a moral space in which all action is judged, or sanctioned, characters are saved or damned according to the will of a Supreme God who militantly intervenes on behalf of "those who are persecuted in the cause of right." [Gustavo Gutiérrez, in his *The Power of the Poor in History*, 1984].

Cardenal himself is a self-declared, renowned liberation theologian; however, his writings on the subject have been mainly applied in nature. His three-volume collection titled *Evangelio en Solentiname*, for example, is a series of transcribed meditations on the Bible by numerous individuals from the viewpoint of liberation. For this reason, we turn to Gustavo Gutiérrez, the pre-eminent theologian from Peru, who offers a succinct explanation of this Biblical interpretation in his book, *The Power of the Poor in History*. Several points that are central to the liberationist perspective deserve mention because they shed light on the operating belief system that informs the explanation of historical events that *El estrecho* offers.

Crucial to this interpretation is the assumption that the Bible tells the story of a people; it is seen as a historical account of the Jews. Furthermore, this history is perceived as a struggle for liberation from Egypt throughout which God reveals Himself and in which humankind proclaims Him. Besides revealing Himself in history, the God of the Bible is a God who not only governs history, but who orients it in the direction of the establishment of justice and right. He is more than a provident God, He is a God who actively sides with the poor and the afflicted in their struggle for liberation from misery, poverty, slavery and oppression.

This history from which Faith springs, argues Gutiérrez, is an open-ended history; it is open to the future. Its core—the Jews' struggle for liberation from Egypt—is an event that should be read and re-read for it prefigures other historical interventions of Yahweh. To find such interventions of Yahweh, finally, Gutiérrez insists that readings of history must be undertaken from the viewpoint of the poor, the oppressed and the enslaved. Claiming that "the history of humanity has been written with a white hand," he calls for the recovery of the memory of the struggles of "the scourged Christs of America" (which is how Bartolomé de las Casas referred to the Indians of the American continent), adding that "this memory has never died and has a latent existence in the cultural expression and resistance against the institutionalized church." Re-reading history from the viewpoint of those in the struggle, finally, makes the subversion and the re-making of history possible:

. . . *rereading history* means *remaking* history. It means repairing it from the bottom up. And so it will be subversive history. History must be turned upside down from the bottom, not from the top. What is criminal is not to be subversive, struggling against the capitalist system, but to continue being "*super*versive"—bolstering and supporting the prevailing domination. It is in this subversive history that we can have a new faith experience, a new spirituality— a new proclamation of the Gospel.

Cardenal's *El estrecho dudoso* is a brilliant and creative articulation of these concepts. It is a rereading/remaking of history of the Spanish Conquest of America, told from the vantage point of those struggling for freedom rather than from the viewpoint of the victors and perpetrators of violence and injustice. Using authoritative historical documentation, the poem explores God's presence and alliance with the victims in their struggle for life and renewal. The author remakes a history where God exhibits a clear "preferential option" for the underdogs in the struggle for justice and right. In this history, His name is proclaimed and Faith in Him and the future is renewed. He intercedes on behalf of the gravely afflicted, promising them a better world to come. Canto XVII of *El estrecho*, citing fragments of the book of prophecies of *Chilam Balam*, prophesies to the afflicted Maya that the dawning of a new age is at hand:

Es ella la insignia de Hunab-ku erguida;
el tronco del árbol enhiesto vendrá a anunciar a las gentes
que surge la nueva aurora para el mundo.

As is appropriate to the serious nature and subject of his story, Cardenal emplots the series of events into a discernible epic structure that most resembles a Christian contrast epic. In it, one series of actions involves characters in ironic human situations, and another outlines the origin or continuation of a divine society. Fragments are selected and recombined to reveal a cycle with close metaphorical identification with the Biblical structure, where the movement is from a situation of apparent exile from God toward the arrival of messengers of faith, and finally to a sign of God's redemption and revelation.

The ironic pole in *El estrecho* results primarily from an elaborate and innovative development of the quest theme. As the title of the poem suggests, *El estrecho dudoso* devotes particular attention to what may be deemed in retrospect as the Spanish obsession, particularly during the XVIth century, with locating an interoceanic waterway—un "estrecho"—that would enable them to navigate west directly to Calicutt and the Moluccas, avoiding the hostility of the Portuguese (who had virtual control over the African route to *La Especiería*). "El estrecho dudoso" is in fact "un estrecho ansiado." In Cardenal's poem, the elusive strait constitutes a pivotal object of desire; it is the object of repeated quests, the motivation for complicated and violent action, and the cause of war. The quest for the delusive strait, moreover, becomes metaphorically identified with the con-quest, that is, with the subduction of the "other" and the corruption of power which ensues. These are ultimately revealed, however, as the unattainable, as false objectives, misguided quests that invariably result in catastrophic action.

These episodes typically involve a materialistically inclined explorer on a perilous journey that promotes a temporary *agon* and a subsequent death struggle, or *pathos*, that he is rarely able to survive. The struggle pits these individuals' grossly idealized preconceptions and fabricated illusions regarding the still unexplored and unknown totality of the New World against the overwhelming, diverse, and threateningly harsh and cruel reality of the American continent. In an ironic reversal, the greedy expectation of a materialistic utopia is met instead by a hellish world of chaos and anarchy marked by labyrinthine marshes, impenetrable tropical forests, catastrophic earthquakes, volcanic eruptions and fierce maritime storms. Where the Spanish explorers hope to find gold and emeralds in infinite abundance, they instead encounter death. Extremes of heat or cold kill them off in the most grotesque manner or simply drive them to a lonely, pathetic insanity. Thirst and hunger lead the few survivors to drink sea water and eat poisonous plants and raw shellfish. Some resort to cannibalism.

A related field of action associated with the ironic pole of the contrast epic in *El estrecho dudoso* is one involving the events of war. Here again the action entails a quest, but the quest moves beyond the desire to control geographical territory to include that of conquering peoples. Hence the confrontation between man and nature is substituted for the violent confrontation between two opposing peoples.

Cardenal draws from segments of Bernal Díaz's *Verdadera historia*, and from Francisco Fuentes y Guzmán's *Recordación Florida* to develop this quest series. Hernán

Cortés, the conqueror of México, and Pedro de Alvarado, the conqueror of Guatemala, are the central figures in these episodes. They are initially portrayed as individuals of heroic dimensions, marked by their overall strength, character and daring. They invariably appear flanked by a loyal entourage of soldiers, pages, messengers, cooks, and priests. Their stature is further enhanced by colorfully waving flags, pennants and banners.

The primary obstacle the conquerors face is the resistance of the Native American peoples. Unlike the aforementioned life-threatening struggle with an antagonistic nature, this one concludes with a relatively easy Spanish victory. The domination of the Native population in these episodes is facilitated by a combination of Spanish military superiority and aggressiveness, Amerindian collusion with the conquerors (La Malinche being the classic case—Canto VIII), and the generally well-meaning and peaceful Amerindian predisposition.

The success of the conqueror, however, turns against itself when the Amerindian becomes the irreversible underdog and victim. Unable to measure their power, the conquerors become perpetrators of prolonged and unnecessary brutality. This is exemplified by the unwarranted execution of Cuauhtemoc in Aclan ordered by an over-suspicious Cortés and narrated in Canto VIII, or the ruthless burning of villages and people alike by Alvarado in his conquest of Guatemala, narrated in Canto XIII. These "executive-type" episodes are supported by the more "deliberative-type" episodes involving the speeches and letters of figures such as Bartolomé de las Casas and Antonio de Valdivieso, which graphically describe the injustices being committed and are a reminder of their moral consequences.

The successful conqueror's remarkable achievements and heroic dimensions appear, therefore, marred by the fundamental imperfection inherent in his misguided and unbridled power. This shortcoming is signalled by the introduction of an omen such as "el más extraño quetzal," which haunts Alvarado in Canto XIII. The devices utilized portend an eventual fall. The conqueror's transgression, which elicits Divine disfavor of fatal consequence, is his abuse of power in the service of oppression.

Finally, the ironic pole in *El estrecho* reaches its highest level of expression in the actions described that involve the foundation and government of cities by the Spanish in the New World. To this series belongs the ominous centrality of the governor-tyrant figure, represented by Pedrarías Dávila, Rodrigo de Contreras, and his two sons, Pedro and Hernando de Contreras.

Under the supposed aegis of the governor, life takes on nightmarish proportions. Cities are founded on greed in commercial ventures requiring extensive exploitation of the native population and resources. Mining and pig farming, metaphorically degrading tasks, are promoted as the major sources of revenue, along with the trading of slaves. Simply put, the governor-tyrant violates all the ethical codes of Christian governorships. He is the antithesis of the ideal ruler.

The turning point in *El estrecho* comes in Canto XXIV, when Hernando de Contreras, one of Rodrigo de Contreras' sons, seeks revenge against Antonio de Valdivieso for his role in ousting Rodrigo de Contreras from the Nicaraguan governorship. Hernando Contreras savagely murders the bishop in the town of León in the wake of a more generalized rebellion against Spain in 1550. Valdivieso, represented as a messianic figure selflessly devoted to delivering Nicaragua from evil, emerges at this point as a hero, introducing the anagnorisis.

The triumph of the hero is dramatically supported by the closing Canto of the poem. In an episode inspired by a segment of Fray Antonio de Remesal's, *Historia de las Indias Occidentales,* the Canto narrates the "excommunication" of the accursed city of León, Nicaragua, site of the murder of the bishop who is, like Christ himself, a "servant of God." God hands down his wrathful judgement in the shape of darkness, storms, plagues, periods of infertility, violent earthquakes, and consequent torrential landslides that virtually submerge the city in a murky sea of sulphuric-smelling mud.

From amidst the sinking city, however, emerges a sign of redemption. The text closes and the story ends with the image of a wall stained by the bloody handprint of the murdered Antonio de Valdivieso. . . . The image of the bloodstained hand is a reminder of the violence suffered by Valdivieso, but it also signals vengeance, repossession of the city, its deliverance from sin and the dawn of a new era, thus fulfilling the earlier mentioned prophecy from the *Chilam Balam* which appeared in Canto XVII. The closing, both terrible and wondrous, coincides with an episode of the Book of Revelations, which reads as follows:

And the Angel whom I saw standing on sea and land lifted up his right hand to heaven and swore by him who lives for ever and ever, who created heaven and what is in it, and the sea and what was in it, that there should be no more delay, but that in the days of the trumpet call to be sounded by the seventh angel, the mystery of God, as he announced to his servants the prophets, should be fulfilled. (Rev. 10: 5–7)

Concurrent with the narration of the deluded Colonial quest, its progressive corruption and ultimate self–destruction is the contrasting field of action narrating the origin and continuation of a divine society.

In Cardenal's poem, the original society is the society of the New World, in other words the society that the Spanish found in place when they reached what they believed to be the Indies. It is portrayed well within the realm of the divine community struggling against a sudden onslaught of Spanish injustice, disease and oppression, threatening their very survival and existence. How-

ever, the *Estrecho* goes beyond the superficial treatment of the topic of the noble savage in its adherence to Bartolomé de las Casas' argument that the Amerindian is a creature (and a creation) of God, and as such, should be embraced freely and indiscriminately into His flock. In *El estrecho dudoso*, the emphasis is overwhelming on those qualities (both individual and societal) of the Native peoples of America that point to their rightful membership to the human race and the Christian community at large.

The *Estrecho* thus undermines and ultimately inverts the stereotypical savage/civilized opposition. The Amerindian is portrayed as the virtuous, civilized and Christian victim of the lawless, fierce, godless Spanish tyrant. A selection from the XVIIIth Canto of the *Estrecho*, which draws almost entirely on Las Casas' *Brevísima relación de la destrucción de las Indias,* refers to this inversion very directly, using animal imagery reminiscent of the Biblical Psalms in opposing the wolf and the tiger (the oppressors) to the lamb (the oppressed): "Y los españoles llegaron como lobos y tigres, / como lobos y tigres donde estas ovejas mansas . . . "

It would be inaccurate to limit the portrayal of the American Indian in *El estrecho* to the extreme consequences of this inversion, which would render what would really amount to a romanticized or allegorical characterization of limited complexity. The inversion, an overcompensation and reverse stereotipification, functions on one level as a reminder of the indigenous peoples' deserved membership in the community of man and of Christ. In assuming this membership, the text assumes its implications. Once the Amerindians are inscribed in the community, their words are uttered, their voices are heard, and their actions carry a weight beyond the "othering-type" of discourse of manners and customs. Their utterances, ranging from moral judgements to prophetic messages, the most notable being speeches of Panquiaco (Canto IV), Nicaragua (Canto VI), Cuauhtemoc (Canto VIII), and Lempira (Canto XVII), and their actions (including the abortive attempts of armed resistance by Lempira in Canto XVII and the defeat of Cortés by the Aztecs in Canto XXI) become a vital component, a resisting force, in the complexity and violence of colonial reality as the *Estrecho* reads it.

Like the afflicted children of Israel, the Amerindian peoples, finally, are portrayed as a chosen people of God. Through a fragment selected from the Mayan book of prophecies by Chilam Balam, a selection which in itself reveals the poem's commitment to the idea that the native Americans were in fact "the scourged Christs of the Indies," It is revealed that, following a sustained period of discord and anarchy, one just and merciful God will come to guide and protect the people of Itzá, marking the dawn of light and the age of renewal. The inclusion of this millenial prophecy and others like it suggests a metaphorical identification with the Babylonian captivity, in that they both deal with a community experiencing a seemingly endless period of servitude and captivity, infernal darkness, victimization and destruction preceding the coming of a new heaven and a new earth.

> Adoradla, oh Itzalanos. Debéis adorar esa insignia enhiesta
> y creer en la palabra del verdadero Dios
> que viene del cielo a hablaros.
> Multiplicad vuestra buena voluntad oh Itzalanos,
> ahora que está el nuevo amanecer por iluminar universo
> y la vida está por entrar en una Edad Nueva.
> Tened fe en mi mensaje, yo soy Chilam Balam
> y he interpretado la palabra del verdadero Dios.

"La palabra del verdadero Dios" is brought to the chosen Native American society by two exemplary messengers of Christ, Antonio de Valdivieso and Bartolomé de las Casas. Profoundly committed to the community which the Spaniards had thus far considered insignificant, irrelevant, nameless and disposable, Las Casas and Valdivieso dedicate their Christian ministry to the renewal of the life and wellbeing of a culture and a people who, since the advent of the Conquest, have been systematically denied the right to life, freedom and cultural integrity.

The Defender of Indians emerges well within the dimensions of a Messianic hero, whose divinely inspired messages and actions struggle to rescue a beleaguered society from the demonic control of tyranny restore peace, order, and fertility in a world of hellish confusion on the brink of death.

Valdivieso, as was mentioned earlier, dies in the struggle as a murder victim of a threatened enemy, Hernando Contreras. His death shares close parallels with Christ's crucifixion in that Valdivieso dies symbolically for the repossession of life, justice, and peace in the midst of a decaying and violently corrupt society. Las Casas lives on in the struggle, leaving the reader with some degree of confidence and hope in the continued fight for a better world to come.

The poem displays the characteristic expansiveness of the epic, achieved primarily through the theme of the quest. On the one hand, the materialistically motivated discoveries and explorations, the quests for (to use the Augustinian model) "the city of man," its conquest and colonization lead the reader through an ample and heterogeneous physical territory ranging from coastal areas, jungles, forests, swamp lands and estuaries, to more populated spaces: villages, towns and cities. These quests could be said to constitute the horizontal spatial axis in the text. On the other hand, and projected onto this horizontal spatial axis, is a quest of a moral kind—the divinely inspired quest for the just and the right—"the city of God"—which is engendered through the figures of Las Casas and Valdivieso. It constitutes a vertical spatial axis in its metaphorical identification with heaven and hell. The vertical spatial axis and its thematic associations—God/Satan, good/bad, order/disorder, darkness/light, barrenness/fertility—modify the quality and desirability of the horizontal spatial axis and combine with it to create a poem that embraces an eschatological world. This world embraces both history and myth; it is both physical and spiritual, human and providential. (pp. 111–20)

Tamara R. Williams, "Ernesto Cardenal's 'El estrecho dudoso': Reading/Re-writing History," in *Revista Canadiense de Estudios Hispánicos,* Vol. XV, No. 1, Fall, 1990, pp. 111–21.

RUSSELL O. SALMON
(essay date 1992)

[In the following excerpt from his introduction to *Golden UFOs*, Salmon discusses Cardenal's poetic technique in the *Indian Poems* and his view of the poet as an agent of psychic wholeness.]

Poetry for Ernesto Cardenal is permanence. In the *Indian Poems* the poet situates illuminating moments in a mosaic, and like the lines in an ancient wall painting or codex his words gain permanence. Motifs in his language—the UFO, Machu Picchu, pyramid, peace, community, wisdom, fire/water, utopianism, unity—these links to themes, serve to liberate. Language is liberation. We discern this best in the poet's use of ideograms, borrowed from Ezra Pound and the Chinese poets. An ideogram is the superimposition of images, in this case often a juxtaposition of past and present, of the Indian past and modern time. Two different (or in some cases ironically identical) images when superimposed create an unsuspected third image which is powerfully dynamic—it becomes the basis of the prophetic vision of the poet-priest who has a revolutionary vision. This synergistic projection often consists of a jumble of contemporary images with an underlying mythic reality that is foreign to "modern" cultural standards. "**The Secret of Machu Pichhu**" has this quality, and once the relationship between the mythic and modern elements is understood, their juxtaposition becomes enlightening, even a revelation.

Cardenal adjusts vocaulary to the situation, and often its shock effect brings the reader to the synergistic reality the poet sought to inscribe. Or even more common is a "bleed through" effect, as seen in "**Mayapán.**" While describing the demise of ancient Mayapán in terms appropriately imitating ancient texts, Cardenal uses the vocabulary of contemporary realities to describe what happened: centralism, totalitarianism, control, dictatorship. Another type of ideogram is a juxtaposition of the dual realities of priest and revolutionary, as when the poem is an incantation, a prayer, and at the same time a call to action.

In the *Indian Poems*, Cardenal provides us with an alternative vision of the role of the poet: a link between the esthetics of the work and the ethics of the vision. As we read the *Indian Poems* we become aware of the radical dissent from the dominant values of Western society—it is the view of a religious contemplator joined with that of Indian myth and history. His poetry synergizes elements of many cultures into a coherent, stable vision, a vision derived from experience—physical, vicarious, and mystical—which is transformed into wisdom. It is a poetic integration of various forces, and even various levels of awareness, a search for unity, a need to locate and name a centering force. A sense of fragmentation manifested in the language creates a longing for a unity of consciousness, a concern for the mythical modes of thought which are attained by the style itself.

The two overriding themes of *Golden UFOs* are love and America. In this respect he follows the two great American poets José Martí and Pablo Neruda. It is a poetry both intimate and public. Asked in an interview if this poetry is religious, Cardenal replied to Mario Benedetti (1970), "the religious aspect I have expressed more indirectly, through political poems, or economic ones [**"Tahirassawichi in Washington"**; **"The Economy of Tahuantinsuyu"**], or social ones, or I have expressed one reality which is political, economic, social, religious, and mystical all at the same time. . . .

Ultimately, the poet is the keeper of the Word, and Cardenal's poetry in its expression of exterior stimuli and internal responses creates a synergetic system of unparalleled wisdom about the future values of America. Ernesto Cardenal has unearthed the lost mythic structure which is American, a prophetic vision for the future of our America. (pp. xxxiii–xxxv)

Russell O. Salmon, in an introduction to *Golden UFOs: The Indian Poems* by Ernesto Cardenal, translated by Carlos Altschul and Monique Altschul, Indiana University Press, 1992, pp. ix–xxxv.

SOURCES FOR FURTHER STUDY

Cohen, Jonathan. Introduction to Ernesto Cardenal's *With Walker in Nicaragua and Other Early Poems, 1949-1954*, translated by Jonathan Cohen, pp. 3–17. Middletown, Conn.: Wesleyan University Press, 1984.

> Overview of Cardenal's life and career.

Elias, Edward. "Prophecy of Liberation: The Poetry of Ernesto Cardenal." In *Poetic Prophecy in Western Literature*, edited by Jan Wojcik and Raymond-Jean Frontain, pp. 174–85. London: Associated University Presses, 1984.

> Examines how Cardenal communicates a prophetic message by mixing historical documents, the language of pre-Columbian civilizations, biblical quotations, and colloquial Spanish in his poetry.

Gibbons, Reginald. "Political Poetry and the Example of Ernesto Cardenal." *Critical Inquiry* 13, No. 3 (Spring 1987): 648–71.

> Presents Cardenal within the context of Latin American politics, contending that, although the poet wrote in a given historical circumstance, his verse exhibits a wider cultural conscience.

Johnson, Kent. "Interview with Ernesto Cardenal." In Ernesto Cardenal's *A Nation of Poets: Writings from the Poetry Workshops of Nicaragua*, translated by Kent Johnson, pp. 7–24. Los Angeles: West End Press, 1985.

> Interview in which Cardenal discusses his work as Nicaraguan Minister of Culture, the poetic tradition of Latin America, and the relation of literature to political revolution.

Pring–Mill, Robert. Introduction to Ernesto Cardenal's *Marilyn Monroe and Other Poems*, translated by Robert Pring-Mill, pp. 7–32. London: Search Press, 1975.

> Outlines Cardenal's life and career, focusing on his poetry's changing style and content.

Randall, Margaret. "Talking with Ernesto Cardenal." *Fiction International* 16, No. 2 (Summer/Fall 1986): 47–60.

> Interview in which Cardenal discusses his literary influences, the Nicaraguan revolutionary struggle, and the relation of poetry to spiritual life.

Schaeffer, Claudia. "A Search for Utopia on Earth: Toward an Understanding of the Literary Production of Ernesto Cardenal." *Crítica Hispánica* IV, No. 2 (1982); 171–79.

> Examines "the totality of Cardenal's literary production as a continuous and developing historical praxis which pursues both personal and artistic orientation in contemporary social structures, and which offers not absolute solutions but provides an impetus to the continuing forward movement of his search."

———. "Peace, Poetry, and Popular Culture: Ernesto Cardenal and the Nicaraguan Revolution." *Latin American Literary Review* XIII, No. 26 (July–December 1985): 7–18.

> Analyzes the political and nationalistic dimensions of Cardenal's poetry and its contribution to the 1979 Nicaraguan Revolution.

Valdes, Jorge H. "The Evolution of Cardenal's Prophetic Poetry." *Latin American Literary Review* XI, No. 23 (Fall–Winter 1983): 25–40.

> Contends that Cardenal's poetry has a dual purpose: it announces the emergence of a new world order and outlines the way to achieve it.

Additional coverage of Cardenal's life and career is contained in the following sources published by Gale Research: *Contemporary Authors*, Vols. 49–52; *Contemporary Authors New Revision Series*, Vols. 2, 32; *Contemporary Literary Criticism*, Vol. 31; *Hispanic Writers*; and *Major Twentieth-Century Writers*.

Alejo Carpentier

1904–1980

(Born Alejo Carpentier y Valmont) Cuban novelist, journalist, essayist, musicologist, poet, and short story writer.

INTRODUCTION

Carpentier is a commanding figure in Latin American and Caribbean literature for his importance in shaping the twentieth-century novel. He was briefly associated with the Surrealist movement in Paris but eventually renounced it, developing his own concept of *lo real maravilloso* ("the marvelous real"), the presence of a kind of magic he saw as indigenous to the physical world of Latin America. Carpentier lived outside his homeland for a number of years, and his expatriate experience supplied the stimulus for his novels, which portray the encounter of European culture with the mystery and primitivism of the untouched New World. Alongside his renown as a novelist and short story writer, Carpentier enjoyed a reputation as a distinguished journalist and musicologist during his lifetime.

Carpentier's family background and cultural world were representative of the most evolved cosmopolitanism of Latin American society. He was born in Havana to a French architect father and a Russian mother who had studied medicine in Switzerland. As a youth Carpentier studied in Paris at the Lycée Jeanson de Sailly, where he achieved an advanced level of musical training. He returned to Cuba in 1920 and began studies in architecture at the University of Havana. He had already begun contributing articles and criticism to Havana newspapers when his need to earn a livelihood forced him to abandon his university studies and to support himself exclusively by journalism. The youthful Carpentier contributed music and theater criticism and short fiction to numerous experimental reviews, and in 1927 collaborated in founding *Revista de avance*, the most influential of the organs of the Cuban *vanguardismo*. In 1927 Carpentier was jailed in Havana for signing a manifesto against the Cuban dictator Gerardo Machado y Morales. While in prison he wrote his first novel *¡Écue-Yamba-Ó! Novela afrocubana*, which was published in 1933. After his release in 1928, Carpentier fled Cuba for Paris, where he spent the following eleven years working as a journalist and a sound-effects specialist for French radio. During this period he experimented with new media, such as radio plays and works that mixed text and musical components. He also collaborated on musical programs with avant-garde composers, among them Heitor Villa-Lobos and Darius Milhaud. Carpentier returned to Cuba in May 1939, but subsequently moved to Caracas, Venezuela to found a radio station; he remained there until 1959. The South American period was one of Carpentier's most productive, when he wrote his first mature novels, as well as his masterwork of musicology, *La música en Cuba* (1946). Following the Cuban revolution of 1959, Carpentier returned to his own country, where he served as director of the Cuban Publishing House in Havana from 1960 to 1967. In 1966 he took up residence in Paris once again as cultural attaché to the Cuban Embassy, a position he held until his death in 1980.

Two distinct periods are recognized in Carpentier's career. The first, comprising the 1920s, 30s, and early 40s, is known as his Afro-Cuban period and includes his early collaborative work with choreographers and composers in Paris. In performance works of mixed media, Carpentier integrated text, music, and dance in experimental formulations. His earliest works were collaborations with the composer Amadeo Roldan on librettos and scores for experimental Afro-Cuban ballets and choreographic poems of folkloric character, the most important of which is "El milagro de Anaquillé," written in 1927 but not published until 1937. The Cuban *vangardismo*, with which Carpentier aligned himself after 1939, revolutionized modern art by its emphasis on the black African heritage within Cuban culture. Carpentier became fascinated with African religious beliefs, art, and music, as they were transplanted to the Europeanized Cuban culture, and his earliest short stories, as well as his first novel *¡Écue-Yamba-Ó!*, evoke the mystery and paradox of this peculiarly Caribbean Africanism. Through the character of Menegildo in *¡Écue-Yamba-Ó!*, Carpentier represents the values of black African society—the power of the primitive and the knowledge of the occult.

Carpentier's *El reino de este mundo* (1949; *The Kingdom of This World*) and his *El siglo de las luces* (1962; *Explosion in a Cathedral*) represent the metaphysical concern with history and its meaning that recurred as a theme in all his mature fiction. In these historical novels about the Haitian Revolution and an uprising in the Antilles during the French Revolution, Carpentier sets the values of the European Enlightenment up against the intensity of Caribbean culture, with its supernatural and magical aspects. Carpentier

achieves an apocalyptic climax in *Explosion in a Cathedral* that has suggested to some readers the terrors of Goya's etchings entitled *The Horrors of War*. Carpentier's third novel, *Los pasos perdidos* (1953; *The Lost Steps*) treats another theme of special interest to the author—the theme of modern man repelled by the alienating confinements of civilization. The narrator of the novel is a musician and composer who speaks through the pages of his journal. The narrative of his urban life, diminished in both the professional and personal sense, is followed by his description of a trip by river into the interior of the Amazonian forest to search for authentic musical instruments of the indigenous peoples (the Orinoco River in Venezuela, which Carpentier had visited, may have been the model). In the end the allegorical novel asks whether modern man—and specifically the modern artist or person of ideas—is capable of casting off civilization and reimmersing himself in an unspoiled primitivism. A collection of Carpentier's short stories, published in 1958 under the title *Guerra del tiempo: Tres relatos y una novela* (*The War of Time*), includes early stories from the 1940s, such as "Viaje a la semilla," ("Journey Back to the Seed"), and "Semejante a la noche" ("Like the Passing of the Night"), as well as the carefully crafted "El camino de Santiago," ("The Road to Santiago"). In these shorter works Carpentier takes an understated and enigmatic tone rarely encountered in his novels, while developing some of the same themes of voyage and discovery, exile and return.

Incongruity and paradox, according to Carpentier, are at the heart of Latin American life and the *real maravilloso*. Carpentier stated that it was during a trip to Haiti in 1943 that he had recognized the source of the marvelous real in the virgin landscape, the myths, and the history of the Americas. "After feeling the genuine sorcery of the landscape of Haiti, discovering magic omens along the red roads of the Central Plateau, hearing the Petro and Rada drums, I found myself comparing the marvelous reality I had just experienced with the tiresome pretense of provoking the marvelous that characterized certain literature of the last thirty years [i.e., surrealism]." As the critic Karl Müller-Bergh has explained it, Carpentier viewed the discovery of the Americas as an unprecedented event that fundamentally changed the course of global history. In novels such as *The Kingdom of This World* and *Explosion in a Cathedral*, Carpentier reveals how the historic encounter between the Old and the New Worlds forced upon Europe a new perspective on history in which the celebrated cradles of European civilization could no longer be viewed as historically unique. His writing is considered without parallel in twentieth-century literature for having defined the special role of Latin America and the New World in the mythology of this new universal culture.

CRITICAL COMMENTARY

RAYMOND D. SOUZA
(essay date 1976)

[In the following excerpt from his book *Major Cuban Novelists: Innovation and Tradition,* Souza surveys four of Carpentier's novels, including the early *¡Écue-Yamba-Ó!* which has had little critical discussion in English. Souza analyzes the philosophic and existential pessimism of Carpentier as exhibited in these works and concludes by defining the writer's stature within Cuban and Spanish-American literature.]

Alejo Carpentier is the dean of Cuban novelists. A man of cosmopolitan background and tastes, he has travelled extensively and has resided many years outside of Cuba. Carpentier began his literary career in the 1920s when vanguardism was in vogue, with its marked interest in experimentation and new methods of artistic expression. His first novel, *¡Écue-Yamba-Ó!,* was published in 1933, the year of Labrador Ruiz's experimental novel *El laberinto de sí mismo* and Novás Calvo's novelized biography of a Spanish slave trader, *Pedro Blanco, el negrero.* In 1932, Novás Calvo also published three major short stories, "La luna de los ñáñigos," "En el cayo," and "Aquella noche salieron los muertos." The first years of the 1930s marked a turning point in the artistic development of Cuban narrative fiction.

Carpentier's first novel contains elements that he would expand, refine, and use as the basis of his major works. *¡Écue-Yamba-Ó!* reveals his interest in the documentation of his novels, a technique that he would combine with an appraisal of an individual's subjective way of viewing the reality of his personal existence. Carpentier's novels present an interpenetration of the subjective and objective, of the temporal and the eternal, of man as an individual and man as a member of the species. He accomplishes this coordination by the skillful use of archetypal patterns and structural devices. *¡Écue-Yamba-Ó!* marks the beginning of Carpentier's novelistic efforts to capture the marvellous elements of Latin-American reality.

Labrador Ruiz's *El laberinto de sí mismo,* on the other hand, is an innovative work characterized by extreme fragmentation. It is almost impossible to gain a coherent view of the novel, since the narration, characters, and time are fragmented into a maze of disparate pieces. Novás Calvo's stories appeared in José Ortega y Gasset's prestigious Spanish journal *La Revista de Occidente.* They are stories that utilize a first-person narration, which successfully captures the essence of popular language. The language conveys and creates a magical world that emotionally telescopes the reader back in time, so that he views and experiences the cosmos as man did before the dawn of history. Artistically, Novás Calvo's stories are the most successful creations of Cuban prose fiction during 1932 and 1933. They are indicative of a new awareness of the creative power that language can have, whereas Labrador Ruiz's novel is an early manifestation of the fragmentation that the novel as an artistic form would be undergoing. All of these works foreshadow future accomplishments in Cuban narration.

Novás Calvo's "La luna de los ñáñigos" and Carpentier's *¡Écue-Yamba-Ó!* are narrative manifestations of the growing interest in the Negro, which occurred in Cuba during the late 1920s. In part, this concern was an outgrowth of the rapid development of anthropological data on the African in the Western world. Within Cuba, such folklorists as Fernando Ortiz were largely responsible for the development and dissemination of this information. The blossoming of these interests coincided with the cultural and intellectual turmoil that was occurring in Cuba. The *Revista de Avance* (1927–1930), an important Cuban journal, became one of the focal points of this intellectual ferment that was characterized by a search for a new cultural orientation and a reappraisal of national values. At times these preoccupations centered on the identification of the most autochthonous elements in Cuban culture—an undertaking that also took place in many other Spanish-American countries. In some nations, the Indian became the object of this search for roots; in Cuba it was the Negro. Carpentier has admitted that these ventures were often superficial and tended to center on the picturesque, but he also feels they were a necessary step in the development of a new sense of awareness:

> La posibilidad de expresar lo criollo con una nueva noción de sus valores se impuso a las mentes. . . . Súbitamente, el negro se hizo el eje de todas las miradas. Por lo mismo que con ellos se disgustaba a los intelectuales de viejo cuño, se iba con unción a los *juramientos ñáñigos,* haciéndose el elogio de la danza del *diablito.* Así nació la tendencia afrocubanista, que durante más de diez años alimentaría poemas, novelas, estudios folklóricos y sociológicos. Tendencia que en muchos casos, sólo llegó a lo superficial y periférico, al "negro bajo palmas ebrias de sol," pero que constituía

Principal Works

"El milagro de Anaquillé" (ballet) 1927
["The Miracle of Anaquillé: An Afro-Cuban Ballet," 1980]

Poèmes des Antilles: Neuf chants sur des textes d'Alejo Carpentier (poetry; music by Marius François Gaillard) 1931

¡Écue-Yamba-Ó! Novela afrocubana (novel) [first publication] 1933

"Histoire de lunes" (short story) 1933
["Tale of Moons," 1980]

"Viaje a la semilla" (short story) 1944
["Return to the Seed," 1963; also published as "Journey Back to the Source," 1970]

"Los fugitivos" (short story) 1946
["The Fugitives," 1972]

La música en Cuba (music history) 1946

*El reino de este mundo (novel) 1949
[*The Kingdom of This World*, 1957]

Los pasos perdidos (novel) 1953
[*The Lost Steps*, 1956]

El acoso (novella) 1956
[*Manhunt*, 1959; also published as *The Chase*, 1989]

†*Guerra del tiempo: Tres relatos y una novela* (short stories and novella) 1958
[*The War of Time*, 1970]

El siglo de las luces (novel) 1962
[*Explosion in a Cathedral*, 1963]

Tientos y diferencias (essays) 1964

Literatura y conciencia política en América Latina (essays) 1969

La ciudad de las columnas (architectural history) 1970

Concierto barroco (novella) 1974
[*Concierto Barroco*, 1988]

El recurso del método (novel) 1974
[*Reasons of State*, 1976]

El arpa y la sombra (novel) 1979
[*The Harp and the Shadow*] 1980

La consagración de la primavera (novel) 1979

Obras completas. 9 vols. (collected works) 1983–1986

---

*The English edition of this work lacks the author's "Prólogo."

†Contains "El camino de Santiago," "Viaje a la semilla," "Semejante a la noche," and *El acoso*.

---

un paso necesario para comprender mejor ciertos factores poéticos, mucicales, étnicos y sociales, que habían contribuido a dar una fisonomía propia a lo criollo [*La música en Cuba*].

¡Écue-Yamba-Ó! and "La luna de los ñáñigos" go beyond a mere portrayal of the Negro as a picturesque part of Cuban culture. These works deal with the process that individuals pass through in order to become a member of a group, and in both cases the groups are ñáñigo sects. These sects are secret organizations of African origin, a type of mutual protection society based on religious concepts. Novás Calvo's story is remarkable in that it deals with a white woman's attempts and her success at crossing the invisible boundary of membership in the face of severe opposition. She is accepted into the sect in spite of its opposition, because spiritually and emotionally she becomes one and the same as the group. The delineation between blacks and whites in the story is not based on sociological factors, but on emotional ones. The story captures the aura of the unknown, and the protagonists become linked with the mysteries of the world that surrounds them. Rather than being in opposition to the environment, they become a part of it.

Since Carpentier's work is a novel, it is a more extensive treatment of this theme. It covers the complete life of a single protagonist, Menegildo, a Negro. The novel is divided into three major parts that separate Menegildo's life into three distinct phases. In the first, we view his birth and childhood and the beginning of his movements out of this stage. The second section presents Menegildo's experience as an adolescent with its attendant awakening of powerful emotions and ends when he departs to live in the city. In the third part of the novel, Menegildo becomes an adult and a member of a ñáñigo sect. The individual cycle of existence closes with Menegildo's death, but life goes on in the presence of his son who will bear his name.

¡Écue-Yamba-Ó! is only partially successful. The contents of the novel indicate that the author did extensive research before writing. It contains, for example, a lengthy glossary and even has photographs to introduce the reader to the realm of the ñáñigo sects. Although these elements contribute to the novel's authenticity, they give it a documentary quality that appeals purely to the reader's intellect rather than his emotions. We observe ritual, for example, but we do not experience it and, therefore, gain no emotional appreciation of what it means to its participants. Novás Calvo's story, "La luna de los ñáñigos," is more successful in this respect: the first-person narration and the conversational quality of the story create an intimacy that involves the reader, drawing him into events until he finds himself believing the impossible is true. In *¡Écue-Yamba-Ó!*, rational observation

fails to capture the irrational realities of the ñáñigo world.

Carpentier himself has recognized some of the limitations of his first novel. "Esta primera novela mía es tal vez un intento fallido por el abuso de metáforas, de símiles mecánicos, de imágenes de un aborrecible mal gusto futurista y por esa falsa concepción de lo nacional que teníamos entonces los hombres de mi generación." It is interesting to note that his comments are directed at some of the concepts on which the novel is based and the language that is employed. His observations on language are perhaps the most significant, since the author uses this medium to create a credible world for his reader. If an author is skillful enough in his usage of language, he is apt to convince his reader of the plausibility of what he is relating even when his observations miss the mark. The major thrust of Carpentier's career has been toward making the unbelievable believable. In his view, Latin-American reality is so contradictory and awe inspiring that real events seem bigger than life. He has stated, "For me the American continent is the most extraordinary world of the century, because of its all-embracing cultural scope. Our view of it must be ecumenic" [quoted by Luis Harss and Barbara Dohman, in their *Into the Mainstream: Conversations with Latin American Writers*, 1967]. He has attempted to convey these convictions by painstakingly researching his novels and by developing a rich and flowing language. The writing of *¡Écue-Yamba-Ó!* marks the beginning of the movement toward this goal, and it was an experience that would serve Carpentier well in the composition of future novels.

¡Écue-Yamba-Ó! was written in an early period in Carpentier's career as a novelist. At that time, he was involved in the "vanguardista" movements that swept Cuba in the 1920s. In 1928, searching a more favorable political climate, he left for France, his base of operations until 1939. It was a spiritual pilgrimage that enabled him to learn more about Latin America. It is one of the paradoxes of human existence that geographical separation often heightens our ability to perceive the inner workings of our own society. His stay in France added greatly to his intellectual and artistic formation, for he had direct contact with many groups including the surrealists. He continued to broaden many of his interests such as music that he had cultivated in Cuba. Carpentier is a perceptive critic, and this ability was fully exercised in Europe. In an article he had published in the Cuban journal *Social* in 1932, he identified three of the cultural leaders of arts in the twentieth century when he stated, "Tres creadores de nuestro tiempo se sustraerán, tal vez por mucho tiempo todavía, a los efectos de una reacción de la juventud: Stravinsky, Picasso y James Joyce." This is the type of observation that can establish a critic's career.

Sixteen years elapsed between the appearance of Carpentier's first novel and his second. He returned to Cuba in the late thirties after his stay in France. During his sojourn in Europe, he experienced the Spanish civil war, a tragic and compelling event that attracted and touched the lives of many of the world's writers and intellectuals. In 1943, Carpentier visited Haiti, and this trip provided the impetus for his second novel *El reino de este mundo* (1949). In Haiti there are impressive ruins of Henri Christophe's regal palace Sans-Souci and the mountain fortress he constructed. Christophe is an imposing figure in Haitian history. Born a slave he used the Wars of Independence as a means to fulfill his wildest dreams. He seized power in 1806, and in 1811 he had himself crowned king and ruled with an iron and cruel hand until his death in 1820. His is the classical tale of the revolutionary hero turned tyrant, and he is one of the historical figures that appear in Carpentier's novel.

El reino de este mundo takes place in Hispaniola and relates different phases of the Haitian Wars of Independence. The novel is divided into four main sections, and each chronicles an important stage of the independence movement. The first part narrates the exploits of Mackandal, a Negro rebel who led an early slave uprising that used the poisoning of live-stock and people as a major tactic. Terror gripped those in power as the island became filled with the stench of death, but Mackandal was finally captured and executed in 1758. The second part deals with the outbreak of a rebellion led by Bouckman in 1791. Bouckman suffered the same fate as Mackandal, but the organized Negro forces prevailed and defeated the French in 1803. The third division deals with Henri Christophe, the hero who became tyrant. Under his stern rule, the country became more prosperous, but many of the abuses the Negroes had struggled against were reinstituted. This section ends with the demise of Christophe's reign and his suicide. The final part occurs during the period of the government of the mulatto Boyer (1820–1843), a time of reunification after the collapse of Christophe's government. During Boyer's rule, many of the old abuses are still perpetuated, and there is a definite need for a renewed struggle against tyranny. Ti Noel, a slave who witnessed and at times participated in many of the events in the other sections, is faced with the problem of deciding whether he should use the knowledge he has acquired during the course of many years to answer the needs of his people.

Carpentier uses Ti Noel to bridge the gap between the objective truths of history and the subjective beliefs of the slaves, who fought for their freedom. He spans this dichotomy in order to present his reader with the extraordinary nature of the events that took place in Hispaniola. It was a period that saw black slaves rebelling against and defeating their French masters despite the formidable odds. Even Napoleon Bonaparte's brother-in-law, General Leclerc, was defeated. A slave later became a king and ruled over a royal court of formal and majestic splendor only to succumb to the wrath of his own people. It was a time of bizarre events, when the extraordinary seemed natural and the miraculous appeared normal. One of Carpentier's descriptions of the struggle against the French captures the essence of the times:

> Ahora los Grandes Loas favorecían las armas negras. Ganaban batallas quienes tuvieran dioses guerreros que invocar. Ogún Badagrí guiaba las cargas al arma blanca contra las últimas trincheras de la Diosa Razón. Y, como en todos los combates que realmente merecen ser recordados porque alguien detuviera el sol o derribara murallas con una trompeta, hubo, en aquellos días, hombres que cerraron con el pecho desnudo las bocas de cañones enemigos y hombres que tuvieron poderes para apartar de su cuerpo el plomo de los fusiles.

In the first section of the novel, the rebel leader Mackandal is put to death at the stake in an elaborate ceremony properly designed to impress the Negro slaves. The execution, however, does not have the desired effect, for the slaves believe Mackandal has acquired the power of metamorphosis and that he changed into an insect to escape his executioners. In the last part of the novel, Ti Noel is pictured as having this power. At first he attempts to use it for his own personal use to escape from difficult circumstances, but his search for peace in another realm is thwarted. He then realizes that any powers he possesses must not be used to escape from man but to better man's condition. He is seized by a "cosmic fatigue" and is aware that

> el hombre nunca sabe para quién padece y espera. Padece y espera y trabaja para gentes que nunca conocerá, y que a su vez padecerán y esperarán y trabajarán para otros que tampoco serán felices, pues el hombre ansía siempre una felicidad situada más allá de la porción que le es ortorgada. Pero la grandeza del hombre está precisamente en querer mejorar lo que es.

After this illumination, Ti Noel raises a call to battle and then disappears like so many heroic figures before him. He has unleashed another rebellion in the struggle for a better existence, and another cycle is about to run its course.

The development of *El reino de este mundo* is chronological, but the four sections repeat the story of the transformative role of the hero. We have a presentation of the forward movement of history, but within this chronological progression there are patterns that repeat themselves in an endless process of renewal. Carpentier takes the long view of history, for him an individual lifetime is like a second in a century of time. It is man's continual quest to better his condition that concerns him, a preoccupation that would be further explored in *El siglo de las luces.*

El reino de este mundo as *¡Écue-Yamba-Ó!*, reflects Carpentier's interest in the documentation of his works. The author points out in the introduction to his second novel that his book

> ha sido establecido sobre una documentación extremadamente rigurosa que no solamente respeta la verdad histórica de los acontecimientos, los nombres de personajes—incluso secundarios—,de lugares y hasta de calles, sino que oculta, bajo su aparente intemporalidad, un minucioso cotejo de fechas y de cronologías.

He seems to be stressing that in America reality is more marvellous than the world of the imagination. His works are narrations of the fantastic within the contexts of reality, artistic creations that attempt to unravel the contradictory paradoxes of existence.

El reino de este mundo is greatly superior to Carpentier's first novel, and the reader is more apt to find himself involved in this work than in *¡Écue-Yamba-Ó!*. The language is more authentic, and one feels a movement on the part of the author toward a recognition of the subjective dimensions of his characters. However, the reader senses that Carpentier's emphasis on the verisimilar aspects of this novel caused him to eschew imaginative narration to some extent. The result is that we have an outline of what might have been a major novel. The characters are not well developed; they are really caricatures. There is a multitude of historical events that are only briefly covered in the novel, and this combination of great breadth with little depth precludes the development one would like to see. *El reino de este mundo* does represent a considerably expanded view of Latin-American reality, when contrasted with *¡Écue-Yamba-Ó!*, and this new undertaking must have presented a number of technical difficulties to its author. A few years after the publication of *El reino de este mundo*, the first of Carpentier's two major works appeared, suggesting that the preparation of his chronicle of the Haitian Wars of Independence helped him to deal with and resolve many technical considerations.

In his first two novels, Carpentier deals mainly with characters who do not share his cultural or social background. The appearance of *Los pasos perdidos* in 1953 marks a change in this procedure, for the main protagonist in this novel is a man who shares Carpentier's cultural formation. This would also be true of his portrayal of Esteban in *El siglo de las luces* (1962). Esteban is depicted as an intellectual who questions and sees the flaws in all schemes. Both of these novels evidence an all-encompassing view of mankind. In this respect, they could have been more abstract and removed from the reader than his first two novels. Such is not the case, however, for Carpentier solved the difficulties of presenting an interpenetration of the subjective and objective by allowing his protagonists to be more intimate reflections of a reality he personally knows. This does not mean that his later novels are intimate writings, for Carpentier always maintains a fairly objective stance, but they do reflect more comprehension and understanding of the inner motivations of their characters. Carpentier is a detached writer, and one does not find in his novels the type of examination of the dark recesses of the human soul that a Carlos Fuentes or Ernesto Sábato demonstrates. The novels of Fuentes and Sábato tend to overwhelm the reader with their stark intimacy, as their characters pursue the answers to moral dilemmas. Carpentier's approach is calmer, more detached and ideological, and he is at his best when he is portraying men whose intellectualism or personality keeps them somewhat removed from their own passions. This ability was not used to the best advantage in the first two novels. In fact, it was a decided liability, for he achieved detachment when passionate commitment was required. Fortunately, this distance, which proved to be a weakness in Carpentier's first two novels, became a distinct strength in *Los pasos perdidos* and *El siglo de las luces*.

Los pasos perdidos is Carpentier's most personal book. The novel is presented in the form of a diary, and this first-person narration helps to create a greater sense of intimacy than one is accustomed to finding in Carpentier's works. It should be pointed out, however, that the novel is a narration controlled by the intellect, told by a man whose emotions are subordinate to his thoughts. Carpentier demonstrates a complete command of the language, and the novel is a fully developed, mature work. In *Los pasos perdidos*, he found a way to capture the temporal dimensions of Latin-American reality.

The novel is a journey back through time, a return to the world of Genesis when vital forces were engaged in a struggle against formlessness, imposing order on the chaos of existence during the dawn of creation. The journey is made by a man from the contemporary period, whose life has become an existence without any permanent value. His potentials in music are not being used creatively, and he finds himself debasing his talents to the interests of the commercial world in order to earn a living. His life is a series of unfulfilled promises, dull, and deadening routines. His wife's main interest is her theatrical career, and when she is not involved in professional activities, their sexual life has been reduced to a Sunday ritual. He lives without purpose and is overwhelmed by the urban environment in which he dwells. He seeks solace in a mistress, Mouche, a pseudo-intellectual who earns a living as an astrologer. She is a false solution to a difficult problem. His relationships with Mouche and his wife, Ruth, are indicative of the life he is living. In fact, throughout the novel the quality of his life is revealed by the women with whom he is involved. Ruth's life is a series of theatrical pretenses, and Mouche is a authentic as the astrology she practices. They both exemplify the superficial glamour to which the protagonist is very much attracted.

An opportunity to renew his life comes from an unexpected source. He has a chance meeting with a former mentor, the curator of a museum. During an earlier period of study, the protagonist had developed a theory on the origin of music, and recent findings indicate that he may be correct. The curator offers him the opportunity to organize an expedition to search for musical instruments

that would confirm his theory. At first, he declines the offer, but Mouche's interest in a free trip to the tropics and the prospect of an empty three week vacation that is approaching convince him to accept. Mouche has a friend who is capable of fabricating primitive musical instruments, so the search will be no problem. The protagonist's journey into authenticity begins with deceit and deception.

Once they embark on their trip, the beginnings of a new realm slowly begin to unfold. They first travel to a Latin-American city, and, while there, a revolution breaks out. They leave the city and proceed into the interior, and at each stage of the journey further elements of civilization are left behind. The protagonist becomes increasingly interested in the search for the musical instruments and finds himself gradually being rejuvenated. Just the opposite transpires with Mouche whose personality becomes diminished by each step into the past. She becomes less attractive to the protagonist, as the qualities of the seductive world of illusion she represents are revealed.

It is at this point that Rosario, the third woman in the protagonist's life, appears. Rosario is completely different from Ruth and Mouche. She is free of the superficiality and deception that are apparent in the protagonist's wife and mistress. Rosario belongs to the world of primitive man, and her life is rooted in primordial realities. She is identified with telluric forces, and her elemental beauty attracts the protagonist. Rosario and Mouche have a physical confrontation, and shortly after this episode Mouche returns to civilization. Rosario then becomes the protagonist's companion in his voyage to the beginning of time.

As he and the group penetrate and are engulfed by the jungle, the protagonist frequently finds himself overwhelmed by fear. For him the jungle is "el mundo de la mentira, de la trampa y del falso semblante; allí todo era disfraz, estratagema, juego de apariencias, metamorfosis." It is a place of constant change that threatens him with the specter of formlessness. He is awed by this world that would devour him, and he experiences anew the primordial fear of darkness and the chaos it represents. While in this maze, his attention is drawn to a succession of vertical images that suggest that another realm exists. He notices the upward extension of the trees, the apparent freedom of movement of the birds, and he discovers

> un nuevo mundo de nubes: esas nubes tan distintas, tan propias, tan olvidadas por los hombres, que todavía se amasan sobre la humedad de las inmensas selvas, ricas en agua como los primeros capítulos del Génesis. . . . Esas nubes, rara vez enlazadas entre sí, estaban detenidas en el espacio, como edificadas en el cielo, semejantes a sí mismas, desde los tiempos inmemoriales en que presidieran la separación de las aguas y el misterio de las primeras confluencias.

This vertical fixation of images progresses to the appearance of a massive meseta that rises above the jungle.

For two days they climb its slopes, leaving behind the devouring jungle as they enter into the barren world of rock. The meseta, unlike the jungle, is a place of permanence, and the protagonist terms it the "Capital de las Formas." The stark contrasts between the jungle and the meseta cause him to recognize that he has entered a realm that existed prior to man:

> Lo que se abre ante nuestros ojos es el mundo anterior al hombre. . . . Estamos en el mundo del Génesis, al fin del Cuarto Día de la Creación. Si retrocediéramos un poco más, llegaríamos adonde comenzara la terrible soledad del Creador—la tristeza sideral de los tiempos sin incienso y sin alabanzas, cuando la tierra era desordenada y vacía, y las tinieblas estaban sobre la haz del abismo.

It would seem that the protagonist has returned to paradise. He is rejuvenated in this world of elemental forms, and his creative energies are rekindled. He decides to forget and abandon his past in order to remain in the "Valle del Tiempo Detenido." The people who brought him to this place, which is far removed from the contemporary world, are constantly struggling against the forces of chaos as they establish settlements and begin to give form to existence. The exertion is a collective struggle against primal realities, but the protagonist is a musician, the practitioner of an individual art that does not belong to this time. A sequence of events indicates that the protagonist is an alien in this land of Genesis and that to fulfill his ambitions he must return to his own time.

Despite his general satisfaction with life in primitive society, the protagonist never becomes a complete part of this existence. There is one event in the novel that clearly delineates this separation. At one point Narciso, a leper who lives near the settlement, attempts to violate a young Indian girl. When she appears, running through the village, screaming, and bleeding from the attempted assault, the men immediately search for Narciso. The protagonist accompanies one of the men and carries an old rifle. They discover Narciso kneeling in a clearing, and Marcos, the protagonist's companion, orders the immediate execution of the leper. As he gazes at Narciso, the protagonist finds himself unable to pull the trigger. Marcos brusquely takes the rifle from him and shoots the hapless leper.

Narciso represents the forces of death, and, therefore, he must be instinctively battled and destroyed. However, the protagonist is a man with a civilized concept of morality, and he does not form a part of the collective consciousness of this primitive society. Marcos acts without hesitation or reflection, because he belongs to this world of primal realities. The protagonist's reluctance in taking this decisive act signals his seperation from this realm and the fact that Marcos will eventually be with Rosario. As a representative of the telluric forces of life, Rosario is the antithesis of Narciso.

Shortly after this event, a search party sent by the curator arrives in a plane. They locate the protagonist, and he is confronted by a dilemma as to what he should do. He is unwilling to leave, but to create music he needs adequate quantities of elemental materials such as paper, which the settlement cannot supply. More importantly, he needs an audience that can participate in the creative act and by doing so complete it. He decides to return to civilization to acomplish these goals and to deliver to the curator the musical instruments he has discovered. He also plans to ask Ruth for a divorce. Once these ends are accomplished, he will return to Santa Mónica and Rosario.

Caricature of Carpentier by Pancho Grailles.

The protagonist's reappearance in the civilized world is not a happy one. After a series of confused events, he finds himself disassociated from Ruth and slowly sinking into an aimless existence. By chance he comes across a newspaper article about a friar he had known in the jungle. He discovers that Fray Pedro had ventured into a region of hostile Indians and had been executed. The protagonist perceives that behind this tragic death there exists a commitment to permanent values that he does not have. He decides to return to Santa Mónica and to live again with Rosario. It is a journey that is initiated but is never completed.

The protagonist retraces his former journey only to discover that flood waters block the way to Santa Mónica. He also is informed that Rosario is now living with Marcos and is pregnant. He decides to abandon his attempts to return and begins to understand that he ardently desires to live in another period of human history, but it is a time and place that do not correspond to his own destiny. He does not belong to the age of Genesis for "los mundos nuevos tienen que ser vividos, antes que explicados. Quienes aquí viven no lo hacen por convicción intelectual; creen, simplemente, que la vida llevadera es ésta y no la otra. Prefieren este presente al presente de los hacedores de Apocalipsis."

His intellectuality separates him from the realm of Genesis, but he also feels emotionally alienated from the apocalyptical nature of the contemporary world, for it offers no transpersonal values he can cling to. He speculates that if he had not been a composer, he might have been fully incorporated into Rosario's world. The conclusion suggested by the protagonist's observation is that as a creative artist his task is to reveal to his contemporaries locked within an apocalyptic age the primal truths of the world of Genesis. He then becomes a mediator between the two realms, drawing from one to rejuvenate the other. In this sense, creative works can be regarded as tangible manifestations of the eternal elements of existence, for they bring together the marvellous and the real. They make us aware of the forces that transcend the limits of our personal existence.

Los pasos perdidos allows its reader to consider different types of disorder and formlessness. In its presentation of the contemporary world, we view a civilization that has lost its possibilities and seems on the verge of dissolution. Human existence has become petrified into sets of hollow patterns devoid of vitality, and one senses that all forms will soon crumble into dust. In his journey into the past, the protagonist encounters a reality that is in the process of forming, where vital forces have not yet imposed order on existence. It is a realm of pure potentiality bursting with chaotic energy. The novel moves from a chaos generated by the destructive forces of dissolution to the chaos that precedes the creation of new forms. It should be pointed out that the protagonist's ordeal, as he moves between these two domains, is the main concern of the novel. His voyage and quest occupy center stage in *Los pasos perdidos*. The processes of chaos and the transition from form to formlessness, however, would become major considerations in Carpentier's next novel, *El siglo de las luces* (1962).

The protagonist-narrator in *Los pasos perdidos* is a product of the modern world, a civilized man who has been trained to think and ponder to the extent that his intellectualism almost paralyzes any ability to act. He is swept up into a great adventure more by the forces of circumstance than by the efforts of his own will. In contrast, the main character in *El siglo de las luces*, Víctor Hugues, is a man of action who subordinates philosophical and intellectual considerations to deeds. He is a man of great vigor and will, who greatly influences all those who come in contact with him. In many respects, he is the exact opposite of the protagonist in *Los pasos perdidos*. Despite these essential differences, they do hold one thing in common. They both attempt to overcome the limitations of the present, hoping to bring into being a better and more complete existence. Indeed, this is a quality common to most of the main characters in Carpentier's novels. They are motivated by the desire and conviction that the creation of a better world is within man's grasp, and Carpentier's novels constitute an examination of the many roads taken to realize this goal.

At times this nostalgia and longing for a "Lost Paradise" leads Carpentier's characters into major undertakings. In *El siglo de las luces*, Carpentier examines the revolutionary process as a means to attain this end. The characters in this novel participate in a mass movement, attempting to realize their goals in contrast to the highly individual search conducted by the protagonist in *Los pasos perdidos*. Carpentier returns in *El siglo de las luces* to the collective approach utilized in *El reino de este mundo* but with much greater success. He avoids the fragmentary structure of his second novel by narrating the personal destinies of three main characters during the entire course of *El siglo de las luces*. Their lives span the temporal limits of the work, and this gives it great cohesiveness despite the broad historical context covered.

El siglo de las luces deals with the arrival and spread of the French Revolution throughout the Antilles between 1790 and 1809. The novel is anchored in historical events, and its most important figure, Víctor Hugues, actually existed. Carpentier first learned of Víctor and his role in history during a forced stop in Guadalupe, an island that Víctor governed during a part of the French Revolution. Carpentier found in this remarkable man who had been neglected by history the perfect vehicle for the development and expression of his most consuming concerns. He has stated, "Amo los grandes temas, los grandes movimientos colectivos. Ellos dan la más alta riqueza a los personajes y a la trama." The unusual but forgotten Víctor must have appeared to be an excellent example of the marvellous reality of the New World, which could seemingly swallow and hide in the records of its past such an imposing figure. He exemplifies the incongruities of Latin-American reality and human existence and serves as the embodiment of a collective movement in Carpentier's novel. The writing of this work must have been an exciting and exhilarating experience for Carpentier.

El siglo de las luces opens in Cuba in 1790, as Carlos, a minor character in the novel, is returning from his family's country estate. He discovers that his father has recently died, leaving him, his sister, Sofía, and their cousin,

Esteban, alone in the world. They have been left a comfortable estate, however, and this allows them to lapse into a lax and disorganized existence. Their lives become carefree and chaotic, and they even fall into the habit of sleeping during the day and staying awake through the night. The absence of any adult authority or tradition in their lives seems to reflect the spirit of an age that is groping for a new direction and is about to experience great change.

This state of affairs begins to change shortly after Víctor appears at their home on a business matter. He befriends them and begins to introduce order and direction into their lives. Although he is engaged in commerce, he is also a Freemason, and his ideas are extremely contagious to Sofía and Esteban, who are just emerging from adolescence. For them it is the beginning of a great adventure that will parallel the fortunes of the French Revolution, particularly in the New World. However, it should be pointed out that Carpentier's primary concern in this novel is not to chronicle the course of a particular revolution but to examine and capture the very essence of the revolutionary process. Thus, the novel attempts to fathom man's continual search for a complete existence and the extremes he resorts to in attempting to create it.

After several events, Esteban goes to Europe with Víctor, where they both participate in the French Revolution from 1791 to 1794. Although they keep in contact, their activities separate them a great deal of the time, and this enables Esteban to acquire an objective view of Víctor. In 1794, Víctor returns to the New World and leads an expedition, which Esteban joins, to the Antilles. As their ship plows its way through the open sea during the journey to Guadalupe, Víctor has a guillotine assembled on the deck. Those who would bring equality to all men arrive in the New World with an awe-inspiring instrument of death. Dreams are to be made into reality by nightmarish means.

Víctor reaches Guadalupe, successfully defends it against the British and governs the island for a few years. Esteban's slowly developing disenchantment with the revolution that had begun in Europe continues until he finds himself completely disillusioned with it and Víctor. Esteban is emotionally persecuted on the paradoxes of the revolutionary process. Víctor has decisively influenced his life, but as the revolution wears on and he answers the political needs of the times, Esteban feels that his morality is lost in a maze of political maneuvers. Víctor's consuming dedication to the wielding of power without recourse to moral considerations perplexes Esteban. Víctor's reasoning is coldly impersonal. His devotion to the functional and the practical blinds him to the psychological needs of his fellowmen, and he never fully comprehends their spiritual and emotional demands. This detachment proves to be his ruin as he is swept along by the contradictory currents of the French Revolution. He himself becomes a contradiction, alternately supporting and suppressing

the same things according to the political dictates of the day. Víctor is a perverse force, a distortion that will be annihilated by the dialectical process of history.

Esteban accepts a mission that allows him to return to Cuba, and he arrives at Sofía's home after a long and complicated trip, defeated and disillusioned by the failure of the revolution. It is 1799 and Sofía has been married for a year. He tells Sofía:

> Esta vez la revolución ha fracasado. Acaso la próxima sea la buena Pero, para agarrarme cuando estalle, tendrán que buscarme con linternas a mediodía. Cuidémonos de las palabras demasiado hermosas; de los Mundos Mejores creados por las palabras. Nuestra época sucumbe por un exceso de palabras. No hay más Tierra Prometida que la que el hombre puede encontrar en sí mismo.

Sofía refuses to accept this view, although she acknowledges the excesses of the revolution. It is her conviction that great suffering is an unfortunate but necessary sacrifice to be made in order to transform the world.

When Esteban returned to Cuba, he gave Sofía a personal letter from Víctor. Later they learn that Víctor has survived another political crisis and has been assigned to govern Cayenne. When Sofía's husband becomes ill and dies, she immediately seizes the opportunity to join Víctor. Although Esteban personally deplores this action, he finally accedes to her wishes and foils an attempt by the colonial police to arrest her. Sofía's revolutionary activities have been discovered, and Esteban takes evasive action that saves her but dooms him to prison. Sofía succeeds in rejoining Víctor, but she soon discovers that he no longer is the revolutionary hero he once was. He has changed from a man who challenged unjust authority to one who will take any action to maintain power. Sofía finally leaves him and plans to rejoin Esteban. She has lost her respect for Víctor but not her faith in the capacity of a revolution to transform human existence. Sofía is a unyielding in her belief as Víctor is stubborn in his fanatical clinging to power. They are both overwhelming personalities who are not subject to the vacilation that characterizes Esteban.

At this point in the novel, we lose direct contact with Sofía and learn of her fate only through the investigation of her brother, Carlos. He appears in Spain where Sofía had worked to obtain Esteban's release from prison. She was successful and they lived together "como hermanos" for some years in Madrid. Carlos discovers that they both were killed when they participated in a spontaneous uprising of the Spanish people against forces of Napoleon. It strikes the reader as being a futile effort conducted against hopeless odds, and we are reminded of the reaction of the protagonist in *Los pasos perdidos* when he learned of the death of Fray Pedro. We are puzzled by the depth of the commitment to transpersonal values. In both novels, a level is reached where individual needs are subordinated to a cause that transcends the individual's life, and this attainment seems to be beyond rational understanding.

Carpentier opens and closes *El siglo de las luces* with Carlos. Through this narrative device, the reader is exposed to an objective view of what happens. Since the reader hardly knows Carlos, there is little identification with him, and this makes it possible to have an emotionally detached presentation of events. This distance is further heightened, because the events are presented in retrospect. Carlos discovers that it was Sofía who insisted on participating in the demonstrations against the French. Esteban had attempted to resist Sofía's spontaneous impulse to action, but he joined her when he saw she was determined to leave without him. It is significant that Sofía overcomes Esteban's resistance. He represents, as much as any character in the novel, the individual who attempts to understand the world in rational terms. Sofía's passionate and uncompromising commitment to the improvement of man's social condition is an instinctive force that overcomes Esteban's intellectual reservations. Instinct overcomes rational judgment as individuals are swept along by the forces of history. The reader is left with little faith in the individual's capacity to control the forces that operate on him. Carpentier's use of a particularly objective presentation at the end of the novel intensifies the emotional impact that this revelation has on the reader. It is one of the novel's paradoxes that those who most employ reason—Víctor and Esteban—should become embodiments of subjectivism, while the impetuous Sofía becomes a representative of an objective truth that operates in history. In this respect, Sofía's idealism reflects a wisdom that transcends our understanding of existence.

Some critics feel that Carpentier evidences in his novels an ambivalent attitude toward revolution. Harss points out that "revolutions, in Carpentier's books, are always short-term failures but, as he goes to great pains to assure us, harbingers of greater things to come." Reaction within revolutionary Cuba to *El siglo de las luces* was, as one might suspect, mixed. It is not difficult to make the transition from the guillotine to the firing squad. A thorough study of *El siglo de las luces* will produce contradictory evidences in favor of and opposing revolution. Actually, it is doubtful that Carpentier had any intention of espousing a moral or utilitarian view of revolution. The presence of contradictory positions towards revolution in the novel is due to the interpenetration of subjective and objective views.

From an individual's subjective outlook, a particular revolution is either good or bad. Seen from a historical perspective, a revolution is simply an agent of change, one of many patterns within a cyclic evolutionary process. One finds in Carpentier's works the conviction that there is a progression of meaning and order in history, and he conveys this by the way he organizes his novels. The impression that existence is chaotic and without meaning emanates from the individual's subjective view with its temporal limits. Within a historical context, chaos is often presented as a stage in the process of dissolution, a process which simultaneously signals the death of one order and the birth of another. Carpentier tends to emphasize the objective by avoiding as much as possible the personal aspects of his characters. We all have ideas and attitudes that do not belong to us as individuals but to the age we live in. They originate in the world that is exterior to us and form part of the collective experience of our times. It is this part of the individual that Carpentier stresses in his works.

Carpentier's career marks the international acceptance of the Cuban novel. He is the most consistently successful Cuban novelist, and his work has won him an enviable international reputation. His achievements have given the Cuban novel a degree of prestige as never before, and in many respects he helped prepare the way for novelists such as Cabrera Infante, Lezama Lima, and Severo Sarduy, by establishing a record and tradition of excellence. Mexico's distinguished novelist Carlos Fuentes has stated that Carpentier is "uno de nuestros primeros novelistas profesionales." His assertion is an eloquent testimony of the esteem that Carpentier has attained and the influence he has had outside of Cuba on the development of the Spanish-American novel.

Carpentier shows in his novels a dedicated sense of discipline and rigorous intellectual control. They are thoroughly researched and minutely planned before they are written, and his books rely greatly on the presentation of visual reality. This results in the creation of well-structured works deftly directed and controlled by the author, but it also reduces their spontaneity. Although Carpentier is interested in the process of dissolution and the role of disorder and chaos in human existence, these concerns are largely treated thematically and never become technically incorporated into his novels. It should be noted that he has been much more experimental in some of his short stories such as **"Semejante a la noche"** and **"Viaje a la semilla."** In the first work, he presents a juxtaposition of events greatly separated in time and space, and in the second he reverses the direction of the flow of time, going backward in the narration of a character's life. Until the appearence of *El siglo de las luces*, however, his novels have tended to be more innovative thematically than technically.

If one wished to single out the most outstanding faction of Carpentier's art, careful consideration would have to be given to his style. His language is elegant, polished, and a testimony of his knowledge. He is a consummate craftsman and the very essence of his work is reflected in his style. Fernando Alegría observes on Carpentier's use of language in *Los pasos perdidos*. "El idioma de Carpentier se levanta como una catedral en la selva, se asienta o vuela, se ilumina o se ensombrece, se enjoya hasta cegarnos, se retuerce o se estiliza, resuena en infinitas cadencias, estalla en colores, o se afirma en pátina de pintura antigua." [*Historia de la novela hispanoamericana*, 2nd ed., 1965.] It is a language that charms and inspires as it flows on, bringing into the world of reality the marvellous and incredible. It beguiles us into accepting a realm in which the particular illustrates the general, and permanent values are discovered in the midst of disorder and chaos. For Carpentier there is much comfort in regarding the tribulations of human existence from the long view of extended time. It is a lofty perspective that few can achieve let alone convey, and the skill with which it is presented in Carpentier's novels testifies to the unifying forces operating in his work. Carpentier searches for the absolute without falling into the trap of offering absolute certainties, for he is aware that human existence will always be tempered by limitations. His is a dispassionate voice in a time of extremes, and in his search for permanence Carpentier has created novels that will be with us for a long time.

Raymond D. Souza, "Alejo Carpentier's Timeless History," in his *Major Cuban Novelists: Innovation and Tradition*, University of Missouri Press, 1976, pp. 30–52.

Carpentier on the discovery of the Afro-Cuban culture by the avant-garde artists of his youth in Havana:

For the very reason that it offended the sensibilities of old-fashioned intellectuals, we gleefully went to *ñáñigo* initiation rites, the secret black fetishist cults similar to voodoo, and praised the dance of the "diablito," the small, ritual dancing devil. Thus was born the Afro-Cuban mode that provided subject matter for poems, novels, folkloric and sociological studies for more than ten years. Often it tended to remain at a superficial, local color level, the black man under sun-drenched palm trees; nevertheless, it also constituted a necessary first step to understand better certain poetic, musical, ethnic, and social factors that have contributed to and given a special character to the "criollo," the creole, the quintessence of Cuba.

Alejo Carpentier, in Klaus Muller-Bergh's "Alejo Carpentier," *Latin American Writers*, Vol. III, Scribner's, 1989.

Dust jacket for Carpentier's early Afro-Cuban novel *¡Écue-Yamba-Ó!*.

ROBERTO GONZÁLEZ ECHEVARRÍA
(essay date 1983)

[González Echevarría's important study, *Alejo Carpentier: The Pilgrim at Home*, launched him to the forefront of Carpentier criticism in 1977, a position since enhanced by his numerous shorter studies in Spanish and English, as well as an annotated bibliography of the writer (co-edited by Klaus Müller- Bergh, 1983). The following essay by the Cuban-born American scholar focuses on two of Carpentier's novels *Explosion in a Cathedral* and *The Kingdom of This World*. According to González Echevarría, the larger themes of both novels concern deeply held European beliefs about history and the profound unsettling of these beliefs that came with the discovery of New World cultures and civilizations.]

Latin American history has always been a competition among warring versions of history. The chroniclers of the discovery and conquest of America were the first to realize that the existence of the New World unsettled their notions of history. As they met the natives, they asked themselves who these people were, and how their magnificent civilizations could have been left out of the Bible. From whom did they descend? How was their history linked to the biblical histories and to classical history? Why had the Fathers not spoken of them? The theological, philosophical, and political dilemmas opened by the discovery and conquest of the New World violently shook the foundations of European thought. The first indigenous historians faced similar dilemmas, but from a different perspective. Garcilaso de la Vega, el Inca, born in Peru of a Spanish father and a noble Indian woman, wrote that Cuzco was "another Rome" in order to signify that Incaic civilization should take a place next to Greek and Roman cultures. In other words, while the Incas were heathens, they were civilized and quite prepared to receive Christianity, at least as prepared as the Ancient World had been. Felipe Guaman Poma de Ayala, a full-blooded Indian, was bolder. He maintained that the Incas had known Christianity before the arrival of the Spaniards, thereby removing the theological justification for the conquest and at the same time inserting the history of his people into the mainstream of world history. In the New World, particularly in the part we today call Latin America, the employment of history has never been an innocent activity.

By the time America was discovered, the history of Africa had been given a place in the overall scheme of world history. Africa had been known to Europeans since the most remote of times, and for them, Africans had been part of the unfolding of human history. But it was not until large numbers of Africans were brought to the New World that their role in post-Christian history began to assume a larger significance. Once Africans had been transported to the New World, they too became part of the problem of how to narrate history. Like the Incas, the Mayas and other pre-Columbian cultures, Africans had their own version of history, a version which soon began to include their fate in the New World. Enough work has already been done to know that African versions of history incorporated a possible return to Africa after the ordeal of New World slavery. It is also known that Neo-African cultures soon began to develop in the Americas and they, of course, had their own accounts of African history in the New World. These versions further enriched the multiplicity of those versions of history already present in America, a mulplicity of competing histories each attempting to find the master-version.

Garcilaso, Guaman Poma, and other historians including the Spaniard Bartolomé de las Casas, saw clearly and early the magnitude of the dilemma these differing versions of history raised. They also saw how the competition among them was linked to conflicts whose ultimate consequences would amount to radical changes in mankind's conception of religion, politics, and art. Garcilaso's answer to this issue was to adopt what Juan Bautista Avalle Arce has called *uniformismo*, a term he derives from Lovejoy's unwieldy *uniformitarianism*. In essence, Garcilaso—an early Lévi-Strauss, or perhaps a Toynbee or a Spengler—believed that all peoples were endowed with the same reason; therefore, their cultures were uniform in developemnt and structure. For Garcilaso's cool and elegant mind, history consisted of a harmonious evolution that culminated with Christianity. Guaman Poma, who was of a more contentious spirit, argued for a restoration, maintaining that the conquest had been an illegal act. He advocated vehemently the superiority of his people over the Spaniards in a number of areas, not the least of which was morality. Las Casas, a medieval mind who fought against Hapsburg Renaissance imperialism, conceived of an orderly Christian community in which the asperity of differing cultures would be smoothed over by charity and the peaceful conversion of non-Christians. His view of history was thoroughly medieval and his conception of the roles various peoples should play in it so anachronistic that it appeared to his contemporaries as a form of far-fetched libertarianism, when it was in fact quite conservative. But history, for Las Casas, was Christian history.

By the eighteenth century the unsettling of European thought brought about by the discovery and conquest of America and the importation of large numbers of Africans, provoked a radical questioning of European beliefs, a process that has come to be known as the Enlightenment. America was a powerful agent in generating the questions asked by *philosophes*, as has been persuasively argued by Arthur P. Whitaker ["The Dual Role of Latin American in the Enlightenment," in his *Latin America and the Enlightenment*, 1942]. Carpentier's *Explosion in a Cathedral*, called in the original *El siglo de las luces*, that is to say, *The Age of Enlightenment*, centers on that moment when the various versions of history are again pitted against each other in an attempt to reach a master version.

Published in 1962, the importance of *Explosion in a Cathedral* for the Latin American literary tradition is the way in which it explores the dilemma of what constitutes American history and how to narrate it. For Carpentier, the core of that dilemma is how Blacks are part of the history of the New World, how their presence undermines mainstream political thought and, in so doing, reveals the very problematic nature of any understanding of American history. This process of undermining is accomplished not simply by showing the political impact of Blacks in the course of events during the eighteenth century and the beginnings of the nineteenth, but more ambitiously by defining the presence of Blacks in the New World as a break in history that repeats a larger, archetypal split. In a sense, Carpentier is repeating Garcilaso's gesture by showing that there is a certain uniformity to history. His meditation in *Explosion in a Cathedral* is as wide-ranging as Garcilaso's, and it implies much more than the issue of how to narrate history. It is a proclamation of an American poetics whose energy is found in the relation of Neo-African cultures in the New World to European notions of history. The subversion promoted by Blacks is not merely a repetition of that provoked earlier by Indians; it is a subversion whose compulsive repetition is the essence of American history and more broadly of American culture.

Prior to Carpentier's works, Blacks had appeared in the Latin American novel only as individual characters. The Cuban anti-slavery novel gives us fine portraits of rebellious slaves, and various other narratives include important black characters. But it was Carpentier, with *¡Écue-Yamba-Ó!* (1933) and particularly *The Kingdom of This World* (1949), who showed that the presence of Blacks in Latin America was an important historical difference, a force that had to be reckoned with in any writing or rewriting of Latin American history. In *Explosion in a Cathedral* Carpentier goes further by incorporating the presence of Blacks into an historical paradigm that transcends the New World as historical event.

The Kingdom of This World had already introduced the conflict between different versions of history: the European one, in which the central event is the French Revolution, and the Afro-American one, in which the central event is the Haitian Revolution. How are they related? Does the first cause or determine the latter? In *The Kingdom of This World* European history is not given priority; in fact, it appears inauthentic in relation to the New World. European history has as its highest representative Pauline Bonaparte, who surrenders to sloth and sensuality in the tropical heat, while Afro-American history is represented by the various *loas* who incarnate in the black revolutionaries. The Haitian Revolution appears as an echo of the French, yet at the same time the novel shows that the slave revolts had begun much earlier. If the latter are echoes of the former, they are distorted, false repetitions that in some way deny the causality of the apparent relationship. *In The Kingdom of This World* the competition between the various versions of history is not resolved. At the end, Ti Noel, senile yet lucid, speaks of the tasks man must accomplish while on this earth, but he is being brutalized by the Mulattoes, who have adopted the repressive policies of the former colonists. The Mulattoes do not simply repeat history. They become a poor copy of the white regime. There is an obvious gap between Ti Noel's grasp of history and the turn that events take in the novel. It is that gap which represents the divergence between a European and an African, Afro-American, conception of history.

Explosion in a Cathedral, a book in which Carpentier returns to the historical landscape covered in *The Kingdom of This World*, is an effort to find a common ground for the warring versions of history present in the earlier text. This is evident not only in the expansion of the fictional world to include most of the Caribbean as well as France, but more importantly in the way in which the Caribbean and European worlds are presented in relation to each other. *Explosion in a Cathedral* is a vast geographico-historical experiment whose goal is to discover the prime movers of universal history and also how history turns to text. The slave rebellions in *The Kingdom of This World* anticipated the Haitian Revolution and were contrasted to the French Revolution. In *Explosion in a Cathedral* the slave revolts are paradigms of an overall unfolding of history that includes the French Revolution. *Explosion in a Cathedral* is a hermeneutical machine that attempts to interpret the master tropes of history, particulary but not exclusively, American history.

To begin with, the novel is at pains to suggest the essential unity of European and Afro-American cultures through the demonstration that both have a similar approach to knowledge, even if European thought pretends that it is different and unique. This theme is present, above all, in Ogé, the doctor and philosopher who cures Esteban. Ogé's magical interpretation of medicine is successful in finding the cause of Esteban's respiratory difficulties where conventional doctors had failed. Ogé's cure is highly instructive in that it shows how Carpentier initially contrasts European with Afro-American beliefs. The cause of Esteban's malady is a garden kept by the black servant Remigio in a secret part of the backyard of the house:

> The sight that now met their eyes was very surprising; parsley, nettles, mimosa and woodland grasses were growing in two long parallel beds around several very flourishing mignonette plants. A bust of Socrates, which Sofía remembered having once seen, as a child, in her father's office, was set in a niche, as if displayed on an altar, surrounded by curious offerings, such as magicians use for their spells: Cups full of grains of maize, sulphur stones, snails, iron fillings. "*C'est ça,*" said Ogé, contemplating the miniature garden as if it had great meaning for him.

In spite of Sofía's smug doubts, Esteban recovers quickly after Ogé pulls out the plants in the garden and burns them. For Remigio, who bitterly protests the destruction of his garden, Socrates was the Lord of the Forests, while for Ogé the cure would be accomplished because "certain illnesses were mysteriously connected with the growth of a grass, a plant or a tree somewhere nearby. Every human being had a 'double' in the vegetable kingdom, and there were cases where this 'double' to further its own growth, stole strength from the man with whom it was linked, condemning him to illness while it flowered or germinated." Whereas in *The Kingdom of This World* there was irony implicit in the imbalance between the beliefs and practices of blacks and a given reality (Mackandal is burnt), here the irony has been reversed, for we can easily discover the "scientific" foundation of Ogé's diagnosis—allergies are the cause of Esteban's asthma.

The presence of the bust of Socrates in the midst of the garden is, of course, full of implications. It is obvious that the whole garden can be taken as an emblem of the mixture of European philosophy with Afro-American beliefs and, more specifically, of the conjunction in America of Neo-classical art and thought with nature. But there are further implications. Socrates, the Master of Reason, of discourse, of logos, has been turned by Remigio into the Lord of the Forest, presiding over the medicinal powers of plants. In a sense, Remigio has restored to Socrates, or more specifically to logos, its ambiguous power as purveyor of both poison and medicine. In the beginning, Socrates and Osain, Lord of the Forest, have a similar function. The codification of plants in Remigio's garden is flawlessly true to Afro-Cuban lore, and the deification of Lord of the Forests, of *el monte*, is at the very center of Afro-Cuban beliefs. In *The Kingdom of This World* the plants used by Mackandal only poisoned whites; here they both poison and cure. *Explosion in a Cathedral* seeks an American hermeneutics, one that will allow a reading of American history in all its variety and conflict. The occult is the real knowledge as opposed to reason, which posits an ideal order. The occult is both knowledge and desire, or knowledge de-formed, *warped* by desire. In this sense, both Whites and Blacks practice occultism as pragmatic interpretation of reality. This is, as we shall see, what unites them in American history and poetics. Reason is the *urtext*, whereas the occult is the *text*; the former, paradoxically, turns out to be a sort of heuristic device of the latter.

Against the ideal order of reason *Explosion in a Cathedral* pits the disorder of revolution, or perhaps better, the real order of revolution. The French Revolution, as viewed by Esteban and as lived by Víctor, consists of a series of movements and counter-movements, rituals and counter-rituals that bring to power or topple from power various leaders and groups. Symbols are exchanged for other symbols, but the symbolic nature of the social process is never really altered. As an event in the novel, the French Revolution appears not as the logical product of an historical progression, but as the expanded version of the domestic revolution that takes place in the house of the protagonists after the death of the father. Events are repeated, expanded, distorted, not inserted into a causal relationship. Things become intelligible in their various relationships to others on a symbolic level, not as objects of a real order or as events in a given teleology. Even the arrangement of characters in the novel obeys a secret kabbalistic code, not necessarily a mimetic representation of human relations. Everything in *Explosion in a Cathedral* threatens to become significant, legible, if only the reader can find the proper code, or perhaps, the mastercode. Like Ogé, we stand before a complex text, traversed by various codes whose intersection we must find.

The persistent reversal of revolutionary ideals belies the European notion of history as the progression toward a perfect society. The liberators soon become oppressors, and the guillotine turns justice into inquisitorial *auto*. In Guadeloupe, the recently freed slaves are forced to return to work with the same methods of coercion used earlier by the slave masters. In Cayeene, Víctor is the jailer of many former revolutionaries. Lives, careers, whole historical movements are turned upside down or run backwards. The intended purpose of revolutionary language is often betrayed, as when Billaud Varenne's lan-

guid mulatto mistress fans her breasts with an old copy of *La décade philosophique*. History turns out to be the error, the errancy inherent in all action, as opposed to theory or intention. Just as gnosticism is knowledge twisted by the force of desire, so history is intention bent by reality. What *Explosion in a Cathedral* pretends to do is show the errancy of history as well as the latent analogy between history, viewed in this manner, and the writing of history.

If in *Explosion in a Cathedral* doors become magical thresholds, guillotines enigmatic symbols, and the bust of Socrates appears in the midst of medicinal herbs, historical events are linked through an associative method whose coherence is hardly the product of reason. Although there is no more telling historical event in the novel than the French Revolution, what Carpentier offers are mostly the echoes of the Revolution as its shock waves reach the Caribbean. But are they echoes? Do they signify or represent the Revolution? Can one understand the Revolution through a reading of these peripheral events? The fact is that even in Paris itself, all Esteban and Víctor can perceive are the marginal rituals, the liturgical manifestations of the new order. Action itself is never to be seen, save for what appear to be its reactions. In the Caribbean, the echoes of the Revolution are presumably distortions, but distortions of what ideal model? The laws enacted by the revolutionary government suffer a fate similar to the Spanish laws directed to the New World during the colonial period—*se acatan, pero no se cumplen*; their authority is acknowledged, but they are not put into practice. Besides, by the time the laws reach the French possessions, the government that passed them has often already been toppled. They are emanations from a locus of power that has disappeared, texts whose only validity lies within themselves, for their source has vanished and their link to reality is tenuous at best.

Throughout *Explosion in a Cathedral* Blacks upset the course of history, and set off unexpected side effects. But are these side effects? On the side of what do they appear? Not only do Blacks upset history; they question its central tenets, or better yet, the myths about its centrality. By burning down Víctor's store in Le Cap, Blacks thrust him into political action, and by burning down the whole city they force the metropolitan government into taking action against them. The very same government that frees the slaves and confers French citizenship upon them has to send troops to quell their rebellion. The freedom proclaimed in Europe does not translate into liberty for the slaves in the Caribbean, as if crossing the ocean meant entering a world where everything is inverted. In a discussion with Esteban, Billaud Varenne and Brottier, the Swiss colonist Sieger emphasizes the magnitude of the gap between revolutionary law and the actions of the slaves: "'All the French Revolution has achieved in America is to legalise the Great Escape which has been going on since the sixteenth century. The black didn't wait for you, they proclaimed themselves free a countless number of times.'" In one of the most memorable passages in the novel, Sieger goes on to enumerate the important slave revolts in the New World from the sixteenth century to the time when the action of the novel takes place. Freedom as taken by the rebellious slaves is quite different from the freedom magnanimously bestowed upon them by the white rulers. Historical action differs radically from the course the French revolutionaries try to give history: a chasm opens between the text of the law and the actions of Blacks. Within that chasm there lie the transformations, the tropes through which American history is made and written. Reading must take into account this opening, this discontinuity wherein inversion and perversion take place. That gap, that no-man's land, is the ground on which the warring versions of history that make up American history meet.

In my own formulation of the process there are inevitable traces of a *retruécano*, a rhetorical inversion, a Baroque figure that here, as it nearly always does, resembles a specular movement in which it is impossible to tell what takes precedence over what, what is the reflection of what. The *retruécano* displays itself both in its inherent repetition and difference, in its reiteration and desired simultaneity. The inversion can be read in either direction, both ways meeting somewhere in a virtual center where appearances are reversed; in most inversions that virtual fulcrum is precisely an ellipsis. American history, American writing, and, therefore, the reading of American writing, must allow for the manifestation of such inversions, must practice such inversions; it is its system. To understand this, the more abstract significance of the presence of Blacks in the novel, we must turn to a scene that apparently has little to do with our topic: the one in which Sofía and Caleb Dexter visit the tomb of the grandson of the last Byzantine emperor in Barbados.

On her way to meet Víctor in Cayeene, Sofía stops over in Barbados. In the island she takes a carriage ride with Caleb Dexter, all the way to

[T]he little rocky bastion of St. John, where, behind the church she found a tombstone with an inscription that referred unexpectedly to the death on the island of a person whose name bore a crushing weight of historical association: *Here lie the remains of Ferdinand Paleologue, descendant of the last Emperors of Greece— Priest of this parish—1655–1656.*

The bottle of wine he had drained during the journey had made Caleb Dexter somewhat emotional, and he uncovered himself respectfully. In the dusk, whose light was turning the waves red as they broke in a great spray against the rocky monoliths of Bathsheba, Sofía decorated the grave with some bouganvillaea which she had cut in the garden of the presbytery. The first time he visited the house in Havana, Victor Hugues had spoken at length about this tomb of the unknown grandson of the Ecumenical Patriarch who

had been killed during the final resistance of Byzantium, having chosen to die rather than fall into the sacrilegious hands of the conquering Turks. And now she had found it, in the place he had indicated. Across the grey stone, marked with the Cross of Constantine, a hand now followed the course which another hand had followed years before, searching out the hollows of the letters with the tips of its fingers.

To cut short this unexpected ritual, which he felt had already lasted long enough, Caleb Dexter remarked: "And to think that the last rightful owner of the Basilica of Saint Sophía should have ended up on this island."

Víctor had indeed mentioned during his first visit to the house in Havana, during a tirade about the marvels to be found in the Caribbean, that there was in "Barbados, the tomb of a nephew [sic—*nieto*] of Constantine XI, the last emperor of Byzantium, whose ghost appeared to solitary wayfarers on stormy nights." The context in which Víctor mentions this is significant, for the theme of the Caribbean as generator of strange, odd shapes and forms is quite germane to the issue of the unfolding of history in the novel. The linking of these two moments in the novel is also relevant to our discussion, insofar as they both occur at breaking points in the plot: the first appearance of Víctor, and Sofía's voyage to return to him. One can add to all this that Carpentier himself visited Barbados and wrote a piece about the tomb of Constantine's grandson for *El Nacional* in Caracas which undoubtedly had an impact on the genesis of *Explosion in a Cathedral*. But there is a lot more to this scene.

The existence of this tomb in Barbados would merely be one of those instances of the marvelous that Carpentier liked to cite, were it not for the fact that throughout the novel there is a sense that what occurs in the Caribbean is a repetition (though a skewed one) of what took place earlier in the Mediterranean. Are not Víctor and the others replaying in the Caribbean the roles already performed by Robespierre and other revolutionaries in Paris? There is even a direct allusion to the Caribbean as a new Mediterranean that leaves little doubt about the importance of this theme in *Explosion in a Cathedral*. The passage is part of one of Esteban's meditations as he travels in the corsair ship under Captain Barthelemy.

I shall have to quote the original Spanish here because the translation into English has erased important features of the way in which the Caribbean and the Mediterranean are paired. I will then quote the translation and, by way of a critique of its failings, underscore the relationship I have in mind: "En Francia había aprendido Esteban a gustar del gran zumo solariego que por los pezones de sus vides había alimentado la turbulenta y soberbia civilización mediterránea—ahora prolongada en este Mediterráneo Caríbe, donde proseguíase la Confusíon de Rasgos iniciada, hacía muchos milenios, en el ámbito de los Pueblos del Mar." The English version reads: "Esteban had learned in France to appreciate the noble juice of the vine, which had nourished the proud and turbulent civilization of the Mediterranean, now spread into this Caribbean Mediterranean, where the blending of characteristics had for many thousands of years been in progress within the ambit of the peoples of the sea." Fortunately the binomial Mediterranean Caribbean has been retained in English without mediating elements, for this superimposition is the way in which the relationship must be viewed; the only thing separating the two is literally the gap between the two names. But "blending" does not translate "Confusíon," and the elimination of the capitals takes away the cosmic sense of what the text proposes: this Confusion of Features is a single event setting in motion a series of historical echoes that refer back to their own dynamic movement of joining and dispersing, of blending and separating. (Carpentier likes to capitalize these "mastermoments," these *Mastermotions* of history, a practice that may be more offensive to English readers than to Spanish ones, though in the latter language such capitalization is not common either. Another vexing change introduced in the translation is the breaking up of the text into paragraphs, something that Carpentier did not do in Spanish, also contravening common practice.) The superimposition of the Caribbean on the Mediterranean allows the reader to realize the significance of the tomb in Barbados and of Sofía's gesture. The superimposition reveals the larger design of history that unfolds behind the plot of *Explosion in a Cathedral,* for, if the Caribbean is like the Mediterranean, then the history of the former is a repetition of the latter: the Byzantine Empire is to the Roman Empire as Caribbean history is to European history. In brief, America is to Europe as Constantinople is to Rome. If the fissure in the Roman Empire was its contact with the Eastern World, in America the break occurs through the presence of Africa.

If we turn again to the scene in Barbados, we notice that the text refers specifically to the grandfather of the man buried as he "who had been killed during the final resistance of Byzantium," that is to say, in the event—the fall of Constantinople—which caused, albeit indirectly, the discovery and conquest of the New World. This suggestion assembles at once a structure of repeated breaks: The formation of the Eastern Empire, the Fall of Constantinople, and the Independence of America, the major break already prefigured by the slave rebellions. All of these breaks, which are in consonance with those in the plot of the novel that bring the characters to Barbados, repeat the Confusion of Features mentioned above. I would like to think of this Confusion of Features in terms of the *retruécano* discussed earlier in connection with how things are transformed by crossing the ocean.

Like the famous Basilica of the same name, Sofía is the hinge between different worlds that are distorted mirror-images of each other, and it is, therefore, appropriate that she be the character to be placed in front of the tomb in Barbados. She also incarnates a secret form of knowledge, a mystical, gnostic understanding. Thus she mediates between the contemplative Esteban and the active Víctor. Given these characteristics, we can now surmise what her running her fingers on the letters of the epitaph means—"a hand now followed the course which another had followed years before, searching out the hollows of the letters with the tips of its fingers." At least three hands have preceded Sofía on the epitaph: Víctor's, the person who chiseled them on the tombstone, and probably also Carpentier's. There are three dots after "dedos" in the original, Carpentier's conventional winking of the eye when he is referring to himself. In all three cases, Sofía is acting out the process of reading—she is following a contour already inscribed by another. But she overcomes the secondariness of this act by seeking the hollow of the letters, that is to say, by looking behind the writing. Through this act she is reading the inverted shape of the letters, their specular image, at the same time that she is delving into the gap, the fissure that precedes them. Sofía is reaching into the Confusion of Features, of marks, searching out in the back of the letters their secret meaning which is not apparent on the visible surface. What Sofía is looking for is the "de-forming" by which Roman art becomes Byzantine art, the "mis-shaping" at the core of the Latin American Baroque.

This process of changing something into something else appears to Esteban as characteristic of the Caribbean. The proliferation of shapes changing constantly into something other forces the language to hyphenate words in order to be able to designate the continuous act of changing, of being transformed:

Carried into a world of symbiosis, standing up to his neck in pools whose water was kept perpetually foaming by cascading waves, and was broke, torn, shattered, by the hungry bit of jagged rocks, Esteban marvelled to realise how the language of these islands had made use of agglutination, verbal amalgams and metaphors to convey the formal ambiguity of things which participated in several essences at once. Just as certain trees were called "acacia-bracelets," "pineapple-porcelain," "wood-rib," "tisane-cloud," and "iguana-stick," many marine creatures had received names which established verbal equivocations in order to describe them accurately. Thus a fantastic bestiary had arisen of dog-fish, oxen-fish, tiger-fish, snorers, blowers, flying fish; of striped, tattooed and tawny fish, with their mouths on top of their heads, or their gills in the middle of their stomachs; whitebellies, swordfish and mackerel; a fish which bit off testicles—cases had been known— another that was herbivorous; the red-speckled sand-eel; a fish which became poisonous after eating manchineel apples—not forgetting the vieja-fish, the captain-fish, fish with its gleaming throat of golden scales; or the woman-fish—the mysterious and elusive manatees, glimpsed in the mouths of rivers where the salt water mingled with the fresh, with their feminine profiles and their siren's breasts, playing joyful nuptial pranks on one another in their water meadows.

The shape of these fish, of these creatures, is not given by the second term in the hyphenated word, but by the very process of changing one into another, by the hyphen itself. This movement from one order to another, from model to distorted copy, is also evident in the painting that serves as emblem of the novel and gives its title to the English version: *Explosion in a Cathedral*. Ramón García Castro has rightly noted that this painting—which he had not been able to see—has much in common "with other Romantic paintings. It reminds one, because of the flames, of Turner's (English, 1775–1851) *Fire in the Parliament*, which dates from 1834, a date later than the canvas in the house of the protagonists. Also, because of its violent lights, it is related to another painting from after the end of the eighteenth century, *Pandemonium*, by John Martin (English, 1789–1854)... Also, because of the sun rays and the houses about to be razed, the painting could be related to Carl Brullov's *The Last Day of Pompey* ["La pintura en Alejo Carpentier," *Tláloc*, No. 7 (1974)]. There is no doubt that there is a Romantic conception of art at the core of Carpentier's works, and one can feel a certain *Sturm und Drang* in the catastrophe depicted by Monsu Desiderio. But there is more than destruction in this painting, which, thanks to my colleague Verity Smith, I am able to include in this essay.

The actual painting is not called *Explosion in a Cathedral*, but *King Asa of Judah Destroying the Idols*. While in the first description of the painting the emphasis is on the row of columns breaking down, in the second the existence of an unbroken row of columns is also mentioned. It is easy to think only of the destruction of the church, particularly when we think that the novel deals with revolution, but the painting is in fact more complex than that. The second description of the painting reads:

Esteban suddenly stopped, stirred to the very depths, in front of the *Explosion in a Cathedral* by the anonymous Neapolitan master. In it were prefigured, so to speak, so many of the events he had experienced that he felt bewildered by the multiplicity of interpretations to which this prophetic, anti-plastic, un-painterly canvas, brought to the house by some mysterious chance, lent itself. If, in accordance with the doctrines he had once been taught, the cathedral was a symbol—the arch and the tabernacle—for his own being, then an explosion had certainly occurred there, which, although tardy and slow, had destroyed altars, images, and objects of veneration. If the cathedral was the Age, then a formidable explosion had indeed overthrown its most solid walls, and perhaps buried the very men who had built the infernal machine beneath an avalanche of debris. If the cathedral was the Christian Church, then Esteban noticed that a row of sturdy pillars remained intact, opposite those which were shattering and falling in this apocalyptic painting, as if to prophesy resilience,

Carpentier on *lo real maravilloso* in the Americas:

It is found at every step in the lives of men for whom dates are recorded in the history of the Continent . . . from the seekers of the Fountain of Eternal Youth and the Golden City of Manoa, to certain rebels of the first hour or certain modern heroes of our wars of independence. . . . And the fact is that, because of its virgin landscape, its formation, its ontology; because of the Revelation its recent discovery constituted, the fertile crossbreedings it produced, America is far from having exhausted its wealth of mythologies.

Alejo Carpentier in *Myth and History in Caribbean Fiction: Alejo Carpentier, Wilson Harris, and Edouardo Glissant*, edited by Barbara J. Webb, University of Massachusetts Press, 1992.

endurance and a reconstruction, after the days of destruction and of stars foretelling disasters had passed.

While the interpretations suggested by Esteban are correct, looking at the picture we cannot fail to be struck by the broken symmetry, by the fact that the collapsing row of columns on the right is/was the specular image of the unbroken one on the left. In other words, the row of columns on the right is a *deformation* of the row on the left. What the painting suspends is not so much a catastrophe as the very process of transformation, of troping, by which one thing becomes another. American history, culture and poetics is not the "de-formed" right row of columns but *both*. The best example of this kind of superimposition is the text of the novel itself. If we simply read along, we are sure to miss the repetitions in the plot of the novel and the larger historical repetitions that are suggested. Like Byzantine art, *Explosion in a Cathedral* appears to have a conventional, classical shape, only slightly askew, but as one looks closer, larger, more significant distortions begin to appear. The novel demands that we, like Sofía running her fingers on the epitaph of Constantine's grandson, look beyond the surface shape of the letters to the hollow behind them, to the gap; that we, without losing sight of the contour of the signs, without ceasing to relish their very materiality, seek the hidden meaning.

Because in the end, what is most remarkable about *Explosion in a Cathedral* is that the text of the novel itself shares characteristics of Latin American culture and history as (mis)shaped by African culture. The text is not composed of letters which, like the French revolutionary law, presume to give history an ideal course. The text of the novel, like a ritualistic object, has its own value as a system of symbols, as access to an arcane gnosis wherein its complicated numerology and emblematic quality are more important than the ebb and flow of concepts. The text does not simply "side" with a Neo-African American culture; it seeks to show that all symbolic activity, including literature, operates in this fashion. History, particularly written history, is not so much elucidation as cultural self-recognition and celebration. Enlightenment, *Aufklärung*, is a clearing, a demolition of local idols and an investiture of idols who will some day be meaningful to all mankind. By making Blacks the catalyst for this meditation on history, Carpentier is echoing Nicolás Guillén's renowned statement that Africans came to the New World to "give man his definitive profile"; only that what is unchanging about that profile is that it is an agent for change.

Carpentier's wide-ranging meditation on history is, in effect, a manifesto of an American poetics. Only by taking into account the warping through repetition displayed in *Explosion in a Cathedral* and its suggested analogon in Byzantine art can we really begin to understand the nature of such American Baroque artists as Wifredo Lam and Aleijandinho. In fact, some of Lam's elongated figures and Aleijandinho's angular and tortured prophets display clearly a Byzantine "mis-shaping" that is the very essence of the Latin American Baroque.

By reflecting on Carpentier's vast geographico-historical experiment we can also understand that similar intellectual and artistic adventures by Garcilaso, Guaman Poma and others are not mere coincidences, but part and parcel of every American effort to narrate history, not an elimination of warring versions of history, but a superimposition: Cuzco on Rome, the Caribbean on the Mediterranean. Carpentier was perhaps the first to posit this self-consciously as a key to the narrative of America, a vision so powerful in its conception and execution that it has indelibly marked the works of other American writers, such as Carlos Fuentes in his *Terra Nostra*, Severo Sarduy in his *Maitreya*, and Gabriel García Márquez in his *One Hundred Years of Solitude*.

Explosion in a Cathedral also demonstrates that American narrative is never merely story-telling, or history re-telling, but an activity that is akin both to philosophical meditation and religio-cultural ritual. It is a mutual recognition sought through an understanding of symbolic exchange, of the process by which history as shared symbols of becoming and being are activated, rendered meaningful. Who knows how much this owes to Afro-American cultures specifically? What we do know is that it owes much to their integration into the larger process of American culture and certainly of American writing. Carpentier is urging us not to look beyond the symbols to the blank stare of Socrates' bust among the weeds of Remigio's garden, but to the forest of symbols that surrounds it.

Roberto González Echevarría, "Socrates Among the Weeds: Blacks and History in Carpentier's 'Explosion in a Cathedral'," in *The Massachusetts Review*, Vol. XXIV, No. 3, Autumn, 1983, pp. 545–61.

SOURCES FOR FURTHER STUDY

Adams, M. Ian. "Alejo Carpentier: Alienation, Culture, and Myth." In his *Three Authors of Alienation: Bombal, Onetti, Carpentier*, pp. 81–105. Austin: University of Texas Press, 1975.
    Discusses Carpentier's definition of the Latin American novel, with primary focus on *The Lost Steps* and its theme of alienation.

Brotherston, Gordon. "The Genesis of America: Alejo Carpentier." In his *The Emergence of the Latin American Novel*, pp. 45–59. Cambridge: Cambridge University Press, 1977.
    Faults Carpentier for perceived contradictions in the writer's philosophic and artistic attitudes towards the New World experience. Brotherston focuses on Carpentier's mature novels—*The Kingdom of this World, The Lost Steps*, and *Explosion in a Cathedral*.

Gikandi, Simon. "The Deformation of Modernism: The Allegory of History in Carpentier's *El siglo de las luces*." In his *Writing in Limbo: Modernism and Caribbean Literature*, pp. 139–67. Ithaca, N.Y.: Cornell University Press, 1992.
    Follows Roberto González Echevarría, as well as more recent deconstructionist theory, in interpreting the major preoccupation in Carpentier's fiction with Eurocentric history and its confrontation with Latin American-Caribbean culture.

Gonzalez, Flora. "Exile as U-topia in Carpentier's *El Recurso del Metodo*." *The Centennial Review* XXX, No. 2 (Spring 1986): 251–59.
    Alludes to an image drawn by novelist and critic Henry James—the window as a metaphor for the fictional viewpoint—to point up the complexity of Carpentier's theories of the narrator in the novel *Reasons of State*.

González Echevarría, Roberto. *Alejo Carpentier: The Pilgrim at Home*. Ithaca: Cornell University Press, 1977, 307 p.
    Characterizes Carpentier's literary enterprise as the evocation of Latin American modernism and the subverting of the reality constructed by European descriptions of history.

Harss, Luis, and Barbara Dohmann. "Alejo Carpentier, or the Eternal Return." In their *Into the Mainstream: Conversations with Latin-American Writers*, pp. 37–67. New York: Harper & Row Publishers, 1967.

A biographical and critical sketch of Carpentier's development, observant of the dual European and Latin American elements of his literary art.

Janney, Frank. *Alejo Carpentier and His Early Works*. London: Tamesis Books Ltd., 1981, 141 p.

Treats the short fiction and the novel *¡Écue-Yamba-Ó!* of Carpentier's early Afro-Cuban period.

Macdonald, Ian. "Magical Eclecticism: *Los pasos perdidos* and Jean-Paul Sartre." In *Contemporary Latin American Fiction: Carpentier, Sabato, Onetti, Roa, Donosa, Fuentes, Garcia Marquez*, edited by Salvador Bacarisse, pp. 1–17. Edinburgh: Scottish Academic Press, 1980.

Maintains that Carpentier's *The Lost Steps* discloses the writer's engagement with European existentialism of the 1930s and 40s. Macdonald contradicts traditional interpretations of the novel by denying a closely autobiographical identification between narrator and author.

Peavler, Terry J. "Alejo Carpentier and the Humanization of Latin American Fiction," *Hispanofila* 25, No. 74 (January 1982): pp. 61–78.

Discusses the introduction of more humanized character types as an important ingredient of the "new Latin American novel."

Priestley, J. B. Introduction to *The Lost Steps* by Alejo Carpentier, translated by Harriet de Onis, pp. 5–11. New York: Avon Books, 1979.

The British novelist and critic regards Carpentier's novel as a journey through inner and outer worlds with an end in the primeval and the archetypal.

Shaw, Donald L. *Alejo Carpentier*. Boston: Twayne Publishers, c. 1985.

An important monograph in English on Carpentier.

Van Ghent, Dorothy. "The Race, the Moment, and the Milieu." *The Yale Review* XLVI, No. 2 (December 1956): 274–88.

An early English-language review of *The Lost Steps*, wherein Van Ghent compares Carpentier's energetic and sweeping style to that of novelist Honoré de Balzac.

Vazquez Amaral, José, "The Return of the Native: Alejo Carpentier's *The Lost Steps*." In his *The Contemporary Latin American Narrative*, pp. 95–119. New York: Las Americas Publishing Co., 1970.

Recounts the plot of Carpentier's novel and interprets its seeming reality as symbolic action.

Webb, Barbara J. "*Lo real maravilloso* in Caribbean Fiction." In her *Myth and History in Caribbean Fiction*, pp. 13–25. Amherst: The University of Massachusetts Press, 1992.

Discusses Carpentier's concept of *lo real maravilloso* and its meaning within the new literature of Latin America exemplified by Jacques Stéphen Alexis, Nicolás Guillén, Aimé Césaire, Jacques Roumain, and Edouard Glissant.

Weber, Frances Wyers. "*El acoso*: Alejo Carpentier's War on Time." *Publications of the Modern Language Association* LXXVIII, No. 1 (March 1963): pp. 440–48.

Identifies time as an essential theme of Carpentier's fiction in an article now considered a classic of Carpentier criticism.

Rosario Castellanos

1925-1974

Mexican poet, novelist, essayist, short story writer, and play-wright.

INTRODUCTION

Castellanos is one of Mexico's most respected writers, especially known for her treatment of issues pertaining to women and Indians in that country. Focusing on the role of language as a subtle means of subjugating both women and indigenous peoples in Spanish culture, Castellanos's competent literary versatility allowed her to discuss these social and political themes in a variety of genres.

Born in Mexico City, Castellanos was raised on her parents' estate in Chiapas. Shunned by her parents in favor of her brother, Castellanos witnessed her brother's suicide and became a solitary child who retreated into literature. After her family's estate was appropriated by the government in the 1941 land reform plan, Castellanos began her studies in the College of Philosophy and Letters at the National University of Mexico in 1944. While there she joined an international group of Hispanic writers who came to be known as the Generation of 1950. Following her parents' deaths in 1948, Castellanos published her first long poem, *Trayectoria del polvo,* on the subject of death. In 1950 she received her master's degree in philosophy, writing a thesis entitled *Sobre cultura femenina,* and subsequently serving as the cultural program director of Chiapas. In 1957 she married a university professor and gave birth to their son, Gabriel; Castellanos then worked as the information director of the National University of Mexico from 1960 to 1966. She traveled to the United States in 1967 as a visiting professor of Latin American literature at the universities of Wisconsin, Indiana, and Colorado, and chaired the Comparative Literature Department at the National University of Mexico upon her return. Now divorced, in 1971 she was named Ambassador to Israel by President Luis Echeverría. While in Israel she taught Mexican literature at the Hebrew University in Jerusalem and continued to write poetry, short stories, essays, and a play—all of which involved women's issues. Castellanos died accidentally of electrocution in 1974. Her body was returned to Mexico City, where she received a state funeral and was buried in the Rotunda de los Hombres Illustros—a tomb reserved for Mexico's most respected leaders and heroes.

The foundations of Castellanos's literary career were laid in *Sobre cultura femenina*, a collection of essays addressing the role of women in Mexican culture. Castellanos's *Balún-Canán* (1957, *The Nine Guardians*), her first novel, focused on the racial and cultural oppression of indigenous people in Mexico, and was told through the eyes of a seven-year-old Indian girl. *The Nine Guardians* incorporates many of Castellanos's own childhood memories as well as Tzotzil Indian myths from her native Chiapas. The plight of the Indian and of the Mexican woman are also the subject of *Oficio de tinieblas* (1962). Often considered her best novel, its central character is an Indian woman who becomes a priestess and healer. The plot revolves around an actual Indian uprising which Castellanos employs to emphasize her point that the Spanish language is a powerful, primary tool used to exploit various elements of Mexican society that are dominated by a male elite. Returning to the essay genre, Castellanos published *Mujer que sabe latín* in 1973, where she discusses the responsibility of writers to represent women in new and realistic ways—ways which challenge the patriarchal constraints that manipulate and control women in western society. Many of these same concerns were the focus of two short story collections entitled *Los convidados de agosto* (1964) and *Album de familia* (1971), as well as a collection of poems entitled *Poesía no eres tú; Obra poética (1948–1971)* (1972).

Castellanos has received widespread international attention for her literary acumen. Some scholars note the importance of her difficult early life in fostering her writing career and formulating her literary themes. Others remark that her adept use of humor throughout her works helps to present more effectively the sensitive issues surrounding women's lives and the exploitation of the Indian. Several commentators have asserted that her commanding use of language deftly leads her readers towards an understanding of how language itself is the key to determining the social stature of people within Mexican society. Regarding her poetry, critics have suggested that Castellanos's earlier poems, such as "Lamentación de Dido" (1957), are sometimes impersonal and abstract, while her later poems, as in *Materia memorable* (1969), introduce the reader to a more colloquial style which mirrors the rhythms of ordinary speech. Nevertheless, many of these same critics generally agree that her poetry is on the whole less effective than her prose works. *El eterno femenino* (1975), Castellanos's dramatic farce set in a beauty parlor where the hair driers and other beauty paraphernalia are devices used to keep women in their proper place, is considered her best work for the stage because of its effective humor and dialogue, but reviewers note that Castellanos's lack of a sense of stagecraft hinders the overall presentation.

Although she died at the height of her career, Castellanos nevertheless was an enormously productive and influential writer who initiated the beginnings of a changing attitude towards women in Mexican society. As Naomi Lindstrom has written, "in her eagerness to convey female experience, she created fictional voices which spoke of their own relegation to lesser status. . . [and] demonstrated that the re-examination of sex roles . . . can move beyond specific grievances to provide new perspectives in literature and culture."

CRITICAL COMMENTARY

MARY SEALE VÁSQUEZ
(essay date 1980)

[In the following excerpt, Vásquez surveys Castellanos's oeuvre, especially focusing on her literary style and themes.]

Within Castellanos' rich and varied literary production,

the genre most consistently and abundantly cultivated was poetry. It is also, perhaps, the truest key to an understanding of Rosario Castellanos. "'Yo creo que la Rosario más íntima está en su poesía ya que aun en los mayores desengaños ella podía levantarlos a la altura de una formulación poética,'" said close friend Raúl Ortiz.

Castellanos left twelve titles that she herself compiled as *Poesía no eres tú* (1972), which incorporated her

Principal Works

Apuntes para declaración de fe (poetry) 1948

Trayectoria del polvo (poetry) 1948

Sobre cultura femenina (essays) 1950

Balún-Canán (novel) 1957
   [*The Nine Guardians,* 1959]

Ciudad real: Cuentos (short stories) 1960

Oficio de tinieblas (novel) 1962

Los convidados de agosto (short stories) 1964

Juicios sumarios: Ensayos (essays) 1966

Materia memorable (poetry) 1969

Album de familia (short stories) 1971

Poesía no eres tú: Obra poética 1948–1971 (poetry) 1972

Mujer que sabe latín (essays) 1973

El uso de la palabra (essays) 1974

El eterno femenino: farsa (drama) 1975

Meditación en el umbral: Antología poética (poetry) 1985
   [*Meditation on the Threshold: A Bilingual Anthology of Poetry,* 1988]

The Selected Poems of Rosario Castellanos (poetry) 1988
   [*A Rosario Castellanos Reader,* 1988]

previously published books, as well as poems separately published. The volumes of major works which stand individually are: *Trayectoria del polvo* (1948), *Apuntes para una declaración de fe* (1948), *De la vigilia estéril* (1950), *Presentación al templo* (1951), *El rescate del mundo* (1952), *Poemas 1953–1955* (1957), the dramatic poems *Judith y Salomé* (1959), *Al pie de la letra* (1959), *Lívida luz* (1960), *Materia memorable* (1969), and *Poesía no eres tú.* The last-named volume included most of Castellanos' poetry to 1971, with the exception of **"Ponderación de provincia,"** a very few isolated poems . . . , and the unknown poetry of Castellanos' period in Israel.

The abstract-concrete, idea-image, prose-poetry oppositions that run through the body of Castellanos' thought and literary production inform her poetry, nearly always in creative, rather than destructive, tension. Often they are conciliated; the concerns which sent Castellanos to prose nourished, in turn, her poetry, as her prose is enriched by lyricism.

Rosario Castellanos' poetry, in the line of Sor Juana, Octavio Paz and Gorostiza, evolves from the declamatory, rhetorical tone of her early work to the colloquial, tongue-in-cheek, understated approach found in later collections;

from the long poem to the condensed *pincelada;* from the personal declaration in a wide, even cosmic context to a concern with the rendering of the objects which surrounded her, to a final involvement with humankind, a view of the other as bearing upon the self and of the meaning of that self in the commonality. Love, solitude, destiny, death and, finally, comfort and affirmation are repeated themes. With full attainment of her own poetic voice her stance becomes markedly feminist; it is this feminism from which Castellanos reaches to touch humanistic concerns, moving from protest and lament to a posture of creative change. Humor becomes the instrument she employs to reveal the ridiculous and celebrate the magical, to laugh at herself and at humanity—and sometimes cry with it.

Castellanos' poetic voice was, not surprisingly, hard-won. Following *Trayectoria del polvo* and *Apuntes para una declaración de fe*—both judged severely by Castellanos herself and the latter by critics as well—she began to move away from the long poem and from abstraction, with which she had become impatient. Viewing as excessive the intellectualizing tendency in Mexican poetry, she saw her own poetic nature in quite different terms: "'. . . No deseaba escribir poemas intelectuales. Quería crear poemas si no emotivos por lo menos con imágenes referidas a cosas concretas'." she remembered. The result was *De la vigilia estéril,* though Castellanos later judged herself as still too prolix—and too abstract.

More successful, in Castellanos' later view, was *El rescate del mundo,* in which she had attempted to control her tendency toward a proliferation of images. "'. . . Traté de aprehender un objeto mediante un chispazo: dos o tres imágenes referidas al mismo tema'." But it was with *Poemas 1953–1955* that she felt most satisfied in her trajectory to that date. Castellanos felt two continuous influences in her poetry: the emotive current of Gabriela Mistral and the more intellectual one of Guillén. Here the Guillén influence is marked in the effort toward a transparency of form which would reveal, intact, the object. The concern with the rendering of objects expressed in connection with *De la vigilia estéril* continues here, imbued with a kind of celebration. "'Traté de encontrar entre los objetos que me rodeaban aquéllos que fueran más significativos, más esenciales, los que me permitieran integrar mi propia visión del mundo'," which she described as "'una vivencia religiosa del mundo, [un] sentirme ligada a las cosas desde un punto de vista emotivo y. . . considerarlos como objetos de contemplación estética'."

It was in *Al pie de la letra,* she wrote, that "I began to recognize my own voice . . . and could see three cardinal points to develop: humor, solemn meditation and contact with my carnal and historical roots. And everything bathed in that stark light of death, which makes all matter memorable." **"Monólogo de la extranjera"** was her favorite poem from that key 1959 collection.

En el momento de hacerlo no fui consciente de eso, creía que estaba contando la historia de otra mujer y al terminar me di cuenta de que estaba hablando de mí, de que era mi historia, que la había otra vez transfigurado y usado en forma oblicua de referencia que es lo que pone distancia entre el objeto y la expresión. . . quizá es la distancia estética.

The collection is made up of word portraits described by Castellanos as "'reminiscencias prosística'." She had moved in the direction of prose impelled by the complex of childhood memories stirred by her return to Chiapas. The exercise of that medium now made itself felt in her verse: "'Desde que comencé a escribir prosa, ésta se reflejó en mi poesía'."

The poems of *Lívida luz* mark an evolution in the direction of engagement with the human community, their deeply-felt humanity contrasting with the deliberate coldness of tone. *Materia memorable* and *En la tierra de en medio* continue this expression of commitment, rendered often in the very personal terms of the self and "el otro," the loved fellow human, *tú*. Between the two lies, in some of the poems, the impossible barrier, while in others they form together a promise of continuity.

Castellanos considered the three groups of previously uncollected poems written after 1969 which form the last three sections of *Poesía no eres tú*, under the titles of *En la tierra de en medio, Otros poemas* and *Viaje redondo,* as her most complete and mature poetry. In these poems, she said:

> . . . Tomo una serie de anécdotas o de incidentes o de experiencias que no son las que de una manera muy formal se consideran como poéticas. Me siento ya en libertad de salirme del canon y de encontrar fuera algo que a mi modo de ver es válido. . . La última parte me gusta en general por la libertad que tiene, el no preocuparme más si esta palabra es lícita, si es aceptable, sino simplemente es la palabra necesaria, la palabra exacta. Y además son vivencias en un plano de consciencia, en un plano de madurez que espero que haya pasado al poema.

Here Castellanos' favorite discourse structure is the dramatic monologue of a feminine poetic voice that probes essential questions through ironic humor, a vein she pursued in her play, *El eterno femenino*. What is a woman's perception of her experiences? How does the woman artist see herself? What are the roles of women in our society? Which ones are imposed by history and custom? "Custom holds that a man has to be very 'macho' and a woman very self-sacrificing. The complicity between executioner and victim is so old that it is impossible to distinguish who is who." The poem **"Lecciones de cosas"** traces that process of internalization of the Golden Rule as a maxim of self-sacrifice, while **"Post-Scriptum"** gives the lie to the traditional solution of adjustment. A musing on a typically "unpoetic" Castellanos event, the clipping off of a fingernail, **"De Mutilaciones"** looks at loss of identity. **"Mirando a la Gioconda"** is a good example of how Castellanos used a frivolous vehicle, in this case her "dumb little tourist lady," to set up dramatic irony of scene that conveys her very serious point that women's problems are also cultural and political. Castellanos' *ars poetica,* **"Poesía no eres tú,"** is more than just a latter-day reaction to the poetic ideal of a Bécquer: "What happened is that I developed very slowly from the most closed subjectivity to the disturbing discovery that the other existed, and finally to the rupture of the pattern of the couple to integrate myself into the social ambit which is the one in which the poet defines, understands and expresses herself."

The reflection in mode of expression of the idea-image opposition and synthesis running through Castellanos' creative life is the cross-nourishment of prose and poetry. She had composed prose along with poetry "'from the beginning'." Viewing the two as complementary, she did, however, seek in prose what she referred to as a possibility for discipline lacking in the more elusive poetic genre, as well as a mode for expression of another kind of reality. "'Deseaba contar sucesos que no fueran esenciales como los de la poesía: sucesos adjetivos'." The concerns encountered and expressed in her practice of each of the two media enriched, in turn, the other. In form, Castellanos brought to narrative the lyricism found, especially, in *Balún Canán* and took back to her poetry qualities of prose.

Castellanos' recounting of "adjectival happenings" came to fill five volumes. There are three novels—*Balún Canán* (1957), *Oficio de tinieblas* (1962) and *Rito de iniciación*, announced as a forthcoming publication by Fomento de Cultura Económica in 1964 but never published — and three volumes of short stories: *Ciudad Real* (1960), *Los convidados de agosto* (1964), and *Álbum de familia* (1971).

In the cases of novel and short story alike, the first two books in the chronology deal with Chiapanecan themes, while the third does not. Both *Balún Canán* and *Oficio de tinieblas* — to be treated separately here as the culmination of Castellanos' narrative art — powerfully evoke the social reality of Chiapas and the mythic structure of its indigenous culture. The poetic prose of the former work is laced through with the fantasy which characterized Castellanos' own childhood years. Its lyricism fits the imaginative capacity of the child narrator, as it does the strong mythic content of Tzeltal and Tzotzil culture. Time moves for the girl much as it does for the indigenous peoples; for each, the measure of time is a function of the sense made of it. Castellanos' approximation of the two worlds, through structurally imperfect, is forceful. (Castellanos herself saw as flaws of *Balún Canán* an unconvincing conclusion and roughness in the intercalation of the middle section, narrated in the third person, between the first and third, which have the child narrator.)

The consensus of Mexican critics judged *Balún Canán* the best novel to appear in Mexico in 1957. It brought Castellanos the Premio Chiapas the following year.

The experience of writing *Balún Canán* was for Castellanos a central one which altered the direction of her art. The re-encounter with childhood memories and with the dichotomized *indígena-ladino* reality that framed them was powerful. Castellanos' view of her literary vocation began to change. In her poetry she would move from seeing the world around her as "'an object of aesthetic contemplation'" whose components she wished to render through a form as crystalline, as transparent as possible, and toward a position as *escritora situada* bound up in the workings of a world of struggle: its injustices, hopes, dreams and what became of them. Castellanos' prose already involved, in *Balún Canán* and the **"Primera revelación"** story which preceded it, such a concern with the human community and its fate. Continuing narrative activity, culminating in *Oficio de tinieblas,* developed this commitment. In the nine stories which comprise *Ciudad Real,* set in the bicultural ambience of San Cristóbal de las Casas, Castellanos focuses vividly upon the perspective of both Indian and *ladino* and upon the problematical co-existence of the two. The later *Los convidados de agosto* was the last work in Castellanos' Chiapas cycle. The stories of *Album de familia,* of highly sophisticated construction, are in a different vein. Their setting is urban and contemporary, their tone the ironic, even biting one of such late poems as **"Kinsey Report"** and **"Jornada de la soltera."**

Different from its predecessors, too, was *Rito de iniciación,* about which Castellanos spoke at length with critic Joseph Sommers shortly before the novel was due to be published. "*Rito de iniciación* is a novel of personal search and discovery, tracing the human process by which an adolescent girl finds her way to the vocation of literature," he wrote [in "The Present Moment in the Mexican Novel," *Books Abroad* (Summer 1966)]. The novel was set in the Mexico City of the 1940's, in the Universidad Nacional which antedated the huge, modern institution of today. An autobiographical novel, then? No, Castellanos told Sommers, adding that because her autonomous protagonist's process of self-discovery is "more intellectual than emotional . . . the work deals more in concepts and in the clash of ideas than in detailed psychological analysis of moods or states of mind." "Conventional" in structure, *Rito* was distinct from Castellanos' previous novels in style as well, emphasizing "precision and abstract language, rather than imagery and lyrical tone."

The lack of reader and critical access to *Rito de iniciación* is unfortunate especially so since Castellanos had, in her second novel, *Oficio de tinieblas,* moved into command of the novel genre, overcoming some of the difficult structural problems which had troubled her in the composition of *Balún Canán* and in later reflection upon that novel.

The narrative axis of *Oficio,* which won Castellanos the Sor Juana Inés de la Cruz and Xavier Villarrutia prizes for literature, is an actual Chamula revolt of the Juárez era, transferred by the novelist to the Cárdenas period and, ultimately, to a mythic sphere where time has ceased to be linear. The difficulties encountered in the novel's elaboration were such that the process took more than six years:

> Tuve que modificar la época, tuve que interpretar todos los hechos históricos a la luz de otros aspectos meramente estéticos; porque en el curso de las páginas fue imponiéndose la exigencia propia de la literatura sobre los sucesos de la historia.[Rhoda C. Dybrig, *Rosario Castellanos: biografía y novelística,* 1965.]

The results of such labors are impressive; the novel's depth and force of effect are sustained through a balance and a unity of complex elements which point to a high degree of mastery of the novelistic craft. Joseph Sommers emphasized the importance of *Oficio's* demythification function in its challenge to officially promulgated truths regarding the Cárdenas era and pointed out the attention accorded to female characterization. Castellanos herself had denied membership in the indigenist current of Mexican literature, judging that the indigenist writers had presented too simplistic a view of all-good *indígena* and nefarious *ladino* and had paid insufficient heed to style — defects which surely do not characterize the Castellanos of either *Balún Canán* or *Oficio de tinieblas.* In Sommers' view, however, *Oficio* did display traces of paternalism and "cultural pessimism," "el tratar al indio como un sujeto incapaz de entender su pasado o de analizar su presente, y al ladino como alguien que permanece congelado en un inalterable y rígido sistema social de corte capitalista y agrario." He views the novel, for all its strengths, as an example of the best "critical narrative."

Taken together, the contribution of Castellanos' narrative art stand out for the range of themes treated; the control evident particularly in the later stories and in *Oficio de tinieblas;* the grace of style; the completeness of the novelistic worlds created.

Castellanos' drama writings began in the early Fifties, when Emilio Carballido, Luisa Josefina Hernández and Sergio Magaña — friends and fellow members of the Generation of 1950 — urged her to try her hand in that genre. The result was *Tablero de damas* a bitingly satirical portrayal of the female literary sub-culture of Mexico which provoked considerable commentary among members of the literary set, a number of whom Castellanos later acknowledged, had indeed been the models for *Tablero's* characters. The play and its aftermath of resentment eventually led to the dissolution of *América: revista antológica,* where the work had been published.

Aesthetically, *Tablero* had not pleased Castellanos: "'Su argumento pudiera haber sido interesante pero el diálogo no funcionaba, los personajes no se conjugaban uno con otro'." Carballido's suggestion that Castellanos employ verse as her medium of dramatic expression yielded three one-act verse plays; *Judith, Salomé* and *Eva,* all free-from interpretations of the biblical characters suggested in the titles. A drama group at the UNAM did *Salomé* and *Judith* on stage and in a campus radio broadcast. Other verse dramas followed: *Vocación de Sor Juana,* in two acts, and the three-act *La creciente.* Castellanos was dissatisfied with these works, and no evidence exists that they were ever published: "'No funcionaban dramáticamente porque [yo] era incapaz de mover a mis personajes y, sobre todo, de darles un motivo para sus acciones'."

In search of assistance in dramatic technique, Castellanos took a drama course with Rodolfo Usigli in 1954. The course disappointed her, but she did compose one prose play, *Casa de gobierno.* Her aim had been creation of a realistic work, Mexican and political in theme. Finding, however, that her play was "an exact copy" of Usigli's *El gesticulador,* she destroyed the manuscript.

Castellanos abjured theater work, and seemed to discount narrative as well, after that experience: "'Veía entonces como las únicas possibilidades para mí en el campo literario, la lírica y la critica. Ningún otro género me parecía accesible'." *Balún Canán* was published three years later.

Nor was *Casa de gobierno* to be Castellanos' last dramatic work. In the early Seventies actress Emma Teresa Armendáriz contacted Castellanos, impressed by an *Excélsior* column by Rosario. The two met, discovered that they shared deep feminist concerns, became friends. The actress urged Castellanos to write for her a dramatic vehicle of feminist theme to be staged in Mexico City, with Armendáriz' husband, Rafael López Miarnau, as co-producer and director. Eventually Castellanos did indeed compose such a work, sending it from Israel with Raúl Ortiz. A production of *El eterno femenino* (1975) was mounted as planned in 1976, but when financial backing was suddenly withdrawn after only a few weeks of performances, the play was forced to close.

El eterno femenino is in the ironic vein of Castellanos' later poetry and the stories of *Álbum de familia.* Set in a Mexico City beauty salon, the play presents, through a series of representative characters, a highly effective commentary on the institutions and stereotyped attitudes which imprison women.

It is an imprisonment in which women are shown to be active collaborators. Castellanos' characters speak, but there are no true conversations, their lack a function, surely, of isolation. "Rosario hubiera querido dialogar," comments Elena Poniatowska, "pero sus personajes estuvieron siempre solos, de ahí que sólo produzca largos monólogos; los diálogos no se dan en la obra de Rosario, no hay una conjunción del yo y del tú que ella buscó tanto" [from a personal interview with Emma Teresa Ar-

mendáriz, and Rafael López Miarnav in 1974]. In *El eterno femenino* the lack is not a defect, serving, rather, to buttress the work's themes of entrapment and loneliness. But the usual necessity for dialogue in drama may well be one reason for Castellanos' enduring discomfort with that genre; such a requirement may have seemed inappropriate within an *oeuvre* which has as one of its major motive forces precisely the yearning for communion.

Following the Hispanic tradition which sees as parallel and complementary the crafts of the journalist and the creative writer, Castellanos was active in journalistic labors for *Novedades, Siempre!* and *Excélsior,* as well as for such periodicals as the *Revista de la Universidad de México* and *La palabra y el hombre.* In addition to *Sobre cultura femenina* (1950) and the four volumes of Castellanos' collected essays,. . . [there are] ninety uncollected Castellanos pieces belonging to the essay genre. Her philosophy studies had, she wrote, imparted to her the habit of questioning; the essays contained in *Juicios sumarios* (1966), *Mujer que sabe latín* (1973), *El uso de la palabra* (a selection by José Emilio Pacheco of Castellanos' *Excélsior* columns, 1974) and *El mar y sus pescaditos* (1975) indeed reveal an intellectual curiosity of impressive range and, in her expression of it, concision, a capacity for synthesis, a marked sense of humor inclined, as in her work in other genres, toward the ironic. Topics range over the cultural scene of Mexico, other Latin American countries, the United States, Europe, the Middle East, the Orient.

The last two pieces of Rosario Castellanos' writing known to exist are a column, **"Jerusalén celeste, Jerusalén terrenal,"** mailed to *Excélsior* on July 30, 1974 and printed on August 11th, and a loving, whimsical **"Recado a Gabriel donde se encuentre,"** written by Rosario while her son was away that summer and found among her papers after her death. It, too, appeared in *Excélsior.*

Castellanos also may have left a journal, mentioned by her in connection with her girlhood years in Chiapas and Mexico City. After Castellanos' death, Nahum Megged commented, "Quizá haya conservado su diario, no lo sé. O quizá ya no creyó en él" [*La cultura en Mexico,* September 4, 1974]. (pp. 26–35)

Mary S. Vásquez, "Rosario Castellanos, Image and Idea," in *Homenaje a Rosario Castellanos, Vol. II,* edited by Maureen Ahern and Mary Seale Vásquez, Albatros Hispanofila, 1980, pp. 15–40.

HELENE M. ANDERSON

(essay date 1983)

[In the following essay, Anderson investigates what Castellanos regards as the traditional three views of womanhood in Mexican society; she also comments on the relationship between the plight of the woman and that of the Indian, and on language as the "key to taking possession" of Mexican society.]

In 1950 Rosario Castellanos (1925–1974) presented a thesis on feminine culture which has come to be considered the intellectual point of departure for the women's liberation movement in Mexico. According to Mexican essayist, Carlos Monsiváis, no one up to that time had expressed so clearly what it meant to be both a woman and a Mexican [in a footnote, the critic refers the reader to José Emilio Pacheco's introduction to Rosario Castellanos's *El uso de la palabra* (Mexico: Excelsior, 1974), p. 7]. This became, in effect, the central line of Castellanos' work, but always from a very particular perspective: the relationship of women to their culture within the broader relationship in Mexican society of those with power to those deprived of it.

Although her 1973 book of essays, *Mujer que sabe latín . . . (Woman who Knows Latin . . .)* is considered the first provocative Mexican analysis of the image of women within the framework of Western culture in general and Mexican culture in particular, it is well within a national tradition of polemical literature which has existed since the seventeenth century. In this tradition Castellanos examines the issues of image and reality, and submission and domination from a consistently unique, female perspective.

The feminine ideal of Western culture, according to Castellanos, is that of the strong woman of the Scriptures whose strength is defined in terms of her prenuptial purity, marital fidelity, devotion to her children, dedication to domestic obligations, and her prudent administration of a patrimony which she herself is not permitted to inherit or possess. Her virtues are, therefore, constancy, loyalty, patience, chastity, submission, humility, unobtrusiveness, and above all, self-sacrifice. All of these qualities are even more pronounced within Mexican culture. In fact, Castellanos proposes three female archetypes as typical of the Mexican reflection of woman's image: La Malinche, La Virgen de Guadalupe, and Sor Juana Inés de la Cruz.

La Malinche is an Indian woman who was given to Cortés, after he established contact with the first Indian towns on the coast, to serve as his slave, his interpreter, and ultimately, his concubine. Since she knew both the language of the coastal Maya area and the language of the central valley of Mexico (Nahuatl), she became—with the collaboration of Jerónimo de Aguilar who knew both Spanish and Maya—the key instrument by which Cortés was able to open his way into the Mexican interior. This is very significant because La Malinche and Cortés represent, symbolically, Mexico's "ancestral couple," responsible for the "fall" of the Indian nation and the configuration of the Mexican future. Thus, she is the Mexican counterpart of Eve, and through her knowledge she facilitates the penetration and violation of Mexico. These terms are used with purposeful consciousness of their sexual overtones when talking about La Malinche in Mexican history for she is, in fact, the "Dark Lady" of sinister sexuality. She not only facilitates the violation of her own people, but also becomes the mother of the violator's child. Interestingly enough, however, she can never be the "legal" mother because, historically, the Spanish crown did not recognize the legality of any relationship between Indian women and Spanish men, nor did it confer legitimacy on offspring resulting from such a relationship without the man's express stipulation. Of even greater significance for the symbolic overtones in the figure of La Malinche, she can never be considered the "legal" mother because true motherhood in the Catholic context implies an "immaculate" conception rather than a carnal one. As concubine to Cortés, she represents sexuality. This already sets up, symbolically, a conflictive tension between womanhood and motherhood. The maternal ideal cannot possibly encompass a figure like La Malinche.

The ideal of motherhood has to be La Virgen de Guadalupe, another Mexican legend. The figure of the Virgen Morena that appeared to an Indian, miraculously, became the emblem and symbol of Mexican nationhood during the struggle for Independence. Therefore, nation—or children as future nation—becomes identified with the emblem of motherhood which is untainted by the sexual implications of the Malinche figure: the maternal ideal as a figure unrelated to sexuality.

The third symbolic image of woman in Mexican culture is Sor Juana Inés de la Cruz, the poet-nun who lived in the seventeenth century and who is seen to embody intellectual activism. She entered the convent because only there could she have access to study, to writing, to the kind of activity for which there was no place within the traditional roles for Mexican women in that era. By confronting choice and its consequences rather than waiting to "be chosen" as (sweetheart or wife), she rejected the accepted norm. Moreover, by embodying intellectuality in the figure of a nun, Sor Juana symbolically conveys an image of intellectuality as a negation of both motherhood and sexuality.

For Castellanos, therefore, the three elements which are a symbolic synthesis of woman's image and reality in Mexican culture are sexuality, or betrayal leading to the fall of (Mexican) man; motherhood, which is chaste and excludes any recognition of sexuality; and intellectuality, which is a negation of both motherhood and sexuality. These elements, whose equivalent counterparts are considered integrative in the male, are thus displaced and fragmented in the image of woman in Mexico.

Rosario Castellanos has stated that, when she wrote *Mujer que sabe latín* . . . her purpose was to raise consciousness, to awaken the critical spirit, to disseminate it and make it infectious, and not to accept any dogma until one is sure it is capable of "resisting a good joke." The "good joke" is perpetrated by the author in her play *El eterno femenino (The Eternal Feminine)*, a farce set in modern Mexico which satirizes the typical female roles in Mexican society and visualizes projects of defiance and rebellion against them. Ironically, all of the action takes place in a beauty parlor under a hair dryer.

In *El eterno femenino* there are those female characters who do not wish to challenge the status quo, who have managed to adapt to the "cult of the venerated slave"—that comfortable role of mother, wife, or lover. They play the roles of innocent virgins, analytical, pragmatic wives, and self-sacrificing mothers. The fantasy counterparts of these women are the characters who have rejected all stereotypic and conventional behavior, women who establish either tacitly or overtly the necessity of finding another way of being human and free. These are key words in Castellanos' work; it is precisely because she deals with the question of women within the larger context of questions of freedom and liberation, that there is, in her work, an important synthesis of social issues that goes beyond the female and has to do with the fundamental structures of power and the theme of domination and submission within society.

In the beauty salon that serves as the setting for *El eterno femenino,* a device is being sold by an agent for use by women while under the dryer. This device is guaranteed to avoid what the salesman considers to be the greatest danger to which women are susceptible while doing nothing—that is, thinking. Thought in itself is dangerous and must be avoided at all costs. The little device plugged into the dryer triggers a series of scenes which are, in fact, projections of distorted and surrealistic situations in which women either contemplate wild extrapolations of their own image of their roles as proper wives and mothers, or else they are fantasies which absolutely destroy all traditional roles.

Castellanos uses techniques of the theater of the absurd to project fantasies through the little device in the hair dryer. She also inserts herself into the world of her play by having the characters express a variety of speculations on what the author's purpose is in setting up these absurd situations. One character says:

> Do you realize that our most venerated traditions, our dearest symbols, are right now objects of mockery in a theater in the Capital? Against whom are they speaking out? Against one who is the pillar of our society, the one who transmits the values that sustain all of us to future generations, against the one who is the source of our strength and wholeness—the Mexican woman. . . . The attack is specific: and is against the self-sacrifice of mothers, the chastity of sweethearts, the virtue of wives, that is, against all our proverbial attributes. These are attributes in which our most solid institutions are rooted—family, religion, country.

By having a character comment on the dire consequences of allowing a play-wright to mock the very pillars of society, Rosario Castellanos takes the question of women out of a limited focus and sets it in a more general perspective: the way in which women are conditioned to uphold the structures of power and how, therefore, within the family unit one finds a symbolic synthesis of the social, economic, and cultural structures of society at large. As in her other essays, novels, and short stories, Castellanos goes beyond the limits of conventional discourse on feminist questions and examines the whole question of social justice and economic exploitation, not unlike the concerns of Simone Weil, a writer she greatly admired. This is precisely the preoccupation that binds together the themes of the woman and the Indian in Castellanos' work.

Neither women nor Indians are given the privilege of choice. As an instrument of repression, the mythification of the traditional role models for Mexican women has glorified the negation of choice as one of the most desirable qualities in a "proper" woman:

> Mexican women do not choose. We wait modestly for a man to cast an eye in our direction and note our marvelous qualities. All that follows goes according to fairly rigorous rules. . . . If we manage to wait long enough, if we are finally chosen, the rest flows with mathematical precision. . . . We manage to be satisfied with someone . . . who accepts marriage as a valid institution which one does not treat lightly and within which the wife has a role and must be given that role. . . . Our cardinal virtue is patience, and if we exercise it, we will be rewarded. . . .

Mexican literature has perpetuated this legacy of the feminine ideal in a series of archetypal characters, reflecting the fact that Mexican reality seems not to have changed its attitudes toward women since 1839 when the wife of the first Spanish Ambassador wrote that Mexican women were devout nuns, impeccable housewives, docile daughters, and dedicated mothers. But the other side of the coin, she observed, was to be seen in the mental asylums and prisons where most of the cases of madness in women had been brought on by abandonment or amorous deceit, sometimes involving the murder of lovers and spouses. These were women who had reached a *situación límite* (a point of ultimate desperation) at which, according to Castellanos, echoing Sartre, nothing is forbidden because nothing matters anymore.

Castellanos' approach to the vital dilemmas of her characters has been substantially influenced by her reading of Simone de Beauvoir, Agatha Christie, Virginia Woolf, and Doris Lessing. It was in de Beauvoir's work that she first encountered female reality discussed not as biological destiny, but as choices influenced by religious, moral, and intellectual factors behind which were specific economic interests. These interests and the systems of exploitation that express them are encapsuled in the structure of the family, for their efficiency depends to a great degree on the dose of dogmatism that can be inculcated in its dependent members. Castellanos found a similar awareness of the intimate relationship between larger economic and social structures and race or gender relationships in the work of Rhodesian-born Doris Lessing. She saw in Lessing's exploration of black and white in Africa an essential point of contact with her own concern for the relationship between Indian and white in Mexico, not to mention the analogous implications this held for the question of women. Castellanos fully appreciates Lessing's perception of the inextricable knot of humiliation, remorse, and mutual dependency that characterizes the relationships between these groups. Indians, blacks, and women share a common reluctance to break that knot for fear of confronting a cold and impersonal alternative. On the other hand, what interests Castellanos even more is Lessing's subordination of the importance of color to economic motives in explaining the African situation. Any exploitative system depends for its survival on creating and sustaining an "inferior," exploitable sector, and in this sense, Indians, blacks, and women have shared a common fate.

Because Rosario Castellanos sees both women and Indians as occupying a confined space within Mexican society, the small town of Comitán in Chiapas becomes the perfect emblem of this confinement. Castellanos spent a good part of her early life in the southern Mexican region of Chiapas, an area deeply permeated by Indian (Tzotzil) culture. It is alive in the stories, traditions, and legends passed on from generation to generation in the language which is still spoken by a majority of the population there. It has also been rocked by repeated political and economic upheavals due to the confrontation between the landless Indian peasants and the white landed gentry. This area is also extremely provincial in its attitude toward the roles of male and female in society. Thus Comitán becomes the natural setting for Rosario Castellanos' narrative. It is here that the dominant problems of Mexican society intersect in the theme of submission vs. liberation.

The utilization of a restricted space to examine larger, hidden tensions draws Castellanos to the work of another woman author, Agatha Christie. In Christie, she admires the ability to detect beneath the apparent placidity and respectability of small English towns, the stifled ambitions, buried resentments, and skeletons hidden in country closets. Castellanos applies a similar optic to the town of Comitán. Delving into the "lives of the obscure"

in this remote town, she writes about people of no great social, political or economic import. They are those who consider themselves *gente decente* (proper citizens). Basically, they are small voices heard in a minor key. Yet it is precisely this dramatic counterpoint between the obscurity of the voice and the emblematic magnitude of the situation that gives such force to Castellanos' narrative.

In *Los convidados de agosto* (*The Guests of August*), a collection of short stories, various female characters in the town of Comitán confront their *situación límite*. These characters, reflecting the archetypes Castellanos discusses in her essays, are, among others, restless adolescents on the threshhold of womanhood, impatient to claim its experience and rewards; or spinsters who, in a desperate attempt to break the structures that enclose them, surrender themselves on summer nights to strange men, "without resistance, without enthusiasm, without sensuality, without remorse," but in some last effort to give meaning to their lives which, "like water, seem to filter through the fingers of the hand." They are women left at life's periphery, abandoned by fathers and lovers, whose role it is to wait, for there is nothing more dishonorable than initiating a thrust into life. Time and again the female characters in Castellanos' stories wait.

When, as in the case of a story entitled **"Vals capricho"** (**"Waltz Caprice"**), a young girl, Reinerie, invades the lives of two maiden aunts who have made their peace with static marginality, the repercussions are immediate. Reinerie has been sent to her aunts by their brother who has, up to then, cared for his daughter alone in a remote jungle region of Mexico; he now wishes her to be educated and made into a proper young woman by his two maiden sisters. When she erupts into their lives, she is all unselfconsciousness and unbridled movement; her knowledge of nature's ways, her initiative of action, her sensual response to the world, her rebellious attitude are all a threat to the social codes which have been established to contain women. As Castellanos points out, a man generally counts on a woman's ignorance and innocence so that she may depend on him and be grateful to him for revealing life to her. Reinerie, however, needs no masculine interpreter of experience or dispeller of ignorance since she has lived in intimate contact with the physical world in the hinterlands. Thus, her presence causes general consternation not only in the lives of her aunts but in the life of the town as a whole. The center of the story becomes the conflict that arises as the aunts attempt to restrain, condition, and mold this young woman according to traditional female roles. Her very name, Reinerie, upsets the aunts for it bears no relationship to conventional names to which they are accustomed. In the course of the story she is called by a series of names simultaneously—Claudia, Gladys—all of which represent approved possibilities of womanhood for this young, untameable woman. In the end, Reinerie leaves, having reappropriated the same state of natural abandon in which she appeared, but not without suffering the consequences of a painful confrontation with her aunts, who are also wounded in the process.

The *soltera*, or spinster, is a prominent figure in Castellanos' stories because if the duty of woman is to wait passively to be chosen, the ultimate embodiment of waiting is the maiden lady. In the title story of *Los convidados de agosto*. Emelina, a spinster of thirty-five, is caught between the possibility of life and the abandonment of hope. In a last desperate attempt to break out of the structures that have confined her to a sterile waiting, she impulsively decides to attend the fair that is being held in honor of the patron saint of the town. Her solitary flight to freedom and an encounter with a stranger dissolves into public humiliation as her brother takes a very inebriated Emelina home by force. Protesting that the stranger did not do anything to her, that he was just going to teach her how to live, she is berated by her brother who sees her behavior as an ineradicable stain on the honor of his name. One final, composite image in the story—very much in keeping with Castellanos' critical vision—is Emelina howling in the streets with the description of an animal, while her brother, after satisfying the affront to his honor, is seen knocking at the door of the town brothel.

For Castellanos, spinsterhood within the confines of a small Mexican town is the constant recollection of time, the constant aspect of time slipping away and death slipping in. (In this aspect her stories are not unlike those of Sherwood Anderson's *Winesburg, Ohio.) Soltería* is the absolute opposite of everything that constitutes energy, activity, and affirmation of lie. The anguished point in the lives of these characters is the approaching moment when hope and resignation lie in the balance. It is within this moment, with its desperate awareness of being the last chance for a thrust into life, that many of her *solteras* are fixed. These women—the unmarried, the abandoned, the aged—will never be free of the conflict between a potential for life that they still feel, and the social impositions that forever determine the channels of their existence.

Castellanos' novel *Balún-Canán,* fuses the theme of the Indian and the woman. It is set in Chiapas during the time of the presidency of Lázaro Cárdenas when Mexico undertook a program of land redistribution. It was a time of anticlerical legislation as well as of the division of large expanses of land into smaller parcels to be distributed to the Indians, and was thus a time that threatened all the traditional power structures. This novel deals with the repercussions of these events on both the relationships in Chiapas between Indians and ladinos (persons of Indian-Spanish racial origin, or mestizos, who identify with the dominant culture), and the relationships between men and women.

An important character is the Indian woman, Catalina Díaz Pantelhó who suffers the knowledge of her inability to bear children. Within the Indian tradition, her husband would have the right to abandon her. Her anguish is intensified by not knowing when her husband will pronounce the words of repudiation. Ultimately, her attempts to harness all the forces at her disposal—both natural and supernatural—to remedy her condition, invest her with the aura of an *ilol,* a seer or sacred spirit. As she becomes more and more obsessed by the need to find a solution to her barrenness, she also becomes transfigured by it. She seems to undergo a process of "dematerialization" whereby her role of woman as potential mother is gradually replaced by that of woman as sacred spirit, preoccupied with things that transcend the immediate problem of motherhood. Her impassioned commitment to the mythic forces that mold the universe of the Tzotziles eventually leads her to galvanize the Indian community around her and to offer, as a kind of sacrifice to the gods of social justice, the illegitimate child she has raised as her own. Suddenly the initial dilemma of the Indian woman takes a turn in another direction: it is precisely the denial of her maternity which frees her to become the catalytic agent of the Indian insurrection when the local landowners refuse to carry out the mandate of the Cárdenas reform. This is an interesting Castellanos twist on the notion of motherhood, not as liberation, but as imprisonment within an alternative role bequeathed to Catalina. The moment that she finally denies the possibility of motherhood she becomes the agent of true liberation.

Another female figure in the novel dares to challenge traditional roles Julia Acevedo, La Alazana, a stranger to Comitán, defies custom and walks through the streets alone, her red hair insolently loosened. She has been raised to support herself by a mother abandoned by her husband, and for fear of becoming enslaved, she wants no children of her own. For yet another character, Idolina, passivity itself becomes an instrument of control. Her paralyzing illness is the mechanism of power she comes to exert over those at whose mercy she has always been.

Another aspect of the structures of power, as they relate to Indians and to women, is brought out in *Balún-Canán* when an Indian nursemaid says to the little girl who is the narrator and the daughter of a well-to-do ladino family: "It is very bad to love those who rule, those who possess." When the child, who worships this woman who raised her, looks at her father dismissing his Indian workers, she thinks of him for the first time as "one who rules, one who possesses." The newly raised consciousness in the child's perception of her father's role is Castellanos' way of pointing to the family structure as a microcosm of society as a whole. The same young narrator, for example, finds a notebook in her father's desk which contains a text, obviously taken from an Indian source, which recounts the conquest and suffering of the Indians under the *caixlanes,* or ladino overlords. The child reads it furtively. When her mother discovers her, she admonishes her for playing with things that are part of her brother's inheritance. In other words, the knowledge of the world around her, as represented by the text, is denied to her. It can only be filtered to her through her male counterpart.

In yet another revealing incident in *Balún-Canán,* a ladino visits his family ranch at Chactajal. The owner of the ranch has "inherited" his Indian laborers as well as his property. He boasts to his visitor of the Indian women at his disposal, the number of children he has had with them and the advantages this entails, since the children stay close to the big house and serve with loyalty. Thus, the Indian woman—akin to La Malinche—becomes a mechanism for perpetuating the servitude of her people and the structures of colonialism. Hers is a double submission—as Indian and as woman.

Castellanos signals the fusion of the Indian and the woman's theme in other ways as well, such as in the selection of quotes from Indian texts to serve as epigraphs to her stories. In *Balún-Canán,* she chooses the following lines from a Mayan text:

> We are only returning. We have fulfilled our task. Our days are finished. Think of us. Do not erase us from memory. Do not forget us.

The Indian vision of life is as part of a continuity of the past in the present; one's life is part of an inherited, collective experience. For non-Indians, life is unique and individual, ending in nothingness, thus heightening the panic felt by the lonely spinster. The Indian woman, on the other hand, is transformed by the consciousness of being part of a process that has preceded her and will survive her. By deriving strength from her ancestors as well as from contemporaries, she is better able to confront her *situación límite.*

Rosario Castellanos' awareness of herself as an articulator of the dilemmas of Mexican culture, as a responsible and committed writer, is summed up by some comments she made about the profession of writing and the nature of language in a collection of articles entitled *El uso de la palabra* (*The Use of Words*). Language, for Castellanos, is an instrument of command over one's self and one's reality. She interprets the literary vocation as being rooted in profound levels of human experience. By virtue of having written the words, tensions are released and a sense of liberation achieved.

Language is also a structure of power. When one of her Indian characters speaks in Spanish to the ticket-taker at the ferris wheel, the ladino comments mockingly: "Just listen to him, this Indian who thinks he's equal. He's speaking Spanish! Who ever gave him the right?" Spanish, says the narrator, is a privilege that belongs to us (the ladinos), and we use it by addressing our superiors as *usted,* our equals as *tú,* and Indians as *vos.* One of Castellanos' Indian characters, as he is learning to read and write, thinks "What a feeling, to discover the names of things, to pronounce them, to write them, and to take possession of the world!"

It is this consciousness of the significance of language as a key to taking possession of the world that in-fuses all of Rosario Castellanos' work. It is through her language as an author that Mexican women and Mexican Indians finally break the invisible space to which they have been confined and, by clamoring to be heard, claim their portion of the world. (pp. 22–31)

Helene M. Anderson, "Rosario Castellanos and the Structures of Power," in *Contemporary Women Authors of Latin America: Introductory Essays,* edited by Doris Meyer and Margarite Fernández Olmos, Brooklyn College Press, 1983, pp. 22–32.

MARTHA LAFOLLETTE MILLER

(essay date 1985)

[In the essay below, Miller examines the role of humor in Castellanos's poetry, arguing that it is used as a feminist weapon against male-dominated Mexican society.]

José Emilio Pacheco, in a prologue to a collection of newspaper columns by Rosario Castellanos published shortly after her death, remembers her as *"dos personas distintas"*: on the one hand, as a charming, ever-smiling friend, and on the other, as the author of "los poemas más trágicos y dolorosos de la literatura mexicana." Although Pacheco does not stand alone in describing her work as tragic, her poetry is more appropriately characterized, like her personality, as double-sided; her poems, though unremittingly serious, are often more apt to cause us to laugh or smile than to cry. Critics have sometimes downplayed Castellanos' humor (Beth Miller [in "The Poetry of Rosario Castellanos: Tone and Tenor," *Homenaje a Rosario Castellanos,* 1980] terming it only *"occasional,"* stresses the author's *"essential seriousness"*); nevertheless it lies at the heart of the reaction as a woman to an uncomfortable existence in a male-dominated society and of her skepticism regarding human institutions. Castellanos herself considered humor (along with "la meditación grave" and "el contacto con la raíz carnal e histórica") to be one of her poetry's main threads, and as some of her essays indicate, she saw it as a tool that could serve in conveying some of her deeply held values and in subverting societal norms with which she disagreed. As I hope to show in analyzing her poetry, it was her acute sensitivity to language and to other forms of societal discourse that allowed her to create the humor that she judiciously but effectively uses.

The complexity of humor in general has spawned a myriad of competing theories regarding its functions and uses, and some of these are relevant to the attempt to discover the mechanisms of the comical in Castellanos' poetry. Though the idea that humor helps to maintain social structures and is thus a conservative force has sometimes been advanced, other theories lend support to Castellanos' vision of laughter as a force for changes in the power structures of society. Freud's classic psychological study of jokes, with its claim that humor both saves psychic energy by short-circuiting pity and anger and discharges aggressive and sexual impulses in a safe way might be said to support the notion of humor as a stabilizing force. Yet in recognizing the importance of the identity of the listener in humorous interactions, Freud confirms the significance and dynamism in humor production of the relationship between joker and audience. Other theorists have recognized humor's value in creating bonds between group members, in softening messages, and in cajoling interlocutors. These ideas, in implying that the social roles, power, and status of those creating and responding to humor are important components of the joking process, suggest humor's significance for the understanding of political relationships, including those between males and females in society. Because questions of gender differences in writing obey political imperatives, humor is highly relevant to the study of the feminist perspective of Castellanos and other women writers. As Regina Harrison MacDonald [in "Rosario Castellanos on Language", 1980] and Sandra Messinger Cypess [in "*Balún Canán*: A Model Demonstration of Discourse as Power," *Revista de Estudios Hispanicos*, 1985] have shown, Castellanos in fact understands the power of language and the political structures embedded in its forms. Her humor, in calling attention to the structures of language, inevitably has a critical function that relates to societal structures themselves. As my analysis of specific texts will show, furthermore, her work frequently exhibits a feature typical of comedy by women as well as of many types of political writing-liminality, a state of existing outside the ordinary categories of society.

In the essay **"La participación de la mujer mexicana en la educación formal,"** Castellanos herself characterized humor as a liberating tool in the struggle for equality and freedom. Advocating humor as the best means of combatting outmoded notions of male and female roles, she suggests:

> una campaña: no arremeter contra las costumbres con la espada flamígera de la indignación ni con el trémolo lamentable del llanto sino poner en evidencia lo que tienen de ridículas, de obsoletas, de cursis y de imbéciles. Les aseguro que tenemos un material inagotable para la risa. ¡Y necesitamos tanto reir porque la risa es la forma más immediata de la liberación de lo que nos oprime, del distanciamiento de lo que nos aspirsiona!

Laughter, Castellanos' works indicate, can subvert both rigid, clichéd forms of language and rigid, clichéd social structures.

Humor in Castellanos' poetry, though ranging in form from almost gratuitous punning to the parodic monologue exemplified by such poems as **"Kinsey Report"** and **"Economía doméstica,"** is often based on ruptured expectations and on the incongruity that many long-standing theories describe as the cornerstone of jokes in general. At times Castellanos startles her readers by violating, on some level, the linguistic or cultural norms and formulas that they have previously assimilated and armed with which they approach her works. Her mastery over the rhetoric of her language and her culture is in fact precisely what allows her to create humorous surprises through the effective misuse of such rhetoric.

A close look at several of Castellanos' poems shows both linguistically and socially subversive uses of humor, revealing as well her evolution from word play on the sentence level to social parody achieved through speaker point of view. **"Apuntes para una declaración de fe"** (1948), one of her first published poems and one she later uses to open her collection *Poesía no eres tú*, represents an early stage in her use of humor. This long poem is full of grammatically or culturally inappropriate combinations, that whether they merely border on humor or qualify as full-fledged jokes, attest both to Castellanos' acute sense of the absurd and to her desire to demythify. In the following passage, she refers to Eve's serpent:

> Tal vez no debería yo hablar de la serpiente
> pero desde esa vez es un escalofrío
> en la columna vertebral del universo.
> Tal vez yo no debiera descubrirlo
> pero fue el primer círculo vicioso
> mordiéndose la cola.
> Porque esto, en realidad, sólo tendría importancia
> si ella lo supera.
> Pero lo ignora todo reptando por el suelo.
> dormitando en la siesta.

Here the description of the serpent as a chill down the spine of the universe could almost be taken seriously, despite the grotesquely disproportionate nature of the terms of the comparison, but in the image that follows, of the snake as "el primer círculo vicioso mordiéndose la cola," humor at some level is inescapable. Both the absurd coincidence between a figurative phrase and its concrete incarnation and the fact that on both abstract and concrete planes the description is unmotivated by logic (Why, in the first place, should the serpent be termed a vicious circle? Why, furthermore, is it biting its tail except to form a circle and thus fit into the cliche?) preclude a totally serious reading of the passage. As often is the case in Castellanos' writing, here the humorous effect stems partly from the cumulative effect of several separate, drily understated bits of humor.

The poem contains various other snippets of humor. Describing humanity's banishment from Eden, Castellanos refers to a God with udders, certainly a portrayal that, in its implications of earthy, maternal nourishment violates the traditional Old Testament image of a severe male deity who tempts, tests, and punishes His creatures.

Later in the poem, in describing a Martian's weekend visit to Planet Earth at some time in the future, she ruptures reader expectations by juxtaposing the relative, arbitrary, and culturally defined concept of the weekend with the cosmic context of extraterrestrial beings:

> Puede ser que algún día
> invitemos a un habitante de Marte
> para un fin de semana en nuestra casa.

The Martian, equipped like any other tourist with photographic equipment, will, the poet declares, visit "lo típico" in Europe, but her list of the sights he will see does not fit our image of the usual fodder for tourists:

> alguna ruina humeante
> o algún pueblo afilando las garras y los dientes.
> Alguna catedral mal ventilada,
> invadida de moho y oro inútil
> y en el fondo un cartel: "Negocio en quiebra. . . "
>
> los vientres abultados de los niños enfermos,
> las mujeres violadas en la guerra,
> los viejos arrastrando en una carretilla
> un ropero sin lunas y una cuna maltrecha.

Castellanos caps this dreary litany with a phrase that though carrying out perfectly the touristic formula is grotesquely inappropriate to the sights she has just described: "Y luego le diríamos: / 'Esto es sólo la Europa de pandereta'." This misapplication of a cliche about flashy tourist attractions creates a bit of black humor, first through its unexpected incongruity and then through the resolution found in its implication that the evils enumerated are only the superficial ones.

Thus in **"Apuntes"** Castellanos exploits her awareness of cultural and linguistic formulas, skillfully manipulating them to create humor. Her intention, she claims, was to paint "un panorama negro del mundo contemporáneo" and to counterpose this black vision to a more promising future based in the New World.

Her humor in this poem succeeds in demythifying Western civilization by exposing its spiritual bankruptcy and the fallacy of its faith in progress and technology; but Castellanos nevertheless repudiated the work in her essays, naming among its defects its "vocabulario abstracto" (**"Si poesía no eres tú, entonces ¿qué?"**), her tendency to lose her train of thought in the abundant imagery, and, most importantly, her misplaced confidence, which she terms "absolutamente gratuita," in the New World ("Una tentativa de autocrítica"). In this early work, Castellanos' jokes and puns, though clever, are not as well integrated into the poem as is her humor in later works, and thus they contribute to the work's disjointedness. And though they serve the cause of her desire to demythify, their effect is at odds with her advocacy of a new myth at the end of the poem. In later poems she overcomes such problems, integrating her humor more fully into each poetic unit, and refusing to allow new myths, formulas, or conventions to replace those that she has destroyed, through ridicule, in the name of liberation.

If in **"Apuntes"** Castellanos twists clichés and presuppositions, in other poems her mixture of the lofty with the lowly creates a demythifying sense of disproportion. In **"Mala fe,"** representative of a later stage in the author's poetic development, a speaker struggles with metaphysical questions, dignifying her musings from the outset by comparing herself to Kant. As she sketches her view of humankind's place in the vast scheme of the universe, absurd juxtapositions undermine the validity of her inquiry and reveal the anthropocentric arrogance underlying much of Western thought. She exults over

> . . . Orugas, tempestades,
> hiedras alrededor de una columna
> a medio derruir,
> casitas suburbanas, tractores, incunables,
> abrelatas, tratados de paz, mesas de bridge,
> piedras semipreciosas, recetas de cocina
> y más y más y más.

The humor thus created colors her subsequent references, to humankind's supreme importance in the universe and to herself as the apex of creation:

> Y yo erigiéndome
> en el centro del mundo
> y sintiéndome el foco de la atención de todo
> lo que existe o de aquel que lo creó
> si es que lo que existe ha sido creado.
> Y yo, coronación de siglos. . .

This grand vision collapses with the metaphor she employs to describe the evolutionary process:

> Se llama evolución. Y yo soy la cereza
> puesta sobre la punta del helado.

Castellanos' juxtaposition of the large and the small, the trivial and the transcendent, the timeless and the fleetingly faddish and contemporary create, in sum, the humorous vision that undermines the metaphysical hierarchies created by male-dominated Western civilization, suggesting that our search for ultimate meaning is perhaps a misguided one.

In **"Mala fe"**, then, Castellanos ridicules human philosophical pretensions through combinations that according to norms of discourse are inappropriate to the elevated level of her discussion. In other poems she uses humor both as a means of dealing with painful personal reality (exemplifying the Freudian principle of the short-circuiting, or "conservation", of pity, mentioned earlier) and as a weapon against social structures she views as undesirable. As the poems **"Autorretrato"** and **"Kinsey Report"** demonstrate, Castellanos is keenly aware of societal value systems and the power they exercise over individuals, whose view of the world is often nothing more than a set of clichés, clichés that her humor frequently exposes. As she states in an essay, her poetry consists of "algunos atisbos de la estructura del mundo, el señalamiento de algunas coordenadas para situarme en él, la mecánica de mis relaciones con los otros seres. Lo que no es ni sublime ni trágico. Si acaso, un poco ridículo" ("**Si poesía no eres tú, entonces ¿qué?**").

Thus Castellanos uses humor both to expose and to cope with harsh realities. In many cases she places this double edged sword in the hands of a female speaker whom she herself resembles. In "**Monólogo de la extranjera**", from the collection *Al pie de la letra* (1959), Castellanos combines black humor of the type seen in her poetry since the early "**Apuntes**" with an awareness of the relationship of language to societal structure and a skillful manipulation of linguistic formulas. In this poem, fundamentally a very serious one (and reputedly Castellanos' favorite from the collection as well), a woman reviews her development from a sensitive child into a misfit adult. Language is present in the poem as a *"moneda"* and a *"herramienta"*, i.e., as an instrument of both economic exchange and political hierarchies. The speaker, whose status outside the discourse of society is underlined by her characterization as a monologuist, as mute, and as an instrusive and transgressive animal that scandalizes crowds at social rites and ceremonies ("perro / que ofende con su sarna y su fornicación / y su ladrido inoportuno, en medio / del rito y la importante ceremonia"), at one point intentionally misuses words to create a wry joke that displaces her anguish: "La juventud, / aunque grave, no fue mortal del todo." In this phrase, she evokes at once two grammatically possible but incompatible utterances: one that might take the form "La juventud, aunque triste, no fue mala del todo," and the other, "La enfermedad, aunque grave, no fue mortal". Her juxtaposition produces the ungrammatical locution "no mortal del todo", ungrammatical in its implication that an illness can be partly mortal or that one can be partially dead. This attribution of degrees to an adjective that, like *"perfect"* or *"pregnant"*, does not logically admit them, functions as a grim joke, following the typical joke pattern of incongruity followed by a resolution (when we realize that the poem depicts the speaker's life as a kind of death) that theorists assign to jokes in general. Castellanos' bending of logical discourse reinforces the poem's central metaphor of death in life by transforming the speaker from an outsider whose incompatibility with societal norms creates a scandal into a spiritually dead participant in society's structures.

Castellanos' speaker in this poem, by appearing in the window of her house as a challenge to community norms ("para que. . . interroguen lo oscuro en mi persona"), exhibits a quality that critic Judy Little has described as characteristic of women's cosmic writing-liminality. Little [in her *Comedy and the Woman Writer: Woolf, Spark, and Feminism*, 1983] describes liminality as "a threshold (limen), a transition, a borderline area or condition" that often involves inverting hierarchies. She cites Virginia Woolf for having recognized one aspect of liminality characteristic of women writers—the taking seriously of what men consider insignificant, and the treating as trivial of what they think important. This type of liminality, as well as another example of black humor as a defense against anguish, can be seen in Castellanos' poem "**Autorretrato**". Here Castellanos' speaker engages in self-parody, describing herself in terms that reveal her awareness of the role society plays in shaping our responses. At the beginning of the poem she ridicules the social pressures that lead women to overvalue marriage and society to judge a woman more according to her marital status than for her accomplishments:

> Yo soy una señora: tratamiento
> arduo de conseguir, en mi caso, y más útil
> para alternar con los demás que un título
> extendido a mi nombre en cualquier academia.
>
> Asi, pues, luzco mi trofeo y repito:
> Yo soy una señora. . .

As she continues her self-portrait, she counterposes her societal persona to what lies beneath it. Like an actress she assumes an appearance that belies her personal reality and changes with her make-up:

> Rubia, si elijo una peluca rubia.
> O morena, según la alternativa.
> (En realidad, mi pelo encanece, encanece).
> Soy más o menos fea. Eso depende mucho
> de la mano que aplica el maquillaje.

Her role in life has certain rules, and she defines herself in relation to them. At times she breaks them:

> Sé que es obligatorio escuchar música
> pero la eludo con frecuencia, Sé
> que es bueno ver pintura
> pero no voy jamás a las exposiciones
> ni al estreno teatral ni al cine-club.

But at other moments, she is compelled to follow her script, which, as it happens, is an unhappy one:

> Sería feliz si yo supiera cómo.
> Es decir, si me hubieran enseñado los gestos,
> los parlamentos, las decoraciones.
>
> En cambio me enseñaron a llorar. . .

She is a mechanized puppet, but one who does not always respond as society demands because, as she explains it, she is out of order, a misfit, or in Little's terminology a liminal creature:

> . . . el llanto
> es en mí un mecanismo descompuesto
> y no lloro en la cámara mortuoria
> ni en la ocasión sublime ni frente a la catástrofe.
>
> Lloro cuando se quema el arroz o cuando pierdo
> el último racibo del impuesto predial.

In this poem, as in "**Apuntes**" and "**Mala fe**", humor lies in the rupture of reader expectations. Here, however, this rupture has to do more with the poetic form Castellanos chooses than with verbal or conceptual play. In consistently portraying her speaker as mechanized, she subverts the principle of individuality that underlies the autobiographical form she chooses. She demonstrates the power of social forms, which themselves might be considered a sort of language, in determining what we do and say. The poem is one more example of her recognition of the power of social structure, which, rather than our own individuality, shapes our interpersonal relationships and our world view to the point that our actions might be described as mechanical.

The liminal motifs and the attacks on Western culture's myths and social institutions are not found only in Castellanos' poetry but are evident in her other writings as well. In the *corrido* with which Castellanos closes her play *El eterno femenino,* she creates a classically *"liminal"* text that overturns a cultural myth. Here she addresses the notion of male supremacy by ridiculing one of Western society's cherished traditions—that of the creation of Eve from Adam's rib. As a response to the conventional view that Eve, created as an afterthought, was a secondary and inferior creature, she offers the following reinterpretation of the Bible, based on a different logic:

La Biblia dice que Dios
cometió un gran desatino
cuando al hombre lo formó
con lodo medio podrido
y sin ninguna experiencia
le salió como ha salido.

Un día que estaba durmiendo
en los prados de Edén,
Dios le quitó una costilla
para hacer a la mujer;
como ya le sabía el modo
resultó a todo meter.

This poem depends for its energy on making males, in their presence, the butt of a joke. The poem may or may not be funny to men, but women laugh with Castellanos in part because men form part of her audience.

Liminality is fundamental to Castellanos' novels as well. As Sandra Cypess has shown, Castellanos structures *Balún-Canán* precisely on a reversal of patriarchal values, endowing a young girl (whose status as such would normally exclude her from what Michael Foucault has termed the "fellowship of discourse") with narrative power. Similar targets and techniques may be found in her essays, in which, as in the *corrido,* she often uses masterful humor to soften her darts. In **"La participación de la mujer mexicana en la educación formal"**, she employs a descending incongruity to ridicule the idea that the unmarried woman is one whom "ningún hombre consideró. . . digno de llevar su nombre ni de remendar sus calcetines". In **"La liberación de la mujer, aquí"**, humor disguises her anger at women's marginalization in a male-dominated world; she describes masculine attitudes towards women's liberation as ranging from "el repudio irracional hasta esa condescendiente benevolencia con que se observan los vanos esfuerzos que hacen los cuadrúpedos para mantenerse el

mayor tiempo posible en sólo dos pies" [in *El uso de la palabra: Una mirada a la realidad*]. Liminality plays an important role in the essay **"A pesar de proponérselo"**, where she uses an ungrammaticality similar to that seen in "Monólogo de la extranjera" to establish herself as an outsider. Here, as in her novel, she takes the risk of breaking patriarchal rules:

En Israel nadie (aparte de mí, hace tres años y pico) habla un solo idioma. Todos hablan de tres para arriba. . . todo el mundo es de lo más poligloto. (¡Zas! ¿Qué es ese ruido? Es el portazo que, una vez más, me da en las narices la Academia Mexicana de la Lengua por el no sé si impropio, pero sí inseguro uso de un vocablo. No importa. Al cabo ya me acostumbré a "permanecer en los umbrales"). (*El uso de la palabra*)

In this article, written from her ambassadorial post in Tel Aviv for publication in the Mexican newspaper *Excelsior,* Castellanos demonstrates the same creativity and sensitivity to grammatical categories that she shows in her poetry; her use of the word "*poligloto*" in this case is as ungrammatical as that of "*mortal*" in **"Monólogo de la extranjera"**. Here, however, unlike in that work, she comments explicitly upon her violations of linguistic conventions and on their political significance. Through her reference to the Academy of the Language, as in a sense in the poem above, she brings the issue of grammar into a wider arena than that of simple word usage. Her vision of herself as an outsider reveals a notion of the poet as one who operates from without societal institutions, performing a critique of these institutions that is not always welcome.

Castellanos' use of the term "umbrales" here underlines her liminality, etymologically a threshold status. It also describes particularly aptly her peculiar position in Mexican society, as an ambassador and, simultaneously, a woman. Unlike the typical male writer, who as Simone de Beauvoir points out [in her *The Second Sex*] can take his gender for granted, she speaks from her femaleness, as the fact that so much of her humor involves gender-based social roles would indicate. At the same time, however, though she claims to be an outsider, she enjoys a status within the Mexican cultural establishment that allows her to speak in man's world, to send messages to males from a position of equality, and thus actually to discharge her anger on behalf of women rather than simply to voice her complaints to an audience made up solely of other outsiders—her fellow females. She herself recognized both the hierarchies of exclusion that she was up against and her own ability to overcome those hierarchies, as she shows in the comments she makes to explain the familiar tone with which she addresses consecrated male writers: "Hay que reír, pues. Y la risa, ya lo sabemos, es el primer testimonio de la libertad. Y me siento tan libre que inicio un 'Diálogo con los hombres más honrados' es decir, con los otros escritores. Al tú por tú. ¿Falta de respeto? ¿Carencia de cultura si cultura es lo que definió

Ortega como sentido de las jerarquías? Puede ser. . . " ("**Si 'poesía no eres tú, entonces ¿ qué?**"). Because in part she operates within the power structures of society, Castellanos is not just willing but is also able to put humor at the service of liberation from the injustices of those very structures.

Nevertheless, the celebration of Castellanos' liberation through humor needs to be qualified. If she sometimes uses humor as a subversive weapon and at others as a defense against her own feelings, she also employs jokes at times to soften the criticism she aims at male domination. In such texts as the *corrido* examined above she uses humor to makes less strident her anger at the relegation of women to a position of inferiority. Like liminality, this use of humor is typical of women, in whom the scathing irony often used by male writers might be deemed unbecoming

in a woman or even unacceptable. Just as Castellanos appeared "ever-smiling" to her friends, it might be said that as a writer she sometimes channeled her despair and anger into humor in the same way that her speaker in "**Autorretrato**" has to hide her aging behind make-up and wigs. Thus the liberation that Castellanos finds in humor is no doubt an ambiguous and relative one. Nevertheless, because of her achievements and her stature, and her ability to reach a large audience, she clearly succeeded in using humor to break new ground in male-female relationships and to pave the way to a more liberated future. (pp. 61–72)

Martha Lafollette Miller, "Humor, Power and in Female Condition in the Poetry of Rosario Castellanos," in *Revista/Review Interamericana*, Vol. XV, Nos. 1–4, 1985, pp. 61–72.

SOURCES FOR FURTHER STUDY

Lindstrom, Naomi. "Women's Expression and Narrative Technique in Rosario Castellanos's *In Darkness*." *Modern Language Studies* XIII, No. 3 (Summer 1983): 71–80.

Examines the novel *Dark Service,* focusing on Castellanos's use of narration, interior monologues, and commentary in her exploration of the status of women and Indians in Mexican society.

Macdonald, Regina Harrison. "Rosario Castellanos: On Language." *Homenaje a Rosario Castellanos,* edited by Maureen Ahern and Mary Seale Vásquez, pp. 41–64. Spain: Hispanofila, 1980.

Focuses on Castellanos's assertion that the power of language fosters gender, racial, and cultural prejudices in Mexican society.

Miller, Beth. "The Poetry of Rosario Castellanos: Tone and Tenor." *Homenaje a Rosario Castellanos,* edited by Maureen Ahern and Mary Seale Vásquez, pp. 73–83. Spain: Hispanofila, 1980.

Assesses the tone (attitude) and tenor (use of metaphor) in Castellanos's poetry, centering on their ability to convey social and ethical ideas.

Miller, Martha Lafollette. "A Semiotic Analysis of Three Poems by Rosario Castellanos." *Revista/Review Interamericana* XII, No. 1 (Spring 1982): 77–86.

Examines Castellanos's poems "Economia doméstica," "Tan-tan, ¿Quien es?," and "Telenovela," assessing the ungrammatical structures used to emphasize her social and political themes.

Nigro, Kirsten F. "Rosario Castellanos' Debunking of the *Eternal Feminine*." *Journal of Spanish Studies: Twentieth Century* 8, No. 1–2 (Spring/Fall 1980): 89–102.

Analyzes Castellanos's drama, *Eternal Feminine,* with particular emphasis on the use of comic situations and visual effects to present the problems of women in a male-oriented society.

Rodriguez-Peralta, Phyllis. "Images of Women in Rosario Castellanos' Prose." *Latin American Literary Review* VI, No. 6, (Fall/Winter 1977): 68–80.

Investigates Castellanos's demythologizing of the role of the Mexican woman and her creation of a new feminist image.

Schlau, Stacey. "Conformity and Resistance to Enclosure: Female Voices in Rosario Castellanos' *Oficio de Tinieblas [The Dark Service]*." *Latin American Literary Review* XII, No. 24 Spring/Summer 1984): 45–57.

Discusses Castellanos's picture of the controlling power of language in *Dark Service.*

Scott, Nina M. "Rosario Castellanos: Demythification through Laughter." *Humor* 2, No. 1 (1989): 19–30.

Examines the way in which Castellanos used the technique of humor to teach women the importance of the power of language and through which "she probed, questioned, and exposed to view the absurd myths and social inequalities endemic to women's roles in Mexico."

Sommers, Joseph. "Changing View of the Indian in Mexican Literature." *Hispania* XLVII, No. 1 (March 1964): 47–55.

Compares *Dark Service* with Bruno Traven's *La rebelión de los calgados,* contending that Castellanos adeptly blends style and themes, while Traven allows his similar social themes to dominate the literary style of his novel.

Additional coverage of Castellanos' life and career is contained in the following sources published by Gale Research: *Contemporary Authors*, Vol. 131; *Contemporary Literary Criticism*, Vol. 66; *Dictionary of Literary Biography*, Vol. 113; and *Hispanic Writers*.

Fidel Castro

1927–

(Born Fidel Castro Ruz) Cuban politician.

INTRODUCTION

A master of the spoken word, Castro has written relatively little in the course of his long political career. However, the controversial Communist leader has engendered a vast literature about himself and his regime, and many collections of his speeches and interviews have been published. Probably no other living political figure has been so thoroughly documented, analyzed, praised, and vilified in print as Castro —a testimony to the Cuban leader's forceful political personality and the intense passions he arouses in having been the first to introduce Communism to the Americas.

Born the illegitimate son of a poor Spanish immigrant who became a wealthy sugarcane planter, Castro received an upper-class education, distinguishing himself even in his early years as a charismatic and powerful orator. He began his political career when he entered the University of Havana to study law in 1945, a tumultuous period of Cuban democracy which saw the formation of violent political action groups that sought control of the country's civil institutions. Determined to become a student leader, Castro found himself obliged to join one of these associations, the left-populist Union Insurrectional Revolucionaria. Packing a pistol and eluding several assassination attempts, Castro won the leadership of the law students' federation. His magnetic personality and effective oratory helped launch him into national politics as a founding member of Eduardo Chibas's liberal reformist Partido del Pueblo Cuban in 1947. Several of Castro's speeches and manifestos from his university days are collected in *Revolutionary Struggle, 1947–1958* (1972), which also includes a detailed introduction to the complex Cuban politics of the 1940s. After earning his law degree in 1950, Castro set up a private practice in Havana, where he often represented workers and the poor for no fee. He ran for

Congress two years later, but found his political ambitions frustrated when Fulgencio Batista assumed power in a military coup that year and canceled the elections. After several unsuccessful attempts to have Batista removed through constitutional means, Castro organized an armed force of rebels and launched a night attack on the Moncada military barracks in Santiago de Cuba on 26 July 1953. The assault was quickly repulsed and failed to spark the anticipated civil insurrection, but Castro's extraordinary daring made him famous throughout Cuba. He conducted his own defense at a secret trial and delivered an impassioned speech on the right of the people to revolt against tyranny that was later circulated clandestinely as a pamphlet under the title *La historia me absolverá* (1954; *History Will Absolve Me*), which helped build support for the revolutionary movement. After serving two years of his fifteen-year sentence, Castro was released from prison under a general political amnesty in May, 1955. Finding Batista still intent on keeping power, Castro, with his brother Raúl and other supporters, fled to Mexico to organize a new revolutionary armed force. Taking the name "26th of July Movement" to commemorate the Moncada assault, the insurrectionists—including Argentine doctor Ernesto "Che" Guevara—launched a guerrilla attack against the Cuban army in December, 1956, from the north coast of the Oriente province, a region which has a long tradition of peasant rebellion. Demoralizing Batista's ill-trained conscript army by their bold military tactics, Castro's eight hundred insurgents mounted a multi-front offensive in mid-1958 that defeated Batista's thirty-thousand-strong army, driving the dictator into exile on 1 January 1959. Castro's record as a guerrilla leader may be studied in *Revolutionary Struggle, 1947–1958,* which contains some of the rebel commander's most important field orders, letters, proclamations, and decrees.

After the revolutionary victory, Castro briefly cooperated with moderate liberals in a provisional government and was named prime minister of Cuba. His popularity and control of the armed forces gave him almost total power, however, and he swiftly steered the Cuban Revolution sharply to the left. Historians have long debated whether Castro was a secret Marxist before the revolution or whether he was radicalized by a series of confrontations with the United States in the early 1960s. The United States had treated Cuba as a virtual colony for most of the century and reacted to Castro's early reforms—including an extensive agrarian redistribution plan and the nationalization of some foreign-owned industries—as a threat to American political and economic interests. Castro's refusal to hold early elections and his cultivation of relations with the former Soviet Union also upset the Americans, who broke diplomatic ties with Cuba in January, 1961. The United States-sponsored Bay of Pigs invasion—in which fifteen hundred CIA-trained Cuban exiles attempted un-

successfully to overthrow Castro's government—and Castro's declaration of the "Marxist-Leninist" character of the revolution later that year sealed American enmity. Historical evidence has suggested that the aggressive stance of the United States probably hastened the consolidation of the leftist regime in Cuba, but that socialism had long been Castro's ultimate political objective. The Cuban leader later told interviewer Frei Betto that he had a Marxist-Leninist concept of political struggle several years before 1951, but adopted a nationalist and populist program to ensure the broadest popular support for the revolution. "I believe my contribution to the Cuban Revolution consists of having synthesized [Cuban independence leader José] Martí's ideas and those of Marxism-Leninism and having applied them consistently in our struggle," Castro observed in *Fidel and Religion: Castro Talks on Revolution and Religion with Frei Betto* (1987).

The political ferment and social experimentation of the Cuban Revolution's early years is well documented in *Fidel Castro Speaks* (1969), the first volume of speeches by the Cuban leader to be published in the United States. A voluble but seldom boring orator, Castro made important policy pronouncements and addressed concrete problems in public speeches often lasting four hours and longer. Cuban policy in the mid-1960s was characterized by a strong effort to develop revolutionary consciousness and cooperative social relations among the Cuban people and by material and political support for revolutionary movements abroad, particularly in Latin America. Influenced by Che Guevara, Castro stressed moral over material incentives in building Cuba's new socialist economy and criticized the Soviet Union for failing to aid third-world revolutionary movements. *Fidel Castro Speaks* includes the famous "Second Declaration of Havana" that Castro delivered after Cuba's expulsion from the Organization of American States in 1962, wherein the Cuban leader denounced United States imperialism in Latin America and defiantly pledged to assist leftist rebellions in the region. Castro's militant stance earned him great prestige with leftists all over the world but strained his relations with the Soviets, on whom he relied for vital economic and military support. Cuba's growing dependency coincided with severe economic problems and the collapse of the Latin American guerrilla movements after Che Guevara's death, prompting Castro to adopt a more cautionary stance in the 1970s. The first volume of *Fidel Castro Speeches: Cuba's Internationalist Foreign Policy, 1975–80* (1981–85) details this new foreign policy, which centered on military support to such established third-world leftist states as Ethiopia, Angola, and Nicaragua; extensive material aid programs that sent Cuban doctors, teachers, technicians, and construction workers to many corners of the globe; and leadership of the Non-Aligned Movement of nations.

A second volume of speeches, subtitled *Our Power Is That of the Working People* (1983), focuses on Cuban politics and government and attempts to meet criticism of Castro's regime as personalistic and authoritarian. Among other topics, the Cuban leader discusses the "People's Power" system of popular input in political and economic decision making. Castro also defends Cuba's form of government in *Fidel and Religion,* insisting that "our system is a thousand times more democratic than the capitalist, imperialist system of the developed capitalist countries" because it protects the interests of workers and fosters active participation in local government. While acknowledging that he enjoys great personal authority and influence as the leader of the Cuban Revolution, Castro has maintained that a broader collectivity actually decides government and Communist party policy in Cuba. Observers of Cuban politics have affirmed that the system permits some genuine—if limited—grassroots initiative and criticism of the leadership within the parameters of Castro's Marxist-Leninist doctrines. However, the unrelenting hostility of the United States has contributed to a permanent siege mentality among Cuba's leaders that tends to identify the regime with revolution and refuses to countenance any organized political opposition, even one committed to socialism. The Cuban Communist party, led by Castro since 1965, remains the country's sole political party and the Cuban press is among the most tightly controlled of any socialist state.

Castro's speeches amply document the Cuban Revolution's social restructuring and economic reforms: since 1959 Cuba has raised educational and health standards to levels that rival and often exceed those prevalent in developed countries. Some critics have argued, however, that in light of the loss of civil freedoms and the routine rationing of basic necessities, the average citizen has benefited minimally from Castro's policies. In addition, Castro has made little advance in diversifying the Cuban economy from dependence on sugar exports, most of which were once purchased by the former Soviet Union at prices well above the world market rate. Deprived of access to the American market by a longstanding embargo and abandoned by his Soviet-bloc patrons, Castro has shown no interest in decentralizing the Cuban economy and promoting the domestic market mechanism. Despite Cuba's deepening economic crisis, Castro still remains a popular figure for many Cubans who appreciate the revolution's social welfare measures and Castro's defiance of the United States. His moderating of foreign policy and curtailment of direct support to insurgent movements have also earned him increased respect among mainstream statesmen in Latin America and elsewhere, although the United States continues to view him with suspicion. Nonetheless, historians and biographers have found Castro an intriguing and charismatic subject, acknowledging him as one of the most influential and important political figures of the twentieth century.

CRITICAL COMMENTARY

FIDEL CASTRO

(speech date 1953)

[The excerpt below is from Castro's *History Will Absolve Me* oration, which was delivered in 1953 and published as a pamphlet under that title the following year. Here, he outlines the objectives of the Moncada assault, insisting on the people's right to revolt against tyranny.]

In the summary of the proceedings there must be the five revolutionary laws that were to have been proclaimed and broadcast by radio to the nation immediately after the

fall of the Moncada Barracks. It is possible that Colonel Chaviano deliberately destroyed those documents, if he has, it does not matter, I still remember them.

The first revolutionary law would return sovereignty to the people, proclaiming the Constitution of 1940 as a true supreme law of the state until such time as the people would decide to modify or change it. And in order to reestablish the Constitution, mete out exemplary punishment to all those who have betrayed it, there being no organization for holding elections to carry this out, the revolutionary movement, as the momentary incarnation of that sovereignty which is the only source of legitimate power, would assume all the faculties inherent

Principal Works

La historia me absolverá (speech) 1954
  [*History Will Absolve Me,* 1960]

Fidel Castro Speaks (speeches) 1969

Fidel in Chile: A Symbolic Meeting between Two Historical Processes (speeches) 1972

Revolutionary Struggle, 1947–1958 (speeches) 1972

*Fidel Castro Speeches. 3 vols. (speeches) 1981–85

Women and the Cuban Revolution: Speeches and Documents by Fidel Castro, Vilma Espin, and Others (speeches) 1981

Fidel Castro: Nothing Can Stop the Course of History (speeches) 1986

Fidel and Religion: Castro Talks on Revolution and Religion with Frei Betto (interview) 1987

† *To Speak the Truth: Why Washington's 'Cold War' against Cuba Doesn't End: Fidel Castro and Ernesto Che Guevara* (speeches) 1992

*These speeches have been published in three volumes: *Cuba's Internationalist Foreign Policy, 1975–80* (1981), *Our Power is that of the Working People* (1983), and *War and Crisis in the Americas, 1984–85* (1985).

†This work is a compilation of speeches given at the General Assembly of the United Nations (1960–1979) and the Geneva Development and Trade Conference (1964).

pensate landowners on the basis of the average income they would have received from said land over a ten-year period.

The third revolutionary law granted the workers and employees of all the large industrial, mercantile, or mining concerns, including sugar mills, the right to 30 percent of the profits. Companies classified as agricultural were excepted because they would come under other agrarian laws to be implemented.

The fourth revolutionary law would have granted all planters the right to share 55 percent of the sugar production and also allotted a minimum grinding quota of 900,000 pounds of cane to all small planters who had been growing sugar cane during the last three years or more.

The fifth revolutionary law ordered the confiscation of all the wealth of those who had misappropriated public funds in previous regimes, as well as those of their heirs and legatees. This law was to be enforced by a special court with full legal access to all sources susceptible to investigation, said court being endowed with the right to intervene for the above purposes in all corporations registered or operating in Cuba, wherein or under the cloak of which ill-gotten gains might be concealed, and to request from foreign governments the extradition of persons and the embargo of property. Half the value of property thus recovered was to go to the retirement fund of workers and the other half to hospitals, asylums, and orphanages.

We stated also that the Cuban foreign policy in America would be one of close solidarity with the democratic peoples of the continent and that those persecuted because of their political beliefs by the bloody tyrannies which oppress brother nations would find generous asylum and brotherly love and food in the country of Martí, in direct contrast to the persecution, hunger, and betrayal which is found here today.

These laws would have been proclaimed immediately and were to be followed, once the battle had ended and after a minute study of their contents and scope, by another series of laws and measures, all fundamental, such as the agrarian reform, the integral reform of the educational system, the nationalization of the electric trust and telephone trust, calling for the restitution to consumers of the illegal excess which these companies have been charging and for the payment to the Public Treasury of all monies which these companies have failed to pay.

All these and other laws would be inspired by the strictest fulfillment of two of the most essential articles of our constitution, the first of which directs that latifundia be proscribed, and to that end the law should define the maximum amount of land that any person or entity may own for each kind of undertaking, adopting the necessary measures to revert all lands to the Cubans. The other article categorically orders the state to employ all the means

in sovereignty (such as the powers to legislate, to enforce the laws, and to judge), except that of modifying the Constitution itself.

This measure and its purposes could not be more clearly stated or freer of sterile charlatanism. A government acclaimed by the mass of combatants would receive and be vested with the necessary power to proceed to establish effectively the will of the people and true justice. From that moment, the judicial power which since March 10 has placed itself against the Constitution and outside the Constitution would recess as such, and we would proceed to an immediate and total purification of it before it would again assume the faculties which the Supreme Law of the Republic concedes to it. For if we place the custody of the Constitution in the hands of those who dishonorably gave in without taking these prior measures, the return to legality would be a deceit, a hoax, and a new betrayal.

The second revolutionary law would have granted property, non-mortgageable and nontransferable, to all planters, tenant farmers, renters, sharecroppers, and squatters holding parcels of five *caballerías,* the state to com-

within its reach to provide work for all those who might need it, and to assure dignified living to every manual and intellectual worker.

Neither of the two laws, therefore, can be labeled unconstitutional. The first government to come out of the first free election held would have to abide by these laws, not only because it would have a moral obligation toward the nation, but also because when people achieve what they have eagerly sought through various generations there is no force in the world strong enough to take it away from them.

The problem of land, the problem of industrialization, the problem of housing, the problem of unemployment, the problem of education and the health of the people—there we have, concretely, the six points toward which, together with the return of public liberty and political democracy, we would have resolutely directed all our efforts. (pp. 184–87)

The future of the nation and the solution of its problems can no longer depend on the selfish interests of a dozen financiers, nor on the cold computation of profits by ten or twelve magnates in their air-conditioned offices. The country cannot continue on its knees, begging for a miracle from some golden calf like that of the Old Testament which the wrath of the prophet cast down. The golden calf cannot perform miracles of any kind. The problems of the Republic can be solved only if we devote ourselves to fighting for it with the same energy, honesty, and patriotism as did our liberators in creating the Republic. It is not with statesmen like [defeated 1944 presidential candidate] Carlos Saladrigas, whose statesmanship consists of leaving everything as it is, mouthing nonsense about the "absolute freedom of enterprise," "guarantees for the investment of capital," and "the law of supply and demand," that we are going to solve our problems. The bones of those who today demand urgent solutions will turn to dust while those ministers happily chat in some Fifth Avenue mansion in Havana. In the real world, no social problem is solved by spontaneous generation.

A revolutionary government with the support of the people and the respect of the nation, once it cleans out all venal and corrupt office-holders, would proceed immediately to industrialize the country, mobilizing all inactive capital (currently over 1,500 million dollars) through the National Bank and the Bank for Industrial and Agricultural Development, submitting that giant task to the study, organization, planning, and final realization by technicians and men of absolute capability, free from political meddling.

A revolutionary government, after making the 100,000 small farmers owners of the land for which they now pay rent, would proceed to end the land problem once and for all. This would be done first by establishing, as the Constituon orders, a limit to the amount of land a person may own for each type of agricultural undertaking,

acquiring any excess by expropriation; by recovering the lands usurped from the state; by improving swamplands; by setting aside zones for tree nurseries and reforestation. Second, it would be done by distributing the rest of the land available among rural families, preferably to those large in number; by promoting cooperatives of farmers for the common use of costly farm equipment, cold storage, and technical-professional guidance in the cultivation of crops and the breeding of livestock. Finally, it would be done by making available all resources, equipment, protection, and know-how to the farmers.

A revolutionary government would solve the problem of housing by lowering rent 50 percent, by giving tax exemption to houses inhabited by their owners; by tripling the taxes on houses built to rent; by substituting the ghastly one-room flats with modern multistory buildings; and by financing housing projects all over the island on a scale never before seen, which would be based on the criterion that if in the rural area the ideal is for each family to own its parcel of land, then in the city the ideal is for each family to own its house or apartment. There are enough bricks and more than enough manpower to build a decent house for each Cuban family. But if we continue waiting for the miracle of the golden calf, a thousand years will pass and the problem will still be the same. On the other hand, the possibility of extending electrical power to the farthest corner of the Republic is today better than ever before because today nuclear energy applied to that branch of industry, lowering production costs, is already a reality.

With these three initiatives and reforms, the problem of unemployment would disappear dramatically, and sanitation service and the struggle against disease and sickness would be a much easier task.

Finally, a revolutionary government would proceed to undertake the complete reform of the educational system, placing it at the same level as the foregoing projects, in order to prepare adequately the future generations who will live in a happier fatherland. Do not forget the words of the apostle Martí:

> A grave error is being committed in Latin America. In nations which live almost completely off the products of their land, the people are educated exclusively for urban life and are not prepared for life on a farm.
>
> The happiest people are those who educate their children in how to think for themselves and on how to guide their sentiments.
>
> An educated people will always be strong and free.

The soul of education is the teacher, and teachers are now poorly paid in Cuba. Yet there is no one more in love with his vocation than the Cuban teacher. Who of us did not learn his alphabet in a public school? It is high time to stop paying with alms those men and women to whom is entrusted the most sacred mission in the world today and tomorrow–the mission to teach. No elementary teacher should earn less than $200, and no secondary school teacher should receive less than $350 if we want them to devote themselves entirely to their high mission free of want and privation. Moreover, the teacher who works in the rural districts should be given free transportation, and every five years, at least, all teachers should be given a six-month leave with pay in order that they may attend special courses here or abroad to keep up to date on the latest pedagogical trends, thus improving constantly their programs and systems. Where can we get the necessary money? When there is an end to robbery, when there are no corrupt public officials who let themselves be bribed by big companies to the detriment of the public treasury; when the great resources of the nation are mobilized and the state ceases to buy tanks, bombers, and cannons to oppress the people in a country which has no frontiers; and when the state decides it wishes to educate instead of killing—then there will be money enough.

Cuba can support splendidly a population three times larger than it now has; there is no reason then for the misery among its inhabitants. The markets should be flooded with produce, pantries should be full, all hands should be industriously producing. All this is not inconceivable. It is inconceivable that there are men who go to bed hungry while there remains one inch of uncultivated land. It is inconceivable that there are children dying without medical assistance. It is inconceivable that 30 percent of our farmers do not know how to write their names, and that 99 percent of them do not even know Cuba's history. It is inconceivable that the majority of the families on our farms are living under worse conditions than the Indians Columbus found when he discovered the most beautiful land that human eyes have ever seen. For those who call me a dreamer because I say these things, I tell them as Martí did,

A real man does not look around to see on which side he can live better, but rather on which side duty lies. That man is the only practical one; his dream today will be law tomorrow, for he who has set his eyes on the universal and has seen peoples boil up inflamed and blood drenched from the cauldrons of centuries knows that the future, without exception, is on the side of duty. (pp. 189–92)

It looked as if the apostle Martí was going to die in the year of the centennial of his birth [1953]. It looked as if his memory would be extinguished forever, so great was the affront! But he lives. He has not died. His people are rebellious, his people are worthy, his people are faithful to his memory. Cubans have fallen defending his doctrines. Young men, in a magnificent gesture of reparation, have come to give their blood and to die at the side of his tomb so that he might continue to live in the hearts of his countrymen. Oh, Cuba, what would have become of you if you had let the memory of your apostle die!

I conclude my defense, but I shall not end it as all lawyers for the defense do, asking for acquittal of the defendant. I cannot ask for acquittal when my companions are already suffering in the ignominious prison on the Isle of Pines. Send me there that I may share their fate. It is conceivable that honest men should be dead or in prison when the president is a criminal and a thief!

To you, Your Honors, my sincere gratitude for having allowed me to express myself freely, without base coercion. I feel no rancor toward you. I recognize that in some aspects you have been humane and I know that the presiding judge of this court, the man of unimpeachable background that he is, cannot disguise his repugnance for the reigning state of things which forces him to dictate an unjust verdict.

There still remains for the court a graver problem to solve. I am referring to the seventy cases of murder which should be more aptly called the greatest massacre we have ever known. The guilty ones are still at large carrying their weapons, and that is a perennial threat to the lives of citizens. If the full weight of the law does not fall on them because of cowardice or because the court cannot do anything about it and as a consequence thereof all the judges do not resign to a man, I bemoan the honor of your names and I weep for the unprecedented stain that will besmirch judicial power.

As for me, I know that jail will be as hard as it has ever been for anyone, filled with threats, with vileness, and cowardly brutality but I do not fear this, as I do not fear the fury of the miserable tyrant who snuffed out the life of seventy brothers of mine.

Condemn me, it does not matter. *History will absolve me!* (pp. 220–21)

Fidel Castro, "History Will Absolve Me," in *Revolutionary Struggle, 1947-1958*, Vol. 1, edited by Rolando E. Bonachea and Nelson P. Valdés, The MIT Press, 1972, pp. 164–221.

FIDEL CASTRO WITH FREI BETTO
(interview date 1985)

[A Brazilian Roman Catholic priest and Castro admirer, Betto spent four years in prison in his native country for his political activism. In the following interview conducted in 1985, Castro defends Cuba's form of government, asserting that "our system is a thousand times more democratic than the capitalist, imperialist system of the developed capitalist countries."]

[Betto]: *Commander, the people in some Christian environments admire the Cuban Revolution's social and economic*

Castro speaks to the revolutionaries prior to attacking the Moncada Barracks on 26 July 1953:

In a few hours you will be victorious or defeated, but regardless of the outcome—listen well, *compañeros!*—regardless of the outcome, this movement will triumph. If you win tomorrow, the aspirations of Martí will be fulfilled sooner. If the contrary occurs, our action will set an example for the Cuban people, and from the people will arise young men willing to die for Cuba. They will pick up our banner and move forward. The people of Oriente Province will support us; the entire island will do so. Young men of the centennial [of Martí's birth], as in 1868 and 1895, here in Oriente we make our first cry of "Liberty or Death!"

You know already the objectives of our plan; it is a dangerous plan, and anyone who leaves with me tonight will have to do so willingly. There is still time to decide. Anyway, some of you will have to stay behind because we do not have enough weapons.

Those who are determined to go should move forward. The watchword is not to kill except as the last resort.

Fidel Castro, in his "This Movement Will Triumph," speech, in *Revolutionary Struggle, 1947–1958*, The MIT Press, 1972.

achievements, its achievements in education and health care, but say there's no democracy in Cuba—as there is in the United States and Western Europe, where people can vote in an election and change their government. What would you say to this? Is there or isn't there democracy in Cuba?

[Castro]: We could talk about this for a long time, and I think our interview is rather long already. I don't want to take too much of your time or try the patience of the people who will read this interview. I think that all that alleged democracy is nothing but a fraud, and I mean this literally.

I was asked that question not long ago.

By whom?

A fellow from the United States—rather, there were two interviewers, a congressman and a professor, who wanted to publish some articles and a book. He said that some people thought I was a cruel dictator. He said some other things too.

Just imagine! What could I say? I had to resort to logic. I analyzed what a dictator was. In the first place, I said, "It's somebody who makes one-man decisions, who governs by decree." And I said, "Then you could accuse [President Ronald] Reagan of being a dictator." With all due respect, I went on and said, "You could even accuse the pope of being a dictator, because the pope governs by decree; he makes decisions, concerning the appointment of ambassadors, cardinals and bishops; they're all the pope's unilateral decisions, and nobody has thought of saying that the pope's a dictator." I've heard critcism of the Church's inner system, its inner workings, but I've never heard anybody say the pope is a dictator.

I explained about Cuba, that I didn't appoint Ministers, ambassadors or anybody else—not even the least important employee in this country–didn't make unilateral, individualistic decisions; and didn't govern by decree. I explained that we had a collective leadership–I've spoken to you about this. We've always discussed all basic problems collectively, right from the beginning, ever since our Movement was founded. And I added, "What I do have is the right to speak and to present my arguments in the Central Committee, the Political Bureau, the Executive Committee of the Council of Ministers and National Assembly, and I really don't want any other rights." I didn't deny that I had authority and prestige, just as many other comrades have authority and prestige in the Party and among the people, and their views carry weight in our country. Other people listen to them, and I'm the first to do so. I like to listen to others and take their views into consideration.

After explaining all this, I said, "Well, then, and what is cruelty?" I told them that men who have devoted their lives to the struggle against injustice, crime, abuse, inequality, hunger and poverty and to the struggle to save the lives of children and the sick, to find jobs for all the workers and to provide food for every family—men who have devoted their lives to this couldn't be cruel. I asked, "What is it that's cruel? The capitalist system, that's responsible for so much poverty and calamity; capitalist selfishness; and capitalist exploitation."

Imperialism is cruel; it has caused the deaths of millions of people. How many were killed in World War I? Somebody said 14, 18 or 20 million. How many were killed in World War II? Over 50 million. And who promoted those deaths and those catastrophes? In addition to the dead, there are the maimed, the blinded, the crippled and countless other victims. How many were orphaned, how much property was destroyed and how much human labor was wiped off the face of the Earth? Who was to blame for that? The imperialist system, the capitalist system, and the struggle for markets and colonies in World Wars I and II. They were responsible for those tens of millions of deaths.

Who is cruel, then? Those who struggle for peace? Those who struggle to put an end to so much misery, so much poverty and so much exploitation? Those who struggle against the system? Or is it the system and those who support and uphold it? Who are the cruel ones? The U.S. troops killed millions of human beings in Vietnam and—as I said before—dropped more bombs on that small country, which was fighting for its independence, than were used in World War II. Isn't that cruel? Can that system be called democratic?

I also explained that Reagan won an election in which barely half of the U.S. population voted. He was elected by 30 percent of the voters in that alleged democracy. And Reagan has powers that not even the Roman emperors had, because a Roman emperor, a madman like Nero, could cause Rome to be set on fire—I don't know if Suetonius told the truth or not, if it's a historic fact or if it was a fable made up by a historian who said that Nero set Rome on fire and then played the lyre. It seems to be true that all of the emperors joined in those games at the circus, where—according to all the historians—they made gladiators kill each other or had Christians devoured by the lions. These modern emperors have more power than the earlier ones; Reagan could set off a nuclear conflagration that would be much worse than what may have happened in Rome under Nero.

A nuclear holocaust may incinerate Catholics, Buddhists, Muslims and Hindus; the followers of Confucius, Deng Xiaoping and Mao Zedong in China; Christians, Protestants and Catholics; the rich and the poor, multimillionaires and beggars; the young and the old, children and the elderly; men and women; farmers and landowners; workers and industrialists; businessmen and proletarians; and intellectuals and professionals. The whole world may disappear in a nuclear holocaust, though I don't believe that Reagan would have time to play the lyre while the world was going up in smoke, for scientists have already determined that all life would be wiped off the face of the Earth in a matter of minutes, hours, days or even months—with the possible sole exception of certain insects that can withstand nuclear radiation better. They say that cockroaches have great resistance. So, Reagan could turn this world into a world of cockroaches. He has a locked briefcase in which he keeps nuclear codes, and it's said that, if he issues a coded order, a nuclear war would start. So the emperors of our times have much more power than did the emperors of the past. And that's what they call a democracy, and it isn't considered cruel. All those countries that you've mentioned—England, West Germany, Italy, Spain and all the others—which praise democracy so highly are also members of NATO and share in that unbelievable notion. And they're called democracies. It's democracy characterized by unemployment: Spain has 3 million unemployed; France has 3 million; England, 3 million; and Germany, 2.5 million. There's unemployment in all those countries.

But I don't want to go into details. I admit that progress has been made and that Europe isn't the same now as it was during the Middle Ages—it's not the Europe of the Conquests, the Europe that burned religious dissenters alive; it's no longer the Europe of colonial times. It's the Europe of neocolonialism, of course; it's the Europe of the imperialist system. But I'm ready to admit there's been some progress. I don't know what they're so proud of, though; I don't know if they take pride in the progress that was made some years ago, when they emerged from fascism and the massacres that took place during the two World Wars they unleashed. What I still haven't seen is a clear, unambiguous admission and criticism of the long centuries of slavery, exploitation and atrocities they imposed on the world. I see that they're still subjecting the world to great exploitation, because, in the first place, their development was financed by the Third World. They financed everything with the gold they wrested from their old colonies, plus the sweat and blood of men, women and children that went into the establishment of capitalist society—which, as Marx said, came into the world dripping blood from every pore.

I don't see what they can feel so proud of or how they can possibly consider themselves more democratic than we, the former slaves, the formerly colonized, the formerly exploited; we, the survivors of the peoples they nearly exterminated; we who live in the lands that the big U.S. companies and those of other imperial powers had forcibly seized, just as they took away our countries' mines and other resources. Those who, like us in Cuba, have struggled hard against and freed ourselves from this situation; we who now own our wealth and the fruits of our labor; we who not only enjoy what we have but are willing to share it with other countries; we who are no longer the slaves or the colonized or the illiterate or the sick or the beggars of the past; we who, through a genuine social revolution, have united the people, all the people—workers, farmers, manual and intellectual workers, students, the old and the young, men and women—we have always had the resolute support and the confidence of the vast majority of our fellow citizens, because we have dedicated our lives to serving the people's interests.

It cannot be said of the so highly praised Western governments that they are generally backed by the majority of the people. At times, they have that majority for a few days after the election, but, for the most part, they win with a minority vote. Let's take Reagan, for example. In his first election, only about 50 percent of the voters cast their votes. There were three candidates, and with the votes of less than 30 percent of the total number of U.S. voters, Reagan won the election. Half the people didn't even vote. They don't believe in it. Half of the U.S. voters didn't vote. He may have gotten a few more votes, but when he won his second presidential election, Reagan wasn't supported by much more than 30 percent of the U.S. people with the right to vote.

Others get a majority of 50 percent plus one of the votes, which is far from being the total of the voting population, and, as a rule, that backing lasts for a few months, or maybe one or two years at the most. The people's support immediately starts to decline. It doesn't matter whether it's the Prime Minister of Great Britian, the President of France, the Prime Minister of Italy, the Chancellor of West Germany, the Prime Minister of Spain or the head of state of any other Western country—models that are referred to constantly—after a few months in office, they're backed by a minority of the people.

An election every four years! The people who elected Reagan four years ago had no other say in U.S. policy, simply because Reagan could draw up a military budget, concoct the Star Wars weapons program, produce any kind of missile or other weapon, make complications of all kinds, invade or intervene in the internal affairs of other countries and send Marines anywhere without having to consult anybody. He could cause a world war without consulting with the people who voted for him, just by making one-man decisions.

In this country, one-man decisions are never made on important basic issues. We have a collective leadership that analyzes and discusses all those things. More than 95 percent of the voters take part in our elections. The candidates who run for office at the grass-roots level, to be delegates of the voting districts (in which every 1,500 citizens in the case of the big cities—in some cases, 1,000 or fewer citizens—in rural areas or in special voting districts, depending on the territory—elect a delegate), are nominated by their neighbors. There are around 11,000 voting districts in the country, so there's a delegate for every 910 citizens. Those delegates aren't nominated by the Party; they are nominated directly in the neighborhood assemblies. Each voting district may have from two to eight candidates. If none of them receives at least half the votes plus one, then a runoff election is held between the two who got the most votes in the first round. Then, those delegates are the ones who elect those who exercise state power in Cuba; they elect the members of the municipal bodies of People's Power—who, in turn, elect the members of the provincial bodies of People's Power, who elect the members of the National Assembly. More than half the members of our country's National Assembly are delegates who were elected at the grass-roots level and nominated by the people. For example, I'm not a delegate at the grass-roots level. I'm a member of the National Assembly who was nominated and elected by the delegates of a municipality—Santiago de Cuba, where we began our revolutionary struggle.

The delegates who are elected at the grass-roots level are practically slaves of the people, because they have to work long, hard hours without receiving any pay except the wages they get from their regular jobs. Every six months, they have to report back to their voters on what they've done during that period. Any official in the country may be removed from office at any time by the people who elected him. All this implies having the backing of most of the people. If the Revolution didn't have the support of most of the people, revolutionary power couldn't endure.

Our entire electoral system presupposes the support of most of the people, and our revolutionary concepts are also based on the premise that those who struggle and

work for the people, those who carry out the work of the Revolution, will always have the support of the vast majority of the people, because, no matter what is said, nobody is more grateful than the people; nobody appreciates the efforts that are made better than the people. In many countries, people vote for a lot of individuals who don't deserve their votes, but, when there's a revolution that identifies itself with the people, a power that identifies itself with the people—a power that is their power—they always give it their wholehearted support. As I already explained, any Cuban citizen can truly say "I am the state," because he's the one in charge, he's the one with authority, he is the army, he is the one who has the weapons, who has the power. When you have this kind of a situation, it's impossible for a revolution not to have most of the people behind it, regardless of the mistakes the revolutionaries may make, as long as they correct them quickly and are honest men and women and as long as it's a real revolution.

That's why I say that everything that's being said is nothing but a big lie, because there can be no democracy and no liberty, without equality and fraternity. Everything else is fiction; everything else is metaphysical, as are many of the so-called democratic rights. For example, when you speak of freedom of the press, you're really talking about the freedom to own the mass media; a true dissenter from the system won't be allowed to write on the most renowned U.S. newspapers—*The Washington Post, The New York Times* or whatever. Look at the two parties that take turns governing the United States, that run candidates for all the government posts and monopolize them. You won't see a single Communist in their midst, nor will you find him writing for *The Washington Post, The New York Times* or any other important U.S. newspapers or magazines. Nor will you hear him on the radio or see him on coast-to-coast television programs. Those who really dissent from the capitalist system will never have access to those mass media. That freedom exists only for those who agree with the capitalist system. They're the ones who shape public opinion; they create opinion; they even create the people's political convictions and beliefs. Yet they're called democracies.

We're a little more honest. There's no private ownership of the mass media here. The students', workers', farmers', women's and other mass organizations; the Party; and the state—each has its own publication. We develop democracy through our own methods of election to positions of power and, above all, through constant criticism and self-criticism, collective leadership, and constant participation and support by the masses of the people.

As I already explained, I don't appoint any ambassadors here—though I can give my opinion when one is proposed—or even any low-ranking civil servants, because we have a system of promotion to higher posts and responsibilities that's based on capacity and merit. I don't appoint anybody. I can't, I don't want to, and I really don't need to make any one-man decisions to appoint even a low-ranking civil servant.

In other words, I believe—I'm being perfectly frank with you—that our system is a thousand times more democratic than the capitalist, imperialist system of the developed capitalist countries—including the NATO countries, which plunder our world and ruthlessly exploit us. I believe that our system is really much fairer and much more democratic. (pp. 285-92)

Fidel Castro and Frei Betto, in an interview in *Fidel and Religion: Castro Talks on Revolution and Religion with Frei Betto*, Simon and Schuster, 1987, pp. 261-312.

FIDEL CASTRO WITH JEFFREY M. ELLIOT AND MERVYN M. DYMALLY
(interview date 1985)

[Elliot is an American educator and journalist who has interviewed many nationally and internationally renowned figures in world affairs and American politics; Dymally has held numerous elective offices, including lieutenant governor of California and state senator, and has served on the Foreign Affairs Committee in the United States House of Representatives. In the interview below, Castro discusses the qualities of effective leadership, maintaining that it is not the individual who makes history but the people and objective circumstances.]

[Dymally]: *What qualities make for a great leader? Do you believe you have those qualities?*

[Castro]: I think I have the qualities to do what I'm doing.

Now, what makes a great leader? What does the concept of a great leader imply? Moses was a great leader; Christ was a great leader—here, I'm referring to spiritual leaders. I think Mohammed was a great leader. They were personalities in history who are known as leaders, because each had a doctrine, founded a doctrine, and was followed by multitudes. Even when they started out, they were backed by a few. Christ, it's said, was followed by twelve apostles at first, then by millions of believers. He was a spiritual leader, as was Mohammed. They were religious leaders—but leaders, nonetheless.

I have an idea of what a leader is. Ho Chi Minh was a great leader. And, for me of course, the one with the most extraordinary qualities as a political and revolutionary leader was Lenin. Lincoln was a leader, a really great leader. There were many leaders in the history of Latin America. Without a doubt, Bolívar was a great leader, both politically and militarily. Throughout the history of

Latin America, there have been many leaders who have led their countries under difficult conditions. In this century, Roosevelt was a leader, that's beyond question. I'm referring to the Roosevelt of the New Deal.

There have been many religious and political leaders. History is full of leaders. Wherever a human community has existed, a leader has emerged. The times determine what is required of them. Certain qualities are needed at one time, others at another. In the Napoleonic era, it seems that it was military qualities that were required: battles, prestige, glory. The French revolution itself had many outstanding leaders. Under certain circumstances, the important thing was the ability to wage war; in others, it was the ability to think, to reason; in still others, the gift of expression, to make speeches, to convince others; in yet others, the capacity for action; and, in still others, the ability to organize. In short, you can't describe a leader with any one model.

Now, I'm going to talk about a current leader: Jesse Jackson. He certainly has the qualities of a leader. His ability to communicate, deep convictions, ethics, and courage in the milieu in which he lives and works—the United States is a very difficult one—all bear witness to his leadership qualities.

Each epoch, each society, each historical moment demands certain qualities. It's possible that leadership qualities in the future will differ from those needed in times of revolutionary struggle: the imagination and audacity that were required at a given moment. Perhaps some other time will demand cooler-headed, less intuitive, more methodical people—another type of man, the right man to lead society in a different phase of its development. But a certain amount of creative spirit and imagination will always be needed. Regardless of how much a society develops, there will always be room for improvement and change.

The qualities required at one moment are not necessarily the ones needed at another. We're talking about serious leaders, aren't we? We're not talking about demagogues or electioneering politicians, because sometimes they have to be good demagogues, have good publicity, a good public image, and even be good looking, to get votes—a lot of votes. Then they've got to have television and special advisers. Advertising specialists can make leaders. That's not what I had in mind. I'm talking about men who are capable of generating ideas, of inspiring confidence, of directing a process, of leading a nation in difficult times. That's what I'm referring to. I think the characteristics vary greatly from one situation to another, from one time to another, from one people to another. There are many.

If you ask, "What about the qualities of a revolutionary leader?" I could go into it a little deeper. I might have a litttle more to say about that. I think a revolutionary leader needs to have a lot of conviction, passion, for what he's doing. He also needs to have great confidence in the people. He must be tenacious and cool-headed and have a sense of responsibility and of identification with what he's doing and with the people. He also needs some training, some clear ideas. Well, there you have a few elements.

I'd like to add one more qualification to the concept of a revolutionary leader. He should also have a great sense of human solidarity, great respect for the people. He should view the people not as an instrument, but as a protagonist—a real protagonist—the subject and hero of the struggle. Now, I don't mean to suggest that those qualities are technically indispensable for leading a process of change. There may be a leader who has all of the other qualities and yet views the people as an instrument, an object, rather than as the main protagonist and real hero. That could happen. It might. That would be more of a moral assessment than an evaluation of the intrinsic characteristics that a leader needs.

Other men have proved capable of leading regressive processes in history. Take Hitler: he was a leader, at least technically. He had some of the characteristics required for being a leader—but, of course, not a revolutionary one. He was a fascist leader, a reactionary leader, who communicated with the masses and stirred people's passions, their resentment, their hatred. He appealed to the lower instincts of man and rallied multitudes. Morally, he was no leader at all.

I'm thinking, rather, of revolutionary leaders; about what is required of a leader who is to make a positive mark on history. I mentioned the German case, the demagogue, as an exception—an example of an individual who, under certain circumstances and using certain methods, can rally people behind a bad cause. I'd prefer that type of demagogue be excluded from the concept of a leader.

There's something else I want to say about this. I think that many people have leadership qualities. It's a mistake; a serious mistake, to think that these qualities are rare or infrequent. I'm convinced of this. For a leader to emerge, the only thing needed is the need for a leader.

In revolutions, leaders emerge. The masses produce an infinite number of people with great qualities.

If we talk about the independence struggles in Latin America, for example, dozens of political and military leaders emerged. If we talk about the French revolution, a great many leaders emerged from the masses, people who no one had heard of the day before. They were brilliant, capable, excellent orators, such as Danton and Mirabeau; great pamphleteers, such as Marat; and rigorous, methodical military chiefs, such as Robespierre—all ephemeral, in keeping with the dynamic and complex nature of the process itself. Great leaders also emerged in the thirteen colonies and led their people to independence. Many people have leadership qualities. Circumstances determine which of them becomes more prominent than others. These circumstances are often fortuitous; chance

is a factor. For instance, in the history of the independence struggles, those who organized a struggle often died and then others with great capabilities emerged. Thay's why I maintain that all that's needed for leaders to emerge is that there be no leaders.

I recall our experience during the war. After our initial victories, we had a column of 80 to 100 men. You had to urge each of the men in charge, every day, to insist on discipline, vigilance, and the maintenance of a permanent state of alert, stressing that there be no carelessness. Later, when you chose some of the comrades who excelled and assigned them the responsibility of commanding a new column, they then established discipline and saw to every detail. If you assigned them to an area of action, they really excelled. That is, when they were given important missions and assumed responsibility, many people showed what they could do. It was a small group, and many outstanding leaders came from it. This means that a man needs responsibility to develop his potential.

Let me give you some examples. Indira Gandhi was a great leader. She knew the problems of India, the psychology of her people, and characteristics of the country. She did an excellent job. What was the determining factor, however? Her family ties with Nehru. That was the factor which gave her opportunity. Right now, the same is true of Rajiv Gandhi. I believe he's doing his job—which isn't an easy one in that huge, complex country—with a great sense of responsibility. In his case, too, the opportunity arose because of family ties.

What I mean is, it can't be assumed that leadership qualities are exceptional. I think it was Aristotle who said that man was a political animal. Political genius is more widespread than artistic genius.

There's something else. I'm convinced of this, and it's easy to prove: the emergence of leaders is determined by the historic moment and objective conditions. Let me cite several examples. If Lincoln had lived today, he might be a simple farmer in the United States, and nobody would have heard of him. It was the times in which he lived, the society in which he lived, that made a Lincoln possible. If George Washington had been born fifty years after independence, he might have been unknown; the same holds true if he had lived fifty years previous to it. The conditions at that historic moment were what made a Washington possible. Let's take Napoleon, a great military leader. What would have been his lot if he had been born fifty years earlier? He might never have left his small Corsica. If Lenin, with all his exceptional ability, had been born at the beginning of the past century, he would have been unknown in history.

I believe that human beings, all human beings, have a great capacity for political leadership. What must have happened on countless occasions is that the possibilities for developing those abilities did not arise, because the person lived in a different era, under different circumstances.

I maintain that, wherever there are 1,000 cadres, there are many potential leaders.

Take my case, for example. If I hadn't been able to learn to read and write, what role could I have played in the history of my country, in the revolution? Where I was born, out of hundreds of kids, my brothers and sisters and I were the only ones who had a chance to study beyond the first few grades. How many more people were there among those hundreds of kids, with the same or better qualities for doing what I did, if only they had been given the opportunity to study? The first thing that eliminates many talented and capable people is the social factor; they simply didn't have the least opportunity to study.

One of the 100 best poems in the Spanish language tells of how often genius lies dormant in one's innermost soul, awaiting a voice that would call out, "Arise and go!" This is true; I believe this deeply. That is why I believe that the qualities for leadership are not exceptional; they are to be found among the people.

The Cuban revolution itself is the best proof of this. In this country, for example, there were hundreds—thousands—of prominent people: political leaders, ministers, deputies, senators, and mayors. There was an enormous number of political and military figures who were well known and recognized in that social milieu. Then the revolution came along and not a single one remained in public office. Virtually everyone who took charge of running the country later on—who became political leaders, military leaders, administrative leaders, and cadres at all levels—was completely unknown. Five, three, or two years before the revolution, the people knew few, if any, of the farmers, workers, professionals, or students—the humble citizens who later shouldered the responsibilities of leadership. No, in order to be absolutely precise, I should say that half a dozen comrades from the old Communist Party were known throughout the country, but none of them held public office.

The entire leadership of Cuban society was replaced with people who came from the masses. Around 200,000 new professionals have graduated from our universities since the triumph of the revolution: men and women who are engineers, doctors, economists, and professors, with much more theoretical training. And millions of people have obtained incomparable levels of political training.

On one occasion, when a comrade [Camilo Cienfuegos] who had had an outstanding record in the war died— he disappeared in a plane accident—I spoke about it on television and said, "There are many Camilos among the people; many men like him will emerge from the people." He'd been living in California at the time we were in Mexico, and he came and joined our ranks. He participated in the landing and was one of the men in the small group that survived and continued the struggle. What did I first think of him? At that time, we were all going hungry. He had a tremendous appetite, and, if any food was left when the others finished, he was always the first one to ask for seconds, although he did so in a very disciplined manner. The only thing I remember about him at that time was his voracious appetite. No one could have imagined the extraordinary military, political, and revolutionary qualities he possessed—which were brought out only after the fighting, after the military operations began.

The same was true of Che Guevara. Che—we called him that because he was Argentine—came as a doctor. Nobody then could have imagined his talents as a solider, as a revolutionary thinker, his remarkable integrity. Che left Argentina immediately after medical school. He arrived in Guatemala, witnessed the overthrow of Arbenz, and then moved to Mexico, where I met him. What I said earlier was again borne out; if he hadn't run into us in Mexico, or if he'd been killed in the difficult early moments, only a few of us would have known him. The Che we all know wouldn't have existed, for we wouldn't have known who he really was.

What does this mean? There are potential values everywhere that only need an opportunity to develop. This is also true of military figures. If it weren't for the circumstances that gave rise to a great world conflagration, few would have heard of Eisenhower, Patton, MacArthur, or any of the others who achieved renown in the United States during the last world war. Without that war, who would have known of the existence of de Gaulle?

There is a fabulous potential capacity in the human mind and heart. It's said that people use only 5 or 6 percent of their mental capacity—there are scientists who are doing research on this. No one can imagine the kind of computer man has in his head.

Why am I saying this? I've noticed, especially in the West, that there's a great tendency to associate historical events with individuals. It's the old theory that individuals make history. There's also a tendency in the West to view the leader of any Third World country as a chieftain. There's a certain stereotype: leader equals chieftain.

I'm amazed that, in the West, where you suppose that there are cultured societies and that people think, there's such a strong tendency to associate historical events with individuals and to magnify the role of the individual. I can see it myself, in such phrases as: "Castro's Cuba," "Castro did this," "Castro undid that." Almost everything in this country is attributed to Castro, Castro's doing, Castro's perversities. That type of mentality abounds in the West; unfortunately, it's quite widespread. It seems to me to be an erroneous approach to historical and political events. (pp. 30–8)

Fidel Castro with Jeffrey M. Elliot and Mervyn M. Dymally in an interview in *Fidel Castro: Nothing Can Stop the Course of History,* Pathfinder Press, 1986, pp. 30–8.

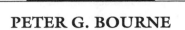

PETER G. BOURNE

(essay date 1986)

[A distinguished psychiatrist who has had an extensive career in politics and foreign affairs, Bourne has served as Assistant Secretary of the United Nations and as a special assistant on health care issues to former president Jimmy Carter. In the following excerpt from his critically acclaimed work *Fidel: A Biography of Fidel Castro* (1986), Bourne elucidates the background of Castro's *History Will Absolve Me* speech (1953), citing the oration as the "classic document of the Cuban revolution."]

The trial began on September 21, 1953, before the Urgency Court of Santiago de Cuba in the ornate Palace of Justice that Lester Rodríguez, [Castro's brother] Raúl and their men had so successfully captured. During his two hours of testimony on the opening day, Fidel, assertive and gesticulating, seized the initiative from the prosecutor, and while freely admitting his role in the attack, used the forum of the crowded courtroom to give his version of it. He persuasively articulated his motives, and before an audience that included journalists, lawyers, and opposition politicians, he ridiculed the government's contention that he was part of a conspiracy involving Prío or any other political figure. "The only intellectual author of the attack on the Moncade is José Martí, the apostle of our independence," he declared. Before the end of the first day's testimony, Fidel requested and received permission to act as the lawyer in his own defense. (p. 91)

[On 16 October,] Fidel, vigorous and unbowed by his confinement, was brought to trial again, together with Fidel Labrador, who had been badly wounded in the attack and was unable to attend the first trial. The hearing was held in the nurses' lounge of the Santiago Civil Hospital, where the authorities thought they could carry out the proceedings in relative secrecy. . . . In his own defense, Fidel made a two-hour speech, largely unrelated to the charges against him, in which he analyzed the human suffering and social ills that afflicted Cuba, and argued that revolutionary change was necessary. But it was not just the content, but his manner of delivery that stunned the court. Later known by the closing phrase, "History will absolve me," the speech represents the simplest and probably the most accurate statement of Fidel's political beliefs. Fidel had worked on the speech for several days and had tried it out the night before on a fellow prisoner, Gerardo Poll Cabrera, a railway worker, who had been put in Fidel's cell now that the other conspirators had gone.

[Journalist] Marta Rojas recalls the startling impact of his speech on the court.

There was something very unusual in *History Will Absolve Me*. I was simply carried by his words. . . . It was the first time I was listening to such things. I had heard nothing similar to that before. The same was true with the guards. I was watching the guards standing with their weapons loose. . . listening, carried away by Fidel. . . . They were simply absorbed and engrossed by his words. When Fidel was through with his speech, there was silence, and he had to slap on the table and say something like, 'Well, I finished. This is all.'

At that point, the stunned and flustered judge rang his bell and called; "Order! Order!" even though there was silence. Fidel walked around the table to his lawyer and old friend, Baudilio Castellanos, handed him a book he had borrowed, and asked what he thought of his speech. The court was in disarray, taken aback by the unprecedented oratory and commanding behavior of the defendant. Finally, however, reasserting control, the judge declared Fidel guilty and sentenced him to thirteen years. As he was leaving the room, Fidel asked Marta Rojas, "Did you take notes?" "Yes," she replied, and he smiled.

In sentencing the original twenty-six men and two women, the court had ordered that the men serve their time in la Cabaña Fortress in Havana. On October 13, they took off from Santiago de Cuba in two DC-3s, handcuffed in pairs and sitting on benches with their backs to the windows. As the planes approached Havana they turned left and flew south over the Gulf of Batabanó to the Isle of Pines. A last-minute decision had been made by the minister of interior, Ramón Hermida, to incarcerate them instead at the Presidio Modelo (Model Prison) on this island sixty miles off the southwest coast of Cuba. From there, both in prison and exile, they could not so easily continue to foment discord and revolution among young sympathizers as they could had they been imprisoned in Havana.

At the dusty landing strip, they were met by Lieutenant Pedro Rodríguez Coto, director of internal order at the prison. He was a tall, thin man with stooped shoulders and a large hooked nose. His eyes were masked by large dark glasses, and out of his back pocket protruded a coiled whip. He and a group of guards took delivery of the male prisoners, and the planes took off again to fly the two women to the National Women's Prison in Guanajay, in Pinar del Río Province.

The men were isolated from the other prisoners in a wing of the prison hospital. They slept in a long gallery, 120 feet by 24 feet. Whitewashed walls reflected the light of three bare 500-watt bulbs that burned twenty-four hours a day. Their iron beds lined the walls on either side. In the day they had access to a large courtyard. Discipline was strict and they were roused from bed every morning at 5 a.m. for a head count. Their only contact with the rest of the prison population was with two prisoners who brought in a sack of bread and a large can of milk for breakfast at 7:30 a.m. and returned at 11:00 with lunch and again at 5:00 p.m. with dinner. In the first few days, the leaderless group suffered from despondency adjusting to the new surroundings, reconciling themselves to their long sentences, and worrying about the plight of their families. They also anticipated that Fidel would be held apart from them as he had been at Boniato.

There was therefore great joy when, on Sunday, October 17, 1953, Fidel walked into Building 1 of the prison hospital and embraced his comrades, trying to hug them all at once. Immediately he started to reassert his authority and began organizing their activities. Their role in prison, he told them, was to be combative; they were not there merely to serve their sentences, but rather to use the time to prepare themselves for the continuing struggle after their release. They agreed to pool their few pesos and scanty supplies from relatives to meet the group's needs. They set up procedures for holding meetings, and established, under Fidel's direction, the Abel Santamaría Academy. Each morning, sitting at wooden tables at the edge of the courtyard in the shade of the overhanging roof, they gave instruction to one another in history, political theory, literature, geography, and mathematics. Fidel, however, did much of the teaching. In the afternoons they played chess, Ping-Pong, and volleyball. If any of the men had had the idea that once their sentence was over they would end their revolutionary career, Fidel had quickly dissuaded them.

By most accounts, the school was only a modest success because most of the men did not have the same academic interest or intellectual curiosity as did Fidel. He sought to galvanize their commitment to education by admonishing them with a quote from Martí: "A fortress of ideas is worth more than a fortress of stone." The idea was that they would be creating a fortress of ideas for themselves while in prison. But most of their efforts came out of loyalty to Fidel rather than any deep commitment to knowledge.

The opportunity for intellectual maturation that prison offered had a profoundly greater effect on Fidel than on the others. The setting was really not very different from the life he had lived in the Jesuit schools, and he found it relatively easy to commit himself to intensive study. As was the case in school, the external discipline of the prison system helped him to focus his own motivation and self-discipline on the task he had set himself. It was a crucial period in the development of his political philosophy and the crystallization of his dedication to revolution. After months of reading and contemplation, he would write in a letter, "I have rounded out my view of the world and determined the meaning of my life."

The prisoners were able to receive books, and they established the "Raúl García Gómez Library," named for their comrade who had been murdered in front of

Melba and Haydée. By the time they were released twenty months later, thanks to the generosity of friends, relatives, sympathizers, and several university professors, the library contained more than a thousand volumes. Fidel read voraciously. During the first six months in prison his letters, mainly to Luis Conte Agüero and Naty Revuelta, contained lists of the titles he had read; added together they revealed his wide range of intellectual interests.

In a letter written in November, he mentions the works of Shakespeare, A. J. Cronin's *The Keys of the Kingdom*, André Maurois's *Memoirs*, García Llorente's *First Lessons in Philosophy*, Romain Rolland's *Jean-Christophe*, Victor Hugo's *Les Misérables*, Karl Marx's *The Eighteenth Brumaire of Louis Bonaparte*, and Axel Munthe's *The Story of San Michele*, the recounting of a physician's life-long commitment to the struggle against social injustice and human suffering, a book that made a significant impression of Fidel.

"When I read the work of a famous author," Fidel wrote,

the history of a people, the doctrine of a thinker, the theories of an economist or the theses of a social reformer, I am filled with the desire to know everything that all authors have written, the doctrines of all philosophers, the treatises of all economists, and the theses of all apostles. I want to know everything, and I even go through the bibliographies in the books treasuring the hope of reading those books someday. Outside I chafed because I did not have enough time; here, where there seems to be too much time I am still chafing.

The Jesuits had done a good job inculcating in him a fascination with ideas.

In a letter dated December 18, 1953, he mentioned William Thackeray's *Vanity Fair*, Ivan Turgenev's *A Nest of the Gentry*, Jorge Amado's *Luis Carlos Prestes, Champion of Hope*, A. J. Cronin's *The Citadel*, Eric Knight's *Fugitives from Love*, the Dean of Canterbury's *Secret of Soviet Strength*, and Karl Marx's *Das Kapital*. A later letter referred to the works of Martí as his constant companion, which he was alternating with Victor Hugo's *William Shakespeare*, Honoré de Balzac's *The Magic Skin*, Stefan Zweig's *Biography of Little Napoleon*, Rómulo Gallegos's *On Equal Footing*, A. J. Cronin's *The Stars Look Down*, Somerset Maugham's *The Razor's Edge*, four of the eighteen volumes of *The Complete Works of Sigmund Freud*, and Dostoevski's *The Brothers Karamazov*, *The Insulted and the Humiliated*, *Crime and Punishment*, *The Idiot*, and *The House of the Dead*. These books represented only a sample of the literature he devoured during those first six months.

By March 1954, the scope of Fidel's self-tutoring program aimed at creating a thoroughly educated intellect was increasingly narrowing to the field of political theory. In a letter that month he wrote, "I have rolled up my sleeves and taken on a study of world history and political doctrines." He read a great deal of Marx and Lenin, but also a range of other political theorists, and on April 15 was desperately asking friends on the outside to get him information about Franklin Roosevelt.

Roosevelt. I mainly want information on him: in agriculture, his price raising policies for crops, the protection and conservation of soil fertility, credit facilities, the moratorium on debts and the extension of markets at home and abroad; in the social field, how he provided more jobs, shortened the workday, raised wages and pushed through social assistance to the unemployed, the old and the crippled; and in the field of the general economy, his reorganization of industry, new tax systems, regulation of the trusts, and banking and monetary reforms.

It is the custom today, both among the Cuban leadership and, ironically, right-wing politicians in the United States, to suggest that Fidel's Marxism long antedated the Moncada attack. That he early had strong ideas about social justice based on his Christian understanding of right and wrong is evident, but there is little to suggest that he had an ironclad commitment to any particular political theory. He continued to identify strongly with historic figures, but it was the conception of revolution, especially the French model, and the mastery of power that dominated his thinking. It was during this period in prison that he expanded his awareness of political ideology and began to formulate an independent set of political beliefs. Yet he found it very difficult. He saw the protean nature of political theory, and felt it had to be adapted to the times to achieve concrete goals. In a letter of January 27, 1954, Fidel expresses lucidly his sense of the expediency of political ideology:

Human thought is unfailingly conditioned by the circumstances of the era. In the case of a political genius, I venture to affirm that his genius depends exclusively on his era. Lenin in the time of Catherine, when the aristocracy was the ruling class, would necessarily have been a champion of the bourgeoisie, which was the revolutionary class at the time, or could have simply been ignored by history. If Martí had lived when Havana was seized by the English, he would have defended the standard of Spain alongside his father. What would Napoleon, Mirabeau, Danton, and Robespierre have been in the times of Charlemagne?. . . Julius Caesar would never have crossed the Rubicon in the early years of the Republic before the intense class struggle that shook Rome was sharpened and the great plebian party developed.

Fidel saw political ideology as a pragmatic tool to be adapted by "political geniuses" in the service of historic achievement. He made the further point in this letter that creative geniuses were not dependent for their recognition on the circumstances of their times. A great work of art was a great work of art in any era. Making that distinc-

tion, he said, "A literary, philosophical or artistic genius has a considerably broader field in terms of time and history than that offered by the world of reality and action which is the only arena for the political geniuses." These views explain a great deal about what would later seem such enigmatic ideological positions. Pragmatism in the pursuit of power was clearly the underlying concept that he embraced. (pp. 92–7)

Shortly after his arrival on the Isle of Pines, Fidel started to reconstruct the speech he had given in his defense at the trial. *History Will Absolve Me* has been quoted in a variety of different forms, but the final version that appeared as a pamphlet in 1954, although a substantial elaboration of the original speech, contained almost verbatim what he had said at the trial. Writing with lemon juice between the lines of legitimate correspondence, or smuggling tracts between the double bottoms of matchboxes, Fidel was able, bit by bit, to get out the entire text.

Melba and Haydée had a list of people to whom Fidel was corresponding. They would retrieve the letters and after ironing them to make the words written in lemon juice legible, they would transcribe the material, which Melba's father, an excellent typist, would then type up. Marta Rojas was at Melba's house almost every day, and says that she was amazed, comparing the material with the notes she had taken in Santiago, at the accuracy with which Fidel had been able to repeat his speech.

Edited into this basic text was additional material contained in a long letter to Luis Conte Agüero, which Fidel had been able to send earlier in his confinement.

Fidel told Haydée and Melba to get 100,000 copies printed and distributed. The cost was prohibitive for an organization virtually without resources. "What is the difference between twenty-five and one hundred thousand, only paper and ink," Fidel responded when they argued the impossibility of the task. In the end they produced ten thousand and Fidel was very satisfied. "That is why I asked you to get out one hundred thousand," he said. "If I had told you to print five hundred you would have aimed for five hundred and never printed ten thousand." It was quintessential Fidel, believing that accomplishment was limited only by the inadequacy of one's own vision. He characteristically set goals that most would never have the audacity to suggest, and then expected heaven and earth to be moved to achieve them.

The pamphlets were distributed all over Cuba by several loyal friends, including Gustavo Ameijeiras, who traveled in an old jalopy begging money for gas wherever he could.

History Will Absolve Me is the classic document of the Cuban revolution. Fidel began by reviewing the difficulties he had encountered in preparing his defense, and the ways in which the government and the prosecutors had violated the judicial system. He then gave a detailed account of the entire Moncada event. It was in effect a full admission of everything with which he was charged, but it served, at a time when only the government version could get into the newspaper, as a way to tell his side of the story both for immediate political benefit and for history, the latter being particularly on his mind.

The strategy, he said, had been based on the belief that if they were successful in capturing Moncada the people would rise in their support. "When we speak of the people we are not talking about those who live in comfort, the conservative elements of the nation, who welcome any oppressive regime, any dictatorship, any despotism. . . we mean the vast unredeemed masses, those to whom everyone makes promises and who are deceived by all." There then followed a detailed documentation of the extreme poverty, deprivation, and suffering in which most Cubans lived: six hundred thousand Cubans without work (in a population of about six million), five hundred thousand farm laborers living in miserable shacks, two hundred thousand peasant families without a single acre of land on which to grow food, while half of the productive land in the country is owned by foreigners. He then detailed the levels of illiteracy, parasite infestation, malnutrition, and what amounted to indentured servitude under which most rural workers lived. He decried the lack of health care, education and social services, and those which did exist, usually staffed by dedicated professionals, were weighed down by corruption at the top. All of this he contrasted with the lavish lifestyle of the millionaires and others in power, most of whom had acquired their wealth not by honest work, but by graft and corruption.

He offered as a remedy five "revolutionary laws":

Return the power to the people and proclaim the 1940 Constitution the Supreme Law of the State, until such time as the people should decide to modify or change it. [This last phrase would later have particular significance.]

Give nonmortgageable and nontransferable ownership of the land to all tenant and sub-tenant farmers, lessees, sharecroppers, and squatters who hold parcels of five *caballerías* of land or less. [One *caballería* is approximately 33 acres.]

Grant workers and employees the right to share 30 percent of the profits of all large industrial, mercantile, and mining enterprises, including sugar mills.

Grant all sugar planters the right to share 55 percent of all sugar production and a minimum quota of forty thousand *arrobas* for all small tenant farmers who have been established for three years or more. [One *arroba* is about 25 pounds.]

Order the confiscation of all holdings, all ill-gotten gains of those who had committed frauds during previous regimes, as well as the holdings and ill-gotton gains of all their legates and heirs.

He went on to describe the terrible abuse and torture to which his men had been subjected after their capture, and he detailed the cold-blooded murder of several dozen of them. He tied responsibility for this directly to Batista, accusing him of being one of the most despicable tyrants in the history of the world.

Finally, citing extensively from Montesquieu, Thomas Aquinas, Martin Luther, John Locke, Rousseau, Thomas Paine, the United States Constitution, and other sources, he carefully laid out a legal and historical rationale to justify his right to try to overthrow an unjust dictator who held power illegitimately. Under such circumstances, he argued, he could not possibly be guilty of any crime.

Woven throughout the document is the thread of Cuban history and the story of the great Cuban heroes who had struggled against great odds for justice and national independence. Quoting, among others, Martí and General José Miró Argenter, chief of Antonio Maceo's general staff, Fidel lavishly wraps himself in the folds of Cuban patriotism, elevating himself to the stature of these revered national heroes.

History Will Absolve Me has been attacked by critics as unoriginal and a distillation or hodgepodge of existing ideas. It has even been suggested that it was lifted almost entirely from the work of another Cuban writer. In later years, Fidel was accused of betraying many of the ideals it contained as he made Cuba a Marxist state. There is some validity to these arguments. However, such criticism misses the fact that whatever its inspiration, the document, in describing the social ills that afflicted Cuba and a program of reform, represented exactly what Fidel believed at the time. In addition, having survived Moncada, even if unexpectedly, Fidel needed to begin orchestrating the future of the movement. *History Will Absolve Me* was a political document promulgated for very specific and carefully thought-out strategic purposes. It was intended to enshrine the Moncada attack in a cloak of idealism to counter any perception that it was an impulsive act of political frustration, albeit by brave men. In this respect it was an important answer to the Communists, who had denounced the attack in exactly these terms, describing it as a "putsch." It was vital to Fidel and his ambitions to have Moncada understood as one event within the context of a long-term struggle to achieve revolution in Cuba around a set of clear ideals. It must be remembered that in 1953 most Cubans saw Moncada as a failure, and Fidel, facing thirteen years in prison, as finished politically. Thus, it was essential to create an image of himself as the leader of a viable movement.

History Will Absolve Me was to serve as a core around which such a movement could be created. It was a way of giving potential supporters access to Fidel while he remained physically confined. He had an intuitive understanding of the importance of propaganda, describing it as "the soul of every struggle." While *History Will Absolve Me* caused apoplexy among the Cuban wealthy elite and United States investors, it was a document carefully crafted to mobilize the broadest possible support while at the same time offending the smallest number of potential backers. It was acceptable to the Communists (indeed, some of the statistical material seems to have come from a book by Blas Roca), but avoided mentioning communism, Marxism, or even socialism. It identified what most educated Cubans knew in their hearts were the great injustices in their country, without threatening them with either the time frame or the methods for redress. There was no attack on the United States and there was no call to revolution. It was intended to draw to his cause the idealistic youth of the country, whether they were currently affiliated with the Communists, the Ortodoxos, or, as in most instances, were independent. It never reached the mass of the population, and even within the educated community its impact fell far short of Fidel's grandiose fantasies. But it was stunningly successful in the quality of commitment it elicited from a relatively small group of new followers who were enough to form the basis of "The Movement." Vilma Espín, who later became a central figure of the organization, and who married Raúl, has said, "The tremendous impact of *History Will Absolve Me* must be stressed. . . . I was in the laboratory when someone gave me a copy. . . . We were all fascinated. It spoke a new language and it set out a clear program around which we could all center our struggle, an advanced program that was attractive to young people."(pp. 98–102)

Peter G. Bourne, in his *Fidel: A Biography of Fidel Castro*, Dodd, Mead & Company, 1986, 332 p.

TAD SZULC

(essay date 1986)

[A former *New York Times* correspondent, Szulc first interviewed Castro in 1959, the year of the Cuban Revolution, and toured the swamps and beaches of the Bay of Pigs with the dictator to hear his personal story of the battle. In the excerpt below from his comprehensive biography *Fidel: A Critical Portrait* (1986), Szulc discusses Castro's powerful loquacity, focusing particularly on his propagandistic use of television and the press.]

Fidel's loquacity is a legend. . . . He holds forth anywhere, anytime. Once after an American television-interview taping session with his big brother at the Palace of the Revolution in Havana in 1985, Raúl Castro was asked whether he had watched the full five hours before the cameras.

Oh, my God, no, no . . . , Raúl, who has much more of a sense of humor than Fidel (the big brother does not

---

> **Castro addresses the General Assembly of the United Nations, 12 October 1979:**
>
> I address myself to the rich nations, asking them to contribute. And I address myself to the poor nations, asking them to distribute.
>
> Enough of words! We need deeds!
>
> Enough of abstractions! We need concrete action!
>
> Enough of speaking about a speculative new international economic order that nobody understands. We must speak of a real, objective order that everybody understands!
>
> I have not come here as a prophet of revolution. I have not come here to ask or to wish that the world be violently convulsed. I have come to speak of peace and cooperation among the peoples. And I have come to warn that if we do not peacefully and wisely resolve the present injustices and inequalities, the future will be apocalyptic.
>
> The sounds of weapons, of threatening language, and of prepotent behavior on the international arena must cease.
>
> Enough of the illusion that the problems of the world can be solved by nuclear weapons. Bombs may kill the hungry, the sick, and the ignorant; but they cannot kill hunger, disease, and ignorance. Nor can they kill the righteous rebellion of the peoples. And in the holocaust, the rich—who have the most to lose in this world—will also die.
>
> Let us say farewell to arms, and let us in a civilized manner dedicate ourselves to the most pressing problems of our times. This is the responsibility and the most sacred duty of all the world's statesmen. This, moreover, is the basic premise for human survival.
>
> I thank you.
>
> Fidel Castro, in his "I Speak on Behalf of the Children of the World" address in *To Speak the Truth: Why Washington's 'Cold War' against Cuba Doesn't End*, edited by Mary-Alice Waters, Pathfinder Press, 1992.

laugh at himself unless *he* makes the joke), replied in mock annoyance. "I think I've heard Fidel talk enough to last me for the rest of my life. You know, when I was moved into Fidel's prison cell where he had been in isolation for about a year—this was at the Isle of Pines Presidio late in 1954, when we were serving our sentences for the Moncada barracks assault—he didn't let me sleep for weeks. Having been alone all that time, he just talked day and night, day and night. . .

Moreover, Fidel Castro demands undivided attention when he addresses a visitor on a one-to-one basis. He often prefers to stand rather than sit down during conversations—he also tends to pace rapidly when he is excited by an idea or an indignity he believes he has suffered in some context of world politics—and if the visitor is not riveted by his words, he might suffer a punch in the arm or the chest.

Castro can also be a superb listener when he is interested in the subject or the speaker. And he is a great questioner, centering swiftly on the heart of the matter under discussion. One often does feel that he may be dying to speak out, but his courtesy and curiosity usually prevail—and Fidel will remain silent for very long minutes, fiddling with his cigar, lit or unlit (before he abruptly quit smoking late in 1985), or twisting his beard with his fingers between his chin and lower lip in characteristic gesture of thoughtfulness. (p. 35)

Indeed, Fidel Castro's revolution—or, at least, the selling of this revolution to Cubans—might not have succeeded without the medium of television. From the first day, in fact, Castro has governed through television, the first such massive use of this technology in the craft of government as distinct from campaign politics. While he does have a natural rapport with his audiences and he used this symbiotic emotional relationship in the first years of his rule by addressing crowds as large as one million, television was vital in carrying the face, the voice, and the message beyond the meeting plaza to Cubans in their homes. Later, television became the regular channel of communication between Castro and the population.

By Latin American and even United States standards, Cuban television was quite advanced technically early in 1959 when Castro forced Batista's ouster, and the number of sets in the country was relatively high, especially in the cities. But what mattered the most was that Castro, whose revolutionary concept was always built on communication with the masses, instantly understood that he and television were made for each other. Actually, Cuba had a tradition of the use of the radio in politics, and Fidel had been very effective with the microphone on the limited occasions when he was allowed to get near one. In the second and last year of the guerrilla war, Castro installed a radio station—Radio Rebelde—at his headquarters atop the Sierra Maestra, rapidly turning it into a superb instrument of propaganda and the dissemination of coded operational orders. He often addressed Cuba over Radio Rebelde.

The switch to television was thus natural, and Castro's ideal on-camera presence and his rich dramatic gifts did the rest. The Cuban propaganda apparatus is so well honed that the nation may be treated to a Castro speech carried live (always in its entirety) as well as to a number of taped rebroadcasts over the two national channels, sometimes over a period of days. Additionally, every public appearance by Castro is either carried live in special reports or as part of the regular television news programs (the radio, of course, carries the Fidel sound as well).

It may be difficult to believe that Castro, who seems to adore public speaking, actually fears it before the first words are out. He told the Cuban magazine *Bohemia* that "I confess. . . I suffer from stage fright when I speak in Revolution Square. . . . It is not at all easy for me." As a young man, he forced himself to deliver speeches in front

of a mirror in his room until he was satisfied they were adequate to encourage him to pursue a career in law and politics. On most occasions, Fidel begins his speeches in a low, almost uncertain voice, talking quite slowly—until he has that sudden feeling of having established rapport with his audience. From there on, it is Fidel Castro, the great orator. Other famous orators never conquered the initial fear, among them Gladstone and Winston Churchill.

Castro is fascinated by the art of public speech. He has reminisced that when he was a high-school student he became friendly during summer vacations with a well-educated Spaniard in Oriente who told him that in order to overcome his speech difficulties, Demosthenes used to place a pebble under his tongue. This led Fidel to recount that, still in high school, he began collecting speeches by other great classical orators, but that he subsequently concluded that he disliked their oratory because "it was too rhetorical and grandiloquent, depending too much on wordplay." Moreover, he says, today Demosthenes and Cicero would "have great problems if they had to face concrete realities and explain their society," Castro's point being that he ceased to admire Athens' democracy when he understood that it meant that a "tiny group of aristocrats met in public place to make decisions." Fidel's favorite speaker, it turns out, was Emilio Castelar, the brilliant Spanish statesman and thinker who headed Spain's short-lived First Republic in 1873, but as "marvelous" as Castelar's parliamentary speeches had been, "today he would have been a complete fiasco in any parliament." In the end, Castro decided to practice the exact opposite of what all the great orators in history had done, creating his own fiery yet chatty style. It is unlikely that there is another Communist ruler in the world nowadays who delights in dissecting classical oratory, or is capable of it.

There have also been "secret" Castro speeches, unknown in number, delivered before Communist party or armed-forces leadership groups, and unpublished *charlas* (chats) at meetings of, say, the Cuban Women's Federation or the Committees for the Defense of the Revolution. Additionally, all the top revolutionary leaders—Castroites and "old" and "new" Communists alike—engage in a permanent flood of oratory to keep rallying the nation behind Fidel, to demand new efforts, and confess past errors. It is like living in an echo chamber, and inevitably words lose meaning and coherence.

But it is untrue that nowadays Castro's speeches turn the Cubans off. First, there still is a sense of fascination with him and his oratory; second, nobody in a society as tightly and rigidly organized ideologically as Cuba—it is more so than Eastern European Communist countries—can afford *not* to know what the President of the Republic is saying. Ideological indoctrination (*Fidelismo*, Cuban history, and Marxism-Leninism skillfully blended together by Castro) is so important that soldiers, workers or students must study his speeches as promptly as possible after delivery, and be able to explain, preferably in his words and slogans, the views he holds on domestic and foreign problems. (pp. 39–41)

In real life . . . , Castro insists on being posted on just about everything, and consequently even relatively minor decisions may be delayed or postponed until the Commander in Chief can catch up with the problems in the midst of his other interests and commitments. His frequent speeches confirm that he is abreast of all aspects of every problem in Cuba: He touches upon all of them as he preaches the virtues of hard work and the tremendous need to save resources. The printing of the Communist party's official daily newspaper, *Granma,* the voice of the regime, may be held up until dawn hours while Castro personally edits a lengthy policy speech he had delivered extemporaneously the previous day, or a major policy editorial (he writes some of the page-one unsigned editorials, his style being unmistakable for its color and subtle invective).

Fidel Castro's style of government is based on what he calls dialogue or rapport with the population. In practice, it means oratorical hard sell of new policies or an insistence on the fulfillment of old ones. This is usually done through televised speeches delivered before large audiences that applaud Castro and reply affirmatively when he asks whether they approve of what he proposes. (In this fashion, Cubans since 1959 have "approved" executions of Batista-regime torturers, the military presence in Angola, multifarious social and economic sacrifices, and even the transfer of the port town of Moa from Holguín province to Guantánamo province in eastern Cuba.)

Crowds have never said no to Castro, and this technique of popular "consultation" was refined by Fidel at the outset of his rule. He says it is "direct democracy," preferable to old-fashioned elections, and it remains his most powerful political weapon in any crisis—the recourse to the masses. Chants of "Fidel, Fidel!" punctuate the mass rallies as he whips the audiences into a frenzy of enthusiasm.

Mass-circulation newspapers and magazines—as well as specially printed booklets of interviews granted by Castro to foreign radio and television networks and publications—are another facet of government-by-verbiage. After *Playboy* printed a long, boring Castro interview in August 1985, an expanded text in Spanish was published as a special pullout section in *Granma,* but it carefully avoided any reference to *Playboy* as the magazine in which it had appeared. Instead, *Granma,* provided only the names of the two American interviewers. Fidel Castro is still prudish, at least concerning his image at home, and image is what counts the most. (pp. 65–6)

Tad Szulc, in his *Fidel: A Critical Portrait,* William Morrow and Company, Inc., 1986, 703 p.

ALAN RIDING
(review date 1987)

[Here, Riding offers a favorable assesment of *Fidel and Religion,* Castro's first interview on the subject since the 1959 Cuban Revolution, finding that the dictator has adopted a conciliatory attitude toward faith and the Roman Catholic Church—an institution that has undergone, in Castro's opinion, a "political conversion."]

When Fidel Castro and the July 26 Movement seized power in Cuba in 1959, it proved relatively easy to install *La Revolución,* with its wealth of dogma, martyrs and missionaries, as the country's new religion. "Most of the active Catholics were well-to-do, supported the counterrevolution and left the country," Mr. Castro recalls in *Fidel and Religion,* his first interview on the subject. Further, since the Roman Catholic Church had lost touch with poor workers, farmers and peasants; it controlled no "masses" who could re-enact, say, the Cristero uprising against socialism in Mexico in the 1920's. Thus weakened and isolated, the church rapidly faded into insignificance. Mr. Castro himself, reared by a devoutly Catholic mother and educated by strict Jesuit fathers, had long since renounced any religious faith. "Those who believed in God" were also excluded from the new revolutionary party, though "as potential counterrevolutionaries, not Catholics." As the regime consolidated its power, the church was not among its problems.

Yet the Cuban Revolution helped set in motion a process that, 25 years later, would lead Mr. Castro to view Catholicism in Latin America in a new light. Just as the United Stated moved to shield the region's poor from Havana's revolutionary message by launching the Alliance for Progress, events in Cuba alerted influential Catholics to the fact that the church's traditional association with ruling cliques had cut it off from most of the faithful. Empty churches, a falling number of new vocations and the dramatic growth of Protestant fundamentalist sects were simply symptoms of a deeper crisis in an institution that for more than 400 years had taken its power for granted. If Catholicism were to survive in a changing political climate, it had to learn to compete.

Over the last two decades, then, an important part of the Roman Catholic Church in Latin America has undergone a kind of political conversion. A highly active minority now adheres to what is known generically as "liberation theology," while even the Catholic mainstream accepts the church's new "option for the poor." Today, thousands of bishops, priests and nuns across the continent dedicate—and in many cases sacrifice—their lives to opposing rightist dictatorships, defending human rights, organizing trade unions and fighting for land reform. And, in the process, they have rescued the church's traditional role as a major social and political force. In many countries, in fact, the church is now considered the new "enemy" of conservative establishments, viewed more as a partner than a competitor of the left.

Stuck with its historical image of a reactionary church, however, the Latin American left was slow to recognize this change. In the 1960's and early 1970's, a host of Cuban-style guerrilla movements appeared, but religion had not been included in Mr. Castro's revolutionary formula. In fact, not until the late 1970's did it become apparent that sectors of the church, with Jesuits prominent among them, were playing a central role in the growing movement for social change in El Salvador, Guatemala and Nicaragua. Where they still educated the children of the rich, for example, priests began teaching them to challenge the inequities of their societies. Still more important, as repression fed support for guerrilla movements, priests often served as a bridge between upper- and middle-class revolutionary "vanguards" and the instinctively anti-Communist "masses" whom the revolutionaries had such difficulty in reaching.

But it apparently took the triumph of the 1979 Nicaraguan revolution to prompt Mr. Castro to revise his views of the Latin American church. Not only had Nicaragua's bishops publicly justified a popular uprising against the Somoza regime's tyranny just days before the rebels launched their final offensive, but many priests and nuns worked alongside Sandinista activists in mobilizing workers and peasants to participate. After the revolution, the church—along with Nicaraguan society—divided, with Miguel Cardinal Obando y Bravo of Managua eventually emerging as a powerful opposition voice. But, risking the wrath of the Vatican, three priests became and remained Sandinista ministers, while other clergy promoted a new Peoples Church that had liberation theology as its creed. Further, despite their subsequent clashes with Cardinal Obando, the Sandinista leadership never failed to emphasize that the revolution embraced Christianity.

Mr. Castro, then, drew several lessons from the Nicaraguan experience. He recognized that—unlike in Cuba, where the number of active Catholics was relatively small—religion was so ingrained in the popular culture of Nicaragua and many other Latin American countries that atheist revolutions were not feasible. At the same time he concluded that while liberation theology was "one of the most important events of our time," its importance lay not in its religious message but "in its profound impact on the political views of its followers." It had therefore become possible—indeed recommendable—for revolutionaries to forge strategic alliances with activist sectors of the church in order to achieve common moral and political objectives.

Fidel and Religion, the transcript of 23 hours of interviews in May 1985 between Mr. Castro and Frei Betto, a Brazilian Dominican friar and advocate of liberation theology, is the ultimate proof that the subject now merits his attention. In realilty, the subject doesn't get his full attention here: Mr. Castro, known for his prolific opinions on every imaginable subject, devotes more than half the interview to reminiscences about his childhood, youth and days as a guerrilla leader and to answering journalistic questions about whether Cuba is a democracy or "exports" revolution. Nonetheless, it is a fascinating document, which, since it was first published in Spanish and Portuguese, has become a massive best seller throughout Latin America. Its publication in English will be welcomed by anyone interested in Fidel Castro, Cuba, Latin America, the Roman Catholic Church or revolution. It is well translated by the Cuban Center for Translation and Interpretation.

The fact that the interview was given to a priest, especially one who spent four years in jail in Brazil for his political activism, can be no coincidence. Mr. Castro was talking to an admirer. He could also count on sympathy when he noted that the church's historical position "on the side of the conquerors, oppressors and exploiters" explained why "the revolutionary ideas that emerged in the struggle against those age-old injustices had an antireligious spirit." But perhaps most of all, Mr. Castro wanted endorsement of his claim that the church had changed in order to share his point of view and, in doing so, had recognized the moral and ethical qualities of his revolution.

At one point, he argued that it is not possible to practice "non-belief as a philosophy," yet he described his beliefs in religious terms, such as the "revelation" of his discovery of "the irrefutable truths of Marxist literature." He noted: "I think that religious martyrs were generous selfless men; they were made of the same stuff of which revolutionary heroes are made. Without those qualities, there can be no religious or political heroes." And he added: "I believe that Karl Marx could have subscribed to the Sermon on the Mount." In the end, in fact, the message he seemed most anxious to convey was that he and his revolutionaries are better Christians than most Christians. Not surprisingly, he showed little interest interest in the evangelical aspects of liberation theology.

Alan Riding, "God and Man in Latin America," in *The New York Times Book Review,* June 14, 1987, p. 15.

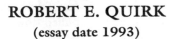

ROBERT E. QUIRK
(essay date 1993)

[An American educator and editor, Quirk has written extensively on Latin American history and politics. In the following excerpt from his recent biography *Fidel Castro,* he assesses the Cuban President's declining status as a world leader.]

Few leaders in the post-World War II era have spoken as often as [Castro], with such colorful language, and at such great length, up to five or six hours in his public speeches and in his private or televised interviews. A clear pattern emerged, from his earliest to his latest pronouncements, a pattern of death and destruction, of obstinacy, of fighting in the "trenches of the world," of a people, he insisted, willing to die rather than capitulate to any enemy. From an early age he had exhibited a fascination with violence and with weapons—the larger the better. Not yet ten, he took aim at his mother's chickens with a shotgun. In primary school he pummeled classmates and hit a priest in the stomach. At an elite Jesuit academy he threatened a fellow student with a pistol. As a university student he joined a "gangster" group that engaged in intramural battles. Fighting in the mountains with his Rebel Army, he prized, most of all, his famous rifle with its telescopic sight. And as Cuba's Maximum Leader he assembled the most modern and powerful army and air force in Latin America. In 1962 he allowed the Soviets to install strategic missiles on Cuban soil that threatened the security of the United States. His favorite title was commander in chief. And in 1993, after more than thirty years in power, he was still speaking of trenches and of the bitter struggles that would endure far into the twenty-first century. He alone, in Cuba, wore the fatigues and the combat boots of the guerrilla leader. He adopted a new phrase for his public speeches—"Socialism or Death!" Whatever the pressures from outside, he would not change. (p. x)

. . . . .

An election year in the United States [1992] was no time to talk about improving relations with Castro's Cuba. When an Army War College report recommended a normalization of relations between the two countries, a spokesman for the Bush administration countered: "Don't even waste your time on a new policy for Cuba. It's a non-issue." With the country in a prolonged recession, the chief campaign issues were domestic—the state of the economy, the character of the candidates. Still, Florida could be important in a close election, and both major candidates took opportunities to identify themselves with the hard-liners in Miami's exile community.

George Bush told a meeting of Cuban-Americans that he planned to be the first American president to walk the streets of a free Cuba. And the Democratic challenger, Governor William Jefferson Clinton of Arkansas, who wanted to be called "Bill", charged that the Republican administration, for more than three years, he said, had missed opportunities to "put the hammer down" on Fidel Castro and his communist regime. Ten days before the election, with the Republicans trailing badly in the polls, Bush went to Miami to sign into law legislation that tightened the economic embargo. Clinton protested that his opponent was grandstanding. The Democrats had backed the measure from the start, he said, while the president had initially opposed it. He did not reveal that he too had talked with members of the Cuban American National Foundation, who had made a handsome contribution to the Democratic campaign. They were glad to play the game on both sides of a busy street. Still, the Democrats lost the state.

There seemed to be no end to the crises in Cuba. Lights were going out in the cities. More factories closed. Others operated only during the day. Bus routes were cut. The country was running out of gasoline, of paper, of new clothing, of vital foodstuffs. Children over seven were no longer guaranteed milk. Black markets flourished, and everyone tried to get illegal dollars. A woman in Havana told Jo Thomas, a correspondent for the *New York Times,* that her family had had no meat for over a month. Another woman remarked bitterly that "it might have been different with Ochoa." And a civil engineer, who had always supported the revolution, asked: "How is it possible that today we have nothing?" Cuba was "Jonesville", said a young poet. In October 1992 the Russian government announced that the long-promised aid to complete a nuclear power plant for Cuba would not be forthcoming. The Castro government had no hard currency to pay for the equipment. At the same time the American Chevron Corporation agreed to spend up to ten billion dollars to develop oil fields in Kazakhstan. The former Soviet republics preferred to sell their petroleum in the West. Castro responded by removing his son, Félix Fidel, from his post as head of the Atomic Energy Commission. He was not the first—or the last—high official to go. Julio A. García Oliveras, head of the Chamber of Commerce, and Carlos Aldana, the party's ideology chief, were both summarily sacked. Castro was relying more and more on the old guard, the apparatchiks, who were not insisting on changes. Spectacular escapes, by air and by sea, indicated a breakdown in the country's security system. Antigovernment graffiti appeared in public places. At the end of February 1993 Castro hinted to Diane Sawyer of ABC News that he "might" step down in five years—if the economy improved and the United States ended its economic " blockade". He was tired he said. But this was the "other" Castro, who conversed reasonably and agreeably with women reporters. He refused to make any promises or to mention any possible successors. Two weeks later he was "elected" to a new five-year term as president of the Council of State. Work harder and remain patient, he advised the people. Time is on our side.

Afflictions multiplied. The March 1993 storms that ravaged the East Coast of the United States produced extensive losses in Cuba as well—as much as a billion dollars in destroyed crops and buildings. Already the economy had declined in the 1990s an estimated 40 percent. At the same time a mysterious disease appeared that threatened blindness for tens of thousands across the island. Some complained of motor disorders also and of sharp pains in their legs and arms. Medical doctors in the capital speculated that perhaps the "neuropathic epidemic" had been caused by vitamin deficiencies. Government officials recommended that farmers raise more sweet potatoes, and they appealed to the World Health Organization for assistance. Radio Havana, in daily broadcasts, called for international protests against the American "blockade", while *La Tribuna de la Habana* charged that the United States was the "principal ally of the epidemic and its consequences."

"Socialism or death!" Fidel Castro no longer spoke of the Marxist paradise on earth. In the last decade of the twentieth century the future was a blur. He lived with monuments to dead dreams and "dead angels", to irrelevant heroes—Ernesto ("Che") Guevara, Camilo Cienfuegos, José Martí, Vladimir Lenin. Like the North Koreans, he could even find reasons to invoke the name of Joseph Stalin. Elsewhere in the Western world the old communist rituals had lost their meaning. Yet Cuba continued to celebrate the anniversary of the Russian Bolshevik revolution, and thousands of workers marched on May Day. No one in Havana pulled down statues. Outmoded slogans remained in the streets. Castro had become a caricature of his earlier self. The bulging army fatigues. The querulous voice. The sui generis mannerisms, long cultivated—his scowls, his pursed lips, the twisting of his face, as he squinted at something he was reading, the impatient jerking of his hands. Gestures and words that had once brought shouts of approval and of "To the wall!" from a half million Cubans in the Plaza of the Revolution now seemed merely silly for one who had aspired to international leadership. Fidel Castro too had become irrelevant. He had stayed too long. At the Moncada trial he had prophesied that history would vindicate him. Forty years later, history had passed him by. As his people desperately contemplated disaster, he waited stubbornly for the miracle that would save him, searched for just one more panacea. By all appearances the Maximum Leader would see Cuba destroyed, before he gave up his power and his prerogatives. (pp. 838–40)

Robert E. Quirk, in his *Fidel Castro,* W. W. Norton & Company, 1993, 898 p.

SOURCES FOR FURTHER STUDY

Bender, Lynn Darrell. *The Politics of Hostility: Castro's Revolution and United States Policy.* Hato Rey, Puerto Rico: Inter American University Press, 1975, 156 p.

    Examines the volatile relationship between Cuba, the Soviet Union, and the United States, from the Cuban Revolution to the mid-1970s.

Draper, Theodore. *Castroism: Theory and Practice.* New York: Frederick A. Praeger, 1965, 263 p.

    Discusses Castro's political ideology and its relation to the Communist movement, drawing attention to his changing economic policies and their practical results. As the critic states, this book "attempts to define a living political phenomenon which by its nature does not yet lend itself to easy definition."

Halperin, Maurice. *The Rise and Decline of Fidel Castro: An Essay in Contemporary History.* Berkeley: University of California Press 1972, 380 p.

    Details the successes and failures of Castro's Communist regime.

———. *The Taming of Fidel Castro.* Berkeley: University of California Press, 1981, 345 p.

    Continues the author's 1972 work.

Karol, K. S. *Guerrillas in Power.* Translated by Arnold Pomerans. New York: Hill & Wang, 1970, 624 p.

    Historical analysis of the events surrounding the "26th of July Movement" and the Cuban Revolution.

Landau, Saul. "After Castro." *Mother Jones* 14, No. 6 (July/August 1989): 20–6, 46, 48–9.

    Chronicles the changes in Castro's economic, social and political policy from 1960 to 1989, particularly focusing on the dictator's effort "to convert Cuba from a colonized playground into a proud nation."

Mankiewicz, Frank. *With Fidel: A Portrait of Castro and Cuba.* Chicago: Playboy Press, 1975, 269 p.

    Contains interviews conducted with Castro in July and October 1974.

Martin, Lionel. *The Early Fidel: Roots of Castro's Communism.* Seacaucus, N.J.: L. Stuart, 1978, 272 p.

    Elucidates Castro's early years and their influence on his political perspectives.

Oppenheimer, Andres. *Castro's Final Hour: The Secret Story Behind the Coming Downfall of Communist Cuba.* New York:

Simon & Schuster, 1992, 461 p.
    Discusses Cuba's economic and social decline since
    the fall of Soviet Communism in 1991.

Smith, Wayne S. *The Closest of Enemies: A Personal and
Diplomatic Record of U.S.-Cuban Relations since 1957*. New
York: W.W. Norton, 1987, 308 p.
    Documents the tumultuous relationship between Cuba
    and the United States over the course of three decades.

Suchlicki, Jaime, ed. *Cuba, Castro, and Revolution*. Coral
Gables, Fla.: University of Miami Press, 1972, 250 p.
    Analyzes the Cuban Revolution's impact on the coun-
    try's politics, social conditions, and foreign relations.

Additional coverage of Castro's life and career is contained in the following sources published by
Gale Research: *Contemporary Authors*, Vols. 110 and 129; and *Newsmakers: The People Behind Today's
Headlines*, 1991 Cumulation.

Camilo José Cela

1916–

Spanish novelist, short story writer, travel and nonfiction writer.

INTRODUCTION

*C*onsidered a pivotal figure in twentieth-century Spanish literature, Cela is best known for his stylistically diverse works of fiction that convey the political, social, and psychological legacy of the Spanish Civil War. His early novels, *La familia de Pascual Duarte* (1942; *The Family of Pascual Duarte*) and *La colmena* (1953; *The Hive*), secured his reputation as a compassionate yet severe analyst of a Spanish underclass debased by social injustice and personal deficiencies. Cela is also credited with broadening the range of Spanish literary language through his meticulous reproduction of working-class speech and his continuous experimentation with revolutionary modes of expression.

Cela was born in northwest Spain, the son of Spanish geography teacher and a Spanish-born Englishwoman. He studied philosophy, medicine, and law—without taking a degree—from 1933 to 1936 and from 1939 to 1943. At the outbreak of the Spanish Civil War in 1936, Cela fought in the ranks of the right-wing Falangist party and was wounded in battle. He later became an anti-Fascist and moved to Mallorca where he ran *Papeles de Son Armadans*, a literary magazine which featured young anti-Franco writers. Having been employed as a bullfighter, painter, actor, and civil servant, Cela earned critical acclaim as a writer at the age of twenty–six with his first novel, *The Family of Pascual Duarte*. Although his early novels met with strong opposition from Spanish censors, Cela became a member of the Academy of the Spanish Language in 1957. In 1977 King Juan Carlos appointed him to a seat in the Spanish parliament and in the following year the writer helped to draft Spain's new constitution. In 1989 Cela was awarded the Nobel Prize in Literature.

In *The Family of Pascual Duarte* the title character composes his memoirs while awaiting execution for murder. A victim as well as a criminal, Pascual describes his squalid upbringing by an abusive, bitter mother whose other children turned to prostitution or proved mentally incompetent. Pascual also recounts his descent into violence, beginning with the killing of animals and culminating in the murder of his mother. At the novel's end, faced with the death penalty for yet another homicide, Pascual refuses to blame society for his downfall and instead attributes his actions to fate and his own innate sinfulness. Cela's grotesque portrayal of what he viewed as the vulgar, repulsive aspects of Spanish society initiated a literary trend in Spain later termed *tremendismo*. Often compared to the existentialism of Albert Camus and Jean-Paul Sartre, *tremendismo* graphically depicts the perversion of morality by oppressive social forces. Cela, however, eschewed this mode of expression in his following novel, *Pabellón de reposo* (1943; *Rest Home*), which examines the private anguish of tuberculosis patients confined to a sanatorium, and in *Nuevas andanzas y desventuras de Lazarillo de Tormes* (1944), a modernized version of the sixteenth-century picaresque narrative *Lazarillo de Tormes*. While these novels did not garner the widespread critical attention of *The Family of Pascual Duarte*, both are regarded as perceptive explorations of contemporary Spanish society. Cela's subsequent novel, *The Hive*, is generally considered his greatest work. Set in working-class Madrid immediately following World War II, *The Hive* chronicles three days in the lives of approximately three hundred people who frequent a seedy cafe. Devoid of traditional plot structure or character development, the novel intricately combines the experiences of maids, beggars, bakers, prostitutes, and poets to achieve a panoramic yet intimate portrait of a society reduced to avarice and vice through poverty and oppression.

While Cela's later novels have not achieved the international renown of the *The Family of Pascual Duarte* and *The Hive*, several are recognized as inventive explorations of the novel form. *Mrs. Caldwell habla con su hijo* (1953; *Mrs. Caldwell Speaks to Her Son*) contains over two hundred short, unrelated chapters constructed around the rambling letters of an elderly Englishwoman to her dead son that reveal her incestuous love for him. In *Historias de Venezuela: La catira* (1955), an ironic reevaluation of the romantic novel, Cela nar-

rates the adventures of an independent woman on the Venezuelan frontier. In *San Camilo, 1936: Vísperas, festividad y octava de San Camilo del año 1936 en Madrid* (1969), Cela employs a stream-of-consciousness narrative style through the perspective of a young student to examine the events leading up to the Spanish Civil War. Amongst his nonfiction works, Cela is well known for his travel sketches that recount his *vagabundajes*, or "vagabond journeys," through the Iberian Peninsula. His first such work, *Viaje a la Alcarria* (1948; *Journey to the Alcarria*), garnered critical accolades for its atypical approach to the travel genre. Cela's other well regarded travel writings include *Judíos, moros y cristianos* (1956), which examines the diverse cultures of southern Spain, and *Viaje al Pirineo de Lérida* (1965), a description of the mountainous Pyrenees region at the Spanish-French border. Cela gained further notice for his works by combining his own commentary with photographs or drawings by other artists; the best known of these is *Gavilla de fábulas sin amor* (1962), a collaborative effort with Pablo Picasso, and *Izas, rabizas y colipoterras* (1964) which depicts the life of Barcelona prostitutes. Cela also published dictionaries of vulgar sexual terms, including *Diccionario secreto* (1968–70), and *Enciclopedia de erotismo* (1977), that oppose the moralistic concerns of traditional Spanish society.

Cela's innovative writings have been viewed by critics as both a synthesis of Spain's experience in the twentieth century and as an artistic watershed which flouted the reactionary conformity advocated by the Francisco Franco regime. Regarded as the founding father of *tremendismo* and the *vagabundaje* genres, Cela has had an enormous impact on the younger generation of Spanish writers. Indeed, *The Family of Pascual Duarte* has been called the most widely read Spanish novel since Miguel de Cervantes's *Don Quixote* (1605). Although several critics who considered Cela's later work derivative of his earlier fiction objected to the choice of Cela for the Nobel Prize, most commentators concur with the Nobel Committee, which stated: "Cela has revitalized the language as few people have done in these times. He has joined the ranks of such masters of the Spanish language as Cervantes, Góngora, Quevedo, Valle-Inclán, and García Lorca."

CRITICAL COMMENTARY

SAUL BELLOW

(essay date 1953)

[Recipient of the Nobel Prize in Literature in 1976, Bellow is one of the most prominent figures in contemporary American fiction. Among his most celebrated novels are *The Adventures of Augie March* (1953), *Herzog* (1964), and *Humboldt's Gift* (1975). Bellow is noted as an artist who upholds the moral values of humanism and the literary conventions of Realism, thus opposing the trend toward a modern literature that is nihilistic by temperament and experimental by conscious design. In the following excerpt, Bellow favorably reviews Cela's *The Hive*.]

Camilo José Cela, the only considerable novelist to appear in Spain since the end of the civil war, fought in Franco's Army and was a member of the Falange party, and yet the censorship system forced the withdrawal of his first novel, published in 1942. That book, *Pascual Duarte's Family*, is the story of a murderer told by himself, and its characters are for the most part as barren as the district they come from, semi-starved and violent. After its Argentinian success *Pascual Duarte's Family* was allowed to reappear in Barcelona. Its fourth edition contained a preface by Cela in which he thanked his enemies "* * * who have given me so much help in my career." "If a place smells," he added, "the best way to attract attention is not to have the same smell only more so, but to change the smell." *The Hive* has not been published in Spain.

It is not to be wondered that the Franco censorship disapproves of Cela's novels. Life in Madrid as he portrays it is brutal, hungry and senseless. Hypocrisy, fear and oppression are in command. Cela's political loyalties may be conservative or reactionary but his literary affiliations are of the most radical; they are with Camus and Sartre, with Moravia, with Zola and French naturalism. Only Cela has very little of the theoretician about him and has no existential, sexual or political message to deliver. It is in his directness and lack of squeamishness that he resembles Sartre and Moravia.

Cela writes: "My novel *La Colmena* [*The Hive*], the first book of the series 'Uncertain Roads,' is nothing but a pale reflection, a humble shadow of the harsh, intimate painful reality of every day. They lie who want to disguise life with the crazy mask of literature. The evil that corrodes the souls, the evil that has as many names as we

choose to give it, cannot be fought with the poultices of conformism or the plasters of rhetorics and poetics."

In practice, Cela does not ramble so much as he jumps. Now we are with the powerful Dona Rosa, who tyrannizes over her waiters and customers; now with a cafe musician; now with a mediocre nonconformist poet; then with a tender-hearted money lender; then with the bookkeeper of a black-marketeer; with old maids and prostitutes, with singers and seducers. An old woman is murdered. A man finds his wife's lover hiding in the laundry hamper. A father meets his daughter on the stairs of a house of assignation. The wife of a dying man is already planning to marry her first lover and to make him rich. All of this is rather abruptly and sketchily represented, it is forceful and it is bald.

One sympathizes with Cela in his impatience with literature. Probably he is attacking his conformist contemporaries within Spain. But there is a great deal to be said for his attitude. Literature is conservative; it is "behind the times," and it does not easily cope with certain familiar modern horrors. One asks one's self how Goethe would have described a concentration camp, or how Lope de Vega would have dignified a black-marketeer. Journalists and writers of memories rather than imaginative writers have told us most of what we know of these and other phenomena of contemporary life. Apparently, however, these reporters do not satisfy the highest demands of the imagination. Attacking literature and writing novels, the talented Señor Cela puts himself into a rather paradoxical position.

Saul Bellow, "The Evil That Has Many Names," in *The New York Times Book Review*, September 27, 1953, p. 5.

PAUL ILIE

(essay date 1964)

[In the following excerpt, Ilie discusses Cela's literary career, paying particular attention to his travel sketchbook *Journey to the Alcarria*.]

In one of Camilo José Cela's autobiographical moments he wrote of himself:

Principal Works

La familia de Pascual Duarte (novel) 1942
[*The Family of Pascual Duarte*, 1964]

Pabellón de reposo (novel) 1943
[*Rest Home*, 1961]

Nuevas andanzas y desventuras de Lazarillo de Tormes (novel) 1944

Esas nubes que pasan (short stories) 1945

Viaje a la Alcarria (travel essay) 1948
[*Journey to the Alcarria*, 1964]

La colmena (novel) 1951
[*The Hive*, 1953]

Mrs. Caldwell habla con su hijo (novel) 1953
[*Mrs. Caldwell Speaks to Her Son*, 1968]

Historias de Venezuela: La catira (novel) 1955

Judíos, moros y cristianos (travel essay) 1956

*La cucaña: memorias (memoirs) 1959

Gavilla de fábulas sin amor (nonfiction) 1962

Izas, rabizas y colipoterras (travel essay) 1964

Viaje al Pirineo de Lérida (travel essay) 1965

Diccionario secreto. 2 vols. (nonfiction) 1968–70

San Camilo, 1936: Vísperas, festividad y octava de San Camilo del año 1936 en Madrid (novel) 1969

Oficio de tinieblas 5; o, novel de tesis escrita para ser cantada por un coro de enfermos (novel) 1973

Enciclopedia de erotismo (nonfiction) 1977

Cristo versus Arizona (novel) 1988

**A portion of this work was reprinted as *La rosa* in 1979.

An excerpt from *La rosa*:

To be tied to several geographies does not seem to me, at least for a writer, at all inconvenient. Some bloods or lineages file down the harshness of others, and the mixture of all of them allows things to be seen with a certain serenity, with the necessary coolness and sufficient perspective.

I, who feel very truly and deeply Spanish, believe that I see and know and love Spain with more common sense than the majority of my Spanish friends. Perhaps this reality is supported by the fact that the mixture of blood is simplicity itself compared to what is foreign, because what is foreign feels familiar and close, quotidian and common, usual and domestic. I do not know. In any case, I am satisfied not being pure-blooded. I do not think there are any purebreds left in the world except for the Bantus, the Zulus, and the pure Aryans, who if they were not, would manage to believe they were.

Camilo José Cela, *La rosa*, excerpted and translated in *Contemporary Authors Autobiography Series*, Vol. 10.

I was born in Iria-Flavia, a tiny village in the province of La Coruña [Galicia], on May 11, 1916, of a Spanish father, an English mother, and an Italian grandmother. I've done nothing of any use in my life, or at least nothing that would be recognized as such, and I've traveled more or less to the same places that every other Spaniard has. Writing is the only activity that distracts me and makes me forget the very unfunny drama of every-day existence.

This capsule confession reveals many things about Cela's ironic, offhand manner, his dry, detached style, and his attitudes towards literature, his country, and the meaning of life in the post-war era. All of these issues are pertinent to the aims of Cela's work in general. . . . Above all, their treatment in [*Journey to the Alcarria*] is a major statement about the nature of both contemporary Spanish life and the condition of all men in the modern World.

Cela belongs to the generation of Spaniards whose first significant cultural experience was the Civil War. As a historical event, the war sharpened and darkened the intellectual perspective of this generation of 1936, whose outlook was to grow skeptical, bitter, and confused. And as a trauma of the collective psyche, the war dulled the nation's nerve centers, along with the individual fibers that were their human constituents. The result in literature was an emotional listlessness that clung wearily to an equally drab traditionalism. . . . This, of course, is understandable, for the tenor of the age has been one of caution and isolation. The political scene required silence, harmony was society's watchword, and withdrawn recuperation was by necessity, not choice, the highest national value. More important than immediate entry into the European literary community was the re-establishment of Spain's cultural identity, and the healing of deep spiritual wounds.

Out of the moral numbness of the war's aftermath came the bold, disruptive voice of Cela to jolt Spain from her much-desired tranquillity. He wrote with precision, authority, and ruthlessness. His cold objectivity toward pain spoke volumes. And yet his acrid tone permitted a faint touch of tenderness. In all of this, Cela was not only the unrelenting goad of his country's tired body, but the conscience of its divided soul, and he described without self-pity or remorse the physical and moral condition of his fellow men. He burst forth upon the intellectual scene in 1942 with his shocking first novel, *The Family of Pascual Duarte*, which described the passions and crimes of an inarticulate and otherwise naïve man. This tale of violence and primitivism, so clearly a symbolic product of the brutality underlying Spain's fratricidal history, gave Cela instantaneous title to the literary leadership of his generation. He still holds this position, not because, as he once said cynically, the competition was so easy, but because of his audacious originality and his superb prose style. He is today, after twenty-five years and as many books, Spain's foremost writer. . . . (pp. vii–viii)

Cela's work falls into two categories, fiction and travel sketches, Both groups are characterized by the same sophistication, technical brilliance, and overt or subtle stylization. The novels are unique, revealing little continuity among them of either theme or form, and showing even less artistic progress or emergence of an individual technique. On the contrary, they are all distinct from each other and full-grown, with no two alike in anything except their excellence. Cela has tried, as none of his contemporaries have, to experiment with a different novelistic theory in each successive narrative. As a result he achieved a disturbing esthetic of violence in *The Family of Pascual Duarte*, a state of pure contemplation in *Rest Home*, and a structural fragmentation in *The Hive*. Other novels indicate still other forms: surrealism, linguistic innovation, the picaresque, but in all of them it is the formal problem which eventually expresses the author's intellectual position. That is, instead of providing an ideological content for the subject matter of the novel itself, Cela allows certain inferences to be drawn from the structural form and technique. Thus, the removal of all action in *Rest Home*, and the conversion of its chapter sequences into a tableau of interior monologues, suggest that solitude is the basic form of existence, and that social and historical man has lost his significance in a world of incommunicability. Similarly, the treatment of gratuitous violence and primitive mentality in *The Family of Pascual Duarte* indicates the incapacity of modern man to make others understand his sense of impotence and absurdity.

The Hive is one of the best Spanish novels of the century, and probably the most spectacular. Banned in Spain because of its devastating social critique, it gained unanimous acclaim in the Hispanic world for its technical accomplishment, verbal perfection, and richly drawn characterization. It is similar in construction to Dos Passos' *Manhattan Transfer*, and traces the "uncertain paths" of a number of lives that criss-cross or touch each other tangentially within a three-day period which is cut up, as a film strip might be, and restructured without regard to chronological time. Thus the disintegration of temporal order parallels the purposeless drift of the characters. The real protagonist of the novel, however, is the city of Madrid, dirty, vice-ridden, and throbbing with vitality. Her inhabitants, living in the impoverished misery and moral bankruptcy that followed the war, reveal nevertheless the vital impulses and frailties that are universally recognized as the common human denominator. Thus the novel's pathos consists first of the visible waste of men's lives desensitized by poverty and spiritual anguish, and second, of the silent and desperate hopelessness found in the characters' action and even inaction. As a pitiless incision into the tissue of Madrid society, *The Hive*'s realism

is immediate and graphic. Its language is racy, poetic, and incredibly faithful to colloquial speech, while its personages are memorably individualistic even as they are typical of middle and lower-class life.

I have dwelt this long on the first category of Cela's literary work because if *The Hive* is the crowning point of his novels, the *Journey to the Alcarria* is its jeweled counterpart among the travel sketches. In both works the sociological relevance is the same, the linguistic fidelity equally dazzling, and the philosophical undertones similar, but of different intensity. The *Journey to the Alcarria*. . . is probably the best of Cela's *vagabundajes*. It is also the first of a number of excursions into various regions of the peninsula which, as real acts in the author's life, become a symbolic expression of an intellectual position. As a literary form it has the dual purpose of gaining a direct and intuitive understanding of the nature of the Spanish personality, and of presenting a cultural anatomy of the nation's most fundamental social stratum: its provincial life. (pp. viii–x)

The *vagabundaje*, which is Cela's term for a book of travels named after its central figure, is actually a picaresque narrative made subjective and lyrical by the vagabond's consciousness of the landscape. Whether Cela journeys to the Alcarria, Andalusia, or Galicia, the technique is the same. The autobiographical form of the picaresque becomes a fictionalized biography in the third person; the peripatetic compulsiveness of the wanderer continues; and the constant preoccupation with food and lodging claims first attention. But in the process a great change occurs. The structure of life is reduced to its basic simplicity. People are met and engaged freely, with purity of intention. And a certain direct knowledge of individuals and their customs is acquired. Hence the value of the journey with respect to glimpsing the essence of human experience, while also providing an insight into the life sources of Spanish civilization.

Cela sets out to accomplish so much, and finally does, that it is almost as if he has a theory of the travel sketchbook. He himself is the vagabond, an urban resident, an intellectual, and a Spaniard in search of self-identity. In the wake of a disastrous civil war, the problem of who the Spaniard is and what his national values stand for has become a critical and urgent concern. There have been many images of Spain, all accurate in part, yet none satisfactorily illuminating her complete face. But in the contemporary period it is impossible to deduce anything from life in the great cities, which are in the midst of social upheaval due to population shifts and economic changes. The writer must go to the rural areas, where there is not only stability but a carefully preserved character as old as tradition itself. (pp. xi–xii)

The result of this quest for Spain's identity is a kind of rough literary vignette which Cela has called a bittersweet etching. It either describes with irony and stylized exaggeration an interesting person encountered during a trip, or else consists of an invented composite of a few real or probable "types." In many cases these people are Castilians, traditionally considered both the political unifiers of the land and the group that most firmly impressed its personality upon the national climate. Cela's main object is to capture the human drama, but in the process of travel other advantages also accrue. His conversation turn up bits of local history and folklore, and his descriptions subtly introduce sociological details worthy of more formal studies. In addition, we see the contrast between the external and transitory history of society and what Unamuno called the intrahistorical life of the people, the profound and unchanging emotional experience of humanity that triumphs over all events.

But in addition to this cultural purpose, Cela has a private one that is open to interpretation. His rejection of metropolitan life for a more simple form suggests a dissatisfaction with the growing artificiality and complexity of technological civilization. The cities are corrupt, spontaneity is replaced by more self-conscious styles of living, and the loss of contact with nature is no less tragic than the increasingly impersonal forms of communication among men. Modern man has in fact become isolated, and this solitude is represented in the figure of the vagabond, who escapes from the empty routines of the city, but who is condemned to a rootless existence, moving from town to town. Furthermore, his vagabond rôle is a kind of activist anti-intellectualism. Sensing his position as an outsider in society, the intellectual attributes his alienation to an oversensitive awareness of himself in relation to the values of the group. He reacts against this contemplative state by engaging physically in the most tiring of activities: rugged travel. He enshrines country simplicity not only because it is innocent of the fruitless rituals of the mind, but because its own actions are so fatiguing that they consume all of the traveler's energies, allowing him to forget his loneliness. These physical acts, of course, are themselves converted into ritual by the vagabond Cela, who, after all, is really a writer. But the esteem in which he holds them is significant proof of the judgment he has made. Nevertheless, his renunciation of intellectualist values cannot really convert him into an ingenuous rustic. And so the literary genre of the *vagabundaje* which he has perfected becomes an act of artifice in the face of its own artlessness. (pp. xii–xiii)

[Cela has said of *Journey to the Alcarria*] that it was an orthodox book of travels, conceived according to the old and venerable laws of narration: truth, simplicity, and the gratifying vision of the unforeseen. The fact that he wrote it in the third person does not diminish its biographical origin, but since the narrator is so subordinated to the material that he is recording and reflecting, the question of veracity is unimportant. In Cela's definition of the travel-sketch genre, the itinerant writer must react with genuine and simple surprise to what he sees, and jot it down without inventive alteration. There is no room for the novelesque, the discursive, or even the interpretative. Everything that is not straightforward becomes pedantic in a world whose mental dimension is neither analytical nor imaginative. (pp. xiii–xiv)

But if the travel sketchbook has its own precepts, there are also certain requirements of the traveler himself. He must not have a preformed idea of the direction of his excursion, except, of course, for the general outline. . . . Furthermore, he rids himself of evil thoughts on leaving the city, and encounters other men without ulterior motives. But above all, he accepts the world as it is offered to him good and evil, for "all things are to be found in the vineyard of the Lord."

Nevertheless, Cela's disposition runs strongly to pessimism. If he reaches a strange village in the evening, he prefers to leave its inspection for the next day, in the belief that "the morning light is preferable and more propitious for this matter of wandering through a town." In fact, "it even seems that in the mornings people look more favorably on a stranger," whereas "at night people are tired and the darkness makes them fearful, mistrustful, and guarded." This says much about human psychology, but it is also indicative of the author's own attitude toward social relationships. He is a sentimentalist, but also a melancholic. . . . He suppresses bits of romantic verse that come to mind, his farewells become "laden with unrecognized sorrow," and he resists the "dangerous drowsiness" that overcomes him when he is "entirely too comfortable." Part of his vagabond philosophy consists of a promise not to sleep in the same place two nights in a row, and since "roads are made for walking on. . . it gets to be a bad habit to sit by the roadside talking to people."

It is to our advantage that Cela is so restless, for otherwise his pensiveness might have restricted the wealth of detail that is offered in the book. Yet it is important to recognize that the dozens of motifs about the Alcarria that are found here have been chosen from an infinity of possibilities, motifs determined by Cela's own psychological framework. The reality which emerges, therefore, does exist in fact, but its objectivity is impaired by virtue of being selective. For example, many of Cela's favorite, and sometimes obsessive, themes appear in these pages: the child, the village idiot, the beggar, and other "types" such as the old wanderer and the peddler. In some cases the scenes are presented in cheerful terms, but more frequently the people are described pessimistically as long-suffering individuals who are leading lives of quiet desperation. (pp. xiv–xv)

The affinity between the intellectual outsider and these social pariahs is clear enough, but Cela's presentation of such themes is less apparent. *The Journey to the Alcarria* is deceptively easy to read, and its observations are so casual that incidents can slip by unnoticed because they are always supplanted by fresh detail. The tiny tragedies of each day seem minimal for the sophisticated reader, but they are the only events of importance that occur in the Alcarria. . . . Even more disturbing is Cela's manner of expressing the sorrow of existence. He tells of several young bar girls who "already seem to have in their eyes that special patient sorrow that one sees in hired animals, dragged hither and yon by bad luck and evil intentions." There is one child who looks "as timid as a whipped dog.". . . In these and many other details, the weariness and futility of existence are evoked in a less than human, sometimes primitive, undertone.

Part of Cela's artistry belongs to the Goyesque tradition, not just in that certain deformed types catch his attention, but also in his use of the ugly as an esthetic category. Such descriptions are more than intense realism, for cases like the sheep-shearing scene, or the fly-plagued, bleeding donkey, or the references to garbage are graphic parallels in the concrete physical world to the spiritual despondency of the people. Perhaps in the most significant area of Cela's accomplishment—his style—is this dual effect best realized. His imagery above all, the similes and metaphors which pierce the delicate prose texture, combines sympathy and horror in an uneasy symphony of pathos. In speaking of Madrid, he says that the city's "inhabitants are still asleep and its pulse, like an invalid's beats quietly as if ashamed of being heard." At dawn in the capital "the street doors of the houses are still closed, like stingy purses," whereas at a similar hour the traveler lets his imagination wander freely so that "it flutters like a slow, dying butterfly." (pp. xvi–xvii)

These examples, along with the muted sorrow pervading the book, are engrained in the fabric of the prose and contribute to the general mood of the journey. Nevertheless, the great sweeps of Cela's brush contrast strongly with the dark lines of his detail. His skillful use of innuendo and understatement, which leave much of what is unspoken to the reader's imagination, has a counterpart in the distinct atmosphere of buoyancy that emerges. . . . This is partly because of the lightness of the style, but due also to the sense of space and daylight that is imparted by the setting. Very little occurs at night, and still less within four walls. Cela dispenses with the nocturnal element in the re-creation of typical scenes, land-scapes, or village topography, and stresses amplitude. (p. xvii)

One major aspect of the *vagabundaje* is the landscape itself, and no statement about it can replace a reading of the entire text. There is a poetic purity to be found in the magic naming of the thistles and sprigs, in following the minute movements of insect life, and in tracing the scents and sounds of a countryside trembling with sensation. The beauty of these descriptions is beyond praise, for it is essentially artless, and the scenes, stripped of adornment, leap forward unexpectedly from the tedium of travel and the emptiness of conversation. In such circumstances it is possible for Cela to affirm an absolute happiness, in which "his imagination was flooded with a swarm of golden thoughts" and an inner peace steals over his heart.

Finally, and most far-reaching, are the two contributions made by Cela to contemporary Spanish literature. One is a general feature: the image of Spain that takes form clearly and faithfully, both in its sociological relevance and in its vision of a lost grandeur and a newly found dignity. The Alcarria is still backward compared to Madrid; its values are conservative, its community structure monolithic, and its living standards very low. During his reportorial moments Cela offers many examples to confirm this, and yet they all somehow recede before the more affirmative image of historical Spain. Here too the view is pessimistic, but with the pride of discovering a still visible cultural heritage that is worthy of a modern metamorphosis. (pp. xviii–xix)

This first contribution, however, would not be possible were it not for the greatness of Cela's style. It is his verbal brilliance which has given him much of his fame, and his use of language has indeed invigorated modern Spanish prose. . . . Cela's style is not only so colloquial that it resists translation, its very transparency is contrary to the texture and rhythm of English prose. . . . [To successfully translate his works] is most difficult, for Cela can combine in one expression not only an entire folkway, but a personal lyricism and a sly irony as well. His prose is fluid and deceptively simplistic. It is sometimes tart and frequently wistful. Never does it lack the ingenious juxtaposition of colloquial, non-abstract vocabulary alongside of metaphorical innovation. And yet whether in the humor, snatches of song, slang phrases, or nicknames, the purity and poise of its linguistic dignity is constant. From the land comes Cela's language, and from the people, his book. (p. xix)

Paul Ilie, in an introduction to *Journey to the Alcarria* by Camilo José Cela, translated by Frances M. López-Morillas, The University of Wisconsin Press, 1964, pp. vii–xix.

DAVID WILLIAM FOSTER
(essay date 1990)

[In the following essay, occasioned by Cela's reception of the Nobel Prize in Literature in 1989, Foster provides an overview of Cela's career.]

[It] is difficult to imagine what Spain was like in 1942, when Camilo José Cela published *La familia de Pascual Duarte*. Barely three years after the cessation of one of the bloodiest conflicts of the twentieth century (the Spanish Civil War has often been called the dress rehearsal for World War II), Cela's novel appeared in the midst of some of the bleakest years in Spanish history. On the one hand, daily life was dreadfully difficult, as Spain, with its back to the war being fought in the rest of Europe, experienced both the scarcity occasioned by the interruption of a complex economy by its own civil war and the unavailability of many essential products from its former trading partners, now themselves at war. On the other hand, the triumph of the fascists unleashed one of the worst examples of sociopolitical repression in modern Europe, a mechanism both of revenge and ideological confirmation clearly modeled after what Hitler had exemplified in Germany and in concert with numerous international models of how to bring—or at least how to attempt to bring—order out of the chaos of a multifaceted twentieth-century society. Franco's Spain in the forties was unswervingly committed to dictating a new social order based on the fantasies of reactionary Catholicism, and there was little room for even the slightest manifestations of dissent from this program, which El Caudillo himself touted as divinely inspired and the only way to save Spain from the evils of the modern worlds.

Tyrannies whether from the right or from the left, never seem to learn the lessons of history: cultural expression cannot be effectively silenced, nor is it possible to impose, no matter how Draconian the methods employed, a totalitarian cultural ideology. Culture, by its very nature, embodies an opening toward the contestatorial, the demythificational, the deconstructive, and the disruptional. Even the sincerest attempts to toe the line of ideological uniformity fail in speaking clearly with one voice, and one of the few hopes for humankind in the nightmare of its contemporary history is the fact that culture cannot be other than now a reluctant, now a shameless reflection on the failures of the social contract.

Cela and his publisher, although hardly standing alone among an underground of voices from the pre-Franco cultural legacy (a period of intense brilliance in Spain) and from those both excluded by the system of revenge or simply unable to assimilate to a prescribed cultural voice, were able to prevail against the many formal and informal mechanisms of censorship to bring out *Pascual Duarte* at a time when Spanish readers were hardly disposed to contemplate a rewriting of their social body that went so dramatically against the grain of the official versions of Catholic Spain, the sanctity of the family, the benevolent nature of the social hierarchy, and the acquiesence of individuals in the face of their assigned lot in life. Or at least, the Franco cultural establishment assumed there could not be—ought not to be, was not probably—any space in the new Spanish consciousness of *Pascual Duarte*: the official versions were viewed as so patently self-evident and so persuasively prevalent that such a narrative could only be viewed as fanciful, as so much a distortion of reigning social reality as to be fantastic at best and scurrilously prevaricating at worst.

Such was not to be the case: Cela's novel so effec-tively challenged the fantasies of the mythic never-never land of Franco's image of Spain for export—the bargain-basement Spain that he tried successfully to sell for business investments, military bases, neo-Hollywoodian film-making, and gum-chewing tourism—that it inaugurated the entire tradition of anti-Franco cultural honesty which has affirmed itself with such emphasis in present-day constitutional, socialized Spain. A cultural producer like Pedro Almodóvar may be the international darling of the hour because of his audacious film interpretations of the social myths that still cling like lint to the Spanish social fabric, but it must be understood that it was authors like Cela who made the first strategic moves to defy and to counter a cynical cultural policy that rewrote in overpowering large letters whatever reality Spain was in fact experiencing in those intolerable days fifty years ago.

Pascual Duarte is the story of a young man who is a witness to all the unrelenting brutality of social life and who, in turn, becomes yet one more unreflecting instrument of that brutality. The fact that Pascual narrates his own story is a dramatically ironic index of his essential separation from any awareness of the dynamics of his social existence, while at the same time allowing for some glimmer of an inherent redemptive grace beyond the swagger of his words. An assassin of both his mother and the local patriarch, potent symbols in the mythology of the nuclear and social family, Pascual, as his name suggests, is a sacrificial victim to a system of justice that condemns and punishes the crime but is incapable of reflecting on the sources of the antisocial behavior to which it attests. That the local patriarch, no matter how benevolent, is a token of an oppressive economic order and that his mother is, in her maliciousness, the antithesis of the Marian image cannot be computed in the calculus of Pascual's behavior—or so at least it would seem on the surface of the relentless chronicle of the harsh facts of life he has witnessed and his own deeds that defy the institutionalized code of Christian charity.

Cela's novel, of course, is a challenge to his readers to perceive the fissures in the social discourse that surrounds them in the carefully orchestrated rhetoric of Franco's eternally Catholic Spain. Against the first hypothesis that Pascual Duarte is the sort of sinner who must be extirpated in order to consolidate the triumph of traditional morality and the reciprocal social order it implies, the novel postulates a counter-discourse, especially in its unremittingly stark descriptive and narrative registers, whose effective resonance must be both the recollection of the social injustices that culminated in the civil war in the first place and the terrible social contract its aftermath sought to enforce. It is not so much that Cela's was a lone voice. Indeed, the forties and fifties in Spain present a rich inventory of cultural producers in all genres who cast light on the darkest corners of the Franco social edifice. The stark naturalism of *Pascual Duarte,* however, its unrelenting reality effect, so to speak, was an especially forceful articulation of the horrors of life in Spain at the time, particularly in its most impoverished regions like Extremadura, where the novel takes place, as it signaled the recovery in Spanish fiction of a registry of colloquial authenticity that official discourse both diligently belied and strove to drown out.

Authenticity in the literary representation of social discourse is, in fact, a key to much of Cela's subsequent writings. It has often been stated that the themes and characters in Cela's works are grotesque, verging on the repugnant, and exemplary all too often of gross vulgarity. Such a complaint derives from the abiding conflict between an ethics of culture that proposes to contemplate unflinchingly the life humankind is obliged to live and an ethics of culture that postulates a Utopia of society reconstructed or redeemed. The latter is always a valid program for culture, as long as the Utopia it proposes makes some sort of sense within the concrete physical and social parameters of existence. Clearly, for Cela and the many other writers who spoke against the official discourse of the tyranny, the romantic myth of an eternally Catholic Spain, sanitized whenever necessary as the gaily painted scrim of the tourist industry (medieval castles, stomping Gypsy dancers, black-clad reverent peasants, and taut-liveried bullfighters), simply had nothing to do with the daily lives of the battered Pascual Duartes.

Pascual Duarte provided the rural dimensions of life in Franco's Spain. The neorealist novel *La colmena* (1951; Eng. *The Hive*, 1953) turned attention to the more contemporary reality of the difficulties of urban existence. Combining images of the migration of people into the cities (the consequence of both the devastation of the countryside by war and the concentration of the postwar economy on city-based capitalist expansion), of the meanness of quotidian human commerce as the reflex of the scarcity of jobs and goods, of the omnipresence of moral righteousness as a mechanism to enforce irreflective conformity, and of all manner of degrading exploitation in the context of a social reality that did not have much to do with the Christian virtues routinely invoked by the righteous defenders of the faith, *La colmena*, not surprisingly, was banned in Spain, to be published in Buenos Aires.

The title of Cela's novel invokes the socialist icon of the beehive as the buzzingly harmonious abode of a smoothly integrated and productive society, with every member-individual given over selflessly to the pursuit of the common weal. Perhaps such was one of the fantasies of Franco's new order, and the icon of the beehive has an indisputable eloquence within the fascist mythology of the frictionless social hierarchy. Nevertheless, the tenement that is the real-life manifestation of the apian icon is instead a cockroach—and fly-infested dungheap where the sweet harmony of the productive bees is replaced by the hideous noises of the pariahs in a world in which the distinction between those who were bestialized because

of their spiritual corruption and those who are bestialized because they have been victimized is a sentimental nicety to which this mosaic of urban chaos gives short shrift.

The portrayal of social intercourse as cacophony is one of the most powerful dimensions of Cela's writing, as well as it is one aspect of both his expressive range and the sense of the grotesque that emanates from his texts. No writer in twentieth-century Spain since Ramón del Valle-Inclán (1866–1936) has had the command over the vast lexicon of Spanish evinced by Cela's writings. The *Diccionario* of the Spanish Royal Academy affords only a minimalist's appreciation of the semic wealth of the Spanish language along its multiple regional, class, and stylistic dimensions. Indeed, one of the goals of the Academy has been traditionally to codify—that is, to circumscribe—this wealth in favor of the fixed (if yet still flexible) standard required by contemporary socioeconomic needs: language too is a capital that must be rationally controlled. Cela's confrontation with this goal has been threefold.

In the first place, in consonance with his depiction of the vast panorama of social reality that overflows the narrow confines of the Franco and sundry other neofascist containments, he has assumed the task of demonstrating the cynical manipulation of language in the interests of that containment and the mythologies it propagates; this is the case, certainly, of his handling of the icon of the beehive and its derivations, or of his deconstruction of pastoral tropes in *Pascual Duarte*. Second, in repudiating the tinny sounds of a Spanish language denatured by bureaucratization and the exigencies of a repressive official discourse, Cela has worked indefatigably to recover the echoes of Spanish as it is actually used by people all of whose languages, verbal as well as not linguistically symbolic, have been excluded from the new order. This means not only calling things by their rightful names, as in his outrageous picturebook on whores and the lexicon of their trade (*Izas, rabizas y colipoterras*, 1964) or when his characters speak a language that denotes, in painfully graphic detail, the humiliations of their life, as well as evoking at the same time, with joyful ebullience, the ways in which popular language creatively metaphorizes the processes of daily existence. Concomitantly, Cela's *Diccionario secreto* (1968), easily his most ambitious and original undertaking, is an impressive interpretive compilation of the history and derivation of taboo words in Spanish, sort of the lexical outhouse of the Royal Spanish Academy and an eloquent demonstration of all the real-life manifestations of language that such institutions, by their very nature, cannot address. One interesting example of Cela's commitment to non-Academic Spanish has been (and in this he also follows Valle-Inclán) an exploration of the complex projections of the language outside Spain, as in his Venezuelan novel *La catira* (The Blonde; 1955) and his American novel *Cristo versus Arizona* (Christ versus Arizona; 1988).

Finally, Cela himself has been an assiduous contributor to the evolution of the Spanish language. His writings abound with neologisms, complex figures of diction that both reproduce the metaphorical processes of the language of everyday people and add their own poetic dimension to the ongoing project of finding adequate linguistic expression for the intricacies of daily experiences, and the ingenious deployment of fruits of his philological fieldwork among all the strata of spoken and written Spanish. Cela's writing oscillates (not always felicitously) between the poles of a naturalistic depiction of the richness of Spanish as it is used by his characters to speak their lives and what often verges on a Byzantine *préciosité*, a vertigo of linguistic foregrounding that brings the reader back to the inevitable—and, of course, salutary—realization that what is being read is a highly acculturated text and not, after all, social reality itself. If there is any significant ideological slippage in Cela's writing, it may well be found in the perhaps unresolvable tension between a commitment to rewriting for the reader the Book of Life for post-civil-war Spain and in indulging in all the feverish enterprises (here concentrated in linguistic pyrotechnics) late capitalism promotes. This is evident not only in the enormous verbal energy unleashed by his writing, but also in the dizzying frequency with which he startles the reader with shifts in the structure of his works and his experimentation with the considerable range of narrative models offered by modern fiction. (The foregoing observation probably means that one should talk about Cela as the paradigmatic Spanish postmodernist, as far as literature is concerned, but it is not crucial to pursue such a critical option as this point.)

I have stated that one might consider the *Diccionario secreto* to be Cela's masterpiece, not only because of the philological research it implies but, more important, for its central role in his view that the Spanish language must be rescued from the Academy and from the repressive bureaucratization of culture—linguistic in the first instance, comprehensive in the final analysis—that the Academy serves. (The Academy is, after all, an official government entity, as are the universities and other scientific institutions with which it enjoys interdependence; Cela, in the usual evolution of cultural history, is now a member of the Spanish Royal Academy and has held employment as a servant of the government, serving also as one of the king's appointed senators.) Still, the *Diccionario secreto* has rarely been given more than passing commentary in studies of Cela's writing, as though it were somehow parenthetical to his major titles. The same can be said of Cela's extensive bibliography of travel sketches, which were inaugurated in 1948 with *Viaje a la Alcarria* (1964; Eng. *Journey to the Alcarria*) and extend through the early 1970s.

These books were, at least in the beginning, based on Cela's journey by foot through areas he describes, and their importance lies in the implied effort to recover in another dimension an authentic image of Spanish society

An excerpt from Cela's Nobel Prize acceptance speech, "In Praise of Storytelling":

We know that we think, and indeed, we think because we are free. We are like the dog that chases its tail or, rather, like the dog that is eager to capture its tail; for being free is as much an immediate consequence of thought as it is an essential condition. By thinking, we can detach ourselves as much as we wish from the laws of nature; we can accept them and subject ourselves to them, of course, and chemists who have surpassed the limits of phlogiston theory will base their success and prestige on that servitude. But in thought, the kingdom of nonsense lies next to the empire of logic, for we can conceive of more than what is real and possible. The mind is capable of shattering its own machinations and then recomposing them in an image that is novel to the point of aberration. For this reason, rational interpretations of the world that are subject to empirical events may be succeeded by as many alternative views as the whim of a thinking mind entertains, especially if that mind is free. Free thought, in this restricted sense, opposed to empirical thinking, is translated into stories. And the ability to tell a story would appear, then, to be a third companion of the human condition, added to freedom and thought, thanks to that pirouette of making truth out of what was not even a simple lie before its story was created.

Camilo José Cela, "In Praise of Storytelling," *PMLA*, January, 1991.

beyond the confines of a new order that either flattened out the rough texture of lives conducted in the only way they could be conducted under the difficult circumstances of the time or repressed whatever those lives contained that did not conform to the official sociocultural ideology that had been securely locked into place. Cela sought to listen to the real language of the people, with all its rough edges, and he sought to provide a nonromanticized depiction of what they lived by, what they thought, and what the contradictions of their not always, not usually lovely existence were. Although these sketches have not enjoyed the fame his novels have, the latter being written in conformance with the contemporary priorities of "elaborted" art, they too constitute very significant elements in Cela's enterprise of countering the totalizing official discourse.

One can be pardoned for entertaining many objections to Cela's works published during the last twenty years, although some come near to reproducing the brilliance of his early production. Perhaps this is only because there is so much outstanding writing coming out of Spain in recent decades, as well as from the many other Spanish-language countries. The over-whelming coherence that can be attributed to Cela's writing from its earliest manifestations, however, and the role his work has played in defining what literary culture in Spain might be since the worst days of the postwar period lend his texts the singular distinction the Nobel Prize serves to confirm. (pp. 5–8)

David William Foster, "Camilo José Cela: 1989 Nobel Prize in Literature," in *World Literature Today*, Vol. 64, No. 1, Winter, 1990, pp. 5–8.

CHRISTOPHER MAURER

(essay date 1990)

[In the following excerpt, Maurer assesses Cela's oeuvre, focusing on *The Family of Pascual Duarte*, *The Hive*, *Journey to the Alcarria*, and *Mrs. Caldwell Speaks to Her Son*.]

Cela has long been a household word in Spain, though not a polite one. No Spanish writer since Francisco de Quevedo, who died in 1645, has been so identified in the popular imagination with verbal scandal. Spain's foremost man of letters, the seventy-four-year-old winner of last year's Nobel Prize in literature is also a connoisseur of four-letter words, particularly those that designate genitals. Cela's two-volume *Diccionario secreto* (1968–71) devoted over 200 pages to the testicles, and one of his proudest achievements as a member of the Royal Spanish Academy has been to persuade it to include the word *coño* (from the Latin *cunnus*) in the most recent edition of its dictionary. Spanish writing has drifted too far from popular speech, he likes to argue, and has forgotten the "lexical violence" of its origins. (Twelve centuries ago, an Asturian monk could call the archbishop of Toledo a "*cojón* of the Antichrist.")

Cela's lifelong war on euphemism explains only a part of his notoriety. His literary output is vast: an early book of poems; collections of short stories; books of essays and lectures; an oratorio and a play; reprintings of his columns for the Madrid daily *El País*; transcriptions of his weekly television talk show; travel literature; philological writing on eroticism; modernized versions of Spanish classics; *costumbrismo* (the sketch of manners); memoirs; and eleven novels. Whatever the subject, he has strong opinions, and he airs them regularly on television and in the press. Most important, perhaps, he has been widely criticized for his political past, and this has influenced the reception of his work. Spain's socialist minister of culture, the novelist Jorge Semprun, was conspicuously absent from the ceremonies in Stockholm last fall.

Camilo José Cela was twenty years old in 1936, at the outbreak of the Civil War. A year later he left Republican Madrid, enlisted with Franco, was wounded in battle, and was discharged. In a much reprinted letter of March 1938, Cela offered his services to the security apparatus of Franco's "Glorious National Movement," and asked to be assigned to the capital: "Having lived uninterruptedly in Madrid for the past thirteen years, [the undersigned] believes himself able to provide useful facts on the conduct of certain persons. . . ." The offer was not accepted. In the lean years following Franco's victory, however, Cela accommodated himself to political circumstance: he wrote for the Nationalist press, was protected in official literary circles, and eked out a living as a censor of trade magazines and an employee of the national textile syndicate. In its offices he began *The Family of Pascual Duarte,* which he was able to publish without problems in 1942.

Within a few years, however, Cela's relations with officialdom went sour. The censor himself began to be censored. Both the second edition of *Pascual* (1943) and his second major work, *The Hive,* were banned in Spain. After he published the latter in Buenos Aires in 1951, Cela was expelled from the Madrid Press Association. The royalties from a paperback edition of J. M. Cohen's English translation (it appeared in 1954 and is reprinted now with minor revisions) helped Cela make ends meet while he set up shop on the island of Mallorca. There he published *Papeles de Son Armadans* (1956–79), an excellent literary monthly that was hospitable to many of the exiled writers and critics who were ignored or silenced by the "official" press. Whatever his political beliefs, it seems fair to say that Cela's work on behalf of free expression has overshadowed his early service to the Franco regime. "Love," says the cynical Spanish proverb, "is deeds, not fine words."

Critics have often praised Cela's stylistic "restlessness" and his love of "experimentation." In fact, Cela's roots as a novelist and an essayist may be found in nineteenth-century European realism, and in a literary movement known as the Generation of 1898, a group of individualistic Spanish writers who sought to redefine their country's identity and its relation to Europe after the humiliation of the Spanish-American War. Reading Cela, one is reminded of Spain's almost self-enclosed literary tradition, of its isolation in the 1940s and 1950s.

Cela's yearning to make Spanish more supple and more inclusive resembles the project of Miguel de Unamuno (1864–1936), whose unorthodox views on the novel Cela took to heart in his early work. Cela's description of the Castilian countryside draws on the poetry of Antonio Machado (1875–1939); in what Machado called a bare "corner of the planet," both men have glimpsed "the shadow of Cain." And still more important for the evolution of Cela's work was the truculent realism of Pío Baroja (1872–1956), a novelist almost unknown in English but much admired by Hemingway, and Ramón de Valle-Inclán (1869–1936), with his aesthetic of the grotesque and his satirical novels about nineteenth-century Spanish society. No modern Spanish writer is a more skillful imitator than Cela, a more gifted disciple of the past, a more complete man of letters. An inventor of language, however, he is not: Cela has altered the lexicon, but the words he has added to it have not been his own. His linguistic ideas can be traced to Unamuno and Valle-Inclán who believed that Castilian would have to be re-created if Spain was to be rescued from intellectual stagnation, though Cela has neither their sense of social mission nor their inventiveness, their power over words.

Cela's first . . . novels—*The Hive* and *The Family of Pascual Duarte*—were attacked in Spain for what was called their *tremendismo*. It is a vacuous term that has pursued Cela as doggedly as "magical realism" has pursued García Márquez. The word refers confusedly both to style and to subject matter. It denotes, briefly, the unflinching description of anything revolting and grotesque.

There is a classic example in *Pascual Duarte*: when Pascual's brother Mario was four years old, we are told, "his luck turned, turned against him for good. Though he hadn't done a thing, though he hadn't bothered a soul or tempted God, a hog (begging your pardon), chewed off his ears." Wondering how to dispose of a human fetus that is stashed in a shoebox under yesterday's newspaper, a grandmother in *San Camilo, 1936* (1969) stokes up the kitchen stove and forces the box through a burner-hole onto the coals. ("Spaniards," another character will remark, "are fonder of fire than water.") Dogs and cats fare worse still: they are drowned or stoned senseless, and street urchins like to poke at them with sticks. One of Cela's characters amuses himself by using a razor to "separate" a pair of copulating dogs. Humans are indifferent to the suffering of animals, and vice versa: cockroaches are never fatter and brighter, they glow "like patent leather," than at the morgue.

Tremendismo is not easy to master. At its best, it is an appeal for mercy. When it is used gratuitously, as it sometimes in the *The Hive*, shock turns into schlock. The historical meaning of Cela's *tremendismo* has been much debated. In the '40s conservative Spaniards found it indecent. "*Pascual Duarte*," wrote a reviewer of a Catholic newspaper in 1942, "has a repulsive realism. Everything, even what is unchaste, is expressed with the same crude brutality. The novel is contaminated by Russian fatalism, and its characters commit crimes against their wills." Outside Spain, however, *tremendismo* was seen as an expression of postwar trauma: as a bleakly pessimistic reaction to violence and bloodshed, as a way of rendering the immoral atmosphere of a totalitarian society. Whatever the case, the description of cruelty is a constant in Cela's work, even in his most recent novels. Of course, Spanish artists (Quevedo, Goya, Valle-Inclán, Buñuel) have always lavished talent upon the grotesque. Cela himself has insisted, as authors of the grotesque often do, that he invents nothing, that reality itself is deformed, that most people will tolerate in life the cruelty that they will not bear in literature.

The Family of Pascual Duarte arose from Cela's fascination with the narrative tone—the strange blend of irony and naïveté of respect and irreverence—of the anonymous sixteenth-century picaresque novel *Lazarillo de Tormes,* a first-person epistolary narrative that portrayed the scandalous "case" of a social outcast. Together with the confessional nature of his narrative, Cela inherited from this early modern work a perennial philosophical question—the role of fate and free will in human conduct—as well as certain readerly expectations. Like Lazarillo's story, Pascual's story could be expected to be a judgment on an entire social milieu.

Pascual, a field worker from Extremadura, the poorest region of Spain, seems (as the critic Gonazalo Sobejano once remarked) like the "Paschal lamb" (*cordero pascual*) sacrificed by his family: that is, by all of Spanish society. Pascual's crimes of passion—the killing of a dog, or a mare, of his sister's pimp, of his own hated mother—culminate in the act for which his is awaiting execution: the murder of a rich rural landowner. The murder of the Count of Torremejía lies outside Pascual's own narrative. It is mentioned, almost in passing, by the transcriber of his confessions, who refuses to speculate about the motives for the deed. The reader learns only that Pascual repented, sought counsel from the prison chaplain, and died an almost exemplary death.

The murder, however, occurs in 1936. For that reason, it has often been seen as a symbolic act of social aggression, as an attack on the conservative rural aristocracy that would unite behind Franco. Using the dates supplied by the narrator, the reader deduces that Pascual's repentance occurred in what would have been a fascist jail, and that he was pardoned by a Catholic Church allied to the regime. Pascual's "case" can thus be understood as a tacit apology for the right. Cela, some argued, was praising the new regime for having pardoned its "prodigal sons" and regenerated Spanish society.

The existence of competing historical interpretations of Cela's work must not be mistaken for evidence of political courage. Politically he is protean, elusive, sometimes inscrutable. He made his peace with fascism, and then made it with socialist democracy. In this respect, too, he has fallen painfully short of the fiery Unamuno. Cela's thoughts on the "Spanish identity" can be read with interest, but unlike Unamuno's, they will never be read with passion. And yet one cannot but admire his skill as a narrator. *Pascual Duarte* is as indestructibly ambiguous as *Lazarillo*, and equally "anonymous"; and those qualities are considerable literary achievements.

Not the least of Cela's triumphs lies in having hidden himself so completely, in having prevented his readers and his censors from assigning definitive blame or putting together a convincing social thesis. Early in the book, for example, Pascual struggles with the accusatory stare of his dog:

The bitch went on peering at me with a fixed stare, as if she had never seen me before, as if she were on the point of accusing me of something terrible at any moment, and her scrutiny roused the blood in my veins to such a pitch that I knew the moment was near when I would have to give in. It was hot, the heat was stifling, and my eyes began to close under the animal's stare, which was sharp as flint. I picked up my gun and fired. I reloaded, and fired again. The bitch's blood was dark and sticky and it spread slowly along the dry earth.

This is not, as some have written, a "senseless" killing. It is, instead, another reminder of Cela's inscrutability, which is his signature. And perhaps also of his hostility to the reader: Pascual's hatred comes pulsing through the page. It is as though he had leveled his gun at the reader, who has been staring expectantly, perhaps accusingly, since the story began.

However one reads this book, it is an unforgettable encounter with loneliness, hatred, and cruelty. The political meaning of *The Hive,* by contrast, is far less ambiguous. The setting is Madrid during three days in December 1942 or 1943, in the sordid, corrupt society that (as Raymond Carr has noted ironically) Franco "saved." *The Hive* is a discontinuous, fragmented narrative—a cellular, hivelike one—with a cast of over 300 characters who live out their dreary, honeyless, "realist," war-ravaged existence. The most important of them, a lonely writer with vague "social ideas," is sought by the regime, presumably for his minor role before the war in organizing leftist students. The tone is unrelentingly somber, and there is only an occasional glimpse of human kindness:

> There are people whom it amuses to see others having a bad time. To get a close view of it, they haunt the slums, they take battered old things as gifts to dying people, to consumptives huddling under a vile blanket, to anemic little children with swollen bellies and soft bones, to girls who have become mothers at the age of eleven, to whores in their forties, eaten up by pustules and looking like . . . Indian chiefs with the scab.

The interest of this book, which is more dated and less memorable than *Pascual Duarte,* lies in Cela's skill at showing the uncertain and unforeseen ways in which human lives touch one another, and in his tireless observation of the seamy side of urban life. In a prologue to the first edition, Cela calls his novel a "slice of life, drawn without charity." A passage about street benches illustrates the book's scope, and the maudlin quality of its *tremendismo:*

> Street benches are a sort of anthology of every form of trouble and of nearly every form of good fortune: the old man seeking to ease his asthma, the priest reading his breviary, the beggar delousing himself, the bricklayer lunching together with his wife, the consumptive panting for breath, the madman with huge, dreaming eyes, the street musician resting his horn on his knees—each one of them with his urge, great or small, impregnates the planks of the seat with the stale smell

of flesh. . . . And the young girl recovering from fatigue after her deep moan of pleasure, and the lady reading a long novel about love, and the blind woman waiting for the hours to pass, and the little typist gulping her sandwich of sausage and coarse bread, and the woman with cancer fighting her pain, and the moron with her gaping mouth dribbling softly . . . and the little girl who likes nothing so much as to watch men peeing.

It is as a patient observer of the city and countryside that Cela will probably leave his mark on Spanish literature. His best descriptive writing lies outside the novel, in travel sketches and essays that carry on, and emulate, the tradition of *costumbrismo,* a genre that has its roots in the nineteenth-century belief that a nation's "character" is best captured in scenes from daily life, by detailed description of its customs, dress, speech, and so on. The best-known and most charming of Cela's travel sketches is *Journey to the Alcarria,* which appeared in 1948, a third person account of a walking trip through an austere, hilly region to the northeast of Madrid.

"The traveler," the author's alter ego, has promised himself not to sleep for more than one night under the same roof. And here, as in the *The Hive,* Cela's liberal apologists have found grist for a redeeming "historical" reading. "The traveler" makes his trip in 1942, the very year in which *The Hive* takes place. Here is the rural portion, the other "hive," of the Spain that Franco saved. The Alcarria is known for its honey. The region is extremely poor, and many of its inhabitants are illiterate, maimed, or idiotic. Most are either indifferent to Spain's glorious past (many a palace and castle is in ruins) or feel defeated by it. "Past splendor overwhelms and in the end exhausts the people's will," the traveler tells himself, "and without force of will . . . they leave current problems unsolved."

Decades after writing the book, Cela insisted that a travel writer ought to limit himself to description, and guard against history and sociology, "foreign elements" that often spoil the genre. Therein lies some of *Journey's* charm. Read today, in Frances M. López Morillas's comfortable translation, it seems less like an interpretation of Spanish history and character and more like a version of pastoral. The traveler's senses awaken as he leaves Madrid and takes to the open road. The air is so still that the flame of his lighter scarcely wavers, and the smoke from his cigar "rises slowly, straight up, occasionally forming tenuous blue spirals." In the silence he gathers sense data that nobody else attends to: the "harsh, wild, sweetish taste" of goat's milk; the breath of a child that "smells like a baby calf's, a little suckling calf's"; the gloom of a village that "seems to have no business being surrounded by green fields." In the fragrant shade of a hawthorn tree, "an adolescent goatherd and a member of his flock are sinning one of the oldest of sins."

As in Cela's novels, chance and necessity tug at each other in an almost palpable way. And "the traveler" seems always to strike the right balance between the observation of particulars and the impulse toward generality. Cela is less sentimental here than in *The Hive*: his attentiveness to place names and to nicknames opens his eyes to all sorts of idiosyncrasy. The hard-working inhabitants of one village "are called 'Squatters' . . . the rumor goes that they sleep in a squatting position so as to be able to get up early and go to the fields." The fat-legged folk of another are mocked, for miles about, as "Fat-Calves," and "while he is having a smoke with the cart driver," the traveler learns of town-dwellers referred to as Misers, Itchies, Tricksters, and Mangies. Those from Hontanillas are "'Trough-Eaters,' because they eat from the pig's trough so as not to get the plates dirty."

Cela's guiding intuition has always been that truth dwells in particulars, and it has usually kept him from renaming people and objects. In *Journey,* metaphor, which is rare in his work, would have seemed especially irreverent. The domain of "the traveler" is, rather, gentle simile:

An old light-colored ox with long horns and a sharp thin face like a knight of Toledo is drinking from the basin of a brimming fountain beside the washing place, barely dipping his grizzled muzzle into the water. When he has finished drinking he lifts his head and passes behind the women, humble and wise. He seems like a loyal eunuch, bored and discreet, who guards a harem. . . . The traveler follows the animal's slow, resigned progress with perplexed eyes. Sometimes the traveler feels completely transfixed by things he cannot possibly explain.

This lyricism burns still more brightly in the novel *Mrs. Caldwell Speaks to Her Son* (1953), now back in print in J.S. Bernstein's competent, though badly edited, translation. This is the diary of an eccentric English widow, who pours out her incestuous love for her only son, who drowned in the Aegean Sea before the story begins. Like *The Hive, Mrs. Caldwell* is arranged in fragments; like *Pascual Duarte,* the narration belongs virtually to the epistolary genre. (The son is so vividly present in his mother's thoughts that the diary fragments have the feel of short letters.)

Mrs. Caldwell's progression from lucidity of madness (she dies in an insane asylum) allows Cela to display the whole range of his lyrical gifts. As always, a "classical" Spanish writer is silently evoked and emulated: the first half of the book is an implicit and very brilliant tribute to the metaphorical powers of Ramón Gómez de la Serna (1891–1963), a novelist remembered for his humorous aphorisms. While still lucid, Mrs. Caldwell takes her dead son on an imaginative, wide-ranging tour of "reality," and seems capable of bringing all things—from colored pencils to chrysanthemums, from well-bred neighbors to seal hunters—within the reach of humoristic metaphor. The wit of Gómez de la Serna (and perhaps of Wilde) is emulated in observations like these:

[S]hipwrights . . . resemble industrious and happy coffinmakers.

Family life is the drug that makes families stupid.

In a better world. . . , in a more just and reasonable world, pigeons would live on deserted and distant islands.

Yet the miscellaneous and impersonal nature of the aphorism never threatens the intimacy and the unity of this lovely book. Mrs. Caldwell's imagination returns always to her son, bringing him the little gifts of poetic analogy that she has gathered. Sails, for example, remind her of bedsheets, and bedsheets make her remember her son:

If you and I lived in the days of sailing ships, oh! if you and I lived! / In the sailing days, the sea resembled a bedroom in which—what a shame to have been born too late!—you and I would have met!. . . / In the sailing days, Eliacim, the sea pretended to be a forest of amorous trails, a jungle which had lost its virginity for love./ Today, no longer.

As the heroine drifts toward madness, her powers of metaphor wane. Yet the novel only gains in poetic interest. Mrs. Caldwell's madness lies in the abandonment of a public domain (humor, metaphor) for a private one: a hell of impenetrable images. These, too, are bizarre and memorable. Half dead of tuberculosis, the heroine often coughs up blood in her sleep. The stains on her pillow have the shape of her dead son's head. "I cut them out carefully," she says, "and so that they do not ravel, I usually make a little hem all round them; this is how I spend almost my whole day now." When she dies, she hopes to be wrapped in a shroud stitched together from "all the portraits of you that I spit out each morning." "Madness," writes Cela in an afterword, "embodies a logic as subtle as it is elusive, before which we must with humility confess our impotence." The same is true of good poetry, as *Mrs. Caldwell* reminds us.

Only Cela's earliest work is available in English; all four of these books were written before 1953. In his most recent and untranslated novels, from his Civil War saga *San Camilo, 1936* (1969) to *Cristo versus Arizona* (1987), Cela has experimented with the possibilities of soliloquy, with what Gonzalo Sobejano has called narrative "litany." In these works, observes Sobejano, an individual voice appeals to what is sacred, or what can transport us toward the sacred, while evoking "the multitudinous evils of an inhuman, subhuman, or 'too human' world: misery, violence, aberration."

If Cela's many writings share a theme, it is loneliness. All of his novels pit the individual against the collectivity, and probe the solitude of the traveler, the infirm, the writer, the madman, the social outcast. And as with characters, so with words: Cela has befriended the language that has been expelled from polite society. His prodigious lexicographical work—a sort of scholarly *tremendismo*—is a glossary of his own essays and fiction, a protective wall surrounding them, an assurance that his own work will be understood.

He has seen himself, rather flatteringly, as a misunderstood, solitary figure. In the '50s Cela called himself the greatest novelist since the Generation of 1898, and added: "It scares me to think how easy it has been." His individualism and his sense of isolation are a perfect image of pre-democratic Spain, that outsider to Europe, whose literary scene he dominated. Perhaps the judges in Stockholm thought of him as a symbol. If so, they were wrong. Cela stands at the end of a chapter of Spanish literary history. He is a grim survivor, a keeper of tradition. For decades he kept the novel alive in the country that gave birth to it, listening, more attentively than others, to the ghosts of an introspective, violent past. (pp. 41–4)

Christopher Maurer, "The Tremendist," in *The New Republic*, Vol. 203, No. 10, September 3, 1990, pp. 41–4.

CAMILO JOSÉ CELA WITH MARIE-LISE GAZARIAN GAUTIER

(interview date 1991)

[In the following interview, Cela discusses his writing methods and the influence of Medieval and Golden Age Spanish literature on his work.]

[Marie-Lise Gazarian Gautier]: *You have been a reporter, a poet, a bullfighter, a movie actor, a painter and a vagabond (these are the words with which you are described in* Who's Who in Spanish Letters). *Why did you become a writer?*

[Camilo José Cela]: It is not true that I have been all these things, although I have tried my luck at all of them. I never wanted to be a bullfighter or a soccer player. I enjoyed seeing bullfights and soccer games, as well as acting in several very poor movies. But to draw the conclusion that I have been a bullfighter, a soccer player, or an actor is highly inaccurate. To say that I was journalist is a different story, because I did write. I contributed short stories and essays to newspapers and magazines. In that sense, I was a journalist but not a news reporter.

Do you still write articles?

Yes, I write long articles for *El Independiente*, which takes me three days every week. If I go on a trip or have some other commitment to fulfill, then I don't have the time for that. I call my column "Desde el palomar de Hita" (From the Pigeon-House in Hita), after the name of the town where the great medieval poet, the Archpriest Juan Ruiz, lived. It's a generic heading, but everything fits under it. The articles are more literary pieces than critical

essays, so there is a lot of narration with some thought also thrown in, of course. I try to express my views on some issue or another, I cover many topics.

You have said, "The writer is a man whose soul needs every kind of nourishment." Do you find themes for your books in your own experience or from the world that surrounds you?

I find my material everywhere. I observe some aspect of reality, which my mind transforms, forcing me to move the pen upon the paper, which in turn produces the phenomenon we call literature. Of course, I do not think that initial reality can be recognized in my books. First of all, it would be unfair merely to imitate a passerby. Secondly, it would be dangerous artistically. Finally, that reality had become remote, because the work has been fictionalized through the imagination. Someone took an inventory of the real and fictitious characters in *The Hive,* and the real characters outweigh the fictitious ones by a margin of 3 percent.

What is realism for you?

Realism for me is everything that can be perceived with the senses or intuited. It can be assumed that realism encompasses surrealism and subrealism. Not just what man is aware of, but what came before and what will come after. Whether we are able to reflect this is another question. The subconscious is also a form of reality, even though we may not be able to articulate or interpret it.

How would you define the worlds contained in a book then?

I think they reflect particular aspects of reality, from one end of the spectrum to the other. These reflections are what make up the novels, which very often have little anecdotes as the vessels that link the action, although this is not necessary. I have written some novels with no plots, such as *Oficio de tinieblas 5*, where I locked myself in a dark room to elicit the necessary feelings of anxiety.

You have compared literature to a ship, saying, "It is a pirate vessel, without a flag and without lifeboats . . . . It is a ship that sails because God so wishes." But you also write, "It is a boat without destination . . . in which each man rows as he is so inclined." Are you religious? Do you see literature as divine inspiration or as a profession in which one never rests?

As neither. I do not believe that God makes us write. I think that there are very few people, perhaps none, who write under divine inspiration. To write, one must work hard, be patient and persistent. But writing should not be considered strictly a profession, because the writer would turn into a caricature of himself if he decided to do nothing more than put out a certain number of pages a day. That would be unfortunate, particularly if it led to his demise. There have been many writers throughout the history of literature who have written their own epitaphs because they do nothing but plagiarize themselves. Because of this, I try to use a different technique in each of the novels that I write, so as not to fall into a regular pattern or become sterile. But to get back to your question, the only profession I would want as a man is precisely to be a man, a human being. Everything else would be secondary.

Your books are all different in terms of techniques.

I think the technique of a book is like to scaffolding used to build a cathedral, something necessary which later disappears. When the cathedral stands, it is time to take the scaffold down. In a book, the technique is absorbed, otherwise it would remain a mere experiment.

So the technique is there, but it cannot be seen . . .

Or it shouldn't be seen, or not too much, but of course it does exist.

You are both a lyrical and comic troubadour, and seem almost embarrassed to express your tender feelings. Why do you cover them up with irony and caricatures?

I don't know. It may be a defense mechanism that prevents me from exposing myself, but I am not sure. I would have to study myself objectively. In any case, it seems to be a constant in my work that many critics have pointed out, but which I did not think I should redress. Something similar happened to Cervantes with *Don Quixote*. Each time he used an elegant adjective, he followed it with a colloquial synonym, thinking that the reader would perhaps understand it better.

Picasso once said, "When one is truly young, one is young for one's whole life."

Picasso told me this when he celebrated his ninetieth birthday. I said to him, "I find you very young, Pablo," and he replied, "You are wrong, Camilo José; when a man is young at heart then he is young for his whole life." This is beautiful because he died at a very old age and still he was young at heart.

How did you manage to recapture the freshness of your childhood years in **La rosa,** *where you recount the first six years of your life with great sensitivity and grace?*

It is a biography of my early childhood and my wonderfully foolish family. I hold that memory dear because I was a very happy little boy who lived a golden childhood. I remember those years fondly and nostalgically. My aunts used to ask me, "What would you like to be when you grow up?" and I would cry because I did not want anything—I did not want to grow up. I was very content just being a little boy. I would have been happy to remain five or six years old forever in beautiful, pastoral, rustic Galicia.

What does Galicia mean for you?

A lot, of course. A person is never born in a vacuum. One is not just Galician, Greek, or Chinese by birth; we carry that heritage with us all our lives, for better or for worse. In my case, I trust that it was all for the good, of course. Since we are all products of the family we were born into, an my mother was British, my father was Galician, and my grandmother Italian, all those elements have influenced my development.

How do you feel being a mixture of those three elements?

Very comfortable, very comfortable.

Do you feel more Galician or Spanish?

Both, they are two different spheres. Although one remains the same, the diameter of the sphere increases, from Iria Flavia to Padrón, Galicia, the Kingdom of Spain, Europe, and finally the world.

The Galicia West Railway was designed by your great-grandfather Camilo Bertorini, and your grandfather John Trulock was its manager. Since the train played such an important role in your family, have you ever thought of writing a story, novel, or poem in which it would be the main character?

I don't know if I have not already used it somewhere. The train was my great-grandfather's property. It was the line that ran from Pontevedra to Santiago, an eighty-kilometer run. The railway sustained the family. Later, a young engineer was brought over from England. His name was John Trulock, my grandfather-to-be, and he married the owner's daughter, which was the normal, sensible thing to do, because everything remained in the family that way. This is a great idea, and I think that young engineers should always marry the daughter of the owners.

You have said that before you learned how to write, you were already dictating verses to others. If poetry was your first love, why did you abandon it, even though not completely, to write in prose?

As a matter of principle. One is never faithful to one's first love. Very often we prose writers begin by writing poetry, although there have been many who have not written a single verse in their lives. I started out writing in verse, and I enjoyed it, until some of my friends who ran the literary section of a magazine in Madrid heard me tell some anecdotes in a café. They asked me, "Why don't you write some stories?" This was at the end of the Spanish Civil War. "I don't know," I replied, "I think that I am a better poet," to which they said, "We insist that you write at least one story." I then wrote **"Don Anselmo."** They liked it, and asked me for more. That's how I began to develop a liking for prose. These first stories prior to **The Family of Pascual Duarte** are collected in a book entitled *Esas nubes que pasan.* They are included in my complete works. I have never rejected a single page I have written because I do not like the attitude of writers who have complete works that are not really complete.

You see poetry and prose as two branches of the same tree. Could you talk about that relationship?

The novel encompasses poetry and, in some way, all poetry also encompasses the novel. *El cantar de Mío Cid,* for instance, is a very long poem, but it is also a chronicle or a novel because it gives an account of many events. The same thing is true of Jorge Manrique's "Coplas a la muerte de su padre" (Eulogy at the Death of His Father). Medieval poets were extraordinary. They have greatly influenced me and everyone else. Let's not forget that, contrary to what is claimed by literary historians, Boccaccio's *Decameron* was not the first novel to be published; it was *El Conde Lucanor,* by Prince Don Juan Manuel. I have never believed in literary genres, and I do even less as time goes on. These genres are very comfortable for professors and critics; they are a sort of literary etymology, a way of pinning a little tag on us with a Latin name on it, if at all possible. But that is a lie.

Is that the reason why rhythm is so important in your novels?

Of course, as it should be in any work. I have always said that to be a prose writer one has to have a far better ear than a poet or a musician, because the rhythm of prose is considerably more mysterious than that of music, which usually follows a set pattern.

Do you speak out loud what you write?

I write by hand and usually read my text aloud as I put it together, because that way I can catch many stylistic imperfections, repetitions, and discordant sounds. These things are more discernible through the ear than through the eye.

How can you explain the affinities between your work and the picaresque novel?

I think it was Virginia Woolf who said that all later novels are derived from the Spanish picaresque novel. I think literature is culture, not just the spontaneous product of a generation. Every generation carries the torch as far as it can, and then it hands it over to the next one. Technically speaking, writers today know far more than authors of the seventeenth, eighteenth, and nineteenth centuries. Whether they are as good now as they were back then depends on the talents of a particular writer. But any high school student knows about the circulatory system, which Hippocrates and his great school of doctors in Greece were unaware of. Culture is transmitted, and the picaresque novel has its place for various causes and reasons. The picaresque novel is astonishing, from *Lazarillo de Tormes* (although some people argue it is not a picaresque novel) to a more erudite work like Quevedo's *El Buscón.* However, I don't believe in labels very much.

Do you think Cervantes handed you his torch?

Yes, but all the writers in between us also carried it. The torch was around even before Cervantes, of course. It has been passed from generation to generation, and I will probably hand it to someone, whoever he is. It's like a relay race.

Do you identify with Cervantes in any way?

Don Quixote is a perfect work, a true wonder. I never tire of admiring it; so yes, I do identify with its author. If I could speak to him, I would congratulate him and tell him of my healthy envy at his having produced such a masterpiece.

If you could speak to another great writer from the past, whom would you choose?

Quevedo. I think he is the most astonishing writer the Spanish language has ever had. I would undoubtedly ask him how he was able to achieve this and master all the things he knew.

Do you have followers?

I don't know. When people ask me the opposite question of who my influences were, I always reply that they were all the authors who wrote before me, not just in Spanish but even in languages I don't know. All writers have undoubtedly influenced me, and we will all probably influence those who come after us.

Who are some of the people who helped you when you started out as a writer?

The three people who helped me the most were Pablo Neruda, Maria Zambrano, and Pedro Salinas. Maria Zambrano paid particular attention to me, encouraging me to keep writing. She is still alive, although the others have died.

Your first works were published in Argentina, for political reasons. Do you think that sometimes censorship can have a positive effect on the development of imagination because it causes mental exercises worthy of a tightrope walker?

My first poems were published in Argentina by pure chance. This was before the Spanish Civil War. They were poems written when I was eighteen or nineteen years old (in 1935), and they were first published in *Argentino,* a newspaper of Río de la Plata, and then in a literary magazine called *Fábula.* They had been sent to Luis Enrique Délano, director of those publications. But *The Family of Pascual Duarte* was published in Buenos Aires in 1944 for political reasons, because the second edition, published in Spain in 1943, was not allowed to circulate. Later, *The Hive* was also published there, when it was censored in Spain. Each time I lost a fight with a censor, I considered it a personal failure. When words and sentences were crossed out from my manuscripts, I felt I was being persecuted. I can't forget how the chief censor in Spain boasted that as long as he held his post, "Mr. Cela would never publish a single book."

Wasn't Luis Enrique Délano a friend of Gabriela Mistral?

He was the Secretary of the Chilean Consulate, first under Gabriela Mistral and later under Pablo Neruda. He was a fellow student in the Universidad Central of Madrid. The last time I saw him he was living in exile in Mexico because he had been the Chilean ambassador to Sweden during the time of Allende. Naturally, when the Allende regime fell he did not return to Chile.

You have said that the writer has two rules: to write and to wait. His best accomplice is time. Upon publishing **The Family of Pascual Duarte** *in 1942, did you think it would bring about the revival of the Spanish novel and that you would become the most illustrious of prose writers?*

No, not at all. I did not even write this novel with the intent of having it published. Actually, I was writing a chapter a day because a sister of my wife, who was my girlfriend then, was sick and I used to read her the novel. Each time she would grow worse, poor thing. It was not a soothing balm but the complete opposite. I did not think it would be published because at first all the editors refused it. Publishing is the profession that produces the most jackasses in the entire world. I can now say with pride that *The Family of Pascual Duarte* is the most translated Spanish work after *Don Quixote*. It has even been translated into Latin. I carried my manuscript under my arm for two years, and publishers told me the same old nonsense they always tell young writers: "You are young, you can still change professions. Thank you very much. You must understand that this is a business enterprise and that your book could barely sell ten or twelve copies. I am sorry." And so it was for two years, until it was published thanks to Rafael Aldecoa, who was the son of General Ibañez de

Aldecoa, the owner of a very conservative and conventional publishing house. Rafael lived in Madrid and that month his father had not sent him any money because they had quarreled, and he told me, "Since my father is never aware of what is published in his firm, let's pull this one on him to teach him." And that's how the novel was published by Aldecoa. Its success came later and I was the first one to be pleased by it, of course.

You do not like the title of "father of tremendismo *" that has been applied to you. Would you be against being called a chronicler of your time and your people?*

No, this is what I would aspire to be. *Tremendismo* is a sexton's terms that was created to be used against me by one of the so-called very proper critics in my country, with the purpose of picking a quarrel with me. Later on, people in foreign countries used that term affectionately when they spoke of me, so it has now turned against him and in my favor. But I think the term does not mean anything. This attitude attributed to me is a constant in all Spanish literature, even as far back as the sixteenth and seventeenth centuries. There is such a thing as chronological order which should be respected. (pp. 81–7)

Camilo José Cela with Marie-Lise Gazarian Gautier, in an interview in *Interviews with Spanish Writers* by Marie-Lise Gazarian Gautier, Dalkey Archive Press, 1991, pp. 77–96.

SOURCES FOR FURTHER STUDY

Herzberger, David K. "Cela and the Challenge to History in Francoist Spain." *Ojácano*, No. 5 (April 1991): 13–23.
> Analysis of "the way in which Camilo José Cela's fiction pertains to the understanding of history, and how it is enriched if we perceive it in relation to Francoist historiography."

Kirsner, Robert. *The Novels and Travels of Camilo José Cela.* Chapel Hill: University of North Carolina Press, 1963, 187 p.
> Critical analysis of Cela's works, maintaining that the "art of Cela mirrors the inner truth of the Spanish people, as it captures the essence of post-Civil War life."

Labanyi, Jo. *Myth and History in the Contemporary Spanish Novel.* Cambridge: Cambridge University Press, 1989, 283 p.
> Study of the mythologizing of history in the modern Spanish novel, containing a detailed discussion of Cela's *San Camilo, 1936.*

Penuel, Arnold M. "The Psychology of Cultural Disintegration in Cela's *La familia de Pascual Duarte.*" *Revista de Estudios Hispanicos* XVI, No. 3 (October 1982): 361–78.
> Examines *The Family of Pascual Duarte* as "a vision of the Spanish soul which . . . illuminates some of the significant psychological, social, and historical forces culminating in the Spanish Civil War."

Schwartz, Ronald. "Cela and *La colmena* (1951)." In his *Spain's New Wave Novelists, 1950–1974,* pp. 32–49. Metuchen, N. J.: The Scarecrow Press, 1976.
> Study of the modern novel in Spain, containing a discussion of Cela's *The Hive.*

Thomas, Gareth. *The Novel of the Spanish Civil War (1936–1975).* Cambridge: Cambridge University Press, 1990, 273 p.
> Discusses the extent to which the Civil War informed twentieth-century Spanish literature.

Additional coverage of Cela's life and career is contained in the following sources published by Gale Research: *Bestsellers; Contemporary Authors,* Vols. 21–24; *Contemporary Authors Autobiography Series,* Vol. 10; *Contemporary Authors New Revision Series,* Vols. 21, 32; *Contemporary Literary Criticism,* Vols. 4, 13, 59; *Dictionary of Literary Biography Yearbook, 1989; Hispanic Writers; Major 20th-Century Writers.*

Denise Chávez

1948–

Chicana dramatist, poet, and novelist.

INTRODUCTION

Chávez is widely regarded as a leading Chicana playwright and novelist of the American Southwest. She has written and produced numerous one-act plays since the 1970s; however, she is best known for *The Last of the Menu Girls* (1986), a poignant and sensitive novel about an adolescent girl's passage into womanhood.

Born in Las Cruces, New Mexico, Chávez was reared in a family that particularly valued education and self-improvement. The divorce of her father, an attorney, and her mother, a teacher, in 1958 was a painful experience for Chávez which led her to remark in retrospect that she "grew up knowing separation as a quality of life." She was raised in a household of women that included her mother, two sisters, and a half-sister, and has acknowledged that the dominant influences in her life—as well as in her work—have been women. From an early age Chávez was an avid reader and writer. She kept a diary in which she recorded her observations on life and her own "physical, spiritual, and emotional ups and downs." During high school she became interested in drama and performed in several productions. Regarding her discovery of the theater, Chávez has stated: "It was like a revelation for me. I told myself, this is it. I can extend myself, be more than myself." She wrote her first play while a senior in college: originally entitled *The Waiting*, it was renamed *Novitiates* when it was produced in 1971. A story about several persons in transitional periods in their lives, her play won a prize in a New Mexico literary contest.

From 1973 to 1984 Chávez composed and collaborated on some twenty-one dramas, ranging from one-act children's theater pieces to tragic dramas that explore religious or existential themes. New Mexico generally serves as the backdrop for her plays: "My work is rooted in the Southwest, in heat and dust, and reflects

443

a world where love is as real as the land. In this dry and seemingly harsh and empty world there is much beauty to be found." Although background is significant in Chávez's work, Martha E. Heard has contended that the "inner transformation [of characters] is more important than external setting." Critics have noted that Chávez's plays typically focus on the characters' self-revelation and developing sense of their place in the community. *Mario and the Room María* (1974), for example, is a play about personal growth: its protagonist, Mundo Reyes, is unable to develop emotionally due to his refusal to confront painful experiences in his past. Likewise, *Sí, hay posada* (1980) depicts the agony of Johnny Briones, whose rejection of love is the result of emotional difficulties surrounding Christmas. While Chávez's plays most often concentrate on her characters' inner lives, some deal with external and cultural elements that impede social interaction. In *Plaza* (1984) she contrasts two characters who have different impressions of life in the town square. Iris, a lonely and resentful woman who grew up "being told what to do, who to talk to, who to marry" because her parents were so "very Spanish," fears the plaza that she sees from her window, viewing it as a hangout for disreputable types; young Benito, on the other hand, finds it a stimulating place where he can converse and meet people. As he advises his friend Cris: "you don't get lonely here. There's always something going on. Someone to talk to. Someone you know. Someone you don't know. Whether old friend or new, one can help out." Though they range in age, the protagonists in Chávez's plays are frequently positioned at a pivotal period in their lives that calls for a decision or a leap in self-understanding. Critics have observed, however, that Chávez's characters defy conformity to any fixed pattern since she goes to great lengths to portray each figure as an individual. Her use of detailed descriptions, strong dialogue, and linguistic nuances taken from the lingo of the Chicano community help Chávez to delineate her characters and to distinguish one from another. "I feel," she has said, "that as a Chicana writer, I am capturing the voice of so many who have been voiceless for years. I write about the neighborhood handyman, the waitresses, the bag ladies, the elevator operators. . . . My work as a playwright is to capture as best I can the small gestures of the common people." Though some critics have cen-

sured the loose structure of her plays, most consider Chávez a perceptive and inventive dramatist.

Many of the themes pervading Chávez's plays are echoed and drawn together in her novel, *The Last of the Menu Girls*. Composed of seven related stories, it explores the coming of age of Rocío Esquibel, a New Mexico college student. In the opening story, Rocío goes to work handing out menus in a hospital, where she is exposed to many different people and experiences. Her impressions are shaped, in large part, by the ordinary individuals whom she daily encounters: the local repairman, the grandmother, and the hospital helper, among others. Confronted by the basic facts of hardship, pain, and death, she begins to plan her future. Rocío is especially attentive to women's voices and concerns, and questions the narrow roles assigned to them. Taking stock of her family and society, Rocío denounces feminine stereotypes and decides to become a writer so that she may, in the words of the noted Chicano author Rudolfo A. Anaya, "give meaning to the emotionally turbulent lives of the people she has known." The novel concludes with Rocío's mother challenging her to write another *Gone with the Wind:* "You don't have to go anywhere. Not down the street. Not even out of this house. There's stories, plenty of them all around. What do you say, Rocío?"

Commentators have admired the way in which Chávez has interwoven the seven stories that comprise the novel in order to emphasize the human need for *compadría*, or community. Although some scholars have found her style to be disjointed and flawed, most have lauded her lively dialogue, revealing characterization, and ability to write with insight. They have also extolled the way in which the novelist incorporates elements of American Southwest culture, such as traditional folk stories and poetry, into her work, helping to root her characters more firmly in their social and geographical context. Chávez does not look upon *The Last of the Menu Girls* as a novel, but as a series of "dramatic vignettes" which explore the mysteries of womanhood. In fact, she envisions all her work as a chronicle of the changing relationships between men and women as women continue to avow their independence. This assertion has led critics like Anaya to hail Chávez as a "feminine voice" that is contributing "a new vision and dimension to the literature of [the Chicano] community."

CRITICAL COMMENTARY

BEVERLY LYON CLARK

(essay date 1986)

[In the following review of *The Last of the Menu Girls*, Clark commends Chávez's literary debut, regarding her as a promising Hispanic novelist.]

Does [*The Last of the Menu Girls*] mark the emergence of a Hispanic woman writer of the stature of Toni Morrison or Leslie Silko? Not quite. Not yet. But Denise Chávez does show promise. The interrelated stories in this first collection sketch the coming of age of Rocío Esquibel, as the adolescent girl examines available models of womanhood, tries out roles, comes to terms with the clutter of her past and emerges as a writer. The stories are of two types: lyrical meditations on everyday objects and montages of dialogue that swiftly reveal character. The former strain too hard for lyricism. The latter, though, show Ms. Chávez's strengths in dialogue and in juxtaposing evocative scenes. The title story, for instance, shows 17-year-old Rocío working in a hospital delivering menus to patients, touched by the lives of those she encounters: a beautiful, bitter woman suffering something mysterious, something to do with sex; an illegal alien who has lost his nose in a barroom fight; a hunchbacked dietitian proud of his iced tea. **"Compadre"** tells of moments in the life of the neighborhood handyman, whose repairs are never quite right, but also of moments in the life of Rocío, from whose perspective, variously snobbish, exasperated and compassionate, the story is told. It concludes with Rocío's mother encouraging her to write another *Gone With the Wind*, which Rocío doesn't do, but also giving advice that she will follow in writing her own stories: "You don't have to go anywhere. Not down the street. Not even out of this house. There's stories, plenty of them all around."

Beverly Lyon Clark, in a review of *The Last of the Menu Girls*, in *The New York Times Book Review*, October 12, 1986, p. 28.

RUDOLFO A. ANAYA

(essay date 1986)

[Anaya is a prominent Chicano novelist and short story writer. In the following excerpt from his introduction to *The Last of the Menu Girls*, he praises Chávez's first novel and summons the reader "to enter the rich and imaginative world which she portrays with such feeling and insight."]

With the publication of *The Last of the Menu Girls*, Denise Chávez joins the ranks of writers who are rounding out the parameters of Chicano literature. The feminine voice adds a new vision and dimension to the literature of this community. Clearly, a new vanguard is here, and its name is woman.

In this collection, the reader will savor the poignant experiences and dreams of Rocío, a young girl whose rites of passage into womanhood give unity to the collage of stories. At the beginning of the novel Rocío cries out against the traditional serving roles which society has prescribed for women, and she opts for the life of the artist. By the novel's end she has found her calling, and that is to give meaning to the emotionally turbulent lives of the people she has known. It is Rocío's mother who wisely counsels and dares her daughter to write the story of their lives.

Denise's novel reflects her particular sense of place, revealing the depths of the world of women and the flavor of southern New Mexico. The central metaphor of the novel is the home. The family, the known neighborhood and the role of women in this context are Denise's concern as a writer. Her eye for detail is sharp; the interior monologues of her characters are revealing; and Denise's long training as a dramatist serves her well in creating intriguing plot and dialogue. In short, all the strengths of a writer are here.

Rocío's yearning is to write a great novel from the lives of those people she knows best. It is the same dream Denise Chávez has followed, challenging us to let go of familiar patterns and to enter the rich and imaginative world which she portrays with such feeling and insight.

Rudolfo A. Anaya, in an introduction to *The Last of the Menu Girls* by Denise Chávez, Arte Público Press, 1986, p. ix.

Principal Works

Novitiates (drama) 1971

Mario and the Room María (drama) 1974

The Flying Tortilla Man (drama) 1975

The Adobe Rabbit (drama) 1979

Nacimiento (drama) 1979

Life is a Two-Way Street (poetry) 1980

Santa Fe Charm (drama) 1980

Sí, hay posada (drama) 1980

El camino (drama) 1981

El santero de Córdova (drama) 1981

Hecho en México (drama) 1982

El más pequeño de mis hijos (drama) 1983

Plaza (drama) 1984

The Last of the Menu Girls (novel) 1986

Novenas narrativas (drama) 1986

Face of an Angel (novel) forthcoming 1994

RAYMUND A. PAREDES
(essay date 1987)

[In the following excerpt, Paredes describes *The Last of the Menu Girls*, noting flaws in Chávez's writing, but lauding her ability to realistically depict the human condition.]

Denise Chávez's *The Last of the Menu Girls* [is] a collection of seven related stories that chronicle, in several narrative voices and dialects, the experiences of a young New Mexico woman, Rocío Esquibel. In the title story, Rocío is a college student whose first job, in a hospital taking meal orders from patients, serves as her initiation into a human drama as acted out by a variety of hospital characters. The hospital is a microcosm of the larger world Rocío barely knows and it is here that she, confronted by the essential facts of pain and death, begins to plan her life.

Like [Chicano writer] Gary Soto, Chávez is attracted to the literary potentiality of ordinary events. She writes of summers in west Texas, of childhood games around a willow tree. But whereas Soto's narratives are snapshots, Chávez's are more elaborated, "continual speculations" as she calls them, "into the mysteries of womanhood." As Soto celebrates the camaraderie of

boys, Chávez celebrates her memories of "all those women, all of them . . . girls, girls, the bright beautiful girls. . . ."

[Chicana writer Ana] Castillo's narrator [in *The Mixquiahuala Letters*, 1986] never quite feels at home in either American or Mexican culture but Chávez's various narrators seem to settle comfortably on any part of her fictional landscape. Chávez assumes her various identities gracefully, whether Spanish or English speaking, Mexican American or Anglo. For her, to be a Mexican American implies not a haunting sense of marginality but an ability of move easily from one cultural environment to another.

Ultimately, Chávez offers her readers an expansive view of the human community, rich and poor and Anglo and Mexican alike: Chávez's literary technique—the suddenly shifting narrators and scenes—initially creates a sense of disjointedness but eventually characters and lives intersect and sometimes blend. This technique corresponds with Chávez's view of the human condition. We seem, at first glance, to be a world of many peoples in many communities with apparently little in common. But if we look beyond superficial differences, we find ourselves joined together by the inescapable facts of life and death and the awareness that loneliness is the least tolerable of human circumstances. Chávez's final story, **"Compadre"** — from the Spanish term that identifies the Mexican principle of the extended family—depicts the longing for community elegantly and poignantly.

Chávez is a young writer and a flawed one but her sense of herself as an artist is what the best Mexican American writing is about. Drawing from the resources of two cultures and languages, rooting her fictions in folk experience and belief, and defying traditional notions of gender, Chávez fashions stories that are at once distinctive and broadly appealing. (p. 128)

Raymund A. Paredes, in a review of *The Last of the Menu Girls*, in *Rocky Mountain Review*, Vol. 41, Nos. 1–2, 1987, pp. 124–28.

DENISE CHÁVEZ
(essay date 1987)

[In the following essay, originally composed in 1987, Chávez explores the familial, religious, and ethnic influences which shaped her writing.]

My first childhood recollection is of heat. Perhaps because I was born in the middle of August in Southern New Mexico, I have always felt the burningly beautiful intensity of my dry, impenetrable land. Land not often relieved by the rain—that wet, cleansing, and blessed catharsis. I remember as a little girl sitting waist-deep in the cool, grassy water that had been channeled from the irrigation ditch behind our house. The heat, then the rain, and the water were my first friends.

My other friend was my imagination that invented an extended family of loving, congenial spirits who wandered with me nighttimes in my dreams—into the other worlds I inhabited as vividly and completely as I did my own waking existence as middle daughter in a family of three girls, one mother, Delfina Rede Faver Chávez, a teacher divorced by my father, E. E. "Chano" Chávez, one lawyer, long gone.

These friendships with spirits were real to me, and still are. The spirits were voices of people, people I'd known and not known, feelings I felt and couldn't at that time conceive of feeling. I had no way to explain my creative world to anyone, could not even explain it to myself. All I know is that my life was rich and deep and full of wonder.

I always felt advanced for my age, somehow different. I always thought I *thought* more than people of my own age. My imagination was a friend at first, and later a lover, a guide, a spirit teacher.

I grew up in a house of women. That is why I often write about women, women who are without men. My father divorced us early on; he was a brilliant lawyer, but an alcoholic. My mother was incredibly intelligent, with a keen curiosity and love of life and people. Their minds were compatible, their spirits and hearts were not. I grew up knowing separation as a quality of life—and this sorrow went hand in hand with extensions—for despite the fact my parents were apart, both families were an everpresent part of my life. So I grew up solitary in the midst of noise, a quality I didn't know then was essential to my work as a writer.

People always ask me how and when I started writing. The answer never varies. From an early age I kept diaries, some with locks, locks I kept losing or misplacing, others with no locks. I'm sure my mother read my diary. I'm positive my younger sister did. . . . Somehow, looking back on myself in these diary entries, I am aware of myself, even then, as an observer of life. Without my diaries, I don't think I'd ever have become a writer. I now see that 1958 was a hard year, the breakup of my parent's marriage, a devastating time for all of us. I see the order I began to put into my life, the need to account for, evaluate, assess. Time was of significance, my life of value. Religion was important then as spirituality is to me now. I wanted to grow up so badly, to be an adult, to understand. My life was rich then, I see that too, with much experience that was to feed me for years to come.

I see that I was not a good student, ever. I rarely did homework. I would study in bed, usually lying down, waking up the next morning, the light on, in my clothes, very hot and clammy, dry mouthed, Mother yelling for me to wake up, to find the History or Math book mashed into my face. I would race to school, then fly back to enter the latest news into my diary. Painful accounts were entered, then torn. Did *I* tear them, and if not me, who? My mother, my sister? Or that other girl, the me who wanted to be happy? I note with interest my early stream of consciousness technique (not a technique then), my disinterest in chronological time (critics take note), I see the roots of my still poor grammar and spelling, and observe the time I begin to sign my writing—Denise. The writing had become a statement for someone other than me. What I had to say, suddenly, to me "mattered."

I see also the many gaps between entries, and that too is of significance. I see that I wrote on sad, happy, elated, and depressed days. The regular days were entryless. Writing was a gauge of my personal life. It was a record of my physical, spiritual, and emotional ups and downs. I enjoyed writing, always have, the actual physical movement of pen or pencil across a piece of paper. I enjoyed/enjoy the mind-eye-to-hand-acting-out-delineation of internalness. I practiced my handwriting constantly.

I see now that I was training myself unconsciously to "write" efficiently, quickly. A sort of "scales" for the writing self/hand. Rolling letters, moving them through space, limbering up mechanically so that later I could use my hand like a tool, limbered, unrestrained. I still find myself practicing the alphabet on random sheets of paper, testing letter style, still looking for a more effective fluid line. Much flight time on the white canvas of my constantly emerging movement toward my work as a writer. I didn't know it then. I didn't know it when I got a notebook and started copying other people's poems, songs. But this was later, because first there were books, books, and more books to read, like my favorite childhood book called *Poems of Childhood* by Eugene Field, with scary-wonderful poems like "Seein' Things."

I was a voracious reader. Anything. Everything. I went on binges. My mother would hide our books in the summertime so we would help her with the housework. My sister would lock herself in the bathroom with a book, heedless of my mother's cries. It never occurred to me to do that. Everyday my book would be missing, I'd find it, read awhile, then find it missing. It went on like that. I read fairy tales. Mysteries. Nancy Drew. You name it. Later on it was Ian Fleming's James Bond, D.H. Lawrence, Thomas Mann, Thomas Wolfe, Chekhov, Eugene O'Neill, Samuel Beckett. Now it's the *Enquirer*. I love the scandal sheets and movie mags and bowling and soap operas in the middle of the day, and so much of what everyone else considers pedestrian, sub-mainstream culture. Director John Waters calls Baltimore the Hairdo capital of the world. New Mexico/Texas was and is Character Capital of the Universe. Unbelievable stories, lives. I have always been a talker, friendly to strangers, and so invariably people tell me about their lives. It's a gift to listen to so many of these stories. The *Enquirer* has nothing over New Mexico/Texas or the world I see every day!

But this sense of wonder came early. I began to copy my favorite passages, poems. One of the earliest was a cowboy song. I loved the rhythm. Sang it to myself. Later on I copied Gibran and the Black poets, wrote angry poems to the nuns at Madonna High School, where I attended school for four years, poems they refused to publish in the *Mantle*, the school newspaper. Once, as a joke, I invented a quote for the "Quote of the Day" for World Literature class: "Christmas is the flowing of honey on a mound of cold, white snow." Mrs. Baker, lovely, frail, intelligent, and wispy-haired, loved it. I didn't know what the hell it meant. I was playing the rebellious know-it-all, making up my own poems and quotes. I didn't know writing was becoming a facile thing. Then it was just a joke. The other day I heard a writer say, "All those lies, writing all those lies—I love it!" I didn't say anything. For me, writing is no longer a facile joke, a prank to be played on a well-meaning and unsuspecting reader, nor is it a lie. I have said to writers I have taught: Don't lie. And to myself: You may lie in other things, but never in this. It's a sacred covenant I have with myself. Honesty. And no meanness. Sometimes it's been hard. Lies always surface, don't you know?

I never thought of lying in my writing. It would have been like hiding in the bathroom to read.

I could never lie to those voices, to those spirits, to those voices I hear clearly. Voices like my mother, who always spoke in Spanish, or my father, who mostly spoke in English. Mother grew up in West Texas, moved to New Mexico as a widow and met and married my father. My father, as a child, was punished for speaking Spanish in the school yard. He decided to beat the Anglos at their game. He went and got a law degree from Georgetown during the Depression. And he became, in his mind, more Anglo than those Anglos who had punished him. I remember my mother saying, "I never think of your father as Mexican." My mother was, though, in her heart and soul. She studied in Mexico for thirteen summers, was a student of Diego Rivera. She'd been widowed for nine years, all that time wearing black, when she met my father, just returned from the Big City. Both my parents were very intelligent, perceptive, sensitive people. My mother's grandparents were the first Spanish-speaking graduates of Sul Ross State College in West Texas. All of them became teachers. Both my grandfathers were miners, all-around men, carpenters, teamsters, fixer-uppers, workers with their hands. They used their brains and their hands to support their large families. The women were independent, creative, and did most of the child-rearing, alone. The Chávez men are painters now, artists with canvas and paint, or architects, builders of some kind. The Rede Family (my mother's clan) are educators, fighters for human rights, communicators, and believers in the equality of all people.

I grew up between and in the middle of two languages, Spanish and English, speaking my own as a defense. My mother always said I "made up words." Speaking Spanish to the Redes or English to the get-ahead Chávezes and Spanish to the traditional Chávezes and English to my Rede cousins was all taken in stride. We went back and forth, back and forth. My mother taught Spanish and she was always correcting, in any language. When I asked how to spell a word, she would tell me to sound out the syllables, and to find a dictionary. "There she goes again," I'd think, "teacher-ing me." I was lazy, still am. My English needs work and so does my Spanish. I can't spell, punctuate or understand the possessive. My multiplication is a mess and I can't tell time. I was absent the day we kids learned the 7, 8, and 9 multiplication tables. I have gaps—huge ones. But I've taught myself what little grammar I know, what math I know, and how to type. I can take any vacuum cleaner apart and fix it and my pen hand is very fast at the draw. I really write according to what I hear—sometimes English, sometimes Spanish, sometimes both. As a writer, I have tried to capture as clearly as I am able *voices*, intonation, inflection, mood, timbre, pitch. I write about characters, not treatises, about life, not make-believe worlds. If my characters don't work, I will go back and make them work. Without them, robust and in the living flesh, there is no story for me. Readers should stop looking for traditional stories, ABC. Writing, to me, is an assemblage of parts, a phrase here, an image there, part of a dialogue.

Suddenly it occurs to me that Jesusita Real, the not-so-mousy spinster in my play, *Novenas Narrativas,* should wear green tennis shoes, and so I add them to the script. When she finally does walk, it will be in comfort, with support from the ground up. I work with my characters in the way an actress or actor assumes a role, slowly, carefully, with attention to physical, emotional, and spiritual detail. I may read the material out loud, speak it into a tape recorder, play it back, rewrite it, and then tape it again. My years as a theater person have helped me immensely. I have acted, directed, and written for the theater. I have done props, hung lights, performed for all types of audiences, young, old, handicapped, drunk, aging, for prisoners, in Spanish and English. My work has always been for alternative groups, the people who never get much, for the poor, the forgotten. My writing as well is about the off-off Main street type of characters. My short stories are really scenes and I come from the tradition of the traveling *cuentista*. I believe stories should captivate, delight, move, inspire, and be downright funny, in a way. The "in a way" is what I try to do with all my heart. But always, I go back to the characters and their voices. I see them: flat feet, lagañas, lonjas, lumps, spider veins, and all. From the feet up and back down and around the other side. And I love them. Dearly. But I don't excuse them nor will I lie for them.

I write for you. And me. And Jesusita with the green tennies, spinster owner of Rael's Tiendita de Abarrotes, active member of the Third Order of St. Francis, and for

An excerpt from *The Last of the Menu Girls*

In the hazy half-sleep of my daily nap, the plaster walls revealed a new face. Behind all the work of growing up, I caught a glimpse of someone strong, full of great beauty, powerful, clear words and acts. The woman's white face was reflected in the fierce, mid-day sun, the bright intensity of loving eyes. Who was that woman?

Myself.

I thought about *loving* women. Their beauty and their doubts, their sure sweet clarity. Their unfathomable depths, their flesh and souls aligned in mystery.

I got up, looked in the mirror and thought of Ronelia, my older sister, who was always the older woman to me. It was she whom I monitored last. It was she whose life I inspected, absorbed into my own.

It was my sister's pores, her postures that were my teachers, her flesh, with and without clothes, that was my awakening, and her face that was the mirror image of my growing older. To see her, was to see my mother and my grandmother, and now myself.

I recalled Ronelia standing with her back to me, in underwear. How I marvelled at her flesh, her scars. How helpless she was, how dear! It was she who grabbed me when I was fearful that I would never be able to choose, to make up my mind. One time she and another young married cornered me, picked over me, my skin. Her friend hissed at me to tow the womanly line. "For godsakes, Rocío, stand up straight, and do *something* about your hair!" I felt hopelessly doomed to vagueness. Everything seemed undefined, my hair, my skin, my teeth, my soul. I'm incapable of making decisions, Ronelia, I thought. Leave me alone. Why are you attacking me? Go on with your babies and your fetid errands! But instead of crying out, I sat forward, bit my lip, and allowed these two young matrons to attempt a transformation of me, an indecisive girl with bumpy skin.

The charting of my sister's body was of the greatest interest to me. I saw her large, brown eyes, her sensual lips (always too big for her) soften and swell into dark beauty. At the same time, I checked myself, measuring *my* attractiveness and weighing it against my other models: Eloisa, Diana and Josie. Looking in the mirror, I saw my root beer eyes (my sister's phrase) in front of me monitoring flesh and its continuance.

I never spoke of growing old, or seeing others grow older with any sense of peace. It was a subject that was taboo, a topic like Death.

I knew that we grew older, but how could I imagine that all the bright young girls, the Jennies and the Mary Lous, the Eloisas and Dianas and the Josies, with their solid B-cups, their tangle of lovers, their popularity and their sureness, would one day become as passing shadows on the white canvases of late afternoon dreams?

The turning, plaster waves revealed my sisters, my mother, my cousins, my friends, their nude forms, half dressed, hanging out, lumpish, lovely, unaware of self, in rest rooms, in the dressing rooms, in the many stalls and the theatres of this life. I was the monitor of women's going forth. Behind the mirror, eyes half closed, I saw myself, the cloud princess.

I addressed my body, the faint incandescent loveliness of its earliest but not dearest blooming. Could I imagine the me of myself at age twenty-one and thirty-one and so on . . .

I turned the mirror to the light. The loveliness of women sprang from depthless recesses; I thought, it was a chord, a reverberation, the echo of a sound, a feeling, a twinge, and then an ache . . .

Always there is the echo of the young girl in the oldest of women, in small wrists encased in bulky flesh, in the brightest of eyes surrounded by wrinkles. There is beauty in hands tumultuous with veins, in my grandmother's flesh that I touched as a child, flesh that did not fall, but persisted in its patterning. Her skin was oiled old cloth, with twists and folds and dark blue waves of veins on a cracked sea of tired flesh. On my dream canvas my grandmother pats her hands and says, "Someday, someday, Rocío, you'll get this way."

Denise Chávez, in her *The Last of the Menu Girls*, Arte Público Press, 1986.

the people: Anglo, Hispanic, Black, you name it: anybody out there who doesn't know Jesusita is alive, inside her little store, swatting flies, and wondering aloud about Prudencio Sifuentes, the only man who asked her to marry him.

I write for the viejitas at the Save-And-Gain in black scarves, for the tall blond man testing tomatoes, for the Vietnamese cashier, and for the hot dog man outside the electric door. For me, it is a joy to carry my bag full of stories.

Naturally I write about what I know, who I am. New Mexico. Texas. Chicanismo. Latinismo. Americanismo. Womanismo. Mujerotismo. Peopleismo. Worldismo. Peaceismo. Loveismo.

Writing has been my heat, my accounting, my trying to understand; and rain has been my prayer for peace, for love, and mercy. August in Southern New Mexico is very hot, for many, unbearable. It has been my blessing in this life of mine to share that heat. And to remember the rain. (pp. 29–32)

Denise Chávez, "Heat and Rain (testimonio)," in *Breaking Boundaries: Latina Writing and Critical Readings*, edited by Asunción Horno-Delgado and others, Amherst: The University of Massachusetts Press, 1989, pp. 27–32.

MARTHA E. HEARD
(essay date 1988)

[In the following excerpt, Heard surveys Chávez's dramatic oeuvre. Although she finds the plays deficient in plot, she commends Chávez's characterization and dialogue, concluding that "Chávez must be considered *the* chicana play-wright from New Mexico."]

New Mexico's most prolific playwright is Denise Chávez. From 1973 through 1984 she wrote and collaborated on some twenty-one works. Her plays range from one-act children's theatre to full-length contemporary tragedy and vary in theme from religious to existential. The wealth of memorable characters, lively dialogue, poetic insights imaginative staging make Chávez—according to José Rodríguez, former director of La Compañía de Teatro de Albuquerque—New Mexico's most promising play-wright. In 1984 La Compañía chose Chávez to write the play they would present at the Edinburgh International Arts Festival and the Festival Latino de Nueva York.

Chávez' previous association with La Compañía had proven mutually fruitful. She wrote three of their Christmas productions; *Nacimiento* (1980), *Sí, Hay Posada* (1981), and *El más pequeño de mis hijos* (1983) and for the Feria Artesana in the summer of 1981 she wrote *El Santero de Cordova.* For the Edinburgh Festival she used *Santa Fe Charm* which had been a project of the Santa Fe Actors Lab as a seminal piece. *Plaza* which brings together six Hispanic characters who frequent the plaza in Santa Fe was the result. Another work which La Compañía requested, *El camino* (1981), has not been produced to date.

Since her days at Madonna High School in Mesilla, New Mexico, Chávez has been involved in all aspects of play production. She began her acting career as Antigone and has played such roles as Mauyra in *Riders to the Sea,* Anne Boleyn in *Royal Gambit,* and the Bride in *Blood Wedding.* Commenting on her discovery of the marvel of theatre, she told Jim Sagel in an interview [in *Journal North* (4 August 1982)]: " It was like a revelation for me. I told myself, this is it. I can extend myself, be more than myself." She went on to write plays and direct them— her own as well as work from standard and experimental repertoires. For both acting and directing she has received awards and her playwriting has brought her numerous grants and scholarships. (p. 83)

Chávez' theatre dramatizes interior landscapes against a New Mexico backdrop. From jagged rocks and mountains to brown deserts, from small town plazas and cafes to barrio living rooms, New Mexico is usually present in Chávez work. Yet the inner transformation is more important than the exterior setting. In an O'Neill fashion (Chávez admits a direct influence here), the characters reveal their inner lives. They strive to become more than what they are. The Tortilla Man tells Carlos in *The Flying Tortilla Man*, "Things can't be too easy for us or we don't appreciate them. We don't grow that way." They must choose; and if they refuse to do so, they are left to stagnate. For example, in *Mario and the Room María* Mundo Reyes is celebrating his third wedding anniversary in the De Vargas Hotel in Cuchillo, New Mexico. Because he will not confront the ghosts of his past, he remains "fossilized"—neither loving nor hating, just getting by in a world where "everything is okay." On the ninth night of the Posadas, Johnny Briones, the Vietnam vet, in *Sí, Hay Posada,* comes to terms with his past. After a powerful scene in which the actors representing different animals return to their essential human condition, Johnny accepts the love he had rejected.

The dramatic action in many of Chávez' plays centers around the unmasking of the character. "Caras vemos, corazones no sabemos," Cris tells Iris in *Plaza.* Iris tends to form hasty impressions of people as she sees them from her store window. She has warned Cris against Benito and Wilfred who hang out in the town square. Chávez shows that rigid social boundaries keep people from getting to know each other. This social conformity can also injure the person who has not been able to express his own feelings and desires. Iris grew up "being told what to do, who to talk to, who to marry" because her parents were so "very Spanish." Now resenting her unhappy marriage, she has turned against her culture and herself. Having no desire to reach out to others, she leads a lonely, purposeless life.

In *El camino* the characters are also in fixed patterns, unable to reach other. In this play the struggle becomes more intense when the characters engage in a life/death conflict. The eight characters come together in a small New Mexican town, Cruz Blanca. Existential in nature, they are brought to life in order to reach beyond their mundane selves and choose to help each other out of a sense of responsibility. In order to effectively dramatize the conflict, Chávez has chosen a carnival scene to portray animated motion that "reaches a wild, colored ferocity and whirling pace, and then falls off." Chairs are set in a circle to depict a "progressive dissolution of geometric form, life." They also represent carnival rides—the merry-go-round, the hammer or the tilt-a-whirl. As these characters move in circles slowly then faster and faster, the people at the booths become masked figures, representing youth at its fullest. In the following scene, Delia and Eloy are going to walk around the carnival leaving Lino on his own:

(He turns away and as they go off, they circle, in a different speed—slow, building to fast, the top winding down then up. ROSE leaves the mice booth, runs excitedly to them. They stand in the center of the chairs as the chairs become the merry-go-round. The people at the booths, SMILEY, LINO, RAMONCITA become figures, with masks, the style of these masks is similar to the Roman masks worn by mummies, with large luminescent eyes and a head of thick hair . . . The masks are an equation of that fixed moment of well-being, youth. One has the feeling when you look at the mummies' faces that, underneath, the body is a sham: shriveled, diseased, now dust . . . During the carnival whoever is not directly involved in the scene will wear the masks and act as participants in the ride—the faceless crowd. The scene progresses with excitement, rapidity, the rides should be full of energy and fast.)

The feeling of anticipation with which the scene began ends with a frenzied motion, life rapidly turning into death. Eloy, a drug addict, tries to rob Orpha, who runs into the street and is hit by a passing car.

Eloy then sits in a chair, his car, pantomimes shooting up, he also drinks, and then a simulation of the scene in the Hammer, it is his death, the Hammer, and he dies, in slow motion, seated, he jerks, his face contorts, he talks to himself, mumbles things. . . .

ELOY: Eeehhh! I did it, this is it, man, I did it . . . the hammer, man, Eloy Varenal, man, this is it, this is it, eh, man, cold, the Hammer, man . . . the Hammer, Delia, I did it . . . I did it . . .

(He O.D.'s. Pantomine slow motion, then stillness.)

As he dies, Eloy imagines himself in the Hammer. For the characters in *El camino,* like Eloy, who are unable to communicate to each other, the road of life becomes a journey to death.

Other characters like Benito in *Plaza* know how to be open with others. He feels the intensity of life in the plaza where he can talk and interact with people. To Cris, his new, young friend he explains: "The plaza. Como le decía a mi compadre, Librado, que descanse en paz, you don't get lonely here. There's always something going on. Someone to talk to. Someone you know. Someone you don't know." Whether old friend or new, one can help out. "That's what we're here for," he has told Cris. In such cases, a character is able to assist another with philosophical advice. These 'gems of wisdom' often provide an ideological base to the play. In *The Flying Tortilla Man,* the wise Tortilla Man tells the troubled Carlos, a twelve-year-old orphan, who is complaining about his job in the tortilla factory:

There you go again. It's not what you do but how you do it. And as for having a family, you have people who love you and you have yourself. So many people don't have themselves, Carlos, so what does it matter how

many brothers and sisters you have, why, all of us are brothers and sisters! We're all fellow countrymen!

Even though Carlos will have to face some tough times when he is unjustly accused of illegal entry into the tortilla factory, he will not feel totally abandoned. The Tortilla Man helps Carlos in the sometimes torturous process of growing up, as Benito has assisted Cris.

The passing of time is seen in Chávez plays in the clearly defined ages of the characters. Frequently the characters represent different stages in life, as in *El camino* which has characters playing the roles of the Old Woman, the Young Woman, the Young Man and the Young Girl. The women in *Nacimiento* range from the seventy-four-year old grandmother to the nineteen-year-old Lillie. In *The Flying Tortilla Man*, the boys are in precise stages of adolescence from twelve to twenty, but the Tortilla Man, a magical figure, is ageless. In plays with many characters like *Sí, Hay Posada* and *Mario and the Room María* all ages are represented, particularly in *Posada*, where family and neighbors play important roles.

The characters are not stereotypes. Chávez fleshes out each character giving him or her individuality. Some of her characters, such as Benito, reflect her Chekovian interest. They are caught up in the whims of history. In notes preceding the plays she frequently gives detailed descriptions of the nature of the characters. She once stated in an interview [in 1984] that she wanted to write dramas in which "actors relished their roles." Such characters as Benito in *The Plaza,* Mida, la abuela, in *Nacimiento,* Orpha in *El camino,* and Carlos in *The Flying Tortilla Man* do live on in the minds of the spectators afterwards. The author's affection for her characters is transmitted to her public.

For the director/reader of her plays, a complete description of the characters is included. These short narrations give family history, past events, daily routines, inner thoughts, secret dreams—the total person. After reading these descriptions, one's curiosity is aroused. What is going to happen to this person to whom we have just been introduced? From these narrative descriptions and from the dialogue, it is clear that Chávez knows her characters well.

Through language the essence of the character is depicted, whether in casual chit-chat or premeditated speech. Chávez' ear for the nuances of language is evident in the dialogue which captures the character's individuality, his social status, and his culture. She particularly catches that language of the Chicano community in which Spanish flows freely into the syntactic patterns of English. The dramatic tensions also are portrayed through dialogue. In a scene from *El camino* Smiley, the town crazy, quietly urges Orpha, a cranky, old woman who lives in the past, to get off the bus at the rest stop. In this masterful scene the tension between reality and fantasy is dramatized:

SMILEY: The window.

(No answer from Orpha)

SMILEY: The window. (She looks at him, the window) You got to sit by the window.

ORPHA Yes.

SMILEY: In the back of the bus.

ORPHA: The bathroom smells. Alguien no flochó bien . . .

SMILEY: Onde fuites?

ORPHA: (As if having taken an imaginary trip) A ver a mi Mamá, y mí Papá, en el CIELO, it was so pretty. Little fat angels and Mamá en su vestido azul. The one she was buried in, her favorite. . . .

SMILEY: ¿Y cuándo llegaste?

ORPHA: Hoy, hace un ratito . . . I got back to Cruz Blanca, it was a long trip. . . .

SMILEY: Por qué no vas a la casa a descansar? You must be tried . . .

ORPHA: No, I was looking out the window. It was a long trip, all the time I could see the people and the lights. One time I fell asleep, but then I woke up and I was hearing, "Cruz Blanca, rest stop." I knew I was home.

SMILEY: (Going to her and helping her up) Venga, ya es tiempo para lonchar . . . Y los perros tienen hambre. . . .

ORPHA: (A flicker of recognition) Los perros . . . Oh, si, los perros . . . I have to go home . . . (getting up) Go home. (She goes to the door, gets off, engrossed. Smiley follows her; at the door she stops, looks at Smiley, she smiles, she goes on, picks up a stone, to place at the *descanso* ; to herself): Go home. . .

Smiley enters into Orpha's world, while retaining a foothold in his own, and helps her mitigate between present and past. Looking out the window in the back of the bus, Orpha dreads stepping into the outside world where she is considered a crazy old woman, a witch. She prefers her flights of fantasy into the "golden" world of the past: Her childhood when her parents were still alive. Smiley gently prods her back into the real world with his questions: "Onde fuites?" "Y cuándo llegaste?" "Por qué no vas a la casa a descansar?" His sympathy toward her enables her to return home. At the end of the play she is the first one back on the bus—the first to die. She had died in a hit-and-run accident after Eloy tried to rob her. When Smiley saw the two of them dead, he temporarily lost his mind:

SMILEY: (Incoherently) On the road . . . Orpha and Eloy, Orpha and Eloy! Orpha in front, and Eloy in the back, dogs, her dogs with chains and bells, they were running by the side of the road . . . the dogs, the dogs. Eloy and Orpha!!! Orpha! Eloy! (He is very agitated).

Smiley is the only character in the play who does not die. In his other role (all the characters represent two selves), he is the bus driver who chauffeurs the others when they were dead persons, bringing them to the place of the living. Thus, he goes back and forth from the world of the living to the world of the dead in the same way he traversed reality and fantasy in the bus scene with Orpha.

Not only do characters develop through dialogue, the varied sounds of speech are important to the over-all audial effect. In *Nacimiento* the characters, all women, are identified through specific sounds. From Cuca to Juanita they grow louder, more toneless. Chávez even recommends to the actresses that they search for a vocal litany. Dramatic rhythm is also created with verse and song. In the children's plays, *The Flying Tortilla Man* and *The Adobe Rabbit*, there is much singing and light verse. In more serious plays, Chávez introduces poetry which conveys vivid, surrealistic images. In *Mario and the Room María*, Mundo's daughter Carmen, upon being told her father is dancing, recites these lines to herself:

His little legs, dancing,
dancing.
Shuffle along, your sad
body in step as best you can,
dearly,
childfeet in rhyme and flowing
the sail of your legs in cloth,
racing to be done.

Your little legs
Dancing.
Dancing.

In these lines describing defeated movement—racing to be done—Carmen catches the hopelessness prevalent throughout the play.

In spite of her believable characters and flowing dialogue, Chávez sometimes has difficulty in structuring the action. The plot wanders, getting lost in unimportant monologues, unnecessary dialogues. *Mario and the Room María*, written in the early 70s, loses its focus. There is no central character, no main action. There are too many characters and too many side actions. Rich in content, it explores the many problems and fantasies of the world of Mundo Reyes. There was more said about the characters in the "chapters" than could be discerned from the dialogue and action on stage.

Chávez needs to work with a good director who can assist her in dramatizing her vision. Then the numerous rewrites and restructuring which her plays undergo during production would be fruitful. Since many of Chávez's plays are written for special occasions, upon request, production deadlines must be met. She would not feel, as she does, that she is never able to totally finish a play if she could work more frequently with a compatible director.

When Chávez bases a play on a particular celebration, she gives that play special roots in time and place with universal dimensions. Two of the unproduced works, *Mythical Uncle Willy* and *All Your Brothers on Your Mother's Saint's Day*, were based on a wedding and a

Saint's day respectively. Mundo Reyes and Mae are celebrating their third wedding anniversary in *Mario and the Room María.* In *Nacimiento* Cuca and Mida reenact a scene from *Los Pastores,* the traditional Christmas play. Both Mida's family and the Briones family are digging into their pasts on that special night, Christmas Eve, during festivities with Hispanic traditions.

A drawback to the play of celebration is the forced resolution. In *Sí, Hay Posada,* the final act begins with a transformation scene. The characters wear animal masks to represent the essential human condition. Through them Johnny Briones works out his past emotional hangups about Christmas. Suddenly, the animals revert back to humans and the Christmas merriment resumes. Johnny joins in wishing everyone a merry Christmas. But has Johnny really changed? He only appears to have been swept up into the Christmas spirit.

A celebration contributes to the visual effect of a play. The set, for Chávez, is the visual underlining of the theme. The final scene in *The Flying Tortilla Man* is a pageant celebrating Oñate's founding of a colony in New Mexico. Chávez' description shows her concern with staging. Splashes of color, scenic movement, and costumed Spanish soldiers contribute to the spectacle. A carnival scene in *El camino* is also full of movement. As in *The Flying Tortilla Man,* there are booths in a circle. Eloy is trapped in the hammer (a carnival ride) which represents his approaching death.

When she describes the scene for *Nacimiento,* she indicates her knowledge of theater and set design. Taking from the medieval, she wants "mansions" to show time or place in order to add "spatial and psychological intensity." She continues:

> The main set piece is the Slab; a moving raked platform that alternately transforms into a cart, stone slab, couch, altar, possibly a fountain, the river, a Nacimiento, a confessional, a grotto, a picture frame, an altar piece, and possibly even a representation of Tlaloc, the Rain God.

Chávez indicates that the style of the mobile made of light wood from which hang *milagritos* is pure constructivism or nonrepresentational. Her command of the visual setting is seen in a sketch of the places of action in El Cuchillo for *The Flying Tortilla Man. Mario and the Room María* also occurs in El Cuchillo, but the set is distinct. The action occurs in the delapidated De Vargas Hotel. Chávez describes the scene in minute detail:

> On the walls are "faded sarapes" and "dusty-glassed photographs of wild bug-eyed men." In the bar area is "a brightly colored juke box with a pastoral theme on the front, lush tones." Near the women's restroom is a couch of sorts, a sculpture of sorts, with a shiny enameled wood Negro lying supine with a wondrous grin on his face and his curved and deliciously smooth ass sticking up to the beams, the richly stained vigas.

For *The Adobe Rabbit* Chávez specified a simple set, "suggestive of the areas in the state of New Mexico." Chávez ranges from classic to modern, from realistic to impressionistic in her set designs. For Chávez spatial relations reflect the interior. Stage set and dramatic action complement each other.

At this time, Chávez must be considered *the* chicana play-wright from New Mexico. Consistently active in the theater since the early seventies, she has written more plays and had more plays produced than any other Hispanic playwright. Her plays reflect different segments of New Mexican society; her characters talk and act like people familiar to all Hispanic New Mexicans. She celebrates the traditions and customs of Hispanic New Mexico. The *sabor nuevomexicano* serves to root the plays in time and place. Yet there is a universal quality which makes these plays produceable outside of New Mexico (*Plaza* was a success at the Edinburgh Festival in Scotland). The inner conflicts of the characters are common to all humanity; so are their triumphs and defeats. Chávez' characters are masterful conceptions. They live on after the curtain has come down. For this reason, above all, Chávez is on her way to becoming an outstanding and original playwright. She is someone whose works are worth seeing and therefore deserves more recognition and support. (pp. 84–91)

Martha E. Heard, "The Theatre of Denise Chávez: Interior Landscapes with 'Sabor Nuevomexicano'," in *The Americas Review*, Vol. 16, No. 2, Summer, 1988, pp. 83–91

DENISE CHÁVEZ WITH LYNN GRAY
(interview date 1988)

[In the following interview Chávez discusses the influences on her works, comments on the critical reception of *The Last of the Menu Girls*, and touches on other literary projects in which she is presently engaged.]

[Lynn Gray]: *Are the stories in* **The Last of the Menu Girls** *taken from diaries that you kept, or do you just have a good memory for what it was like to grow up?*

[Chávez]: I have a good memory, and also I did keep journals. I think they provided a way for me to write down things that I was dealing with, but when I'm writing now I work a lot with the senses; I specifically hone in on sensual images and memories. I break down my work into tactile or sensual images and these key images, like a smell or whatever, help to flesh out the story.

"The Willow Game" and **"Evening in Paris"** (from *The Last of the Menu Girls*) were written earlier than the rest in the collection and in a way they are mood pieces, meditative reminiscences. Later on I wrote more structured things, but I'm not interested in plot so much as I am in characterization. To me my stories are dramatic in the sense that they are presented as scenes. I'm waiting for someone to come up with a terminology to better describe *The Last of the Menu Girls.* It's like a series of scenes more than short stories; it's not a novel. Maybe dramatic vignettes is a better description.

Your word choices and the economy of language in your work makes me wonder if you ever wrote poetry. Did you work mainly on plays before writing the pieces in **The Last of the Menu Girls?**

I wrote plays and skits in high school, but for a long time I would just write things down as they came to me on loose pieces of paper and then staple them together—just ruminations or thoughts that I guess I believed had some validity or were pretty good, you know—and I'd hand out these little bunches of stapled papers to people, as gifts.

As far as my progression as a writer, I would say that I work very organically. I started off with the diaries, then went to the little note-books. I enjoyed copying down things that other people had written and that I like. I liked the physical act of writing itself—penmanship. I used to practice handwriting a lot. I love all the physical accouterments of writing: paper, pens, the hand. Anyway, I went into acting, then directing, and finally writing plays. When I was a senior in college I wrote my first play, sitting in my room, which was freezing cold, with a blanket over my head, picking out this thing on the typewriter because I didn't know how to type, and just having a wonderful time. The play sort of burst out of me. It was a leave-taking play, called *Novitiates,* about a brother leaving home.

You consider yourself a "performance writer." Some of your stories are largely dialogue with minimal outside narrative and in that sense become very close to being plays.

I included a few poems in *The Last of the Menu Girls* because I like the combination of different genres in writing. I'm interested in the overlap of various kinds of writing, creating different effects. In the same way I'm also interested in how things appear on the page, in the amount of white space and how things are laid out. As you say, it's really the way the narrative is placed on a page that determines, sometimes anyway, whether we call it prose or poetry or drama.

In this new book I'm working on, *Face of an Angel,* I'm trying to do some interesting things with space, bending the space, so I can combine dramatic scenes with poetry within the structure of a novel. I want to have voices in one section and straight narrative in another. I'm hoping to experiment with that rectangular space of the page to see what I can work into it.

As evidenced early in your career when you handed out bundles of papers as gifts to people, it seems that you consider art a thing to be shared.

That is true. It's important for me to present these things. Sometimes when I write a play I take it to the local senior center or the prison and share it. Though I'm now teaching a class in Chicano drama at the University of Houston, I still do workshops in the elementary schools, talking about writing. I like working with different age groups. When I go into a class of third graders I throw at them all kinds of characters, my gay bag lady, everything, because these characters are life, this is what's out there. And their reactions are wonderful, even these little kids; they're very sharp.

I think that writers need to train themselves to "hit the streets." This is what I try to do in my drama class. The students create the scenes, act them out, and then take them to the public. The important thing is being able to communicate, making that connection between the writer and the audience. It's not enough to write something.

I write to communicate, to share, and to order my own thoughts and background and experience. It's also a very healing thing. It's a catharsis, a transcendent process, and a means of bringing forward something that you hadn't realized was there.

Do you think that sharing your work helps people who don't write to experience some of that catharsis and transcendence?

Oh I do. It's interesting the number of people who come up to me and say how much they want to write. It stirs up something in people. They tell me that they didn't realize everyday life could be so fascinating or that they have stories that they didn't think had any validity. It's wonderful and I encourage them, especially women, to come out of the woodwork, so to speak, and write down their stories.

I was on an open-microphone radio show not too long ago and all the calls I got, I tell you, I felt like Dr. Ruth. The stories people tell you, it's so stimulating to me to hear these things. A prisoner who heard me on the radio sent me some things and we started a correspondence, so you never know what kind of feedback you're going to get.

What is your reaction to criticism? I know **The Last of the Menu Girls** *has gotten rave reviews. . .*

Let me tell you, talk about criticism. I got the pit of a review in my own hometown! One of the graduate students at the university reviewed *Menu Girls* and said things like "ambitious work chokes on fluff." That was the headline. I was devastated. All my relatives saw it and I felt no one in town would buy the book, you know. But finally I thought, well, you learn something from everything. I learned that even in the heart of a culture, one could be insensitive to it. The use of Spanish in the book scared him. It scares other people too. Why? Isn't it about time that we shared our languages with each other? The use of Spanish is my reality. Why is it other writers can intersperse

French or Latin or German in their work; isn't it the same thing? The criticism bothered me for a week or so, then I released it. Often critics have insights that are valuable, so I try to look for that.

I do get the comment, "Where's the plot?" That doesn't concern me and I feel that one writes what one writes. You have to keep in mind what you're trying to do and weigh that against the criticism.

Do you, or did you, write in Spanish or English?

My poetry I write often in Spanish, because it seems to me to be a more lyrical language, more moody, heavier, if you will. I selectively choose Spanish words or phrases to include in my English books when it seems appropriate. It's a wonderful asset to know another language, because when one of them fails you then you can fall back on the other. Or sometimes there's a perfect word in Spanish that's untranslatable, so I leave it in Spanish. There's a power in that, in having that choice.

You were mentioning of a recent reading the difficulty of moving from an oral to a written form of expression, especially in regard to all the things that get lost on the page: intonation, nuances of inflection and rhythm and so on. You compensate for that when you are able to "perform" your stories, but do you find it frustrating to lose so much on the page?

I like to get that sense of voice, but that comes from my dramatic training. When you're reading this stuff for yourself then I guess it just stays however you hear it in your head. But from my very first reading I was becoming the characters, speaking in their individual voices.

Let me tell you a story. I was in an all-girl high school and one of the nuns gave me The Passion to read during Holy Week. So I really got into it, you know, I was crying and it was just a very dramatic performance of the passion of Christ. The next day sister came up to me and said, "Denise, we really want you to do this reading, but do you think next time you could not read it *quite* so dramatically?" I really get into anything I pick up, it's just part of me. When I get on stage I plug in.

Could you say something about the **Novena** *piece that you're working on?*

Five women (a potter, weaver, a tinsmith, an actress, and myself) put together a collaborative piece based on a sculpture called Our Lady of Milk and Good Childbirth (*Nuestra Señora de Leche y Buen Parto*). The madonna figure was placed on an altar. These altars, which are traditional in Catholic culture, are coming into a kind of status here now as art pieces. We artists made this pregnant, singing madonna and around her I wrote a theater piece. There are nine women in this piece; it's comprised of the lives of nine women, from a nine-year-old girl who has been sexually abused, to the gay bag lady who has been in prison, a spinster who runs a little shop, the wife of a Vietnam veteran, an old woman in a nursing home who has Alzheimer's disease, several other characters, and

a narrator. Kika Vargas is the actress who plays all these roles, and she is currently touring, performing this hour-and-a-half long program.

It depicts very powerfully the lives, the spirituality, of all women. This spirituality is grounded in everyday life—the dreams and hopes and sorrows of these women are portrayed, and they relate to the great mother-spirit that is the center of all life, and of this piece. We artists surrounded this traditional, handmade, hand-dyed, hand-worked madonna with *recuerdos* which are objects from our own lives that mean something to us. It's a piece of folk art; it combines so many traditions: song, theater, handcraft.

Could you describe the descansos *piece that you mentioned at your reading?* [*Note:* Descansos, *which means "resting places," are the white crosses that are found along the side of the road in the Southwestern United States and other countries that mark the spot of a fatal-auto accident. They sometimes are decorated with flowers, dolls, a car bumper, or other mementos, and are considered an homage to the victim more than a memorial to death.*]

I had been driving on the highway from Santa Fe to Albuquerque with a friend of mine and we started talking about how eerie it was to come upon these crosses, especially on a stretch of road that doesn't look dangerous at all. We began to think that maybe death has a path, that there are certain areas that death touches down. My friend, Esteban Arellano, began taking pictures of these *descansos* and I wrote a piece to accompany each one. Some of this writing is research, some is rumination, some I wrote after visiting the spot and knowing something about the history of that *descanso*.

It's kind of fitting that when you look for *descansos* you can't find them, but when you aren't thinking about them they rise up out of the dark in your headlights. But these crosses on the highway are not a morbid thing; it's just a corollary for the road of life. The name of our book is ***Descansos: An Interrupted Journey.***

The women characters in your work are very strong; they're survivors. They are also women upon whom not only others depend but in whom the culture abides.

Well, my father divorced my mother when I was very young and my mother filled the role of both parents; I used to give her gifts on Father's Day because she was such a good father. She was a very strong person. My grandmother's (my mother's mother) children were the first Hispanic graduates of Sul Ross University in Texas, and the women in my family were always striving. One of my aunts was Texas Mother-of-the-Year, *twice*. So I come from a lineage of strong women, and I feel the voices of these women, of *all* women, are very, very important. (pp. 2–4)

Denise Chávez and Lynn Gray, in an interview in *The Short Story Review*, Vol. 5 , No. 4 , Fall, 1988, pp. 2–4 .

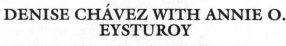

DENISE CHÁVEZ WITH ANNIE O. EYSTUROY

(interview date 1988)

[In the following interview conducted in 1988, Chávez discusses how her cultural background molded her writing. She particularly cites the inspiration of women she has known, adding that she regards herself as a transmitter of an "authentic female voice."]

[Eysturoy]: *Where were you born?*

[Chavez]: I was born in Las Cruces in 1948, in what later was to become my bedroom; I think I was the last child born at home. My mother was a teacher and had moved from West Texas. She was a widow and met my father in Las Cruces. His family was originally from Socorro and around there; they were farmers. I was the first child of that union. My mother had an older child, my half-sister. I have two sisters. My parents divorced when I was ten years old, so I basically grew up in a house of women, and I think that has probably affected my writing quite a bit.

I never felt that I was really connected to the United States; I never knew what it was to me. Las Cruces was a world unto itself, and to me that world included the Organ Mountains, which I could see directly from the street, and the world of the ditches. At that time in Las Cruces they had a very large ditch system and we played there and hung out in the trees. They had to spray the ditches for the mosquitos that would spread encephalitis—I haven't really written about that—but it was a magical time in a way, because people would come by wearing this futuristic head gear and would spray, and all the little kids would run inside the house and the whole street would be filled with this spray. Now I think that was probably not very healthy, to spray it out just like that.

My mother's family comes from the Big Bend area in West Texas. They were Mexicans who had originally come from Chihuahua, so we are *mexicanos.* They had come up through the Rio Grande and settled in a town called El Polvo, the dust; so that is where my mother's family originated, in the dust. They came into the area in the late eighteen hundreds. Settlers were wanted, so people were given money to come over and settle this place that nobody wanted to live in. After my parents were divorced, we spent a lot of time in Texas with my mother's relatives. My grandfather and my grandmother were alive then, and there were a lot of elderly relatives, male and female; so I was around a lot of old people from a very early age, and I think that has been a blessing.

I remember taking my grandmother to the bathroom, cleaning her, and attending to a lot of older men and women, and that is good, because I don't think a lot of young people do that any more; just ship them off to the nursing home.

So I grew up with a lot of people of different ages and different environments, and I think all those images of dust and rain and heat and wild flowers and wild land and mountains and sky certainly affected my writing.

Is there any particular part of your cultural background that has most strongly influenced your writing?

Well, my mother was a great influence. She was such a strong woman. Her family were the first Hispanic graduates of Sul Ross College in Texas. All of them were voracious readers, and they forged ahead in a time and a place where, I tell you, it was not done. One of my aunts was Texas Mother of the Year for several years. My grandmother's English was impeccable, and that naturally gave her an advantage; so when she got older she became the post-mistress of the small town.

There was always a yearning for education and improvement in the family, so my mother instilled this into us. She taught Spanish for many years. She was always challenging us to look up words or to read and she instilled a love of the culture and the traditions. She was also a very devout Catholic. I went to Catholic school for twelve years, so I grew up with *los pastores,* the traditional folkplays, *las posadas.* I can remember going with my mother to *las posadas,* and on Good Friday going to Church and doing *las velorios,* waiting at night and praying, and all the other customs; later on I was in that miracle play myself. We also always put out *luminarias* for Christmas. My mother was an influence, and so were all the people I happened to be around. My father's relatives were very artistic; I come from a family of artists on both sides. On my father's side I have many cousins, male particularly, who are painters. Some of my father's cousins have enormous farms, and it is a sense of loss, I think, for me to know that that land at one point was my grandfather's land; now the Reyes and Chavez farms have all the chile. But I buy chile from my cousins, and I am very proud of them; maybe that was not the path for our family.

My mother passed away five years ago, and as I went through her things I found many poems; she did write and I am finding a lot of her material. It is very interesting to me that after a person dies you know them. Now I feel that I really didn't know her before.

I was, like I said, in Catholic elementary and high school. One of my stories is based on a May Day procession. All of the children in the neighborhood had to collect flowers, and they would spread out this white satin sheet and the kids would bring the flowers. Laying flowers at an altar made a beautiful scene. That was the time when

Latin was spoken and there was a magic and mystery to those cultural things that we experienced.

Many of your stories, and particularly your plays, seem to take a point of departure in religion. Has religion been a major influence, maybe inspiration as well?

Like in the novel? Yes, absolutely so. The novel I am working on now has a chapter called "Saints" where I talk about all the different saints; I felt very connected to the patron saint of the mentally ill and to Saint Martin de Porres, a saint who is beloved by Hispanics even though they would never allow their daughters to marry a black man. That was, I think, a starting point in this particular chapter, my exploration of what did sainthood involve. This was instilled in us; what can you do to evolve and become fully yourself spiritually? What is your purpose in life? I think those things had a fundamental influence on me.

But at the same time I was also skeptical. Even as a young child I scrawled my initials out in the wooden pews during Mass; I did that like all the other kids did, drawing hearts and things. In high school I took another form of rebellion. I remember reading *Lady Chatterley's Lover* in Mass. The thing was to get by the nuns and get away with as much as you could. One of the biggest pranks that year was when two of the seniors switched the statues on the altar around when the nuns were not looking. I have written a play about elementary school and one about high school; they are all hilarious, wonderful experiences that give me great joy, and I laugh at them now and I see how crazy it was. There were twelve girls in this graduating class of Madonna High School, and we referred to ourselves as the apostolettes. I still see some of those women. We had a reunion last year, and we still get together. We are now very different, but there is that part of us that we still know.

I started doing a lot of creative work in high school; I started acting, took drama courses, and was always writing little skits and plays. It was such a small school you could do anything you wanted; if you had any creative bent you were free to do that.

It was there you started your writing?

Well, I probably started while I was in elementary school, in my diary at that time; I started early and was just writing all the time.

So your diary writing developed into writing the skits, et cetera?

Yes, and then I would act and perform the skits. I majored in drama in high school and won a drama scholarship for a role I did in a high school play. I took a playwriting class when I was a senior in college, and the first play I ever wrote won a prize in a New Mexico State literary contest. It was the first money I had ever earned in my life with my writing—fifteen dollars—and I kept that receipt for a long time.

I wrote it in the winter, in the room where I was born, and I remember it was so cold back there that I had a blanket over me. I didn't know how to type—I eventually taught myself how, but at that time I was still picking out the letters—and in that freezing back room I wrote this play. It was originally called *The Waiting* and it is interesting now, because I was doing a play on waitressing, and I had not thought about that connection. Later on when I was in graduate school somebody produced the play and I changed the name to *Novitiates*, which is the period of time that one has to go through, like a trial period, on your road to priesthood, or the sisterhood. So the play is about characters in some kind of transitional period, going from one thing to another. There is a brother and a sister, a mother and grandmother; it is a very interesting play, it ambles all over the place. No one has seen this play, but I did send a copy of it to the UNM library, so it is there in the files. I just recently sent a massive amount of things to the library, and that play is in there. It was my first, and I was very proud of it.

Do you ever go back and use diary writing for your creative writing?

I do that all the time. I have a lot of characterizations and many poems there. I have a shelf of journals, and sometimes I go back there if I am working on something I want to remember. If I want to do something on the sixties, I might go back and reread some of the sixties stuff. I should go back and clean it up, because there is a lot of work there I am sure I could use and poems I probably should type up that have never seen the light of day.

In **The Last of the Menu Girls** *you say somewhere that going back is going forward. Is that what you are doing when you go back . . . or how would you explain it?*

Well, I do explain it that way. I think it is very true. You never understand a situation or experience or relationship when you are in the midst of it; you have to step back from it and look again, and that may be a matter of going back in time, or analyzing what that experience did to you. I will use an example: I mentioned my parents were divorced, and recently I found a diary. There is a book coming out of Smith College in which I have written a chapter about my origins as a writer, and that chapter has some excerpts from this diary. It wasn't until I worked on that chapter last year that I realized I was able to see myself as that ten-year-old going through a major life change. So you go back and you go forward.

Do you think that is true culturally as well?

Yes, to use the traditions and cultures and language; I pay great homage to that.

Particularly in New Mexico, maybe?

Yes, and in the Southwest and in other cultures, too, the South and the cultures that have a sense of family and connections to the land, that give a reverence to the cultural traditions, songs and music; I like to use those elements. I will sometimes use some of the old songs, the forms, the dances.

What about the oral tradition?

Oh, very much so; yes, I like that.

Did you grow up with a lot of storytelling?

Oh, my God, yes. My mother was a great story-teller, and we were around a lot of people who were great storytellers. Everybody old and young had their stories, especially when we went to Texas; it was a small town of under fifty people, and we would sleep outside because it was so hot. There was nothing to do there, so everybody was outside, mind you, on their cots and sweating out there; and we just started talking to each other, so there was always a lot of conversation going back and forth. My mother would take us to these places and there would be a lot of people telling their stories.

She was a humanitarian and she would collect rum-mage. We could never get anything into the trunk of her car because it was jam-packed full of stuff for other people; all the neighborhood would bring her their used clothing, and she would even take things to people in Juárez.

I grew up with maids because my mother was a teacher, and I have paid homage to them in a work called **Hecho en Mexico** where I talk about all those wonderful women who brought me up and taught me language and everything. So I now find myself driving around, and my husband gets upset with me; I always have something for the Goodwill or I will call the Vietnam Veterans, or I will take something over to the senior citizens. Like I said, I have been cleaning out my mother's house and I just gave away twelve enormous boxes of clothing material. I feel that if you have something you should give it to people, so I guess I am a bag lady like my mother was, too.

Talking about influence—what about the southwestern landscape? Has it been an important influence on your creativity? How do you relate to it?

Oh, very intimately; to me it has been a lover, mother, sister, any sort of relationship that you might have with a human being and even with God Himself, perhaps. I remember just sitting on the front porch, talking to the trees out there, sitting in the darkness and watching the darkness grow and just seeing the trees come to life; or hiking in the mountains, collecting wild flowers like I talk about in one of the stories—or waiting for the rain, a sign of release. We waited for the rains in the summer. We loved to go out there and play around; the irrigation ditch behind us would be really high and we children would play out in that water.

I am still very connected. When I am tired and have been writing, I go out and look at the landscape and it soothes me, particularly the mountains. I have written a lot about this in my poetry; I talk about the stone breath of horizons moving, and I think in a lot of my work I talk about the rain; the dust, the heat; I mean it was hot and it

is still hot during the summer in Las Cruces, 110 degrees. You have to pay respect to that weather, because if not it just is too much for you.

There have been times when I have had a garden, but I have not been able to the last few years. I like going out there and puttering around, watching things grow, talking to my trees. I love nature and it has fed me in so many ways.

Are you a religious person?

Yes, I am. I did grow up as a Catholic, and I still go to church, probably not on a regular basis but I have a great spiritual nature, and I am seeker, too. I am always searching out my heart, and I have gone through a lot of different experiences in the Church; I have gone on many retreats and gone through healing experiences and participated in charismatic work, I guess you might say, interdenominational to me. I don't feel it is necessary to have one particular religion. But I am a spiritual person and am drawn to people who have that; it makes all the difference in the world. For example, this weekend I am staying with a Native American healer. The altar is there and every day I go and I say my prayers. When you are in an environment of people like that you celebrate eating, celebrate everything you do; there is a sense of joy then which I think certainly makes life a lot fuller. But that is not to say that I don't have my personal demons or struggles.

You grew up in Las Cruces, which is on the border of Mexico, and **Hecho en Mexico** *deals with relationships between Mexico and the U.S. Is that relationship a central concern of yours?*

Yes, and I want to write more about it. Like I said, we grew up with women who came *como criadas;* they were servants. No, not servants, they were never servants; they were like an extended part of the family, so we knew their lives, we took them back to Mexico, we shared with them, we ate dinner with them; we knew their families, we went back and forth, and there was an exchange between us. It was very common for us to go to the *mercado*, buy our food, go shopping for the feastdays and do things; to have our hair done. I went to my first beauty salon in Juárez. I was going to a dance so I had my hair done with all these little curls.

We traveled in Mexico sometimes. My mother had studied at the university and traveled for thirteen summers in Mexico. She instilled in us a love for the country and the people and the literature, so when I go back to Mexico I feel that I am truly home. I love Nuevo Mexico, but I always do feel that is where I really came from. As opposed to some people who say they are Spanish, I say that I am a *mexicana*, although it is true that Chávez is a name which has Spanish roots.

I have been talking to a very good friend, the bishop in Las Cruces—he is a *mexicano*—and I asked him what themes can be explored now. So we started talking about these laborers who got to a certain destination, a spot, to be picked up at two and three o'clock in the morning and are taken over state lines to work all day on the farms and then taken back home about six o'clock. They catch whatever sleep they can get, or food, or rest, and then are back out on the streets again about two o'clock. And, you know, I think a lot of things can be said about the *maquiladores* and what is happening now with the Immigration Bill. In Houston, where I am now, I am connected with a group called La Resistencia which is demonstrating against this bill.

So I would like to pursue some of these other things in my work. But of course, I also do realize that you have to go around political themes with a certain sense of humor. I am not a didactic person, and hopefully not in my writing; whatever theories or philosophies I have to expound would be done in a different sort of way. **Hecho en Mexico** was about women who work as maids, but I was more focused on the characters of the women, on the suffering they had. We did show *la migra* and the aliens lined up, but you have this one alien—this was at the time of E.T.—the only alien who can get by is this E.T. with his greencard; he is the only one who has a greencard. You have to make statements, especially in theater, with a certain perspective that does not cut you off from the people you want to reach. I try to show the characters as they are, even one character who is a horrific woman, who although she has had a hysterectomy destroys her daughter's relationship with this teacher. Even if she is an awful woman, she suffers great, great pain; so I try to balance out the evil in that character with the great suffering she has had to endure.

Is the Chicano relationship to the dominant culture something that you find you want to explore?

I think so. Now when I teach, the students say to me that they want to hear about contemporary people, and it is the middle class they want to hear about now, you know. I have made a statement to the effect that we have written the *curanderas* out. We have those people who still work in that world, and healing is certainly a part of our lives—my mother was a *curandera* in many ways and other women I have known—but people now have a need to address some of the contemporary situations, divorce for example, and what is happening to the family. I have never seen adequate treatment of the high incidence of alcoholism in Hispanic families. I know that every male in my family was an alcoholic, and now the younger generation is into drugs. What character traits or circumstances cause these men to do this?

This has been an oppressed culture and so the oppressed have to oppress as well, and it has usually fallen on women, or those who have dark skin, or the people who are laborers and so on and so forth. This cycle of oppression continues, and I am exploring a lot of those themes in my current novel [**Face of an Angel**].

In your new novel do you focus on the issues that are relevant to the contemporary Chicano community?

Yes, I am enjoying that. There are themes of interest to myself as well, for instance the changing relationship between men and women as women are coming into their own. Our grandmothers did not have voices. My mother's voice was a cry, perhaps, a moan; it was a sad voice. Our voices are hopefully stronger, and we can sing our stories and other women's stories as well.

You have taught a lot of different groups in New Mexico. Do the voices you hear in those workshops and classes become a source of inspiration to you? Are they the contemporary Chicano community, perhaps, that you relate to?

Well, yes, but not only Chicanas and Chicanos. Like this woman who had murdered her two children and would only play a cat character . . . but in a writing class she wrote a poem called "Sea Child." She was from Washington, she had grown up in that wild environment, and she saw herself as the sea child. I want to write a play about that woman. And then there are some of my experiences working with the women prisoners at the Radium Springs Center for Women. There were a lot of gay women there, and I myself would be gay if I were there—and even if not there I certainly might be gay anyway—but many of the women were gay, and there were two women who wanted to get married. One of them was a really rough type. She was a younger version of one of my characters, Corine, *la Cory* Delgado. *La Cory* had shaved her eyebrows, completely erased them, but the stubs were coming out while about the middle of her forehead to the side she had painted eyebrows very high up there; so you had these low eyebrows and high eyebrows, and then her hair was dyed blond. She had been married, had kids, and gone through that whole scenario, you know. She had everything, but it just wouldn't work for her, and here she was in prison and her play was going to be a wedding play; she was working on a play about a wedding between herself and this other woman. The concept in her work was really fascinating. She was an amazing woman, very resilient and powerful, and I admired her; she had a great sense of humor, but she was a tough cookie.

You have mentioned women several times. Do you gain a lot of your inspiration from women? Are you trying to create an authentic female voice?

I think so, yes. I am a transmitter of the woman's voice, a voice that may or may not have been heard; in the greater, larger world it has not been heard. And so I feel particularly close to many of my characters who are women, but I also have many men characters, too. In **Plaza**, the little *viejito* on the park bench, Benito Sieta, watches the world as it comes and goes, and he philosophizes. But I do think that my focus has probably been on female characters.

You mentioned your grandmother, and your great grandmother, and your mother; is that something you are very conscious of, that you are trying to channel their voices through yourself?

I am. I have been working on a book called **Rio Grande Family** in which I go back to the past. I have tried to enter the voice of my various relatives, to actually become the voice of my grandmother—I have certain facts and I do talk about those things—or the voice of my mother, or my uncle, or my grandfather, and it has been very interesting because it is a family history, but from a different point of view; I try to get inside those people.

You have mentioned that relationships were very important to you.

Oh, yes, like I am writing in this novel now. The character is a woman, a forty-five-year-old waitress. She works for a living, but she has somebody that comes in and cleans her house; that is her luxury. She gets in there and works just as hard as the cleaning woman, but she won't deal with that horrible substance you use to clean stoves. She comes to the realization that it is all right for the other person to do it, or it has been up till now, but she won't touch it; it is like it is all right if *she* does the toilet, but *I* cannot do that. She realizes that she is not totally being equal, feeling that way.

When I go to Mexico, I cannot understand *los mexicanos* in that way; they just throw the garbage out in the street. It is the concept that it is not our land, it is somebody else's. That is the theme in my new novel. I am exploring this woman's relationship to garbage; not the relationship between men and women, which you can go on with forever, but the relationship to a stove. This woman realizes she cannot do that to the other person.

The relationship among women is clearly a theme in **The Last of the Menu Girls.**

Yes, and the relationship to our spirit, to our dreams, to our alter ego, to ourselves; the relationship to ourselves when we are young. It is like there are all these different personalities and we have all these relationships to the me of this time and the me of that time.

The protagonist of the novel says at one point, "What does it mean to be a woman?" Is that something in your unconscious mind when you are writing?

Right. In that short story, **"Shooting Star,"** she talks about all her models and her disillusionment with them. It is a naive disillusionment, in a way, because it has been a naive world of imagining.

In my latest book I am also questioning what it means to serve. Women have traditionally been in service, so I think it is about time that we question it. I have one chapter called "Mothers Teach Your Sons," because I think it is very important. Unless mothers and women take the opportunity to teach male children what it is to clean house, to cook, to take responsibility, the cycle will go on as before.

My own husband is very sensitive, but he will say, "We did not do anything today except clean house," and I say "We didn't do anything? This is work." Cleaning house is a balance to the writing world and the creative world. I am the one who does the dishes and the laundry; he cooks, and we are working on that balance of what each of us does, that I do certain things and you do certain things. For the most part, women don't have that balance, and it has been unfortunate, but I blame the women equally, or even more than the men. So I am challenging women in this book, and it should be interesting how it comes out; I am sure I am going to get a lot of reaction.

So you explore what it means to serve, both for the recipient and the giver, and what kind of relationship that creates?

You can take that into the metaphysical or the spiritual, whatever. What is a life of service? Then what is work? Is it not in a way service, too? And what is meaningful work? I mean, here is a woman who is working as a waitress; most people don't find that to be a meaningful profession. An older waitress whom I worked with happened to be one of the strongest women that I have ever known, and she was a therapist. She may not have seen herself as a therapist, but she helped many people.

We talked about the question of what it means to be a woman; that is also a search for identity. Rocio in **The Last of the Menu Girls** *goes off to become a writer. How closely do you think the search for identity is connected to the urge toward creativity, the urge toward writing? Is it the same kind of search?*

Oh, I think so. Whatever your life's work is, if you are a plumber, if you design flower baskets, there is always that search for order and clarity in whatever you do; even if you make a salad it can be creative. It is the sense of love and devotion and commitment that you put into your work that I celebrate. Like this handyman in **The Last of the Menu Girls;** his work is slipshod, but he gets such delight out of this fountain—it does bring delight to him and to the mother; to her it is the beauty of the fountain, of being able to sit out in the early evening when the birds are there and look at that beauty. So I try to show those people, the nurses or whoever, who have a commitment to work, because it is a creative life and it should be, or else you have no business doing it. Too many people, I think, are in the wrong profession, doing something that is uncreative to them. I am lucky because I have almost always been able to do what is meaningful to me. Not always; I have had a lot of uncreative jobs, too, but you see that there is an end to it, you see that it has a purpose and even if it is painful or whatever, you can use it; nothing is ever lost, really.

So in that search for clarity, in that process, you also clarify yourself?

I think so. Definitely. Writing is a healing process. A writer told me she was working her way toward mental health. Not that one has to be crazy, or that you have to be schizophrenic or anything, but it is a healing process.

A large bulk of your work has been drama. Was the transition to fiction difficult or did you find drama a useful background for writing fiction?

There has really never been too much separation, because I use the monologue in the dialogue form. I can literally lift up scenes from my book and read them as theatrical pieces. I can cut out a few "she saids" or "she retorteds" and then I have the whole bulk of the scene there. I look at my characters as actors in the sense that I go in and I know them. I study their lives, do biographical sketches on my characters and know about their past. In this book I have been working on, I have this genealogical chart that has gone on forever, and the nicknames of the people, and the grandparents and where they came from; it is so involved and complex, this novel. What does the father do for a living? He wanted to be a plumber, his dream was to become a plumber, but he is a janitor. I mean, people might not think that dreaming to become a plumber is a big deal, but to him it was.

To me, the pieces in *The Last of the Menu Girls* are scenes; I don't know if they are short stories, I don't know if it is a novel. You have to come up with some kind of term that deals with what these pieces are. They are scenes in some way. But it has that dramatic element. I won't say that I rehearse my lines as an actor does, but I move toward my characters with the same kind of intensity. I have so many different worlds; I have the world of the restaurant, I have the family world, which is very extended, and I have the world of the character and her people and friends.

Do you feel that you're taking a new direction in your new book?

Yes, and it is scary. I have jumped from one chapter to another, and I sometimes don't know if I am connecting, or the linkages are seamless enough. I have three stories going on at the same time; I have broken it down into eight different phases so I have all those different environments, and then I am trying to remember who the people are, remember their names and how old they are and everything. It is just this enormous tapestry of things that I have to spread out on the wall, and I sometimes have to literally go up there and look at who a person is.

You are obviously moving into a new direction technically, but do you feel that you are moving into new areas thematically as well?

Yes, I think so. I think that *The Last of the Menu Girls* was in a sense a book that all writers have to write, a coming-of-age book. Perhaps my concern is a woman of thirty-nine because number one, I am growing older. I feel comfortable with myself, I feel I am becoming the person I am; sexuality is a very important theme to me, rela-tionships between men and women, women and women, men and men. Just looking at some of the myths of sex, and I don't mean just the act of making love, but like I said, the face of an angel; women are to be this, we are to harness ourselves. We wear angel face powder, and we are angels. One of the voices in the book is the brother of the main character, Hector; he is the manager of a car park and he has got three women pregnant at the same time, the one he is to marry, the maid of one of the relatives, and a girlfriend on the side. His sister overhears him saying that—this is where the title of the book comes from—she has the face of an angel, but she likes to fuck. And his sister is so shocked, she doesn't know which woman he is talking about; in a way she understands too well what he means, but in a way she cannot understand what he means. The fact is that if one enjoys any kind of sexuality, intimacy, for women it is immediately put into a certain category and we have this myth to deal with and these lies, really, these lies that we have lived with for so long. Just basic things; my mother wore girdles for years, and when I started wearing pantyhose, I was skinny and I had to wear a girdle, too, and that was torture. The whole girdle mentality crippled many women; my mother had a very large bust and she had indentations from carrying around this load of her sex. People used to tease her all the time; she was like Dolly Parton and had a very good sense of humor about it. But she was harnessed; her yoke was her breasts and her girdle. She had very bad legs, and I am sure that the girdle contributed to that, but it got to the point where she could not take it off because her body was so stuck into this mold, and we as women have been stuck in this mentality. Fortunately women are not that way so much any more, but many women still are; we are stuck with this image and perception of how we should be and how our children should be.

You mean that the physical girdle has been removed, but the psychological girdle is still there?

Yes, right, and so we teach our children that way, our male and our female children, and perpetuate the cycle.

So you see yourself as moving into areas that are central to you as a woman of thirty nine?

Yes.

To someone who doesn't know your work in its totality, how would you describe its unifying theme? Is there such a theme?

I think that there might be. I don't know, it is hard to say. One of the themes would be to impart a sense of acceptance and merciful love for characters. I try to portray people with problems and failings; they could be the handyman, or the nurse's aide or whoever, but each character has an existence that is sacred and I try to show that. I think I have a commitment to show characters who are strong, who endure. A central theme might be that one must endure and to do that we have to love and be merciful because we are human beings and are not perfect.

Do you have any particular Chicana perspective in your writing?

Yes, I try to bring that in the use of language, the situation. Talking about *compadrazco, comadrazco,* dealing with themes of that nature that maybe other people might understand, what *that* relationship is; talking in this new book about feast days and saints' days and all of those things that are cultural givens; the land, the wedding where they use the *lazo* and they pin the money on the bride's veil; just cultural traditions. As a Chicana I think I am very alert to what is, but I also have a very great respect for what was and what will be. Perhaps I am just a transmitter. I see myself as somebody who has been given a gift, something I never asked for. I am here to have this stuff move through me, and it is a responsibility and a commitment; I feel that I just need to do

that. I think I try to demystify happiness as well, because what is happiness? We should not expect to be happy; we should expect to do our work, and I think that whatever happiness or state of contentment or peace one finally comes to—my characters are always looking for peace—it is a lonely, sad peace. But a strong peace. I think all human beings have to go through this because eventually, inevitably we are alone and there is that peace that no one can give you, really, other than you coming to grips with and confronting your own life and your own destiny, what work you have done and what you need to do. (pp. 159–69)

Denise Chávez and Annie O. Eysturoy, in an interview in *This Is about Vision: Interviews with Southwestern Writers,* William Balassi, John F. Crawford, Annie O. Eysturoy, eds., University of New Mexico Press, 1990, pp. 157–69.

SOURCES FOR FURTHER STUDY

Soete, Mary. Review of *The Last of the Menu Girls. Library Journal* 111, No. 12 (July 1986): 106.
> Favorable review of the novel, particularly noting Chávez's ability to write "feelingly of things she obviously knows well."

Additional coverage of Chávez's life and career is contained in the following sources published by Gale Research: *Contemporary Authors,* Vol. 131; *Dictionary of Literary Biography,* Vol. 122; and *Hispanic Writers.*

Sandra Cisneros

1954–

American short story writer and poet.

INTRODUCTION

*D*rawing heavily upon her childhood experiences and ethnic heritage as the daughter of a Mexican father and a Chicana mother, Cisneros addresses poverty, cultural suppression, self-identity, and gender roles in her fiction and poetry. She is perhaps best known for her award-winning *The House on Mango Street* (1983), a collection of short fiction focusing on adolescent rite of passage and the treatment of women in a distinctly Chicano community. Critics have lauded this book and Cisneros's most recent collection, *Woman Hollering Creek* (1991), for their realistic depiction of the condition of Hispanic women and for their innovative compositional style; in fact, commentators have credited Cisneros's collections—which exhibit the overall completeness of a novel, the dynamic energy of a short story, the pointedness of a vignette, and the lyricism of poetry—with transcending the boundaries of traditional literary genres.

Born in Chicago, Cisneros was the only daughter among seven children. Assuming that she would adopt a traditional female role, her brothers attempted to control her life; as a result, Cisneros often felt like she had "seven fathers." The family frequently moved between the United States and Mexico because of her father's homesickness for his native country and his devotion to his mother who lived there. Consequently, Cisneros often felt homeless and displaced. She has claimed that "because we moved so much, and always in neighborhoods that appeared like France after World War II— empty lots and burned-out buildings—I retreated inside myself." As a child, Cisneros read extensively, finding comfort in such works as Virginia Lee Burton's *The Little House* and Lewis Carroll's *Alice's Adventures in Wonderland.* She wrote poems and stories throughout her adolescence and her college years at Loyola University but did not discover her literary voice until attending the University of Iowa's Writers Workshop in the late 1970s. During a discussion of French philosopher Gaston Bachelard's *The Poetics of Space* and his metaphor of a house as a realm of stability, Cisneros realized that her experiences as a Chicana woman were unique and outside the realm of dominant American culture. She observed that with "the metaphor of a house—*a house, a house,* it hit me. What did I know except third-floor flats. Surely my classmates knew nothing about that. That's precisely what I chose to write: about third-floor flats, and fear of rats, and drunk husbands sending rocks through windows, anything as far from the poetic as possible." Shortly after participating in the Iowa Workshop, Cisneros returned to Loyola, where she worked as a college recruiter and counselor for minority and disadvantaged students. Troubled by their problems and haunted by conflicts related to her own upbringing, she began writing seriously as a form of release.

Noted for their powerful dialogue, vivid characterizations, and well-crafted prose, Cisneros's short story collections are unique in that they incorporate several genres. Of her short fiction, Cisneros has written: "I wanted to write a collection which could be read at any random point without having any knowledge of what came before or after. Or, that could be read in a series to tell one big story. I wanted stories like poems, compact and lyrical and ending with a reverberation." Therefore, while each story within her collections is complete in itself, it is bound to the others by common themes that focus on Hispanic women, divided cultural loyalties, feelings of alienation, sexual and cultural oppression, and degradation associated with poverty. *The House on Mango Street* features a semi-autobiographical Chicana adolescent named Esperanza who, humiliated by her family's poverty and dissatisfied with the repressive gender values of her culture, overcomes her situation by writing about her experiences on Mango Street. She claims: "I put it down on paper and then the ghost does not ache so much. I write it down and Mango says goodbye sometimes. She does not hold me with both arms. She sets me free." Esperanza then suggests that her writing will someday enable her to leave Mango Street but adds that she will return for the women she left behind—"the ones who cannot get out." *Woman Hollering Creek* features twenty-two narratives that in-

volve numerous Mexican-American characters living near San Antonio, Texas. This work follows a structural and thematic pattern similar to *The House on Mango Street,* but the female protagonists are maturer and more complex. Ranging in length from a few paragraphs to several pages, the stories are first-person narratives of individuals who have been assimilated into American culture but feel a divided sense of loyalty to Mexico. In "Never Marry a Mexican," for example, a young Hispanic woman expresses feelings of contempt for her white lover fuelled by her emerging sense of inadequacy and guilt resulting from her inability to speak Spanish. Although Cisneros is noted primarily for her fiction, her poetry has also garnered attention. In *My Wicked Wicked Ways* (1987), Cisneros writes about her native Chicago, her travels in Europe, and, as reflected in the title, sexual guilt resulting from her strict Catholic upbringing. A collection of sixty poems, each of which resembles a short story, this work further evidences Cisneros's penchant for merging various genres.

Critics of Cisneros's short fiction point out that for several reasons she has yet to be fully embraced by the American literary community. They have argued that because Cisneros's prose combines elements of several genres, it diverges from generally accepted literary patterns in American fiction. Some commentators have also considered Cisneros's dialogue overly simplistic, especially in *The House on Mango Street,* where she often incorporates children's speech and games into her stories. Further, a number of critics have contended that her recurrent portrayal of male violence toward women in her fiction presents an unflattering view of Hispanic life. Many commentators, however, have lauded these same elements is Cisneros's fiction, asserting that her distinctive literary style and innovative techniques have been greatly unappreciated and that her concentration on cultural imperialism and women's issues has universal appeal. According to these critics, it is these aspects, in addition to her skillful prose, striking realism, and dynamic characterizations, that have established Cisneros as an emerging literary figure. While Cisneros's poetry has received little recognition, her *The House on Mango Street* earned the Before Columbus American Book Award in 1985, and *Woman Hollering Creek* has further consolidated Cisneros's reputation as an important voice in American fiction.

CRITICAL COMMENTARY

JULÍAN OLIVARES
(essay date 1988)

[Olivares is an American educator and scholar of Spanish literature whose writings include *The Love Poetry of Francisco de Quevedo* (1983). Here, Olivares illustrates the differences between Cisneros's treatment of the house metaphor in *The House on Mango Street* and Bachelard's in *The Poetics of Space,* centering on Cisneros's representation of Hispanic women.]

In some recent essays collectively titled **"From a Writer's Notebook"** [*The Americas Review,* Spring 1987], Sandra Cisneros talks about her development as a writer, making particular references to her award-winning book, *The House on Mango Street.* She states that the nostalgia for the perfect house was impressed on her at an early age from reading many times Virginia Lee Burton's *The Little House.* It was not until her tenure at the Iowa Writers Workshop, however, that it dawned on her that a house, her childhood home, could be the subject of a book. In a class discussion of Gaston Bachelard's *The Poetics of Space,* she came to this realization: "the metaphor of a house, *a house, a house,* it hit me. What did I know except third-floor flats. Surely my classmates knew nothing about that." Yet Cisneros' reverie and depiction of house differ markedly from Bachelard's poetic space of house. With Bachelard we note a house conceived in terms of a male-centered ideology. A man born in the upper crust family house, probably never having to do "female" housework and probably never having been confined to the house for reason of his sex, can easily contrive states of reverie and images of a house that a woman might not have, especially an impoverished woman raised in a ghetto. Thus, for Bachelard the house is an image of "felicitous space . . . . the house shelters daydreaming, the house protects the dreamer, the house allows one to dream in peace . . . A house constitutes a body of images that give mankind proofs or illusions of stability." Cisneros inverts Bachelard's nostalgic and privileged utopia, for her's is a different reality: "That's precisely what I chose to write: about third-floor flats, and fear of rats, and drunk husbands sending rocks through windows, anything as far from the poetic as possible. And this is when I discovered the voice I'd been suppressing all along without realizing it."

The determination of genre for *Mango Street* has posed a problem for some critics. Is *Mango Street* a novel, short stories, prose poems, vignettes? Cisneros herself states:

I recall I wanted to write stories that were a cross between poetry and fiction. I was greatly impressed by Jorge Luis Borges' *Dream Tigers* stories for their form. I liked how he could fit so much into a page and that the last line of each story was important to the whole in much the same way that the final lines in poems resonate. Except I wanted to write a collection which could be read at any random point without having any knowledge of what came before or after. Or that could be read in a series to tell one big story. I wanted stories like poems, compact and lyrical and ending with a reverberation.

She adds that if some of the stories read like poems, it is because some had been poems redone as stories or constructed from the debris of unfinished poems. The focus, then, on compression and lyricism contributes to the brevity of the narratives. With regard to this generic classification, Cisneros states:

I said once that I wrote *Mango Street* naively, that they were "lazy poems." In other words, for me each of the stories could've developed into poems, but they were not poems. They were stories, albeit hovering in that grey area between two genres. My newer work is still exploring this terrain.

On a different occasion, Cisneros has called the stories "vignettes." I would affirm that, although some of the narratives of *Mango Street* are "short stories," most are vignettes, that is, literary sketches, like small illustrations nonetheless "hovering in that grey area between two genres."

I should like to discuss some of these stories and vignettes in order to demonstrate the manner in which Cisneros employs her imagery as a poetics of space and, while treating an "unpoetic" subject—as she says, expresses it poetically so that she conveys another element that Bachelard notes inherent to this space, the dialectic of inside and outside, that is, *here* and *there,* integration and alienation, comfort and anxiety. However, Cisneros again inverts Bachelard's pronouncement on the poetics of space; for Cisneros the inside, the *here,* can be confinement and a source of anguish and alienation. In this discussion we will note examples of (1) how Cisneros expresses an ideological perspective of the downtrodden but, primarily, the condition of the Hispanic woman; (2) the process of a girl's growing up; and (3) the formation of the writer who contrives a special house of her own.

This book begins with the story of the same title: **"The House on Mango Street":**

We didn't always live on Mango Street. Before that we lived on Loomis on the third floor, and before that we lived on Keeler. Before Keeler it was Pauline, and before that I can't remember. But what I remember most is moving a lot. Each time it seemed there'd be one more of us. By the time we got to Mango Street we were six—Mama, Papa, Carlos, Kiki, my sister Nenny and me. . . .

They always told us that one day we would move into a house, a real house that would be ours for always so we wouldn't have to move each year. . . .

But the house on Mango Street is not the way they told it at all. It's small and red with tight little steps in front and windows so small you'd think they were holding their breath. Bricks are crumbling in places, and the front door is so swollen you have to push hard to get in. There is no front yard, only four little elms the city planted by the curb. Out back is a small garage for the car we don't own yet and a small yard that looks smaller between the two buildings on either side. There are stairs in our house, but they're ordinary hallway stairs, and the house has only one washroom, very small. Everybody has to share a bedroom—Mama and Papa, Carlos and Kiki, me and Nenny. (pp. 160–62)

Mango Street is a street sign, a marker, that circumscribes the neighborhood to its latino population of Puerto Ricans, Chicanos and Mexican immigrants. This house is not the young protagonist's dream house; it is only a temporary house. The semes that we ordinarily perceive in house, and the ones that Bachelard assumes—such as comfort, security, tranquility, esteem—, are lacking. This is a house that constrains, one that she wants to leave; consequently, the house sets up a dialectic of inside and outside: of living *here* and wishing to leave for *there*.

The house becomes, essentially, the narrator's first universe. She begins here because it is the beginning of her conscious narrative reflection. She describes the house from the outside; this external depiction is a metonymical description and presentation of self: "I knew then I had to have a house. A real house. One I could point to." By pointing to this dilapidated house, she points to herself, House and narrator become identified as one, thereby revealing an ideological perspective of poverty and shame. Consequently, she wants to point to another house and to point to another self. And as she longs for this other house and self, she also longs for another name. But she will find that in growing up and writing, she will come to inhabit a special house and to fit into, find comfort, in her name.

In **"My Name"** the protagonist says: "In English my name means hope. In Spanish it means too many letters. It means sadness, it means waiting . . . It is the Mexican records my father plays on Sunday mornings when he is shaving, songs like sobbing." In this vignette Esperanza traces the reason for the discomfiture with her name to cultural oppression, the Mexican males' suppression of their women. Esperanza was named after her Mexican great-grandmother who was wild but tamed by her husband, so that: "She looked out the window all her life, the way so many women sit their sadness on an elbow. . . Esperanza, I have inherited her name, but I don't want to inherit her place by the window." Here we have not the space of contentment but of sadness, and a dialectic of inside / outside. The woman's place is one of domestic confinement, not one of liberation and choice. Thus, Esperanza would like to baptize herself "under a new name, a name more like the real me, the one nobody sees. Esperanza as Lisandra or Maritza or Zeze the X. Yes. Something like Zeze the X will do." That is, Esperanza prefers a name not culturally embedded in a dominating, male-centered ideology.

Such a dialectic of inside / outside, of confinement and desire for the freedom of the outside world is expressed in various stories. Marin, from the story of the same name, who is too beautiful for her own good and will be sent back to Puerto Rico to her mother, who wants to work downtown because "you . . . can meet someone in the subway who might marry and take you to live in a big house far away," never comes out of the house "until her aunt comes home from work, and even then she can only stay out in front. She is there every night with the radio. . . Marin, under the streetlight, dancing by herself, is singing the same song somewhere. I know. Is waiting for a car to stop, a star to fall. Someone to change her life. Anybody." And then there is Raphaela, too beautiful for her own good:

On Tuesdays Rafaela's husband comes home late because that's the night he plays dominoes. And then Rafaela, who is still young, gets locked indoors because her husband is afraid Rafaela will run away since she is too beautiful to look at.

One way to leave house and barrio is to acquire an education. In **"Alicia Who Sees Mice,"** a vignette both lyrical and hauntingly realistic, the narrator describes her friend's life. Alicia, whose mother has died so she has inherited her "mama's rolling pin and sleepiness," must arise early to make her father's lunchbox tortillas:

Close your eyes and they'll go away her father says, or you're just imagining. And anyway, a woman's place is sleeping so she can wake up early with the tortilla star, the one that appears early just in time to rise and catch the hind legs hidden behind the sink, beneath the four-clawed tub, under the swollen floorboards nobody fixes in the corner of your eyes.

Here we note a space of misery and subjugation, a dialectic of inside / outside, a latina's perception of life—all magnificently crystallized in the image of the "tortilla star." To Alicia Venus, the morning star, does not mean wishing upon or waiting for a star to fall down—as it does for Raphaela, nor romance nor the freedom of the outside world; instead, it means having to get up early, a rolling pin and tortillas. Here we do not see the tortilla as a symbol of cultural identity but as symbol of a subjugating ideology, of sexual domination, of the imposition of a role that the young woman must assume. Here Venus—and the implication of sex and marriage as escape—is deromanticized, is eclipsed by a cultural reality that points to the drudgery of the inside. Alicia "studies for the first time at the university. Two trains and a bus, because she doesn't want to spend her whole life in a factory or behind a rolling pin . . . Is afraid of nothing except four-legged fur and fathers."

There are two types of girls in *Mango Street.* There are those few who strive for an education, like Alicia and the narrator, but most want to grow up fast, get married and get out. But these, like Minerva, usually have to get married, and they leave a father for a domineering husband. Such is the fate of Sally in **"Linoleum Roses"**:

Sally got married like we knew she would, young and not ready but married just the same. She met a marshmallow salesman at a school bazaar and she married him in another state where it's legal to get married before eighth grade. . . She says she is in love, but I think she did it to escape. . . .

[Her husband] won't let her talk on the telephone. And he doesn't let her look out the window. And he doesn't like her friends, so nobody gets to visit her unless he is working.

She sits at home because she is afraid to go outside without his permission. She looks at all the things they own: the towels and the toaster, the alarm clock and the drapes. She likes looking at the walls, at how neatly their corners meet, the linoleum roses on the floor, the ceiling smooth as wedding cake.

The title is an oxymoron expressing an inversion of the positive semes of house and revealing a dialectic of inside / outside. "Linoleum Roses" is a trope for household confinement and drudgery, in which the semes of rose—beauty, femininity, garden (the outside)—and rose as a metaphor for woman are ironically treated. The roses decorate the linoleum floor that Sally will have to scrub. This is an image of her future. The image of the final line, the "ceiling smooth as wedding cake," resonates through the story in an ironical twist, a wedding picture of despair.

Such images as "tortilla star" and "linoleum roses" are the type of imagery that perhaps only a woman could create, because they are derived from a woman's perception of reality; that is to say, that this imagery is not biologically determined but that it is culturally inscribed. A woman's place may be in the home but it is a patriarchic domain.

With regard to the poetics of space and the dialectic of inside / outside and as these apply to the process of growing up, I shall give only one example, but one that also touches on the formation of the writer. It is taken from the story **"Hips,"** in which the process of a girl's growing up is initially described as a physical change, the widening of the hips:

One day you wake up and they are there. Ready and waiting like a new Buick with the keys in the ignition. Ready to take you where?

They're good for holding a baby when you're cooking, Rachel says turning the jump rope a little quicker. She has no imagination. . . .

They bloom like roses, I continue because it's obvious I'm the only one that can speak with any authority; I have science on my side. The bones just one day open. Just like that.

Here, then, Esperanza, Lucy and Rachel are discussing hips while jumping rope with little Nenny. At this point the kids' game turns into a creative exercise as the older girls take turns *improvising* rhymes about hips as they jump to the rhythm of the jump rope. Esperanza sings:

Some are skinny like chicken lips. Some are baggy like soggy band-aids after you get out of the bathtub. I don't care what kind I get. Just as long as I get hips.

Then little Nenny jumps inside but can only sing the usual kids' rhymes: "Engine, engine, number nine." Suddenly, the awareness of time passing and of growing up is given a spatial dimension. Esperanza, on the outside, is looking at Nenny inside the arc of the swinging rope that now separates Nenny's childhood dimension from her present awareness of just having left behind that very same childhood: "Nenny, I say, but she doesn't hear me. She is too many light years away. She is in a world we don't belong to anymore. Nenny. Going. Going." Yet Esperanza has not totally grown out of her childhood. She is still tied to that dimension. Although we perceive a change in voice at the end of the story, she is still swinging the rope.

Indications of Esperanza's formation as a writer and predictions of her eventual move from home and Mango Street are given in two stories related to death, suggesting perhaps that creativity is not only a means of escape from the confines of Mango Street but also an affirmation of life and a rebirth. The first story is **"Born Bad,"** in which Esperanza reads her poetry to her aunt who appears to be dying from polio. The aunt replies:

> That's nice. That's very good, she said in her tired voice. You must remember to keep writing, Esperanza. You must keep writing. It will help keep you free, and I said yes, but at the time I didn't know what she meant.

In **"The Three Sisters"** three mysterious women appear at the funeral of a neighbor's child. Here Esperanza begins to fit into the cultural space of her name. These women seek out Esperanza for special attention:

> What's your name, the cat-eyed one asked.
> Esperanza, I said.
> Esperanza, the old blue-veined one repeated
> in a high thin voice. Esperanza . . . a good name. . . .
> Look at her hands, cat-eyed said.
> And they turned them over and over as if
> they were looking for something.
> She's special.
> Yes, she'll go very far. . .
> Make a wish.
> A wish?
> Yes, make a wish. What do you want?
>   Anything? I said.
> Well, why not?
> I closed my eyes.
> Did you wish already?
> Yes, I said.
> Well that's all there is to it. It'll come true.
> How do you know? I asked.
> We know, we know. (pp. 162–67)

In this paradigm of the fairy godmother, Esperanza receives a wish that she does not understand. How can she leave from *here* to *there* and still be Mango Street? How can she come back for the others? What is the meaning of the circle? Esperanza thought that by leaving Mango Street and living in another house, one that she could point to with pride, she would leave behind forever an environment she believed to be only temporary. A mysterious woman embeds in Esperanza's psyche a cultural and political determination which will find expression in her vocation as a writer. Esperanza will move away from the confining space of house and barrio, but paradoxically within them she has encountered a different sort of space, the space of writing. Through her creativity, she comes to inhabit the house of story-telling. Although she longs for **"A House of My Own"**—

> Not a flat. Not an apartment in back. Not a man's house. Not a daddy's. A house all my own. With my porch and my pillow, my pretty purple petunias. My books and my stories. My two shoes waiting beside the bed. Nobody to shake a stick at. Nobody's garbage to pick up after.

—it is clear, nonetheless, that a magical house is had through the creative imagination: "Only a house quiet as snow, a space for myself to go, clean as paper before the poem."

The realization of the possibility of escape through the space of writing, as well as the determination to move away from Mango Street, are expressed in **"Mango Says Goodbye Sometimes"**:

> I like to tell stories. I am going to tell you a story about a girl who didn't want to belong.
>
> We didn't always live on Mango Street. Before that we lived on Loomis on the third floor, and before that we lived on Keeler. Before Keeler it was Pauline, but what I remember most is Mango Street, sad red house, the house I belong but do not belong to.
>
> I put it down on paper and then the ghost does not ache so much. I write it down and Mango says goodbye sometimes. She does not hold me with both arms. She sets me free.
>
> One day I will pack my bags of books and paper. One day I will say goodbye to Mango. I am too strong for her to keep me here forever. One day I will go away.
>
> Friends and neighbors will say, What happened to that Esperanza? Where did she go with all those books and paper? Why did she march so far away?
>
> They will not know I have gone away to come back. For the ones I left behind. For the ones who cannot get out.

I do not hold with Juan Rodríguez that Cisneros' book ultimately sets forth the traditional ideology that happiness, for example, comes with the realization of the "American Dream," a house of one's own. In his review of *Mango Street*, Rodríguez states:

> That Esperanza chooses to leave Mango St., chooses to move away from her social/cultural base to become more "Anglicized," more individualistic; that she chooses to move from the real to the fantasy plane of the world as the only means of accepting and surviving the limited and limiting social conditions of her barrio becomes problematic to the more serious reader.

This insistence on the preference for a comforting and materialistic life ignores the ideology of a social class' liberation, particularly that of its women, to whom the book is dedicated. The house the protagonist longs for, certainly, is a house where she can have her own room and one that she can point to in pride, but, as noted through this discussion of the poetics of space, it is fundamentally a metaphor for the house of storytelling. Neither here in the house on Mango Street nor in the "fantasy plane of the world"—as Rodríguez states, does the protagonist indulge in escapism. Esperanza wants to leave but is unable, so she attains release from her confinement through her writing. Yet even here she never leaves Mango Street; because, instead of fantasizing, she writes of her reality. Erlinda Gonzales and Diana Rebolledo confirm that the house is symbolic of consciousness and collective memory, and is a nourishing structure so that "the narrator comes to understand that, despite her need for a space of her own, Mango Street *is* really a part of her—an essential creative part she will never be able to leave"; consequently, she searches in (as narrator) and will return to (as author) her neighborhood "for the human and historical materials of which [her] stories will be made." On the higher plane of art, then, Esperanza transcends her condition, finding another house which is the space of literature. Yet what she writes about—"third-floor flats, and fear of rats, and drunk husbands sending rocks through windows, anything as far from the poetic as possible"—reinforces her solidarity with the people, the women, of Mango Street.

We can agree, and probably Cisneros on this occasion does, with Bachelard's observation on the house as the space of daydreaming: "the places in which we have experienced daydreaming reconstitute themselves in a new daydream, and it is because our memories of former dwelling places are relived as daydreams that these dwelling places of the past remain in us for all time." The house that Esperanza lives and lived in will always be associated with the house of story-telling—"What I remember most is Mango Street"; because of it she became a writer. Esperanza will leave Mango Street but take it with her for always, for it is inscribed within her. (pp. 167–69)

Julián Olivares, "Sandra Cisneros' 'The House on Mango Street' and the Poetics of Space," in *Chicano Creativity and Criticism: Charting New Frontiers in American Literature*, edited by Maria Herrera-Sobek and Helena María Viramontes, Arte Publico Press, 1988, pp. 160–70.

ELLEN McCRACKEN

(essay date 1989)

[In the following excerpt, McCracken examines Cisneros's Chicano ideology and language, as well as the role of women, in *The House on Mango Street* to demonstrate how the collection varies from traditional canonical standards of literature.]

Difficult to find in most libraries and bookstores, [*The House on Mango Street*] is well known among Chicano critics and scholars, but virtually unheard of in larger academic and critical circles. In May 1985 it won the Before Columbus Foundation's American Book Award, but this prize has not greatly increased the volume's national visibility. Cisneros' book has not been excluded from the canon solely because of its publishing circumstances: major publishing houses are quick to capitalize on a Richard Rodríguez whose widely distributed and reviewed *Hunger of Memory* (1982) does not depart ideologically and semantically from the dominant discourse. They are even willing to market an Anglo writer as a Chicano, as occurred in 1983 with Danny Santiago's *Famous All Over Town*. Rather, Cisneros' text is likely to continue to be excluded from the canon because it "speaks another language altogether," one to which the critics of the literary establishment "remain blind."

Besides the double marginalization that stems from gender and ethnicity, Cisneros transgresses the dominant discourse of canonical standards ideologically and linguistically. In bold contrast to the individualistic introspection of many canonical texts, Cisneros writes a modified autobiographical novel, or *Bildungsroman,* that roots the individual self in the broader socio-political reality of the Chicano community. As we will see, the story of individual development is oriented outwardly here, away from the bourgeois individualism of many standard texts. Cisneros' language also contributes to the text's otherness. In opposition to the complex, hermetic language of many canonical works, *The House on Mango Street* recuperates the simplicity of children's speech, paralleling the autobiographical protagonist's chronological age in the book. Although making the text accessible to people with a wider range of reading abilities, such simple and well-crafted prose is not currently in canonical vogue.

The volume falls between traditional genre distinctions as well. Containing a group of 44 short and interrelated stories, the book has been classified as a novel by some because, as occurs in Tomas Rivera's *. . . y no se lo tragó la tierra*, there is character and plot development throughout the episodes. I prefer to classify Cisneros' text as a collection, a hybrid genre midway between the novel and the short story. Like Sherwood Anderson's *Winesburg, Ohio*, Pedro Juan Soto's *Spiks*, Gloria Naylor's *The Women of Brewster Place*, and Rivera's text, Cisneros' collection represents the writer's attempt to achieve both the intensity of the short story and the discursive length of the novel within a single volume. Unlike the chapters of most novels, each story in the collection could stand on its own if it were to be excerpted but each attains additional important meaning when interacting with the other stories in the volume. A number of structural and thematic elements link the stories of each collection together. Whereas in *Winesburg, Ohio,* one important structuring element is the town itself, in *The House on Mango Street* and *. . . y no se lo tragó la tierra* the image of the house is a central unifying motif.

On the surface the compelling desire for a house of one's own appears individualistic rather than community oriented, but Cisneros socializes the motif of the house, showing it to be a basic human need left unsatisfied for many of the minority population under capitalism. It is precisely the lack of housing stability that motivates the image's centrality in works by writers like Cisneros and Rivera. For the migrant worker who has moved continuously because of job exigencies and who, like many others in the Chicano community, has been deprived of an adequate place to live because of the inequities of income distribution in U.S. society, the desire for a house is not a sign of individualistic acquisitiveness but rather represents the satisfaction of a basic human need. Cisneros begins her narrative with a description of the housing conditions the protagonist's family has experienced:

> We didn't always live on Mango Street. Before that we lived on Loomis on the third floor and before that we lived on Keeler. Before Keeler it was Paulina, and before that I can't remember. But what I remember most is moving a lot . . .

> We had to leave the flat on Loomis quick. The water pipes broke and the landlord wouldn't fix them because the house was too old. . . . We were using the washroom next door and carrying water over in empty milk gallons.

Cisneros has socialized the motif of a house of one's own by showing its motivating roots to be the inadequate housing conditions in which she and others in her community lived. We learn that Esperanza, the protagonist Cisneros creates, was subjected to humiliation by her teachers because of her family's living conditions. "You live *there*?" a nun from her school had remarked when seeing Esperanza playing in front of the flat on Loomis. "*There*. I had to look where she pointed—the third floor, the paint peeling, wooden bars Papa had nailed on the windows so we wouldn't fall out. You live *there*? The way she said it made me feel like nothing. . . ." Later, after the move to the house on Mango Street that is better but still unsatisfactory, the Sister Superior at her school responds to Esperanza's request to eat lunch in the cafeteria rather than returning home by apparently humiliating the child deliberately: "You don't live far, she says. . . I bet I can see your house from my window. Which one?. . . That one? She said pointing to a row of ugly 3-flats, the ones even the raggedy men are ashamed to go into. Yes, I nodded even though I knew that wasn't my house and started to cry. . . ." The Sister Superior is revealing her own prejudices; in effect, she is telling the child, "All you Mexicans must live in such buildings." It is in response to humiliations such as these that the autobiographical protagonist expresses her need for a house of her own. Rather than the mere desire to possess private property, Esperanza's wish for a house represents a positive objectification of the self, the chance to redress humiliation and establish a dignified sense of her own personhood.

Cisneros links this positive objectification that a house of one's own can provide to the process of artistic creation. Early on, the protagonist remarks that the dream of a white house "with trees around it, a great big yard and grass growing without a fence" structured the bedtime stories her mother told them. This early connection of the ideal house to fiction is developed throughout the collection, especially in the final two stories. In **"A House of My Own,"** the protagonist remarks that the desired house would contain "my books and stories" and that such a house is as necessary to the writing process as paper: "Only a house quiet as snow, a space for myself to go, clean as paper before the poem." In **"Mango Says Goodbye Sometimes,"** the Mango Street house, which falls short of the ideal dream house, becomes a symbol of the writer's attainment of her identity through artistic creation. Admitting that she both belonged and did not belong to the "sad red house" on Mango Street, the protagonist comes to terms with the ethnic consciousness that this house represents through the process of fictive creation: "I put it down on paper and then the ghost does not ache so much. I write it down and Mango says goodbye sometimes. She does not hold me with both arms. She sets me free." She is released materially to find a more suitable dwelling that will facilitate her writing; psychologically, she alleviates the ethnic anguish that she has heretofore attempted to repress. It is important, however, that she view her departure from the Mango Street house to enable her artistic production in social rather than isolationist terms: "They will know I have gone away to come back. For the ones I left behind. For the ones who cannot get out."

Unlike many introspective writers, then, Cisneros links both the process of artistic creation and the dream of a house that will enable this art to social rather than individualistic issues. In **"Bums in the Attic,"** we learn that the protagonist dreams of a house on a hill similar to those where her father works as a gardener. Unlike those who own such houses now, Esperanza assures us that, were she to obtain such a house, she would not forget the people who live below: "One day I'll own my own house, but I won't forget who I am or where I came from. Passing bums will ask, Can I come in? I'll offer them the attic, ask them to stay, because I know how it is to be without a house." She conceives of a house as communal rather than private property; such sharing runs counter to the dominant ideological discourse that strongly affects consciousness in capitalist societies. Cisneros' social motifs undermine rather than support the widespread messages of individualized consumption that facilitate sales of goods and services under consumer capitalism.

Another important reason why Cisneros's text has not been accepted as part of the dominant canonical discourse is its demystificatory presentation of women's issues, especially the problems low-income Chicana women face. Dedicated "A las Mujeres/To the Women," *The*

House on Mango Street presents clusters of women characters through the sometimes naive and sometimes wise vision of the adolescent protagonist. There are positive and negative female role models and, in addition, several key incidents that focus the reader's attention on the contradictions of patriarchal social organization. Few mainstream critics consider these the vital, universal issues that constitute great art. When representatives of the critical establishment do accord a text such as Cisneros' a reading, it is often performed with disinterest and defense mechanisms well in place.

Neither does *The House on Mango Street* lend itself to an exoticized reading of the life of Chicana women that sometimes enables a text's canonical acceptance. In **"The Family of Little Feet,"** for example, Esperanza and her friends dress up in cast-off high heels they have been given and play at being adult women. At first revelling in the male attention they receive from the strangers who see them, the girls are ultimately disillusioned after a drunken bum attempts to purchase a kiss for a dollar. While capturing the fleeting sense of self-value that the attention of male surveyors affords women, Cisneros also critically portrays here the danger of competitive feelings among women when one girl's cousins pretend not to see Esperanza and her friends as they walk by. Also portrayed is the corner grocer's attempt to control female sexuality by threatening to call the police to stop the girls from wearing the heels. Cisneros proscribes a romantic or exotic reading of the dress-up episode, focusing instead on the girls' discovery of the threatening nature of male sexual power that is frequently disguised as desirable male attention and positive validation of women, though what is, in fact, sexual reification.

Scenes of patriarchal and sexual violence in the collection also prevent a romantic reading of women's issues in this Chicano community. We see a woman whose husband locks her in the house, a daughter brutally beaten by her father, and Esperanza's own sexual initiation through rape. Like the threatening corner grocer in **"The Family of Little Feet,"** the men in these stories control or appropriate female sexuality by adopting one or another form of violence as if it were their innate right. One young woman, Rafaela, "gets locked indoors because her husband is afraid [she] will run away since she is too beautiful to look at." Esperanza and her friends send papaya and coconut juice up to the woman in a paper bag on a clothesline she has lowered; metonymically, Cisneros suggests that the sweet drinks represent the island the woman has left and the dance hall down the street as well, where other women are ostensibly more in control of their own sexual expression and are allowed to open their homes with keys. The young yet wise narrator, however, recognizes that "always there is someone offering sweeter drinks, someone promising to keep [women] on a silver string."

The cycle of stories about Esperanza's friend Sally shows this patriarchal violence in its more overt stages.

Like Rafaela, the young teenager Sally is frequently forced to stay in the house because "her father says to be this beautiful is trouble." But even worse, we learn later that Sally's father beats her. Appearing at school with bruises and scars, Sally tells Esperanza that her father sometimes hits her with his hands "just like a dog . . . as if I was an animal. He thinks I'm going to run away like his sisters who made the family ashamed. Just because I'm a daughter. . . ." In **"Linoleum Roses,"** a later story in the Sally cycle, we learn that she escapes her father's brutality by marrying a marshmallow salesman "in another state where it's legal to get married before eighth grade." In effect, her father's violent attempts to control her sexuality—here a case of child abuse—cause Sally to exchange one repressive patriarchal prison for another. Dependent on her husband for money, she is forbidden to talk on the telephone, look out the window, or have her friends visit. In one of his fits of anger, her husband kicks the door in. Where Rafaela's husband imprisons her with a key, Sally's locks her in with psychological force: "[Sally] sits home because she is afraid to go outside without his permission."

A role model for Esperanza, Sally has symbolized the process of sexual initiation for her younger friend. Two stories in the cycle reveal Esperanza's growing awareness of the link between sex, male power, and violence in patriarchal society. In **"The Monkey Garden,"** Esperanza perceives her friend Sally to be in danger when the older girl agrees to "kiss" a group of boys so that they will return her car keys; ". . . they're making her kiss them," Esperanza reports to the mother of one of the boys. When the mother shows no concern, Esperanza undertakes Sally's defense herself: "Sally needed to be saved. I took three big sticks and a brick and figured this was enough." Sally and the boys tell her to go home and Esperanza feels stupid and ashamed. In postlapsarian anguish, she runs to the other end of the garden and, in what seems to be an especially severe form of self-punishment for this young girl, tries to make herself die by willing her heart to stop beating.

In **"Red Clowns,"** the story that follows, Esperanza's first suspicions of the patriarchy's joining of male power, violence, and sex are confirmed beyond a doubt. She had previously used appellation throughout the first story in the Sally cycle to ask her friend to teach her how to dress and apply makeup. Now the appellation to Sally is one of severe disillusionment after Esperanza has been sexually assaulted in an amusement park while waiting for Sally to return from her own sexual liaison:

> Sally, you lied. It wasn't like you said at all . . . Why didn't you hear me when I called? Why didn't you tell them to leave me alone? The one who grabbed me by the arm, he wouldn't let me go. He said I love you, Spanish girl, I love you, and pressed his sour mouth to mine . . . I couldn't make them go away. I couldn't do anything but cry . . . Please don't make me tell it all.

This scene extends the male violence toward Esperanza, begun on her first day of work, when an apparently nice old man "grabs [her] face with both hands and kisses [her] hard on the mouth and doesn't let go." Together with other instances of male violence in the collection—Rafaela's imprisonment, Sally's beatings, and the details of Minerva's life, another young married woman whose husband beats her and throws a rock through the window—these episodes form a continuum in which sex, patriarchal power, and violence are linked. Earlier, Cisneros had developed this connection in the poem "South Sangamon," in which similar elements of male violence predominate: "he punched her belly," "his drunk cussing," "the whole door shakes/like his big foot meant to break it," and "just then/the big rock comes in." *The House on Mango Street* presents this continuum critically, offering an unromanticized, inside view of Esperanza's violent sexual initiation and its links to the oppression of other women in the Chicano community.

Cisneros does not merely delineate women's victimization in this collection, however. Several positive female role models help to guide Esperanza's development. Minerva, for example, although a victim of her husband's violence, makes time to write poetry. "But when the kids are asleep after she's fed them their pancake dinner, she writes poems on little pieces of paper that she folds over and over and holds in her hands a long time, little pieces of paper that smell like a dime. She lets me read her poems. I let her read mine." Minerva's artistic production is reminiscent of Dr. Reefy in *Winesburg, Ohio*'s "Paper Pills," who scribbles words of wisdom on scraps of paper he crumples up, finally sharing them with a patient. It is also similar to the character of Rosendo in Soto's *Spiks*, a barrio artist who can only find space to paint an idyllic scene on the crumbling wall of his tenement bathroom and whose wife, acutely aware of the pressing economic needs of their young children, cannot afford the luxury of appreciating this non-revenue-producing art. Like Dr. Reefy, but unlike Rosendo, Minerva succeeds in communicating through her art; exchanging poems with Esperanza, she contributes to the latter's artistic development while at the same time offering a lesson in women's domestic oppression and how to begin transcending it.

Also supportive of Esperanza's artistic creativity in her invalid aunt, Guadalupe: "She listened to every book, every poem I read her. One day I read her one of my own... That's nice. That's very good, she said in her tired voice. You just remember to keep writing, Esperanza. You must keep writing. It will keep you free...." Although the aunt lives in squalid, poor surroundings and is dying from a disease that has disfigured her once-beautiful body, she listens to the girl's stories and poems and encourages Esperanza's artistic talent. The story, "Three Sisters," recounts the wake held for the baby sister of Esperanza's friends Lucy and Rachel and is also the theme of Cisneros' earlier poem, "Velorio," in the collection entitled *Bad Boys*. Expanding upon "Velorio," however, this story introduces the figures of "the aunts, the three sisters, *las comadres*," visitors at the *velorio* who encourage Esperanza to see her artistic production in relation to the community: "When you leave you must remember always to come back ... for the others. A circle, you understand? You will always be Esperanza. You will always be Mango Street.... You can't forget who you are." Although Esperanza doesn't understand the women's message completely, the seeds of her socially conscious art have been planted here through the directives these women give her at the baby's wake.

Alicia, another positive role model who appears in "Alicia Who Sees Mice" and "Alicia and I Talking on Edna's Steps," also counsels Esperanza to value Mango Street and return there one day to contribute to its improvement: "Like it or not you are Mango Street and one day you'll come back too." To Esperanza's reply, "Not me. Not until somebody makes it better," Alicia wryly comments "Who's going to do it? The mayor?" Alicia had previously appeared in the collection as a university student who takes "two trains and a bus [to the campus] because she doesn't want to spend her whole life in a factory or behind a rolling pin." Rebelling against her father's expectations of her, that "a woman's place is sleeping so she can wake up early ... and make the lunchbox tortillas," Alicia "studies all night and sees the mice, the ones her father says do not exist." Fighting what the patriarchy expects of her, Alicia at the same time represents a clearsighted, non-mystified vision of the barrio. As a role-model and advice-giver to Esperanza, she embodies both the antipatriarchal themes and the social obligation to return to one's ethnic community that are so central to Cisneros' text.

Cisneros touches on several other important women's issues in this volume, including media images of ideal female beauty, the reifying stare of male surveyors of women, and sex roles within the family. In an effort to counter the sexual division of labor in the home, for example, Esperanza refuses one instance of women's work: "I have begun my own quiet war. Simple. Sure. I am the one who leaves the table like a man, without pulling back the chair or picking up the plate." Although this gesture calls critical attention to gender inequities in the family, Cisneros avoids the issue of who, in fact, will end up performing the household labor that Esperanza refuses here. This important and symbolic, yet somewhat adolescent gesture merely touches on the surface of the problem and is likely, in fact, to increase the work for another woman in Esperanza's household.

The majority of stories in *The House on Mango Street,* however, face important social issues head-on. The volume's simple, poetic language, with its insistence that the individual develops within a social community rather than in isolation, distances it from many accepted canonical texts. Its deceptively simple, childlike prose and its emphasis on the unromanticized, non-mainstream issues of patriarchal violence and ethnic poverty, however, should serve precisely to accord it canonical status. We must work toward a broader understanding among literary critics of the importance of such issues to art in order to attain a richer, more diverse canon and to avoid the undervaluation and oversight of such valuable texts as *The House on Mango Street.* (pp. 63–71)

Ellen McCracken, "Sandra Cisneros' 'The House on Mango Street': Community-Oriented Introspection and the Demystification of Patriarchal Violence," in *Breaking Boundaries: Latina Writing and Critical Readings*, edited by Asunción Horno-Delgado and others, Amherst: The University of Massachusetts Press, 1989, pp. 62–71.

SANDRA CISNEROS AND PILAR E. RODRÍGUEZ ARANDA

(interview date 1990)

[In the following interview, Cisneros discusses the content of her poems and short stories, particularly focusing on autobiographical elements in her works.]

[Rodríguez Aranda]: *Lets start with what I call the soil where Sandra Cisneros' "wicked" seed germinated. Your first book,* **The House on Mango Street**, *is it autobiographical?*

[Cisneros]: That's a question that students always ask me because I do a lot of lectures in Universities. They always ask: "Is this a true story?" or, "How many of these stories are true?" And I have to say, "Well they're all true." All fiction is non-fiction. Every piece of fiction is based on something that really happened. On the other hand, it's not autobiography because my family would be the first one to confess: "Well it didn't happen that way." They always contradict my stories. They don't understand I'm not writing autobiography.

What I'm doing is I'm writing true stories. They're all stories I lived, or witnessed, or heard; stories that were told to me. I collected those stories and I arranged them in an order so they would be clear and cohesive. Because in real life, there's no order.

All fiction is giving order to that . . .

. . . to that disorder, yes. So, a lot of the events were composites of stories. Some of those stories happened to my mother, and I combined them with something that happened to me. Some of those stories unfortunately happened to me just like that. Some of the stories were my students' when I was a counselor; women would confide in me and I was so overwhelmed with my inability to correct their lives that I wrote about them.

How did the idea of **Mango Street** *turn into a book?*

The House on Mango Street started when I was in graduate school, when I realized I didn't have a house. I was in this class, we were talking about memory and the imagination, about Gustave Bachelard's *Poetics of Space*. I remember sitting in the classroom, my face getting hot and I realized: "My god, I'm different! I'm different from everybody in this classroom." You know, you always grow up thinking something's different or something's wrong, but you don't know what it is. If you're raised in a multi-ethnic neighborhood you think that the whole world is multi-ethnic like that. According to what you see in the media, you think that that's the norm; you don't ever question that you're different or you're strange. It wasn't until I was twenty-two that it first hit me how different I really was. It wasn't as if I didn't know who I was. I knew I was a Mexican woman. But, I didn't think that had anything to do with why I felt so much imbalance in my life, whereas it had everything to do with it! My race, my gender, and my class! And it didn't make sense until that moment, sitting in that seminar. That's when I decided I would write about something my classmates couldn't write about. I couldn't write about what was going on in my life at that time. There was a lot of destructiveness; it was a very stressful time for that reason, and I was too close to it, so I chose to write about something I was far removed from, which was my childhood.

So you are and you're not "Esperanza," the main character in **The House on Mango Street**. *Now, at some point she says to herself that she's bad. Is that something you felt when you were her age?*

Certainly that black-white issue, good-bad, it's very prevalent in my work and in other Latinas. It's something I wasn't aware of until very recently. We're raised with a Mexican culture that has two role models: La Malinche y la Virgen de Guadalupe. And you know that's a hard route to go, one or the other, there's no in-betweens.

The in-between is not ours. All the other role models are outside our culture, they're Anglo. So if you want to get out of these two roles, you feel you're betraying you're people.

Exactly, you're told you're a traitor to your culture. And it's a horrible life to live. We're always straddling two countries, and we're always living in that kind of schizophrenia that I call, being a Mexican woman living in an American society, but not belonging to either culture. In some sense we're not Mexican and in some sense we're not American. I couldn't live in Mexico because my ideas are too . . .

. . . progressive?

Yeah, too Americanized. On the other hand, I can't live in America, or I do live here but, in some ways, almost like a foreigner.

An outsider.

Yes. And it's very strange to be straddling these two cultures and to try to define some middle ground so that you don't commit suicide or you don't become so depressed or you don't self explode. There has to be some way for you to say: "Alright, the life I'm leading is alright. I'm not betraying my culture. I'm not becoming anglicized." I was saying this last night to two Latinas in San Antonio. It's so hard for us to live through our twenties because there's always this balancing act, we've got to define what we think is fine for ourselves instead of what our culture says.

At the same time, none of us wants to abandon our culture. We're very Mexican, we're all very Chicanas. Part of being Mexicana is that love and that affinity we have for our *cultura*. We're very family centered, and that family extends to the whole Raza. We don't want to be exiled from our people. (pp. 64–6)

Even in the eighties, Mexican women feel there are all these expectations they must fulfill, like getting married, having children. Breaking with them doesn't mean you are bad, but society makes you feel that way . . .

Part of it is our religion, because there's so much guilt. It's so hard being Catholic, and even though you don't call yourself Catholic anymore, you have vestiges of that guilt inside you; it's in your blood. Mexican religion is half western and half pagan; European Catholicism and Precolumbian religion all mixed in. It's a very strange Catholicism like nowhere else on the planet and it does strange things to you. There's no one sitting on your shoulder but you have the worst censor of all, and that's yourself.

I found it very hard to deal with redefining myself or controlling my own destiny or my own sexuality. I still wrestle with that theme, it's still the theme of my last book, *My Wicked Wicked Ways,* and in the new one that I've started and the one that comes after, so it's a ghost I'm still wrestling with.

Talking about ghosts, would you say that writing is a way of getting rid of your guilt, of saying: "You might think I'm wicked, but it's not about being wicked, it's about being me." Some kind of exorcism . . .

I used to think that writing was a way to exorcise those ghosts that inhabit the house that is ourselves. But now I understand that only the little ghosts leave. The big ghosts still live inside you, and what happens with writing—I think a more accurate metaphor would be to say—that you make your peace with those ghosts. You recognize they live there . . .

That they're part of you . . .

They're part of you and you can talk about them, and I think that it's a big step to be able to say: "Well, yeah, I'm haunted, ha! There's a little ghost there and we coexist."

Maybe I'll always be writing about this schizophrenia of being a Mexican American woman, it's something that in every stage of my life has affected me differently. I don't think it's something I could put to rest. I'll probably still be writing about being good or bad probably when I'm ninety-years old.

It didn't seem to me that in My Wicked Wicked Ways there was a conflict over being a Hispanic woman. What I saw was the telling of different experiences, memories from childhood, travels, love affairs . . . of course you can't get away from the fact that you are Mexican and that you experience life in a certain way because of this.

These are poems in which I write about myself, not a man writing about me. It is my autobiography, my version, my life story as told by me, not according to a male point of view. And that's where I see perhaps the "Wicked Wicked" of the title.

A lot of the themes for *Mango Street* are repeated: I leave my father's house, I don't get married, I travel to other countries, I can sleep with men if I want to, I can abandon them or choose not to sleep with them, and yes, I can fall in love and even be hurt by men—all of these things but as told by me. I am not the muse.

Some men were disappointed because they thought the cover led them on. They thought it was a very sexy cover and they wanted . . . I don't know what they wanted! But they felt disappointed by the book. The cover is of a woman appropriating her own sexuality. In some ways, that's also why it's wicked; the scene is trespassing that boundary by saying: "I defy you. I'm going to tell my own story."

You see, I grew up with six brothers and a father. So, in essence I feel like I grew up with seven fathers. To this day when any man tells me to do something in a certain way, the hair in the back of my neck just stands up and I'll start screaming! Then I have to calm down and realize: "Well, alright, okay, you know where this came from, you don't even need an analyst to figure this one out!"

In Mango Street there's a story called "Beautiful and Cruel," where Esperanza obviously feels an admiration towards the woman in the movies who was "beautiful and cruel," the one "with red red lips" whose power "is her own." Is that why you colored your lips on the black and white photograph of the cover of My Wicked Wicked Ways?

I never thought about that. I was looking at women who are models of power. I suppose that for someone like Esperanza the only powerful women she would see would be the same type that Manuel Puig idolizes, those black and white screen stars. People like Rita Hayworth, the red-lip women that were beautiful. They didn't have to cling to someone, rather they snuff people out like cigarettes. They were the ones in control, and that was the only kind of role model I had for power. You had to have beauty, and if you didn't have that, you were lost.

The cover was trying to play on the Errol Flynn years of film, the lettering and everything.

I got a lot of objections to that photo. People said, "Why did you paint the lips? It's a good photo." The photographer himself didn't want his photograph adulterated. But then, if the lips weren't painted then you'd think I was serious. (pp. 66–8)

When did you realize that you wanted to be a writer or that you were a writer?

Everytime I say I'm a writer, it still surprises me. It's one of those things, that everytime you say it . . . me suena muy curioso. It's like saying "I'm a faith healer." Sounds a little bit like a quack when you say it; something a little immodest, a little crazy, admitting you're a writer.

I guess the first time I legitimately started saying that's what I was instead of that's what I wanted to be was when I was in graduate school, when we all had the audacity to claim our major as what we were. But you never get used to saying it because we've always had to make our living other ways. I had to be a teacher, a counselor, I've had to work as an Arts Administrator, you know, all kinds of things just to make my living. The writing is always what you try to save energy for, it's your child. You hope you're not too exhausted so that you can come home to that child and give it everything you can.

It's hard to claim in this society that that's what you are. I feel a little more legitimate saying it these days after I've been doing it professionally for more than ten years. When I'm riding on a plane and I'm off to do a lecture somewhere and the person to the right of me says: "Well, what do you do?" I don't say "I'm a professor," because I only started doing that recently and that doesn't have anything to do with writing. I say "I'm a writer." And the next question always is: "Oh, do you publish?" That really makes me mad like you have to have your vitae with you. But it's nice to say, "Yes, I do." (p. 70)

There's a story in The House on Mango Street *where Esperanza goes to the fortuneteller, who tells her she sees a home in the heart. Did it become true for you, this home in the heart?*

The story impressed me very much because it is exactly what I found out, years after I'd written the book, that the house in essence becomes you. You are the house. But I didn't know that when I wrote it. The story is based on something that happened to me when I went to see a witchwoman once. Going to see that woman was so funny because I didn't understand half the shit she told me, and later on I tried to write a poem about her. The poem didn't work, but a lot of the lines stayed, including the title, so I decided, well, I'll write a story to include in *House on Mango Street*. Her response is at the end when Esperanza says: "Do you see anything else in the glass for my future?" and she says: "A home in the heart, I was right." I don't know where that came from. I just wrote it, and thought: "That sounds good. Kind of sounds like

'anchor of arms' and the other ambiguous answers that the witchwoman is giving the girl."

Two years after I wrote that, when the book finally came out, I was frightened because I had no idea how these pieces were going to fit together. I was making all of these little *cuentitos*, like little squares of a patchwork quilt, hoping that they would match, that somehow there wouldn't be a big hole in the middle. I said, "I think it's done but, *quién sabe!*" So when I saw the book complete, when I opened it and read it from front to back for the first time as a cold thing, in the order that it was, I looked and said, "Oh my goodness, *qué curioso!*" It is as if I knew all of these symbols.

I suppose a Jungian critic would argue: "Yes, you always do know in some sense. This writing comes from the same deep level that dreams and poetry come from, so maybe you're not conscious of it when you're writing, but your subconscious is aware."

It surprised me, and it's also a strange coincidence that I would write the things that eventually I would live. That, yes, I did find a home in the heart, just like Elenita, the witchwoman predicted. I hope that other women find that as well.

What is your home of your heart made of?

I've come this year to realize who I am, to feel very very strong and powerful, I am at peace with myself and I don't feel terrified by anyone, or by any terrible word that anyone would launch at me from either side of the border. I guess I've created a house made of bricks that no big bad wolf can blow down now.

I didn't feel that by the end of My Wicked Wicked Ways *you had that house yet.*

No, because, see, those poems were all written during the time I was writing *The House on Mango Street,* some of them before. They're poems that span from when I was twenty-one years old all the way through the age of thirty. It's a chronological book. If anything, I think that the new book, the *Loose Woman* book is more a celebration of that house in the heart, and *My Wicked Wicked Ways* I would say is in essence my wanderings in the desert.

The last poem in the book is the only one in Spanish. When I read this poem, maybe because my first language is Spanish—but I don't think it is only that—it felt to me the most vulnerable. Your language was more simple, direct, straight to the heart. The poem is called "Tantas Cosas Asustan, Tantas."

"So Many Things Terrify, So Many."

Do you write more in Spanish?

I never write in Spanish, y no es que no quiero sino que I don't have that same palate in Spanish that I do in English. No tengo esa facilidad. I think the only way you get that palate is by living in a culture where you hear it, where the language is not something in a book or in your dreams. It's on the loaf of bread that you buy, it's on the radio jingle, it's on the graffiti you see, it's on your ticket stub. It must be all encompassing. (pp. 73–4)

You have two books published now and you're working on four.

I really have three books. I have a chap book, **Bad Boys,** that preceded this book of poetry and it's out of print now.

So, you are always getting some kind of criticism, comments, etc. How does that affect you? When you write, are you aware of an audience?

Well, sometimes, but not really. Poetry is a very different process from fiction. I feel in some ways that I'm more conscious of my audience when I'm writing fiction, and I'm not conscious of them when I'm writing poetry, or hardly. Poetry is the art of telling the truth, and fiction is the art of lying. The scariest thing to me is writing poetry, because you're looking at yourself *desnuda*. You're always looking at the part of you that you don't show anybody. You're looking at the part of you that maybe you'd show your husband. The part that your siblings or your parents have never even seen. And that center, that terrifying center, is a poem. That's why you can't think of your audience, because if you do, they're going to censor your poem, in the way that if you think about yourself thinking about the poem, you'll censor the poem, see? That's why it's so horrible, because you've got to go beyond censorship when you write, you've got to go deeper, to a real subterranean level, to get at that core of truth. You don't even know what the truth is! You just have to keep writing and hope that you'll come upon something that shocks you. When you think: "Oh my goodness, I didn't know I felt that!" that's where you stop. That's the little piece of gold that you've been looking for. That's a poem. It's quite a different process from writing fiction, because you know what you're going to say when you write fiction. To me, the definition of a story is something that someone wants to listen to. If someone doesn't want to listen to you, then it's not a story.

I was reading an article discussing how there could be more audience for poetry, that one mistake is thinking that poetry is not storytelling.

Poetry can be storytelling. As a critic said, my poetry is very narrative, and is very poetic. I always denied when I wrote **House on Mango Street** that I was a fiction writer. I'd say: "I'm a poet, I just write this naively." But now I see how much of a storyteller I've always been. Because even though I wasn't writing stories, I was talking stories. I think it is very important to develop storytelling abilities. The way I teach writing is based on the oral word. I test all my stories out with my class. When I have every student in that class looking up and listening to me, I know I've got a good story. There's something in it that makes them want to listen. I ask my students, "Do you take notes in my class when I tell you stories?" They go, "No." "How

many stories that I've told you, since the beginning of this semester, can you remember?" Ooooah! They all came back with these stories, they could remember them! "You didn't have to take notes. You didn't have to study, right? Why? See how wonderful stories are? You remember!"

You remember the ones that are important to you or that affect you, and you filter out the ones que no te sirven. It's just a nice thing about fiction. To me that's a test of what a good story is: if someone listens to you and if it stays with you. That's why fairy tales and myths are so important to a culture; that's why they get handed down. People don't need to write them down! I think that, even if we didn't have them written down, they would be alive as long as they fulfilled a function of being necessary to our lives. When they no longer spoke to us, then we'd forget.

I've always been interested in trying to understand the function of the myth. It's still kind of a puzzle to me. The way I see it now is that we're sort of in a crisis partly because we don't seem to have that many contemporary myths.

I think that there are urban myths, modern myths, only we can't tell which ones are really going to last. I think that maybe the visual is taking the place of the oral myth. Sometimes I have to make allusions in my class. If I said, "Now, do you remember when Rumple . . . ?" They'd say: "Who?" or they more or less would know the story. Or if I'd make an allusion to the "Little Mermaid" or the "Snow Queen," which are very important fairytales to me, and an integral part of my childhood and my storytelling ability today! . . . ¡ No hombre! They didn't know what I was talking about. But if I made an illusion to Fred Flintstone, everyone knew who Fred Flintstone was. Ha, ha! It's kind of horrible in a way that I have to resort to the television characters to make a point. That was our common mythology, that's what we all had in common, television.

You've said a lot of positive things about your teaching, what else is in it for you, and does it sometimes get in the way of your writing?

I complain about my students and say how they're always sucking my blood. Ha! But they would never kill me or suck my blood if I didn't let them. I will work very hard for students that work hard for me; it's a contract thing, you know, you have to work for each other. I tell my students all the time that teaching and writing don't have anything to do with one another. And I say that because when I'm writing on a weekend, then that following week I'm kind of half-ass as a teacher: I didn't read through their stories well enough, I didn't have time to read them ahead of time, I read them in class for the first time, and so I have to steal their time in order to be a writer. When I'm teaching and doing a really kick-ass job that week, my private time gets stolen because I can't write. My creativity is going towards them and to my teaching and to my one-on-one with them. I never find a balance. I can't have it both ways, they don't have anything to do with one another.

On the one hand, I get encouraged to be a writer. They like it that I'm a writer, they like that I publish, that I lecture. Everywhere I've worked writing's always been kind of an interruption to my other duties. On the other hand, as a writer, I can't understand the priorities that academia has towards titles and towards time and deadlines, I don't work like that.

It helps that I call myself a writer because they think: "Oh well, she's just a writer, that's why she can't get her grades in on time," or "That's why she wears those funny clothes and has her hair so funny . . . she's a writer." The way universities are set up is very countercreative. The environment, the classroom, the times; the way that people have to leave when you're in the middle of a sentence to go to another class is countercreative. The fact that I have to be there on time boggles me. My students would get all upset if I'd come fifteen minutes late, and I'd say, "What are you so upset about? If I was in a cafe, would you leave?" They'd say, "Nooo." "I would wait for you. What are you all so upset about?" You'd have to be there a certain time or right away they'd want to leave. That inflexibility with time to me doesn't make sense. I know that some of them might have to go to another class but that's not the way that I would like to do it. I would like to start the class when I get there and finish when we finish. Usually we don't run out ready in two hours, I want to go on. And I want to go out and drink with all of them, and have some coffee or beer after class, because I think the real learning keeps going.

We talk about that, we talk about what would we like if we could have any type of environment we would choose, and any kind of schedule. Sometimes we spend a whole class talking about what's important in making ourselves more creative and we come up with a whole, exaggerated list of demands, which we give to the chair: "We want a house by the country . . . " It's fun to talk about those things because you start articulating what's important to you. Maybe we can't have a house in the country, but we realize we need a quiet space to write; alright, maybe we can't all go out and spend a weekend in Europe but we could take a trip to the next town by ourselves. I always feel that when we get off the track like that on a subject in class, it's important. I say: "Forget about my lesson plan because we're going to get on the track by going off the track." Some of my students don't like that about me, that I'll throw the lesson plan, or I won't have a lesson plan or I'll throw the whole syllabus out the window and say, "Well, that's not going to work, I've changed my mind." But it is precisely because I come from an anti-academic experience that I'm very good at teaching writing. (pp. 75–8)

In The House on Mango Street *you were "bad," then you went through the times of figuring out who you were and you came out "wicked," and now you say you're working on being a "loose woman," how does that fit in with your solid brick house?*

I love that title: *Poemas Sueltos.* I was thinking of Jaime Sabines' book: *Poemas sueltos, Loose Poems,* because they didn't belong to any other collection. I started writing these poems after being with other women this last spring, and getting so energized. I had a whole series that I continued on through the summer and I thought: "These loose poems don't belong anywhere." I was in the bathroom in Mexico City, sitting on the pot and thinking, "What can I do with these poems, what would I call them? They're loose poems. But they're loose 'women' poems." You see? I'm reinventing the word "loose." I really feel that I'm the loose and I've cut free from a lot of things that anchored me. So, playing on that, the collection is called *Loose Woman.*

It is because your home in the heart is now so strong that you can be loose.

Yes. Like there is a poem called **"New Tango,"** it's about how I like to dance alone. But the tango that I'm dancing is not a man over a woman, but a "new" tango that I dance by myself. Chronologically it follows the books as a true documentation of where the house of my heart is right now. (pp. 79–80)

Sandra Cisneros and Pilar E. Rodríguez Aranda, in an interview in *The Americas Review,* Vol. XVIII, No. 1, Spring, 1990, pp. 64–80.

JIM SAGEL
(interview date 1991)

[A recipient of the Casas de las Americas literary award, Sagel is a bilingual poet and short fiction writer who has written *Tunomas Honey* (1981), a collection of short stories concerning cultural dissonance. In the following excerpt, drawn from an interview with Cisneros, Sagel surveys *The House on Mango Street* and *Woman Hollering Creek,* noting that "Cisneros's literary landscape teems with characters who live, love and laugh in the flowing cadences of the Spanish language."]

Taped to her word processor is a prayer card to San Judas, a gift from a Mexico City cabdriver. Her two indispensable literary sources are mail order catalogues and the San Antonio (Tex.) phone book. She lights candles and reads the *Popul Vuh* before sitting down to write long into the night, becoming so immersed in her characters that she dreams their dialogue: once she awoke momentarily convinced she was Inés, bride of the Mexican revolutionary Emiliano Zapata.

Cisneros on her motivations as a writer:

If I were asked what it is I write about, I would have to say I write about those ghosts inside that haunt me, that will not let me sleep, of that which even memory does not like to mention. Sometimes it seems I am writing the same story, the same poem, over and over. . . .

Perhaps later there will be time to write by inspiration. In the meantime, in my writing as well as in that of other Chicanas and other women, there is the necessary phase of dealing with those ghosts and voices most urgently haunting us, day by day.

Sandra Cisneros, in her "Ghosts and Voices: Writing from Obsession." *The Americas Review* (Spring 1987).

Such identification with her characters and her culture is altogether natural for Sandra Cisneros, a writer who has always found her literary voice in the real voices of her people, her immediate family and the extended *famiulis* of Latino society.

"I'm trying to write the stories that haven't been written. I feel like a cartographer; I'm determined to fill a literary void," Cisneros says. With the Random House publication of her new collection of stories, ***Woman Hollering Creek***, . . . and the simultaneous reissuing of her earlier collection of short fiction, ***The House on Mango Street***, in a Vintage edition, Cisneros finds herself in a position to chart those barrio ditches and borderland arroyos that have not appeared on most copies of the American literary map but which, nonetheless, also flow into the "mainstream."

The 36-year-old daughter of a Mexican father and a Chicana mother, Cisneros is well aware of the additional pressure to succeed with this pair of books that represent the opportunity for a wider readership, not only for herself but for scores of other Latina and Latino writers right behind the door that she is cracking open.

"One of the most frightening pressures I faced as I wrote this book was the fear that I would blow it," Cisneros says, sweeping a lock of her closely cropped black hair from her forehead as she sips a midmorning cup of coffee. "I kept asking myself, What have I taken on here? That's why I was so obsessed with getting everybody's stories out. I didn't have the luxury of doing my own."

Coupled with that "responsibility to do a collective good job," is Cisneros's anxiety about how her work will be perceived by the general reading public. Universal as her themes are, Cisneros knows her characters live in an America very different from that of her potential readers. From her friend Lucy, "who smells like corn," to Salvador, whose essence resides "inside that wrinkled shirt, inside the throat that must clear itself and apologize each time it speaks," Cisneros's literary landscape teems with char-

acters who live, love and laugh in the flowing cadences of the Spanish language.

Yet, unlike her character Salvador, Cisneros offers no apologies when she speaks. Energetic and abounding with *gusto*—only the Spanish word will do to describe her engaging humor—Cisneros relishes the opportunity to startle the jaded reader and poetically unravel stereotypes, especially those that relate to Latinas.

"I'm the mouse who puts a thorn in the lion's paw," she says, with an arch smile reminiscent of the redlipped *sonrisa* on the cover of ***My Wicked Wicked Ways***, . . . a collection of poetry celebrating the "bad girl" with her "lopsided symmetry of sin / and virtue."(p. 74)

[In ***The House on Mango Street***] Cisneros discovered what she terms her "first love," a fascination with speech and voices. Writing in the voice of the adolescent Esperanza, Cisneros created a series of interlocking stories, alternately classified as a novel and as a collection of prose poems because of the vivid and poignant nature of the language. Since its first publication in 1984 by Arte Público Press, *Mango Street* has sold some 30,000 copies. The book is used in classes from junior high school through graduate school in subjects ranging from Chicano studies to psychology to culture, ideas and values at Stanford University, where it has been adopted as part of the "new curriculum."

Mango Street was also the catalyst that drew Cisneros to her literary agent or, to be more accurate, that led Susan Bergholz to Cisneros. Bergholz was so moved after reading the book that she did something she had never done before: she set out to track down the writer. "It was a delightful chase," Bergholz recalls, in spite of the fact that it took some three to four years to accomplish.

Ironically, even while Bergholz was enlisting the aid of Richard Bray of Guild Books to contact Cisneros, the writer was going through what she calls the worst year of her life, 1987. She had spent the previous year in Texas through the auspices of a Dobie-Paisano fellowship. Though the experience had convinced her to make Texas her permanent home, the writer found herself unable to make a living once the fellowship expired.

While her boyfriend waited tables, Cisneros handed out fliers in local supermarkets and laundromats, trying to scrape together enough students to teach a private writing workshop. At last, she was forced to leave her newly adopted home, her confidence shaken and her outlook on life darkened.

The depression she sank into followed her to California, where she accepted a guest lectureship at California State University in Chico. "I thought I couldn't teach. I found myself becoming suicidal. Richard Bray had told me Susan was looking for me, but I was drowning, beyond help. I had the number for months, but I didn't call. It was frightening because it was such a calm depression."

An NEA fellowship in fiction revitalized Cisneros and helped her get on her feet again, both financially and spiritually. Finally calling that Manhattan phone number stuffed in her pocket, Cisneros sent Bergholz a small group of new stories. With only 39 pages in hand, Bergholz sold *Woman Hollering Creek* to Joni Evans and Erroll Mcdonald at Random House/Vintage; Julie Grau became the book's enthusiastic editor.

Then, of course, the real work began for Cisneros, whose previous output had been about one story every six months. "There's nothing like a deadline to teach you discipline, especially when you've already spent your advance. *Susto* helps," Cisneros says, explaining that fear motivated her to put in eight-to-12-hour days. Though exhausting, the experience was genuinely empowering.

"Before, I'd be scratching my *nalgas*, waiting for inspiration. Now I know I can work this hard. I know I did the best I could."

That's not to say Cisneros believes she's done the best work of her career. "I'm looking forward to the books I'll write when I'm 60," she observes. She's also looking forward to the contributions other Latina and Latino writers will be making in the future. "There's a lot of good writing in the mainstream press that has nothing to say. Chicano writers have a lot to say. The influence of our two languages is profound. The Spanish language is going to contribute something very rich to American literature."

Meanwhile, this self-described "migrant professor" plans to continue her personal and literary search for the "home in the heart," as Elenita the Witch Woman describes it in *Mango Street*. As "nobody's mother and nobody's wife," Cisneros most resembles Inés Alfaro, the powerful central character in **"Eyes of Zapata,"** the story Cisneros considers her finest achievement.

Small, but "bigger" than the general himself, Inés is the woman warrior, the *Soldadera* who understands what the men will never comprehend, that "the wars begin here, in our hearts and in our beds." She is the *bruja*, the *nagual* who flies through the night, the fierce and tender lover who risks all, the eater of black things that make her hard and strong.

She is, in short, a symbol of the Latina herself, the Mexican woman whose story is at last being told, a story of life and blood and grief and "all the flower colors of joy." It is a story at once intimate and universal, guaranteed to shove a bittersweet thorn into the paws of literary lions everywhere. (p. 75)

Jim Sagel, "Sandra Cisneros," in *Publishers Weekly*, Vol. 238, No. 15, March 29, 1991, pp. 74–5.

LORENZO CHAVEZ
(essay date 1991)

[In the excerpt below, Chavez offers a brief overview of *Woman Hollering Creek,* praising the collection's language, humor, and realistic depiction of barrio life.]

Poet/short fiction writer Sandra Cisneros once again compresses truth into every line in *Woman Hollering Creek,* a collection of 22 short stories. Like her previous work, *The House on Mango Street,* these stories describe, in the author's words, "the schizophrenia of being a Mexican American woman." Cisneros' deceptively simple language illustrates the Hispanic woman's struggle to constantly redefine herself. But unlike the author's *Mango Street,* which depicts life in a Chicago *barrio,* the characters in these stories inhabit small, dusty, but quaint South Texas towns.

In the book's title story, Cisneros provides a view of Cleófilas, a powerless, Mexican-born woman trying to survive a wife-beating husband in a macho world where the menfolk's highest form of entertainment is to gather at the local ice-house to drink, laugh loudly, and belch. No bowling alleys here. Destiny rules, or so it seems, until a determined and suddenly independent Cleófilas takes drastic action.

"La Fabulosa" is a brief, but hilarious tale of the extra-curricular exploits of Carmen, a big-busted Chicana legal secretary from San Antonio. Some readers may accuse Cisneros of reinforcing negative stereotypes, but her blatant, larger-than-life caricatures are drawn so humorously out of proportion that they shatter, rather than perpetuate negative images. We laugh and wonder, "Could such people actually exist?"

In **"One Holy Night,"** a naive teen loses her virginity to a man claiming to be descended from Mayan kings. Later, we discover he is a mass murderer. Cisneros avoids romanticizing the hardships of barrio life. Instead, she injects humor: "It's a good thing we live in a bad neighborhood," says the young protagonist, "There are always plenty of bums to blame for your sins."

Cisneros' gift with language is felt throughout the entire volume, but especially in **"Eleven,"** a poignant story of how an eleven-year-old's birthday is ruined by an insensitive teacher. Cisneros has a good ear for recreating the voices of three different stages of life: innocent but seemingly wise children, unlucky and confused teens, and world-weary but comically cynical adults living life near the border.

Lorenzo Chavez, in a review of "Woman Hollering Creek and Other Stories," in *Hispanic*, April, 1991, p. 52.

MERRIHELEN PONCE

(essay date 1991–92)

[In the following essay, Ponce offers a laudatory overview of *Woman Hollering Creek,* claiming that, unlike Cisneros's earlier fiction, this collection "resonates with voices of wiser Mexicanas/Chicanas."]

This new collection, [*Woman Hollering Creek and Other Stories*], by the *enfant terrible* of Chicana letters, author of *House on Mango Street,* is an important addition to fiction by ethnic American women. While Amy Tan (*The Joy Luck Club*) examines mother-daughter relationships and Gish Jen (*Typical American*) explores ethnicity in America, Cisneros' stories strafe Texas-Mexico boundaries that, for those with strong ties to Mexico, are nothing less than imaginary borders.

Cisneros's *gente* (people) are full of life, resilient, and funny. Treated like second-class citizens because of skin color, lack of English, and a tendency to cling to Old World customs, they struggle to bring some semblance of order to their lives and loves. Still, images of those caught in a culture of poverty, as in **"Salvador, Late or Early,"** are unsettling: "Salvador . . . inside that forty-pound body of boy with its geography of scars, its history of hurt in that cage of the chest where something throbs with both fists and knows only what Salvador knows."

Salvador, alias "savior" attempts to survive the poverty that has made him old before his time. In **"Little Miracles, Kept Promises,"** true believers light votive candles and beg *un milagro* from a favorite saint: "Thank you for helping us when Chapa's truck got stolen . . . he needs it to get to work . . . he's been on probation since we got him to quit drinking . . . Please send us clothes, furniture, shoes, dishes. We need anything that don't eat. Since the fire we have to start over. . . . Lalo's disability check don't go very far."

A petition to San Antonio de Padua is particularly humorous — and touching. A woman asks "Can you help me find a man who isn't a pain in the nalgas/ass? There aren't any in Texas. . . . Especially not in San Antonio."

The strongest work in this collection is **"Eyes of Zapata,"** and is based on the enduring relationship between Mexican General Emiliano Zapata and Ines Alfaro Aguilar, his common-law wife, to whom Zapata returns in between other liaisons. Cisneros evokes Ines's pain at

loving and losing the man who led the agrarian revolt during the 1910 Mexican Revolution, a man often tired of being a leader: "You say you can't sleep anywhere like you sleep here . . . always having to be el gran general Emiliano Zapata. The nervous fingers flinch, the long elegant bones twitch . . . waiting for the assassins's bullet."

"Eyes of Zapata" weaves romance and history against the harsh Mexican landscape of the 1900s, with a lyricism reminiscent of Mexico's Nelly Campobello. It captures Ines's intense love for her handsome general: "I put my nose to your eyelashes . . . the skin of the eyelids soft as the skin of the penis, the collarbone with its fluted wings, the purple knot of the nipple, the blue-black of your sex, the thin legs."

Unlike *The House on Mango Street,* which is dominated by the child-voice, this book resonates with voices of wiser Mexicanas/Chicanas: a flip high school teenager and a smart-aleck tough, who is **"La Fabulosa."** In **"Bien Pretty,"** we sense the cultural ambivalence of Lupe, a bored Chicana who falls for a Chicano exterminator—built like the Aztec God Popocatepetl—who puts aside notions of social class in favor of a live *vato.*

An inherent danger for writers of the ethnic American experience is the tendency to trivialize folk customs, language, or plot. One wonders if the current popularity of ethnic women's literature is predicated on race and class differences. Must Latinas be portrayed as passive, fatalistic, *foreign?*. . . For Cisneros however, this is not a problem. We laugh and weep along with her *mujeres:* strong, resilient women who celebrate life to the fullest.

Merrihelen Ponce, "A Semblance of Order to Lives and Loves," in *Belles Lettres: A Review of Books by Women*, Vol. 7, No. 2, Winter, 1991–92, pp. 40, 44.

MARY B. W. TABOR

(essay date 1993)

[In the following excerpt, Tabor presents a biographical and critical overview of Cisneros and her short fiction, commenting on the author's distinctive literary voice and discussing her Latino philosophy.]

On a rainy winter afternoon, the writer Sandra Cisneros stands before a ragtag group of children and adults in the tiny Brownsville branch of the Brooklyn Public Library, and with orange and black cat-eyed glasses perched atop her head, begins her song of life in the barrio.

One hand clutches her open book. The other moves passionately, as does her face, which she scrunches into a knot and then opens with delight as she reads aloud of wise children and foolish adults, of tangled Latino and American cultures, of noise and silence and Proustian moments, of intense love and intense anger.

Then she passes around her fifth-grade report card. "I have C's and D's in everything," she says. "The only B I had was in conduct. But I don't remember being that stupid."

The teachers, she explains to the students who strain to see the yellow card, just did not understand what to do with a working-class Mexican-American girl from the South Side of Chicago. "They thought I was a dreamer," she says.

In some ways, she still is a dreamer. But after two fellowships from the National Endowment for the Arts, and with a six-figure publishing contract from Turtle Bay Books, a division of Random House, this 38-year-old poet and short-story writer now has few questioning her abilities.

Cited by critics as an important new author with a vigorous and original voice, Ms. Cisneros is one of only a handful of Latina writers to make it big on the American scene, along with the likes of Julia Alvarez, a Dominican-American, and Cristina Garcia, a Cuban-American. In 1991, she won praise for *Woman Hollering Creek,* a collection of short stories and sketches that survey the condition of women.

In December, Turtle Bay published a hardcover version of a collection of poems, *My Wicked Wicked Ways,* first published in paperback in 1987 by Third Woman Press. Its first printing of more than 5,000 sold out, the book is in its second printing.

Her works are filled with young girls coming of age, dejected brides and powerful, passionate women. And just as the report card seems an odd mirror for one whose writings have made their way into hundreds of curriculums and more than a dozen anthologies, Ms. Cisneros, who can be both fiercely feminine and androgynous, idealistic and deeply cynical, is herself a study in contradiction.

Before her audience at the library, which she visited as part of a three-city tour promoting *My Wicked Wicked Ways,* she cuts a sophisticated figure in a long, sleek crushed velvet outfit, boots and short dark hair. But her expressions are whimsical, her voice small and childlike.

Her writing is lean. Her conversation style is chatty and rambling. Though she speaks with passion about her collection of boyfriends, she lives alone as "nobody's mother and nobody's wife." She is a self-described "terrorist," "anarchist" and "Chicana feminist," though in the same breath she says she knows little about "-ists or -isms."

"I am a woman and I am a Latina," she says over a plate of pancakes and bacon the next morning at Good Enough to Eat, on the Upper West Side, lacing her sentences with Spanish words that roll over her tongue. Her voice is deeper when she speaks Spanish. "Those are the things that make my writing distinctive. Those are the things that give my writing power. They are the things that give it sabor, the things that give it picante."

But it is finding the middle ground between the Latin and the American that has provided the most creative tension for Ms. Cisneros. The first resolution of such tension, she says, was making it through school. The second was moving away from home and her Mexican father, Mexican-American mother and six brothers.

"The house on Mango Street is ours," she writes in her book *The House on Mango Street,* "and we don't have to pay rent to anybody, or share the yard with the people downstairs, or be careful not to make too much noise, and there isn't a landlord banging on the ceiling with a broom."

Pausing over her breakfast, she says: "I always felt that we were victims of a fairy tale, that somehow some spell had happened. I thought it was just temporary hard times."

Those hard times have made her success seem so sweet. "Every time someone asks me to sign a book, I feel like laughing," she says. "It's so wacky. I was the girl with the C's and D's. I was the girl in the corner with the goofy glasses from Sears. I was the ugly kid in the class with the bad haircut, the one nobody would talk to. I was the one that never got picked to be in the play."

Having spent most of her adult life living hand to mouth, Ms. Cisneros says the publishing contracts have allowed her to buy a new Victorian house in San Antonio, where she has lived off and on since 1984. Unlike Chicago, where her family still lives, San Antonio allows her to straddle the Mexican-American border and culture.

But those early hard times have also served to forge a clear political agenda for Ms. Cisneros, who has refused to appear in ads for the Gap or to allow her work in anthologies that use the word "Hispanic."

"'Hispanic' is English for a person of Latino origin who wants to be accepted by the white status quo," she says. "Latino is the word we have always used for ourselves."

Now, besides working on a new collection of poetry, *Loose Woman,* and a novel, *Caramelo,* Ms. Cisneros says she serves as an informal spokeswoman for Latinos.

"I don't have to dream anymore about how to give insulin shots or how to give out condoms from planes," she says. "I can do my terrorist activities now by staying home and writing. I have the power to make people think in a different way. It's a different way of defining power, and it is something that I don't want to abuse or lose. I want to help my community."

"I'm a translator. I'm an amphibian. I can travel in both worlds. What I'm saying is very important for the Latino community, but it is also important for the white community to hear. What I'm saying in my writing is that we can be Latino and still be American."

Mary B. W. Tabor, "A Solo Traveler in Two Worlds," in *The New York Times*, January 7, 1993, p. B2.

SOURCES FOR FURTHER STUDY

Cisneros, Sandra. "Ghosts and Voices: Writing from Obsession." *The Americas Review* XV, No. 1 (Spring 1987): 69–73.
Discusses early influences and their impact on her poetry and fiction.

———. "Notes to a Young(er) Writer." *The Americas Review* XV, No. 1 (Spring 1987): 74–6.
Comments on her motivations and development as a writer.

González-Berry, Erlinda, and Rebolledo, Tey Diana. "Growing Up Chicano: Tomás Rivera and Sandra Cisneros." *Revista Chicano-Riqueña* XIII, Nos. 3–4 (Fall–Winter 1985): 109–19.
Comparative study of the differing narrative modes found in Rivera's and Cisneros's *bildungsromans*. The critics especially focus on the differences and similarities between Rivera's male and Cisneros's female protagonists.

Kingsolver, Barbara. "Poetic Fiction with a Tex-Mex Tilt." *Los Angeles Times Book Review* (28 April 1991): 3, 12.
Observes the poetic elements of *Woman Hollering Creek*.

Julio Cortázar

1914–1984

(Also wrote under pseudonym of Julio Denís) Argentine novelist, short story writer, poet, essayist, critic, and translator.

INTRODUCTION

Cortázar is one of the seminal figures of the "Boom," a surge of excellence and innovation in Latin American letters during the 1950s and 1960s. Like Gabriel García Márquez and other contemporary Latin American writers, Cortázar combined fantastic and often bizarre plots with commonplace events and characters. Much of his fiction is a reaction against the Western tradition of rationalism and is an attempt to create new ways in which literature can represent life.

Cortázar was born in Brussels, Belgium. In 1918 he moved with his parents to their native Argentina, where they settled in a suburb of Buenos Aires. An excellent student, Cortázar began writing at a young age and completed a novel by the time he was nine years old. After earning a teaching degree, he taught high school from 1937 to 1944. During this time Cortázar began writing short stories, and, in 1938, under the pseudonym Julio Denís, he published *Presencia,* a book of sonnets exhibiting the influence of French Symbolist poet Stéphane Mallarmé. In 1944 and 1945 Cortázar taught French literature at the University of Cuyo in Mendoza. He resigned from his post after participating in demonstrations against Argentine president Juan Péron, moving to Buenos Aires, where he began working for a publishing company. In that same year Cortázar published his first short story, "Casa tomada" ("House Taken Over"), in *Los anales de Buenos Aires*, an influential literary magazine edited by Jorge Luis Borges. Between 1946 and 1948 Cortázar studied law and languages to earn a degree as a public translator. Cortázar has stated that the arduous task of completing this three-year course in less than a year produced temporary neuroses that are reflected in his fiction. One of his phobias, a fear of eating insects hidden in his food, inspired the short story "Circe," a tale about a woman who feeds her suitors cockroaches in the guise of candies. In 1951 Cortázar published *Bestiario,* his first collection of short stories, and also received a scholarship to study in Paris, where he became a translator for the United Nations Educational, Scientific, and Cultural Organization (UNESCO). In 1953, collaborating with his wife, Aurora, Cortázar completed translations into Spanish of Edgar Allan Poe's prose works. Throughout his life Cortázar traveled extensively—primarily between Argentina, Cuba, Nicaragua, and the United States—often lecturing for social reform in Latin America. A number of Cortázar's works explicitly reflect his strong concern for political and human rights causes. For example, the novel *Libro de Manuel* (1973; *A Manual for Manuel)* is in part an exposé of the torture of political prisoners in Latin America. Both in his fiction and in his essays, he was an advocate of socialism and a vocal supporter of the Cuban and Nicaraguan revolutions. He died in 1984.

Among Cortázar's early works are three short story collections: *Final del juego* (1956; *End of the Game, and Other Stories),* *Historias de cronopios y de famas* (1969; *Cronopios and Famas),* and *Todos los fuegos el fuego* (1966; *All Fires the Fire).* Many of these stories feature extraordinary characters and events. "Axolotyl," one of Cortázar's most famous stories, is told by a man who has been transformed into a salamander after spending several days watching salamanders in an aquarium. While not overly fantastic, Cortázar's first novel, *Los premios* (1960; *The Winners),* also represents a strange set of circumstances for which no rational explanation is offered. In this work, passengers on a luxury cruise begin to feel threatened when they are restricted to certain areas of the ship and forbidden to communicate with the crew. Cortázar examines the diverse ways in which the passengers react to this enigmatic situation. *Rayuela* (1963; *Hopscotch),* Cortázar's best-known work, has been called Latin America's first great novel for its complex and inventive narrative structure. Described by Carlos Fuentes as "one of the great manifestos of Latin American modernity," this novel consists of one hundred and fifty-five chapters that can be read in at least two logical sequences to create variant narratives. Cortázar uses this technique to encourage the active participation of the reader and to emphasize his disdain for traditional narrative.

Cortázar's later works include two short story collections, *Alguien que anda por ahí y otros relatos* (1977; *A Change of Light and Other Stories* and *Queremos tanto a Glenda* (1980; *We Love Glenda So Much),* and a novel *Un tal Lucas* (1979; *A Certain Lucas). A Change of Light* reflects the range of Cortázar's fiction, from stories of political oppression to tales of fantasy. The stories in *We Love Glenda So Much* examine the nature of reality and those patterns and forms that people impose upon the world to maintain a sense of order and definition. In the title story, members of a fan club murder their favorite actress because her films do not meet their standards. *A Certain Lucas* is divided into three sections composed of short musings and observations. The first and third sections describe dreams and episodes from the life of Lucas, an aging Argentine writer. The middle section contains some of Lucas's own writings. Through Lucas, Cortázar ruminates on many of the ideas that were important to him throughout all of his writings: the nature of reality, the exploration of literary form, and the search for new ways to view the world.

CRITICAL COMMENTARY

CARLOS FUENTES

(essay date 1967)

[Fuentes is a prolific, versatile Mexican writer noted for his innovations in language and narrative technique. His concern for affirming a viable Mexican identity is revealed in his allegorical and thematic use of his country's history and legends, from the myths of the Aztecs of the Mexican Revolution. In the following essay, first published in Spanish in *Mundo Nuevo* in 1967, he examines the themes and narrative technique of *Hopscotch*.]

Hopscotch is a Latin American novel; it is so because it is infused with the magic atmosphere of a pilgrimage that never arrives. Before it was discovered, America had already been invented in the dream of a Utopian quest, in Europe's need to find a *là-bas,* a blissful isle, a city of gold.

Principal Works

Presencia (poetry) 1938

Los reyes (poetry) 1949

Bestiario (short stories) 1951
[*End of the Game, and Other Stories,* 1967 (partial translation); also published as *Blow-Up, and Other Stories,* 1968]

Final del juego (short stories) 1956
[*End of the Game, and Other Stories,* 1967 (partial translation); also published as *Blow-Up, and Other Stories,* 1968]

Las armas secretas (short stories) 1959
[*End of the Game, and Other Stories,* 1967 (partial translation); also published as *Blow-Up, and Other Stories,* 1968]

Los premios (novel) 1960
[*The Winners,* 1965]

Historias de cronopios y de famas (short stories) 1962
[*Cronopios and Famas,* 1969]

Rayuela (novel) 1963
[*Hopscotch,* 1966]

Todos los fuegos el fuego (short stories) 1966
[*All Fires the Fire, and Other Stories,* 1973]

El perseguidor y otros cuentos (short stories) 1967

La vuelta al día en ochenta mundos (nontification and poetry) 1967
[*Around the Day in Eighty Worlds,* 1986]

62: Modelo para armar (novel) 1968
[*62: A Model Kit,* 1972]

Ultimo round (nonfiction and poetry) 1969

Pameos y meopas (poetry) 1971

Libro de Manuel (novel) 1973
[*A Manual for Manuel,* 1978]

Octaedro (short stories) 1974
[*A Change of Light, and Other Stories,* 1980 (partial translation)]

Vampiros multinacionales: una utopía realizable (short stories) 1975

Los relatos. 4 vols. (short stories) 1976–85

Alguien que anda por ahí y otros relatos (short stories) 1977
[*A Change of Light, and Other Stories,* 1980 (partial translation)]

Un tal Lucas (short stories) 1979
[*A Certain Lucas,* 1984]

Queremos tanto a Glenda (short stories) 1980
[*We Love Glenda So Much, and Other Tales,* 1983]

Deshoras (short stories) 1982

Nicaragua tan violentamente dulce (sketches) 1983
[*Nicaraguan Sketches,* 1989]

Salvo el crepúsculo (poetry) 1984

Is it any wonder that the most significant feature of Latin America's literary imagination should be the questing after El Dorado—Carpentier,—of a patriarchal paradise—Rulfo,—of an original identity—Asturias,—or of a frozen mythification—Borges—to be found somewhere beyond the historical nightmare and cultural schizophrenia of a world dreamed up in Utopia and degraded in the epic? But, while that imagination has up to now been born of an awareness of the decomposition of history and society, Cortázar makes his pilgrimage inward, to implode in upon himself so that, with luck, he will be able to "move beyond" the figures of his literature. At any rate, Cortázar does not presume to place society at issue without having first placed reality at issue.

At the most obvious level, *Hopscotch* offers a structure and a story, both booby-trapped. The book is divided into three parts. The first part, "From the Other Side," is Buenos Aires and the coming together of Oliveira and Talita, La Maga's double, a circus cat keeper and later a madhouse nurse. The third part, "From Diverse Sides: Expendable Chapters," brings together a collage of quo-

tations, newspaper clippings, signs and ads that range from academic to pop.

A "Table of Instructions" completes the structure only to begin transforming it; the novel may be read for the first time straight through, and a second following the table of instructions. But this second reading only opens the door to a third, and, we suspect, to the infinite numbers of the true reading. Cortázar, we realize, is setting forth something more than a narration. His purpose is to exhaust all the possible formulations of an impossible book: a book that would radically supplant life or, rather, would turn our lives into one vast reading of all the combinations of what has been written. An "incredible" project, as Borges would say, equivalent to imagining the total negation of the total recuperation of time.

"Would I find La Maga?" The first words of *Hopscotch* give us the key to this search never to be finished, "incredible," cut off before the book is written, represented by Oliveira in the ceremony of the writing of the book.

Because only the book will allow him to get back with La Maga, that "nebula swirl," a little naïve, a little perverse, continually remembered and foreseen in a present tense of literature becoming then the third death of real time. Three things are killed off in *Hopscotch:* the death of remembered presence, the death of foreshadowing, and the death of the written book as compensation for the absence of La Maga, the indispensable companion in the uninterrupted, desacralized childhood game. Only the couple, that "incredible" attempt to win negation and salvation, can negate and save the fatality of heaven and hell in the game of hopscotch. Oliveira is given over to exodus, to the search of the "final island" representing the lost place, to the pilgrimage toward the "kibbutz of desire" in which one can live—or believe oneself living—with substitutes for a lost unity of loving.

A novel of bridges between the lost and the salvageable, *Hopscotch* begins under the Seine arches and culminates atop a few rickety boards stretched between the windows of a Buenos Aires boardinghouse. Oliveira's odyssey takes him to Paris (the original model), then to Buenos Aires (the false homeland). Buenos Aires is the cave where the shadows of being are reflected. The reality of Argentina is a fiction; the authenticity of Argentina is its lack of authenticity; the national essence of Argentina is the imitation of Europe; the city of gold, the isle of bliss is nothing more than the shadow of the settlers' dream. Oliveira returns to Buenos Aires to come together with Talita, the double of the La Maga lost in Paris. But La Maga, necessarily, comes with a double of Oliveira; Traveler, who hates to be named that, since he's never traveled beyond the River Plate. Talita and Traveler, degraded reflections of La Maga and Oliveira, have the same pick-up sort of a life: expatriate.

Bohemia, intellectual tripping-out, all this becomes, in the context of the "home country," the stuff of the circus, the madhouse and the hospital. Downfall? Nothingness? Yes, but not with the tragic will of an awareness contemplating the downfall of *something*. The fall, in *Hopscotch,* is that of some Buster Keaton of the Pampas, willingly comic, buffoonish, grotesque; it's the fall of someone who has no place to fall because he never got up; it's the nothingness of the Latin American world, confronted with nothingness before being or having anything. Or, rather, after having only a dream: would I find La Maga? But did Oliveira ever meet La Maga, or does he only hope to encounter her in the words that Oliveira says and Cortázar writes?

The irony of Cortázar's spiritual journey is that, like every quest for being, it is born out of a solitary awareness that cannot be maintained in isolation. Oliveira tries every alchemy of substitution. And each one gives him a dry, tragicomic caricature of the splendorous unity he dreams of, a cuckold sex maniac alongside the desired and detested companion, La Maga. At this level, the "dispensable chapters" become indispensable. Morelli, an old,

failed writer, possibly an alter ego of the writer, is the magister ludi of this cultural flea market, of this Porta Portese bazaar of ideas, cluttered with the discards of reason ("a whorehouse of virgins, as if such a thing were possible"), society ("this dead-end serving the Great Idealist-Realist-Spiritualist-Materialist Infatuation of the West, S. R. L."), history ("It may well be there's a thousand-year reign, but if we ever get there, it won't be called that anymore") and intelligence (". . . the very fact of being thinking about it instead of doing it proves it's wrong"). Cortázar here sets down a true list of what not to take with you to a desert island.

But Oliveira already is, settled in with masochistic joy, on a desert island. His dream, La Maga, Madonna and lover, is gone. He cannot rely on the insubstantial shadow of the cavern, Buenos Aires. All he has left is what he drags along with him: the castoffs of rationality, the pianos stuffed with dead donkeys in *Un Chien andalou.* Oliveira renounces the words of this garbage heap ("To war against the word, to war, whatever it takes, even if it means renouncing intelligence"), in favor of actions. But actions must be described in the words of the author, Julio Cortázar: "The violation of man by the word, the proud vengeance of the word against its father, tainted each of Oliveira's meditations with bitter suspicion; he was forced to turn to his own enemy to gain access to a point where perhaps he could rule on his enemy's case and then move on from there—how and by what means, through what white night, or inky day?—toward a total reconciliation with himself and with the reality he lived in."

The real piecing-together of *Hopscotch* begins with this taking-apart of words to make up the acts the novelist will need to describe. Michel Foucault says that "Don Quixote reads the world in order to demonstrate books . . . the promise made by books is incumbent upon him." Cortázar shows the opposite at work. With Morelli as his spokesman, he declares his intention to make a novel, not a written one, but dis-written. To dis-write, Cortázar invents a counter-language capable, not of replacing images, but of going beyond them, to pure coordinates, figures, constellations of characters. "Trap them, grab them by the tail, squeal, you whores," Octavio Paz says of words: this is exactly what Cortázar does. With both fists, breathlessly, with erratic blasts of conceptual dynamite, rhythmic, onomatopoeic, he blows the language of his own novel sky-high and atop the total ruins flies—a blown-to-bits triumph with wings aflame—the author, the last angel of this anti-paradise and anti-hell in which God and Devil are a single paradox: the more is created, the more is damned. *Hopscotch* is to Spanish prose what *Ulysses* is to English prose.

This coming-together of actions and the counter-language capable of dis-writing them forces Oliveira into a "non-behavior," a pointless accumulation of motions foreign to the language that traditionally has described them. The conflict leads straight to mockery, farce and absurdity. The outsize joke, worthy of Rabelais and Sterne, seizes hold of the book. Putting out the planks in Buenos Aires, where failed intentions are so numerous that failure becomes the whole point of the undertaking. The death of Rocamadour, La Maga's son, in the middle of a literary orgy. Descending into the refrigerated morgue, into the searing ice of hell. The rewriting and reordering of the world in the notebooks of the distinguished Uruguayan madman, Don Ceferino Piriz. These are profound keys of *Hopscotch,* of its basis in the extreme illumination of the surrealists, of its unsettled dialogue between the Bretonian sphinxes of humor and happenstance.

Marginal language and action become counter-language and action-beyond-action in Oliviera's search. The pilgrimage takes him to his own double, Traveler. And facing one's double in the flesh, there are only two responses: murder or madness. Otherwise, Oliveira would have to accept that his life, not being unique, lacks value and meaning; that another person, who is he himself, thinks, loves and dies in his stead and perhaps Oliveira is only his double's double and only living the life of a doppelgänger. Oliveira attempts murder by terror. Not a true murder, since murdering one's double would be suicide, but rather a criminal "attempt" that will open the doors to madness. Or, at least, that will make others believe Oliveira mad. There, at the end, in the madhouse and hospital that are the only kibbutz chance guarantees, the virtue and the need of the Oliveiras of this world is that they can live in absurdity without justifications or contradictions. One can, in the end, multiply unreality by inventing everything the world seems to lack. Oliveira belongs to that line of genius-idiots who, from Louis Lambert to Pierrot le Fou, create the indispensable order of the dispensable. In the madhouse and the hospital, the final harbor of the Nietzsche we could all be, is located the center of the hopscotch; heaven and hell are one and freedom can be exercised starting from a perpetual clamor of something lacking, some lack of satisfaction.

"Here it is now," says Oliveira. To this being-here-now, the novelist gives only the mortal urge, the leap toward the probable island of desire become reality. True being lies elsewhere, and the novelist is the prophet who would lead us out of the captivity of discourse, history and psychology.

A contemporary grandmaster of the *ars combinatoria,* Julio Cortázar has written a novel faithful to the author's deep conviction: "Apart from our individual destinies, we form part of figures that we cannot know." And the constellations of *Hopscotch,* finally, speak to us of time and liberty. Together with Octavio Paz and Luis Buñuel, Julio Cortázar represents today the vanguard of contemporary Latin American thought and culture. With Paz, he shares the incandescent tension of the instant as a supreme high point in the tides of time. With Buñuel, he shares the vision of freedom as the aura of permanent desire, of an

unauthorized dissatisfaction that is, for that very reason, *revolutionary.* (pp. 86–8)

Carlos Fuentes, "'Hopscotch': The Novel as Pandora's Box," translated by Naomi Lindstrom, in *The Review of Contemporary Fiction,* Vol. 3, No. 3, Fall, 1983, pp. 86–8.

ALFRED J. MAC ADAM
(essay date 1977)

[In the following excerpt, Mac Adam analyzes *Hopscotch,* focusing on its significance in the history of the Latin American novel.]

Julio Cortázar's *Rayuela* [*Hopscotch*], the work that put both its author and Spanish American literature into a position of prominence in Western culture, is a deliberately essayistic text. It attempts to enact a coming to grips with the problem faced by all authors, the relationship between what the author talks about and how he talks about it. . . . [*Rayuela*] dramatizes the problem any author faces when he writes—which elements he will select and which reject, and how he will use those he selects, whatever elements his culture supplies to him. At the same time, Cortázar represents the same sort of problem, the dialectical or nondialectical relationship of "tradition and the individual talent," on a philosophical level by creating a protagonist who tries to evade a life of preordained patterns.

The metaphorical relationship between *Rayuela's* two sides, the conscious mirroring of the ethical and the esthetic, is further complicated by the protagonist's also being his own narrator. This is, the text simultaneously writes and "unwrites" itself as it grows. A word might be said about the two reading methods offered to the reader at the beginning of *Rayuela:* the reader may choose to follow either the "Tablero de Dirección" or to read the text as an ordinary book (or, if he disdains both options, invent his own reading method). If he chooses the short reading, he omits the chapters designated "From Other Sides/Omissible Chapters." Immediately the reader is challenged by the text: to choose the easy, "feminine" (in Cortázar's terminology) route or to choose the complex, possibly baffling route seemingly suggested by the text itself. This is a kind of existentialist "either/or" tempest in a teapot which plays not only on the reader's self-esteem but also on his snobbery (who would admit to having chosen the feminine plan and abandoned a third of the book?). Notwithstanding this crux, it is advisable to read the book both ways and then experiment, simply to see how Cortázar's sense of composition works, how what is disarticulated neatly in the long reading is rather ambiguously articulated in the short reading.

Articulation is indeed the dominant metaphor in *Rayuela:* how a character imagines his life to be defective because the pieces do not cohere as he would like, and how Cortázar would like to break down a traditional plot by fusing it with meditations on narrative problems. It is rather like a cubist still life in which we see all sides of a given object at the same time, something impossible except in the work of art. But let us note at the same time that Cortázar's experiment is not without precedents. Saporta's *Composition No. 1* and Huxley's *Eyeless in Gaza* are also forays into new forms of discourse. What we have in *Rayuela* is a melange derived from Breton's *Nadja,* Sartre's *La Nausée,* Beckett's *Murphy,* with a touch of Céline's *Voyage au bout de la nuit,* reworkings all of the story of the soul's journey to enlightenment, of the same kind we find in Apuleius's *Golden Ass* or Bonaventura's *Itinerarium Mentis in Deum.* Cortázar, following Breton and Sartre, develops this model on a less obviously religious plane (although it is nevertheless a religious plot) and combines it with esthetic speculation. To what end? The clearest object in view is the reader himself, whose views on literature and life Cortázar has long been trying to change.

Cortázar's dissatisfaction with the status quo, or what he imagines the status quo to be, of occidental narrative, what he consistently calls "the novel" has been long lived. In fact, his earliest utterances on "the novel" are testimonies of this dissatisfaction. But there is more to the situation than esthetic impatience. In reality Cortázar is a genuine sufferer from what Harold Bloom has called the "anxiety of influence." Simply stated, this anxiety, which Bloom sees operative in all modern poetry, is caused by the unavoidable influence of the poets of the past on the creative ability of later writers. There is no moment of their work which is not warped by a backward glance at their "forefathers," and the result of this constant rearguard action is *"a history of anxiety and self-saving caricature, of distortion, of perverse, willful revisionism without which modern poetry as such could not exist"* (italics in original). Modern writers, to rephrase Bloom's thesis, are born with oedipal problems which they resolve in the ways just described.

Without seeing Cortázar in the light of the anxiety of influence theory, it is difficult to understand just what it is he finds so oppressive about the literature, specifically the narrative literature, of the past. What he calls the traditional novel is something that exists, if at all, only marginally in English and American literature and seems peculiarly French. In fact, Cortázar's attitude as an avant-garde writer seems almost to be a serious rendition of the ironic distinctions Borges makes between French and English literary history in "The Paradox of Apollinaire." In that essay, Borges notes that French literature seems to be a product of French literary history, that instead of being written by people, it consists of "schools, manifestos, generations, avant-gardes, rearguards, lefts, rights, cells, and references to the tortuous destiny of Captain Dreyfus." Cortázar too looks at the novel (without ever distinguishing between the major genres) in the same way. There are good writers, of whom he approves, and bad ones, whose work he attacks. The major object of his literary assaults is the mythical "traditional novel," analogous to the one Ortega attacks in *The Dehumanization of Art.* It is clear that Cortázar needs a straw man so that he can overcome his anxiety of influence, just as he needs a mythical "good-father" author, one, naturally, he creates himself, the novelist Morelli in *Rayuela.*

The creation of a "father" by an author is an act which ought to have elicited a torrent of critical speculation. The opposite is in fact true, and the sad reality of most Cortázar criticism is its pious repetition of what the author or his surrogate (Morelli) says about literature. Criticism becomes repetition. Morelli does have, however, a significance beyond Cortázar's own immediate need for a master. He is the master absent from Hispanic culture in general (especially since Spanish Americans, like their Peninsular counterparts, scrupulously avoid reading Brazilian or Portuguese authors, thereby excluding Machado de Assis or Eça de Queiroz from their spectrum). The single Spanish author who might, through sheer output, have vied for such a place of honor, Pérez Galdós, is held up to ridicule by Cortázar. In chapter 34 of *Rayuela,* the protagonist, Horacio Oliveira, reads a passage from *Lo prohibido,* and the text is so arranged that one line of Galdós is followed by a line of Oliveira's thoughts. The juxtaposition is ironic, and Galdós suffers, perhaps unjustly, in the process.

The creation of Morelli is important also because Cortázor not only shows him as a text (the characters comment on his works) but also as a character. One thinks of Plato's relationship with Socrates, the often commented control the younger philosopher had over his master when he turned him into a character. Perhaps Cortázar is showing something more than he realizes: if Morelli is a master, he is more like Cortázar himself than any living figure. And if this is true, he is relegating himself to the position of innovator, one who writes for the history of literature, and not necessarily to be read. To a certain extent this is true. *Rayuela* has aged, not so much in its abstract sense as an experiment with discourse, but in its style and its cultural accouterments. It is in this sense a rather banal *Summa* of the early 1950s, existentialism-cum-mysticism. Borges's remark in the Apollinaire essay about the fact that, although Apollinaire and Rilke are of the same generation, Rilke's work seems fresh while Apollinaire's has become a collection of period pieces, holds true for Cortázar as well. To write in order to change the "now" of literature is to situate oneself prominently at the beginning of another "now."

It is therefore in a double perspective that we should consider *Rayuela:* what it did as a phenomenon in literary history remains; what its accomplishments are as a work of art remain to be seen. Above all else, *Rayuela* altered the sociological status of the Spanish American writer. The Spanish American writer of the 1960s became almost as great a celebrity as his political counterparts. To be sure, writers of an earlier generation, such as Neruda or Borges, were famous, as were such poets as Octavio Paz or César Vallejo, but the publication of *Rayuela* inaugurated a period of wide dissemination and, more importantly, of wide exposure of writers to a primarily Spanish American public. Cortázar's text was an international Latin American success and broke down barriers which long kept, for example, Mexican readers from sharing reading experiences with Argentine readers.

A serious obstacle fell, the idea that in order to be understood by the Spanish speaking world in general a writer had to use a kind of B.B.C. Spanish. *Rayuela* is an Argentine book in the way Cabrera Infante's *Tres tristes tigres* is a Cuban book or Guimarães Rosa's *Grande Sertão: Veredas* is a Brazilian book. This is a step perhaps difficult to understand for an Anglo-American audience. Faulkner was not, we assume, afraid of not being understood by Scotch readers. Something may be lost, but how much more was lost when writers had to become grammarians to produce a work of art? No longer would a writer hesitate to use either localisms or street talk of any sort.

The relaxation on the linguistic level has its counterpart on the sexual plane as well. Cortázar's characters talk about sex, practice it with an almost Henry Miller–like verve, and regard it as a part of everyday life. This frankness was not common in the Spanish American world before 1963. There were exceptions of course, but, again, Cortázar's text made sex into a subject for all Spanish American writers, a matter which no longer had to be treated elliptically. That this corresponds to a change in the attitude of the reading public (and is not therefore a cause *per se*) is a matter for consideration. It would seem, as Emir Rodríguez Monegal states in his study of the "Boom," that Cortázar and the social change mutually complemented each other.

Important for the non-Latin American reader of Cortázar is the kind of culture Cortázar displays. Borges and Bioy Casares had spattered their texts with allusions and quotations, but Cortázar carries this display of cultural material to an absurd point. Like a baroque writer of the seventeenth century, Cortázar stuffs his text with references; his characters talk about religion, philosophy, art, literature, and history in a professional way, as if their lives were spent in galleries and libraries. At the same time, this manifestation of culture, though accomplished by an international cast, seems very Argentinian, indeed, very Latin American. To "know" French, English, and American literature is not rare in Latin American middle-class life, and an educated Argentinian would not shock his friends by referring to Baudelaire. At the same time, this same person would be familiar with his own literature, so that Cortázar can refer to Raymond Roussel, Musil, and

Roberto Arlt in the same passage without hesitating. It is this, for us, bizarre mixture—which we find in Borges as well—that makes *Rayuela* seems so dazzling. At the same time, the tendency toward the encyclopedic is typical of satire, so that in a sense culture and genre complement each other in a quite natural way.

The idea that culture is nothing more than a skin, a surface that desensitizes and isolates the bearer, is taken up in *Rayuela* during the Parisian phase of Horacio Oliveira's life. The myriad possibilities that present themselves to Oliveira, the conflicting religions, philosophies, and literary schools are proof to him that he will not find what he wants through them. This situation is Augustinian in origin in that illumination, the kind of ontological security Oliveira seeks, is something given, not something acquired. In other terms, Oliveira is seeking grace, which cannot be acquired through works alone. The Paris section of his life is therefore a progressive discarding of his cultural baggage, a separation from his milieu, which includes his friends and his lover Maga, the Nadja of *Rayuela*.

This renunciation is accomplished through a series of parallel deaths, suicides, and sacrifices which make most of the characters in Paris doubles for Oliveira. The death of Rocamadour, Maga's child, the event which precipitates Oliveira's banishment from Paris, is the symbolic death of Oliveira's humanity, the side of him that arouses pity in others. At the same time, Morelli is dying in a hospital, and another of Oliveira's lovers, Pola, is dying of cancer. These deaths underline the mind-body dichotomy which puts arbitrary limits on the protagonist's search, and, at the same time, they make him aware of his need to die in one sense in order to be reborn. Again, the text is a chronicle of how an individual passes from one state to another: in Machado, Brás Cubas is reborn in his text; in Bioy a man dies so that a text may be born; and here in Cortázar a fictitious but exemplary life is transformed into words on a page.

Oliveira's most significant renunciation, the one of which he repents almost immediately, is his giving up Maga, the women he loves. This enactment of the idea that one always destroys what one loves most is extremely important to Oliveira because it makes manifest his desire for salvation, no matter what the cost. Again, the parallel to Augustine in this sundering of personal ties to the world in order to save one's soul is clear. Since Maga cannot give him what he wants (although she seems to possess it), she must be sacrificed. In the same way, when he feels his enlightenment is at hand, Oliveira does not hesitate to use his friend and spiritual double, Traveler, as a means to reach it. Whether he does in fact reach his goal is not clear, but it is the goal that justifies the process and the sacrifices.

There is certainly nothing new, either in content or in style, in Oliveira's history. We must then turn to the other side of the text in order to see what made it so explosive. And, again, if we look carefully here, we shall see that the interpolation of material alien to the protagonist's story (though related to it thematically) is not new at all. The kind of moralizing digressions in Mateo Alemán's *Guzmán de Alfarache* or Defoe's *Robinson Crusoe* parallel the various sorts of interpolations Cortázar utilizes. His book does not disorder plot, not even the epic sense of beginning *in medias res;* it simply makes the straight line into an arabesque.

Plot may be understood either as an element of the work of art or as an aspect of the psychology of composition. In the first sense, plot is the arrangement of events; strictly speaking, their arrangement to show causality. This does not, as Aristotle or Borges would have us believe, mean that paratactic texts like the *Golden Ass* or the *Lazarillo de Tormes* are not "plotted." They obey a different order, one in which causality is generally removed from the realm of ordinary human logic and left in the hands of fate or a divinity. They follow a process of accumulation which leads to some sort of culminating moment, a hierophany in the *Golden Ass,* an ironic discovery of identity in the *Lazarillo.* We might also note that in *La Nausée,* the same sort of trajectory is found.

Rayuela displays two sorts of organization, the type we see in Sartre's text, and another, one in which the reader "sees" the author selecting those elements which will constitute the book's "best of all possible worlds." Oliveira's story is that of Roquentin; the text's own "story" is its assimilation of all sorts of heterogeneous material (newspaper clippings, almanac quotations, passages from other literary texts). The reader may not be "correct" in his utilization of the materials Cortázar has brought together under the one roof of the text, correct here being merely an approximation of the author's own wishes. But these wishes are irrelevant because the mere act of assemblage suffices as *prima facie* evidence of a wish to create an order. Despite the ironic quotation from Bataille's *Haine de la poésie* (chapter 136) about the author's own inability to explain why he brought together certain materials, the fact remains that the materials have been gathered. They are now in the hands of the reader, whose reading will connect the pieces. All plots are "replotted" by the reading, which accounts for all loose ends.

Cortázar seems to have overlooked this aspect of reading in his desire to work some sort of disordering magic on the reader's sensibility. Like the surrealists, whose work he has long admired, he forgets that interpretation is a weapon which turns the text against its creator. Like the monster in Mary Shelley's *Frankenstein,* the work, once in the world, acquires characteristics unimagined by the creator. It may horrify or delight him, but it will no longer be his property. What Cortázar wishes, therefore, is not something an artifact can give: he wants to change his reader, but he uses a tool that the reader will twist into something different. Whatever changes occur in the reader as he reads will be modified when the work is reconstructed in memory. There it will be organized and transformed, turned into an image of the reader's, not the artist's, mind.

What happens to *Rayuela* reminds us of what has happened to the didactic satires of the eighteenth century. When we read Swift or Voltaire, it is obvious we are not reading them as their original readers did. We see simultaneously more and less in both texts than did their age. Does Voltaire really teach us anything? Perhaps, but the thrust of his philosophical arguments is meaningful only to those readers who can reconstruct the extratextual milieu that surrounded *Candide* when it first appeared. *Gulliver's Travels* (which even had a different title) is more a hallucinatory experience for today's readers, more an anatomy of the soul than a satire directed against specific targets. The error of Cortázar's didacticism is its naïve faith in the ability of the work of art to retain his intentions when placed in alien hands. To be sure, *Rayuela* should be read as one of Stanley Fish's *self-consuming artifacts:* "A self-consuming artifact signifies most successfully when it fails, when it points *away* from itself to something its forms cannot capture. If this is not anti-art, it is surely anti-art-for-art's sake because it is concerned less with the making of better poems than with the making of better persons," but the question of whether Cortázar's enterprise is worth the trouble or not remains unanswered. To read him fairly we must forget the banality of his ideas and consider the goals he sets both for himself and for us.

He fails, perhaps, but there is grandeur in his failure. The experiment with narrative, the attempt to point out what might be done with narrative, and the risks involved—all of this constitutes a noble endeavor. Whatever else *Rayuela* may have done, it certainly made the Latin American literary world aware of new possibilities. A good example of the kind of book Latin America was prepared for by *Rayuela* is Cabrera Infante's *Tres tristes tigres.* This is in no way a suggestion that Cabrera Infante is a follower or imitator of Cortázar. Far from it. And yet, when we realize that *Tres tristes tigres* is an assemblage, a kind of verbal scrapbook, then we must inevitably recall Cortázar's art of assemblage in *Rayuela.*

Rayuela must also be remembered whenever language, narrative structure, or the depiction of the artist within the work of art are discussed. *Rayuela* is a point of crystalization for so many subjects that one is tempted to set it at the head of a movement. This of course would be a falsification. Authors like Machado de Assis, Bioy Casares, Roberto Arlt, Juan Carlos Onetti, and Felisberto Hernández, dead, forgotten or simply ignored for one reason or another, all did what Cortázar did. His importance lies in having done it all at the moment when he was able to make a huge impression on a new generation of readers and writers. Drawing lines between the writers of different generations is not difficult, especially in Latin

America where two genres, satire and to a lesser extent romance have held such sway. That is, since most writers are working within the confines of a single genre, the essential traits of that genre soon begin to be common currency. What *Rayuela* is, then, is not so much an innovation as a gathering place in which an entire catalog of innovations is put on display. (pp. 51–60)

Alfred J. Mac Adam, "Julio Cortázar: Self-Explanation & Self-Destruction," in his *Modern Latin American Narratives: The Dreams of Reason,* The University of Chicago Press, 1977, pp. 51–60.

JOYCE CAROL OATES
(essay date 1980)

[Oates is an American fiction writer and critic who is perhaps best known for her novel *them*, which won a National Book Award in 1970. Her fiction is noted for its exhaustive presentation of realistic detail as well as its striking imagination, especially in the evocation of abnormal psychological states. As a critic, Oates has written on a remarkable diversity of authors—from Shakespeare to Herman Melville to Samuel Beckett—and is appreciated for the individuality and erudition that characterize her critical work. In the following excerpt, she commends Cortázar's collection *A Change of Light, and Other Stories.*]

A Change of Light is Cortázar's eighth book of fiction to appear in English, and it is in many ways a change: of tone, of manner, of style, of emphasis, of "light" itself.

Here one does not find the lush and motile openness of *Hopscotch*, or the risky, funny, ceaselessly inventive predicaments of *End of the Game* (1967). The penchant for exploring obsessions—the more futile, the more fertile for the ravenous imagination—that was a thematic undercurrent in *All Fires the Fire* (1973) is given in these 20 stories an unexpected delicacy, a surprising Jamesian dignity, by the elegiac tone of Cortázar's language and a less hurried (and more dramatic) pace.

"You who read me," one of Cortázar's typical narrator-protagonists says, "will think that I'm inventing; it doesn't matter much, for a long time now people have credited my imagination for what I've really lived or vice versa." In **"The Faces of the Medal"** the narrator Javier—a man who "doesn't know how to cry"—attempts to free himself from nightmares of loss and impotence by "writing texts that try to be like nightmares . . . but, of course, they're only texts."

Throughout *A Change of Light* one is always aware that a story, an artifact, is being created. The political context is sometimes in the foreground, sometimes an ominous assumption, but at all times we are aware of the words that constitute the story as words, for the most part judiciously chosen. "He" frequently shifts to "I" and back again to "he" and then again to "I." The narrator may suddenly announce his own befuddlement. One of the more self-consciously literary of the stories, **"Footsteps in the Footprints, "** is prefaced, not altogether unfairly, by the author's terse summary, as a "rather tedious chronicle, more in the style of an exercise than in the exercise of a style, say that of a Henry James who might have sipped maté in some Buenos Aires or Mar del Plata courtyard in the twenties"; the least satisfactory story, **"The Ferry, or Another Trip to Venice, "** written in 1954, is "revised" here in a high-spirited gesture of defiance—the author, acknowledging the story's inferiority, is nevertheless intrigued by it and cannot let it go: "I like it, and it's so bad." (Cortázar, following the possibly infelicitous examples of Nabokov, is intermittently tempted to take himself very seriously indeed—as a literary phenomenon, a cultural figure whose every utterance, "bad" or not, is of value. Or is the pomposity really playful? Are the prefaces themselves jokes? Cortázar says: "Ever since I was young I've been tempted by the idea of rewriting literary texts that have moved me but the making of which seemed to me inferior to their internal possibilities. . . . What might have been attempted [however] through love would only be received as insolent pedantry." But even the most willfully self-conscious stories, even the "bad" story, are so finely written, sentence by sentence, and the author's melancholy intelligence so evident in every line, that the actual reading of *A Change of Light* is an invariable pleasure. And the incursions of fantasy, of improbability and nightmare, do not deflect from the stories' "realist" emotional authority: Several stories in this collection have the power to move us as Kafka's stories do.

In **"Summer"** . . . the pleasurable monotonous marriage of a quite ordinary couple is interrupted, perhaps fatally, by the overnight visit of a young daughter of a friend. The girl is innocent enough, a mere child, yet she appears to be accompanied by an enormous white horse who gallops snorting around the house, a ferocious white blur, a "rabid" creature, or anyway one maddened enough to want to enter a house. The white horse has stepped magnificently out of a dream recorded in Kafka's diary for 1914 (the year of Cortázar's birth, incidentally), and in this eerie parable of ritual monotony and ritual violence he acquires a new menacing authority: "In the window the horse rubbed his head against the large pane, not too forcefully, the white blotch appeared transparent in the darkness; they sensed the horse looking inside, as though searching for something. . . . He wants to come in, Zulma said feebly." In fact the horse does not enter the house, though the little girl—accidentally or deliberately—leaves the front door open for him. But the marriage has been altered, the "new day that had nothing new about it" has been irrevocably lost. Cortázar's most

Julio Cortázar on *Hopscotch*:

I have read enough books by young authors to suspect that *Hopscotch* has meant to many people what one might call an existential shock rather than a literary experience, so that its influence has been extraliterary rather than technical or linguistic, as its author intended when he wrote what has been described as an anti-novel. The noticeable bewilderment the book caused many critics obviously came from the fact that it would not fit into any more or less usual category, and it was significant that they failed to realize that any close comparison of *Hopscotch* to literature involved losing contact completely with the central ideas of the book. Petrus Borel used to say "I'm a republican because I can't be a cannibal." For my part I should say that I wrote *Hopscotch* because I could not dance it, spit it out, shout it, or project it as any form of spiritual or physical action through any conceivable medium of communication.

Julio Cortázar, in Rita Guibert's *Seven Voices: Seven Latin American Writers Talk to Rita Guibert*, translated by Frances Partridge, Alfred A. Knopf, 1973.

ing. And no story is so irresistible, so immediately engaging as the classic **"Axolotl"** of *End of the Game*—my favorite Cortázar tale. But the risks of psychological realism, of genuine emotion, of the evocation of human beings enmeshed in plausible cobwebs of friendship and enmity make this volume all the more valuable. "I know that what I'm writing can't be written," one of Cortázar's narrators says in despair, and in any case, as the unhappy protagonist of **"Footsteps in the Footprints"** learns, one is always writing autobiography, however disguised; and the autobiography is always distorted. Perhaps writing is "social revenge" of a sort? Or an attempt, necessarily doomed, to compensate for the fact that one doesn't know how to cry? Nevertheless the writing is triumphant, and Cortázar's text survives tears or the lack of tears. It transcends both game and ritual to become art. (pp. 34–5)

Joyce Carol Oates, "Triumphant Tales of Obsession," in *The New York Times Book Review*, November 9, 1980, pp. 9, 34–5.

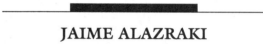

JAIME ALAZRAKI
(essay date 1983)

[In the following excerpt, Alazraki surveys the development of Cortázar's short stories.]

There was a time when Cortázar's readers argued over the merits of his novels vis à vis the quality of his short stories. Since his short fiction came first, the heresy of measuring his newly published novels against his more established stories was inevitable and equally aberrant. Today very few readers—if any at all—will argue with the fact that he is an unsurpassed master of both genres. Furthermore, he has written some of the most powerful essays in the Spanish language: a recent collection—*Territorios* (1978)—places him as one of the most gifted and original essay writers to have emerged from Latin America in the last few decades. Cortázar, the poet, is still waiting to be discovered, but a few perspicacious and daring readers have already expressed their strong preference for the poet. This slow, and yet steady, recognition of his work is understandable. He is not a popular writer—in spite of his popular subjects—and he has resisted the temptations of facile professionalism and bestsellerdom. Like all genuine artists, his first loyalty is to his own perceptions and beliefs, and to forms and textures that match those perceptions. A new book by him is neither a rehash of nor an easy sequel to a previously gained momentum. It is, instead, a new effort to explore those few passions and obsessions haunting the consciousness of a true writer. When one has published eight collections of short stories in a period of less than thirty years, a new one might

sympathetic people are those who believe in compulsions (which they call rituals or games) as a response to death and nothingness—"fixing things and times, establishing rituals and passages in opposition to chaos, which was full of holes and smudges." But no ritual can accommodate the snorting white horse, or even the overnight visit of a friend's child. (p. 9)

This collection's most compelling stories are unambiguous elegies. The narrator of **"Liliana Weeping"** imagines not only his own poignant death but a future for his wife that guarantees her survival; the narrator of **"The Faces of the Medal"** addresses a woman he has loved but to whom he cannot, inexplicably, make love—

We didn't know what to do or what else to say, we didn't even know how to be silent . . . find each other in some look. It was as if Mireille were waiting for something from Javier that he was waiting for from Mireille, a question of initiatives or priorities, of the gestures of a man and the compliance of a woman, the immutability of sequences decided by others, received from without . . . . It would have been preferable to repeat together: we lose our life because of niceties; the poet would have pardoned us if we were also talking for ourselves.

And in the volume's title story two "lovers" are victims of their own self-absorbed fantasies about love: They are real enough people, but not so real as their obsessive dreams.

There are one or two stories here that seem out of place in the volume—fairly conventional "suspense" stories that dissolve to sheer plot, despite the fastidious writ-

unavoidably run the risk of being either overlooked or taken for granted. Such seems to be the case with *We Love Glenda So Much*. . . .

In this new volume, one can recognize themes and motifs found in previous collections. **"Orientation of Cats"** brings to mind Cortázar's fondness of cats purring and pawing throughout his writings. **"We Love Glenda So Much"** reenacts the paroxismal admiration for an artist that borders on the collective hysteria treated earlier in **"The Maenads."** The unexpected twist that closes **"Story with Spiders"** reminds one of a similar situation and ending in **"Condemned Door."** Cortázar's attraction to subways as the scene of bizarre encounters and dramas, previously explored in **"Throat of a Black Kitten"** and **"Manuscript Found in a Pocket,"** is once again probed in **"Text in a Notebook."** **"Press Clippings"** deals with violence in terms reminiscent of his famous story **"Blow-Up."** His penchant for plots about triangular relationships—most memorably treated in **"The Idol of the Cyclades," "The Motive,"** and **"All Fires the Fire"**—is evinced here in **"Return Trip Tango."** The exquisite structure of **"Clone"** based on that of Bach's *Musical Offering*, reveals a close affinity with *Hopscotch*'s intricate patterning, and at the level of theme, it restates Cortázar's fascination for groups as the framework of his novels: all of them resort to this constellational coterie for the development of situations and characters. **"Stories I Tell Myself"** pivots around the twilight zone where reality yields to dream, so characteristic of a good segment of his short fiction and so brilliantly captured in **"The Night Face Up."** **"Moebius Strip"** is more a motif than a "state of mind": Cortázar's intuition of an uncharted order where opposites coalesce and harmony follows.

That a writer writes and rewrites those few obsessions that form the backbone of his/her creation is neither new nor uncommon. One begins to be suspicious of a writer whose range of themes is unlimited since what determines the limits to his craft is the same limitation that underlies his human experience. García Márquez has said and repeated that he had been trying to write *One Hundred Years of Solitude* since he began writing, but he had first to write several novels before he was able and ready to write his famous novel. Borges' entire fiction is but the reformulation—over and over—of a handful of subjects. If a subject is too complex, it requires by necessity not one but several formulations, as if its intensity overflows the capacity of a single version and calls for new ones. Successive variations on a given theme aim at capturing new angles of the same face. If **"Blow-Up"** is an exploration of evil and violence, **"Press Clippings"** ventures into the same area, but the difference in treatment between the first story and the second is the same difference that separates Cortázar's art when he wrote *End of the Game* in 1959 and this last collection twenty years later.

Cortázar's handling of the short story has gone a long way. Although the stories of his first collection—

Bestiary (1951)—display a rare perfection for an author who was making his first strides in the genre, his subsequent collections have been a relentless endeavor to push the medium's power to its utmost limits. Cortázar has refused to capitalize on what he calls, quoting Gide, the acquired "élan." Instead of relying on previous success, he has sought new roads, new challenges, new peaks to climb, reaching unsuspected heights. Since his beginning as a writer, he distrusted realism. He felt that realism and reality had little to do with each other. Realism had to do with convention, with an accepted code that acted as a surrogate of reality. One may say that all art forms are conventions seeking to represent reality; realism, on the other hand, posed as the embodiment of reality. Cortázar endorsed, instead, a motto written on one of Artaud's drawings: "Jamais réel et toujours vrai." He was subscribing, of course, to the surrealist effort "to discover and explore the more real than real world behind the real." But if he recognized in its philosophy his own outlook on art, he never joined the verbal experimentalism of its magus and iconoclasts. His stories invariably present a world we recognize as our own, a world that seemingly does not depart from that of realism: the same routines, duties, ceremonies and institutionalized games; the same problems and situations, stereotypes and conflicts. Yet, his stories do not point at those surfaces we associate with realism, but rather at cracking them, at forcing them to yield to a hidden face. It is as if we mistakenly took the mask for the face, and the story proceeds to subtly remove that mask so that for a fleeting second the true face can be glimpsed. Another way to describe his approach is contained in a passage from Clarice Lispector's *Close to the Savage Heart* quoted as the epigraph for **"Moebius Strip"**: "Impossible to explain. She was leaving that zone where things have a fixed form and edges, where everything has a solid and immutable name. She was sinking deeper and deeper into the liquid, quiet, and unfathomable region where vague and cool mists like those of morning hovered." Although the passage fits more accurately the situation of the story where it has been inserted, it is also applicable to most of his stories. Most of them struggle to explain what "is impossible to explain" by means of language's conceptualizations, simply because language deals with those surfaces we habitually identify with reality. When language faces those cracks in its own makeup, it naturally closes them in the way skin heals its wounds. Why not peep through those cracks? How to make language enter that zone where things no longer "have a fixed form and edges," to become, instead, "a liquid and unfathomable region?" That is the province where most of his stories travel to. Of course the question is *how* to get there. If language, as the master tool of reason, has constructed the world we inhabit, it follows that to abandon the logic of language entails abandoning also the logic of our world. Confronted with this alternative, Cortázar broke with surrealism. In *Hopscotch*, one of the characters retorts: "The surrealists hung from words instead of brutally disengaging themselves from them. . . . Language means residence in reality, living in a reality. Even if it's true that the language we use betrays us, wanting to free it from its taboos isn't enough. We have to relive it, not reanimate it." Reliving language meant for him what it has always meant to literary art: converting the signs of its code into means of expression of a new code, that of literature. A notion or situation inconceivable in the language of communication—a person turned into an insect—becomes possible through the language of fiction. Fiction speaks where language remains silent. Furthermore, fiction dares to enter that *region* which is out of language's reach: a space irreducible to physical scales, a time outside the clock's domain, emotions not yet recorded in psychology manuals.

To explore that region, Cortázar resorted first to fantastic event (a man who vomits rabbits, noises that evict homeowners from their house, a tiger roaming freely through the rooms of a middle-class home, etc.). I am referring to the stories collected in *Bestiary*. In all of them, the conflict presented through their plots comes to a resolution by means of this fantastic "crack" on the realist surface of the story. This is far from being fantastic fiction as understood in the nineteenth century, since their ultimate effect is not to assault the reader with those fears and horrors that have been defined as the attributes of the fantastic. In addition, the technique of mounting suspense gradually leading to a sudden break in our rational order—someone dead who is alive—characteristic of the fantastic tale, does not operate here. Instead, the fantastic event can appear at the very beginning of the story, purporting not to frighten or horrify the reader but rather to offer a metaphor. A metaphor is a sign, or group of signs, that stands for a meaning other than the normative one represented in that sign. The rabbits vomited by the character in **"Letter to a Young Lady in Paris"** stand for something else, pointing to a tenor contextualized in the story but never quite named or openly disclosed. Metaphors assist the poet in naming what conventional language cannot name, at least not quite in the same way. For Cortázar, these stories were a form of describing those perceptions which, coming from "an unfathomable region," defy conventional language. Their irrational images transcend realism to explore a territory loosely labeled as the fantastic.

Without totally abandoning this literary artifice, most of the stories in his next collection—*End of the Game* (1956)—respond to a different narrative strategy. The fantastic element reappears in the form of a classical Greek myth—**"The Maenads"** and **"The Idol of the Cyclades"**—through a metamorphosis of sorts (**"Axolotl"**) or by means of an unyielding silence (**"After Lunch"**), but the rest of them abandoned altogether the weird side manifested in the fantastic break. Not that the fantastic ceases to act in these stories; it does act, but in a different way. We have no longer uncanny metaphors,

as in the first collection. The fantastic dimension of the story must be sought now at the level of its organisation; not so much in its theme as in the way that theme has been treated. In each one of these stories, there are two stories that have been craftily integrated. In **"Continuity of Parks,"** one story deals with an estate owner, and the other with two lovers plotting to murder the estate owner. In **"The River,"** there is a narrative about a middle-class couple and a second one about the wife's suicide. In **"After Dinner,"** there are two juxtaposed versions as to what happened during a friends reunion. A similar juxtaposition of two versions of the same event occurs in **"The Friends."** There is a third juxtaposition; yet in **"The Motive,"** one triangular love affair, which ends in a killing, is understood and solved in the context of a second mirroring triangle. In **"Axolotl,"** the narrator's vision of the axolotl overlaps the axolotl's vision of the narrator. **"End of the Game"** has also this contrapuntal quality: the perception three girls have of an outsider collides with the outsider's perception of the three girls. This technique attains to virtuosity in **"The Night Face Up"** where the story of a motorcycle accident interlocks with the story of a Moteca Indian sacrificed by the Aztecs.

If there is a fantastic side of these stories, it does not depend on any fantastic event, but rather on the way the two stories or points of view have been amalgamated. There is nothing uncanny or particularly disturbing in each of the two stoties if they are taken separately. But by coupling them in one single narrative where one bears a close adjacency with the other, the two stories can generate a meaning absent in each of the two individually. It goes without saying that braiding the two stories is not a haphazard or mechanical operation. It is precisely in this interweaving where Cortázar's art lies. By creating a net of intrinsic interrelations between the two stories, he has forced them to say something denied to each one in isolation. There is nothing appealing or appalling in the story of a motorcyclist having an accident, being rushed to a hospital, and undergoing surgery. Nor is there anything unusual in the second story of a Moteca Indian fleeing hunting Aztecs during the "war of the blossom" and brought finally to a pyramid's altar to be sacrificed. Both stories are narrated in that compelling and liquid style that has become Cortázar's trademark, but what makes the story a narrative feat is the masterful articulation of the two stories in a single structure. By cunningly presenting the second story as a dream of the character in the first story, and by gradually reversing the condition of dream from the second to the first character, this short story achieves a magic that challenges causality. Its impact lies somewhere between the two stories: in that space or interstice that their interlacing has created. The fantastic aura that the story may have stems from that point of intersection where one tale is cleverly linked with the other: what was a dream becomes reality and what was reality becomes a dream. For the motorcyclist, the sacrificed Indian is a dream caused by his own delirium after the accident; for the Moteca Indian, the motorcyclist and his accident in a Paris street is a dream caused by his own delirium before the Aztec priest lowers his arm with a stone knife in his hand to open his chest. We readers shall never know who is the dream and who is the dreamer. There is here a reverberation of that old piece of wisdom uttered by Shakespeare—"Life is a dream." There is also an echo of that dilemma that has troubled generations of Chinese readers: Was it Chuang Tzu who dreamed that he was a butterfly or was he a butterfly dreaming that it was Chuang Tzu? A third reading points to the confrontation of two civilizations, one attempting to understand the other, one unfailingly appearing as a dream of the other. Jacques Soustelle expressed this idea in a lapidary and intense sentence: "The reality of one civilization is the dream of another." These interpretations and many others constitute a multiplicity of meanings embodied in the story and underline its nature of metaphor capable of manifold tenors. If in the previous collection only the fantastic event bears the metaphorical weight, in *End of the Game* the entire story has become, by virtue of its narrative organization, a metaphor. Cortázar has moved from reliance on fantastic events interpolated in the plots in *Bestiary*, to situations that depend no longer on *what happens* at the level of plot but on *how* the story has been structured in this second collection. In the first case, he resorted to a fantastic resolution; in the second, to a compositional solution. The second choice required, beyond any doubt, a greater skill in the handling of the genre.

In this next collection, *Las armas secretas (Secret Weapons)*, 1959, he avoided cashing in on the accomplishments of his previous volumes. Instead, he left behind the fantastic metaphors of the first and the structural virtuosity of the second, to seek new possibilities, new questions, and new answers. Of that period, he said:

> When I wrote **"The Pursuer,"** I had reached a point where I felt I had to deal with something that was a lot closer to me. I wasn't sure of myself any more in that story. I took an existential problem, a human problem which was later amplified in *The Winners*, and above all in *Hopscotch*. Fantasy for its own sake had stopped interesting me. By when I was fully aware of the dangerous perfection of the storyteller who reaches a certain level of achievement and stays on that same level forever, without moving on, I was a bit sick and tired of seeing how well my stories turned out. In **"The Pursuer"** I wanted to stop inventing and stand on my own ground, to look at myself a bit.

Is there a better definition of the nonconformist artist, of the writer indifferent to the temptations of the book market and only true to his own convictions? With *Secret Weapons*, Cortázar found new tones and inflections for his voice, new preoccupations and themes for his fiction, and new forms of expression to tackle more effectively those new concerns. His stories became longer—an average of 30 to 40 pages as opposed to the 3 to 10 page story in the earlier collections—less focused on the exactly structured plot and closer to the breadth of the novel, less geared to situations and more concentrated on characters, more vital and less dependent on plot. All this should suffice to prove the constant process of renovation in his art, his tireless search for new forms and narrative modes, his commitment to the short story as a genre capable of inexhaustible regeneration. What we have seen thus far brings us also to the question of his most recent collection, *We Love Glenda So Much*, and to its place in Cortázar's production as a short-story teller.

A good point of departure is his view of the short story as a sister genre to poetry. In an essay devoted to the former and included in his book-collage *Ultimo round* (*Last Round*, 1969), he stated that "there is no genetic difference between the brief short story and poetry as we understand it since Baudelaire"; to further explain:

> The genesis of the short story and the poem is basically the same. Both are born out of a sudden estrangement, out of a *displacement* that alters the normal state of our consciousness. At a time when labels and genres are on the verge of bankruptcy, it is worth insisting on this affinity that perhaps others will find fictitious . . . . My experience tells me that, in a way, a brief short story does not have a *prose structure*. Each time I had to check the translation of one of my stories (or I had to translate stories by others, like those by Poe), I have felt, to a high degree, that the short story's effectiveness and meaning depend on those same elements that bestow a specific character to poems as well as to jazz: tension, rhythm, internal beat, the unexpected within expected parameters, that *fatal freedom* that does not tolerate alteration without an irreparable loss.

Cortázar alludes to the nature of literary artifact of the short story or poem: autonomous and precise organisms capable of breathing on their own, and of communicating their charge of experience thanks to their sensitive and delicate machinery. The narratives of this new collection share with earlier ones the same effort addressed to capturing an experience or perception or feeling incommunicable by means of ordinary language. They also share the condition of extended metaphors in the sense that while they tell a well-crafted story, they also open in the body of the narrative a double bottom, a second meaning awaiting to be detected in the same way that a poem offers a message that goes beyond its immediate text. We cannot have an exact translation for the rabbits vomited by the narrator in **"A Letter to a Young Lady in Paris,"** just as the ultimate message conveyed by the two merged stories in **"The Night Face Up"** escapes a single and rigid interpretation. In the end, the reader of these stories is confronted with a silence which represents its most powerful message. In reading them, one has the distinct feeling that the narrative has been woven around that silence, as its habitat, as the only way of transmitting its implications and resonances. The whistling wind one hears in the nautilus shell is not the shell, but without its spiral shape and its air-filled chambers there would not be that sea whistle one hears. This is not a mystic silence; it is literary silence similar to the one elicited by poetry, hence the brotherhood between the two genres Cortázar referred to. The new in the stories from *Glenda* is the way that that silence has of existing. Like poems, which convey their meaning through the interplay of images and through the music-filled lines of their linguistic patterns, these stories too emit messages through narrative patterns of imagery, rhythm and fictional diction.

The first three stories have in common an elliptic quality that accentuates their kinship with poetry. What do cats see when their look is lost in an invisible point? What does a woman see when she looks at images of a painting? How to explain that the admiration for an artist could be so strong as to destroy the very object of admiration? Is there a point where a rapist and his victim could have reversed their times and turned the heinous crime into a human experience? Are dreams and reality just different manifestations of the same substance? How to answer these questions without falling into the traps of common sense and correct syllogisms? What *Glenda*'s stories seek is not to provide answers but simply to explore questions, and they do that in the same way a piece of music explores an emotion and a poem encodes a charged silence. Yet the medium of fiction is not music or verse. Its task is to tell a story, but Cortázar tells it in the way a poem exudes poetry and a musician plays music. So much so that "Clone" was patterned following the model of Bach's *Musical Offering,* and "Orientation of Cats" reads like a prose poem. What approximates these stories to other art forms, however, is not their dress but their substance. Powerful short stories loyal to their medium, they share with other art forms the same matter that becomes music at one point, painting, at another, and poetry, at a third: messages devoid of rational meaning.

What we have said thus far might give the impression that *Glenda*'s stories suffer from an excessively aesthetic proclivity. This will be, of course, a wrong impression. They are, quite the opposite, deeply rooted in the most immediate experiences of everyday life, but they avoid the triteness and the stereotype of its mechanics to focus on what we suspect lies underneath that ocean of practicalities; not what a truck driver does, but what he dreams; not what a cat eats or breaks, but what she sees with her eyes lost in some invisible sight; not a rape as reported by a newspaper, but as examined from within; not the entries of a couple's diary vacationing on an island, but the only entry omitted in that hypothetical diary. Cortázar is a wizard of those ellusive spaces, unrecorded experiences, unmeasurable times. The butterflies caught in his fictional net are either rara avis or extinguished species.

At the same time, and paradoxically, he is one of the most courageous writers to have emerged from Latin America. He comes from a country where military torture and murder have become the only laws. Argentina under the military rule has been turned into a prison, a slaughterhouse, a swindled, deceived and frightened nation. Italo Calvino has recently said about the writer's involvement in politics: "I am interested in writers who say something that ordinary politicians don't say." But since Argentina and other similar Latin American countries do not have politicians—they have been either killed or gagged—writers become the de facto spokesmen of their people. Since repression has silenced all freedoms, silence has become a form of complicity with the repressors. To speak up, though, one has to be outside their reach, in exile. "Press Clippings" is one of the most powerful literary texts written about that form of crime that Amnesty International has called "political killings by governments." The 30,000 people who have "disappeared" in Argentina can no longer be dismissed: they are public information. We haven't been able yet to measure the human suffering and horrors implied in that abstract figure. Their story is beginning to unfold painfully. How to deal with such an explosive subject without turning literature into a political pamphlet? How to approach this horrible tragedy without trivializing it? How to shout the horrors and stay at the same time within the bounds of art? Julio Cortázar has performed this tour de force with skill, verve, and integrity. In "Press Clippings" we recognize all the marks of his craft: mastery over his medium; the exactness, vivacity, and dignity of his language; the text folding over itself to say the unsayable. At the same time, he has confronted with unusual courage not only the murderers, but also himself as a human consciousness witnessing those murders. Should violence be met with violence? The story's answer is neither passionate nor legalistic, neither intellectual nor rhetorical. It is an existential one that chooses to elucidate the question rather than to provide answers. The narrator is swept away by violence, and she herself falls into its vortex before she can reflect: "How could I know how long it lasted, how could I understand that I too, I too even though I thought I was on the right side, I too, how could I accept that I too there on the other side from the cut-off hands and the common graves, I too on the other side from the girls tortured and shot that same Christmas night. . . ". Facing violence, the narrator is forced to act, and yet, by acting, she falls herself into the nightmare of violence. There are no blacks and whites: white turns black and vice versa. The reader is confronted with the inevitability of violence on the face of violence: evil cannot be witnessed impassively. At the same time, reacting to violence with violence puts us on the side of the criminal. The criminal has succeeded in turning us into criminals. Human values and human rights have disappeared, force has replaced laws and institutions, the stronger destroys the weaker and the weaker seeks to defend himself with the only weapon his oppressor understands: more violence. Savagery. Jungle. People turning into beasts.

Although Cortázar does not present a clear-cut answer, in poignantly enlightening the question, he has given his reader all the insights needed for a human response. This has always been art's task: not to dictate answers but to illuminate the question, not to solve the presented problem but to unveil its ins and outs. Catharsis still remains the only answer to which art accedes. To go any further amounts to distorting it and, consequently, to its denial. Cortázar understands too well this dangerous borderline. He knows that literature's power lies not in transgressing its boundaries, but in accepting them and pushing against them until those limits become the hidden source of its own strength and the secret fulcrum of its leverage. In *We Love Glenda So Much,* he put into practice his wisdom and craftsmanship as a storyteller. These stories prove, once again, that he can break his own record. It matters not if the story ponders on what a cat sees, or if it dares to venture into the hells of political killings; if it traces a literary counterpart to Bach's *Musical Offering,* or if it depicts the city subways as our modern purgatory. In all of them we sense the hand of a master telling us what perhaps we once knew and forgot. (pp. 94–9)

Jaime Alazraki, "From 'Bestiary' to 'Glenda': Pushing the Short Story to Its Utmost Limits," in *The Review of Contemporary Fiction*, Vol. 3, No. 3, Fall, 1983, pp. 94–9.

AMARYLL B. CHANADY

(essay date 1984)

[In the excerpt below, Chanady provides a retrospective of Cortázar's literary career.]

Cortázar started writing at a very early age. By his own account, he completed his first novel when he was nine and wrote love poems at 12. But apart from a collection of poems strongly influenced by Mallarmé that appeared in 1938 under the pseudonym Julio Denís and a "dramatic poem" brought out in 1949, Cortázar published almost nothing until 1951. Nevertheless he had been assiduously writing short stories for some time. In that year, he published his first collection of stories, *Bestiario,* which contains some of his best-known short prose. These carefully structured and polished narratives introduce two themes that reappear in his later work—the presence of the mysterious and unusual in our everyday world, and the stifling force of convention. In **"Omnibus,"** a young girl boards a bus in which all the passengers are carrying flowers on the way to the cemetery. Since the girl, Clara, and a young stranger who sits beside her are the only people without flowers, all the other travellers stare at them with hostility. After all the passengers with flowers have left the bus,

Clara and her companion are physically threatened by the driver at every stop until they escape at their destination. There they immediately buy flowers and are happy that they are like everyone else again. Read on a literal level, the story is a suspenseful narrative about an extraordinary and frightening experience, but on the symbolic level, it illustrates people's intolerance towards what is different, and depicts the distress of the outsider. **"Carta a una señorita en París"** can also be read on this double level. More than just a fantastic story about a man's stay in an apartment that is progressively destroyed by the rabbits he vomits at regular intervals, it is also a symbolic account of rebellion against the fastidiously tidy and well-furnished home of a financially successful friend. It is not a liberating rebellion, but one that leads to the protagonist's insanity and suicide. In **"Lejana"** (**"The Distances"**), a young and wealthy Buenos Aires socialite, Alina Reyes, feels that she is being suffocated by an endless round of parties and cocktails with their superficial conversations and conventional rituals. She imagines she has a double in Budapest, a beggar who shivers in the cold and leads the authentic life that is denied to the materially comfortable Alina Reyes. On a subsequent trip to Budapest, Alina meets her double, exchanges identities and casts off her former self to become the beggar. **"Bestiario"** is the story of a family that inexplicably keeps a tiger roaming freely through the house, while the inhabitants are careful to stay out of its way. A young relative who comes for a visit upsets this order when she lies to the family about the tiger's location and thus causes the death of her uncle. Another well-known story in the 1951 collection is **"Casa tomada"** (**"House Taken Over"**) in which an elderly couple is driven out of their home by mysterious noises. In all these narratives, the supernatural and the extraordinary appear as an integral part of life. They are neither questioned nor rejected as implausible by the narrator or the characters, and are seen by the reader as a forceful expression of hidden impulses and social tensions.

In his next volume of short stories, *Final del juego* (1956), Cortázar continues to juxtapose the natural and the supernatural. **"Axolotl"** is the story of a man who pays daily visits to an aquarium in order to stare with fascination at the axolotl, a type of larval salamander, until he himself is transformed into one. In **"El idolo de las Cícladas" ("The Idol of the Cyclades")**, two men are mysteriously coerced by the statue of a pagan goddess to commit human sacrifice. In this anthology, we also see the emergence of a theme that reappears frequently in Cortázar's fiction—that of the *figure*. According to the Argentinian author, people and events are united in "constellations" or "figures," that are often unknown to the individuals. A *figure* may be created by the resemblances between two strangers, the relationship between a man and a woman, or the meeting of a group of people. In **"Una flor amarilla" ("A Yellow Flower"),** a middle-aged man recognizes his double in the fourteen-year-old Luc, and realizes that instead of dying, he will be reincarnated in an infinite series "of poor devils repeating the *figure* without knowing it, convinced of their liberty and free will." When Luc dies, the protagonist is happy that his unsuccessful life will not be continued by subsequent doubles. But the sight of a yellow flower suddenly reminds him of the horrible threat of nothingness, since he knows that after his death there will be no reincarnated double to appreciate the beauty of flowers. **"La noche boca arriba" ("The Night Face Up")** also depicts a *figure,* that of the resemblance between an injured man on a twentieth-century operating table and a sacrificial victim of the Aztecs many centuries earlier. After alternating presentations of both scenes, the modern protagonist is finally described as the sacrificial victim.

Those entertaining and stylistically sophisticated stories do not yet contain the theme of anguished search for the mystical "centre" or "absolute" that runs through much of Cortázar's later work. This theme first appears in **"El perseguidor" ("The Pursuer")** in 1959. The protagonist of this portrait of existential quest and tormented awareness is a brilliant jazz musician called Johnny Carter (based on the historical Charlie Parker), who submerges himself in drugs and alcohol and tries to commit suicide twice in his despair at not being able to find the elusive absolute for which he is looking. Existential searching is completed by what the author calls a "crack" in reality which permits us a glimpse of the absolute. Profoundly influenced by his readings about Zen Buddhism and the Vedanta, Cortázar frequently deplored the Western world view that restricts reality to what is logical and empirical, and divides everything in binary fashion. He believed that fantastic literature provides us with a brief view of a different reality that is obscured by our ordinary rationality. Several of Cortázar's protagonists try to break away from the sterile and stifling conventional reaction towards the world. Johnny Carter, for example, sometimes finds in his music the illumination that enables him to see a dimension of reality usually hidden to us. But he is incapable of grasping it, and finally dies of excessive drink and drugs. (pp. 46-9)

One of Cortázar's most popular and humorous publications is *Historias de cronopios y de famas* (1962), which, in spite of its lighthearted tone, further develops the fundamental theme of escaping from convention. In the first selection of the volume, the world is described as a "glutinous mass" which is tedious and unchanging unless we force ourselves to see things differently. . . . In the final selections of the 1962 collection, Cortázar introduces the mythical famas, cronopios and esperanzas. The green and viscous cronopios with their unconventional behavior are counterparts of the rebellious family on Humboldt street in the first part of the book. One of them invents a thermometer for measuring lives and finds out that the fama, who most resembles ordinary people, belongs to the category of "infra-life," while the professor of languages is characterized as "inter-life" (**"El almuerzo",** or **"The Lunch")**.

Cortázar develops most of the themes from his earlier fiction in his major novel *Rayuela (Hopscotch),* published in 1963. The innovative style, experimental structure, erudite references and intellectual digressions force the reader to participate in the creation of fiction. Instead of starting on page one and passively perusing an engaging plot to its tidy conclusion, the reader must jump from chapter to chapter and constantly leave the primary plot to ponder the lengthy opinions about literary aesthetics expressed by the fictitious writer Morelli. Parallel to the author's search for authenticity in stylistic experimentation is the protagonist's search for what he calls the "kibbutz of desire" through unusual experiences. Horacio Oliveira, torn between Paris and his native Argentina, rebels against the absurdity of life by immersing himself in absurd situations. On one occasion he has a sexual encounter with a physically repulsive beggar on the bank of the Seine and is taken away by the police. On another he extends a wooden plank between two multi-storied apartment buildings so that his friend Talita can bring him some nails without having to climb up and down several flights of stairs. His unsuccessful search for the absolute and an authentic expression of his self ends in insanity and possible suicide.

Hopscotch, however, is not just the personal search of the failed writer Oliveira, who never reaches the square of the hopscotch figure that symbolizes the sky. It also contains the author's proposal for a new way of writing in which conventional categories of time, space and psychological motivation will disappear in a more authentic presentation of reality. In 1963, Cortázar published *62/modelo para armar (62: A Model Kit),* where he put into practice the literary proposal outlined in chapter 62 of *Hopscotch.* Instead of a logical plot, the novel contains a succession of actions that are frequently absurd and unmotivated, and take place simultaneously and consecutively in London, Vienna and Paris. The characters are all connected in *figures* or "human constellations" as they travel and form groups and couples in various combinations, determined by destiny. (pp. 49–50)

Many protagonists in Cortázar's fiction are dissatisfied with life and desire a more authentic existence. Inability to find it often leads to death, as in the case of Johnny Carter. The flight attendant Marini in **"La isla a mediodía"** (**"The Island at Noon"**) dreams about living in idyllic seclusion on a Greek island, and finally dies there when the plane crashes. Marcelo in **"Lugar llamado Kindberg"** (*Octaedro,* 1974) drives his car into a tree when he realizes that his career as a travelling salesman robs him of freedom and spontaneity. The middle-aged couple in **"Vientos aliseos"** (*Alguien que anda por ahí*, 1977) commit suicide when they find out that their marriage will never be anything but a tedious ritual. Other characters search for meaning in life through political awareness and involvement. Andrés in *Libro de Manuel* (1973, translated as *A Manual for Manuel)* joins a group of Latin American revolutionaries. The protagonists of **"Alguien que anda por ahí"** and **"La noche de Mantequilla"** in *Alguien que anda por ahí* both become involved in secret missions and are killed. (p. 51)

In *Deshoras,* the last collection of short stories that Cortázar published before his death, the characters are no closer to reaching personal fulfilment than in the earlier narratives. Apart from the eulogy to Glenda Jackson in **"Botella al mar,"** the stories do not paint very uplifting scenarios. . . . [The] narrator/protagonist of **"Diario para un cuento"** tries unsuccessfully to write about Anabel, a woman he knew in the past. At the end of this last story, the narrator gives up in frustration when he realizes that he can only describe himself, but never the real Anabel. In a depressing conclusion he writes: "It is so sad to write about myself." He had already explained this sadness a few pages earlier. After telling us that Anabel, although ignorant in many ways, was often able to glimpse what she called "life," the narrator/protagonist admits that life for him was "a forbidden territory that only the imagination or Roberto Arlt could give him vicariously," and that the really innocent people are those, like the narrator, "with a tie and three languages." Can we draw parallels between the protagonist of **"Diario para un cuento"** and Cortázar himself, whose hyperintellectualism may have distanced him from what we often call "reality" and whose life consisted mainly of the reading and writing of fiction? His characters never successfully completed their quest, in spite of their anguished attempts. But Cortázar's work, although often difficult and disquieting, yet always original and stimulating, is a magnificent monument to his own quest. (p. 52)

Amaryll B. Chanady, "Julio Cortázar's Fiction: The Unfinished Quest," in *The Antigonish Review*, No. 57, Spring, 1984, pp. 45–53.

SOURCES FOR FURTHER STUDY

Alazraki, Jaime, and Ivask, Ivar, eds. *The Final Island: The Fiction of Julio Cortázar.* Norman, Okla.: University of Oklahoma Press, 1976, 199 p.
    Collection of critical essays by well-known critics of Cortázar's fiction; also includes reprints of a short story and two essays by Cortázar.

Bennet, Maurice J. "A Dialogue of Gazes: Metamorphosis and Epiphany in Julio Cortázar's 'Axolotl'." *Studies in Short Fiction* 2, No. 1 (Winter 1986): 57–62.
    Analysis of the protagonist's transformation in "Axoltl" as a complete blending of man and animal.

Boldy, Steven. *The Novels of Julio Cortázar.* Cambridge: Cambridge University Press, 1980, 220 p.
    Highlights three recurrent elements in Cortázar's novels: the *doppelgänger*, or the relationships between double characters; the *figura*, or the structural relationships between episodes and characters; and the "double text," or the presence of two discourses or narrators within one work.

Garfield, Evelyn Picon. *Julio Cortázar.* New York: Frederick Ungar Publishing Co., 1975, 164 p.
    Critical biography based chiefly on interviews with Cortázar.

Gyurko, Lanin A. "Narcissistic and Ironic Paradise in Three Stories by Cortázar." *Hispanofila* 50 (1974): 19–42.
    Posits that ironic destruction awaits protagonists whose inward searches for self-fulfillment are narcissistic in the short stories "Las puertas del cielo," "La isla a mediodía," and "El otro cielo."

Neyenesch, John. "On This Side of the Glass: An Analysis of Julio Cortázar's 'Axolotyl'." In *The Contemporary Latin American Short Story,* edited by Rose S. Mine, pp. 44–60. New York: Senda Nueva de Ediciones, 1979.
    Discusses the immobility of several protagonists in Cortázar's short stories as a recurring motif suggestive of Western humanity's desire to escape reality.

The Review of Contemporary Fiction 3, No. 3 (Fall 1983): 5–106.

An issue devoted primarily to Cortázar; includes essays by Carlos Fuentes, Evelyn Picon Garfield, and Cortázar.

Standish, Peter. "Cortázar's Latest Stories." *Revista de Estudios Hispanicos* XVI, No. 1 (1982): 45–65.

Explores thematic and technical elements within stories collected in *Alguien que anda por ahí* and *Octaedero,* and identifies recurring characteristics evidenced in these collections and earlier works.

Additional coverage of Cortázar's life and career is contained in the following sources published by Gale Research: *Contemporary Authors,* Vols. 1–24 (rev. ed.); *Contemporary Authors New Revision Series,* Vol. 12; *Contemporary Literary Criticism,* Vols. 2, 3, 5, 10, 12, 13, 15, 33, 34; *Dictionary of Literary Biography,* Vol. 113; *Major 20th-Century Writers;* and *Short Story Criticism,* Vol. 7.

Victor Hernández Cruz

1949–

Puerto Rican poet, essayist, and short story writer.

INTRODUCTION

Considered one of the leaders of the Neorican movement, a branch of Hispanic literature derived from Puerto Rican culture and language, Cruz is known for his collections of poetry and prose that examine the status of Puerto Ricans in America and the reality of life in Spanish Harlem. He imbues his work with a combination of Spanish and English ("Spanglish") diction and syntax, nature imagery, historical references, and the rhythm of Latin American popular music. Cruz's poetry, maintains Corinne E. Bostic, "is filled with humorous, angry, brilliant imagery that makes him one of America's finest young poets."

Cruz was born in Aguas Buenas, Puerto Rico. Because of difficult economic conditions, his family migrated to New York City in 1955 and settled on the Lower East Side of Manhattan, one of the areas designated as "el barrio." When he was about fourteen years old Cruz began to write verse, and at seventeen composed his first collection of poetry, entitled *Papo Got His Gun! and Other Poems* (1966). Cruz and his friends duplicated the collection on a mimeograph machine, distributing five hundred copies to local bookstores to sell for seventy-five cents each. Cruz's official career began somewhat fortuitously when an avant-garde New York magazine, the *Evergreen Review*, featured several poems from *Papo Got His Gun* in 1967. His first major poetry collection, *Snaps* (1969), depicts life on the gritty streets of the East Harlem barrio using powerful, simple language. Abrupt rhythms and realistic imagery create a series of "photographs" that vividly illustrate aspects of barrio street life: friendship, machismo, "hanging out," alienation, and death. *Mainland* (1973), his second book of poetry, chronicles Cruz's travels as he moved from New York to San Francisco and contains more eclectic, sustained imagery and themes than his earlier work. Cruz returned to the New York City barrio milieu to research and compose *Tropicalization* (1976), in which he utilized humor and energetic language as well as more experimental structures in order to capture the spiritual side of barrio life. In his poetry and prose collections *By Lingual Wholes* (1982) and *Red Beans* (1991), Cruz combines Spanish and English diction and syntax to create Span-glish, a language that also relies on the rhythm of Latin-American music. Drawing from a wide range of historical events and characters to explore his Puerto Rican heritage, Cruz incorporates African, Native American, and Spanish cultural motifs in both of these works.

Critics have acknowledged Cruz's growth as a poet from *Snaps* to *Red Beans*, lauding the increasing depth of his language, humor, and imagery. His early work, and especially the snapshot technique used in *Snaps*, was derided by most reviewers as monotonous and derivative, though some approved of its unconventional form and realistic portrayals of street life. In regarding his later verse, commentators have praised both the wider thematic scope and increased stylistic experimentation, particularly Cruz's use of Span-glish, popular Latin American musical rhythms, and his handling of nature imagery and wit. Cruz's nonfiction has also been lauded for its reflections on the author's Hispanic heritage; according to Ann C. Bromley, Cruz's essays enlighten "readers who need to be reminded of the rich diversity of influences that come to American poetry from sources other than the Anglo-European tradition." Nonetheless, some commentators argue that Cruz's nonfiction overlooks the concerns of Hispanic women; according to reviewer Jose Amaya, his nonfiction "deteriorates at times into a sexist vision of Hispanic culture and literature."

Cruz's vibrant, often humorous examination of themes concerning street life and the status of marginalized cultures in America has earned him a diverse and growing audience. Summarizing his overall standing, Pamela Masingale Lewis has asserted that "certainly Cruz's poetry and prose are important to the American literary scene, for they explore and expose American society, and they use human imagination to break down cultural barriers, to create new perceptions of reality, and to formulate new visions for the future."

CRITICAL COMMENTARY

NANCY SULLIVAN
(essay date 1970)

[Below, Sullivan examines the imagery and language of *Snaps*.]

Victor Hernández Cruz is twenty. He was born in Puerto Rico, and has lived in New York City for fifteen years. The poems in *Snaps* remind me in their subject matter of the taped conversations made by Oscar Lewis for *La Vida*, his sociological-anthropological study of a group of poor, oppressed Puerto Ricans in New York and San Juan. Cruz has lived in the same miserable New York tenements Lewis explores, ridden the same clacking subways to 114th Street and the Bronx, eaten the same kind of

---

Principal Works

Papo Got His Gun! and Other Poems (poetry) 1966

Snaps (poetry) 1969

Mainland (poetry) 1973

Tropicalization (poetry and prose) 1976

The Low Writings (short story) 1980

By Lingual Wholes (poetry and prose) 1982

Rhythm, Content and Flavor: New and Selected Poems (poetry) 1989

Red Beans (poetry and prose) 1991

---

rice and beans, felt-up similar girls, smoked pot and sold it as did the confused young men interviewed for *La Vida*. But Cruz's language is something else again. While Lewis honed and sterilized his subjects' conversations, Cruz allows the staccato crackle of English half-learned, so characteristic of his people, to enrich the poems through its touching dictional inadequacy. If poetry is arching toward the condition of silence as John Cage and Susan Sontag suggest, perhaps this mode of inarticulateness is a bend on that curve. See it at work in a poem called **"How You Feel"**:

> the rats took over
> the store downstairs
> eddie called & said
> a herd of dogs
> chased him into
> a woman's bathroom
> the afternoon dying
> with this poem
> a quart of beer
> & some cake
>
> how you feel?

or here in this excerpt from **"Their Poem"**:

> WE TOOK WILLY HOME   WITH HIS EYES
>   DRAGGING   ON THE STAIRS
> he gave Barbara a baby & she left him & married
> now has a house in Brooklyn & Perry Como records
> she plays for her guests she won't come around
> because it's too dirty her husband is stupid
> bought a big car he didn't know them white folks
> like little ones to put liberal magazines on the back
>   seats
> they even have pancakes for breakfast.

Cruz's visual images are like snapshots—spontaneous, hurried photographs, often a little out of focus, as though taken with a $2.98 Brownie camera; his sound patterns are abrupt like the snapping of fingers to the beat of a marimba. Cruz's language is sub-language used to detect life (*la vida*) in a sub-culture, the sepia ghetto of Spanish Harlem. Cruz has no interest in metaphor, sim-

ile, or established forms as poetic devices. What have they ever done for him? Who needs a simile in describing a gang-bang? For Cruz, the instant, the moment the shutter snaps is *it*. Such a poetic procedure has its limitations, of course: spareness and monotony; but it also has this great advantage: the shock of reality. I think that Cruz is writing necessary poems in a period when many poems seem unnecessary. Let necessity lead him *toward* not *away*, toward with a Rolleiflex zooming in on his territory once his Brownie is broken. (pp. 120–22)

Nancy Sullivan, "Snap Judgments," in *Poetry*, Vol. CXVI, No. 2, May, 1970, pp. 120–25.

CHOICE
(essay date 1977)

[In the following review, the critic discusses the stylistic provenance of Cruz's surrealistic collection *Tropicalization*.]

You can very precisely predict the style/tone of Hernández from the names of the mags where some of these poems [in *Tropicalization*] have been published: *Yardbird Reader* and *Invisible City*. Call it the "ethnic avant-garde." Hernández is a Puerto Rican American, and his poetry is a stunning batter of "Spanglish" (Spanish & English) with its ultimate stylistic roots in the far-out surrealism of Garcia Lorca—especially Lorca's *The poet in New York* (1955). This is very vital, energetic, fresh, innovative poetry, and it treats English just the way it should be treated—as its own kind of amalgam capable of easily incorporating into itself huge quantities of new words-syntaxes. Cruz is a poet to watch.

A review of "Tropicalization," in *Choice*, Vol. 13, No. 12, February, 1977, p. 1594.

RICHARD ELMAN
(essay date 1983)

[In the following excerpt, Elman notes the humor and eccentricity of language in Cruz's *By Lingual Wholes*.]

> Lucy Camancho is an artist
> art this
> She makes all the Stars in Hollywood
> seem like flashlights which have
> been left turned on for a week.

She had a frenisi
A friend in C
A friendinme

Bilingual since childhood, Mr. Cruz writes poems about his native Puerto Rico and elsewhere which often speak to us with a forked tongue, sometimes in a highly literate Spanglish. He gives things their proper names (bodega, *bacalao*). He's a funny, hard-edged poet, declining always into mother wit and pathos: "So you see, all life is a holy hole. Bet hard on that."

In *By Lingual Wholes*, his fourth collection of Spanglish poems, Mr. Cruz uses wit to defend an odd, almost eccentric disability of sensibility. He compares his mambos to the rhythms of "Choicer" and the Earl of Surrey in one poem, and then presents us with a variety of transformations in which English is made to seem almost Spanish and vice versa. The amalgam poetry which emerges is finely drawn, without apology or inhibition:

> The first corner has become a
> bodega whose window is full of
> platanos who have traveled
> miles to rest in that reality
> green with splashes of black
> running down their spines.

Mr. Cruz's poems are funny and bitter, warped by their humor and their tenderness. In a prose herbal, he depicts the effects of taking *pasote*: "One step at a time you enter the veins of the leaf . . . down this funnel you are going like water in a tube. The passage puts you on the other side of flesh, or an eyeball coming out of a cliff."

Reading the poetry of Victor Hernández Cruz brings to mind images digested from a similar herb. With a decoction of English, Spanish and the Arawak language, he serves up the guava villages.

Richard Elman, "Three American Poets," in *The New York Times Book Review*, September 18, 1983, p. 36.

FRANCES R. APARICIO
(essay date 1989–90)

[Here, Aparicio delineates the role of popular Latin American music in Cruz's poetry.]

Latin popular music, and *Salsa* in particular, imbues Victor Hernández Cruz's urban poems *Snaps* (1968), his first collection of poetry, already illustrates the central role that *Salsa* will play in Cruz's repertoire of poetic images and motifs. As Barry Wallenstein has already observed [in his "The Poet in New York: Victor Hernández Cruz," *The Bilingual Review*] regarding *Snaps*, "Cruz's work, when read aloud, sounds like jazz poetry. And it is like

a jazz poet that Cruz triumphs. The underlying sense of beat and polyrhythms, informed by jazz or Latin music, gives structure to Cruz's minimal poems, his "city snaps" and "clips," as Wallenstein describes them. Music appears in scenes of parties and as an integral part of drug experiences, both visually evoked as memories about growing up in the Bronx. In **"Coming Down,"** the poetic self evokes images of the neighbors in the area, subway trains and trips, drugs (implied by the title), music, and girls: "walking walking till 116th/up high stairs/a door/music." Here the sequence of verses creates a visual *diminuendo* (the number of words is reduced from one verse to another, from four words to one final word, "music"). Simultaneously, one imagines the spatial experience of going up a narrow stairs having done drugs (up *high* stairs), opening a door, and being inundated with the sounds of music blasting from the inside.

Yet Latin music is much more than just another aspect of urban life. **"Megalopolis,"** a poem about traveling by car in the urban sprawl of the East Coast, concludes with an act of singing: "singing magic words of our ancestors" is counterposed to the inauthentic discourse of advertising: "billboards of the highway are singing lies." This ancestral song offers him a sense of continuity with his cultural past, differentiating him from that particular urban scape which he crosses and in which he sees himself only as a spectator, not as a participant.

Traveling is an experience dear to the poet, and it serves as a dynamic poetic motif related to the mythical search of the self as well as to the reality of (im)migration and displacement. Throughout *Snaps* one finds the constant movement of subways in New York City, the uptown/downtown and inside/outside references, and numerous indications to walking and driving in the city. *Mainland* (1973) begins with poems in and about New York, then the Midwest, California, the Southwest, ends in Puerto Rico, Cruz's native island, and then returns to New York City. According to Nicolás Kanellos [in his *Victor Hernández Cruz y la Salsa de Dios*, 1979] the return to *Borinquen* in the last section of *Mainland*.

> represents the culmination of the poet's search for the
> origin of that vitalizing energy which is the music that
> he loves and the poetry that he writes. He has returned
> to the mother, the source, the tropical cradle, and he
> has found God.

Though such reading may well be valid—a return to the native island is, at a mythical level, a return to the origins—the poetry of Cruz eludes an all-inclusive mythic-religious interpretation. If the ethnic identity of Latinos is reaffirmed in poetry *vis à vis* the appropriation of our cultural products by dominant and economic institutions, such return would suggest an imagined reappropriation of the immigrants' own culture, a re-centering of the self within the reality of urban life in New York. **"The Man Who Came to the Last Floor,"** the last poem in

Mainland, reveals through the codes of a surrealist humor the underlying poetics of Cruz: a tropicalization of the American cultural urban scape from within, originated in the Latino community itself, as opposed to the tropicalizing efforts of Hollywood and the mass media in previous decades. The mango seeds which "accidentally" fall from up above onto a cop's head and which subsequently grow into a mango tree, were actually thrown by the Puerto Rican immigrant who came "to the last floor" and who, at the end, confessed he had never felt that he had left the island. Having experienced geographical, spatial, cultural and linguistic displacements, immigrants recenter themselves not only by living in areas ethnically defined, but by bringing along, and subversively "planting," seeds, objects that afford them cultural continuity. Among these, one finds ethnic symbols such as food (mangoes) and music. That the Puerto Rican man "fell into song/and his head was in motion" when he "started flinging the/seeds of tropical fruits down to/the earth," indicates the power of music as a catalyst in this planting of cultural "seeds."

In *By Lingual Wholes*, Cruz's 1982 collection of poetry and prose, there is a short poem that reads: "Put Seeds into the *Maraca*/So That It Could Sound." The image of seeds, then, becomes semantically polyvalent: from those contained in tropical fruits, such as mangoes, to "seeds" that produce music and, consequently, political and cultural awareness in the audience. In contemporary *Salsa*, Rubén Blades and Willie Colón's famous song "Siembra" (Sow) employs the image of planting seeds in overtly political terms, following an already clear tradition of "seeds" as a metaphor for the revolution (Cuba, Nicaragua) within the New Song Movement (*La Nueva Trova*) in Latin America.

While to an outside reader the "*maraca*" poem may suggest a didactic or moralistic aphorism, to many readers/listeners of the poet's generation these two verses constitute an English translation of an *estribillo* (refrain) made famous by Cheo Feliciano in the mid-'70s. From the song "El ratón" ("The Mouse"), the refrain says: "*échale semilla a la maraca/para que suene.*" While it refers on one level to the need for rhythm and *sabor* in music-making, this line was supercodified during those years and it was employed by the Latino youth to refer to marijuana smoking. Historically, then, "seeds" gain yet another semantic value: that of the marijuana plant and of drug-induced experiences. Thus, the recognition process which the in-group reader undergoes in not simply identifying lyrics and songs in a playful way, but a personal reading which invites a historical remembrance, a knowledge both of the self and of the community at the time. It becomes a musical experience repeated in the literary page which, in turn, establishes "predictability."

While pondering about this short text, I asked myself: Why did the poet translate the verses into English; why didn't he leave them in the original? The title of the book, *By Lingual Wholes*, may partly explain this decision. Its bilingual texture exhibits a complex dynamic between English and Spanish that extends beyond the oppositional linguistic dialectic prevalent in the earliest bilingual poetry of United States Latinos. One dynamic level between English and Spanish in this book consists of imagery, verses or phrases which are in English but which have a Spanish sub-text. Literal translations of proverbs such as; "*lo que no mata engorda*" ("what doesn't kill you gets you fat") constitute part of Cruz's imagery in English. Thus, the two verses: "Put seeds into the *maraca*/so that it could sound" illustrate this strategy, what could be deemed as the "tropicalization" or hispanification of American poetry at the surface structure. Beyond this linguistic description, the choice of English expands the semantic field of the utterance: by isolating it from its musical context and from the song in which it appears, the poet suggests that reading, as a creative act, involves the categories of whole/hole, totality/absence. The image itself, an empty *maraca*, is a metaphor for the preliminary possibilities of artistic creation. The seeds may be read as inspiration, *sabor*, or even the material resources needed for any aesthetic production. In the song interpreted by Cheo Feliciano, it certainly refers to the need for *sentimiento* and *sabor* in music making, the essential criterion which makes or breaks a performer, according to many musicians. Either you have it, or you don't. This quality, expressed through the image of "seeds," is clearly ethnic.

The *semillas* (seeds), then, become a central image out of which a constellation of various meanings emerge: ethnic identity, the musical rhythm and *sabor* of *Salsa* and fast dancing, the subversive and political powers of ethnicity, and the drug experiences. The powers of music are analogous to the visionary or "mystical" effects of hallucinations or drug-induced states. Cruz describes dancing to Ray Barretto's music, for instance, as an experience of self-unfolding (*desdoblamiento*), of coming out of oneself, of a trip beyond one's own consciousness, of a seeing oneself seeing;

> you marching in space
> you talking   you
> flying
> you already there
> nothing stopping you
> you are magic
> magic
> magic
> espiritu libre
> espiritu libre

In "latin and soul," the poetic voice asks where all this movement/dancing/traveling is leading to:

> they should dance/dance
> thru universes
> leaving-moving
>   we are traveling
> where are we going
> if we only knew

The last two lines reveal that the object of knowledge is not as important as the searching for it: the acts of dancing or of traveling and displacement through space, whether exterior (travel), interior (drugs), or both (dancing). Perhaps there is no place to go, since for immigrants movement itself becomes a constant in life. **"After the Dancing"** suggests that knowledge is congealed as the aftermath of the act of dancing—knowledge as trace, like the "coming down" in drug-induced states. The poem begins with the following verses: "we move/to the whispering/after the dancing" and concludes with an empowerment implied in the syntactic change from an indirect to a direct object: "we move/ the whispering/after the dancing." Empowerment occurs as a result of the recognition—ac-knowledgement—of one's own power, a process which makes up the core of the poem:"do you sometimes wonder/if you let go/if the walls move/if the floor cracks/if the ceiling lights up/. . . if the judge say/your boogaloo is ammunition/."

That "boogaloo" is viewed as "ammunition" proposes a new perspective on the powers of music. Though in other poems by Cruz, Latin music appears as a soothing, comforting alternative to urban violence, for the dominant culture and the outsider, Latin popular music may be disturbing, charged with violence, subversive: "stereo music/pucho & the latin/soul brothers/disturb/anglo-saxon/middle-class/loving/americans." Disturbances created by any type of loud music disrupt an ideal order of tranquility sought by a middle-class sector who, indeed, flee to the suburbs escaping the noises and disruptions found in the inner city and in densely-populated areas. Yes, latin popular music is disturbing. It throws the listeners into a state of apparent disorder, as perceived in the musical and acoustic elements, in the polyrhythmic structures, in the centrifugal textures of the lyrics, and, of course, in its dancing. From an order to a disorder, to chaos and violence as Cruz described with surrealistic humor in **"descarga en cueros,"** a poem whose title translates into English **"jamming with drums"** as well as **"jamming naked"** (*en cueros*), both subversive in their implications. In this poem music, the source of all destruction, is alluded to as "the vibrations":

> at the bar people's drinks flew out they hands the vibrations knocked people to the floor/& the lights began to bust/& the floor to crack. . . the floor began to rock people fell off the balcony/t.p. was smiling/his face ready to rip/o.k. you win/hands in the air ready to fly/hands outside beyond the buildings.

The verse "o.k. you win" implies that a musical performance may be a contestatory struggle, a war in which the drumming rhythms are invested with a power to which people submit. The violence and destruction described in terms of a natural catastrophe, such as an earthquake, find their tenor in the dancing movements provoked by the drums, centrifugal movements, going

out of oneself, which the poet hyperbolizes to the utmost extremes. Thus, in Cruz's poetry the potential for violence and destruction of Latin Music, its "disturbing" quality, orginates in the poetic strategy of making literal the fears of the Other, the middle-class, peace-loving American who understands neither the lyrics in Spanish nor the polyrhythmia, both of which, indeed, contest the traditional order of musical balance, harmony and lyrical beauty.

On the other hand, this movement towards disorder, chaos and violence also holds a transformational power with strong political and epistemological implications. Victor Hernández Cruz's poetry is consistently systematic in its presentation of music and dancing as forms of knowledge. His play with words such as *sabor* (taste)/*saber* (knowledge), a clear example of "*differánce*," and verses such as "Think with your body/and dance with your mind" undermine the traditional boundaries between feeling, thinking and acting. For Cruz, feeling music, perceiving it, is truly a form of knowing. To dance with the mind suggests forms of thought that embrace our body's senses, intuitions and emotions as an integral part of reasoning. In the title **"Listening to the Music of Arsenio Rodríguez is Moving Closer to Knowledge,"** the act of listening to music is defined in the poem as an epistemological experience. With his particular surrealistic humor, the poet suggests that music possesses a transformational power. People dance to Arsenio's music and its effects are extreme; *se liquidan* (liquidate), they literally turn to water (a pun with the associated signified, *matarse*—to be killed, or destroyed—*destruirse*—). In the poem, a group of researchers comes into the room, asking questions such as "Where is everybody?" "Are the windows opened ?" "Has it rained?"—questions that only address superficial phenomena from a logical, rational point of view.

Popular music evokes a sense of cultural empowerment in the listener/dancer/reader. Empowerment follows the knowledge and self-knowledge brought about by mystical and hallucinatory experiences and "trips" and by acts of "ac-knowledgement," the moving closer to our knowledge about our own power and authority as a community in the development of a dynamic, ethnically and aesthetically complex, cultural expression.

In this respect, the image of the *maraca* seeds again holds epistemological and cultural repercussions throughout Cruz's work. In *Tropicalization* the poetic voice ponders:

> Sitting on the Brooklyn Bridge at night
> Looking at the electrical lights
> Midtown a fire
> I think of the many seeds inside a maraca
> If each seed was like a light
> All holding hands
> Then the world would become a horse
> Start to gallop

We can mount it
We can ride.

In an idealistic and hopeful posture more prevalent in his earlier poetry, Cruz envisions that the demographic reality of Latinos in the United States, combined with collective efforts ("light/All holding hands"), could translate into a sense of true empowerment, mounting and riding that "horse" which is the world and also the United States. In *By Lingual Wholes*, however, cultural empowerment assumes a less simplistic or idealistic expression. It becomes effective mostly in the sense of continuity and "predictability" that the musical intertext in poetic discourse may offer the in-group reader, as was discussed earlier in the case of the *maraca* poem.

Dancing (*el baile*) is another act of acquiring knowledge and self-knowledge. Though secular to our contemporary sensibility, Afro-Cuban dancing, and the basic rhythms of *sones* and *rumbas*, find their origins in African religious ceremonies and rituals. When Cruz talks about "*la salsa de Dios,*" or states that "when you dancing God can't be far," the act of dancing recovers its religious genesis. Whether a mystical experience, as the poet implies about dancing to Ray Barretto's music (**"Free Spirit"**), or as a more secular act of reaffirmation of the Self and of our ethnic identity (*By Lingual Wholes*), dancing to *Salsa* becomes a vehicle for acknowledgement. For the masses and for working class communities, it is something they can truly call their own. Like the *maraca* seeds, composing, performing, and dancing to *Salsa* differentiates the Latino from the rest of North American society.

Throughout Caribbean history, popular music has served as a vehicle of empowerment for the Latino community. The *merengue*, for example, was banned in Puerto Rico at the end of the nineteenth century because of its apparent "lascivious" nature (see Hernández Cruz's short prose piece entitled **"Merengue in History,"** *By Lingual Wholes*). Despite consistent efforts by the Church and the government to ban so-called pagan, lascivious and primitive forms of music—such as *la guaracha* and *la rumba*—and to keep them from entering mainstream society, Afro-Caribbean dances and rhythms have historically survived as collective acts of ethnic reaffirmation, as ethnicity. In fact, it has already been suggested that playing the drums in Cuba under the structures of slavery was an act of cultural resistance. "Do it to them Mongo/do it to them Mongo," says Miguel Piñero in "Reflections on Dirty Windowpanes," alluding to the power of drums associated with *Santería* and to the possibility of taking vengeance on the Other. The drums are called upon to wake up the community and to revitalize the Latino individual in the midst of New York's dirt, poverty and abandonment. When Piñero's poetic speaker addresses Mongo Santamaría and Machito, asking them to "bring it back to me Mongo/bring it back to me Machito," the "it" clearly refers to the Latin roots in him, to his sense of being unique and different, of

---

Cruz on his recent poetry:

Red Beans is a significantly different book. Between its covers I included both poetry and essay, dance and instruction. Much of the prose was written while I was still in California. The poetry was written in Puerto Rico. In one sense it is a history book. More than ever I poeticize the forces of history. The poems set up a telescope at the intersection where civilization encounters the person, whose interior is nowhere on the societal program. It is a hybrid cuadra-cultural communication where the creative surges pursue their stimulus, to engorge them with self-awareness. Selfs meeting selfs.

Sinking into the caves as far as possible with the light of Germanic English, passing the torch over to the Latin Spanish. Writing in Spanish is seeing the scars of the body, its lyrics full of swords and whips. Merely to speak it is an act of violence, it bellows out with much more force than the English can ever gather up. As I vaporize into the meaning, into the patterns, each day I feel more at home. There is a lot to do. Writing is a responsibility to self and to the epoch. There are so many circles, squares, pyramids, ovals, pentagons, lines, and colors making up the mandala—that there is no time to waste. We need to start tracing the etchings on the *quiros* (gourds). Listening to it—dancing. That is life. *Eso es la vida.*

Victor Hernández Cruz, in *Contemporary Authors Autobiography Series*, Vol. 17, Gale Research Inc., 1993.

---

belonging to a particular community with its own musical, linguistic and cultural roots. That is, indeed, the same sense of comfort which Colón recalled, a comfort that comes from an acknowledgement of the power of his own community to create artistic and cultural products.

The tropical *barriada* on 139th Street that Willie Colón remembers was initially defined not only by an appropriation of a particular urban area or space, but mostly by a consistent, persistent ethnicity: drinking Café Bustelo, speaking Spanish and Spanglish, and listening to *descargas* throughout the night. When Hernández Cruz states in **"Free Spirit,"** a poem dedicated to Ray Barretto, that "the bronx is ours" and that "the piano plays *our* memories/*our* dreams/*our* loves," he attests to the continuity and survival of music as an ethnic symbol which holds the key to knowledge, self-knowledge and acknowledgement. Hernández Cruz, as do many other Nuyorican poets, recalls, reclaims, and recognizes the authority of the Latino community (indeed as collective author and audience) in the development of *Salsa* music, an authority that history has tried to snatch away from El Barrio. Moreover, both *Salsa* and Nuyorican poetry in the United States have had an impact well beyond the Latino community, as we witness an emerging "tropicalization" of American

On SNAPS.

"Cruz speaks of himself, about himself, from himself about what he sees, feels, hears. His poetry is not an easy poetry, but even on first reading, something comes through which brings you back a second and third and fourth time."

Julius Lester

"Victor Hernández Cruz is an original American poet. He is young, together and his work is heavy pagan feet crushing the necks of the imperial dead (x's for eyes) metaphors, allusions, symbols and images that characterize the American poetry establishment and—forgive me, religious fanatics—anti-establishment. . . . If you can imagine Mongo Santamaria and early Supremes making it together, then you can hear the picture. You can dance to these poems. . . . For formfreaks there is a careful and astute craftsman at work here with his own system and resources; but the most remarkable thing about these poems are the nowness the newness and ownness and the passion."

Ishmael Reed

"Poesy news from space anxiety police age inner city, spontaneous urban American language as Williams wished, high-school street consciousness transparent, original soul looking out intelligent Bronx windows."

Allen Ginsberg

MAINLAND
poems by VICTOR HERNÁNDEZ CRUZ

RANDOM HOUSE

Dust jacket for the 1973 poetry collection in which Cruz chronicles the American experience from the Puerto Rican point of view.

popular culture and literary discourse, a transformation that originates in the Latino writers and musicians themselves, out of which Victor Hernández Cruz is a central figure. This phenomenon is yet another topic that merits further analysis. (pp. 49–56)

Frances R. Aparicio, "'Salsa,' 'Maracas,' and 'Baile': Latin Popular Music in the Poetry of Victor Hernández Cruz," in *MELUS*, Vol. 16, No. 1, Spring, 1989–90, pp. 43–58.

ELIZABETH ALEXANDER
(essay date 1991)

[In the following essay, Alexander provides an overview of Cruz's life and career.]

Página is a better word than *page*: the English word just sits there, while the Spanish moves like—well, like flipping pages. *Escribimientos* is rather cumbersome in con-

trast to its English cousin, *scribblings*, which looks, on the page, like what it is. *Guayaba* stays the same in either language (depending on how you speak it), but what does it mean to someone who has never seen the fruit's elemental curve, or tasted its pink?

These are the linguistic waters Victor Hernández Cruz navigates in *Red Beans*, a collection of poems and prose musings which marks his 22nd year as a published writer. Random House brought out his first full volume, the Nuyorican classic *Snaps*, in 1969, when Cruz was 19 years old and a self-described "teeny-bopper" from the Lower East Side. His published work since then includes *Mainland* (1973), *Tropicalization* (1976), and *By Lingual Wholes* (1982).

"Migration is the story of my body, it is the condition of this age," Cruz writes in the essay **"The Bolero of the Red Translation,"** in the beginning of *Red Beans*. He is currently living *"campesinamente"* in Aguas Buenas, Puerto Rico, where he was born in 1949, a town "bombarded by . . . insectology of the strangest biologies and at night the sound of distant brewing." Cruz moved to New York at age five and then, as a young adult, to the Bay Area, where he lived until this last move. He remains, in his written words, "a body of migration, an entity of constant change."

Cruz writes in an English that incorporates—in the exact sense of the word—Spanish as well. The early argot of *Snaps* might be called "Spanglish" or "Nuyorican" (with a West Coast dollop). In a recent telephone interview from Aguas Buenas, Cruz called it "a combination of Puerto Rican slang and Black English, and then there's that Jewish lilt that everybody gets in New York." He is an acute observer of the Englishes of fellow writers like Conrad and Kosinski, languages bred in a world where "bilingualism is the norm rather than the exception"

Cruz insists that multilingualism has always been the state of the art for writers. "Look at Ezra Pound, he used 13 languages in the Cantos. He even had Chinese characters in there," Cruz says. "[U.S.] television always had the phrase, 'see you pronto.' If you name the mountains, and the valleys, and the rivers, and the towns in the Southwest, you're practically speaking Spanish, so I think Spanish is an integral part of the North American experience at a much larger level than people are admitting. My poetry is very North American in that sense."

Cruz's poetry over the years has always been clever and filled with word and sound play. He wields narrative at a storyteller's leisurely pace even as the poems snake down the page. The poems move with Cruz's migratory imagination from New York to Hawaii, San Francisco to Amsterdam. Puerto Rico is both real and imaginary, a place where things happen as well as a mythological motherland remembered. Cruz is knowledgeable about the history and culture of the creolized Caribbean and its pre-diaspora roots; he claims African, Indian, and Iberian kin by weaving music and legends throughout the poems. When one of his women wonders, "what is rice if it doesn't fluff," or reaches out the window for a letter, daily rituals snap into focus as culture fighting to perpetuate itself in different accents and on different turf. He draws people, places, customs, and history on the head of a pin, as in **"El Club Tropical"**.

> . . . Pito
> Pito of the shiny green shirt   with
>   all his African Powers
> hanging from his neck...
> What time was it   was it time for
>   another day to be born to
> originate in the middle of quiet valleys
>   to come and eat us like
> moving fog   It was a warm night
>   when you dancing God can't
> be far.

The poems in **Red Beans** are lean, clean, and historical. In **"Snaps of Immigration"** he remembers his mother caressing parsley in the supermarket and new English "Like trumpets doing yakity yak." Many of the poems contemplate the color red, in roosters, red dirt, the Red Sea, red beans, of course, and "[t]he hidden/Red

pepper/ In a stew/Not the thing itself/But the shadow." The tight rhythms in Cruz's poems reflect his own listening, from doo-wop to *guaguancó* via "[m]arimba tango samba/Danza Mambo bolero/ . . . Maraca güiro and drum/ Quicharo maraca y tambor/ Who we are / Printed in rhythm and song."

Though Cruz has published fiction and nonfiction prose before, **Red Beans** is the first of his books to contain so many essays. In our interview, he spoke about the difference he sees between poetry and prose. "If I bring a question up I feel I have to answer it in prose, whereas poetry is more suggestion. . . . The prose is like a map. I want to take them to a specific place and have them see a specific opinion I have." The most powerful essays in **Red Beans** emerge from between the "map" and the sound-conscious dreamworld of a poet who would "never put 'mango' next to 'technology.'"

The section entitled **"Morning Rooster"** contains prose odes to salsa music, Old San Juan, and *Mango Mambo*, Adal Maldonado's book of photographic portraits of Latin musicians. Cruz's passions are eclectic; he offers sober musings on the approaching 500th anniversary of Columbus's voyages to the Americas a few pages after narrating a poetry bout between himself and Andrei Codrescu in Taos, New Mexico. "The gladiator spirit exists in poetry at many levels, so why not focus it with a poetry reading bout?" Cruz asks. The two jousted before an audience of 500, some of whom bet cash on the outcome. A victorious Cruz riffs like his own Bundini Brown: "So gua-gua-gua. I say to my possible opponent next year she or he better bring rhythm, content and flavor, for I am sharpening the nails of my rooster, and I don't care where their content is from, for I am a Caribbean frog —and those jump every-which-a-way."

"The Bolero of the Red Translation" is a memoir of migration in which "[m]en with huge wavy pants and shoes like boats stood in clusters smoking cigarettes pointing towards the sky suggesting other dimensions." Once Cruz was in New York, where Spanish was forbidden in school and English "sounded like bla-bla-bla," culture still replicated itself in "story sessions in that grandiose manner known to all Latin Americans, el cuento campesino, phantasms arrived through coffee pots, pictures shook on walls and dead relatives peeled off."

"Bolero" then becomes a tract on poetry, an addition to a long line of Ars Poeticas. "Poetics is the art of stopping the world," he writes, "asking it the basic question: Where are you coming from? Putting a mirror in front of its big face, deciphering its emotional ingredients, speculating on its intent."

The "big face" of the world has long fascinated Cruz, even before he was a Lower East Side teenager mining Gotham for inspiration and adventure. "I come from the old New York, the old neighborhood New

York," he told me. "I was able to get a classic New York upbringing—stickball, kick the can, the street life. You could walk in the streets, you could go get yourself a knish and bring it back to your house and put the knish next to your rice and beans. You could go to Avenue A and get yourself a pizza, and you knew the numbers people, and everything had its patterns." At 16 he published his first chapbook, *Papo Got His Gun*, on a mimeograph machine used by the 11th Street Block Asociation to print rent strike leaflets, then sold it to bookstores around town for 75 cents a copy.

Cruz kept writing and fell in with a group of African American writers that included Ishmael Reed, David Henderson, and Clarence Major. "Every time they'd start to publish, they'd say, what to do with Cruz? And I was of course young, and my sense of coming from a *criollo* culture, my sense of racial separation, would be different from an Anglo kid, so I said yeah, here's the poem." He published in the late lamented *Negro Digest* and *Umbra* as well as in magazines like *Progressive Labor* and *Evergreen Review*. "I'm a *criollo* person," he says, "in blood and culture."

Cruz is now at work on a new novel, *Time Zones*, which emerges from his sense of change in different sites of migration. "The whole sense of change here [in Puerto Rico] is different. Some people are still into the boleros of the '30s and '40s. Some people—they call them *roqueros*—they like metal rock. Some people like the salsa of the '60s, some people are at the turn of the century. There's less uniformity. Here, there's the possibility that some people might be in the last century with those ideas and fears, a sense of life."

Puerto Rico has been the right place for him to explore those zones. The poetry he's writing is in Spanish—though, perhaps, a Spanish as hybrid as North American English. "I wanted to write in Spanish," he said, "which is full of Arabian words, it's full of African words, it's full of those rhythms and patterns, and when I write in Spanish, no matter what the poem is about it's full of history, because one word would remind me of the history of that word, not just the sound of the word, and the poem then becomes a crowd of stuff, of history and psychology and energies."

What would be treacle in the hands of lesser souls in quirky and utterly lovely in *Red Beans* and in Victor Cruz. His nostalgia is a way of remembering as well as an avenue of response to the present. "I remember," he says once again, and I'm in another time zone, too, "seeing *jíbaros* in the plaza with those hats. You know, there was a sense of hat on the island. You see the old pictures from the '40s here of meetings and groups, and all the men had these straw hats and those *pra-pras*—you remember those flat-top hats? With the ribbon around them? This place was rampant with beautiful straw hats. You don't see that as much now, but I remember when I was a kid here, everybody had that sense of hat, a sombrero."

Now I'm telling him about my grandfather's "sense of hat," how I remember him sitting on a bench, studying his *Amsterdam News*, wearing his grey felt brim with the little red feather, down the street from the Harlem Y in Cruz's "old neighborhood New York," where writing painted on the wall by the playground still reads, "Harlem Plays the Best Ball in the World." Puerto Rican *pra-pras*, New York red beans and knishes—all survive in the urban Atlantis of Cruz's poetry, awaiting rediscovery.

Elizabeth Alexander, "Living in Americas," in *VLS*, No.100, November, 1991, p. 36.

JOSE AMAYA
(essay date 1991)

[Below, Amaya traces the influence of Cruz's Puerto Rican heritage on his collection of poems entitled *Red Beans*.]

Victor Hernández Cruz is singing to us again and sounding better than ever. Much like Jose Vasconcelos, a Mexican scholar who felt that a *Raza Cosmica*, comic race, would generate new advances in civilization, Cruz experiments with the vast linguistic and cultural possibilities of "indo-afro-hispano" poetry and comes up with a strong vision of American unity. *Red Beans* constitutes his poetic investigation into a historical land of memory, which for Cruz is both affirmation and condemnation of Spanish influence in the culture of the Americas.

> For the children the toys were the insects
> and sing songs from the time of Spain
> Closer than Spain was the pain
> The Spaniards came with so much
> embroidery
> Our virgins were naked
> This is a climate for flesh

('New/Aguas Buenas/Jersey')

Like the earlier New Jersey poet, William Carlos Williams, Cruz reaches back into his Puerto Rican background (Williams' mother was born in Mayaguez) for those deep voices whose vibrant sound still resonates within the poetic space that Cruz inhabits. Cruz's work is redefining the poet's need for artistic freedom and takes up the poetic challenge to "take the thing and make it new."

> I love the quality of the spoken thought
> As it happens immediately
> uttered into the air

('An essay on William Carlos Williams')

The poetic work which has gone into **Red Beans** represents an emergent American sensibility that anticipates changes in English which will "give it spice, Hispanic mobility." These qualities seemed to have entered his poems: a reminder that not only North Americans sing songs of America:

This is the greatest flavor
The earth has to offer
Marimba tango samba
Linda America just rise and take off your
clothes. . .

('**Areyto**')

But Cruz is at his best in **Red Beans** when he portrays, as in the poem **"Was is,"** the distinct sounds and voices of Caribbean life which crash into his poetic consciousness like a wild ocean surf. Clearly, those scenarios of sounds and color that injected life into his previous work remain components of Cruz's poetry; but the poetic message has matured, and is now ready for the twenty-first century.

The humor in Cruz's poetry has matured as well. Since Cruz acknowledges the fact that "Red-beings" can't get along on "red beans" alone, we get him playing with the ironic and absurd comedy of the Americas:

A campesino told me;
With hurricanes it's not the wind
or the noise or the water. . .
It's the mangoes, avocados
Green plantains and bananas
flying into town like projectiles.

How would your family
feel if they had to tell
The generations that you
got killed by a flying Banana.

('**Problems With Hurricanes**')

Cruz's book also includes several prose works on Columbus's enterprises in the New World such as, **"Thoughts As We Approach the 500th Anniversary of the Discovery of the Americas,"** which provides a satirical historical window on earlier voyages of Columbus:

It is well documented
that Spanish authorities emptied many
prisons and gave the prisoners an offer
they couldn't refuse.
Either you go off with this Genovese
racketeer to wherever
or you stay in that cell.

Since Cruz's poems will emerge on the eve of the 500th anniversary of Columbus's journey to the New World, he could be accused of jumping on the Quincentenary bandwagon. Yet too much in his work stands out as distinctive to carry out this charge. Cruz's poems present a bicultural presence that can't be easily faked. Like all Hispanos in the New World, Cruz cannot forget the atrocities the Spanish committed against the Indians and, as if to counteract history, his essay celebrate the uniqueness of American culture.

Some of the essays, like **"Mountains in the North,"** assert that Carribean criollo language is "full of passion and opinion," because Carribean inhabitants are "sons and daughters of campesinos, fishermen, farmers. . . cutters of cane. . . " But Cruz seems to often forget the achievements of women in the Carribean. His construction of the "hottest tropicality" deteriorates at times into a sexist vision of Hispanic culture and literature.

Yet Cruz has enough good work in this collection to overlook the flaws in the essays and does showcase the range of his carefully tuned poetic voice here. And if you keep the blend of Spanish and English in Cruz' work waiting, you might find yourself left behind.

Jose Amaya, "Marímba tango samba: Poetry of the Américas," in *San Francisco Review of Books*, Vol. 16, No. 3, 1991, p. 16.

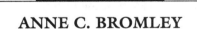

ANNE C. BROMLEY

(essay date 1992)

[Here, Bromley praises the diversity of influences and traditions manifest in *Red Beans*.]

In **Red Beans**, a collection of poetry and prose, Hernández Cruz embraces the mixed traditions within Puerto Rico: the "red beans" are a pun on "red beings," the characters from Hernández Cruz's native Puerto Rico: indigenous (Taino and through them the whole of the pre-Columbian American World), Spanish (which includes Arabs, Gypsies, and Jews), and African (the Yorubas). "Migration is the story of my body," he says, exploring the difficult marriage between "Northern Americana" and the "Hispano-Criollo-Caribbean" cultures when they clash on the streets of New York City. He remembers the town of Aguas Buenas in Puerto Rico, his place of birth, and the great Puerto Rican migration toward New York that moved his family from one island to another: "A world of awesome gray velocity, an air of metallic coldness, a cement much more cemented than any which we had previously observed. Another language which sounded like bla-bla-bla." Yet through these "migratory entaglements" Hernández Cruz has found a poetry that keeps alive lyrics and rhythms that used to emanate from coastal Caribbean beaches and towns, traditions that extended into the mists of Spain and Africa.

Hernández Cruz brings poetry back in many ways to its earlier public functions. His are poems that remember, poems that declaim, poems that celebrate language as a pathway into and out of dreams. The poems of *Red Beans* are not private poems in the sense that a personal "I" figures as the controlling voice. It is instead the voice of a troubadour that emerges out of a poem such as **"Corsica,"** in which Hernández Cruz links Puerto Rico and Spain by way of plate tectonics:

Underneath with the geologic plates
Puerto Rico and Corsica
Are holding hands
Both hands with gold rings
Sweating each other's palm
The same moon is seen
From both islands
The light of the sun
Upon the mother
The seaman's stories of migration
Like whispering olives within
Red beans.

Although he writes in English, Hernández Cruz seasons this language with Spanish. In a provocative essay on Hispanic writing in the United States, he says, "National languages melt, spill into each other." Spanish revitalizes English as a poetry that can "dance on the edges." Broadcasting the kaleidoscopic qualities of Puerto Rican culture, he celebrates the variety with new hybrids:

he writes about Salsa, guava, and all that embodies the organic, succulent, explosive energy that has infused the urban centers of the United States with the essences of rural villages of the Caribbean. *Red Beans* celebrates a migratory poetics that is self-reflective, lyrical, lush, and often dead-pan humorous as Spanish and English dance a lambada through its pages.

Through his lyrical narratives (essays, stories, and manifestos on poetics), Hernández Cruz offers himself as an "informant" to readers who need to be reminded of the rich diversity of influences that comes to American poetry from sources other than the Anglo-European tradition. In truth, as consumers of American poetry, we are, in many ways, still colonized by that tradition. Hernández Cruz would ask us to be receptive to other traditions, other ways of regarding language, other ways of regarding art and its relationship to community and spirituality:

I wait with a gourd full
of gasoline
for a chip to fall from
The festival fireworks
to favor me
And set me on fire.

(pp. 26–7)

Anne C. Bromley, "The Poetics of Migration," in *The American Book Review*, Vol. 13, No. 6. February–March, 1992, pp. 26–7.

SOURCES FOR FURTHER STUDY

Leibowitz, Herbert. "The Muse and the News." *The Hudson Review* XXII, No. 2 (Summer 1969): 502–03.
Mixed review of Cruz's *Snaps*, asserting that "the half-articulate intensity of his language" is revealing, yet a "relatively limited vehicle."

Nyren, Dorothy. Review of *Mainland*, by Victor Hernández Cruz. *Library Journal* 98 (15 February 1973): 549.
Maintains that Cruz's "juxtaposition and intermingling of Latin and Anglo ways of seeing things gives an inner tension to the verse that makes it continually surprising and interesting."

Review of *Red Beans*, by Victor Hernández Cruz. *Publisher's Weekly* 238, No. 40 (6 September 1991): 99.
Addresses Cruz's thematic scope and syntax in his collection *Red Beans*.

Ratner, Rochelle. Review of *Tropicalization*, by Victor Hernández Cruz. *Library Journal* 102 (1 January 1977): 113.
Contends that Cruz "is a poet who grows with every book."

Torrens, James S. "U.S. Latino Writers: The Searchers." *America* 167, No. 2 (18–25 July 1992): 39–42.
Discusses several Latino writers, asserting that Cruz and his contemporaries "say what they see—a numbing poverty, struggles for dignity, tears and clamors, the importance of thinking 'us' instead of 'me'."

Additional coverage on Cruz's life and career is contained in the following sources published by Gale Research: *Black Writers*; *Contemporary Authors*, Vols. 65–68; *Contemporary Authors Autobiography Series*, Vol. 17; *Contemporary Authors New Revision Series*, Vols. 14, 32; *Dictionary of Literary Biography*, Vol. 41; and *Hispanic Writers*.

Rubén Darío

1867–1916

(Pseudonym of Félix Rubén García Sarmiento) Nicaraguan poet, short story writer, journalist, critic, essayist, autobiographer, and novelist.

INTRODUCTION

*O*ne of the great names of Hispanic poetry, Darío is recognized as the embodiment of Modernism in Spanish letters. His entire oeuvre, as critics have affirmed, is an expression of the principles of technical innovation, iconoclastic imagination, and artistic audacity. In fact, Darío, who coined the Spanish term "modernismo," is credited with bringing the spirit of Modernism to Spain.

Darío started his literary career early in life; he was already a writer by the time he was fourteen, when he started signing his works with his pseudonym. In 1886 he travelled to Chile, the first of his journeys in a life entirely dedicated to travel and literary pursuits. *Azul*, Darío's first critically acclaimed work, was published two years later. Consisting of stories, prose sketches, and verse, and graced by a style of extraordinary verbal brilliance and sensuality, *Azul* marked, as Octavio Paz has written, "the official birth of Modernism." Although influenced by the "art for art's sake" aesthetic of French Parnassian poets, Darío's book was hailed as the fundamental work of Spanish Modernism. Darío visited Spain in 1892 on a diplomatic mission; the following year he was named Colombian Consul to Argentina. Having travelled to Buenos Aires via New York and Paris, where he often met with the French literary elite, he arrived in the Argentine capital with an aura of wordliness and literary prestige. Buenos Aires, a cosmpolitan city with an effervescent literary life, provided many opportunities to the young writer. When the Colombian consulate was closed in 1894, Darío turned to journalism, also writing fantastic stories which reflected his interest in spiritualism, theosophy, parapsychology, and other occult disciplines. As critics have noted, the representative work of this period is *Prosas profanas y otros poemas* (1896; *Prosas Profanas and Other Poems*), in which the poet boldly experimented with prosody in an effort to attain the formal purity of music. Critics have regarded this collection as a pivotal work. For instance, Paz has singled out the last poem of the collection as "both a resume of [Darío's] aesthetics and a prophecy about the future course of poetry." According to Paz, the poem's "first line is a definition of his verse: 'I seek a form that my style cannot discover.' He seeks a beauty that is beyond beauty, that words evoke but can never state. All of Romanticism—the desire to grasp the infinite—and all of Symbolism—an ideal, indefinable beauty that can only be suggested—are contained in that line."

In 1899, in the aftermath of the Spanish-American War, Darío arrived in Madrid as a correspondent of the Buenos Aires newspaper *La Nacion*. From Spain he also traveled to France and Italy. Named Nicaraguan Consul to France, the poet resided in the French capital from 1903 to 1907. A significant work of his Parisian period, *Cantos de vida y esperanza* (1905) turns to personal, social, and political issues. The outstanding achievement of the last decade of Darío's life, during which the poet tirelessly journeyed from the New World to Europe and back, is the *Poema del otoño,* published in *Poema del otoño y otros poemas* (1910). In this work, Darío meditates on life and death, forging a passionate, life-oriented pantheism as a resolution of his religious and metaphysical conflicts, and also embracing death as the pinnacle of life.

In 1914, ailing and troubled by financial difficulties, Darío returned to his homeland. But he resumed his travels the following year, embarking on a lecture tour throughout the Americas. Upon reaching New York, however, Darío was forced by illness to give up his plans; soon thereafter he returned to Nicaragua, where he died.

Critics, with the exception of those traditionalists who viewed Modernism as an abomination, have generally greeted Darío's works with enthusiastic praise, and fellow poets and readers have been seduced by the opulent imagery and mellifluous sonority of his poetry. Commentators have also agreed that Darío, by dint of his verbal imagination, breathed new life into the Spanish language, opening unseen horizons for younger Hispanic poets. However, the critical response to Darío has not been uniform. While earlier criticism emphasized Darío's extraordinary poetic talent and technical virtuosity, later commentators have suggested that the poet's formal splendor sometimes lacks substance. Thus C.M. Bowra wrote that much of what impressed the reader of Darío's poetry as strikingly original was derivative, revealing the poet's profound knowledge and appreciation of modern French poetry. Yet, as scholars strove to arrive at a fuller understanding of Darío's oeuvre, they have found that despite the eclectic, even superficial, nature of many of his works, his writing reveals a poetic vision resulting from a pronounced spiritual impulse. As Paz has written, Darío's multifaceted work sprang from the poet's acute awareness of the world, and also from his profound desire—evidenced by his interest in occult traditions and esoteric teachings—to probe the deepest secrets of the universe and to understand humankind's cosmic destiny.

CRITICAL COMMENTARY

C.M. BOWRA

(lecture date 1951)

[Bowra was an eminent English critic, literary scholar, and translator whose studies of classical and modern literature are known for their erudition, lucidity, and straightforward style. His books include *The Heritage of Symbolism* (1943) and *The Creative Experiment* (1949). In the following essay, originally delivered as a lecture in 1951, Bowra provides a comprehensive view of Darío's poetry. Observing that Darío's fame may have exceeded his achievement, Bowra posits that the poet's aesthetic and literary goals hampered his natural talent, which "was better suited to a less elaborate, less sophisticated, and less ambitious art."]

Rubén Darío (1867–1916) presents a signal case of a man who had a remarkable influence on poetry but whose own achievement may seem in retrospect not fully to deserve its first renown. That he, more than anyone else, was re-

Principal Works

Emelina [with Edouardo Porier] (novel) 1887

Azul . . . (short stories and poetry) 1888

Los raros (essays) 1893

Prosas profanas, y otros poemas (poetry) 1896
    [*Prosas Profanas and Other Poems,* 1922]

Peregrinaciones (travel essays) 1901

Cantos de vida y esperanza (poetry) 1905

Opiniones (criticism) 1906

El canto errante (poetry) 1907

Poema del otoño y otros poemas (poetry) 1910

Autobiographia (autobiography) 1912

Canto a la Argentina, y otros poemas (poetry) 1914

Eleven Poems of Rubén Darío (poetry) 1916

Selected Poems (poetry) 1965

Poesia (poetry) 1980

sponsible for the dazzling revival of Spanish poetry with the generation of 1898 is beyond question. At the time when Spain lost to the United States the last remnants of her once world-wide empire this stranger from Nicaragua brought a ringing message of confidence and a range of verbal melodies such as Spain had never heard before. His metrical innovations, his rippling, lucent language, his unquestioning devotion to his art, did something to comfort Spain for her territorial losses by providing her with a new poetry. Through him men of pre-eminent gifts like Antonio Machado and Juan Ramón Jiménez found their true selves and inaugurated an era of creative activity which lasted till the Civil War. Yet, great though Darío's influence undoubtedly was, its results were paradoxical. The poets whom he inspired reacted against his methods and were in no sense his disciples. There is no trace of his mellifluous ease in the Castilian austerity of Machado or the delicate impressionism of Jiménez. Nor has his reputation for originality weathered the years. It is true that he did something that had never been done before in Spanish and that he handled the language with a dexterity which first shocked, and then enthralled, a generation which had come to believe that poetry was dying from inanition, but we can now see that much of his work was not ultimately original but a brilliant transposition into Spanish of French images and cadences. He absorbed with uncommon skill the most prominent qualities of French poetry from Hugo and Gautier to Mallarmé and Verlaine and presented them in an alluring Spanish dress, but the substance remained French. Even in this Gallicising task Darío was not influenced by those who were the greatest forces in the development of modern poetry. Rimbaud, Corbière, and Laforgue meant little or nothing to him,

and though he was an ardent apostle of the Symbolists, we may doubt if he understood their essential aims. His achievement was largely derivative, and that no doubt is why he has lost some of his first glory.

It is not necessarily true that, because Darío's poetry is to some extent second-hand, it is therefore second-rate. European poetry presents many examples of men who have learned foreign manners and adapted them so skillfully and sincerely to their own languages that their work has a lasting appeal. The case against Darío is not so much that he derived his art from France as that he was too much concerned with the more superficial and more ephemeral qualities of his chosen masters. His metaphysical swans and butterflies, his Columbines and Pierrots, his figures from Greek myth, his *femmes fatales* like Herodias and Cleopatra, his scenes from Chinese vases and Japanese prints, his transposition of Catholic ritual to secular, erotic purposes, all betray their origins too candidly and suggest that Darío thought them to be essential elements of pure poetry, when in fact they were the fleeting fashions of an age whose other and richer resources escaped his attention. It is true that his debt to Verlaine was largely determined by a similarity of temperament, that Darío really had something of 'le pauvre Lelian' in his vagabond habits, his oscillations between gaiety and grief or between sin and repentance, and his childlike outlook on the world, but this similarity must not be pressed too far or made to justify too much. For Darío differed from Verlaine in several important respects. He was not a Parisian, not a European; he had nothing of Verlaine's cunning or love of mischief; his Catholicism was far less conscious and far less sophisticated; his literary training owed little to friends concerned with the same artistic problems as himself. If he was drawn to Verlaine by some similarity of personality and experience, he admired him chiefly because of his art. Much of Darío's poetry has lost its first appeal because, despite his unfailing technique, his excellent ear and abounding vitality, too much of it is concerned with matters which no longer touch us seriously but have passed into the limbo of lost curiosities.

Yet, when all this is said, something in Darío's work is still alive and compelling and undeniably serious; something still has more than a personal or historical interest and holds its own as original poetry. Amid all the flaunting stylishness, which has now rather faded, we come upon pieces which ring entirely true and have the authentic touch of a unique individual. But this individual has been misrepresented by false parallels and inapplicable standards. It is easy to think of Darío as yet another gifted wastrel of the Nineties, a Bohemian genius, who wrecked his health with drink and trailed a sordid entourage of mistresses from one place to another, whose air of innocent candour was no more than the impertinence of an overgrown urchin, and whose lack of any central philosophy was the defiant gesture of a sceptical and defeated age. It is no less easy to treat him as the typical poet of Latin

America, who turned to the mother country and to Paris, the capital of the world, because he believed that in them he could find roots and feel at home, and whose success in Europe was a tribute paid to a prodigal son who brought back to Spain some return for what she had spent in the extravagance of imperial expansion. Neither of these views is right. Darío was a Bohemian only because he came from a simpler, less organised, less departmental, and less self-conscious world. His self-indulgence was that of a child of nature confronted with unexpected opportunities for pleasure, and he found no difficulty in combining it with hard work and the friendship of the best Spaniards of his time. His lack of philosophy is the natural condition of a man who has given his first love to art in a country where art hardly exists, and who for that reason treasures it beyond everything else and feels no call to look outside it. Nor is he the national voice of Latin America. There were indeed times when he spoke nobly for it, but they were almost incidental. Spain and France meant quite as much to him as his own country, and the world of his dreaming fancies meant more than any of them. To see him in his right perspective we must remember that he was a stranger from an undeveloped land, that he had Indian blood in his veins and lacked the complexity and the sophistication which would belong to a European of his gifts and tastes. He differs from European poets of his time because he speaks for human nature at a very simple level and takes things as they come without shaping his life to a plan. Even his assumption of Parisian airs betrays his tropical love of bright colours and his desire to do the smart thing with rather too much emphasis and display.

Because Darío formed his art far away from Europe and saw in European models all that poetry ought to be, it was almost impossible for him to surrender gains which had been made at so much cost to himself and with so proud a sense of achievement. That no doubt is why he persisted almost to his death in writing verses which repeat the mannerisms of *Prosas profanas* (1896). This kind of poetry was not only an ingrained element in his life but a consolation for his personal troubles. If for long periods Darío retired into a secluded universe of dreams, he was well aware of it and not in the least ashamed. In his view this was all too natural and too necessary in a world which wounded and depressed him. In defending his art against the critic José Enrique Rodó, Darío is perfectly frank about his position:

> El dueño fui de mi jardín de sueño,
> lleno de rosas y de cisnes vagos;
> el dueño de las tórtolas, el dueño
> de góndolas y liras en los lagos. . . .

> (I was the master of my garden of dreams,
> full of roses and wandering swans,
> master of the turtledoves, master
> of gondolas and lyres on the lagoons.)

Though this withdrawal into imagination won for Darío his first renown, it was not responsible for his best work.

When he writes on these subjects, he usually lacks the full strength and conviction of which he is capable, and his comparative failure is yet another proof that it is the apparently most attractive and brilliant qualities of poetry which perish first, while its more solid and less obvious worth survives.

That Darío should wish for an escape into imaginary worlds was natural enough. He was troubled not only by his own temperament but by the society into which he had been born. Those who saw in him a laureate of Latin America must have been painfully shocked when they read his poem **"A Colón,"** which he wrote in 1892 for the fifth centenary of the discovery of America by Columbus. For an occasion which might all too easily have been drenched in sentimental rhetoric Darío paints a melancholy, even tragic picture of the New World which the great captain called into being. He dwells on its perpetual discords and wars, its perfidious ambitions and betrayed liberties, its destruction of ancient habits and its failure to put anything in their place. He cries out that it would have been better if Columbus had never sailed:

> ¡Pluguiera a Dios las aguas antes intactas
> no reflejaran nunca las blancas velas;
> ni vieran las estrellas estupefactas
> arribar a la orilla tus carabelas!. . .

> (Would that the waters hitherto untouched
> had never reflected the white sails;
> would that the stupefied stars had not seen
> your caravels come to shore.)

Then indeed the aboriginal Americans might have been left to their primitive occupation of hunting pumas and bisons in the forests and on the mountains. In such a world even the introduction of Christianity means nothing; for Christ is neglected, while Barabbas enslaves the people. And as for the gifts of civilisation, what can be said for it when it has given over to panthers the ancient cities of Chibcha, Cuzco, and Palenque? Darío sums up this sorry history:

> Duelos, espantos, guerras, fiebre constante
> en nuestra senda ha puesto la suerte triste:
> ¡Cristóforo Colombo, pobre Almirante,
> ruega a Dios por el mundo que descubriste!. . .

> (Afflictions, terrors, wars, and constant fever
> miserable chance has set upon our way;
> Christopher Columbus, poor Admiral,
> pray to God for the world that you discovered.)

With time Darío was indeed to modify his views, and in his **"A Roosevelt"** to set against the crude ambitions of the United States his own Latin America with its Christianity, its tenderness, its ancient ceremonies. But his lines to Columbus spring from something deep in his being, his appalled realisation of the world to which by birth he belonged; and that is why this poem is more impressive than his challenge to Roosevelt, which somehow asserts too much and fails to carry us with it.

With this background behind him, and with all the music of French poetry in his head, Darío inevitably retired into fancies of his own making and was comforted by the thought that all over the world other poets were doing the same thing. He accepted from the start the view that poetry is an escape from the squalors of existence and must offer some harmonious alternative to them. When a poet does this, there is always a danger that his work will fail because it is insufficiently related to ordinary existence and lacks the substance which comes from a close contact with common life. When this poetry of escape succeeds, as it does in Coleridge's "Kubla Khan" or in Keats' "La Belle Dame sans merci," it is because the dream becomes a vehicle for something else which belongs to the waking consciousness, and expresses through forceful imagery what the considering mind expresses less happily through analytical abstractions. Poetry of this kind needs an intimate relation to events of every day and must appeal as a heightened, purified form of them. However ever mysterious and impalpable it may be, we must assume that it speaks of something intelligible and has a message of some importance. In the last resort the poetry of escape, of a search for an ideal order or a 'beyond', must reflect some deep need in ourselves and provide for it a satisfaction which is not mere dream or mere fancy but is more solid and more absorbing than what we find in the daily round. In this respect Darío often fails. Though his desire for escape was often prompted by powerful motives, he did not often write about it in its full strength, but disguised it in the imaginary scenes in which his fancy delighted but which were liable to omit much of the experience which preceded their creation. Indeed these scenes are some times insufficiently imagined. Neither by temperament nor by conviction was Darío really fitted to follow Mallarmé in his search for a mystical or ideal 'beyond'. He felt that he was committed to a search, but he did not always know what he sought, and was liable to be led astray by his august masters and to feel that quite ordinary objects of desire were more remarkable than they actually are.

It would not be untrue to say that at its best Darío's 'beyond' was like the pleasure which children find in fairy-tales. He was able to lose himself in vivid fancies and not to ask for any meaning in them beyond the most obvious and most immediate. When he followed this impulse, he was able to put all his resources of rhythm and imagery to good use and to create something which stands on its own in some fascinating Never-Never-Land. So when he wanted to give pleasure to a young girl called Margarita Debayle, he wrote a delicate fairy-tale which surely pleased her and certainly pleased him. In it a young princess picks a star. Her father is furious and accuses her of a mad and godless caprise. Then Christ appears and tells her that she can have it. The king capitulates handsomely, and, when he sees white robes in the sky, sends out four hundred elephants to the sea-shore to pay homage. It is a trifle of gossamer, a toy for a child, but within its frail limits faultless. It succeeds because Darío's princess is just like other children and her picking of a star is what any child might in the right circumstances do:

Las princesas primorosas
se parecen mucho a ti;
cortan lirios, cortan rosas,
cortan astros. Son así. . .

(Beautiful princesses
are much the same as you.
They pick lilies, pick roses,
pick stars. That's what they do.)

Darío succeeds because he is perfectly at home in this world of childhood and confines himself carefully to it. We do not look for any ulterior meaning, and we would not find one if we did.

Darío naturally could not and would not always so restrict himself, and his art would have suffered greatly if he had. He wished to advance beyond fairy-tales to situations in which vivid shapes stand for something else and give contour and significance to it. In this he struck an obstacle common enough in such poetry. It is difficult to make the poetical meaning emerge in its full strength without either being lost in the individual images or coming out too starkly in purely intellectual language which defies and defeats the symbols. Such a task requires an excellent judgment and a firm notion of what the central theme really is. Darío, perhaps with Mallarmé's "L'Apres-Midi d'un Faune" in his mind, attempted a symbolical poem of some length in his **"Coloquio de los Centauros"** in which he uses the Greek Centaurs to discuss fundamental issues of life and death. The sensuous richness of the decoration has something in common with Mallarmé's sultry afternoon, but the Centaurs have no very marked individualities, and their interchange of speeches is no more than a device to let Darío think aloud. That he claims a high symbolical intention is clear when he makes Chiron say:

toda forma es un gesto, una cifra, un enigma;
en cada átomo existe un incógnito estigma;
cada hoja de cada árbol canta un propio cantar
y hay un alma en cada una de las gotas del mar. . .

(Every form is a gesture, a cipher, a riddle;
in every atom exists an unknown sign;
every leaf of every tree sings its own song
and there is a soul in every single drop of the sea.)

Here Darío surely had in mind Baudelaire's famous sonnet "Correspondances," where natural things are said to be symbols of other, more mysterious realities. But Darío, with his simpler and plainer outlook, does not go so far as this and contents himself with saying that every natural thing has its own individuality. It is a perfectly tenable view, but it is not necessarily tied to the use of symbols or to the cult of the ideal. At the start Darío uses this elaborate method to suggest that he is probing a deep mystery, but what he says makes us think that he may not after all be pursuing any very remote or intangible end.

As the poem proceeds, it becomes clear that this is so. So far from using his Centaurs for remarkable states of mind or to display some remote, almost inexpressible reality, Darío conducts a poetical discourse on the ends of life, and when, after discussing song, love, and strength, he decides that the most important thing is death, we are a little disappointed and feel that the presentation is too grandiose for so clear and emphatic a conclusion. Darío has made the mistake of allowing his conclusion to emerge too easily from the enveloping symbols, and we feel that the decoration is largely there for its own sake and has no functional purpose. The truth is that the technique which Darío uses here was intended by its inventors to deal with mysteries beyond the reach of exact description and with a mystical vision which can be conveyed only by hints and allusions. Dario had no such vision. Though he talked about the Beautiful and the Ideal, his concept of them had little of the range and magnificence which Mallarmé found in 'le Néant'. His natural simplicity, which rejoiced in the pictorial attraction of such symbols as the swan or Pegasus, shrank from giving them their full implications. If Darío was a Symbolist, his Symbolism was not of the most advanced or most authentic kind, since he used his symbols for matters which he could easily convey through plain statement and to which he could even give names, whereas the essence of French Symbolism is that it conveys realities which have no names and are beyond the reach of direct description.

Darío was more successful when he set firm limits to his subject and did not try to make too much of it. In **"Sonatina"** he tells a story very close to fairy-tale, of a young princess who lies sunk in day-dreams of a perfect love. Darío tells the story so gaily and so brilliantly that we hardly look for an ulterior or secondary meaning. He builds up his situation with affectionate care and fully indulges his taste for bright, luscious things. While the princess dreams in her golden chair, the peacocks parade in the garden, the buffoon pirouettes in his scarlet dress, and the swans float on the azure lake. Her dreams are of impossible splendours and unrealisable hopes:

> ¡Ay! la pobre princesa de la boca de rosa
> quiere ser golondrina, quiere ser mariposa,
> tener alas ligeras, bajo el cielo volar;
> ir al sol por la escala luminosa de un rayo,
> saludar a los lírios con los versos de mayo,
> o perderse en el viento sobre el truento del mar. . . .

> (Ah, the poor princess with her rosy mouth,
> wishes to be a swallow, to be a butterfly;
> to have light wings, to fly under the sky;
> to go to the sun by the gleaming stair of a sunbeam,
> to salute the lilies with the verses of May,
> or to lose herself in the wind above the sea's thunder.)

The poem passes beyond fairy-tale because it has more conviction and more passion than such a tale needs. Darío

brings off a success in a very difficult medium because his details, however brilliant in themselves, contribute to a single, complex effect. The inner world of the princess is as rich and radiant as the outer world which she ignores, and between the two she is revealed as a creature very rare and precious and far removed from ordinary existence.

"Sonatina," however, is more than this. The princess's day-dreams prepare the way to a resounding climax, in which Darío passes beyond the mere story to something else:

> ¡Calla, calla, princesa—dice el hada madrina:—
> en caballo con alas hacia acá se encamina,
> en el cinto la espada y en la mano el azor,
> el feliz caballero que te adora sin verte,
> y que llega de lejos, vencedor de la Muerte,
> a encenderte los labios con su beso de amor!. . .

> (Silence, silence, princess—says the fairy godmother—
> on a winged horse travels hither,
> sword on his belt and hawk in his hand,
> the happy knight who adores you without seeing you,
> and who comes from afar, conqueror of death,
> to set your lips aflame with his kiss of love.)

Skilfully and carefully, but with true dramatic effect, Darío raises the end to a symbolical significance. The knight, who has defeated death, is the symbol of ideal love, and his arrival gives a new dimension. What was only an imaginative story becomes a myth in which the old notion of a love stronger than death takes a new form. Though even here Darío is far from finding an ideal comparable in scope and mystery to Mallarmé's 'le Néant', he finds a substitute in love, and he is wise to do so, for this is a matter which he understands and is able to present with a full wealth of poetry. He has turned his own dreams to good account by attaching them to other and older dreams and relating them to a notion which, however fantastic, still appeals to something deep in the human heart.

In poems like this Darío built his secret defences against the blows of circumstance. He needed such protection and felt happy with it, but he was aware that it was not unassailable, that he could not completely escape from common life or his own darker moods. Much though he cultivated his day-dreams, he felt that they were not everything and that as an honest artist he must pay proper attention to the actual world and face the consequences. In his poem to Rodó he gives something like a spiritual autobiography, in which he tells how he has moved from his first deliberate absorption in fancies to a condition closer to common day. He explains his early withdrawal as a revolt against 'the world, the flesh, and Hell', and though he does not in the least regret it, he knows that no man can maintain such a seclusion for ever and that he must sooner or later abandon it for something else, for truth and simplicity; that he must allow his soul to go naked into the mysteries of the eternal harmony and nourish its inner flame on 'life, light, and truth'. He recognises that in the last resort truth may be beyond reach and perfection unattainable, but he sees the way towards them:

> Por eso ser sincero es ser potente;
> de desnuda que está, brilla la estrella;
> el agua dice el alma de la fuente
> en la voz de cristal que fluye d'ella. . . .

> (For that reason to be sincere is to be powerful,
> it is because it is naked, that the star shines;
> the water tells the soul of the fountain
> in the voice of crystal which flows from it.)

When Darío speaks of sincerity, he reminds us of the great change which came over such poets as W.B. Yeats and Alexander Blok when they gave up their first, entrancing dreams to face naked facts. Darío's intention resembles theirs, but he differs from them because his decision demands a much less violent break with his earlier outlook. For him dreams are still a part of truth so long as the poet speaks truthfully of them. In his career there is no such abrupt division as there is in that of Yeats or Blok. None the less he knew that dreams were not enough and must not be indulged in entirely for their own sake. They must be tempered by truth, and this in his own way he tried to do.

If Darío reached these decisions through natural honesty, his personal experience sometimes force him into a poetry very different from that which he most delighted to write. When he was not on the wings of dreams, he was liable to be assailed by dark melancholy, which was all the darker because he tried to assuage it with drink. At such times he felt himself unarmed against the attacks of circumstance and attributed his very vulnerability to his poetical calling. He, who was naturally so sensitive to impressions of many kinds and who attached such importance to receiving them and translating them into poetry, found that this task was at times almost more than he could bear. The effort which it demanded, the extreme uncertainty which obsessed him during it, the contrast between his inner life and the brutal facts around him, made him feel that he was the victim of a terrible curse, a man set aside for a peculiarly painful and exhausting task. To adjust his inspiration to his art demanded and took everything from him, as he says in **"Melancolía"**:

> Hermano, tú que tienes la luz, dime la mía.
> Soy come un ciego. Voy sin rumbo y ando a tientas.
> Voy bajo tempestades y tormentas
> ciego de ensueño y loco de armonía.

> Ese es mi mal. Soñar. La poesía
> es la camisa férrea de mil puntas cruentas
> que llevo sobre el alma. Las espinas sangrientas
> dejan caer las gotas de mi melancolía.

> Y así voy, ciego y loco, por este mundo amargo
> a veces me parece que el camino es muy largo,
> y a veces que es muy corto. . . .

> y en este titubeo de aliento y agonía,

> cargo lleno de penas lo que apenas soporto.
> ¿No oyes caer las gotas de mi melancolia?

> (Brother, you who have the light, give me mine.
> I am like a blind man. I go without direction and
>   grope in the dark.
> I go under tempests and torments
> blind with dream and mad with harmony.

> This is my curse. To dream. Poetry
> is the iron shirt of a thousand bloody spikes
> that I wear over my soul. The bloodstained thorns
> make fall the drops of my melancholy.

> And so I go, blind and mad, through this bitter world;
> at times I think that the way is longer,
> and at times that it is shorter . . .
> and in this staggering between breath and agony,
> I bear full of afflictions that which I scarcely support.
> Do you not hear the drops of my melancholy fall?)

In a crisis like this Darío, with his untutored simplicity and his complete lack of irony, is able to speak with a force beyond the range of many more gifted and more sophisticated poets. His whole being is absorbed in his predicament, and he feels it so strongly that nothing comes between him and its complete presentation.

If his creative task placed special burdens on Darío, they aggravated troubles that were already his. Inevitably at times he felt that he had wasted his life and failed to fulfil his promise or his hopes. He was tortured by shame and guilt and found, especially when he was alone at night, that he could not withstand or placate the sharp pangs of conscience. Like Baudelaire, he draws from such humiliating moments a poetry of special intimacy and candour, but he differs from Baudelaire in the character of his response. Baudelaire is dominated by disgust at himself and feels that only God can deliver him by enabling him to master it by courage and intellect:

> Ah! Seigneur! donnez-moi la force et le courage
> De contempler mon coeur et mon corps sans dégoût!

Darío's mood is less sharp and more despairing. He seems to have no hope and to see no way out; so dominated is he by his sense of failure. Here too his simplicity gives a remarkable force to his poetry. On such a matter he speaks straight from the heart and indulges in no illusions:

> Y el pesar de no ser lo que yo hubiera sido,
> la pérdida del reino que estaba para mí,
> el pensar que un instante pude no haber nacido,
> ¡y el sueño que es mi vida desde que yo nací!. . .

> (And the weight of not being that which I could have
>   been,
> the loss of the kingdom that was waiting for me,
> the thought that an instant might not have been born,
> and the dream that is my life since my birth.)

To appreciate Darío's treatment of this theme we may compare it with lines in which Rossetti, who indulged similar appetites and suffered from similar remorse, expressed himself:

> Look in my face; my name is Might-have-been;
> I am also called No-more, Too-late, Farewell.

The grand style exalts the theme and makes it less personal, and in so doing diminishes some of its authentic horror. But Darío, who speaks with perfect frankness because he cannot deceive himself about the melancholy facts, touches us more intimately and more poignantly.

Though Darío was in no sense a philosopher, his depressions sometimes forced him into statements in which he looks at the scheme of things and passes judgment against it. His condemnations, delivered with an apt imagery and consummate restraint, recall those moments when the Greek poets at some sublime and tragic crisis proclaim that it were best not to have been born. But whereas they say this because circumstances prove too hard for man and make all his ambitions futile, Darío speaks from a painful, personal situation in which his tortured consciousness makes him hate to be alive. This is the burden of one of his most impressive poems, **"Lo Fatal"** (**"Doom"**), in which, with measured solemnity and no trace of rhetoric or display, he leads from a quiet start to an agonised conclusion:

> Dichoso el árbol que es apenas sensitivo,
> y más la piedra dura proque esa ya no siente,
> pues no hay dolor más grande que el dolor de ser vivo,
> ni mayor pesadumbre que la vida consciente.
>
> Ser, y no saber nada, y ser sin rumbo cierto,
> y el temor de haber sido y un futuro terror . . .
> y el espanto seguro de estar mañana muerto,
> y sufrir por la vida y por la sombra y por
>
> lo que no conocemos y apenas sospechamos,
> y la carne que tienta con sus frescos racimos,
> y la tumba que aguarda con sus fúnebres ramos,
> ¡y no saber adónde vamos
> ni de dónde venimos. . . !

> (Happy the tree that scarcely feels,
> and happier the hard stone because it does not feel at
>   all,
> since no pain is greater than the pain of being alive,
> nor affliction heavier than conscious life.
>
> To be, and to know nothing, and to be with no sure
>   goal,
> and the fear of having been, and a terror to come. . .
> and the certain horror of being dead to-morrow,
> and to suffer for life, and for the shadow, and for
>
> what we know not and hardly suspect,
> and the flesh that tempts us with its fresh clusters,
> and the tomb that waits with its funeral wreaths,
> and not to know whither we go,
> nor whence we come . . .)

This is not emptiness or guilt but despairing fear, the heart-cry of an extremely sensitive man who looks with horror on his human state and sees no hope in the future to atone for the ghastly present. Unlike Leopardi, who plumbed similar depths, Darío does not regard death as a merciful deliverance but finds its daily menace yet another misery in life. Most men shrink from asking what death really means, and to think of it too precisely is to feel the reason unseated, but Darío, in applying his whole mind to it, catches the very essence of its terror, which is precisely that it cannot be understood or imagined and therefore cannot be faced.

"Sonatina" on the one hand and **"Lo Fatal"** on the other mark the poles between which Darío's genius moved, and show the contrast and the discord between his soaring fantasies and his moments of abasement. They illustrate how difficult it was for him to maintain his early conception of poetry as an ivory tower which protected him from himself. He oscillated between the two extremes, and if he writes more often about his exalted than about his depressed moments, it is the latter which provoke the stronger poetry. This is perhaps because the scale of his catastrophes summoned his deepest powers to work and eliminated much that flourished only on the surface of his consciousness. To bridge the gap between the two states presented problems both personal and artistic; he must face his own situation, and then he could transform it into art. In his own way Darío solved both these problems. Despite long bouts of dissipation, *delirium tremens*, and prolonged bad health, he lived to be nearly fifty without seriously impairing his mental or poetical powers. He was fortunate in his friends, who looked after him with devoted care, and in his own temperament, which was able to recover with remarkable resilience from his blackest moods. How he did this can be seen from **"No obstante"** (**"Notwithstanding"**), in which he tells how he feels an earthquake in his mind and fears that he may see the abyss which haunted Pascal in his last days or the 'wing of idiocy' which struck Baudelaire. But he is not dismayed. He gathers his strength and chooses to live:

> Hay, no obstante, que ser fuerte;
> pasar todo precipicio
> y ser vencedor del Vicio,
> de la Locura y la Muerte. . . .
>
> (I must, notwithstanding, be strong;
> pass every precipice
> and be conqueror of Vice,
> of Madness and Death.)

Darío sees the situation quite simply and makes his decision with admirable fortitude. A man, who faced his own problems in this way, was not likely to shirk similar problems in his art.

The dualism of Darío's character and life made it difficult for him to put the whole of himself into any single poem. Yet if he was to realise the full promise of his gifts, this was necessary, as he himself knew. Between dream and despair, between order and chaos, he had to find some compromise or adjustment. This was in the main a question for his art. In his own life he could turn to his Catholicism and find the consolation and the forgiveness which he required. Towards the end of his life, when the First World War brought home to him the hideous anarchy of human society, he resorted more consciously to his faith and shaped it into a more coherent structure. But this did not affect his poetry very profoundly. His last poems have indeed a touching simplicity, but they lack his earlier force and suggest that in his final years his creative impulse had begun to lose some of its drive. But in the heyday of his powers, though sometimes he wrote poems of an exquisite and lucid Christianity, as when he describes the angelus in the dawn or tells of the Three Wise Men, these are not very close to his inner struggles. More important are those pieces in which he faced his troubles with courage and candour and saw that what he found in himself was something that permeated the whole world and deserved to be spoken of with all the sincerity that he could summon. By an apt choice of a subject which illustrated his own discords he was able to give his complete self to poetry and to show of what scope he was capable.

One means of resolving his discords which appealed to Darío was to deny that in the last analysis they existed, to assert that the contradictions and discrepancies which ordinary men denounce do not matter for the artist, who moves in his own world by his own laws. In asserting this Darío felt that he was speaking for the oppressed and the misunderstood against the dogmas and conventions which harass them. This was of course no final solution to his problem, but it was at least a brave and conscious attempt to see what the problem was. So in **"Letanía de Nuestro Señor Don Quijote"** he applies the method of Baudelaire's "Les Litanies de Satan" and addresses a prayer to the wonderful character who stands for so much in the Spanish consciousness. Of course the Don is totally unlike Baudelaire's Satan, but he is none the less a suitable figure to invoke for the causes which Darío has at heart. Darío indeed makes rather too much of him and assumes that he must necessarily share all his own pet aversions, such as Nietzsche's Superman, Academies, and the rule of the crowd. But in effect Darío speaks for the life of the imagination, which resolves political and ethical discords and provides a system of behaviour based on personal honour. Of course the Don appeals to him because he too is a dreamer, but he is much more than that, and in praising him Darío asserts the power of dreams to inspire courageous action. He sees something holy in the Don's chivalrous outlook and regards him as a true hero who tilts against all the wrong assumptions and restricting categories of the modern world. He sees that such a man defies the ordinary distinctions of truth and falsehood, but thinks that he is all the better for it, because he stands for the life of the spirit and the imaginative approach to experience:

> Noble peregrino de los peregrinos,
> que santificaste todos los caminos
> con el paso augusto de tu heroicidad,
> contra las certezas, contra las conciencias,
> y contra las leyes y contra las ciencias,
> contra la mentira, contra la verdad. . . .

> (Noble pilgrim of the pilgrims,
> you have sanctified every road
> with the august passage of your heroism,
> against certainties, against consciences,
> and against laws, and against sciences,
> against falsehood, against truth.)

This poem represents a position which Darío undeniably held at time, but it is rather the climax of his attachment to dreams than the beginning of his search for truth. By denying the need for truth, he may indeed speak for his own cause, but he cannot defy the forces of reality which break into his life and compel him to pay attention to them. In the figure of the Don Darío speaks for the aesthetic outlook. It is his most remarkable statement of it, but he was not ultimately content with it.

Against this poem we may set another, which represents a different point of view. In **"Los Motivos del Lobo"** (**"The Motives of the Wolf"**) Darío takes the story of St. Francis and the wolf of Gubbio and makes it the myth for something that troubled and touched him deeply. Aware as he was of the beauty of holiness, and equally aware of the limitless corruption of men, he found in this story a myth for his own divided feelings. St. Francis, with his 'heart of lily, cherub's soul, and celestial tongue', was in his very simplicity and warmth of heart dear to Darío. He tells how the Saint wins over the terrible wolf, who puts out his paw in friendship and comes to live in the convent. For a time this happy association lasts, but then the wolf disappears, and once again stories reach the Saint of its violent ravages. He seeks it out on the mountains and appeals to it to return, but the wolf gives a terrible answer. He was, he says, happy in the convent, but he found that life there was just as evil as elsewhere, and his account of it is not unlike Darío's earlier account of Latin America:

> Hermanos a hermanos hacían la guerra,
> perdían los débiles, ganaban los malos,
> hembra y macho eran como perro y perra,
> y un buen día todos me dieron de palos. . . .

> (Brothers made war on brothers,
> the weak lost, the wicked gained,
> woman and man were like bitch and dog,
> and one fine day they all took sticks to me.)

The wolf, true to St. Francis, does not resist, because it believes that all creatures are its brothers. None the less it is beaten and thrown out. So it resumes its old life of rapine and feels that it is at least better than those who have persecuted it. It concludes by telling the Saint that they must go their separate ways:

Déjame en el monte, déjame en el risco,
déjame existir en mi libertad,
vete a tu convento, hermano Francisco,
sigue tu camino y tu santidad. . . .

(Leave me on the mountain, leave me on the cliff,
leave me to live in my liberty,
go to your convent, brother Francis,
follow your way and your sanctity.)

The wolf speaks for Darío, who believed that the dichotomy between holiness and corruption is almost absolute and that in an evil world it is all but necessary to be evil. But from this Darío creates poetry, because he sees the situation fairly and freely from both sides, and reaches a conclusion which is tragic in its very inconclusiveness. Here, as in the poem to Don Quixote, his solution is not philosophical but artistic. He presents a situation which we can accept and understand, but to which we can see no end. The conflict which he dramatises he knows both from other men and from himself, and he set it out with an impressive and touching pathos. So far as his art is concerned, he has closed the gap between competing and opposite tendencies in himself.

In these two poems Darío accepts certain facts about human life and shows his personal approach to them. They show a wider understanding than either **"Sonatina"** or **"Lo Fatal"** and prove that at time he could attain what Yeats called a 'unity of being'. For though the discords remain unresolved, he has mastered them in his art. But once at least Darío did more than this, and united all his different and discordant forces in a single complex experience, showing that he could sometimes transcend his inner struggles and make everything in himself work to a single end without losing its individuality. This he does in what is surely his finest poem, **"Canción de Otoño en Primavera"** (**"Song of Autumn in Spring"**). It is the history of his loves, but it is much more than that. It is a series of brilliant and touching variations on an elegiac theme, which is presented at the start and recurs four more times in the poem:

¡Juventud, divino tesoro,
ya te vas para no volver!
Cuando quiero llorar, no lloro,
y a veces lloro sin querer. . . .

(Youth, divine treasure,
you go, never to return!
When I wash to weep, I do not weep,
and at times I weep without wishing.)

On this basis Darío builds his story of three women whom he has loved, and to each he gives a mixture of lyrical exaltation and realistic irony, without allowing either to spoil the other. He paints each woman in a few deft strokes and displays with a tolerance that is half regretful and half humorous their illusions and his own, from his first timid love for a girl whom he saw as Herodias or Salome, to another who nursed his dreams and killed them, and a

third, who, in the excess of physical passion, hoped to discover some Eden of the flesh and took no thought for the passing of love and youth. Nowhere else does Darío choose his images with such point and such detachment. He recaptures the atmosphere in which he once lived, and enjoys again the old enchantment, while he laments its passing. Into this poem Darío has put the whole of himself, his illusions and dreams, his irony and melancholy, his eye for the significant detail and his irrepressible gift of song.

The conclusion of the poem is Darío's solution of his own conflicts so far as he ever solved them in his art. He knows that his dreams bear very little relation to life and that he can never realise them. He confesses his defeat, and then almost immediately admits that he has no intention of abandoning his search for a perfect love:

En vano busqué a la princesa
que estaba triste de esperar.
La vida es dura. Amarga y pesa.
¡Ya no hay princesa que cantar!

Mas a pesar del tiempo terco,
mid sed de amor no tiene fin;
con el cabello gris, me acerco
a los rosales del jardín. . . .

(In vain I searched for the princess
for whom I was weary of waiting.
Life is hard. Bitter and burdensome.
There is no princess to sing!

But in spite of stubborn time
my thirst for love has no end;
with gray hair I approach
the rose-trees of the garden.)

If here regret seems to be Darío's dominant note, yet it is countered by his candid confession that he cannot give up his old ways, and still more by his finale, when, after repeating his refrain, he finishes with the single line:

¡Mas es mía el Alba de ora! . . .

(But the Dawn of gold is mine!)

In this way he triumphs over his failures, his depressions, his disillusionments. And the triumph is won through poetry. What survives is just his imaginative approach to life, his taste for the affections and the mirages which they create, his many-sided understanding of the human temperament with its moods and vagaries and contradictions.

It was Darío's fortune to be born at a time when the poetry of his own language had nothing to teach him, and he turned for help and inspiration to France. He found them indeed in abundance, and they made him a poet. Yet he was not altogether lucky in this, since his simple, natural character was better suited to a less elaborate, less sophisticated, and less ambitious art. His French schooling imposed on his extremely receptive spirit a manner which he wore with a remarkable brilliance and variety but which at times his inner life forced him to modify or to reject. This hampered the development of his talents and made him seem a minor disciple of the Symbolist school, when he might well have been something more original. More than this, his French attachments strengthened him in his desire for escape and his cult of dreams. Yet just because he cherished this, it provoked a conflict in him which was responsible for his best work, whether he spoke from the depths of melancholy about his falls from imaginative grace or wove together all the strands of his passionate personality into enchanting patterns of song. (pp. 242–64)

C.M. Bowra, "Rubén Dario," in his *Inspiration and Poetry*, Macmillan & Co. Ltd., 1955, pp. 242–64.

OCTAVIO PAZ

(essay date 1965)

[An author of works on literature, art, anthropology, and politics, Paz is primarily recognized as one of the most important Spanish-American poets. His writings include *El laberinto de la soledad* (1959); *The Labyrinth of Solitude: Life and Thought in Mexico*, (1961), *A Draft of Shadows and Other Poems* (1979), and *Convergences: Essays on Art and Literature* (1987). In the following excerpt, he places Darío in the context of Hispanic literature and praises his poetry as a rich expression of Modernism's restless, passionate, and inventive spirit.]

According to the textbooks, the sixteenth and seventeenth centuries were the Golden Age of Spanish literature. Juan Ramón Jiménez has said that they were not gold but gilded cardboard. It would be fairer to say that they were the centuries of Spanish rage. During that period the Spaniards wrote, painted, and dreamed in the same frenzy in which they destroyed and created nations. Everything was carried to extremes: they were the first to circumnavigate the earth, and at the same time they were the inventors of quietism. They raged with a thirst for space, a hunger for death. Lope de Vega was prolific, even profligate: he wrote something over one thousand plays. San Juan de la Cruz was temperate, even miserly: his poetical works consist of three longish lyrics and a few songs and ballads. It was a delirium, whether boisterous or reserved, bloodthirsty or pious. The lucid delirium of Cervantes, Velázquez, Calderón. Quevedo's labyrinth of conceits. Góngora's jungle of verbal stalactites.

And then, quite suddenly, the stage was bare, as if the whole performance had been illusions rather than historical reality. Nothing was left, or nothing but ghostly reflections. During all of the eighteenth century there was

no Swift or Pope, no Rousseau or Laclos, anywhere in Spanish literature. In the second half of the nineteenth century a few faint signs of life began to appear—for instance, Bécquer, whom Rubén Darío imitated in his early **Rhymes**—but there was no one to compare with Coleridge, Hölderlin, Leopardi, no one who resembled Baudelaire. And then, toward the close of the century, everything changed again, just as suddenly, just as violently. The new writers had not been expected (most certainly they had not been invited) and at first their voices were drowned out by the jeers. But a few years later, through the efforts of the very figures whom the "serious" critics had called Frenchified outsiders, the Spanish language was on its feet, was alive again. It was not as opulent as it had been during the Baroque period, but it was stronger, clearer, better controlled.

The last major Baroque poet was a Mexican nun, Sor Juana Inés de la Cruz. Two centuries later, the revival of Spanish literature—and of the language itself—was also accomplished, or at least begun, here in the New World. The movement known as Modernism, of which Rubén Darío became the leader, had a double importance in the literature of the Spanish-speaking world. On the one hand, it produced four or five poets who linked up the great chain that had come apart at the end of the seventeenth century. On the other hand, to change metaphors, it smashed windows and broke doors so that the fresh air of the times could revive the dying language. Modernism was not merely a school of poetry: it was also a dancing class, a gymnasium, a circus, and a masked ball. Ever since, Spanish has been able to put up with the most raucous noises, the most dangerous escapades. And the influence of Modernism has not ended: everything written in Spanish afterward has been affected in one way or another by that great renascence. Modernism began in about 1880 and flourished until about 1910. (pp. 7–8)

At first, Modernism was not an organized movement. There were isolated poets in widely separated parts of the Americas, from Darío, then in Chile, to the Cuban Jose Martí in his New York exile. They soon came to know each other, however, and to realize that their individual efforts were part of a general change in sensibility and language. Little by little they formed groups and published their own magazines, and the various tendencies united in a movement that had two centers of activity, Buenos Aires and Mexico City. The period has been called the "second generation" of Modernism, with Rubén Darío as the bridge between the two periods. The premature death of most of the precursors, plus his gifts as critic and stimulant, made him the acknowledged leader of the movement. With increasing clarity the new poets understood that their work was the first truly independent expression in Spanish-American literature. They were not intimidated when traditional critics called them outsiders: they knew that no one finds himself until after he has left his birthplace.

The French influence was not exclusive—for example, José Martí knew and loved English and United States literature— but it was predominant. The first Modernists turned from the French Romantics to the Parnassians. The second generation, while not abandoning what had been learned from the Parnassians, turned to the Symbolists. Their interest was intense and extensive, but often their very enthusiasm clouded their judgment. They were equally impressed by Gautier and Mendès, by Heredia and Mallarmé. This is made especially clear in the series of literary portraits that Darío published in an Argentine newspaper: Poe, Villiers de l'Isle Adam, Leon Bloy, Nietzsche, Verlaine, Rimbaud, and Lautréamont are jumbled together with minor or now-forgotten writers. It is necessary, of course, to add other names to the list: first, Baudelaire, and second, Jules Laforgue, both of them decisive in the development of the second Modernist generation; the Belgian Symbolists; and among others, Stefan George, Wilde, and Swinburne. Whitman should also be mentioned, not as a direct model but as an example and stimulus. Although his idols were not all French, Darío once said—perhaps to annoy the Spanish critics who accused him of "mental Gallicism"—that "Modernism is nothing else but Castilian prose and verse passed through the fine sieve of good French prose and verse." But it would be a mistake to reduce the movement to an outright imitation of France. The originality of Modernism does not lie in its mastery of influences but in its own creations.

As they searched for a modern, cosmopolitan language, the Spanish-American poets, by a process that looks intricate but was actually natural, rediscovered the genuine, central Spanish tradition—rhythmic versification—which is something quite different from what the traditionalists were defending. The wealth of rhythm in Modernist poetry is unique in the history of the Spanish language, and among other things it opened the way for free verse and the prose poem. Their rediscovery of the true tradition was far from casual, and what they discovered was not merely a rhetoric: it was also an aesthetic and, above all, a way of looking at the world, a way of feeling it, knowing it, and speaking of it. The Modernists accomplished more than a job of restoration; they added something new. The world, the universe, is a system of correspondencies under the rule of rhythm. Everything connects, everything rhymes. Every form in nature has something to say to every other. The poet is not a maker of rhythm but its transmitter. Analogy is the highest expression of the imagination. This longing for cosmic unity is an essential characteristic of the Modernist poet. So, too, is his fascination with cosmic diversity. Forms, colors, and sounds all fly apart; feelings and meanings come together. Poetic images are expressions, both spiritual and sensory, of that single-plural rhythm. It has been said that Modernism is a poetry of sheer emotion. I think it would be more accurate to say

that the Modernist poet, despite his sometimes annoying egoism, was speaking, not of his own soul, but of that of the world as a whole.

To repeat, Rubén Darío was the bridge between the precursors and the second generation of Modernism. His constant travels and his generous activity in behalf of others made him the point of connection for the many scattered poets and groups on two continents. He not only inspired and captained the battle; he was also its observer and critic. The evolution of his poetry, from **"Blue"** to **"Poem of Autumn,"** corresponds with that of the movement, which began with him and ended with him. But his work did not end with Modernism: he went beyond it, beyond the language of that school and, in fact, of every school. Darío was not only the richest and most ample of the Modernist poets: he was one of the great modern poets. At times, he reminds us of Poe; at other times, of Whitman. Of the first, in that portion of his work in which he scorns the world of the Americas to seek an otherworldly music; of the second, in that portion in which he expresses his vitalist affirmations, his pantheism, and his belief that he was, in his own right, the bard of Latin America as Whitman was of Anglo-America.

Darío loved and imitated Verlaine's poetry above all other, but his best poems have little resemblance to those of his model. He has superabundant health and energy; his sun is stronger, his wine more generous. Verlaine was a Parisian provincial, Darío was a Central American globetrotter. His poetry is virile: backbone, heart, sex. It is clear and rotund even when it is sorrowful. It is the work of a Romantic who was also a Parnassian and a Symbolist. The work of a hybrid, not only because of the variety of his spiritual and technical influences but also because of the very blood that flowed in his veins: Indian, Spanish, with a few drops of African. A phenomenon. A pre-Columbian idol. A hippogriff. (pp. 9–12)

Although Darío found rationalist atheism repugnant—his temperament was religious, even superstitious—it cannot be said that he was a Christian poet. Fear of death, the horror of being, self-disgust, expressions which appear now and then after *Songs of Life and Hope*, are ideas and feelings with Christian roots; but the other half, Christian eschatology, is absent. Darío was born in a Christian world, but he lost his faith and was left, like so many of us, with the inheritance of a guilt that no longer has reference to a supernatural sphere. The sense of original sin impregnates many of his best poems: ignorance of our origins and our end, fear of the inner abyss, the horror of living in the dark. Nervous fatigue, made worse by disorderly living and alcoholic excesses, together with his constant coming and going from one country to another, added to his uneasiness. He would wander aimlessly, driven by his anxieties; or he would sink into lethargies that were "brutal nightmares" and in which death seemed alternately a bottomless well or a glorious awakening. In the poems of this nature, written in a temperate and reticent language, varying between monologue and confession, I am especially moved by all three of the nocturnes. The first and third conclude with a presentiment of death. He does not describe death and only names it with a pronoun: She. In contrast, he sees life as a bad dream, a motley collection of grotesque or terrible moments, futile actions, unrealized projects, flawed emotions. It is the anguish of a city night, its silence broken by "the rumble of distant wheels" or the humming of the blood: a prayer that becomes a blasphemy, the endless reckoning of a solitary as he faces the blank wall that closes off the future. But all would resolve into a serene happiness if She would appear. Darío's eroticism never ceased, and he even made a marriage of dying.

In **"Poem of Autumn,"** one of his last and greatest works, the two streams that feed his poetry are united: meditation on death and pantheistic eroticism. The poem is a set of variations on the old, worn-out themes of the brevity of life, the necessity of seizing the moment, and the like, but at the close the lone becomes graver and more defiant: in the face of death the poet does not affirm his own life but that of the universe. Earth and the sun vibrate in his skull as if it were a seashell; the salt of the sea is mingled in his blood as it is in that of the tritons and nereids; to die is to live a vaster, mightier life. Did he really believe this? It is true that he feared death; it is also true that he loved and desired it. Death was his Medusa and his siren. Dual death, dual like everything he touched, saw, and sang: his unity is always dual. That is why, as Juan Ramón Jiménez said, his emblem is the whorled seashell, both silent and filled with murmurs, an infinity that fits in one's hand. A musical instrument, speaking in an "unknown voice." A talisman, because "Europa touched it with her sacred hands." An erotic amulet, a ritual object. Its hoarse voice announces the dawn and the twilight, the hours when light and darkness meet. It is a symbol of universal correspondency, and also of reminiscence: when he presses it to his ear he hears the surge of past lives. He walks along the beach, where "the crabs are marking the sand with the illegible scrawl of their claws," and finds a seashell: then "a star like that of Venus" glows in his soul. The seashell is his body and his poetry, the rhythmic fluctuations, the spiral of those images that reveal and hide the world, that speak it and fall silent. (pp. 16–17)

Octavio Paz, in a prologue to *Selected Poems of Rubén Darío,* translated by Lysander Kemp, University of Texas Press, 1965, pp. 7–17.

CATHY LOGIN JRADE
(essay date 1983)

[In the following excerpt, Jrade discusses significant esoteric elements in Darío's poetry. According to Jrade, Darío's poetry was an attempt to arrive at a comprehensive spiritual vision of the universe.]

Though the centrality of esoteric Pythagoreanism to Darío's poetic creation has generally been overlooked, the importance of his search for unity and harmony has not. Pedro Salinas, in the conclusion to his *La poesía de Rubén Darío* [1948], finds the common ground that unites the three diverse themes of love, art, and society in Darío's frustration with the inadequacies of the human condition—especially in the face of time—in his struggle with fate, and, finally, in his increasing longing for peace. Miguel Enguídanos, taking Salinas as a point of departure, sees the tension generated by this constant dissatisfaction with human destiny as the source of Darío's artistry ["Inner Tensions in the Work of Rubén Darío," Miguel Gonzale-Gerth and George D. Schrade, eds. *Rubén Darío Centennial Studies,* 1970]. In his own terms, Enguídanos emphasizes Darío's refusal to accept the imperfect world that he was given to live in. Both critics therefore indirectly highlight Darío's continuation of the Romantic and Symbolist longing for the paradise from which the modern individual has been exiled. The poet struggles to discover the hidden order of the cosmos—an order that he trusts to be, in its essence, ideal music and beauty—and to incorporate that order into his life and works. Tension results from the possibility of failure: the possibility that he will fail either to recognize the pulse of creation or to control the human frailties that disrupt it. Darío eventually finds a philosophic framework for his hopes and fears in esoteric Pythagoreanism.

Like the Romantics and Symbolists before him, the youthful Darío rejects the dominant ideologies of the day, for they offered few solutions to his sense of alienation and fragmentation. He turns instead to an older conception of the universe. His sensitivity to the lush tropical environment that surrounded him from his birth and his religious and even superstitious character combined to produce a propensity to see God in nature. As early as 1879 Darío links nature and God by describing the roar of the sea as "el eco tremendo / de la voz del Señor." He also perceives the entire world as a living organism, for in the sea's "seno profundo / fuerte palpita el corazón del mundo." In 1880, in **"Desengaño"** he wrote (first ellipsis in original):

> Era en fin, todo armonía;
> era todo allí grandeza;
> sonreía Naturaleza
> al contemplar aquel día . . .
>
> Pero del Sol asomó
> la faz pura y soberana
> y entre celajes de grana
> la aurora se disipó,
>
> y derramó los fulgores

de su lámpara esplendente,
dando vida a la simiente
y fecundando las flores. . . .

Here Darío adapts *Genesis* I: 31, "And God saw every thing that he had made, and, behold, it was very good," to his pantheistic notion of the fusion of God and nature. The harmony described derives from the unity of life manifested in the well-working union of sun and earth. In **"El año lírico"** of *Azul* (1888), Darío transforms the Pythagorean universal monochord into a "lira universal" and envisions the song of birds in sympathetic resonance with one of its chords. In this brief but telling passage, he reaffirms his faith in the musical order of the universe that may be hidden but that can be recovered and reestablished as the basis of poetry and life.

Darío found support for this intuitive response to and poetic interpretation of the universe in the intellectual currents coming to him from Europe. His youthful tendency to a pantheistic view of the world was given impetus by his early familiarity with the writings of Victor Hugo and, shortly thereafter, by his extensive readings of Romantic and Symbolist poets. These readings were soon complemented by his own zealous immersion in occult doctrine. . . . As a result of the confluence of literary and esoteric traditions, Darío's early attitudes began to jell into a coherent conception of the universe as a single living being animated by a single divine soul. This belief that God is the One that is everything is the foundation of esoteric Pythagoreanism and the key to Darío's vision of unity. Through it he discovers not only the unity of all the elements of creation but also the unity of male and female and the unity of life and death.

Esoteric Pythagoreanism holds that the whole universe is God, and since the Great Monad is composed of harmony, the entire universe is considered one harmonious unfolding of his divine being. Though God is one, he acts as a creative Dyad, the union of the Eternal Masculine and the Eternal Feminine. Because both individuals and the universe are thought to have been made in the image of God, primordial man is conceived as a cosmic androgyne who has fallen into the material and bisexual world. It is necessary to understand the harmony of the macrocosm in order to imitate it and establish a similar divine order in the microcosm, thereby becoming "orderly of soul" and approximating the undivided primordial ancestor.

Although Pythagoreans maintain that God is omnipresent, they imagine that all the elements of creation are set up in a hierarchy based on their degree of spirituality and resemblance to God. In order for the human soul to have attained its present position, it had to traverse all the kingdoms of nature, gradually becoming developed through a series of innumerable existences. Furthermore, it is believed that the soul becomes aware that the link between it and its external companion, Spirit, is insoluble even though death breaks the soul's attachment to the body. Accordingly, death is viewed as a "new sleep" or a "delightful swoon" during which the soul receives the hierarchical teaching of the circle of divine love. The alternation between life and death is, therefore, necessary for the development and purification of the soul.

All these tenets are based on and are inextricably linked to the belief in the unity of life. This belief forms the philosophic backdrop to Darío's entire poetic production and underlies his faith in an ordered, intelligent, decipherable universe. While it seldom appears in isolation, it stands solidly at the core of seven major poems written between 1895 and 1908. In these poems Darío explores, through the concepts derived from esoteric Pythagoreanism, the possibilities of human perception and attainment of perfect harmony. Darío recognizes that people aspire to be reintegrated into the order of the cosmos, but he is also aware that their disruptive nature makes failure likely. The resulting tension, alluded to earlier, is at times blatantly expressed in admonitions, but, more generally, it is subtly contained within wishes and self-directed commands. In **"Coloquio de los centauros,"** Darío's first sophisticated recourse to occultist mythology and doctrine, the figure of the centaur, a composite creature that embodies the polar elements of intelligence and bestiality, underscores the poet's awareness of the uncertainty of human destiny. Though some centaurs speak on behalf of immoderate behavior, anger, and discord, Darío optimistically joins ranks with Quirón, the voice of harmony, order, and wisdom. In some later poems, Darío's view of his own fate is less confident. (pp. 25–8)

[In **"Coloquio de los centauros"** Dario for the first time] focuses on and explores at length the question of the unity of life and all its ramifications, or, as he himself wrote several years later, he examines "las fuerzas naturales, el misterio de la vida universal, la ascensión perpetua de Psique" [*Historia de mis Libros*]. For this examination, Darío astutely turns to the centaur, for few figures are more suited to discuss the kinship of life than this creature that is half human and half horse.

Like the Egyptian sphinx and the Assyrian man-bull, the centaur signifies for occultists spiritual evolution, for in it the human form rises from the body of the beast. As the sign of Sagittarius, the centaur, generally shown with a bow and arrow in hand, is a symbol of aspiration and ambition. Just as it aims its arrow toward the stars, every human being aims at a mark that is beyond his or her reach. In the poem, the composite nature of the centaur is emphasized by Folo:

El biforme ixionida comprende de la altura,
por la materna gracia, la lumbre que fulgura,
la nube que se anima de luz y que decora
el pavimento en donde rige su carro Aurora,
y la banda de Iris que tiene siete rayos
cual la lira en sus brazos siete cuerdas; los mayos
en la fragante tierra llenos de ramos bellos,
y el Polo coronado de cándidos cabellos.

El ixionida pasa veloz por la montaña,
rompiendo con el pecho de la maleza huraña
los erizados brazos, las cárceles hostiles;
escuchan sus orejas los ecos más sutiles;
sus ojos atraviesan las intricadas hojas,
mientras sus manos toman para sus bocas rojas
las frescas bayas altas que el sátiro codicia;
junto a la oculta fuente su mirada acaricia
las curvas de las ninfas del séquito de Diana;
pues en su cuerpo corre también la esencia humana,
unida a la corriente de la savia divina
y a la salvaje sangre que hay en la bestia equina.
Tal el hijo robusto de Ixión y de la Nube.

Since the centaurs are said to have been the offspring of Ixion and, cloud, the more spiritual aspects of their character are supposedly inherited from their mother. Their baser emotions are from their father, whose incorrigible behavior was severely punished by Zeus. The split in the centaurs' personality emphasizes the fusion of contraries. It also parallels human nature and the tension within Darío' poetry.

Like Darío, the centaurs aspire to comprehend the heavenly phenomena of lights, clouds, rainbows, and seasonal changes at the same time that they respond with unrestrained sensual delight to their physical surroundings. Though Darío has them perceive the harmonious order of the universe in the seven bands of the rainbow which recall the seven strings of the lyre and the music of the spheres, he also captures, in the second half of the section quoted the centaurs' potential for destructiveness. They assert their freedom by crushing the "intractable thicket" that holds them like "hostile jails" as they surge across the landscape. This unbridled energy is coupled with unlimited sensuality. They hear, see, touch, and taste with the greatest acumen and pleasure, and their desirous looks "caress" the nymphs of Diana's retinue. But it is the unity of their being that is emphasized in the concluding lines: "pues en su cuerpo corre también la esencia humana, / unida a la corriente de la savia divina / y a la salvaje sangre que hay en la bestia equina.

In his usual, summary manner, Quirón, the pivotal figure of the poem, confirms Folo's emphasis on the unity of opposites: "Sus cuatro patas, bajan; su testa erguida, sube." The verbs "bajar" and "subir" highlight the poles of the centaur's behavior. He aspires toward the divine but may fall toward the bestial. In effect, the poem grows out of the search both for the reconciliation of the tension within the centaurs and for their reintegration into a harmonious and well-working universe. They discover on the magical "Isla do Oro" the hidden order of the cosmos, which, in turn, illuminates the proper role of sexuality and death. As a result, **"Coloquio"** represents a paradisiacal interlude in the harried, modern world, or, in other words, a poetic utopia. The resolution of strife and discord is directed by Quirón, the wisest of all centaurs, who, according to Reto, is the source of the truth sought by the human race.

The conspicuous placement of the word "harmonía" as well as the carefully constructed description of the poem's setting underscore from the very beginning the underlying harmony of nature to which the centaurs will strive to attune themselves. The entire colloquy takes place "En la isla en que detiene su esquife el argonauta / del inmortal Ensueño, donde la eterna pauta / de las eternas liras se escucha." The argonaut who sails the seas alone in search of the immortal Dream and who stops only at the island where the fundamental accord of existence is felt is the poet. This association of the poet with an argonaut continues throughout Darío's poetry and may have its roots in the Romantic connection linking the visionary with the prodigal son, who wanders in search of "home." Certainly the word "esquife" carries with it overtones of Rimbaud's "Le bateau ivre." (pp. 28–30)

The pulse of celestial music sensed by the poet is echoed in the rhythmic gallop of the centaurs and in the throbbing movement of the ocean, to which the centaurs are instinctively attracted. The sea is more than an ornament in the verbal picture of the poem's location, and Darío's own statement about **"Coloquio"** underscores its importance: "Y bajo un principio pánico, exalto la unidad del Universo en la ilusoria Isla de Oro, ante la vasta mar" [*Historia de mis libros*]. As Alan S. Trueblood, in his article "Rubén Darío: The Sea and the Jungle" [*Comparative Literature Studies*, 1967], observes, the sea holds a unique place in Darío's poetic imagination, for from the beginning of his career, he senses in it in the beating of a giant heart. Trueblood's conclusions regarding the symbolism of the cicada apply equally to the image of the sea.

> [It] leads us to the genetic core of Darío's art, a zone where nature, man's sentient life, and his creative impulse become coordinated in a kind of symbiosis from which the poem takes its life. The beat and echo of human hearts, the stresses and sonorities of the poet's lines, the pulsating call of the insect, and the lappings on the ocean's shore are rhythms and sounds belonging ultimately to a single harmony and it is this music which the poet seeks to apprehend. We detect here a pre-disposition on Darío's part to the Pythagoreanism which will become marked later on in his view of art, life and spirit and of their essential concordance, and we see an early intimation of the "harmony of the spheres" to which he will seek to attune his art.

In **"Coloquio"** the sea recalls the single pulsating heart of the world which echoes throughout the universe and within Darío's poetry. Darío relays the message of this universal pulse in the staccato rhythm of the second, third, and fourth strophes. The beat of these lines and the description of the thundering sounds of the approaching centaurs serve as a drum-roll introduction to the colloquy and emphasize its basic theme: all life is one harmonious extension of God.

This sense of harmony is reinforced by the sound patterns established throughout the poem. The rather rigid *alejandrino pareado* is given new life and flexibility in **"Coloquio"** through various forms of enjambment as well as through the free alteration among various alexandrines. Trochaic uniformity disappears, and Darío relies upon the *alejandrino mixto* to express movement and speed and upon the *alejandrino dactílico* in more musical passages. In addition, the rhythmic recurrence of the sounds of the paired consonantal rhymes evokes the ordered pulse of the cosmos.

The fundamental accord among the elements of the universe that is alluded to and suggested acoustically in the first twenty-two lines is demonstrated immediately. Quirón's attempt to open the colloquy is assisted by nature; the Tritons and the Sirens grow silent and the winds die down. He proposes to discuss: "la gloria inmar cesible de la Musas hermosas / y el triunfo del terrible misterio de las cosas." His injunction reflects certain basic assumptions. The glory of the Muses is unfading, for the arts that they represent like the attractive goddesses themselves, embody the eternal harmony of the universe. As a result, the female form serves as one more example of the universal order that the poet must strive to emulate in his creations. This association of the female body with poetry is particularly strong for Darío. [Creation]— poetic or otherwise—is conceived of in sexual terms. He therefore, links language, the "flesh" of poetry, with woman. To become poetry language must be inseminated with "ideal music." Therefore, the glory about which Quirón wishes to speak is present only in those cases where the artist has succeeded in inseminating the materials of artistic creation with ideas that sustain the perfection of the cosmos. This perfection is the "mystery of all things"; it is rooted in the unity of all life in and through God.

Quiron's suggestion is taken up after Reto's speech praising him with allusions to the stories that surround his death. Chiron was known everywhere for his goodness and wisdom, so much so that the distinguished heroes of Grecian mythology, like Jason, Achilles, and Aesculapius, the great physician, were entrusted to him. Hercules, too, was his friend; but while fighting with the other centaurs he inadvertently injured Chiron, who, although immortal, chose to die. He gave his immortality to Prometheus, who, in one story, was being punished for arranging that human beings get not only fire but also the best part of the animals sacrificed. Prometheus had been warned that there would be no end to his suffering until a god would freely die for him. Although it seemed unreasonable to expect such a sacrifice from another, Chiron offered himself, and Zeus accepted him as a substitute. After his death, Chiron was placed among the stars as Sagittarius.

These introductory remarks about Quirón are picked up toward the end of **"Coloquio."** The later references to Quiron's death bring the poem full circle and shed light on the role of mortality within the Pythagorean vision of life. Discussion of this perspective, which continues throughout the poem, is initiated by Abantes, who, following Quirón's command, begins by praising Nature, the womb of existence, and the seed of life:

Himnos a la sagrada Naturaleza; al vientre
de la tierra y al germen que entre las rocas y entre
las carnes de los árboles, y dentro humana forma,
es un mismo secreto y es una misma norma:
potente y sutilísimo, universal resumen
de la suprema fuerza, de la virtud del Numen.

Genesis is again imagined in sexual terms with all matter as the womb of creation. With the implantation of spirit, the divine seed of life, the inanimate becomes animate, the trees come alive and have flesh like their kin of the human race. The germ that lies at the heart of all mineral, vegetable, and animal life is one, "un mismo secreto." It is the extract, the essence of the supreme deity that permeates all.

Quirón supports and elaborates upon Abantes's statement:

¡Himnos! Las cosas tienen un ser vital: las cosas
tienen raros aspectos, miradas misteriosas;
toda forma es un gesto, una cifra, un enigma;
en cada átomo existe un incógnito estigma;
cada hoja de cada árbol canta un propio cantar
y hay un alma en cada una de las gotas del mar;
el vate, el sacerdote, suele oír el acento
desconocido; a veces enuncia el vago viento
un misterio, y revela una inicial la espuma
o la flor; y se escuchan palabras de la bruma.
Y el hombre favorito del numen, en la linfa
o la ráfaga, encuentra mentor:—demonio o ninfa.

Quirón emphasizes the presence of life everywhere, even in what is normally regarded as inert matter. The kinship that exists between "inanimate" objects and people is further reflected in Darío's choice of a humanizing vocabulary. They have appearances, looks, and gestures; the leaves sing, the wind enunciates, and the foam reveals. These human qualities not only point out natures sympathetic relationship with people—which makes it possible for it to communicate its message to them. They also suggest that "humanity" is rooted in the lower forms of life and is perfected through the transmigration of souls.

It is, of course, the poet/magus who is most sensitive to the signs of life and harmony present in all things. It is the *vates* who can "read" the gesture, the sign, or the puzzle of external forms a indications of the order of the universe and the immanence of God both of which are generally hidden from human experience. The difficulty of this apprehension is highlighted by the adjectives used in this section. The signs of nature are odd, mysterious, unknown, and unfamiliar. Yet the poet understands them like his own language. He sees in them a text to be interpreted and translated.

The final two lines summarize the points made in this twelve line section. The poet is God's favorite, for wherever he looks whether in water or in the air, he finds a guiding spirit that will teach him the secrets of the cosmos. The "linfa" and "ráfaga" are correlated in reverse order with the previously mentioned "viento" and "espuma." Darío capitalizes on the images connected with these two elements. The wind is often linked with life by virtue of its association with creative breath or exhalation. The foam of the sea recalls the ebb and flow of the ocean and the throbbing of a giant's heart. Together they evoke the natural pulse and movement of the universe and convincingly assert the presence and unity of life.

In the next two sections, the unity of life is discussed from the perspective of apparent discord. First Folo, in the section already examined, deals with the split in the centaur's personality. Then Orneo outlines the problem of good and evil in the traditional Western manner:

> Yo comprendo el secreto de la bestia. Malignos
> seres hay y benignos. Entre ellos se hacen signos
> de bien y mal, de odio o de amor, o de pena
> o gozo; el cuervo es malo y la torcaz es buena.

Orneo segregates all creatures into absolute, dualistic categories: goodness and evil, love and hate, pleasure and pain. Quirón disagrees and insists upon the basic oneness of life. He holds that all creatures are manifestations of a single life force. "Ni es la torcaz benigna ni es el cuervo protervo: / son formas del Enigma la paloma y el cuervo."

As in an actual conversation, where a single word occasions a series of responses, the word "enigma" calls forth remarks by both Astilo and Neso. As used by Quirón, the "enigma" was the apparent paradox of Pythagoreanism: what is in essence one is in appearance many. Astilo reminds the assembled centaurs that the underlying unity is found in mathematics and music. His comment is: "El Enigma es el soplo que hace cantar la lira." The impersonal "viento" mentioned previously becomes a "soplo," a "puff" exhaled by some invisible anthropomorphic force that activates the universal lyre and causes celestial music. Similarly, this "breath" infiltrates the soul of the artist, driving him to translate universal harmony into music or poetry. The connection between artistic creation and the harmonious order of the universe is clear. Neso's response to Astilo draws attention to their link with woman. "¡El Enigma es el rostro fatal de Deyanira!" Skyrme's conclusion is thus supported: "Whatever physical stimulus the man may have found in woman, the poet certainly saw in the female body the incarnation of the enigma of the universe, and in the act of love a sacrament of communion with its motive spirit, music and mystery in one. . . . Love is a means to knowledge, and in this sense Darío's erotic images are metaphors for mystical cognition" [Raymond Skyrme, *Rubén Darío and the Pythagorean Tradition*, 1975].

But as much as love is a means to knowledge, passion is a means to destruction. This dichotomy in the nature of love and in the relationship between man and woman is explored in the sections spoken by Neso, Eurito, Hipea, Odites, and Quirón. These sections draw heavily upon the account of the battle between the centaurs and the Lapithae described by Ovid in *The Metamorphoses*, book 12. Neso begins with recollections of his encounter with Deianira.

According to the myth, Nessus met Deianira when she was on her way home after he marriage to Hercules. The newlyweds came upon the river where the centaur acted as ferryman, carrying travelers over the water. He took her on his back and in midstream insulted her. She shrieked, and Hercules shot Nessus as he reached the other bank. Before Nessus died, he told Deianira to take some of his blood and use it as a charm if Hercules ever loved another woman more than her. When she heard about Iole, she anointed a robe with the blood and sent it to Hercules. As he put it on, he was seized with excruciating pain, but he did not die. To relieve the suffering, he ordered the construction of his own funeral pyre.

It is only in the context of this original story that the meaning of the adjective "fatal" can be understood. Deianira's beauty aroused a passion that led to the death of her suitor. Neso actualizes the memory of this meeting with Deianira and makes her a presence that is just barely removed by stating: "Mi espalda aún guarda el dulce perfume de la bella; / aún mis pupilas llama su claridad de estrella." He continues: "¡Oh aroma de su sexo!, ¡oh rosas y alabastros!, / ¡oh envidia de las flores y celos de los astros!" His uncontrolled emotions are reflected in the final two lines, in the breakdown of sentence structure and in the projection of envy and jealousy onto the flowers and stars.

On the other hand, Quirón directs the discussion away from the baser emotions aroused by women by turning to the figure of Venus, who represents the feminine attributes of the godhead. He does not reject Neso's claims on behalf of feminine beauty. He simply highlights its integration into the harmony of creation. Quirón takes Neso's sensual phrase "¡oh rosas y alabastros!" and develops a unified vision of woman's role in the cosmos. The erogenous pink and white of the female body are related to the genesis of Venus, who sprang from the white foam of the sea impregnated by Uranus's red blood.

> Cuando del sacro abuelo la sangre luminosa
> con la marina espuma formara nieve y rosa,
> hecha de rosa y nieve nació la Anadiomena.

Her marine birth places her within a context that is for Darío laden with rhythmic and harmonious associations: the curves of the sea-horses are echoed conceptually in the curling green waves and Venus's well-rounded hips; these "ondas" are echoed aurally in the "redondas" describing the goddess's feminine shape.

> Al cielo alzó los brazos la lírica sirena;
> los curvos hipocampos sobre las verdes ondas
> levaron los hocicos; y caderas redondas,
> tritónicas melenas y dorsos de delfines
> junto a la Reina nueva se vieron. . . .

The rhythmic undulations of the verbal picture, which . . . has many possible sources, spotlights Darío's novel conclusions regarding Venus's impact upon the world.

For the poet, Venus's creation is identified with the birth of her concept or with her being named; both acts fill the void with a deep, resonant harmony of meaningful existence and communication, a dual phenomenon that can only be compared with poetic creation:

> . . . .Los confines
> del mar llenó el grandioso clamor; el universo
> sintió que un nombre harmónico, sonoro como un
> verso,
> llenaba el hondo hueco de la altura: ese nombre
> hizo gemir la tierra de amor: fué para el hombre
> más alto que el de Jove, y los númenes mismos
> lo oyeron asombrados; los lóbregos abismos
> tuvieron una gracia de luz. ¡VENUS impera!

The mention of her name sends a sympathetic moan of love throughout the earth, and the gloomy abysses are filled with light. Venus, indeed all women, illuminates the path to consonance. She is the Eternal Feminine in God, the divine substance of creation, and the embodiment of harmony. She is "the living earth and all earths, along with the bodies they enclose, into which souls are incarnated. . . . [She is] the great Soul of the World who gives birth, preserves, and renews. . . .":

> Ella es entre las reinas celestes la primera,
> pues es quien tiene el fuerte poder de la Hermosura.
> ¡Vaso de miel y mirra brotó de la amargura!
> Ella es la más gallarda de las emperatrices,
> princesa de los gérmenes, reina de las matrices,
> señora de las savias y de las atracciones,
> señora de los besos y de los corazones.

Beauty, as epitomized by Venus, is the manifestation of divine perfection and universal accord. She is "la lírica sirena" because the harmonious proportions among her parts and her consonance with the cosmic order reveal her essence to be music. She is, for this reason Darío's standard for artistic achievement, and, like poetry, she is able to convert all bitterness into honey and myrrh. She leads man away from discord toward the goal of the assimilation of the music of the spheres. In addition, as the feminine aspect of the godhead, Venus is also the universal source of the vital fluid of existence ("las savias") that flows throughout all the elements of nature. This image reinforces the underlying associations of the first few lines of this section. If Darío senses in the ocean the beating of a giant heart that attests to the perpetuation of life, he establishes in love and in resulting quickened heartbeats a microcosmic parallel. Venus, born of the ocean, contains within herself the lifeblood of creation that continues to flow because of her human counterparts, women, and the emotions that they arouse.

These emotions mean but one thing for Eurito, for his thought about women revolve exclusively around his abduction of Hippodamia, whom he carried off at her wedding to Pirithous, starting the battle between the Lapithae and the centaurs. The Lapithae, mythical people inhabiting the mountains of Thessaly, were governed by Pirithous, who, being a son of Ixion, was a half brother of the centaurs. When Pirithous married Hippodamia and invited the centaur to the marriage feast, the latter attempted to carry off the bride and other women. The bloody conflict evoked led to the defeat of the centaurs. For this season, Hipea angrily denounces women as cunning, traitorous, and deadly.

> Yo sé de la hembra humana la original infamia.
> Venus anima artera sus máquinas fatales;
> tras los radiantes ojos ríen traidores males;
> de su floral perfume se exhala sutil daño;
> su cráneo obscuro alberga bestialidad y engaño.

It is, according to Hipea, woman's external grace and apparent accord with creation that hide her true bestial and deceitful nature. Her amphoral shape and her laughter, which recalls a rippling, iridescent brook, belie her poisonous temperament. Therefore, in Hipea's judgment, she is worse than the female of any other species.

> Tiene las formas puras del ánfora, y la risa
> del agua que la brisa riza y el sol irisa;
> mas la ponzoña ingénita su máscara pregona:
> mejores son el águila, la yegua y la leona.
> De su húmeda impureza brota el calor que enerva
> los mismos sacros dones de la imperial Minerva;
> y entre sus duros pechos, lirios del Aqueronte,
> hay un olor que llena la barca de Caronte.

As physical heat saps physical strength, the heat of passion that emanates from woman's "humid impurity" weakens man's powers of reason. The consequent irrational behavior manifests a complete disregard for life. As a result, Hipea describes female breasts as lilies from the river Acheron, the river of woe that flows toward the outer limits of the underworld. They have the same odor as the boat that Charon uses to ferry the souls of the dead across the water to the adamantine gates of Hades: they smell of death.

The contrast between Hipea's speech and Quirón's underlines the fundamental split in the centaurs' perception of woman. Whereas Hipea asserts that woman is the cause of discord, destruction, and death, Quirón upholds that she is the origin of harmony, art, and life. The resolution of this conflict is not found, as suggested by Odites, in earthly woman's enchantingly attractive features. Rather it is discovered in the oneness of the universe. Quirón is the first to return to this primary theme. He does so by introducing the esoteric belief in the androgynous nature of human beings.

According to esoteric doctrine, though God is one, he acts as a creative Dyad and contains within himself the Eternal Masculine and the Eternal Feminine. Adam is similarly imagined as androgynous since he was made in God's image. His fall into evil is identified with his entrance into the material and bisexual world. A return to the union of male and female becomes a means of perceiving the prelapsarian bliss of unity and of intuiting the divine state. In general, marriage is the way humans reattain the original androgynous states or, as Quirón expresses it, the way Cinis [*sic*] can become Ceneo. This image, like many others of the poem, is derived from the tale of the battle between the centaurs and the Lapithae. Caeneus was originally a maiden named Caenis who was beloved by Poseidon and who was, upon her request, changed into a man by this god:

> Por suma ley, un día llegará el himeneo
> que el soñador aguarda: Cinis será Ceneo;
> claro será el origen del femenino arcano:
> la Esfinge tal secreto dirá a su soberano.

According to Quirón's statement, the marriage that the visionary awaits and that is ordained by the highest law of the universe will place sexual love within the context of universal accord. It will restore human beings to their original androgynous state and allow them to comprehend the order of the cosmos. One who comprehends the other of the cosmos will understand the role of woman and be master of the Sphinx's secret—traditionally an ultimate meaning which remains forever beyond human comprehension. This individual will have achieved a degree of spiritual perfection that approximates his or her original, noncorporeal existence in union with God and will be prepared for immortality, which is a theme of central importance to the concluding sections of the poem.

The question of the unity of the sexes brings the colloquy back to the discussion of the oneness of creation. Clito holds that humans are the highest form of life on earth and the goal of all earthly evolution. Of all individuals, visionaries are the most elevated because they perceive the hidden meaning of existence. But Caumantes rejects this emphasis on humanity. Instead he holds that all creatures, though externally divergent, are forms of a single life force. He therefore turns to the figure of the monster, which represents the unity of creation despite apparent diversity. His only concession to Clito comes in the final three lines of his speech:

> Naturaleza sabia, formas diversas junta,
> y cuando tiende al hombre la gran Naturaleza,
> el monstruo, siendo el símbolo, se viste de belleza.

Monsters—or composite beings—are created by an intelligent nature that willfully choose to join divergent forms. Though nature tends toward human status through a series of incarnations, the monster is the symbol of the spectrum of life, a symbol that is beautiful in its eloquence or, as Darío states, "El monstruo expresa un ansia del corazón del Orbe."

The composite beings to which Caumantes refers are, in addition to the centaur, the satyr, Pan, the siren, and the Minotaur. In Greek mythology, satyrs are woodland deities represented as men with the characteristics of a goat and associated with the luxuriant vital powers of nature. Pan, a merry, musical god, resembles the satyr in

that he also has goat's horns and goat's hooves instead of feet and lives in the wild thickets, forests, and mountains. Sirens are sea nymphs who lured sailors to their destruction by their sweet singing; they have come to be identified with mermaids, legendary marine creatures with the head and upper body of a woman and the tail of a fish. The Minotaur, the fruit of the union of Minos's wife Pasiphae with a bull, is half man and half bull. Caumantes sees in all these creatures the fusion of opposites: animal and human life are united in the centaur, sexual passion and harmonious fury in the satyr, the harmony of rustic life and rhythm of the cosmos in Pan, bewitching incantations and idyllic music in the voice of the siren, Pasiphae and the bull in the Minotaur:

> en el Centauro el bruto la vida humana absorbe;
> el sátiro es al selva sagrada y la lujuria:
> une sexuales ímpetus a la harmoniosa furia;
> Pan junta la soberbia de la montaña agreste
> al ritmo de la inmensa mecánica celeste;
> la boca melodiosa que atrae en Sirenusa,
> es la fiera alada y es de la suave musa;
> con la bicorne bestia Pasifae se ayunta.

The contrasting elements that form the center of Caumantes's argument are carefully selected to exemplify the apparent, though fallacious, diversity of life. "La selva sagrada" is contrasted with "la lujuria," "sexuales ímpetus" with "la harmoniosa furia," and "la soberbia de la montaña agreste" with "el ritmo de la inmensa mecánica celeste." As Darío makes clear in "Yo soy aquel que ayer no más decía," the introductory poem of *Cantos de vida y esperanza*, the sacred forest is where the initiate can sense the palpitation of the divine heart and learn from it the art of harmony and rhythm:

> Mi intelecto libré de pensar bajo,
> bañó el agua castalia el alma mía,
> peregrinó mi corazón y trajo
> de la sagrada selva la armonía.
> ¡Oh, la selva sagrada! ¡Oh, la profunda
> emanación del corazón divino
> de la sagrada selva! ¡Oh, la fecunda
> fuente cuya virtud vence al destino!

The "sagrada selva" is a forest in which the wild movements of life have been disciplined and made to beat in rhythm with the divine heart (which also appears in the first line of Caumantes's speech). It is united with the concept of "lujuria" in that it is an enlightened, rhythmic development of the lower form. The same is true for "la harmoniosa furia" and "sexuales ímpetus," which parallel the former pair. A similar correspondence is found between "la soberbia de la montaña agreste" and "el ritmo de la inmensa mecánica celeste." The perfect order that is the rhythm of the celestial mechanism is, in a rougher, less refined state, the pride of the rustic mountain. The same life pulse is present both on the distant mountaintop and in the magnificent structure of the heavens.

These paired comparisons also underscore again the underlying tension that is central to Darío's work and to

"**Coloquio**". They highlight Darío's awareness that human beings have within themselves the power— indeed the responsibility—to ascend, to become more spiritual, divine, and orderly of soul or the capacity to descend toward the bestial and uncontrolled.

Whereas Caumantes's speech focuses on the resolution of contraries in composite beings, Grineo directs his attention further down on the scale of existence. He speaks of inanimate objects, which he claims to love as much as Hesiod, the great poet of the simple life. Quirón supports Grineo's unusual affection by reaffirming the most fundamental belief of esoteric Pythagoreanism: the entire universe is permeated by a single, divine soul. Grineo's response to Quirón explains his attachment to stones and rocks:

> He visto, entonces, raros ojos fijos en mí:
> los vivos ojos rojos del alma de rubí;
> los ojos luminosos del alma del topacio,
> y los de la esmeralda que del azul epacio
> la maravilla imitan; los ojos de las gemas
> de brillos peregrinos y mágicos emblemas.
> Amo el granito duro que el arquitecto labra
> y el mármol en que duerme la línea y la palabra.

Grineo does not perceive the stones and rocks as inanimate; rather he sees locked within them inchoate beings that peer out, attempting to communicate with higher forms of life. They are "pilgrims" about to begin their journey through the evolutionary process made possible by the transmigration of souls. He sees the fiery gems as sparkling eyes through which— like human eyes—their souls make contact with others. Moreover, as the granite is worked by the architect and the marble by the sculptor, a special relationship arises between the artist's soul and that of the stone. The hidden figure and word through which nature speaks are released from their stony confines by art. The artist who understands the order of creation awakens the sleeping "linea" and "palabra."

The discussion regarding the presence of the universal soul in stones and rocks is continued in Quirón's reference to the Greek myth of the destruction of the world. When Zeus resolved to destroy the degenerate race of human beings, the pious Deucalion and his wife Pyrrha were the only mortals saved. Deucalion built a ship in which he and his wife floated in safety during the flood of nine days that killed all other inhabitants. At last the ship rested. Deucalion and Pyrrha consulted the sanctuary of Themis as to how the population might be restored. The goddess directed them to cover their heads and throw the bones of their mother behind them. Interpreting the cryptic message to refer to the Great Mother of all creatures, Mother Earth, Deucalion and Pyrrha picked up loose rocks and cast them behind them. From those thrown by Deucalion there sprang up men, from those thrown by Pyrrha, women.

The occultist reading of this allegory strengthens the connection between Grineo's comments and Quirón's brief remark. It holds that the story of Deucalion and Pyrrha epitomizes the mystery of human evolution. Spirit, by ensouling matter, becomes the indwelling power that propels the mineral to the status of the plant, the plant to the plane of the animal, the animal to the dignity of humanity, and humanity to the glory of the gods. This interpretation of the myth also sheds light on the speech by Abantes that opened the discussion regarding the unity of life. The "vientre" is the womb of the Great Mother where the "germen," spirit, is implanted. The seed develops until it is liberated from matter and returns to the godhead.

These beliefs regarding the origin and destiny of the human soul bring the poem to its final theme, namely, the proper role and function of death. The esoteric view of death, alluded to throughout the poem, ties together all the ideas already examined. It is introduced by Lícidas with a reference to lemurs, the name give by Romans to disembodied spirits associated with ghosts and apparitions:

> Yo he visto los lemures flotar, en los nocturnos
> instantes, cuando escuchan los bosques taciturnos
> el loco grito de Atis que su dolor revela
> o la maravillosa canción de Filomela.
> El galope apresuro, si en el boscaje miro
> manes que pasan, y oigo su fúnebre suspiro.
> Pues de la Muerte el hondo, desconocido Imperio,
> guarda el pavor sagrado de su fatal misterio.

Darío once again brings inanimate elements to life, this time by mixing Greek mythology with his own view of nature. Atys is remembered as a youth who was driven into a frenzy by a jealous Agdistis and who, in that moment of wild abandon, castrated himself. Zeus thereupon turned him into a fir-tree. A similar story of metamorphosis is the background to Darío's reference to Philomela. Philomela was a princess of Athens who was raped by her sister Procne's husband, Tereus, who also cut out her tongue. In revenge Procne killed her son, Itys, and fed him to her husband. When Tereus was about to kill both of them, they were turned into birds, Philomela into a swallow and Procne into a nightingale, whose song is the sweetest of all birds because it is the saddest. Roman writers, however, got the sisters confused and identified Philomela with the nightingale. Darío, like the Greeks, sees nature populated by human forms struggling to express human emotions. The forest is, therefore, taciturn as it listens to Aty's wild shouts of pain heard in the whining of the fir-trees or to Philomela's marvelous song. In spite of this sympathetic relationship with nature described by Lícidas, the centaur quickens his pace whenever he sees the manes, the spirits of the dead, pass by. Death remains frightful to him. The concluding speeches respond to Lícidas's fear.

The myth that underlies all the responses recounts Chiron's willful surrender of his immortality so that Prometheus might be freed from his unending punishment. Though any number of literary works with their individual interpretations of the myth may have brought the tale of Chiron's generosity to Darío's attention, his rendering of the myth departs from the traditional and follows instead esoteric doctrine. Quirón finds that "La Muerte es la victoria de la progenie humana" because it is through death—or the deaths that precede and make possible each new, more advanced reincarnation—that one is able to attain union with God.

This statement clarifies what is meant by Arneo's statement: "La Muerte es de la Vida la inseparable hermana." It also explains Medón's description of death: "No es demacrada y mustia, / ni ase corva guadaña, ni tiene faz de angustia." Death is not horrible or fearsome as in traditional Christian iconography; rather "es semejante a Diana, casta y virgen como ella," because it is unsullied by the flesh, by matter. The "palmas triunfales" represent death's victory over life and the "agua del olvido" the forgetfulness which separates birth from death.

In this context, it is reasonable for Quirón to conclude, "La pena de los dioses es no alcanzar la Muerte," and for him to give up his immortality to Prometheus, who is mentioned in this last section by Eureto [*sic*] in relation to the creation of human beings. Legend states that Prometheus created man out of earth and water and gave him a portion of all the qualities possessed by the other animals. Eureto, therefore, suggests that if human beings, through Prometheus, could steal life, they should be able to understand the key to death that is presented, in conclusion, by Quirón:

> La virgen de las vírgenes es inviolable y pura.
> Nadie su casto cuerpo tendrá en la alcoba obscura,
> ni beberá en sus labios el grito de la victoria,
> ni arrancará a su frente las rosas de su gloria.

By supernatural communication or intuitive accord with nature, the centaurs conclude the colloquy as Apollo, the sun god, rises to the highest point in his journey through the sky. At the same time, the thundering sounds that are produced by his passage through the heavens (an adaptation of the image of the universal monochord) are echoed by the ocean. The winds that died down begin to blow, and the various sounds of nature replace the sounds of voices. The light rustle of the west wind is pierced by the strident song of the Greek cicada, the voice of inextinguishable life:

> Mas he aquí que Apolo se acerca al meridiano.
> Sus truenos prolongados repite el Oceano.
> Bajo el dorado carro del reluciente Apolo
> vuelve a inflar sus carrillos y sus odres Eolo.
> A lo lejos, un templo de mármol se devisa
> entre laureles-rosa que hace cantar la brisa.
> Con sus vibrantes notas, de Céfiro desgarra
> la veste transparente la helénica cigarra,
> y por el llano extenso van en tropel sonoro
> los Centauros, y al paso, tiembla la Isla de Oro.

The conclusion of the poem is, thus, a perfect echo of and balance to the introduction. In both sections Darío un-

derscores the rhythms and sounds that ultimately belong to the single harmony of the universe, to the rhythmic pulse of the life to which the poet aspires to attune his life and art.

Shortly after composing **"Coloquio de los centauros,"** Darío wrote a series of thirteen poems entitled **"Las ánforas de Epicuro,"** which he added to the 1901 edition of *Prosas profanas*. Four of the thirteen deal with occultist themes; two (**"La espiga"** and **"Ama tu ritmo . . . "**) center on the Pythagorean concept of the unity of life. In the first of the series, **"La espiga"**, the peaceful tone of the harmonious accord is the same as in **"Coloquio."** The setting, however, is different. The Greek temple and mythological figures disappear. What is left is a scene of timeless, natural beauty undefined as to period or style. Indeed, time stands still, and, unlike **"Coloquio,"** which provides a harmonious interlude limited to the confines of the poem, **"La espiga"** takes place in an eternal setting of idyllic and unchanging peace. Moreover, with the disappearance of artistic intermediaries, Darío declares his confidence in his ability to perceive the order of creation directly from nature. (pp. 30–45)

In the first three lines of the sonnet, Darío establishes the scene in which the underlying concepts of the poem germinate. A sign is seen in the movement of a plant which is being stirred by "los dedos del viento." The sign is subtle, noticed only by the enlightened poet, who now directs the reader's attention to it. He sees the swaying plant as a golden brush with which the fingers of the wind paint upon the blue canvas of the sky. They sketch "el misterio inmortal de la tierra divina/ y el alma de las cosas." In other words, it is in all the elements of nature working together in universal harmony that the poet perceives the mystery of the divine and the soul of all things.

The pantheistic belief that God is present throughout creation is reinforced by the transitional ninth line, "Pues en la paz del campo la faz de Dios asoma." Darío concludes the poem on a syncretic note by introducing standard Christian symbols, which clarify his previous allusions to the Eucharist. He is thus able to reconcile Catholic doctrine with his pantheistic vision.

As **"La espiga"** unfolds, Darío builds upon the elements present in the initial scene, preparing the way for the final, syncretic image. The elements gradually become more and more invested with supernatural and religious significance. In contrast to this deepening religious experience of **"La espiga,"** in the fifth sonnet of **"La ánforas de Epicuro,"** **"Ama tu ritmo. . . "** Pythagorean pantheism is seen through a cool, calculating, mathematical eye. Not that religion and mathematics represented to Pythagoras opposing points of view. Rather they were two inseparable factors in a single world view. The central notions which held these two elements together were those of contemplation, orderliness, and purification. By contemplating the order revealed in the universe, especially in mathematics, music, and the regular movement of the heavenly bodies, and by assimilating themselves to that orderliness, individuals are progressively purified until they eventually escape from the cycle of birth and attain immortality.

As [we know], Pythagoras derived the fundamental doctrines of his philosophy from observing the mathematical ratio that exists between the lengths of string required to produce different notes at a particular tension. Indeed, the key Pythagorean view that the real and comprehensible nature of things was to be found in proportion and number came to him largely from these observations, which formed the basis of both the belief in universal harmony and the image of celestial music. Many times these various ideas became fused into a simplified conception of Pythagoreanism as holding that the universe is regulated by rhythm.

In **"Ama tu ritmo. . . "** one senses, through the poet's use of self-directed commands and the shorter, eleven-syllable lines, the imperative quality both of his desire to attune himself to the all-pervading pulse of the universe and of the universal beat itself. No longer, as in **"La espiga,"** is the setting idyllic or the unity of life immediately evident; rather the poet must strive to perceive and to achieve harmony. Thus the lyricism of the previous poem gives way to crisp, assertive tone; its long, flowing lines to short, abrupt phrases; and its pastoral scene to arithmetic and geometric signs and symbols. The poet tells himself: "Ama tu ritmo y ritma tus acciones/bajo su ley, así como tus versos." He feels an obligation to obey the rhythm of the universe—seen here as divine law—because he has singled himself out as the most capable of integrating himself into this rhythm, thereby achieving harmony in his life and in his poetry.

Since Pythagoreans hold that from the moment that God is manifest he is simultaneously indivisible essence and divisible substance and that the physical manifestations of God, both human beings and the universe, are made in his image, Darío's conception of himself and his works is enhanced. This traditional solution to the problem of the One and the Many and its implications are elaborated and reworked in lines 3 through 8 of **"Ama tu ritmo. . . ."**

eres un universo de universos,
y tu alma una fuente de canciones.

La celeste unidad que presupones,
hará brotar en ti mundos diversos;
y al resonar tus números dispersos
pitagoriza en tus constelaciones.

The poet is told that he is a universe of universes, for he is a microcosm which ideally should be a perfect reproduction of that harmonious macrocosm. His soul is a source of songs, for the enlightened poet distills and transforms into poetry the music of the spheres that reverberates within him. Yet clearly the poet's accord with the universe does not stop there. As Darío contemplates the divine unity, he assimilates its productive qualities and becomes the origin of new life and diverse worlds. Since these diverse worlds of art and beauty are patterned on universal harmony, their fundamental nature is proportion and number. Hence, at the same time that the celestial unity is harmoniously reflected within the constellations of Darío's poetic worlds, the reading of Darío's poetry causes his "números dispersos" to re-echo within the universe. In this way, Darío establishes within the quatrains a series of parallel mirrors in which the harmonious universe is reflected in the artist and his or her works while the artist's image and views of the universe are reflected back. Acoustically Darío communicates the sensation of echo through the purposeful use of repetition throughout the poem. The word "versos" reappears in "uni*verso* de uni*versos*" and in "di*versos*," "divina" reappears in "a*divina*," and "urna" in "noct*urna*" and "tacit*urna*." In addition, "dispersos" echoes "diversos" in the second quatrain.

After the normal pause, the sonnet "resumes" with a series of commands that continue the injunctions of the first line and maintain the imperative tone of the poem.

Ecucha la retórica divina
del pájaro del aire y la nocturna
irradiación geométrica adivina;

mata la indiferencia taciturna,
y engarza perla y perla cristalina
en donde la verdad vuelca su urna.

Once again the poet is told to attune himself to universal harmony: to listen to the enlightened song of the bird and to solve the riddle of the geometric movement of the stars. The chiasmus of the first tercet and the greater fluidity of these lines suggest that Darío senses that he is approximating his goal. The commands remain as a warning that he always be vigilant. For this reason the poem concludes with an appeal that the poet eliminate silent indifference and neglect and that he string together "perla y perla cristalina/en donde la verdad vuelca su urna." The final imagery is more fully understood in light of another of Darío's poems, **"Lírica"**, written in 1902:

Todavía está Apolo triunfante, todavía
gira bajo su lumbre la rueda del destino
y viértense del carro en el diurno camino
las ánforas de fuego, las urnas de armonía.

As the later poem indicates, Darío envisions the sun as a giant urn of truth and harmony. In **"Ama tu ritmo . . . ,"** the poet is told to string together his crystalline creations, which, like the pearls of a necklace, catch and reflect the light of the sun. The ultimate mission of the enlightened poet is, as implied in the quatrains, to produce works that mirror the truth and harmony that he perceives around him.

Approximately seven years later, in April, 1908, Darío wrote another sonnet, **"En las constelaciones,"** which bears a strong resemblance to **"Ama tu ritmo . .**

. ." but which reflects a fundamental change in attitude. The undefined "nocturna irradiación geométrica" reappears as "constelaciones pitagóricas,"and the repetition, with minor variations, of the words "constelaciones," "Pitágoras," and "leía" recalls the repetition within the first line of **"Ama tu ritmo. . . ."** More importantly, the poet's concern with following the rhythm of the universe is the same in both sonnets. But the differences are crucial. In the earlier of the two, one senses the poet's recently awakened awareness of the universal law of harmony and his faith—perhaps at times a bit shaky—in his ability to follow his own commands. In the later poem, he seeks to explain—or to justify—his often unsuccessful attempts to do so. He no longer tells himself what to do; the "tú" of the earlier poems is now a "yo," and the imperatives are now indicatives. The poet states:

> En las constelaciones Pitágoras leía,
> yo en las constelaciones pitagóricas leo;
> pero se han confundido dentro del alma mía
> el alma de Pitágoras con el alma de Orfeo.

The "but" of line 3 marks the introduction of the poet's explanation of his loss of harmony—both with nature and within himself. The use of the adjective "pitagóricas" to describe the constellations emphasizes this loss. When Darío tries to read harmony in the stars, he loses touch with them; they become Pythagorean and alien. "En las constelaciones" relates the poet's internal struggle and his attempt to overcome the chaos within his soul by reestablishing contact with the order inherent in nature, an order that he seeks to re-create in his poetry.

As Erika Lorenz points out [in *Rubén Darío: "Bajo el divino imperio de la musica,"* 1960], it certainly is not surprising that Pythagoras and Orpheus should become confused in Darío's syncretic imagination, for both serve a dual, musical-religious function. Pythagoras, who is, of course, closely associated with the "music of the spheres," also symbolizes the "rhythm of all that exists." Thus, the Pythagorean law which demonstrates the unity of all life in number and proportion is linked with Orpheus's magic song, which fuses all that exists in a unity of feeling.

Darío does not deny that great beauty can be created under the aegis of feeling. He does find, however, that in his life feelings often turn into wild impulses which interfere with the pursuit of harmony. To illustrate this point, the two facets of Darío's soul that are alluded to in the first quatrain are delineated in the second as opposing forces of dissonance and consonance and as the result of two antithetical incarnations (ellipsis in original):

> Sé que soy, desde el tiempo del Paraíso, reo;
> sé que he robado el fuego y robé la armonía;
> que es abismo mi alma y huracán mi deseo;
> que sorbo el infinito quiero todavía . . .

On the one hand, Darío feels that his permanent, reincarnating soul has been sinful since the beginning of time and, as a result, that he has been an outcast. On the other,

he believes that he is aspiring and benevolent and deserving of paradise—a fact signaled by his appropriation of both fire and harmony. This split recalls the split in the personality of the centaurs and the other composite beings of **"Coloquio."** It is emphasized by the repetition of the initial "sé"of lines 5 and 6 and by the parallels established in lines 7 and 8. The "abismo" that is his soul is contrasted with the "infinito" that he is able to absorb, thereby attaining communion with the soul of the world, and his wildly uncontrollable and destructive desire is contrasted with his open-ended aspiration.

The anguish caused by the struggle within his soul is clear in the choppy, almost disjointed, structure of the first tercet, and his confusion is apparent in the use of the extended rhetorical question that begins with: "¿qué voy a hacer . . . ?" The fundamental problem, as Darío sees it, is that he cannot satisfy both aspects of his being simultaneously, and he therefore always wishes to be different from what he is. The path toward reconciliation and harmony is indicated in the second tercet by the "tortuga de oro," which shows the poet God's will.

> En la arena me enseña la tortuga de oro
> hacia dónde conduce de las musas el coro
> y en dónde triunfa, augusta, la voluntad de Dios.

As previously indicated, Darío learned from esoteric Pythagoreanism that because the entire universe is the visible unfolding of God in space and time, there is life everywhere, even in what is generally regarded as dead and inert matter. It is most often the enlightened poet who can interpret the external signs that indicate deeper meanings and internal life. Consequently, it is not unusual that the tortoise should lead Darío to the choir of the Muses or show him where God's will triumphs. Similarly, in an earlier sonnet, **"La tortuga de oro . . . ,"** written in 1900, it is the tortoise—through the signs that it traces on the carpet, the enigma that is engraved on its carapace, and the circle that is drawn in its shadow— that identifies the God that usually remains unnamed and unrecognized. In both poems, Darío concludes with a reference to the underlying music of reality and, by extension, to the universal harmony to which he seeks to attune himself in spite of his "pecho süave" and his "pensamiento parco." **"La tortuga de oro . . . "** also shows the close linking of God's will with the concept of the eternal return, an association which is only alluded to in **"En las constelaciones"** in the reference to reincarnation.

God's will is seen not in the ploddings of a tortoise across the sand but in the sweep of the birds across the sky in **"Pájaros de las islas,"** written on the island of Mallorca during the winter of 1906.

> Pájaros de las islas: en vuestra concurrencia
> hay una voluntad,
> hay un arte secreto y una divina ciencia,
> gracia de eternidad.

Here again the elements of nature reveal "la única Verdad," that is, the oneness of the universe in and through God, and once again Darío aspires to learn the divine wisdom captured in their flight in order to establish in his poetry and his soul the idyllic harmony unseen by most people.

Darío finds in the graceful movement of the birds a sign or "cifra" of a perfectly ordered and proportionate universe. He also responds to their flight aesthetically, by proclaiming it a work of art. Although ordinarily these two points of view are considered incompatible—one based on a mathematical or scientific grasp of the universe, the other on an intuitive reaction to it—Darío, following in the tradition of the Romantics and Symbolists, is able to reconcile these two approaches to nature. Harmony, which within esoteric Pythagoreanism is based on number and proportion, is for Darío an artistic standard associated with divine perfection, the Good, and the Beautiful. Nature is the supreme work of art, in which the divinely gifted and inspired poet recognizes the perfect proportions of universal harmony. By drawing upon the harmony behind the dis-organized appearance of external realities, the poet is able to capture the essence of the supernatural in his art. In this way, the complementary pairs established in stanzas 1, 2, and 5—"arte"/"ciencia," "academia"/"signos," "dicha de mis ojos"/" problemas de mi meditación"—deal with a single truth about the birds.

Darío's desire to imitate their flight and thereby capture in his poetry the secret art and divine wisdom that they embody becomes clear in the final stanza. Artistically he has achieved this objective throughout the poem. The alternating glide and flapping of the birds' wings is captured by the alternation between fourteen- and seven-syllable lines, and the oxytone rhyme in the shorter lines, all but one of which are end-stopped, contributes to a feeling of calm and order.

At the same time it is evident that the attainment of harmony is more than an artistic goal. It is a means of achieving inner peace, accord with all life, and, in turn, immortality through reunion with the single soul of the universe. For this reason, in addition to "una voluntad," "un arte secreto," and "una divina ciencia," Darío sees "gracia de eternidad" in their sweep across the heavens. He more closely joins the image of the birds with the concept of immortality by drawing upon traditional symbolism which links the soul with winged creatures. In the last stanza, Darío represents his soul as a bird that aspires to fly in unison with the others that had previously been described as "almas dulces y herméticas." As his soul is metaphorically converted into a bird, the birds are metaphorically changed into souls that have, for ages, flown in harmony with nature: "a vuestras alas líricas son las brisas de Ulises, / los vientos de Jasón." It is in this way that Darío underscores the evolutionary aspect of "la única Verdad," namely, the doctrine of transmigration of

souls, at the same time that he relates his sense of elation as his soul takes flight "con las alas puras de mi deseo abiertas/hacia la inmensidad."

The fusion of the diachronic and synchronic aspects of the oneness of the universe is evident in **"Filosofía,"** published in *Cantos de vida y esperanza* (1905) not long before the composition of **"Pájaros de las islas."** The first of the two four-line stanzas is directed to the lower creatures of the world who are informed that, because of the kinship of all life and the resulting laws of reincarnation, they can except to advance on the scale of existence and even, perhaps, attain reunion with God. For this reason, they should be grateful that they are alive. The tone of optimism and exaltation is established by the initial phrases of lines 1 and 2: "Saluda al sol, araña, no seas rencorosa./Da tus gracias a Dios, oh sapo, pues que eres." The spider and the toad are to turn skyward and to speak to the sun and to God, respectively. Yet, because the harmonious unity of life has a punitive aspect, Darío reminds these creatures that they can descend as easily as ascend on the scale of existence. The prickly crab is linked to the rose by its thorns, and mollusks have reminiscences of women. The graphic connection between women and mollusks appears to indicate that it is the sexual facet of women that has caused their return to a lower form of life.

In the second stanza, Darío once again turns to the discussion of the signs of nature and introduces the concept of "norms," which are probably demiurgic emanations of divine thought (ellipsis in original):

Sabed ser lo que sois, enigmas, siendo formas;
dejad la responsabilidad a las Normas,
que a su vez la enviarán al Todopoderoso . . .
(Toca, grillo, a la luz de la luna, y dance el oso.)

The demiurge acts on behalf of the supreme being by putting into "formas" God's concept of the world, "el enigma." Neither the forms nor the norms, which are merely divine agents, have responsibility, for all is passed on to the all-powerful. The final, fantastical commands underscore the poet's belief that it is by becoming attuned to the rhythm of life and to the music of the spheres that universal harmony can be achieved.

Most of the "signs" of the oneness of life examined so far come from the land. But in **"Marina," "Caracol,"** and **"Revelación"** the universal life force is seen in the rhythmic movement of the sea and the beating of its great heart, both of which serve as models for the poet's art and soul. Detailed studies of these three poems are presented in the article by Trueblood cited earlier. In tracing the development of the symbol of the sea from **"Sinfonía en gris mayor"** (probably from 1889) and **"Tarde del trópico"** (1892) to **"Marina"** and **"Caracol"** (both from 1903) and **"Revelación"** (1907), he discovers that "behind the various marine rhythms which Darío carried into the beat of his lines, behind the sea-sounds he transposed into verbal music, lay in addition all the sense of a single limitless life which the sea more than any other force in nature arouses." Thus it is in all the elements of nature—on land, on sea, and in the sky—that Darío perceives the single soul of the universe.

In the seven poems analyzed, Darío aspires not only to affirm the unity of life and the harmony of existence but also to integrate himself and his poetry into the hidden order of creation, thereby translating the perfection of the cosmos into a language more generally understood by humanity. He relies upon the creative use of images, acoustical patterns, verbal effects, and figures of speech in his struggle to illuminate the harmonious and living nature that—perhaps through no fault of his own—he fears he might not be able to emulate. This fear haunts him and affects his perception of his ultimate fate. As a poet and interpreter of the orderly universe, he trusts that he is among a chosen few. Yet the possibility of failure—because of the intractability of language or because of his own spiritual weaknesses—is forever present. (pp. 45–53)

Cathy Login Jrade, "Esoteric Pythagoreanism in Darío's Vision of the Universe," in her *Rubén Darío and the Romantic Search for Unity: The Modernist Recourse to Esoteric Tradition*, University of Texas Press, 1983, pp. 25–53.

SOURCES FOR FURTHER STUDY

Cardwell, Richard A. "Darío and *El Arte Puro:* The Engima of Life and the Beguilement of Art." *Bulletin of Hispanic Studies* XLVII, No. 1 (January 1970): 37–51.
    Examines philosophical attitudes in Darío's work.

Davies, Catherine. "Woman as Image in Darío's *Prosas profanas.*" *Romance Quarterly* 36, No. 3 (August 1989): 281–88.
    Analyzes Darío's use of mythological symbolism in *Prosas Profanas*, noting that the feminine "images of Western humanist culture are used to express a complex aesthetic undertaking fraught with underlying spiritual and moral conflict."

Dixon, Paul B. "Rebirth Patterns in Several Short Stories by Rubén Darío: A Distinctive Feature." *Hispanic Journal* 7, No. 2 (Spring 1986); 87–91.
    Comments on the manifestations of rebirth archetypes in Darío's stories, noting that according to the writer's view of rebirth, it is the essence of life, and not a particular subject, that survives physical death.

Ellis, Keith. *Critical Approaches to Rubén Darío.* Toronto: University of Toronto Press, 1974, 170 p.
    Commentary on various types of Darío criticism, including bibliographical criticism, structural analysis, and general assessments. Also includes an appendix, "Rubén Darío as a Literary Critic."

Fiore, Dolores Ackel. *Rubén Darío in Search of Inspiration: Greco-Roman Mythology in His Stories and Poetry.* New York: Las Americas Publishing Co., 1963, 178 p.
    Scholarly investigation of Darío's familiarity with the classical languages and myths. According to Fiore, Darío knew the classical sources primarily through French and Spanish translations.

Fitzmaurice-Kelly, James. "Some Later Poets." In his *Some Masters of Spanish Verse,* pp. 53–84. London: Oxford University Press, 1924.
    Believes that Darío's chief accomplishment was extending the possibilities of meter in Spanish poetry.

Jrade, Cathy L. "Socio-Political Concerns in the Poetry of Rubén Darío." *Latin American Literary Review* XVIII, No. 36 (July–December 1990): 36–49.
    Discusses the political implications of Darío's rejection—from the standpoint of spiritual values—of the materialism dominating human affairs.

Paz, Octavio. "The Siren and the Seashell." In his *The Siren and the Seashell and Other Essays on Poets and Poetry,* pp. 17–56. Austin: University of Texas Press, 1976.
    A poet's appreciative overview of Darío's work. In commenting on the fundamental themes, sources, and archetypes of Darío's poetry, Paz sheds light on "the current of occultism that pervades Darío's work."

Rodriguez-Peralta, Phyllis. "Christian Elements and Aesthetic-Philosophic Expression in Darío's Poetry." *Kentucky Romance Quarterly* 32, No. 2 (1985): 185–99.
    Analyzes the syncretic philosophic-religious background of Darío's poetry, positing that "Christian beliefs are interwoven on all levels of his poetry and prose."

Watland, Charles D. *Poet-Errant: A Biography of Rubén Darío.* New York: Philosophical Library, 1965, 266 p.
    Well-documented and detailed survey of Darío's life and works.

Additional coverage of Darío's life and career is contained in the following sources published by Gale Research: *Contemporary Authors*, Vol. 104; and *Twentieth-Century Literary Criticism*, Vol. 4.

Abelardo Delgado

1931–

(Full name Abelardo Barrientos Delgado; also writes under the pseudonym Abelardo) Mexican-American poet, essayist, short story writer, and novelist.

INTRODUCTION

Delgado is regarded as one of the most important literary voices to emerge from the Chicano Movement of the late 1960s and early 1970s. His poetry embodies the aims of the movement, advocating social reform for the betterment of the Chicano community and expressing anger at social injustice. Almost all of Delgado's works have been published by his own press, Barrio Publications, often in inexpensively produced editions that have not received wide distribution; as a result, his poetry has attracted little critical attention. Nevertheless, he is widely anthologized, and most collections of Chicano literature include at least one of his poems. Juan D. Bruce-Novoa has stated: "If his books have not become as widely known and read as those of Alurista, Sergio Elizondo, or Ricardo Sánchez, it is surely due to the problems of poor distribution inherent in small-scale publishing, because several of his poems, found in anthologies, must be included among the most popular and most often quoted in Chicano literature."

Delgado was born in the rural village of La Boquilla de Conchos in the state of Chihuahua, Mexico. In 1943, when he was twelve years old, he and his mother emigrated to the United States, where he later became a naturalized citizen. He attended elementary and secondary schools in El Paso, Texas, growing up amid the squalor of the area known as the Segundo Barrio, or "Second Neighborhood." After graduating from high school and marrying, Delgado worked at various jobs before being employed in 1955 as an activities director of a youth center, where he worked with underprivileged children from the barrio for the next ten years. Donaldo W. Urioste has quoted Delgado as saying that during this time he "pledged a lifetime commitment of love and struggle for those afflicted with the social illness of poverty." Delgado received a bachelor's degree

538

in secondary education from the University of Texas at El Paso in 1962, and since that time has worked for health and human services organizations and as an educator.

Unhappy with the attitude of major publishers toward Chicano authors whose work might not prove profitable, Delgado established Barrio Publications as a vehicle for issuing his own work and that of other writers. Its first publication was Delgado's *Chicano: 25 Pieces of a Chicano Mind* (1969), which contains his best-known poem, "Stupid America"—a succinct, tersely worded statement of the Chicano community's frustration at being denied creative expression in American society. Charles M. Tatum has described it as " a warning to Anglo-America to recognize and encourage the potential of the Chicano people lest it explode and be wasted." Since its inception, Barrio Publications has released more than ten additional volumes of Delgado's poetry, including *Bajo el sol de Aztlán: 25 soles de Abelardo* (1973), *Under the Skirt of Lady Justice: 43 Skirts of Abelardo* (1978), and *Unos perros con metralla (Some Dogs with a Machinegun): 25 Dogs of Abelardo* (1982).

The desire to promote social reform is a major theme in Delgado's poetry, much of which criticizes American society and its values. His work reflects the concerns of migrant and undocumented workers and the residents of the nation's barrios, and it explores the defining concepts of Chicano culture. Francisco A. Lomelí and Urioste have claimed that Delgado's poetry depicts a universalized barrio as the central focus of the Chicano experience: "He has known so many barrios that he has resolved to extract a spiritual essence from their common denominators." Delgado's stylistic approach reflects his view of himself as a poet of the common people: his language is non-metaphorical, almost prosaic, and he attempts to reach the reader with ideas rather than imagery. Written in a mixture of Spanish and English, his poetry reflects the speech patterns of the barrio. In Delgado's view, "Chicano literature's main characteristic is that it is a literature that is naturally at ease in the way that Chicanos express themselves, and that is a natural bilingualism. . . To write using natural bilingual style is a very vivid affirmation that we are here, that we are alive and well, thinking and writing in both idiomas [languages]." Delgado has also written what some critics have called an epistolary novel, *Letters to Louise* (1982), which many commentators consider to be largely autobiographical. The work is comprised of a series of letters from Santiago Flores, telling of his travels throughout America as he works to resolve the problems of migrant workers while writing and promoting Chicano literature. Delgado received the first annual Tonatiuh Prize for literature in 1977 when *Letters to Louise* was published in periodical form.

Through poetry readings given across the country, Delgado has acquired a favorable reputation in the Chicano literary community despite the absence of mainstream critical acclaim for his work. Often cited as an influence by other Chicano poets, he is highly respected for his continuing commitment to the aims of the Chicano Movement. In the view of Lomelí and Arcadio Morales, "even when he is introspective, his social commitment to humanistic and egalitarian goals is quite evident. In short, his *ars poetica* represents one of the best examples of the socially committed poetry in Chicano literature, deserving of careful literary analysis."

CRITICAL COMMENTARY

ABELARDO DELGADO

(essay date 1971)

[In the following essay, Delgado objects to the attitude of major publishers toward the Chicano community and states the need for Chicanos to develop their own publishing outlets.]

Among the institutions in this country that have either purposely or unintentionally damaged and obliterated our culture is book publishing. The dispensers of textbooks— texts that have been literally shoved down the throats of Chicanitos (whose inner sense tells them to spit them out)—have also criminally profited by these ventures. The immediate reaction of publishers in general, when confronted with such charges, is the biblical question, "When did I do all these things?" We quickly respond: When you neglected to acknowledge us, as a continuous identifiable

Principal Works

Chicano: 25 Pieces of a Chicano Mind (poetry) 1969

The Chicano Movement: Some Not Too Objective Observations (essay) 1971

Bajo el sol de Aztlán: 25 soles de Abelardo (poetry) 1973

It's Cold: 52 Cold-Thought Poems of Abelardo (poetry) 1974

A Thermos Bottle Full of Self-Pity: 25 Bottles of Abelardo (poetry) 1975?

Reflexiones: 16 Reflections of Abelardo (poetry and short stories) 1976

Here Lies Lalo: 25 Deaths of Abelardo (poetry) 1977; revised edition, 1979

Under the Skirt of Lady Justice: 43 Skirts of Abelardo (poetry) 1978

Totoncaxihuitl, A Laxative: 25 Laxatives of Abelardo (poetry and fiction) 1981

Letters to Louise (novel) 1982

Unos perros con metralla (Some Dogs with a Machine-gun): 25 Dogs of Abelardo (poetry) 1982

*This work was originally published in the journal *El Grito del Sol* in 1977.

community. This has made us invisible to the Anglo community and the Anglo, in turn, has accepted the verbatim invisibility of our Raza.

Because of you, the Anglo knows us not. Your texts, which our children learn from, have tried to make us in your image. But in the face of your constant acculturation bombardment through all media, is the word of mouth of our parents. Here, handed down to us, is a whole heritage seldom captured in a written form. For this last reason, we have a legitimate quarrel with all textbook publishers in that we want that heritage put in written form and presented—primarily from the preservation of our Chicano culture, and secondarily as a contribution of a way of life, which ultimately may be a value to offset the materialistic, destructive trend of your society.

In our anger we tried to be exponents of the lies that have been shoved upon us, and sometimes we forget that in the publishing companies now existing lies the power to make corrections and reparations. We feel that we must speak of a mutual effort to bring a needed freshness of approach and historical validity to those texts in your galley proofs. We suggest that now the Chicanos be counted as competent writers at all levels and in all fields—and that the efforts to scout out Chicano writing talent fall upon the publishing establishment. We are not hung up about

your getting a reasonable profit out of your effort. We do, however, question anything you do that is double talk or tokenism. We say there are options: either you do a job in which Chicanos have an editorial review role, or you assist us in developing parallel institutions of our own to insure that knowledgeability and sensitivity will portray our own Chicano heritage with fidelity.

More than making us invisible, your texts and other printed media have portrayed us as an unproductive and servile population. This has insured that we will play out these roles.

Our talents have not only been ignored. We have been forced to take a pseudonym and to crash into the cubicle of oppression, so that we have lacked the models that would help us to escape the *barrios* and the *campos*.

Publishers even today continue to commit the crime of presenting our *Chicanismo* through white colorless minds and through eyes which see blue in our brown. We do resent having to read about our own Raza from the [Stan] Steiners of the book world. The gentleman's skill as a writer and his knowledge of the subject is not at question but rather the snubbing attitude of publishers to rely on him to even quote what we write. In his book, *La Raza*, he mentions me and devotes some space to quoting some lines of my poetry. I wrote the company that published him. I said, we know you are making out on this book, how about a couple of thousand dollars to publish ourselves and a couple of hundred complimentary copies for the Chicanos in the *barrio* who could not afford the seven dollars for a book. A polite reply in the mail . . . we are referring your letter to the proper persons. That was months ago, and since then not a word. And you ask, what's your bitch?

That's our bitch.

As a closing statement, let me recall a recent incident in which a big publishing company invited some Chicanos in a community to a luncheon and at the end handed each a questionnaire to outline our woes (in 25 words or less). Some of us, sensing the insult, demanded that a different approach be offered and that higher-ups in the company talk to us. It happened days later, that a couple of them offered to talk with us.

My own poem **"Stupid America"** best cries out these complaints.

> stupid america, see that chicano
> with a big knife
> on his steady hand
> he doesn't want to knife you
> he wants to sit on a bench
> and carve christfigures
> but you won't let him.
>> stupid america, hear that chicano
>> shouting curses on the street
>> he is a poet
>> without paper and pencil
>> and since he cannot write

he will explode.
stupid america, remember that chicanito
flunking math and english
he is the picasso
of your western states
but he will die
with one thousand masterpieces
hanging only from his mind.

We Chicanos are at that stage of development in which we are highly cognizant of the social discrepancies which our country has rendered us. For this reason we will develop our own publishing outlets at the risk of investing our very meager resources, but we Chicanos are also wise to the game by now. We will not allow the publishers to profit at our expense or do any injustice to our *causa* in our *own* country.

For most of us, more is at stake than a few of us making a few bucks by literally selling out our talents, since our prime concern happens to be social improvement for all, rather than literary advancement for a few.

Abelardo Delgado, in *Publisher's Weekly*, Vol. 199, No. 11, March 15, 1971, p. 38.

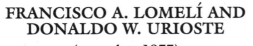

FRANCISCO A. LOMELÍ AND DONALDO W. URIOSTE

(essay date 1977)

[In the following excerpt from an essay which was originally published in Spanish in *De Colores*, Lomelí and Urioste consider how Delgado's poetry reflects the Chicano experience of life in the barrio.]

[Abelardo Delgado] stands out as an errant troubadour who collects emotive and geographical impressions from his journeys. He has set out on an odyssey, having outgrown his own place of origin in order to embrace the meaning of the total Chicano experience. But he ventures out only to find himself in the "other," and returns recovered from the flagellations he has suffered: "vuelo sin plumas y sin mapa y con una ala mala ["**Atardecer un junio**"]. As a quixotic sower of hopes, he scatters seeds throughout Aztlán. Abelardo commits himself to an altruistic messianism to benefit Man with what he calls: ". . . mi arma es más potente, es un violento amor" ["**La violencia**"]. Through his persistent travels, he traces an experiential 'road map' as he explores places and subjectivizes what he has observed. The power of his poetry lies in the fact that he becomes inspired from his journeying, which urges him to recall the circumstances of his people. He puts in Chicano terms everything that he sees with a collective eye. He sees a Barrio with a capital letter, that is, Aztlán. For that reason he has named one of

his poems "**Dondequiera que nos paramos el suelo es nuestro.**" He always carries the barrio inside him, as an integral part of his innermost self, even though he may not refer to it directly. He does not confine the barrio within physical boundaries, though it is obvious that he has nourished himself from the spatial element. He has known so many barrios that he has resolved to extract a spiritual essence from their common denominators. His barrio is the conceptualization of a belief which preaches respect for cultural pluralism.

Abelardo is troubled by a basic preoccupation when he writes "I'm worried about my soul. . . it's cold" ["**From Lewiston To Boise**"]. By this it should not be understood that his soul is cold; rather, the poet feels a coldness and lack of understanding overtaking his soul little by little. He decries the current social phenomenon by which the Chicano is made marginal in two ways: first as a man in contemporary times, and secondly *vis-à-vis* the insensitive Angloamerican society. He does not address his poetry to a strictly Chicano reader/audience because he claims that a people cannot liberate itself alone. He is determined to solve the social dialectics of exploited and exploiters by offering humanizing values through his barrio conscience, for example, carnalismo (meaning more than brotherhood). To achieve this objective, Abelardo tries to persuade with moderate and logical reasoning, without resorting to the rhetoric that he scorns without hesitation. His vindictive efforts, nevertheless, at times lead him to escape, for an instant, away from the outside world to strengthen his sense of mission and thereby to continue the 'divine' struggle. When he vacillates, he goes within himself even more, to find 'the authentic' in his dreams:

> . . . ya no quiero pintar mi verso gris
> ya que no quiero escribir
> de lo que veo sino de lo que sueño.
>
> [*Ya no*]

He seeks the inner reality that originated in his mental barrio, lived in experience. It is here that Chicano intrahistory is glorified with lightstrokes. He focuses on a future and almost never looks back. In this manner he attempts to recreate society according to a reconstructed social-ethical base. For instance, his poem **"Why am I here?"** describes the desired ideal without making distinctions.

> my spirit seeks noble and worthy fulfillment of my
>   dreams,
> a place where no one against another any longer
>   schemes
> and where the word 'underprivileged' is buried,
> yea, carnal, if i'd known earlier i'd have hurried.

In Abelardo we see an active protagonist of his time. His poetry is not phrased in overly worked metaphors but in a prose style. He thinks in terms of ideas, not images. Furthermore, the use of frequent rhyme—remembered easily by the reader—lends itself to oral recitation as well as to individual reading. As a poet he is conscious of becoming a spokesman and a medium of truth. In his poem **"The Poet as a Mirror,"** he assumes the function of a mirror and of what he calls "a human x-ray machine." He believes himself to have surpassed the capabilities of an x-ray machine because he transcends a single function: not only does he reproduce images, but also he interprets them or facilitates their interpretation:

> . . . the poet/mirror interprets
> what's not there
> visible to the unpoetic eye.

He plays out the role of the artist who elucidates what is out of focus so that others may see it as it is. Up to this point, we have shown a poet who assimilates the positive from the barrio, but this changes radically in the poem entitled **"El barrio,"** where he vitalizes it in a direct manner. Here he develops the radiography of a cobweb atmosphere, consumed by the most extreme state of oppression. As he personifies it, the barrio unfolds as an infernal vicious circle, as "progress' sore thumb." It does not appear idealized. On the contrary, it is seen as an internal colony, ignored and considered inferior by the macrocosm that encircles it: "I am that piece of land 'la ciudad' is trying to hide." Due to its alienation, the barrio has not been able to become incorporated into the mainstream; moreover, it has suffered something worse than invasion by evil forces: abandonment. Its cries for help

are answered only by forces that exploit its depressed condition. The barrio-narrator exposes a shocking reality to impact the reader/listener, hoping that its desperate pleas may be heard. It is implicit that the barrio will strip itself of infra-human elements when stagnation is eliminated. With this poem Abelardo criticizes the lack of opportunity, indicating that the barrio has been subjected to the lie of the American Dream, to neglect and to its own venom. (pp. 12–16)

Francisco A. Lomelí and Donaldo W. Urioste, "The Concept of the Barrio in Three Chicano Poets: Abelardo Delgado, Alurista and Ricardo Sanchez," translated by Francisco Lomelí and Sonia Zuñiga, in *Grito del Sol*, Vol. 2, No. 4, October–December, 1977, pp. 9–24.

ABELARDO DELGADO WITH JUAN D. BRUCE-NOVOA

(interview date 1978)

[In the following interview, conducted by mail in the summer of 1978, Delgado discusses his views on Chicano literature. The interview is prefaced by Bruce-Novoa's analysis of "Stupid America" as a characteristic example of Chicano poetry.]

One of the most succinct examples of Chicano protest poetry is Abelardo Delgado's **"Stupid America."** Textual analysis establishes many of the characteristics of Chicano poetry.

> stupid america, see that chicano
> with a big knife
> in his steady hand
> he doesn't want to knife you
> he wants to sit on a bench
> and carve christfigures
> but you won't let him.
> stupid america, hear that chicano
> shouting curses on the street
> he is a poet
> without paper and pencil
> and since he cannot write
> he will explode.
> stupid america, remember that chicanito
> flunking math and english
> he is the picasso
> of your western states
> but he will die
> with one thousand masterpieces
> hanging only from his mind.

The poem violently laments the wasting of aesthetic talents through ignorance on the part of the United States. Time is telescoped to encompass the past and future, while centering on the present. The Christ-carving sculptor evokes the image of the *santero*, the traditional carver of religious statues in Spanish Colonial provinces occupying the present Southwest of the United States. Abelardo recalls a centuries-old art form unfamiliar to the majority of Americans, Anglo-Americans and Chicanos alike. The reference is a synecdoche for the Hispanic society of the Southwest, unified through religious belief and cultural tradition. By extension, Abelardo challenges the misconception of the Atlantic coast origins of U.S. culture perpetuated in biased textbooks and popularized by "How the West Was Won" type propaganda. The future is evoked through Picasso, the epitome of the modern artist and, of course, a Spaniard of universal influence. The reference projects the santero's cultural tradition into a futuristic time zone from the perspective of the stereotypical image of the backward Chicano. The apparently gratuitous image of Picasso is adroitly pertinent—it challenges the U.S. claim to leadership in modernity, for this country has no artist to rival Picasso. Picasso revamped art, first by defining modern multiperspectivism—Cubism—then by reviewing and renewing traditional art forms through a series of actualizing parodies. Moreover, the santero and Picasso share what is the essence of Chicanismo, the art of synthesis. The santero adopted European aesthetics to the rather primitive, limited conditions of the peripheral colonies, creating a distinctive art through practical synthesis. The fact that synthesis also involved indigenous influences is significant. Picasso, in his parodies, synthesized traditional and modern trends to create a forward-moving art at a time of general cultural crisis. Abelardo subtly, implicitly proclaims the Hispanic capacity for progress through regeneration, without the chaotic rejection of the past so associated with U.S. culture. Thus Abelardo offers the United States a possibility of salvation.

Between the sculptor and the painter, in the center, and by implication at the present moment, stands the poet, referenceless except as the author's persona. The poet desires to transform his "oral" expression into written form, but America obstructs him by refusing to provide materials—an image of economic/racial oppression. America wastes the significant contribution that the Chicano could make. The reference to "flunking math and english" underscores a constant leitmotif in Chicano literature: the school system as the hostile agent of socialization, intolerant of alternative forms of American culture.

The poem rises above commonplace protest doggerel through its imagery, which concentrates, in each section of the poem, on the hand as a creative or destructive instrument. The outcome is left in the balance, to be decided in the future—will the hand be allowed to constructively contribute to America or be forced to destroy it? The poem didactically instructs the majority culture to look beyond appearances, to overcome its racist paranoia, to cease being stupid, and to open itself to the positive contribution of Chicano culture. At the same time, it implicitly instructs the Chicanos to redirect their aggression into constructive pursuits, ones which are not alien, but traditionally Hispanic. (In passing, it should be noted that the poem alludes to the contrast of U.S. culture as technological ["math"] and Chicano culture as artistic or aesthetic. This appeal to the aesthetic order is found also in the works of Rodolfo Gonzales, José Montoya, Tino Villanueva, Ricardo Sánchez, and Alurista.)

By centering the frustration and the poetic space in the poet's dilemma, Abelardo creates a truly Chicano image. At the heart of the matter he places a divided self caught between apparently opposite poles—here, methods of expression: oral or written—which in truth are two aspects of the self: the mouth and the hand. At the same time, the division is between the Mexican—oral tradition—and the American—written tradition. Yet the Chicano has a right to both. Chicanos must learn from the images offered by the poem and synthesize a new unity of oral and written expressions, the curse and art, the mouth (spirit) and the hand (body). Otherwise they will remain divided and, in turn, undermine the society in which they live; from the perspective of U.S. society, if the Mexican culture is not allowed its legitimate place, the divided society will self-destruct. Chicanismo is the positive answer.

Finally, in a manner characteristic of the most significant Chicano works, this poem responds to itself by the fact of its own existence. The poem states the Chicano's frustration at not being permitted expression in U.S. society. The poem, however, is the author's realization of expression within the written medium denied his poetic persona; it is the sign and proof of his recuperated unity. It should be noted that the written poem maintains the shouted curses of the oral expression—"stupid america!" Abelardo shouts in violent lament when he recites the poem. Moreover, the realization of the goal of writing does not cancel out the original situation; America ignores santeros and the Hispanism of Picasso, and it will ignore Abelardo's poem. Yet the poem transcends the stupid rigidity of U.S. culture by claiming a space for itself in the U.S. written tradition—the fact that it is in English is not coincidental—while remaining faithful to Chicano concerns and its oral origins. The poem is thus revolutionary in its challenge of unyielding "stupidity" and its seizure of the space denied the Chicano artist.

This synthesis of apparent opposition without abandoning one's ethnic heritage is the most Chicano note of all. Abelardo synthesizes cultures apparently hopelessly at odds. Not that he falsifies reality—no, the poem faithfully reflects the conflict and even ends on a pessimistic note. But the fact of the poem's existence is already a step toward transcending the impasse. By applying the method he evokes—aesthetic and cultural synthesis—Abelardo achieves his poem, a lesson in Chicanismo. (pp. 11–14)

. . . . .

One of the most prolific of the quality Chicano poets, Abelardo, as he is usually referred to, has published to date four books of poetry *(Chicano: 25 Pieces of a Chicano Mind,* 1969; *Bajo el sol de Aztlán: 25 soles de Abelardo,* 1973; *It's Cold: 52 Cold Thought-Poems of Abelardo,* 1974; and *Reflexiones,* n.d.); has contributed a major portion to *Los cuatro,* 1970; has published pieces in many magazines; and has been anthologized in several Chicano collections.

If his books have not become as widely known and read as those of Alurista, Sergio Elizondo, or Ricardo Sánchez, it is surely due to the problems of poor distribution inherent in small-scale publishing, because several of his poems, found in anthologies, must be included among the most popular and most often quoted in Chicano literature. **"Stupid America," "La Causa," "The Organizer," "El Vendido," "El Chisme,"** and **"The New Cross"** are now classics. Among Chicano poets Abelardo is often spoken of as a model and inspiration, and in my conversations with them, several have called him an influence—thematic, technical, and spiritual—on their work. At another level, his enthusiastic readings still excite and move audiences as they used to in the late 1960s, when no mass demonstration of Chicanos in the state of Colorado was complete without Abelardo's voice screaming his poetic synthesis of the Chicano Movement at its emotional peak. As Alurista says, Abelardo's true genre is declamation.

For some years Abelardo has been writing a type of epistolary essay (which someone should study as a possible influence on Ricardo Sánchez's particular hybrid writing). His prose manuscript was awarded the first annual Tonatiuh Prize for literature in 1977. The work, *Cartas a Louise,* is made up of a series of writings in the vein of Abelardo's letter/essays, with the difference that now he has created a fictional character, Santiago Flores, who bears more than a casual resemblance to Abelardo. Flores's letters, with some poetry interspersed at times, are presented as if Louise had given them to Abelardo, who then enters them in the Tonatiuh contest with the hope that by winning, Santiago Flores will be drawn back into public life, after having disappeared into despair and anonymity. This award may bring Abelardo his long overdue recognition.

A first draft of this interview was published in the *Revista Chicano-Riqueña* 4, no. 4 (Fall 1976). It appears here completely revised and greatly extended. Abelardo's responses can be dated from the summer of 1978. The translation of Spanish portions was done by Maricela Oliva.

[Bruce-Novoa]: *When and where were you born?*

[Delgado]: I was born in La Boquilla de Conchos, Chihuahua, Mexico, November 27, 1931. Funny how one always seems to find the time to talk about oneself. . . I would lie if I were to say I remember La Boquilla, the little village where I was born. Because of that I made it a point to visit and get a grown-up view rather than a child's memory. It is a church and a few adobe houses plus the customary kiosk. It is a tourist place because of the famous Boquilla bass which can be caught behind the Boquilla dam. My padrino [godfather], if he is still alive, has a boat for rent in a restaurant-bar called El Tigre. My two abuelas [grandmothers] constantly would talk of La Boquilla and consequently I believe myself to know it. It does occasionally and subconsciously emerge in some of my versos [poems] or prosa [prose]. Because the images of what is true are so blurry they become fantasies at times.

Describe your family background and your present situation.

All of my family consisted of two females, an abuela [grandmother] and a mother. I'm an only son on my mother's side, and have seven half brothers on my father's side. They and my father live in Mexico. Never had a real father but had my share of those who assumed that role. I did get to be greatly influenced by a great-grandmother a lot. I have tried to capture these two abuelitas [grandmothers] in a couple of poems. My mother lives in Santa Paula, California, but is still a Mexican national. She and I came into the U.S. in 1943. Since 1943 to 1969, plus one year that I came back, sums up my actual time spent in El Paso. This bridges the tail end of the Pachuco era. The caló [slang] fascinated the hell out of me and I made it a point to study it even at that early age, even though I did not know that was what I was doing. I would ask people, my Pachuco carnales [brothers], why they used this word and what meaning lay behind it. Most certainly such a huge chunk of my life is the bulk of my pool of experiences from which episodes can be drawn plentifully. Ten years of heavy influence by the Catholic Church, as I worked for a Jesuit priest for that length of time. That religious influence, which ranges from the fanatic to the very pragmatic (the Jesuit priest is German), constantly shows up in my writings. I can very easily use all kinds of space elaborating on my various involvements and present activities, so I hope you bear with me as I try to capsule them out. . . I presently am doing research on farm workers, computers and all of that. . . we are gathering data on one hundred thousand farm workers. This work keeps me moving throughout the nation. I work with the Colorado Migrant Council; back in '69 and the next two years I was the executive director of this outfit. I have taught three years in Utah, one in UTEP [University of Texas at El Paso], and some summers here in Boulder. I have also worked in the northwest getting a health consumer corporation off the ground. I do a lot of readings and a lot of training work plus involving myself with all kinds of pertinent issues. . . such as the undocumented workers' struggle and the Bakke thing. Basically I show and share a lot of enthusiasm in trying out new ideas and that is where I feel more at home, thus creating programs, alternative education options, dreams that at times crumble into plumitas [feathers]. . . I have come to the conclusion that much value lies in merely gathering and disseminating information, so that I have been doing that on the side.

Presently I'm married to the former Dolores Estrada and have eight children. The eldest, 23, is married and lives in El Paso, Texas. My youngest daughter is seven years old. I have two grandchildren.

When did you first begin to write?

I think the earliest I can pinpoint my writing efforts dates back to my elementary school years when I edited a newspaper in the third grade and wrote short cuentos [tales] and verses as well as essays. Later on in junior and senior high school I began to win some prizes for essays and letters, as well as to collect some of my poems. My early experiences in writing were mostly all Spanish or all English. I did not think mixing both was cool.

What kind of books did you read in your formative years?

If by my formative years you mean my childhood years, they were spent in Mexico, where I taught myself to read and write in Spanish. During these years my readings were limited to two daily comic books with continuous stories. They were *El Pepín* and *El Chamaco Chico*. Once in the U.S., I hurried up to learn English to enjoy the variety of comic books of those days, '43 to '50 approximately. I did not have preferences when it came to comics; I took them all. I did go after Classics and others that showed more depth in their plots; without knowing it then I was yearning for literary satisfaction out of those monitos [comic books]. I do not see any influence from those comics. I have always been drawn by the human dilemma, which is plentiful now as it was then.

In school I was exposed to the regular assigned readings: ". . . And Tell of Time," *A Tale of Two Cities*, and Shakespeare. My sister gave me *El Quijote* about then, and another friend, *The Brothers Karamazov*, which I read previous to my going to college. I got interested later on in Mickey Spillane and other paperbacks. I always read particularly that which was prohibited, like *The Tales of the Decameron* and *Forever Amber*. When it comes to books, I cannot honestly say that much remains, as I believe I have always read for the sheer enjoyment and not to see what I get out of books. It is obvious that all that reading has helped me to augment my expression, literary as well as simply communicative. My taste range is so weird that I cannot single out specific books. I go from pornography to religious and I guess the only thing that turns me off about books in general is the darn time it takes me to read just one. I am a very slow reader and read thirty or so pages at a time. I would advise my Chicano carnales [brothers] in general to match their taste to some set of authors and to exhaust their material so that the influence can really be beneficial. Those with inclinations to be poets or writers I would advise lots of care that you do not get into the trap of wanting to be like so and so, and that you develop your own style and say what is really yours to say and quit any attempts at imitation. The world has enough mimics; we need more creative minds.

What is the extent of your studies?

I have gone through a Bachelor of Science degree and some postgraduate courses, as far as my formal education.

Has formal education helped or hindered you as a writer?

I would say education has helped me in two great ways, by expanding the necessary vocabulary in both English and Spanish, and secondly by giving me a general range of challenging basics to write about and exposing me to a few stimulating professors with beautiful minds and hearts as well as a creative spirit. Other than that, my own life experience is the basic source of inspiration and material from which I draw, as well as a vocabulary I would not necessarily have picked up in my formal education.

I would recommend to those who want to indulge in the curse of the pen to write and write every chance they have. Rather than any specific subject I would recommend exercises which can be done without maestros [teachers] or schools, such as doing profiles of people, trying to describe their manners, their physical highlights, their moods, etc., etc. I find driving in a bus much more creative than the whole bunch of creative writing courses I have seen. The writing and writing bit I recommend is for writers to arrive by that process at their own style and their own forte and then cultivate that strength. Of course as you write and write you will also notice your weaknesses. Rather than asking anyone what they think of your writings, just share them and learn to read their expressions as they read it.

Which was the predominant language in your home as a child? Which do you speak more fluently now?

The predominant language in my home has always been Spanish and I'm certain that continues to be the language in which I express myself best; yet my command of English is such that comparatively speaking the vocabulary inventory in English may be as extensive.

When I write it is a very special process. I literally give birth to the ideas which wiggle in me wanting to come out. To see in front of you, on paper, ideas that were but moments earlier all disarranged in your mind is quite a feeling of accomplishment which is more fuel and more inspiration for those of us who write. We have our dry spells in which for whatever reasons nos tapamos [we block ourselves] and nothing comes out. Those moments, long as they may be, are also part of the total process. The spirit is creative and spontaneous, at least it is that way in me, and when you gotta write you gotta write even if the tools are an old crayon and a napkin. I have just said that when an idea is ready to out and become a short story, a novel, or a short verso [poem] it is almost kicking out of me; thus it has already its gender. We can ovulate as well in English or in Spanish, or mixed. . . you can say the genes are there and we at times do not know what we will be creating until it is in front of us. It is like a pregnant woman who knows she has a baby en la panza [in her belly] but does not know if the baby will be a boy or a girl and prieto or quero [dark or fair]. The background I can give you about my personal writing habits is that I tend to be prolific and turn out great quantities of stuff. In doing this I sacrifice quality and turn out a lot of junk; among the junk once in a while, sometimes, I turn out something that impresses even me. I know I will never be a good writer because I am basically too lazy to polish what I do, but I also know that few people have the ability to present so many ideas in so many ways as I do. I began to learn to speak English at the age of twelve when my vocabulary was actually zero, despite the fact I used to love movies (with subtitles in Spanish; thus I never paid much attention to the sound). I started at the age of twelve and now at the age of forty-six I am still learning. This was in El Paso along with other Chicanos chorreados como yo [bedraggled like myself] who really did not realize that learning the language well could have some payoffs in the long run.

Does Chicano literature have a particular language or idiom?

Chicano literature's main characteristic is that it is a literature that is naturally at ease in the way that Chicanos express themselves, and that is a natural bilingualism, with the influence of English naturally predominant, as that is the language in which all Chicanos are educated. As far as an idiom, if I can detect the thin difference applicable to Chicano literature, we can say that Chicano literature is heavily spiced with caló [slang] and a sort of regionalism, and even ungrammatical standard expressions which give it flavor peculiar to Chicanos. To write using natural bilingual style is a very vivid affirmation that we are here, that we are alive and well, thinking and writing in both idiomas [languages], and that there are many like us out there in that mythical Aztlán who also think and talk and write as we do. To list writers and explain by examples of their writings this phenomenon is a bit redundant and causes a problem of saying that those carnalitos and carnalitas [brothers and sisters] writing monolingually in either Spanish or English no andan en la onda [are not in step]. Among Chicano writers some of us tend to favor mixing the two languages, at times naturally or at times calculatedly, for effect, and se vale [it's O.K.], but it is no big deal. Let it suffice to repeat that in the total sum of Chicano literature, bilingualistic mix, even more than two languages at times, is a trademark too big to ignore.

How do you perceive your role as a writer vis-à-vis: (a) the Chicano community or Movement; (b) U.S. society; (c) literature itself?

The way I perceive my role vis-à-vis the Chicano community (Movement) is in a triple-whammy manner.

One role is that of a recorder for Chicano events, happenings, victories, defeats, struggles from a poetic perspective absent from newspapers and prose journals. The other role is that of "animator" to give spirit and even at times philosophical direction and criticism. And yet a third role is to serve as a model in our own communities for other writers to follow in developing their own creative spirits. I could say that not all writing that I do can be considered literature per se, but a lot of my efforts have been dedicated to writing proposals, evaluations, letters of recommendation, teaching modules, etc., etc. I certainly do make a distinction between the Chicano community and the Chicano Movement. Therefore the role of a Chicano writer may very well be viewed from various perspectives. When I write I keep them all in mind.

As far as my role in relation to U.S. society, I do not see how the dominant segment affecting our lives can be ignored either as an audience or as a subject. It is not necessarily the intent, at least mine, to limit my literary expression to theme or audience. The thing is, we as Chicanos are very much a part of U.S. society, and being absent from the literary scene is but one of the calculated, forced exclusions we have experienced and are trying to correct.

As far as literature itself, it must be considered from an artistic and universal perspective, and my role is to introduce myself as part of the continuous process and even impose myself as a contemporary and future influence.

What is the place of Chicano literature within U.S. literature?

The question bothers me, since U.S. literature is not an abstract box which other literatures are fitted in; but Chicano, Black, Native American, and Asian American literary expression, long absent from American literature, have designated by their absence American literature as an incomplete representative of American literary efforts. A true fact is that Chicano literature is an emerging and imposing form needed to make American literature truly complete. Chicano literature does not bring any thing to American literature because it too is American literature. This was not a good question, I am afraid; I cannot field it without getting a bit angry that you would even ask it. What it brings, not to literature but to the dominant world of Anglos, is a chance for them to look at us as we look at ourselves, and that is a minor part of the total Chicano effort to be acknowledged as equals in the full sense of the word without the bullshit of affirmative action.

What is the relationship of Chicano literature to Mexican literature?

The relationship is a very natural one, as among Chicano writers a great portion of us have our native roots in la Madre Patria [Mother Country]. Some Chicano writers are Mexican or at least extensions or descendants of Mexicans making great literary contributions. Again the question of the movement is relevant here in that a stronger bondage is felt by those who have dedicated themselves to the question of using literature as a vehicle of social protest, whether Chicanos or Mexican nationals. Some of us Chicanos envy the way our brothers to the south handle the Spanish word, and they must laugh at times at our shortcomings in that respect, but all in all the brotherhood is a felt and real one. Lately, exchanging articles, poetry, and publications has become a more extensive effort. I would have to say that of all the carnales and carnalas I know who write, very few, if any, are influenced by Mexican writers. I for one do not even know who they are. Not that they are not important and that we should not read them, make efforts even to read them, but right now those chains are not too well built. The fault may lie in the crazy Spanish departments of all U.S. institutions of higher learning who have a bias against Mexico and pump us full of Spain and Latin America before they acknowledge the literary forces of Mexico.

The question of "crítica" [criticism] is a valid international question in which we can develop international critics in both English and Spanish. By international critics I have in mind first of all creating a bond between writers and poets from here and writers and poets from Central and South America, and then exchanging books and material for comment, and ultimately identifying people who can offer crítica [criticism]. The function that they would serve would firstly go to weeding out bad material from quality works and relating Chicano literature in a much wider, international, context. It would be understood that from among Chicano writers some critics would emerge. By now, that I write this, there are already a good dozen individuals whose specialty of work is criticism of Chicano lit and among them some who also criticize works of writers south of the border.

Do you perceive yourself and your work as political?

Whether I do or do not see myself and my writings as political is really not important; the truth is, all writing and person are political in one way or another. In my case it certainly is a more calculated way of life, and my work can easily be identified in the areas of raising questions both inside and outside the Chicano community which are socially and politically motivated. When I inspire my Chicano brothers to rid themselves of all oppression and to rid themselves of hang-ups and complexes, when I speak directly to the dominant oppressive society and point to their neglect and abuse, I am being very political, but you could easily substitute the word "Christian" for "political."

Does the Chicano writer have anything in common with the majority group writers? Differences?

Some of us Chicanos have had some occasion to share expressions and jointly do readings, conferences, or seminars with other writers, with the majority group writers. These occasions are yet few and far between and most of us continue very much on the fringe, some by

design and some by choice. We have found that the majority of Anglo writers are very much in tune (or us with them) when it comes to using literature, poetry in particular, to criticize the obvious abuses that are committed world-wide by our country and all the social neglect, insensitivity, and racism. They too write of a better America, a better world, a real humanity, a start for the use of our divinity. The differences we have, at least those I have noted, have to do with the styles, handling of subjects, and of course the different cultures, values, life styles, and experiences, and most certainly the vocabulary. By being Chicanos, writers contrast with Anglo writers in that certain themes can only be handled vividly by them and Anglos would be at a disadvantage at trying to refer to them with realism and feeling. One obvious one would be the experience of discrimination by Anglos themselves. Most certainly Anglos do not discriminate against other Anglos. There is the white goddess complex, or racially mixed love affairs; only the Chicano can feel and write about such experience and describe what Chicanos feel. The barrio growing-up thing is netamente [genuinely] a Chicano subject. The styles in which these themes are handled are again subject to phrases and words which are part of the Chicano totality of experience and which are used by Anglos only as second-hand observers. When it comes to values it is a new ball game. Chicanos and Anglos both bear the brunt of society in general and both at times have the same value outlook on things and both can write about love, war, life, death, success, and depending on the degree of acculturation of the Chicano, writers offer us a different interpretation of similar episodes. Three novels exemplify this: *Bless Me, Ultima, The Revolt of the Cockroach People*, and *Peregrinos de Aztlán.*

Does Chicano literature share common ground with Black literature? Differences?

Chicanos and Blacks, Native Americans, too, for that matter, have in common the obligation of amplifying in their literature, of dramatizing, las quejas de su gente [the protests of their people], the misery, the struggle, and the heroic survival they undergo. The style of writing and the degree of imitation of the whiteman's literature as a model varies. Most of us do not go around just reading other Chicanos, so that we tend to read what those writers from the dominant culture are writing. Some of us knowingly or subconsciously get influenced by what we read. After all the English language is no sole domain of theirs and whatever we write is bound to look like what someone else wrote. I would say because Blacks do not have another language pool to draw from other than English, in contrast to Chicanos and Boricuas, they would be subject to greater influence form Anglo writers on the pure use of language and plot than we would. The influence is neither positive or negative but depends on what it is we copy or use from any particular Anglo writer.

Another major difference has to do with our own audiences and the degree to which our literature is appreciated and well received by our own people in contrast to the dominant society. People who read what we Chicano writers write are either other Chicanos or minorities or the dominant society in general. It is obvious that the two audiences or readerships are looking at who we create with different eyes and minds. Even among those Chicanos who read what we write there are degrees of acceptance, rejection, relating, as they come from various strata in our own communities. You cannot expect a Chicano banker to relate to a compesino, or a businessman to a pinto [convict] or tecato [drug addict] poem or story. The question of art and the question of how effective we are with what we create are two questions which determine the impact we have. The truth is that we can make classes and races relate to each other and use our works as bridges for them to meet.

Is there any relationship with the literature of other Spanish-speaking groups?

The literature of Portorriqueños is quite similar to that of Chicanos in theme and style. There is a great resemblance to that of other revolutionary people in South America. Some of the Chicano writers, having been educated formally, pick up Spanish (from Spain) poets and authors of the magnitude of Cervantes and Lorca, and consciously or subconsciously, go on to imitate those styles. The short cuento [story] and the poetry have more in common with each other than do novels, generally speaking. Rather than give you examples I will only refer you to *Revista Chicano-Riqueña*, in which the Boricuas and the Chicanos are often placed page to page and one can immediately find the strong resemblances of styles and themes. In the recent Canto al Pueblo festival in Corpus [Christi, Texas, 1978], about five Portorriqueños got up to read, and for some of us who do not get a chance to listen to them it was quite a treat. They take characters from the barrio, or from the drug culture, or the struggle, who are easy to interchange with Chicanos. In exchanging opinions with those who have traveled to Cuba and to other parts of S.A., as Morton and Raúl Salinas do constantly, they rediscover a direct relationship with revolutionary poets and writers. The other art form of canción de protestas [protest songs] brings forth these relationships much better.

Does Chicano literature have a distinct perspective on life? What effect does it have on the literature?

The main criterion from which to recognize Chicano literature, other than the author having told you he is Chicano, is the very distinct perspective on life; our culture, which is, after all, our values or perspectives on life, is different, so we naturally have to express those differences. Because of the great dominance and influence of the Anglo value system, some of our literature cannot help but reflect warped perspectives at times and speak of this cultural struggle constantly.

If you are a Chicano writer you are bound to be in a constant struggle with yourself to sort out what it is that you say that has actually been influenced by the way the Raza you represent thinks. The other side of that coin is that we are constantly influenced, and to a greater degree at times, by the way Anglos think. That struggle is bound to be reflected in what we write. If it is about suffering; the dolor [pain] of the people who lose children at the hands of uncaring schools, prisons, medical systems, the army, has got to be a unique Chicano experience. The humiliation of having to be at the mercy of a crumb-throwing society and even the acceptance of the role of adopting nueva lengua [a new language] and the idea of being on your own soil as a foreigner. . . all of these things have to be a set of themes with universal relationship, but with a very peculiar Chicano flavor. We drown in two cultures and when we come up for air for a third time we do not know whether to yell for help or auxilio [help].

Does Chicano literature improve communication between Chicanos and Anglo Americans?

Because of the intimate nature of communicating with other people via literary efforts, relationships do tend to improve, to increase our levels of tolerance and understanding. There is the danger that those with no minds and no hearts, bent on racist, oppressive, and elitist ways, will see our literature as a polarizing medium which works away from their aim of Americanizing everybody and everything. To these people Chicano literature is an opposing, threatening, and dangerous force.

We as writers carry an added responsibility. Some of us are even very dangerous individuals in that we can confuse readers and speed up the acculturation which often appears in our own writings. This was the subject of some of the crítica [criticism] presently leveled at some writers. If they write and tell people who are suffering that it is cute to suffer and that we must be machos and aguantar las jodas sociales bajo las cuales vivimos [bear the social ills under which we live]. We are worse than sellouts, we are the vocinas [spokesmen] of the dominant culture, the agents of doom and acceptance, we are the social tranquilizers. We are not any longer talking of making people accommodate or survive in an Anglo world, we are talking about revolution, about us not having to change to live in dignity and get our due as true contributors of this land of plenty. Communications are improved all over if there is honesty in the writers. If we are truly artistas and we paint with words fantasies or realities, we are mirrors in which many can come and look at themselves. If we are phony, those mirrors are tinted and no one can truly see himself in us. Thus, communications can improve internally among our own Raza first and secondly we can begin to dialogue with el enemigo [the enemy].

Does Chicano literature reevaluate, attack, or subvert the value system of the majority society? Is it a revolutionary literature? Thematically? Technically?

Both technically and thematically Chicano literature

is a revolutionary force in that it advocates a change not necessarily solicited, welcome, or wanted, by the dominant culture. Chicano literature is revolutionary in that it imposes itself forcefully rather than sit back for natural evolution to invite it in. Most of our initial efforts took the shape of attacks upon a system that has historically been abusive, oppressive, insensitive, and closed to us and our needs. It is cowardly and unnatural for a true artist not to use his talents for this purpose.

One technical revolutionary theme or element presently identified in Chicano literature is that a negation of the "realist" school is strongly emerging among Chicano and other Mexican writers. It is as if we have a nation of people who are fed up with being fed realism and now want a menu full of fantasies. We can deliver fantasies with un poquito de chile [a little dash of spice]. . . but. . . there is danger there, too. Chicano wit, or humor, is found more and more. . . the cabula [word play] that is ours can be a major tool to also combat the hipocrecía [hypocrisy] found among us and certainly among those who profess to lead this nation. Chicano writers have matured significantly since the fifteen or more years that we have been macheteándole a las tristes [beating the sad] typewriters. . . We have weeded out clichés and slogans and now busy ourselves with another bigger mandate [order] than fighting the oppressors, and that is what do we offer by way of strategy to eliminate our social woes and what do we see as a possible Aztlán, rather than a mythical one. We have even directed a few word fregasos [lashings] among ourselves, Chicano leaders and other would-be poets and writers who compromise themselves a vuelta de esquina [just around the corner]. To go on narrowing down fictitious enemies so that we can truly destroy them and an oppressive system which tricks and connives the weak into staying weak—and the goal is so keep before us the beauty of our humanity and anything that is dehumanizing. . . pos a darle matarili [well eliminate it].

What problems have you encountered in publishing? Were they racially founded?

My personal problems in getting published have been and continue to be major ones. In my case I would not wait, so I created Barrio Publications to print my works and those of upcoming writers. Barrio Publications uses the financial support of those carnales who wish to see our works printed and invest their own meager resources. Although my poems appear in almost any existing anthology, major publishers are still afraid to invest in us. Other than a few breakthroughs, I would conclude that racist misreadings on the quality and need of our literature still govern the thinking of major publishers who have a commercial rather than a social concern.

Are Chicanos at a disadvantage in trying to practice the art of writing?

Chicano writers, and other minorities for that matter, are at a set of disadvantages when it comes to the art of writing. Most of us tend to be deficient in two languages rather than proficient in both, as we should be, or as hopefully bilingual programs will prepare us to be. This tends to give us a sense of insecurity when we express ourselves orally and in written form. This tendency to feel unable is reinforced in schools, where our sparks of creativeness are often suffocated. Our homes do not often have the abundance of books, periodicals, and magazines, to inspire in us a love for the written word, and even the beautiful Chicano art of conversation lacks as our parents struggle for mere survival and are often too tired or worried to tend to it. Later on in life, as is the case with some of us, time becomes our worst enemy in that I do not know any Chicano writer who gives writing his best attention; rather we have to do it when we can. The costly question of having our work typed, xeroxed, or properly edited is a luxury. As long as writing is but one of our sidelines, as we work and involve ourselves in El Movimiento [The Movement], it will suffer a bit in that we really do not give it our best effort. Sacrificing time and energy and being involved have a positive side, too, as our work is more relevant and also more precious in nature as it is an artistic birth of our struggle, so that what I state is not truly a complaint but a set of facts.

What are the most outstanding qualities of Chicano literature? Weaknesses?

The most outstanding qualities of Chicano literature have to do with introducing in greater quantities a set of values and perspectives on life so long admired and misunderstood by the dominant society, while at the same time sharing them with our own community, who at times are on the verge of forgetting or ignoring them themselves. These values are in strong contrast with those of the dominant society, and this clash is a healthy one which is long overdue to produce a rainbow of values in the pluralistic society in which we live. Many Anglos have told me personally that they admire our way of life. I am sure others have confessed such. What is it that they admire—our poverty, our misery? No. They admire the way we cope with life and enjoy it. They admire our capacity to suffer and to enjoy. In a way they admire our freedom to be not so concerned with the damm future and with all these material possessions and trinkets which abound. The sense of loyalty to our familias and to friends. Even the rascal qualities we seem to have are at times admired, because we can be dishonest with flair rather than in the dark. They are coming around, with the energy crisis and with the ecological movement, to where we have always been, to a love and respect for mother earth, to a way of using solar energy. . . los tendederos, ese [the clotheslines, man]. Some of our writings express well Indo-Precolumbian thoughts, which ecologically speaking are so in tune with today and offer answers to our personal anxieties and fatigues, so that we can, in fact, say that Chicano literature has in itself a curative effect for our present confusion and despair. Since our raíces [roots] are in themselves indo-ecological, we carry in us a sacred admiration of food and food-producing earth. The idea of poisoning water and earth which give us life is certainly not in our culture. While we acknowledge death as a very natural part of life, we do not go around bending backwards to create it in mass with nuclear plants. The curative effects of Chicano literature frankly is that it offers us a bit of healthy insanity, a valve to let out some of the frustrations of living as we do in America, nay, in the whole world, today. Not many other carnales have picked up on the onda [the notion] that we can be remedeial with our works. Dig on how poetry is part of a psychotherapy now. . . we've known that all along and say it jokingly que de poetas y locos todos tenemos un poco [there is a little bit of poet and madman in everyone]. Unless we know this we are bound to be creating the same kind of anxiety in our works and that same feeling of apathy and hopelessness so abundantly present nowadays. To weave these philosophies into our poetry and our cuentos [stories] without having them appear as moralizing messages is art.

The only weaknesses in our literature that I presently see are by way of danger, that is that we as writers drown and perish in a sea of hate created by ourselves for our lot and against our oppressors. This translates in making every piece we write a slogan, a chicote [whip] to whip our enemies with, a cry, a bellyache for our hunger and misery, leaving out the artistry of expression and the universality of our message. I'm not saying this should not be done, but that it should be done in the medium we have chosen ourselves, which is "literary art."

Critics are not superhumans, they are as desmadrados [messed up] as the writers at times, if not more, in that they have Anglo measuring sticks, or European ones which they were given in academia, and if we as writers had been trained to write in academia also, all would be cool. They are measuring oranges with a tomato scale, and that just won't do. The other set of critics are on a political onda [trip] that overblinds them to writing as an artform; everything is measured by a Marxist yardstick, and if what you are writing does not have gunpowder and lead all masses to overthrow the burgueses [bourgeoisie], olvídate, porque ni te van a criticar estos carnales y admirables carnalas [forget it, because those brothers and admirable sisters are not even going to criticize you]. I have challenged critics to develop their own standards in keeping with what they are trying to criticize, and they think I am nuts. They are right, as that thing we call literature must of necessity have some univesal standards to be measured by, or else a bunch of different measuring instruments would be quite confusing. Chicano literature is bound by these universal standards and by the art standards established long ago. . . those standards, I believe, are subject to revolution also.

What are the milestones so far in Chicano literature?

Oddly enough they have nothing to do with literature per se but with the taste for it aroused, with the demand for Chicano literature courses which constantly grow and demand new materials, new works from us. The biggest milestone is that our barrios, our farmworkers, our pintos [brothers in prison], our still uneducated and impoverished masses have accepted our work. How it happened that Chicano literature emerged and that some became interested in creating it and others in accepting it and even demanding it is the question of the steady diet of Gabacho [Anglo American] literature to which we had been subjected for many years. The item suddenly appeared on the literature menu and people started to taste it and order it again. It is obvious that certain conditions had to exist; the question was one of an explosive readiness on everyone's part. What has been extremely difficult is that we have no Wall Street backers or Madison Avenue promoters, and the few garage printer efforts are few and far between. Since I personally have been in the business of disseminating, I know first-hand how hard it is. Presently I am getting a book out which costs thirty-eight hundred bucks. . . not many of us, none of us have that kind of bread to invest in books, even if they do sell. Los festivales como [the festivals like] Flor Y Canto and now Canto al Pueblo have done much to inspire new writers, particularly young writers, women writers, and the many other art forms from our communities. These festivals have some built-in dangers; they can become too phony and too commercial, too much entertainment and not enough concern for who we are and what we are all about, too much of a forum for all the old prima donnas to promenade in a non-Chicano spirit competitively among each other. As for publishing houses, pos cuales [which] other than Quinto Sol and now the other one [Justa]. . . that is not enough and the dumb Chicanos running Chicano studies, who are in a position to help, continue to buy Gabacho products and foreign, so it is a wonder that they are still operating. If it is not possible on the part of eight million Chicanos to create literature for themselves and to promote it, I say we are in a damn sad state of affairs and maybe ready for another few hundred years of silence and obscurity. There are many things we can do to prevent this self-created doom.

Rayas is one answer. Three or so years ago some of us thought of creating a vehicle to promote Chicano literature in all levels and aspects. It plays a role in identifying writers and doing críticas [criticism] on them. It seeks to identify markets and resources; it seeks to establish communications on an international level and to begin to address ourselves to the question of turning out quality works and doing them in a professional way. Just because La Raza está pobre [the Chicano People are poor] is no excuse to give them crap. . . they themselves deserve the best we can produce, and they know quality from crap as well as any critical genius. We suffer from the same mickey mouse regional and personal tirades that others in the Chicano communities suffer, and so we move slowly and carefully and defensively.

What is the future of Chicano literature: distinctiveness, or the de-emphasis of the distinctive characteristics?

The futue of Chicano literature is precisely dependent on what I have just said. If it continues to be relevant to our gente [people], it will continue to live and give fruit and flower. The danger is also eminent that if we make it a mere toy of the elite or the academician, or bury it in libraries and bookstores, it may not receive the necessary sun, it will die. I take the action of deemphasizing or modifying the characteristics of Chicano literature as equal to accommodating ourselves to the norms of the dominant society and losing ourselves in the process.

Who are the leaders among Chicano writers, and why?

There are by now a good number of Chicano authors well recognized throughout Aztlán. They are liked and oftentimes imitated and even surpassed in effort by young writers. A recent Flor y Canto brought many of us face to face with each other, and yet many remain unread, undiscovered, with shelves full of beautiful manuscripts. To say who the leaders are in our fraternity of artists and writers is a dangerous task, as it only indicates preferences and like, and is not truly reflective of in-depth comparison and crítica. Also, since Chicano literature can be said to be in its embryonic stage, it may now be very easy to be among the first and best, whereas in years to come this might well be a giant task for experts. Three names come to mind who are generally considered geniuses in the art form: Ricardo Sánchez, Rudolfo Anaya, and Oscar Zeta Acosta. We had for a long time the genius of John Rechy from El Paso, Texas (*City of Night*), whom few knew to be a Chicano novelist of great stature. Poets like Alurista and Nephtalí are now giants in the field, while the most-read poem, "Yo Soy Joaquín," cannot be ignored and places its author among these creative brothers. There are technical writers like Rudolfo Acuña, who treats history to our advantage, who can easily be considered great. I'll conclude by giving my own preferences regardless of stature: Miguel Méndez, *Pere-*

grinos de Aztlán; María Mondragón, unpublished poetess from Alamosa, Colorado; the late Heriberto Terán and Magdaleno Avila, who writes with the pen name of Juan Valdez; Pacheco, Contreras, Raymundo Pérez (El Tigre), and Tep Falcón—only some of those I myself consider leaders. As to why I consider them so, the answer may be found in the beauty, the sensitivity, the simplicity, the craft, the heart, the fidelity to our cultural values, the enojo [anger] I find when I read them. Javier Pachecó, José Antonia Burciaga, Lorna Dee Cervantes, Amy López, Bernice Zamora.

I would like to conclude by emphasizing what I consider terribly important. I'm referring to instilling in our young Chicanitos a love for the written word. This word in itself, when it is truly their own and not someone else's, has a liberating power equal to none. In the school and in the home we should do all we can to expose the child to the written word, to equip him with an ample vocabulary and to add variety to his expression and give free vent to the creative spirit so naturally inherent in most Chicanos. Secondly, I foresee a need for developing our own literary critics who can assist in evaluating and prompting our works as well as adding to our improvement by criticizing and pointing out areas of weakness. Thirdly, I would like to see a few more Quinto Soles (a Chicano owned and run publishing house in California), who would help us publish and recognize our works, and more distributing houses and a whole front of educators fighting to crash the racist barriers which continue to keep our materials out of textbooks and out of the schools. The Chicano book belongs in primary and secondary schools and not only at the college and university levels. By the same token, some of us must begin to write for children and put the beautiful cultural values we have into our writings. (pp. 95–114)

Abelardo Delgado and Juan D. Bruce-Novoa, in an interview in *Chicano Authors: Inquiry by Interview* by Juan D. Bruce-Novoa, University of Texas Press, 1980, pp. 3–30, 95–114.

SOURCES FOR FURTHER STUDY

Lomelí, Francisco A., and Morales, Arcadio. "Delgado, Abelardo ('Lalo')." In *Chicano Literature: A Reference Guide*, edited by Julio A. Martínez and Francisco A. Lomelí, pp. 199–205. Westport, Conn.: Greenwood Press, 1985.
    Provides a critical overview of Delgado's writings.

Steiner, Stan. "The Unfrocked Priests." In his *La Raza: The Mexican Americans*, pp. 339–53. New York: Harper & Row, 1970.
    Includes a brief sketch of Delgado in his role as head of a juvenile delinquency center in El Paso, Texas.

Additional coverage of Delgado's life and career is contained in the following source published by Gale Research: *Dictionary of Literary Biography*, Vol. 82.

José Donoso

1924–

Chilean novelist, poet, short story and nonfiction writer.

INTRODUCTION

Donoso is a prolific and internationally renowned author whose fiction frequently depicts the discrepancies between the upper and lower classes of his native Chile. He is best known for *El obsceno pájaro de la noche* (1970; *The Obscene Bird of Night*), a structurally complex novel which, like much of his work, is noted for its nightmarish atmosphere of psychological disorder. *The Obscene Bird of Night* firmly established Donoso's reputation as one of the finest Latin American authors of the twentieth century.

Donoso was born into an upper-middle-class family in Santiago, Chile. He was educated in Santiago until 1943, when he dropped out of high school to seek employment; over the next four years, he worked on a sheep farm in the southernmost region of Chile, and as a dockworker in Buenos Aires, Argentina, before returning to Santiago to complete his high school education and attend college. Donoso received a scholarship to study English literature at Princeton University, where, at the age of 25, he began to write short stories for a student publication. After receiving a bachelor's degree, Donoso traveled throughout North America in 1952 before returning to Chile, where he worked as a teacher and a journalist while continuing to write fiction. His first book, a collection of short stories entitled *Veraneo y otros cuentos*, was published in 1955 and received Santiago's annual Municipal Short Story Prize that year. Over the next three decades, Donoso published more short stories, seven novels, and as many novellas while living and teaching in Mexico, Spain, and the United States. In 1982, he returned to his native Santiago where he continues to write and publish.

A number of themes recur in Donoso's fiction, including the moral decay of Chile's upper classes, the individual's search for identity, and the experience of existential despair. Stylistically, his narratives are characterized by utilization of multiple points of view and un-reliable narrators. Thus, while not all of Donoso's work has the overtly hallucinatory quality of *The Obscene Bird of Night*, his more conventional tales also present subtle challenges to traditional literary realism. For ex-ample, while some reviewers in Chile have praised Donoso's first novel, *Coronación* (1957; *Coronation*), as a realistic depiction of Chile's decadent upper class, Donoso has stated that his intention for its conclusion was to abandon the restraints of realism by dwelling on madness and the grotesque. The novel depicts a repressed, middle-aged bachelor, obsessed with main-taining a rigidly ordered existence in the mansion of his grandmother, who suffers from vivid delusions. Upper-class decadence is also a prominent theme in both *Este domingo* (1966; *This Sunday*) and *El lugar sin límites* (1966; *Hell Has No Limits*). The plot of *This Sunday* involves an affluent but ineffective middle-aged profes-sional named Don Alvaro, his wife, and a chambermaid who is also his mistress; the narrative, divided among the points of view of these characters, delves into their obsessive personalities. *Hell Has No Limits,* written while Donoso was residing in Mexico at a home owned by author Carlos Fuentes, is set in an isolated small town owned by Don Alejo, a powerful, all-knowing, self-ish aristocrat whom many reviewers saw as the satirical embodiment of an unfeeling God.

The Obscene Bird of Night, regarded by most commentators as Donoso's best and most complex work, is narrated by Humberto, an unsuccessful writer who becomes the retainer to a decaying aristocratic family and the tutor to their only son and heir. The child, monstrously deformed, is sent with Humberto to live in a decrepit convent owned by the family, where he is surrounded by equally deformed persons and other castoffs of society. Throughout the novel, past and present are intermingled and characters undergo bizarre transformations. Many critics have viewed the novel's disjointed, non-chronological narration as the product of Humberto's deranged mind. In this view, Humberto is a schizophrenic who freely mixes reality with his fantasies, fears, and resentments of the world; his many transformations reflect his disintegrating per-sonality as he picks up and discards various identities in an effort to define himself. Charles M. Tatum, for exam-

ple, has described the work as "a delirious creation of the male protagonist whose own personality becomes fragmented and his narrative progressively more inco-herent." Other scholars have found a parallel between the novel's form and its content: Amalia Pereira has asserted that "the novel's tortuous, distorted structure functions as a mirror image or plastic symbol of the chaos and terror of existence."

Pereira has noted that the fiction Donoso has writ-ten since the publication of *The Obscene Bird of Night* is marked by "a greater sense of calm [and] a return to less complex forms." *Casa de campo* (1978; *A House in the Country*) has been described by some critics as a political allegory. Set in an aristocratic household in Chile, the novel depicts the chaos that results when the estate is temporarily left in the hands of an uncle, the owners' children, and some of the local people. When the owners return, they use the servants to ruthlessly re-establish the status quo. Though some commentators have faulted the novel for being too intellectual and emo-tionally detached, others have found it highly relevant and involving. *La desesperanza* (1986; *Curfew*), written after Donoso had returned to his native country after many years abroad, is a depiction of life in Chile under General Augusto Pinochet's rule. Though the book de-scribes both Pinochet's torturers and the dispossessed poor, its principal focus is the country's well-educated, dispirited political left. Donoso has called *La desesper-anza* "probably the most realistic of my novels, and the most Chilean."

Donoso has been censured by some writers of the Chilean left for his reluctance to take a firm politi-cal stance in his writings, but some commentators have suggested that his refusal to offer a solution to the prob-lems that he surveys allows his work to transcend the regional concerns of Chilean society. Similarly, the pes-simistic outlook of much of his fiction has been cred-ited with increasing its universality. In the opinion of George R. McMurray, "some readers may be depressed by Donoso's recurring insinuations of impending doom, but few will fail to appreciate his astonishing imagina-tion, aesthetic sensitivity, and profound insight into the terrifying realities lurking beneath the surface of today's world."

CRITICAL COMMENTARY

ALEXANDER COLEMAN
(essay date 1971)

[In the following essay, Coleman explores the themes in Donoso's early works.]

It is quite interesting that the work of José Donoso (b. Santiago de Chile, 1925) has often been described as traditionalist, traditionalist, that is, in the English sense, admiring as he does James and Austen. There has even been mention of the word *costumbrismo*, referring to the genre very much dear to nineteenth-century Spanish writers generally considered to be minor—except Larra, of course. This is confusing, and needlessly so. Such a generally sensible critic as Mario Benedetti, for example, in commenting upon Donoso's first collection of short stories, *El veraneo y otros cuentos* (1955), noted his preoccupation for Chilean reality. Benedetti also underlined the inclusion of many national "types" in these stories, praising the tangible qualities of the very real streets, *barrios*, etc. The stories unquestionably give every evidence of a modest and perfectly calculated king of realistic literary practice. But to see nothing more than this in the stories is to hide their insidious and quite beautifully disguised thematics.

In the title story, for instance, the whole nightmare of marital infidelity is reflected in a perverse and distorted way through the relationships of the various servants of the triangle, and through the way in which the appropriate children manipulate not only each other, but also the servants in turn. The result is a complicated and perfectly executed depiction of intricate human domination, alleviated only when a realm of feeling between the children cuts through the vertical social structures of hate and authority that the adults have created for their children and which they wish to pass on to them.

And so, too, for the language—apparently odd chatter between servants and children and amongst the children themselves, but in reality a linguistic mask for one of Donoso's nuclear fantasies, the alternance and conflict between Life and Authority. Donoso is able to suggest the variegated power of one over another by the subtlest means— at times it is the power of song, where one child can command the other to laugh or cry according to the tune sung, or at times the barely inferred mystic power of a child with a slingshot.

At times the basic obsession in these early stories is inferred in a more pointed way, as in the echoes of the Quetzalcoatl myth in the story **"El Güero"** from the same collection. Here the elements are perhaps purposefully complicated by Donoso, for it is set in Mexico, with a couple from the (North American) groves of academe who are condemned to spend time in a small village while the husband finishes an erudite volume that will crown his academic career in the United States. The husband, Howland, as depicted by Donoso's narration is dull, hopelessly out of style, and severely circumscribed by the nature of his occupation, a limitation that effects the personal disintegration of the wife.

The counterfigure to this immensely limited couple is their son Mike, who grows in primitive power and audacity as his contact with the local myths and tales becomes deeper and more dominant within himself. He begins to dream, and the natural life takes hold of him until "everything mysterious and everything that vibrates with hidden force came to be his own natural element." As a final dénouement to the implosion of the life force in Mike, he sets off upstream in search of the "blond gods," accompanied by torrential rains, thunder, and lighting, never to be seen again. Beneath the impeccable order and spiritual agony of a marriage in the final throes of its own destruction, the death of the child brings forth a new and higher order of vitalism within the couple. All this is artfully transcribed by a sympathetic narrator as Mrs. Howland returns to the village where all this took place long ago.

Other stories in the collection, such as **"Una señora"** and **"Fiesta en grande,"** are superb set pieces that again are expressive of Donoso's essentially urban sensibility. The polarities of "civilized" and ordered existence finally break down, and man is confronted with an overwhelming sense of the violence of nature and man and consciously throws himself into a maelstrom of unconscious, inhuman, and murderous void.

Any discussion of Donoso's thematics must also take into consideration the tone—violently Romantic in spite of everything—which characterizes the evolution of his characters from constriction to expression. If we take such a definition as that of Henry James, where the romantic stands "for the things that. . . we never can directly know; the things that can reach us only through the beautiful circuit and subterfuge of our thought and our desire," we are at least at the beginning of an appreci-

---

Principal Works

El Veraneo y otros cuentos (short stories) 1955

Dos Cuentos (short stories) 1956

Coronación (novel) 1957
[*Coronation*, 1965]

El charleston (short stories) 1960
[*Charleston and Other Stories* (enlarged edition), 1977]

Los mejores cuentos de José Donoso (short stories) 1965; also published as *Cuentos,* 1971

Este domingo (novel) 1966
[*This Sunday*, 1967]

El lugar sin límites (novel) 1966
[*Hell Has No Limits* published in *Triple Cross: Holy Place-Carlos Fuentes; Hell has No Limits—José Donoso; From Cuba with a Song—Severo Sarduy,* 1972]

El obsceno pájaro de la noche (novel) 1970
[*The Obscene Bird of Night*, 1973]

Historia personal del boom (nonfiction) 1972
[*The Boom in Spanish American Literature: A Personal History*, 1977]

Tres novelitas burguesas (novellas) 1973
[*Sacred Families; Three Novellas*, 1977]

Casa de campo (novel) 1978
[*A House in the Country*, 1984]

La misteriosa desaparición de la marquesita de Loria (novel) 1980

El jardín de al lado (novel) 1981
[*The Garden Next Door*, 1992]

Poemas de un novelista (poetry) 1981

Cuatro para Delfina (novellas) 1982

La desesperanza (novel) 1986
[*Curfew*, 1988]

Taratuta; Naturaleza muerta con cachimba (novellas) 1990
[*Taratuta; and, Still Life with Pipe: Two Novellas,* 1993]

---

portrait of a society in which the etymological meaning of *travesty* is fully explored, a world where all objects are signs to their opposites, a terrifying confusion of doubleness. But in spite of the confusion of identity purposefully practiced by Donoso in his short stories, one is often left with a unique vision of the central character of the story—the old man in **"Ana María,"** hypnotized by the eyes of a three year old child, finally determining to flee with her to an unknown and probably dreadful future; the pathetic Aunt Matilde in **"Paseo,"** who gradually abandons the spinster's role automatically imposed upon her by society and disappears into the Buenos Aires night, never to return; the frustrated bureaucrat Santelices, in **"Santelices,"** convinced that the garden outside his window is populated with fierce animals, throws himself into this imagined hell that is at the center itself of all that is deathly.

Against the rigidities of society, there is an ever-present oceanic sense in Donoso into which his heroes plunge. These pathetic and at times comic figures are pilgrims of their own brand of truth, vague searchers for a freer self and society, constantly at odds with the reality of their own spiritual suffocation. A groping for a sense of transcendence, a whole process that inevitably entails the encounter with the monster that is within them, engendered out of the mathematical rigidities with which societies function in apparent order. As Emir Rodríguez Monegal has pointed out in his brilliant study of Donoso, it is precisely this discovery of violence that is the obsessive and often repeated theme. It has also been pointed out that there are rarely any valid paternal figures in his work—it is very much of a matriarchy, but one in which masculine and feminine roles function nonetheless, all to the detriment of those concerned. And often, too, above all in a few of the early stories, a good story is robbed of its impact by a too obviously psychological explanation in lieu of an ending. Such a story is **"Fiesta en grande,"** where a "Napoleonic" national pistol champion, after having engaged in some tragicomic antics at an office picnic, is lulled to sleep by his ancient mother after she has rather obviously gone through his jacket to remove the pistol, which is, of course the cause of all the trouble. But such moments are rare in Donoso's short pieces.

But certainly our sensibilities are constantly engaged by Donoso's stories—above all, because of the sheer power of the inarticulate that underlies them all. He is always careful to draw for us a miniature portrait of a society, often from the point of view of a child-like narrator who is sensitized to the significance of every detail. What draws us out as readers is the power of the unspoken in him, the deadly attraction of nothingness. It would seem that his work, glanced at in a cursory fashion, does more than its share of the reader's work, because it is so evidently a refraction of a society, but this aspect can only cloud our vision of this wholly contemporaneous literary achievement. The carefully appointed society with which

ation of the multiple planification of reality that Donoso constantly practices. It is at times a rather brutal fashion, as in his early novel *Coronación*, where the world of the ruined bourgeois as represented by Misiá Elisa Grey de Abalos and her debilitated son Andrés Abalos is counterpoised by the servant class in the old mansion, who apparently serve but actually dominate the exhausted lives of the fading aristocracy.

In two later novels, *El lugar sin límites* and *Este domingo*, both of 1966, this multiple dependence and relationship of class is delineated in a masterful fashion, a

Donoso began to depict in *Coronación* and in the stories is for us a functioning lie possibly pointing to a truth; the words surround rather than express a reality. If they denote anything, one would have to mention a society that is itself inauthentic and false. Sartre justly observes of Nathalie Sarraute's books that

> they are filled with these impression of terror: people are talking, something is about to explode that will illuminate suddenly the glaucous depths of a soul, and each of us feels the crawling mire of his own. Then, no: the threat is removed, the danger is avoided, and the exchange of commonplaces begins again. Yet sometimes these commonplaces break down and a frightful protoplasmic nudity becomes apparent.

In many senses this is the essence of the best of Donoso, too, for daily life has rarely taken on such traumatic resonances as occur so frequently in his stories. As Severo Sarduy states toward the end of his notable analysis of Donoso's *El lugar sin límites,* "The essence (*fondo*) of a work is to be considered as an absence, metaphor as a sign without basis." (pp. 155–58)

Alexander Coleman, "Some Thoughts on Jose Donoso's Traditionalism," in *Studies in Short Fiction*, Vol. VIII, No. 1, Winter, 1971, pp. 155–58.

CHARLES M. TATUM
(essay date 1973)

[In the following essay, Tatum maintains that the central theme of *The Obscene Bird of Night* is the deterioration and downfall of Chile's landowning aristocracy.]

José Donoso's most recent novel, *El obsceno pájaro de la noche* [*The Obscene Bird of Night*] marks his joining the recent "boom" of Spanish American prose fiction, a literary renaissance that includes such novelist as Julio Cortázar, Mario Vargas Llosa, and Gabriel García Márquez. Eight years in the writing, the work is prodigious, representing a high point of Donoso's artistic creation. Selected by Seix-Barral to receive the "Premio Biblioteca Breve," and confiscated by the Spanish government for alleged censorship violations, the novel has already raised some eye-brows in literary circles. The scant criticism that has so far appeared has been hard pressed to describe, analyze, and interpret it. In the words of one reviewer [Adolfo Drigani in *Visión*, 27 March 1971]: "Será difícil, en efecto, encontrar un punto de referencia literaria con el cual cotejar y enjuiciar esta obra. Ella será la que marque un nuevo hito, un nuevo punto de referencia, una nueva y profunda dimensión" [It will, in fact, be difficult to find a literary point of reference with which to compare and judge this work. The work itself will establish a milestone, a new point of reference, a new and profound dimension].

The complexity of the work can be hinted at when one describes it as a delirious creation of the male protagonist whose own personality becomes fragmented and his narrative progressively more incoherent. *El obsceno pájaro de la noche* is awesome for its variety, richness, and difficulty as the writer confuses myth with reality, logic with absurdity, primitive rites with sophisticated Chilean upper-class ceremonies, [in Drigani's words] "múltiples ingredientes que Donoso echa en el caldero mágico, cuece a fuego lento, agita febrilmente y sirve en un torrente de hechos y sueños, de palabras e imágenes" [many and varied ingredients that Donoso puts into his magic caldron, boils slowly, stirs feverishly, and serves with a torrent of acts and dreams, words and images]. The temporal and spatial complexity of the novel is made more bewildering by the inclusion of the dreamed or fictionalized reality in the form of a biography with no definite end or beginning.

There is, however, a central theme, the demise of a feudal society, to which the reader can relate the many loose strands he picks up during his journey through the fictional maze. Don Jerónimo de Azcoitía, a powerful member of Chile's traditional landholding class, marries his cousin Inés who belongs to the same social elite. Their union produces a monstrously deformed child, Boy, whom don Jerónimo's male secretary, Humberto Peñaloza, is ordered to educate at the family *fundo* of la Rinconada. After an indefinite period, Humberto begins creating his own reality, a fictional microcosm revolving around the master's life. It is through his deranged, disoriented mind that we view the demise of the feudal aristocracy. When the secretary grows old he is sent (as all the retired Azcoitía servants have been for generations) to la Casa de Encarnación [the House of the Incarnation], a joint establishment of the family and the Church. Here, he takes on the guise of a deaf-mute, el Mudito, and in a long delirium he tells his own biography.

Around his basic plot line of the novel Donoso weaves Humberto's fantasy-ridden interpretation of don Jerónimo's life as well as the equally exaggerated recreation of his own. Both versions are filtered through the secretary's distorted view of people and events, creating a surrealistic world populated by grotesque members of a meaningless feudal existence.

The novel begins and ends at la Casa de Encarnación but what transpires between commencement and finale falls into no logical sequence. The old people's home and la Rinconada serve as the poles of the work, each a kind of labyrinth and each an equally horrifying symbol of the decay of an oligarchical system. The temporal and spatial disarrangement is basic to *El obsceno pájaro de la noche* as it contributes to the overall impression of chaos, the inversion of values and myths of a way-of-life that is seen on the verge of extinction.

An essential aspect of the central theme of the novel is the Azcoitía's traditional relationship to the Church. The members of the family conceive of their function within a divinely ordained plan in much the same way in which European kings held that their royal authority descended directly from God. Don Jerónimo's uncle, el reverendo Padre don Clemente "más político que eclesiástico, más mundano que místico" [more political than ecclesiastical, more worldly than mystical], feels obliged to carry his divine mission into the realm of the politics of the large landowners. He reminds his nephew, "Defender tu propiedad mediante la política es defender a Dios" [To defend your property through politics is to defend God].

Don Clemente's statement becomes increasingly more ironical when the reader discovers the perversion and grotesqueness of don Jerónimo's attempt to act out what his uncle has described to him as his Holy Duty. In this novel what seems moral on the surface, becomes ugly and distorted. The heavenly-ordained Order of which the old "señorón criollo" [the grand old Creole gentleman] speaks is, in fact, chaos, the Garden of Paradise irretrievably lost to evil and inhabited by suffering beings, deformed both physically and spiritually.

Corresponding to the Azcoitías' place of prominence in the affairs of the Church and the nation is a family legend they refer to, myopically, as "la niña-beata" [the pious young girl]. Throughout generations the family has stubbornly preserved the version they believe will cast them in the best possible light and will more firmly cement their ties with Divine Power. In contrast, the peasants of the *fundo*, who refer to the legend "la niña-bruja" [the child-witch] tell about the mysterious metamorphosis of a land-owner's daughter into a terrible bird-like head brought about through the intercession of her *nana* [nursemaid]. In both versions, the witch, who takes on the form of a yellow dog, is killed while the girl is bundled off to a convent. The contemporary re-enaction of the legend involves don Jerónimo's wife Inés and her nurse and relative, la Peta Ponce. Donoso uses the legend to heighten the cyclical struggle between the feudal aristocracy and those elements that have traditionally threatened its authority and power.

Specifically, don Jerónimo considers Peta a threat to the order and permanence of his class. She gradually becomes fused with the image of "la perra amarilla" [the yellow she-dog] the symbol of fate throughout *El obsceno pájaro de la noche*. Linked genealogically to Inés, and supernaturally to the ancient version of "la niña-bruja," Peta thus is the counterpart of the legend kept alive in the present in which the aristocracy is pictured in a state of decay. The frequent appearance of the old lady and she-dog is a leitmotif that signals the horrifying demise of this society.

Another important aspect of the novel is the mythological element that comes into play in several ways. It can be seen, on one level, as the struggle between Good and Evil, between the elite upper-class alliance with Catholicism and the supposed forces of the devil that are trying to subvert their power. But the work is a topsy-turvy world where good is perverted and the traditional system of values inverted. The reality presented in the novel is one of turmoil and ambiguity, a reality that, in the end, presents little difference between don Jerónimo and Peta Ponce except that the former claims to live according to divine guidance and authority. Caught in the middle of this power struggle is Humberto Peñaloza whose destiny is inextricably bound up with that of the two contending forces.

Humberto is the central character of *El obsceno pájaro de la noche*, the fragmented personality whose consciousness in present throughout the novel, either in the form of his fantastic biography or the delirious recalling of his struggle to establish an identity. Although he can be viewed sympathetically as a victim, probably more correctly, Humberto is as despicable as don Jerónimo, caught up in the false values and aspirations of his own class. He becomes the aristocrat's secretary because he desperately desires to become part of his master's world of gentility. Beset by an inferiority complex, Humberto feels that to obtain a true consciousness of self, an authenticity, he must first acquire "una máscara magnífica, un rostro grande, luminoso, sonriente, definido, que nadie deje de admirar" [a magnificant mask, a large, luminous, smiling, prominent face that nobody would fail to admire]. Specifically, his father insists that the only face which will give him validity as a person is "uno de caballero." The face or mask is used by Donoso to deal with the theme of Humberto's search for self-importance. It is used literally when the protagonist (as el Mudito) dons a horrible card-board head to become acceptable to a common street whore, and, figuratively, when he pretends to be a talented writer.

Humberto's quest leads him to try to assume the personality of don Jerónimo. He take his place during a violent confrontation with a group of striking miners in order to experience vicariously the power and respect never before afforded him. In a private, more personal way, Humberto yearns to replace his master in the act of procreation. Peta Ponce, acting as a kind of Celestina, arranges a meeting between him and done Jerónimo's wife, Inés, the outcome of which results in one of the high points of the novel.

In a complicated substitution of personalities Humberto is convinced he can replace don Jerónimo while the old lady plans to use the secretary to perpetrate her own evil design on the aristocrat. Several possibilities are suggested by Donoso: the night of sexual intercourse has been the product of el Mudito's delirium; Humberto has either dreamed it or he and Inés did have relations from which a child was conceived; Peta Ponce deceived him by substituting herself for Inés; don Jerónimo copulated with the old lady or with his wife in Peta's bed.

The scene involving the four characters is an excellent example of the ambiguity that is essential to *El obsceno pájaro de la noche*. Basic to this overall impression the novel creates is the fragmentation, mystery, and chaos of Donoso's description of la Casa de Encarnación where Humberto is sent to spend his final years. Because he has taken on the guise of the deaf-mute the view of the house and its inhabitants is a distorted reflection that results from his deteriorating mental condition.

The convent that had been the refuge for "la niña-beata" has been enlarged over the generations to include countless rooms, hallways, patios, and hidden passages, all of which contribute to the maze-like character of la casa:

> Cuidado con esa grada, Madre, es grada, no sombra, y desembocamos en otro patio que no es el patio donde vivía la Brígida así es que hay que seguir por más pasillos, otra pieza vacía, hileras de habitaciones huecas, más puertas abiertas o cerradas, más piezas que vamos atravesando, los vidrios astillados y polvorientos, la penumbra pegada a las paredes resecas donde una gallina picotea el adobe secular buscando granos. Otro patio. El patio del lavado donde ya no se lava, el patio de las monjitas donde ya no vive ninguna monjita porque ahora no quedan más que tres monjitas, el patio de la palmera, el patio del tilo, este patio sin nombre, el patio de la Ernestina Gómez, el patio del refectorio que nadie usa porque las viejas prefieren comer en la cocina, patio y claustros infinitos conectados por pasadizos interminables, cuartos que ya nunca intentaremos limpiar.

> [Watch that step, Mother. It's a step, not a shadow and we are going into another patio that is not the patio where la Brígida used to live, so we have to continue through more corridors, one more, another empty room, rows of hollow bedrooms, more open or shut doors, more rooms that we are passing through, chipped and dusty glass, half-shadows glued to brittle walls where a hen pecks at the secular adobe looking for grain. Another patio. The washingroom patio where washing is no longer done, the patio of the little old nuns where nobody lives anymore because now there are only three little old nuns, the patio of the palm tree, the patio of the linden tree, the nameless patio, Ernestina Gómez's patio, the patio of the refectory that nobody uses because the old ladies prefer to eat in the kitchen, an infinite number of patios and cloisters connected by interminable passageway, rooms that we will no longer try to keep clean.]

Reminiscent of Borges's labyrinths, the image in Donoso's novel has the effect of creating of mood of unreality, horror, and uneasiness. The phantasmagoric impression produced by the novelist's description of the house of refuge alerts the reader to the Poe-like world that exists within its walls, a world of decrepit old ladies and decay. Also, as a representation of the inner life of man, the labyrinth has always symbolized his insecurity and efforts to propitiate, control, or possess the powers that seem to decide his destiny. Thus, the labyrinthine aspect of the house corresponds to the old female servants' and el Mudito's attempts to forestall their own fate.

La Casa de Encarnación, inhabited by sterile, embittered, and senile former Azcoitía servants, represents (along with la Rinconada) the aberrations of a feudal existence, extensions of the family itself. As the last male heir, don Jerónimo maintains a rigid control over the house, suggesting a kind of God-Creature relationship. He eventually surrenders control of the house to the Church, and the old women and el Mudito are forced to seek shelter elsewhere.

La Casa de Encarnación is stripped of its furnishings, the Eucharist is removed from the chapel (symbolizing ultimate spiritual abandonment), and the residents prepare to leave. The last pages of the novel consist of a stream-of-consciousness of el Mudito who imagines himself sewn up into several layers of bags, the terrible figure of an *imbunche*, an unrecognizable, living corpse with all its orifices stuffed shut which cotton, nameless, speechless, and sightless. Forgotten in a corner by the old women, the bags are finally removed from the house, then emptied, and burned. Humberto Peñaloza's destiny is one of total obliteration, symbolizing his failure to achieve a true identity.

The abandonment of la Casa de Encarnación spells the end of the myth of perfect order on which the Oligarchy has relied as a source of strength. The servant class with its own system of false values likewise disappears. Another facet of this putrefaction of an antiquated feudal system is explored by Donoso in the monstrous world of la Rinconada.

Humberto's own fictional creation serves as the core of the longer novel around which is constructed the essential plot line as well as el Mudito's delirious narration in la Casa de Encarnación. His fantastic account of the conversion of the Azcoitía family estate into a closed, tightly controlled refuge for monsters bears a strong resemblance to the classical myth of Theseus an the Cretan labyrinth. However, Donoso reverses the myth as its instigator King Minos (don Jerónimo) and its architect Daedalus (Humberto) are both consumed by the maze which, in *El obsceno pájaro de la noche*, can be interpreted as the protagonists' failure to prevent their certain fate.

Since the mask of writer is important to the secretary's psyche, it is natural that he express himself through the medium of fiction. He thus creates in his mind a "paraíso de monstruos" [a paradise of monsters] at la Rinconada around the supposedly deformed son of don Jerónimo and Inés. The reader is struck by the bizarre quality of his description as well as the opening sentence which establishes the mythical perspective of this section of the novel. The scene of the father seeing his abnormal son for the first time suggests the classical counterpart of King Minos as he views the terrible offspring of his wife and the bull. In this case, the child is the product of an equally abnormal union involving the participation of Peta Ponçe. Like the king, don Jerónimo decides not to kill the monster-child:

> Cuando Jerónimo de Azcoitía entreabrió por fin las cortinas de la cuna para contemplar a su vástago tan esperado, quiso matarlo ahí mismo: ese repugnante cuerpo sarmentoso retorciéndose sobre su joroba, ese rostro abierto en un surco brutal donde labios, paladar y nariz desnudaban la obscenidad de huesos y tejidos en una incoherencia de rasgos rojizos. . . era la confusión, el desorden, una forma distinta pero peor de la muerte.

[When Jerónimo de Azcoitía finally parted the curtains of the crib to look upon his long-awaited descendant, he wanted to kill him on the spot: that repugnant gnarled body writhing on its own hump, that face parted by a horrible furrow where the lips, palate, and nose revealed the obscenity of bones and tissue in an incoherent mass of reddish features. . . it was confusion, chaos, a form different but worse than death.]

The child is a negation of the father's hopes, a perversion of the normalcy that has always been a part of the Azcoitía world. The family line, instead of purifying itself to produce a perfect heir, has been polluted by the imagined forces of evil it has always fought against. Don Jerónimo recognizes the implications of the abnormality of his son but instead of following his first impulse to destroy him, he schemes to use the monster for the further glorification of himself. Don Jerónimo instructs Humberto to create a world of deformed beings at la Rinconada where his son will live protected, never coming in contact with normal persons.

A hierarchy of monsters evolves, an elite with its own servant class of "submonstruos" [submonsters], a parody of the decadent aristocracy and its social inferiors. Both don Jerónimo and Humberto eventually are caught up in the web of intrigue created by the freaks who are intent on protecting their refuge. The secretary becomes a victim of his own fictitious characters as he imagines them exchanging his blood for theirs. This nightmarish process of *monstruificación* [monsterification] and don Jerónimo's suicide (when he realizes that his handsome figures is even more monstrous than the unsightliness of his creatures) brings the chronicle of life at la Rinconada to a close.

The reader is never sure if Humberto's biography of the aristocrat ends here, but what is important is that the "paraíso de monstruos" [paradise of monsters] at la Rinconada together with la Casa de Encarnación represent the demise of the aristocracy and the disintegration of the lower-class characters who, lacking their own true identity, seek to model themselves after their masters.

Through the use of myth and the fantastic creation of the deranged and fragmented personality that produces the surrealistic world of labyrinths, deformity, and mental aberration, Donoso explores the conditions of a waning feudal society. There is no salvation for any member of this anachronistic social and political system as its very underpinnings crumble and give away beneath generations of falseness and internal corruption. (pp. 99–105)

Charles M. Tatum, "'El Obsceno Pajaro De La Noche': The Demise of a Feudal Society," in *Latin American Literary Review*, Vol. I, No. 2, Spring, 1973, pp. 99–105.

AMALIA PEREIRA WITH JOSÉ DONOSO
(interview date 1986)

[In the following interview, which was conducted at Donoso's home in Santiago, Chile, in August, 1986, the author discusses his work, his life in Chile and abroad, and other Latin American writers.]

[Pereira]: *Some of your earliest stories, such as "The Poisoned Pastries" and "The Blue Woman," were written in English when you were a student at Princeton University. Being a very young man, how were you affected by this immersion of the North American intellectual and cultural world?*

[Donoso]: Well, for me it was really the English world that I became immersed in when I came to study at Princeton. I studied English literature, and I also did read some American literature; for one thing I was introduced to Henry James, for example. But I was most impressed with the sensation that "this was the real thing," and that I was a part of it. I studied with great scholars, and I felt involved in the original thing; in contrast, in Chile my studies has always seemed like the shadow of all this. It was a very exciting time. . . .

Many important Chilean writers have spent long periods of their literary careers outside of Chile. (Neruda, Mistral, Huidobro, Donoso, for example.) Do you think there are any common reasons or circumstances that impelled these writers to practice their profession abroad?

The most common reason, naturally, is the political reason. In the case of, for example, the English Romantics like Byron, Shelley, Keats, the reason, though not precisely political, had to do with the dissatisfaction with the social life and customs of the age, don't you think? In the case of Byron, especially, enamored as he was with the libertarian ideals of the epoch. Later on, in the Twenties, let's say, there was a sensation among writers of the need to go abroad; among the Latin Americans who went to Paris, for example, there were Huidobro and Rubén Darío. There was a need for a sense of perspective on their own countries. A need for a more cultured, more complicated world, a world more culturally complex.

Do you mean something similar to wanting to be immersed in "the real thing"?

I'm not sure if that's true in the case of Rubén Darío, for example, because he did not have that sensation that we had of living with copies. Modernism grabbed hold of him, the idea of modernism, after reading Verlaine and the other writers of that circle. He read them for the first time when he was here in Chile.

What constants do you see in Latin-American narrative, starting with the so-called literary "boom" up until today?

Well, quite a number of things. A grandiosity of concepts, in the first place, and a need to experiment. . . . These are novels about identification, about the exploration of identity: the problem is one of identity, a search for national identity and for personal identity is behind all of them.

In your book **A Personal History of the "Boom,"** *you mention various Latin-American women writers as members of the literary boom of the 60s and 70s. Why haven't these writers reached the high level of recognition that some of the male writers have attained? (Beatriz Guido, Sara Gallardo, M. Aguirre)*

Simply for socio-economic reasons, I would say. Most of these women have not been solvent enough to really practice writing as a profession; being married and having children must make it difficult.

Do you mean that the women writers don't receive the same editorial support?

No, they all have that. There is no one that I know of that does not have editorial support. But they themselves, the events of daily life swallow them. The women, I mean. In addition, they don't have the training, the habit of working as a writer. They are somewhat bourgeois, these women that I am talking about, they belong to the upper middle classes; and since most of the women of the upper classes do not have the habit of working, they never get beyond a certain point.

So, writing is sort of a "pastime" for these women?

Right, an adornment, something ornamental. They themselves do not take themselves seriously.

What did you feel with the death of Borges?

Well, the disappearance of a friend, in the first place. I knew him rather well. And, well, what can one feel in the face of the death of a man who has more than completed his life? He had completed his life both in terms of age and in terms of his profession. Borges did not lack anything.

He was a friend, and I felt the pain and sadness that comes with the disappearance of a friend, and the sadness at the disappearance of the most prophetic writer in Latin-American literatures, to be sure.

You discovered Borges when you were quite young, didn't you?

Not so young. But Borges was totally unknown then. In my youth I read an Argentinian writer who was at that time much more famous than Borges, a contemporary of his, a writer called Eduardo Mallea. I adored Eduardo Mallea, really; I liked his books very much. I discovered Borges ten years latter.

Today there are many people who say they know his work but I don't know if they have really read his books, or they just know the name.

It is true, yes, Borges' name has an enormous magic.

You lived your childhood and adolescence in Chile. What influence do your memories of these first stages of your life have in your work.?

They are very important. Let us say that it is like the great stewpot from which all the broths of my creation issue. The memories, the sorrows, the frustrations of that age, the joy—they are all materials which transformed, become the idiom of literature.

Did you keep a diary, or are these just remembrances?

No, just memories. My diary begins only in 1958.

You once commented in an interview: "My experience has been very limited by my emotions and my tastes." What relation does this observation of yours have with one of the most characteristic traits of your work, the experimentation with masks and disguises, both real and symbolic?

Well, there you have a desire to broaden one's scope of action, one's scope of knowledge and vitality. One desires to live more lives, everyone desires to live more than one life. And so, these five-minute masks, which are, as you say, imaginary or real, are always symbols of the multiplication of lives, and consequently, of the multiplication of death.

The publication of **Casa de Campo** [*A House in the Country*] *signified a new stage in the recognition of your work in the U.S. Now there are two principal points of reference for those that study your works:* **The Obscene Bird of the Night** *and* **A House in the Country***. What developments have there been in you work between and including these two novels?*

I see my work as something I am much more conscious of. At times *The Obscene Bird of the Night* was for me a way of becoming aware of the form of what I was doing. I do not mean that I was not conscious of the form that I was taking with my writing—this is already clear in **A Place Without Boundaries** mainly, and also in **Este Domingo** [*This Sunday*]. But most certainly, in *The Obscene Bird of the Night,* the form becomes part of the narrative itself. The form is the argument, let us say.

Something like in Ulysses?

Right. This coincides with the most intense moment in novelistic experimentation in Latin America. All of the writers of that time are experimenting with the form of the novel, and I include myself a bit in that.

Was that a conscious decision on you part?

Oh yes, by all means. Each one of us knew what we were doing. In the ten years that follow, between one novel and the next, there occurs a change of form, of aesthetic intentions of my writing, basically because what is so evident in *The Obscene Bird of the Night* no longer exists; that is, a sense of disquietude towards human existence with respect to the existence of the novel. In my earlier novels, these elements balance and unbalance themselves; they create and destroy, and then once again recreate themselves and each other. This process comes to its solution—I resolve it, let us say—in *The Obscene Bird*. Afterwards, my novels become much more even and level, "planar," if you will, until *A House in the Country*, in which once again I reflect upon the form "Novel."

The way in which you ponder this issue in **A House in the Country** *differs from that in* **The Obscene Bird.**

Yes, they do differ markedly; I would say that my approach to this problem in *The Obscene Bird of the Night* is a modernist approach, while the form this approach takes in *A House in the Country* is a post-modernist one.

You write a great deal about the Chilean upper middle class. And, as a Chilean professor once commented to me, you really drag them through the mud. (Laughter) Do you think that the people of the Chilean high society read your books, and if they do, what must they think of the ways in which you represent the bourgeois class?

I couldn't care less. (Laughter)

After living abroad for seventeen years, has your perception of Chile changed in the six years that you have been back?

Yes, it has changed a great deal. Before returning to Chile, I did not believe that we had the ability to degenerate as much as we have degenerated. We have fallen so low, and in a way so iniquitous, that I did not believe we were capable of it. No, I had never imagined such abject faculties as existing among the Chileans, such as I have seen now. Something like the betrayal of judicial power, for example, which is one thing the Chileans have done that I simply cannot grasp inside my head. I still have not been able to metabolize this.

Do you think that you or your writing have become "Chilenized" in some way after living here these past six years?

Yes, but I hope that my work has not become limited, that it has not been "Chilenized" in the sense of becoming limited. I hope that it has remained universal.

What was it like for you to collaborate with the theatre group ICTUS in the theatrical production that they did of your story, "Sueños de mala muerte" ["Dreams of a Bad Death"]?

It was one of the most marvelous experiences that I have had in this country. I think that writers in general lack the experience of working in a group, of having colleagues. Being a writer is a very solitary profession. Working with the theatre group was wonderful in the sense that I felt companionship, and in the sense that I always had a job to go to, with other people, and with continuous feedback. It was an excellent experience.

Have you given this experience as advice to other writers?

(Laughs) I do not think that solutions can be passed along; I think that solutions are totally personal, unique.

It is not usual for you to be referred ta as a writer who utilizes folkloric concepts in your work. Nonetheless, a variety of popular and folkloric Chilean symbols can be found in your novels. What conception do you have, not necessarily as a writer, of the Chilean people and their folklore?

I know very little about Chilean folklore. I know it inasmuch as it was told to me by the servants in my house when I was a small boy. I do not know the Chilean common folk, almost. I am familiar with the upper middle class, with the intellectual class and with the servants' class. Therefore, my contact with the common folk has always been through the servants; the servants are the ones who related the folkloric stories to me. In general, the servants here are originally from the country, and they are brought to Santiago by their employers. These women were the ones who told me about these things. It has something to do with becoming emotionally close to them. The memories I have are very affectionate, very loving. These stories are surrounded by a world of affection for me.

Do you have memories of spending time in the country, of going to a summer house?

Yes, my family spent the summers in the country, near a place called Talca, where my family is from. We have had property there since the colonial period. Not that we still have it; it has been sold off through the years. But we did have land there, and that's where we would summer, in the houses of my uncles, of my grandparents.

Your novel **A Place Without Boundaries,** *for example, contains many popular, or folkloric symbols, and also themes that have come to be regarded as typically Latin-American, such as the wealthy landowner, the exploitation of the peasant, the "machista" society. This demonstrates a profound understanding of the life of the popular classes.*

Probably so, but it is an understanding absorbed through intuition, let us say. . . through intuition, through "flashes," and not through actual experience. Through poetic transmittance, let us say, more than through information. I could not give you any statistics on Chilean country folk, for example.

What role does the writer, the intellectual, the artist play in today's Chilean society?

I suppose that the answer has to do with preserving some of the human qualities in a world that is purely a struggle for power. It has to do with preserving human qualities such as the faculty for understanding, and for measuring and balancing. The writer's role has to do with conserving pleasure, and knowledge for knowledge's sake.

How does the turbulence that Chile is now experiencing affect the process of writing?

It is impossible to write about anything else. We are all condemned to this. I cannot stand writing about it, but nonetheless I cannot write about anything else. I find myself so completely obsessed by this problem, that I have no other option. May it be damned! But what other option is there?

Can you tell me something about the novel you have just finished writing, **La Desesperanza**?

La Desesperanza is probably the most realistic of my novels, and the most Chilean. It is a novel that begins during the wake of Matilde Neruda, Pablo Neruda's wife, who died about a year ago. The second part of the novel is about a couple and an excursion they make throughout Santiago during the curfew hours, which ends up at Matilde's funeral. Everything occurs within eighteen hours, and, well, the novel has a sense of great urgency. The novel is significantly committed to the actual situation of the country. I both enjoyed and suffered very much writing it.

You taught at the Iowa Writer's Workshop for two years in the late Sixties. Here in Santiago you have conducted a literary workshop for a number of years. How do these experiences compare?

Here in Chile my classes are very elemental; the students are not widely read, and they have little literary training. In contrast, in the U.S., writing students have made the separation between literature and real life, and they understand very well what they are doing. A literary professionalism exists there. Here that does not exist.

The number of publishing houses in Santiago has recently increased, and it seems that there is increased support for the new generation of Chilean writers. Writers such as Diamela Eltit and Raúl Zurita, for example, receive a fair amount of attention in the press. What is your impression of the new generation of Chilean writers and of the literary world in Chile today?

Well, I find it to be somewhat shabby, if you want the truth of the matter. And this is for one reason: basically because of economic problems. For example, the number of books of short stories that are published in Chile is immense. Thin little books of stories, about eighty pages long, of short little stories. This is certainly an economic problem; the problem is the dismantling of the actual society in Chile, in the sense that people do not have the time nor the money to be able to write something longer, broader. I do not mean that the short story is inferior as a literary form to the novel. But there is something more of a commitment to writing a novel, and that commitment cannot be assumed by writers because of economic reasons, because of a sense of social insecurity. Because of this I think that Chile will remain for a time a country of writers of short story books—fifty pages long, of poetry books thirty pages long, those that can be read in one sitting. It is very sad if one compares this to the very large number of novelists my age who were beginning to write a generation ago. There were really a great number of novelists, and they had an enormous impact on the country. In contrast, there is no one like that now.

Except for Isabel Allende, who must have a great influence on other Chilean writers.

No, not really, she has not become a very significant influence. The problem is that she was a momentary flash; she did not continue, although they say that she is writing something else now.

Who are the young writers that most interest you?

For me, the term "young" is such an ample one (laughs); for me, at sixty, almost everyone is young. There is an Argentine writer that I like, called Juan Carlos Martín; there is a Cuban writer I like called Reinaldo Arenas.

Are you familiar with the works of contemporary North American writers like Alice Walker and Raymond Carver?

Well, of Alice Walker I have read the same work that everyone else has read, *The Color Purple*. I read it a year and a half ago, and it impressed me very much. But it is not a style of writing that I like very much.

Another American writer that I like a great deal is John Edgar Wideman.

John! John! He was a student of mine!

John Edgar Wideman?

Yes, of course! In the Writer's Workshop. Is he very well-known now?

Well, he won the PEN/Faulkner Award in 1985.

Oh, how wonderful! And for what novel?

A wonderful novel called Sent For You Yesterday.

Would you believe that my wife and I always wonder: what happened to John Wideman, has he stopped writing, has he fallen into obscurity? This news you've given me brings me great happiness. He was an intimate friend of ours, intimate, intimate. Adored personage! We have a series of photographs from the last time we were in the United States, of my daughter Pilar with his children. We were looking at them yesterday and wondering, What has happened to our friend John! We commented that, well, we had lost contact with him like with so many others.

I almost did not mention him because I thought that you would not know his work.

Of course, but he was a personal friend. What wonderful news you have given me!

You have traveled a great deal as part of your profession. What are your sensations when you leave Chile?

To breathe, to breathe, to move, to rejuvenate myself. Chile is a country that ages one, that causes one to age. There exists a great deal of sadness in this moment; I hope that it is not always like this.

What do you miss when you are away from Chile?

Probably that which caused me to escape (laughs). It is a vicious circle, don't you think?

You mean that what you don't like about Chile is also a part of what you are?

Right, exactly. . . .

What do you miss when you are away from Latin America?

The language, of course, the language not only meaning Spanish but also signifying a series of symbols that come into being through the participation within a culture. There are certain symbols that exist in Latin America that cannot be found outside of the Americas. There is a certain facility for expression, a certain joyousness, a certain ease that you find neither in the U.S. nor in Europe.

There is a significant number of writers, both from Latin America and from other parts of the world, that have been exiled or have self-exiled themselves from their countries for political reasons. What are your impressions of these writers and of the literature that proceeds from political exile?

Well, I think that it is quite necessary for this literature to exist. Political exile is one of the great themes of this generation. I think that it has performed quite brilliantly on various occasions. The elements of blame and nostalgia that are a part of the experience of exile have to make good material for a novel.

It is common for writers in exile to write about their countries even though they cannot return to them.

Sure, notice that all of the well-known novels of the "Boom" were written not in exile, but by writers working outside of their countries. One has only to realize that Mario Vargas Llosa wrote *The City and the Dogs* in Paris, that Cortázar wrote *Hopscotch* in Paris, that García Márquez wrote *One Hundred Years of Solitude* in Mexico; everyone wrote their novels abroad; it was a way of recovering one's birthplace, one's native land, from without.

Have you ever discussed why this was so with any of these writers you've mentioned?

No, no.

You will be going to the U.S. soon for a few months. What do you find attractive about living and writing in the U.S.?

I do no know if I am attracted to living and writing in the U.S.; I like the idea of being in the U.S. for a time. There is something invigorating about the U.S; it is a country that is not totally obsessed by the political phenomenon; it is a country that enjoys freedom. A country that is obsessed by the political phenomenon is a country that does not enjoy freedom. And here in Chile we are obsessed by the political phenomenon.

So in the U.S. you feel that you can breathe more easily?

Right. I have a sense of freedom. Also, many more things are accessible in the U.S., things that are not accessible here in Chile.

What about the literary world in the U.S.; are you familiar with it?

I know something of the literary world in New York; I know Vonnegut, Sontag, Doctorow. I know John Irving, who was also a student of mine. Some of these people are good friends, but in general, I participate very little in the "literary" life. I don't know why, really; I have never been attracted to the "public" thing. The demands, the exigencies have always been distasteful to me. "To be a Personality!": the Americans call it Personality! I can't stand it; I hate it!

You mean you consider it to be a facade?

Yes, it is so false!

"The Imagination of the Writer and the Imagination of the State": this was the theme of the 1986 PEN Conference. What ideas does this theme provoke for you?

It is a very long and painful theme for one; imagine, writers do not have a place in the actual state of Chile. In Chile today we are peripheral to the system. And so, of course, all of this is horrible for me. We do not have the right to participate in public life. In the past it was quite to the contrary; one of the characteristics of the Latin-American writer was his tendency to become involved. It was expected of him to take part in public life; the South American writer has always been a tribune. Now this is no longer so, at least in this country in which I live. It seems that is different in other countries; but here, this is what we have.

What are the greatest satisfactions of being a writer?

Well, it is always the most usual ones, the satisfactions are the most common ones, really: recognition, respect, admiration, money, and being able to earn a living doing what one has a vocation for.

That must bring you a great deal of satisfaction.

It is something very ordinary, if you will, a very modest satisfaction, but it is very fine, after all. The recognition is very good also. I think that one has a right to it. Things become different with age. The satisfactions change; one looks for other satisfactions, don't you think so, different from those one looked for as a young person?

How does one feel when this happens, when things change like this?

It is a part of the evolution of each person. I mean, people adapt to time, to exterior time and to interior time. I think that this is a part of it: it is a pretty phrase, at least! One goes through changes; there is no reason for one to be the same person always. I find myself to be a completely different person from what "I set out to be."

What did you set out to be?

Oh, I set out to be violent, and a rebel, and scandalous. My evolution was, no, things did not turn out badly. . . . What's more, at my age, I can say that all of the objectives change.

Do you think that one gets to know oneself better with age?

Naturally, there is an important element, which is that one's opportunities get more and more limited; the world becomes more limited to a person of greater age. But it becomes limited in terms of breadth, not in terms of depth. That is to say, that which was ample, is transformed into something more profound. Therefore, one no longer has one thousand friends, you see, or calls thirty people, or is intimate with fifty people. One has two, three friends, but these friends are enough, and that is the change. I used to be quite gregarious, very, very gregarious. I knew all kinds of people. I am still very curious about people, but if you get down to it I am less gregarious. For example, this upcoming trip to the U.S. has me up to here; I don't have any desire to go. I will have to meet people, whom I don't know if I wish to meet. So you see, I am no longer so outgoing.

But that does not mean one loses interest in the people one already knows. . . ?

Not in the people one knows.

. . . or the people one loves. . . .

Or those that one loves, or even new people that one meets. One becomes more choosy, that's all. One wants to have time. . . . And have time more for oneself.

Do you think that you are more aware of time?

Very much so, very much so. How to use it; to use it and not to use it up. To inscribe oneself in time, and not allow it only to pass. To do things without urgency, to look for a harmony.

That's all. . . .

Is that all? Ah, well, it's very short.

Thank you very much.

Thank you. You are very welcome. (pp. 57–67)

José Donoso and Amalia Pereira, in an interview in *Latin American Literary Review*, Vol. XV, No. 30, July–December, 1987, pp. 57–67.

George R. McMurray on the universality of Donoso's fiction:

Although the literal sketches of Donoso's short fiction impart an overall impression of traditional realism, his characters' placid lives are frequently disturbed by impulses over which they have little or no control. Their irrational emotions tend to prevail in the later works, suggesting the author's deepening disenchantment with the rigidly conceived world of reason which he lampoons by uncovering the other face of reality. In the process of carrying out his attacks against false values based on absolutes, he has evolved a more subjective style and experimented extensively with avant-garde novelistic architecture, point of view and treatment of time. The result is a shift to metaphoric expression which through implication and comparison lends depth and ambiguity to objective reality. These aesthetic preoccupations tend to minimize the importance of the Chilean scene and elevate the works in question to a more abstract realm of universality. Thus, whereas **Coronation, This Sunday** and most of the short stories convey an unmistakable flavor of Chilean reality, in **Hell Has No Limits** and **The Obscene Bird of Night** the setting and culture of the author's native land, though ingeniously integrated into the fictional texture, are blurred through a prism of poeticized myth and fantasy. In a somewhat similar but more straightforward manner, the Barcelona setting of **Sacred Families** provides a backdrop for numerous scenes typifying upper-middle-class life throughout the occidental world.

George R. McMurray, in his *José Donoso*, 1979.

PHILIP SWANSON
(essay date 1987)

[In the following essay, Swanson divides Donoso's writings into two phases, each characterized by the method the author uses to challenge conventional realism.]

José Donoso's literary production can be divided roughly into two phases: the first is characterized by an increasing mood of anguish, disintegration, and disorder, matched by a parallel increase in the complexity of style and form, peaking in 1970 with one of the classics of the Boom, *The Obscene Bird of Night,* where the novel's tortuous, distorted structure functions as a mirror image or plastic symbol of the chaos and terror of existence. After *The Obscene Bird of Night,* however, the pattern changes sharply. Donoso's subsequent work is much less tormented, much less complex. Much of it is indeed—on the surface—easily digestible and eminently readable.

Why does this change take place? One reason is related to the author's attitude to the Boom. It is interesting to note that *The Obscene Bird* was published at the end of the 1960s: that is, at the time of the split within the Seix Barral publishing house which, in Donoso's view, may be one of the factors marking the end of the Boom. Of course, it would be ridiculously simplistic to suggest that the Boom ended with the appearance of *The Obscene Bird*; but nevertheless, a transition of sorts clearly was underway round about the turn of the decade of the sixties— and one not confined to the work of Donoso alone. A new group of young writers was beginning to emerge; and at the same time certain changes were taking place in the work of more established writers such as Borges and Vargas Llosa (and later Carpentier and Fuentes). In any case, as far as Donoso was concerned, the Boom was over. He makes this clear in his *The Boom in Spanish American Literature: A Personal History* and in his semi-and quasi-autobiographical novel *The Garden Next Door* (*El jardín de al lado*).

But why did Donoso, having struggled to incorporate himself into the mainstream of the Boom, suddenly turn his back on it, as it were?

A clue to his position may be found in a newspaper article by him [in *El mercurio: artes y letras*, 14 November 1982], in which he asks:

When did we Latin Americans leave behind our bodies to be transformed into philosophizing, generalizing and experimenting abstractions? It is incredible that even novels which cannot be considered first rate. . . suffer from this "totalizing" ambition, which in the very recent past we considered to be the outstanding, glorious registered trademark of the novel of this continent, but which is now beginning to appear a bit tiresome to us. Can it be enough simply to construct complex edifices of words to ask ourselves who we are or to prove that we are this or that? Have we not arrived, all of a sudden, at a dead end for the useful novel, for the exploratory novel that seeks to break new ground, and is not time, perhaps, for the "person" novel?. . . Has not a moment of breaking away or change arrived for the contemporary Latin American novel, so that it can be reborn from the ashes of so many "totalizing" novels saturated of meaning and worn out with experimentation which are printed every day. . . ?

The conclusion to be drawn from this piece is that Donoso feels that the Boom has exhausted itself. Though the "new novel" was essentially a reaction against a perceived staleness in conventional realism, many of the formal experiments and innovations of modern fiction have themselves become standardized features of modern writing, leading to another form of traditionalism where one set of stereotypes has been replaced with another. Donoso

therefore posits the idea of a return to more simple forms, formulating the paradoxical notion of innovation through traditionalism. In this sense the return to simple structures can be seen as innovative in the modern context.

However, it this were all there were to Donoso's post-Boom strategy, it would not be terribly revolutionary or terribly exciting. The real point is that the simplicity of the later work is only apparent. Borrowing from Cortázar's distinction between the "lector-macho" (manly reader) and the "lector-hembra"(feminine reader), Donoso [in *Literatura y sociedad en American Latina*, 1981] has himself said of *A House in the Country*, for example, that "it is laid out as if it were a feminine novel, surrendering itself to the reader, but one soon realizes that it is not a feminine novel." This leads us to an important idea: Donoso's post-1970 work continues to attack the assumptions of the "feminine novel" and the realist novel—but in a different way from texts like Cortázar's *Hopscotch* or his own *The Obscene Bird of Night*. Rather than attacking realism head-on via outlandish structural distortion, the post-1970 fiction tricks the reader into accepting the novels as "realistic" or—at least—as straightforward, but only to break down each novel's apparent pattern of development as it progresses. Thus we can establish a contrast between the earlier Boom-oriented tendency to create *alternative* narrative structures, and Donoso's current efforts to subvert traditional realism from *within* by undermining the very realist patterns upon which his later novels appear to be based. In this sense, the later work may be seen not as an out-and-out rejection of the principles of the Boom, but rather as a sophisticated renewal and development of its methods.

A brief analysis of *The Mysterious Disappearance of the Young Marchioness of Loria* (*La misteriosa desaparición de la marquesita de Loria*), written in 1980, should help elucidate this new, post-Boom approach. Readers of the novel might be excused for seeing it as a trivial, light-hearted piece of fluff. It does indeed smack of simplicity, both in terms of content and in terms of style and form. The linear plot, chronological sequences, and standard third-person omniscient narration conspire to give the effect of a traditional novel—with all its implications of comfort and order. The gentle 1920s nostalgia, the pleasing pieces of sexual titillation, and the element of intrigue also contribute to the impression of an unproblematic "good read." Indeed, despite the occasional comic excess, the style of the novel is overwhelmingly realistic in tone, in that it presents us with an amusing tale that the reader accepts as "true"—within the fictional context—and that does not at first appear to question his attitudes too scathingly. This sensation of security is strengthened by the presentation of the story of the Marchioness of Loria as a kind of case history, employing a documentary style which gives an impression of the reporting of facts about events that really did take place.

As I have indicated elsewhere, however, this cozy

format tends to be subverted. The interventions of the narrator take on a hue that becomes increasingly tongue-in-cheek, while his language develops in the direction of artifice and exaggeration (as, for example, in the self-mocking cheeriness of the traditional summing-up of the fates of the other characters in the novel's spoof epilogue). Such narratorial games even find a place at the climax of the novel: following the marchioness's disappearance, her chauffeur is said to rush to the police station "where he recounted what the author of this story has just recounted, a story he is about to finish off." This blatant intrusion by the author seems designed to satirize the very style that the novel purports to employ undermining the illusion of realism it seeks to create.

The entire novel is, in a sense, reliant upon the principle of deconstructing its own apparent system, for it lacks the "colle logique" (logical glue) that Barthes in *S/Z* sees as fundamental to the "readerly" text. The effect of the title is to set forward an enigma: what is the reason for and the nature of the young marchioness's disappearance? The answer is never given in the text. We are faced with an incomplete hermeneutic code, an open-ended enigma. The title suggests a detective or mystery story format, but this is also broken down. The pleasure of reading such tales usually relies upon a gradual evolution toward the resolution of the puzzle, yet, just as Borages's detective stories confront the protagonist with the futility of detection, so too does Donoso deny the reader the comfort and satisfaction of a logical conclusion to his tale. The technique is to dupe the reader into the false security of the realist novel, only to weaken that sense of security by systematically questioning the presuppositions upon which the text itself appears to be based.

This is reflected in the very plot, which asks more questions than it answers. A jovial account of youthful sexuality gives way to the opaque symbolism surrounding the dog's eyes and the imperspicuity of the protagonist's vanishing into thin air. This introduction of a confusing motif and the disturbing distortion of the climax—both within a pseudo-realistic context—are even more discomforting than the hallucinatory complexities of *The Obscene Bird.* In that novel the reader is plunged into nightmarish world from the start; in *The Marchioness of Loria* the shock is all the greater, for the reader is projected from one extreme to the other; he is allowed to experience a sense of order, only to be then confronted with the falsity of that position and faced with the reality of chaos. This tension of opposites is dramatized in the novel's closing pages. The account of the other characters' settled lives may be reassuring, but Donoso stabs at the reader's smugness in the last line: Archibaldo and Charo are always "followed by Luna, their great, loyal, grey dog." This raises all sorts of questions, for Luna, after, apparently, abandoning his master, faded out of the action at the time of the marchioness Blanca's disappearance. What is he now doing with Archibaldo? The answer is that we simply do not

know. Donoso allows his readers to relax, but only to reintroduce the enigma of the dog on the very last line. We are thus made to close our copies of *The Marchioness of Loria* in a mood of confusion and disquiet.

The overturning of the internal logic of realism is even more evident in Donoso's following novel, *The Garden Next Door.* However, there is another element that also needs to be emphasized here. Whereas the works up to 1970 were characterized by fear and existential torment, the novels since that date are more ambivalent. It is enough to consider the contrasts within *Sacred Families* (the rather uncensorious humor of **"Chatanooga Choo-choo,"** the positive outcome of **"Gaspard de la nuit,"** yet at the same time the peculiar mixture of comedy with horror in **"Green Atom Number Five"**) or *The Marchioness of Loria* (a non-malevolent treatment of character combining with an intriguing blend of jocosity and nihilistic symbolism). *The Garden Next Door* expresses the fusion of these opposites: the achievement of tranquillity through an acceptance of the absurdity of life. Though the protagonists, Julio and Gloria, recognize the frustrations underlying their existence, they do not sink into despair. Their lives appear to be heading for a major crisis, but they survive it and gain contentment. Hence the final chapter reveals that Julio does *not* disappear into an abyss of darkness, as was hinted previously, while his once suicidal wife is left to reflect that: "I'm aware of how things have calmed down, taking their place within this perspective, which might seem false and dreamy, but which I now dare to accept as my own." This peaceful synthesis is also reflected at the level of structure and style. Realist and nonrealist elements combine in the novel: the subversive aspect questions the validity of our assumptions about the meaningful nature of reality, while the traditional aspect conveys a mood of new-found solace and quietude.

It is usually emphasized that the tone of the novel is predominantly that of traditional psychological realism. But, as was suggested earlier, as is implied in the novel, this use of a traditional form may be in itself a method of renovating what Donoso [in *Hispamérica* 21 (1978)] sees as the spent forces of the "new novel" which—paralleling the transition of the hippies of *The Garden Next Door* from nonconformism to effective conformism—"aims to destroy the classical novel but forges another type of classical novel." Equally, however, the return to traditionalism relates to the quest for inner peace. In the quotation cited near the beginning of this essay Donoso rejects the large-scale "totalizing" tendencies of the "new novel" in favor of a simpler form he calls the "person" or "personal" novel. This narrowing of focus can be seen quite clearly in *The Garden Next Door,* with its heavily autobiographical content and its self-declared intention, via the opening dedication, to "contemplate. . . domestic or familiar shores." Moreover, the relief Julio feels on finishing his novel—as if he has extracted an irritating, malignant tumor that leaves behind a lingering pain—obviously mirrors Donoso's own oft-stated position after the completion of *The Obscene Bird*: having liberated his obsessions, he feels deliverance tinged by a residual element of angst. The achievement of inner peace from turning to a more traditional, personal literature is personified by Gloria's change of rôle. She says that, while Julio is obsessed by imitating from other contemporary sources, she has found a sense of salvation in assuming a perhaps unfashionable "low-key tone." If the chaotic structures of works like *The Obscene Bird* exemplify the terror of life and the chaos of the universe, then the more gentle, orthodox style of *The Garden Next Door* is seen to embody a calmer, more resigned attitude. Gloria's own words sum up the relationship between changes in narrative technique and attitude, when she says of writing:

> It isn't a solution, but, at all events, it helps me to carry on and stop thinking all the time about the corrosive effects of uselessness. Now that's something at least.

The construct of art is, if not a passport to fulfillment, then at least a means of evading anguish.

But despite the novel's apparently traditionalist orientation, there are several references that actually appear to question the reliability of realist narrative. For example, when Gloria locks herself in the bathroom, Julio raps the door:

> "Open the door!" I shouted.
>
> No. That's not true. I didn't shout. Nor did I bang the door. I only turned the handle, murmuring:
>
> "Gloria, please. . . "

After Julio's subsequent diatribe against his wife, he confesses:

> I may, or I may not have said these thing (I'm inclined to think probably not), while outside the bathroom door. . . I might possibly have said them, though not as set out here, but rather in a fragmented fashion, in the form of interjections, barely emblematic of my edginess.

Julio's novel, meanwhile, is said to consist of "questionable truths" and he himself is earlier seen to make a completely incorrect interpretation of events. The effect, of course, is to cast doubt upon the writer's ability to observe reality accurately.

This skepticism toward realism is reflected, not in the creation of an alternative labyrinthine or chaotic structure, but in the subversion of what appears to be traditional realist structure. The bulk of the novel employs a familiar, orthodox first-person narrator and develops in a normal linear pattern. However, everything changes in the last chapter. It transpires that the narrator is not who we thought it was but, in fact, his wife: thus everything in the first five chapters is called into question; the novel has undermined the realist principles on which it

appeared to be based. This sudden structural turn-about comes as even more of a surprise than the disappearance of Blanca in *The Marchioness of Loria*: indeed, its very unexpectedness is its most subversive quality. Once again, Donoso is seen to negate the omniscient claims of traditional realism, not via the methods normally associated with the "new novel," but via a form of internal structural inversion.

The novel's structural-thematic duality emerges quite clearly. On the one hand, radical techniques invalidate the suppositions upon which realism is based (that is, the notion of ordered reality, a structured, meaningful existence.). On the other, realist techniques are themselves employed to demonstrate man's eventual need to adopt a construct and come to terms with the nature of life.

This duality can be seen in the novel's overall structural pattering. The key section of the opening chapter is the third. The incident at La Cala, where Julio strikes Bijou, powerfully illustrates Julio's problems of age and frustration. Interestingly, the third section of every chapter except the last contains a similar dramatic episode that highlights the apparent hopelessness of Julio's situation: the tense, illegal telephone call home, made with the aid of Bijou in chapter 2; the humiliating encounter with Marcelo Chiriboga in chapter 3; the fiasco of their attempt to paint over the offensive "Red assholes" slogan in chapter 4; and the rejection of Julio's book and his consequent stealing and selling of one of Pancho Salvatierra's paintings in chapter 5. Furthermore, chapters 4 and 5 have only four sections in each. In both of these chapters the fourth section also contains an unfortunate occurrence: Bijou's theft of a painting and Gloria's suicide attempt in chapter 4; and the frightening beggar episode in Tangiers in chapter 5. Thus the novel's patterning repeatedly hammers home the theme of frustration, culminating climactically in the final two chapters of the sequence with a double helping of pessimism. Yet despite all of this, the final chapter overturns the pattern: the negative structure—and therefore the negative outlook—is seen to disintegrate. The fact that the last is the only chapter not to be fragmented into sections implies a unity of attitude that was missing in the previous ones: the confusion of chapters 1 to 5 has given way to a dominant mood of measured philosophic resignation in the sixth.

The structural inversion noted in *The Garden Next Door,* then, seems to point to three salient features of Donoso's post-Boom fiction: a greater sense of calm, a return to less complex forms, and a pattern of internal rather than external subversion. Though space has limited our attention here to two novels, it should be said that these elements are visible, in varying combinations, in all of Donoso's novelistic production since 1970. In *Sacred Families* Anselmo finds satisfaction in life (even if he remains unaware of the secret machinations of his wife), while the creation of family harmony is uppermost at the end of the final novella in the collection. On a formal level, each of the three novellas in the book employs a recognizably realistic style which is counteracted by the introduction of fantasy. Indeed, Ronald Schwartz [in his *Nomads, Exiles and Emigrés*, 1980] described it as "an 'anti-anti-novel',. . . a form that perhaps marks the new direction for Latin American novelist and narratives for the 1980s." *A House in the Country* displays similar characteristics. Humorous and perhaps containing a hint of political optimism at the end, it also employs an accessible narrative technique, but one that it set against exaggeration, artifice, and constant narratorial intervention and uncertainty—an attack on all forms of orthodoxy in a way that echoes the spirit, if not the classic narrative methods, of the "new novel" of the Boom.

As for Donoso's first work following his return to Chile, *Four for Delfina* (*Cuatro para Delfina*), similar considerations apply. In each of the first two novellas of this collection, one narrative mode is offset by another: the build-up to a wedding and to the acquisition of property is subverted by death and the acquisition of a mausoleum as property in one story, while the realistic format of the second is disrupted by the introduction of obscure beggar symbolism and an enigmatic ending. The other two tales in the collection are closer to *The Garden Next Door.* In "Things Past" (inspired by Proust) the evolution from evasion to resignation is expressed through the replacement of Proustian fantasizing with "a realist perspective"—in effect the narrative stance of the novella itself. This sense of resignation is also in the foreground in "Jolie Madame." Here the protagonist, Adriana, seems to use artifice positively in order to come to terms with life: in the words of her friend, she, like Gloria of *The Garden Next Door,* seeks not to "find deep fulfillment," but recognizes that one's "aim in life was more modest," and she thus achieves satisfaction through stoicism and acceptance. Moreover, this novella puts Adriana's transition across strongly by means of a narrative transition in the form of internal subversion. A very straight forward

piece of realism is turned inside out via the injection of a wealth of bizarre symbolism involving Adriana's friend, her daughter, and her perfume (the Jolie Madame of the title).

Of course, any overall statement of Donoso's post-Boom strategy must be, at best, tentative. Though there are clear common threads in his later fiction, there are also many differences or variations. What seems plain, however, is that since the 1970s Donoso has not felt the need to identify himself with the Boom. While his work up to that point was part of a process of increasing integration with the convention of the "new novel," his writing since then has freed itself from those conventions. Hence, in a recent conversation with me, he felt able to describe his latest novel, *Hopelessness* (*La desesperanza*), as one that "has nothing to do with my other works," mischievously calling it a work of the "post-post-Boom." He went on to say that he felt "a liberation from the need to belong to anything" that "it is no longer important. . . to belong to the Boom or not to belong to the Boom." Certainly this freedom has yielded fruitful results in Donoso's case. Rather than repeating the same formulae or producing what in *The Garden Next Door* he calls "a new novel stew," he has gone beyond the Boom to develop a new way of challenging his readers to scrutinize their assumptions about life and literature. As the author himself explains to Silvestre Ventura in *A House in the Country*, he changed his style of writing after *The Obscene Bird* in order "to see whether it might serve me in creating an equally portentous universe: one that might similarly reach and touch and call notice to things, though from an opposite. . . angle." This is as good a summary of Donoso's post-Boom technique as any critic can give. (pp. 520–28)

Philip Swanson, "Donoso and the Post-Boom: Simplicity and Subversion," in *Contemporary Literature*, Vol. 28, No. 4, Winter, 1987, pp. 520–29.

SOURCES FOR FURTHER STUDY

Adelstein, Miriam. "The Insubstantial Country of the Mind: *Cuentos* by José Donoso." *Critica Hispanica* V, No. 2 (1983): 97–106.
    Surveys the characters and themes of Donoso's short stories.

Bacarisse, Pamela. "Donoso and Social Commitment: *Casa de campo.*" *Bulletin of Hispanic Studies* LX, No. 4 (October 1983) : 319–32.
    Explores the social and political implications of *A House in the Country.*

——————. "El obsceno pájaro de la noche: The Novelist as Victim." *The Modern Language Review* 81, No. 1 (January 1986): 82–96.
    Examines the linguistic features of the text and contends that the author and the narrator of *The Obscene Bird of Night* are "virtually one and the same."

Feal, Rosemary Geisdorfer. "'In my End Is My Beginning': José Donoso's Sense of an Ending." *Chasqui* XVII, No. 2 (November 1988): 46–55.
    Examines the conclusions of *The Garden Next Door,*

La misteriosa desaparición de la marquesita de Loria, and the novellas of *Sacred Families* and *Cuatro para Delfina.*

Gautier, Marie-Lise Gazarian. "José Donoso." In her *Interviews with Latin American Writers,* pp. 55–78. Elmwood Park, Ill.: Dalkey Archive Press, 1989.

Donoso provides his views on writing fiction.

González, Flora. "The Androgynous Narrator in José Donoso's *El jardín de al lado.*" *Revista de Estudios Hispanicos* XXIII, No. 1 (January 1989): 99–113.

Analyzes the male and female narrative voices in *The Garden Next Door.*

Lipski, John M. "Donoso's *Obscene Bird:* Novel and Anti-Novel." *Latin American Literary Review* V, No. 9 (Fall/Winter 1976): 39–47.

Explores how language shapes the narrative structure of *The Obscene Bird of Night.*

Mac Adam, Alfred J. "José Donoso: Endgame." In his *Modern Latin American Narratives: The Dreams of Reason,* pp. 110–18. Chicago: University of Chicago Press, 1977.

Discusses *The Obscene Bird of Night,* focusing on its satirical aspects, its multiple-layered narrative, and its blurring of the distinction between narrator and narrative.

Magnarelli, Sharon. "The Baroque, the Picaresque, and *El Obsceno pájaro de la noche* by José Donoso." *Hispanic Journal,* No. 2 (Spring 1981): 81–93.

Characterizes *The Obscene Bird of Night* as a neobaroque example of the picaresque novel.

Swanson, Philip. "José Donoso: *El obsceno pájaro de la noche.*" In *Landmarks in Modern Latin American Fiction,* edited by Philip Swanson, pp. 183–206. London: Routledge, 1990.

Examines ways in which the "bewildering" narrative of *The Obcene Bird of Night* overturns social and literary expectations.

Additional coverage of Donoso's life and career is contained in the following sources published by Gale Research: *Contemporary Authors New Revision Series,* Vol. 32; *Contemporary Literary Criticism,* Vols. 4, 8, 11, 32; *Dictionary of Literary Biography,* Vol. 113; *Hispanic Writers; and Major 20th-Century Writers.*

Ariel Dorfman

1942–

Argentine-born Chilean novelist, nonfiction writer, essayist, journalist, short story writer, poet, and playwright.

INTRODUCTION

Dorfman is considered one of Latin America's most original social critics and fiction writers. He is best known for essays, short stories, and novels in which he examines such topics as exile, life under authoritarian rule, the influence of popular culture on social and political values, and the interaction of power, language, and ideology. Pat Aufderheide has commented: "Like many Third World writers, Dorfman denies the neat division between art and politics; more impressive, he also refuses to collapse the two categories into one."

Born in Buenos Aires, Dorfman was two years old when his family was forced to flee to the United States because of his father's opposition to the Argentine government. Dorfman spent the next ten years in New York City, where his father worked for the United Nations, before his family settled in Chile in 1954. After completing his education at the University of Chile, Dorfman became a naturalized Chilean citizen in 1967. A year later, while working as an activist, journalist, and writer, he published his first book, *El absurdo entre cuarto paredes: El teatro de Harold Pinter,* a critical analysis of English playwright Harold Pinter. Following the overthrow of Chilean president Salvador Allende by Augusto Pinochet in 1973, Dorfman was forced into exile, intermittently living in Argentina, France, the Netherlands, and eventually the United States. As a contributor to English and Spanish journals and a frequent guest on television news programs, Dorfman has remained an active participant in Chile's political and social affairs. He returned to Chile in 1990 after Pinochet relinquished his position to his popularly-elected successor Patricio Aylwin.

The intersection of culture and politics is a recurrent theme in Dorfman's nonfiction. In *Para leer al Pato Donald* (1972; *How to Read Donald Duck: Imperi-*

alist Idealogy in the Disney Comic) and *Reader's nuestro que estás en la tierra: Ensayos sobre el imperialismo cultural* (1980; *The Empire's Old Clothes: What the Lone Ranger, Babar, and Other Innocent Heros Do to Our Minds*), Dorfman argues that such forms of popular literature as cartoons, comic books, picture novels, children's stories, and the magazine *Reader's Digest* subliminally promote capitalist ideology and encourage passivity. Although some critics have faulted Dorfman for failing to place his analyses within a firm social context, others have praised his insights on a rarely studied topic.

Dorfman often focuses on Chilean political life in his fiction and plays. Published the same year as Pinochet's overthrow of Allende, the novel *Moros en la costa* (1973; *Hard Rain*) explores the appropriateness of writing in the midst of mass murder, exploitation, and poverty. *Viudas* (1981; *Widows*) centers on the struggle between an autocratic government and thirty-seven women who suspect that their missing husbands were abducted and killed by the authorities. Although Dorfman set the novel in occupied Greece during the 1940s to avoid censorship, he changed the setting to Chile when he adapted it for the stage. The stories in *Cría ojos* (1979; *My House Is on Fire*) examine how people retain a sense of hope living under a repressive military regime, while *Death and the Maiden* (1992), a play about a woman who believes she has found the man who tortured her years earlier, addresses the questions of morality and justice in post-Pinochet Chile.

Although some commentators have criticized his short stories as simplistic and unimaginative, most critics consider Dorfman's novels highly original for their narrative techniques. For instance, *La última canción de Manuel Sendero* (1983; *The Last Song of Manuel Sendero*) combines narratives told from several different perspectives: unborn fetuses who refuse to enter a world filled with violence and fear, two exiled Chilean cartoonists and characters within the cartoonists' comic strip. Dorfman uses similar techniques in *Mascara* (1988) wherein he incorporates the monologues of a voyeuristic photographer, an amnesiac woman with multiple personalities, and a plastic surgeon whose operations provide politicians with the faces that the public expects. Concerned with human identity and the paranoia created by authoritarian regimes, *Mascara* has been hailed by critics as an innovative political allegory and has been compared to the work of Franz Kafka and Günter Grass. As Robert Atwan has commented: "[One of] Dorfman's main achievements in fiction has surely been his ability to create methods of storytelling that enact, not merely record, a political vision, [and] that fuse both the political and the literary imaginations."

CRITICAL COMMENTARY

ANDREW HACKER

(essay date 1983)

[In the following essay, Hacker reviews Dorfman's collection of essays *The Empire's Old Clothes*, faulting his critique of popular culture as overly "single-minded."]

In each successive stage of history, Friedrich Engels wrote, "the most powerful, economically dominant class . . . acquires new means of holding down and exploiting the oppressed class." Religion has served this end, as has purblind patriotism. In our time there have emerged "more highly developed instruments"—also Engels's phrase—to cloud the public's mind with illusions and delusions. So runs Ariel Dorfman's thesis in *The Empire's Old Clothes* and he has chosen three of these instruments for detailed scrutiny: Babar the Elephant, the Lone Ranger and *Reader's Digest.*

Mr. Dorfman proposes to demonstrate how our consciousness is shaped. He does so by examining a set of children's books, the adventures of a hero for preadolescents and the workings of the world's most widely read adult magazine. A further feature of *The Empire's Old Clothes* is that the author is a Chilean exile, offering us a picture of ourselves as seen by an outsider. Mr. Dorfman was a professor of journalism and literature in Chile until Salvador Allende fell; an earlier book of his, *How to Read Donald Duck*, has been published in 13 languages.

Principal Works

El absurdo entre cuatro paredes: El teatro de Harold Pinter (criticism) 1968

Imaginación y violencia en América (essays) 1970

Para leer al Pato Donald [with Armand Mattelart] (non-fiction)1972
[*How to Read Donald Duck: Imperialist Ideology in the Disney Comic*, 1975]

Moros en la costa (novel) 1973
[*Hard Rain*, 1990]

Ensayos quemados en Chile: Inocencia y neocolonialismo (essays) 1974

Superman y sus amigos del alma [with Manuel Jofré] (essays) 1974

Culture et resistance au Chile (essays) 1978

Cría ojos (short stories) 1979
[*My House Is on Fire*, 1990]

Pruebas al canto (poetry) 1980

Reader's nuestro que estás en la tierra: Ensayos sobre el imperialismo cultural (essays) 1980
[*The Empire's Old Clothes: What the Lone Ranger, Babar, and Other Innocent Heroes Do to Our Minds*, 1983]

Viudas (novel) 1981
[*Widows*, 1983]

Missing (poetry) 1982

La última canción de Manuel Sendero (novel) 1983
[*The Last Song of Manuel Sendero*, 1987]

Hacia liberación del lector latinamericano (essays) 1984

Dorando la píldora (short stories) 1985

Patos, elefantes y héroes: La infancia como subdesarrollo (essays) 1985

Pastel de choclo (poetry) 1986
[*Last Waltz in Santiago, and Other Poems of Exile and Disappearance*, 1988]

Mascara (novel) 1988

Widows (drama) 1988
[adaptor; from his novel]

Some Write to the Future: Essays on Contemporary Latin American Fiction (criticism) 1991

Death and the Maiden (drama) 1992

Babar wends his way to Paris, where he is adopted by a wealthy woman. Under her tutelage he is soon sleeping in a bed, bathing in a tub and even driving a car. He also learns how to read and write and how to dress in elegant style. His education over, Babar returns to Africa, where the other elephants, awed by his accomplishments, crown him their king.

For Mr. Dorfman, Babar's story is a lesson in colonialism with racist overtones. "The child," he writes," has come into contact with an implicit history that justifies and rationalizes the motives behind an international situation in which some countries have everything and other countries almost nothing." As soon as Babar becomes "civilized," he returns (in reality, is sent back) to prepare the natives for the new imperialist hegemony. In this parable, white overlords never appear. Babar does their work for them, adding a liberal veneer by showing that *some* savages can learn Western ways. "Babar's history," Mr. Dorfman tells us,"is none other than the fulfillment of the dominant countries' colonial dream"—domination without tears.

The Lone Ranger, Mr. Dorfman says, reaches older children with action-filled homilies set closer to home. In a typical adventure, the masked rider and his Indian companion (always a few yards behind) defend honest settlers from land barons and their hired thugs. The subtlety here is in casting greed as the villain, acknowledging that excesses exist. But the system is self-correcting, with the Lone Ranger representing capitalist morality. Mr. Dorfman quotes a scriptwriter: "If there are some very rich or powerful ranchers who are trampling on the rights of little people, the Ranger will have to convert them so that they can see the error of their ways." In this mission he is often helped by the land baron's son, who stirs repentance in his dad. Still, the bottom line remains: "The Ranger doesn't have anything against rich people—if they've made their money honestly."

Mr. Dorfman explicates these episodes and stories at academic length. He even deciphers the racial and sexual symbolism of Zephyr the monkey and Silver the stallion. For authority, he cites such authors as György Lukács, Antonio Gramsci and Frantz Fanon, blending in the psychoanalytic leaven found in much Marxist writing. Of course, childhood eventually ends (although "infantilization" does not), so capitalist society must fashion new forms of fantasy for adults. For Mr. Dorfman, *Reader's Digest* clearly fills this bill.

The *Digest's* American circulation is a little more than 18 million; the magazine enters almost one in four of this nation's homes. Subscribers tend to treat it as a family member, and it is easy to see why. In tone and message, the magazine congratulates its readers on what fine folk they are: independent, self-reliant, eager for improvement. Out there, it implies, are others who gripe about the system and look for a free ride; *Digest* people do their bit to make the world work. Mr. Dorfman

---

The Babar books are aimed at young children; they are meant to be read aloud by parents or teachers. Although the authors are French, the series has had a broad appeal. It runs to 32 books, and five million copies have been sold in the United States alone. The books concern an African elephant who is orphaned when his mother is shot by a "wicked hunter." After his mother is killed,

calls this attitude "feverish individualism," an ideology for solid citizens.

According to *The Empire's Old Clothes*, the Digest's politics transcend its conservative stance on unions, welfare programs and the Communist threat. By emphasizing the human element, the magazine deflects attention away from the injustices capitalism creates. Typically, a problem "is placed before our eyes so we can see how, in some model place together with the inspiration of some exemplary citizen, that problem has found a path toward solution." Thus in an article on pollution, we learn of a young Californian who advocates tree planting as a way to combat smog. Or we read about a retired sea captain who reforms young delinquents by teaching them how to sail. All this benevolence blinds the *Digest* reader to the system's contradictions.

Even on its own Marxist terms, Mr. Dorfman's critique takes too effortless a route. He sticks to textual analysis, with no attempt to set his interpretations in a social context. But the *Digest* addresses itself to a specific segment of the population—largely lower middle class Americans who have done sufficiently well to be willing to identify with the established order. Parsing magazine articles, however, does not tell us how the American economy came to foster the creation of such a group of people or why its members take so uncritical a view of the system. (Interestingly, the upper middle class tends to be far less accepting of it.) This is not to say that Mr. Dorfman should have written a sociological survey. Still, insofar as he is claiming that the *Digest* and Babar and the Lone Ranger have succeeded in winning the hearts and minds of Americans, he is obliged to relate his subjects to their intended audiences.

In this connection, I am not persuaded that either the educated elephant or the masked rider has made that much of an impression. (The Lone Ranger has long been displaced as an American broadcasting staple.) If there is anything that shapes and expresses the current consciousness of young people, it is the music that looms so large in their lives from a very early age. When we examine rock or its sundry variations, we find that the music's message is implicitly subversive, invoking a dissociation from adult society. Even those young people who seek careers and success are less loyal to the system than appearances suggest. This is not to say that they think in revolutionary terms, simply that there is a lot of disaffection out there. A Marxist analysis might view these young people as constituting a class without an economic role apart from consumption. This would explain their political alienation and their search for sensual gratification. But there are no such hints in *The Empire's Old Clothes*, Mr. Dorfman shows little curiosity about young people or their intellects. As it happens, since the 1960's America has witnessed a ferment among the young that Mr. Dorfman would probably applaud. Unfortunately, his view of popular culture is so single-minded that he cannot see it. (pp. 15, 28)

Andrew Hacker ,"Who Was That Masked Capitalist?" in *The New York Times Book Review*, May 8, 1983, pp. 15, 28 .

ARIEL DORFMAN
(essay date 1986)

[In the following essay, Dorfman relates events surrounding the false report of his murder in Chile in 1986 and reflects upon the dictatorship of Augusto Pinochet.]

"The reports of my death are greatly exaggerated." From the time I heard Mark Twain's famous phrase, I had always thought it would be extremely amusing to be able to quote it. When that opportunity finally came a few weeks ago however, it was not so amusing as I had imagined: a telephone call on September 12 announced that I had been murdered in Chile.

The news came at the end of one of the most depressing weeks in my country's history. After the failed attempt on his life, on September 7, Gen. Augusto Pinochet, our dictator for the past thirteen years, went wild. This was the pretext he had been waiting for to crush an opposition that had been mounting a campaign of protracted civil disobedience against him. He declared a state of siege, shut down six magazines and a couple of news agencies, raided shanty towns, expelled foreign priests. His secret policemen picked up a number of prominent dissidents. Some of those were lucky. They were carted off to an official jail—paradoxically, one of the only secure places to be if the death squads are also out to get you. Others were arrested by men without warrants, and their bodies, riddled with bullets, began turning up several days later all over Santiago.

Thousands of miles away, in North Carolina, where I spend each fall semester teaching at Duke University, I anxiously awaited the identification of the bodies, and learned with horror that one of the executed men was a friend. Journalist José Carrasco had been my literature student at the University of Chile many years ago. I had taught him *Don Quixote*. We had talked on a couple of occasions since my return to Santiago to settle down after twelve years of exile in December of 1985. The last time I saw him was at a funeral march for a murdered student. After spending some years in a Chilean concentration camp after the 1973 coup, he had gone into eight years of exile in Mexico and now, like me, had come back to live in his own land. He showed me his two sons, who felt more Mexican than Chilean. "This is the man," he said to them, pointing at me, "who taught me to joust with windmills." We didn't finish our conversation because, as usually happens at funerals in Chile, more dangerous than mere windmills, the police had arrived to interrupt the procession, and in the pandemonium that ensued, we lost sight of each other.

Now it was his funeral that would be disrupted, and I, of course, would not be there. Once again the country was being destroyed, and I was far away. The horror was compounded by its familiarity: it was as if we were all caught up one more time, in the endless repetition of the 1973 coup. The terror was widespread. When I called on the phone, my friends did not answer. They had gone into hiding. It was enough for the police to be hunting an undetermined 500 to induce thousands of others to leave home, sleeping in their clothes at night, just in case Carrasco had been taken out in his underwear. "Don't put on your shoes," they had said to him, "You won't be needing them." Suddenly to the new despair about what was happening to my country was added the old, bitter feeling of impotence that had haunted the long years of my exile, before Pinochet had allowed me to return home: a funeral is being held, a boot is breaking down the door to your friend's house, a woman in a slum who gave you tea is watching troops shatter her windows and bayonet her mattress, a priest who stood in front of tanks to stop a raid is being put on a plane while his parishioners sing at the airport so that at least he will be able to hear them one last time. If there was finally something you could do.

The next day, however, when a reporter from United Press International called to inform me that a wire dispatched from Buenos Aires had just announced that one of the other corpses found in Chile had now been identified and was none other than my own, I was brutally reminded that distance from one's country when a dictator rules is not only a curse; it can also confer the ambiguous relief of safety.

As a child, I always wanted to survive my own death. I desired no more than a couple of hours. It would be fun, I thought, to witness how people reacted.

But just let that childhood dream come true, and you will realize that there is nothing to recommend the experience. Besides the pain to one's family and friends, the feverish calls all around the world, what is hard to dismiss is the sensation that in some odd way you may, indeed, have died.

That could be why I automatically reached for my Mark Twain phrase. Those wryly elegant words still serve today, as perhaps they did when they were first pronounced, to give you time to get used to a strange feeling of ghostliness. After all, somewhere in the world there is someone who already thinks of you as past and fixed and irretrievable, and thinks it strongly enough to have scattered the news to the four winds. Humor at least allows you to pretend you are not worried about that day when, inevitably, you will not be around to make your disavowals.

But no amount of quipping and joking could dispel the undeniable death of somebody else back in Santiago, the news of whose killing was, unfortunately, not in the least exaggerated. And there was also the matter of making sense of the whole macabre affair. Was I receiving a warning from the Chilean government, a not-so-subtle way of suggesting that I should not return to my country, as I had been planning to do again, at the end of this year? It would be consistent with all sorts of verbal incursions that had escalated against me in the past months; an attack by Jesse Helms on the Senate floor, accusing me of being "one of the prime disinformation agents of the radical Chilean left"; several denunciations in Chile's right-wing media, along with a barrage of hate mail, some of it with a decidedly anti-Semitic tint. The secret police back home discovered long ago that a threat against somebody's life is often as effective as an outright assault on it and does not exact as high a political cost. Now, I surmised, they were applying their wisdom to me. A few calls to Argentina quickly banished that idea. News of my death had appeared in several Buenos Aires newspapers the morning of September 12. The previous night there was a gigantic solidarity rally for Chile in one of the city's stadiums. One of the orators, Jorge Lavandero, a Chilean left-wing Christian Democrat, had, according to journalists present, denounced my brutal murder in Santiago. Several hours later Lavandero issued a disclaimer: he had been reading one of my poems to the multitude, and members of the press, unable to hear well because of the shouting of slogans, had misinterpreted his words and forthwith ousted me from this world. The corpse had, in fact, been identified that very night as that of Abraham Mustkablie, an accountant abducted from his home by a group of agents wearing ski masks at dawn on September 8.

And, yet, to ascertain that the news of my death originated in journalistic bumbling has not helped me put the affair behind me. I cannot shake the certainty that there could be some sort of warning in that news dispatch.

I have learned that in order to live under a dictatorship you must tame your imagination. Signs of violence and forboding are everywhere, and if you do not want to be paralyzed by fear, you must learn to shut those signs out. I can remember being awakened many times in the silent dawn of curfew in Santiago by the approaching sound of cars —and returning to sleep without giving the matter a second thought, pretending that there was no danger. There is no other way to keep sane when death is an everyday possibility.

One month before he was burned alive by soldiers in a Santiago slum, 19-year-old Rodrigo Rojas de Negri attended the funeral of a 19-year-old student shot by troops in the streets. The photographs Rodrigo snapped that day have survived him, and they are haunting. It is as if you were looking through his now-dead eyes not only at what he saw then but at what he would have seen if he had photographed his own funeral a month later, when the police beat up the mourners, tried to steal the coffin and tear-gassed the crowd on the way to the cemetery.

Did Rodrigo have the slightest notion that he was taking pictures of his own burial? I doubt it; such thoughts would have unnerved him, leaving the military firmly in control of his dreams and the rhythm of his life. He clicked the camera and shut his eyes to the gray prefigurations of his own fate.

A year and a half before, in March 1985, human right activist José Manuel Parada was investigating a paramilitary squad. "I think they're about to kill somebody," he told Andrés Domínguez, executive secretary of the Chilean Human Rights Commission. He did not dare to guess that the somebody in question was himself. Three days later, just as he had dropped his kids off at school, a group of men kidnapped him. The next day his body along with those of two other Communist professionals was dumped by the wayside, not a mile from where Rodrigo Rojas would be thrown by the soldiers who burned him. Their throats had been slashed.

From where did those anticipations of their own death come? From the future that they refused to acknowledge, from the shadow of violence that was already engulfing them? It could well be. Living under Pinochet, I have learned not to laugh at those who, in order to survive treat the universe as if it were a hidden book which the imagination can decipher. I am not, after all, applying any rationality to my own case.

Even though the news of my death might be fraudulent its possibility was all too real. Everybody who had read the Buenos Aires papers had found it quite natural that I, or any Chilean for that matter, could be murdered. Ever since the coup that terminated democracy in Chile, I have been living on borrowed time—trying either to escape that death or to ignore it. My exile thirteen years ago was a way of avoiding it; my return to Chile at the end of last year, while Pinochet was still in power, was a way of making believe it would not touch me. And so, when the news of my murder arrived, it took its place in a long series—one more in a chain of horrors, all the deaths flowing into the slow and endless death of Chile itself. I am contaminated. That is the final message of the death that brushed by my body and did not settle there. I find it difficult to remember a time when there were other forms of passing away, that people can die of old age or of sickness or in car accidents.

I regret to say that Mark Twain's quotation is less apt than I originally believed. The reports of my death have not, alas, been that greatly exaggerated. (pp. 370, 372, 374)

Ariel Dorfman ,"Reports of My Death," in *The Nation,* New York, Vol. 243, No. 12, October 18, 1986, pp. 370, 372, 374.

ARIEL DORFMAN WITH PEGGY BOYERS AND JUAN CARLOS LERTORA

(interview date 1986)

[In the following interview, originally conducted in December 1986 on the campus of Skidmore College in Saratoga Springs, New York, Dorfman discusses the relationship between art and ideology and the nature of exile.]

[Lertora]: *At the beginning of your career as a writer and sociologist, you published an analysis of comic strips,* **How to Read Donald Duck.** *Recently in* Contraviento Vargas Llosa *caricatured what he calls the "chic intellectual," in Vargas Llosa's terms somebody who finds ideology in comic strips, in the visit of the Boston Symphony Orchestra to Lima, in films, only then to apply for a Guggenheim fellowship and take up a position in the United States. What do you think about this condition? Does it sound familiar?*

[Dorfman]: Well, I don't know whether Mario was thinking of me, because he's never said this to me to my face and he's a straightforward person. It's certainly, in any case, a valid question. First, let's talk about the first part of what you asked, about finding ideology everywhere.

Yes, I do think that there is ideology in everything, but not everything can be reduced to ideology or be explained by it in every aspect. When we find ideological patterns in Donald Duck comics, what we are doing is revealing the underlying political message of an apparently innocent piece of entertainment. It's not a coincidence that Donald and his nephews are incessantly rushing off to Third World countries and siphoning off their treasures and suggesting to the savages there how to become successful in the modern world. There is a hidden thesis in Disney's works and in many other mass media expressions—I've studied *Babar the Elephant, The Reader's Digest,* the superheroes, *E.T.*—about development, growth, values. And by pointing that out, you are making a subversive reading of a dominant, official language. But this look underneath, this exploration of what we are being massively fed, does not exhaust the meaning of Donald Duck. He can mean many different things. You can even find forms of social criticism in some comics of Donald. It is, therefore, a caricature of my position to suppose that all I am doing is reducing everything to mere ideology.

But there is a second aspect I'd like to confront in what you said. There is, undoubtedly, a good deal of ideology in art as well. But I don't think that what is good in art is precisely ideology. What makes art so harrowing and liberating is that it is such an anti-ideological form, a form which breaks up ideology. To reduce everything an artist does to his or her ideology is to incarcerate that artist, to exclude him or her—and to prepare the way for doctrines and, who knows, commissars. The best way of answering art that you disagree with is with your own art.

The second part of the question is whether there is a conflict beteen criticizing an empire and living off that empire. You know the argument: why is it that these exiled intellectuals seldom if ever choose to live in the countries they defend, namely Cuba, or the USSR?

In my case, there are a number of quite concrete reasons which may, or may not, be the same for others. For many years, paradoxically, I resisted coming to live in the States—my politics had little to do with my decisions. You see, I had been brought up as a kid in the U.S. and was incredibly involved in American culture. But I said to myself, after the coup, if I go somewhere where I feel that much at home, maybe someday I won't want to go back to Chile—and I needed to tell myself that I would return as soon as possible. I think I subconsciously kept myself—which certainly was not fair to my wife, Angelica, who has accompanied me so faithfully in all our wanderings these years—from settling down. We went to Paris first, and then to Amsterdam and when we finally came here, it was to spend a year in Washington on a Wilson Center Fellowship, where Vargas Llosa, incidentally, was finishing *The War at the End of the World*. I intended to go on to Mexico—where we could bring up our kids in Spanish and where we would be nearer to the struggles of Latin America, but the Mexican government denied me a visa and so we got stranded in the States. But beyond the anecdotal aspect of this decision, it is worth asking what it means to apply for one of these fellowships. I think what matters is that you should not change what you write or what you stand for in order to receive this sort of help. If you ask for one of those fellowships, being who you are, and they give it to you, I see no problem. You just have to be sure enough in what you believe and not sell yourself.

I didn't hide what I was going to write when I applied to work on *The Last Song of Manuel Sendero*—a book narrated by revolutionary fetuses, about exiles who discuss how to deal with defeat after having tried to change Chile under Allende. I didn't cover up the comic book sequences where a country is turned into a laboratory experiment for the multinationals. I wrote what I promised to write in my project. And if I wrote it with money from the country that is considerably responsible for my exile because it intervened with its secret services

in my country and destroyed our democracy, well, then maybe there's something fair in that.

But there are other aspects of this supposedly sacreligious journey to the North which should be confronted. People should be free to travel where they want—and the U.S., which is the dominant power in our lives, constitutes an enormous attraction. The influence you can have here in relation to our continent exceeds any influence you can have elsewhere. Not to mention what you can learn! And then, of course, you are not only coming to the country which destabilized your own democratic government. Am I coming to the land which created the Underground Railroad in the last century or the Sanctuary Movement recently? Or am I coming to the land that supports the contras?

[Boyers]: *I'd like to come back to the issue we discussed earlier, namely, the connection between ideology and art. Camus once wrote of feeling "more than a writer." Do you feel yourself to be more than a writer? Do you ever fear that your political involvements and activities distract you from your "real work," making you less rather than more than a writer? And is it possible to be only a writer, now, not just for you, but for other Latin American writers?*

All my life I have been trying to work out a fertile relationship between literature and politics. There have been times when I have felt very comfortable with the relationship I have established and other times when I have lived in real anguish. At this moment, you're catching me in the midst of what I might call a soul-searching crisis. I've been reading Dante a lot:"in the middle of life, I lost my way ..." I've been wondering about where I go next in my literature and my life. And, as Pepe Donoso is here in our audience, I'd like to bring him into this. Just this year I was having dinner with him in Chile and he asked me what I was busy with and I told him I was writing a long piece for the *New York Times Magazine* and he looked at me and asked—it was a wonderful question: "What for?"And of course I gave him a series of reasons: this was the way of explaining Chile to an enormous audience, this was how I explored the country that had been denied to me for so many years of exile. And all that was true—that article did, in fact, have considerable importance politically in helping to further knowledge about the iniquities of Pinochet and the dilemmas of the opposition, but later I asked myself that very question: "What for? Ariel, why are you writing this?" Because I spent six months on that, perhaps as a pretext not to do other things—it may have been a way of keeping busy while I settled down to what was supposed to be my definitive return to Chile. Up until then I had felt I could do my best immediate political work, my work as a citizen, let's say, as a journalist (or a spokesperson) and that, right next to that, I could explore the deeper relationship between power, language and imagination in my fiction, my poetry and some essays. But I had begun to feel that the immediate tasks of finishing with Pinochet were strangling my possibilities of expressing myself in other dimensions. Not only because the politics is so time-consuming, but because it focuses you excessively on the immediate task and not on the more profound sort of meditation that is needed. What would happen if I wanted to begin to write as if Pinochet did not exist? On the other hand, can I write without taking into account that my country is held hostage? I have coined a phrase for the sort of literature I want to do: socialist irrealism. It sounds better in Spanish, *irrealismo socialista* . Maybe I now have to dip into the real meaning of that phrase.

Do you mean by "socialist irrealism" an attitude that informs your writing with an "unrealistic" hope founded on a utopian ideal rather than on an acknowledgement of what is possible or even likely?

I think the main word there is "hope." Writing itself is an act of extraordinary hope and faith. There is no rational reason why I should have any hope, or why my characters should, or why anybody in this world should. I look at the situation in Chile and I have to agree with Donoso that it's *"la desesperanza."* But at the same time, I do not forget that there was a period in the history of Chile, full of mistakes, full of problems, the Allende years, when the people in my country who had been told all their lives they were nothing and less than nothing, lazy and no good, when those people who had been told that the only way to get out of that situation was for them to compete, when those people decided to take their destiny into their own hands and became the protagonists of History. That is one certainty in a very confusing world: I don't want to betray what I learned from those people. Because if they can do it, those peasants, those workers, the excluded women, then I don't know why I should not be able to do it. History is full of silent people who in fact have created a very vibrant, strong culture of their own. And I have kept, in a corner inside me, the burning sense that that memory, those people, are still alive, that we will one day come to the surface again, step forth from the shadows. This has kept me alive or should we say perpetually resurrected— during these years.

And this has to do with exile. I see exile as a terrible loss, the pain of being distanced from everything that gives you a meaning. There are two basic myths that come out of humanity's experience of that loss. One is the foundational myth. You break the past, you rupture the umbilical cord of the past to found a new society. You create something new—no matter what problems that new vision or society or life cause you. And the other myth of exile, the other form of redemption that exile offers, is the opportunity to go back, to return and with what you have learned outside, to renew your original society. One myth speaks of birth, the other of rebirth. I can't believe that our species would have kept those myths of Eden and Utopia alive all these millenia if they had not been the product of profound needs—although later these needs and these myths have been manipulated and sugared and

packaged and sold. People have the need for their community, the old one renewed or the new one to be created, a place where they can find some sort of redemption. I would not like someone to come away from reading one of my books and feel that there is no hope for human beings. But I will tell you, when I began *The Last Song of Manuel Sendero*, I started out with a sense of extraordinary despair, trying to find the threads of hope in the midst of that despair. There is no rosy optimism in my stories, in the poems of missing people, in *Widows*. If we are going to overcome, as the song suggests, it's going to be difficult. Nobody guarantees that we can find our way out of these tunnels. You don't know if you can come out of the labyrinth once you've gone into it. And the same goes for the labyrinth of language, which you also explore to find something with which to light your way and that of others. I would not want the horrors of life that I have witnessed or uncovered to contradict the hope I feel about life. Many exiled writers, such as Kundera or Naipaul, find only a desolate barrenness. And if that is how they feel, that is the truth they must tell. But I don't see why people should dismiss my politics because they cannot find, in their lives, the basis for hope. Nor is that hope the rosy and false hope of Donald Duck or the superheroes or the *Reader's Digest* or the ducky optimism of a President Reagan.

There is a passage in Borges about the ideal library in which the books of one's dreams would affirm everything, deny everything, confuse everything. Would you be pleased if readers of **The Last Song of Manuel Sendero**, *for example, came away with that sort of experience of it?*

That novel and much of my work is "open," in the Umberto Eco sense of the term, and that leaves a lot of the interpreting up to the reader. But even though there is a constant mixing of different languages and dimensions of reality, the fairy-tale, the "realistic," the scholarly footnotes, the mass media expressions, this should not be understood as a postmodernist gliding over surfaces all of which have identical value. I think that in the midst of all the confusion, there are certain ethical certainties which guide us or should guide us. I don't impose these on the text, or at least I hope I don't. You know, something similar happens in my second play, **Reader**—which is based on the story you are publishing in *Salmagundi*. The play develops at length, as the story did not, the way in which the person—who is reading and suppressing a book in which he is secretly the central character—confuses fiction and reality, is forced to live the anguish of not being able to distinguish between his fears and his everyday life. In the story I am implying, and in the play I am more than implying, that if you lose your values you will not be able to tell the difference between your inner and your outer life, between the fictions that others weave around you and your own consciousness. It begins by being about a man who is an accomplice in a Latin American dictatorship and ends up by being about a man who lives in a society where the boundaries of reality have evaporated—not that different from what you find in ordinary people in the United States, in fact, where there is not a dictatorship. But in *Reader*, and *The Last Song*, and in *Mascara*, my latest novel, it is the reader who must discover this need for anchoring his reality in certain human values—this is not something I have decided for the reader. There is a difference, at any rate, between telling the reader what to think and how to act, and creating a world and a language complex enough so that he must draw—or be unable to draw, perhaps—his own conclusions.

[Lertora]: *Sometimes, not necessarily in your case, exile favors the writer's career. In what way has exile affected you? Do you think your writing would have been different had you not had to go into exile?*

It would certainly have been different. If I hadn't gone into exile, in fact, my writing would have been so different that it would have been non-existent, because I would have been killed. Later, in fact I did die—my body was found in Chile in 1986 according to newspapers—while of course I was still alive. Perhaps those who read the story I told about this in *The Nation* or *El Pais* will remember the episode. At any rate to be dead would have affected my writing considerably. But to answer the question about how exile affected me, first let me quickly sketch out my life, because that is related directly to language. I was born in Argentina in 1942; at two and a half, my family went to the States where I spoke only English until I was twelve, when we went to Chile, for many years. I felt an irrepressible nostalgia for the States. It was as if I was exiled from the States, looking back at it, from Chile. But when I finally settled down in Chile, began living deeply in that country, it seduced me—and one woman in particular, who was to be my wife, Angelica, and who is Chilean, enchanted me. I fell in love with a country. And that is the place where I feel the most hope for the future. Even the vices of Chile I feel as if they were my own. In a sense, you could say that I feel at home there. So when I had to leave the country, I left with an extraordinary sense of guilt. Others were dying there, my brothers and sisters in arms (or without arms, in fact, because we were confronting the Junta in a peaceful resistance). And it was also my adopted land, a land I had originally not even wanted to come to. My first writings in exile—after a first period of two, almost three years of shocked silence—were all as if I were still there. My poems (collected in English in *Last Waltz in Santiago*) and the stories (*My House Is On Fire*, forthcoming in English) are written from the perspective of somebody who has not left the country. These writings circulated clandestinely in Santiago, and people would say to me, when they came out, "you're writing as if you were still in the country. How can you know what we're living here?" So my first writing is based upon a refusal to consider myself an exile, to make believe I was back home.

Widows is the first step towards the acceptance of exile. I wanted a piece of fiction on the disappeared to circulate in Chile and the whole Southern Cone—so I wrote it under a pseudonym, attributing the book to a Danish resistance fighter during the Second World War and set the action in Greece. That double distancing—of mediation through an author who was not me and a country which was not my own—allowed me to write an allegory which is simultaneously realistic, a literary solution to the problem of how to write about overwhelming horror and sorrow. But exile is already structuring the book, its form, its language: the fact that in order to write about a home which was already far in time and space, I had to use indirection and obliqueness.

[Boyers]: *And that is now transformed into a play. What differences are there between the novel and the play?*

Generic differences, to begin—and I spent many years simply trying to work these out. It wasn't until I had effectively destroyed the novel in my head that I could really write the play. I only wrote one version of the novel—with revisions, you know, as I went along, but the version people read is from beginning to end the one I sent to the publisher. On the other hand I must have written some twenty or so finished versions of the play. What to do with the inner life of the characters, their monologues, how to create a chorus, what to do with the magic that in the novel is in the lyrical vision of the characters, but that in the play must function as action and conflict? But there were other, perhaps more interesting problems. For the play to work I decided to set it in Latin America, and therefore to destroy the basic distancing premise that had given a form to the novel. That made it more immediately political—in the most politically ignorant society in the world, the United States. And at the same time I wanted to keep the universality, the fact that this is happening right now, that it happened a thousand years ago, that unfortunately it may well happen tomorrow. For that I had to descend into myth more than I think I did in the novel. And of course there is also the fact that to work on a play, and to write it in English, is in a way to accept that you have a community outside your country, that you are speaking primarily to an audience which is not necesarily the one back home. This can only happen if you have somehow become—perhaps this is not the right word, but here it goes—reconciled to exile, have found out that exile can also fertilize you, be a form of growth.

[Lertora]: **The Last Song of Manuel Sendero** *is openly about exile.*

Yes, I started to write the voice of the fetus, of the son of Manuel Sendero, and around the fourth chapter, another voice, that of Eduardo, the baby's rival, began to attack the fetus, his fairy-tale style, demanding that the real story be told, with people we can identify with, that we can compare to those who lived that period. So a pair of exiles, David and Felipe, were born—in a Mexican traffic jam, which is a terrible place to be born and have to live out your existence forever. I look the dilemmas and sorrows of exile directly in the face there. It was as if I were accepting what had been done to us, what we had done to ourselves, what we had allowed to be done to us in defeat and before defeat by blinding ourselves to reality. But to make sure that readers understood this was, in itself, a construction, and that the mythic world of Manuel Sendero was as real as the supposedly recognizable and immediate world of David and Felipe, I invented a series of footnotes, a sort of academic spoof, which commented on the exiles' dialogue as if it were an extant manuscript discovered by archeologists thousands of years in the future. That also is related to the way in which time and language are constructed in the novel.

[Boyers]: *At least one reviewer of* **The Last Song** *compared it to* The Tin Drum. *I wondered if you had Grass in mind when you wrote your book.*

I admire Grass enormously and his book may have influenced mine significantly. But there was not a conscious attempt to take his basic premise of a child who refuses to grow up one step further by creating a revolution by babies who will not be born until adults show themselves to be responsible. Originally, when I was planning the novel, I had a singer, Manuel Sendero, who had lost his voice in a concentration camp and comes out and finds his wife has fallen asleep. Then I decided it would be more dramatic if she were pregnant and ever so slowly I came to realize that it was the baby that would be telling the story and when the baby began to speak—and I mean this literally, the characters simply take over, to my enjoyment and often to my dismay—he decided that enough was enough, that we mature people had made a total mess of things and it was time for the unborn—who are, after all, at least potentially, the majority—to have a say. And did he have a mouthful! (pp. 150–60)

Ariel Dorfman, Peggy Boyers, and Juan Carlos Lertora, in an interview, in *Salmagundi*, Nos. 82–3, Spring–Summer,1989, pp. 142–63.

EARL SHORRIS

(essay date 1987)

[In the following review, Shorris discusses Dorfman's *The Last Song of Manuel Sendero*, describing it as a "novel in which the sorrows of exile and disappearance are told with jokes, puzzles and extravagances to enable the reader to feel once more a human response to modern evil."]

There is a sameness to political tragedy in our time, as villains know technology makes the horrors repeatable and reproducible, an assembly line of burns and shocks

---

Dorfman on political repression in Latin America:

Forty years ago, Hitler conjured up the technique of making people disappear. He ordered French *résistants* to be deported to the *Nacht und Nebel* of Germany, to be executed. There was a twisted, demoniac logic to such repression: the *résistants'* unmarked graves could not be used as rallying points or memorials. And their friends and relatives were condemned to uncertainty about the fate of the ones they loved. Now, decades later, Latin Americans are refining this technique of demoralization. The armies that are committing these crimes are not foreign, though they treat their own people like a conquered populace. They speak the same language and laugh at the same jokes.

Ariel Dorfman, in his "Fictionalizing the Truth in Latin America," *The Nation* (25 June 1983).

---

of electricity, of drowning moments and disappearances. It happens in the neighborhood: Argentina, Brazil, now Guatemala, El Salvador, and still in Chile, since 1973 in Chile. What shall the writer say? It is not strangeness that boggles the mind; the imagination stumbles over sameness, repetition leaves a man mute. For the 253d reporter on the scene it is very difficult to get a moral scoop.

Contemporary political novelists, faced with a problem once limited to the depiction of happy families, seem to believe they have no choice but to abandon realism if they wish to be heard above the din of technological silence. Ariel Dorfman, a Chilean exile best known in Latin America for his investigation of the cultural and political meaning of Donald Duck, wishes to be heard. To that end he has written a novel in which the sorrows of exile and disappearance are told with jokes, puzzles and extravagances to enable the reader to feel once more a human response to modern evil.

Like many novels trying to deal with phenomena that seem like madness to the rational mind, *The Last Song of Manuel Sendero* relies on one overarching joke on reality: "Who could have believed that a year and a half after the child had been conceived . . . the kid had still not made its appearance into this world, was still waiting there, inside, refusing to come out?" Yes, in Mr. Dorfman's novel the fetuses have revolted, refusing to be born until the grown-ups end political and economic oppression and permit people their human rights. Among their demands: "Instead of freedom of prices, freedom of food must be declared," the stock of big weapons destroyed, and "Everybody has to take off his clothes." All this to prove the sincerity of the Government's declaration of its "own immediate dissolution."

In the hands of a political satirist, the revolt of the fetuses might have been good for a paragraph or two, a chapter at most, but Mr. Dorfman's unborn are well-rounded fetuses, capable of fear and ambition—hopeful, analytical, political, anxious and decent. And two of them are in love. Through their interuterine network the fetuses discuss the major question raised by their revolt, which is whether the world can be changed from without (that is, by their remaining unborn) or only from within (by their being born and participating in the political life of the society).

The desire for light and breath cannot be overcome, however, and the rebellion begins to fail as the fetuses choose to be born, descending in the elevator that traverses the path from conception to life to death. One after another, they are born and lose the wisdom of the womb. At last, only the lovers, the son of Manuel Sendero and the sweet Pamela, are left in utero, talking over the question of being born, observing what has happened to those who preceded them. When Pamela is born, the revolt ends, for the son of Manuel Sendero loves her too much to remain in another state of being.

If that were the whole story, a simple displacement, tragic and straightforwardly imagined, like Mr. Dorfman's first novel, *Widows,* it would be interesting, an important step forward from the relentlessly dour moralizing of that first effort, but insufficient, thin. *The Last Song of Manuel Sendero* is anything but thin. It refracts the life of Ariel Dorfman and his country into a dozen mirrors scattered across thousands of years. The son of Manuel Sendero is both the teller and the tale, born and unborn, fetus and grandfather. His is but one incarnation of the ethical dilemma of the exile: to punish by withholding one's love and participation or to return. It is, as the novel implies, the central question for all who have become estranged, for fetuses and singers and cartoonists and patriarchs and even for messiahs of all kinds.

The problems of exile and return are confronted here most directly by two cartoonists, David and Felipe, whose realistic story weaves in and out of the tale of the fetuses. The young men plan to produce a magazine in Mexico for Latin American exiles and intellectuals. It will feature a cartoon strip about Carl Barks or Marx or Sparks, an octogenarian from the state of Washington who travels to the land of Chilex with his aged wife, Sarah. Will Sarah give birth to a child in the country that just might be the analogue of the place where the fetuses are in revolt?

As the comic strip is written, the writers argue the merits of returning to Chile. The Government has told David he may come home on the condition that he give an interview to the newspapers, telling of the difficulties of life in exile. Curiously, it is not Felipe, the native Chilean, who is drawn back to his homeland, but David Wiseman, a Jew whose parents brought him out of Nazi Germany to Chile when he was 2 years old. One diaspora illuminates another.

The story within the cartoon proceeds, the lives of the exiles complicate—there are children, David has a *gringa* wife, and there are memories of the beginning and the end of the Allende years. Carl Sparks and Sarah become another refraction of the fetuses and are in turn refracted into their biblical analogues. Ishmael and Joseph are exiles; among the fetuses who refuse to be born are a set of twins; David and Felipe, whose arguments may be the contentions within a single mind, are really deciding whether to be born.

And all the while there is the question of the last song of Manuel Sendero. Who is this man, this singer? Here is one part of one of many descriptions of him that appear in the novel:

> Manuel was real as long as the dispossessed marched beside him, as long as they held him up like a banner. It was necessary to convert the unwary, so there wouldn't be even one dissenter near him. Often, during this crusade, Manuel didn't even argue: he distributed kisses, shook hands, painted rosy pictures, and the people believed in him, more than in his ideas. He was like a fetus too, said Eduardo, when he himself was one and wanted to stop being one and the sooner the better, said Eduardo, when he recognized the danger that his companions might stay in the uterus forever, yes, like a fetus that wants everything around him to be walls of milk and of love. Manuel believed in paradise, in the Promised Land, in the Golden Age.

The speaker is complaining about Manuel Sendero, using this description to urge the fetuses to be born; it is the analytical mind attacking the creative urge of the people as embodied in Manuel Sendero.

Should we connect Manuel Sendero in Victor Jara, the enormously popular singer of the Allende period who was killed after Gen. Augusto Pinochet came to power? Who is David Wiseman and how is he different from Ariel Dorfman, who produced cartoons and popular radio and television programs during the Allende years, who cares so much about the meaning of popular culture he has not only investigated Donald Duck but also written a book, *The Empire's Old Clothes*, analyzing Babar the Elephant and the Lone Ranger?

This Manuel Sendero, whose child refuses to be born, is mute now. Some say they heard him sing his last song and others say there never was such a song in Chile. And how is it that such an utterly preposterous complex of stories, burdened by too many echoes of the Latin American magic realists and their Yanqui cousin Thomas Pynchon, engages the reader so that David Wiseman's decision becomes important and Manuel Sendero's song achieves meaning?

To agree with the politics of a novel is the beginning of affection, and I agree with this writer, who is one of those gentle leftists for whom no murder can be excused. After this moral connection has been made, after the complications of plot and puzzle have done their work, the richness of the invention breaks through the gate of reality, and the reader touches congruently the soulful imagination of Ariel Dorfman.

Earl Shorris, "Gestation with a Vengeance," in *The New York Times Book Review*, February 15, 1987, p. 9.

MICHAEL UGARTE

(essay date 1990)

[In the following essay, Ugarte favorably reviews Dorfman's collection of short stories *My House Is on Fire*, praising its "humane yet critical treatment not only of children but of those who encircle them: parents, other relatives, even authorities."]

Consider a passage from Mother Goose that appears as an epigraph for the title story of Ariel Dorfman's new collection of short narratives in English translation, *My House Is on Fire*: "Lady bug, lady bug, /Fly away home./Your house is on fire./Your children will burn." From the perspective of the child, what does this gentle ladybug represent—that is, of course, if she is gentle? Is she a mirror image of the child, or a mother figure? What is the significance for the child of the ladybug's house? What thoughts kindle the speaker's sense of urgency and fear that the house is on fire? And how does the child read that curious semantic contradiction, "Fly away home"? Questions such as these on the nature of fairy tales and children's rhymes are difficult, and although there have been many attempts by psychiatrists, psychologists, anthropologists and literary critics to offer responses, the meanings remain mysterious.

As a Chilean, a writer of fiction, a professor, an activist who worked to elect Salvador Allende and later participated in his government, and as an exile, Dorfman may not provide answers, but he continues to ask pressing questions about the children of dictatorship and their families. He has always been concerned with images and myths that serve political ends, and what better foci to study these cultural artifacts than those embedded in the minds of children and adolescents: Donald Duck and the entire gamut of Disney characters; Superman; the Lone Ranger; and even *Reader's Digest*, which, as Dorfman explained in his *The Empire's Old Clothes*, infantilizes its readers in offensive and oppressive ways. These were the objects of Dorfman's scrutiny in his early essays, and in his fiction he has continued to approach political problems through the perspective and study of the young mind (as in his most ambitious novel, *The Last Song of Manuel Sendero*, in which would-be children rebel by refusing to be born until adults buckle down and solve the world's problems).

My House Is on Fire is yet another example. Although its treatment of children is by no means its only concern, youngsters of all varieties populate this *House*: sons and daughters of dictatorship's *persona non grata*, young soldiers, adolescents caught in a web of oppression and thought control, and children of a not-too-remote past now struggling as adults to deal with a tragic political reality. The collection is typical of Dorfman (a true *mensch* of a writer) in its humane yet critical treatment not only of children but of those who encircle them: parents, other relatives, even authorities.

In "Crossings," a haunting tale of espionage and fear, the reader must play the role of a child listening to a bedtime story to decipher the plot. The identity of the characters and their motivations are not readily available, never made explicit. Through an imagined dialogue between a man in an airport and an unknown woman on a plane whose arrival he awaits impatiently, we learn of other characters: a poor woman dressed in black accompanied by her children; lovers in a passionate embrace; and two men furtively observing certain people as if they were prey. Yet there is a story within the story. The speaker also imagines a man on the plane telling his son a tale of a muleteer who risked his life crossing the Andes more than a century ago to give messages to the troops fighting the Spanish for Chilean independence. Through this children's story the identities of the other characters begin to take shape, and the woman on the plane becomes a modern version of the muleteer, a messenger in service of the resistance against Pinochet.

Fear is clearly the watchword in "Crossings," as it is in several other stories. In "My House Is on Fire" two children hide under a blanket as the authorities come to their house looking for their parents. The brother reassures his younger sister that they are playing a game, so that she won't be frightened, but the reader is never sure if in fact the children *are* playing a game, if they are rehearsing for a time when the police will come or if the person who finally weeds them out is a friend or an enemy. This childlike uncertainty lies at the root of a horrific situation; as Dorfman shows us, to be a child is to be riddled with fears of all types, and in a police state the terror increases tenfold.

These youthful fears manifest themselves in a variety of ways, including in the acts of young males who collaborate with the dictatorship. Dorfman deals earnestly with the mentality and the contradictions that lead to compliance, treating these characters with sympathy and critical understanding. In the story that opens the collection, "Family Circle," a young man is terrified at how his progressive, salt-of-the-earth father will react to his having become a soldier, and worse still, to his having been assigned as a guard in a prison for political transgressors. Near the story's end, at home, the son clutches the handle of a pot of boiling stew and announces that if anyone tries to escape while he is on duty, he will shoot "full-blast."

Dorfman skillfully leads to that pathetic declaration with the image of fire, a constant motif in the collection. The father helps his son carry the pot to the table, but neither of them will let go. The son observes his father's movements: "His hands moved implacably over the metal, they must be burning by now; it must be singeing his skin, sinking to the bone; his blood had to be boiling." Dorfman has penetrated a father's disgrace and a son's shame in the midst of a regime that turns innocent people into killers.

Dorfman's stories are by no means single-minded or preachy, even though his writing exposes its own ideology, unlike that of other Chilean dissidents, such as Antonio Skármeta and Jorge Edwards, who have not been as committed as Dorfman to imagining progressive alternatives to capitalist and neocolonialist culture. The object of Dorfman's political search is a language that is open but never arbitrary or without motive, dialogical but never vacuously pluralistic. Dorfman is interested in relations. Although the women are not given the same depth as the men, all his characters are developed in conjunction, in collusion or in conflict with others: sons with their fathers, brothers with their sisters, children with their families, rebels with their enemies, exiles with those who stay to continue the battle, adolescent soldiers looking for a good time with North American prostitutes—who refuse to give it to them because they are boycotting all Pinochet's merchandise. This last situation occurs in **"Putamadre"**("whore-mother"), a story titled after the nickname of its male protagonist. Although there is something of the myth of the Happy Hooker in the tale, Dorfman underscores the clash between men who think of women as whores and real prostitutes who are wiser and more politically sophisticated than their johns.

The burning question of *My House Is on Fire*, of course, is the future, especially for Chile, with its new political and social possibilities as it cautiously (perhaps too cautiously) returns to democracy. Is Dorfman's sense of urgency dated in the wake of the recent Chilean elections? Is his house no longer on fire—is it merely smoldering in Pinochet's ashes? The answers, or the suggestions of answers, might be found in the final story of the collection, **"Backlands,"** in which the protagonist insists on protecting a dreamlike castle as everything around him burns. He refuses to gaze at the flames of "the city,"concentrating instead on the castle and imagining possibilities for it in spite of the advice of those few left around him to let it burn: "The city's savage breath beats at my back, like an oven lit by a man gone insane. It was then I decided not to turn around. The fire would die out, finally there would be nothing left to burn. The flames would lap at my walls, like bound, like tamed ocean waves. Let the enemy squeeze the city till it was only a rind. Could not a new fruit be dreamed from the peelings?" And sure enough, the dream seems closer to reality than we readers would have thought. Almost as a prediction of the return of Chilean exiles, the protagonist imagines his departed brother back from wherever he has been speaking "a different language," imagines him unable to recognize his family. As he passes by, the protagonist calls his son to witness the event: "And then, taking my son by the hand, I will let my brother disappear into the distance. And then, yes, at that moment, I will turn around to look our city in the face." These culminating words of the collection could be read as a synthesis of the present political and social reality of Chile.

In **"Backlands,"** an allegorical yet open-ended story, Dorfman, like the protagonist, is unwilling to let his house burn in spite of the damage done by the flames of the police state. The appearance of the son, the last of Dorfman's children, is an affirmation that if the ladybug and the brother do as the rhyme admonishes, if they "fly away home," face the house, the children will not burn. (pp. 245–47)

Michael Ugarte, "The Children and the Flame," in *The Nation*, New York, vol. 250, No. 7, February 19, 1990, pp. 245–47.

MICHAEL WOOD
(essay date 1991)

[Wood is an English educator and critic who has written extensively on Hispanic literature. In the following excerpt, he reviews Dorfman's novel *Hard Rain*.]

Ariel Dorfman's *Hard Rain* was written in the last months of the Allende government in Chile and published in 1973, the year of the coup which brought Pinochet to power. For this translation, Dorfman has altered the title (courtesy of Bob Dylan) and shortened the text, but has not, he says, interfered with the original mood of his book: "It is as prophetic and as blind, as hopeful and as anguished, as fervent and as experimental, as it was when I first hurriedly wrote the words . . . ". The book is actually funnier and friskier than those rather complacently balanced clauses suggest, but not a lot funnier. It takes the form of a series of imaginary reviews, conversations, letters, encyclopaedia entries, readers' comments, interviews, student essays, all circling round a "final project" that never comes to completion. The method recalls that of Julio Cortázar's novel *Hopscotch* or his compilation *Last Round*, but Dorfman is less incisive, less inventive, a different, milder stage on the road from Borges to Umberto Eco.

Michael Wood, "Final Project," in *The Times Literary Supplement*, No. 4582, January 25, 1991, p. 19.

LOUISE DOUGHTY
(essay date 1992)

[In the following review, Doughty finds the stories collected in Dorfman's *My House Is on Fire* "redemptive as well as frightening."]

The publication of Ariel Dorfman's new collection of stories, *My House Is on Fire*, follows his award-winning play *Death and the Maiden*. . . . The setting for both is Pinochet's Chile, the subject matter the survival of the human spirit. Dorfman goes beyond the facts—the horror of torture, the bleak realities of oppression—to offer us human details; how to register the birth of a child when the father has been arrested, where to find money for the ingredients of chicken soup. The strength of his writing lies in these particularities. He gives us the biographies behind the grim reports from Amnesty International, acknowledging that dreadful things are done not by monsters but by ordinary people. Within this terrifying truth there lies hope as well as tragedy, for ordinary people sometimes find the extraordinary courage necessary to survive.

Strangely, the collection opens with the least accomplished story. **"Family Circle"** is about a young conscript home on leave. "Any sonofabitch would have better luck than I do", the narrator begins, and this hard-nosed American tone continues through curses and digressions which prevent the reader working out who is who and what is going on. The alienated (and alienating) narrator is a common literary device, but idiosyncratic voices such as this require an identifiable rhythm. It would be interesting to know how much influence has been exerted by the translator from the Spanish. In places, the grammar becomes almost incomprehensible. The soldier follows his father as they walk through the neighbourhood, remembering similar walks when he was a child: "Except that back then he had held my hand, I had felt his magnificent shadow protecting me." Dorfman is at his least interesting when he is experimenting. Another story, **"Trademark Territory"**, is about a doorbell designed to repel beggars with electric shocks. It is making a serious point but, in the absence of characterization, didacticism looms large.

These are isolated examples in an otherwise compelling collection. Another story, **"Reader"**, has as its protagonist a censor who is scanning a novel for signs of "attack on the government". The main character is a bureaucrat who begins to show uncanny similarities to the censor. As he wonders whether to allow publication, he is determining his own fate. This story includes a fine example of the illogicality of oppression. The censor edits a volume of poetry and permits it to be distributed, "approved with changes". He has replaced the word "lion" with "sheep" four times, to "serve as a warning to the publisher".

The bleak humour of totalitarianism also appears in **"Lonely Hearts Column"**, a story consisting of a letter to an agony aunt named Rosalyn. How can I stop my husband meddling in politics, a woman wonders. Rosalyn replies "the solution to your dilemma is just around the corner", and thanks her for including her address. The light-hearted tone sends a chill down the spine. Dorfman's gift is to bring home the full force of brutality without needing to be explicit. He describes a torture victim chatting casually to his tormentors during a tea-break and we feel every inch of his terror. **"Consultation"** describes such a session, where an imprisoned doctor advises the lieutenant who has just beaten him to avoid bread and jam if he wants to lose weight. He is trying to build up a relationship with his tormentor but the plan misfires, precipitating a horror worse than any blow he has received so far. He will be asked to tend other victims of torture, to keep them alive for further agony. The story is written in the second person, and the reader is invited to share "the ambiguous joy of your own existence".

Dorfman finishes the collection with the gutwrenching **"Backlands"**. A fighter waits in a deserted city, a final survivor holding out for his brother to return, kept company by a ruined woman. The situation seems hopeless. Even if he comes, he won't recognize us, the woman says. So the man teaches his son the word "uncle". Even if they are gone, the boy will know. It is this core of optimism that makes this volume readable as well as informing, redemptive as well as frightening.

Louise Doughty, "Under the Oppressor," in *The Times Literary Supplement*, No. 4656, June 26, 1992, p. 22.

SOURCES FOR FURTHER STUDY

Brustein, Robert. Review of *Death and the Maiden*. *The New Republic* 206 (May 11, 1992): 32.

> Faults Dorfman's play for its "preposterous plot" and its failure to resolve the issues which it raises.

Graham-Yooll, Andrew. "Dorfman: A Case of Conscience." *Index on Censorship* 20, No. 6 (June 1991): 3–4.

> Interview in which Dorfman discusses Chile's transition from dictatorship to democracy as well as his plays *Death and the Maiden* and *Reader*.

Hyde, Lewis. "Ducks of the World, Arise!" *The Nation* 237, No. 8 (24 September 1983): 250, 252.

> Review of Dorfman's essay collection *The Empire's Old Clothes*, stating agreement with the author's politics while finding fault with many of his critical assumptions.

Incledon, John. "Liberating the Reader: A Conversation with Ariel Dorfman." *Chasqui* XX, No. 1 (May 1991): 95–107.

> Interview with Dorfman treating such topics as exile, the relationship between reader and writer, and Marxism.

Pineda, Cecile. "Plastic Sorcery." *Los Angeles Times Book Review* (30 October 1988): 3.

> Favorable review of Dorfman's first novel written in English, *Mascara*, maintaining that this work "places Dorfman in the exalted cultural Parnassus inhabited by Franz Kafka and Kobo Abe."

Smith, Wendy. "Ariel Dorfman." *Publishers Weekly* 234, No. 17 (21 October 1988): 39–40.

> Interview in which Dorfman comments on his novel *Mascara*.

Additional coverage of Dorfman's life and career is contained in the following sources published by Gale Research: *Contemporary Authors*, Vols. 124, 130; *Contemporary Literary Criticism*, Vol. 48; and *Hispanic Writers*.

Carlos Fuentes

1928–

Mexican novelist, dramatist, short story writer, scriptwriter, essayist, and critic.

INTRODUCTION

*F*uentes is widely regarded as Mexico's foremost contemporary novelist. His overriding literary concern is to establish a viable Mexican identity, both as an autonomous entity and in relation to the outside world. In his work, Fuentes often intertwines myth, legend, and history to examine his country's roots and discover the essence of modern Mexican society.

Born in Panama City, Panama, Fuentes is the son of a Mexican career diplomat. As a child, he lived in several Latin American countries and spent much of the 1930s in Washington, D.C. He attended high school in Mexico City and later entered the National University of Mexico. While studying law there, he published several short stories and critical essays in journals. After graduating from law school, Fuentes traveled to Geneva, Switzerland, to study international law and in 1950 began a long career in foreign affairs that has included service as Mexico's ambassador to France from 1975 to 1977.

In the late 1950s and early 1960s Fuentes gained international attention as one of the most important contributors to Latin American literature. Along with such authors as Gabriel García Márquez and Julio Cortázar, Fuentes published works that received international acclaim and spurred a reassessment of Latin American literature. Fuentes's work, "el Boom," is technically experimental, featuring disjointed chronology, varying narrative perspectives, and rapid cuts between scenes, through which he creates a surreal atmosphere. For example, in his first novel, *La región más transparente* (1958; *Where the Air Is Clear*), Fuentes uses a series of montage-like sequences to investigate the vast range of personal histories and lifestyles in Mexico City. This work, which provoked controversy because of its candid portrayal of social inequity and its socialist overtones, expresses Fuentes's perception of the Mexican Revolution's failure to realize its ideals. The frustration of the revolution, a recurring theme in his writing, forms the basis for one of his most respected novels, *La muerte de Artemio Cruz* (1962; *The Death of Artemio Cruz*). The title character of this work is a millionaire who earned his fortune by ruthless means. Using flashbacks, the novel shifts between depicting Cruz on his deathbed, his participation in the Revolution, and his eventual rise in business. Through this device, Fuentes contrasts the exalted aims that fostered the Revolution with present-day corruption.

In the novella *Aura* (1962), Fuentes employs bizarre images and elements of the fantastic. This novel involves a woman who mysteriously begins to resemble her aged aunt. Fuentes employs a disordered narrative in *Cambio de piel* (1967; *A Change of Skin*) to present a group of people who relive significant moments from their past as they travel together through Mexico. His concern with the role of the past in determining the present is further demonstrated in *Terra nostra* (1975), one of his most ambitious and successful works. Many critics believe that this novel exceeds the scope of his earlier fiction, extending the idea of history as a circular force by incorporating scenes from the future into the text. Beginning with the Spanish conquest, Fuentes depicts the violence and cruelty that spread in the Mediterranean area and was perpetuated in Mexico through Spanish colonialism.

In *La cabeza de la hidra* (1978; *The Hydra Head*), Fuentes explores the genre of the spy novel. Set in Mexico City, this work revolves around the oil industry and includes speculations on the future of Mexico as an oil-rich nation. Fuentes's later fiction investigates Mexico's relationship with the rest of the world. *Una familia lejana* (1980; *Distant Relations*), for example, involves a Mexican archaeologist and his son who meet relatives in France; on another level, however, this work probes the interaction between Mexican and European cultures. In the novel *El gringo viejo* (1985; *The Old Gringo*), which examines Mexican-American relations, Fuentes creates an imaginative scenario of the fate that befell American author Ambrose Bierce after he disappeared in Mexico in 1913.

Cristóbal nonato (1987; *Christopher Unborn*), a novel often described as verbally extravagant, continues Fuentes's interest in Mexican history. This work is narrated by Christopher Palomar, an omniscient fetus conceived by his parents in hopes of winning a contest to commemorate the quincentenary of Christopher Columbus's arrival in the Americas. According to contest rules, the male baby born closest to midnight on October 12, 1992 and whose family name most closely

resembles that of Columbus will assume leadership of Mexico at the age of twenty-one. The novel's nine chapters symbolize Christopher's gestation and allude to Columbus's voyage, which Fuentes views as a symbol of hope for Mexico's rediscovery and rebirth. Narrating from his mother's womb, Christopher uses wordplay, literary allusions, and grotesque humor, combining family history with caustic observations on the economic and environmental crises afflicting contemporary Mexico. *Christopher Unborn* satirizes Mexico's government and citizenry, warning that the country's collapse is imminent if there is no change. Fuentes returned to the historical novel with *La campaña* (1990; *The Campaign*). Set in early nineteenth-century Latin America, this work chronicles the adventures of Baltazar Bustos, the naive, idealistic son of a wealthy Argentinian rancher, who becomes embroiled in the revolutionary fervor then sweeping the region. Considered less complex than Fuentes's earlier works, *The Campaign* has been praised for its incisive portrait of a tumultuous period.

In addition to his novels, Fuentes has written several plays, including *Orguídeas a la luz de la luna: comedia mexicana* (1982; *Orchids in the Moonlight: A Mexican Comedy*), and has published the short story collections *Los días enmascarados* (1954), *Cantar de ciegos* (1964), and *Chac Mool y otros cuentos* (1973). He is also the author of respected essays on a wide variety of subjects, including literature, art, and politics.

In assessing Fuentes's work, critics often emphasize his ability to fuse myth and history into compelling and brilliantly wrought narratives. In addition, commentators generally agree that Fuentes, particularly in his novels, weaves a wealth of thought-provoking ideas, historical perceptions, and mythological allusion into his stories, thus creating literary texts of extraordinary depth and richness. From a stylistic point of view, as critics maintain, Fuentes's works display the author's brilliant verbal inventiveness and profound understanding of the vast expressive resources of his language. Widely praised, Fuentes has received the warmest accolades from many preeminent Hispanic and European literary figures. For example, the Czech novelist Milan Kundera has lauded Fuentes's ability to construct convincing contexts for his narratives, noting in particular *Terra Nostra*, in which the story, set in the future, assumes the timeless quality of myth without leaving the framework of historical time. Finally, as Kundera and others have asserted, Fuentes's works evince the kind of thematic, philosophical, and psychological universality—as seen in his moving portrayal of humankind's tragic struggle with history— that is the distinctive element of great literature.

CRITICAL COMMENTARY

JUAN GOYTISOLO
(essay date 1976)

[Goytisolo is a prominent Spanish novelist whose books include *Juan sin tierra* (1977; *Juan the Land-less*, 1977), *Makbara* (1980; *Makbara*, 1981), and *Paisajes desoues de la batalla* (1982; *Landscapes After the Battle*, 1987). In the following excerpt, he comments on Fuentes's accomplishment as a novelist, remarking that "Fuentes' ambitious novelistic exercise is a deliberate exploration of the literary space opened up by Cervantes."]

One of the usual tactics of critical terrorism (whether or not it is legitimized by the power of the State) is to create a scarecrow-image, either of the author . . . or of the work, making it out, for instance, to be an impenetrable, confused, chaotic hodge-podge . . . so that the potential reader comes to associate it in his mind with the label "unreadable." The ambition, difficulty, and deliberate excesses inherent in *Terra Nostra* thus make it the ideal candidate for transformation into a scarecrow-image of a work, which is quoted from (in order to tear it to pieces) but not read, and the mausoleum of an author whom the penny-a-liners would like to see interred in it once and for all. But these overeager grave-diggers forget that *Terra Nostra* belongs to that category of novels that, like *Ulysses* or *Under the Volcano*, little by little create, through the text alone, an audience of fanatically devoted readers. (p. 6)

Fuentes alternates the expression of a historical pessimism on the part of his characters and a much more nuanced vision which, while taking into account the repeated failures of the past, nonetheless does not resign itself to fatalism or passivity. . . . From the point of view of the narrators, the repetition of the cycles of history is not necessarily absolute or inevitable: the need for revolution, for the material and moral progress of mankind continues, as strong as ever, despite the failures, the errors, the blood baths that it has everywhere left in its wake. To call them to mind is not a sign of helpless resignation, but precisely the contrary. As one narrator, Guzmán, remarks: ". . . nothing is forgotten as quickly as the past, nothing is repeated as often as the past." The awareness of this is therefore an indispensable step to be taken on the steep, arduous path that will one day permit history not to repeat itself. (p. 8)

The ideological debate that runs through the pages of *Terra Nostra* cannot leave us indifferent, inasmuch as it takes up many problems that those of us who believe in the ideals of justice and progress must necessarily confront. The attentive reader will glimpse between the lines a subtle denunciation of the compensatory mechanisms employed by those who justify today's avoidable evils in the name of imaginary future paradises. Over and against the familiar—and false—assertion that "new worlds are born only through sacrifice" and "that there have always been men who have been sacrificed," there rings out, like a cry of hope, the impassioned invocation of the *hic et nunc* by the rebel leader: ". . . my history, neither yesterday nor tomorrow, I wish today to be my eternal time, today, today, today." Justice and freedom here and now, won painfully, step by step, without allowing a single inch of them to be given up in the name of some supreme later perfection; taking as the point of departure the fact that the real, concrete man is irreplaceable; living and glorifying the instant, through the daily struggle for an immediate terrestrial heaven that does not waste and destroy human beings for the well-being of future generations; abandoning the Christian notions of guilt and sacrifice in favor of the reappropriation of the body and the attaining of a social order whose aim is to promote physical, material, and moral well-being for all rather than the conquest and monopoly of power for the benefit of the few. . . . The historical thought in which the events of the novel are steeped—set forth from the shifting, contradictory points of view of the various characters who alternately take on the role of narrator—appears to oscillate. . . between two diametrically opposed ideas—the necessity and the failure of revolution—without ever definitely opting for either one. (pp. 9–10)

The novel is above all a cruel and penetrating vision of Spanish history and its prolongation in the New World through the Conquest. Here too the accusations of pessimism and fatalism— reality seen as a "sick dream"— that have been leveled against Fuentes would appear to have some foundation. . . According to the novelist's detractors, Fuentes paints far too dark a picture. But let us consider a few examples and judge for ourselves. The history of Spain: "the chronicle of inevitable misfortunes and impossible illusions"; Spaniards: "heroes only because they would not disdain their own passions but rather, would follow them through to their disastrous conclusion, masters of the entire realm of passion but

---

Principal Works

Los días enmascarados (short stories) 1954

La región más transparente (novel) 1958
  [*Where the Air is Clear*, 1960]

Las buenas consciencias (novel) 1959
  [*The Good Conscience*, 1961]

Aura (novella) 1962
  [*Aura*, 1965]

La muerte de Artemio Cruz (novel) 1962
  [*The Death of Artemio Cruz*, 1964]

Cantar de ciegos (short stories) 1964

Cambio de piel (novel) 1967
  [*A Change of Skin*, 1968]

Zona sagrada (novel) 1967
  [*Holy Place*, 1972]

Paris: La revolución de mayo (essays) 1968

Cumpleaños (novella) 1969

Tiempo mexicano (essays) 1971

Chac Mool y otro cuentos (short stories) 1973

Terra nostra (novel) 1975
  [*Terra Nostra*, 1976]

Cervantes: o la crítica de la lectura (essays) 1976
  [*Cervantes: or, The Critique of Reading*, 1976]

La cabeza de la hidra (novel) 1978
  [*The Hydra Head*, 1978]

Una familia lejana (novel) 1980
  [*Distant Relations*, 1982]

Orguídeas a la luz de la luna: comedia mexicana (drama) 1982
  [*Orchids in the Moonlight: A Mexican Comedy*, 1982]

El gringo viejo (novel) 1985
  [*The Old Gringo*, 1985]

Cristóbal nonato (novel) 1987
  [*Christopher Unborn*, 1989]

Myself with Others: Selected Essays (essays) 1988

La campaña (novel) 1990
  [*The Campaign*, 1991]

The Buried Mirror: Reflections on Spain and the New World (essays) 1992

---

mutilated and imprisoned by the cruelty and the narrowness of the religious and political reasoning that turned their marvelous madness, their total excess, into a crime: their pride, their love, their madness, their dreams—all punishable offenses"; our appointed destiny over the centuries: "to purify Spain of every plague of infidels, to tear it out by the roots, to mutilate her limbs, to have nothing left save our mortified but pure bones"; the ideal of our leaders: "servitude, slavery, exaction, homage, tribute, caprice, our will sovereign, that of all the rest passive obedience, that is our world"; . . . Hispanic America: "the same social order translated to New Spain; the same rigid, vertical hierarchies; the same sort of government: for the powerful every right and no duty; for the weak, no right and every duty.". . . (pp. 10–11)

When *Terra Nostra* was published in 1975 the panorama offered by the Spanish-speaking world was not one that inspired much hope. . . A national awareness of their wretchedness on the part of the Spanish-speaking peoples is not a recent phenomenon: to limit ourselves to the Hispanic Peninsula, the work of our best writers, from Blanco White and Larra to Cernuda and Luis Martin-Santos is steeped in it and nourished by it. (p. 11).

To scoff at Fuentes's historico-poetic vision as being evasive and unrealistic is to fall into the error of accepting the canons of a shallow and mechanistic realism which continually confuses life and literature, thus demonstrating that it does not understand either of them very well. (p. 12)

As the reader makes his way through [*Terra Nostra*'s] fascinating hall of mirrors that reflect both the world and each other, he never loses sight of real history. Though the novelist has thoroughly assimilated the admirable precept of Goya and put it to striking use, he nonetheless remains scrupulously faithful to the rational and objective vision of the historians. Even though it takes on the appearance of a dream or madness, his historical nightmare never employs these latter as a substitute for real past history. At each step of the way the reader is able to return to real history, and then plunge once again into the novelist's deliberately distorted and often grotesque perception of things. Even in the most delirious and most dreamlike passages—the magnificent scenes, for instance, in the rotting-chamber of the Hapsburgs with the Madwoman, the dwarf Barbarica, and the doltish Prince—there appear, at times as a sort of sudden brief powder-flash, at times in the form of parody or incantation, reminders of a real and specific history with which the novelist—as well as the Spanish reader—is perfectly familiar. . . . "History shares the methods of science and the vision of poetry," Octavio Paz has written. This fundamental vision or intuition of Castro's has demonstrated its seminal power not only in the field of historiography but also in that of literary creation. When I say this, the first case that naturally occurs to me is my own, but that of *Terra Nostra* is even more obvious. In no way does the novelist's stimulating and unconventional method of confronting our past, his interpretation of tradition, at once critical and creative. . . preclude our interpretation of real history. . . . (pp. 12–13)

It goes without saying that the novelist can allow himself to take a number of liberties with the past that would be unthinkable in the case of the historian. Hence *Terra Nostra*'s author performs sleight-of-hand tricks both with chronology and with the real-life existence of historical figures. (p. 13)

For Fuentes history and literature become one: history can be read as literature and literature as history. By weaving the fabric of his novel with threads from both, the novelist demonstrates to us "his wish to use, with no exceptions and no scruples, all of reality as a work tool." . . . The liberties that Fuentes takes with our cultural patrimony are the sign of an omnivorous creative appetite. His imaginary museum impartially houses novels and chronicles, paintings, legends, sciences, myths. But these liberties are much less gratuitous than they might appear to be at first glance. The normal relation with history, we repeat, is always present as a point of reference, in the form at times of what would seem to be the most trivial novelistic details. . . . All the precepts of realism are applied with great felicity in the novel, though they are incorporated and juxtaposed in such a way as to be unrecognizable to those who refuse to stray from the well-worn path of tired literary convention. Fuentes' meticulous reconstruction of historical reality takes as its point of departure not only chronicles and annals but also literary texts and above all certain major or minor Spanish, Flemish, and Italian paintings. We will find the best example of this "unreal realism" . . . in the extensive passages in the novel devoted to the necropolis of the Escorial and the hallucinatory cortege of the specters of kings and queens of the dynasty and the fierce, monstrous, or ridiculous figures in their retinue.

The cult of death, the fatalism disguised as serenity of spirit, the stiffness of movement, the frozen, motionless ceremonial in which the Hapsburg dynasty slowly immures itself, are described by Fuentes with the pen of a master. . . . [What] might be taken to be a lugubrious invention of the novelist is in fact the literary expression of a historical reality. (pp. 13–14)

[The] Spanish past frequently defies all reason and surpasses our powers of imagination. The monarchs of the Hapsburg dynasty appear to have had a secret obsession: to build "a hell on earth" in order "to ensure the need of a heaven" to compensate themselves and their wretched subjects for the paralyzing horror of their lives. . . . We thus discover that as in Goya's painting of Charles IV and María Luisa, Fuentes has not used too dark a palette at all: sheer fidelity to reality has permitted both painter and novelist to enter the realm of the fantastic and the hallucinatory. (p. 15)

Fuentes' historical imagination is not simply an oneiric game that masks reality and perpetuates myths, as our incorrigible defenders of a superficial, one-dimensional reading have written of García Márquez's *One Hundred Years of Solitude*. Many crimes have been committed in the past, are being committed today, and will be committed in the future in the name of ideology, and perhaps the gravest and most infamous of them lies in the fact that—just as patriotism is the last refuge of scoundrels and the priesthood frequently that of fools—it is used as a shield or a bunker by zombies in order to conceal from the eyes of the public their abysmal lack of ideas and their insufferable lack of sensibility.

Fuentes' creative imagination—like that of Lezama in *Paradiso*—is often nourished by a vast imaginary museum of oils, frescoes, engravings. Some of these are readily identifiable: El Greco's "Dream of Philip II," Signorelli's "Last Judgment," Hieronymus Bosch's "Garden of Delights," Goya's "Royal Family of Charles IV." Others belong to that common heritage or store of memories shared by all of us whose daydreams or reconstructions of our history were first inspired by the plates and reproductions that customarily illustrate grammar-school textbooks. Once again, the novelist's pen, sketching in as it does a wealth of minute detail intended to create an "unreal realism," succeeds in portraying a series of unforgettable scenes in which the prose appears to take on the concrete texture of a fabric, becoming a canvas saturated with color, light, movement, sensuousness. (pp. 16–17)

Fuentes' pictorial prose, his appeal to the visual memory of readers are particularly noticeable in the hunting scenes and in his many evocations of a bestiary whose plastic values are once again mindful of the genius of Lezama: portraits of the mastiff Bocanegra lying at the feet of the Lord and Master; of a pack of famished hounds, "a river of glistening flesh, with tongues glowing like sparks"; of the Lady's mind-haunting falcon: "Such is the union of the avian feet with the woman's gloves that the birds's talons appear to be an extension of the greased fingers of the gauntlet." In other passages, the phantasmagorial discourse of the narrator transports us to the canvases of Velázquez and El Greco, to Goya's *caprichos*, and to Buñuel's films. . . . (p. 17)

One of the most striking and most successful devices is the abrupt shift in narrative point of view (at times without the unwary reader's even noticing), passing from first-person narration to second, and even to a personal narration (since in the final analysis that it what the recounting of events from the point of view of the novel's "he" is equivalent to), and simultaneously rendering objective and subjective reality in one and the same passage with patent scorn for the rules of discourse that ordinarily govern expository prose. . . . (pp. 17–18)

[This] pluridimensional narrative that situates us simultaneously inside and outside the consciousness of the characters. . . achieves its greatest success and reaches its high point in the pages devoted to the rebellion of the *comuneros*—a multidimensional space in which different voices come together and speak in turn, assuming one after the other the task of relating events from different perspectives. . . . The multiple perspective, the story that reflects itself and appears to contemplate itself brings us back once more to Velázquez, whose seminal influence is transparent in one of the most highly charged and meaningful moments of the book—the sequence entitled "Todos mis pecados" ("All My Sins"), devoted to the contemplation of a painting from Orvieto (in reality Signorelli's "Last Judgment"). . . . The novel, like the friar's composition in the style of Velázquez, is a hall of mirrors in which the intruder—the reader—is reflected and lost in the vertigo of an infinite duplication of his own image. (p. 18)

The rich repertory of narrative resources that Fuentes sets before us with such bravura is almost never employed gratuitously: the novelist does not dissociate what (for mutual understanding though with little conceptual rigor) we ordinarily term "form" and "content" by resorting, as do so many mimetic avant-garde writers, to the use of complex narrative devices to express simplistic ideas devoid of either daring or vitality. *Terra Nostra* is a synthesis, achieved by a form of writing that makes no distinction between the two terms: a work that emerges and takes shape, as Pere Gimferrer notes in his discerning review [in *Plural*, July, 1976], through the active intervention of a literary architect of a new type: the *voyeur*, the intruder, the reader. . . .

Fuentes' ambitious novelistic exercise is a deliberate exploration of the literary space opened up by Cervantes. The man from La Mancha, Fuentes reminds us, is not only a hero in a novel born of the reading of novels of chivalry: he is also the first character in fiction who knows that he is read and who changes his behavior as a function of this reading. (p. 19)

Like *Paradiso, Three Trapped Tigers*, and other works that are clearly descendants of *Don Quixote*, *Terra Nostra* contains numerous references and statements of the author regarding the structure of the novel that he is writing—a characteristic which, as we have said elsewhere, distinguishes literary language from everyday language governed by norms that we automatically obey. . . . The narrative space of *Terra Nostra* is a free space, open to dialogue and the intervention of the reader aware of the fact that "nothing is beyond belief and nothing is impossible for poetry, which relates everything to everything." Like García Márquez and the authors of novels of chivalry, Fuentes believes in the pleasure of improbable fantasies. . . . Metamorphoses, transformations, anachronisms that instead of controverting the order of the real, confirm it and enlarge it—a "total" realism, in the sense in which Vargas Llosa employs the term: objectivity and subjectivity, acting and dreaming, reason and miracle. (p. 20)

Fuentes engages in a systematic "sacking" of the whole of Spanish culture. For one thing, he borrows entire phrases from Fernando de Rojas, Cervantes or the chroniclers of the Indies and incorporates them in his own narrative (a trick typical of the author of *Don Quixote*); for another, he transforms the world of the novel into an imaginary museum in which the paths of all manner of disparate literary characters meet and diverge (thus bringing us back once again to *Don Quixote*). . . . In his literary voracity, Fuentes does not scorn the use of age-old devices characteristic of storytelling in all times and places, but—and herein lies the difference as compared to conventional novelistic narration—he employs them to weave a radically new overall pattern, a sort of dizzying *summa* of storytelling. Manuscripts found in a sealed bottle are used, for just one instance, to interpolate a story of the same type as . . . inserted by Cervantes in *Don Quixote*; and above all there is Fuentes' vast gallery of story-tellers, whose function consists of extending to infinity the Chinese-box technique of the story within a story within a story. . . .

As in *Don Quixote* once again, the one possible reading offered by traditional works of fiction is superseded by alternative or multiple interpretations that preserve our freedom of choice and judgment, thus conferring on what would appear to be merely an esthetic undertaking a profound moral justification that quite obviously goes beyond the limits of literature. (p. 21)

The beginning and the end of *Terra Nostra* . . . represent the working-out of a curse or a prophecy whose fulfillment is at once the cabalistic key of all of history and the organizing principle of the novel. I am here anticipating the outcry that will be forthcoming from ideologues who cling to the certainty that time is progressive, linear—as they have a perfect right to do. But to scornfully dismiss the "circularity" imposed upon real history for the purpose of constructing a work of literature that "bites its own tail"— an artistic convention likewise employed most effectively by García Márquez in the final pages of *One Hundred Years of Solitude* and by the author of the *Divine Comedy* long before him—as simply an attempt to "erase from the reader's mind all recollection of reality" and to "perpetuate ignorance and myth," as has been written of the Colombian novelist's work, is to be hopelessly blind to the distinction between reality and novelistic technique. . . .

As Carlos Fuentes says by way of one of his characters: ". . . every human being has the right to take a secret to the grave with him; every storyteller reserves the right not to clear up mysteries, in order that they may remain mysteries; and anyone whom this displeases may ask for his money back." (p. 24)

Juan Goytisolo, "Our Old New World," translated by Helen R. Lane, in *Review*, Winter, 1976, pp. 5–24.

LUIS LEAL
(essay date 1982)

[Leal is a Mexican-born American literary scholar whose writings include *Breve historia de la literatura hispanoamericana* (1971), *Juan Rulfo* (1983), and *Aztlan y Mexico: Perfiles literarios e historicos* (1985). In the excerpt below, he provides an overview of Fuentes's novels, stating that these works "can be considered as mythical approaches to history, or creative history."]

Carlos Fuentes has stated that fiction can be useful in looking at history from new perspectives, and this is precisely what he has done in most of his novels, wherein he has presented a vision of history that cannot be gathered from the reading of history books. And, even more, he has reinterpreted history to present a new version of its development, a version reflected by a mind keenly conscious of the significance of past events in the shaping of the contemporary course of human events. In most of his novels he has gone one step further, to the recreation of history by the combination of realistic and mythical structures. The purpose of this essay is to trace the intrusion of history and myth upon Fuentes' narrative, and to observe how he has solved the technical problems involved and yet has managed to produce novels that are aesthetically satisfying. (p. 3)

One of the characteristics of the writers of the new Spanish American novel . . . is the tendency to create pure fiction. One of the leaders of this trend has been Carlos Fuentes. He, like other new novelists (García Márquez, Cortázar, Rulfo, etc.), has moved in this direction by combining two narrative modes, the realistic (historical) and the mythical. Northrop Frye has discussed these two modes at length [in his *Anatomy of Criticism*, 1957], and he differentiates between them by saying that realism is the art of verisimilitude, the art of implied similarity, and myth the art of implied metaphorical identity. However, he says that the presence of a mythical structure in realistic fiction "poses certain technical problems for making it plausible, and the devices used in solving these problems may be given the general name of *displacement*." (pp. 3–4)

[In the story **"Chac Mool"** from his first book, *Los dias enmascarados*], Fuentes solves the problems of displacement by the use of realistic motifs: the action takes place in Mexico City and Acapulco; the two characters are clerks in a government office; and Filiberto, the protagonist, purchases a statue in a well-known market. To introduce historical fact, the technique of the diary, in which conversations are recorded, is used. The fictitious Filiberto writes about historical events in his diary, such as the introduction of Christianity after the Conquest and the effect it had on the conquered people. In the other aspect of the story Fuentes recreates the myth of the eternal return by the illusory transformation of the statue of the god which Filiberto had placed in the basement of his home. Chac Mool comes back to life with the coming of the rains and takes control of Filiberto's life, finally driving him to suicide. Thus Fuentes skillfully blends the historical and the mythical into a continuous narrative form which derives its structure from the tension created by the interaction between two different cultures, that of ancient Mexico, represented by Chac Mool, and the contemporary, represented by Filiberto.

The technique used in this early story was soon perfected and expanded in the novel, and it has become the distinguishing mark of Fuentes' fiction. The models that he followed for this mode of fiction he found principally in William Faulkner, Malcolm Lowry, and Miguel Angel Asturias. From them he learned the art of utilizing myth, either as form or theme in the context of the realistic novel. (pp. 5–6)

The novels of Fuentes, with some exceptions, can be considered as mythical approaches to history, or creative history. The success of his novels is due in great part to this use of myth to interpret history; for history, as Ernst Cassirer has observed [in *The Philosophy of Symbolic Forms*, 1955], is determined by the mythology of a people. . . . In his first major work, **Where the Air is Clear**, Fuentes presents a mythical history of Mexico City and its four million (1958) inhabitants. The characters who represent the historical aspects of the novel are products of the Mexican Revolution and, at the same time, representative of Mexican society during the 1950s: Robles, the revolutionary turned into a conservative banker; his wife Norma, the social climber who marries for money; Zamacona, the brooding intellectual who becomes one of the sacrificial victims; the decadent Bobó, from the new upper middle class; Gabriel and Beto, the displaced *braceros* back from California; and the Ovando family, the impoverished representatives of the dethroned porfiristas.

In the novel, the representatives of its mythological counterpart are found in the old lady Teódula Moctezuma and Ixca Cienfuegos. They symbolize Mexico's past, a mythical Mexico that still survives and believes in ritual, in sacrifice as the only way for man to redeem himself. The Mexican people have been chosen by the gods to feed the sun and keep it moving so that mankind can survive. Without sacrifices this would be impossible. Displacement in the novel takes the form of parallel action in the fictional world representing history. Both Norma and Zamacona are sacrificed to modern gods. This revelation of the mythical nature of Mexican history is accomplished by the use of image and metaphor. The characters, the description of the city, the action, and the plot are all expressed by uniting two worlds, that of the remote past and that of the present. The interaction between the characters representing both cultures becomes the central technique of displacement. Mythical episodes are used by Fuentes to give his work a pure, literary quality. History and myth balance each other to give the novel equilibrium. (pp. 6–7)

The Death of Artemio Cruz and *Aura* were published the same year, 1962. While in the latter work the mythical predominates, the historical elements surface in *The Death of Artemio Cruz*, but even here mythical aspects are evident in the structure of the subject matter and the characterization of the hero. After writing the social history of Mexico City in *Where the Air Is Clear*, Fuentes continued and recreated the history of modern Mexico in *La muerte de Artemio Cruz*, approximately from the era of Santa Anna to the 1950s, with the period of the Revolution receiving the most attention. Historical personages are freely mentioned, as are historical facts and events. . . It is also a history, as seen through the eyes of Artemio Cruz, an unreliable character. The mythical structure is found in the use of the myth of the descent into hell to depict the career of the hero who recreates in his mind, just before he dies in the hospital, the twelve most important moments of his life. These twelve days represent the twelve circles of Dante's *Inferno*, as well as the twelve months of the year. This mythical motif is repeated in the temporal structure of the novel, in which the narrative time covers the last twelve days in the life of Artemio. (p. 8)

In the novels published after *The Death of Artemio Cruz*— *Aura* (1962), *Zona sagrada* (1967), *Cambio de piel* (1967), *Cumpleaños* (1969), *Terra Nostra* (1975), *La cabeza de la hidra* (1978), and *Una familia lejana* (1980), Fuentes has given more emphasis to the mythical than to the historical, but never forgets history or the social condition, which underlies all his fiction.

In *Aura* he gives expression to the historical and the mythical by creating characters symbolic of both forms of thought. Two male characters—Llorente, a general of the period of Maximilian's Empire, and Felipe Montero, a young contemporary historian who later turns out to be the general's double— represent the historical component in the novelette. For balance, there are two additional archetypes, both female—Consuelo (Llorente's wife and a sorceress), who conquers time by recovering her youth, and Aura, her counterpart as a young girl. (pp. 8–9)

[Some of the mythical elements in *Zona sagrada* occur] in the thematic content, the relation between Claudia Nervo, the mother, and Guillermo (Guillermito, Mito), the son. The first chapter, entitled "Happily Ever After," narrates the myth of the sirens in the story of Ulysses, but in a present-day context—a football game which is played in a sacred zone, the staked field. In the last chapter, "Zona sagrada," Mito is transformed into a dog. While

in *Where the Air Is Clear*, the beginning and the ending of the novel are in opposition (mythical introduction, historical epilogue), in *Zona sagrada* they are parallel. The novel ends with the episode of Circe, the sorceress who changes men into animals. Since Claudia Nervo is associated with Circe, the transformation of Mito into a dog becomes a part of the myth. As a theme, the myth of Ulysses has also been recreated, for the characters represent Penelope and her son Telemachus. Even Telegonus, the son of Ulysses and Circe, is there, under the name of Giancarlo. The historical part of the novel is based on the life story of a famous Mexican movie star.

Cambio de piel (A Change of Skin) signals a change of attitude in Fuentes as a novelist. Here for the first time he builds a purely fictional construct. . . . Displacement is achieved by introducing numerous realistic motifs, starting with the date when the events in the novel begin—Palm Sunday, April 11, 1965. On that precise, historical day two couples leave Mexico City in a Volkswagen on their way to Veracruz, taking the old road and stopping at Cholula, where the rest of the action takes place, at a second-rate hotel and inside the great pyramid. This, however, is preceded by a prologue with a displacement function and in which the destruction of Cholula by Cortés and his men is recreated. (p. 10)

[The theme of *A Change of Skin*] is the mythification of history. In history there is no progress, time has been abolished, as in myth. This explains why the violent acts occurring at the end of the novel—the death of Franz and Elizabeth in the center of the pyramid, the killing of Isabel by Javier in the hotel—are structured in parallel trajectories with some of the most violent events in history: the destruction of Cholula by Cortés, the massacre of the Jewish people. (p. 11)

Cumpleaños (1969) is the first novel by Carlos Fuentes in which the action takes place outside of Mexico. It is also the first that transcends his preoccupation with Mexican history and myth, being based, instead, on European history and myth. However, there are, as in his first novels, both historical and fictitious personages. Also, in *Cumpleaños*, as in previous novels, there is a sacred place, where the theologian, accused of heresy, takes refuge to escape his enemies. This place becomes a bedroom in a contemporary London house where the old man, Nuncia, and [a] boy live. Both places merge into one labyrinthian residence symbolic of the universe. In the bedroom the old man remembers his past life which extends back to the thirteenth century, since he is the reincarnation of Siger de Brabant, a theologian from the University of Paris persecuted for his ideas by Etienne Tempier and Thomas Aquinas. In the present he is George, an architect in London, husband of Emily and father of Georgie, whose tenth birthday they are celebrating that day. This novel is the least realistic of those written by Carlos Fuentes; yet, even here, there are historical elements in the plot, in the artistic motifs, and in the description of the milieu: books read by the boy (*Treasure Island, Black Beauty*, etc.); realistic descriptions of London. . . . (pp. 11–12)

In *Cumpleaños* all traces of Mexican history have disappeared, but the same is not true of *Terra Nostra, The Hydra Head*, and *Una familia lejana*. *Terra Nostra* deals with the history of Spain during the Renaissance period, but in the second of its three parts, "The New World," the subject is pre-Hispanic Mexican myth and the conquest of the land. By the use of history and myth Fuentes attempts to apprehend the meaning of the age of Philip II and, therefore, the destiny of the Hispanic people, both in the Old World and in the New World, and even in "The Other World," the title of the last part of the novel. As a technique he superimposes several historical periods, going back to the age of Tiberius and pre-Hispanic Mexico, and forward to the end of the century. By this means he creates a new historical reality which, although it is purely fictional, is based on empirical fact and real historical personages. The figure of Philip II, however, becomes an archetype, since it is a composite of several Spanish rulers who have exercised absolute power, and it is this obsession with power on the part of Philip II that gives universality to the novel.

Terra Nostra opens with a scene in Paris on a precise day, July 14, 1999, and ends there on the last day of the same year, the end of the millennium. Thus, the entire narrative partakes of the apocalyptic myth. In the second part, Fuentes creates a space in the New World where historical, fictional, and mythical characters act their roles in a purely mythical time. But even here are found the everpresent historical references, presented with the techniques of fiction. (p. 13)

[In] *The Hydra Head* and *Una familia lejana*, history plays a secondary role to fiction. A current event, the struggle for the control of Mexican oil deposits, is the subject of the first, a detective novel. The protagonist, Félix Maldonado, is patterned after a present-day mythical archetype, James Bond. In *Una familia lejana* Fuentes tries to establish, in a minor way, the cultural relations between Mexico and France, as he had done with Spain in *Terra Nostra*, but in a more personal way. The protagonist, Mexican archeologist Hugo Heredia, husband of a French girl, Lucie, and father of two sons, Víctor and Antonio, delivers a long, historical essay in the first part of chapter 20. At the same time, the author identifies himself with the protagonist, thus becoming the hero of his own novel. . . .

Mythical elements in [*Una familia lejana*], which predominate, are given expression by means of several devices: the association of the characters with the mythical past of Mexico (Lucie as La Llorona); the use of the double (Heredia and "Heredia"); the use of motifs related to the "Día de Muertos" (November 2); and, especially, the use of fiction itself as myth. (p. 14)

In general, then, it can be said that the narrative of Carlos Fuentes swerved strongly at the beginning toward the historical, and strongly after 1969 toward the mythical, but never in a pure form. His idea of history, however, is not that of the empirical historian, but goes beyond fact to a reality that includes myth and legend, so important in the shaping of the Mexican mind. Quite often he fills the lacuna of the historical record with oral history, legend, or myth. His fiction reveals that history itself often becomes myth; and although it is based on a collection of facts, the mythical consciousness of the author is ever present before the facts are verbalized. . . By fusing history and myth in his novels (and the same can be said of his play, *Todos los gatos son pardos*), Fuentes has been able not only to reveal important aspects of the mind and character of the Mexican people, but also to project his own hopes and aspirations, one of which is not to kill the past. (pp. 15–16)

Luis Leal, "History and Myth in the Narrative of Carlos Fuentes," in *Carlos Fuentes: A Critical View*, edited by Robert Brody and Charles Rossman, University of Texas Press, 1982, pp. 3–17.

WENDY B. FARIS
(essay date 1983)

[Here, Faris explores some of the ways in which Fuentes captures "the cacophony of modern Mexico," including his use of multiple narrative perspectives, different kinds of time frames, and intertextual allusions.]

For many years the French anthropologist Marcel Griaule studied the Dogon people of Mali and brought to light their sophisticated cosmology. After his death he was given a moving funeral ceremony by the subjects of his research. During the Dogon funeral rites the principal tool of a man's earthly labors is broken, then placed on a ceremonial pile with other relics. Normally a man leaves his hoe, a woman her shuttle. But for Griaule, his friends chose "the tool that they had always seen in the hand of he who had listened to their elders, a pencil." And so they marked their appreciation of his sensitivity to their voices.

Carlos Fuentes might one day merit a similar ceremony, for his writings show a remarkable capacity to transmit the voices of Mexico. His pencil too is a sensitive recording instrument. Griaule listened for the complex but finally harmonious story of Dogon mythology; Fuentes has set himself the more difficult task of capturing the cacophony of modern Mexico. The pages of his fiction are often traversed by multiple narrative voices, which express a "plurality of meanings." Though certain

Milan Kundera on Fuentes's *Terra Nostra*:

If Fuentes has known how to find that spot [from which one can see the past but not the future]—that incontestable locus of the apocalypse—it is thanks to great artistic ruse (or wisdom); he did not search in real history but in myth. The watchtower from which he views history is called the year 1999, the end of the millennium. His description of the apocalypse will thus not be contradicted by the reality of the real year 1999, because Fuentes is talking about a mythic date, not a real one.

It is not the political predictions of the author which are at the root of *Terra Nostra* but something more profound. "Historical time is stretched so taut that it is hard to see how it will not snap," [E. M.] Cioran writes. This "tension of historic time" (of that time which today hurtles on, accumulating events, approaching a paroxysm), and the personal experience Fuentes has of this tension, is, it seems to me, the hidden source, the subterranean force of the unbelievable, apocalyptic dream which is *Terra Nostra*.

Milan Kundera, in his "Esch Is Luther," *The Review of Contemporary Fiction*, Summer, 1988.

of his works reflect the pervasive influence of surrealism on Latin American writing (Fuentes himself remembers that "Breton called Mexico the preferred land of surrealism"), Fuentes's pencil cannot be said to practice any simple kind of automatic writing. It is rather as if an "alternating current" (to use Octavio Paz's phrase) of different voices flows through it as it transforms them. The different voices contribute to Fuentes's dialectical mode, to his oppositions and shifts of perspective. (pp. 185–86)

Fuentes's writing often approaches a kind of literary anthropology, a portrait of the patterns of interaction that compose Mexican society. His most successful novel, *The Death of Artemio Cruz*, locates typical patterns of behavior in the society at large yet projects them through an individual, in this case a fictional character. But unlike a traditional anthropologist, Fuentes hopes that his work will lead the community it describes toward a greater self-awareness. This, in fact, explains Fuentes's insistence that the anthropologist Oscar Lewis's often unfavorable portraits of Mexican life must be read in Mexico. (p. 186)

[The] most striking "multivocal" feature of Fuentes's fiction is the formal shift of narrative stance in many of his works. The device often reveals multiple perspectives even in the treatment of one character, like Artemio Cruz, allowing the reader different views of him, and, through him, of the class he represents. As Cruz is a victim, a product of history and society and the neuroses they engender, we identify and temporarily pardon; as he is an executioner, a powerful manipulator who chooses to dominate at any cost, we distance ourselves and condemn.

The narrative voice in *A Change of Skin* undergoes a different set of changes, shifting both the receiver and the time frame of its discourse frequently. Third-person narration dominates *Where the Air is Clear*, but . . . in the last section of the novel first and second-person stances compose a kind of universal song, and varied monologues reveal multiple inner voices in Mexico City throughout the text. *Terra Nostra* contains the most extensive shifts in narrative voice; there we move between third, second, and first persons, and even hear narration by a painting.

Throughout Fuentes's work, different voices may represent different times in the life of an individual or of a civilization. The three kinds of time that Fuentes discerns in Mexico—utopian, epic, and mythic, often exist simultaneously in his work. As a complement to this synchronic use of superimposed layers of time, each with its own "voice," Fuentes recognizes the diachronic movement of change through time, and its effect on the processes of writing and reading: "the world that the work reads is a changing world; the work wishes to be fixed. Fortunately, it doesn't succeed. The changing world also multiplies its readings of the work."

Fuentes's shifts of narrative voice parallel a variety of other multivocal elements in his work. They all attest to the basically cumulative nature of his technique; as he says, he is a "*puter-inner*, not a taker-outer." First of all, characters often undergo an imaginative doubling or tripling in the text. This process of multiplication may also include condensation and metamorphosis. Artemio Cruz on his deathbed imagines himself in the place of his son; earlier he has usurped the place of Gonzalo Bernal. In *Holy Place*, Guillermo eternally renews the image of his mother—doubles it, triples it, quadruples it—in the series of film clips he projects. Elizabeth's multiple names in *A Change of Skin* expand her identity to include all women in their battle with men. In *Terra Nostra*, Agrippa Posthumous is multiplied by three, and perhaps even more, as Tiberius's slave suggests. Like the mirrors and masks in Fuentes's texts, these personal multiplications and transformations suggest national and individual quests for identity.

A third type of multivocality in Fuentes's work appears when one text echoes another. The echo may exist on the surface of the text in the form of a name or an allusion, or it may be hidden "above or below the normal sound"—a kind of "cry under the water" (*Holy Place*). Fuentes himself explains his extensive use of intertextual allusion as a desire "to recapture a past that seems dead but is really very much alive." Just as one character may recapitulate several, so one narrative is often traversed by others. This idea of voices that come and go in a text is suggested by a pile of sea-polished stones Elizabeth has just gathered on the beach in *A Change of Skin*: "You sort your pebbles out. You know that each of them will change color as the sun moves. Noon's yellow becomes orange as the afternoon lengthens, it is red at twilight, beneath the moon violet, a fusion of red and blue.". . . [The] earlier narratives we glimpse behind the story we are reading often are Aztec or, less frequently, classical myths. Ixca and Teódula reactivate the myth of Huizilopochtli and Coatlicue, the narrator of *A Change of Skin* that of Xipe Totec; Claudia reinterprets the triple role of the goddess Tlazolzéotl and those of Penelope and Circe as well. The chiastic designs throughout Fuentes's works often structure the returns of these voices from the past. (pp. 186–88)

[These] mythic ancestral presences in Fuentes's work project the message that they are present and that they are not to be played with carelessly. Guillermo is held in thrall by the devouring goddess Claudia, who in turn has destroyed much of her own personal happiness in acquiring celluloid divinity. The characters in *A Change of Skin* are trapped inside an ancient pyramid after having wandered there in a frivolously touristic mood. The clearest warning of this kind emerges from the short story **"Chac Mool,"** when Filiberto realizes that the old deity has begun to assert its power: "My original idea was entirely different: I would dominate the Chac Mool as one dominates a toy; it was, perhaps, an extension of my childhood security." His "toying" with the spiritual powers of the past eventually results in his death.

The textual voices that cross Fuentes's work are not always myths. Intertextual allusions encompass other art forms, or other kinds of narrative. References to familiar paintings can instantly evoke a particular tone and style; such is the case when a triptych by Hieronymous Bosch appears near the end of *Terra Nostra*. Many of that novel's characters come directly from earlier literary texts—Celestina, Don Juan, the Knight of the Sorrowful Countenance—or from history, another grand text; the novel also contains lengthy quotations from the gospels, as well as shorter fragments of other books—including Fuentes's own *Cervantes or the Critique of Reading*. Popular songs resonate throughout *Where the Air is Clear* and *A Change of Skin*, whose narrator is a composite of earlier literary voices. In *The Hydra Head*, quotes from Shakespeare and film images proliferate. Fuentes's use of film is especially striking. Just as paintings do, films can evoke a particular mood, an era, a style, which has shaped a character like Elizabeth in *A Change of Skin* or Felix in *The Hydra Head*. The predominantly American titles of many of the films in Fuentes's works represent an intrusion of a foreign voice in the cultural language—acknowledged, often enjoyed, yet also disturbing, even resented. Furthermore, . . . the persistent intertextual intrusions also suggest that literature is, to a large extent, made out of other literature.

Characters who take their identities from other texts, whether mythic, literary, or popular, imply a "multivocal" concept of literary character itself. People in Fuentes's novels are not so much observed in their individualities as composed of different parts. The many voices of history, art, film, even the tape recording of his own voice that Cruz plays over and over on his deathbed, present the individual invaded by his environment.

With regard to social problems as well, Fuentes's texts often speak with more than one voice. His thought is dualistic in nature, alternating between a tragic and a reforming spirit. Fuentes's early novels, in particular, reveal a strong impetus toward social reform, though they propose no concrete plans for its implementation. This potentially constructive social criticism coexists with a tragic view of life. Sacrifices continue, yet conditions do not improve. The answer, as Fuentes himself has suggested, is that even though it may seem hopeless, one must continue to work for reforms. The two tendencies represent two poles of his thought; he has said that his anarchistic subconscious believes—with Bakunin and Buñuel—that there is no good government, but that his conscious life leads him to fight for his government to be less bad.

Finally, Fuentes's sensitivity to the many voices within a text extends to his essays on literature. In *Cervantes or the Critique of Reading*, Fuentes reencounters a Spanish literary voice in order to exorcize the "panic" out of the "hispanic time" ("tiempo is pánico") that used to dominate his part of the new world, achieving a kind of reconquest, or conquest in reverse. Thus the idea of "de-I-ification," which Fuentes explicitly develops in this essay and in his later fiction, is anticipated by the unusual receptivity of his early fiction to the different voices of Mexico and by the narrative strategies he develops to accommodate them.

Fuentes shows individual voices dying into, strengthening a communal literary voice. The process is certainly less brutal than the ritual sacrifice of victims to keep the sun alive. Yet it continues the utopian ideal of commitment to a community that Fuentes cherishes for the new world. He locates this multivocal imperative in Mexico's cultural tradition: "Rejected, the polyvalent, sculptural space of our indigenous past persists beyond the univocal, frontal space of the rationalist project through which Mexico has tried to suppress the unfinished histories that line the far shore of its destiny." Fuentes's creation of many voices allows him to explore these "unfinished histories," this variety of times, places, theories, and images in the world and in the imagination in his texts. In doing this, he approaches what is for him the great truth of literature, that "all the imaginary becomes possible and all the possible becomes universal." (pp. 188–91)

Wendy B. Faris, in her *Carlos Fuentes*, Frederick Ungar Publishing Co., 1983, 241 p.

CYNTHIA DUNCAN

(lecture date 1984)

[In the following excerpt from a lecture delivered in 1984, Duncan assesses elements of the fantastic in two stories from Fuentes's first published short story collection, *Los días enmascarados*.]

In 1954, the literary career of Mexico's most celebrated contemporary novelist, Carlos Fuentes, sprang to life with a modest collection of short stories entitled *Los días enmascarados* (*The Masked Days*). Of these early works, only two presage the grace and skill of the mature writer: "Tlactocatzine, of the Flemish Garden" and "Chac Mool." Both have become classic examples of the fantastic in Mexico and have yet to be surpassed in their treatment of the theme of the living past.

"Tlactocatzine" is presented in the form of a diary by a nameless first-person narrator. Classic motifs, such as the haunted house and the enchanted garden, create an atmosphere reminiscent of nineteenth-century horror tales. Structurally, the house and garden function as a bridge between two worlds for, as we discover, the narrator-protagonist is trapped between the past and the present, Europe and Mexico, the dead and the living, and the fantastic and the "real" world.

The protagonist is an ordinary man, out of step with society, who lives a solitary life built around dreams and disillusions. Accustomed to a quiet, meditative existence, he welcomes the opportunity to withdraw from the outside world when a wealthy acquaintance asks him to act as the caretaker of a charming old mansion dating back to the reign of Maximilian and Carlotta. The narrator immediately feels a spiritual union with the house and the century it represents. He feels a tender melancholy for days gone by and spends most of his time lost in idle daydreams which spring from his active imagination. The small, walled garden at the rear of the house especially fascinates him because it is so different from anything he has seen in Mexico. The trees and flowers were imported from northern Europe and reflect the changing seasons, which normally go unnoticed in warmer climes. Very gradually, the narrator is overcome by the strange sensation that he is not in Mexico at all, but instead in some private world. At the same time, he becomes aware that he is not alone, for an elderly, darkly clad woman begins to make regular but inexplicable visits to the house and garden. Something about the woman strikes fear into the narrator, yet he cannot muster the will to leave the house. Instead, he attempts to exorcise his fear through logic and reason. As always, he is more inclined to thought than action, and it

is this inability to act that ultimately traps him in a static existence.

The fantastic suddenly erupts and overwhelms the narrator as he discovers that he is unable to escape when the terror reaches unbearable levels. The doors have been sealed and he is trapped for eternity in the Flemish garden with a madwoman. Even more horrifying is the realization that she is not a living being, but the ghost of the Empress Carlotta, who believes the narrator to be her dead husband, Maximilian. The motif of the sealed door reinforces the idea that the protagonist cannot return to the other side once he has crossed over into the world of the fantastic.

Many clues are given throughout "Tlactocatzine" as to the identity of the mysterious old woman, but the clues are subtle and aimed at the well-informed reader. For example, *Tlactocatzine*, of the story's title, is a Nahuatl word meaning "leader," and was the form of address used by Mexico's indigenous population to address the Emperor Maximilian. Both Maximilian and Carlotta had strong affiliations with Flanders, the place mentioned in the title of the story. Carlotta was, by birth, a Belgian princess, and Belgium has occupied, since 1830, part of the territory previously known as Flanders. Maximilian's family, the Hapsburgs, ruled Flanders and the lowlands for three hundred years. Many other fleeting references are made in the text to Flanders, Belgium, and the Hapsburg seat of power, Austria.

In "Tlactocatzine," Carlotta symbolized the seductive quality of foreign cultures that have lured Mexico away from the development of an autochthonous heritage and led the nation into a mad course of action: from the conquest through the twentieth century, Mexico has aped foreign models and defaced national pride. Although of a much shorter duration than the conquest, the epoch of the French intervention also left lasting marks on Mexico. Long after the French were expelled and Maximilian executed, many Mexicans continued to look to Europe for standards in culture and knowledge. The narrator of "Tlactocatzine" exemplifies those Mexicans who do not feel at home in Mexico. His love of European culture and his nostalgia for the past make him easy prey for Carlotta, who sensed in him a strong attraction for a lost era, and a growing lack of interest in his contemporary world. Carlotta, however, is a victim as well, and her crimes do not go unpunished. At the end of the story, in her madness, she lapses into the Nahuatl tongue, a reminder that the indigenous forces, though buried, remain alive in Mexico and will exact vengeance from all who turn away from them.

"Chac Mool" is also set in contemporary Mexico City and features as its protagonist a seemingly "ordinary" inhabitant of the capital, who blends in with the thousands of white, westernized Mexicans who are his neighbors there. But suddenly and unexpectedly, the fantastic invades his life, destroying his complacency and reminding him of the "other," indigenous Mexico, which has been left to smolder beneath the surface of the modern-day nation. In this case, his confrontation with the past does not invoke the ghostly figures of Maximilian and Carlotta, but rather an ancient Mayan rain god who gives the story its title.

"**Chac Mool**" begins with the announcement: "A little while ago, Filiberto died, drowned in Acapulco." A friend of the hapless Filiberto goes to the coast to collect the body and transport it back to the capital. As he sorts through Filiberto's possessions, the friend discovers a diary in which Filiberto had recorded the final months of his life. This diary, narrated in the first person from Filiberto's point of view, provides the central narrative thread of the story, while the friend's comments and reactions to Filiberto's death and the events described in his journal present another point of view. Structurally, the friend's first-person narration acts as a counterpoint to Filiberto's bizarre revelations.

Filiberto, a lonely, middle-aged bureaucrat, allows himself few luxuries in life, but he enjoys collecting indigenous Mexican art. He is delighted one day to find a life-size replica of Chac Mool, a pre-Columbian rain god, in a flea market where he is able to buy the object at a modest price because of its doubtful authenticity. Filiberto takes the statue home and installs it in the basement of his house, where he keeps his other trophies, but Chac Mool seems to bring him bad luck. Filiberto notices, for example, that soon after the statue's arrival, the plumbing in his house stops working, the pipes constantly break, and the basement is always flooded. The perpetual dampness causes the statue of Chac Mool to take on a repulsive but oddly human appearance. When Filiberto starts to hear strange noises at night, his worst fears are confirmed: he awakens one night from a troubled sleep to find Chac Mool alive and hovering over him.

After the initial shock of this encounter wears off, Filiberto overcomes his terror and accepts Chac Mool as a companion. Chac Mool slowly assumes the dominant role, however, and Filiberto is resentful of the former statue's tyrannical behavior. Filiberto becomes a prisoner of the rain god and, when he finally manages to escape, Chac Mool brings about his death.

The second narrator is incredulous as he reads about these events. He attempts to explain Filiberto's remarks as the ravings of a mentally unstable man but, to his surprise, he is greeted at the door of Filiberto's house by a strange being who so closely resembles the description of Chac Mool that the formerly rational narrator is left shaken and doubtful. The reader has been lulled into a sense of false security by the second narrator, who was convinced that Chac Mool did not exist. At the end of the story, when this narrator comes face-to-face with a person who is apparently Chac Mool, the narrator hesitates, and so does the reader. Unlike Filiberto's testimony, no previous warning has been given, no hints have been dropped to prepare the

reader for a shock. Unlike Filiberto, who states outright that Chac Mool transformed himself from a statue into a human being, the second narrator's concluding remarks are vague.

Chac Mool is portrayed by Filiberto as a character who is bitterly resentful of the present. He was once a god, a highly respected deity, but in the intervening centuries he has been desecrated and forgotten. He resents the attitude of modern Mexicans who have abandoned their nation's indigenous heritage and are ignorant of their cultural history. Filiberto is guilty of this crime; he has purchased Chac Mool as a curiosity piece and has treated him in an irreverent manner. He has no real knowledge of the culture that Chac Mool represents and he feels no spiritual bond to him. Ironically, as Chac Mool gains vitality and becomes a living being, he loses the immortality he had as a statue and begins to grow old and corrupt. He loses his dignity and divine poise, and develops petty bourgeois tastes.

The creature who opens the door to Filiberto's friend at the end of the story appears to be the same tainted and aged image of Chac Mool described by Filiberto earlier in the narrative. Dressed in Filiberto's bathrobe, Chac Mool exudes the odor of cheap cologne and hair tonic, and his face is covered with poorly applied makeup. The humanization process has been one of corruption, for when Chac Mool gave up his ancient ways and adapted to the twentieth century, he lost both his dignity and his identity. He becomes a culturally hybrid character who, rather than benefitting from the blend of two heritages, adopts and maintains the worst characteristics of both. He is treacherous, despotic, and fickle, a pathetic imitation of something totally alien to his essential being.

Symbolically, Chac Mool can be seen as the representative of many contemporary Mexicans. Like them, he turns his back on his indigenous heritage and forgets his ethnic pride. He eventually adopts the values he earlier berated for disparaging the importance of indigenous cultures. The transformation undergone by Chac Mool is not unlike that undergone by millions of Mexicans since the conquest: it is an act of self-deception and self-denial that has spread like a cancer throughout the Mexican psyche.

The fantastic allows Fuentes and other Mexican authors to voice their preoccupations with their nation's turbulent and violent past, and to suggest some ways in which the modern-day Mexican might come to terms with history. The writers treat the theme of the living past in a way that provokes fear and doubt. The protagonists are caught up in the past against their will and are unable to understand the uncanny events that disrupt the placidity of their daily lives and threaten to destroy them. Eventually, they are destroyed, or sacrificed, in keeping with the ancient patterns of violence and aggression that have repeated themselves throughout Mexican history.

The theme of the living past has provided contemporary Mexican writers with an excellent vehicle for self-expression and an effective tool with which to fashion a more authentic national identity. (pp. 143–47)

Cynthia Duncan, "The Living Past: The Mexican's History Returns to Haunt Him in Two Short Stories by Carlos Fuentes," in *The Fantastic in World Literature and the Arts: Selected Essays from the Fifth International Conference on the Fantastic in the Arts*, edited by Donald E. Morse, Greenwood Press, 1987, pp. 141–47.

CARLOS FUENTES WITH DAVID L. MIDDLETON

(interview date 1985)

[In the following excerpt from an interview recorded in 1985, Fuentes discusses his literary works and writing processes.]

[Middleton]: *I would like to know, since you've worked successfully in so many different literary forms, whether you have by now come to favor one over the others? Have you decided that the novel is truly your* métier?

[Fuentes]: Yes, the novel. And short story. And essay (*laughs*). I don't feel comfortable in the theater. I really don't. I know I'm very limited as a playwright.

But you're very good as a short story writer.

I have a lot of short stories coming out.

And those are so different from your novels, so tightly formed and finished. It's hard to believe you don't respond differently to them. Don't you believe that one or the other, the novel or the story, shows your talents better?

I don't know. They're very different. They permit you to express yourself in different ways, and to focus on certain aspects of writing with greater intensity. I have a couple of books of short stories in preparation.

How do you work on them? In relation to your longer fiction, that is? Do you work on short stories for a sustained period of time and then switch over to the novel?

They're "wound" with the novels in a way . . . intertwined. When I'm stumped with a novel, I go into a short story, and then back into the novel. That sort of thing.

Maybe there's a complementary function served for you by that kind of work habit.

They feed one another. They do, they do. I feel comfortable with both forms. There are many things I can't possibly say in a novel. Sometimes I include short stories in a novel. I don't know whether that's good form, but I like doing it.

I have to admit I haven't seen any of the films you are credited with having worked on, but—

You haven't missed a thing (*laughs*).

I'd like to know, though, what your attitude is toward working in film.

I love film. . . . But I've been very unfortunate in my work in films and in adaptions made from my stories.

Aura is a story that Luis Buñuel wanted to make. But he could never finance it. He thought, besides, that the film would only be conveyable through film if it remained very short, no more than half an hour. So then he had to organize a triple film, you know, three short stories, and it became very cumbersome. But I'm sorry he didn't do it. (pp. 343–44)

When the fashion is apparently for ninety-minute-long entertainments on film, or MTV dramatic forms in three-to-ten-minute formats on television, and when the doomsayers cry that the novel is dead and in response we see the appearance of the "antinovel," you go to work and produce an eight-hundred page, densely built novel. Were you consciously trying to work against fashion, and do you consider **Terra Nostra** *to have been a mistake either artistically or commercially?*

Oh, no, no, no. It is no mistake, my book, and my book *is* eight hundred pages long. I didn't do it to be out of fashion. I felt, since I started writing, that one day I wanted to write a book about the Spanish inheritance of Latin America, to mobilize this very heavy baggage we carry with us. To give that some kind of form. It was announced in another small book of mine. It is not that I want to write small books or large books. *Aura* is a very short book, and there Felipe Montero, the character, the "you" in the novel, says, "One day I will sit down and write the whole adventure of Spain in the New World, its myths, its epics, its conquests, the way it named things." (p. 346)

Could we talk a little about your writing process? When you're working on a very subjective part of one of your books, such as the ending of **Terra Nostra**, *what is your composition and revision process like? When you are going over a draft, for example, do you revise in the direction of ambiguity and openness, or toward coherence?*

Both things. I think both things, because there are times when you say, "Hey, this is just ridiculous. I'm trying to do something and it doesn't make sense. I need a straight sentence here." Other times, you say, "This is too obvious," and you must make it more ambiguous. It depends really on what you have done in the second or third draft. And what risk you are willing to take and what lucidity you have on your own work about when you've reached a final stage. It's very tough. It's a difficult part, a challenging part but very enjoyable, I must say.

Do you have a pattern for revision?

I rewrite as I go. I come back and rewrite and go on. Some things I rewrite at the very end. It depends. And it depends on if it's a short story, where you can easily go back over what you've done every day. But if it's a novel, you lose track. Ask Dickens or Balzac the trouble they had keeping up with characters and avoiding non sequiturs and blunders and repetition. Even characters change names in some of those novels and the writer doesn't know it. A novel is *such* a protracted enterprise. God! It takes so many years at times to get it done. I'm in the final mile of a novel I'm writing right now, and I'm extremely worried about the quality of what I've already written and what I have to eliminate, what I have to better. These are problems that are worrying me all day long right now.

How do you keep your faith?

What do you mean?

How do you satisfy yourself about the quality of the work so that you can be reassured and go on?

Oh, you can never. You always know you have lost. Any novelist knows he has always failed. He has always lost. Whatever he has produced is well beneath what ideally he had in mind. Sometimes I think the perfect consonance of what the writer must have had in mind and what came out is very, very great. (pp. 350–51)

I suppose every author wants to consider his next book his best one, but if you look at the body of your completed work, what would you like to be remembered by?

I have no—by everything, because it's all one novel. It's all interconnected, and as the work progresses, I think you will see very clearly that it is one opus with different chapters. (p. 355)

Carlos Fuentes and David L. Middleton, in an interview in *The Southern Review*, Louisiana State University, Vol. 22, No. 2, April, 1986, pp. 342–55.

GABRIEL GARCÍA MÁRQUEZ
(essay date 1988)

[García Márquez is known as one of the greatest representatives of Hispanic literature. Laureate of the 1982 Nobel Prize for Literature, his many acclaimed novels include *Cien años de la soledad* (1967; *One Hundred Years of Solitude*, 1970), *El otoño del patriarca* (1975; *The Autumn of the Patriarch*, 1976) and *El amor en los tiempos del colera* (1985; *Love in the Time of Cholera*, 1988). In the following excerpt, he discusses his friendship with Fuentes, and admires his friend's extraordinary interest in and support of the efforts of young writers.]

My friendship with Carlos Fuentes—which is old, cordial, and also very enjoyable—began at the moment we met, in the heat of August back in 1961. Alvaro Mutis introduced us in that Dracula's castle of the streets of Córdoba, where an entire generation of writers trying to invent a new cinema were casting Manuel Barbachano Ponca into the first and most glorious of so many ruins. I had arrived in Mexico two months earlier, with my head full of novels and movies that couldn't find a way out, and I had read *Where the Air Is Clear* a short time after its publication. This was only natural because the novel had had a very wide reception in Latin America, and it was being spoken of everywhere—with all the reason in the world—as if of a literary event. The surprising thing for me was that Carlos Fuentes didn't have to search his memory to know who I was, and he told me upon entering that he had read the only two novels I had written at that time. I thought, of course, that it was merely one of those courteous formulas that save us so often from social floundering, above all among writers, since my first novel had been published six years earlier in Bogotá in a fly-by-night edition that didn't even make it to the corner, and the entire text of the second novel, still not corrected, had been published the year before in the journal *Mito*, which was as excellent as it was unavailable. The fact that Carlos Fuentes might truly have read them, as I was able to verify immediately, fed my vanity; it didn't take long for me to come down off my pedestal, however, for I realized very soon that Carlos Fuentes's literary curiosity recognizes neither times nor frontiers and that even then it was impossible to surprise him with a novelty in the world of letters. This curiosity was centered in a special way upon first works of writers, as he and I were in those good old days.

Twenty-five years later so many strange things have happened to us, in so many different places, that if one day we were to write our respective memoirs, readers would find themselves with interchangeable pages. In both books, without a doubt, would appear the most depressing chapter of our careers, which occurred many years ago, when we had to suffer night after night of horror for months on end, because a movie director made us undo, every day, the work of the day before, in order to redo it, again, the next day, only because he needed to delay the premiere of the movie in order to honor a previous commitment. That nightmare of literary Penelopes not only consolidated once and for all my admiration and affection for Carlos Fuentes, but also would inspire later on the solitary vice of Colonel Aureliano Buendía, who made and unmade his little gold fish.

Another pragmatic recollection from that time, but very funny as I recall it, is of an afternoon in Prague in the ill-fated year of 1968, when Milan Kundera decided that the only place in the entire city without hidden microphones was in a public sauna. Seated on a bench of fragrant pine, at 120 degrees Fahrenheit, the two of us stark naked and without the slightest sense of the ridiculous, we listened to Milan Kundera's awe-inspiring report on the tragic situation of his country. The most tragic thing for Fuentes and myself, however, occurred at the end, when we realized that there were no showers with cold water, and we had to break the layer of ice on the Moldava river in the middle of the month of December and submerge ourselves in its glacial waters. We did so without further ado, and at the moment of the tremendous immersion I had the lucid and atrocious conviction that Carlos Fuentes and I had died together in that instant, so far from the streets of Córdoba, and in such an absurd way that no one would ever understand it, not even because it had occurred in the homeland of Kafka.

Nevertheless, these flashes of life are not what I am interested in evoking now; instead I want to celebrate the virtue that I most admire in Carlos Fuentes and which is perhaps the one that is least known about him: his bodily spirit. I don't believe that there is a writer more conscious of those who come after him, nor one that is so generous with them. I have seen him wage wars with editors so that they would publish the book of some young writer who had for years carried around an unedited manuscript, as we all did in our own beginnings. Julio Cortázar, overwhelmed by the number of unedited originals that young people sent him, said shortly before his death: "It's a shame that those who send me manuscripts to read can't also send me the time to read them." Well, despite his numerous works and his intense public life, Carlos Fuentes reads the ones sent to him, and he has time besides to encourage and assist their unprotected authors. What happens, in reality, is that he seems to understand very well the Catholic notion of the Communion of Saints: in each of our acts—even though trivial and insignificant—each one of us is responsible for all of humanity. That is the metaphysics of the infinite literary curiosity of Carlos Fuentes. In contrast with so many writers who would like the world to revolve around them, he would like every day to be a celebration that the influence of writers in this world is more and more decisive. I have the impression that he dreams of an ideal planet, inhabited entirely by writers, and by them only. At times I have tried to dampen his enthusiasm, telling him that such a place already exists—it is Hell. But he doesn't believe me, not even in jest (which is how I have to phrase it to him, of course), because his faith in the messianic destiny of letters does not recognize limits. Nor, of course, does it admit jokes. A writer like this, already such a good writer, is twice as good. (pp. 179–81)

Gabriel García Márquez, "Carlos Fuentes: Good Twice Over," translated by Sandra L. Dunn, in *The Review of Contemporary Fiction*, Vol. 8, No. 2, Summer, 1988, pp. 179–81.

OCTAVIO PAZ
(essay date 1988)

[Paz is recognized as one of the most important Spanish-speaking poets. His writings include *El laberinto de la soledad* (1959; *The Labyrinth of Solitude: Life and Thought in Mexico*, 1961), *A Draft of Shadows and Other Poems* (1979) and *Convergences: Essays on Art and Literature* (1987). In the following excerpt, he praises Fuentes's wisdom, inquisitive spirit, and ability to counter malice with laughter.]

Novels, stories, plays, chronicles, literary and political essays: Fuentes's body of work is already one of the richest and most varied of contemporary literature in our language. In spite of the thematic and generic diversity, the question is always the same. Each one of his books is an approximation of an answer, but the question is continually reborn from each answer. It would be presumptuous, in the few minutes I have to speak, to attempt to define or even describe it. It is a very vast question and has many ramifications. Thus I will limit myself to pointing out one of its characteristics—for me, the central one: Fuentes's question does not refer so much to the enigma of the presence of man on Earth as it does to the nature and meaning, no less enigmatic, of human relations. The literature of the world has only two themes: one is the dialogue of mankind with the world; the other is the dialogue of men with men. Fuentes's question is opened, closed, and reopened in the sphere of the second theme. In truth, more than a question, it is a "one-on-one" with reality—at times in combat and at others in an erotic embrace. Because of this the two extreme notes of his work are eroticism and politics: how are erotic ties and social ties made, unmade, and remade? The bedroom and the public square, the couple and the crowd, the lovesick young girl in her room and the tyrant crouched in his den. Double fascination: desire and power, love and revolution. The author of *Aura* is also that of *The Death of Artemio Cruz*. His books are populated with the lovers and with the ambitious; Carlos could say, like André Gide: "Extremes move me."

It was not rare for Fuentes to provoke—by reason of the brilliance of his talent, the resonance of his work, and the nature of the question that he poses to both himself and to us—irritation, anger, and scandal. A passionate and exaggerated writer, an extreme and extremist being inhabited by many contradictions, an extroverted spirit in the introverted country of halftones and small-time swindlers (*chingaquedito*), a paradox in the republic of

I was born on November 11, 1928, under the sign I would have chosen, Scorpio, and on a date shared with Dostoevsky, Crommelynck, and Vonnegut. My mother was rushed from a steaming-hot movie house in those days before Colonel Buendía took his son to discover ice in the tropics. She was seeing King Vidor's version of *La Bohème* with John Gilbert and Lillian Gish. Perhaps the pangs of my birth were provoked by this anomaly: a silent screen version of Puccini's opera. Since then, the operatic and the cinematographic have had a tug-of-war with my words, as if expecting the Scorpio of fiction to rise from silent music and blind images.

All this, let me add to clear up my biography, took place in the sweltering heat of Panama City, where my father was beginning his diplomatic career as an attaché to the Mexican legation. (In those days, embassies were established only in the most important capitals—no place where the mean average year-round temperature was perpetually in the nineties.) Since my father was a convinced Mexican nationalist, the problem of where I was to be born had to be resolved under the sign, not of Scorpio, but of the Eagle and the Serpent.

The Mexican legation, however, though it had extraterritorial rights, did not have even a territorial midwife; and the minister, a fastidious bachelor from Sinaloa by the name of Ignacio Norris, who resembled the poet Quevedo as one pince-nez

resembles another, would have none of me suddenly appearing on the legation parquet, even if the Angel Gabriel had announced me as a future Mexican writer of some, albeit debatable, merit.

So, if I could not be born in a fictitious, extraterritorial Mexico, neither would I be born in that even more fictitious extension of the United States of America, the Canal Zone, where, naturally, the best hospitals were. So, between two territorial fictions—the Mexican legation, the Canal Zone—and a mercifully silent close-up of John Gilbert, I arrived in the nick of time at the Gorgas Hospital in Panama City at eleven that evening.

The problem of my baptism then arose. As if the waters of the two neighboring oceans touching each other with the iron fingertips of the canal were not enough, I had to undergo a double ceremony: my religious baptism took place in Panama, because my mother, a devout Roman Catholic, demanded it with as much urgency as Tristram Shandy's parents, although through less original means. My national baptism took place a few months later in Mexico City, where my father, an incorrigible Jacobin and priest-eater to the end, insisted that I be registered in the civil rolls established by Benito Juárez. Thus, I appear as a native of Mexico City for all legal purposes, and this anomaly further illustrates a central fact of my life and my writing: I am Mexican by will and by imagination.

Carlos Fuentes, in his *Myself and Others*, Farrar, Straus and Giroux, 1988.

commonplaces, an irreverent individual in a nation that has converted its tragic and marvelous history into a lay sermon and that has made of its living heroes an assembly of plaster and concrete statues. Fuentes has been and is the main course of many cannibal banquets, for in literary matters—and not only in this, but in almost all social relations—Mexico is a country for which human flesh is a delicacy. With but a few exceptions, we do not have critics, but sacrificers. Masked by this or that ideology, some practice slander, others contempt (*ninguneo*), and all a hypocrisy at once productive and boring. The literary gangs periodically celebrate ritual feasts during which they metaphorically devour their enemies. Generally those enemies are the friends and idols of yesterday. Our cannibals profess a type of backwards religion, and their banquets are also ceremonies of profanation of the gods adored the night before. It's not enough for them to eat their victims—they need to dishonor them. After each ceremony of destruction, however, Fuentes appears more alive than before. The secret of his resurrections? A weapon better than the magic bow of Arjuna—laughter. Fuentes knows how to laugh at the world because he is able to laugh at himself. Laughter is the wisdom that disperses the cannibals and mangles their poison arrows. After the laughter, the writer returns to himself and to his question. . . . [Fuentes] asks himself, "What is the novel, and what does it mean to write novels?" And the novel

answers him with another question: "What are men, those creatures that only reach full reality when they transform themselves into images?" (pp. 187–88)

Octavio Paz, "The Question of Carlos Fuentes," translated by Sandra L. Dunn, in *The Review of Contemporary Fiction*, Vol. 8, No. 2, Summer, 1988, pp. 186–88.

ROBIN FIDDIAN

(essay date 1990)

[In the following excerpt, Fiddian discusses Fuentes's *The Death of Artemio Cruz* in the context of Mexico's history, its "moral and political dogmas," and its relation to North American values.]

In Latin America, where writing and politics go hand in hand, ideological protest has often been accompanied by linguistic iconoclasm in the novel. Works by the Cuban Lezama Lima and also Roa Bastos, Cortázar and Fuentes, among others, exemplify a search for new norms of literary expression which are intended to deconstruct 'una larga historia de mentiras, silencios, retóricas y complicidades académicas'. If, as Fuentes suggests, 'Todo es lenguaje en América Latina: el poder y la libertad, la dominación y la esperanza', it follows that a creative departure from accepted standards of verbal decorum constitutes a revolutionary act: 'Nuestra literatura', Fuentes affirms, 'es verdaderamente revolucionaria en cuanto le niega al orden establecido el léxico que éste quisiera y le opone el lenguaje de la alarma, la renovación, el desorden y el humor. El lenguaje, en suma, de la ambigüedad' [*La nueva narrativa hispanoamericana*].

Fuentes's own experiments with the forms and language of fiction match this blue-print very closely. Originally misinterpreted as gratuitous exercises in self-indulgence and the 'puerile' imitation of alien (European Modernist) models, the narrative fragmentation, syntactic disruption and discursive openness of novels like *La región más transparente* (1958) and *Cambio de piel* effectively figure forth suppressed, alternative dimensions of experience which belong to the category of 'the Other'. In *Aura, Cumpleaños* and *Una familia lejana* (1980), the Other manifests itself in the themes of reincarnation and the double; in *La muerte de Artemio Cruz* and *Terra nostra*, it is constituted by the possibilities which have been negated in the lives of an individual and the Mexican nation, respectively; in *Gringo viejo* (1985), it is latent in the potentialities of a historical mystery (that of the disappearance of a retired North American soldier during the Mexican Revolution) which conventional historiography has failed to articulate. In *Gringo viejo*, as in *La muerte de Artemio Cruz* and the futuristic pages of *Terra nostra* and *Cristóbal Nonato*, Fuentes is particularly interested in investigating the relationships of alterity, antagonism and complementarity between Mexico and the United States of America. The later novels debate issues of national identity and integrity on a grand scale: in relation to the values and traditions of post-Renaissance Europe (*Terra nostra*) and against the hypothetical backdrop of a North American occupation of Acapulco, Veracruz and other provinces of Mexico (*Cristóbal Nonato*). The broad perspective of these narratives complements the narrow focus, found in earlier works such as 'Chac Mool' and *La región más transparente*, on 'subterranean' indigenous elements which survive in contemporary Mexican culture, contributing something vital and disruptive to a national identity which has engaged Fuentes's attention throughout his career.

La muerte de Artemio Cruz is generally regarded as his first major novel and a landmark in Mexican and Latin American fiction. Written between May 1960 and December 1961 in Havana and Mexico City, it absorbs many of the energies released by the Cuban Revolution, feeding consciously on a newly awakened spirit of solidarity and commitment to the struggle for greater freedom and self-determination in Latin America. Like *Rayuela*, it is a conjunctural text, and one which made an immediate impression on fellow writers like García Márquez

and the Mexican Gustavo Sainz. García Márquez incorporated a reference to its protagonist in the final sections of *Cien años de soledad*: Sainz admitted that 'this book changed me, as the fall from the horse changed Funes the Memorious, in a provocative and highly stimulating fashion. Translated into some fifteen languages, *La muerte de Artemio Cruz* continues to be read in many parts of the world a quarter of a century after it was first published.

Essentially, the novel explores the legacy of the Mexican Revolution of 1910–17, filtered through the fragmented consciousness of Artemio Cruz whom we visualise lying on his death-bed on 10 April 1959. Cruz is 70 years old and the owner of a huge personal fortune amassed without scruple or restraint over the past forty years. The major events of his life are recounted in retrospect, in a disjointed series of twelve fragments that are narrated in the third person; the remainder of the narrative comprises twenty-six fragments divided equally between a first person—YO—and a second person—TÚ—whose interaction provides the necessary dynamics of narrative progression. In part a showcase of technical experimentation, *La muerte de Artemio Cruz* more importantly explores themes of individual psychology and morality, national history and identity, and certain regional and continental concerns. In this essay I shall examine each of these aspects of the novel in turn, paying attention to technical features of the writing when they seem to have a direct bearing on points of interpretation.

As a starting point for discussion, we may consider *La muerte de Artemio Cruz* as a novel of the psyche focused primarily on the maze-like mind of the dying Cruz. Access to this world of jumbled thoughts, memories, perceptions, sensations, feelings and desires provides insights into the minds and motivation of secondary characters including his wife, Catalina, and their daughter, Teresa, but these are strictly subordinate to Cruz's ego, as they have been throughout his life. Cruz's conscious and subconscious minds may usefully be visualised as the site of innumerable conflicts, a theatre in which are played out complex preoccupations with self and identity, affirmation and the will to power, pride and courage, frustration and guilt. These cluster of themes are presented systematically within the broad parameters of an Existentialist enquiry which highlights notions of responsibility and commitment, alienation and authenticity, freedom and identity, chance and destiny.

Beginning *in media res*, the novel depicts Cruz's interior struggle to salvage something of value from a life characterised by political opportunism, intimate personal failure and the abuse of human relationships. After a childhood which is reconstructed by memory as an idyllic age of innocence and ambiguous promise, the teenage Cruz becomes enmeshed in 'el tejido de lo incierto' which obliges him to define himself and choose between multiple courses of action. Armed with indestructible self-confidence and a Nietzschean will to power which drives him ever onwards—'siempre había mirado hacia adelante desde la noche en que atravesó la montaña y escapó del viejo casco veracruzano'—he proceeds to impose himself on his natural and social surroundings, sweeping obstacles aside and creating new rules 'como si nada hubiese sucedido antes, Adán sin padre, Moisés sin tablas'. Just minutes before he is whisked away by ambulance to be operated on in hospital, he finds the spiritual strength to reaffirm his will to live and to feel pride once again in a sexual relationship which had been the source of an ecstatic 'encuentro con el mundo' almost half a century ago. Through a selective operation of memory, Cruz contrives to forget the horror of Regina's death, an event which provoked 'su primer llanto de hombre' and coincided with his first experience of a sense of shame, during a battle in the military phase of the Mexican Revolution when he deserted from his regiment and abandoned a wounded companion whose life he could, and should, have saved. In the overall pattern of his life, this is a crucial turning point when he lost a sense of direction, symbolised by the 'hilo perdido': 'El hilo que le permitió recorrer, sin perderse, le laberinto de la guerra. Sin perderse: sin desertar. . . . El hilo quedó atrás'.

Cruz's desertion is the first in a series of reactions to specific test-situations where he fails to live up to standards of conduct which his son Lorenzo's example proves are a wholly attainable ideal. It is a lapse which has immediate and inescapable consequences, both for the subsequent direction of his life and for the reader's evaluation of him. Straightaway it narrows the range of options open to Cruz, on the basis that a choice between alternative forks on the path of life simultaneously creates and denies experiential possibilities: 'decidirás, escogerás uno de los caminos, sacrificarás los demás: te sacrificarás al escoger, dejarás de ser todos los otros hombres que pudiste haber sido'. And it projects a shadow onto his entire future which will forever be contaminated by the past.

In this latter respect, his experience resembles a fall from grace into a state of existential inauthenticity which is illustrated in various ways. Since 1947 Cruz has led a double life, grudgingly devoting time and attention to his family in their house in Las Lomas, and cohabiting with Lilia in a residence in Coyoacán which he regards as 'mi verdadera casa'. The retrospective episode of Lilia's sexual infidelity in Acapulco at the beginning of their relationship pointedly reveals its foundation in artificiality and pretence. Flanked by two scenes in which Cruz contemplates his reflection uneasily in a mirror, it awakens in him feelings of vulnerability, world-weariness, impotence, suspicion and rage:

> No podía tenerla más. Esta tarde, esa misma noche, buscaría a Xavier, se encontrarían en secreto, ya habían fijado la cita. Y los ojos de Lilia, perdidos en el paisaje de veleros y agua dormida, no decían nada. Pero él podría sacárselo, hacer una escena. . . Se sintió falso, incómodo y siguió comiendo la langosta. . .

Cruz's embarrassment is plainly visible shortly after, when, as he prepares to shave, he turns to the mirror 'quer(iendo) descubrir al mismo de siempre', and sees an image of himself stripped of comforting illusions: 'Al abrirlos, ese viejo de ojos inyectados, de pómulos grises, labios marchitos, que ya no era el otro, el reflejo aprendido, le devolvió una mueca desde el espejo'. The motifs of the mask and the mirror are constant reminders of the fragmented and inauthentic basis of his life.

That lack of wholeness manifests itself in Cruz's inability to establish integrated relationships with other people. The relationships on which he embarks after his personal Fall characteristically pit one person's will and needs against those of another, excluding any harmonious resolution of contraries. His marriage to Catalina is an extreme example. Locked in a conflict of self-assertion and mutual mistrust, Artemio and Catalina are twinned in complex ways: they are identical in their pride, their disenchantment and sense of loss (Catalina senses that they have both been expelled from their respective 'paradisos'); they are potential complements to each other, 'quizás dos mitades y un solo sentimiento'; yet, they are sadly unable to communicate when the occasion demands and remain unreconcilable in their antagonism.

At a further level of psychological analysis each of these characters embodies contradictory features. On the critical night of 3 June 1924, Catalina feels torn between an instinctual sexual desire for Cruz and a vengeful rejection of the man who was responsible for her brother's death: 'Me vences de noche. Te venzo de día', she reflects, later lamenting the division of her life 'como para satisfacer a dos razones' and imploring '¿Por qué no puedo escoger una sola, Dios mío?' For his part, at this stage of their relationship Cruz is still convinced of his love for Catalina and would openly beg her: 'Acéptame así, con estas culpas, y mírame como a un hombre que necesita. . . . No me odies. Tenme misericordia, Catalina amada. Porque te quiero.' But, he lacks the courage to admit his weakness and culpability, and responds to Catalina's recriminations by taking a frightened, compliant Indian girl to his bed, thus reinforcing the barriers between them.

The sequence of events under consideration illustrates Cruz's tragic inability not only to compromise in his relationship with Catalina but also to integrate opposing sides of his personality. This applies particularly in respect of the feminine side of his nature which he resolutely denies, both figuratively and literally, in his relation with his daughter, Teresa. Fuentes probably had the mythological character of Artemis in mind when he chose his protagonist's Christian name. Artemis, a redoubtable huntress renowned for her vindictive and bloodthirsty nature, was a virgin who refused any contact with the opposite sex, in dramatic contrast to the conduct of her brother and alter ego, Apollo. In Fuentes's novel the name 'Artemio' is at once ironic, inasmuch as it reverses the gender of the mythological referent and is a telling comment on Cruz's suppression of half of his sexual being. The surname 'Cruz' reinforces this interpretation: among its many connotations is that of a coin (the Spanish equivalent of English 'Heads or tails' is 'Cara o cruz') flipped to decide who wins and who loses a contest. Here, Cruz turns out to be simultaneously a winner in life's contest for material gains and a loser in the moral and spiritual stakes. A faceless man who has fulfilled only half of his potential, he might also be described as 'Cruz sin cara'.

Cruz reacts to his circumstances in a variety of ways. One reaction consists in redoubling his challenge to the established moral order, in a triumphant reassertion of pride: 'Les gané a muchos. Les gané a todos', he boasts on his death-bed. This diabolical egotism, coupled with cunning and perversity, provides a yardstick with which Cruz may be judged. Crucially, it establishes a perspective from which to evaluate some of the more positive traits of his character such as the courage that he displays on occasions throughout his life (for example, at a political rally when he was fired on by Don Pizarro's thugs and stood his ground, or on the flight from Sonora to Mexico City where a mechanical failure causes consternation amongst all of the passengers except him); the dignity which informs some of his personal relations; and his capacity for experiencing emotions of love, nostalgia and regret, as in a memorable moment, steeped in pathos, when he wishes he could recall every feature of his dead son, Lorenzo: the smell of his body, the color of his skin. . . . It is a measure of Fuentes's grasp of the subtleties of Existentialist morality that he recoils from presenting any of these qualities in a pure, unadulterated state. It may be that Artemio's courage is no more than the mask of aggressive bravado associated with the Mexican *chingón*: his pride is double-edged ('Nos salvó el orgullo. Nos mató el orgullo', he mentally confesses to Catalina); his nostalgia may be a cover for cowardice. Overall, Fuentes's presentation of Cruz captures the internal contradictions of a man who is 'capaz. . . de encarnar al mismo tiempo el bien y el mal'.

Cruz's nostalgia for a lost garden of Eden (cf. 'jardín', 'paradiso') is a second reaction to his Fall, and one which invariably leads to disappointment because, as Catalina learns from experience, there can be no return to the source of purity, no recovery of innocence. Cruz's private realisation that this is so intensifies the pathos of his nostalgia. Yet, the suspicion is never dispelled that his nostalgic attitude may not be yet one more aspect of a general bad faith. That objection does not hold for the third of his reactions, which consists of a mature acceptance of guilt. For, ever since he abandoned the anonymous soldier in December 1913, Cruz has harboured feelings of guilt which he has so far managed to suppress by dint of will and self-deceit. Years of living 'como si no hubiera atrás, siempre atrás, lápidas de historia e historias, sacos de vergüenza, hechos cometidos por [Catalina], por él' have effectively numbed 'la herida que nos causa

traicionarnos' and protected Cruz from the provocations of conscience. However, on 10 April 1959 the voice of that conscience—the TÚ voice—breaks through his defences and visits on him spectres of the past, from which there is no escape. As the twelve sets of narrative fragments unravel like a ball of twine, we witness the gradual return of the repressed, orchestrated by a mind which is straining to come to terms with its history. In the first YO fragment, a minimal and uncontextualised reference to 'Regina Soldado' sets in motion a process of recovery which is sustained in the fourth fragment through a simple repetition, and expanded in the eighth and eleventh with the recitation of a full list of 'nombres muertos' of people who died in order that Cruz might survive: 'Regina. . . Tobías. . . Páez. . . Gonzalo. . . Zagal. . . Laura, Laura. . . Lorenzo'. The exhumation of these names gives Cruz the chance to relive events which took place on days 'en que tu destino. . . te encarnará con palabras y actos' and enables him to face up to the truth about his relationships with other people.

Fuentes seems to envisage a positive outcome to Cruz's experience, 'hoy que la muerte iguala el origen y el destino y entre los dos clava, a pesar de todo, el filo de la libertad'. A prefatory quotation from Montaigne, 'La préméditation de la mort est préméditation de la liberté', had already anticipated the possibility of a secular form of redemption. Yet the message of salvation contained in *La muerte de Artemio Cruz* is a conditional one which allows contradictory interpretations: on the one hand, it asserts the possibility of finally attaining freedom, while on the other, it is shot through with a streak of irony redolent of Jorge Luis Borges's speculations about imminent revelation and mystical enlightenment at the moment of death, as illustrated in the story of Jaromir Hladík in 'El milagro secreto'.

In any case, the promises held out in Fuentes's novel must be weighed against much more sombre insights into the human condition, encapsulated in two other quotations which make up the Preface: these are an *estribillo* from a popular Mexican song which claims that 'No vale nada la vida. La vida no vale nada', and a quatrain from *El gran teatro del mundo* by Pedro Calderón de la Barca which reads 'Hombres que salís al suelo / por una cuna de hielo / y por un sepulcro entráis, / ved como representáis. . . '. Elaborating on these ideas in the text of his novel, Fuentes conveys an often overwhelming impression of the utter worthlessness and fragility of life. The scene in which a fat policeman plays Russian roulette with Cruz illustrates a horrifying contempt for life which is supposed to typify the Mexican outlook, as examined by Octavio Paz in *El laberinto de la soledad* and dramatised by Malcolm Lowry in the *cantina* episode of *Under the Volcano*.

Elsewhere in *La muerte de Artemio Cruz*, the human body is the focal point of Fuentes's wholly conventional but nonetheless striking thoughts about suffering and death. The opening fragment spares Cruz few indignities as it records his physical collapse into a dehumanised state:

> Los párpados me pesan: dos plomos, cobres en la lengua, martillos en el oído, una. . . una como plata oxidada en la respiración. Metálico todo esto. Mineral otra vez. Orino sin saberlo.

This graphic picture of physical disorder confirms TÚ's prophecy that 'serás un depósito de sudores nervios irritados y funciones fisiológicas inconscientes', at the same time as it emphasises Cruz's vulnerability to the ravages of time and sickness. Having previously taken the workings of his body for granted ('vivirás y dejarás que las funciones se las entiendan solas'), Cruz now experiences their ephemerality and acknowledges the shocking vulnerability of what Fernando del Paso in a central chapter of *Palinuro de México* terms the body's 'sacred symmetry'. In this regard, Cruz's perception of fragmented images of an eye, a nose, an unshaven chin and a sunken cheek which are reflected on the surface of his wife's handbag, and his piecemeal account of the sensations he feels in various other parts of his body, underline the vanity of his thoughts about the unity of 'El propio cuerpo. El cuerpo unido'.

A similar mood of disenchantment informs Fuentes's evaluation of human life in relation to the astronomical duration of the universe. At a point when approximately two-thirds of the narrative have elapsed, the TÚ voice insists on the futility of Cruz's previous attempts to stall and buy time, assuring him that 'tu quietud no detendrá al tiempo que corre sin ti, aunque tú lo inventes y midas, al tiempo que niega tu inmovilidad y te somete a su propio peligro de extinción'. And, near the end, it evokes the chilling emptiness of interstellar space where 'los inmensos astros. . . giran en silencio sobre el fondo infinito del espacio', anticipating the ultimate degradation of the universe on a day when 'no habrá ni luz, ni calor, ni vida'. Reminiscent of the final section of James Joyce's *Finnegans Wake* and of Spanish writing of the Baroque generally, these themes reveal a deep-seated pessimism which is at odds with the requirements of humanistic and Marxist philosophies alike.

Turning to Fuentes's treatment of Mexican themes, we note the same acuteness and breadth of vision and the same spirit of passionate debate as evidenced in his exploration of Existentialist concerns. Collective psychology, race, history and culture are the principal foci of an enquiry which is conducted at all three levels of the narrative: the YO voice acts as the vehicle of ancestral memory and collective desire; the TÚ voice ranges over two thousand years of Mexican history and transcends the bounds of national and regional geography; the narrative fragments in the third person, besides following the course of Cruz's life from the cradle to the grave, also survey the history of his family over four generations. These expansive patterns of the narrative are supplemented by allegorical and figurative procedures which serve to deflect the reader's attention away from the particular aspects of Cruz's experience to a broader frame of reference where his behaviour has a more general significance. For, as well as being the protagonist of an individual biography, Cruz represents a class—of bourgeois entrepreneurs—an age—that of burgeoning capitalist investment in mid-twentieth-century Mexico—and successive periods of the nation's history from the late *porfiriato*, through the years of the Revolution to the narrative present when President López Mateos is in charge of the country's affairs.

In the very first fragments of *La muerte de Artemio Cruz*, Fuentes reveals the extent of his character's financial holdings and gives a detailed description of the social values, aspirations and way of life of a bourgeois parvenu. Multiple business interests allied to the political status quo support a life-style which we are asked to believe was typical of the Mexican bourgeoisie after 1940. Cruz's conspicuous consumerism and sophisticated tastes in food, clothes, music, painting and so on, characterise a social type which compensates for its insecurities by aping foreign life-styles and values, in particular those of white urban society in North America. The TÚ voice observes:

> Desde que empezaste a ser lo que eres, desde que aprendiste a apreciar el tacto de las buenas telas, el gusto de los buenos licores, el olfato de las buenas lociones, todo eso que en los últimos años ha sido tu placer aislado y único, desde entonces clavaste la mirada allá arriba, en el norte, y desde entonces has vivido con la nostalgia del error geográfico que no te permitió ser en todo parte de ellos.

The admiration which Cruz and those like him feel for the social and economic achievements of North America is shot through with jealousy and remorse: 'te duele saber que por más que lo intentes, no puedes ser como ellos, puedes sólo ser una calca, una aproximación'. Yet, Fuentes suggests, few Mexicans acknowledge the deep-seated motives and implications of their behaviour as they routinely order waffles with Pepsi Cola or Canada Dry from a waitress 'vestida de tehuana' at Sanborn's; in effect, they are collaborating in their own economic and cultural colonisation.

Fuentes's most pungent satire of the mental set of the Mexican bourgeoisie is contained in the ÉL fragment which describes 'la fiesta de San Silvestre' celebrated on New Year's Eve 1955 in Cruz's house at Coyoacán. This grotesque tableau, worthy of Hieronymus Bosch, portrays the collective greed, pettiness, vanity and *mauvaise foi* of those whom in another context the author deprecatingly calls 'los de arriba'. Antedating the narrative present by only four years, it sharpens the historical perspective of Fuentes's novel.

The actual death of Artemio Cruz occurs at a critical moment in a turbulent period of Mexican history which Fuentes examines in his essay, **'Radiografía de una década: 1953–1963'**. There, Fuentes surveys political events in contemporary Mexico and records 'las luchas obreras de 1958 y 1959, la represión brutal contra el sindicato ferrocarrilero de Demetrio Vallejo y el deterioro de las condiciones de vida y de trabajo de la gran mayoría de los mexicanos'. On the day before he dies, Artemio Cruz flies into Mexico City and is driven to his office along streets impregnated with mustard gas, 'porque la policía acabará de disolver esa manifestación en la plaza del Caballito'. The bloody repression of striking railway workers, which will shortly provide the backdrop to *José Trigo* by Fernando del Paso (1966), is referred to in a conversation between Cruz and a North American, Mr. Corkery, who would like to use Cruz's newspaper to discredit 'los ferrocarrileros comunistas de México.' Cruz manages the interview with Corkery shrewdly and acts quickly to protect his own financial interests by sanitising reports about 'la represión de la policía contra estos alborotadores'. He is thus inextricably implicated in contemporary events.

Delving into the past, the novel traces the immediate roots of Cruz's political and financial influence to the new order which arose out of the Mexican Revolution. When Cruz visits the Bernal household in Puebla in 1919, don Gamaliel, the failing patriarch, reflects: 'Artemio Cruz. Así se llamaba, entonces, el nuevo mundo surgido de la guerra civil: así se llamaban quienes llegaban a sustituirlo'. Don Gamaliel's judgement turns out to be prophetic: Cruz wheedles his way into the home and, by marrying Catalina Bernal, becomes master of the family estate.

Don Gamaliel's lapidary assessment uncovers an allegorical dimension in Cruz's character and fortunes: he is the personification of the Revolution, an emblem of its origins, course and results. Several commentators have documented coincidences between the fictional life of Cruz and the process of the Revolution, positing a common progression from an initial stage of idealism, through corruption and betrayal to an institutionalised atrophy. They accordingly identify the young Cruz with Francisco Madero's principled opposition to Porfirio Díaz's re-election, and chart his faltering course through late December 1913 (the temporal setting of the third ÉL fragment) and October 1915 (the seventh ÉL fragment) up to May 1919 (the second ÉL fragment) when he arrives in Puebla. As the Mexican critic, María Stoopen, observes, '1913 es el año del fin de la revolución y del gobierno de Madero; es el año del golpe de Huerta y del ascenso del traidor; es el año de las lealtades y de las traiciones'. Significantly, Cruz's biography is similarly ambivalent at this time:

> Es Artemio Cruz, en estos momentos, como tantos otros participantes de la lucha armada, un representante del pueblo que no posee una conciencia clara de

movimiento, pero que tiene la intención justa de 'llegar a México y correr de la presidencia al borracho de Huerta, el asesino de don Panchito Madero'.

> (in the words of the text)

By 1915 the Revolution has entered a third phase of partisan military activity which effectively destroys any chance of its radical potential being realised. At this stage of the conflict, Cruz is fighting for General Álvaro Obregón in alliance with the troops of Venustiano Carranza, and is taken prisoner by the *villista* colonel, Zagal. In the circumstances, he appears to face certain death, along with the wounded Indian companion, Tobías, and Gonzalo Bernal, 'enviado del Primer Jefe Venustiano Carranza', who shares their cell in the prison at Perales. But, a combination of treachery and good fortune allows Cruz to escape, leaving behind the corpses of his two cell-mates along with that of Zagal whom he kills in a duel made possible when *carranclán* troops launch a surprise attack on the town.

Maria Stoopen [in her *La muerte de Artemio Cruz: una novela de denuncia y traición*, 1982] interprets Cruz's behaviour in this episode as a triple betrayal, of (1) the Indian peasant class, represented by the *yaqui* Tobías, (2) the popular cause championed by Villa, and (3) untainted revolutionary idealism personified by Gonzalo Bernal who, according to his father, 'Fue siempre tan puro'. Yet, when he learns that Tobías is to be shot, Cruz asks Zagal to spare his life; also, he does not kill Zagal, as he could have, by shooting him in the back during the confusion of the *carranclán* attack, but grants him the chance to fight a duel with loaded pistols across an imaginary line in the prison courtyard. It is therefore wrong to accuse Cruz of blanket treachery: plainly, his treatment of the three men involves different degrees of culpability. His treachery is greatest with Bernal who represents the moral and intellectual direction of the Revolution, a value nicely illustrated in the image of his corpse lying next to that of Zagal: 'El brazo muerto del coronel Zagal se extendió hacia la cabeza muerta de Gonzalo'. In abandoning Bernal to his fate, Cruz simultaneously sacrifices that part of himself which comprises 'ideas y ternuras' and destroys the integrity of the Revolutionary movement.

So, when he visits Gonzalo's family in Puebla in 1919, Cruz is already the standard-bearer of betrayed ideals 'en el mundo destruido y confuso que dejaba la Revolución'. He is also the prototype of instinctive opportunism: 'Todo el camino de Puebla: cuestión de puro instinto', ready to exploit the embattled position of don Gamaliel whom he finds locked in 'una lucha pasiva' with the recalcitrant local peasantry. As soon as they meet, don Gamaliel, who 'se imaginaba a sí mismo como el producto final de una civilización peculiarmente criolla: la de los déspotas ilustrados', seals a 'pacto tácito' with the self-possessed Cruz who, he tells Catalina, can save the old order—'Este hombre puede salvarnos'—by accommodating it within the new regime of land tenure, political influence and power being forged in the early days of post-Revolutionary Mexico. From this point on, the fortunes of the Bernal family and those of Artemio Cruz merge and become a mirror of the motley affairs of the nation.

Cruz's semiotic status as a type is signalled repeatedly throughout the narrative. In an early section, the TÚ-voice, wondering 'cuáles datos pasarán a tu biografía y cuáles callados', answers: 'No lo sabrás. Son datos vulgares y no serás el primero ni el único con semejante hoja de servicios'. Near the end of the novel, the same voice considers Cruz's legacy to the nation in terms which confirm his role as a personification of Mexico: 'legarás este país; legarás tu periódico, los codazos y la adulación, la conciencia adormecida por los discursos falsos de hombres mediocres; tengan su México: tengan tu herencia.'

Other allegorical dimensions of *La muerte de Artemio Cruz* centre on Cruz's family history and origins, which are the subject of the last two fragments narrated by the ÉL voice. At this stage we discover that Cruz is the illegitimate child of a black servant-girl known as Isabel Cruz, and Atanasio Menchaca, the elder son of a *criollo* family settled since the early nineteenth century on a large estate in Cocuya in the province of Veracruz. Atanasio's father, Ireneo, had been an associate of General Santa Anna—the supremo of Mexican politics during the 1830s, 1840s and 1850s—and had lived 'una vida de azar y loterías como la del país mismo'. His wife, Ludivinia, is a symbolic counterpart, having been born in 1810, the year in which Mexico broke its colonial ties with Spain. In January 1903, which is the temporal setting of the penultimate ÉL fragment, Ludivinia still occupies the dilapidated remains of the family estate, whose doors she remembers opening 'al largo desfile de prelados españoles, comerciantes franceses, ingenieros escoceses, británicos vendedores de bonos, agiotistas y filibusteros que por aquí pasaron en su marcha hacia la ciudad de México y las oportunidades del país joven, anárquico'. Clearly, Cocuya is a microcosm of nineteenth-century Mexico, and the Menchacas typical representatives of the nation's tendency to accept *caudillo* figures and submit to colonising forces. It is no accident that these faults reappear in the character of Artemio Cruz a century later: in Fuentes's diagnosis, they constitute a *damnosa hereditas* which hangs like a dead weight around the country's neck.

In the case of Artemio, that heritage is handed down through his father Atanasio, a violent man who drove Isabel Cruz off his estate as soon as she gave birth, and would have killed the baby if Lunero had not made himself available as surrogate father. Interestingly, Atanasio had a brother, Pedro, who differed markedly from him in character and behaviour, striking up a contrast which the narrative mediates through the thoughts processes of their mother, Ludivinia:

Ah—suspiró Ludivinia, encaramada en su lecho revuelto—, ése no es Atanasio, que era como la prolongación de su madre en la virilidad: éste es la misma madre, pero con barba y testículos—soñó la vieja—, no la madre como hubiese sido en la hombría, como fue Atanasio.

In a brilliant analysis of this aspect of the novel, Steven Boldy [in his "Fathers and Sons in Fuentes's *La muerte de Artemio Cruz*," *Bulletin of Hispanic Studies* 61 (1984)] has explained Pedro and Atanasio's role as the first pair in a series of brothers or doubles of opposing tendencies, who represent stark moral and political alternatives between which the nation must choose at crucial moments in its history. Following the sequence through to the fictional present, Pedro and Atanasio are succeeded by Gonzalo Bernal and Artemio Cruz who stand respectively for revolutionary commitment and cynical self-interest; their antagonism, which acquires its most dramatic expression in the prison sequence at Perales, is reproduced in the following generation in the relation between Lorenzo and Jaime Ceballos. As Boldy sees it, this cyclical scheme is intended to evoke 'the unfulfilled, censured promises of the Mexican heritage'. Yet, one might argue just as convincingly that Fuentes paints a profoundly dispiriting picture of recurrent frustration and determinism in Mexican history since 1810: looked at from the vantage point of 1959, Artemio Cruz seems to have been fated to repeat the excesses and shortcomings of his grandfather, Ireneo, and his uncle Pedro. What is more, prospects for the future are glum, since the death of Lorenzo in the Spanish Civil War leaves the way open for the unscrupulous and scheming Jaime Ceballos to inherit Cruz's legacy, setting in motion a new cycle of injustice and sterility.

Cruz's status as Atanasio's illegitimate child yields a further set of meanings which have relevance here. First and foremost, his illegitimacy marks him as an 'hijo de la chingada' who is the very type of his nation, born in 1519 of the conjunction between imperial Spain—its power delegated to Hernán Cortés— and the Aztec empire of Anáhuac to whose seat Cortés gained access by using the political, linguistic and sexual services of an Indian woman known as La Malinche. According to Paz and Fuentes, modern Mexican man's obsession with legitimacy and betrayal follows directly from that founding event which is pictured as a violation of the national psyche and body politic.

In complicated ways, Cruz stand for all three terms in the equation Spain + Anáhuac = Mexico. He is portrayed as a *conquistador* setting foot on Mexico's Gulf Coast at Veracruz, like Cortés in a famous mural painted by Diego Rivera. A New World Atlas, he carries on his shoulders the whole of Mexican antiquity, including its landscapes, languages, customs and civilisations. And, he embodies the Mexican nation's two-pronged obsession with sexual betrayal and abuse, which is summed up in the repertoire of phrases featuring variants of the verb 'chingar.' The immense referential range of this 'palabra de honor' makes it the 'blasón de la raza. . . , resumen de la historia: santo y seña de México'. Used by the malevolent *chingón*, the word is a weapon that can hurt and humiliate, but also one that can be turned against its user. This is exactly what happens in *La muerte de Artemio Cruz* where the TÚ voice turns on the protagonist and reminds him that 'Eres un hijo de la chingada/ del ultraje que lavaste ultrajando a otros hombres.' The ÉL fragments also conspire to shatter Cruz's pretensions to power and respectability, tracing his origins back to the day when he was born and, imaginatively, to the moment of his conception during one of 'los mil coitos feroces, descuidados, rápidos [de Atanasio Menchaca]'. The overall pattern of the narrative thus tends towards the revelation and reenactment of a violation in which the origins of Cruz's personal identity and that of modern Mexico reside.

Comparisons of Cruz with the archetypal figures of Quetzalcóatl and Jesus Christ enhance his significance as an emblem of the nation. In *Tiempo mexicano* (1970) Fuentes represents the Conquest of Mexico as a process of interaction between one mythical and religious type identified with the Mesoamerican tradition, and another central to European culture. Fuentes recalls how in 1519 the Mexican Indians were awaiting the return of their chosen god, Quetzalcóatl, who had earlier fled the country in disgrace. Fortuitously, on the very day when he was expected to return, Hernán Cortés disembarked at Veracruz and instigated a chain of substitutions which caused native Mexicans subsequently to confuse Quetzalcóatl and Jesus Christ: 'México impuso a Cortés la máscara de Quetzalcóatl. Cortés la rechazóe impuso a México la máscsara de Cristo. Desde entonces', Fuentes writes, 'es imposible saber a quien se adora en los altares barrocos de Puebla, de Tlaxcala y de Oaxaca'.

This psycho-historical analysis of the Conquest provides an insight into processes of cultural syncretism in sixteenth-century Mexico and establishes a context for understanding the symbolic portrayal of Artemio Cruz as both a Christ-figure and an avatar of Quetzalcóatl. Parallels between Cruz and Christ are varied and oblique. In the opening pages of the novel Cruz suffers '[un] dolor del costado' which brings to mind Christ's suffering on the Cross. The surname 'Cruz' contributes a vital element to the comparison, connoting the weight of collective guilt which rests on the character's shoulders like the sins of the world on those of Jesus. Indeed, the sum of 'hechos cometidos por todos' is a burden that Cruz finds intolerable: 'Ésa era la palabra intolerable. Cometidos por todos'. In a complicated set of equivalences, Cruz is also likened to God the Father, at the moment when his daughter Teresa remarks, apropos of his relationship with Lorenzo, '¿No envió a la muerte a su propio hijo mimado?' That the analogy is meant seriously and not ironically is confirmed by the author's

declaration to Walter Mauro [in *Los escritores al poder*, 1975] that he was moved to write *La muerte de Artemio Cruz* partly by 'una obsesión trinitaria de la que siempre he sufrido.' In narrative terms, that obsesión translates into the three levels of Cruz's consciousness which correspond to the Holy Trinity of God the Father (YO), God the Son (ÉL) and God the Holy Ghost (TÚ). The figure of Cruz combines aspects of all three in a heretical synthesis which challenges conventional notions of moral authority.

The role of Quetzalcóatl is assigned most conspicuously in the novel to Lorenzo Cruz who is identified with fertility and self-sacrifice and other positive values. As he leaves Mexico to go and fight for freedom on the side of the Republic in the Spanish Civil War, Lorenzo follows in the fabled footsteps of Quetzalcóatl who, in the author's words, 'Huyó, hacia el oriente, hancia el mar. Dijo que el sol lo llamaba'. The manner of Lorenzo's death is suitably heroic, making him a worthy successor of Quetzalcóatl. However, to emphasise Lorenzo's positive attributes and achievements is to overlook the ambivalence of Quetzalcóatl and of Mesoamerican deities in general. For the fact is that Quetzalcóatl symbolises vice as well as virtue, lust as well as chastity, shame as well as honour. Fuentes incorporates these negative traits into the character of Artemio Cruz who cuts a cowardly figure no less reminiscent of Quetzalcóatl than his son Lorenzo. Referring to a legendary event in the god's experience, Fuentes relates how Quetzalcóatl, faced with the reflection of his body in a mirror, 'Sintió gran miedo y gran vergüenza. . . Presa del terror de sí mismo—del terror de su apariencia—-Quetzalcoatl, esa noche, bebió y fornicó. Al día siguiente, huyó. . . '. Cruz's experience overlaps with this account in some important details: he indulges in repeated acts of self-contemplation which cause him to feel disgusted with himself and anxious about his identity; also, he has a substantial record of adultery. In short, he resembles the mortal and fallible Quetzalcóatl whom Fuentes elsewhere compared [*Tiempo mexicano*] interestingly to more familiar archetypes: 'Quetzalcóatl, protagonista simultáneo de la creación, la caída y el sacrificio: Yavé, Adán y Cristo de un mundo sin secuelas históricas, mítico'.

This hybrid characterisation of Artemio Cruz conforms to the dominant patterns of the cultural history of Mexico. Yet is should not be forgotten that the worship of Quetzalcóatl was a regional phenomenon, extending beyond the territorial boundaries of modern Mexico. Similarly, the fusion of Christian and Amerindian traditions was not unique to the colony of New Spain, but typified the cultural *mestizaje* of the New World generally. With these points in mind, we may briefly consider the regional and continental resonances of Fuentes's novel.

A Caribbean perspective linking the Eastern seaboard of Mexico with the 'archipiélago tropical de ondulaciones graciosas y carnes quebradas [de las Antillas]' is defined in the final sections of *La muerte de Artemio Cruz*, tying the history of that part of Mexico in with the slave trade emanating from 'las islas del Caribe' and identifying the Gulf as an important point of intersection where the pre-Colombian civilisations of Meso-America met with a multiplicity of cultures arriving from Africa as well as Europe. The Menchaca estate in Veracruz exemplifies a synthesis of historical, racial and cultural factors which set it apart from the 'México seco [del] altiplano'. In that setting, the figure of Lunero is of special importance. Described by Helmy Giacoman [in *Homenaje a Carlos Fuentes*, 1971] as '[el] primer gran personaje mulato de la novela mexicana', he may be regarded as a fictional cousin of Carpentier's Ti Noel and other black characters who populate the literary landscape of the Caribbean, particularly that of Cuba.

Cuba is in fact a prominent point of reference in *La muerte de Artemio Cruz*. At one moment in the narrative a tape-recording is played back of a conversation between Cruz and Mena in which Cruz comments on the changes that have taken place in Cuba since Batista's departure; the same conversation also mentions General Trujillo whose presidency of the Dominican Republic came to an end in 1960. At another point on the tape, a citizen of the United States who is visiting Cruz's office announces his Ambassador's intention 'to make a speech comparing this Cuban mess with the old-time Mexican Revolution'—a project which reflects ironically both on Cruz, who had seen active service in the Mexican Revolution, and on the Revolution itself, now largely institutionalised and ineffectual. In a very real sense, Fuentes, as he writes from Havana, invites his Mexican readers to look at the achievements of their own revolution through the prism of the new Cuba of 1959–61.

[Events] in Cuba sent reverberations all over the Americas, altering political perceptions and ceating new perspectives on areas of common interest. In such circumstances it was inevitable that certain writers of the period should register a sense of community and take it upon themselves to represent continental opinion. Fuentes's dedication of *La muerte de Artemio Cruz* to C. Wright Mills, whom he salutes as the 'verdadera voz de Norteamérica, amigo y compañero en la lucha de Latinoamérica', indicates a clear and conscious intention to pitch the message of his novel beyond local boundaries, onto a wider plane of significance.

While the text of *La muerte de Artemio Cruz* makes overt references only to Cuba and the Dominican Republic outside Mexico, a supranational perspective may readily be inferred from a range of historical data which are valid for the entire subcontinent. At a general level, these include the experiences of conquest, colonial and neo-colonial status and the consequences of political and economic dependence. More specifically, they embrace the phenomena of *caciquismo* or bossism, government repression of labour organisations, financial corruption and social inequality. As he denounces these and other ills in Mexican society under President López Mateos, Fuentes articulates the grievances of people throughout Latin America, prefiguring his systematic treatment of some of the same themes in *La nueva narrativa hispanoamericana*.

The climax of that essay is an analysis of linguistic alienation north and south of the Rio Grande, where the name of C. Wright Mills is invoked once again to exemplify continental experience. In Fuentes's opinion [in "An Interview with Carlos Fuentes," *Modern Fiction Studies* 18 (1972–73)], the linguistic falsification of reality 'is an enormous fact in Latin America', which he describes as a 'continente de textos sagrados' requiring immediate 'profanation' by writers of an iconoclastic disposition. On the evidence produced in this essay, *La muerte de Artemio Cruz* is a seminal contribution to that enterprise. In it Fuentes mounts a vigorous and coherent assault on moral and political dogmas, with the aid of formal and linguistic procedures which shortly become common currency in the writing of the Boom. A quarter of a century later, when other writers have renounced their faith in formal experimentation, Fuentes retains an unswerving commitment to exploration and iconoclasm, forever producing new and unsettling novels. Histories of the Boom and after will remain incomplete as long as he continues to write them. (pp. 98–117)

Robin Fiddian, "Carlos Fuentes: 'La muerte de Artemio Cruz'," in *Landmarks in Modern Latin American Fiction*, edited by Philip Swanson, Routledge, 1990, pp. 96–117.

SOURCES FOR FURTHER STUDY

Brody, Robert and Rossman, Charles, eds. *Carlos Fuentes: A Critical View*. Austin: University of Texas Press, 1982, 221 p.

  Fourteen interpretive essays on various aspects of Fuentes's writing, focusing on his novels.

Durán, Gloria B. *The Archetypes of Carlos Fuentes: From Witch to Androgyne*. Hamden, Conn.: Archon Books/The Shoe String Press, 1980, 240 p.

  A revised and enlarged edition/translation of Durán's *La magia y las brujas en la obra de Carlos Fuentes* (1976). Discusses the importance of magic in Fuentes's novels, with special emphasis on the role of the sorceress as a guide to the unconscious.

——. "Carlos Fuentes as Philosopher of Tragedy." *The Modern Language Review* 81, No. 2 (April 1986): 249–56.

  Examines the influence of Marxism and existentialism on Fuentes's fiction.

Faris, Wendy B. *Carlos Fuentes*. New York: Frederick Ungar, 1983, 241 p.

  Analyzes Fuentes's novels, short stories, dramas, and essays in separate sections devoted to each of his published volumes.

——. " 'Without Sin, and with Pleasure': The Erotic Dimensions of Fuentes's Fiction." *Novel* 20, No. 1 (Fall 1986): 62–77.

  Discusses the importance of eroticism in Fuentes's writing.

de Guzmán, Daniel. *Carlos Fuentes*. New York: Twayne, 1972, 171 p.

  Critical and biographical study, focusing primarily on Fuentes's novels.

Perez, Janet. "Aspects of the Triple Lunar Goddess in Fuentes's Short Fiction." *Studies in Short Fiction* 24, No. 2 (Spring 1987) 139–47.

  Analyzes the role of the mythic White Goddess in several of Fuentes's stories.

The Review of Contemporary Fiction 8, No. 2 (Summer 1988): 147–291.

  Special issue partly devoted to Fuentes, with essays by Gabriel García Márquez, Octavio Paz, Milan Kundera, and others. Also features a new short story by Fuentes and an interview with the author.

Swietlicki, Catherine. "*Terra Nostra*: Carlos Fuentes's Kabbalistic World." *Symposium* XXXV, No. 2 (Summer 1981): 155–67.

  Surveys some of the major elements of Kabbalism in Fuentes's novel.

World Literature Today 57, No. 4 (Autumn 1983): 529–98.

  Special issue devoted to Fuentes, with essays by Gloria Durán, Margaret Sayers Peden, Wendy B. Faris, and others. Includes a bibliography.

Additional coverage of Fuentes's life and career is contained in the following sources published by Gale Research: *Authors and Artists for Young Adults*, Vol. 4; *Contemporary Authors*, Vols. 69–72; *Contemporary Authors New Revision Series*, Vol. 10; *Contemporary Literary Criticism*, Vols. 3, 8, 10, 13, 22, 41, 60; and *World Literature Criticism*.

Gabriel García Márquez

1928-

(Full name Gabriel José García Márquez; also wrote under the pseudonym Septimus) Colombian novelist, short story writer, and essayist.

INTRODUCTION

García Márquez is internationally known for his skillful use of "magical realism" in his novels and stories. One of the group of Latin American writers of the 1960s who initiated the literary phenomenon known as "El boom," García Márquez is credited for creating a unique connection between the real and the fantastic in his fiction. These stories easily move the reader beyond a merely surface encounter with persons and events towards a deeper understanding of his themes, which range from the political and social, to love and solitude. *Cien años de soledad* (1967; *One Hundred Years of Solitude*), a chronicle of a fantastic jungle village and its people, brought García Márquez international acclaim, and virtually made the literary term "magical realism" not only popular but also synonymous with most of his future literary works.

García Márquez was born in 1928 in Aracataca, Colombia. His first eight years were spent with his grandparents from whom he learned the art of storytelling: his grandmother spoke of the myths and legends of Aracataca, while his grandfather, an ex-colonel in the army, related stories about war and the military. In the late 1940s, García Márquez studied at the Universidad Nacional de Colombia, and the Universidad de Cartagena, during which time he began careers in journalism and writing. As a journalist, García Márquez travelled extensively thoroughout South America, Europe, and the United States. In Colombia itself, he endeavored to learn and write everything he could about the Colombian people, and it was this interest that spurred him on to write his novel and short stories. After the unqualified success of *One Hundred Years of Solitude*, he turned to writing as his primary occupation. However, since his political views were perceived as leftist in Colombia, he decided to move to Mexico City, where he now resides.

García Márquez's first literary success was *La ho-*

yarasca (1955; *Leaf Storm*)—a novella set in the fictitious village of Macondo during the funeral of a disreputable doctor. It explores the themes of solitude, bitterness, and moral decay in Macondo after a period of economic prosperity. In 1961 García Márquez published his novella *El coronel no tiene quien le escriba* (*No One Writes to the Colonel*) which obliquely refers to the 1956 "La violencia" in Colombia. The main theme is the optimism and determination of the central character, the Colonel, whose wit aids him in finding meaning in life's incessant struggles. With the collection entitled *Los funerales de la Mamá Grande* (1961), García Márquez's mixing of fantasy with reality began to play an increasingly important role in his storytelling.

One Hundred Years of Solitude marks a transitional moment in García Márquez's writing career. Set in the jungles of Colombia, the novel introduces the reader to the founders and people of Macondo. From the mysterious figure of the Gypsy Melquíades, to the ancient matriarch Ursula, and her enigmatically ethereal husband José Arcadio Buendía, to the ascension to heaven of Remedios the Beauty, to the profusion of butterflies and flying carpets, to the final apocalyptic moment, when violent winds erase every trace of Macondo and its people forever: the events and characters of García Márquez's novel blend to create a fascinating microcosm of destinies, hopes and aspirations.

In 1972 García Márquez published a collection of short stories entitled *La increíble y triste historia de la cándida Eréndira y de su abuela desalmada* (*Innocent Eréndira, and Other Stories*). The title story, *Eréndira*, utilizes many mythic archetypes—the evil grandmother, Eréndira the captive princess, and Ulises, the good knight who slays the monster (the grandmother who dies in a pool of her own oily green blood). In another book, *El otoño del patriarca* (1975; *The Autumn of the Patriarch*), the imaginary and grotesque blend with the political in a chronicle of the life of a solitary and ruthless dictator, who rules for over two hundred years, employing fantastical atrocities to maintain his iron grip on his people and country. *Crónica de una muerta anunciada* (*Chronicle of a Death Foretold*), written in 1981, focuses on an actual twenty year old murder case concerning a young man killed by the brothers of a girl with whom he allegedly had a sexual encounter. Here we find García Márquez employing his vast journalistic talent to examine the case from a variety of perspectives, exposing the emotional horrors, and the religious and human costs involved. Another novel, *El amor en los tiempos de cólera* (1985; *Love in the Time of Cholera*), sets out to explore the romantic attachment between two octogenarians, and how love transcends age, career, and even death. The atmosphere of this work is redolent of nineteenth-century Romanticism, yet the masterful blending of the real and the imaginary contributes to an insightful understanding of true love and its importance in life.

Critics have generally noted García Márquez's ability to interweave fantastic episodes into the fabric of real life, asserting that this technique heightens the dramatic effect of his narrative. Yet others disparage his use of fantasy, contending that it interferes with any serious consideration of his themes. On this issue, García Márquez remarks that he had to learn to believe in what he was saying as his grandmother had taught him, and that in this way the story with all its so-called fantasy becomes perfectly true and believable.

Solitude is a fundamental theme in García Márquez's works, and critics have observed that he consistently portrays it as ruinous to life. García Márquez explains, however, that solitude is inextricably connected with power—another popular theme—and that the powerful are often condemned to isolation.

Commentators have also noted García Márquez's frequent use of travesty as a method of intensifying the emotional effects of his narratives. For example, in *The Autumn of the Patriarch*, the patriarch serves a traitorous general as the main course for a staff banquet. This parody of communion illustrates a quasi-religious feeding on the essence of power. The narrator then meticulously explains how General Aguilar was placed on a very large platter atop a fresh bed of cauliflower and greens, and how he was decorated with the appropriate vegetable military insignia. Critics have further remarked that García Márquez's journalistic manner of reporting such extravagant events introduces a sense of realism into his works. Some have viewed his prose as purely political tracts; yet García Márquez asserts that he is never politically motivated to write a story, but that many of the characters he creates, such as the patriarch in *The Autumn of the Patriarch* and Colonel Aureliano Buendía in *One Hundred Years of Solitude*, certainly echo his political ideas. Scholars have also contended that García Márquez presents a pessimistic view of life and the contemporary world in his writings, citing the rise and fall of Macondo in *One Hundred Years of Solitude* as a primary example; others, however, find some optimism in such characters as the Colonel in *No One Writes to the Colonel*, Ursula and José Arcadio Buendía in *One Hundred Years of Solitude*, and the lovers in *Love In the Time of Cholera*.

García Márquez's Nobel Prize-winning works have had a worldwide appeal because they deal with universal themes. Addressing psychological and social issues relevant to the contemporary world, his writings continue to attract and compel readers. García Márquez remains a dedicated writer today, and has remarked in an interview with Peter H. Stone: "I'm absolutely convinced that I'm going to write the greatest book of my life but I don't know which one it will be or when. When I feel something like this—which I have been feeling now for awhile—I stay very quiet so that if it passes by I can capture it."

CRITICAL COMMENTARY

RICARDO GULLÓN

(essay date 1971)

[In the following essay, originally published in *Diacritics* in 1971, Gullón extols García Márquez's mastery of the ancient art of storytelling in the development of the characters, tone, rhythm, and setting of his novel *One Hundred Years of Solitude*.]

When speaking of the excellence of **A Hundred Years of Solitude**, it is not enough to say that Gabriel García Márquez has invented an original imaginary world; and yet it should not be forgotten that this is precisely what he has done. The invention is in itself a remakable achievement, and in our day even unusual. It would not be idle to remind ourselves of something so well-known that it is usually forgotten, namely, that the creation of space in fiction is similar to that of sacred space insofar as it implies a transformation of chaos into cosmos and the imposition of order. The first impulse to accomplishing an act of creation is like the laying of a foundation, the tracing of boundaries, the making of a reservation (in the American sense of the word) where the fictional will develop.

That fictional space alternately communicates and does not communicate with the outside world that is, with Life, is easy to understand when we consider the analogy that exists between fiction and sacred space. What has been introduced into, and assimilated by sacred and fictional space has form, whereas what remains outside does not and because of its lack of form continues to appear chaotic. For this and other reasons Gabriel García Márquez is correct in giving us the details of how the foundation is laid together with the foundation itself as indispensable parts of the novel. Macondo becomes and then *is* "the World." In that world the characters are born and from it they overflow. Everything is contained in that world and within its boundaries all the prodigious events occur. Things further removed are less dense, less consistent, almost misty, at times formless.

One wonders how García Márquez came to create a world so similar to our everyday one and yet so totally different from it. Technically, he is a realist in the pre-

sentation of both the real and the unreal. He somehow skillfully handles a reality in which the limits of the real and the fantastic fade away quite naturally.

This feat requires analysis of his resources, beginning with the one which seems to me the most important—narrative tone. García Márquez intuitively grasped the vital relationship that exists between space and tone when he noticed that tone could serve as the main unifying force in the novel. Tone belongs by all rights to the narrator's voice, and the narrator is the Narrator: someone who is removed from his narrative; who knows all there is to know about the events; who reports them as a reporter would—calm and untouched, without comment, and without passing moral judgments on what has happened. He does not doubt or question events or facts. For him there is no difference between what is likely and what is not; he fulfills his mission—his duty—of telling all, speaking as naturally of the dead as he does of the living, associating with the greatest of ease the intangible with the tangible. His steadfastness reveals itself in his unchanging, constant tone. From the first page to the last he maintains the same tone levels, without fluctuation or variation.

Prodigious events and miracles mingle with referances to village and household events. The narrator never allows it to become evident, by interjection or amazement, that there may be a substantial difference between the extraordinary and the commonplace. For example, there is a character who wakes up a ghost (whom he does not see) as he urinates on him. Phantoms may sleep and do other things that make one forget their state, just as the living may at any moment take flight without anyone's attaching the slightest importance to it. In García Márquez' novel, they all communicate easily. And why shouldn't they? They live side by side—immersed in an atmosphere which shelters them indiscriminately, making them equals. In the novel's space, proven and fabulous events are equally true, a fact which all great fiction should show.

In the *Odyssey* the Sirens are neither more nor less real than Ulysses. Understanding this fact, García Márquez breaks with the literary conventions of realism.

Principal Works

La hoyarasca (novella) 1955,
　　[*Leaf Storm* in *Leaf Storm and Other Stories*, 1972]

El coronel no tiene quien le escriba (novella) 1961
　　[*No One Writes to the Colonel* in *No One Writes to the Colonel and Others Stories*, 1968]

Los funerales de la Mamá Grande (short stories) 1961
　　[*Mamá Grande's Funeral* in *No One Writes to the Colonel and Other Stories*, 1968]

La mala hora (novel) 1962
　　[*In Evil Hour*, 1979]

Cien años de soledad (novel) 1967
　　[*One Hundred Years of Solitude*, 1970]

No One Writes to the Colonel and Other Stories (prose) 1968

La increíble y triste historia de la cándida Eréndira y de su abuela desalmada (short stories) 1972
　　[*Innocent Eréndira and Other Stories*, 1978]

Leaf Storm and Other Stories (prose) 1972

El otoño del patriarca (novel) 1975
　　[*The Autumn of the Patriarch*, 1975]

Crónica de una muerta anunciada (novella) 1981
　　[*Chronicle of a Death Foretold*, 1982]

El amor en los tiempos de cólera (novel) 1985
　　[*Love in the Time of Cholera*, 1988]

El general en su laberinto (novel) 1989
　　[*The General in His Labyrinth*, 1990]

Yet he does not stray from the tradition or from fictional reality. And his authentic presentation of events (that is to say, his tone) allows him to dispense with explanations and justifications. There is no need to justify the fact that a character dies, or appears to die, and later comes back to life, or appears to, twenty, a hundred, or five hundred years later; there is no reason to follow the clock's chronology, or the calendar's when the only really important time is the novel's own time. One hundred years of solitude? Might it not be a hundred centuries? Might not the novel's own time be time in its totality, absolute, beginning with the awakening of humanity and ending with its expiration? Would it not be possible to calculate mathematically what the world is, put it in a nutshell and with it all of history, from Genesis to the Apocalypse?

The novel has the circular and dynamic structure of a gyrating wheel. The narrator has seen that wheel turn, and his way of relating the events which he came to see in the wheel's constant turning serves as a unifying force. Narrative authenticity becomes more readily perceptible when what is related oscillates between impossible and everyday occurrences. As an example of this we have José Arcadio Buendía telling Prudencio Aguilar's

obstinate ghost (it insists on appearing and reappearing) to go to hell, just as he would have told a bothersome neighbor.

The narration of events, we are told, was recorded twice. First, in a language unintelligible to the Macondo inhabitants (Sanscrit) by Melquíades, before they actually took place; as prophet-chronicler, he foresees what is to come (unless he has seen it in some other turn of the wheel) and anticipates it in his story. Second, by the narrator (in Spanish), after the events have occurred; he relates the past, recognizing it as such, and on the first page predicts the execution of Colonel Aureliano Buendía, which will not actually take place for years or centuries. Could the narrator be Melquíades' double, or in the terms of this novel, his reincarnation? In any case, we know that there is no discrepancy between his version and the immortal man's; one is a facsimile of the other, the result of a miracle similar to Pierre Ménard's when he unwittingly wrote a *Quixote* identical to Cervantes'. When we read on the last page that Aureliano IV deciphers Melquíades' parchments, we discover that the novel was contained in them—that they are in fact the novel—which is why they cannot be deciphered until the novel ends. The ancient papers do not allow their meaning to become clear until the prophecies are fulfilled, and the narrator describes that fulfillment step by step. He limits himself to the business of narrating: he neither predicts the future nor possesses the key to the past. Melquíades duplicates him and in some ways anticipates him; a mythical and legendary figure, he possesses special powers, and in the novel he plays multiple roles.

We do not know at the beginning what the difference consists of, even though we are aware of Melquíades' uprootedness, his readiness to be absent. We come to feel that he is only passing through Macondo. This gives him the special attribute of a being without a beginning or an end. He is not reincarnataed in other people; he reappears after his spurious deaths, and when he withdraws from the novel he does so because he has played out his role of prophet and scribe. Melquíades is successively and simultaneously alchemist, adventurer, experimenter, scientist, encyclopedic sage; he is mortal and immortal, a resurrected being. But most important, he is the wanderer who circulataes freely through the space of the novel and beyond, crossing without effort the boundaries between one world and another. He serves as link and messenger between the living and the dead.

In the novel only the narrator's voice is heard; such is the demand of tonal unity. Through it the reader apprehends everything the characters say or think, their dialogues and monologues. The narrative voice is, as the tone suggests, friendly and familiar; it is a voice which instills confidence in the listener and succeeds in making itself heard and accepted without objections. The relationship between the narrative voice (that is, the narrator) and the reader is also one of familiarity, and therefore a close one.

Events occur and characters parade before the reader in the most natural manner, nearby, and seemingly at the same spatial and psychological distance from him.

The narrator's speaking unfazedly, calmly (even when describing tragic events), does not prevent him from becoming a centre of consciousness. Quite the contrary. The distance between the narrator and what he narrates reinforces his objectivity and allows him to speak without judging. What is said is ethically qualified because of the way it is said. The characters derive their consistency from the word and the consciousness from which that word springs; the imagery and a unique use of adjectives allow the reader to detect a value judgment which has not been formulated, but merely insinuated. When the army enters Macondo to end the great strike, the narrator says: "Its many-headed dragon-breathing impregnated the midday sunlight with pestilent vapors."

The extremely reduced distance between the reader and the characters, due to the intimacy of the narrative voice, practically disappears when a character, living his normal everyday life, performs the minute actions so familiar to the reader himself. Colonel Aureliano, without ceasing to be a kind of retired mythological figure, urinates at certain times during the day. The Colonel's regularity brings him closer to the reader, who thereby more readily identifies with him and tolerates everything else said about him in that and previous chapters.

The central character is Úrsula Iguarán, wife of José Arcadio Buendía; together they make up the first couple. Ursula is both a mother and The Mother, and is present throughout most of the novel. She articulates some of the key observations: her "normal" domestic activities, constructive and incessant, create a center where decisive events happen and others slowly germinate. That center is charged with the unique atmosphere which Ursula radiates. Ursula's function is to impregnate the fictional space with everyday realities so that the marvelous may enter it smoothly. Thus stabilized and "normalized," the novelistic space assimilates prodigious things and converts them into acceptable phenomena which the reader can easily admit.

García Márquez' success in creating such an atmosphere is more evident if we contrast that atmosphere to the backdrops of Gothic novels and other such narratives. Poe's castles, cemeteries, shadows, thunder, and phantasmagoria produce the opposite effects of those in *A Hundred Years of Solitude;* instead of fusing the extraordinary with the ordinary, such backdrops mark boundaries too sharply, thereby opposing the real to the unreal and preventing them from communicating; in Gothic tales "real" life is distinct from the fantastic episodes related.

There is still more to say about space in the novel. The Buendía house and the city of Macondo are representations of a vast universe where everything has its proper place, including time. Primordial space, which precedes creation, is not organized until the creator comes and gives objects names: "The world was so new that many things lacked names, and in order to refer to them one had to point them out." José Arcadio Buendía is the first to take space and conceptualize it, grasping it intellectually in all its fullness: "When he became expert in the use of his tools, he developed an idea of space which enabled him to sail unknown seas, visit uninhabited lands and engage in relationships with magnificent beings without ever having to leave the room." Together, José Arcadio's imagined space and Ursula's familiar space embrace everything that has ever existed or exists, from nothingness to infinity.

At least one critic, Emmanuel Carballo, has suggested the possibility that Macondo might be an equivalent of Spanish America. But it would be a mistake to narrow the scope of the novel to specific places. Though the novel may suggest parts of Colombia, it clearly transcends physical particularizing and offers instead a parable of creation, man's history and human nature.

The circular structure of the novel leads the reader from the chaos and void where creation occurs to the chaos and void where all ends and is resolved. The presence of a well-defined, concrete geographical space (Macondo) does not lessen its universality; it reinforces it. And the circularity is compatible with the plot, which moves forward in linear development, never retroceding, yet also searches constantly for its origins. The book contains no index and its chapters have no titles; it is a chain of reiterations; it is continuity itself. Names are constantly repeated. There is always a new beginning, a returning—I would almost say a reincarnation—of the characters, whose overwhelming personalities reappear continuously in accordance with the design-destiny of their names: the José Arcadios, the Aurelianos, the Remedios, the Amarantas and the Ursulas. Pilar Ternera, at once priestess and lust incarnate, knows that "the history of the Buendía family [is] a chain of irreparable repetitions, a gyrating wheel that would have continued turning forever had it not been for the gradual and inevitable wearing out of its axle." The gyrating wheel in the quotation is a suitable structural image for this novel. Because Melquíades is both magician and seer, the wheel is superfluous for him; he needs but look into the crystal ball, for in it he sees time in its totality—without duration, without past, without future. In a magical realm, events and worlds appear with a simultaneity and density that, we are told, may be captured only at the moment of death. It is no accident that Melquíades' documents guard their secrets, which may be deciphered only when the narrative concludes.

The wheel never stops; its constant motion, linking the beginning to the end, is visible in the case of Ursula. Her old age is and is not like that of others. As the years—centuries—pass, she becomes progressively smaller, "becoming mummified while alive to the point that, during her last months, she was a mere prune lost in the folds of her nightgown." That powerful image is anticipated when the narrator indicates that Ursula was becoming so "foetus-like" that she looked like "a newborn old lady." Nor is she the only one who ends up the way she started. The signs of repetition multiply in the course of the novel: at the end, the gypsies who had appeared at the beginning (years or centuries earlier) return to the village and bring once again the wonders that had earlier produced such widespread awe: the magnet, the gigantic magnifying glass, the false teeth. These objects are symbols of what is permanent in change or of what changes without ceasing to be identical to what it was. The Arab merchants are where they were before and where they will be again "sitting in the same place and in the same posture as their parents and grandparents, taciturn, fearless, invulnerable to time."

When Aureliano II returns to the house of his mistress, Petra Cotes, after the flood, he finds her worn out, aged, and sickly, but also beginning anew, preparing once again to engage in the activities that helped make their fotune. She was "writing numbers on scraps of paper for a raffle." Later, Ursula finds José Arcadio II in Melquíades' room and is surprised to find herself repeating something that Colonel Aureliano had said to her much earlier when she told him what José Arcadio had just told her. This is the moment of dreadful realization: "time did not pass . . . ; it went around in circles."

The contrast between tone and rhythm, which is characteristic of *A Hundred Years of Solitude*, is one more reason why this novel attracts, convinces and seduces the reader. If the familiar tone makes the suppression of limits between the real and the imaginary tolerable, the rhythm complements it by contrast: vertiginous beneath the apparent calm, the rhythm injects the narrative with a dynamic force that might seem incongruous with the tone. Yet this is not so: the narrator does not allow his pace to be affected by the accumulation of events. Rather, he concentrates, summarizes and equalizes them in his constant talespinning. The kaleidoscope turns, slowly shaping very different situations. So many things are compressed into the space of a few pages that one might say the narrator has overdone it. But no, he has merely reduced things to their essentials—condensed them without sacrificing vitality—and connected them through imperceptible transitions. Events accumulate naturally because of the natural tone. The transition from one delirious state to the next occurs as smoothly as the switch from the unreal to the real. Delirium is presented as trivial reality; in a state of hallucination, Amaranta is not surprised to see death sitting beside her sewing in the hall. Reality, by logical contrast, is delirious. Wars succeed each other so rapidly that war eventually becomes a way of life. The gringos come, fleece and devour the country, destroying everyting, like a plague, and then disappear. The killing of Colonel Aureliano's seventeen sons is a clear case of an event that occurs on the borderline of reality. The event lacks versimilitude yet it *is* "real" and is told with the tonal objectivity and quick rhythm that García Márquez blends so well. In a single page the inhuman killing begins and ends.

This curious rhythm-tone symbiosis implies complete mastery of condensatory techniques, from the oxymoron to synesthesia. An example of the former: "the enchanted region" that José Arcadio Buendía explored when Macondo was founded and where banana plantations were to prosper later, "*was* a marsh of putrefied stumps." The verb "was" (which I have italicized) links the contradictory terms of the sentence. Synesthetic imagery ("delicate breeze of light") enlarges the frame of reference, Similarly, the use of paradox permits transitions to be made with verbal economy: "Ursula allowed decreptitude to drag her into the depths of darkness where only José Arcadio Buendía's ghost continued to be visible under the chestnut tree." Equally effective in the process of condensation is the systematic use of anachronisms, for they unite distant moments of time. By locating in one moment what happened in another, the author is able to stretch the temporal boundaries of his novel in a few lines: "Every time Ursula flew off the handle with rage because of her husband's follies, she skipped over three hundred years and cursed the day Francis Drake attacked Riohacha."

A sustained synthesis, *A Hundred Years of Solitude* covers centuries, perhaps millenia. On the first page alone we find prehistory and Arcadia (whence the "Adam" of the story—Arcadio—takes his name); then come Genesis and the journey to the "un"-promised land; the founding of the city; the plagues that devastate Macondo (insomnia and forgetfulness); the resurrection of Melquíades; and the Flood (which lasts four years, eleven months and two days), imposed as a punishment for man's sins, especially for the greed and pride of the directors of the Yankee banana company who spoil the regularity of the rainy seasons with their agricultural methods. The book contains all of History, synthesizing it in symbolic episodes such as the finding of the Spanish galleon or the arrival of the Magistrate, who brings with him the seeds of violence (of authority) that will later destroy José Arcadio's "Arcadia." Contemporary history is represented in the exemplary episodes of the corruption engendered by American banana interests; the capitalist exploitation; the poor people's strike and their execution by an Army that represents "the Law," that is, the violence which those in power (the uniformed executioners) use against the weak; the sinister black men who "legalize" the spoils; the falsification of the truth by a Government of assassins. And at the end, completing the circle, is the Apocalypse, announced from the pulpit by Father Antonia Isabel, who reads the omens as dead birds rain down, scouring the village (this episode is told in the short story **"A Day After Saturday"** in **Mamá Grande's Funeral**); a Biblical hurricane razes Macondo when the prophecies are fulfilled on the last page.

This feat of condensation takes place in 350 pages. They are taut, although somewhat slackened by the monochord tone; and they are dense, for individual and collective destinies are meshed. Each particular character's life and vital concerns are interrelated with the collective life of the town from the beginning: together they search for Arcadia: together they undertake expeditions and live the fleeting moments of paradise and the eternity of hell. Plague and war afflict them equally, just as the flood blinds them all and violence from without strikes them all. The structural curve is identical for the hero and the masses, and their fall is simultaneous, which is why these fabulous and mythified heroes never cease to be "representative."

Solitude, the novel's central theme, knits personal destinies closely. Whatever their essence, all the characters are born condemned to suffer it. It is a universal law and no one, not even Ursula, the Mother who lives for others, is spared it; her final blindness plunges her into "the impenetrable loneliness of decreptitude." The most obvious example, emphasized by the symbolism of the act, is Colonel Aureliano's order to have traced around him a chalk circle which no one may cross. His is the solitude of power, and in that solitude, as the narrator says, Colonel Aureliano is completely isolated. Later we read that "he locked himself in, as it were, and his family ended up thinking of him as if he had died." This line sums up the meaning of solitude by equating it with death.

Perhaps it is here that the novel—correctly read—yields its meaning and the reason why the living characters can co-exist and converse so naturally with the dead ones. Whoever lives his solitude as these people do, incapable of communication with the other alive-dead souls, is at the same distance from other people as he is from the dead-alive, or dead. Solitude is a common denominator that tinges them with a common sadness; it both unites and separates them as one may note in the realationship between Aureliano IV and José Arcadio IV: "That bond between the two loners of the same family was far from being a friendly one; it allowed them both to bear better that fathomless solitude which simultaneously brought them together and separated them." Aureliano IV is not at all interested in escaping from the confinement to which his grandmother has condemned him. He is content to live within himself, stubborn in his will to unravel the meaning of Melquíades' parchments: it is the duty of a loner.

Solitude is a vocation imposed by birth, in accordance with a law; it is an indelible mark. The successive Aurelianos and Arcadios have in common the family's "solitary look"; Aureliano IV has been "from the beginning of the world and forever branded by the pockmarks of solitude." The solitude of silence is a prison and a refuge. When Mauricio Babilonia is wounded, his lover Meme withdraws in "stony" silence and much later dies

of old age without ever having uttered another word. In this case, solitude is a form of desperation, and in the case of Aureliano II, it is even more extreme; he surrenders to the "bitter solitude of drunken sprees." He loses himself in them in order to escape the solitude of Fernanda, the stern wife who, as an outsider and foreigner to Mancondo, attempts to force the chain of isolation on their home and village. Fernanda wishes to live entombed, faithful "to the paternal decree to be buried alive," as her father had done and as she herself demands of her daughter and grandson. Rebeca does the same thing, but for different reasons: she shoots and kills the thief who attempted to force the door to her place of confinement. (The visit to Macondo by the dead boy's mother is told in **"The Tuesday Afternoon Siesta"** in *Mamá Grande's Funeral*.)

In the case of José Arcadio Buendía, the solitude of madness is accompanied by the failure of language. He suddenly begins to speak in a strange language (which we later learn is Latin) incomprehensible to those around him. He will live for years or centuries tied to the trunk of a chestnut tree in the courtyard, and after his death he will continue to inhabit the same place with a ghostly life scarcely different from his former one. No less incomprehensible, although in a quite different way, is Remedios the Beautiful, impervious "to the language of man," always "wandering in the desert of solitude" and finally rising out of fictional time and space into oblivion.

Amaranta's solitude is that of rancor and death in life. She lives alone with her hate and solely for it. Her communication with Death is normal and no different from that which she has with people around her. Death is neither more nor less than "a woman dressed in blue, with long hair, of a somewhat antiquated appearance and bearing a certain resemblance to Pilar Ternera," who sews by her side and who one day asks her "to please thread a needle for her." Knowing the date of her own departure, she offers herself as messenger to the inhabitants of Macondo to carry news from the living to the dead, thus redeeming the wretched solitude of her hate. Her offer is accepted without objection: "The news that Amaranta Buendía was setting sail for the twilight zone carrying the mail of death spread through Macondo before noon, and by around three in the afternoon there was already a big box filled with letters in the room. Those who were not able to write spoke their messages, which Amaranta jotted down in her notebook with the name and date of death of the addressee." No one doubts that the requests will be carried out.

The Buendías are not the only ones who live as recluses. So do the veterans, whittling away their useless old age waiting for the promised government check that never comes. (In *The Colonel Has No One to Write Him* García Márquez has elaborated on this hopeless waiting.) There is only one way for mortal beings to transcend this common solitude: through love. But love during these hundred years (or centuries) is precarious and always in danger of ending in a catastrophe like the ones that undermine the lives of Amaranta, Rebeca, Mauricio, Meme. Amaranta Ursula and Aureliano IV believe they have conquered solitude by forgetting themselves in frantic love, an erotic passion in which the family's last energies are consumed. Around them the world is destroyed and returned to dust. In Macondo, "forgotten even by the birds [. . .] it was difficult to breathe," but the lovers reconstruct for their passion the fatal solitude that consumes everything, withdrawing "through the solitude of love" into the house that is being devoured by ants—before they devour the last of the Aurelianos. They are the last living creatures in this fictional space: "in an empty universe where love [is] the only daily and eternal reality," in a world where they hear no voices other than those of their dead parents, grandparents, and great-grandparents, they achieve peace, persuaded that death itself will not be able to separate them. The birth of Aureliano V is the end of the novel; in him the prophecies of destruction are fulfilled, and Macondo, reduced to dust, disappears forever and with it the memory of those who made and inhabited it.

Among the unifying devices utilized by García Márquez, the reiteration of certain motifs is important. The motifs reappear at certain intervals and unite various parts of the novel, thus reinforcing the feeling of circularity (the sinister black men, charged with preparing and justifying the Government's pillage; the distant, invisible doctors with whom Fernanda communicates). One motif, of particular interest, accentuates the futility of human actions, and can be seen in the Buendía family's peculiar custom or vice of making things only to destroy them afterwards. Aureliano I falls into this characteristic mode of repetition, as the narrator observes, when instead of selling the little gold fish he makes, he melts them down to remake them and thus continues incessantly. Memories come back to Ursula in a similar way. José Arcadio Buendía keeps busy reading and rereading Melquíades' parchments. Amaranta sews and unsews buttons, and alternately weaves and unweaves her shroud to retard the coming of death. These are solitary games, designed to regain lost time; they are also the novelist's technique of indirectly expressing small but significant details in order to press the creative process.

There is a kind of justifiable excess in the novel, a systematic distortion by means of hyperbole that fits the author's design; a design to create a world of fiction so perfect as to make it ideal. Events and figures contain dimensions, as they should. The novel's beginning is Genesis; its end is the Apocalypse; rain is equivalent to the Flood; wars are War. García Márquez' weakness for hyperbole is decisive when it comes to characterization. Being verbal inventions, the characters necessarily owe their substance to the way in which the author arranges his words; the traditional hypothesis that the novelist faithfully describes characters who exist previous to the narrative is a

metaphor that suggests, at length, the autonomy of the character.

Hyperbole may produce a comic effect, as when Aureliano IV runs about the house "balancing a beer bottle on his inconceivable sex organ," or it may yield lyrical imagery: "His mistress was so close to him and so completely disarmed that Aureliano could perceive the deep murmur of her bones." Again, it may induce a fantastic vision: "The atmosphere was so humid that fish could have come in the doors and exited by the windows, swimming through the air in the rooms." Such hyperboles might be read as metaphor; but in context they should be accepted literally, because of the levelling off between reality and unreality which is characteristic of *One Hundred Years of Solitude.*

A systematic study of the imagery (and the symbols, such as the plague of insomnia and forgetfulness or the indelible ash crosses that single out the Aurelianos for death) would show that it points towards that levelling and indeed contributes to it. The excesses of the Buendías are passed on from one generation to the next. Aureliano II is a Gargantuan, capable of devouring a whole calf; José Arcadio II, who went around the world sixty-five times and like Ray Bradbury's illustrated man had his whole body tattooed, became a cannibal when the moment demanded it. His overindulgence in bed or at the table knew no bounds. "His farts wilted the flowers," reads the expressive image.

War and the general strike are culminations of horror in the novel—nightmares that actually happen yet retain their delirious quality. There is no doubt about their function in the novel. The narrator, as he relates them, erases any differences that might have existed, indeed destroys the very idea of a possible barrier between the real and the imaginary. In the natural order of things, such nightmares fall witin the realm of the possible—they are readily accepted as "historical" and natural events, and for the assassins they are even honorable—but in the novel they are more, rather than less, fantastic and incredible, in their naked brutality, than are specters and monsters. Whoever thinks they can be explained will easily accept the plague of insomnia or the rain of dead birds. There is no substantial difference between those horrors and these unnatural events, even though only the former are man-made. Narrative objectivity undergoes no change, not even when in the end the false version of the story must be told (a falsification occasioned by the criminal's desire to erase all traces of the crime and by man's refusal to recognize the monstrosity of the real).

As García Márquez completes his last fictional circles, he illuminates their and the novel's meaning. The differance between Márquez and other contemporary novelists lies in the fact that the latter may disperse themselves in a welter of techniques: he does not. His need to tell a story is so strong that it transcends the devices he uses to satisfy that need. Technique is not a mere game;

it is something to be made use of. At its best, it serves only to relate the story. Should the novelist get lost in his own creation, it is so he might find himself in it, in that imaginary world which is Macondo—the Macondo which has been compared to Faulkner's Yoknapatawpha county, if for no other reason than that both are relatively pure fictional regions, absolute inventions like Goriot's Paris or Fortunata's Madrid; inventions that are reserved for artists like Márquez who know how to revitalize the ancient and almost forgotten art of storytelling, reserved for those who practice it with the complex simplicity the genre demands. (pp. 129–40)

Ricardo Gullón, "Gabriel García Márquez and the Lost Art of Storytelling," in *Critical Essays on Gabriel García Márquez*, edited by George R. McMurray, G. K. Hall & Co., 1987, pp. 129–40.

RONALD DE FEO
(essay date 1977)

[In the excerpt below, De Feo discusses the motifs of spiritual and physical isolation in García Márquez's works, with particular reference to *The Autumn of the Patriarch*.]

Though he is one of the wittiest and most exhilarating of contemporary Latin American writers, García Márquez has repeatedly created characters who live, to varying degrees, in a state of solitude. From the earliest work, *Leaf Storm*, to the wonderful novella *No One Writes to the Colonel*, to the masterwork *One Hundred Years of Solitude*, we find people existing not only in spiritual isolation but in physical isolation as well: Macondo, the author's miraculous mythical town—the setting of much of his work—has been "condemned" to solitude, and indeed is so remote from the rest of the world that it possesses its very own laws of nature and logic.

The Autumn of the Patriarch . . . is García Márquez' most intense and extreme vision of isolation. In this fabulous, dream-like account of the reign of a nameless dictator of a fantastic Caribbean realm, solitude is linked with the possession of absolute power. The author has worked with this theme before—notably when tracing the career and increasing loneliness of Colonel Aureliano Buendía in *One Hundred Years of Solitude*—but here it receives the grand treatment.

Yet the book is in no way a case history or a psychological portrait of a dictator. It is, rather, a rendering in fantastic and exaggerated terms of a particular condition of might and isolation. As such, it is essentially plotless, though it is stuffed with enough anecdotes and incidents for several novels. When, at the beginning of the book, an unidentified party breaks into the decaying presidential palace and discovers the lichen-covered body of the patriarchal general who has governed the country for well over two centuries, a flood of memories of his incredible reign is released, and it is these memories, both collective and individual, flowing in free-associative, temporally jumbled repetition, that form the entire novel. (pp. 620, 622)

No summary or description of this book can really do it justice, for it is not only the author's surrealistic flights of imagination that make it such an exceptional work, but also his brilliant use of language, his gift for phrasing and description. As with *One Hundred Years of Solitude*, the reader is repeatedly surprised by the grace and ease with which an image is recorded, a phrase is turned.

And yet one must note, regretfully, that for all it brilliance *The Autumn of the Patriarch* is a difficult book to stay with for an extended length of time, difficult not because of the sentences that run on for pages or the absence of paragraphs, but because of an overabundance of riches. At times, the marvelous details accumulate so rapidly that the reader is simply overwhelmed by them. He seeks relief, a subdued passage in which to rest, but the author does not accord him that opportunity. At times, García Márquez's passion for inflation causes him to create a tale that is, even in a fantastic context, a shade too strained and whimsical—such as the account of the two thousand children kidnapped by the government to prevent them from revealing their role in the general's crooked lottery.

Still, of course, it is that very same passion for the absurd and the exaggerated that is responsible for the innumerable grand, witty passages we find—for example, the general discovering the hidden sentiments of his staff through the graffiti in the palace bathroom, or the account of a traitor who is served as a main course to the general's staff ("Major General Rodrigo de Aguilar entered on a silver tray stretched out on a garnish of cauliflower and laurel leaves . . . embellished with the uniform of five golden almonds for solemn occasions"). Here and elsewhere throughout this unique, remarkable novel, the tall tale is transformed into a true work of art. (p. 622)

Ronaldo De Feo, "The Solitude of Power," in *National Review*, New York, Vol. XXIX, May 27, 1977, pp. 620, 622.

GEORGE R. MCMURRAY
(essay date 1977)

[Below, McMurray explains how the narrative design of *The Autumn of the Patriarch* contributes to the successful portrayal of the horrors of political tyranny.]

In spite of the political implications of the plot and the evidence of the protagonist's sadomasochistic tendencies,

The Autumn of the Patriarch is not primarily a political or social-protest novel, nor are its psychological elements of paramount importance. Rather it is a lyrical novel, whose plot and character development are subordinate to its formal design and symbolic imagery. The narrative content is conveyed by a wide variety of rhetorical devices intended to reinforce themes, generate mood, and sustain dramatic movement. (pp. 131–32)

The novel's temporal design can best be described as a spiral consisting of six circular configurations—corresponding to the six units—each of which begins with the death of the patriarch, then evokes a chain of episodes from the past, and finally ends with a major event in his life. The unidentified narrative voice initiating each section is a first-person-plural soliloquy, reminiscent of the chorus in a Greek tragedy, that alludes the conditions surrounding the patriarch's death, i.e., the sight of his corpse, his mythical omnipotence, the decaying physical environment, and the urgent meetings held by leading goverment officials to determine the nation's future course. These motifs, repeated with variations, generate a rhythmic momentum that carries the narrative thread of each unit to a point in the protagonist's life beyond that of the preceding unit until, at the end of the novel, the plot comes full circle.

The following summary illustrates this spiral structure. The first unit deals primarily with Patricio Aragonés's fate and ends with the patriarch's evocation of the Spaniards' arrival in the New World. The second unit narrates the details of the patriarch's rise to power, his brief relationship with the beauty queen, Manuela Sánchez, and her mysterious disappearance. In the third, the struggles for power and the ensuing episode of the flood are punctuated by the gruesome death of General Rodrigo de Aguilar. The fourth is mainly concerned with the demise of the patriarch's mother, her canonization, and, in the final lines, the appearance of his future wife, Leticia Nazareno. In the fifth unit the principal events include the patriarch's marriage, the assassination of his wife and child, the introduction of the sadist, Ignacio Saenz de la Barra, and the one-hundredth anniversary celebration of the patriarch's reign. The last unit depicts the patriarch's extreme loneliness, physical decay, and death.

The novel's structural design is reinforced by archetypal patterns and universal tensions reminiscent of biblical and heroic myths. Although the patriarch's origin remains obcure, "scholarly texts" claim that he was conceived "without male cooperation" and that his "messianic destiny" was revealed to his mother in a dream. According to these same sources, a fortune teller once asserted that because he was born without lines in his hands, he was destined to become a king. His subjects believe him to be invulnerable to bullets and gigantic in stature, having allegedly continued to grow until he was one hundred years old. At the age of 150, moreover, he supposedly cut his third set of teeth. He is also reputed to have fa-

thered five thousand children and to be endowed with the magical ability to converse with animals, cure all kinds of illnesses with salt, and predict the future.

In reality, however, the patriarch embodies all the opposite characteristics of the legendary hero. His life represents an ironic inversion of the quest myth, i.e., the traditional narration of the hero's birth (often attributed to a virgin), his exploits in love and war, and his rise to power and mastery of his kingdom. The patriarch's mother was a prostitute who readily admits her ignorance of his father's identity. Unlike the idealized legendry hero, who achieves love and communion through valor and salf-sacrifice, the patriarch is a lonely tyrant living in terror of an assassin's bullet. Contrary to the idyllic paradise of myth, his residence is invaded by cobwebs, moths, and buzzards, and its grounds, by lepers, cripples, and blind people. The flood, moreover instead of performing its mythical cleansing function, serves to bolster the patriarch's waning authority when he commands the waters to recede, restores the city and is loudly acclaimed by his people. Toward the end of his regime the city is again a mass of ruins and . . . the sea a barren lunar landscape.

The novel's spiral structure conveys an impression of mythical time, i.e., a sense of endless renewal, tending to negate temporal progression, and thus escape from the terrors of history, into a realm of absolute stability. Aesthetically, the end result is a kind of static, timeless continuum in which present and past are joined spatially through the principle of juxtapostiton. This principle is perhaps best demonstrated in the final pages of the first unit when the patriarch visits the mansion where the exiled dictators are lodged and listens to the tales of their glorious past. While enjoying the magnificent panoramic view of the Caribbean from the terrace of the mansion, he recalls an historic Friday in October when he awakened to find everybody in the presidential palace wearing red hats. After numerous inquiries he finally ascertained that a group of foreigners dressed like the jack of clubs had come from across the seas, "jabbering" in a different tongue and offering beads and red hats in exchange for the local merchandise. Confused and intrigued, the patriarch looked out his window and saw the battleship abandoned by the United States marines next to the pier, and "beyond the battleship, anchored far out at sea, he saw the three caravels." This amusing allusion to the Spaniards' arrival in the New World juxtaposed with an image of twentieth-century gringo imperialism, suggests that although specific conditions throughout the course of history may change, the existence of oppressor and oppressed, especially in Latin America, remains a constant factor. The fictitious account of Columbus's voyage also illustrates how a fabulous historical adventure can become imbedded in the collective unconscious and emerge centuries later transformed into poetic myth.

As mentioned above, the patriarch's schizophrenic tendencies profoundly affect the novel's aesthetic quality, creating dramatic tension and tonal modulations through the constant interplay of contrasting, symbolic images and leitmotifs. These stylistic devices, convey the protagonist's incessant wavering between self-assertion, resulting from his overwhelming desire for love and power, and paranoic withdrawal, submission, and death wish, a reaction to his obsessive fear of the hostile world. The following detailed discussion of the third section is intended to illustrate the pendulum-like movement, which can be detected throughout the book.

The introductory passage alluding to the patriarch's decrepitude and death is immediately offset by a description of his youth when he would mingle with his subjects, calling them all by name and visiting their homes to share their meals. On one occasion he even worked for three hours to repair a woman's sewing machine while a group of officials waited for him outside in the street. He was so powerful that when ever he asked what time it was the reply would inevitably be, "Any time you wish, general." One night he had a masochistic dream in which he saw himself surrounded by knife-wielding men who proceeded to carve his body into pieces. However, instead of being afraid, he felt relieved, pure, and even smiled at the prospect of imminent death. Upon awakening he reasserted his authority by dismissing the members of the senate and the supreme court, obliging them to take refuge in foreign embassies. From this moment on, his retinue consisted solely of a machete-armed Guajiro Indian, whose image becomes a leitmotif symbolizing the patriarch's omnipotence and solitude.

During this period of his life the patriarch acquired the habit of visiting fortune tellers, one of whom told him she saw an armed man with a green mask posing a threat to his existence. The patriarch soon "identified" the man as one of his closest aides, and two days later the unfortunate one inexplicably "committed suicide." Another fortune teller had the unique ability to predict the death of her clients by gazing into the "unequivocal waters" of a washbasin. When the patriarch caught sight of his lifeless body reflected in the basin and heard the prediction that he would die between the ages of 107 and 125, he strangled the woman. Subsequently, the oft-repeated references to the "unequivocal waters of the basins" convey his narcissistic withdrawal and obsession with death.

The disappearance of Manuela Sánchez, which occurred at the end of the second unit, continues to irritate the patriarch, causing him to evoke an incident from his past when he entered the home of a recently married couple, had the husband chopped to pieces by his Indian bodyguard, and violated the young woman. He then directs his thoughts to General Rodrigo de Aguilar, his "lifelong friend," but even he, the patriarch suspects, is capable of treachery and perhaps already has gained too much influence. Thus, in order to bolster his ego, he recalls his loyal Indian protector whose cry, "Here comes the one in charge," was always answered by throngs of admirers chanting, "Long live the *macho*!" or "Long live the general!"

Soon thereafter, the patriarch has a premonition of impending disaster. His mounting anxiety is manifested metaphorically by the stench of carrion comming from the sea a flock of buzzards he sees from his window, and the flutelike whistle of his enlarged testicle, an absurd recurring motif representing a barometer of his anxiety. The catastrophe comes in the form of a cyclone accompanied by torrential rains that inundate the city. While surveying the muddy lake covering the streets and houses, the patriarch soothes his feelings of anxiety by concluding that God is really his ally and has sent the flood to make him forget his anguish over the vanished Manuela Sánchez. Then, having caught sight of the cathedral towers rising above the flood waters (probably phallic symbols of sadistic domination), he orders the waters to recede, directs the reconstruction of the city, and once again hears the multitude proclaiming, "Long live the *macho*!" The immediate prospect of addressing "the abyss of the crowd," however, arouses his terror and precipitates his flight to his mother's quarters. There, the image of her wringing a hen's neck "with a certain tenderness" in preparation for the evening meal underscores his renewed masochistic desire for self-annihilation.

The inevitable reaction to this state of mind occurs when the patriarch receives a visit from a young, idealistic adventurer seeking arms to fight wars throughout the hemisphere for the glory of the fatherland. Instead of responding directly to the youth's extravagant request, the patriarch shows him a glass ball he holds in the palm of his hand, exclaiming, "This is something that one either has or one doesn't have, but only he who has it has it, this is the fatherland." In other words, the patriarch perceives the nation he governs as an object to be held firmly in his grasp, never to be relinquished until his last breath. His tight grip on the glass ball, then, is a metaphor of his greed for power and, consequently, of his solitude.

After the cyclone and the ensuing period of reconstruction, the patriarch finds himself once again in such firm control of his domain that he allows all exiles to return except the men of letters, whom he considers more dangerous than priests or politicians. This period of tranquility is soon interrupted by an absurd episode that poses an additional threat to the patriarch. It seems that the national lottery is rigged every week in his favor by having a child draw from a bag of balls the only one that is ice cold. Because it is feared the youngsters will reveal this ruse, they are imprisoned in a fortress where their number eventually reaches two thousand. As parents grow more and more distressed over their missing children, the patriarch has a grotesque nightmare in which he sees the victims not as "two thousand separate children but as an immense, formless animal . . . impossible to destroy." In desperation he has the young prisoners sent by night to the most remote region of the country, publicly denies the rumor of their confinement, and invites a commission from the Society of Nations to investigate the matter. The members of the commission conduct a thorough search, even looking under Bendición Alvarado's bed, but they find all the jails closed for lack of prisoners and therefore conclude that everything is in order. After their departure, however, the problem of what to do with the children remains. For this reason they are sent from the jungle

> to the provinces of perpetual rain where there were no treacherous winds to carry their voices . . . he ordered them to be taken to Andean caves . . . he sent them pearls of quinine and woolen blankets when he learned that they were shivering with fever because they were hidden for days on end in rice paddies with mud up to their necks so that the airplanes of the Red Cross would not find them . . . he sent them showers of candy and ice cream from airplanes loaded with Christmas toys in order to keep them happy until he could think of a magic solution, and thus he put them out of his mind. . . .

Nevertheless, the dilemma of the missing children continues to arouse the patriarch's anxiety, which he attempts to suppress through a sadistic sexual assault on a servant woman gathering eggs. He then retires for the night and dreams he hears a multitude of young voices singing a song about a soldier who went off to war and returned in a velvet-lined coffin. This nightmare precipitates his decision to put an end to the intolerable situation. Before dawn he orders three officers to transport the two thousand prisoners far out to sea and to sink the boat with charges of dynamite. Several days later, when the officers report their mission accomplished, he promotes them, pins medals on their chest, and has them executed "like common criminals because there are orders that can be given but not carried out, goddammit, poor children."

The aftermath of this gruesome episode is an uprising led by General Bonivento Barboza, whose troops occupy the Conde Barracks, causing panic in the palace. In spite of his painfully whistling testicle and his secret desire to abandon the capital for some obscure refuge, the patriarch rejects General Rodrigo de Aguilar's offer to mediate with General Barboza and carefully plots his revenge. A mule cart loaded with six large milk containers is sent from the palace dairy to the Conde Barracks. Though highly suspicious, the rebels finally allow the cart to enter under the condition that the driver will taste the milk. Moments later, as they watch an orderly lift the lid from the first container, "they saw him floating in the ephemeral backwater of a dazzling burst of flames, and they didn't see anything more for centuries and centuries . . . because of the tremendous explosion of the six casks of dynamite."

The peaceful period following the aborted insurrection turns out to be a prelude to the third unit's climax and the novel's most grotesque and macabre episode. During this brief interval the self-confident patriarch makes the mistake of taking fewer security precautions, the result of his negligence being an attempt against his life by a "false leper." He suspects the instigator of the plot to be somebody close to him and spends many sleepless nights pacing up and down "dragging his elephant feet," another leitmotif suggesting his unlimited power. One evening while he is playing dominoes with his "lifelong friend," General Rodrigo de Aguilar, the latter's " thoughtful hand" somehow reveals itself as the long-sought "hand of perfidy." The incident convinces the patriarch that a coup against his regime has been plotted for the following Tuesday, when General Rodrigo de Aguilar is slated to offer the main toast at a banquet honoring the palace guard. That evening the guests drink and chat for several hours while restlessly awaiting General de Aguilar's arrival. As twelve o'clock approaches, the enticing odor of tasty dishes garnished with flowers pervades the hall, heightening the atmosphere of anticipation. Finally, at the stroke of midnight the curtains open and

> the distinguished General Rodrigo de Aguilar made his entrance, stratched out on a silver platter decorated with cauliflower and laurel branches, marinated in spices, browned in the oven dressed up in a unifrom with five golden almonds for solemm occasions and decorations for outstanding valor on his sleeve . . . , fourteen pounds of medals on his chest and a sprig of parsley in his mouth, ready to be served to his comrades by the official carvers . . . and we witnessed without breathing the exquisite ceremony of carving and serving and when there was on each plate an equal portion of minster of defense with piñon-seed stuffing and fragrant herbs, he [the patriarch] gave the order to begin, eat heartily, gentlemen.

As evidenced by the previous discussion of the third unit, *The Autumn of the Patriarch* not only relies heavily on contrasting symbolic motifs to create narrative progression and define characters and themes, but also makes frequent use of fantasy, the absurd, and the grotesque. These aesthetic elements refashion external reality into a seemingly endless picture gallery mirroring García Márquez's highly subjective view of the world and thus contributing to the lyrical quality of the novel.

Though fused with the absurd, two of the most obvious examples of fantasy derive from the death of Bendición Alvarado, the patriarch's mother, and from the theme of gringo imperialism. Immediately after Bendición Alvarado dies from a horrible disease resembling jungle rot, the foul-smelling sheet on which she has been lying displays a beautiful painting of her as a young woman and exudes a penetrating fragrance of flowers. Although the sheet is washed repeatedly, both the painting and the fragrance remain unaltered. Moreover, when her body is transported throughout the country so that all the people can pay their last respects, it becomes rejuvenated and on one occasion she opens her eyes and smiles. The subject of gringo imperialism reaches its climax when the American ambassador, having joined with several European powers to strip the country of everything of value, demands the sea. At first the patriarch refuses to comply. Finally, under the threat of a marine landing, he permits a group of American engineers to pack the water and everything it contains "in numbered pieces" and to ship it to the Arizona desert.

The novel's numerous absurd incidents negate the tenets of reason and convey a lack of meaning and purpose in human existence. The result is an overall impression of chaos, often rendered hilarious by gross exaggeration and the ironic elimination of cause and effect. For example, the palace is in a perpetual state of disorder due to the multitude of humans and animals wandering about, both inside and out. Hens' eggs are found in desk drawers, sharks appear in the reception hall, and the patriarch spends much of his time milking his cows, which appear on his balcony and other unlikely places. During the siesta he usually chooses one of his many concubines "by assault," while "everybody remained petrified with his index finger held to his lips, without breathing silence, the general is screwing." Years later he makes love to uniformed schoolgirls passing by the palace on their way home. Eventually it is revealed that they are really prostitutes in disguise hired by the authorities to keep him in good spirits.

During his final years the patriarch becomes senile, amusing himself with television soap operas made only for his viewing, always with happy endings. Moreover, in ironic contrast to the terror he inspired previously among his subordinates, he is occasionally described as wandering helplessly about the palace grounds taking orders from laborers unaware of his identity: " . . . stay upstairs, sir, because a scaffolding could fall on top of you, and he stayed there, bewildered by the uproar of the carpenters and the fury of the bricklayers who shouted to get out of the way you old fool . . . and he stepped aside. . . . " And shortly before his death, though still wielding absolute power, he himself reveals a momentary awareness of his absurd senility when he exclaims, "I'm just a puppet painted on the wall of this house filled with ghosts." (pp. 133–44)

Like the absurd, the grotesque emerges as a major aesthetic feature of *The Autumn of the Patriarch*, its purpose being to create tension in the reader's mind through the clash between the comic and an incompatible element, usually horror, disgust, or physcial abnormality. The reader's reaction to this unresolved incongruity can range from civilized repugnance or embarrassment to barbarous glee over the flouting of taboos, but the response is always emotional and never intellectual. Probably the novel's best example of grotesque are General Rodrigo de Aguilar's "execution," the national lottery involving the two thousand children, and the patriarch's pumpkin-sized testicle, which, on at least one occasion, whistles like a coffee pot.

A series of scurrilously grotesque events, some of which are narrated by the patriarch himself, occurs during the chaotic period a few years after his rise to power. It seems that at an anniversary dinner attended by the foreign diplomatic corps, General Adriano Guzmán became thoroughly inebriated. Unbuttoning his fly, he proceeded to urinate on the ambassadors' wives, all the while singing impassively amidst the panic, "I am the slighted lover who waters the roses of your garden . . . " Also during this time Commandant Narciso López was caught committing a homosexual act—described in graphic detail—with a dragoon of the palace guard. Shortly thereafter, out of shame, he put a stick of dynamite up his rectum and lit the fuse.

After his mother's death, the patriarch has considerable difficulty with the Catholic Church over her canonization, the result of which is the expulsion from the country of all ecclesiastical personnel. While the patriarch is supervising the depature of the priests and nuns, who are stripped naked before they are allowed to leave, he is greatly impressed with one of the novices, a plain, robust girl with full breasts, large buttocks, and flat feet. Unable to forget her physical charms, he traces her to a convent in Jamaica and has her drugged and brought back to him in a glassware crate marked, "Do not drop. This side up." Two year later, after many hilarious bedroom episodes, Leticia Nazareno becomes his mistress and, subsequently, his wife. The wedding ceremony, which takes place when she is seven months pregnant, is one of the most grotesque scenes of the novel. Moments after they have given their vows before the priest

> Leticia Nazareno bent over sobbing Father . . . have pity on your humble servant who has taken much pleasure in the disobedience of your holy laws and accepts with resignation this terrible punishment, but at the same time . . . she squatted . . . in the steamy puddle of her own water and brought out from among the tangle of muslin the premature infant. . . .

The assassination of Leticia Nazareno and her son occurs several years later when they are torn to bits in the market by a pack of fierce dogs trained to attack Leticia's silver-fox fur pieces. This frightful scene is narrated by one of the patriarch's aides, whose description includes not only the grotesque mixture of the animal and the human, but also poetic images of striking incongruity.

> . . . they ate them alive, general . . . sixty identical dogs that . . . jumped out from between the vegetable stands and fell on Leticia Nazareno and the child without giving us time to shoot for fear of killing the two of them who, it appeared, were drowning together with the dogs in a hellish whirlpool, we saw only the fleeting glimpses of ephemeral hands stretched out toward us while the rest of the body was disappearing piece by piece, we saw fleeting expressions which were at times terrified, at times pitiful, at times jubilant, until they at last sank into the vortex of the scramble and only Leti-

cia Nazareno's felt hat with violets remained floating before the impassive horror of the vegetable vendors.

. . .

The passages involving José Ignacio (Nacho) Saenz de la Barra, the cultured sadist hired to ferret out the murderers of Leticia Nazareno and her son, lend an element of grotesque irony to the novel. The patriarch is awed by the young aristocrat whose French accent, knowledge of seven languages, and impeccable appearance, make him unique among the government official. Thus he easily gains the patriarch's high esteem and, ironically at times treats him like a subordinate. Soon after Nacho assumes his duties as chief investigator of Leticia'a murder, he sends the patriarch a bag of what appear to be six coconuts, advising him to store it in a filing cabinet. Several days later, an unbearable stench leads to the discovery that the bag contains six heads of the patriarch's most bitter enemies. Eventually 918 heads are delivered, one of which the patriarch unhappily recognizes as having belonged to an aide with whom he had enjoyed playing dominoes. Nevertheless, the arrogant Nacho continues his fiendish police operations. He even designs and manufactures instruments of torture, having been told by the patriarch that everything is permitted except "the application of electric shocks to the testicles of children under five years of age in order to elicit confessions of crimes from their parents." As Nacho's power and influence continue to grow, the patriarch's admiration for him predictably turns to suspicion and fear. Therefore he arranges an insurrection against his criminal investigator and looks on with sadistic amusement when the latter's overbearing self-confidence turn to panic and terror. Nacho's horrible fate (he is beaten to a pulp and hanged from a street light with his genital organs in his mouth) becomes an instrument of irony when the masses extol their leader for ridding the nation of a dangerous enemy. (pp. 146–49)

Leitmotifs illuminate important aspects of the major characters, thus fixing them more firmly in the reader's mind. For example, Bendición Alvarado's favorite pastime of painting birds recalls her humble life before she became a prominent figure. Manuela Sánchez usually carries a rose, bringing to mind her youthful beauty, but the fact that the rose withers and dies parallels her loneliness and foreshadows her disappearance. Leticia Nazareno's sexual appeal to the patriarch is expressed by her odor of a "wild animal," while the silver-fox fur pieces she wears after their marriage symbolize the cunning by which she is able to achieve her ambitions. Nacho's beastly nature is paralleled by his ferocious Doberman pinscher, Lord Köchel, which follows him everywhere, even into the patriarch's office. Occasionally leitmotifs define relationships between characters, as for example in the case of the highly ironic phrase "my lifelong friend," which the patriarch uses to express his "affection" for General Rodrigo de Aguilar.

The most frequent leitmotifs, however, allude to the patriach and serve primarily to highlight his schizophrenic bid for power and domination, on the one hand, and, on the other, his withdrawal, submission, and obsession with death. His longing to dominate emerges through the repetition of phrases such as "I am the one who's in charge," "Here comes the one in charge!" and "Long live the *macho*!" This same characteristic is also communicated by the golden spur he wears on his left heel, his tight grip on the glass ball he holds in his hand, his enormous feet, and his custom of throwing salt to the infirm in order to elicit their love, gratitude, and acclaim. His solitude and air of submission find expression through the image of his feminine-appearing hands, often encased in satin gloves, languidly waving a white handkerchief from behind the window of his limousine. His withdrawal and isolation motivated by fear become apparent when, upon retiring, he locks his door with three crossbars, three bolts, and three latches before stretching out on the floor face down, his right arm serving as a pillow. And his obsession with death is accentuated by the "unequivocal waters" of the fortune teller's basin and the terrifying flashes of the lighthouse beacon alternating its beam between the lifeless seascape and his bedroom.

In some cases the motifs are repeated with variation in order to render the illusion of rhythmic movement and reinforce thematic content. The best example of this technique is the image of the patriarch "dragging his elephant-sized feet," at first a sign of his power and animal nature but gradually an indication of fluctuating moods, solitude, and advancing age. Thus in subsequent passages he is seen "dragging his big feet like a lover in hiding" (reflecting his initial unwillingness to marry Leticia Nazareno); "dragging his big, captive-elephant feet." (paralleling his fascination and delight with Rubén Darío's poetry); "dragging his dense, decrepit feet;" "dragging his big senile elephant feet;" "dragging his big feet like a hopeless victim of insomnia;" and, shortly before his death, "dragging his big feet like a specter as he wandered through the immense, dark mansion."

Other motifs allude to secondary social and psychological themes. For example, the oft-mentioned battleship anchored in the harbor underscores gringo imperialism; the absurd image of rich children being ground up for sausage in the slums conveys the deep division between social classes that exists throughout Latin America; the patriarch's fantastic vision of the spectacular volcano in Martinique alongside "the nightmare of Haiti" highlights extremes typical in this part of of the world; and the mechanical toys the patriarch purchases for Manuela Sánchez (the beauty queen) reflect the superficial nature of their relationship.

Additional stylistic devices frequently utilized in *The Autumn of the Patriarch* are paradox and metaphor, their purpose being to foster poetic ambiguity, intensify mood, and, especially in the case of mataphor, to render the abstract more concrete. There are numerous examples. In a moment of anger the patriarch pounds the table with his "rough maiden's hand." The old battleship was "longer and more somber than truth." The patriarch "felt older than God in the semidarkness of dawn." Leticia Nazareno's unborn child speaks to her of "the tender steel of her insides." The patriarch's power is defined as a "mass of slime without shores," and the precariousness of his fate is conveyed by the "quicksand of his power." During the search for Manuela Sánchez's home in the labyrinthian slums, the patriarch wonders which house is hers in "this uproar of peeling walls." The first time he sees Leticia Nazareno, the patriarch becomes aware of her "large blind breasts," and after her return from Jamaica he views her under the "flourlike light" of the mosquito netting. When he finally makes love to her, he weeps, "stunned by the anxiety of his kidneys and the string of firecrackers in his guts." Subsequently, their midday sexual encounters are referred to as "the shrimp broth of the siesta frolic." As he thinks about how to handle a revolt against his regime, the patriarch "inhaled the murmur of recently born roses" and, upon observing the one-hundredth anniversary of his rise to power he sees the crowds as a "torrent of slime."

In the final pages of the novel the patriarch is awakened in the middle of the night by the ghostly image of death standing over him. During the ensuing moments, the last of his life, a first-person-plural narrator asserts that the patriarch's incapacity for love has made him a victim of the "solitary vice of power," a vice that gradually took possession of him and compelled him to commit many wrongs "in order to keep the glass ball in his fist until the end of time." He has realized all along, we are told, that he acquired his power and glory through devious means, but the denial of this knowledge has enabled him to live with it and deceive himself with the belief that lying is "more convenient than doubt, more useful than love, and longer lasting than truth." Thus the unidentified narrator states, the patriarch has been condemned to know only "the reverse side of life," never having felt the sentiments of love or happiness that even his poorest subjects have experienced. The juxtaposition of his hermetic isolation with the spontaneous outpouring of joy triggered by his death sustains to the end the duel of opposites typifying the entire work. (pp. 149–53)

The most puzzling and least convincing part of the novel is its ending. Soon after the image of death appears hovering over the patriarch, the above mentioned first-person-plural soliloquy effects an abrupt change in the narrative tone. This anonymous narrator's rather bland statement to the effect that the patriarch's total alienation has resulted from his lust for power conveys information the reader has gleaned by the end of the first unit, thus making it seem redundant and even detrimental from an aesthetic point of view. Equally perplexing is the narrator's attitude of resignation and conciliation toward the misdeeds of the past, an attitude unlike any expressed heretofore in the book.

> . . . the only feasible life was . . . the one we saw from our standpoint which wasn't yours, general, the standpoint of the poor . . . of our innumerable years of misfortune and our fleeting moments of happiness, where love was contaminated by germs of death but it was still love, general, while you yourself were scarcely a hazy vision of pitiful eyes seen through the dusty curtains of a train window. . . .

This narrative voice could be intended to perform a function similar to that of the chorus in Greek tragedy, i.e., it could represent a final commentary by the citizenry, whose suppressed hatred and rage have been replaced by their forbearance, understanding, and pity, thus indicating the regeneration of love and human solidarity. If this is indeed García Márquez's intention, it would appear that he is attempting to portray his protagonist as a tragic figure, whose suffering and death have had a purifying effect on his nation's collective psyche. Personally, I find this view of the patriarch difficult to accept, for in spite of his filial devotion and agonizing solitude—his only redeeming features—he remains a monstrous specimen of the human race, unworthy of the admiration or compassion usually associated with tragic characters. In my opinion, the novel would have been strengthened both thematically and aesthetically had the tension between poetry and horror been maintained to the end, omitting the first-person-plural soliloquy in the final passage and leaving any possible sympathy on the part of the reader to be gleaned from the scenic action or the patriarch's interior monologues. In this way the cathartic effect of his demise—if such an effect is intended—would be dramatically conveyed instead of tritely stated.

The book's ending is not its only flaw. Its impact would probably be heightened and its artistic value enhanced were it shortened by at least twenty-five pages, half of which could be extracted from the relatively tedious sixth unit. Because of the extremely long sentences and numerous repetitions, those unaccustomed to the stylistic patterns of the lyrical novel may find this one easy to lay aside. Nevertheless, its drawbacks notwithstanding, *The Autumn of the Patriarch* in some respects looms as García Márquez's most memorable literary creation. The work of an astonishing sensibility and prodigious imagination, it tells an outrageous chapter of Latin-American and universal reality, all the while maintaining a remarkable equilibrium between lyrical and narrative art. This jungle view of Latin-American politics, poetically apprehended and recreated symbolically, is only too real in the world of the 1970s. García Márquez's brilliantly stylized portrait of a mythical tyrant playing God but hopelessly trapped in the "darkness of power" is likely to stretch his readers' imagination to the limit. It is not only the most original Latin-American novel to date on the timely subject of political tyranny, but also an ingenious experiment in prose fiction. (pp. 155–56)

George R. McMurray, in his *Gabriel García Márquez*, Frederick Ungar Publishing Co., 1977, 182 p.

JOHN S. BRUSHWOOD

(essay date 1985)

[In the following essay, Brushwood explains García Márquez's fantastic view of the world as the author's characteristic perception of reality. He further points to the fact, affirmed by García Márquez himself, that in Latin America reality itself is fantastic.]

Gabriel García Márquez has always said that his *One Hundred Years of Solitude* is a novel based wholly on reality. More than a few readers have been surprised by this statement, since many of the characters and events seem far removed from ordinary daily routines. The novelist has also said, on occasion, that *One Hundred Years of Solitude* is a metaphor of Latin American reality—not a history. Most recently, when he accepted the Nobel Prize for literature, he equated solitude with the estrangement of Latin America—that is, the reluctance, on part of other nations, to accept the Latin American nations for what they really are.

What García Márquez does not say is that, even though the novel is based on reality, it is conceived in a way that makes reality seem larger than life. The book's people and events range from the extraordinary to the unreal. That's why it seems myth-like. As a consequence, we are tempted to look for an allegorical structure or, at the very least, systematize a few symbols. This undertaking is not entirely wrong, but it can easily be carried too far. Since the novel is based on reality, it must refer to Colombia, and since Colombia is a Latin-American country, it must refer also to the larger area.

A novelist can exploit three sources of narratable material: what he experiences personally, what he is told by others, and what he imagines. Obviously, the products of all three sources influence each other in his narration, just as they influence each other in our ordinary experience. García Márquez once said that nothing interesting had happened to him since he was eight years old, the year he left the home of his grandparents to live with his mother and father. Of course, novelists are not renowned for the accuracy of what they say in interviews, but I think we can be certain that García Márquez's grandfather must have made quite a strong impression on him.

Both grandparents told him stories that he transformed into elements of his narrative. The wonderful thing is that a small child can accept literally something that seems exaggerated or downright impossible to an adult. This kind of credulity, transposed to an adult age level, can explain some of the presumably incredible phenomena in *One Hundred Years of Solitude*.

My own childhood was spent in a milieu similar, in some ways, to García Márquez's. I remember when I was five or six years old, walking from my house to my grandparents' house and hearing my great-grandfather hail me from the front yard of *his* house, saying, "Hey, boy, come on over here where it's cooler." If I were writing a novel in the manner of [García Márquez], I would create two entirely different climates in two front yards separated by a road approximately 25 feet wide. This difference would be incredible, and readers would probably try to find some hidden significance far beyond anything the author had imagined. But inevitably, it would serve to identify a fictional reality. This is one of the techniques the author uses to create a reality that seems larger than life. He treats the commonplace as if it were exceptional and the exceptional as if it were commonplace.

The characters in the novel, like the events, are transformations of reality. Of course, that is true of many novels. The difference, in the world of García Márquez, is in the dimensions of the transformation. Certainly the author's grandparents are, in some sense, in the novel. Something of his grandmother is in Ursula, but the fictional character has her own life. We do not know—nor do we need know—exactly how the transformation changes her. It's a fair guess, of course, that the prototype didn't live to be 145 years old, but a further detailed comparsion of fiction and reality doesn't produce much in the way of satisfactory experience. Ursula, on the other hand, is very much herself, and estimable for what she is in the novel. Much the same may be said for another commonly recognized prototype, General Rafael Uribe y Uribe, the constant revolutionary. His biography by Eduardo Santos, subtitled "El Caudillo de la Esperanza" ("The Caudillo of Hope"), leaves no doubt of the similarity to Colonel Aureliano Buendía. But the differences are considerable, not the least of which is the futility implied by the everlasting task of making gold fishes from gold coins and selling them for gold coins which could be made into more gold fishes, an occupation that never attracted Uribe.

In connection with such aspects of the narrative, we are tempted to allegorize, but it is better to think in terms of metaphor, as suggested by the author. An especially good example is the series of seventeen sons begot by Colonel Aureliano during his protracted military campaigning, all born with crosses of ashes indelibly marked on their foreheads. One inevitably remembers that Colombia is as clergy-ridden as any country in the modern world.

One might also point to this phenomenon as an example of "magical realism," but García Márquez would be the first to point out that you do not have to invent "magical" or incredible reality in Latin America. Almost forty years ago, Alejo Carpentier, a Cuban writer who had lived in France and knew the Surrealists' interest in "the marvellous," set forth the concept of "marvellous reality"; that is, in the Latin American world, you don't have to invent the marvellous, reality itself is marvellous enough for anybody. García Márquez is one of many novelists who have exploited this phenomenon. Although García Márquez is Latin American to the core, with major emphasis on the Caribbean, his travels—and probably his literary associations—add a certain objectivity that causes him to emphasize its idiosyncrasies more than might be the case if he had never left Colombia.

In addition to whatever inscrutable natural tendencies García Márquez may have, we can easily identify three literary influences that cause him to conceive and narrate fictions in his characteristic manner. They are Alejo Carpentier, William Faulkner, and a little known Colombian writer named José Felix Fuenmayor. The two Latin Americans were largely responsible for encouraging the flow of his imagination. Faulkner's works taught him a great deal about narrative point of view, and reinforced the influence of the other two in making [García Márquez] see extraordinary qualities in the commonplace.

William Faulkner is very much in evidence in García Márquez's first novel, **Leaf Storm**. Three alternating narrator voices tell the story of a physician who was ostracized by the town in which he once practiced, and of the campaign waged by one grateful patient to give the doctor a decent burial. There is an interesting suggestion of *Antigone* here, of course, but mainly what one thinks of is *The Sound and the Fury* or *As I Lay Dying*. The voices belong to a small boy, his mother, and his grandfather. The ambience is the oppressiveness of provincial society. Enigma is constantly at work, as the three accounts interweave to reveal slowly, and still continue to tease.

We may guess, though never be quite certain, that this novel was conceived in a way that presupposed the oppressive social ambience and the maverick's struggle to maintain dignity. Certainly that is the conflict which is developed in the narrative, and resolved by the grandfather's persistence, in a climax made dramatic only by its fictional relativism. That is, the climax is not an event that would seem dramatic if we were to experience it without having experienced that narrative itself. Rather, it might seem decidedly commonplace. Only the narrative build-up—the series of events that we put together thanks to the conflict between individual integrity and the demands of society— makes the climax dramatic. The basic conflict that I have pointed out and identified as between individual integrity and the demands of society is the fundamental opposition throughout García Márquez's fiction. It may be expressed in other words that are more specifically appropriate to a given situation, such as the conflict between the dignity of an individual and rejection by society, but the various formulations are very close to each other in meaning.

In all the novels and stories following **Leaf Storm**, this conflict appears in some form. In **No One Writes to the Colonel**, the protagonist's hope of receiving a pension is one of the two phenomena that sustain him. The other is a fighting cock which he keeps tethered to the foot of his bed. (It is important to remember that it is practically impossible to find an ordinary person among the main characters of García Márquez; only some secondary characters seem commonplace.) During the experience of reading **No One Writes to the Colonel**, it seems as improbable that the gamecock will ever fight as it does that the colonel will receive the long awaited letter. While either would alleviate his financial distress, it would also remove the expectation that is his reason for being.

García Márquez begins this narrative at a point following the death of the colonel's son. A prolonged illness of the colonel's wife has left them with virtually no food and even less money. The narrative conflict becomes clear almost immediately as the colonel puts on his best, ludicrously threadbare, clothing, to pay respects to a bereaved acquaintance. Following him through this incident, we discover his lack of self-confidence, born of uncertainty about how others may react to him. Call it alienation, if you will. He is out of touch with the townspeople. He should belong to their society, but he really doesn't. He is different, and this difference is exacerbated by his routinely meeting the mail launch and hoping for a letter. The townspeople see him as an old fool hoping without hope. Against this attitude, he struggles to maintain his dignity. Several incidents that are really metaphors of each other serve to illustrate and intensify this conflict. The incident that many would choose as the climax of the story almost robs him of the hope that is represented by his gamecock. The denouement then unfolds rapidly and satisfyingly, though hardly in the sense of solving his problems.

No One Writes to the Colonel, and García Márquez's next novel, **The Evil Hour**, deal with "la violencia," a term used with reference to a decade of civil strife in Colombia, beginning in 1948. This period was, in some respects, worse than an open confrontation, worse than a clearly defined revolution. It was caused by political intransigence on the part of both conservatives and liberals. Its manifestations were murder, betrayal, brutality—hidden warfare. It produced hate, distrust, general insecurity. Both novels succeed in producing the experience, the feeling, of that awful period, rather than a factual represenation of it. In this respect, they are good examples of what García Márquez means when he says that **One Hundred Years of Solitude** is a metaphor of Latin America.

One Hundred Years of Solitude follows **The Evil Hour** in the story of García Márquez's books, even though it is the starting point for many readers. In fact, it is the climax of the story. A rather simplistic structure of narrative fiction may be handily applied to any one of his narratives: first, the point in the story at which the narration begins; second the statement or suggestion of the conflict, the polarity on which the narrative is developed; third, the incidents that develop the conflict; fourth the climax; fifth, the denouement. The conflict and development, of course, always reveal the extraordinary individual's struggle for dignity against the exigencies of conventionality. It seems to me that one can apply the same structure to García Márquez's work as a whole. (I would not care to push this sort of analogy too for, but I think it may be useful in explaining what he has accomplished.) His work in fiction begins at a point when the author's conceptualization of his material—that is the way the thinks about the subject he is going to write about—already assumes a state of separation on the part of a principal character, a separation created by the character's difference from a social norm. The conflict is between the defense of this difference and the demands of society. García Márquez's fictions develop this conflict in one work after another, just as an individual narrative develops it in one *incident* after another. Each of his novels is to a considerable extent a metaphor of the others. To put it another way, we might say that the deep meaning of his novel is invariable, even though each novel might express it in slightly different terms. If we grant that this is the case, it might seem that García Márquez has wasted his time, saying the same thing over and over. But that is not what happens. This development of a basic opposition, throughout his work, leads to a climax that is *One Hundred Years of Solitude*, and then to a denouement in his more recent work, especially *The Autumn of the Patriarch*. *Chronicle of a Death Foretold* is a coda, a reaffirmation of its predecessors.

The Autumn of the Patriarch, García Márquez's more recent full-length novel, is one of several written about dictators during the 1970s. When I refer to it as a denouement in the trajectory of his work, I do not mean that he writes an entirely different kind of fiction. In fact, we find the same hyperbole, the same humor produced by larger-than-life reality. Who would not be amused by the dictator's mother, a woman of humble origin, hanging out the laundry on the presidential balcony? The juxtaposition of coarseness and elegance generates much of the novel's satire. *Autumn* is more specifically political then *One Hundred Years of Solitude*. It is also a more difficult exercise in reading; that is, it requires a reader to contribute more in order to make the communication effective. To a practical mind, these two qualities seem to be incompatible. If a book is very political, one might expect the author to provide the reader extremely easy access. That is not what García Márquez does in this case. The novel is divided into six parts, each beginning with an awareness of the protagonist's death. This condition emphasizes the notion of the dictator's persistence—the

presence of his power if not of his person. It also requires a reader to adjust, five times, his store of information concerning the pratagonist. The sentences become longer in each section. The last section consists of a single sentence that runs about fifty pages.

Of course it can be followed. But it would be absurd to say that it can be followed easily. A reader can feel swallowed up in a vortex of narration. No doubt it can be argued that a reader is therefore, more committed, more incorporated into the meaning of the novel. "Involved" is the buzz word most appropriate to the condition. However, this involvement, if it is highly valued, must be measured in terms of depth rather than of numbers, since one could hardly expect this book to attract as large an audience as his other, more accessible, novels.

I have trouble reconciling this kind of fiction with the author's political anxiety. On the other hand, the novel's structure does require the reader to become involved in the creation of its fictional world. This involvement is an appropriate denouement in a literary *oeuvre* that is, according to the author, a metaphor of Latin America. It forces readers into contact with the Latin-American difference that García Márquez would have us recognize. In this connection, it appears also that the novelist sees the conflict between the extraordinary individual's dignity and the requirements of society as analogous to the conflict between Latin America's dignity and the requirements of the non-Latin world. In his recent Nobel acceptance speech, significantly entitled *The Solitude of Latin America*, he makes a major point of Latin America's difference. Citing facts of Latin-American history that corroborate the notion of "marvellous reality," he suggests that other countries should accept these differences, accept Latin America for what it is, and so remove it from its state of solitude. (pp. 9–14)

John S. Brushwood, "Reality and Imagination, in the Novels of García Márquez," in *Latin American Literary Review*, Vol. XIII, No. 25, January–June, 1985, pp. 9–14.

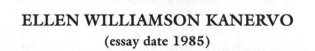

ELLEN WILLIAMSON KANERVO
(essay date 1985)

[In the essay below, Kanervo explores the relationship between García Márquez's journalism and his literary works, especially *One Hundred Years of Solitude* and *Chronicle of a Death Foretold*. According to Kanervo, García Márquez combines a magical perception of reality with traditional newspaper reporting techniques to create a unique vison of the world.]

Gabriel García Márquez was recently asked to comment on his fascination with the relationship between literature and politics. He responded saying "I'm fascinated by the relationship between literature and *journalism*. I began my career as a journalist in Colombia and a reporter is something I've never stopped being" (*Playboy*, February 1983). Then he returned to the question of politics and literature, leaving the reader's curiosity piqued but certainly not satisfied. What does García Márquez see as the relationship between literature and journalism?

Certainly the 1982 Nobel Prize winner is equally at ease as a journalist or as a novelist. He began his career in 1946 as a reporter for Bogota's *El Espectador* and continued working as an editor and foreign correspondent for the newspaper until it was closed in 1955. After that he had editorial stints at several papers in Caracas and from 1959–61 he worked for the Cuban news agency Prensa Latina. In 1961 he moved to Mexico and cut himself off from the monthly paycheck of the reporter, devoting his time fully to writing *One Hundred Years of Solitude*, his best known novel which was published in 1967. Since then he has written several more novels and numerous short stories. However, he still dabbles in reporting as a free-lance writer and says he hopes to start his own newspaper soon. Yet the fact that García Márquez can support himself as a journalist or as a novelist does not really illuminate the question about the relationship between the two fields. (pp. 467–68)

[If] the relationship between journalism and literature that fascinates García Márquez isn't the clean and lean style of the journalist, what does he mean by his statement?

Perhaps he refers to the purposes of journalism and literature. Journalists are supposed to inform their readers about the world around them. And certainly one of the principal reasons one studies literature is to learn about life. But those purposes are so broad that one hardly knows how to begin any kind of fruitful comparison of literature and journalism as they relate to life.

Twentieth-century American literature does have a genre that is somewhat a hybrid of literature and journalism. It influenced and was influenced by the Underground Press of the late 1960s and has been called variously "parajournalism," "gonzo-journalism," or "new journalism." The New Journalists (included in this breed are authors as diverse as Jimmy Breslin, Tom Wolfe, Norman Mailer, Hunter Thompson, and Truman Capote) said that the "old" journalism, with its emphasis on objectivity, failed to inform people about what was truly happening. They maintained that journalists cannot be objective, that, to borrow a phrase from columnist Walter Lippman (*Public Opinion*, 1921), we describe "the world outside" through "the pictures in our heads." Their answer to the journalist's dilemma about objectivity was to let their readers know their biases up front, arguing that readers would then have a better chance of deciding for themselves what really happened. And so, in the interest of accuracy, these writers, to a greater or lesser extent, turned away from describing the world outside and focused more on the pictures inside their heads. In *Armies of the Night* we watched Norman Mailer watching himself watching the anti-Vietnam march on Washington. He was doing the work of a journalist reporting on the march, and at least to some people his quasi-journalism had literary merit since he was also a candidate for the 1982 Nobel Prize in Literature (*New York Times*, 22 October 1982).

One might be tempted to compare Mailer's work with that of García Márquez since the objective world provides a stimulus for both. Mailer's accounts are rooted in real events, and García Márquez has often said that much of his fiction did not have to be invented—that he took most of it from reality.

But García Márquez's reality is very different from Mailer's. While critics of the South American's work have described it as realism or surrealism they more often label it magical realism. The world of García Márquez's fictions is realistic; however, events and characters in that world are often magical; they are outrageous, fantastic, and unbelieveable. For example, in an otherwise realistic small town, a priest will levitate after drinking hot chocolate or a ghost will return to her home to gather the belongings that made her happy in life to comfort her in death. Realism and magic are inextricably entwined.

And indeed García Márquez himself seems not to be at all concerned with where the realism ends and the magic begins. In *One Hundred Years of Solitude*, a town's banana workers go on strike. Three thousand of them are massacred in the town square, and their bodies are shipped in boxcars to the sea. García Márquez says that the episode "is, more or less, based on historical reality." He notes that the strike chronicled in his novel parallels an actual strike that took place in 1928 against the United Fruit Company in every detail but one: in the novel 3000 die during the strike, whereas actually only a very few individuals were killed. García Márquez evidently became aware of his ability to create truth through fiction after the publication of this novel. He told a *Playboy* interviewer: "Let me tell you something very curious about that incident. Nobody has studied the event around the real banana strike—and now when they talk about it in the newspapers, even once in Congress, they speak about the *3000* who died! And I wonder, if with time, it will become true that 3000 were killed. That is why, in the *The Autumn of the Patriarch* there is a moment when the patriarch says, 'It doesn't matter if it is not true now; it will be with time '" (*Playboy*, February 1983).

Journalists flinch at that statement. Truth and accuracy are the cornerstones of the profession. Certainly the journalist may not always attain them, but they are always his goals. And even the new journalists, who scorn attempts at objectivity, say they give subjective accounts in order to be more accurate and more closely to approximate the truth.

So in his magical realism García Márquez seems to go several steps beyond journalists in telling us about our world. The accurate, objective account of what has happened and what is happening is not the best way to inform us about the world we live in, he says. What is important to tell us about is the image, the experience. Those discrete events that we read about in San Salvador or Peoria are not what we need to know in order to understand the world. And those nicely balanced media accounts based on interviews with several principal parties do not really tell us what we need to know. So it is that García Márquez's blend of truth and fiction, of realism and magic is, paradoxically, as fair and accurate an account of the world as the journalist's assemblage of verbatim statements made by individuals intimately involved with an event.

But García Márquez may have had some more specific ideas when he made his statement about the relationship between journalism and literature. Gregory Rabassa (*World Literature Today*, 1982), who translates all of García Márquez's works into English, points out the novelist sees "little difference between reporting and the writing of chronicles." Though he does not give many specifics, Rabassa notes that the format used for the narration of García Márquez's novella, *Chronicle of a Death Foretold* (1983), [is] quite journalistic. A reading of this novella reveals that García Márquez is playing around with the values of journalists and with the ways journalists tell us about the world. The novella is based on historical facts that can be determined from real newspaper accounts. On January 22, 1951, in the Colombian town of Sucre, a man was murdered because he was thought to have been the lover of another man's bride. The victim was an acquaintance of García Márquez, then a young newspaperman in the city of Barranquilla. The bride's two brothers were convicted of the murder but spent only a few years in prison for what was generally regarded as a legitimate defense of their family's honor.

Similarly, García Márquez's *Chronicle of a Death Foretold* is about twin brothers who butcher the man they believe compromised their sister before her marriage. Like the real bride, the young woman of García Márquez's story is returned by her husband to her parents' house on the wedding night. The victim and principal character of the story is Santiago Nasar, whose steps the novel reconstructs until his murder. During the course of the morning, warnings are withheld, paths fail to cross, backs are inopportunely turned. Even the killers waver, hoping for a bloodless way to save the family honor, but no one seems able to keep the victim from his fate. The doomed man's steps lead to a door that should not have been locked. It becomes the altar on which he is hacked to pieces as a sacrifice to the god of honor.

Many of the reviews of *Chronicle* compare the novella to a detective story and the narrator to a detective trying to discover not whodunit but why. But it makes more sense to compare the novella to a news story and the narrator to a journalist trying to write an objective account of the event. Certainly the novella's telling employs many of the elements of journalism. Like a good journalist, the narrator pretty much keeps his own thoughts and feelings out of his narrative. Like a good journalist, he carefully attributes almost every scrap of information he reports. He interviews 34 named people plus "22 people in the market" and "several butchers." He even gets "no comments" from the groom and the bride's mother. García Márquez tells his story through the alternating of direct and indirect quotes from these sources, a time-honored journalistic device. In fact, many journalists seem to define objectivity as quoting from several sources without inserting their own opinions and accuracy as making sure that each quotation represents the exact words of the speaker in context. They worry less about whether the quote from the source represents the true situation. After all, they attribute all information to a source, and they cannot read his mind.

It may not be his main intention, but García Márquez takes pot shots at both journalistic objectivity and accuracy in *Chronicle*. Though he doesn't "editorialize in his news account," a phrase copy editors use when they delete a reporter's opinions in a news story, he nevertheless arranges the words of the townspeople to suggest that they are all guilty of the murder. The mayor claims he took the twins' knives away and assumed they would just go on home. The priest claims he "had forgotten" to tell Nasar's mother of her son's peril. A friend claims he "lost his nerve" and simply patted Santiago Nasar on the back instead of warning him of his impending death. By failing to act, all the townspeople implicitly sanction the murder, and García Márquez's outrage at the town's belief in *pundonor*, point of honor, is implicitly, but clearly communicated.

Also, in weaving his story the narrator gives quotes containing fact, superstition, and outrageous irrelevance equal weight, just as a journalist gives quotes from all parties involved equal weight even if one party is clearly wrong. The narrator records recollections of dreams along with factual statements of what Santiago Nasar did at what time. He records conflicting statements about the weather with great seriousness. He quotes his mother in the middle of her otherwise relevant character analysis of the bride and the bride's sisters as saying that their one fault is combing their hair at night because such an action slows down the seafarers. Such outrageous statements are vintage García Márquez, but in *Chronicle* the method of the narration, the journalist's method, questions whether the quotes journalists use in their accounts bear any more closely on the events they report on than the narrator's do to the murder of Santiago Nasar.

And there is "something very curious" about García Márquez's use of these journalistic techniques. They work. As the use of quotes without commentary gives newspapers a facade of objectivity and accuracy, the same device also gives García Márquez's fiction a facade of objectivity and accuracy. Christopher Lehmann-Haupt, critic for the *New York Times* who reviewed *Chronicle*, said that he expected of the novella "another powerful dose of the fabulous and surreal. But behold! While in no way resembling conventional social realism, *Chronicle* is not nearly so fantastic as García Márquez's earlier novel." He is mistaken. A close reading of *Chronicle* reveals elements of the surreal on every page: a mother blames herself for her son's death because she failed to interpret his dreams accurately; a ghost returns to her home to collect her earthly belongings; a jilted bride writes wild letters to her husband for 17 years until he shows up on her doorstep one day to stay holding a box filled with all her letters—unopened; knives come bloodless out of a body after each stab. García Márquez's writing in *Chronicle* is as magic as ever; it just seems more plausible because of its journalistic form. In fact, when García Márquez quotes one of the twins discussing his pain from an infection, saying, "'I was awake for eleven months,' he told me, and I knew him well enough to know it was true," the reader finds himself wondering whether a person could stay awake for 11 months. Unlike the obviously magical insomnia spell in *One Hundred Years*, this surreal condition is made believable because it appears as a journalist's report.

In his *Playboy* interview García Márquez asserted that because of his "great affection for journalists," he sometimes "may create something" to make sure a reporter gets a different kind of interview. His comment reveals his awareness that these fictions he makes for the benefit of journalists would, when reported, *appear* to be the truth and would indeed *become* the truth when no one will or can gainsay them. That is, the journalist, like the literary artist, does not merely report the truth; he creates it. Fascinated with this relationship between journalism and literature, Gabriel García Márquez chose to emulate the journalist, thus effecting the transmutation of the unbelievable into the believable in *Chronicle of a Death Foretold*. (pp. 468–75)

Ellen Williamson Kanervo, "Gabriel García Márquez: Journalist as Novelist, Novelist as Journalist," in *The Midwest Quarterly*, Vol. XXVI, No. 4, Summer, 1985, pp. 467–75.

JEAN FRANCO
(essay date 1988)

[In the following excerpt, Franco contends that García Márquez's *Love in the Time of Cholera* reveals an ironic and melancholy view of society that has drifted "from the stagnation of colonialism to the devastation of modernity," as illustrated in the author's treatment of the themes of love, aging, and death.]

Set in a stagnant tropical port at the turn of the century, *Love in the Time of Cholera* tells the story of Florentino Ariza's prolonged passion for Fermina Daza, a passion that is finally consummated after fifty years, nine months and four days, when they are both over 70 years old. The consummation takes place on a riverboat that flies the cholera flag in order to protect their privacy. When Fermina undresses, Florentino finds her "just as he imagined her. Her shoulders were wrinkled, her breasts sagged, her ribs were covered by a flabby skin as pale and cold as a frog's"—which does not prevent him from exploring "her withered neck with his fingertips, her bosom armored in metal stays, her hips with their decaying bones, her thighs with their aging veins." The boat cannot land because of the cholera flag, so the couple, enjoying "the tranquil, wholesome love of experienced grandparents," are destined to live out their lives perpetually journeying up and down the river through a calamitous and ruined landscape, clinging hopefully to the last vestiges of life.

The humor of this autumnal romance cannot, however, dispel the odor of mortality. On the very first page, the reader is greeted "with the aromatic fumes of gold cyanide" and the suicide of the Caribbean refugee Jeremiah de Saint-Amour. The doctor who writes the death certificates is Fermina Daza's 81-year-old husband, Juvenal Urbino, who hours later is killed falling from a ladder as he tries to coax a parrot from a tree. It is at the funeral that Florentino renews a courtship he had begun half a century earlier.

The novel retraces the story of their love and separation: Fermina's adolescence under the jealous guardianship of a father who had made his money in contraband and wanted her to be a great lady; her brief engagement to the illegitimate and lowly Florentino; her marriage to the brilliant European educated doctor Juvenal Urbino; and her then exemplary life (marred only by a two-year separation caused by her husband's infidility). Meanwhile, Florentino has a brilliant career with the riverboat company and becomes an impenitent and bizarre womanizer who, when he is over 60, is capable of assaulting a maid "in less time than a Philippino rooster" and leaving her in the family way. His lovers include a 50-year-old widow who receives him stark naked with an organdy bow in her hair, an escapee from the lunatic asylum and, when he is over 70, a school girl "with braces on her teeth and the scrapes of elementary school on her knees."

The humor and pathos of aging and death are subjects that have obsessed García Márquez from his earliest writings. His first novel, *Leaf Storm*, was about a funeral. In *One Hundred Years of Solitude*, there are dozens of tiny vignettes of death—Amaranta Úrsula preparing her own shroud, José Arcadio Buendía's dying dream of walking through room after room until he meets the man he has killed, and the matriarch Úrsula, concealing her blindness from her children before lucidly dying. In *Love in the Time of Cholera* bodies fail long before passions are spent. . . .

Decay is part of the landscape. The colonial Caribbean port where Fermina and Florentino pass most of their lives is familiar García Márquez territory. It was in towns such as this that he wrote his first sketches for a novel in the late 1940s and which he chronicled as a journalist in Barranquilla and Cartagena. It was here that he collected the repertoire of legend, anecodote, small-town boredom and eccentricity that he has drawn on ever since. Not that there is any nostalgia in *Love in the Time of Cholera*, which moves from the stagnation of colonialism to the devastation of modernity in the time it takes to turn a page. Although the cobbled streets of the city recall "surprise attacks and buccaneer landings," "nothing had happened for four centuries except a slow aging among withered laurels and putrefying swamps." On the edge of the town are the old slave quarters, where buzzards fight over the offal from the slaughterhouse. Cadavers are everywhere, some dead of cholera and others in the wars. (pp. 573)

By the end of the novel and its "happy ending," the mood is paradoxically apocalyptic. Fermina and Florentino's love boat, which once had steamed through an idyllic landscape, now passes "calcinated flatlands stripped of entire forests." The manatees "with their great breasts that had nursed their young and wept on the banks in a forlorn woman's voice were an extinct species, annihilated by the armored bullets of hunters for sport." Natural life has almost disappeared, "the parrots, the monkeys, the villages were gone, everything was gone."

For this is the irony of García Márquez's novel—that the genial good humor disguises apocalyptic foreboding. The same civilization that idealizes lovers produces a global wasteland, and the private fantasies of romance are rafts on a sea of public devastation. Fermina and Florentino salvage their own idyll but are themselves part of the destruction, a last nineteenth-century romance that can only find a heart of darkness (not for nothing is Joseph Conrad a character in the novel; he is accused of cheating Fermina Daza's father in a shady arms deal). Fermina and Florentino's love boat, indeed, adds to the devastation, since it has polluted the river waters and consumes the last of the forests on the riverbanks. It is this ambiguous relationship of private felicity and mass destruction that provides the novel with its disturbing undertow.

In his novels, García Márquez constantly returns to one particular historical period—from independence to the first decades of the twentieth century. It is the hundred years of Macondo in *One Hundred Years of Solitude* and of the dictatorship in *The Autumn of the Patriarch*. What fascinates him, evidently, is the meeting of fierce Latin idiosyncrasy with rationalism and modernity. Yet *Love in the Time of Cholera* is not only about the past but also about

the anachronistic life forms that still survive in the ruins left by nineteenth-century progress. In this respect, the novel shares the *fin de siécle* mood of much contemporary Latin American writing. (pp. 573–74)

Jean Franco, "Mementos Mori," in *The Nation*, New York, Vol. 246, No. 16, April 23, 1988, pp. 573–74.

KATHLEEN McNERNEY
(essay date 1989)

[In the following excerpt, McNerney surveys several of García Márquez's early short novels and stories, revealing how he utilizes "fantasy realism" to tell his stories and expound his themes. According to McNerney, these prose "works form an impressive body of literature."]

Though any piece of writing done by García Márquez can stand on its own, certain common themes, characters, and situations make it useful to look at some of his short fiction, particularly the earlier stories, for García Márquez weaves familiar faces and places in and out of these works. This technique has been seen variously as puzzle pieces, episodes that seem to be seeds of other, more developed episodes, or miniatures. The Eréndira who passes so briefly through the pages on *One Hundred Years of Solitude*, for example, becomes the subject of the film and novella she entitles, complete with heartless grandmother and itinerant photographer. Far from being repetitious, the incidents are as intriguing as life. Just when we thought we knew the judge or the priest from one story, he appears in another, and we see a new aspect of his character which explains something that had gone before, as if people we know superficially one day were to tell us their deepest secrets. Like a detail in a photograph blown up many times, the enlargement shows us what was always there but didn't come to our attention before. (p. 98)

García Márquez's earliest stories, written when he was barely twenty and under the influence of his favorite writers, especially Woolf, Hemingway, and Faulkner, were published first in periodicals and finally gathered together under the title *Ojos de perro azul* (*Eyes of a Blue Dog*), the name of one of the stories. The title is characteristic in its bizarre flavor: the stories, for the most part, are excursions into realities and perceptioins, and into irrational, surreal, and sometimes nightmarish states of consciousness. In the least successful stories technique becomes more important than content, as if the author were still a bit too self-conscious. Half the stories are an exploration of death: **"The Third Resignation"** examines the stages, or phases, of death, with many hints of the circular motion of time so perfected in *One Hundred Years of Solitude.* "The Other Side of Death" uses García Márquez's first set of twins in a grotesque look at death and finding one's identity. "Dialogue with a Mirror" repeats the doubling motif with an image reflected in a mirror which gains its own autonomy. The passage of time is mentioned abruptly in "Eva Is Inside Her Cat," a story in which beauty is seen as Eva's enemy, and in which her only contact with the realm of the senses is the desire to eat an orange. In the title story a man and woman who meet only in their dreams cannot remember those dreams upon waking. Perhaps the most Faulknerian of the tales in its atmosphere is "Nabo, the Black Man Who Made the Angels Wait." Nabo, having been kicked by a horse he was grooming, is locked up in the stable because of his resulting madness. His only possible communication is with the retarded girl he had taught how to use the phonograph. The most staightforward of the stories is probably "The Woman Who Came at Six O'Clock," in which a woman who always comes into the bar at six wants an alibi for what she has just done and convinces the barman to say she came at five-thirty that day.

The stories are replete with surprising images and startling cerebral voyages. Mirrors and reflections, doubling, smells and tastes, and a preoccupation with time and death are characteristic threads in these early experimental death tales, threads which are to be picked up and fully developed in other works. (pp. 99–100)

Perhaps the most striking image of dignity in García Márquez' work, however, is the figure of a woman. In the story that opens *Big Mama's Funeral*, which is also García Márquez's own favorite, "Tuesday Siesta," a woman and her daughter, both dressed in black, get off the train during the heat of the day and ask the priest for permission to visit the cemetery. At first the priest resists, because it is siesta time, but her quiet dignity prevails. In answer to the priest's queries, she states, with her head held high, that she wants to visit her son, who was shot last week for being a thief. The contrast between the ineffectual priest and the proud woman is at its peak when he pompously asks her whether she ever tried to get him on the right track:

> "He was a very good man."
>
> The priest looked first at the woman and then at the girl, and realized with a kind of pious amazement that they were not about to cry. The woman continued in the same tone:
>
> "I told him never to steal anything that anyone needed to eat, and he minded me."

The author tells us that his stories often begin with a visual image rather than an idea. He mentions this story as an example, and it is indeed a convincing one. If his early stories were perhaps too metaphysical, the later collections show a certain influence of his growing interest

and experience in film, and more success in capturing certain feelings and sensations. In "One of These Days" the overwhelming sensation is that of a toothache, set against the backdrop of the wars. It is an episode which appears in a somewhat different version in *In Evil Hour*. In the story the dentist is a courageous partisan on the wrong side. But the balance of power is shifted as a result of the mayor's devastating toothache. He orders the dentist to extract it or be shot. The dentist extracts it without anesthesia with the words: "Now you'll pay for our twenty dead men." The balance of power returns to its earlier status as the dentist sarcastically asks whether to send the bill to the town or to the mayor. "It's the same damn thing" is the mayor's succinct, and accurate, reply. The war and civil repression are skillfully understated, or unstated, in the reaction of the child to the mayor's threat to shoot his father: he registers neither fear nor surprise, so accustomed is he to the violence of the status quo.

"There Are No Thieves in This Town" reminds the reader of Spanish literature of a story by nineteenth-century Valencian novelist Vicente Blasco Ibáñez, "El hallazgo" ("The Windfall"), in which a thief hurriedly grabs a pile of quilts from his victims' house, only to find an infant inside when he arrives at home. His heart goes out to the child, and he returns it to the home, but by now it has gotten late and the family catches him. He goes to jail. The thief in García Márquez's story steals billiard balls, not a child, but he finds himself in a similar situation: what can he do with them? At first he hides them. The whole town is talking the theft, and a victim is found to blame. Since the townspeople don't want to believe it was one of them, they accuse a black man who is passing through. The thief still holds his tongue, but since the town's only recreation was the billiard table, he finally decides to return the balls. The owner accuses him of stealing money as well and takes him to the mayor, "not so much for being a thief as for being a fool." The power of gossip, so central to *In Evil Hour*, is an interesting part of this story. When the thief and his wife go to find out what is being said in the town, they are almost convinced of the townspeople's version of the events, because the people tell what they heard with such conviction.

"Balthazar's Marvelous Afternoon" is the triumph of the nobility of a poor man over the meanness of a rich man, and at the same time of art over political power. Balthazar's beautiful cage, which needs no birds for it could sing by itself, was made with little Pepe Montiel in mind, and cannot be sold to anyone else, even when Pepe's father refuses to pay for it. José Montiel's anger at the construction of the cage for his son is heightened by Balthazar's generosity in giving it to Pepe. Balthazar can't bear the child's tantrum, whereas the father doesn't seem to be affected. José Montiel, however, perceives the gift as a threat to his authority and throws the carpenter out. That the cage had been constructed, that he had not been paid for it, and that he had left it behind do not seem important to Balthazar, until he goes to the bar and sees that the supposed sale is important for his peers, who are delighted at the thought of anyone extracting money from Montiel. Balthazar can't bear to let them down, so when they buy him a beer, he buys rounds for everyone. Since the carpenter is unused to the consumption of alcohol, the festivities excite his dream to build thousands of other cages, selling them all to rich people. His understanding of rich people, from what he has seen, is that they all have ugly and contentious wives, and that they are so unhealthy that they can't even get mad, and that they're all about to die, so he must hurry up with his plans to build cages to sell them. Dead drunk but still clinging to his dream at the end, he realizes that his shoes are being taken, but he doesn't want to break the spell of the happiest dream of his life.

But José Montiel does get mad, and dies from it. His widow is the only person in town in **"Montiel's Widow"** who believes he has died of natural causes. So hated is this usurper of people's land that everyone expected him to die from a bullet in the back. The story explores the widow's world of unreality, and how she benefits from his despotism without knowing what is going on. While Montiel murders his poor enemies and runs the rich ones out of town so he can steal their belongings, she sympathizes with the victims. She believes her husband has helped those who had to flee, and chastises him for helping them, since they won't remember him for it. Since her premise is wrong—that her husband helped them— her conclusion is wrong. They will certainly remember him. The usurped lands are in danger of being taken by others when Montiel is no longer around, but the widow is oblivious to everything, never having been in touch with reality. She urges her children to stay in Europe, and the only time she smiles is when she receives a letter from her daughter describing the pink pigs in the butcher shops of Paris: "At the end of the letter, a hand different from her daughter's had added, 'Imagine! They put the biggest and prettiest carnation in the pig's ass.'" She only wants to stop living. It is Big Mama, in whose house she lives, who tells her in a dream that she will die when the tiredness starts in her arm.

"One Day after Saturday" paints the elderly Father Antonio Isabel as a totally methodical man, always absorbed in the temptations of the senses and how to make sermons out of them, a man who connects the dead birds in the town, not with the record-breaking heat, but with the Apocalypse. He has never been able to persuade the equally aged widow Rebeca to reveal to him the mysterious circumstances of her husband's death years before. When Father Antonia Isabel takes a dying bird into her house, he seems to fear her concupiscence more than the suspicions that she is a murderer. The birds cause his Sunday sermon to turn to the appearance of the Wandering Jew, and when he collects money to fight off the terrible apparition, he gives it to the poor young man who has just arrived in the town seeking his mother's pension. In his mind's wanderings he believes that maybe it is possible to be happy, if only it weren't so hot.

"Artificial Roses" shows the intergenerational tensions in a family as a result of repression and hypocrisy. The roses Mina makes and her false sleeves are as unreal as the appearances she must keep up. Her blind grandmother sees better than anyone into Mina's reality, but only to try to control her behavior. In a comment on madness, which García Márquez deals with in depth in *One Hundred Years of Solitude*, this story shows the lucid grandmother as crazy, but as she says herself, "Apparently you haven't thought of sending me to the madhouse so long as I don't start throwing stones."

The title story in this collection, **"Big Mama's Funeral,"** is the first example of an accumulation of hyperbole, a technique García Márquez uses extremely well here and in later works. An enumeration of Big Mama's properties and powers is endless and fanciful, including a brilliant collection of set phrases particularly from the field of journalism. When she dies, it hadn't occurred to anyone to think she was mortal. In a way she is the prototype of the patriarch to come, though her power is inherited from her family, and kept in part because she never married. Matriarch of everyone and "well enough endowed by Nature to suckle her whole issue all by herself [she] was dying a virgin and childless."

The narrator who tells the whole story in all its details sees his role as protector of the truth against distortions and memory loss, and he is anxious to do so before the historians get hold of it and before the garbage men sweep up the garbage from the funeral forever. This grand funeral is to be attended by the pope, for Big Mama died in the odor of sanctity.

When García Márquez wrote the story, a visit by the pope to Colombia was unthinkable, but even so he changed the physical appearance of the President of the Republic in order not to be accused of pointing to anyone in particular. But by the time the real pope came to Latin America, the President of the Republic fit the description in the story. Big Mama dies as a saint, or at least as much of a saint as the mother of the patriarch, Bendición Alvarado, whom he tries to have canonized. Both Bendición and Big Mama also come almost full circle chronologically, since they are presented after their deaths as young women again. In the case of Big Mama, a photograph of her when she was twenty-two and the printed word make her instantly famous even among those who had never seen her. Big Mama had been more powerful than even the government; her secret estate includes forged electoral certificates. A patriotic hero as well as a saint, she is given the honors due a soldier killed in battle. Big Mama had melted into her own legend. (pp. 109–15)

Two of the stories in the original Spanish *Innocent Eréndira* collection have subtitles indicating that they were written for children. Both **"Un Señor muy viejo con unas alas enormes"** (**"A Very Old Man with Enormous Wings"**) and **"El ahogado más hermoso del mundo"** (**"The Handsomest Drowned Man in the World"**) feature adults with whom children can play, as if they were toys. In both cases, however, other adults in the story end up doing most of the playing with these bizarre humanoids. The very old man who falls to earth is thought to be an angel by some, including the wise woman of the town. But he is treated more as a circus freak, and his hosts, Pelayo and Elisenda, make a fortune charging people to see him. The townspeople's suggestions about what to do with him indicate their typical viewpoints: the simplest want to name him mayor of the world, sterner ones think he should be a five-star general, and visionaries feel he should be put out to stud. Father Gonzaga is put off by the creature's inability to speak Latin, but still indecisive, he writes to Rome for instructions. The miracles the angel supposedly performs are as disoriented as he is himself: the blind man doesn't recover his sight but grows new teeth; the paralytic still can't walk but wins the lottery; and the leper's sores sprout sunflowers. In reality the angel's most salient virtues are passivity and patience. He just wants to get as comfortable as possible, get rid of the insects in his wings, and eat eggplant mush. It is only when the circus comes to town with its own freaks that the attention is diverted, and time passes imperceptibly as the angel regains his strength. He is little more than a nuisance when, having recuperated enough to fly, he waits for the wind and the light to be right and becomes "an imaginary dot on the horizon."

The other strange visitor found by children is Esteban, "the world's handsomest drowned man." They play with him until the adults take over, astonished at his size, beauty, and pride. While the men go to neighboring villages seeking clues to his identity, the woman fall in love with him. They try to make clothes for him, but everything is too small; his inner strength even bursts the buttons on his clothing. Delighted that no family can be found to claim him, they adopt him, giving him a mother and a father and a place to come back to in his posthumous travels. For of course they must bury him, sending him back where he came from: the sea.

His personality also allows them to name him. He cannot be Lautaro, as some of the younger women wanted; he must be Esteban. In death as in life, he doesn't know what to do with his oversized body, and spends most of his time trying to stay out of everyone's way. The only clue about his identity is that the vegetation growing on him is from deep, faraway water, lending support to their adoption of him.

In this story García Márquez dabbles with the technique, later developed in *The Autumn of the Patriarch*, of shifting the narrator and point of view within a single line, tracing, for example, the dialogue between a nervous hostess looking for her strongest chair and an uneasy Esteban trying to avoid embarrassment. Esteban leaves behind his memory for the townspeople, along with the gifts of beauty, generosity, hope, and solidarity his visit inspired in them.

The oldest story in the collection, **"El mar del tiempo perdido"** (**"The Sea of Lost Time"**), also involves an underwater adventure. Mr Herbert and Tobías are alive, but during their voyage they meet many dead people, some who had been there a very long time and had finally reached a state of repose.

When the smell of roses invades the town, Jacob's wife takes it as a premonition of death and asks to be buried alive. She dreads the usual mode of burial in the town: being thrown off the cliffs into the sea. Actually, the smell forebodes the arrival of Mr. Herbert, the gringo who exploits the town under the guise of charity. He arrives with all kinds of promises and trunks full of money, which his Protestant ethic won't allow him to give away without some kind of performance in return. Not unlike the foreign companies he represents, he leaves with much more than he came with. In a panorama of time the sea with its dead people is the past; the town with its unnatural smell of roses is the present; and Mr. Herbert's description of glass houses is the only vision of the future.

"Muerte constante más allá del amor" (**"Death Constant Beyond Love"**) is a delicious political satire which appears as a story in the collection, but is incorporated into the *Innocent Eréndira* film as an episode in which Eréndira visits Senator Onésimo Sánchez. In the story the senator and the situation are the same, but the protagonist is not Eréndira but Laura Farina. The favor she wants is papers legalizing her father's presence in the country, and of course her proposed method of payment is inexorably the same. The difficulty is that her father has locked up her private parts in some sort of chastity belt, to which only he has the key. The senator's demise is exactly as predicted, with him raging at dying without her.

The senator's reelection campaign techniques show him for the phony he is; he parades cardboard buildings and even an ocean liner through town. But he also speaks the truth to his supporters: his election is just as important to them as to him, for they live on his power. Shown as a cheap politician building dependencies on himself, he is a possible version of the patriarch in his early days. Nelson Farina, Laura's father, recognizes him for what he is: "le Blacamén [sic] de la politique."

He is referring to the two opposing characters in another story, **"Blacamán el bueno vendedor de milagros"** (**"Blacamán the Good, Vendor of Miracles"**). The narrator claims for himself the epithet "the Good" and refers to his employer as "the Bad." In fact, both Blacamáns are rogues totally without scruples in their dealings with the public and fiendishly cruel to each other. The Bad hires the Good to aid him as a swindler because of his foolish face, very helpful in his trade of selling all manner of deceitful merchandise with proclaimed magical properties to the unwary. After a sadistic torture scene the Good acquires magical properties and takes his revenge, which consists of reviving his dead mentor to live forever within his grave.

Like **"The Handsomest Drowned Man in the World," "Blacamán"** uses long sentences within which can be found shifting narrators with their necessarily changing speech patterns and identifying tags.

A barb at the viceroys is not lacking in this pungent story, as Blacamán's embalming technique makes them govern better dead than when they were alive; the marines, too, come in for attack. Fooled by Blacamán's elixirs, they take after him, killing everyone in their paths, "not only the natives, out of precaution, but also the Chinese, for distraction, the Negroes, from habit, and the Hindus, because they were snake charmers."

The story that develops the shifting narrative technique to the fullest in this collection is **"El último viaje del buque fantasma" ("The Last Voyage of the Ghost Ship")**. Again the narrator is a young man. His goal in life, once he has seen the fabulous, immense liner, is to prove its existence to others, thereby affirming his worth. At sea in his little boat, he spots the ship during the intervals when the beam from the lighthouse is not shining on it, for it disappears with the flash of light. Both Sir Francis Drake and William Dampier make their way into this story, representing death and fear, respectively. The narrator's obsession absorbs the reader with the appearance, once a year on a Wednesday in March, of the phantasmagoric vessel until, to prove his version of reality, he leads the ship to crash in the port as he shouts, "There it is, you cowards, a second before the huge steel cask shattered the ground and one could hear the neat destruction of ninety thousand five hundred champagne glasses breaking, one after the other, from stem to stern." The story, like the last section of *The Autumn of the Patriarch*, is told in a single sentence, and is replete with striking visual imagery, mostly related to the sea,—for example, the "lovemaking of manta rays in a springtime of sponges."

Something of a folk tale with its engagingly long title, its monstrous grandmother with green blood, and the charming, angelic hero Ulises, **"The Incredible and Sad Tale of Innocent Eréndira and Her Heartless Grandmother"** blends legend, myth, allegory, and previous literature into its rich tapestry. Though all four elements of the universe that fascinated medieval readers are evident—the sea as water, the desert as earth, the fire that twice dooms Eréndira—it is the presence of the wind that overwhelms. From the very first line, when the "wind of her misfortune began to blow," it is connected with Eréndira's fate. The missionaries capture her while a wind almost as fierce is blowing, treating Eréndira to a shift in her history of exploitation from her grandmother to the church. The wind of her misfortune blows again before

her fateful attempt to escape with the hapless Ulises, and finally she runs into the wind of the desert, never to be heard from again. The photographer too is subject to the wind, and in fact travels wherever it takes him.

The subjection to nature, specifically the wind, parallels Eréndira's maddeningly passive acceptance of her fate. She is treated as a virtual slave by her grandmother from earliest childhood, and the exploitation of prostitution is merely added on to her other tasks. Her trip to the convent breaks, at least for a time, the endless parade of men waiting for her favors, but her duties within the walls consist of whitewashing the stairs every time anyone goes up or down them. When Grandmother finally devises a way of getting her back, Eréndira has her moment to speak but returns, inevitably, to her. In fact, rebelling doesn't occur to her until Grandmother herself, albeit unwittingly, suggests it; before Grandmother's monologue envisioning Eréndira's future life without her, that possibility hadn't crossed the girl's mind. Afterward it obsesses her. Unable to murder the old lady herself, she enlists the help of her hero, Ulises.

But Ulises is really not much of a hero, and at first the great lady is too much for him. Eréndira is impatient with his failed attempts, and when he succeeds, his painful shouts are more those of a son than of a lover, and Eréndria is gone, forever, with the gold. Eréndira, seeing the face of her dead grandmother, has attained the maturity that eluded her during the twenty years of her misfortune.

Grandmother is a total exploiter, with no redeeming value, not only of Eréndira but of everyone. As if she were running a company store, she deducts so much from the Indians who work for her that they have hardly anything left. She settles accounts with the musicians by her sleight-of-hand figuring, having them play two happy numbers for every waltz, to avoid paying them what she already owes them. She wants the photographer to pay for the music too, even though, as he points out, it doesn't come out in the pictures. She argues with him that it isn't fair to have a poor innocent child paying for everything. Indeed.

Her unremitting evil underscores the irony of her having to get a letter of recommendation for her good character, for the person she gets it from is every bit as degenerate as herself, the very Sentator Onésimo Sánchez. The letter serves its purpose even though the policeman she shows it to when she needs to recapture Eréndira can't read.

Eréndira has few happy moments. When she first hears music, during her stay in the convent, she knows happiness perhaps for the first time. It is not enough to keep her inside, but perhaps it offsets the endless whitewashing of the stairs. The truck loader treats her with tenderness instead of the brutality she is accustomed to, and she makes love with him willingly. But it is Ulises who first makes her laugh. She is charmed, she says, by the serious way the golden lad talks about nonsense. Indeed it seems like nonsense to readers as well as to Eréndira that his father's oranges might be worth 50,000 pesos each, but that is before we find out that each one contains a large diamond. In this exchange, García Márquez might be showing his own penchant for saying outrageous things with deadpan straight delivery, a characteristic, he claims, that he learned from his grandmother and to which he attributes a measure of his success as a storyteller.

One must accuse him of exaggeration only with great caution, however. Clearly he's having great fun at the expense of the mayor, whose job consists of shooting clouds to make it rain. But the *Wall Street Journal* of 6 August 1985 ran a story about Spanish farmers who are convinced that it is sinister planes that come and attack their thunderclouds, keeping them from raining on their parched fields.

The church comes under attack as well, along with its intransigent representatives from the Iberian Peninsula. Just as the priest in *In Evil Hour* argued with the judge's woman that she should marry now to legitimize the child she will have, the priests search the highways, byways, and remotest villages for pregnant Indian women to persuade or force them to marry. The resistance is always for the same reason: they receive better treatment as concubines than as wives. But they finally succumb, usually to treachery or a pair of flashy earrings.

The depiction of the lack of communication within marriage is wryly humorous as well. Ulises's father is Dutch, his mother Indian. Each speaks to him in her or his language and wants to know what the other has said, to which Ulises's usual response seems to be "Nothing special."

Though nearly the entire story is told in third-person narration, García Márquez indulges in a curious example of first-person intrusion into the text, the details of which are accurately autobiographical. Just after the unsuccessful escape attempt, the author begins to tell the story himself, explaining that it was at that point in time that he knew the protagonists. It would not be until much later, however, that he would tell the tale, inspired by the singer Rafael Escalona, who composed one of his pieces about them. Saying that he was there to sell encyclopedias, the narrator blends back into the atmosphere of their greatest splendor, when they attracted the circus with its Blacamán, its girl who had been transformed into a spider for disobeying her parents, and its announcement of the arrival of the astral bat. (pp. 120–29)

With the exception of the very earliest stories, all García Márquez's works usually considered minor are characterized by their very visual imagery. One can easily believe him when he states that his stories usually start with an image in the mind's eye, and can appreciate the influence film has had on his fiction. Some critics have said that all the early works are understudies, sketches, or

outlines for the masterpiece that follows, but each taken separately has its own special quality, and taken together these early works form an impressive body of literature. (p. 130)

Kathleen McNerney, in her *Understanding Gabriel García Márquez*, University of South Carolina Press, 1989, 180 p.

MICHIKO KAKUTANI
(essay date 1993)

[Below, Kakutani reviews García Márquez's collection of short stories entitled *Strange Pilgrims*, comparing its literary style and techniques to his earlier works.]

There are moments in these 12 stories that are instantly, incontestably recognizable as the work of Gabriel García Márquez. In **"María dos Prazeres,"** an aging prostitute picks out her own cemetery plot and teaches her little dog to cry at her grave. In **"I Sell My Dreams,"** a Colombian woman finds permanent employment as the intepreter of dreams for a wealthy family. In **"Light Is Like Water,"** an entire fourth-grade class drowns in an apartment flooded with light.

Such bizarre, hallucinatory scenes in *Strange Pilgrims* will remind the reader of the plague of insomnia and the rain of yellow blossoms in *One Hundred Years of Solitude,* the 1970 masterpiece that first made Americans aware of the astonishing magic acts Mr. García Márquez could perform. The fact remains, however, that that novel—like such later ones as *The Autumn of the Patriarch* (1976), *Love in the Time of Cholera* (1988) and *The General in His Labyrinth* (1990)—grounded its more spectacular acts of sleight of hand in a Faulknerian sense of the past. In these commodious novels, Mr. García Márquez mapped out the spiritual geography of a fictional Latin America, creating history out of the tangled, overlapping stories of his characters' lives, and conjuring myths out of their troubled dreams.

As *Strange Pilgrims* unfortunately demonstrates, the shorter form of the story does not lend itself to such huge, looping narratives. What's more, the tales in this volume are all set in Europe—they more or less concern Latin Americans traveling or living abroad—and most of them lack the fierce, visionary senses of time and place that distinguish Mr. García Márquez's strongest fiction. Indeed, these stories tend to feel like disembodied fairy tales: flimsy, oddly generic tales that for all their charm fail to impress themselves upon the reader's imagination.

In a prologue to the book, Mr. García Márquez points out that the stories were written intermittently over a period of 18 years: some began as journalistic notes, some as screenplays, and one as television serial. They were written and rewritten in starts and stops: some were lost or temporarily abandoned before being reconstructed; all were revised after the author revisited several European cities last year.

This peripatetic history perhaps explains why these stories are so uneven. **"Sleeping Beauty and the Airplane"**—which concerns a traveler's crush on the beautiful woman he's sitting next to on a plane—is a silly sketch that belongs in a notebook, not a published book. And **"The Ghosts of August,"** which concerns a family's encounter with a haunted house, reads like a mediocre parody of Edgar Allan Poe. As for **"I Only Came to Use the Phone"** and **"The Trail of Your Blood in the Snow,"** both are highly contrived O. Henry-like stories that pivot around the same device: a woman's mysterious disappearance into the bureaucratic clutches of an institution—in the first case, an asylum; in the second, a hospital.

The more persuasive stories in *Strange Pilgrims* unfold delicately, like complicated origami constructions, to delineate a character's entire life. Each of these tales is written from the vantage point of old age, and each of them possesses a tone of melancholy wisdom reminiscent of *Love in the Time of Cholera.*

"Bon Voyage, Mr. President" movingly depicts the shabby exile of a former Latin American ruler in Switzerland, and his incongruous friendship with an ambulance driver who had hoped to exploit his nonexistent riches. **"The Saint"** recounts the story of a persistent pilgrim from Colombia, who has come to Rome with the eerily preserved body of his late daughter, hoping to persuade the Pope to make her a saint. And **"María dos Prazeres"** relates the story of a whore who has spent decades trying to transform herself into a respectable Barcelona lady.

These tales knit together Mr. García Márquez's natural storytelling talents with his highly tuned radar for images that bridge the world of reality and the world of dreams. Gracefully written as these stories are, they lack the emotional depth of field found in Mr. García Márquez's novels. They leave the reader beguiled, but hungry for something more.

Michiko Kakutani, "Gabriel García Márquez, Short Form," in *The New York Times*, October 15, 1993.

SOURCES FOR FURTHER STUDY

Bloom, Harold, ed. *Gabriel García Márquez.* New York: Chelsea House, 1989, 306 p.

 A collection of essays touching on numerous aspects of García Márquez's writings, such as his use of scientific paradigms, myths and fantasy, parody, ritual, politics, and his connection with the works of William Faulkner.

Buford, Bill. "Haughty Falconry and Collective Guilt." *The Times Literary Supplement*, No. 4145 (September 10, 1982): 965.

 Contends that García Márquez's journalistic style in *Chronicle of a Death Foretold* successfully creates a "political fable" designed to criticize Latin American social values.

Burns, Graham. "García Márquez and the Idea of Solitude." *The Critical Review* No. 27 (1985): 18–33.

 Analyzes the character development, themes, and structure of García Márquez's *One Hundred Years of Solitude*, contending that the make-believe world of Macondo is a dynamic but compressed vision of the real world.

Byk, John. "From Fact to Fiction: Gabriel García Márquez and the Short Story." *Mid-American Review* VI, No. 2 (1986): 111–16.

Maintains that García Márquez 's extensive use of journalism and magical realism may have obscured his Marxian concern for his people, their history, and the twentieth-century world.

Janes, Regina. *Gabriel García Márquez.* Columbia, Mo.: University of Missouri Press, 1981, 115 p.

 Examines García Márquez's literary creativity—with particular reference to *One Hundred Years of Solitude, The Autumn of the Patriarch, No One Writes to the Colonel*, and *In Evil Hour*—asserting that these imaginative writings reflect no particular political ideas.

Malm, Ulf. "Reading Gabriel García Márquez." *Studia Neophilologica* LXI, No. 1 (1989): 77–88.

 Investigates García Márquez's narrative principles and his use of hyperbole in four of his short stories—"El mar del tiempo perfido," "Un señor muy viejo con unas alas enormes," "El ahogado más hermoso del mundo," and " La incréible y triste historia de la candida Eréndira y de su abuela desalmada."

McMurray, George R., ed. *Critical Essays on Gabriel García Márquez.* Boston, Mass.: G. K. Hall, 1987, 224 p.

 Collected essays on García Márquez and his works, including biography, book reviews, and articles discussing his themes and literary technique, with a particular emphasis on *One Hundred Years of Solitude*.

Ortega, Julio, and Elliott, Claudia, eds. *Gabriel García Márquez and the Powers of Fiction*. Austin: University of Texas Press, 1988, 96 p.

> Collected essays assessing García Márquez's narrative style, his use of myth, and the influence of journalism on his writings.

Pierce, Robert N. "Fact or Fiction? The Developmental Journalism of Gabriel García Márquez." *Journal of Popular Culture* 22, No. 1 (Summer 1988): 63–71.

> Examines the style of García Márquez's novels, comparing and contrasting them with his journalism.

Porter, Lawrence M. "The Political Function of Fantasy in García Márquez." *The Centennial Review* XXX, No. 2 (Spring 1986): 196–207.

Contends that García Márquez uses fantasy to foster his personal political agenda.

Williams, Raymond. "An Introduction to the Early Journalism of García Márquez: 1948–1958." *Latin American Literary Review* XIII, No. 25 (January–June 1985): 117–32.

> Examines García Márquez's writings which "range from political commentary to fiction," detailing journalistic elements, the use of hyperbole, and other writing techniques.

———. "The Visual Arts, the Poetization of Space and Writing: An Interview with Gabriel García Márquez," *Publications of the Modern Language Association* 104, No. 2 (March 1989): 131–40.

> García Márquez reflects on the techniques, ideas, and themes used in the construction of his novels—*One Hundred Years of Solitude*, *The Autumn of the Patriarch*, and *Love in the Time of Cholera*.

Additional coverage of García Márquez's life and career is contained in the following sources published by Gale Research: *Authors and Artists for Young People*, Vol. 3; *Bestsellers* 89:1, 90:4; *Contemporary Authors*, Vols. 33-36; *Contemporary Authors New Revision Series*, Vols. 10, 28; *Contemporary Literary Criticism*, Vols. 2, 3, 8, 10, 15, 27, 47, 55; *Dictionary of Literary Biography*, Vol. 113; *Discovering Authors*; *Hispanic Writers*; *Major Twentieth Century Writers*; *Short Story Criticism*, Vol. 8; and *World Literature Criticism*.

Juan Goytisolo

1931–

Spanish novelist, essayist, short story writer, travel writer, and autobiographer.

INTRODUCTION

Goytisolo is widely considered the greatest modern Spanish novelist. Praised for the power and originality of his prose, he has repeatedly assailed Spanish history and culture, as well as the Spanish language itself. Although the author has spent nearly his entire career in self-imposed exile, critic Michael Ugarte has noted that "Spain is perhaps the most crucial theme in Goytisolo's works, for it is the inspiration for the declamatory and aggressive nature of his novels." Goytisolo himself has claimed, "I don't know of any contemporary author who has pondered Spain's cultural roots as much as I."

Goytisolo was born in Barcelona shortly before the outbreak of the Spanish Civil War. When he was just seven years old, his mother was killed during a Nationalist bombardment. Soon after her death, the family fled the city for a small village, where Juan, his sister Marta, and his brothers José-Augustín and Luis (both of whom are also writers) were raised by their father, a former executive at a chemical company. Goytisolo attended Jesuit schools before enrolling at Barcelona University to study law. After a brief stay there he transferred to the University of Madrid, but soon abandoned his studies to work on his first novel, *Juegos de manos* (1954; *The Young Assassins*). Frustrated by the lack of artistic freedom in his homeland, Goytisolo traveled to Paris in 1957, accepting employment with the Gallimard publishing house; he decided to remain in France and wrote prolifically over the course of the next decade. During this time he met Monique Lange, whom he later married, and also traveled to northern Africa, becoming enamored with its languages, cultures, and natural beauty. He began to explore his own bisexuality, which played an increasingly important role in his writing. Although the rise of democracy in Spain allowed him the option of returning to his native country, Goytisolo has chosen to remain away, lecturing worldwide and dividing his remaining time between Marrakech, Morocco, where he lives with his male companion, and Paris, where he resides with his wife.

Goytisolo's oeuvre, which encompasses novels, stories, essays, and travelogues, displays a wide range of purpose, mood, and style. Critics have typically divided his work into two periods, the first of which precedes the publication of *Señas de identidad* [*Marks of Identity*] in 1966. Following the objectivist approach of his one-time mentor Alain Robbe-Grillet, Goytisolo in his early work sought to present precise, accurate descriptions of social reality. Despite his preference for an objective style, however, Goytisolo believed that the novel should function as social and political commentary. Impassioned by this belief, his work resulted in what Charlene Suscavage has described as "a relentless condemnation of Spanish society." His first novel *The Young Assassins*, for which the author became known as a member of Spain's "restless generation," portrayed a group of bourgeois youths rebelling against the apparent meaninglessness of their privileged existence. Praising the work for its "flavor of genuine tragedy," reviewer David Dempsey wrote that *The Young Assassins* "begins where the novels of a writer like Jack Kerouac leave off." Goytisolo next published *Duelo en el paraíso* (1955; *Children of Chaos*), which has been compared with Anthony Burgess's *A Clockwork Orange* and William Golding's *Lord of the Flies* for its portrayal of a nihilistic adolescent subculture—this time in the aftermath of the Spanish Civil War. Goytisolo followed *Children of Chaos* with "The Ephemeral Morrow," a trilogy consisting of *El circo* (1957), *Fiestas* (1958; *Fiestas*), and *La resaca* (1958). In these works he remained largely true to his objectivist theory of the novel, which he expressed more formally in a collection of essays entitled *Problemas de la novela* (1959). During this early period he also published two politically-oriented travelogues, *Campos de Níjar* (1960; *The Countryside of Nijar*) and *La chanca* (1962; *La chanca*); *La isla* (1961; *Island of women*) a short novel originally intended as a screenplay; and *Fin de fiesta* (1962; *The Party's Over*), a collection of short stories that essentially concluded his objectivist phase.

Marks of Identity marks the beginning of what Goytisolo has called his mature work. His break with realism became evident in that novel's experiments with characterization and narrative structure. According to Abigail Lee Six, "one of the reasons for the shift in the author's style of writing. . . is precisely his awareness that fiction is not fact, that literature is not history and that being a responsible novelist is primarily concerned with taking language and literature seriously, not life, past or present." Goytisolo outlined his new

theories in a collection of essays entitled *El furgón de cola* (1967). *Marks of Identity*, the first novel in "The Mendiola Trilogy," a group of works named for Goytisolo's autobiographical protagonist and narrator, Alvaro Mendiola, portrays the desolation of Spain's sociocultural life; the second novel in the trilogy, *Reivindicación del conde don Julián* (1974; *Count Julian*), attacks Spain itself. Widely recognized as Goytisolo's masterpiece, *Count Julian* inverts Spanish legend in that Julián, traditionally viewed as a traitor who betrayed his country to the Moors, becomes the hero of the story, punishing Spain for its cruelty and hypocrisy. Carlos Fuentes has written that the work is "the most beautifully cruel requiem yet written by a Spaniard for his native land. . . . [Nothing] reaches quite the peak of intense hatred and horror that Goytisolo achieves in this novel." The last work of the trilogy, *Juan sin tierra* (1975; *Juan the Landless*), features Goytisolo's attack on the Spanish language, which he views as the principal weapon of dictatorial oppressors, insisting that it be destroyed and replaced. For Goytisolo, the Mendiola trilogy metaphorically annihilated Spain; while his homeland has not been conspicuous in his subsequent writings, his deep sense of alienation is evident in their relentlessly disorienting portrayals of human nature.

Carlos Fuentes has written that "Goytisolo is obviously out to destroy what he sees as an old and oppressive language, create a new one, and make the novel the vehicle for this operation." In doing so, the author has not only radically deviated from standard narrative structures, but has also incorporated thematic elements that were once taboo—deviant sexual practices, drugs, rape—into his commentary. While some critics have complained about his violent, often repulsive images (Anatole Broyard has remarked of *Count Julian*, "Don Quixote no longer tilts at windmills, but toilets"), admirers view them as an important part of Goytisolo's efforts to subvert conventional language: by desensitizing the reader to the connotations of specific words, he attempts to effect a change in the language itself. Critics have also commented on the "rewriting" of classic texts in his work, debating whether these are conscious manipulations or simply unfortunate misreadings. Ugarte has pointed out that "Goytisolo mimics his predecessors and subverts their intentions. . . he infiltrates a previous text, corrupts its meaning, and disguises himself as an embodiment of the very culture he violates." Goytisolo has identified himself with a literary heritage which includes Miguel de Cervantes, Fernando de Rojas, Laurence Sterne, Luis de Gongora, Marquis de Sade, and Louis Ferdinand Celine, and critics have frequently made comparisons between him and James Joyce, another writer in exile and assailant of traditional language. Fuentes has also linked the two: "Joyce, Goytisolo: exiles condemned to live with the language of their oppressions, digest it, expel it, trample on it, and then resign themselves: these words, returned to the earth, will fertilize the earth and be reborn, hated, transfigured, a necessary object of both the refusal of and the need for communication."

CRITICAL COMMENTARY

CARLOS FUENTES

(essay date 1974)

[Fuentes is a prolific, versatile Mexican writer noted for his innovations in language and narrative technique. His concern for affirming a viable Mexican identity is revealed in his allegorical and thematic use of his country's history and legend—from the myths of the Aztecs to the Mexican Revolution. In the following excerpt, Fuentes offers a favorable review of *Count Julian*, calling the novel "the most terrible attack against the oppressive forces of a nation that I have ever read."]

Count Julian is a shout from the heart and the belly of a modern Spaniard against the triumph of all that killed the promise of freedom and love and joy in Spain. It is a fierce answer to the Spanish decadence that began in the instant of Spanish glory. It is a mockery no other writer has dared make of the hollow imperial gesture by which Spain defeated herself, fatally cut herself off from the human, cultural and economic resources that fled with the expulsion of the Jews and the defeat of the Arabs. It is, at times, the caricature of a caricature; the fruitless energies that Spain, as appointed *defensor fides*, spent fighting against the Reformation; the paralysis and quarantine Spain imposed on herself against the diseases of modernity; the cult of appearances, honor, purity and orthodoxy and the verbal masks created to uphold appearances and give them a semblance of reality; the fading away of the Habsburg and Bourbon dynasties into insanity, hemophilia, syphilis, frivolity and just plain idiocy.

Goya and Buñuel have given us the images of this history. Goytisolo attacks its language. Behind his assault on the consecrated language of Spain linger the voices of the mystics, growing ever dimmer and finally dying for lack of contact with living flesh. Goytisolo is keenly conscious that the last erotic novel written in Spanish was Delicado's "La Lozana Andaluza" (1528). The language of Spain became as hollow as the power it sustained. The sins of poverty and isolation became virtues. Literature celebrated the uniqueness of Spain's proud past and miserable present. The will to empire was ridiculously kept alive in a flame of rhetoric. Ethical superiority was found in empty gestures of honor, cruelty and intolerance. Metaphysical meanings were read into the starkness of a landscape that had voluntarily refused beauty: is there anything more contrasting than the pleasure gardens of the Alhambra and the granite mausoleum of El Escorial?

This is the language that, finally, Spanish Fascism made its own. It's been a long, weary road from Cervantes to the laudatory editorials in the Franco press, and Juan Goytisolo, the foremost novelist of contemporary Spain, is furiously unhappy about it. In *Count Julian*, he takes the totality of Spanish language and history, traps it, imprisons it, encapsulates it, digests it and then expells it. The vehicle of this cannibalistic and excremential adventure is the Count Don Julian, a traitor redeemed. Goytisolo's book is the most beautifully cruel requiem yet written by a Spaniard for his native land.

A traitor redeemed. Gore Vidal has done his antimanichean bit for the arch-villain of American history, Aaron Burr, and now along comes Juan Goytisolo to revindicate Count Don Julian, the super-traitor of official Spanish history who, according to most accounts, in 711 opened the doors of the Peninsula to the Islamic invasion that was to overrun a vast portion of Iberia and create a distinctive Hispano-Arab civilization around such centers as Cordoba, Seville and Granada. Vidal and Goytisolo are both mythoclasts searching for a second truth behind the masks of hypocrisy.

Yet there is an important difference between the American and the Spanish novelist. Vidal can demolish

Principal Works

Juegos de manos (novel) 1954
  [*The Young Assassins*, 1959]

Duelo en el paraíso (novel) 1955
  [*Children of Chaos*, 1958]

El circo (novel) 1957

Fiestas (novel) 1958
  [*Fiestas*, 1960]

La resaca (novel) 1958

Problemas de la novela (essays) 1959

Campos de Níjar (travel narrative) 1960
  [*The Countryside of Nijar* in *The Countryside of Nijar
  and La chanca*, 1987]

La isla (novel) 1961
  [*Island of Women*, 1962; also published as *Sands of
  Torremolinos*, 1962]

La chanca (travel narrative) 1962
  [*La chanca* in *The Countryside of Nijar* and *La chanca*,
  1987]

*Fin de fiesta: Tentativas de interpretación de una historia
  amorosa* (short stories) 1962
  [*The Party's Over: Four Attempts to Define a Love
  Story*, 1966]

Señas de identidad (novel) 1966
  [*Marks of Identity*, 1969]

El furgón de cola (essays) 1967

Reivindicación del conde don Julián (novel) 1970
  [*Count Julian*, 1974]

Juan sin tierra (novel) 1975
  [*Juan the Landless*, 1977]

*Disidencias (essays) 1977

Obras completas (novels, travelogues, short stories, essays) 1977

Libertad, libertad, libertad (essays and speeches) 1978

Makbara (novel) 1980
  [*Makbara*, 1981]

*Crónicas sarracinas (travel narrative) 1982

Paisajes después de la batalla (novel) 1982
  [*Landscapes after the Battle*, 1987]

*Contracorrientes (essays) 1985

Coto vedado (autobiography) 1985
  [*Forbidden Territory: The Memoirs of Juan Goytisolo*,
  1989]

En los reinos de taifa (autobiography) 1986
  [*Realms of Strife: The Memoirs of Juan Goytisolo,
  1956–1982*, 1990]

Las virtudes del pájaro solitario (novel) 1988
  [*The Virtues of the Solitary Bird*, 1993]

La cuarentena (novel) 1991

*Portions of these works have been translated in *Saracen
  Chronicles: A Selection of Literary Essays*, 1992.

---

myths with a prose that is by now proverbially urbane and witty, self-possessed and capable of recreating history critically without a noticeable break in the structure of the language employed. One has a sense of an evolving tradition, of language as a continually and finely honed instrument of upper-class American irony. Vidal is at odds with ideas, not with the language that expresses them.

Goytisolo, on the contrary, must first break with his own language in order to oppose and expose traditional history. His enterprise offers a dual aspect: attack the myths, and do so by assailing the language on which the myths rest. *Count Julian* is, first and foremost, an adventure of language, a critical battle against the language appropriated by power in Spain. It is also a search for a new/old language that would offer an alternative for the future but also a fecund linkage with the outlawed Arab and Jewish strains. *Count Julian* is a book written against all the stylistic rules of the Royal Academy and against the precept set down by the hidebound scholar Menendez y Pelayo: "Tolerance is the easy virtue . . . Intolerance is the forceful law of human intelligence." *Count Julian* turns the tables on this Hispanic dogma and applies to all things deemed pure and orthodox in Spain the same intolerance Spain has inflicted on all things deemed by her to be impure and heterodox.

The American reader of this breathtakingly urgent novel should bear these considerations in mind if he is to read Goytisolo's book fruitfully and admit its unconventional form as a necessity and not as a writer's whim. It would be wise to place *Count Julian* in the perspective of the increasing world literature of cultural revisionism. It should certainly be read and appreciated by Americans with deep second thoughts about their own history, society and culture, for *Count Julian* represents for Spain what a combined critical consciousness of black, Indian, Chicano, Women's Liberation and Gay Power attitudes would represent in the United States. There is a difference, however. The contesting minorities in the United States have questioned a success story. Goytisolo is questioning a failure. The risks he takes are proportionately greater.

From the high belvedere of Tangier, rising above the sounds and noises and smells of the Arab world (and how strongly and beautifully and sadly Goytisolo describes them), the ghost of Count Julian, or his present-day incarnation, looks across the Straits of Gibraltar at the "enemy coast . . . the scar dripping poison on the other shore of the sea," and wishes that like "a new Atlantis" Spain will at last founder and disappear from sight: "a terrible cataclysm, a blessed relief."

The setting and action are deceptively simple. They belong to an instant in the Casbah of Tangier. As in Malcolm Lowry's "Under the Volcano," a few insistent signs fix the scene: a poster for a blood-donating campaign; the queues lined up in front of a theater showing a James Bond movie; a group of American tourists; a beggar boy; a gagged woman. Count Julian is near and far from this scene, as he is near and far from Spain. The coast is "within arm's reach"; history recedes to the time of Julian's treason. The year is 711. The congealed instant is liberated by the streaming consciousness of Julian as he lies next to Tariq, his ally, perhaps his lover, the namesake of the first Arab invader, in a haze of fragrant Kif-pipe smoke, isolated by hallucination and, in his drugged hypersensual mind and body, destroying Spain with a double-edged scimitar of mind and body.

This is the basic structure of **Count Julian** and it reveals Goytisolo's intentions neatly. Count Julian and his Moslem cohorts can only invade Spain again in the imagination and with words, but words and the imagination can be explosively powerful when wielded against a closed society that forbids the invention of another reality, a second reality that is like an acid mirror, dissolving the preserved features of a worn-out hag. Spain is the hag. The novel is the mirror.

What does this mirror offer to the "harsh homeland" that has banned Goytisolo's novel? An image of stone, a fortress of grandeur, the will to empire, honor and purity symbolized in the sacred grotto, the inviolate cave of virginal sex, virginal language, virginal stoicism: a virginal pedigree of essences that date back to Seneca, the Goths, the Cid . . . and culminate in the figure of the Omnipresent Caudillo, Franco, a stock-company *hidalgo* surrounded by the garbage of tourist-raped beaches, crumbling skyscrapers and not-so-hard currencies sent home by migrant workers.

Spain imports tourists and exports chambermaids. Spain is ripe for Count Julian's imaginary invasion. Count Julian has returned to betray contemporary Spain, which has become "the zero of her nothingness." "Tomorrow is another day," he murmurs, almost like a whimsical Scarlett O'Hara. But then he adds: "The invasion will begin all over again," and this time his tone is fierce with the lust for vengeance: Count Julian is an atrocious Count of Monte Cristo.

And like an Edmond Dantés risen from the jails of Spain, he goes about his task of treason by collecting dead insects and then pressing them between the leaves of the

books he hates; the volumes and volumes of rhetoric, purity and intolerance are forever stained by the squashed bodies of flies, bees and fleas. He chops down the rustling elms, the chaste poplars, the dark majestic oaks that are supposed to signify the mystical aureole of Spain. He defiles the stark plateau of Castile and its "obscene metaphysical connotations." He kicks sweet little old ladies riding on fluffy burros.

He severs the ringed fingers of the figurines of the Holy Mother. He introduces hashish in communion wafers. He plays Rolling Stones' records in convents as the nuns unzip their habits, appear in black silk pajamas, dance a collective striptease and flagellate themselves in an orgy of sexual and religious perversity. He transforms a somber Holy Week procession of penitents, crossbearers and hooded flagellants into a conga line and a free-for-all tropical carnival. He destroys the heraldic Spanish he-goat and populates Castile with kangaroos. He gives his infested blood, treacherous and Moorish, to the Red Cross campaign. He exiles from the Spanish language all un-Spanish words and beats the purists at their own game; they cannot even scream *ole!* in the bullring, since it is nothing but the Arabic *wallah!*

Spain fights back; it calls forth all its resources. Seneca is re-elected as the champion of a stoicism that is the natural ally of Christianity, but Seneca is devoured by the immense pile of refuse of the consumer society and the "in" kids wearing Bonnie and Clyde berets and fedoras and Pierre Cardin ties. The essential Castilian, Don Alvaro, takes the podium and recites the lists of Gothic Kings and the imperial territories of Spain as his mask expands and his words shrink and shrink: ethical emanations, metaphysical vistas, are called to the rescue. Alas, the words have become illegible under Count Julian's swarming army of squashed insects.

Back to the caves, then, back to Altamira and its essential bull, back to troglodyte prehistory rather than accept change and infection. Back to the Cave. Count Julian has expected this. The final refuge of Spain is "the Stupid [Vagina]" its "national emblem, sanctuary and grotto, citadel and cavern, bastion and alcazar." Against the Cave, Count Julian wields the Serpent capable of raping the cave and showing Spain to herself as the whore she is.

At this level, Goytisolo's novel achieves a final, sadistic horror and beauty. Once the women of Spain get acquainted with Count Julian's serpent, they reject "the limp as lettuce [penises] offered by the Spanish males." And once he has had the women, Julian goes after the men. To save themselves from the supreme disgrace of sodomy, Spanish males offer Julian their mothers, wives and sisters. To no avail. Count Julian will destroy and defile all.

He will disguise himself as Granny and receive Alvarito, the male adolescent version of the essential Don Alvaro, in his embrace. Alvarito will be dressed in a red riding hood and remark how odd his Granny looks this afternoon: an Arab with tiger's eyes, a handlebar mustache and razor sharp claws "capable of tearing a pack of cards in two." Alvarito shall be sodomized by Count Julian in Granny's garb; then the boy's throat will be slit.

Is this all the destruction that the avenging Count Julian can wreak on Spain? The final pages of this landmark novel of Spanish literature hold a terrifying secret. Count Julian's serpent has violated the grotto of Spanish purity. But once inside the stony fortress, Count Julian himself is ensnared, and from inside the cave, his serpent a blade of stone, his words a putrid marsh, he himself a prisoner of Spain, he proceeds to the final task of destruction from within: a sickness, a rotting, a humiliation that fully realizes the Marquis de Sade's vision of the eternal crime—one that beyond the acts, dreams and even the death of the criminal would continue to breed general corruption.

And so, Count Julian will rest after seven days of destruction. He has infected, mocked and debased the Catholic kings, the Inquisition, the Catholic Church, the Dictionary of the Royal Academy and El Caudillo's silver wedding anniversary. He has wreaked the vengeance of the expelled Jews, the vanquished Arabs, the silenced writers, the repressed lovers. *Count Julian* is the most terrible attack against the oppressive forces of a nation that I have ever read. Nothing that black has written against white, or woman against man, or poor against rich, or son against father, reaches quite the peak of intense hatred and horror that Goytisolo achieves in this novel. That he does it with magnificent beauty and perfect craftsmanship only adds to the power of his invective against his "harsh homeland." It is quite a feat, and quite a risk, for the novelist works with words, yet he is conscious that "violence is mute." (pp. 5–7)

Carlos Fuentes, "A Fierce Answer to Spanish Decadence," in *The New York Times Book Review*, May 5, 1974, pp. 5–7.

JUAN GOYTISOLO WITH JULIO ORTEGA

(interview date 1975)

[In the following excerpt, Goytisolo discusses the relationship between his critical and literary works, noting the undercurrents of alienation, protest, and revolt. He also describes the evolution of his work and comments on the writing of *Juan the Landless*.]

[Julio Ortega]: *The main character in your novel entitled* **Signs of Identity** *is a Spaniard alienated from his milieu. In* **Count Julian,** *your new novel, alienation is even more*

radical: Don Julian is actually in exile. Your recent work on Joseph Blanco White retrieves from oblivion a Spanish intellectual of the nineteenth century who seems to have been ignored by the critics on purpose. One is tempted to relate this process in your critical work with your own attitude as an exile. Maybe you yourself have had need of a tradition that comes to grips with the solitude of exile and an obsession for Spain? It might be interesting, I think, to establish a critical relationship between your literary persona and these other figures which in some way broaden your own discourse in fiction and in criticism. How would you describe the process that led you to assume and include these two historical people?

[Juan Goytisolo]: There is, in fact, a common denominator to the three texts that you mentioned—the two novels and the critical study of Blanco White on which I worked for the last two years—and this common denominator is, as you point out, the problem of exile. *Signs of Identity* is, among other things, the expression of the process of alienation in a contemporary intellectual with respect to his own country. It is the exposition of a moral wound in a man of my generation who has had to live through one of the most sepulchral periods of peace in the lengthy history of Spain, a person who has been in the anomalous situation of growing old without having ever known youth or responsibility (as you well know, the Spanish people live in a perpetual state of legal adolescence since April 1, 1939). In *Count Julian* the process of being dispossessed and breaking with his homeland on the part of the narrator has already taken place. *Saint Dreamgirl* or *The Foster Mother*—as Cernuda used to call his country—is seen from the outside; the moral wound has given place to a vengeful curse. As Professor Vicente Lloréns, the Spanish critic who has contributed the most to reviving the work of Blanco White has pointed out, an expatriate lives generally in a state of anguished isolation. But, this very state of marginality is favored toward the affirmation of his own ideas, liberated in this way from the hypnosis, from the tabus and the blackmail demanded from him by the society in which he lived. For a country is not merely a piece of earth; it is, above all, a compendium of social, cultural, and historical factors which begin to acquire sense and order through the process of writing. The narrator in *Count Julian* has renounced the specific space which comprises his homeland (landscape, earth), but he has not renounced its *discourse* (literary, ideological, etc.) in which his actual identity resides, his historical evolution. With the total freedom which comes from possessing absolutely nothing and having nothing to lose, he wanders like a nomad through eight centuries of Spanish culture, stopping at random wherever his own inspiration dictates, and he picks his intellectual sustenance wherever he pleases. In this manner he integrates in a new and free *discourse* the places, phrases, and words which he extracts from the collective Hispanic discourse and thus invests it with an active and dynamic function. His aggression, vented against the society in which he has had to live, is first and foremost an aggression toward history and language. All of this is possible because of his alienation and estrangement, since we are dealing with a vision from the outside, from Africa, or more specifically, from Tangiers. Naturally, it must be tempting for the literary critic to establish a relationship between my own person, that of the author, and the other "persons" which amplify my own discourse in the novel or in my criticism. It is not an accident that the two Spanish authors who have interested me the most and influenced me profoundly in the last two years are two exiled authors, two pariahs, two execrated authors: Blanco White and Cernuda. While I lived in Spain, and during the first years of exile, my models were those that had thus served my generation: Larra, Machado. When, in the last decade, I began to shed the tabus and myths which continued to mold in Spain the so-called intelligentsia on the Left, my isolation became distressing. I not only lived physically away from my native land, but the values and critical judgments of those closest to me became stranger and stranger. As I began to discover my own truth and endeavored to possess it with clarity, I became more and more alienated from that which my companions held, or professed to hold. My exile was not only a physical one, motivated exclusively by political reasons; it was also a moral, social, ideological and sexual exile. And with each day that passed, the gulf broadened and my isolation became more accentuated. In such a situation, the discovery that my experience was not unique, that it had also been that of other Spanish intellectuals, became very important for me. When I began to study the work of Blanco White, I had the impression that I was re-reading something that I had written myself, so instant was my familiarity with it. In this centrifugal force a certain law of national gravity had taken over in me. His works amplified, as you say, my own discourse; the tone was different, but the voice was so intimately related to mine as that of the fictitious Don Julian is to my own. And it is because a series of elements in Spanish life which operate today the same way as they did in the times of Blanco White made obvious my relationship with him, based on a similarity in Spain's condition.

The most notable aspect in **Count Julian** *seems to me the formal and expressive will which questions the notion of genre and also of colloquial language spoken in Spain. There is a critical plurality (from a poetical point of view) in the novel, much more radical than the one which appears in* **Signs of Identity.** *This invention of a plural language seems to me to originate precisely in the critical and fictional unity that the text possesses, in the very passion that governs its obsessive writing. I would like for you to tell me how you wrote this novel, how it came to you, how it imposed itself upon you.*

In my opinion, the most significant works of the twentieth century are those that rise beyond the conceptual tyranny of genre; they are, at the same time, poetry,

criticism, narrative, drama, etc. A contemporary artist can use the findings of all epochs and all styles, from the most primitive literary expressions up to the most refined products of the baroque. The fundamental purpose of a novel like **Count Julian** is to achieve the unity of object and means of representation, the fusion of treason as scheme and treason as language. **Count Julian** is at the same time a work of criticism and one of fiction, or, if you prefer, of critical praxis. The free use of different expressive forms and literary styles as building elements in new architecture is a reflection of the present aspiration of authors to achieve a totalizing art, an art that will reflect the situation of man in the 20th century confronting a cultural heritage of tens of centuries forced to take into account and to be influenced by that *musée imaginaire* of which Malraux speaks. A mythic interpretation which would justify Spain's history had been obsessing me for years. It is difficult to live in a city like Tangiers, chasing the proximity of the Spanish coast, without evoking the legendary figure of Don Julian, and without musing over a grandiose "treasonous act" as his was. My distance from the official values of Spain had reached such an extreme that the idea of profanation, of symbolic destruction accompanied me day and night. The only problem which faced me was the choice of language with which I was to commit my own "treasonous act." In order to violate Hispanic values, i.e., legends and myths, I had to violate the very language in which they were created, to destroy both with the same violent aggression. Having reached this conclusion the rest was relatively easy; the text began to grow by itself.

I am very interested in another aspect of **Count Julian;** *its close relationship with the new Hispano-American narrative. I would say that* **Count Julian** *is the most Spanish novel that you have written, but it is also the most Hispano-American one, because of its diversity of form and of expression which allows you even to gloss Hispano-American oral language in your novel. What importance has the the Hispano-American prose fiction had for you?*

Of course, **Count Julian** is the most Spanish work I have written. And the reason is simple: its content on a purely verbal level consists of the Hispanic literary discourse from its origins to the present. The attempt to vindicate the treason committed by Don Julian is to refute centuries of hostile history through a kind of vandalic aggression against the written word of our chroniclers, poets, and story tellers. The examples of "plagiarism" which are included at the end of the book may resolve for the erudite scholar the problem of "sources." The real problem, however, is not a problem of sources, but rather of *functions* which I attribute to those "plagiarisms," to the rather free use which I make of them. My approach allows me to engage in an *intertextual* dialogue with authors whom I admire, or to parody or play with the style of those who seem to me not very respectable, etc. All of which leads us to the second part of what you say: my symbolic intellectual nomadic quality does indeed have affinities with the new Hispano-American prose fiction, which is much freer in its relationship with the past than in Spanish prose fiction. In fact, it is also freer with the past tradition of other languages and other cultures. In my opinion, the great pioneer of this attitude is Borges. Without him, neither the new Hispano-American novel nor a work like *Count Julian* would have been possible.

Although the contact between Hispano-American literature and Spanish literature has been rather poor in the last few years, I would say that there is now a new situation. Do you believe that a more modern tradition is now changing the new Peninsular literature, or do you see a more decisive hiatus in it at an earlier period?

This lack of contact does not exist only between Peninsular literature and Hispano-American literature. If the Atlantic separates writers and readers from Barcelona and Madrid from those of Mexico City, Buenos Aires, or Lima, then among the latter there is also a kind of political, psychological, and patriotic Andes barrier separating them, which actually favors compartmentalization and plays right into the hands of imperialism. I believe that to lift cultural blockades, to ferment a real free interchange of ideas, and to combat all kinds of monolithic structures, can contribute decisively to the creation of a literature in the Spanish language without any kind of frontiers or custom houses.

Having said this, I do believe that the new relationship between Hispano-American literature and Spanish literature is irreversible on both parts. One characteristic of Peninsular literature has been its isolation and lack of permeability to ideas and currents from the outside. Hispano-American literature, on the other hand, has suffered from exactly the opposite effect, sometimes incurred through too much acceptance of foreign literature. Today both the tendencies are beginning to correct themselves and to compensate each other, and in this respect it is interesting to observe that the most European of our poets—I am referring to Cernuda—is the one who has most influenced later generations in Spain. These generations are no longer impeded as ours was, by the asphyxiating cult to the authors of '98 and their followers. The paralyzing attention to "Castilianism" with all its narrowness has now lost its prestige, and young writers show themselves to be more internationalist. In the last analysis the world does not stop at the River Guadarrama, at the Gredos Mountains, or at the walls of Avila. The generational gap and the new life forms have really abolished many of the old frontiers.

In your own work, I find that the moment of breaking with tradition is fundamental to an essential reformulation of your creative endeavor. What importance do new critical ideas have in this process? To what extent do you think that an awareness of critical theory can affect the formal nature of a work of fiction?

All creative work is indissolubly linked to the exercise of a critical faculty. *Count Julian* is, simultaneously, a work of fiction and a work of criticism, which defies deliberately a tyrannical conception of genre. The old-fashioned novel (with "round" characters developed psychologically, with its verisimilitude and its "realism," etc.) no longer interests me, and I don't think that I will write such any more (which does not mean that I renounce those I published earlier). The only kind of literature which interests me at the moment is that which lies outside the labels of "novel," "essay," "poem," etc. When I wrote my essay on Blanco White, I also included in it my own autobiography. I have appropriated Blanco White into my own myth. In *Count Julian* I simply proposed to create a text which would allow for diverse levels of reading. My approach is the natural result of a series of critical reflections based, in part, on my reading of the Russian formalists, Benveniste, Jakobson, the Prague Circle, etc. A writer who is unaware of the movements in poetics and linguistics seems to me an anachronism in today's world. The writer cannot abandon himself simply to inspiration, and feign innocence vis à vis language, because language is never innocent.

As we all known, you are known as a literary figure who also has taken an active part in politics. You have gone from a literature of protest, and an involvement in political activity, to literary reflections of culture within an international ideological framework of a totally engagé *nature. But does not* engagement *have its own evolution? What can you tell us with respect to this aspect of your work?*

If we analyze literary history, we will find the alternation between periods in which the individual expression of the artist predominates with others in which literary works reflect rather unanimously what Lukács has called with keen insight the "social charge" of a period. In times when religious or political faith or hope predominates, the writer functions totally in unison with society, and expresses society's feelings, beliefs, and hopes in perfect harmony. This is what happened during the Middle Ages, when no one doubted Christianity or, to take more recent examples, in the great moments of revolutionary strife, in 1789, 1848, 1871, 1917, etc. When the Spanish Civil War broke out, almost all the best writers and intellectuals put aside their personal problems and obsessions and immediately offered their talents to the service of the Republican cause. The same thing occurred in Cuba, I remember, during the dramatic hours of Playa Girón and the missile crisis. But when this faith and hope in the collectivity either becomes weakened or disappears—through a change in circumstances or perspectives or, simply, through fatigue—and the writer no longer feels the urgency of his "social charge," the expression of problems of a social and collective dimension tends to give way to individual expressions of the artist himself. It is for this reason that socialist regimes often impose by decree upon their authors a set of themes which are to be followed because they are convenient for those regimes.

But the mechanism of such creations explains the failure of the so-called "socialist realism." The faith and enthusiasm that a poet possesses cannot be dictated from above. When Christianity was not an empty word, the architects and artisans could construct those marvelous romanesque or gothic cathedrals which today fill us with admiration; today, in a world without God such a religious art is absolutely unthinkable.

In the Europe which was created by the Second World War, divided into two blocks, each in need of a revolution that would end the abuses and injustices of capitalism and the privileges of a bureaucratic caste, collective faith does not exist. Given the difficulty of capturing and expressing the discontent, often vague, and the aspirations, often confused, of the masses, the best writers and painters opt for the expression of their own psyche, for rebellion, sometimes alienated, sometimes schizophrenic, against an age which repels them in its totality.

This vacilation between "social charge" and individual expression functions in the same manner within the work of a painter, a novelist, or a poet, according to the accidents of the historical moment in which he lives. Picasso and Alberti offer us good examples of that fact. I see the same kind of alternation within my own work. After an initial stage (that of *Juegos de manos, Duelo en el paraíso,* and *Fiestas*) in which, rather vaguely even for me, I try to express my obsessions and personal anguish, my own vision of the world (oppressed, as I felt, by a rigid education and traditional values which I felt were invalid), my developing political conscience, the discovery of the brutal injustices of the society which had spawned me, all these factors led me, as they also did many of the writers of my generation, to express the urgent need for social and political change in my country. These conditions forced me to adopt a literary form which was suited to didactic and revolutionary purposes which guided my pen: novels of social theses—*La resaca*; documentaries—*Campos de níjar, La chanca, Pueblo en marcha*; scripts to be used for popular films—*La isla*; political articles, etc. This *engagé* state lasted as long as the reality surrounding us seemed to make possible a revolution that we thought feasible. But when it became evident to me that Spain was modernizing itself, and becoming Americanized, under the present regime, and that this process threatened to last even beyond the death of Franco, I began to weaken. I was at that time well on my way to becoming one of those official writers of world progress, glorious representatives in exile of their country's political plight (a rather comfortable career, I might add, dependent upon closing one's eyes to the defects—ever more visible—of institutionalized revolutions). I remember that in 1963 when I was visiting Cuba, I was introduced to a large popular group in this manner, and while I was being applauded, I perceived with anguishing clarity that the applause was directed toward an official and external person which has little to do with me. Between my real person and applause that I

was hearing there seemed to stand a double, or, as Cavafi says in one of his most beautiful poems, "an inopportune visitor." This experience was an essential one for me because it led me to examine the roots of things, to look at problems in a different way. From that time on I have not ceased to have the need to clear the atmosphere that surrounds me, to explain my real being to others and to myself without worrying about any inconvenient obstacles. *Signs of Identity, Count Julian,* my essay and translation of Blanco White all form part of this new attempt at individual expression, which I have found absolutely necessary to go on living in peace with myself. The book that I am now working on ought to complete in rather definitive form, I hope, this stage. For the last few years I have abstained, sometimes with great difficulty, from participating in an active way in a series of political causes which affect me personally. I want to separate my artistic and human condition from any stricture which might be based on equivocation, inhibition, or censorship. If I am true to myself and recognized as such by others, I will be able to take up causes and be more effective in them. I hope that at that time I will be able to give myself again to an activity which is not "literary."

In this respect, how would you place your own critical confrontation vis à vis the theme of Spain? This is not the place to review it, but I know that your own dissidence is taken seriously by Spanish intellectuals and creates very diverse reactions: from the attempt to bypass it dealing with it as "obsessive" up to the genuine need of assuming it for oneself because the intellectual recognizes himself in his marginality. I think that it might be interesting to have you comment on this.

For many years I wrote regularly a series of articles and notes, some in Spanish, some in French, about Spanish political affairs. Most of them appeared under a pseudonym in *L'Exprèss* and *L'Observateur*. The last one was published in 1964 and was the object of very severe criticism on the part of many of the Spanish opposition within Spain, and above all, in exile. Recently I reread it by chance and, without sounding at all vain, I must say that subsequent events have borne me out in what, at the time, was held by others to be negative and defeatist. These reactions from the Left after a very violent campaign of denigration from the official Right (so similar to that which Blanco White suffered in London after the publication of his articles in favor of the Hispano-American revolutionaries) influenced me to withdraw from Spanish political life. My role in it was never intended to produce either personal gain or a career. It was prompted by strong feelings for my country. The Spanish tragedy—the consciousness of the national tragedy which has been felt so actually by our best intellectuals since the middle of the 18th century—reached its paroxysm during the Civil War of 1936–39, in terms which moved and mobilized the entire liberal and progressive intelligentsia of the world. When I read or meditate on what happened in those years, it is difficult for me to hold back my emotions and not think of what Spain meant to so many writers and intellectuals and to thousands of people of different means and ideologies, races, religions and languages, who left their countries, their work, their families, and their friends in order to fight and die for our country. It is evident that the Spanish cause appealed to a universal conscience in the clear-cut dilemma which was then being faced politically, and that explains the passion and the generous sacrifice of so many lives.

But the Spain which emerged around 1960, beginning with its economic miracle, created by the invasion of tourists, can no longer result in impassioned dedication on the part of its intellectuals, and even less on the part of foreign intellectuals. This does not mean that Spanish intellectuals do not continue to have a reasonable and pragmatic interest in the destiny of their country. What I am saying is that their passion, when it exists, will be channeled in other directions. Let us take, for example, the case of England at the beginning of the nineteenth century. She had obtained religious liberty, resolved religious conflict, begun the Industrial Revolution (full of horrible injustices, of course, but necessary nonetheless) and the result was that its intellectuals began to draw away from the national problem. They continued naturally to intervene in British political life, but their heart was in Greece, in Italy, or in Spain. Everyone remembers the death of Lord Byron defending freedom in Greece. Well, even though the episode is not as well known, the Spanish liberal cause also had its martyrs. Vicente Lloréns has described magnificently the participation of young people like Robert Boyd and the poet Richard Trench in the ill-fated expedition of Torrijos. In the final pages of *The Face of Spain*, Brenan has described with great precision the kind of nomadic sentimentality which his British compatriots feel frequently, as an escape from their countryside more and more devastated by the Industrial Revolution.

What happened in England in the nineteenth century is happening right now in Spain, even though many intellectuals of my generation, and particularly those of previous generations, do not understand the process. Those who do, and very clearly indeed, are the modern captains of industry, those technocrats of the *Opus dei* who have freed Spanish Catholicism from all its shame accumulated during the centuries and now concentrates only on commercial values and money. One might say that the *Opus dei* are our Calvinists, and that explains why they have had such a good reception in Protestant countries. As I wrote in an article in 1964, Spain has lost its dramatic character and hence the attraction that underdeveloped countries have (traits which one finds today, for example, in Mexico or in Morocco), without acquiring through that process the material and moral advantages of richer nations. The fight must continue to acquire political and syndical freedom, the abolition of censorship, the elimination of social injustice, etc. But

today this fight cannot create in Spain the passion and the unlimited dedication which either the Vietnamese or the Palestine cause has elicited in others. Spain's present image approximates more and more that of the other European countries, and just as no intellectual of the French Left can feel passionately about France, no British subject about England, no Dutch citizen about Holland, a loving passion for Spain these days, to my view, would be anachronistic. I have tried to develop these thoughts in my essay on Blanco White. Patriotism on the Left, I say there, is linked to underdevelopment and to the necessity and even the actual possibility of violent change. Clearly this is not the case in Spain today. I can safely say that I have been among the first to see this Spanish problem in a modern light. As British writers have been doing for the last century and a half, I continue to be interested in the cause of liberty and democracy in my country (as I am also interested in that of any other European country), but my passion (not only intellectual, but also "physical, physiological, anatomical, functional, circulatory, respiratory, etc.," as Artaud used to conceive it) is now spent on the revolutionary struggle of the Arab countries. Neither exultation which I felt towards Spain in the decade of the fifties, as a result of my remembrances as a child in 1936–39, nor the repressive political climate which ensued thereafter, obtains any longer for those young people in Spain for whom the Civil War evokes no memory, for those who have been educated in a country converted through an annual tourism of more than 20 million Europeans into a paradise.

Signs of Identity and *Count Julian* *are independent works of fiction, but at the same time they belong to a process which not only presupposes a "destruction" of your previous narrative, but also unleashes its own system, a system which seeks to destroy the novel as a genre. Where do you think that this process might lead you to?*

I have for some time now been working on the continuation of *Count Julian* and, with it, will close the cycle which I began with *Signs of Identity*. I am not dealing, of course, with a continuation of a novelistic world of characters, events, actions, and environments, but rather with a discourse which in each of the three books operates on different linguistic strata. In *Signs of Identity* I was searching for integration of different narrative techniques within the mold of an eclectic, artistic conception in the sense which Broch gives to this term. In **Count Julian** I tried to create a circular work, unified and hermetic, with no loose ends. In the book which I am now writing, I aspire to create an open work, radiating in various directions as with the slats of a fan, and in which the centrifugal force of the various narrative lines will become unified through the use of discursive language. Alvaro, the character who used to speak in *Signs of Identity*, became metamorphosed later into the mythic Don Julian and now haunts time and space as would a ghost, like the Wandering Jew. Spain no longer plays an important

---

An excerpt from *Count Julian*

you are doubtless familiar with the story of Pandora, that woman possessed of a marvelous beauty: as her dowry, she brought her spouse a magnificent gold box, and when the latter opened it, pain and misery and sickness flew out and spread throughout the earth: my dearly beloved young flock, forbidden pleasures are like this gold box that appears to contain splendid treasure: but woe to the imprudent hand that dares to open it!: there is nothing that so predisposes the organism to consumption as sin: like an insatiable leech it sucks your blood, fades the rosy bloom of youth on your cheeks, extinguishes the joyous sparkle in your eyes: a dread disease that even those researchers in the very forefront of science confess they are powerless to cure: the body of the sinner becomes covered with pustules, he suffers constant wracking headaches which give him not a single moment's respite: little by little the telltale signs of his affliction manifest themselves, on his skin, on his eyelids, in his intestines: he is tormented by insomnia despite his desperate craving for sleep: he is helpless in the face of disease, and is overcome by all sorts of physical ailments: in the most acute phase, his palate is pitted with sores: very often the cartilage of his nose rots away and his face is permanently disfigured: he looks like a ghost: his joints become very brittle (as the old man gets the sharp instrument out and refills it and

I'm not hurting you, am I?
no, not in the least
but breathing a sigh of relief when)

nonetheless this is no more than the first step on the path to doom: we have not yet reached the bottom of the mire: there is a law of physics according to which a falling body does not fall at a uniform velocity: rather, the velocity of a falling body accelerates as it approaches the abyss toward which it is being attracted by mysterious telluric forces: this law of gravitation applies not only in the physical realm, but also in spiritual life: the soul has its own insidious tendencies, its own perverse inclinations: as we begin to give in to temptation they begin to impel us, with a more and more irresistible force, toward the obscure abysses of sin: lion cubs are gentle creatures until they see blood: but at the very first bite, they are transformed, they become savage beasts: my beloved sons, famished dogs, bloodthirsty wolves lie hidden in the depths of your nature as fallen creatures: don't offer them food, or they will sink their fangs in your flesh and drink your pure, fresh young blood

Juan Goytisolo, in his *Count Julian*, translated by Haley R. Lane, Viking Press, 1974.

---

role as in **Count Julian**. The phantasmagoric discourse which the text produces no longer has a homeland in a material of spiritual sense. In **Count Julian**, the narrator had renounced Spain, but not yet its history or culture. In this new novel, the process of cultural pruning continues; sometimes it is embodied in the person of a character who failed in his aspirations; other times it adopts the voice of a priest who believes in slavery, or it transforms itself into King Kong or Lawrence of Arabia. The essential *meaning* of the work takes no barriers into account: it jumps from Cuba to Istanbul, from New York to the Sahara Desert, from the past to the present, and then to the future or to Utopia. Everything treated is unbelievable or strange but, as Sklovski saw very well, the more remote the possibility was of justifying a moral or artistic position "the greater the pleasure that the writer takes in developing his examples." The creator of "discourse" changes his voice, and in that manner changes his skin, as easily as a *fregoli*; he is a "mere linguistic character," an authentic man without a country, and that is why I have entitled the novel *Juan sin Tierra*. (I must explain that when Blanco White seeks refuge in London, and begins the publication of his political chronicles in *El Español*, he does it with pseudonym of Juan sin Tierra.) As you might suppose, I use the label "novel" only out of convenience because, as I have said earlier, the only kind of writing that interests me lies outside canonized literary forms. My own praxis (and not just my critical reflection) has shown me the wisdom of Barthes's suggestion, in *Le degré zéro de l'écriture*, that every writer can potentially add to the process of literature.

And it is true that my own birth as a writer coincides in fact with the destruction of my literature, of the literary molds which in routine fashion I took from tradition.

What you say indicates that the natural result of this cycle which you're writing lies in the very code of the text; within a literary construction which seemingly destroys itself. But before we deal with this "zero degree" of the narrative process, I must ask you about "the objective correlative" as an ingredient in the two novels of your present cycle.

When I write now I do not invent situation, characters, or actions, but rather structures and discursive forms, textual groupings which are combined according to secret affinities among themselves, as in architecture or the plastic arts. In fact, the only "novelistic" works which I am interested in now are those which show a new and audacious elaboration; those in which the creative imagination of the writer manifests itself not through an outside referent in reality, but above all, through the use of language.

Actually, there is no contradiction between the desire for personal expression which I have mentioned above and the intention of constructing a discursive texture which can be judged of and by itself. As you know, any literary work has within it several kinds of readings: it is, at the same time, the illustration of certain ideas (political, artistic, philosophic, etc.), the image or reflection of the society in which it is produced, and the expression of the author who creates it. Traditional critics tend to accentuate one of these three factors, sometimes all three; but a literary work is much more than this. In **Count**

Julian there is obviously a desire for personal expression. Nevertheless, the best critical reading is that of the text itself in its relations with the *literary corpus* of the Spanish language. Only an analysis of this sort can reveal its originality, its innovations and relationships, its secret architecture.

You are right. Both **Signs of Identity** *and* **Count Julian** *require in the reading the various levels which you are pointing out.* **Count Julian** *may be read as an answer to the romantic treatment of the theme as treated by the English romantics who also wrote of a legendary Spain using the themes which you do in* **Count Julian.** *But this very disintegration of forms and of themes which seem to culminate in* **Juan sin Tierra,** *might it not imply a "zero degree" of its own, a black page, a silence? If so, how far have you actually advanced?*

I don't know when the novel will be ready. I imagine not for three or four years yet. In contrast to that period in my life when I used to produce a novel a year, now I write very slowly and I am in no hurry at all to publish my work. In recent years I have achieved what I had wanted before and found very difficult to achieve; namely to disappear from the world of publishing, to cease to be a piece of merchandise in that world. Before, when I used to write novels in a few months, these were immediately translated into more than ten languages, and I could live from my royalties. The temptation was great to continue producing at that pace, and to assure myself in that manner a place in the publishing world. But even then I was cognizant of the danger that such a process holds for the development of a creative writer. When I was one of the most translated writers and the majority of my colleagues considered me very fortunate, I felt myself more and more anguished and in need of sabotaging my own position. I came to realize that my own personal growth as a literary writer depended upon my giving up the capacity to earn a living through writing. Now I teach for several months in universities in the United States or Canada, and I can work without any hurry, at my own pace. When the text that I am working on now ceases to grow and its architecture satisfies me, I will publish it. But I do not want to be pinned down about dates.

If young writers were to ask me for advice, the first one that I would give them is that they renounce living from their writings, that they search for parallel activities that might earn them a living. In large measure it is these economic reasons which are responsible for that monstrously irresponsible and repetitious mass of writing which floods the publishing market, converting writers into hens, some of whom lay eggs at an amazing speed. The writers, too, ought to have the right to keep quiet and not to produce. In this sense the silence of Sánchez Ferlosio after publishing his extraordinary work, *El Jarama,* ought to be a lesson to all. His is a much more significant work than the entire "realistic-objective" production of those novelists whose works we have read for a long time.

I hope that when the time comes when I have nothing to say or do not feel like saying anything, I will have the good sense and guts to keep quiet. (pp. 56–68)

Juan Goytisolo and Julio Ortega, in an interview, translated by Joseph Schraibman, in The *Texas Quarterly*, Vol. XVIII, No. 1, Spring, 1975, pp. 56–77.

V.S. PRITCHETT
(essay date 1978)

[An English author, biographer, and critic, Pritchett is respected for his mastery of the short story and for what commentators describe as his judicious and insightful literary criticism. In the following excerpt, he reviews *Juan the Landless*.]

As readers of the Spanish novelist Juan Goytisolo will expect, exile is his continuing subject. It was established in *Marks of Identity* and *Count Julian*; now *Juan the Landless* completes a trilogy. Goytisolo would probably reject the denomination "Spanish," for he is a young Catalan who left Franco's Spain for North Africa: his novels are a sustained skirl of love-hatred for the country he derisively calls "Sunnyspain" of the travel brochures, or "the foul Stepmother." He has the traditional Catalan contempt for the central power of Castilian government and culture, its stagnant bureaucracy, monkish fanaticism, and cruelty—the lifeless formality and obedience to custom which put a lasting puritan gooseflesh on the famous Spanish stoics and saints and on the spontaneous sexual life of the natural man. For him, Spain's classic fiesta was the auto-da-fé. His recalcitrant Catalan is a dramatic, pagan Mediterranean, a descendant of the old Provençal culture, a sensual, volcanic earthshaker—though Goytisolo hates the Catalan bourgeois. Savage digs at the Castilian classics are among the farcical passages of *Count Julian*: there was an element of double-take in Goytisolo's caricature of Seneca reborn as one of Francós vulgar public-relations officers. In that book, the novelist built up the vengeful fantasies of a legendary Arab leader appearing in the desert and crossing the Straits to massacre the dull descendants of the conquistadores. The book was less a novel than a kind of anti-psalm—a chanted autobiography and a work of offensive travel. The evocation of North Africa was unforgettably electric in its images and was provoked by more than a whiff of Indian hemp. There was an exhilarating scorn in that book. In *Juan the Landless*, exhilaration turns to pain in the raw.

It is notoriously difficult to know how to sustain the force of a trilogy in its final volume. A scream will turn into a sob unless one can transpose it into thunderous orchestration, all drums going hard. The end not with a bang but a whimper may have suited the twenties, but it is useless now. There are alternatives: one of them is to give one's personal noise a wider geographical and historical territory. Goytisolo plays the dangerous game of solving his problems by enlarging them—as H. G. Wells did—to make them sound global. The danger is that generalized hate becomes vague and loses the force of the specific, and it must be said that in Goytisolo's final volume rhetorical generalities have weakened the force of his destructive fantasy and wit. To offset this, he, like other modern satirists with a revolutionary turn, has fallen back on obscenity. Here his masters are the homosexual Genet and the fashionable Marquis de Sade—sex and the scatological have their anarchic uses. Politically, the exile turns to Beckett for the *clochard*, the outcast and pariah, and finds a sort of anti-hero in T. E. Lawrence, whose sexual aberrations were a private revolt in the desert. Here Goytisolo is a neo-romantic celebrating the nonchalant freedom of the vagrant Arab sodomite. There are also references to Swift's obsession with excrement and gross sexuality, but a critic is bound to point out that the fantasies of *Gulliver's Travels* are in no sense revolutionary: they are narrated by Gulliver, the most orthodox and plainest of haters. Gulliver the citizen suggests the classical notion of a simple rational norm; Goytisolo never does.

Juan the Landless is really a book about the exile's imagination. Enlarging his scene, he takes a dive into history, and we find him in what reads like a Latin-American sugar plantation, where the master has called his black slaves together to witness a "portentous occasion." The master sits on a decorative throne, surrounded by his tame, *bien pensant* family and attended by priests, who exhort the slaves to give up their natural and incurable sexual appetites in the interests of working harder for the master. The slaves gaze at the throne, which is really that newly invented European marvel the patent flush water closet, and await the miracle of the master's defecation. When it occurs, joy and dancing will begin, while the priests hold forth on the ingenious theological distinctions between stench and the perfumes of privilege and sanctity. Goytisolo is rich in black comedy, and he knows his theology. The whole scene has the raw caricature of a play by Genet. The Christian God is a colonialist: the world is His slave population. We now turn back to Arab Africa. Goytisolo's fantasy is of himself as a pariah travelling to Egypt, Istanbul, Baghdad, Damascus, and back to Fez, at one with the stink and sores of beggars who have found a savage freedom in living outside society. Their opposite numbers are ourselves, the ludicrous tourists with our fatuous questions, our cameras slung around us as a kind of substitute genitalia. The mania for taking pictures is natural to the gaping mechanicals of an ersatz culture who have lost contact with reality and live on tidbits of random information. The pariahs like to shock them with shameless homosexual performances in the streets, and Goytisolo derides his private arch-enemies—the perfect,

timid, sexually incompetent, respectable, and perpetually disappointed Married Couple. They know nothing of the savage and releasing cruelties of the outcast in the dunes or the gutters, or of the abasement that relieved T. E. Lawrence when he was the double agent of the exploiters.

Although Goytisolo is rubbing our noses in his disgusts, he is also lashing himself, for the journeys and scenes he makes so physically vivid may not have occurred. As I have said, the joke is that he is imagining it all in his bleak North African room and is really writing about the imagination peculiar to exile; the exile's only capital, his only luggage, is his language. For the artist, language is "the splendid prerogative of our disguise": language dictates his "protean ever-shifting voices," as it certainly did in another of Goytisolo's masters, James Joyce. His North African room is, intellectually, in the Boulevard Saint-Germain. We get glimpses of the private cause of the narrator's homosexuality—the child's frightened sight of a copulation in a rich, pious, immensely respectable bourgeois family:

> I began to dream of colossal disasters, and swift, magnificent cataclysms which, with the same inexorable force as those which devastated ancient Egypt, would finish my progenitors off once and for all and rid the world of their inane and absurd presence. . . I conjured up in my mind (in the vaguest of ways) fierce, barbarous tribes, with bodies as steely and unyielding as knives, whose coppercolored, enigmatic faces would rival the hardness of a precious stone with dazzling polyhedral, crystalline facets . . . I prayed for the advent of torturers who would subject my progenitors' ridiculous, anemic bodies to the rigors of their harsh pleasure . . .

That is Goytisolo at his Catalonian worst. I trust him in the streets of Fez, in all his ferocious caricatures, and in his satire on brochures, travelogues, and corrupt historical films. I trust his laughing phrases: "the double row of sphinxes pierced like sieves by the cameras of sightseeing tours," and "baritone sightseeing guides. . . recite names, dates, limp spaghetti-like bits of serpentine erudition." I admire his "protean voice" when he is sardonic. But when he is evoking T. E. Lawrence and I see *The Seven Pillars of Wisdom* on his table I know the tortured prose of that work will infect him. I prefer Goytisolo's tricks. I admire his ingenuity as an original narrator who addresses himself as "You," as if "You" were a kaleidoscope he is shaking, or were the half-mocking yet self-entranced audience of his schizophrenia. We have had a considerable cult of the diatribe in poetry, prose, and the theatre in the last decade, and it now begins to be déjà vu; but even if You bring all the Latin gift for rhetoric to Your diatribe, there is still the difficulty of bringing it to an end. Goytisolo returns to the pain of his remark that an exile's only luggage is his language. The pain is real, and he has made it real to us. (We indeed feel a growing sense of mental exile in our own cultures.) But when we find him ending his trilogy with a tormented avant-garde manifesto about the staleness of the realistic novel, the fraud of character drawing, the autonomy of the literary subject as a verbal structure, his incantation falls as flat as a lecture. Listen to the prose traveller prosing on about the need to free language of "its simoniac, ancillary entelechy: transmuting semantic anomaly into the generative nucleus of poetry and thereby uniting, in polysemic harmony, sexuality and writing," and finally resolving, "The secret equation lying behind your two fold deviation: unproductive (onanistic) manipulation of the written word, self- sufficient (poetic) enjoyment of illicit pleasure." (pp. 146–49)

V. S. Pritchett, "An Exile's Luggage," in *The New Yorker*, Vol. LIV, No. 5, March 20, 1978, pp. 146, 149.

MICHAEL UGARTE

(essay date 1982)

[In the following excerpt, American educator and critic Ugarte claims that Goytisolo's "Mendiola Trilogy" expresses the author's desire to divorce himself from his homeland. Ugarte notes that "as [Goytisolo] becomes increasingly aware of the impossibility of ridding himself of this culture, his hatred becomes more poignant."]

The composition of vast books is a laborious and impoverishing extravagance. To go on for five hundred pages developing an idea whose perfect oral exposition is possible in a few minutes! A better course of procedure is to pretend that these books already exist, and then to offer a resumé, a commentary.

Jorge Luis Borges, *Ficciones*

A comparison between Borges and Goytisolo uncovers an underlying difference between the two that is demonstrative of Goytisolo's literary enterprise. This quotation shows Borges's affirmation of the playful nature of writing, the happy subversion of outside texts in which the author assumes the role of an aloof and sardonic commentator of a previous style or text. Goytisolo, on the other hand, does not engage in such playfulness. His task is deadly serious. Not only does he wish to redirect what he considers to be the entire thrust of Spanish history from 711 to the present but he also searches for political, social, and religious, as well as linguistic redemption. He is deeply burdened by a culture that he once embraced but now ridicules and scorns. As he becomes increasingly aware of the impossibility of ridding himself of this culture, his hatred becomes more poignant.

The bulk of Goytisolo's parodies, citations, commentaries, and transcriptions of other texts are manifestations of his attempt to corrupt and contaminate a cultural tradition. The spirit of subversion, however, is marked by a therapeutic quality incongruous with the author's purpose. The literary and biographical relationship among the protagonists of *Señas*, *Don Julián*, and *Juan sin tierra*, on the one hand, and Goytisolo himself, on the other, is perhaps the most telling evidence of an implicit notion of writing as psychoanalysis. *Señas* is an exposition of Alvaro's inner turmoil, a deeply psychological dilemma resulting from a series of social, political, and economic circumstances. In an attempt to relieve himself of his problems, the protagonist drinks excessively, avoids responsibility, and wanders about his country in search of something that he can call his own. But he never discovers that something. In *Don Julián* the attempt to sever the link between the protagonist and his native land takes the form of a reenactment of a historical event: the treasonous crime that opened the doors of the mother country to an alien culture. Linguistic treason becomes the mainstay of *Juan sin tierra* as the author-protagonist rejoices in his new found identity. In all three texts the author-protagonist sees himself as a neurotic and divided individual who defames his culture in order to alleviate his personal suffering. In the last two volumes of the trilogy he no longer reveals his existential anguish, yet he never denies it. The culminating pages of the final volume, the linguistic metamorphosis of Spanish into Arabic, the declaration of a definitive change of identity, are anticlimactic. A translation of the words of *Juan sin tierra* reads:

You who do not understand,
stop following me
our communication has ended
I am definitively on the other side
with the pariahs of always
sharpening my knife

From the beginning of the trilogy to the end, one of the most frequent and significant features is the author-protagonist's state of flux, never-ending division, duplication, and permutation of identities. Yet in the last section of the trilogy's final phase, Goytisolo puts a stop to his own dynamic process of writing. He seems unwilling to view his text as an object whose "condition [according to Edward W. Said in his *Beginnings: Intention and Method*] is that *it must be produced constantly*." Even though intertextuality affirms the ability of a text to change and disguise its identity, the end of the trilogy denies this possibility. In the final words of *Juan sin tierra*, Goytisolo's world seems to freeze. The change is permanent. There is no longer a need to write, for the exploitative, oppressive, and repugnant self (an embodiment of the Spanish language) has been killed. The verbal suicide has accomplished what he wanted: an end to textual and existential multiplicity.

Goytisolo's bitter irony confirms Paul De Man's

definition of irony as an alienating feature of literature that leads to a permanent division of the self. De Man [in his "The Rhetoric of Temporality"] describes this division as a reflection on insanity: "When we speak, then, of irony originating at the cost of the empirical self, the statement has to be taken seriously enough to be carried to the extreme: absolute irony is a consciousness of madness, itself the end of all consciousness; it is consciousness of a non-consciousness, a reflection of madness from the inside of madness itself." Goytisolo's intertextual irony, the textual masks that he wears in order to conceal his subversion of a tradition, intensifies this state of madness. His self is divided not into two but many, a fact that further complicates the deranged nature of his writing.

The "reflection on madness from the inside of madness" cannot take on a therapeutic value. Yet toward the end of the trilogy, Goytisolo shows his unwillingness to accept this maxim. His glorious self-annihilation is intended as an attempt at reconciliation of the plurality of selves. The final act is a mediation between the destruction of sacred Spain inside the act of writing and outside it. In the culminating pages, art is reconciled with the world. The exiled Spanish author longs for this recovery throughout his linguistic journey and truly believes that the search has ended joyously. Goytisolo's sense of his own self-integration, his oneness with the world, unravels, however, when we take into consideration an important consequence of ironic discourse: the awareness of inauthenticity does not presuppose authenticity. Although Goytisolo mimics his predecessors and subverts their intentions; although he praises the literary figures whom he abhors; although he infiltrates a previous text, corrupts its meaning, and disguises himself as an embodiment of the very culture he violates; all these techniques cannot permanently relieve the anguish and alienation that inspired the series of assaults. The perverse pleasure that he receives from these acts of treason is momentary and ultimately heightens the tension that caused them. The eventual result can only be further rebellion and aggression—a perpetual regeneration of linguistic subversion.

A few years after the completion of *Juan sin tierra*, Goytisolo remarked that the "ganas de escribir" ("urge to write") had not affected him since the completion of the trilogy. He believed himself cured of a malady that had plagued him throughout his life. Feeling at one with himself, he spent his time traveling to the corners of the Arabian world that continued to fascinate him. Although he wrote a few essays (*Disidencias*) in which he re-created in coherent and logical prose the themes and concerns of his fiction, he produced nothing that approached the style and scope of *Juan sin tierra*. But this state of self-gratification was short-lived, for Goytisolo had not resolved his problem, he had only created new ones. The texts that he believed he had destroyed, including his own, were not dead. After a brief period of rest, Goytisolo became aware of the contradiction. In the prologue to a new book of political essays, *Libertad, libertad, libertad* (1978), he states:

> In spite of all my efforts to remain in the margins of the problem of Spain, it was impossible to do so. Spain came back to haunt me in my most grave moments with its destructive force. I am referring to the resurgence of my indignation against all that official Spain represented, the same indignation of old, as if the only possible link between myself and my country were, after all these years, that oppressive feeling of frustration, impotence, and rage of which I ingenuously thought myself cured and which, after having poisoned me since adolescence, threatened to escort me to my grave. Being Spanish has always been for me, and probably for many others, a fate both sad and grotesque, an endemic disease that, after a period of insidiously deceptive tranquility, reemerged, at times with irrepressible violence.

In these words lie the seeds of a new linguistic derangement. In the new neurosis, in the new textual mask of *Makbara*, in the new Goytisolo are the remnants of the old. Juan sin Tierra still writes. (pp. 146–49)

Michael Ugarte, in his *Trilogy of Treason: An Intertextual Study of Juan Goytisolo*, University of Missouri Press, 1982, 171 p.

CARLOS FUENTES
(essay date 1984)

[In the following excerpt, Fuentes reviews *Juan the Landless*, comparing Goytisolo to James Joyce. Calling the pair "exiles condemned to live with the language of their oppressions," Fuentes correlates the individual works of Goytisolo's "Mendiola Trilogy" with Joyce's *A Portrait of the Artist as a Young Man, Ulysses,* and *Finnegans Wake*.]

In the Aztec mythologies, the masculine gods, even when they possess more than one attribute—rain, war, fire, sun—are curiously unambiguous. The feminine deities, on the contrary, seem to be equivocal even when their attribute is singular. Their representation is always dual and even multiple; the feminine deities are the bearers of the other, of the contrary. Xochiquetzal has jewels encrusted on her cheeks; from her mouth springs a bouquet of flowers and a sacrificial knife. Her words are poetry and destruction. Chalchihuitlicue is the goddess of uncertainty; she uses a moon on her nose and sings, but between her legs protrudes the head of her rival, the witch Tlazolteotl.

And she, Tlazolteotl, is the most functionally ambiguous woman in the Mexican Pantheon: she wields the

Abigail Lee Six on historiography in Goytisolo's fiction:

Goytisolo's texts lend themselves to postmodern readings of their approach to history. They delegitimate traditional Spanish history, showing it to be one-sided (for it ignores or misrepresents the Semitic component) and flout the rules of historiography by fusing past with present, temporality with timelessness. They reject the dividing-lines between fact, opinion, and imagination; they question the notion of past as something gone which may be recalled or forgotten at will, whether by the individual or a whole culture. But these points are made most powerfully through a discourse on language and literature rather than directly on the outside world. The Moorish influence on the Spanish language—not just Spain—is denied at the language's—not just the nation's—peril; snippets of texts—not just events—from earlier centuries rub shoulders with neologisms, not just modern life. Spain's literary past cannot be obliterated by a bag of dead insects smuggled into a library, any more than its national history can be blotted out by an effort of will.

Abigail Lee Six, in *History and Post-War Writing*, Rodopi, 1990.

broom of the witch and of the housekeeper. She is the deity, simultaneously, of purity and of filth, the scavenger-goddess who devours trash, cadavers, and excreta in order to cleanse the land. She was, moreover, the confessor and shrink of the Aztec world: the warriors, on the eve of battle, would tell her their sins and their dreams so as to meet the enemy without the burdens of fault or desire which, in most repressive societies, tend to be synonymous.

Juan Goytisolo's *Juan sin tierra* seems written under the sign of the goddess of the Indian night: his words both pollute and cleanse, cleanse and pollute, but do not cease to devour all that they find in their way. What they find, indeed, is the corrupt matter of reality first, and then the signs of the literary representation of that reality. Goytisolo's relation to reality is the same as his relation to the narrative text: the narrator's enterprise of social demolition is inseparable from the textual form that allows it to run its course or, even, that congeals it in a fictive succession of instants that aspire to an equal verbal intensity, simultaneous instead of linear. Orthography, syntax, discursiveness are all set in such a way that progression is excluded and all the narrative elements acquire a value of identity that is both equal and actual.

Rarely has the Spanish language, commonly academic and explanatory as a result of its prolonged sickness since the late seventeenth century, been submitted to a narrative form that so severely denies the laws of succession in discourse. Goytisolo is very close in this desire for simultaneity and instantaneity (as well as in many other

things) to some of the great poems of Octavio Paz. *Juan sin tierra*, nevertheless, is a novel in debt to everything it denies. This debt, this dependency on what is denied, is evident to the Spanish reader through the constant intrusion of pet phrases of the Spanish commonplace, elegant turns, archaic formalities, forms of rationalization, adjectives and metaphors that belong (and belong only) to the body (the cadaver) of the very same language that Goytisolo assails and which other writers in overseas-Spanish (I think especially of Cortázar and Cabrera Infante) have definitely abandoned, perhaps because on this side of the Atlantic it is easier to dismiss certain heirlooms of peninsular rhetoric. Goytisolo takes on this peculiar inheritance in order to wage war against it, and this is one of the secrets of the tortured and torturing prose, pure and impure at the same time. (p. 72)

Goytisolo is obviously out to destroy what he sees as an old and oppressive language, create a new one, and make of the novel the vehicle for this operation. His work becomes the bridge which unites two literary movements of identical idiomatic sign but of radically opposite attitudes towards that sign: the peninsular Spanish novel and the Spanish American novel. The modern novelists of Spanish America have centered their work on a renewal of language because, for a Spanish American, to create a language is to have a being. The Spanish American does not feel he owns a language; he feels he suffers an alien language, imposed by the conquistador, the hidalgo and the Academy. The customary way in which a Peruvian oligarch addresses a servant—"cholo de mierda"—deprives the latter of his language and his being. The forms of speech in Mexico—the obsequious circumlocution, the humble diminutive, the aggressive insult—are all manners in which the cultural slave denies his own presence, softens it or brutally affirms it because he feels he does not have it.

The history of Spanish America is that of a dispossession of language: we only own the texts imposed on us to disguise reality; we must appropriate con-texts. For the Spaniard, on the contrary, the problem is not to possess a language, but to dis-possess himself from it, renounce it, become a stranger to his own tongue, recover an unsheltered solitude in the language and then, thanks to all this, transform it once more into a challenge and an exploration, as it was for Rojas, Cervantes, and Góngora. With Goytisolo, the Spanish written in Spain ceases to be the language of the masters and becomes, as in Spanish America, the language of the pariahs.

In *Señas de identidad*, Alvaro, the protagonist, goes to a public library and there squashes flies and bugs between the hallowed pages of Lope de Vega and Azorín. There is no more eloquent act in the modern Spanish novel. Goytisolo's implacable intention is to point out that the moral, economic, and political institutions of Fascist Spain were founded on a certain rhetoric: the values of "purity" and "casticismo" (this extraordinary Castilian word implies the ideas of caste, chastity, orthodoxy, and unmixed blood) were consecrated in order to justify a closed culture and a system of submissive relationships.

Goytisolo rarely counterpoints these realities with their opposite, liberating numbers; his novels prefer the techniques of a permanent and ironical integration. Languages fuse and confuse, periodically; the languages of lyrical description with police reports; the monologues of private angst with the leaden prose of the official press; the pure Castilian tradition with the unconscious camp of Hispanic oratory; the most "brutal" popular language with the truly brutal language of commercial solicitation. Goytisolo contaminates all levels of the written Spanish language and in so doing he radically deprives them of hierarchical security. A solemn mountain becomes a churning river which the author contains within fragile narrative walls.

If Juan Goytisolo is, undoubtedly, the greatest living Spanish novelist, it is because he has not avoided this challenge. He is the prisoner of all the verbal chains of the Spanish language only to make them evident. He is forced to swallow the words he hates in order to excrete them with coprophilous pleasure: did Jonathan Swift, in his time, do something comparable with the English verbal tradition? Swift, Goytisolo; Joyce, Goytisolo: exiles condemned to live with the language of their oppressions, digest it, expel it, trample on it, and then resign themselves: these words, returned to the earth, will fertilize the earth and be reborn, hated, transfigured, a necessary object of both the refusal of and the need for communication. This is then the problem: where does transformation end and death begin? Where does exile end and suicide start ?

Juan Sin tierra seems to form a triptych initiated with *Señas de identidad* and continued with *Reivindicación del Conde Don Julián*. In the three novels, Alvaro, the young-old narrator, Goytisolo's Dedalus, dreamer, and historical clown, liberates a part of his secret autobiography. *Señas de identidad* is his *Portrait of the Artist as a Young Man*—perhaps the great *Bildungsroman* of contemporary Spain. From his Parisian exile, Alvaro reconstructs with more disenchantment than anger the melancholy vision of the Spanish colony in Cuba, slavery as the origin of the family fortunes, his catatonic childhood under Franco's fascist dictatorship, and his voluntary exile. To the other side of the Pyrenees, grown higher than ever, if he is on a collision course with the tourists flocking into Spain, his migration is parallel to that of the servant going into France.

In *Don Julián*, Alvaro sharpens the blades of his vengeance by resurrecting the legendary traitor who opened the doors of Andalusia to the Moors in 712. From a terrace in Tangier, Goytisolo writes his *Ulysses* while he imagines a renewed Arab invasion of Christian and gothic Spain. Accompanied by Julián he burns, sacks, and cuts the throats of all the literary, histori-

cal, and religious traditions of Spain invented by the Catholic monarchs, Ferdinand and Isabella. But the end of the novel prefigures *Juan sin tierra*: Alvaro, once more a child and disguised as Little Red Riding Hood, is sodomized by Julián, the Arab disguised as Granny. Before Bruno Bettelheim, Juan Goytisolo transformed the fairy tale into a key for deciphering psychic and social terrors; the Arab's sex tears through the boy Alvaro in the same way as did the stake traditionally employed by an armed and intolerant Spain against heretics, criminals, and, of course, Indian chieftains in the New World.

Goytisolo's first novel could be as sad and amiable as a page in Chateaubriand; the second one, as savage and gay as a passage in Sade. Both, when they appeared (the evidence was redundant), were classified as attempts in Hispanicide. Indeed, Goytisolo's prose, a ruin amongst ruins, passes as a burnt breath over the shambles of a country wedded to death. How to ruin the ruins; how to assassinate the dead? Goytisolo set fire to the cardboard facades of Franco's gigantic Potemkin village.

In one of the most extraordinary requiems in prose of our times, Juan Goytisolo, a perverse Bossuet, celebrated the death of Franco as the death of a part of Juan Goytisolo's life and of the life of many Spaniards. The world became incredible without the undesired father, the shadow who during forty years silenced the children who then became youths and were now mature men and women who had learned to read without reading, to see without seeing, to live without dying, in the long, parallel coexistence between a longevous dictator and the generation of Spaniards condemned to him and *by* him.

There is a strange coincidence between Franco's death and the life of *Juan sin tierra*. This is an exile's title, but also the title of his exile: the death of the hated father frees it from its immediate critical connotation; it transcends it without denying it, because the title of this exile—Juan the Landless—is the title of all the expulsions from Spain, even since the first landless Juan was exiled in 1492: the Spanish Jew. Freed from Franco but integrated into a historical totality, the land which Juan no longer has is no longer Spain: it is Utopia, the place that is not in space, because its reality happens only in time. But in what time does Utopia happen? Not in any time: only in the time of all. And the only time that belongs to all is the time of the origin, since it is the only duration which prefigures every future and cancels, in one fell ritual, the succession of the calendars.

Goytisolo's biography is profoundly original in the strict sense: *Juan sin tierra* occurs in the eternal present of myth and this is the myth of Utopia impossible in space but possible in the original time identified with (identical to) the texts which conceive it. Tierra: terror.

Goytisolo's textual gestures, simultaneously, partake of what they deny (the terror of the terrestrial, the space that denies Utopia) and oppose it with the utopias of the body, a body liberated *before* history, *before* the law: sodomy, phalolatry, coprophilia, incest, bestialism. Goytisolo sees these operations of the body as perverse and perverted only if seen with the optics of the earth conceived as the space of a false culture developing in a false linear time which simplistically transposes spatial extension to the measurement of time. But these operations are purely ritualistic if regarded with the optics of the original time, previous to the initiation of the culture of laws. Goytisolo does not see anal and phallic rites as the signs of any old decadence, but as the gestures proper to a savage, prehistoric stage of time before time.

Juan sin tierra is thus a voyage to the center of the body, since the body occupies the center of this ritualistic time. The true characters of Goytisolo's novel are names of the body. In *Conjunctions and Disjunctions,* Octavio Paz brilliantly traces the cultural curve that leads to separation between face and ass (divorce between soul and body) and illustrates it with a scandalous gravure by José Guadalupe Posada, the great Mexican artist of the turn of the century: a body with a face of buttocks. *Juan sin tierra* travels between the artistic and moral extremes of Quevedo who, in the seventeenth century, had written, with the surplus humor of the baroque, a litany on the *Graces and Disgraces of the Ass Hole,* and a funambular joke by Buñuel. The Spanish Golden Century, which was the last and late flowering of the Renaissance, devoured, included, related, named. The reductivism (the corporeal shame) of the twentieth century finds its definitive image in this scene by Buñuel: the guests at a sophisticated dinner party eat in secret and defecate in public.

Juan sin tierra is the black Utopia of the body shamed into hiding by anathema. Goytisolo's devaluation of the body is a consecration; it is also a condemnation. *Juan sin tierra,* a phallocratic Quixote, sallies forth to do battle against the windmills of nice sexual behaviour incarnated by the heterosexual, reproductive, and consumering couple that reads *Paris Match* and *Town and Country.* But Goytisolo's ethics, like his prose, support themselves on what they deny: in his fight against orthodox sexual intolerance, he relies on the opposing signs of unorthodox sexual intolerance. This is a profoundly Spanish attitude, to fight intolerance with intolerance. Américo Castro describes it in relation to the Spanish followers of Erasmus in the sixteenth century who attempted to constantly live "in the most exalted expectation of destiny." Nothing could be further from the Erasmian conversation on the relativity of truth, the illusion of appearance, and the ironies of reason and folly. Castro contrasts the spectral gesture of El Greco to the robust sensuality of Franz Hals. Goytisolo assumes all the unorthodox sexualities in order to free them from the spec-

tral condition of El Greco, but he does not lead them to the beer-swilling, sausage-swinging tavern of Franz Hals: he roots them in the same intolerant passion, in the same exalted destiny, of the orthodox Spaniards he detests.

If you wish to incarnate the physiology and the ethics of another forbidden body, you must also have *another* personality: you must be other: yet there is no other *self* without another *culture.* Both Américo Castro and Juan Goytisolo find this otherness for Spain in the Arab culture that represents untrammelled sensual pleasure. Alvaro, the narrator, chooses another body and another personality for himself, and these happen to be the bodies and personalities of those who became others: Fra Turmeda, a Medieval monk who converted to Islam; T. E. Lawrence, who only existed as long as he was disguised as an Arab; and Father Foucauld, the French missionary in the Sahara, who died—disguised as his assassins—in a useless effort to convert them.

And this is the parting of the ways between Alvaro and Dedalus: the Spaniard will not travel to "forge in the smithy of my soul the uncreated conscience of my race." *Juan sin tierra* is Goytisolo's *Finnegans Wake,* more desolate, more terrible because Alvaro shall renounce soul, conscience, and race. And if Dedalus, while searching for them, loses himself in Finnegan's funereal wake, Alvaro, who only searches for the body and its primeval rites, loses himself in a desert without oasis and there he bides, sharpening the knives with which he extirpated the forces of germination from the bodies he loves, as much as he hates the act of their conception. Now he must employ these razors against himself, against his own body: the final refuge of the solitary passion. This is the brief triumph of Onan, in the instant previous to the final castration.

Juan sin tierra is the novel of an exile. This exile leads us everywhere; thus, it leads us nowhere. It is the suicidal novel of the final body as it consumes itself in the pleasure of its own sterility. The fatal figure of the utter transformation is death. This is the beauty and the strength of Goytisolo's work; few artists are willing to risk so much so seriously, so unredeemingly. On the eve of self-destruction, Juan the landless stands alone: without Eve.

Faithful unto itself, *Juan sin tierra* would then seem to signal the end of Juan Goytisolo's literary career. We must think this in order to ask ourselves, immediately, if the suicidal deception is not our own and if Goytisolo's black Utopia is not, truthfully, but the ritual of a time that announces, in spite of itself, perhaps even in spite of Juan Goytisolo, a new legality, a new code, a new history, and a new space for culture.

A ghost then approaches the solitary figure of the desert in *Juan sin tierra*: this figure has breasts, vagina, a mound of Venus, and she too is another, she too is dual, she too devours in order to purify and feasts on refuse in order to conceive. Her name is Tlazolteotl and she is the Goddess of the Aztec night: she is the companion of the exalted Spaniard Juan sin tierra, his Eve covered with excrement and sperm. (pp. 73–6)

Carlos Fuentes, "Juan Goytisolo or the Novel as Exile," in *The Review of Contemporary Fiction*, Vol. 4, No. 2, Summer, 1984, pp. 72–6.

ABIGAIL LEE SIX

(essay date 1990)

[In the following excerpt, English educator and critic Lee Six discusses the themes of betrayal and sacrifice in *The Young Assassins, Children of Chaos,* and Goytisolo's other early works.]

In the first chapter of her excellent study of *Señas de identidad* and *Reivindicación del conde Don Julián*, called *Juan Goytisolo: la destrucción creadora*, Linda Gould Levine looks at the evolution pre-*Señas* of the theme of betrayal, together with the interplay of the figures of executioner and victim. Her analysis is illuminating, the basic thrust being that the early fiction was as preoccupied with the interlinked concepts of betrayal and the executioner-victim relationship, as the Mendiola trilogy would be; but at first, she explains, the elements appeared embodied in separate characters, whereas later, they fused together. Thus, Goytisolo's first published novel, *Juegos de manos* (*The Young Assassins*) is the story of a group of youths, longing to make their mark by rebelling against the regime and their conformist families. They decide to shoot a politician, but the plan fails dismally, when the member of the group chosen to perpetrate the crime is too afraid to carry it out. This person is David, a shy adolescent, unlike his tough, often unscrupulous companions and he has been chosen unfairly through the trickery as a character called Luis. The outcome of the flop is that Agustín, the *de facto* leader of the group and hitherto David's sponsor, feels obliged to kill him. The novel ends as Agustín is being led away by the police, grimly resigned to what the future must hold for him and actually pleased that he has committed himself to a new identity—that of murderer—and truly burnt his boats behind him. As Gould Levine points out, the roles of traitor, executioner, and victim are dramatized in clearly separate characters here, with Luis the traitor, David the sacrificial victim, and Agustín the executioner.

A similar structure can be identified in Goytisolo's second novel *Duelo en el Paraíso* (*Children of Chaos*) (1955), which is set during the Civil War. The main characters are a group of savage Republican children who have been evacuated to a rural boarding-school and their Nationalist neighbours on the estate called 'Paraíso' ('Paradise') consisting of assorted eccentric women and a boy called Abel, who has been sent there for his safety. Bored and lonely, Abel finally overcomes his shyness and snobbery and makes friends with one of the evacuees, a certain Pablo. Together they plan to run away and join the war, but Pablo betrays Abel and leaves him behind. The remaining evacuees then involve him in their war-games, but these turn nightmarishly serious when they decide to execute Abel for being on the enemy side. Again we have a betrayer—Pablo—a sacrificial victim—Abel—whose only crime is to have been born into a Nationalist family, and an implacable executioner, a child nicknamed *Arquero* ('Archer').

In both novels, the three characters seem predestined to play the role assigned to them in the betrayer-executioner-victim triangle, aware of and resigned to their part in the drama. But this is not the only prefiguration of [Goytisolo's] later novels. *Juegos* focuses on the impotence imposed on the main characters by the system: the only one who does succeed in asserting his freedom to some extent is Agustín, the executioner, and ironically, the price he will pay for it is no doubt his liberty, as the ending of the book indicates with his being led away by the police. Yet despite the pessimism of this irony, it conceals a glimmer of hope which will not return until the end of the Mendiola trilogy: by becoming a murderer, Agustín has successfully changed his identity, cast off the blue-eyed-boy shell in which his parents had enclosed him against his will, cut himself off irrevocably from his social background. Of his mother's love for him, he says, 'me envolvía como un ropaje excesivamente prieto' ('it wrapped itself around me like clothes that are too tight'). He feels impelled to rid himself of the constraining garment in such a way that it can never be donned again: 'Me es preciso quemar las naves' ('I must burn my bridges'), he says to David, and once he has done so, by killing him, he feels that he has killed himself too. This is true in the sense that he has killed his former self and taken on a new identity: that of a murderer. All these ideas—the parental vision of oneself resembling a form of imprisonment, the need to murder this virtuous shell, the consequence of the murder expressed as a change of identity—would be reworked and incorporated into the mature fiction, not to mention certain more obvious parallels: the use of masks and play-acting to create changeable identities, the nonconformism of the protagonists, their wish to be pariahs as far as the establishment was concerned, but also to be accepted by other social outcasts whom they admired (there is a more active group of rebels in *Juegos*, that the protagonists wish to impress by murdering the politician).

Duelo introduces the notion, crucial to the later fiction, of a character stigmatized by the accident of birth. The transparent symbolism of the victim-to-be having the name Abel, alerts the reader to his unchosen role; indeed, an air of inexorability hangs over the whole novel, since it is constructed as a flash-back, starting with the discovery of Abel's body. Another concept that appears in this novel and will take on considerable importance in the Mendiola trilogy is the split between the individual's childhood and adult selves. In *Juegos*, it had seemed that this abyss separating the two only existed for characters like Agustín, who had fought hard to create it; in *Duelo*, we realize that it is a natural phenomenon. Abel sees a photograph of his late grand-uncle as a child and wonders 'cómo aquel niño había podido trocarse en hombre viejo' (how that little boy could have changed into an old man). He reasons that 'puesto que no había muerto entonces, debía de andar oculto en algún sitio: los cuerpos de los niños que no morían jóvenes se metamorfoseaban y habitaban sus sueños' (since he had not died then, he must be hidden away somewhere: the bodies of children who did not die young were metamorphosed and inhabited their dreams).

In *Juegos,* we saw that voluntary metamorphosis was possible, as it would be again for Mendiola by the end of the trilogy, in *Duelo,* a more pessimistic vision prevails, for characters want to metamorphose but are unable to do so; Abel's aunt wants to metamorphose into a certain glamorous character called Claude, but 'comprendió la imposibilidad del cambio, el egoísmo obstinado del ser, la terca codicia de la sustancia' (she came to understand the impossibility of the change, a being's obstinate egotism, the stubborn covetousness of substance). (pp. 17–19)

These are fleeting foretastes, appreciable only with the benefit of hindsight. In one important sense, though, the whole plot of *Duelo* prefigures one of Alvaro Mendiola's fundamental problems. Just as Abel was a middle-class child whose bourgeois identity prevented him from being fully accepted by the low-class evacuees next door, the adult Alvaro similarly comes to long to be part of an underclass from which his 'pecado de origen', the sin of his origin, his involuntary white, bourgeois birthright irremediably bars him. When asked why they had killed Abel, one of the evacuees explained that although he had done them no harm personally, 'su familia era propietaria desde hacía muchos años y él tenía dinero en la época en que nosotros pasábamos hambre' (his family had been land-owners for many years and he had money at a time when we were going hungry). As in the Mendiola trilogy, *Duelo* presented this from the point of view of the frustrated member of the 'privileged' class, denied access to the ranks of the lowly. Thus, the relativity of outcast status was already treated in this early novel; the evacuees, called *desplazados*, literally those who are displaced, may have been the outcasts in the 'real' frame of reference of Spain during the Civil War, but Abel was clearly the pariah within the confines of his own self-image.. . . [Alvaro] suffers the same fate exactly, of being the pariah's pariah, rejected by the social outcasts whom he wishes to join.

After *Juegos de manos* and *Duelo en el Paraíso*, Goytisolo wrote a trilogy called 'El mañana efímero' ('Ephemeral Tomorrow'), quoting the turn-of-the-century Spanish poet, Antonio Machado, whose verse, though fiercely patriotic, was also sharply critical of national attitudes and looked to the country's future with ambivalence. The novels that constitute the trilogy, called *Fiestas* (1957), *El circo* (*The Circus*) (1957), and *La resaca* (*The Ebb* or *The Hangover*) (1958), leave the bourgeois perspective behind, focusing on the Andalusian underclass of Barcelona, in the style typical of the decade, which is to say, without authorial commentary and with implicit social criticism embedded in the documentary tone. The hypocrisy of the Church, the bigotry and heartlessness of the Catalonians in their attitudes towards the Andalusians, and the pure misery of poverty and deprivation, causing various characters to retreat into a fantasy world of one kind or another, are among the themes treated. But leaving aside this *engagé* aspect of the three novels, which perhaps seems somewhat dated in the 1980s, there are other elements that merit attention. As with *Juegos* and *Duelo*, the pattern of betrayal, followed by sacrifice of a victim by an executioner continues to feature strongly, as Gould Levine observes. As with *Duelo*, again we find particular attention paid to the world of children, their games, their fantasies, their suffering. But what comes out for the first time here is the special affinity and affection the author feels for Andalusians, the same feelings that led him to visit their home territory and subsequently to write two travelogues based on the time he spent there: *Campos de Níjar* (*Fields of Níjar*) (1960) and *La Chanca* (1962).

Catalonians call Andalusians *africanos* ('Africans'), intending the nickname as a term of abuse, in keeping with the traditional national antipathy towards the Moors. Goytisolo also feels that the Andalusians have something in common with the people of the Maghreb, but in his case, this is a compliment rather than an insult; indeed, he talks about his love affair with North Africa being a 'prolongación natural' (a 'natural extension'), of his relationship with Andalusia. And the literary progression from novels depicting Andalusians in Barcelona, to travelogues describing them at home, to North Africans in the Mendiola trilogy mirrors the author's own order of experience as he relates it in his memoirs.

Although the 'Mañana efímero' trilogy had introduced the sympathy and warmth for the Andalusians to be found in the travel books, by the time he came to write these, Goytisolo had recognized the artificiality of attempting to write with objectivity and omniscience about a society alien to him—that of poverty-stricken Andalusians—and never again would he attempt to write in this mode. The traveller is openly accepted as an enduring outsider presence in both *Campos de Níjar* and *La Chanca*, as well as in a Cuban travelogue called *Pueblo en marcha* (*People on the Move*) (1962). Similarly, two collections of short fiction, *Para vivir aquí* (*To Live Here*) (1960) and *Fin de fiesta* (*The Party's Over*) (1962), plus a short novel originally intended as a screenplay, *La isla* (*Sands of Torremolinos*) (1961) are all about the kind of people Goytisolo knew well, the bourgeoisie, even though his irritation with them had not diminished. He had simply recognized the impossibility of transmigrating his soul into the bodies of people with a radically different background from his own. This is what he said on the subject to Emir Rodríguez Monegal [as recorded in Monegal's *El Arte de narrar: diálogos*, 1968]:

> Si me propongo describir la realidad de un barrio pobre de Barcelona o del sur de España, yo no puedo escribir como si fuese un murciano que vive en las chabolas de Barcelona, un campesino pobre de Níjar o un pescador de La Chanca. Cuando me introduzco en su mundo, para mí estraño, para mi chocante, no puedo renunciar a llevar conmigo una tradición cultural, un medio social, una educación. Si hago un análisis de este mundo, ya sea de una región pobre del sur o de Barcelona, estoy obligado a hacerlo desde mi propio enfoque, desde mi propio punto de vista.. . . . A partir de *La resaca* me di cuenta que, si me proponía reflejar una serie de fenómenos propios de la sociedad española, tenía que . . . aceptar el subjetivismo.

> (If I set out to describe the reality of a poor quarter of Barcelona or of the South of Spain, I can't write as if I were a Murcian [Andalusian] living in the shanty-dwellings of Barcelona, a poor peasant from Níjar or a fisherman from La Chanca. When I go into their world, strange to me, shocking to me, a cultural tradition, a social milieu, an upbringing which I can't renounce comes with me. If I make an analysis of that world, be it a poor region in the South, or Barcelona, I am obliged to do so with my own focus, from my own point of view. . . . From *La resaca* onwards, I realized that if I set out to reflect a series of phenomena peculiar to Spanish society, I had to. . . accept subjectivity.)

In summary then, Goytisolo's early literature introduces certain preoccupations destined to come to the fore in his mature phase: betrayal and the executioner-victim relationship explored by Gould Levine; the nature of childhood and growing up seen as metamorphosis; the desire also to metamorphose at will, to take on a new identity; the plight of the pariah, especially that inverted variety which depicts a social superior rejected by the social inferiors whom he wishes to join. Alongside these issues, we find certain sentiments that will also endure, most notably, the preference for the disadvantaged in society over a smug élite and the desire to leave the native environment. Stylistically, the early novels fit into the realist documentary fashion of the times in which they were written, notwithstanding their use of symbolism and mythological patterns, but there is a marked shift away from attempted objectivity with the travel books, prefigured perhaps in the multiple points of view used in *Juegos de manos* and *Duelo en el Paraíso*, which will develop into the densely introspective, self-conscious narration of the later fiction. (pp. 19–22)

Abigail Lee Six, in her *Juan Goytisolo: The Case for Chaos*, Yale University Press, 1990, 232 p.

SOURCES FOR FURTHER STUDY

Epps, Brad. "The Politics of Ventriloquism: Cava, Revolution and Sexual Discourse in *Conde Julián*." *MLN Hispanic Issue* 107, No. 2 (March 1992): 274–97.

> Argues that Goytisolo's deconstruction of societal values in *Count Julian* leaves in place many troubling features of Spanish culture, most notably the tradition of women's oppression.

Gazarian Gautier, Marie-Lise. "Juan Goytisolo." In her *Interviews with Spanish Writers*, pp. 137–50. Elmwood Park, Ill.: Dalkey Archive Press, 1991.

> Covers a variety of issues, including Goytisolo's status as an exile-writer, his "literary genealogy," and the evolution of his thought and style.

González, B. A. "The Character and His Time: From *Juegos de manos* to *Reivindicación del Conde don Julián*." *Revista Canadiense de Estudios Hispánicos* IX, No. 1 (Autumn 1984): 31–44.

> Examines the changing conception of time in Goytisolo's works.

Henn, David. "Juan Goytisolo's Almeria Travel Books and Their Relationship to His Fiction." *Forum for Modern Language Studies* XXXIV, No. 3 (July 1988): 256–71.

> Comments on *The Countryside of Níjar* and *La chanca* as they relate to Goytisolo's other early work. Henn finds that the travelogues anticipate many concerns common to the author's later work as well.

Jordan, Paul. "Goytisolo's *Juan sin tierra*: A Dialogue in the Spanish Tradition." *Modern Language Review* 84, No. 4 (October 1989): 846–59.

> Maintains that *Juan the Landless* is a re-writing of Span-

ish Golden-Age texts, especially Miguel de Cervantes's *Don Quixote*.

Navajas, Gonzalo. "Confession and Ethics in Juan Goytisolo's Fictive Autobiographies." *Letras Peninsulares* III, Nos. 2–3 (Fall-Winter 1990): 259–78.

Explores the relationship between the self and society in Goytisolo's work.

Pope, Randolph D. "Writing after the Battle: Juan Goytisolo's Renewal." In *Literature, the Arts, and Democracy: Spain in the Eighties,* edited by Samuel Amell, pp. 58–66. Rutherford: Fairleigh Dickinson University Press, 1990.

Discusses *Landscapes after the Battle* as an example of the changing course of Spanish literature following the death of Franco.

The Review of Contemporary Fiction: Juan Goytisolo, Ishmael

Reed 4, No. 2 (Summer 1984): 4–175.

Presents a number of critical studies on individual titles in Goytisolo's oeuvre, as well as samples of his literary criticism.

Schwartz, Kessel. "Stylistic and Psychosexual Constants in the Novels of Juan Goytisolo." *Norte* XIII, Nos. 4–6 (July–December 1972): 119–28.

Highlights narrative techniques and thematic concerns common to Goytisolo's work before 1972.

Ugarte, Michael. "Juan Goytisolo: Unruly Disciple of Américo Castro." *Journal of Spanish Studies* 7, No. 3 (Winter 1979): 353–64.

Presents *Count Julian* as a fictional manifestation of Américo Castro's social and historical theories, which claim that it is myth which lies at the heart of reality.

Additional coverage of Goytisolo's life and career is contained in the following sources published by Gale Research: *Contemporary Authors,* Vols. 85–88; *Contemporary Authors New Revision Series,* Vol. 32; *Contemporary Literary Criticism,* Vols. 5, 10, 23; *Hispanic Writers;* and *Major 20th-Century Writers.*

Che Guevara

1928–1967

(Born Ernesto Guevara de la Sarna) Argentine political theorist and essayist.

INTRODUCTION

*E*rnesto "Che" Guevara, the Argentine-born Marxist revolutionary, remains a potent political symbol more than twenty years after his death at the hands of the Bolivian army. The bearded, beret-clad guerrilla leader, who inspired a generation of radical youth in the 1960s with his call for the defeat of United States imperialism, is still recognised by leftists all over the world as a martyr to the cause of third world revolution. Guevara's near-mythic reputation today rests largely on his military exploits and his personal example of courage, self-sacrifice, and idealism, rather than any major original contributions to Marxist theory and revolutionary practice. Guevara's best-known books are a training manual entitled *La guerra de guerrillas* (1960; *Guerrilla Warfare*) and his posthumously published *El diario de Che en Bolivia* (1968; *The Diary of Che Guevara*), but numerous collections of his speeches and articles on topics ranging from socialist morality to economic planning have also appeared over the years.

Guevara was born into a left-leaning, upper middle-class family to whom he remained close in later life. As a boy, Guevara developed the severe asthma condition that would plague him throughout his life and contributed to his decision to pursue a medical career. Guevara received his doctor of medicine degree from the University of Buenos Aires in 1953 and then traveled around South and Central America, eventually settling in Guatemala, where he worked as an inspector for the agrarian land redistribution program launched by reformist President Jacobo Arbenz Guzmán. Not long after the young physician arrived in that country, a military coup organized and financed by the U.S. Central Intelligence Agency overthrew the Arbenz government. After fruitless attempts to organize local popular resistance to the military takeover, Guevara took asylum in the Argentine embassy, where he remained for two months before fleeing to Mexico. Guevara's first-hand experience of the coup against Arbenz deepened his anti-American sentiments and helped convince him that armed revolution was needed to carry out and defend social reforms in Latin America.

In Mexico Guevara met the exiled Cuban brothers Fidel and Raúl Castro, who were organizing just such a revolutionary movement against the Cuban dictator Fulgencio Batista. Guevara agreed to join the Castros' "26 of July Movement" as the physician and sole non-Cuban among an expeditionary force of eighty-three guerrilla fighters who landed in Cuba from Mexico aboard the boat *Granma* in December of 1956. The Cuban army crushed the force immediately, but Guevara and the Castros were among the twelve survivors who managed to reach the rugged Sierra Maestra mountain range, where they began organizing the infrastructure for a prolonged guerrilla insurgency. Guevara, nicknamed "Che" by his Cuban comrades, took up arms with the rest of the insurgents and displayed such leadership ability that he was named commander of a second guerrilla column composed of local peasant recruits. He also served as a trusted political adviser to commander-in-chief Fidel Castro, headed the insurgent medical corps, and organized military training camps, a radio station, a weapons plant, and a network of schools in the guerrilla zone of control. In late 1958 Guevara's soldiers routed a much larger and better equipped Cuban army contingent at the decisive battle of Santa Clara, which convinced Batista to resign from office and flee the country. Not long afterward, Guevara led the first rebel force into Havana and sealed the revolutionary victory.

Guevara held a series of important positions in the early years of the Cuban revolutionary government, serving first as military commander of Havana's La Cabaña fortress and successively as a top official of the National Institute of Agrarian Reform, president of the National Bank of Cuba, and minister of industries. In the last two posts, Guevara (who was given the full citizenship rights of a native Cuban by the Castro government) became a leader in the immensely complex and difficult task of converting a sugar-based, capitalist economy heavily dependent on the United States into a state-run system with a more diversified production and trading base. In 1960 Guevara helped negotiate an historic trading pact with the Soviet Union, exchanging sugar for capital goods and, after the United States imposed an economic boycott of the island later in the year, he traveled to other East Bloc countries to develop new commercial relations. Better versed in Marxist economic theory than Castro, Guevara envisioned a socialist outcome for the Cuban Revolution, and he encouraged the Cuban leader to take the definitive step toward a state-run system by nationalizing virtually all of the country's industry in late 1960. As minister of

industries, Guevara confronted the daunting task of organizing, administrating, and expanding a broad range of industrial and agricultural enterprises. Determined to break Cuba from its over-reliance on sugar exports, Guevara sought to industrialize the island rapidly with support from the East Bloc, which provided generous aid and advantageous sugar prices. But Guevara believed that the emergence of a new "socialist morality" among the Cuban people would have the greatest effect in developing the island's economy in the long run. For this reason he favored moral over material incentives to raise production and advocated voluntary work programs to strengthen revolutionary consciousness and solidarity.

In early 1965 Guevara mysteriously disappeared from public view amid speculation that he had disagreed with Castro over economic policy and had been purged to placate the Soviet Union. Castro's official explanation that Guevara had freely departed Cuba to advance the cause of socialist revolution abroad was substantiated when he later appeared in Africa with two hundred Cuban troops to assist Congolese rebels. In 1966 he returned to Havana, where he made plans to apply his military expertise to the guerrilla insurgency in South America; Guevara's ultimate goal was to create "two, three, many Vietnams" to challenge what he perceived as the imperialist hegemony of the United States. With Castro's support, he assembled a force of Cuban and Peruvian revolutionaries who secretly entered Bolivia in late 1966. With the addition of some Bolivian rebels, the group began its guerrilla campaign in southeastern Bolivia in March 1967 after its presence was revealed to local peasants. Guevara's far-reaching plans proceeded disastrously, however, as neither the local peasantry nor the Bolivian Communist Party provided the expected support. The Bolivian army, actively assisted by the CIA, finally annihilated the guerrillas. Guevara was captured on 8 October 1967 and, after being identified by Cuban CIA agents, executed the next day.

Guevara's major political works reflect his attempt to adapt Marxist theoretical revolutionary principles to Latin America's unique historical and social conditions. He drew on his combat experience in the Sierra Maestra to write *Guerrilla Warfare,* a manual of guerrilla strategy, tactics, and logistics that was published in Cuba in 1960. In this work the author openly stated his hope that the Cuban example would trigger similar revolutions elsewhere in Latin America and argued that a dedicated guerrilla force of only a few dozen combatants could successfully initiate an insurgency virtually anywhere in the continent. Guevara's guerrilla manual found a readership not only among revolutionaries but also within the ranks of U.S. Army strategists seeking to apply lessons to the growing counter-insurgency war in South Vietnam. Guevara later wrote a series of articles describing his personal experiences in the

Cuban insurgency that were published in book form as *Pasajes de la guerra revolucionaria* (1963; *Episodes of the Revolutionary War*). *The Nation* reviewer Jose Yglesias found this collection "simple, beautiful, and politically prophetic."

Guevara's *Diary* is considered by many critics his most significant work. Seized by the Bolivian army after the destruction of Guevara's guerrilla force, the manuscript created a media sensation, and publishers in Europe and the United States offered bids for it ranging well over $100,000. The matter was settled, however, when Fidel Castro successfully intrigued to acquire the *Diary* and international publishing rights from Bolivia's Minister of the Interior, who subsequently fled the country in the ensuing political scandal. Written in a German calendar notebook in a direct, unadorned style, the *Diary* is an intensely personal account of Guevara's successes, failures, and frustations as he attempted to establish the Bolivian guerrilla movement.

Guevara summarized the group's activities at the end of each month, analyzing what had gone right—as well as what had gone wrong. Scholars agree that the work provides invaluable insights into Marxist revolutionary theory in the field of guerrilla warfare. Guevara further addressed his conception of the socialist "new man" and other political and social issues confronting post-capitalist society in numerous speeches and articles published in Cuban journals. He also wrote a number of papers on international economic topics still current today, such as the problem of third world foreign debt and terms of trade with the industrialized countries and the controversy over "market socialism" versus centralized planning in the non-capitalist world. Many of Guevara's major articles and speeches have been translated into English and appear in the collections *Che Guevara Speaks, Selected Speeches and writings* (1967) and *Venceremos! The Speeches and Writings of Ernesto Che Guevara* (1968).

CRITICAL COMMENTARY

CHE GUEVARA WITH LAURA BERGUIST

(interview date 1963)

[In the following excerpt, Berguist probes Guevara's views on Marxism, world politics, and social reform in Cuba.]

[Laura Berguist]: *Many early Castro supporters certainly didn't have today's Marxist-oriented revolution in mind. When you were fighting in the Sierra Maestra mountains, was this the future Cuba you envisioned?*

[Che Guevera]: Yes, though I could not have predicted certain details of development.

Could you personally have worked with a government that was leftist but less "radical"—government that nationalized certain industries, but left areas open for private enterprise and permitted opposition parties?

Certainly not.

Historically, the extreme Right and Left in Latin America (and Europe) have combined for different purposes, in an effort to topple "centrist" governments like Rómulo Betancourt's in Venezuela. Why does Cuba levy

more violent attacks at Betancourt than at dictator like Paraguay's Alfredo Stroessner.

Paraguay's dictatorship is obvious. Betancourt a traitor; he has sold out to the imperialists, and his government is as brutal as any dictatorship.

But Nasser of Egypt takes help from the "imperialist" West, as well as from the East. Has he "sold out"?

No, he is a big anti-imperialist. We are friends.

You once said Cuba would resist becoming a Soviet satellite to the "last drop of blood." But how "sovereign" were you when Khrushchev arranged with Kennedy for the missile withdrawal without consulting you?

As you know from Fidel's speech, we had differences with the Soviet Union.

You've traveled widely since our last talk—from the Punta del Este Conference in Uruguay to Moscow. Since you call yourself a "pragmatic Marxist" who learns from the "university of experience," what have you learned?

At Punta del Este, I learned in a shocking, first-hand way about the *servilismo* [servility] of most Latin-American governments to the United States. Your Mr. Dillon was a revelation to me.

Principal Works

La guerra de guerrillas (essays) 1960
[*Guerrilla Warfare*, 1961]

Pasajes de la guerra revolucionaria (reminiscences) 1963
[*Episodes of the Revolutionary War*, 1968; also published as *Reminiscences of the Cuban Revolutionary War*, 1968]

Che Guevara Speaks: Selected Speeches and Writings (essays and speeches) 1967

Obra revolucionaria (essays) 1967

El diario de Che en Bolivia: novembre 7, 1966, a octubre 7, 1967 (diaries) 1968
[*The Diary of Che Guevara; Bolivia: November 7, 1966-October 7, 1967*, 1968; also published as *The Complete Bolivian Diaries of Che Guevara and Other Captured Documents*, 1968]

Venceremos! The Speeches and Writings of Ernesto Che Guevara (essays and speeches) 1968

Che Guevara on Revolution: A Documentary Overview (diaries, essays, letters, and speeches) 1969

Obras, 1957–1967 (diaries, essays, and speeches) 1970

El hombre y el socialismo en Cuba (essays) 1973

Che Guevara and the Cuban Revolution: Writings and Speeches (essays and speeches) 1987

I've heard many Cubans refer to the period when Anibal Escalante was a director of ORI as "our Stalin" period. But Anibalistas are still in the government. What can keep them from regaining power?

Escalante was shipped out of the country. He had to go. That period is finished. We are completely reorganizing ORI along different lines.

Bureaucracy seems a plague of most "Socialist" countries. I noticed it in Moscow. Hasn't it also invaded Cuba?

Bureaucracy isn't unique to socialism: General Motors has a big bureaucracy. It existed in Cuba's previous bourgeois regime, whose "original sins" we inherited. After the Revolution, because we were taking over a complex social apparatus, a "guerrilla" form of administration did develop. For lack of "revolutionary conscience," individuals tended to take refuge in vegetating, filling out papers, establishing written defenses, to avoid responsibility. After a year of friction, it was necessary to organize a state apparatus, using planning techniques created by brother Socialist countries.

Because of the flight of the few technicians we had, there was a dearth of the knowledge necessary to make sensible decisions. We had to work hard to fill the gaps left by the traitors. To counteract this, everyone in Cuba is now in school.

During the last mobilization, we had many discussions about one phenomenon: When the country was in tension, everyone organized to resist the enemy. Production didn't lessen, absenteeism disappeared, problems were resolved with incredible velocity. We concluded that various forces can combat bureaucracy. One is a great patriotic impulse to resist imperialism, which makes each worker into a soldier of the economy, prepared to resolve whatever problem arises.

What about Cuba's new school system, which separates many children from their parents? Isn't it completely disrupting family life?

The revolutionary government has never had a definite policy, or dealt with the philosophical question of what the family should be. When the process of industrial development takes place, as in Cuba, women are increasingly at work and less at home caring for children. Nurseries must be established to leave the child somewhere. In places like the Sierra Maestra, where there can be no central schools after a certain age, because pupils are too widely scattered in the countryside, we think it better for the children to receive schooling in a specialized center like Camilo Cienfuegos School City. There they can also train for their later work in life. The child spends his vacations with his family—certainly this is no worse than the "boarding schools" of the wealthy people we knew, who did not see their children for eight to ten months a year. There are the problems of families divided, where half the members are revolutionary, the other half not with the Revolution—even pathetic cases of parents who left for Miami, but whose children of 12 or 14 did not want to go. If we hurt the family, it is because we haven't thought about it, not because we are against the family.

Recently, at a trade-union banquet, you noted that "youth" was conspicuously lacking among "exemplary workers" honored that night. Since this is such a "young" Revolution—why?

Perhaps an artificial division has arisen in the thinking of our people. In the armed defense of the Revolution, young people have always been disposed to heroic adventure. Ask them to make long marches, to take to the trenches or mountains, to sacrifice their lives if need be, and they respond. But when the word "sacrifice" refers to an obscure, perhaps even boring job that has to be done daily with efficiency and enthusiasm, older people of experience still excel them. Socialism cannot be achieved by either armed fight or work alone. We must now create a new authentic national hero—a work hero whose example is contagious, as potent as any military hero's.

Finally, what of claims by Cubans that "socialism" here is "different"?

Perhaps it was more spontaneous, but we are part of the Socialist world. Our problems will be solved by our friends. (pp. 26–7)

Che Guevara and Laura Berguist, in an interview in *Look*, Vol. 27, No. 7, April 9, 1963, pp. 26–7.

CHE GUEVARA
(essay date 1965)

[In the following essay, originally published in 1965, Guevara critiques the meaning and function of modern art from a Marxist perspective.]

People have for a long time been trying to free themselves from alienation through culture and art. While they die every day during the eight or more hours that they sell their labor power, they hope to come to life afterwards in spiritual activities. But this remedy bears the germs of the very alienation they fight during the day: it is as solitary individuals that they seek communion with their environment. They react to their oppressed indivudialities through the medium of art and they react to art as unique beings whose aspiration is to remain forever pure and alone.

This is simply an attempt to escape. The law of value is not just a naked reflection of relations of production under capitalism: the monopoly capitalists—even while using purely pragmatic methods—weave around art a complicated web which converts it into a willing tool of their interests and ideology. A school of artistic "freedom" is created, but its values also have limits even if they are only perceptible when we come into conflict with them—that is to say, only when the real problem of humanity and its alienation arises. Meaningless anguish and vulgar amusement thus become convenient safety valves for anxiety. The idea of using art as a weapon of protest and change is combatted. The condition which has been imposed by bourgeois culture is that one cannot try to escape from the monkey cage.

When the revolution occurred in Cuba there was an exodus of those who had been completely housebroken; the rest—whether they were revolutionaries or not—saw a new road open up before them. Artistic inquiry experienced a new impulse. The paths, however, had already been more or less laid out and artistic escapism hid itself anew behind the word "freedom."

Those countries which had gone through a similar process tried to combat such tendencies by an exaggerated dogmatism. General culture was virtually taboo. It was declared that the acme of cultural aspiration was the formally exact representation of nature, later transformed into a mechanical representation of a "positive" social reality. In other words, an ideal society almost without real conflicts or contradictions which the revolution was seeking to bring into being.

Socialism is young and has made errors. Many times revolutionaries lack the knowledge and intellectual courage to meet the task of developing the new man and woman with methods different from those handed down by custom and tradition, methods stamped with the alienation of the societies which created them. Disorientation is widespread, and the problems of economic development are foremost in a revolution. There are no artists of great authority who at the same time have great revolutionary authority. The party must take up the responsibility and seek the attainment of the main goal, the education of the people.

But the revolutions of the past sought simplification as a means to this end. They wanted an art that would be understood by everyone—the kind of "art" *functionaries* understand. True artistic values were disregarded, and the problem of general culture was reduced to combining some things from the socialist present and some from the dead past (since it was dead, it was not dangerous, they thought). Thus, Socialist Realism arose on the foundations of nineteenth-century art.

But the realistic art of the nineteenth century was also a class art, more purely capitalist perhaps than the decadent art of the twentieth century which at least reveals the anguish of alienated humanity. Why then should we try to find the only valid prescription for revolutionary art in the frozen academicism of Socialist Realism? We cannot counterpose the concept of Socialist Realism to that of complete artistic freedom because the latter does not yet exist and will not exist until the development of the new society approaches completion. But we should not attempt, from the pontifical throne of a "realism-at-any-cost," to condemn all the art forms which have come into being since the first half of the nineteenth century, for we would then be liable to the Proudhonian mistake of returning to a nostalgic past, of putting a straitjacket on the artistic expression of humanity which is being born and which is in the process of making itself anew through revolution. (pp. 117–28)

Che Guevara, "On Art and Revolution," translated by John Beverley, in *Praxis*, Vol. 1, No. 2, Winter, 1976, pp. 117–18.

FIDEL CASTRO
(speech date 1967)

[A leader of the Cuban Revolution together with Che, Castro considered Guevara an outstanding revolutionary leader and intellectual mentor. In the following essay, originally delivered as a speech at a memorial rally for Guevara in Havana's Plaza of the Revolution on October 18, 1967, Castro eulogizes Guevara's literary, military, and political achievements, noting "Che possessed the double characteristic of the man of ideas—of profound ideas—and the man of action."]

Revolutionary compañeras and compañeros:

I first met Che one day in July or August 1955. And in one night—as he recalls in his accounts—he became one of the future *Granma* expeditionaries, although at that time the expedition possessed neither ship, nor arms, nor troops. That was how, together with Raúl, Che became one of the first two on the *Granma* list.

Twelve years have passed since then; they have been twelve years filled with struggle and historical significance. During this time death has cut down many brave and invaluable lives. But at the same time, throughout those years of our revolution, extraordinary persons have arisen, forged from among the men of the revolution, and between those men and the people, bonds of affection and friendship have emerged that surpass all possible description.

Tonight we are meeting to try to express, in some degree, our feelings toward one who was among the closest, among the most admired, among the most beloved, and, without a doubt, the most extraordinary of our revolutionary compañeros. We are here to express our feelings for him and for the heroes who have fought with him and fallen with him, his internationalist army that has been writing a glorious and indelible page of history.

Che was one of those people who was liked immediately, for his simplicity, his character, his naturalness, his comradely attitude, his personality, his originality, even when one had not yet learned of his other characteristics and unique virtues.

In those first days he was our troop doctor. And so the bonds of friendship and warm feelings for him were ever increasing. He was filled with a profound spirit of hatred and loathing for imperialism, not only because his political education was already considerably developed, but also because, shortly before, he had had the opportunity of witnessing the criminal imperialist intervention in Guatemala through the mercenaries who aborted the revolution in that country.

A man like Che did not require elaborate arguments. It was sufficient for him to know that there were men determined to struggle against that situation, arms in hand. It was sufficient for him to know that those men were inspired by genuinely revolutionary and patriotic ideals. That was more than enough.

One day, at the end of November 1956, he set out on the expedition toward Cuba with us. I recall that the trip was very hard for him, since, because of the circumstances under which it was necessary to organize the departure, he could not even provide himself with the medicine he needed. Throughout the trip, he suffered from a severe attack of asthma, with nothing to alleviate it, but also without ever complaining.

We arrived, set out on our first march, suffered our first setback, and at the end of some weeks, as you all know, a group of those *Granma* expeditionaries who had survived was able to reunite. Che continued to be the doctor of our group.

We came through the first battle victorious, and Che was already a soldier of our troop; at the same time he was still our doctor. We came through the second victorious battle and Che was not only a soldier, but the most outstanding soldier in that battle, carrying out for the first time one of those singular feats that characterized him in all military action. Our forces continued to develop and we soon faced another battle of extraordinary importance.

The situation was difficult. The information we had was erroneous in many respects. We were going to attack in full daylight—at dawn—a strongly defended, well-armed position at the edge of the sea. Enemy troops were at our rear, not very far, and in that confused situation it was necessary to ask the men to make a supreme effort.

Compañero Juan Almeida had taken on one of the most difficult missions, but one of the flanks remained completely without forces—one of the flanks was left without an attacking force, placing the operation in danger. At that moment, Che, who was still functioning as our doctor, asked for two or three men, among them one with a machine gun, and in a matter of seconds set off rapidly to assume the mission of attack from that direction.

On that occasion he was not only an outstanding combatant but also an outstanding doctor, attending the wounded compañeros and, at the same time, attending the wounded enemy soldiers.

After all the weapons had been captured and it became necessary to abandon that position, undertaking a long return march under the harassment of various enemy forces, it was necessary for someone to stay behind with the wounded, and Che stayed with the wounded. Aided by a small group of our soldiers, he took care of them, saved their lives, and later rejoined the column with them.

From that time onward, he stood out as a capable and valiant leader, one of those who, when a difficult mission is pending, do not wait to be asked to carry it out.

Thus it was at the battle of El Uvero. But he acted in a similar way on a previously unmentioned occasion during the first days when, following a betrayal, our little troop was attacked by surprise by a number of airplanes and we were forced to retreat under the bombardment. We had already walked a distance when we remembered some rifles of some peasant soldiers who had been with us in the first actions and had then asked permission to visit their families, at a time when there was still not much discipline in our embryonic army. Back then we had thought that possibly the rifles were lost. I recall that the problem was not brought up again and, during the bombardment, Che volunteered, and having done so, quickly went to recover those rifles.

This was one of his principal characteristics: his willingness to instantly volunteer for the most dangerous mission. And naturally this aroused admiration—and twice the usual admiration, for a fellow combatant fighting alongside us who had not been born here, a man of profound ideas, a man in whose mind stirred the dream of struggle in other parts of the continent and who nonetheless was so altruistic, so disinterested, so willing to always do the most difficult things, to constantly risk his life.

That was how he won the rank of commander and leader of the second column, organized in the Sierra Maestra. Thus his standing began to increase. He began to develop as a magnificent combatant who was to reach the highest ranks in the course of the war.

Che was an incomparable soldier. Che was an incomparable leader. Che was, from a military point of view, an extraordinarily capable man, extraordinarily courageous, extraordinarily aggressive. If, as a guerrilla, he had his Achilles' heel, it was this excessively aggressive quality, his absolute contempt for danger.

The enemy believes it can draw certain conclusions from his death. Che was a master of warfare! He was an artist of guerrilla struggle! And he showed that an infinite number of times. But he showed it especially in two extraordinary deeds. One of these was the invasion, in which he led a column, a column pursued by thousands of enemy soldiers over flat and absolutely unknown terrain, carrying out—together with Camilo [Cienfuegos]—an extraordinary military accomplishment. He also showed it in his lightning campaign in Las Villas Province, especially in the audacious attack on the city of Santa Clara, entering—with a column of barely 300 men—a city defended by tanks, artillery, and several thousand infantry soldiers. Those two heroic deeds stamped him as an extraordinarily capable leader, as a master, as an artist of revolutionary war.

However, now after his heroic and glorious death, some people attempt to deny the truth or value of his concepts, his guerrilla theories. The artist may die—especially when he is an artist in a field as dangerous as revolutionary struggle—but what will surely never die is the art to which he dedicated his life, the art to which he dedicated his intelligence.

What is so strange about the fact that this artist died in combat? What is stranger is that he did not die in combat on one of the innumerable occasions when he risked his life during our revolutionary struggle. Many times it was necessary to take steps to keep him from losing his life in actions of minor significance.

And so it was in combat—in one of the many battles he fought—that he lost his life. We do not have sufficient evidence to enable us to deduce what circumstances preceded that combat, or how far he may have acted in an excessively aggressive way. But, we repeat, if as a guerrilla he had an Achilles' heel, it was his excessive aggressiveness, his absolute contempt for danger.

And this is where we can hardly agree with him, since we consider that his life, his experience, his capacity as a seasoned leader, his authority, and everything his life signified, were more valuable, incomparably more valuable than he himself, perhaps, believed.

His conduct may have been profoundly influenced by the idea that men have a relative value in history, the idea that causes are not defeated when men fall, that the powerful march of history cannot and will not be halted when leaders fall.

That is, true, there is no doubt about it. It shows his faith in men, his faith in ideas, his faith in examples. However—as I said a few days ago—with all our heart we would have liked to see him as a forger of victories, to see victories forged under his leadership, since men of his experience, of his caliber, of his really unique capacity, are not common.

We fully appreciate the value of his example. We are absolutely convinced that many men will strive to live up to his example, that men like him will emerge from the peoples.

It is not easy to find a person with all the virtues that were combined in Che. It is not easy for a person, spontaneously, to develop a character like his. I would say that he is one of those men who are difficult to match and virtually impossible to surpass. But I would say that the example of men like him contributes to the appearance of men of the same caliber.

In Che, we admire not only the fighter, the man capable of performing great feats. What he did, what he was doing, the very fact of his rising with a handful of men against the army of the ruling class, trained by Yankee advisers sent in by Yankee imperialism, backed by the oligarchies of all neighboring countries—that in itself constitutes an extraordinary feat.

If we search the pages of history, it is likely that we will find no other case in which a leader with such a limited number of men has set about a task of such importance; a case in which a leader with such a limited number of men has set out to fight against such large forces. Such proof of confidence in himself, such proof of confidence in the peoples, such proof of faith in man's capacity to fight, can be looked for in the pages of history—but the likes of it will never be found.

And he fell.

The enemy believes it has defeated his ideas, his guerrilla concepts, his point of view on revolutionary armed struggle. What they accomplished, by a stroke of luck, was to eliminate him physically. What they accomplished was to gain an accidental advantage that an enemy may gain in war. We do not know to what degree that stroke of luck, that stroke of fortune, was helped along, in a battle like many others, by that characteristic of which we spoke before: his excessive aggressiveness, his absolute disdain for danger.

This also happened in our war of independence. In a battle at Dos Ríos they killed the apostle of our independence; in a battle at Punta Brava, they killed Antonio Maceo, a veteran of hundreds of battles. Countless leaders, countless patriots of our war of independence were killed in similar battles. Nevertheless, that did not spell defeat for the Cuban cause.

The death of Che—as we said a few days ago—is a hard blow, a tremendous blow for the revolutionary movement because it deprives it, without a doubt, of its most experienced and able leader.

But those who boast of victory are mistaken. They are mistaken when they think that his death is the end of his ideas, the end of his tactics, the end of his guerrilla concepts, the end of his theory. For the man who fell, as a mortal man, as a man who faced bullets time and again, as a soldier, as a leader, was a thousand times more able than those who killed him by a stroke of luck.

However, how should revolutionaries face this serious setback? How should they face this loss? If Che had to express an opinion on this point, what would it be? He gave this opinion, he expressed this opinion quite clearly when he wrote in his message to the Latin American Solidarity Conference that if death surprised him anywhere, it would be welcome as long as his battle cry had reached a receptive ear and another hand reached out to take up his rifle.

His battle cry will reach not just one receptive ear, but millions of receptive ears. And not one hand but millions of hands will reach out to take up arms. New leaders will emerged. The men of the receptive ears and the outstretched hands will need leaders who emerge from the ranks of the people, just as leaders have emerged in all revolutions.

Those hands will not have available a leader of Che's extraordinary experience and enormous ability. Those leaders will be formed in the process of struggle. Those leaders will emerge from among the millions of receptive ears, from the millions of hands that will sooner or later reach out to take up arms.

It is not that we feel that his death will necessarily have immediate repercussions in the practical sphere of revolutionary struggle, that his death will necessarily have immediate repercussions in the practical sphere of development of this struggle. The fact is that when Che took up arms again he was not thinking of an immediate victory; he was not thinking of a speedy victory against the forces of the oligarchies and imperialism. As an experienced fighter, he was prepared for a prolonged struggle of five, ten, fifteen, or twenty years, if necessary. He was ready to fight five, ten, fifteen, or twenty years, or all his life if need be! And within that perspective, his death—or rather his example—will have tremendous repercussions. The force of that example will be invincible.

Those who cling to the idea of luck try in vain to deny his experience and his capacity as a leader. Che was an extraordinarily able military leader. But when we remember Che, when we think of Che, we do not think fundamentally of his military virtues. No! Warfare is a means and not an end. Warfare is a tool of revolutionaries. The important thing is the revolution. The important thing is the revolutionary cause, revolutionary ideas, revolutionary objectives, revolutionary sentiments, revolutionary virtues!

And it is in that field, in the field of ideas, in the field of sentiments, in the field of revolutionary virtues, in the field of intelligence, that—apart from his military virtues—we feel the tremendous loss that his death means to the revolutionary movement.

Because Che's extraordinary character was made up of virtues that are rarely found together. He stood out as an unsurpassed man of action, but Che was not only an unsurpassed man of action—he was a man of visionary intelligence and broad culture, a profound thinker. That is, in his person the man of ideas and the man of action were combined.

But it is not only that Che possessed the double characteristic of the man of ideas—of profound ideas—and the man of action, but that Che as a revolutionary united in himself the virtues that can be defined as the fullest expression of the virtues of a revolutionary: a man of total integrity, a man of supreme sense of honor, of absolute sincerity, a man of stoic and Spartan living habits, a man in whose conduct not one stain can be found. He constituted, through his virtues, what can be called a truly model revolutionary.

When men die it is usual to make speeches, to emphasize their virtues. But rarely as on this occasion can one say of a man with greater justice, with greater accuracy, what we say of Che: that he was a pure example of revolutionary virtues!

But he possessed another quality, not a quality of the intellect nor of the will, not a quality derived from experience, from struggle, but a quality of the heart: He was an extraordinarily human man, extraordinarily sensitive!

That is why we say, when we think of his life, that he constituted the singular case of a most extraordinary man, able to unite in his personality not only the characteristics of the man of action, but also of the man of thought, of the man of immaculate revolutionary virtues and of extraordinary human sensibility, joined with an iron character, a will of steel, indomitable tenacity.

Because of this, he has left to the future generations not only his experience, his knowledge as an outstanding soldier, but also, at the same time, the fruits of his intelligence. He wrote with the virtuosity of a master of our language. His narratives of the war are incomparable. The depth of his thinking is impressive. He never wrote about anything with less than extraordinary seriousness, with less than extraordinary profundity—and we have no doubt that some of his writings will pass on to posterity as classic documents of revolutionary thought.

Thus, as fruits of that vigorous and profound intelligence, he left us countless memories, countless narratives that, without his work, without his efforts, might have been lost forever.

An indefatigable worker, during the years that he served our country he did not know a single day of rest. Many were the responsibilities assigned to him: as president of the National Bank, as director of the Central Planning Board, as minister of industry, as commander of military regions, as the head of political or economic or fraternal delegations.

His versatile intelligence was able to undertake with maximum assurance any task of any kind. Thus he brilliantly represented our country in numerous international conferences, just as he brilliantly led soldiers in combat, just as he was a model worker in charge of any of the institutions that he was assigned to. And for him there were no days of rest; for him there were no hours of rest!

If we looked through the windows of his offices, he had the lights on until all hours of the night, studying, or rather, working or studying. For he was a student of all problems; he was a tireless reader. His thirst for learning was practically insatiable, and the hours he stole from sleep he devoted to study.

He devoted his scheduled days off to voluntary work. He was the inspiration and provided the greatest incentive for the work that is today carried out by hundreds of thousands of people throughout the country. He stimulated that activity in which our people are making greater and greater efforts.

As a revolutionary, as a communist revolutionary, a true communist, he had a boundless faith in moral values. He had a boundless faith in the consciousness of man. And we should say that he saw, with absolute clarity, the moral impulse as the fundamental lever in the construction of communism in human society.

He thought, developed, and wrote many things. And on a day like today it should be stated that Che's writings, Che's political and revolutionary thought, will be of permanent value to the Cuban revolutionary process and to the Latin American revolutionary process. And we do not doubt that his ideas—as a man of action, as a man of thought, as a man of untarnished moral virtues, as a man of unexcelled human sensitivity, as a man of spotless conduct—have and will continue to have universal value.

The imperialists boast of their triumph at having killed this guerrilla fighter in action. The imperialists boast of a triumphant stroke of luck that led to the elimination of such a formidable man of action. But perhaps the imperialists do not know or pretend not to know that the man of action was only one of the many facets of the personality of that combatant. And if we speak of sorrow, we are saddened not only at having lost a man of action. We are saddened at having lost a man of virtue. We are saddened at having lost a morally superior man. We are saddened at having lost a man of unsurpassed human sensitivity. We are saddened at having lost such a mind. We are saddened to think that he was only thirty-nine years old at the time of his death. We are saddened at missing the additional fruits that we would have received from that intelligence and that ever richer experience.

We have an idea of the dimension of the loss for the revolutionary movement. However, here is the weak side of the imperialist enemy: They think that by eliminating a man physically they have eliminated his thinking—that by eliminating him physically they have eliminated his ideas, eliminated his virtues, eliminated his example.

So shameless are they in this belief that they have no hesitation in publishing, as the most natural thing in the world, the by now almost universally accepted circumstances in which they murdered him after he had been seriously wounded in action. They do not even seem aware of the repugnance of the admission. They have published it as if thugs, oligarchs, and mercenaries had the right to shoot a seriously wounded revolutionary combatant.

Even worse, they explain why they did it. They assert that Che's trial would have been quite an earthshaker, that it would have been impossible to place this revolutionary in the dock.

And not only that, they have not hesitated to spirit away his remains. Be it true or false, they certainly announced they had cremated his body, thus beginning to show their fear, beginning to show that they are not so sure that by physically eliminating the combatant, they can eliminate his ideas, eliminate his example.

Che died defending the interests, defending the cause of the exploited and the oppressed of this continent. Che died defending the cause of the poor and the humble of this earth. And the exemplary manner and the selflessness with which he defended that cause cannot be disputed even by his most bitter enemies.

Before history, men who act as he did, men who do and give everything for the cause of the poor, grow in stature with each passing day and find a deeper place in the heart of the peoples with each passing day. The imperialist enemies are beginning to see this, and it will not be long before it will be proved that his death will, in the long run, be like a seed that will give rise to many men determined to imitate him, many men determined to follow his example.

We are absolutely convinced that the revolutionary cause on this continent will recover from the blow, that the revolutionary movement on this continent will not be crushed by this blow.

From the revolutionary point of view, from the point of view of our people, how should we view Che's example? Do we feel we have lost him? It is true that we will not see new writing of his. It is true that we will never again hear his voice. But Che has left a heritage to the world, a great heritage, and we who knew him so well can become in large measure his beneficiaries.

He left us his revolutionary thinking, his revolutionary virtues. He left us his character, his will, his tenacity, his spirit of work. In a word, he left us his example! And Che's example will be a model for our people. Che's example will be the ideal model for our people!

If we wish to express what we expect our revolutionary combatants, our militants, our men to be, we must say, without hesitation: Let them be like Che! If we wish to express what we want the men of future generations to be, we must say: Let them be like Che! If we wish to say how we want our children to be educated, we must say without hesitation: We want them to be educated in Che's spirit! If we want the model of a man, the model of a man who does not belong to our time but to the future, I say from the depths of my heart that such a model, without a single stain on his conduct, without a single stain on his action, is Che! If we wish to express what we want our children to be, we must say from our very hearts as ardent revolutionaries: We want them to be like Che!

Che has become a model of what men should be, not only for our people but also for people everywhere in Latin America. Che carried to its highest expression revolutionary stoicism, the revolutionary spirit of sacrifice, revolutionary combativeness, the revolutionary's spirit of work. Che brought the ideas of Marxism-Leninism to their freshest, purest, most revolutionary expression. No other man of our time has carried the spirit of proletarian internationalism to its highest possible level as Che did.

And when one speaks of a proletarian internationalist, and when an example of a proletarian internationalist is sought, that example, high above any other, will be the example of Che. National flags, prejudices, chauvinism, and egoism had disappeared from his mind and heart. He was ready to shed his generous blood spontaneously and immediately, on behalf of any people, for the cause of any people!

Thus, his blood fell on our soil when he was wounded in several battles, and his blood was shed in Bolivia, for the liberation of the exploited and the oppressed, of the humble and the poor. That blood was shed for the sake of all the exploited and all the oppressed. That blood was shed for all the peoples of the Americas and for the people of Vietnam—because while fighting there in Bolivia, fighting against the oligarchies and imperialism, he

> ## Ebon on the origins of Guevara's nickname:
>
> He liked to be called "Che." When Guevara was made a "native-born" Cuban by law, his nickname legally became part of his name. As director of the National Bank of Cuba, he brought his personal and informal touch to the face of all bank notes: they bore his signature, "Che Guevara." "Che" is a hail-fellow expression of camaraderie. He used to call those around him "Che" so often and consistency that they began to use the word back at him. And as "Che Guevara" he has become a symbol in contemporary history. Since his dramatic death in Bolivia, which ended an attempt at guerrilla warfare that was to spread to all of Latin America, the Guevara legend has achieved worldwide proportions. The myth of Che Guevara has set off a responsive vibration among thousands who see him as the gallant revolutionary—a symbol of rebellion—against hypocrisy, injustice, human suffering, and a society without soul.
>
> Martin Ebon, in his *Che: The Making of a Legend*, 1969.

knew that he was offering Vietnam the highest possible expression of his solidarity!

It is for this reason, compañeros and compañeras of the revolution, that we must face the future with optimism. And in Che's example, we will always look for inspiration—inspiration in struggle, inspiration in tenacity, inspiration in intransigence toward the enemy, inspiration in internationalist feeling!

Therefore, after tonight's impressive ceremony, after this incredible demonstration of vast popular recognition—incredible for its magnitude, discipline, and spirit of devotion—which demonstrates that our people are a sensitive, grateful people who know how to honor the memory of the brave who die in combat, that our people recognize those who serve them, which demonstrates the people's solidarity with the revolutionary struggle and how this people will raise aloft and maintain ever higher aloft revolutionary banners and revolutionary principles—today, in these moments of remembrance, let us lift our spirits, with optimism in the future, with absolute optimism in the final victory of the peoples, and say to Che and to the heroes who fought and died with him:

Hasta la victoria siempre! [Ever onward to victory]

Patria o muerte! [Homeland or death]

Venceremos! [We will win]

(pp. 19–29)

Fidel Castro, "Introduction: Che's Enduring Contributions to Revolutionary Thought," in *Che Guevara and the Cuban Revolution: Writings and Speeches of Ernesto Che Guevara*, edited by David Deutschmann, Pathfinder/Pacific and Asia, 1987, pp. 19–32.

Guevara with political ally Fidel Castro.

EMILE CAPOUYA

(essay date 1968)

[In the following excerpt, Capouya reviews Guevara's personal account of the Cuban revolution, focusing on *Reminiscences of the Cuban Revolutionary War* and *Guerrilla Warfare*.]

In order to arrive at a true estimate of men like Ernesto Guevara and his fellow-revolutionary, Fidel Castro, we should first of all have to wake up to the world in which we are living. In that world, there are two hundred million Latin Americans, most of whom are very hungry, and their hunger is a necessary feature of the political and economic arrangements that make us North Americans rich. They are ruled for the most part by armed degenerates whose brutality bears an exact proportion to the

misery over which they preside, and the degenerates in question are subsidized out of the American treasury. In that waking world of hunger and hopelessness, Guevara and Castro took up the cause of the dispossessed. Most unfortunately—by our own standards of social decency, by our own ideals of freedom and personal dignity, by our own humane professions—they are in the right and we are in the wrong. That is what all the shooting is about.

Ernesto Guevara was, next to Fidel Castro, the most influential spirit and the best mind of the Cuban Revolution—both in its military phase and, after the overthrow of Batista, in the phase of intensive social reconstruction that still goes on . . . . Guevara's classic work is *Guerrilla Warfare*. Two translations have been published in this country, both of them technically and stylistically faulty. Guevara was, among other things, a first-rate writer, and no available translation of any of his works does him justice. Readers must be warned, accordingly, that the spirit of the man and sometimes the point and bearing of his ideas are misrepresented in English.

Guerrilla Warfare is more than a treatise of irregular military operations. It is a manual of political struggle in regions ruled as Latin America is ruled. For Guevara, guerrilla warfare is important because it is the most appropriate political instrument—and also the most effective instrument of political education—in countries like pre-revolutionary Cuba, where three general conditions exist: poverty, a predominantly rural economy, and no legal means of reform and redress. For understandable reasons, neither the conservatives nor the adherents of the traditional leftist sects and parties in North and South America are willing to accept the thesis.

Reminiscences of the Cuban Revolutionary War is Guevara's unadorned memoirs of his own service in that struggle. They suffer somewhat from having been set down as occasion offered, and because the author confined himself strictly to what he himself had done or observed. Guevara hoped that other participants in the revolution would write their own accounts in the same sober spirit, and produce collectively an accurate report of that turning-point in the history of the Western Hemisphere. The most interesting sections of the present book are concerned with the hand-to-mouth stage of the revolution, when, after the rout of the *Granma* expedition, the 12 survivors, including Guevara, Fidel Castro, and Camilo Cienfuegos, were fugitives rather than soldiers. Semi-starved, often bivouacking without shelter, for a long time, their object was mere survival and their immediate enemies were the climate and the terrain. Whether we are concerned with political and military history or with the history of particular souls, the transition from the stage of survivors in flight to the phase of effectual rebellion is of the highest interest. Despite the circumstantial character of Guevara's narrative, unfortunately, that transition accomplishes itself offstage, for there is a hiatus in the account precisely at the point where the material and moral current must have shifted to permit the first forays upon Batista's troops.

What does emerge clearly enough is Guevara's personal development in the course of the fighting. When it began, he was an enthusiast for revolution and the next thing to an invalid (he suffered all his life from incapacitating attacks of asthma), and, for all his spirit, hardly a likely soldier, one would think. But he fought along on sheer nerve, bearing severe physical hardship with his comrades, and showing reserves of will that marked him as a natural leader in difficult undertakings. Fidel Castro says of him that his failing as a soldier was excessive disregard of danger, and coming from that authority the judgment is one we had better accept. Yet there is no doubt that Guevara was one of the master tacticians of recent military history.

In that respect, *Guerrilla Warfare* is his witness; it is the only significant work on the subject written in the West—for the good reason that no other writers have had clear strategic notions in the light of which their tactics might be developed. The strategic aims of Western commentators tend to be, as it were, subconscious, and in any case unavowable. But in Guevara's writings, strategy is always conceived in terms of political evolution, and is necessarily more ample, more adequate in terms of reality, than the abstract geo-politics plus games theory that passes for military thought in other places.

For an example of his astuteness as a political analyst, the reader is referred to the epilogue to *Guerrilla Warfare,* in which, writing in 1959, he predicts the manner and means of the invasion of Cuba that was to take place in 1961. Another classic of analysis and polemic is his speech at the Punta del Este conference (reproduced in *Che Guevara Speaks*), called for the purpose of quarantining Cuba and containing the Latin-American revolution by means of the Alliance for Progress. Guevara's exposition of the program's defects, had they been heeded, might have saved Mr. Moscoso from resigning his directorship in despair when time had made clear to everyone what was clear only to the Cuban delegation at Punta del Este.

The present volume ends with 26 remarkable letters written by Guevara, for the most part while he was serving as a bureaucrat of the revolution after the seizure of power. I think it impossible to read those letters—direct, unassuming, austere—and not know that one is in the presence of a rare being, a man of principle, deserving of Castro's eulogy: "Immensely humane, immensely sensitive."

Ernesto Guevara was wounded in the Bolivian mountains, captured, and apparently shot after capture. Then his body was exhibited to photographers by relieved officials. From his point of view, fair enough—he had sought out just such a fate. But our perspective must be different. He was a very great man. He died at 39. In terms of the political evolution of Latin America in this century, the loss cannot be made up. (pp. 110–11)

Emile Capouya, "Che Guevara—the Loss Looms Larger," in *Commonweal*, Vol. LXXXVIII, No. 4, April 12, 1968, pp. 110–11.

NORMAN GALL
(essay date 1968)

[In the following essay, Gall reviews several works by Guevara, tracing the development of his ideological position as revealed in his political essays.]

The capture and murder last October in Bolivia of Ernesto "Che" Guevara was the most significant consequence of his own botched guerrilla insurgency. The story of his death—still subject to final refinement of detail—adds new mythic material to the reverence most Latin Americans feel for martyred guerrilla saints like Mexico's Emiliano Zapata. Nicaragua's Augusto Sandino and Colombia's rebel priest, Father Camilo Torres. Moreover, in Guevara's case, the flame of publicity has lighted candles in the literary salons of New York and Paris, as well as in the official eulogies of the Cuban Revolution and in the imagination of revolutionary youth throughout the world. The shadow, of course, has dwarfed the man; it has been enlarged by canonization and official tribute of the kind easily turned into a lean and flashy song.

The lacquered image of Che Guevara will not be beautified by the anemic spurt of quickie books issuing from his death [*Venceremos!, Reminiscences of the Cuban Revolutionary War, Episodes of the Revolutionary War* and *Che Guevara Speaks*]. Nor, as a result of their publication, will we understand more clearly the mystery of his restless romanticism, which has become an ideal for some of the more dynamic and concerned youth of both Americas. Offered here are diverse collections of the hero's wooden words, yielding little of Che's affecting presence and charm, and even less food for the nourishment of romantic illusion. Instead, human warmth gives way to the stilted, humorless prose of his official pronouncements, articles and speeches published by the Castro regime since 1959.

There are no unguarded moments here, only occasional signs of a momentous intellectual pilgrimage by a wanderer with the noble obsession of forming a pure and just human society, at whatever cost. Unfortunately, no independent editor or scholar has bothered to tell us of the origins and course of the pilgrimage, or of the intellectual milestones along the way. John Gerassi's introduction to *Venceremos!* is not what is needed. It merely provides a thin biographical sketch of the author, without any critical evaluation of his development or his political role.

The spirit shining through these hastily produced volumes is the fervent orthodoxy of the newly converted. They are full of exhortations for Cuban workers to work, to get organized, to produce, to correct the chaotic "errors" of the state-spawned bureaucracy that Che himself helped build to monster proportions. There is urgency throughout, as well as a healthy sense of vindication through the cyclonic social progress of the revolution.

Since Che was one of the key symbols and spokesmen of Cuba's revolutionary government, virtually every word in these books was uttered for its propaganda effect. His public personality shone strongest outside Cuba—and beyond the shadow of Fidel Castro—in cavalier appearances with beard and olive-green fatigues at international conferences such as the Punta del Este meeting of 1961 (when Cuba was expelled from the Organization of American States) and in Geneva at the 1964 United Nations Conference on Trade and Development. On that occasion he offered a modest proposal that, given the declining terms of trade for the Third World, the underde-

veloped nations suspend payments of dividends, interest and amortization "until such time as the prices for [their] exports reach a level which will reimburse them for the losses sustained over the past decade."

Until he landed in Cuba in late 1956 in Fidel Castro's confused but momentous guerrilla expedition, Ernesto Guevara was part of Latin America's permanent floating population of young political bohemians; he had shown scant interest in "Marxist-Leninist" teachings. Relatives report that since his early adolescence he was prodigious in both his sympathy for the unfortunate and in his fondness for the open road.

As a teen-ager, he took marathon bike trips to read poetry to the inmates of a leper colony. His absorbing interest in leprosy and its victims led him, both as a medical student and a young doctor, into extravagant wandering (from the time of his first motor-bike trip across the Andes in 1952) into remote parts of South America to visit leprosariums and participate in anti-leprosy campaigns. By the time he met the Castro brothers in 1955 in Mexico City, where he earned his living as sidewalk photographer, Che already had obtained a much broader Knowledge of Latin America than any of Cuba's top revolutionary leaders were ever to achieve. He had traveled through Bolivia just after the profound and convulsive 1952 revolution, when the tin miners had crushed the Bolivian Army and, in effect, seized the mines, when Indian serfdom was abolished and land and the vote given the hacienda peons. He had wandered about Colombia in the years of the *violencia*, the savage civil war that claimed 200,000 lives, then drifted to Guatemala just in time to witness the C.I.A.-organized invasion of right-wing exiles (conniving with key Guatemala Army officers) that ended the agrarian revolution of President Jacobo Arbenz, whose Communist and other leftist supporters did not rise to his defense. The lessons of these wanderings were hardened in Che's exemplary career as a guerrilla column leader in Cuba's Sierra Maestra, and only after he descended from the hills did the attitudes formed by these experiences begin to take doctrinal shape.

The formal crystallization of his revolutionary belief began when he became a kind of alter ego and lightning rod in Fidel Castro's maneuvers to consolidate his power. The formalization of his ideal was dramatized best in his last published essay, the utopian **"Man and Socialism in Cuba"** (reprinted in *Venceremos* and *Che Guevara Speaks*), which appeared in Uruguay shortly after his widely publicized disappearance in March, 1965, and proposes a new moral motor for socialist society. It underscored a common feeling in the young Cuban leadership that a new kind of Communist is being formed by the revolution, far better in breeding and behavior than the Stalinist party hacks implicated in sordid bargains with the old Batista dictatorship.

Che's last visionary essay foresees the day when "man will begin to see himself mirrored in his work and to realize his full stature as a human being through the object created, the work accomplished. Work will no longer entail surrendering a part of his being in the form of labor-power sold, which no longer belongs to him, but will represent an emanation of himself reflecting his contribution to the common life, the fulfillment of his social duty. We are doing everything possible to give labor this new status of social duty and to link it on the one side with the development of a technology which will create the conditions for greater freedom, and on the other side with voluntary work based on a Marxist appreciation of the fact that man truly reaches a full human condition when he produces without being driven by the physical need to sell his labor as a commodity."

This is the glorification of the "moral incentives" to production—as opposed to material incentives of pay hikes pegged to economic performance advocated by Soviet-oriented Marxists—which under Che's influence have come to dominate the Cuban production ethos. Indeed, this moral formula bears a striking resemblance to that of China's communes and the disastrous "Great Leap Forward," and the analogies between Cuban and Chinese Marxism do not end there.

Just as Mao Tse-tung has been responsible for the adaptation of Marx and Lenin to Chinese cultural traditions, Castro and Guevara have been attempting another major mutation—under Chinese influence—by designing a program of revolutionary armed struggle for Latin America. Curiously, neither Che nor Castro nor Mao made any systematic study of Marxism-Leninism until they had come to power or—in Mao's case—retreated to a secure guerrilla base area.

Mao's peasant origins always have inclined him to a profoundly popular and violent form of revolutionary struggle, which was fed and inflamed by peasant self-defense against the scourge of Japanese invasion in the 1930's. On the other hand, the guerrilla theories of Che and Fidel are more narrowly rooted in the radical student politics of Latin-American universities, and contain the "élitist" flaw of imposing the guerrilla movement—as Che did, fatally, in Bolivia—from outside the peasant area, often with little preparation and less regard for local conditions.

Unfortunately, the anthologies published since Che's death fail to include—and barely mention—his little handbook, Guerrilla Warfare, which is probably the most influential book published in Latin America since World War II, even though its strategic precepts may be wrong and the guerrilla movements it guided may have failed. While Che's strategic formulation has failed so far to change the outcome of Latin America's revolutionary struggle, it has profoundly altered its focus and tone.

Of the four volumes under consideration here, two are separate editions of Che's recollections of the Cuban guerrilla insurrection in the Sierra Maestra mountains of Oriente Province, while John Gerassi's Venceremos anthology contains most of this text. These "reminiscences" were first published as separate articles in the Cuban armed forces magazine, Verde Olivo, for the political orientation of the military establishment. It is a skeletal official history told in the first person, strangely shy of personal reflection or any departure from normative political requirements.

In contrast, for example, to George Orwell's graphic and introspective memoir, in Homage to Catalonia of boredom and filth and starvation in the trenches of Spain, Ernesto Guevara steers clear of the "subjective" literary material that would seem to be of greatest interest: the inner life of the guerrilla band, the doubts, the sufferings, the quarrels, the factions, the diverse strains of human character tied together in a struggle to survive, the give and take of winning the loyalty of frightened peasants and of outwitting Batista's brutal, stupid, pot-bellied army.

As a result, the skirmishes are all here but the war is missing. The soldier-author affects a kind of Hemingwayesque curtness and stoicism, with little interest in personality save for a monotonous and perhaps abnormal adulation of Fidel Castro. Of the spear-carriers we learn little, save that Juan was a peasant who joined the guerrillas and became a good fighter, while José sneaked away one night to betray his comrades to the army, and that Che always knew that Pedro, the quiet one, was also a traitor, since after Castro came to power he went into exile in Miami.

Of the two anthologies reviewed here, the slimmer one, Che Guevara Speaks, has by far the more incisive and luminous selection of Che's writings, and costs much less than the bulky, repetitious and carelessly assembled Gerassi collection. Che in print is important because of his influence on the Cuban Revolution (his public utterances consistently anticipated Fidel's future moves) and his symbolic meaning to much of Latin America. But the warmth and weight of his personality are muffled in his official words, and the evolution of his intellectual character still needs to be described.

Norman Gall, "Guerrilla Saint," in The New York Times Book Review, May 5, 1968, pp. 3, 34–5.

KENNETH MINOGUE
(essay date 1970)

[In the following excerpt, Minogue articulates the principal tenets of Guevara's "concrete and practical" Marxism.]

Che was a Marxist in both his actions and his theories.

His fame in his respect is such as to place him along-side Bernstein, Kautsky, Lenin, Rosa Luxemburg, Tito, Ho Chi Minh and Mao Tse-tung. Most of these leaders combined action with theory, but the theory is mostly subordinate to the action. Such was the case with Che.

What did his Marxism amount to? Here we need to observe the way in which Marxism itself has developed in the first century of its existence. Marxism in the nineteenth century claimed its following because it stood at the opposite pole from the attitudes of a professional revolutionary like Louis Blanqui, or a romantic anarchist like Mikhail Bakunin. Marxism recognised the fact that a man cannot simply 'make a revolution'. It recognised this fact by asserting that a great deal of preparatory work must go into building up the proletarian organisation that will make the revolution. But it developed these 'practicalities' of the activity of making revolutions vastly further, till they had become elaborated into the celebrated philosophy of history known as historical materialism. Every society was seen as a ferment of 'contradictions' working themselves out by a steady process of which the human participants were often quite unaware.

Marx developed this line of thought so far that he reached the conclusion that no society would be transformed by revolution until its potentialities had all been developed. Capitalism, for example, would have to go through a number of stages until everything inherent in it had been worked out. And when that point had been reached, then revolution would come about as part of the natural process. The Protestant reformers and the merchants of northern Europe, for example, had overthrown feudal society quite effectively, in spite of the fact that they had no theory of revolutionary social transformation and their conscious thoughts had been focused on quite different preoccupations. Now this version of Marxism evidently leaves very little room for the conscious making of revolutions. Up to the point at which potentialities had been exhausted, revolution could only fail or generate a monstrosity; and beyond that point, the resistance to revolution was so feeble that it would in all probability be a quick and relatively painless affair.

Now this is the version of Marxism which made it the most important brand of socialism of its time. On the basis of it, nineteenth-century Marxists expected the revolution to come first in the most advanced industrial countries. It took a man as strong minded as Lenin to overthrow this theory. He had already significantly revised Marxism by developing a theory of imperialism to explain why capitalism was lasting longer than had been expected, and a theory of the party as the vanguard of the proletariat in order to build up the revolutionary organisation he thought was needed in Czarist Russia. In 1917 at the Finland Station, he instructed his followers to work directly for an immediate proletarian revolution, in spite of the fact that capitalism was very little developed in the Russia of the early twentieth century.

Lenin was the first really talented revisionist of Marxism, and after his time the history of Marxism is the history of men who showed the theory who was boss. Mao Tse-tung defied Stalin's orthodox advice and built a successful revolution amongst the peasants. And Fidel Castro, along with Che, made a revolution in Cuba which was so much based upon a practical sense of local conditions that it was only some years later, and under the pressure of economic need, that the revolution came to be approximately squared with Marxist theory.

By the 1960s, even Marxists themselves, long immured as they were in Stalinist scholasticism about 'correct' lines of thought, had come to recognise this. Marxism, they began to proclaim, was not a dogma but a method, and for its elucidation they turned to the romantic strain which is prominent in the very early writings and which also appears in some of the very late pieces. Here we find a Marx who is the moral critic of contemporary capitalist society, and who develops the notion of alienation to explain why it is that human life as we moderns know it is so impoverished. The new Marxism of the mid-twentieth century has thrown off the fashionable positivism that Marx had absorbed a century before; it no longer advances Marxism as superior because it is 'scientific' socialism. On the contrary, it throws to the fore the element of Marxism which appeal to hope, and which inflame the will to make revolutions and bring the long awaited terminus to the horrors of capitalism. What remains of the old Marx is the idea that all the evils of the world compose a single system and that each man must fight for the revolution in whatever circumstances he may find himself. The Marxism of Che belongs to this latter kind.

Yet Che does seek to restore the original unity between the romantic and the 'scientific' elements of Marxism, and he does so with a simplicity that can only be regarded as savage, and impatient:

> There are truths so evident, so much a part of people's knowledge, that it is now useless to discuss them. One ought to be "marxist" with the same naturalness with which one is "newtonian" in physics or "pasteurian" in biology, considering that if facts determine new concepts, these new concepts will never divest themselves of that portion of truth possessed by the older concepts they have outdated. . . . The merit of Marx is that he suddenly produces a qualitative change in the history of social thought. He interprets history, understands its dynamics, predicts the future, but *in addition* [my italics] to predicting it (which would satisfy his scientific obligation), he expresses a revolutionary concept: the world must not only be interpreted, it must be transformed. Man ceases to be the slave and tool of his environment and converts himself into the architect of his own destiny. . . . We, practical revolutionaries, initiating our own struggle, simply fulfil laws foreseen by Marx the scientist.

Marxism is, then, taken entirely for granted. A fully conscious revolutionary, as Che understands him, has the same sort of awareness that he lives in a world full of exploitation as the average man has that stones fall down, not up. Revolutionary struggle is as natural to him as walking and speaking; and as he walks and speaks he makes discoveries about the world which happen to correspond to the 'laws' of Marxian ideology. It is here—in the area where theory is related to practice—that the Cuban revolution has made its major contribution to Marxism; it is here that a kind of individualist renaissance has followed the frozen middle ages of Stalinism. This is the contribution of Che, of Fidel, and it was brought to its fullest maturity in the writings of Regis Debray. It amounts to a new version of the supremacy of practice over theory. Latin America had long been equipped with orthodox Marxists, but they had not succeeded in making revolutions. On the other hand, people who *did* succeed in making revolutions did in the end turn into orthodox Marxists. Such, at least, was the official view of the Cuban movement, a view which (it has been plausibly suggested) has allowed Castro to support guerrilla movements in Latin America and to by-pass the existing communist parties whilst yet claiming, for the benefit of his patron the Soviet Union, to be unimpeachably correct in his line.

Che's Marxism, like everything else about him, is concrete and practical. We hear little about historical epochs, and very little analysis of class relations. We do hear a great deal about the guerrilla. Developed into a theory, the guerrilla generates the idea of the *foco* the process of revolutionary detonation by which a small band of guerrillas set up a centre of attraction in the sierras and bring the capitalist or neo-colonialist regime to its knees. It is essential to this theory, certainly as developed by Debray, that the *foco* be regarded as simultaneously military and political. No longer does the commissar fight beside the soldier and guard the purity of his doctrine; for the two figures are fused together by practice, and the guerrilla will learn in the fires of experience what the urban communist has abstractly acquired from his books.

This development of Marxism runs very quickly into a problem which cannot but have struck anyone who has considered the history of Marxism. Marxism, we have seen, has largely been developed by its heretics—the men who knew when to throw aside the book and act on their own political judgment. Further, this has now happened so often that (as we have seen) it has received official recognition in the way in which Marxism is now conceived. The whole notion of orthodoxy, with its apparatus of 'correct' lines, has weakened in the poly-centric communist world of the mid-twentieth century. For those many, however, who wish to repair the fractured unity of theory and practice every break induces a desire to restore the unity. Consequently each change has been followed by a development of theory which purports to learn the lessons of the new experience.

The Russians, the Chinese, the Yugoslavs and the Cubans have all indulged in this exercise. Its logic is of course, inductive. It consists in transposing the most striking facts of the successful experience into abstract terms and generating theory from them. In this way, the successful landing of Castro and his guerrillas in Eastern Cuba, their difficult but successful struggle to survive, and their final overthrow of the Batista regime, turn into the theory of the *foco;* the fact that these men were revolutionaries whose acquaintance with Marxist theory was slim, and that they became increasingly sweeping in their ambition to remodel the social order, turns into the thesis that under guerrilla conditions the military and political struggles fuse together.

This kind of argument is, we have noted, inductive, and inductive argument has been subject to devastating criticism. Why, the critics ask, does the inductive reasoner select *this* set of facts, and out of this set of facts generate *this* set of general principles? For since logically all experiences are very complex, and capable of generating very large numbers of facts and principles, the inductive reasoner must have left out of his account of what he was doing the crucial principle which led him to select (rather than to discover) what he has found. The attempt to learn lessons from practice very frequently gets shipwrecked on this difficulty, and political and military history, no less than that of ideologies, is full of people learning the wrong lessons and being surprised by the reality they encounter.

The Cuban experience, then, began by rejecting a good deal of Marxism as being inappropriate to the special conditions of Latin America. There was good warrant in Marxism itself—indeed in Marx himself—for such cavalier treatment of established principles. But the ideological passion to realign theory with practice led to the production of a revised ideology which *would* be appropriate to Latin American conditions. Such a production is immediately subject to the same criticism as that on which it is itself based: Need we assume that Latin America is homogeneous enough to be covered by such a general theory? Might it not be true that each region of Latin America, or even perhaps each separate country, might have its own particular conditions; might, in other words, require its own special theory? It would seem that Che, who worked hard to develop a Marxism appropriate to Latin America, did not carry his reasoning this far. But his fate has certainly provoked other Marxists to do so.

Here, to understand Che's Marxism, we need to consider the conditions of his Bolivian enterprise. Bolivia is a small and relatively underdeveloped country in the geographical heart of South America; and it seems that it was primarily this geo-political fact which made it attractive to Che as the detonator of the revolutionary liberation of the whole continent. It had a government which (like many in South America) called itself 'revolutionary', but was not so in any respect that Che would recognise;

and it had an army which was small, ill-equipped, and had been savagely mauled back in the 1930s in a war with Paraguay, an even smaller and more primitive state. It had lots of jungle and plenty of peasants, and its economy depended upon tin, the miners of which commodity were frequently in a turbulent condition.

Anyone looking at these conditions with a fresh eye would light upon the tin miners as the evident beginning of a revolutionary movement in Bolivia. But it would seem that Che looked at Bolivia and saw only Cuba; looked at its wild and inhospitable countryside and saw the Sierra Maestra; looked at President Barrientos, and saw only the figure of Batista. What Che established in Bolivia was a carbon copy of what Fidel had done in Cuba. And since Che was, far more than Fidel, a theoretical animal, the conclusion is tempting that Che was the victim of his own theory. He seems to have believed that Cuba was *nothing else but* the first instance of a pattern that could be repeated in other parts of Latin America. He had, like so many figures in history, learned the lessons of experience—the wrong lessons. For what was missing in Bolivia was a thousand particular characteristics—the radical organisation in the cities, the feebleness of the Batista government, and perhaps above all the fact of leadership by the able, articulate, intuitive and entirely native Fidel.

Thinking in international terms, Che clearly thought that a revolution could be induced in Bolivia without a prominent Bolivian leader. No doubt he had to think this, since no serious candidate was available; but even beyond this inevitable deficiency, Che (and Fidel) exhibited an astonishing indifference to local Bolivian sensibilities. They failed to win over the peasants, they alienated the local communist party and they never managed to have more than a few effective Bolivians fighting amongst their picked Cuban veterans.

In this respect, then, Che has run the whole gamut of experience available to a Marxist theoretician. He bucked the theory to make a revolution, reconstructed the theory to fit the revolution he had made, and then proceeded to demonstrate by his actions the inadequacy of his own theory. It is not an enviable odyssey and it is unlikely to be frequently repeated.

Yet the adventures of a man are not the same as the premises of an ideology. The accidents which often lead to fatal consequences in the world of action are a standing *ceteris paribus* clause for an ideology; and an adroit use of this clause will prevent any theory from being refuted. We must therefore qualify our conclusion in two ways: firstly, that Che's failure in Bolivia does not necessarily indicate that the theory of the *foco* must be discarded, for it may simply be the case that ill-luck and poor preparation led to that particular disaster. More importantly, the very failure itself has abundantly the heroic quality which Che often spoke about in his writings and speeches. Whilst the Bolivian episode did—to some extent—refute one part of Che's Marxism, it also illustrated another part, and one

which, although of less interest to practical revolutionaries, is far more important in generating the legend. This part of Guevara's Marxism is his preoccupation with 'the new man'.

The most suitable text for illustrating this preoccupation is **"Man and Socialism in Cuba,"** perhaps the most famous pamphlet he ever wrote. It is here that Che states what may be vulgarly called the ideals of the movement: and the central ideal is the creation of the new man. This figure of the inevitable future is sketched out against the familiar Marxist account of twentieth-century life. Man suffers a kind of death, we learn, during the eight hours of his daily work, and even the artistic creations by which he might express the (presumed) anguish of his environmentally determined situation have been restricted by an ideological conditioning through which the monopoly capitalists prevent art from becoming (what Che thinks it must become if it is to be authentic) a 'weapon of denunciation and accusation'.

Man is exploited, and consequently his moral stature is diminished; but this happens very largely without his awareness. His attention is focused (by the agents of the monopoly capitalists) upon the success of a Rockefeller, and diverted away from the unsavory facts which made such a gigantic accumulation of wealth in the hands of one man possible. Since this is a rhetorical document, it would be unfair to press too hard upon its logical inadequacies. We need merely to note that Che has in full measure the belief common among men of his time that human beings are 'conditioned' by the environment in which they live, and that the adoption of revolutionary Marxism, although not inexplicable in terms of social conditions, is the one form of human behavior in which man throws off his 'conditioning' and embraces freedom. Clearly this is an equivocation upon the notion of 'conditioning', for the conditioning that a man can throw off is no conditioning at all. What is evidently being used here is the commonsense distinction between proceeding thoughtlessly along the paths of habit on the one hand, and becoming more self-conscious and deliberate on the other. This latter is a casual distinction we commonly make; but as transposed into Marxist ideology, it is dressed in a different vocabulary and becomes a pseudo-science of social determination. What Che has to say about it is very little distinguished from the writings of any other exponent of Marxist beliefs; what does distinguish him is his intense interest in the other term of the contrast—the new man who will replace the spiritual cripple of today's capitalist world.

Often, the specification is extremely crude, since it derives from the easy device of inserting the word 'revolutionary' before moral words which are universally regarded as virtues. There are times when Che indulges in what is virtually self-parody, and exhorts us to engage in revolutionary struggle with revolutionary dedication towards revolutionary aims. In the end, the new man does not turn out to be very much more than a revolutionary paragon:

> We are seeking something new that will allow a perfect identification between the government and the community as a whole, adapted to the special conditions of the building of socialism and avoiding to the utmost the common-place of bourgeois democracy transplanted to the society in formation . . . the ultimate and most important revolutionary aspiration (is) to see man freed from alienation.

This freedom is specified in two main ways. The first is that the new man will be the possessor of a highly developed social consciousness. This means, presumably, that the category of the private will disappear from his thinking. It certainly means that the new man will hold the same beliefs about social reality which are already held by Che himself, along with the revolutionary vanguard. In other words, the distinction between agreeing with Che's Marxist interpretation of the world, and disagreeing with it, has been transposed into the distinction between being socially conscious and remaining 'conditioned' and unaware. The doctrine of social consciousness, in other words, is a vehicle of dogmatism by which the promotion of one particular interpretation of social life is being passed off as the only possible thought on the subject.

The new man, then, will be a dedicated communist. His second general characteristic is that he will be a dedicated worker towards the communal goal of building up the community. Since Che speaks for an 'underdeveloped' country, the actual content of the work of building up the community is, quite simply, economic self-sufficiency. What it would be beyond that is very little specified. But there is one part of the revolutionary work which is so powerful that it has infused the entire picture:

> Let me say, with the risk of appearing ridiculous, that the true revolutionary is guided by strong feelings of love. It is impossible to think of an authentic revolutionary without this quality. This is perhaps one of the great dramas of a leader; he must combine an impassioned spirit with a bold mind and make painful decisions without flinching. Our vanguard revolutionaries must idealize their love for the people, for the most hallowed causes, and make it one and indivisible. . . . They must struggle every day so that their love of living humanity is transformed into concrete deeds, into acts that will serve as an example, as a mobilizing factor.

Love is the master passion of the new man. It involves 'doing away with human pettiness' and it will be both higher and more persistent than love found under contemporary conditions: 'There ought to be a spirit of sacrifice not reserved for heroic days only, but for every moment.' Again: 'One ought always to be attentive to the human mass that surrounds one.'

In praising the speech which has supplied these last quotations, Che's editor, Professor Gerassi, writes:

> '. . . the author gently criticizes Cuba's communist youth for its dogmatism, dependence on official directives, lack of inventiveness, lack of individuality—yes, Che was always fostering individualism—and continues with a beautiful, moving definition of what a communist youth ought to be.'

Che's emphasis on the new man may, then, be taken initially as evidence of his attachment to individuality, but to an individuality of a new and more complete kind than exists now. If there is any part of Che's Marxism (by contrast with other features of his career) which is responsible for the legend, it is to be found here. Communism has often been associated with a soulless collectivity, a kind of endless *corvée* directed towards some remote and abstract goal. But here is a major exponent of communism outflanking the appeal of capitalism on its own individualist ground.

Significantly enough, perhaps, it is in passages like this that Che sounds most like an old-fashioned Christian preacher; and he may easily be presented as a man trying to fuse the best of the old moral ideals with the most complete attention to the social realities which religious exhortation in the past has often ignored. Nor can this theme in Che be dismissed as merely the attractive rhetoric of a man who was, after all, something of a poet. For in his enjoyment of power, Che showed a powerful and continuous hostility to the capitalist device of material incentives, because he believed that such incentives split people off from one another; he believed that they stood in the way of developing the only truly socialist motive for working harder—socialist emulation.

Yet before we take Che's devotion to individuality entirely at its face value, we must consider two important qualifications. The first arises immediately if we ask: What exactly does Che mean by 'individuality'? A man like John Stuart Mill, who in his essay *On Liberty* supplied the classic account of individuality, believed that each person has his own unique thoughts to think and lines of action to pursue; and in what Che would call a capitalist society, which Mill would call a liberal one, the laws and governing institutions should be so framed as to permit the greatest possible development of such resources of individuality. But we can hardly believe that Che is thinking anything remotely like this when we read:

> Thus we go forward. Fidel is at the head of the immense column—we are neither ashamed nor afraid to say so—followed by the best party cadres, and right after them, so close that their great strength is felt, come the people as a whole, a solid bulk of individualities moving toward a common aim; individuals who have achieved the awareness of what must be done; men who struggle to leave the domain of necessity and enter that of freedom.

These are individualities only in the sense that a tray of buns straight from the baker's oven contains a collection of individualities. Each is separate, but in all essential respects they are made up of the same materials, they have the same awareness of the same 'what must be done'. And if we pursue this line of thought further we shall find many occasions on which Che speaks exactly like an old-fashioned Stalinist agitator—or 'orientator' as Fidel guilefully renamed the function: he harangues the workers to produce more and to rise above their personal preoccupations in order to join in the common struggle. Indeed, this theme becomes at times so obtrusive that the inspiring notion of the 'new man' looks like nothing so much as a carrot to induce people to drive tractors more carefully, or to ease pining for luxuries like chewing gum and lipstick which are no longer imported from the United States. And although it is perilous to extract a doctrine from writings which are fundamentally rhetorical, we must conclude that although Che makes use of the appeal of individualism, his view of the matter is consistently the one he expressed when he discussed revolutionary medicine:

> Individualism, in the form of the individual action of a person alone in a social milieu, must disappear in Cuba. In the future, individualism ought to be the efficient utilization of the whole individual for the absolute benefit of a collectivity.

There could be no better illustration than this of the way in which an ideological thinker appropriates an attractive term for propaganda purposes, and changes the meaning so that it means precisely the opposite of what once made it attractive.

The second qualification we must make to Che's individualism is closely related to the first. One of the most important differences between current capitalist society and the revolutionary society of the future is that the first has a government which must repress the people whilst the second has only leaders, or a vanguard, who are one in love and feeling with the people. The desire to eliminate politics from life, to create a community in which no one shall be rendered alien by his exercise of power, is as old as Rousseau and (in this century) as wide as the seven seas. It is by no means confined to Marxism, but it is a very powerful motor of that doctrine. To anyone who stands outside this current of thought, the aspiration can only seem delusory, the more so because it is precisely the leaders speaking most about love who have perpetrated some of the worst excesses of our time. The love which is supposed to unite Fidel and his people, for example, has had to emerge out of the early apparatus of televised executions and the constant hostility of some hundreds of thousands of Cubans who have preferred exile to the benefits of such a love.

We may go further: virtually all modern politics is an exercise of ventriloquism, in which the rulers speak *on behalf of* a populace which is most of the time necessarily mute. In the countries conventionally recognised as democratic—countries like Britain and America—this muteness is qualified by periodic elections, and by a fairly constant ferment of discussion and criticism. Nevertheless, it is of the nature of authority that whoever holds it must in the end make a pronouncement which shall be accepted as the political decision of the populace involved. Now most ideologies are devices by which this ventriloquial act may be carried on with virtually no interference from the puppet whatever. A democratic government, having to face elections, must come to some terms with the political opinions of its working class. But a Marxist government does not have a working class: it has a proletariat, whose consciousness may (by the rules of the ideology) be objectively determined, and instead of a political problem the government is faced by a pseudo-educational one: how to make the people conscious of what it *must* be thinking (but actually may not be). A great deal of what Che has to say is part of this kind of ventriloquial performance. The justification of it—as given to a group of communist youth—goes as follows:

> If we—disoriented by the phenomenon of sectarianism—were unable to interpret the voice of the people, which is the wisest and most orienting voice of all; if we did not succeed in receiving the vibrations of the people and transforming them into concrete ideas, exact directives, then we were ill-equipped to issue those directives to the Union of Young Communists.

In politics at least, a posture of humility often disguises arrogance; and those whom men wish to control they first drown in flattery. The 'concrete ideas' which the Cuban government articulates from the 'vibrations' of the people are indistinguishable from the practices of all the other countries in which Marxism has become the official creed. Here is Che discussing the central problem that arises from the pretence that there is no gap between a government and its people:

> And today . . . the workers consider the state as just one more boss, and they treat it as a boss. And since this [Che is referring to the new Cuba] is a state completely opposed to the State as Boss, we must establish long, fatiguing dialogues between the state and the workers, who although they certainly will be convinced in the end, during this period, during this dialogue, have braked progress.

This is one more version of the Stalinist argument that no safeguards (such as an opposition) are needed in a communist society, because the only oppression is class oppression, and classes have been abolished. It is a Quixotic argument in the most literal sense, for no intelligent worker is going to be taken in by propaganda pictures of Che or Fidel out in the fields humping bags of sugar. And it is particularly Latins who will, once the excitement of the moment is past, treat with amusement such exhortations as that of Che to 'raise our voices and make Fidel's radio vibrate. From every Cuban mouth a single shout: "Cuba si, Yankees no! Cuba si, Yankees no!'" The political problem is that when the puppet does get restless, and the 'dialogue' fails, the ventriloquist generally resorts to clouting him.

Our conclusion must be that although Che had a journalistic flair for the concrete detail, and although he was supremely sensitive to the intellectual and emotional atmosphere of his time, his Marxism is really very little distinguished from that of other Marxists. In the field of revolutionary guerrilla tactics, he will no doubt be remembered for a variety of devices and observations; he is the inventor, for example, of the 'beehive effect' whereby one of the leaders, 'an outstanding guerrilla fighter, jumps off to another region and repeats the chain of development of guerrilla warfare—subject, of course, to a central command.' But in the field of theory he has contributed very little, which is not surprising, since he was man who wrote gestures, postures, promises and exhortations, rather than arguments of any depth. (pp. 23–38)

Kenneth Minogue, "Che Guevara," in *The New Left: Six Critical Essays*, edited by Maurice Cranston, The Bodley Head, 1970, pp. 17–48.

SOURCES FOR FURTHER STUDY

Berger, John. "Che Guevara." In *The Look of Things: Essays by John Berger,* edited by Nikos Stangos, pp. 42–53. New York: The Viking Press, 1974.

> Considers the meaning of the recorded images of Guevara following his execution by the Bolivian army in 1967.

Ebon, Martin. *Che: The Making of a Legend.* New York: Universe Books, 1969, 216 p.

> Biographical study focusing on Guevara's career as a revolutionary activist.

Gerassi, John. Introduction to *Venceremos!: The Speeches and Writings of Ernesto Che Guevara,* edited by John Gerassi, pp. 1–22. New York: The Macmillan Co., 1968.

> Surveys Guevara's political career, noting that Che "was primarily a doer, a revolutionary activist."

James, Daniel. Introduction to *The Complete Bolivian Diaries of Che Guevara and Other Captured Documents,* edited by Daniel James, pp. 11–69. New York: Stein and Day, 1968.

> Reviews "the background and course of the Bolivian campaign so that the reader will be able to grasp the import of the diaries and documents which make up the rest of the book."

————. *Che Guevara: A Biography.* New York: Stein and Day, 1969, 380 p.

> Biographical study that concludes with an assessment of Guevara's political influence.

MacIntyre, Alasdair C. "Marxism of the Will." In his *Against the Self-Images of the Age: Essays on Ideology and Philosophy,* pp. 70–5. New York: Schocken Books, 1971.

> Investigates Guevara's unique perspective on Marxist-Leninist theory, arguing that "in Guevara, although questions of organisation are treated with intellectual respect, it is the voluntarist component of Leninism which is appealed to as never before."

Additional coverage of Guevara's life and career is contained in the following sources published by Gale Research: *Contemporary Authors,* Vols. 111, 127; and *Hispanic Writers.*

Nicolás Guillén

1902–1989

Cuban poet, journalist, and editor.

INTRODUCTION

*G*uillén has been recognized as one of Cuba's finest poets and as an important figure in contemporary West Indian literature. Named National Poet of Cuba by Fidel Castro in 1961, Guillén chronicled the turbulent social and political history of his native land. He is also credited as one of the first poets to affirm and celebrate the black Cuban experience. Robert Márquez characterized Guillén's work as "a poetry which is explicit, deceptively simple in style, militant in its assumptions, one which reaches out to the Third World and looks forward to liberation, then peace."

Guillén, a mulatto from the Cuban provincial middle class, was born in Camagüey to Argelia and Nicolás Guillén. His father, a journalist and Liberal senator, was assassinated in a political skirmish in 1917. According to Vera M. Kutzinski, after his father's death "the young Guillén became increasingly interested in poetry and journalism." He graduated from high school in 1920 and then attended the University of Havana, where he planned to study law. Guillén left school after a year, however, and founded the literary magazine *Lis* while also writing for various Cuban newspapers and magazines. In 1937 Guillén joined the Communist Party, and he was a candidate for various political offices throughout the 1940s. He became president of the Cuban National Union of Writers and Artists in 1961, a position he held for twenty-five years. His honors include the Lenin Peace Prize from the Soviet Union in 1954 and the Cuban Order of José Martí in 1981. Guillén died after a long illness in 1989.

The majority of Guillén's poems are informed by his African and Spanish heritage, often combining the colloquialisms and rhythms of Havana's black districts with the formal structure and language of traditional Spanish verse to address the injustices of imperialism, capitalism, and racism. Guillén's first acclaimed volume of poetry, *Motivos de son* (1930), introduced to a literary audience the *son*, a sensual Afro-Cuban dance rhythm. In this collection Guillén utilized the rhythmic patterns of the *son* to evoke the energetic flavor of black life in and around Havana. Although some readers accused him of displaying negative images of black Cubans, Guillén was more often praised for originality and for blending Afro-Cuban idioms and traditional verse. Guillén expanded his focus in his next volume, *Sóngoro cosongo* (1931), to include poems depicting the lives of all Cubans, with emphasis on the importance of mulatto culture in Cuban history.

Following the demise of the corrupt government headed by Gerardo Machado in 1933 and the increasing industrial and political presence of the United States in Cuba, Guillén began to write poetry with overtly political implications. In *West Indies, Ltd.* (1934), a collection of somber poems imbued with feelings of anxiety and frustration, he decried the social and economic conditions of the Caribbean poor. Guillén attacked imperialism through his recurring description of the region as a vast, profitable factory exploited by foreign nations. The poet's commitment to social change grew when he traveled to Spain in 1937 to cover the civil war for *Mediodia* magazine and participated in the anti-fascist Second International Congress of Writers for the Defense of Culture. That year he joined the Cuban Communist Party and produced an extended narrative poem chronicling the Spanish Civil War entitled *España: Poema en cuatro angustias y una esperanza* ("Spain: A Poem in Four Anguishes and a Hope"). In 1937 Guillén also published *Cantos para soldados y sones para turistas* ("Songs for Soldiers and *Sones* for Tourists"), a volume of poetry denouncing the escalating military presence in Cuban society. He employed biting satire in poems that contrast the darkness and squalor of Cuba's ghettos with the garish atmosphere of downtown tourist establishments.

Guillén spent much of the 1940s and 1950s—the height of the Fulgencio Batista y Zaldívar regime—in exile in Europe and South America. His works of this period reflect his opposition to Batista's repressive policies and denounce racial segregation in the United States. The poems in *La paloma de vuelo popular: Elegías* (1959) favor revolution, praising the activities of such political figures as Castro and Che Guevara. Guillén returned to Cuba following Batista's expulsion in 1959, and in 1964 he published *Tengo*. In this volume, he celebrates the triumph of the Cuban revolution and the abolition of racial and economic discrimination.

Many commentators have distinguished between Guillén's early *poesía negra,* or Afro-Cuban-influenced poems, and the political poems he produced after converting to Communism. There is little agreement, however, among critics who have attempted to place him in a specific group or category of writers. As Richard Jackson noted, "Some critics have focused on Guillén as an exponent of Afro-Cuban poetry while others have viewed him as a poet having little to do with Africa. Some perceive a black aesthetic in his poetry; others say he is the most Spanish of Cuban poets. Some see him as a poet who stopped writing black poetry; others declare that he never wrote black poetry at all." Despite controversy concerning Guillén's treatment of racial themes and his status as a political poet, many scholars have found coherence in his oeuvre. Kutzinski argues: "Perhaps the best way to describe Guillén's poetic ventures is as processes of unraveling the intricate hieroglyphics of Cuban (and Caribbean) culture: his poetic texts are engaged in the forging of a literary tradition from the many disparate elements that constitute the cultural landscape of that region, and he is well aware that such a tradition can be established only on the basis of a perpetual reconciliation between black and white cultures."

CRITICAL COMMENTARY

LLOYD KING

(essay date 1975)

[In the following excerpt, King examines the social and political content of Guillén's poetry.]

Nicolás Guillén is Cuba's most honoured poet. There is little doubt that most of his aspirations as a political activist and 'social protest' poet have been realized since the Cuban Revolution. Within Cuba itself his most popular collection of poems is his *Songs for Soldiers and Ballads for Tourists (Cantos para soldados y sones para turistas)* which he originally published in 1937. These poems are anticipatory blueprints of the relationship between the people's militia, formed since the Revolution as part of Cuba's embattled response to U.S. aggression, and the Cuban people. Written at a time when the soldier seemed

Principal Works

Motivos de son (poetry) 1930

Sóngoro cosongo: Poemas mulatos (poetry) 1931

West Indies, Ltd.: Poemas (poetry) 1934

Cantos para soldados y sones para turistas (poetry) 1937

España: Poema en cuatro angustias y una esperanza (poetry) 1937

Cuba Libre: Poems by Nicolás Guillén (poetry) 1948

Elegía a Jacques Roumain en el cielo de Haití (poetry) 1948

Versos negros (poetry) 1950

Elegía a Jesús Menéndez (poetry) 1951

Elegía cubana (poetry) 1952

La paloma de vuelo popular: Elègías (poetry) 1958

Buenos días, Fidel (poetry) 1959

Prosa de prisa; crónicas (prose) 1962

Poemas de amor (poetry) 1964

Tengo (poetry) 1964
   [*Tengo,* 1974]

Ché Comandante (poetry) 1967

El gran zoo (poetry) 1967
   [*¡Partia o muerte! The Great Zoo and Other Poems by Nicolás Guillén, 1972*]

Cuatro canciones para el Ché (poetry) 1969

El diario que a diario (poetry) 1972

Man-Making Words: Selected Poems of Nicolás Guillén (poetry) 1972

La rueda dentada (poetry) 1972

El corazón con que vivo (poetry) 1975

Poemas manuables (poetry) 1975

Prosa de prisa: 1929–1972 (prose) 1975–76

Cerebro y corazón (poetry) 1977

Por el mar de las Antillas anda un barco de papel (poetry) 1977

Música de camara (poetry) 1979

Páginas vueltas: Memorias (memoirs) 1982

Sol de domingo (poetry) 1982

terness towards him as an insane but all too visible symbol of the rigorous and painful grip on Cuba's monoculture economy by American imperialist-capitalist interests.

As is well known, the Cuban Revolutionary leadership ran out the tourists and the capitalists and aligned itself with the Cuban Communist Party, of which Guillén had been a member since the thirties. The Revolution also acted swiftly to eliminate a feature of Cuban life against which Guillén had campaigned both in verse and prose, namely racial discrimination; it desegregated the schools and the beaches and provided equal educational opportunity for all. Guillén has expressed his recognition of this reality in a poem **"Tengo"** (**"All is mine"**) . . . . (p. 30)

When Guillén wrote **"Tengo"** in the post-revolutionary period, it must have seemed to him that he and other militant Cubans—artists, trade unionists, ordinary folk—had reached the end of a long process of struggle and desperate affirmation during a dark night of dictatorship and violence, to bring in the dawn of a socialist state in the Americas. For Guillén it was a process which had always had to do with the achievement of an integrated national personality, based on a discovery of the common Cubanness of whites and blacks in Cuban society. But equally Guillén realized that this objective could not possibly take shape until external capitalist interests were tamed along with their capacity for disruptive activity. Thus the two constants of his verse were related to internal racial integration and socialist militancy. His verse therefore came to be prophetic of some of the main objectives of the Cuban Revolution itself. (p. 31)

[In 1930], Nicolás Guillén published eight 'negrista' poems in the newspaper *Diario de la Marina* with the general title *Son Motifs (Motivos de son)* and in 1931 included them again with others in book form, with the title *Sóngoro Cosongo.* Guillén was immediately recognized as a writer who had his finger on the pulse of folk sensibility. . . . Guillén seemed instinctively to realize the opportunity to blend the scribal and oral traditions and derived the rhythms of his verse from a popular musical form, the 'son', which had been born of the contact between African rhythms and the creole environment, a form which had long been frowned on by polite Cuban society. In one long magical moment Guillén came to prefigure some of the obsessions of future Caribbean writing. (pp. 35–6)

The poems of *Son Motifs* explored a variety of folk urban situations. Two of the poems **"Ay negra si tu supiera"**, (**"Aye, black lover, if you only knew"**) and **"Búscate plata"** (**"Go and look for bread"**) deal with women abandoning their lovers because they have no money, a situation related to the effects of the Depression. Two others **"Ayer me dijeron negro"** (**"Yesterday I was called nigger"**,) and **"Mulata"** refer to the antogonism between mulatto and black. In **"Yesterday I was called nigger"**, Guillén strikes what was to be a recurring

rather to be the tool and guardian of U.S. interests and the power hunger of Fulgencio Batista, they yet called on the soldier to recognize his links with the ordinary folk who were the victims of exploitation and political gimcrackery, and the need to forge fraternity with the oppressed masses. The *sones para turistas* expressed the repugnance felt by many Cubans towards the insensitive American tourist, and sought to dramatize the resentment and bit-

note of his verse suggesting to some person who passed for white that he has African/black blood:

> Tan blanco como te bé,
> y tu abuela sé quién é.
> Sácala de la cocina,
> Sácala de la cocina,
> Mamá Iné.
>
> (As white as you look
> I know your grandma (the cook)
> Bring her out of the kitchen
> Bring her out of the kitchen
> Mamma Inés.)

This Caribbean picong uses the sharp-edged social barb to puncture the pride along the colour and class line. The most disturbingly ironic of the poems is **"Negro Bembón"** (**"Thick-lipped Nigger"**). The speaker, Caridad, is presented telling her Negro boyfriend with thick lips not to allow himself to be wounded by the mocking intent of those who call him 'negro bembón', and seeking to turn the epithet into a term of endearment. Hers is in a certain sense a Négritude position, for she urges the man to assume freely a term which the society uses in a 'denigratory' manner:

> Por qué te pones tan bravo.
> cuando te dicen negro bembón
> se tienes la boca santa
> negro bembón.
>
> (Why do you get so vexed
> When people call you big-lipped nigger
> Since your mouth is very attractive
> You thick-lipped nigger, you?)

However the poem cannot sustain a Négritude interpretation because in the last two lines we learn that the 'negro bembón' is really living off his mistress's earnings, whatever her line of work may be.

When he widened the collection of poems in *Sóngoro Cosongo,* it was noticeable that many of the poems dealt with the self-contained violence of the low-life of Havana. **"Velorio de Papá Montero"**, (**"Wake for Papa Montero"**) was inspired by a popular 'son' of the time, and evokes with a mix of irony and sadness the death in a drunken brawl of a folk character. **"Chévere"** (sweetman) is a short dense image of concentrated violence, orchestrating the movement of a man's rage till he slices his unfaithful woman to death. (pp. 36–7)

Guillén's ghetto images were not calculated to win the approval of coloureds who were seeking to project an image of respectability, and in an interview with Antonio Fernández de Castro in the newspaper *La semana,* we find him denouncing those who were unwilling to acknowledge the 'son' as a part of their culture. These attitudes of shame and self-contempt were particularly striking, Guillén noted, since the 'son' was popular in Paris and even in Cuba was now accepted in the most exclusive

society, and yet many Negroes demonstrated public hostility to this popular art form because it was lower-class and 'incompatible with their spiritual delicacy and their grade of culture'. (pp. 37–8)

One of the most hostile critics of the influence of Afrocuban folk forms on the wider Cuban sensibility was Rámon Vasconcelos, a Cuban journalist resident in Paris. A self-styled watchdog of Cuban culture, he wrote from Paris to discourage Guillén from the idea that the Cuban 'son' could be used and become popular in the way that the American 'blues' had been, since it was not at all suitable for social commentary or serious purposes . . . . Vasconcelos's attitude was so outrageous that one would have expected a stinging reply, but Guillén's answer was quite mild. He explained that his use of the 'son' was simply in line with the world-wide interest in popular forms, and that the 'son' poems were not in the majority in *Sóngoro Cosongo.* He even went on to lament that it was a pity that to use the speech rhythms of the folk seemed to require heroism.

This moderate reply to Vasconcelos exposes the weakness in Guillén's mulatto position. One senses that he has always been a little afraid of being called a black racist. Thus in an interview with Keith Ellis, published in the *Jamaica Journal* in 1973, Guillén, when asked about his attitude to Négritude, at first dismissed it contemptuously, then went on to admit that the assertion of blackness and of neo-African values was certainly necessary in a colonial situation. But he sees it as above all 'one of the manifestations of the class struggle'. In other words, he felt that 'black assertiveness' in post-revolutionary Cuba was wrong, but even before this he always rejected the use of the term 'Afrocuban'. One need not be a black racist in order to question Guillén's attitude. (pp. 38–9)

It is not a little amazing that Guillén was never tempted to adopt a Négritude position, particularly as even sympathetic white Cuban critics were not persuaded by his claim that Cuba's was mulatto. (p. 39)

In *Sóngoro Cosongo,* Guillén had captured something of the downbeat of ghetto life, a sense of its cynicism and violence, the rhythms of its speech. His next collection of poems, *West Indies, Ltd.* (1934) shows that his political awareness had sharpened, for these were the years of the Depression and of the inept and brutal dictatorship of General Machado who finally fell from power in 1933. Behind him, there was already the example of another mulatto poet, Regino Pedroso, who had been converted to Marxism and the Communist Party in the twenties. In one of his better known poems, "Hermano Negro" ("Brother Black"), Pedroso called upon his black brothers to acquire a right consciousness and to recognize that race prejudice was secondary to economic exploitation. They ought to reconsider their role as entertainers for the western world and understand that they were a part of the exploited proletariat . . . . Once Guillén got the message, his folk characters assume the elemental posture of exploited men. The poet's own posture is that of a member of the revolutionary vanguard, sharpening the consciousness of the masses. The movement in tone and perspective anticipates the classical transferral of aggression which Fanon analyzed in *The Wretched of the Earth,* whereby that violence which the sub-culture practiced against itself, as exemplified in poems such as **"Chévere"** and **"Velorio de Papá Montero",** must now be directed outwards against the colonialist exploiter and the bourgeoisie. Such poems as **"Caminando"** and **"Sabás"** reflect this new mood and show Guillén undertaking the task of political education. In **"Sabás",** the poet calls upon Sabás, servile because reduced to penury in the Depression days, to recognize his moral and economic rights and to understand that when the society will not allow him the dignity to survive as a human being, he must be prepared to claim his right violently if necessary. The irony is both sharp and bitter:

> Porqué Sabás la mano abierta?
> (Este Sabás es un negro bruto)
> Coge tu pan pero no lo pidas;
> Coge tu luz, coge tu esperanza cierta
> como a un caballo por las bridas.

> Why Sabás do you hold out your hand?
> (This Sabás is really a foolish nigger)
> Take your bread, don't beg for it
> Take hold of your senses, take firm hold of your
>   hopes
> As of a horse under sure command.

In 1937, Guillén published his *Cantos para soldados y sones para turistas,* and although his earlier collection *West Indies, Ltd.* (1934) and later *El son entero* (1943) have a better selection of poems, they were not greeted with as good a press as the *Songs for soldiers.* Guillén's Party colleague Juan Marinello. . . hailed the *Songs for soldiers* as a definitive triumph of the American melting pot. What strikes one about this claim in relation to the poems is the fact that Guillén here abandoned the Afrocuban stance which is so easily picked up in the other collections. One must therefore conjecture that there was possibly some pressure on the poet to move away from his 'negrista' image, perhaps to come closer to Marti's dictum that 'Cuban was more than black, more than white'. Perhaps also a bland poem like **"Balada de los dos abuelos" ("Ballad of the two grandfathers")** in which slave-owning conquistador grandfather and enslaved African grandfather are reconciled in the poet's dream, has been played up by some critics for the same kind of reason. There was a lot of truth in Cintio Vitier's judgment on Guillén that 'the new theme is not just a fashion, a subject for literature, but the living heart of his creative activity'. But because he has always been sensitive to the charge of black racism and to the ideological posture of the Party in Cuba, he has also had to react to the association of his name with Négritude.

This is confirmed by a poem **"Brindis" ("Cheers!")**

which he wrote in 1952 but which has never appeared in book form till the recent publication of his *Obra poética.* **"Brindis"** is addressed to the famous black American singer Josephine Baker who in her day was the toast of Paris and who met with racial discrimination on returning to the United States. In disgust and anger, the poet tells la Baker that she might well have been lynched and he introduces a mood of violence which again anticipates one response of black militants which eventually came to pass. . . . In a few lines, Guillén evokes the long hot summer, the incendiary fury which would take a place in ghettos like Watts years later. What is equally interesting, however, is that Josephine Baker had also visited Cuba, and there had also been refused a hotel room by a racist management. But the Cuban incident had drawn from Guillén an article written in sadness rather than in anger. It can be argued, and quite rightly, that Cuba did not have a Ku Klux Klan and that white Cuban racism was milder; but it is also clear that it was felt to be 'politic' to focus on the more extreme brutalities which occurred in the United States. The poet could both deliver a blow against racism and associate it with imperialistic capitalism.

One way in which Guillén tried to hit at the Cuban bourgeoisie was by insisting that most of its members had some concealed African ancestry, for example in the poem **"Canción del bongó" ("Bongo song"):**

> Y hay titulos de Catilla
> con parientes en Bondó.

> (There are those with patents of nobility from
> Castille. Who yet have relatives in Bondó.)

Guillén in such poems was striking an embarrassing note for whereas in Latin countries those who can pass for white are considered white, in the United States a drop of African blood makes a man black. The Cuban bourgeoisie who identified their interests so closely with American capitalists and American standards would therefore not particularly appreciate what the poet was taking pains to advertise.

In 1943, Guillén published *El son entero* with a number of negrista poems, **"Sudor y latigo" ("Sweat and the whip"), "Ebano real" ("Royal ebony"), "Son número 6" ("Son No. 6"), "Acana",** and even a rather embarrassing poem which calls upon Shango and Ochun to guard Stalin whom 'free men accompany singing, "Una canción a Stalin"'. These poems do not add anything new to his output although they show once again how strongly influenced by the oral tradition Guillén was. A much more interesting later poem is **"El apellido" ("The surname")** in which Guillén again worries about the way in which the African connection is vulnerable to the Hispanic mould, even in such things as names. . . . Finally one must mention a not-too-good poem **"Qué color"** which was provoked by a comment of the Russian poet Yevtushenko on the death of Martin Luther King that his soul was white as snow. Guillén insists rather that Luther King's soul was as black as coal, 'negro como el carbón'. **"Qué color"** shows the way in which Guillén and the Cuban Revolution are solid supporters of men who struggle against oppression and imperialism everywhere. Amílcar Cabral and Angela Davis are very popular in Cuba. Nevertheless, Guillén would never write of a *Cuban* that his soul was black as coal, on the basis that the Revolution has abolished the emotive connotations of colour.

The Marxist attitude to colour, which is Guillén's own attitude, is that it is irrelevant in a socialist state. It counts upon Revolutionary policy of equal opportunity to reverse a variety of instinctive attitudes about race, bred during more than one hundred and fifty years of Cuban history in the context of the white racist attitudes of western civilization. At the primary level of what we accept as the basic human needs and rights, the right to a balanced diet, educational development, etc. no one can disagree with the Cuban perspective. However, at a second level of reference, that of cultural formation and a variety of subtle attitudes, this writer, whose experience is that of the English-speaking Caribbean (where black men have attained the highest offices) and who has seen how readily a Euro-oriented environment can twist and confuse men of African ancestry, must express some reservations about the Cuban Revolution's desire to straighten out the kinks and achieve a determined uniformity in Cuban cultural life. (pp. 40–4)

Lloyd King, "Nicolás Guillén and Afrocubanismo," in *A Celebration of Black and African Writing,* edited by Bruce King and Kolawole Ogungbesan, Ahmadu Bello University Press, 1975, pp. 30–45.

KEITH ELLIS

(essay date 1983)

[In the following excerpt from his book *Cuba's Nicolás Guillén: Poetry and Ideology,* Ellis examines Guillén's use of a variety of poetic forms.]

The scrupulousness about forms that Guillén has shown in conveying this historically based poetry is arrived at by a consciousness of the responsibility for producing elevated, though not hermetic, expression. The theoretical framework that has informed this approach was formulated early in Guillén's career and was expressed in his article, **'Emma Pérez: poesía y revolución' ('Emma Pérez: Poetry and Revolution'),** of 1937, where he writes:

Social poetry has had a similar fate [to that of the so-called vanguardist poetry]: offering verses, and at times hardly verses at all, full of party sectarianisms, of invocations to Lenin and Marx, of apostrophes to the capitalists, of bad oratory, high sounding and hollow. The

cliché then flourished and the *cliché* brought the standard poem, mass production, super production: soon we were drowned, sepulchered in a thick wave of 'revolutionary' songs, made up simply of words, shouts, wild gesture. What is the result of this? Very simply, the only survivors are those who in addition to being revolutionaries are poets and bring to their art, cleansing it, making it the substance of beauty, the conflict between a world that is disappearing and another that is being born. In this way revolutionary poetry stops being basically party slogans and transforms itself into a human concern without contradicting the slogans; and as for form, the already known—and often forgotten!— Horatian difficulty of simplicity must finally be faced. It is necessary to talk to the man in the street in a direct language, with clean energetic words that he himself knows how to use, and that becomes evident when we have a human, imperative message to transmit to him. We have been constructing a rhetorical poetry that is unintelligible to the worn-down being to whom it is addressed. Why don't we get closer to him and, abandoning the apocalyptic tone that frightens and confounds him, speak to him in his own simple way?

In 1961, in his report to the First Congress of Writers and Artists, Guillén demonstrated the consistency of his views by suggesting that no writer would be able to win many readers among the people by catering to the lowest levels of intelligence or by supplying political slogans and books that rely solely on revolutionary themes, and he added: 'No, it is not true that it is necessary to talk down to the people in order to please them. We must give to the people the best of our spirit, of our technique, of our intelligence, of our work, in the certainty that they understand and know what they are giving them, acknowledging it with gratitude' ["Informe al Congreso de Escritores y Artistas," *Islas,* Vol. 4, 1962]. Both statements consider form by presupposing that the transmitted content has potential and engaging importance for the reader, but with the awareness that even such content may be debased by inadequate attention to form. These views are similar to (and predate by two decades) those of García Márquez, examined in the first part of this study. The great emphasis placed on artistic quality is the distinguishing feature between them and views expressed by Mario Benedetti and others who believe the sacrifice of artistic finery in times of urgency to be worthwhile.

The breadth of formal means exhibited by Guillén is unusual among twentieth-century poets. At the service of the comprehensiveness of his poetic world is a variety of techniques relating to point of view that are so wide in their embrace as to incorporate aspects of other genres. Not only is the whole range of personal points of view employed in his poetry, but within each one the possibilities are fully exploited. This is exemplified in his widespread use of the first person. A lyrical 'I' in monologue functions in a work such as **'Un poema de amor'**('A Love

Poem'). An 'I' that speaks explicitly and authoritatively as poet to an assumed public appears in others such as 'Unión Soviética' ('Soviet Union'). An 'I' representative of the oppressed is used in 'No sé por qué piensas tú' ('I Don't Know Why You Think'). 'Tengo' ('I Have' illustrates one that functions with eclectic collectivity to represent the formerly oppressed. One representing the implied poet in dramatic monologue is exemplified by 'Frente al Oxford' ('Facing the Oxford') and 'Búscate plata' ('Go Get Money',) provides a case of an 'I' representing a character in dramatic monologue. The first-person plural, normally used to represent the oppressed in various attitudes as in 'West Indies, Ltd.,' 'Canción de los hombres perdidos' ('Song of the Lost Men') and '*España* . . .' is also used with irony to represent positions antithetical to the norm in Guillén's work, as in 'Llanto de las habaneras' ('Lament of the Women of Havana'). All this makes obvious the error of necessarily identifying the first-person pronouns with Guillén himself and dictates the procedure of referring to the speaker of individual poems, a procedure that permits an enhanced view of the workings of the poems. The numerous poems written in the second-person singular, such as 'Negro bembón' ('Thick-lipped Negro'), and 'Responde tú' ('Answer!'), and in the plural, 'La sangre numerosa' ('The Numerous Blood'), enjoy a dramatic intensity, which is achieved elsewhere in Guillén's poetry by dialogue, both within poems and in full-fledged dramatic pieces such as 'Poema con niños' '(Poem with Children') and 'Floripondito.' Also, in addition to the third-person poems that do not depend on irony (such as the 'Retratos' ['Portraits']) are those in which irony reigns, as in many of *El Gran Zoo* and *El diario que a diario.* The variety of points of view is one of the means by which the range of objective correlatives is made impressive in Guillén's poetry. It is a fundamental device for making the presented experiences, their emotional charge, and the ideology underlying them arise from the poems themselves.

Because the *son* is Guillén's strikingly original contribution, the reader is apt to imagine it to occupy a more dominant place in his poetry than it actually does. He employs, with balance, the gamut of verse forms, including *redondillas, quintillas,* quartets, tercets, *romances, coplas,* sonnets, *silvas,* and *décimas,* often using them in innovative ways. The sonnet 'Sictransit . . .' ('Thus passes . . .'), for example, possesses not only an *estrambote* or tail but also, inserted in the middle of the second quartet, a playful indication of time lapse—'Pausa de 15/segundos a / un año'('A pause of 15/seconds to/one year'). In addition, the rhythmic variety in his poems is unsurpassed.

Verse form and rhythm in turn facilitate the creation of various moods in Guillén's poetry. The moods are distinct from each other, like those evoked in the poems 'Hay que tené boluntá' ('One Must Have Willpower'),

'Sensemayá,' 'La sangre numerosa' ('The Numerous Blood'), the poems of the section 'Salón independiente' ('Independent Salon') of *La rueda dentada,* in those of *El Gran Zoo,* and the moods evoked within the 'Elegía a Jesús Menéndez' ('Elegy to Jesús Menéndez'). Besides, the laughter / crying polarity encompasses a wide spectrum of emotions—joy, hope, faith, love, pathos, curiosity, incredulity, dismay, indignation, loss, grief. These emerge from the poems, affirming the authentic humanity they project. The polarity, while present in many of his poems, is thus compelling as an overall effect throughout his poetry.

Just as it would be possible to make separate collections of Guillén's poems on the basis of verse forms, so it would be possible to make or divide anthologies of his work on the basis of categories such as political, folkloric, black, love, satirical, elegiac, epic, lyrical, nature, or children's poetry. But while such a procedure carries the advantage of emphasizing Guillén's versatility, it is ultimately unsatisfactory because his poems are not contained by these categories. A crucial part of the meaning of the individual poems, the part that contributes most to the central character of his poetry, would be obscured. It was shown in the course of analyses that poems, at first glance belonging to any one of these groups, on closer examination exceeded those bounds to embrace aspects of the other categories. Beyond that, in their broad representation of life, particularly Cuban life, the poems have contributed to shaping the ideology of the Cuban revolution from its earliest stages. The breadth of relevance that makes Guillén's poetry specific and general, concrete and comprehensive, and (as the symbolic 'guitarra' of *El son entero* was described) 'universal y cubana' is in great part due to the poetry's simultaneous involvement with different generic categories while dealing with well-defined subjects. Thus when Guillén is properly spoken of as a social poet, 'social' is not to be understood as a sub-category of poetry but as a strategy in which an unusually wide range of poetic modes are made to merge, with consummate skill, in the conveyance of worthy and uncompromising human sentiments and aspirations.

This appealing distinctiveness within Guillén's work rests largely on its semantic features. Here his characteristic comprehensiveness is also in evidence. His expression ranges from the popular to the standard to the classical and the archaic. He creates words and draws from several languages and from all sectors of human activity over a vast historical expanse. One conspicuous feature of his use of figurative language is his preference for creating meaning by means of metonymy, which functions through contiguity, rather than metaphor which functions through contrast. This preference is a part of his broad inclination to avoid hermeticism, to regard poetry as communicative rather than cryptic, to keep it close to historical reality, and to enhance its didactic possibilities. A lesson often presented in Guillén's poetry—that man is the controller of his destiny and of his environment—has its repercussions in the function of language in his poetry. Thus, because man is capable of change and of altering his social systems, no pattern of linguistic signs will constantly represent his activity. Consequently, a semiological approach to the criticism of his poetry will be ineffective, as was shown in my analysis of the '**Elegía a Jesús Menéndez**.'A structural analysis of the language of Guillén's poems is beset by paradoxes that can be resolved, as they were in that poem, only by taking into account the values attached to the participants in the struggle between progress and reaction. 'Metal' associated with Casillas is antithetical to 'metal' associated with Menéndez, and in this and other poems 'serpiente' may be an image of imperialism or of the fascination held by the locks of the loved one's hair. This kind of usage is a further indication of the fact that the generative principle at work in Guillén's poetry is dialectical rather than metaphysical. A reading of the '**Elegía a Jesús Menéndez**' and of poems subsequent to it reveals that out of the conflict of 'metal' versus 'metal' comes a different form of reality, in which the 'metal' representative of Menéndez gains the ascendancy and evolves continuously in response to new challenges. The natural appeal that the struggle between progress and reaction holds for readers who are sympathetic to the idea of social progress is in itself one of the factors that prevents whatever difficulties may arise in Guillén's poetry from reaching the level of the hermetic. Even though potential hurdles to ready understanding such as archaisms and hyperbaton are functioning in his poetry at the semantic and syntactical levels respectively, these usages are fitted to engaging social contexts that elicit commitment, creating the impetus for and facilitating their resolution.

Guillén has found fitting forms in the macro sense at all stages of his poetry. For example, the *son* and popular speech provide appropriate forms for the newly emerged content of the *Motivos de son;* the newspaper, the keeper of the social record, itself satirized, conveys artistically the chaos of pre-revolutionary times in *El diario que a diario;* and post-revolutionary works tend to be characterized by a greater degree of difficulty reflecting the broader experience presented and the growing sophistication of his readers. He has also varied his forms considerably from one poem to the next. Thus in '**Guitarra en duelo mayor**' "(**Guitar in Grief Major**') and '**Lectura de domingo**' ('**Sunday Reading**'), which are two perspectives on the same event, different forms are fully operative in the different meanings, including the suggestions of the different levels of audience for which the poems are immediately destined. From the *Motivos de son* to *El diario que a diario* Guillén's unfailing sense of how to say what he has to say has led to the special appeal of his comprehensive achievement.

It has caused many of his poems to attain a degree of popularity that has made them part of the national oral tradition. At the same time, recondite features of his

work—the unobtrusive artistic elements, his place within literary history, his creation of new expressive possibilities for use by his fellow practitioners—give him outstanding stature. (pp. 205–09)

Keith Ellis, in his *Cuba's Nicolás Guillén: Poetry and Ideology*, University of Toronto Press, 1983, 251 p.

GUSTAVO PÉREZ-FIRMAT
(essay date 1987)

[Pérez–Firmat is a Cuban-born American poet and critic, whose critical studies include *Idle Fictions: The Hispanic Vanguard Novel, 1926–1934* (1982) and *Literature and Liminality: Festive Readings in the Hispanic Tradition* (1986). In the following essay, he discusses Guillén's use of the sonnet form.]

Nicolás Guillén, best-known as a composer of *sones*, has also favored the sonnet. Although the fame of the author of *Sóngoro cosongo* (1931) rests primarily on his innovative nativist verse, from his earliest poems Guillén has shown a special predilection for traditional poetic forms, and particularly for the sonnet. Indeed, almost half of the poems written before *Motivos de son* (1930) are sonnets. His first collection, *Cerebro y corazón,* completed in 1922 but not published until 1965, already contains twenty-two of these compositions. In Guillén's literary career, the sonnet preceded the *son;* the mature *sonero* grew out of the juvenile sonneteer. Beginning with *Motivos de son,* sonnets appear less frequently in his work, but they never disappear altogether. One finds sonnets in *West Indies, Ltd.* (1934), in *Cantos para soldados y sones para turistas* (1937), in *Elegía a Jacques Roumain* (1948), in *La paloma de vuelo popular* (1958), in *Tengo* (1964), and in *Poemas de amor* (1964). In his recent poetry, Guillén has continued to resort to this form with some frequency; *La rueda dentada* (1972) includes eight sonnets, and there are sonnets also in *El diario que a diario* (1972) and *El corazón con que vivo* (1975).

In spite of Guillén's persistent use of the sonnet and other traditional forms, the critical consensus seems to be that Guillén's "learned" poetry is less significant than his vernacular verse. Ezequiel Martínez Estrada, for one, does not find much interest in the Guillén of the sonnets [in *La poesía afrocubana de Nicolás Guillén*]:

El poeta conoce y maneja con maestría el verso regular; usa de la rima y escande como cualquier aventajado escolapio de la Poética Didascálica. Ha compuesto, a veces, intercalados con piezas vernáculas y aborígenes, impecables sonetos, silvas, romances, madrigales y

tioner of onomatopoetic, incantatory verse. I am interested in a more elusive Guillén, one who does not quite fit the image of Cuba's "black Orpheus." I am interested in the poet who, alongside such poems as **"Sensemayá"** and **"Canto negro,"** composed sonnets and madrigals. Guillén's "white" verse, or the "white" strain in his vernacular verse, is undoubtedly the least studied aspect of his poetic production. Although a great deal has been said about his "mulatto" poetry, this discussion has generally drawn attention to the black ingredient in the mix. And yet, as Nancy Morejón has mentioned [in *Nación y mestizaje en Nicolás Guillén*, 1982] (not without some exaggeration perhaps), Guillén "is the most Spanish of Cuban poets."

Guillén's use of the sonnet is not only persistent but varied. He has written sonnets in hendecasyllables, in alexandrines, and in free verse. At times he employs consonance (with varying rhyme schemes), at other times assonance. In the choice of subject matter there is also considerable diversity. His sonnets deal with a whole gamut of topics, from the political to the culinary. One memorable instance of the latter is a sonnet entitled **"Al poeta español Rafael Alberti, entregándole un jamón,"** which reaches heights of sybaritic indulgence worthy of Baltazar de Alcázar. It begins:

Este chancho en jamón, casi ternera,
anca descomunal, a verte vino
y a darte su romántico tocino
gloria de frigorífico y salmuera.

Quiera Dios, quiera Dios, quiera Dios, quiera
Dios, Rafael, que no nos falte el vino,
pues para lubricar el intestino,
cuando hay jamón, el vino es de primera.

[This calf-sized pig, turned into a huge haunch of ham, came to see you and give you its romantic bacon, the glory of refrigerators and salts. May God, may God may God, may God, Rafael, provide us with wine, since, when there's ham, the intestines need to be lubricated with a fine wine.]

As I have already indicated, Guillén's earliest sonnets appear in *Cerebro y corazón*. Nearly all of the poems in this volume demonstrate his debt to the poetry of the *modernistas*, making plain the young poet's apprenticeship in the works of Darío, Silva, Casal, Nervo, and other figures of the turn of the century. A typical example of this youthful poetry is a sonnet entitled **"Tú."**

Eres alada, y vaporosa, y fina:
hay algo en ti de ensueño o de quimera.
como si el alma que te anima fuera
la musa de Gutierre de Cetina.

Tu piel es porcelana de la China;
tus manos, rosas de la Primavera
y hay en la gloria de tu voz ligera
un ruiseñor que, cuando cantas, trina. . .

hasta tercetos a la manera de Dante. No es ésa, naturalmente, la poesía que nos interesa de él, pues aunque de méritos artísticos incomparablemente más altos, carece de otros valores que no acierto a calificar mejor que con dos polabras griegas de expendio libre: *ethos y ethnos,* en que reside su fuerte personalidad humana y poética.

[The poet knows and handles with mastery regular verse forms; he uses rhyme and he scans like any bright student of Didascalic Poetry. At times he has composed, interspersed among his vernacular and aboriginal works, impeccable sonnets, *silvas,* madrigals and even tercets in the manner of Dante. But, obviously, this is not the poetry that interests us, since although it has incomparably higher artistic merits, it lacks other values that I can only, describe with two Greek words: *ethos* and *ethnos,* where Guillén's strong human and poetic personality resides.]

In my view, however, the interest of these poems *fechos at itálico modo* lies precisely in their combination of *ethos* and *ethnos* with traditional forms like the sonnet or the madrigal. Guillén's sonnets and madrigals are worthy of attention because they mark the point of intersection between his "white" literary formation and his attempt to develop a vernacular literary idiom. Indeed, one could say that Guillén's project of creating a poetry with "Cuban color" (as he put it in the prologue to *Sóngoro cosongo*) finds its definitive challenge, and perhaps its consummate accomplishment, in genres like the sonnet and the madrigal. To write a mulatto madrigal or a *mestizo* sonnet is to transform, to transculturate, two of the "whitest" literary forms, two genres whose whiteness extends even to their conventional content, the stylized portrait of a limpid *donna de la mente.* Guillén's achievement, as we will see, is to add color, and even local color, to the pallid outlines of this conventional figure.

The Nicolás Guillén who will appear in these pages, therefore, is neither the social reformer nor the practi-

Un torrente es tu loca cabellera,
y tu cuerpo magnífico de ondina
bambú flexible o tropical palmera. . .

Y eres alada, y vaporosa, y fina
como si el alma que te anima fuera
la musa de Gutierre de Cetina.

[You are winged, and vaporous, and refined: there's something dreamlike or chimeric about you, as if the soul that animated you were Gutierre de Cetina's muse. Your skin is Chinese porcelain; your hands are Spring roses; and in your glorious, light voice there's a nightingale that trills when you sing. . . . Your wild hair is a torrent; your magnificent, undine-like body is a flexible bamboo or a tropical palm. And you are winged, and vaporous, and refined, as if the soul that animated you were Guitierre de Cetina's muse.]

The author of **"Sensemayá"** is nowhere to be found in these vaporous and vapid verses. The one vernacular note is the passing reference to the "tropical palm," though even this insinuation of the poet's real-life environment is vitiated by being made of a woman with the body of a water-sprite, a creature that has never graced the fauna of Cuba. Rather than a flesh-and-blood woman, the lady of the poem is only a tissue of descriptive commonplaces that, as the references to Gutierre de Cetina attest, go back to Renaissance Petrarchism. More than a *mujer,* this lady is a *mujer-cita.* As the speaker himself recognizes, she is nothing but a chimera—an entity built from disparate scraps and thus lacking a distinct identity. Even though the sonnet begins as a straightforward definition "Eres . . . "), with the adjectives that follow — "alada, y vaporosa, y fina" — it becomes clear that the woman's insubstantiality precludes further specification. In fact, all of this lady's attributes lead *away* from her: her skin comes from China; her hands belong to the Spring; her voice is like a nightingale; she has the body of a sprite; and her soul belongs to Gutierre de Cetina, her spiritual daddy. By the end of the enumeration, **"Tú"** has been emptied of any individualizing content, and the word itself is less a "personal" pronoun than an impersonal marker of Guillén's debt to a certain literary tradition and its attendant conception of woman. What Guillén "addresses" in this poem is simply a constellation of commonplaces.

Using **"Tú"** as a term of comparison, let me now take a look at the first sonnet of Guillén's mature work, **"El abuelo,"** which appeared in *West Indies, Ltd.* (1934).

Esta mujer angélica de ojos septentrionales,
que vive atenta al ritmo de su sangre europea,
ignora que en lo hondo de ese ritmo golpea
un negro el parche duro de roncos atabales.

Bajo la línea escueta de su nariz aguda,
la boca, en fino trazo, traza una raya breve,
y no hay cuervo que manche la solitaria nieve
de su carne, que fulge temblorosa y desnuda.

¡Ah, mi señora! Mírate las venas misteriosas;
boga en el agua viva que allá dentro te fluye,
y ve pasando lirios, nelumbios, lotos, rosas;

Que ya verás, inquieta, junto a la fresca orilla,
la dulce sombra oscura del abuelo que huye,
el que rizó por siempre tu cabeza amarilla.

[This angelic lady with septentrional eyes, who lives attentive to the rhythm of her European blood, ignores that in the depths of that rhythm a black man beats the taut skin of hoarse drums. Beneath the outlines of her small nose, her mouth, with a delicate contour, traces a brief line, and there is no crow to stain the solitary snow of her skin, which glows tremulous and naked. Oh, my lady! Look into your mysterious veins; travel in the living waters that flow inside you; go by lilies, nelumbiums, lotuses, roses; and you will see, restless, next to the fresh shore, the sweet, dark shadow of your fleeing grandfather, the one who permanently curled your yellow head.]

There are significant affinities between this sonnet and the previous one. Both poems derive from the tradition of Petrarchan love poetry, a fact that shapes the appearance of the women as well as the manner of description. **"El abuelo"** begins by actually quoting this tradition, since "mujer angélica" is a transposition of *donna angelicata,* one of the epithets applied to the Lauras and Beatrices of Medieval and Renaissance poetry. This little lady is no less a *mujer-cita* than "tú." In addition, the description in both instances follows a downward path, from the head to the torso, as was prescribed by classical rhetoric. In **"El abuelo"** the descending trajectory generates a fairly detailed catalog of traits. The lady, perhaps, is naked before a mirror, and we watch as her glance inspects her physical charms, beginning with her light-colored eyes and ending with her limpid skin.

The tradition of Renaissance love poetry is also present in the subtle insinuation of the motif of vassaldom, an essential element in the thematics of courtly love. By addressing her as "mi señora," the speaker adopts the conventional posture of a lover subjugated by an indifferent mistress. These connections with the Petrarchan tradition are reinforced by the fact that **"El abuelo"** follows rather closely the structural format of the Italian sonnet, since it divides into two metrical and conceptual units (the two quartets and the sestet) separated by a *volta,* that is, a change or modulation in the line of argument. Here the *volta* is punctuated by the exclamation with which the first tercet begins: "¡Ah, mi señora!" Upon reaching this point, the sonnet "turns" in a number of directions: the speaker modulates from a description in the third person to a direct address, from "esta mujer" to "mi señora"; he abandons the catalog of physical charms in favor of a description of her state of mind; and he brings to an end the downward trajectory in order to peer into his lady's soul. Psychological intimacy replaces physical intimacy. The speaker proposes now to accompany the woman on a journey into the innermost recesses of her being, and the two verbs of sight which appear in the tercets, "mírate" and "verás," have to do less with physical sight than with spiritual vision. In the two quartets the description had gone from top to bottom; in the sestet the direction is not down but in, from the lady's skin to her soul, from her physique to her psyche.

This movement inward is accompanied by a retrospective glance, by a kind of flashback. Since by peering into her soul the speaker discovers his lady's ancestry, looking in means looking back. Thus, the tercets are successively introspective and atavistic. They take us from the here and now of the lady's resplendent skin to the *illo tempore* of her place of origin. As we move from her boudoir to the African jungle, the modern world gives way to the colonial epoch. The poem as a whole shifts from inspection to introspection to retrospection: from the lady's snowlike skin to her heart of darkness to the dark shadow of her fugitive grandfather. We should recall that in the earlier sonnet there was also a movement away from the woman's immediate physical presence, but it only led into the rarefied realm of literary convention. Here the displacement takes us to very different surroundings and has a very different effect, for this is not a voyage of escape but of discovery, and even, as the reference to the slave trade suggests, of entrapment. This journey back to the source concludes in the last line of the poem, which suddenly redirects our gaze back to the body of the woman, to her "cabeza amarilla." We return to the woman's body, and specifically to her upper body, which had been the sonnet's point of departure.

The phrasing at the end suggests, however, a marked switch in focus. In the last line of the poem the speaker employs not the metaphorical language of amorous encomia, but the prosaic lexicon of impassive description. In "Tú" the "wild hair" of the woman had been compared, with typical hyperbole, to a torrent. At the end of "El abuelo" the hyperbolic torrents have been replaced by a "yellow head." One can summarize the argument of the poem by juxtaposing its opening words with its closing ones: "mujer angélica" and "cabeza amarilla." On one level, the two phrases are nearly synonymous, since angel ladies are always blond. But these two phrases reflect diverse ways of looking at the woman's blond hair. In one instance, idealization and hyperbole; in the other, sobriety and simplicity. As happens with numberless love sonnets, this poem recounts the transformation of the poet's lady, but in a direction contrary to the traditional one, for there is no idealization or sublimation. By the end of the poem the earth-angel of the opening lines has been transformed into a flesh-and-blood woman whose blood pounds to the beat of African drums. The subject of "El abuelo" is not blanching but coloration. Guillén adds color, Cuban color, to the *versos blancos* of the Petrarchan sonnet.

Another point of contact between "Tú" and "El abuelo" is their attention to genealogy. "Tú" may be seen as an exploration of the protagonist's genealogy, which goes back to Gutierre de Cetina, for it turns out that this winged lady ("alada, y vaporosa, y fina") has flown in from the Renaissance. In other words, Cetina is the "grandfather" of "Tú." By the same token, "El abuelo," from the title on, makes evident its interest in the lady's ancestry, though here the regress leads back to a workhorse of a different color. A black slave now occupies the position assigned to Cetina in the other sonnet. But the claims that "Tú" makes for Cetina's influence on the lady are similar to the claims made on behalf of the black ancestor. In both instances the forebear infuses his descendant with vital breath; just as Cetina "animates" the protagonist of "Tú," the black ancestor determines the very pulsations in the veins of his granddaughter, whose apparent whiteness is revealed as mere illusion, as a kind of *engaño de los ojos.* With his typical wit, Fernando Ortiz once remarked that there were Cubans so light-skinned that they could pass for white. He must have been thinking of someone like this angelic woman, mulatto in head and heart but white everywhere else. At any rate, the mixed heritage of the lady is crucial not only because it symbolizes Cuba's *mestizo* culture, but also because it marks the spot where Guillén deviates from the literary tradition that animates his own poem. The intrusion of that dark, fleeing shadow represents what one might term the "barbaric" moment in the poem, that is, the point at which Guillén has grafted foreign matter—be it lexical or, as in this case, racial— unto the European family tree. In "Tú" there is no question of barbarism, since this poem prolongs or perpetuates tradition in a pure, unproblematic way; but in "El abuelo" Guillén departs from his earlier sonnet as well as from its models by injecting into the poem a "barbaric" or foreign ancestry.

The transculturation of the angel-lady into a Cuban mulatto entails important alterations in the rest of the poem. One of the dogmas of formalist criticism is that changing one element in a system alters it as a whole. Something of this sort happens in "El abuelo," where the transfiguration of the lady transfigures other elements as well. Foremost among these is the motif of vassaldom. Once it has been transferred from the never-never-land of courtly love to Cuban territory, this conventional gesture acquires a profoundly human dimension, since it can now be construed as a reference to the institution of slavery. What appeared initially as a deference to literary usage now becomes a reference to a deplorable historical reality. As a result, the speaker's exclamation, "¡Ah, mi señora!," acquires an unsuspected pathos. As by anamorphosis, the entire scene suddenly changes complexion: no longer does a suitor address a fickle lady, but a slave addresses his mistress. Seen from this perspective, "El abuelo" enacts one of the paradigmatic scenes in Cuban literature (and in Cuban history as well), the depiction of an interracial romance. Moreover, by relating the speaker of the poem to the grandfather, Guillén suggests that, if the suitor is being spurned, the reason lies perhaps in the lady's aversion to her own black background.

Another element that is altered by the lady's mixed ancestry has to do with the place of this poem in the tradition of the sonnet. As its name indicates, the sonnet was initially a musical from; a *sonnetto*, literaly, is a brief song, or—to express in terms closer to Guillén—a brief *son*. As the paranomasia suggests, the Cuban *son* and the Italian sonnet are distant relatives, for both are musical forms. The *son* is Cuba's native sonnet, and the sonnet is Italy's native *son*. In the first stanza the speaker states that in the depths of this woman one can hear the sound of African drums; but this percussive beating constitutes, of course, the most important antecedent of the Cuban *son*. Those drums are beating out the rhythms of an ancestral *son*, a chant whose echo is perhaps audible in the assonance of *hondo* and *ronco* in lines three and four. What the angel lady carries within her is the deep beat of a *son*. What a sonnet carries within itself, also, are the vestigial echoes of a "sonnetto," a *son*. By referring to the lady's origins in musical terms Guillén has collapsed her genealogy with that of the sonnet. Just as the woman travels back to her African origins, the sonnet itself may be said to travel back to its acoustic origins.

The role of music in **"El abuelo"** makes it perfectly compatible with Guillén's "folkloric" poetry. In fact, this poem may be read as an Italiante version of the "Canción del bongó." Both poems make the same point: that all Cubans are mulatto, if not ethnically ("cueripardos"), then culturally ("almiprietos"). Therefore, all Cubans, regardless of social class, are susceptible to the call of the African drums.

Esta es la canción del bongó:
—Aquí el que más fino sea,
responde, si llamo yo.

[This is the song of the bongo drums: When I call, everybody here answers.]

The essential subject of **"El abuelo"** is the angel-lady's belated response to the sound of the bongo, represented in the sonnet by the atavistic *atabales*. In spite of superficial differences (and let us not forget that the theme of **"El abuelo"** is the deceptiveness of surfaces), **"Canción del bongó"** and **"El abuelo"** are cognate works—the sonnet is a "white" version of what the *son* renders in mulatto. In more general terms, it may be said that the *son* and the sonnet are the two opposite but mutually implicated poles of Guillén's poetry, the two terms in his Cuban counterpoint. In the case of the *son*, he needs to impose poetic form on native rhythms, to turn the beat of the bongo into a "song." In the case of the sonnet, he needs to infuse a traditional form with indigenous vitality, to highlight the "son" in the sonnet.

If we listen a little longer to what may now be called "el son de la dama," we will notice that the first stanza is

not the only place in the poem where the distant *atabales* resound. The densest, most charged word in the poem is the adjective "inquieta" in the first line of the closing tercet:

que ya verás, *inquieta*, junto a la fresca orilla
In dulce sombra oscura del abuelo que huye,
el que rizó por siempre tu cabeza amarilla.

[. . . and you will see, *restless,* next to the fresh shore, the sweet, dark shadow of your fleeing grandfather, the one who permanently curled your yellow head.]

Marking the precise spot of the lady's anagnorisis and underscoring it with the chocking sound of a plosive consonant, "inquieta" summarizes the poem's meaning, since it brings about the reunion of granddaughter and grandfather. At first glance "inquieta" seems to modify the "tú" implicit in "verás". The woman feels restless, perturbed, upon discovering that she is mulatto, and the adjective highlights her disquieting realization. But it is equally plausible to read "inquieta" as a description not of the woman but of her grandfather, the fleeting and fleeing shadow that moves across the last lines. The sense would now be: "que ya verás [la sombra] inquieta . . . del abuelo que huye." The lady is restless or troubled because of her impending realization; the grandfather is troubled or restless because of his flight from the slave traders. Separated by centuries and circumstances, granddaughter and grandfather join in a shared anxiety, albeit one with very different roots.

This second reading of *inquieta,* of course, supposes that the adjective is displaced, distanced from the noun it modifies. This hyperbatonic placement is not inconsistent with the poem's meaning. Hyperbaton names the separation of sentence parts that normally go together; it is a form of syntactical displacement, of grammatical dislocation. But displacement and dislocation are precisely what this poem is about. What does the poem describe if not the black grandfather's own dislocation, his enslavement and exile? The dislocated syntax functions as an analogue of his historical dislocation. Or, to reverse the analogy, exile itself is a sort of hyperbaton, an existential dislocation that shatters the concinnity of self and surroundings. Slavery disjoins the grandfather and his African home just as the hyperbaton disjoins adjective and noun.

"Inquieta," therefore, has an ambiguous referent, as it can apply both to the woman and to her grandfather. This ambiguity is a cypher of the poem's meaning, which is simply that the black slave and the white lady, in a profound sense, are indistinguishable. "Inquieta" joins the grandfather with his granddaughter, grammatically and affectively. From this arises a certain ironic parallelism between lives of the two relatives: the granddaughter, like her ancestor, tries to escape; but that from which she flees is her grandfather. There is a double, failed flight in the sonnet: the grandfather attempts to flee from the slave trader but, as the lady's curls attest, he does not succeed; the girl attempts to avoid her black origins but, as the grandfather's shadow attests, she also does not succeed. If he is enslaved by a white man, she is "trapped" by her black ancestor.

The poem contains yet another foiled escape. Although in modern Spanish *inquieta* only means restless or perturbed, etymologically the word has an acoustic grounding, as is evidenced by *quieto's* etymological doublet, *quedo*. *Quieto* goes back to *quietare*, to silence, to make quiet. In its phonic sense, *inquieto* means noisy, not silent. That is to say, the word resonates with the beating of the *atabales* of the opening stanza. "Inquieta" marries sound and sense, *son* and sense, sound and sonnet. Although the sonnet as a genre has all but forgotten its musical origins, in **"El abuelo"** these origins are noisily retrieved. Much like the poem's protagonist, the genre recalls its own ancestry. In a kind of metaleptic reversal, Guillén's transculturated sonnet is actually closer to the source, more "primitive" than its predecessors.

This means that *inquieta* not only links grandfather and daughter, but also makes explicit the figurative bond that unites them—the sound of the *atabales*. In this voluble word, the poem voices the acoustic conceit with which it began (the equation of the lady's negritude with the beating of the African drum). In order to ascertain Guillén's revisionary use of the sonnet form in **"El abuelo,"** it is enough to remember that in **"Tú"** the "light voice" of the girl had been likened to a "nightingale that trills." By comparing the girl's voice to a nightingale's song, Guillén is still working with the commonplace metaphors of traditional love poetry. However, by substituting the percussive drums for the melodious nightingale, he is incorporating into this network of imagery an entirely uncommon place (Africa), a place foreign to the tradition of the sonnet as a whole but very much a part of this sonnet's historical background. Those African drums also mark the spot of Guillén's deviation from tradition, his "literary barbarism." In fact, the drums are "barbaric" in the genuine sense of the term, for the messages they send are surely incomprehensible to the girl. Like the girl's mulattoness, of which they are the phonic metaphor, the *atabales* bear loud witness to Guillén's daring, noisy intervention in the Western literary tradition.

My discussion of this poem demonstrates that Guillén's "learned" poems do not lack, as Martínez Estrada claimed, *ethos* and *ethnos*. **"El abuelo"** is an "ethnic" sonnet, as it were, and one could show that Guillén's use of other traditional forms is similarly innovative. Even when Guillén begins from a constellation of received attitudes and themes like the stylized portrait of an ethereal woman, he manages to give it a sound and sense all his own. A more accurate way of looking at Guillén's poetry, it seems to me, is contained in the following statement by Juan Marinello, which appeared in an early review of *West Indies, Ltd.*:

Hay en el poeta de *West Indies* una milagrosa capacidad para insuflar su potencia natural en moldes de la mejor calidad tradicional. El perfecto maridaje entre el soplo primitivo y la expresión culta de viejas sabidurías es la clave del valor de estos poemas. Nunca, en nuestra lírica, la voz múltiple de la masa ha encontrado vestiduras como éstas, a un tiempo fieles y transformadoras.

[The poet of *West Indies, Ltd.* has a miraculous capacity for wedding his natural potency to the finest traditional moulds. In the perfect marriage between primitive breath and old, learned forms of expression lies the key to the worth of these poems. Never before in our lyric poetry has the multiple voice of the people found vestments like these, at once faithful and transforming.]

Guillén's sonnet fits this description well, for it is both faithful and transforming, traditional and innovative—as if Gutierre de Cetina also played the *bongó*. (pp. 318–28)

Gustavo-Pérez Firmat, "Nicolás Guillén between the 'Son' and the Sonnet," in *Callaloo*, Vol. 10, No. 2, Spring, 1987, pp. 318–28.

IAN ISIDORE SMART

(essay date 1990)

[In the following excerpt from his critical study *Nicolás Guillén: Popular Poet of the Caribbean*, Smart examines the synthesis of European and African cultural influences in Guillén's poetry.]

Mulatez is a cultural concept of direct artistic relevance, which involves an awakening to the full importance of the African cultural heritage. This new awareness engenders conflict in every cultural sphere, be it social, political, economic, or psychological—the inevitable conflict between Eurocentered and Afrocentered realities. In Guillén's view, the conflict of thesis and antithesis must be faced and resolved through the harmonious blending or synthesis of the opposing elements. In a real sense, there is conflict at the heart of Guillén's creativity; it is the very fount of that creativity. Without the tensions generated by the clash between Europe and Africa, Guillén's best and most characteristic work would have no emotional core.

The concept of *mulatez* finds direct expression in several of Guillén's poems. The most significant is, perhaps, the **"Balada de los dos abuelos."** This work, from the collection *West Indies, Ltd.*, is written predominantly in octosyllabic lines, combined with five- and three-syllable lines. There appears to be no regular rhyme scheme, but an assonance in *e-o* imposes itself throughout the entire poem. Significantly, this is the assonance in the words *abuelo*, *negro* and *veo* (I see), the last word of the first line. By the same token, the assonance *a-o*, as in *blanco* (white), is also frequently employed. The stanzas are irregular in length. The poet is clearly not making any great effort to stay within the well-worked traditions of Hispanic verse. However, this poem is not a *son*; it is close to the innovative, somewhat rebellious, spirit of contemporary Hispanic poetry and, in this regard, looks more to the *abuelo blanco* than to the *abuelo negro*.

The *abuelos* are introduced as *sombras* (shadows) and then presented in a series of paired images that symbolize and characterize them. In the second strophe, "lanza con punta de hueso" (lance with a bone tip) and "tambor" (drum), associated with the *abuelo negro*, are paired with "Gorguera en el cuello ancho" (Ruff on a wide collar) and the "gris armadura" (gray armor), associated with the *abuelo blanco*. Then in the third stanza, "Africa de selvas húmedas" (Africa with its damp jungles) is contrasted with the "galeón ardiendo en oro" (galley ablaze with gold). Of the two *abuelos*, one is dying and the other is tired. One is associated with the sun and the other with the moon.

In the fourth stanza, the historical and geographical context of their confrontation is clarified further. The opening lines evoke images of ships, black people, sugarcane, the whip, and the slaveholder. Then the horrors of slavery are suggestively presented:

Piedra de llanto y de sangre,
venas y ojos entreabiertos,
y madrugadas vacías,
y atardeceres de ingenio,
y una gran voz, fuerte voz
despedazando el silencio.

(A stone of tears and blood,
veins and eyes wide open,
and early morning emptiness,
and dusks at the sugar mill,
and a great voice, a loud voice
ripping the silence to shreds.)

These images are based on the implied, in fact preconscious, complicity of the reader, who thereby enters into the creative process with the poet. This aspect of Guillén's creative technique is, of course, consistent with the major trends in nineteenth-century and contemporary Western art.

In the penultimate stanza, the *sombras* metamorphose into more material existence. They become individuals with names, Don Federico and Taita Facundo— the "Don" that immediately precedes the given name is the traditional Hispanic formula for showing respect, and "Taita" has the same force as "Uncle," in "Uncle Remus" or "Uncle Tom" for example. The last line of this penultimate stanza manifests the powerful force of poetic volition and effects the synthesis, the harmonious blending of Europe and Africa, in the stark **"Yo los junto" (I join them)**. The counterpoint carried on throughout the poem thus attains its intellectual peak.

The rhythm of the final stanza intensifies, mostly through the repetition of the line "los dos del mismo tamaño" (the two of the same stature). The new urgency of the rhythm gives the impression of an erotic coupling that is resolved in the climatic two-syllable line "Cantan" (they sing) with which the poem concludes, peaking affectively. A most appropriate final stanza for this ballad, it reads:

—¡Federico!
¡Facundo! Los dos se abrazan.
Los dos suspiran. Los dos
las fuertes cabezas alzan;
los dos del mismo tamaño,
bajo las estrellas altas;
los dos del mismo tamaño,
ansia negra y ansia blanca,
los dos del mismo tamaño,
gritan, sueñan, lloran, cantan.
Sueñan, lloran, cantan.
Lloran, cantan.
¡Cantan!

(—Federico!
Facundo! The two embrace.
The two sigh. The two
raise their strong heads;
the two of the same stature,
under the far-off stars;
the two of the same stature
black and white, both longing,
the two of the same stature,
they shout, they dream, they cry, they sing.
They dream, they cry, they sing.
They cry, they sing.
They sing!)

The rhythmic pattern is, of course, the familiar one of the *son* poems, the most effective rhythm of the poet's repertoire and the artistic element that accounts for much of the beauty of this poem. The poem represents the realization of *mulatez*, speaking through technique as well as theme to the fundamental relationship, the partnership, between Europe and Africa, the two *abuelos*. The harmonious aesthetic union in both form and content effectively symbolizes the cultural union that is *mulatez*.

Many other poems directly address the concept of *mulatez*. In fact, the image of the shadowy *abuelo* is used in the poem **"El abuelo"** of the same book, *West Indies, Ltd.* It is an alexandrine sonnet with a twist, entirely worthy of the Caribbean master bard who was also the consummate smartman. The first line presents:

Esta mujer angélica de ojos septentrionales,
que vive atenta al ritmo de su sangre europea,
ignora que en lo hondo de ese ritmo golpea

un negro el parche duro de roncos atabales.

(This angelic woman with her northern eyes,
who lives attentive only to the rhythm of her European
   blood,
in ignorance of the fact that deep within this rhythm
   a black
beats the coarse skins of raucous drums.)

The shadowy element is essential to the thrust of the sonnet, for the punch line in the final tercet reads:

que ya verás, inquieta, junto a la fresca orilla
la dulce sombra oscura del abuelo que huye,
el que rizó por siempre tu cabeza amarilla.

(One day you will see, to your chagrin, close to the
   cool bank
the sweet dark shadow of the fleeing grandfather,
the one who put that permanent curl in your yellow
   hair.)

The blonde female so proud of her European heritage is reminded by the poet, in his inimitably picaroon style, of the ubiquity of *mulatez*. These lines recall those of an earlier poem, **"La canción del bongo"** (The song of the bongo) from *Sóngoro cosongo:*

siempre falta algún abuelo,
cuando no sobra algún Don

(There's always either a grandfather missing,
or some noble title slipped in.)

Both poems depend for their effectiveness on the readers' understanding of, if not familiarity with, the whole question of race relations in Cuba—and, indeed, in the Americas in general. They could be written only by a poet honest enough to include into his poetic universe elements from both the thesis and the antithesis which create the synthesis that is Cuban culture.

The poem **"Dos niños,"** (**"Two children"**), again from *West Indies, Ltd.*, also explicitly addresses the question of the relationship between the sons of Europe and Africa in Cuba. In **"Poema con niños"** (A poem with children) from *El son entero,* the poet presents in dramatic form a conflict among four children, one Jewish, one European, one Chinese, and one African. The mother of the Euro-Cuban child resolves the conflict by invoking the principle of *mulatez*. **"Son número 6,"** (**"Son number 6"**), also from *El son entero,* begins with a resounding proclamation of the persona's African heritage:

Yoruba soy, lloro en yoruba. . . .
Yoruba soy, soy lucumí,
mandinga, congo, carabalí.

(I am Yoruba, I weep in Yoruba. . . .
I am Yoruba, I am *lucumí* [a Yoruba speaker]
Mandingo, Congo, *carabalí* [*Ibo*].)

However, the theme of the racial blend that constitutes the Cuban ethos is also presented and, in fact, becomes paramount. The abiding image of the work is contained in the following lines from the central *son* portion of the poem:

Estamos juntos desde muy lejos,
jóvenes, viejos,
negros y blancos, todo mezclado;

(We have been together for quite a long time,
young, old,
blacks and whites, all mixed together.)

The Martinican critic Alfred Melon has been particularly struck with how often these, or remarkably similar, images turn up in Guillén's poetry (he uses the term *obsession* in his analysis) [in *Recopilación de textos sobre Nicolás Guillén*, edited by Nancy Morejón]: "The constant juxtaposition in fraternal solidarity of blacks and whites, rather, their constant mixing, is perhaps Nicolás Guillén's greatest obsession, and it is not mere sentimentality for it bespeaks a constructive efficacy and force." Since the mulatto is biologically at the crossroads where Europe and Africa meet, his physical duality has frequently been accompanied by sociological and psychological dysfunction. His identity is frequently assailed in the most fundamental fashion by external pressures and, indeed, intense internal pressures too. [In a footnote the critic adds: Carl N. Degler, *Neither Black nor White: Slavery and Race Relations in Brazil and the United States,* confirms my assertion. Although he is speaking principally of the Brazillian situation, it is clear that the Cuban situation could not have been very different. The situation in Trinidad and Tobago, my native country, has been similar in many ways to that described in Degler's book. It seems quite reasonable to assume that analogous patterns would have developed in countries as similar as Cuba, Trinidad, and Brazil, along with many others that have had similar historical experiences in the matter of race relations. Degler asserts poignantly, with more than adequate demonstration, "The lot of the mulatto in Brazil can be anxiety-producing. Not white, yet often wanting to be so, the mulatto nevertheless can be classed as a black at any time a room clerk or maitre d'hotel chooses to treat him as such. This, too, is the negative side of the mulatto escape hatch." There is evidence that at least some of this turmoil was experienced by Guillén, and it is borne out in his remark about being a "mulato bastante claro 'y de pelo.'"] Neither black nor white, the mulatto's metaphysical alienation is likely to give him a clearer insight into the primordial contradiction of the human condition. Guillén seems to have developed the potential of this difficult position. He avoided the pathological pitfalls of his own biological and sociological *mulatez,* and, by elaborating on its positive aspects and incorporating these into his active artistic and psychological life, he converted a potential nightmare into poetic inspiration. The artist often builds beauty out of his own psychoses and neuroses; however, in this case, the aesthetic profit appears to have been made only after the destructive *mulatez* was transformed into a positive force.

Melon, being a Marxist critic, is naturally partial to the idea of synthesis and sees Guillén as "el poeta de la síntesis" (the poet of synthesis), a view he defends with masterful arguments [in his "El poeta de la síntesis" in *Recopilación*]. He asserts, for example, that the poet's "synthesizing vocation" was already evident in his earliest works, and he cites the following lines from **"La balada azul"**:

> Frente al mar, viendo las olas
> la quieta orilla besar,
> los dos muy juntos, muy juntos

> (Facing the sea, seeing the waves
> kiss the still shore,
> the two of us together, close together.)

Of course, the image of "los dos muy juntos" is natural in a love poem. However, Melon attaches special significance to it. He points out that it is repeated later in the same poem:

> al pie de la fuente clara
> juntos, muy juntos los dos.

> (At the foot of the clear fountain
> together, the two of us close together.)

He cites this as yet another example of "the obsession with pairs, the reiteration of the expressions *de dos en dos, los dos juntos, muy juntos*," in Guillén's poetic work.

Samples of these recurring images of pairing and togetherness can be seen in the poems I analyzed previously in this [essay]. Melon cites many other examples, especially in the poem **"No sé por qué piensas tú"** (**"I don't know why you think,"**) from the collection *Cantos para soldados y sones para turistas,* which was first published in Mexico in 1937. Perhaps the most aesthetic example of Guillén's obsession with duality, this poem is a clever and moving play on "tú" (you) and "yo" (I). All the lines, except three, end with "tú" or "yo." The three exceptions act as the strong link, like two strong hands firmly clasped, uniting "tú" and "yo." Two exceptions come from the line "si somos la misma cosa" (if we are the same thing), which is repeated to heighten its intensity, and the third exception is the only line in which the pivotal "juntos" is articulated, "juntos en la misma calle" (together in the same street).

Much of the effectiveness of the poem, and this is often the case with Guillén, comes from its simplicity. It begins:

> No sé por qué piensas tú,
> soldado, que te odio yo,
> si somos la misma cosa
> yo,
> tú.

> (I don't know why you think
> soldier, that I hate you

> if we are the same thing
> I,
> you.)

Written in 1937, the year Guillén joined the Communist party, the poem evokes deep emotions of revolutionary solidarity between the divided, and conquered, oppressed groups. It represents what Frantz Fanon called the Radicalization phase, when the native artist or intellectual participates in the real revolutionary struggle. Guillén tries to persuade the soldier, who is one of the Cuban people, to open his eyes, become aware of, and desist from his complicity in the brutal oppression of his brothers, a complicity that is a necessary, and indeed sufficient, condition for the colonial process. In the stanza quoted above, three octosyllabic lines are joined to the two one-syllable lines, "yo" and "tú," to take the strophe beyond the limits of the traditional, and very popular, romance form. The special structure is intimately bound to the content, with that impressive matching of form and content that always attends good art.

Building through the rhythmic interplay of "tú" and "yo," the final stanza comes to a climax:

> Ya nos veremos yo y tú
> juntos en la misma calle,
> hombro con hombro, tú y yo,
> sin odios ni yo ni tú,
> pero sabiendo tú y yo,
> a dónde vamos yo y tú. . .
> ¡No sé por qué piensas tú,
> soldado, que te odio yo!

> (One day we'll meet, I and you,
> together on the same street,
> shoulder to shoulder, you and I,
> with no hatred either in me or in you,
> but knowing, you and I,
> where we're going, I and you. . .
> I don't know why you should think,
> soldier, that I hate you!)

The obsession with pairing reaches its highest pitch of intensity in this last strophe, since not only are "tú" and "yo" matched by being the final words of the lines and hence the basis of the rhyme, but also, in most of the lines, they are actually joined as well: "tú y yo." The only line that does not enter into this pattern is the one that contains the very significant image "juntos." In fact, the sense of "juntos" is reaffirmed by the "misma" (same) that qualifies "calle," and so a double idea of unity is employed to bond "tú y yo."

Duality is at the core of reality. Guillén himself posited *mulatez*, an expression of duality and the creative dialogue between Africa and Europe, as the core of his art. [It] is this precisely *mulatez* that links Guillén's art so closely to the Caribbean sensibility and culture, for this same duality is at the core of West Indianness or Caribbeanness. Every Caribbean artistic expression examined in [this study]—from the Cuban *son* to the kaiso from Trinidad and Tobago or the Colombian *vallenato*—results from some synthesis of African and European elements. For example, the particular process that produced the carnival in Trinidad and Tobago (with its accompanying kaiso) was seen to be a rich, complex synthesis uniting various European elements—Spanish, French, and English, in particular—with African culture, which was itself the end product of the synthesizing processes of New World slavery.

Anyone interested in forging, or merely exploring, a common Caribbean sensibility, in order to remedy the pernicious fragmentation imposed by the colonial experience, must, then, take the carnival kaiso from Trinidad and Tobago into very careful consideration. However, the *mulatez* at the core of Guillén's poetry is, in fact, synthesis enough—it provides an area of cultural communality within the fragmented Caribbean. It is interesting that, although this region is populated overwhelmingly by African-ancestored peoples; the fragmentation is found mostly in the European element, the most important element of diversity being the various European languages spoken in the area. The original African ethnic groups and their corresponding cultures quickly lost their functional specificities under the barbaric treatment meted out by the Europeans. However, the Africans' experience with the process of cultural synthesis will bear fruit in the Caribbean, through *mulatez*, as has already happened in Guillén's poetry. Thus, the creative dialogue, which generated this poetry by overcoming the stony silence imposed by Europe's cultural hegemony, must in time grow to fill the entire region with its rich cadences, to banish forever the hostile, self-serving, limitingly egocentric silences that once prevailed. (pp. 164–72)

Ian Isidore Smart, in his *Nicolás Guillén: Popular Poet of the Caribbean,* University of Missouri Press, 1990, 187 p.

SOURCES FOR FURTHER STUDY

Benítez–Rojo, Antonio. "Nicolás Guillén and Sugar." *Callaloo* 10, No. 2 (Spring 1987): 329–51.

  Analyzes Guillén's social poetry, addressing the economic, political, and cultural problems associated with Cuba's sugar industry.

Coulthard, G. R. *Race and Colour in Caribbean Literature.* London: Oxford University Press, 1962, 152 p.

  Explores various treatments of the theme of race in Caribbean literature and includes discussion of Guillén's poetry.

Prescott, Laurence E. "A Conversation with Nicolás Guillén." *Callaloo* 10, No. 2 (Spring 1987): 352–54.

  A 1984 interview in which Guillén shares his views on politics and literature in Cuba.

Spicer, Eloise Y. "The Blues and the *Son:* Reflections of Black Self Assertion in the Poetry of Langston Hughes and Nicolás Guillén." *The Langston Hughes Review* III, No. 1 (Spring 1984): 1–12.

  Evaluates several early poems from *Motivos de son,* comparing Guillén's development of the *son* rhythm in his poetry with Langston Hughes's poetic use of the blues musical form.

Williams, Lorna V. *Self and Society in the Poetry of Nicolás Guillén.* Baltimore: Johns Hopkins University Press, 1982, 177 p.

  Discusses Guillén's perspective on the Afro-Cuban experience of colonialism.

Additional coverage of Guillén's life and career is contained in the following sources published by Gale Research: *Black Literature Criticism,* Vol. 2; *Black Writers; Contemporary Authors,* Vols. 116, 125, 129; *Contemporary Literary Criticism,* Vols. 48, 79; and *Hispanic Writers.*

Oscar Hijuelos

1951–

American novelist and short story writer.

INTRODUCTION

*D*rawing heavily upon his ethnic heritage as the son of Cuban immigrants, Hijuelos writes realistic novels about Cuban-Americans noted for their eloquent prose, energetic narratives, powerful characterizations, and overall sensuality. Best known for his *The Mambo Kings Play Songs of Love* (1989), which was awarded the Pulitzer Prize for Fiction in 1990, Hijuelos's novels are lauded by critics for their universal thematic value. According to Edith Milton, Hijuelos "is less concerned with the trials of immigrant life generally presented in fiction than with questions of identity and perspective."

Born in New York City, Hijuelos was raised in an urban environment rich with Hispanic culture. He was profoundly influenced by the mambo music popular in his youth and played in several Latin American bands throughout his adolescence and early adulthood. After receiving his master's degree in creative writing from the City University of New York in 1978, Hijuelos wrote several short stories while working for an advertising agency. In 1983 he completed his first novel, *Our House in the Last World*, which depicts the experiences of a Cuban family living in New York City during the 1940s. The book was well-received and shortly afterwards Hijuelos began writing full-time. In 1989 he published his second novel, *The Mambo Kings*, which recounts the lives of two Cuban-American brothers, named Cesar and Nestor, from their arrival in New York City in 1949, to their brief moment of fame as guest musicians on the "I Love Lucy" television show, and finally, to their subsequent decline into anonymity. "Basically the first image I had for the book was of a superintendent who played music," recalls Hijuelos. "He was a wonderful bolero singer. I'd listen to him and think, 'This guy could be famous. What happened?' . . . So I had this idea of incredibly talented people who never made it." *The*

Mambo Kings was followed by *The Fourteen Sisters of Emilio Montez O'Brien* in 1993. While different from Hijuelos's earlier works in many respects, *The Fourteen Sisters* has achieved some success among critics for its insight into family life and relationships, thus consolidating Hijuelos's reputation as a leading author of Hispanic literature.

Lauded by commentators for their colorful and moving portraits of Cuban-Americans, Hijuelos's books center on the American dream of upward mobility—yet in all of his works this dream is never fully realized. In *Our House*, Alejo and Mercedes marry and move to New York City from Cuba seeking a better life than the one they left behind, but the novel ends tragically when, after years of disappointments, poverty, and failed relationships, Alejo dies. Alone, Mercedes is left with memories of her youth in Cuba which, according to Edith Milton, is treated like a "lost, misremembered Eden," providing a sharp contrast to Mercedes's present reality. Several critics have noted that *Our House* is not really about the plight of Cuban-Americans but rather about the universal conditions of alienation and loss. Ellen Quinn has observed that "the first English phrases Mercedes sets herself to learn—'I am alone,' 'I come from another country,' and 'I am lost'—reflect the family's difficulties in making a success of their American life, and their inability to come to terms with one another." In many ways a realistic novel, *Our House* also contains numerous mythical, magical, and surrealistic elements derived from Hijuelos's Latin heritage.

Similar to *Our House* in many respects, *The Mambo Kings* is noted for its bold expression of sexuality and its realistic depiction of a time in which American popular culture was profoundly influenced by Latin music. The theme of music is so prominent in *The Mambo Kings* that it even determines the structural framework of the book: each chapter was written as a different song on a record. According to Hijuelos, "I wanted to move atmospherically. . . . That's why I needed the device of the hotel, with Cesar sitting in The Hotel Splendor at the end of his life, listening to an old Mambo Kings record, and as different songs come on he has different thoughts, going forward, going back. It does drift around, I have to admit; . . . but I wanted that improvisational feel in part of the book, like a horn line." Critics suggest that despite the novel's treatment of many themes—love, death, music, and sex—the most important focus of *The Mambo Kings* is on self-awareness as Hijuelos's protagonists eventually develop a sense of identity through the aid of family and friends.

The Fourteen Sisters of Emilio Montez O'Brien, as Michiko Kakutani has asserted, "is less concerned with loss and missed opportunities" than Hijuelos's first two novels. Centering almost entirely on women, *The Fourteen Sisters* opens as Nelson O'Brien, a photographer of the Spanish-American War, meets and marries Mariela Montez while in Cuba; the couple then settle in a small Pennsylvania town where they raise fourteen daughters and one son. Most of the plot revolves around the lives of the fourteen daughters and their battles with such problems as alcoholism, drug addiction, death, illness, and divorce. Some reviewers have found Hijuelos's numerous protagonists underdeveloped and often limited to stereotypes. Nonetheless, critics laud the novel for its colorful depiction of family life; Kakutani has observed that, in comparison to Hijuelos's other works, *The Fourteen Sisters of Emilio Montez O'Brien* "takes a longer view of family life . . . and its vision is ultimately more redemptive, concerned in the end . . . with the cyclical nature of time, and the enduring possibilities of love."

Overall, critical response to Hijuelos's novels has been enthusiastic. While the characters of *Our House* are considered somewhat predictable, Milton has argued that they are simultaneously "touching" and that "as they decline from hope to resignation, from romance to nagging, they are not just material for a literary exercise but the subject of a loving and deeply felt tribute." Criticism of *The Mambo Kings* has been more severe. Nicolás Kanellos has noted that the work "drags in the middle and towards the end, without the benefit of a hard-driving plot," adding that "its insistence on detailing the culture and spirit of the times and its repetitive reminiscence are somewhat tiring." Peter Matthews has suggested that "reading this book induces a strange, drugged elation"; "only later perhaps may one feel mildly cheated by the smoothly processed quality of the colours." Nonetheless, most reviewers have praised *The Mambo Kings* for its compelling characters and skillful prose. These characteristics, in addition to the poignant themes and striking realism of his fiction, have established Hijuelos as an emerging and significant figure in Hispanic literature.

CRITICAL COMMENTARY

EDITH MILTON
(essay date 1983)

[In the excerpt below, Milton examines the characters, themes, and general style of *Our House in the New World*, distinguishing Hijuelos from other contemporary novelists by asserting that he is "less concerned with the trials of immigrant life generally presented in fiction than with questions of identity and perspective."]

Oscar Hijuelos is less concerned with the trials of immigrant life generally presented in fiction than with questions of identity and perspective. His *Our House in the Last World*'s strengths are in its characters and the sheer energy of its narrative, which centers on the Santinio family, come to New York from Cuba in 1944 to make their fortune. Its particular focus is Hector, the younger of the Santinios' sons. Since his father, Alejo, expects him to be manly and "Cuban" and his mother, Mercedes, smothers him with her anxieties, he is unable to find a life and persona of his own.

Our House in the Last World is a novel of great warmth and tenderness. Written from the perspective of innocence, it reflects the wonder and confusion of an immigrant family and the bewilderment of a child trying to sort out his world. It begins at the ticket window of the Neptuna theater in Holguín, Cuba, in 1939. Mercedes, who is 27 and almost past hoping for a husband, is selling tickets to an Edward G. Robinson double feature when Alejo, debonair but disastrously undirected, happens by and woos her with flowers he picks from beside the road. They are married. They move to New York, where they share an apartment with relatives in Spanish Harlem. Other Cubans move in, get rich and move on. The Santinios stay poor and stay.

History, in the personages of Joe DiMaggio having a drink and Fidel Castro driving by in a motorcade, comes close but does not touch them, though Alejo, who has become a cook in a big hotel, once serves a chocolate sundae to the visiting Nikita Khrushchev. "Only in America," Mr. Hijuelos observes in homage to the great cliché of novels about immigrants, "could a worker get so close to a fat little guy with enormous power."

Alejo has become a drunk, a glutton, a man too weak to resist the vindictive campaign waged by his oldest sister against poor Mercedes, who is a woman lost in illusions. Her heart, given early to sentimental recollections of her dead father, is transferred to Alejo only at the novel's end, after he has had the grace to drop dead from heart failure and allow her the freedom of her dreams.

The couple has two sons. Horacio, the older, evades his mother's ambitious fantasies by accepting a Cuban model of manhood: He fights, he womanizes, he identifies with his father. Finally he escapes into the Air Force. Hector, in whose voice one seems to hear the author's own, is not so lucky. When he is 3, on holiday in Cuba, he catches a near-fatal infection and spends months in a hospital for terminally ill children. This makes him suspicious not only of Cuban bacteria but of all things Cuban, and his frailty gives Mercedes a lifetime's claim to him. Enslaved by her anxieties and his own terror of the *micróbios* lying in wait, he is the helpless witness of his father's drunken excesses and his mother's growing hysteria, too fearful to make a dash for freedom.

In time his parents' inability to change begins to seem perverse; the childlike dreams, frustrated, turn to self-pity. The world too is less hopeful: Castro's victory, at first welcome, turns sour, and Cuba the beautiful, the lovingly remembered, becomes Paradise Lost. As the "Last World" of the title suggests, with its play on "last" to mean both final and previous, the novel's central tension is between this lost, misremembered Eden and the ultimate reality, first of contemporary life and in the end of death.

There is more than a touch of satire in Mr. Hijuelos's writing, but he never loses the syntax of magic, which transforms even the unspeakable into a sort of beauty. He describes children being treated at Hector's hospital as being stuck with rods "so cold and violating that the children's bones would leave their bodies and walk around in the outer hall." Of Horacio's departure into the Air Force he writes, "Before Hector's eyes, Horacio dissolved and became a few lines of scribble on blue airmail paper." And his account of Hector's first brief foray into freedom is couched in the most seductive language I have ever seen used in the service of brute aggression.

But what gives *Our House in the Last World* its aura of affection and gentleness is its people; they are members of the family, irritating, predictable and ours. Their insanities are touching and somehow genial. And as they decline from hope to resignation, from romance to nagging, they are not just material for a literary exercise

---

Principal Works

Our House in the Last World (novel) 1983

The Mambo Kings Play Songs of Love (novel) 1989

The Fourteen Sisters of Emilio Montez O'Brien (novel) 1993

---

but the subject of a loving and deeply felt tribute. (pp. 12, 22)

Edith Milton, "Newcomers in New York," in *The New York Times Book Review*, May 15, 1983, pp. 12, 22.

PUBLISHERS WEEKLY

(essay date 1988)

[Here, the reviewer discusses the principal themes and overall structure of *The Mambo Kings Play Songs of Love*, as well as Hijuelos's motivations as a writer.]

The Mambo Kings Play Songs of Love tells the story of the brothers Cesar and Nestor Castillo, Cuban-born musicians who come to New York in 1949 to find their fortunes, or perhaps to escape them. In any event, their exploits—musical, amorous and gustatory—taking place as they do in Latin nightclubs, crowded kitchens and lonely hotel rooms, provide a lively narrative upon which the author hangs his sometimes somber meditations.

Although *Mambo Kings* has many themes—music, sex and love, pain and death, not to mention TV—Hijuelos's inspirations clearly spring from the self-awareness won through family and friends.

"I was born in New York. I grew up on 118th Street, just a few blocks from here. I was always in a band, mostly with Puerto Rican guys; we played Top-40 stuff and some Latin things," he says of his teenage years and early 20s. As for schooling, Hijuelos describes it in a somewhat dismissive fashion: "Catholic school, public school, public school." He finished at City College of New York.

His parents hail from Oriente province, "the easternmost province in Cuba, home to Desi Arnaz, Fidel Castro, Batista, Jose Lima; Alejo Carpentier. They came here in the 1940s, which is what my first novel, *Our House in the Last World* was about—an ambitious people from a nonprofessional class coming to America."

That first book, published in 1983, was roundly praised for its tender portrait of émigré life. *Mambo Kings*, though not centered on Hijuelos's family, had its origins nonetheless in the details of his life.

"Basically, the first image I had for the book was of a superintendent who played music," says Hijuelos. "I got that image from Pedro, one of the elevator operators in this building who used to come up and play music with me. He was a wonderful bolero singer. I'd listen to him and think, 'This guy could be famous. What happened?'" In the novel, the elder brother, Cesar, after a long career as a modestly successful bandleader, humbles himself by accepting the superintendent position in his building, only to dignify the post with disarming pride.

"I also have a cousin named Angel who was a bolero singer in Cuba, although I didn't know it. I was at his house and he started singing, and he was beautiful. And he became a mechanic. So I had this idea of incredibly talented people who never made it."

"In a way," he adds, "the whole book was formed by listening to music and dwelling on personalities."

The sharply drawn figures of the Mambo King brothers are more than mere amalgams of real people, however, "Cesar and Nestor are archetypes. There's the flamboyant Cesar who's really very troubled, and there's the troubled Nestor who's really very soulful. I guess it's mostly invention rather than portraiture. I hope that anyone who has the greatest lust for living can relate to Cesar, and anyone who has lost a love can relate to Nestor."

And anyone who has seen *I Love Lucy* will be able to relate to an event that wends its way throughout the book—a guest appearance by Cesar and Nestor on the then-top-rated TV show featuring America's favorite Cuban bandleader and his madcap comedienne wife. From their knock on Lucy and Ricky Ricardo's apartment door (to which Lucy responds "I'm commmmmming") to Ricky's "Gee, it's swell you fellas could make it up from Havana," to their performance—as Ricky's Cuban cousins—at the Copacabana, a legend, at least among family and friends, is made. Nephews of Cesar and Nestor are called to the TV whenever neighbors spot the Mambo Kings episode coming on; from such a brief event posterity is born, and it occasions one of the book's more philosophical, or perhaps spiritual, themes.

"I was really thinking of the TV appearance as being about memory, and memory being about immortality," says Hijuelos. "And the thing about a book is that it should have a cumulative effect; some novels go for the quick knockout, and I wanted to write a book where, at the end, you would know what someone feels like who really cares for someone and thinks about them. In the end of the book, when I replay the appearance of the brothers on the *Lucy* show, for me, that's what memory is about—you love someone, you feel for them, you remember them. It's like a re-run in your head."

"Desi and Lucy themselves have become cultural icons," he continues. "Desi is very typically Cuban to me, and I was very interested in the uniting of American and Cuban culture. When I used to watch the show I thought that Desi was the star! I was in Italy when he died and I couldn't continue the book for awhile. And now Lucy is gone. And just yesterday in the Albany train station, I found a 'poor-Lucy-we-loved-you' magazine on the seat. There's a quote in there by Bob Hope: 'One of the greatest gifts to mankind is laughter and one of the greatest gifts to laughter is Lucille Ball. God has her now, but thanks to television we'll have her forever.'"

In *Mambo Kings*, considerations of the hereafter barely hold their own against the enticements of the here-and-now—the book's atmosphere is thick with sexual desire.

"I intended a little bit of parody of the super-sexual virility that men are obsessed with in the macho cultures," says Hijuelos. "I was having fun with it. Also, for me, it's a play on mortality, and on the body and how one can be hyperphallic—built like the Empire State Building—and it won't make any difference to the ultimate issues of love or family or death. I wanted to write a book that had meat in it," he says with a laugh, "but which was also nourishing, with a provocative understructure. A lot of themes are repressed in the book but the sex is not; it actually covers other layers. The sex balances the pain of the book."

Clearly, the challenge of structuring a novel to incorporate Hijuelos's many passions must have been daunting. But Hijuelos knew what he *didn't* want to do—"an elaborate plot—ABCDEFG, with atmosphere, character introduction, dramatic tension, denouement, all that. In a way, I think I avoided it, and honored the idea that life doesn't always work that way."

Instead, Hijuelos settled upon a simple, open organization, one that is familiar to anyone who listens to music—the book has two parts, Side A and Side B.

"The formal idea was sort of like having a record going round and round. You know how sometimes when you listen to music and the song cuts off and you're into another feeling? I wanted to move atmospherically. I saw the chapters as different songs. That's why I needed the device of the hotel, with Cesar sitting in The Hotel Splendour at the end of his life, listening to an old Mambo Kings record, and as different songs come on he has different thoughts, going forward, going back. It does drift around, I have to admit; the reader is not always aware of being with Cesar, but I wanted that improvisational feel in part of the book, like a horn line."

Choosing this structure also allowed Hijuelos to promote another of his passions—the music itself. "It is *the most fun* music in the world," he says, hopping up and into another room to turn on his electric keyboard. "It is soulful, it combines Spanish lyric beauty and almost maudlinness with a sort of hipness. I was listening to a Talking Heads record, *Naked*, and the hippest track on the whole album is a straight mambo vamp. If people listened to the source of that stuff, they'd go nuts."

Hijuelos leans seriously into his keyboard playing. "If you've read the book, you've at least heard *of* this tune." He plays "Beautiful María of My Soul," the song that, in the novel, is rewritten 22 times by the long-suffering Nestor in memory of a lost love; it is the Mambo Kings' only hit, and the song that grabbed Desi Arnaz's attention. Indeed, it is soulful to this listener's ear. To the question of composition (the words and music appear in the book), Hijuelos admits co-authorship with a friend, "I write songs all the time."

The strains of seeing this book through publication have been hard on Hijuelos. "After a while you become indistinguishable from your book," he laments. "I'm getting out of the country—to Portugal—so I can think again." As for his next book, he says that, "Surprisingly, at least to me, writing this book made me want to write a book about women. My next book is about 14 sisters."

There is a particular atmosphere in *Mambo Kings* that fascinated Hijuelos even as he was writing. Certain of the female characters, like the cooly independent Dolores who suffers through a rape attempt by a gum salesman before becoming Nestor's wife, completely grabbed him. "I was sorry to have to leave Dolores. I could have written an entire book about her," he says.

Despite all the male bravado, and the decidedly male melancholy in the book, *The Mambo Kings* has a convincing female camaraderie, in which the women seem to outwit the fates that all the men fall prey to. Hijuelos attributes those scenes to a period in his life just after college.

"When I got out of school I worked in an office researching trends in advertising. Some of the atmosphere in the book came from that job. The women's gossip was distilled from hanging out with the girls from the office. Women often go through incredible trips with men. For some reason they used to tell me about it. I love that whole life—the gin mill life. We used to go to clubs at night. Disco was the craze, not the mambo, but it's all the same. People want to go out and have fun—they want to find magic and romance and they want to find poetry and fall in love and be loved to death. People live this dream and then they hit real life again. And there are arbiters of that dream—that's what entertainers are about. They are that dream all the time. And I think novelists and poets, or the worlds inside their works, are too. What I want to do is entertain and give readers something that can help them live more happily, just like characters in a song of love." (pp. 42, 44)

Publishers Weekly, Vol. 236, No. 3, July 29, 1988, pp. 42, 44.

PETER WATROUS

(essay date 1989)

[In the following excerpt, Watrous discusses Hijuelos's sources for *The Mambo Kings Play Songs of Love*.]

As he dies slowly in a seedy New York hotel, Cesar Castillo, a onetime mambo musician and the central character of Oscar Hijuelos's new novel, *The Mambo Kings Play Songs of Love*, remembers the arc of his life.

He mulls over his youth in Cuba and his immigration in 1949 to the United States. The wild life of clubs, music and dancing, the sway of the shiny, romantic and intense music, his melancholy brother, Nestor, the brothers' appearance on "I Love Lucy," where they played their minor hit, "Beautiful María of My Soul," which Nestor wrote and rewrote 22 times—all these images flash and overlap in a dense evocation of the 1940's and 50's in New York City, a glorious period for Latin American culture.

At the end of his life, Cesar is a building superintendent. But he has no regrets: he is still a celebrity in his neighborhood, he is respected by other musicians and he has lived a full live through his music, even though the flash of his early career quickly waned. The music, even in seedy clubs, was sustenance, never work.

These images have won acclaim for Oscar Hijuelos, but they have also made him feel trapped and more than a bit stereotyped as an immigrant Hispanic author.

"Welcome to my mambo apartment," said Mr. Hijuelos the other day in a mocking tone that indicated his experience with interviewers since *Mambo Kings* won almost unanimous critical applause. He has been asked if he goes dancing every night (And why not? interviewers demand when he says no). He has been queried about good Cuban restaurants in his neighborhood on the Upper West Side of Manhattan. And he has been asked to comment on the political situation in Cuba.

After putting aside his guitar—the 38-year-old Mr. Hijuelos jams with musician friends whenever he has the chance—he got down to the business of talking about himself and his book.

"This is not an immigrant novel, though it might seem like it," he said fervently as he sat in his apartment, which is filled with books by authors like Joseph Campbell, William James and Rimbaud. "It's true that immigrant novels have to do with people going from one country to another, but there isn't a single novel that doesn't travel from one place to another, emotionally or locally.

"In the case of *The Mambo Kings*, I had to get the characters from A to B, Cuba to New York, but the brothers' spirits were neither desperate nor needy. They would have done well if they stayed in Cuba. The immigrant novel implies a desperate need. So the book is about all kinds of change, even though it may be more about emotional change than literal change. There's struggle in the novel but it's creative struggle." It is not, he said, the bleak struggle of day-to-day existence.

The era portrayed in the book, post-war America through the 1950's, is the period when Latin music had a strong impact on culture in the United States. It wasn't the first time Latin culture had made itself felt here: Hispanic music, whether from Cuba, Argentina or Mexico, had been infiltrating the music scene in the United States since the 1880's, when a Mexican marching band visited New Orleans and local musicians picked up on the rhythms.

Since then waves of Hispanic music and culture have crashed on the shores in the form of tangos, sambas, rhumbas, mambos and the boogaloo, influencing Tin Pan Alley, Broadway, jazz and popular music.

In the 1940's and 50's Latin performers like Desi Arnaz and Xavier Cugat became household names in America. The majestic, exciting orchestras of Machito, Tito Puente and Perez Prado spread the sound and movement of a culture romantically and gracefully, and a mambo craze, with the music's joyous rhythms and horn-powered melodies, swept the nation. Nightclubs like the Palladium in midtown Manhattan became magnets where people of all races and ethnic groups came together to hear the Latin beats and show off on the dance floor what they spent long hours perfecting in their neighborhoods.

In Mr. Hijuelos's book, the nightclubs of Havana and New York become rich symbols for the fertility of Cuban culture and by extension the power of the imagination.

"Nightclubs are the equivalent of a Catholic Church in a poor country," he said. "You hear a lot of stuff about churches filled with gold while the people are starving. But what elitists don't get is that for poor people, the church is their own mansion. Nightclubs fill the same function. The music, the dress, the language of nightclubs are all creativity and splendor. Dancing is pure creativity. It's an outlet."

Mr. Hijuelos, a second-generation Cuban-American, grew up in Manhattan; his father was a cook at the Biltmore Hotel and his mother wrote poetry. He graduated from a public high school on West 84th Street, went to Bronx Community College for a year, completed his undergraduate degree at City College and continued with graduate studies there. Donald Barthelme and Susan Sontag were among his teachers. To a certain extent, the culture he writes about is learned; he was born just after the Mambo Kings arrive in New York.

"I grew up hearing about New York in the 40's from relatives," he continued. "When I was about 12, I went to a dance in the neighborhood and there was a mambo band playing 1960's songs. This guy was shaking the maracas and now and then the band would break into these 60's tunes with a mambo beat. One guy was so flamboyant and great-looking, I said, 'This guy is where it's at.' And yet I realized they were just trying to make 50 bucks. It never left me."

Seeking out the details that enrich *Mambo Kings*, Mr. Hijuelos interviewed scores of people involved in Latin music and recalled his own memories of growing up on 118th Street in Manhattan.

"I talked to people who went to the ballrooms," he said. "When I hear certain songs; Nelo Sosa's 'Cuchero Para el Tren,' for example, I hear Havana as it was in 1942. Or Puerto Rico 1955 in 'Lamento Boriquén,' or Manhattan 1964 in 'Bang Bang' by Joe Cuba. The person from whom I got the biggest fix on the music scene was Chico O'Farrill, a band leader and arranger who did one of the greatest albums on earth with Machito, 'Afro-Cuban Jazz,' which has the 'Manteca Suite.' He described the club scene in Havana in the 40's."

Some of the information in the book he stumbled across. "About a year before the book was finished," he said, "I went to a Santería place on 110th Street."

Santeria is the African-derived religion native to the Spanish-speaking Caribbean that mixes Catholicism with worship of West African deities. It is practiced by many Spanish-speaking people of Caribbean descent in New York.

"The whole apartment was in blue," he recalled. "You come in and pay obeisance, put money in a basket and lie down and make a wish. Machito had just died and I had wanted to talk to him. I made a wish: 'I hope everything works out with this music stuff in the book.'

"I got up and sat at a table and three women walked in. One was an 8-year-old saint—in Santería, people thought to have special gifts, like the power to heal or the ability to see the future, are called saints. Another was an older saint and the third was Machito's widow, and she sat down right next to me and talked about what it was like in the ballrooms."

Mr. Hijuelos's meeting with Machito's widow happened upon his return to New York after two years in Europe, where he had been traveling after receiving a Rome Fellowship in Literature from the American Academy of Arts and Letters for his first novel, *Our House in the Last World.*

The Mambo Kings Play Songs of Love, like *Our House* in 1983, is an extended meditation on the power of memory. Over and over Nestor's son, Eugenio, watches the episode of "I Love Lucy" in which the Mambo Kings perform, as if to hold on to both his father and his culture.

It doesn't work. Eugenio slowly inches away from his Cuban background; he stops dancing. Assimilation creeps up on the people in the book; Cesar becomes a superintendent in his building; his last love affair is with a woman who, after he becomes ill, is less a lover than a helper. He turns away from the possibilities of the future—even the present—toward the past and memories.

"Latins are predisposed to thinking about the past," Mr. Hijuelos said. "Catholicism has a lot to do with it because Catholicism is a contemplation of the past, of symbols that are supposed to be eternally present.

"Transpose that sensibility onto the culture, and people will dispense with time. People die but they're still there. I listen to 1940's music but I feel like I'm listening to conversations which are just taking place."

For Cesar, Mr. Hijuelos explained, "music allowed escape, expression and certain freedoms he might not have had otherwise."

"A man who is personally shy can be sexually flamboyant on stage," he said. "A man who is personally flamboyant can be introspective.

"What would it feel like, turning around when you're 60 years old and finding your life behind you? We're all like flowers, we have our bloom, and then we pass the bloom. When you pass the bloom you think about it. But music transcends that, it is a constant bloom. So music is a way of transcending existence. That's corny, but true, because music is emotional expression, an aspect of inner personalities and potentials." (pp. C17, C19)

Peter Watrous, "Evoking When Mambo Was King," in *The New York Times*, September 11, 1989, pp. C17, C19.

NICOLÁS KANELLOS

(essay date 1990)

[Kanellos is a Puerto Rican-born American scholar of Hispanic literature who has founded the *Americas Review* magazine and has written numerous works on Hispanic literature, including *A History of Hispanic Theatre in the United States* (1990). Below, Kanellos comments on the resounding success of *The Mambo Kings Play Songs of Love*, lauding the novel as "the best Hispanic book ever published by a large commercial press."]

Let's talk about promotion and marketing first. *The Mambo Kings* may be the most highly promoted Hispanic book in history by a major press. With a 40,000 copy first hard-cover printing, a $50,000 national marketing campaign, 100% national co-op advertising, rights

---

An excerpt from *The Mambo Kings Play Songs of Love*

For me, my father's gentle rapping on Ricky Ricardo's door has always been a call from the beyond, as in Dracula films, or films of the walking dead, in which spirits ooze out from behind tombstones and through the cracked windows and rotted floors of gloomy antique halls: Lucille Ball, the lovely redheaded actress and comedienne who played Ricky's wife, was housecleaning when she heard the rapping of my father's knuckles against the door.

"I'm commmmmming," in her singsong voice.

Standing in her entrance, two men in white silk suits and butterfly-looking lace bow ties, black instrument cases by their side and black-brimmed white hats in their hands—my father, Nestor Castillo, thin and broad-shouldered, and Uncle Cesar, thickset and immense.

My uncle: "Mrs. Ricardo? My name is Alfonso and this is my brother Manny . . . "

And her face lights up and she says, "Oh, yes, the fellows from Cuba. Ricky told me all about you."

Then, just like that, they're sitting on the couch when Ricky Ricardo walks in and says something like "Manny, Alfonso! Gee, it's really swell that you fellas could make it up here from Havana for the show."

That's when my father smiled. The first time I saw a rerun of this, I could remember other things about him—his lifting me up, his smell of cologne, his patting my head, his handing me a dime, his touching my face, his whistling, his taking me and my little sister, Leticia, for a walk in the park, and so many other moments happenings in my thoughts simultaneously that it was like watching something momentous, say the Resurrection, as if Christ had stepped out of his sepulcher, flooding the world with light—what we were taught in the local church with the big red doors—because my father was now newly alive and could take off his hat and sit down on the couch in Ricky's living room, resting his black instrument case on his lap. He could play the trumpet, move his head, blink his eyes, nod, walk across the room, and say "Thank you" when offered a cup of coffee. For me, the room was suddenly bursting with a silvery radiance. And now I knew that we could see it again.

Oscar Hijuelos, in his *The Mambo Kings Play Songs of Love*, Farrar, Straus & Giroux, 1989.

---

sold in advance to England, France, Finland, Germany, Holland and Italy, extensive exposure at the American Booksellers Association . . . it's great to see an Hispanic book at the top of the list. And it has paid off, with glowing reviews in all of the right places, from *Time* and *The New York Times* to *Publishers Weekly* and *Kirkus;* and the first Pulitzer prize for fiction to a Latino.

And *The Mambo Kings* is worth it. This is the best Hispanic book ever published by a large commercial press. Not your typical ethnic autobiography which charts a protagonist's search for the American Dream, *The Mambo Kings* instead is an evocation of the period when one segment of Hispanic culture heavily influenced American popular culture, dancing its way right into the heart of the mainstream. The novel is set in the 1940's and 1950's and recalls the American craze for Afro-Caribbean music. *The Mambo Kings* succeeds in recreating the euphoria, the optimism and the texture of the times, while following the fortunes of Cesar and Nestor Castillo from their youth in rural Cuba to their jobs in a Manhattan meat packing plant and their domestic life in Spanish Harlem, to the eventual rise of their band—from playing seedy clubs and dance halls to even touring the towns of the Midwestern cornbelt—highlighted by the brothers' hit record and their appearance on the *I Love Lucy* show that brought a version of Hispanic culture into American livingrooms for years, to the tragic death of Nestor in a car accident while on tour, to an aging Cesar's degeneration into an incorrigible and unrepentent alcoholic living at the flea-bag Hotel Splendour, spending more of his waking hours re-living the glories of his now passé music, his

numerous amorous conquests and his romances killed by his lack of commitment, the warm camaraderie of Latin musicians and the high regard they held for his music.

Hijuelos researched his subject well and proves himself to be more than a serious writer, an intellectual, in this well documented chronicle, which is a far cry from his first novel that opened the door of the literary establishment for him: the somewhat predictable Cuban-American version of the ethnic autobiography, *Our House in the Next World*. If *The Mambo Kings* sins, it is through excess. The novel drags in the middle and towards the end, without the benefit of hard-driving plot. Its insistence on detailing the culture and spirit of the times and its repetitive reminiscence are somewhat tiring.

But there is no doubt that *The Mambo Kings Play Songs of Love* is worth reading for pleasure and for knowledge, and it should become a welcome addition as a text for literature classes. (pp. 113–14)

Nicolás Kanellos, in a review of *The Mambo Kings Play Songs of Love*, in *The Americas Review*, Vol. XVIII, No. 1, Spring, 1990, pp. 113–14.

MICHIKO KAKUTANI

(essay date 1993)

[In the following excerpt, Kakutani compares *The Fourteen Sisters of Emilio Montez O'Brien* with Hijuelos's earlier novels, pointing out their similarities but also suggesting that *The Fourteen Sisters* "takes a longer view of family life" and "is ultimately more redemptive, concerned in the end . . . with the cyclical nature of time, and the enduring possibilities of love."]

Like his first two books, *Our House in the Last World* (1983) and *The Mambo Kings Play Songs of Love* (1989), Oscar Hijuelos's latest novel, *The 14 Sisters of Emilio Montez O'Brien,* is a family saga, one of those commodious, emotionally generous books that immerse us in a well-upholstered fictional world. Once again, we are given a richly colored portrait of immigrant life in the United States; once again we are shown how familial hopes, dream, yearnings and sadnesses are handed down generation to generation.

Whereas *Mambo Kings*, which won the 1990 Pulitzer Prize for fiction, was an insistently male book focusing on the sexual and romantic adventures of two Cuban immigrant brothers, *The 14 Sisters* is a novel about women, a novel examining the lives and loves of the Montez and O'Brien women.

Though many of its central characters suffer from a lingering melancholy reminiscent of that possessed by Nestor, one of the two brothers in *The Mambo Kings*, the book is less concerned with loss and missed opportunities than its predecessor. Death, divorce and illness all take their toll here, but *The 14 Sisters* takes a longer view of family life than *The Mambo Kings*, and its vision is ultimately more redemptive, concerned in the end, like Gabriel García Márquez's *Love in the Time of Cholera*, with the cyclical nature of time, and the enduring possibilities of love.

Moving back and forth in time, *The 14 Sisters* begins, more or less, with the story of Nelson O'Brien, a young Irish boy, whose dreams of America are based on the penny novels he has read about Wild Bill Hickok and Jesse James. In time, Nelson emigrates to the United States, settles in a small Pennsylvania town and in 1898 after the death of his beloved sister Kate, goes to Cuba to take photographs of the Spanish-American War.

There, Nelson meets the beautiful, dreamy 16-year-old Mariela Montez, and for 27 Sundays in a row he pays her court. He tells her about his house in Pennsylvania "deep in the heart of America, where people could do as they pleased and there was no war," and she dreams of a good life with this earnest, sad-eyed man. For their wedding, Nelson gives her a telescope so that she might gaze upon the stars, and he introduces the shy young woman to the unexpected pleasures of his bed.

Their passion is enthusiastic, and almost mythically fecund. In the ensuing years in America, Mariela will have 14 daughters, and finally, after all these girls, a son. . . In relating the tangled history of the O'Brien-Montez

clan, Mr. Hijuelos moves confidently from one character's story to the next, leaping ahead in time to foreshadow the future, then jumping backward in time to show us the seeds of hope and despair. He subtly reveals the ways in which the sisters' choices echo—or counterpoint—the choices of their siblings, and he demonstrates, as well, the ways in which their lives both embody and contradict the dreams of their parents.

Toward the end of the book, Mr. Hijuelos's narrative becomes a little rushed, and his quickening litany of developments in the sisters' lives—alcoholism, addiction to Valium, subscriptions to spiritist newsletters, affairs with younger men—can sound suspiciously like an inventory of topics on a talk show. The reader, however, never really minds, so persuasive and generous is his delineation of the family's life. Indeed, one finishes *The 14 Sisters* reluctantly, the way one finishes a long letter from a beloved family member, eager for all the news not to end.

Michiko Kakutani, "Family Has Lots of Women and Love," in *The New York Times*, March 2, 1993, p. B2.

THOMAS MALLON
(essay date 1993)

[An American author and educator, Mallon is best known for his novel, *Arts and Sciences: A Seventies Seduction* (1988). Here, Mallon reviews *The Fourteen Sisters of Emilio Montez O'Brien*, noting weaknesses in its plot and characterizations but concluding that "the overall effect is luscious and life-loving."]

Oscar Hijuelos has made the gutsy decision to follow up his Pulitzer Prize-winning 1989 novel with something like its opposite. While *The Mambo Kings Play Songs of Love* was a propulsive ballad of Cuban-American fraternal machismo, *The Fourteen Sisters of Emilio Montez O'Brien* is the author's paean to femininity, an exuberant history of a Pennsylvania household so vital with food and music and decoration as to be, literally, magnetic: "Over the years a thick maple tree, standing out in the yard, had been the scene of numerous accidents: men were thrown from their horses or, begoggled and yet blinded by what they may have taken as the sun, skidded their Model T's, their Packards, their sporty sedans off the road into a ditch, axles bent and crankcases hissing steam."

The 14 sisters of the title are born between 1902 and 1923 to Mariela Montez and Nelson O'Brien, an Irish photographer who met his wife when he went to Cuba to take pictures of the Spanish-American War. Later he and Mariela immigrate to the town of Cobbleton, Pa., where Nelson operates both a photography studio and the local movie theater. Mariela, who writes poems and dreams of life on other planets, lives to some extent in "linguistic solitude," afraid of the town beyond the house. She is "a fragile, changeable being," but awesome in her generative power: "She worked at motherhood as if the fecund interior of her body, thick with organs and tissue and blood, was a cavernous workhouse."

Mr. Hijuelos uses the oldest and youngest of the Montez O'Brien children to bracket his capacious story, making these bookends sturdy with disproportionate amounts of narrative attention. Margarita's life, which begins aboard the ship carrying her parents from Cuba to America, spans the 20th century. She spends so much of its early years mothering her younger sisters that her later childlessness seems fated. But her own daughterhood is so rich that almost any later experience has to be uninvolving: during her lonely first marriage, to an emotionally mangled WASP named Lester Thompson, she wishes she could once more be "driven insane by the happy chaos of the meals" she remembers at home. Eventually she recaptures her selfhood and sexuality, blooming toward a regal old age of wisdom and usefulness.

The baby of the family, Emilio, arrives, to his father's disbelief, in 1925. Weighing "as much as a bronze altar bell," he descends "out of the heaven of his mother's womb, through clouds of Cuban and Irish humors, slipping into this feminine universe" to be dandled and doted on as few boys have ever been. Only when he nears adolescence does his maleness become a "form of exile," the thing that takes him off to combat in Italy during World War II. But he also survives, to return home and try his luck at being an actor, first in New York (during the 1940's, an era Mr. Hijuelos evoked so well in *The Mambo Kings*) and then in Hollywood, where he becomes "a good B actor" until drinking and scandal (Errol Flynn calls to console him) and the death of his wife and daughter bring him close to ruin.

With so many other Montez O'Brien offspring to raise, Mr. Hijuelos is inevitably reduced to overly vivid shorthand characterizations. He usually relies on a single trait to keep each sister distinct. Isabel is moralistic, Veronica compassionate, Patricia psychic, Irene gluttonous—and so on. Even the sisters' gravest predicaments must often be telegraphed in cliches: thus Helen becomes "the beautiful high-society dame," trapped in a dull marriage, popping pills on Park Avenue. Nevertheless, once Mr. Hijuelos has the whole operetta going, the effect seems marvelously complicated.

It hardly suffices to call *The Fourteen Sisters of Emilio Montez O'Brien* bountiful. It is overstuffed to the point of giddiness. Mr. Hijuelos relies on Rabelaisian catalogues to truck all its earthly objects to the reader: "There were bassinets and cribs everywhere, ironing boards and laundry baskets piled high with dampened underdrawers and diapers, menstrual 'rags,' as they were called at that time, camisoles and flannel gowns, simple cotton dresses and dresses made of crinoline and muslin and lace. Bon-

nets and stockings which Helen or the plump Irene were stoically ironing." Sometimes all the goods are sloppily warehoused, and Mr. Hijuelos's additions of period detail could use more stirring into the text; but the overall effect is luscious and life-loving. There are moments when one has to laugh, appreciatively, at the book's sheer plenitude, as when Mariela shows Nelson the planet Saturn through her telescope: "It hung there with the weight of a cow."

Like Mr. Hijuelos's earlier books, this one is boldly sexual, from its depictions of Margarita's youthful dreams to her deliberate pleasuring of a final suitor around the time of her 90th birthday. Mr. Hijuelos overreaches with some lyrical scatology, but his novel remains beautifully fecund, a word he likes almost as much as D.H. Lawrence did, though he uses it without Lawrence's programmatic urgency; here it is uttered with a wonder and amusement that seem almost childlike.

The sprawling narrative is sustained by the author's leniency in enforcing whatever conventions he adopts. Its pace speeds up and slows down, depending as much, it seems, on Mr. Hijuelos's mood as his material. Sometimes this is Margarita's book, sometimes Emilio's, and sometimes it belongs to no one in particular. The changing degree of connectedness discernible among the characters and plot lines mirrors nothing so much as family life the way it is actually lived, by both great broods and small. The magic-realist touches at the opening (those bewitched car crashes) are never much carried through: the book is in most respects a realistic chronicle that edges toward the tall tale, a story lived at a higher sensory pitch than life usually allows itself to be. Envelopes arriving from Cuba are, for example, "always scented with the tropics and the perfume of blossoms." It is only, of course, the novelist's imagination that permits these aromas to survive the journey to Pennsylvania; and yet just 50 pages into the book, where this description occurs, one already knows it would be more a violation of reality—the reality of Mr. Hijuelos's created world—to have the envelopes smelling of mailbags and glue.

The children of Nelson O'Brien and Mariela Montez suffer disappointments and tragedies, but not so many that one would judge them to be anything but a happy family, uniquely and Tolstoy-defyingly so. The book they inhabit is not only satisfying but brave. The author's nervy male celebration of femininity is carried out despite the risk of his being told—in that chillingly trite current phrase—that he "just doesn't get it." Perhaps even braver is Mr. Hijuelos's suggestion that the local Mennonite farmer who likes to ask Margarita "Isn't it a nice day?" and then explain it's so "because it's the work of the Lord" may be simply, and clarifyingly, correct. Oscar Hijuelos "gets it" all right, and he serves it up with surpassing joy.

Thomas Mallon, "Ripening in Pennsylvania," in *The New York Times Book Review*, March 7, 1993, p. 6.

SOURCES FOR FURTHER STUDY

Coates, Joseph. "When Cuban Musicians Dream the American Dream." *Chicago Tribune Books* (13 August 1989): 6–7.
> Discusses the theme of the unrealized American dream in *The Mambo Kings Play Songs of Love.*

Edwards-Yearwood, Grace. "Dancing to the Cuban Beat." *Los Angles Times Book Review* (3 September 1989): 1, 10.
> Brief overview contrasting the two central characters in *The Mambo Kings Play Songs of Love.*

Fein, Esther B. "Oscar Hijuelos's Unease, Worldly and Other." *The New York Times* (1 April 1993): B2.
> Article in which Hijuelos reveals autobiographical elements in his works.

Fernández, Enrique. "Exilados on Main Street." *The Village Voice* XXXV, No. 18 (May 1,1990): 85–6.
> Reviews *Our House in the Last World* and *The Mambo Kings Play Songs of Love*, finding that both works present an inaccurate and unfavorable view of Cuban-American life.

Hornby, Nick. "Cuban Heels." *The Listener* 123, No. 3158 (29 March 1990): 33.
> Considers *The Mambo Kings Play Songs of Love* sexually excessive, "wildly underedited," and replete with "two-dimensional static images."

Shacochis, Bob. "The Music of Exile and Regret." *Book World—The Washington Post* (20 August 1989): 1–2.
> Analyzes Hijuelos's treatment of the Cuban-American immigrant in *The Mambo Kings Play Songs of Love.*

Additional coverage of Hijuelos's life and career is contained in the following sources published by Gale Research: *Best Sellers*, Vol. 90, No. 1; *Contemporary Authors*, Vol. 123; *Contemporary Literary Criticism*, Vol. 65; and *Hispanic Writers.*

Rolando Hinojosa

1929–

(Born Rolando Hinojosa-Smith) Chicano novelist, essayist, and poet.

INTRODUCTION

Considered one of the most prominent and prolific Chicano writers today, Hinojosa is best known for his sequence of novels identified as the Klail City Death Trip series. This chronicle thus far features eight works that trace the lives and everyday events of the residents of Belken country—a fictional region of Texas's Rio Grande Valley. Many of these novels constitute a series of interwoven *estampas,* or sketches, that incorporate Hinojosa's rich imagery, masterful use of folk humor, and brilliant experimentation with multiple narrators to animate the people of Belken County and its central town, Klail City. Regarding the Klail City Death Trip series, Charles Tatum has asserted that Hinojosa's "creative strength and major characteristic is his ability to render [a] fictional reality utilizing a collective voice deeply rooted in the Hispanic tradition of the Texas-Mexico border."

Hinojosa was born in Mercedes, Texas, to a Mexican-American father and an Anglo mother. As a child, he attended private schools and was taught by Mexican exiles who were employed by the town's Spanish-speaking parents to introduce their students to Mexican culture. Hinojosa entered a public school at the age of six; although his fellow students were Chicanos, the instructors were exclusively Anglo. In fact, he did not come into contact with Anglo children until he attended junior high school. Hinojosa first demonstrated an interest in writing while he was in high school when he published stories and essays in the annual literary magazine *Creative Bits.* Upon graduating in 1946, he enlisted in the army, where he served for two years. He enrolled in the University of Texas, Austin, but was reactivated by the army in 1950 to fight in the Korean conflict. After completing his tour of duty, Hinojosa returned to the University of Texas, where he graduated with a degree in Spanish in 1954. He taught high school in Brownsville, Texas, for a short time and worked in a chemical processing plant before undertaking graduate studies at Highlands University in Las Vegas, New Mexico, in 1960. After obtaining a master's degree in Spanish, Hinojosa entered the Spanish doctoral program at the University of Illinois at Urbana. Since receiving his doctorate in 1969, he has taught at Trinity University in San Antonio, Texas, Texas A & I University in Kingsville, the University of Minnesota, and the University of Texas. Hinojosa has written extensively since 1970, earning such awards as the Quinto Sol prize in 1973 for his first novel, *Estampas del valle y otras obras* (1972; *The Valley*), the Premio Casa de las Américas in 1976 for his second novel, *Klail City y sus alrededores* (1976; *Klail City*), and the Southwestern Conference on Latin American Studies prize in 1982 for *Mi querido Rafa* (1981; *Dear Rafe*).

Hinojosa's works reflect his adherence to unconfined experimentation and risk taking: he has said, "show me a writer who goes to apologize and I'll show you a writer in trouble." Probing a wide variety of artistic methods in his writing style, Hinojosa endeavors to create an atmosphere in which the quotidian experiences of his countless singular characters converge to create one protagonist—the community. These methods include intentionally blurring conventional literary genres and techniques, constructing ambiguous and fragmented temporal and spatial schemes, and, perhaps most importantly, placing a discerning and many-faceted emphasis on dialogue. As Tatum has observed, "Hinojosa's multiplication of points of view breaks down some of the barriers between reader and character reducing the narrative distance between them. This technique also allows him to give vitality to the fictional present as well as give palpability to the fictional past. The work—the community of Klail City—is thereby transformed into a living rather than literary experience for the reader." Many of Hinojosa's most highly regarded works, including *The Valley, Klail City,* and *Claros varones de Belken* (1981; *Fair Gentlemen of Belken County*), employ this unique blend of multiple narrators to preserve the naturalness and local flavor of the author's subject matter. Hinojosa's disregard for generic conventions is perhaps nowhere more evident than in *Korean Love Songs from Klail City Death Trip* (1978). In this work, the author merges the tradition of British World War I poetry with the novel form to create a verse novel about the Korean conflict. Hinojosa has also experimented with the epistolary style in *Dear Rafe* and with the detective genre in *Partners in Crime* (1985), manipulating literary conventions to conform to his unaffected and spontaneous writing style. Hinojosa's most recent work, *Los amigos de Becky* (1990; *Becky and Her Friends),* explores the Chicano notion of *la mujer nueva,* or the woman who renounces her traditional role in the Hispanic culture and asserts her freedom and individuality. In this novel, the author presents twenty-six monologues that explore the various ways in which the community responds to Becky's decision to divorce her husband and go into business for herself.

Critics have maintained that within the scope of each relatively short Klail City Death Trip novel, Hinojosa provides a skillful, densely packed mixture of characters, many of whom have a distinct voice in the overall community structure. Several scholars have pointed out that the author achieves this effect by using a terse, compact writing style, as well as by employing the *estampa* medium to invent hundreds of characters that may appear briefly in one sketch but resurface more prominently in other vignettes or novels. In addition, commentators have asserted that Hinojosa's adept handling of colloquial language and folk humor contribute to his vivid representation of characters and events, especially in such works as *Klail City, Dear Rafe,* and *Fair Gentlemen of Belken County.* Arthur Ramírez, examining *Klail City* in particular, has noted that Hinojosa's multiple narrators "offer partial views of some central situations, resulting in an interlocked view of reality. The stress is on oral storytellers . . . The vision of life is subtle and ironic, with a perceptive sense of humor. The language is supple and muscular, economically performing multiple functions." Based on these observations, it is perhaps not surprising that critics have often found many striking similarities between the form and content of Hinojosa's novels and those of William Faulkner. While commentators have nearly unanimously praised Hinojosa for his compelling evocation of the Rio Grande valley milieu, several have also pointed out that many of his themes transcend regional issues and explore the larger implications of both the Chicano and human experiences. Both *Korean Love Songs* and *Dear Rafe,* for example, convey the emotional and psychological ramifications of warfare on the individual, and *Becky and Her Friends* illustrates how women who endeavor to surmount traditional social roles can be perceived cynically by members of their own community. Hinojosa's novels address these ubiquitous concerns, according to Arnold Williams, because the author "has an expert feel for the pulse of community. He can weave a social fabric that is interesting, surprising, realistic and still entertaining."

Because Hinojosa is a Chicano author, many critics have viewed his works as his attempt to come to terms with the often contradictory cultural influences of Mexico and the United States. Many have even suggested that Belken county—located near the border between these two countries—can perhaps be seen as a symbol of Hinojosa's concerns about assimilation. Yet some commentators, such as Juan Bruce-Novoa, have contended that Hinojosa and his novels are too sublime and complex to be so easily classified; in his words, "Hinojosa the man is a reflection of [his] work: eloquent, lucid, intelligent, ironic, with the constant good humor of a man who knows human nature and loves his fellow man without idealizing him."

CRITICAL COMMENTARY

CHARLES M. TATUM
(essay date 1982)

[In the following excerpt, Tatum discusses the early novels of Hinojosa's Klail City Death Trip series, noting how their imagery, dialogue, and structure make vivid the Chicano experience.]

Rolando Hinojosa has established a solid reputation as a Chicano novelist with the publication of four novels, all of which form a part of the same fictional world of a Chicano community in south Texas in the 1960s and the 1970s: *Estampas del valle y otras obras* (1973), *Klail city y sus alrededores* (1976), *Claros varones de Belken* ["The Illustrious Gentlemen of Belken"] (1981), and *Miquerido Rafa* ["My Dear Rafa," 1981]. In addition, he has published two other books: *Korean Love Songs* (1978), a narrative poem about the Korean conflict, and *Generaciones, notas, y brechas* ["Generations, Notes and Impressions"] (1980), a collection of some of his miscellaneous works.

Hinojosa is the first Chicano writer to win an important international literary award and the first American citizen to be honored by the distinguished group of Latin American intellectuals who comprised the Casa de las Américas panel of judges. The judges' comments on *Klail City* are all applicable to the other works in his trilogy. The novel was cited for its importance as a testimonial to the collective experience of the Chicano community in this country, and in terms of artistry, it was praised for its richness of imagery, its sensitively created dialogues, its collagelike structure based on a pattern of converging individual lives, and the masterful control of narrative time.

Hinojosa's first novel, *Estampas*, is a series of sketches forming a tapestry of the Chicano community in and around Klail City. Each *estampa* forms an integral part of the complex of lives, joys, tragedies, and struggles of the community and to consider each separately would destroy the overall effect of the author's literary creation. Hinojosa warns us at the outset of his work that his *estampas* are like individual strands of hair matted together with the sweat and dirt of generations of human toil. To separate them would be to interrupt the flow of vitality and spontaneity which surges through the work.

Estampas contains a wide range in tone, from a terse, direct presentation to a rich and subtle folk humor. The work alternates between the omniscient author and the first-person narrator. It begins at an indefinite point in time and place with the marriage of Roque Malcara and Terre Tapia and then expands rapidly, growing progressively more intricate as the writer, in every sketch, adds a new character or reveals a different facet of one already presented. Over twenty-five characters appear in the work's relatively few pages.

Hinojosa intentionally obscures relationships between characters, does not identify his narrator, and blurs characterization in order to create a total impression of the community of Klail City. Only a few characters reappear throughout the pages of the novel and they serve to provide threads of unity among the many sketches.

The reader does not discover for several pages even the general location of the community described (Texas) or the time period in which the work is set. It seems to be the author's intent to create, in the place of specific time and place, the traditions and values that his Spanish-speaking community has shared for many generations and at least for as long as any of the characters in the novel can remember.

This summary of the major narrative characteristics of *Estampas* provides a helpful perspective for a consideration of *Klail City* which represents the author's mastery of the techniques utilized in the first novel. He has become more adept in manipulating temporal and spatial fragmentation and the constant refocusing of the narrative on a few central figures who serve as anchors to give the work its cohesiveness. More importantly, Hinojosa

Principal Works

Estampas del valle y otras obras (novel) 1972
[*The Valley,* 1980]

*Klail City y sus alrededores (novel) 1976
[*Klail City,* 1987]

Generaciones, notas, y brechas/Generations, Notes, and Trails (nonfiction; bilingual edition) 1978

Korean Love Songs from Klail City Death Trip (verse novel) 1978

Claros varones de Belken (novel) 1981
[*Fair Gentlemen of Belken County,* 1987]

Mi querido Rafa (novel) 1981
[*Dear Rafe,* 1985]

Rites and Witnesses (novel) 1982

Partners in Crime (novel) 1985

Los amigos de Becky (novel) 1990
[*Becky and Her Friends,* 1990]

*This novel was also published as *Generaciones y semblanzas* in 1977.

is more successful in the second novel in creating a total ambience in which he allows the reader to participate through techniques such as the multiplication of point of view, convergence of individual destinies, and the use of memory as a narrative device. Structurally, *Klail City* is more complex than *Estampas.* We marvel that the author has packed into his relatively short novel over one hundred fictional beings and has succeeded in weaving them in and out of his narrative in a way that enhances reader participation and leaves the impression of complete naturalness and spontaneity.

Only a few characters stand out in relief: Esteban Echevarría, the old-timer with a prodigious memory who is Klail City's closest thing to a wise man and *raconteur;* Jehú Malacara, who recalls for us his youthful adventures with the fundamentalist preacher Tomás Imás; Rafa Buenrostro, a silent but ever-present narrator through whom we learn of the struggles of a young Chicano in school and, later, in the military; the good Chicano cop Don Manuel Guzmán, respected by the Chicano community for his role as counselor and friend of drunks and other unfortunate "down-and-outers"; Choche Markham, the Anglo politician who becomes a benevolent Chicano-lover during elections; the evil Leguizamón family, who were responsible for the death of Rafa Buenrostro's father, Jesús, many years ago; and a few others such as Pedro Zamudio and Celso Villalón. These few central characters give the work its continuity but they do not emerge as separate or even more important than the others. We know them better because they appear more often, but

they possess little of the stuff of literary heroes or even antiheroes.

Hinojosa tells us that he wrote *Klail City* in order to keep alive the memory of his youth, a memory which has taken on added importance as a new and changing world removes him further and further from his past. He does this through the use of different literary techniques. We have already discussed his effective creation of an ambience in which the reader immerses himself. By suppressing the role the individual characters play in the novel and by highlighting the function of the collective protagonist of Klail City, we are able to relate more easily and more personally to a multitude of names, relationships, happenings, etc. Further, Hinojosa's multiplication of points of view breaks down some of the barriers between reader and character reducing the narrative distance between them. This technique also allows him to give vitality to the fictional present as well as to give palpability to the fictional past. The work—the community of Klail City—is thereby transformed into a living rather than primarily a literary experience for the reader.

Through constant temporal and spatial fragmentation, the past continues to invade the present. The present is contaminated not only by memories of the past recalled in the fictional present but by the rapid alternating back and forth between the two temporal poles. The structure of the novel is neither circular nor concentric but intermingled. Characters, spaces, and times touch each other—we touch them—either casually or directly. Memories float in and out of the present, often becoming confused with it for their vividness. The novel is filled with echoes, partial glimpses of characters, snatches of dialogue, whole scenes and parts of scenes, interesting characters and some not so interesting, important events and most not so important.

In the end, the composite of the above emerges as the hermetically sealed world of Klail City and its surroundings in which we have been asked to enter and to participate not as readers by as witnesses, listeners, and friends. We, too, overhear conversations, witness scenes, listen attentively to others as they tell us about their lives or those of others we have never met. As Rafa Buenrostro, we sit and listen patiently, respectfully, in the bar as Echevarría goes on interminably about Jesús, about Choche Markham the crafty politician, about the scheming Van Meers, and about others we have never heard of or will never hear of again.

Hinojosa's recently published *Claros varones de Belken* forms the third part—the fourth part of his long narrative poem *Korean Love Songs* is included—of the series about Klail City. In this work the author continues telling us about Rafa Buenrostro, Esteban Echevarría, Jehú Malacara, and several minor characters. Rafa leaves the valley to go to the university in Austin, graduates, is called up in the reserves for duty in Korea, and returns safely to Belken County. Jehú becomes an itinerant

Baptist missionary, but his religious activities are momentarily interrupted for service in Korea. Esteban Echevarría grows older and weaker; however, his memory is as clear as ever as he continues to tell Rafa about the valley's past. *Claros varones de Belken* ends sadly with Echevarría's long lament on time and change, which have ravished the collective life of the Chicano community. There is no resolution at the end of the latest segment of Hinojosa's continuing saga; rather, we close the book knowing that the novelist will continue to unravel the lives of the characters in works that will certainly follow this one. (pp. 120–24)

Charles M. Tatum, "Contemporary Chicano Novel," in his *Chicano Literature*, Twayne Publishers, 1982, pp. 102–37.

MARK BUSBY

(essay date 1984)

[In the essay below, Busby examines the stylistic and structural similarities between the novels of Hinojosa and those of William Faulkner. According to the critic, "while Hinojosa has not yet created a body of work comparable to Faulkner's, he has effectively merged some of Faulkner's techniques with his own experience as a Mexican-American who grew up in Texas' Rio Grande valley."]

Rolando Hinojosa has said that William Faulkner is probably his favorite author, and an analysis of his work, especially *The Valley,* clearly reveals Faulkner's influence. Hinojosa and Faulkner use mythical counties populated by characters that appear in various works. Despite the fictional place names, the places are recognizable, and the factual sense of place is very strong in their work. Both writers similarly highlight significant historical developments in their areas with a mixture of delight and sorrow. Stylistically, Faulkner and Hinojosa shun using traditional plot structures and concentrate on fragmentary chapters to build tapestries that are ultimately nearly seamless. Finally, both writers concentrate on the theme of human endurance.

Faulkner's mythical place was, of course, Yoknapatawpha County, Mississippi, with its fictional county seat of Jefferson. Once Faulkner's imagination seized his "little postage stamp of native soil," he returned to it in novel after novel. He traced the history of several families like the Compsons, the Sartorises, the McCaslins, the Sutpens, and even the Snopeses. Individual characters such as Quentin Compson appear in stories such as "That Evening Sun" and then reappear in the novels *The Sound and the Fury* and *Absalom, Absalom!* On the map

included in *Absalom, Absalom!* William Faulkner is identified as "Sole Owner & Proprietor," and the country is described as having an area of 2400 square miles with the "Population, Whites 6298; Negroes, 9313."

Hinojosa's mythical county is Belken County, Texas, on the border of Texas and Mexico. Where Faulkner's major city is Jefferson, Hinojosa's is Klail City; but just as Faulkner maps out the other nearby communities such as Mottstown and Frenchman's Bend, Hinojosa also has Belken County's other towns figure in his novels. Relámpago, Jonesville-on-the-Rio, Ruffing, Flora, San Pedro, Bascom, Edgerton, and Flads are clearly drawn on the map of Belken County that appears in the front of *The Valley.*

It has long been apparent to Faulkner scholars how similar Yoknapatawpha County was to Faulkner's home county of Lafayette and its principal city of Oxford. Hinojosa's Belken County, however, seems to merge Cameron County at the tip of south Texas to the county to the east, Hidalgo. Hinojosa was born in Mercedes in Hidalgo County, and he has relatives and friends throughout the valley. Jonesville-on-the-Rio is most certainly based on Brownsville. Geographically, then, Klail City seems to be based on San Benito, Ruffing on Harlingen, both in Cameron County, and Edgerton suggests Edinburgh and Flora seems to be Mercedes, both in Hidalgo County. Hinojosa locates a fictional Relámpago just south of Flora, and there is a real Relámpago, Texas, just south of Mercedes.

Hinojosa also returns again and again to the same characters in his novels. The Buenrostros and the Malacaras are important families who appear in several of the works. Rafa Buenrostro is an important character in *Estampas del Valle y otras obras* (1972) and the English version written by Hinojosa, *The Valley* (1983). He is also the title character of *Miquerido Rafa* (1981). Like Rafa, Jehú Malacara is a significant reappearing character. *Rites and Witnesses* (1982) is mainly concerned with Jehú's life as a south Texas banker, but throughout there are chapters concerning Rafa's experiences in Korea. Just as Faulkner uses a materialistic and generally dislikable family, the Snopeses, so Hinojosa presents the Leguizamón family who, like the Snopeses, are a family of leeches who turn against the people of the valley for their own personal gain. Like the Snopes' name, *Leguizamón* is a pejorative, oozy name that suggests the despicability of the members of the family. Also like the Snopeses, the Leguizamóns came late to the Valley with an eye on making money:

> The second generation of Leguizamóns came and went, and they're the ones who grabbed the land they first nestered in. The original mexicano families said it was all right with them since there was enough land for everybody. A third generation came along, and lost part of the land, but the fourth generation got it back in spades and is still hanging on to it.

Like Faulkner, Hinojosa peoples his fictional county with characters who have a long history. In fact, "Braulio Tapia," the first chapter in *The Valley,* suggests the significance of family history. As Roque Malacara comes to ask don Jehú Vilches for his daughter Tere's hand, don Jehú sees himself asking his late father-in-law, don Braulio Tapia, for Tere's mother, Matilde's hand. And as the chapter ends, don Jehú indicates the importance of historical continuity by wondering, "Who did don Braulio see when he walked up these steps to ask for his wife's hand?"

For both Faulkner and Hinojosa a strong sense of place provides the framework for their fiction. This sense of place includes the physical and the historical details of the area. Faulkner was keenly aware of the fecund black earth of Mississippi, the compelling presence of the river, and plants such as the honeysuckle that become central to works like *The Sound and the Fury*. He was also greatly aware of the history of his part of the country, particularly the antebellum South, the Civil War, and the modern world's readjustments. Hinojosa, too, has a strong sense of place. In fact, in a recent essay originally presented at a Texas literature conference in Austin, he noted: "For the writer—this writer—a sense of place was not a matter of importance; it became essential." For Hinojosa, the physical details of place, the flora and fauna, are less important than the people. While there are few details about the specific plants of the region, Hinojosa is keenly aware of the presence of the Rio Grande, but he is more concerned with the people who populate the place and with their history. He commented that "place is merely that until it is populated, and once populated the histories of the place and its people begin."

In **"This Writer's Sense of Place"** Hinojosa specifies the history of his place:

> For me and mine, history began in 1749 when the first colonists began moving onto the southern and northern banks of the Rio Grande. That river was not yet a jurisdictional barrier and was not to be until almost one hundred years later; but, by then, the Border had its own history, its own culture, and its own sense of place: it was Nuevo Santander, named for old Santander in the Spanish Peninsula.

In *The Valley* Hinojosa also makes it clear that the river's artificiality as a jurisdictional barrier came late in the history of the region, as he says in **"The Old Revolutionaries"**:

> It may be curious for some, but it's all perfectly understandable and natural for lower Rio Grande Valley borderers, as is the lay of the land on both sides of the border; and, if one discounts the Anglo Texas, well, the Texas Mexicans—or mexicanos—and the Mexico Mexicans—the *nacionales*—not only think alike more often than not, but they are also blood-related as they have and had been for one hundred years before the Americans had that war between themselves in the

1860's; the river's a jurisdictional barrier, but that's about it.

This view of the border's culture suggests another point of comparison between Faulkner and Hinojosa. For Faulkner the central event in his characters' past is usually the Civil War. Characters such as Thomas Sutpen in *Absalom, Absalom!* are directly affected by the war; other characters such as Quentin Compson in both *Absalom, Absalom!* and *The Sound and the Fury* attempt to come to terms with the effects of the Civil War. For Hinojosa's borderers, the significant era is the time around the Mexican Revolution of 1910 or "la bola," as Hinojosa's characters call it. Admirable characters such as don Braulio Tapia, Evaristo Garrido, and don Manuel Guzmán (who is based on Hinojosa's father) all fought with the revolutionaries even though they were born in the United States.

Associated with the mexicano's participation in the Mexican Revolution is the antagonism between them and the Texas Rangers. The latter were notorious for trying to take Mexican land grants away and for killing any Mexicans they came across along the border in their attempts to control raids by revolutionaries into Texas. In *The Valley* the old revolutionaries had stood together at the "Toluca Ranch shoot-out" and the Carmen Ranch engagement. Just as the Civil War serves as the historical focal point in much of Faulkner, so the Mexican Revolution and the associated trouble become central to Hinojosa.

Not only is Hinojosa's work similar to Faulkner's through a strong sense of place, but the two writers' styles are quite similar in several ways. First, both eschew traditional structure, particularly chronology. Faulkner, for example, presents a series of disconnected fragments in *As I Lay Dying*. Likewise, *The Valley* is a series of seemingly disconnected fragments, but to Hinojosa his work has a clear unity:

> [M]y stories are not held together by the *peripeteia,* or the plot, as much as by the *what* the people who populate the stories say and *how* they say it; how they look at the world out and the world in; and the works, then become studies of perceptions and values and decisions reached by them because of those perceptions and values which in turn were fashioned and forged by the place and its history.

In one of the epigraphs Hinojosa indicates the intertwining nature of these pieces: "The etchings, sketches, engravings, *et al.* that follow resemble Mencho Saldaña's hair: the damn thing's disheveled, oily, and, as one would expect, matted beyond redemption and relief." While this statement on the surface seems uncomplimentary, beneath it is a combination of humility, with (similar to Mark Twain's famous epigraph against a moral in *The Adventures of Huckleberry Finn),* and an acknowledgment of the humanity that Hinojosa has attempted to present, some-

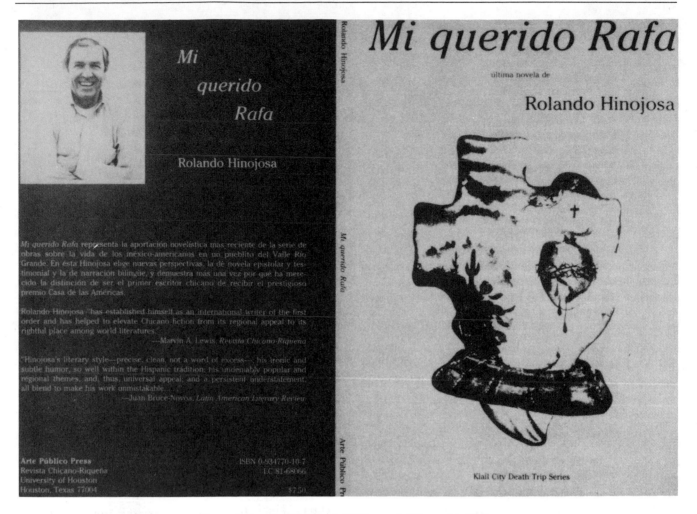

Cover design for Hinojosa's 1981 novel, *Mi querido Rafa.*

thing akin to the "truth with ragged edges" that Herman Melville sought in *Billy Budd*.

A second stylistic device in *The Valley* that is reminiscent of Faulkner is the use of multiple points of view. *Absalom, Absalom!* is probably Faulkner's masterpiece of multiple points of view. Here the Sutpen story is told by Misa Rosa Coldfield, by Quentin Compson's father, and then by both Quentin and his roommate Shreve. The third section of *The Valley,* titled "Sometimes It Just Happens That Way," concerns Balde Cordero's stabbing of Ernesto Tamez, and it is presented from several points of view: from the newspaper's, from Balde's, from Balde's sister Marta's, and from Beto's, his brother-in-law. In each story, the truth shifts. From the newspaper's point of view, the death seems a stereotypical fight over a woman. From Balde's point of view, he cannot say why he stabbed Tamez. From Marta's viewpoint, the fight no doubt had to do with Tamez' infatuation with her in school. Beto's deposition is much more concerned with the details of his own life than with the stabbing.

The third stylistic similarity between Faulkner and Hinojosa concerns the use of folklore and folktales.

Faulkner often incorporates older tales into his own work. His famous story, "The Bear," in *Go Down, Moses,* for example, owes much to Thomas Bangs Thorpe's "The Big Bear of Arkansas" and the oral tradition out of which it grew. In **"This Writer's Sense of Place"** Hinojosa points to the importance of the oral tradition in his own work:

> The history one learned there was an oral one and somewhat akin to the oral religion brought by the original colonials of 1749. Many of my generation were raised with the music written and composed by Valley people, and we learned the ballads of the Border, little knowing that they were a true native art form.

The final stylistic device that indicates the similarity between Faulkner and Hinojosa is the two writers' use of humor. From his earliest work to his last novel, *The Rievers,* Faulkner often employed humor to lighten his predominantly tragic narratives or broadly as in "Spotted Horses." Hinojosa, too, depends on humor. The humorous story of Bruno Cano and Melitón Burnias depends upon a comment misheard. As Bruno digs , he say to Melitón, "'I said we're getting close here.'" Melitón, however, misunderstands, thinking that Bruno has said "a ghost near," and takes off running. Throughout *The Valley* Hinojosa's healthy sense of humor appears in many forms and is one of the most appealing aspects of the novel.

The final point of similarity between Faulkner and Hinojosa comes from the two writers' emphasis on the positive nature of human endurance, particularly the type of endurance brought on by hardship and travail. Faulkner's final comment on Dilsey, the most admirable character in *The Sound and the Fury*, is "They endured." Hinojosa also stresses the theme of endurance in *The Valley*. In the final chapter, "The Squires at the Round Table," as the old men sit around recalling the family histories of characters such as Rafa and Jehú, one of them says, "I don't know of too many things the four of us can't handle." While Hinojosa makes it clear that age and death will take them all, it is also clear that their enduring spirits have helped them to prevail; there's nothing such characters can't handle.

When I taught *The Valley* in my "Life and Literature of the Southwest" class, several of my students were at first perplexed by the book, finding it seemingly disorganized and pointless; to some it was a formless mass of disconnected sketches. These same students, though, knew of Faulkner's reputation as America's preeminent twentieth-century writer. When I then pointed to the similarities between Hinojosa's work and Faulkner's they began to recognize the purpose and integrity of Hinojosa's work. By this comparison, however, I do not mean to suggest that Rolando Hinojosa's work is comparable to Faulkner's. Faulkner wrote twenty novels and scores of stories, and several of those works are now American masterpieces. What I do want to indicate is that Rolando Hinojosa is a serious writer, a writer who is conscious of his craft, and one who consciously draws from a distinguished literary tradition. While Hinojosa has not yet created a body of work comparable to Faulkner's, he has effectively merged some of Faulkner's techniques with his own experience as a Mexican-American who grew up in Texas' Rio Grande valley. Within him is a deep sense of the spirit of the place, the importance of its people's lives, and, among other subjects which need attention, Hinojosa is especially good at rendering the Mexican-American's ability to endure. These are, to be sure, great American themes, and Hinojosa's work shows every sign of a long life. (pp. 103–08)

Mark Busby, "Faulknerian Elements in Rolando Hinojosa's 'The Valley'," in *MELUS*, Vol. 11, No. 4, Winter, 1984, pp. 103–09.

HELENA VILLACRÉS STANTON
(essay date 1986)

[In the following essay, Stanton maintains that Hinojosa's treatment of death is informed by his experience as a Chicano. In the critic's opinion, Hinojosa "synthesizes his heritage and his environment through a style which, though uniquely his, betrays his Mexican origins, and a concern which he shares with other Chicanos, survival in his native land, the United States."]

Death has served as an artistic inspiration from time immemorial. Most of this impulse has resulted from the fear and frustration created by the knowledge of the inevitability of human demise. To avoid its presence many in the Western world attempt to repress its reality, to pretend that it can be avoided. This thought, however evident among modern European and American societies, is not universally shared by all the inhabitants of this continent.

Mexicans not only look at it face-to-face, they display an attraction that some have described as a cult, "a term which readily calls to the mind of anyone who is familiar with Mexico and her culture the unusually constant place of death in the minds and lives of the Mexican people." [Barbara Broadman, *Mexican Cult of Death in Western Literature*, 1976]. This phenomenon, which has inspired many investigations, has been attributed to the confluence of the two cultures that form the Mexican being, the Hispanic and the Nahuatl, and, according to Merlin Foster [in his *La muerte en la poesía mexicana*, 1970]: ". . . ha producido en el México moderno la peculiar actitud íntima, festiva y obsesiva hacia la muerte" [. . . has produced in modern Mexico an attitude toward death which is peculiarly intimate, festive, and obsessive]. The intimate and festive mood indicated by Foster is reaffirmed by the thinker and poet Octavio Paz, as he explains [in his *Labertino de la Soledad*, 1959]:

El mexicano. . . la frecuenta, la burla, la acaricia duerme con ella, la festeja, es uno de sus juguetes favoritos y su amor más permanente. Cierto, en su actitud hay quizá un tanto de miedo como en la de los otros; más al menos no se esconde ni la esconde; la contempla cara a cara con impaciencia, desdén o ironía . . . [The Mexican . . . visits it often, mocks it, caresses it, sleeps with it; it is one of his favorite toys, and his most permanent love. True, in his attitude, as in other people's, there may be fear, but at least he does not hide it, or hide from it; he studies it face to face with impatience, disdain, and irony.]

The dialectic of fear and curiosity implied in Paz's words

brings with it a fearful irreverence toward death, evident in the toys and candles made depicting it, in the festivities connected with the "Día de los Muertos," and in the mummified remains displayed in the city of Guanajuato.

It is to be expected that an impulse of his magnitude should have manifestations in art and literature. Innumerable works of art, created by Mexico's most famous painters, prominently display images of death. And in literature, writers like Juan Rulfo, Carlos Fuentes, Rosario Castellanos, Emilio Carballido, José Revueltas, to name only a few, have embraced the topic of death in their production. Although the perspective from which each writer approaches the subject is different and unique, some find in it a motive for humor. Many works of Mexican literature display a comical treatment of death, which at times borders on black humor. Juan José Arreolas, quoted by Paul Westheim [in his *La Calavera*, 1953], states:

El pueblo mexicano en su expresión artística ha tomado a la muerte en broma. . . . Expresa la alegría de vivir frente a la muerte, el propósito de alzarse contra ella mediante el ejercicio de los instintos que defienden la vida. [Mexicans in their artistic expression have taken death in jest. . . . They express their joy of life in front of death, the purpose of rising against her.]

According to Arreola the mocking attitude shown by some artists is a demonstration of rebellion and daring, with which they hope to intimidate death into delaying its arrival. If the Mexican fear of demise is as intense as that experienced by the rest of the Western world, the attitude taken to deal with this anxiety is notably different. Mexicans do not avoid its presence. On the contrary, they look at it, and often poke fun at it.

The purpose of this paper is to analyze Rolando Hinojosa's view of death, by studying to what extent the Mexican attitude forms a part of his thinking while assessing the degree to which other ideologies may influence his view. Two of his works will be studied for this purpose, *Estampas del Valle y Otras Obras* and *Generaciones y Semblanzas*. Although these books stand as separate works and can be studied independently, they are so closely connected with regard to character and topic development that they will be addressed here as two volumes of the same novel.

Mexican influence in Chicano literature has been indicated by several critics, including Rolando Hinojosa. In **"Mexican-American Literature: Towards an Identification"** [*Books Abroad* 49 (1977)] he explains, "Chicano literature, as an externalization of the will, has it roots in Mexican literature, and Mexican-American writers have their roots in Mexico as well — some deep, others superficial . . . " Charles Tatum, while agreeing with Hinojosa's appraisal, stresses the depth of the influence. He points to the close geographical proximity between the United States and Mexico as creating a constant infusion of Mexican culture in Chicano literature. And the proximity to Mexico is closest in the Rio Grande Valley of South Texas, where Rolando Hinojosa was born, and which has been established as the site of fictional Belken County. This is an area of which Carlota Cárdenas de Dwyer states [in "Cultural Regionalism and Chicano Literature," *Western American Literature* 15 (1980)]: "Possibly nowhere else in the United States is the Mexican quality of Chicano life purer and more intact." Using Hinojosa's terminology we must assume that his Mexican roots run "deep."

Mexico, however, is not the only source for Chicano philosophical influence. An author's physical and aesthetic surroundings become an integral part of his world view, and therefore his inspiration. Ortega y Gasset's famous declaration, "yo soy yo y mi circunstancia" is reaffirmed by Hinojosa as he continues with the tree analogy:

Roots, however, are not to be confused with the trunk of the tree itself or with the branches that spring from it. For despite the Mexican influence, the Mexican-American writer lives in and is directly influenced by life in the United States. To date, the one prevalent theme in Mexican-American writing is the Chicano's life in his native land, the United States. (**"Mexican-American Literature."**)

A study of Hinojosa's view of death, therefore, must take into account his life in this country as an artistic preoccupation. His Mexican roots cannot be searched in isolation but as an integral part of his ontological being as a Chicano. With this in mind, this paper will attempt to clarify how the author, using the topic of human finitude, synthesizes his heritage and his environment through a style which, though uniquely his, betrays his Mexican origins, and a concern which he shares with other Chicanos, survival in his native land, the United States.

The importance he gives to death is manifest throughout his work. In the two books under discussion, its presence is emphasized by the sheer numerical abundance of references to people who have died, and the repetition of these references from several perspectives. Many of the allusions are detailed accounts of death or cemetery scenes. The reader is left with the sensation that death is an active force in the life of Belken County.

Estampas del Valle y Otras Obras, as explained by several critics, begins with a series of vignettes of different lengths, developed in an arbitrary time sequence, without chronological order. The first sketch includes the memory of a gentleman no longer living who was father-in-law to the narrator, Jehú Vilches. In the short scene, we learn that Roque Malacara has come to request in marriage the hand of Jehú's daughter, Teresa. One page later, with Roque as narrator, we are left to infer that the marriage and several deaths have taken place; the first narrator's and three little girls'. ". . . Amén del suegro, hemos perdido tres mujercitas." [. . . in addition to my father-in-law, we've also lost three little girls. . . (*Estampas*).] One child is alive, a little boy, Jehú: "Si la gente vuelve a nacer, diría yo que mi hijo y su abuelo son la misma persona." [If people are reborn, I'd say that my son and his granddad are the same person (*Estampas*).] The boy, then, not only bears the grandfather's name, but also resembles him.

The next sketch, "Huérfano y al pairo," narrated by young Jehú, begins thus: "Conocí la muerte y su finalidad cuando no había llegado a los siete años de edad." [I met death and its finality before I was quite seven years old (*Estampas*).] He goes on to explain that his mother died first and his father two years later. The boy's loneliness and his helplessness are emphasized when he relates his experiences with an aunt.

La cosa es que así que sepultamos a papá, a mí me dejaron solo esa tarde y no teniendo más que hacer fui a casa de la tía Chedes . . . [Ella] empezó a llorar y hacer sus papeles . . . Al rato se le quitó el llorido y. . . como la pobre es tan bruta, luego luego me preguntó que qué andaba haciendo por la vecindad. Por poco me echo a reír pero me detuve y le dije que venía a jugar con mis primos . . . [Ella] me trajo un vaso de agua fría. Metió el dedo cordial en el vaso, me hizo la señal de la cruz en la frente y dijo: "Bébetela de un jalón mientras rezo un padre-nuestro al revés y hoy conocerás a tu nuevo padre."

[As soon as we buried Dad, I was left alone and, not having anything better to do, I went over to Aunt Chedes . . . She began to cry and carry on as usual . . . After a while, she stopped crying, . . . and since the woman was such an idiot, she immediately asked me what was I doing in the neighborhood. I almost laughed but I stopped myself and told her that I had come to play with my cousins. . . . She brought me a glass of cold water. She stuck her middle finger in the glass, made the sign of the cross on my forehead and said, "Drink this down in one gulp while I say an Our Father backwards and this day you will meet your new father."] (*Estampas*)

In spite of the humor of the scene, or perhaps more poignantly because of it, we understand that the child is alone. It so obvious that his aunt does not plan to take responsibility for his upbringing, and is politely telling him to look for a home somewhere else.

He does find a father, though, in don Victor Peláez, the owner of a circus which was in town when Jehú's father died. A short time later, this man, too, dies.

Tres años como un día . . . Esta vez sí lloré, como cuando murió mamá. El día siguiente la Carpa Peláez hizo los preparativos para irse rumbo a Ruffin y yo decidí quedarme en Flora; otra vez la muerte, otra vez huérfano y nuevamente al pairo.

[Three years as if they were just a day . . . This time I did cry, just like when my mother died. Next day, the Peláez circus made arrangements to go to Ruffing and I decided to stay in Flora; once again death, once again an orphan, and once more looking ahead.] (*Estampas*)

From age eleven Jehú Malacara roams Belken County holding different jobs. While people seem nice to him, one must surmise that no one, not even one of his relatives, takes responsibility for raising him.

As seen so far, death constitutes despair, the one suffered by those who are left behind. It evinces the pain of bereaving. The same point of view is demonstrated through other characters. We are told, for instance, by a character, Marta Cordero de Castañeda, on her brother's imprisonment, of the great need she now has of her husband, ". . . gracias a Dios que todavía nos hundimos mamá y yo sin un hombre en casa. . . " [. . . thank God I still have Beto . . . if anything were to happen to him . . . mom and I will really be ruined without a man in the house (*Estampas*).] A few pages after establishing the women's helpless condition, we are told that Beto Castañeda, the woman's husband, has died. It appears in the form of an announcement by a friend. After describing the man's accomplishments, the article ends, "Se le despidió en el cementerio católico mexicano . . . Beto Castañeda, 1941–1971, amigo cabal, q.e.p.d. [Everyone paid last respects to him at the Mexican Catholic cemetery. Beto Castañeda, 1941–1971, a great friend, may he rest in peace (*Estampas*).] The depth of the wife's anguish is set forth more vividly by the simplicity of the announcement. In it, nonetheless, there is a review of the loneliness of the two women. It brings to the reader's memory the desperate situation verbalized by the wife previously. The pain brought to her by his death is underlined.

Hinojosa presents a perspective on death which in some ways resembles Gabriel Marcel's when he states, "What counts is not my death, nor yours, but the death of those we love" [Jaques Charon, *Death and Western Thoughts*, 1963]. For Jehú and Marta, death signifies the sorrow of bereavement.

Pain, however, is not the only sentiment expressed by those affected by the demise of others. There is also guilt and anger. In the two examples which follow, the deceased are responsible for their fates. They die by their own design at the hands of others, who stand by helplessly unable to avoid the consequences.

In one case, la Julie, a prostitute, kills her husband in self defense and turns herself in to the kindly Chicano policeman, Don Manuel. Although the dead man created the situation that killed him, she is taken to the local jail. While there is no other reference to the incident, we can assume that she was prosecuted.

The other example is more interesting because it is given with more detail and with several references. Part two of *Estampas del Valle*, POR ESAS COSA QUE PASAN, is dedicated to the killing of Ernesto Támez by Baldomero Cordero. Ernesto is portrayed as a troublemaker by different people, including Rafa, a narrator, who recalls after the confrontation, "El menor de los Támez, Ernesto encontró de pura suerte y con la ayuda de sus hermanos."

[The youngest of the Tamezes, Ernesto, finally caught up with death after what seemed a determined search; seeking her many times he had eluded her, by sheer luck or thanks to his brothers' help (*Generaciones*).] This dispassionate assessment of the man's behavior makes him responsible for his death. The actual killing takes place through what Sergio Elizondo calls "a clinical case of personal tragedy" as he asserts the inevitability of the killing, which took place as a result of an insult on Cordero's honor. ["Myth and Reality in Chicano Literature," *Latin American Literary Review* 5, No. 10 (1977)]. According to Elizondo the killing was deterministic and Baldemar was forced to act as he did: ". . . His reaction to Ernesto's insult could have no other result but the immediate and total retaliation resulting in the death of Ernesto." Baldomero's words corroborate this theory, "Hice mal, lo reconozco, pero a veces también pienso que si Ernesto me insultara de nuevo, pues de nuevo lo mataría." [What I did was wrong, I'll admit that, but sometimes I also think that if Ernesto were to insult me again, well, hell, I'd kill him again (*Estampas*)] Unquestionably, Támez caused his own demise, he deserved to die as he did. He was not a good person, and in the Mexican world view, according to Paz, ". . . Cada quien tiene la muerte que se busca, la muerte que se hace. Muerte de cristiano o muerte de perro son maneras de morir que reflejan maneras de vivir." [Each one gets the death he seeks, the death that he makes for himself. A Christian death, or a dog's death, is a way of dying which reflects a way of living.] Ernesto's violent death reflected his life. Yet, Cordero was the instrument of this death. In frustration he wonders about his own fate, "Al Ernesto ya le tocaba anoche y yo tenía que ser el que lo iba a despachar." [Ernesto had it coming and I just happened to be the one to give it to him (*Estampas*).] Helplessly he becomes the actor in a violent man's demise. If we consider the symbolism of the name Cordero, lamb, his role in the tragedy becomes clear; he is the victim. He draws a fifteen-year sentence.

The little sympathy shown for Támez seems to indicate Hinojosa's agreement with Mexican thinking as defined by Octavio Paz in the last paragraph. This view is redefined by our author in other situations as well. Echeverría, an old man, tells the story of two men who killed each other for the love of a woman who didn't pay any attention to them. And he remembers with anger the way people wanted to make her responsible for their deaths. In this case, however, by keeping herself aloof and distant, she was not directly affected by their violence.

Another incident involves a feud between two prominent Chicano families. Alejandro Leguizamón was a wealthy Chicano. He was not a good person, though. He allied himself with Anglos, stole land from other Chicanos, and paid to have don Jesús Buenrostro, a respected gentleman, killed. Through different references to Alejandro's death, we learn that he was killed by Julian Buenrostro to avenge his brother's death. What really killed Leguizamón, though, was his sense of power and his womanizing. One night, not expecting retaliation, he waited for a woman outside a church. The next day, not expecting retaliation, he waited for a woman outside a church. The next day he was found: ". . . llevaba una espátula núm. 4 bein sumida en el cráneo." [. . . with a no. 4 spatula stuck deep inside his head (*Generaciones*).] The funeral was held with the casket closed because it was impossible to take away ". . . la mueca de asco que llevaba." [. . . its contorted expression of disgust (*Generaciones*).] The word "llevaba"—to wear or carry (which cannot be translated directly here)—in both quotes emphasizes the dead man's active involvement in his demise. Furthermore it implies the disgust he felt toward others. The latter point is made explicit in the epitaph: "El Alejandro Leguizamón tuvo mucha vida ye debió algunas." [Alejandro Leguizamón led a full life, but he took several others as well (*Generaciones*).] Don Jesús Buenrostro's death, then, was one more on the list of crimes committed by Leguizamón. He is, therefore, responsible for his own death.

The seriousness demonstrated toward death, up to now, is not always evident in Hinojosa. At times, loyal to his Mexican heritage, he shows an open and mocking irreverence toward human finitude. Bruno Cano's death is a case in point. This man was a wealthy, tight-fisted individual, who died of a heart attack. A narrator relates a story of how he died. In fact the town priest, don Pedro Zamudio, caused the man's heart attack with prayers, in retaliation for insults. The rather complicated story can be summarized in this manner: for not very honorable reasons, Cano finds himself in a hole in the middle of the night. When the priest happens by, the man asks him to help him out; rather than do this the priest insists on an explanation. Cano's patience, always short, is exhausted, and he insults the priest. The scene that ensues is one of the most irreverently funny in the novel:

Sáqueme ya con una chingada. !Andele!
!Pues que lo saque su madre!
!Chingue la suya!

Don Pedro se persignó, . . . y se puso a orar aquello de ". . . recoge a este pecador en tu seno" cuando Bruno Cano le mentó la madre otra vez . . . Don Pedro a la vez sacó el rosario y empezó con la misa de muertos; esto puso a Cano color de hormiga y estalló con otra chingue a su madre tan redondo y tan sentido como el primero . . . Don Pedro se levantó extendiendo los brazos en cruz . . . "tomad a este pecador en tu regazo." Entonces Bruno Cano dejó de hablar y sólo se oían unos soplidos como fuelles. Se acabó el rezo y don Petro asomó la cabeza y preguntó: "¿No ve? Con los rezos se allega a la paz . . . " Bruno Cano había echado el bofe entre uno de los misterios del rosario y una de las madres. Entregando, así, su alma al Señor, al Diablo, o a su madre; a escoger.

[". . . Get me out, goddamit! C'mon,"
"Let's see your mother get you out!"

"You shithead, go fuck your own mother!"

Don Pedro made the sign of the cross, . . . and began to pray ". . . take this sinner into your breast . . . " when Bruno Cano cursed his mother again . . . Don Pedro, in turn, took out his rosary and started on the Mass for the Dead; at this Cano got beet-red and burst out with another thunderous "go fuck your own mother" as round and resonant as the first . . . Don Pedro arose extending his arms in the form of a cross while reciting "take this sinner into your breast." At this point Bruno Cano stopped talking and all that could be heard were deep gasps like bellows whooshing. Don Pedro ended the prayer, leaned over the hole and said: "Don't you see? Prayer brings you peace . . . " Bruno Cano had kicked the bucket between one of the mysteries of the rosary and one of his curses, surrendering his soul to God, the Devil or his mother; whoever wanted him. (*Estampas*)]

In the battle between the two men, Cano and the priest, each used his weapon, his tongue and his prayers. And the prayers won. With them, in fact, don Pedro kills Bruno Cano. In the end, though, Bruno Cano has his revenge. The priest is conned by Bruno's friends into conducting funeral rites in the cemetery. The scene turns into a true pageant, narrated by Jehú:

La cosa duró cosa de siete horas . . . La concurrencia, y yéndose por lo bajo, no era menos de cuatro mil almas. . . . Don Pedro tuvo que aguantarse y rezó no menos de trescientos Padrenuestros. . . . Cuando se pusa a llorar (de coraje, de histeria . . .) la gente, compadecida, rezó por don Pedro.

[The affair lasted about seven hours . . . Estimating conservatively, the crowd was at least four thousand strong. . . . Don Pedro had to put up with all this and recited at least three hundred Our Fathers. . . . When he began to cry (whether from anger, hysteria . . .) the people, taking pity, prayed for him. (*Estampas*)]

Ironically, the choir finally sings the resurrection music of Easter. Bruno Cano was redeemed. The irreverence shown toward two imperatives, death and church, normally addressed solemnly, is brought about through the narrator's earthly, matter-of-fact imagery. The result is a delightfully funny story which exemplifies Hinojosa's ironic wit at its best.

While the preceding scene presents the most detailed description of a man's death and funeral, it is not the only one; there are several more. Pioquinto Reyes, it is reported, died in a motel. Though he had lived a spiritless existence, he ended his life enjoying it. In the motel, ". . . estaba de huesped . . . El Pioquinto cuando oyó el trompetazo anunciando su día del juicio estaba montado sobre Viola Barragán . . . Estiró la pata, es un decir, en plena acción, entregando el arpa como cualquier hijo de vecino." [. . . He was a guest . . . When he heard the last trumpet announcing his day of judgment. Pioquinto was mounted atop Viola Barragán . . . Pioquinto kicked the bucket, so to speak, in full swing, taking up the harp like anybody else (*Estampas*).] The humor in this case is created by the contrast between the man's life and his death. Many of the words used, through, "trompetaxo," "plena acción," betray approval toward the man. After all he died while living.

At other times the images are more animalistic. This is the case in the story of the death of Dr. Agustín Peñalosa, who died trying to prove the effectiveness of the medicine he had prescribed to a dead woman. He drinks the potion:

. . . Se echó e líquido al buche. No, pues casi nada: Peñalosa puso turnios los ojos, estiró el cogote y luego, naturalmente, la pata . . . Los ojos se le pusieron como los de las truchas: pelones y sin puntería. No tenía ni qué: estaba más merto que la ambición en casa de putas.

[He gulped the medicine down. No, not much: Peñalosa first went crosseyed, his neck stiffened and stretched out and he collapsed. . . . His eyes bulged with a blank stare; he looked like a trout. There were no two ways about it: he was as dead as ambition in a whorehouse. (*Generaciones*)]

Hinojosa's sharp humor is most vividly exemplified when describing death scenes. The last illustration to be presented will focus, not on a death scene, but on a man's burial. This man, by his own request, was buried standing up. The dialogue between the dead man's brother and Lucero, the gravedigger, introduces the story:

?Dice usted parado, señor Anciso?
Eso. De pie.
?Y quiere el pozo redondo . . . como pozo de barbacos?
Ajá, así, sólo que más hondo.

["Did you say standing up, Mr. Anciso?"
"That's right. Standing up."
"And, do you want the hole to be round . . . something like a barbeque hole?"
"That's right. Exactly . . . only deeper." (*Generaciones*).]

And they continue matter-of-factly discussing a most unusual funeral arrangement. The scene is later elaborated in a conversation between Jehú and Lucero. After relating that the wreaths had to be stacked up like rings one over the other, Lucero explains to Jehú what happened when the casket was lowered:

Pos sí . . . cuando ladeamos la caja, el difunto se resbaló dentro de la caja . . . no lo habían sujetado, ?saben? Bueno, se resbaló un poco . . . y así lo echamos y más al rato lo cubrimos. Los monaguillos se veían uno al otro y se aguantaron la risa porque Dios es grande . . . que si no . . .

["Well, . . . when we lowered the coffin, the deceased slipped inside the coffin . . . they hadn't tied him down, you see. Weil, so he slumped a bit . . . and we laid him down that way and filled the hole. The acolytes kept their mouths shut . . . I tell you if they hadn't. . . ." (*Generaciones*)]

The simplicity of the man in describing the performance of his job, and his indifference, give this scene an unrealistic quality, which is intensified later. In an explanation, which can easily be described as an example of black humor, the gravedigger tells how they buried the man wearing his wig:

Pues sí, así se le sepultó, con peluca y todo. La peluca
la sujetamos con una tachuela . . . un !zas! del
martillo de tachuelas y fue todo; así no se caen.
H'mbre, ¿y por qué no usaron pegadura?
Pos no había . . . y de perdido lo que aparezca . . .

["Well, that's how he was buried, wig and all. We nailed the wig on with a thumb tack . . . You know, just a tap with the hammer and that was it; that's the way to keep them on, by the way."
"And, why didn't you use glue or something?"
"There wasn't any . . . Anyway, we always use what's available." (*Generaciones*)]

In spite of the dehumanizing quality of this scene, and its unreality from an intellectual perspective, the treatment given by the author to this and the other humorous examples is based on folk reality. The vocabulary used throughout: "color de hormiga," "soplidos como fuelles"? "estiró la pata," "buche," "estiró el cogote," is that of the people and is used in the context of popular sayings. The concepts presented, then, are also part of the popular folklore.

There are other evidences of Mexican thinking as well. Some of the characters stoically accept the inevitability of death. The following illustrations represent statements which appear interspersed throughout the novel: "El hombre propone y la tierra se lo come." [Man proposes, but the earth encloses (*Estampas*).] "Unos suben y otros bajan pero, al fin, todos mueren y, al llegar la hora de la hora, aquí no ha pasado nada señores: el muerto al pozo y el vivo al gozo . . . " [Some make it to the top and others fall to the bottom, but in the end, they all die and in the final outcome nothing matters, ladies and gentlemen: let's bury the dead and get on with the business of living . . . (*Generaciones*)], and "Para Lucero, hombre soltero, lo mismo es un hoyo que otro; el que de la luz original como el que la apaga." [For Lucero, a bachelor, one hole is the same as another; the one you first come out of and the last one you go into (*Generaciones*).] Of these examples, the first demonstrates a pessimistic acceptance of death; the second, while declaring the reality of human demise, emphasizes the joy found in human life; and the last reaffirms the possibilities of human existence by reminding the reader that regardless of his mournful profession, the gravedigger is a sexual, fertile man. The latter point is underscored by the symbolism of the gravedigger's name, Lucero, brilliant star.

It is evident, then, that if death is accepted as natural, it is not desired.

Like other Mexican and Chicano writers, Hinojosa uses death as an inspiration for the development of mischievously funny scenes, real jewels of ironic humor. This, however, is not his only perception of demise. He also shows it as a painful separation, the pain suffered by those who bereave. While this view expresses a universal concern defined earlier by Gabriel Marcel, the Chicano writer adds despair to the sadness of separation. Marta Cordero de Castañeda and Jehú Malacara do not only suffer the pain of their loss, they also anguish over the practicalities of survival, illustrated in the expression, "nos hundimos" and "huérfano y al pairo," used by the two characters.

Against this view, the novelist presents dying as timely and deserved. Following Mexican thinking, he believes that violent people deserve to die violently. These people's deaths, therefore, have a very limited importance. They matter only with regard to the lives of the persons who were instrumental to their deaths. Because they sometimes suffer the consequences of their actions, they are seen as the victims of tragedies, not the perpetrators. Julie, the prostitute, and Balde Cordero kill their malefactors on an impulse to remove their oppression and, because they act rashly, they once more fall prey to their malevolence. The name Cordero is particularly symbolic in this respect. Not all those who retaliate are victimized, however. Don Julian Buenrostro avenges his brother's murder successfully. He follows a careful plan and uses Alejandro Leguizamón's weaknesses to set up a trap in which the latter falls. This action provides peace of mind for Julian and a renewed hope for Chicanos in the area, who comment with admiration and confidence on the inability of the police to solve the killing.

The contrast in the results brought on by the actions of the two men, Buenrostro and Cordero, the success of the first and the misfortune of the latter, does not depend on the extent to which each of them uses violence, but on the degree of premeditation with which the two protagonists carry out their acts. That is to say, impulse and blind passion produce continued suffering, careful consideration and sagacity attain freedom and good fortune. Although the author shows an understanding for the impelling force of frustration, he emphasizes that succumbing to its force is counter-productive and demonstrates that honor and freedom are better achieved through calculated and well-devised action.

Careful planning, then, is necessary in order to overpower a malefactor in death. In the cases discussed, this was accomplished through violence. Force, however, is not always necessary. Revenge may also be achieved through careful waiting. In a story which opens *Generaciones y Semblanzas,* subtitled "(Marcando Tiempo)," the main character, Jovita de Anda, redeems her family honor as she survives her father-in-law. We learn that Jovita de Anda is pregnant and must marry Joaquín

Támez. His father, don Salvador Támez, a domineering man, takes charge of the wedding. He relegates the bride to a room and does not allow her family to attend the wedding. He takes advantage of the fact that don Marcial of Anda, her father, is a peaceful man and will not protest.

Later in the book we realize the meaning of the episode's subtitle, for Jovita bides her time until the father-in-law dies and then retaliates against him. She does it in two ways. Of her four children, she names only the oldest after her mother-in-law, who died before the wedding. She gives the other children the names of her own father and brothers. And, more ironically, she takes her father to live in the Támez home. In the house he was not allowed to enter for his daughter's wedding, the old gentleman is cherished by his daughter and by his Támez grandchildren. Jovita cunningly marks her time and uses its power. "!Quién lo diría! Tan bravos los Támez y tan mansos los de Anda . . . don Salvador y Ernesto en el pozo; y don Marcial meciéndose en el corredor de la casa de su hija . . . " [Who would have thought it? The Tamezes were so bold and the de Andas were so meek . . . don Salvador and Ernesto in the grave; and don Marcial now rocks himself on his daughter's porch . . . (*Generaciones*).] Time gave the victory to the gentle de Andas because they knew how to use its might to their advantage.

People's efforts to counter the offenses of those who die bear directly upon them, depending on the degree of intelligence used in the process. People who move on impulse and blind anger suffer added indignities. Conversely, persons who operate astutely and with intelligence gain from the act. To the biblical promise that the meek will inherit the earth, Hinojosa advances an alternative. He declares that the witty will endure and recommends that cunning and determination be used to benefit and overcome.

This same message is directed to life within the larger society. Though interactions in "Belken County" take place primarily among Chicanos, the author also presents examples of Anglo injustice. Of these, we have the case of Ambrosio Mora, a World War II veteran who was unjustly killed by a deputy sheriff, Van Meers. As can happen in reality, in this fictional situation the establishment protects the deputy, who is exonerated. The victim's father lives in pain and anger, but with an obsession which sustains him. He will outlive his son's killer. Though he is twenty-five years older than Van Meers, don Aureliano Mora swears that he will attend his funeral. And his determination is so strong that the narrator is obligated to assure the reader: "No se equivoque nadie, no, a don Aureliano no lo tumbarán ni el viento ni los anõs hasta que asista al entierro de Van Meers. De juro y de esta cruz." [But make no mistake, don Aureliano will not be sent tumbling down by any breeze nor by the years until he attends Van Meers' funeral. I swear to God (*Genera-*

ciones).] The narrator's trust in the force of the older man's determination is a declaration of faith in the power of the will to survive.

As we have seen, Hinojosa demonstrates a deep concern over survival. Paradoxically, he also presents an antithetic disregard toward the end of human life. Following Mexican tradition, he pokes fun at death and creates delightfully funny dying and funeral scenes, with characters who display a complete indifference toward their own finitude. In all the references made to the end of life in the novel, there is not one single instance in which an individual expresses a fear of its approach. Additionally, he gives us situations in which life and death, the two antagonists, are brought together in single thoughts and in unlikely settings. We may recall that the chorus sings resurrection music during Bruno Cano's funeral, that Lucero, which means brilliant star, is the name of the gravedigger, whose duties and sexuality are described in one same sentence, and that people join sequentially the two antonyms, life and death.

This same evidence, which at first appears contradictory, a demonstration of a polarization in the novelist's ideological make-up, actually implies a unity of perspective, revealed more clearly in the treatment of three important characters in the novel. Through the development of these three characters, a respected gentleman, don Manuel Guzmán, and two young boys turned men, Rafa Buenrostro and Jehú Malacara, Hinojosa emphasizes the correlation he sees between life and death, and declares that individual finitude is acceptable and necessary only in its role in the process of renewal.

Don Manuel is introduced early in *Estampas del Valle,* on the event of his death. From then on, however, because of the liberties the author takes with chronology, the good man appears in good health, fighting in the Mexican revolution, helping people and influencing Chicanos with the strength of his integrity. The fact of his death, then, is readily discounted by the force of the presence of the man. He weaves in and out of the pages of the novel, always as a benefactor. His legacy is more important than his death.

Rafa Buenrostro is one of the narrators and the son of don Jesús Buenrostro, who as stated was murdered by Leguizamón and avenged by his brother. The death scene resembles the richness of this man's life: "Una noche de abril cuando las flores de los naranjos querían reventar . . . " [One night in April when the orange trees were ready to blossom, . . . (*Generaciones*).] The fertility portrayed here is more concretely demonstrated through the life of Rafa, the son. The younger man's life is a continuation of the father's. The similarities between the father and the son, are pointed out by other characters, who address the inheritance of the father's good qualities by the son. The older Buenrostro's strengths are perpetuated, and don Jesús lives in Rafa.

The last example to be cited is the most important, because, through the life of Jehú Malacara, Hinojosa develops his message most pointedly. As we might recall, this study began with a review of his misfortune. He was left helpless, to fend for himself without resources. At a very early age he had to hold many jobs to earn his keep. As we see him through the novel, his character develops. He becomes an intelligent young man with a pragmatic sense of humor. He uses intuition and cunning to overcome the obstacles that come before him. He is a survivor. He is also loyal, honest, and has an excellent sense of pride. Years later he is taken in by don Manuel, finishes high school, and goes to college. The following quotation summarizes his development: "es un muchacho espabilado y carancho . . . ese muchacho conoce mucho mundo . . . Dicen que se fue a la universidad . . . " [He's a smart kid and real clever . . . that kid has traveled around a good bit. . . . They say he went off to the university . . . (*Generaciones*).] He becomes a teacher in the same high school in which he had been a student.

This experience he explains casually as he remembers the negative treatment given to Chicanos in the school by Anglo teachers and students. One such student was Elsinore Chapman, a rich Anglo girl. Twenty years later, he retrospectively identifies her future of twenty years back: "Elsinore ignora que en poco más de veinte años estará casada y divorciada y que seremos colegas (maestros de inglés) acquí en Klail high." [Elsinore doesn't know that in a little over twenty years she will be married and divorced and that we'll be teaching together (as English teachers) here at Klail High (*Generaciones*).] The social difference of their adolescent years have disappeared, they have both become teachers; time has been on his side. *Estampas del Valle,* the first book in the novel, begins with Jehú's childhood, *Generaciones y Semblanzas,* the second, ends with reference to Jehú the man. That this is done in a novel which generally disregards chronological order is indicative of the author's purpose for the development of the character and his symbolism.

Jehú's role is underscored when we look at his lineage. Though his parents were poor, he is descendant of an old Chicano family, the Vilches, who lost their possessions through Anglo encroachment. The last of the Vilches was Jehú Vilches, who was the boy's grandfather, after whom he was named. Young Jehú's kinship with the Vilches is mentioned intermittently and his similarity to the grandfather is stressed by his father in the statement quoted earlier: "Si la gente vuelve a nacer, diría que mi hijo y su abuelo son la misma persona" [If people are reborn, I'd say that my son and his granddad are the same person (*Estampas*).] He represents the once important Vilches family and his success is their vindication. In spite of this humble beginning, or because of it, he develops the cunning and intelligence which the novelist believes Chicanos need to survive in an often hostile environment. His

ability to adapt and prevail, then, symbolizes the strength of the Chicano in a quest for endurance in today's world.

In conclusion, Rolando Hinojosa uses the topic of death as an affirmation of life, which transcends finitude by prolonging existence in future generations. The life the author asserts is that of the Chicano, whose capacity to survive is exemplified in the two young men, Rafa Buenrostro and Jehú Malacara. Despite the difference in their lots, humorously identified with their names, Buenrostro and Malacara, they both become strong, intelligent, and life-loving individuals. Through them, and all the other characters who succeed through intelligence and cunning, the writer asserts his faith in Chicano survival.

Hinojosa's interpretation of human mortality reflects his reality as a Chicano. Through this theme he synthesizes his Mexican heritage and his circumstance in the United States. As a consequence of having this nation as his native land, he is preoccupied with Mexican-American survival. His emphasis on its affirmation manifests this anxiety. Because of his ancestry he expresses this concern as Mexicans often do, through the theme of death, which he treats at times mockingly and disrespectfully. In the manner, he pokes fun at death as a dare aimed at intimidating it. He uses the topic of human demise, then, as a defense of Chicano life, whose continuation he asserts while he demonstrates the strengths which are required to endure. (pp. 67–81)

Helena Villacrés Stanton, "Death in Rolando Hinojosa's Belken County," in *MELUS*, Vol. 13, Nos. 3–4, Fall-Winter, 1986, pp. 67–83.

AMY L. ROOT

(essay date 1990)

[In the essay below, based on an interview with Hinojosa, Root relates his discussion of his career as a novelist and his motivation for creating the Klail City Death Trip series.]

For nearly twenty years, Rolando Hinojosa's writing has given the Rio Grande Valley an authentic, if little-heard, voice in the realm of Texana publishing. But word of his Klail City fiction series is spreading: *Publisher's Weekly* recently dubbed him one of the premier Mexican-American authors in the country, and James Ward Lee highlighted two Hinojosa selections in *Classics of Texas Fiction.*

"I don't think my books would sell in the popular market," Hinojosa states plainly. "People are used to the big, thick, fat books that have a nice, readable style. . . . I'm not even sure that they would like the people I write about." Hinojosa's compact novels defy cookbook-formula plots, and his form varies from book to book. Hinojosa engages readers through lively, off-beat characters and scenery so detailed and comfortable that a standard central conflict is unnecessary.

Hinojosa lets residents of the fictional Klail City and its surrounding Belken County towns tell their own story. *The Valley* combines first-person descriptions and memories, gossipy third-person tales, and even paragraphs from mock newspaper clippings to create what Hinojosa calls a "photographic variorum" that spans generations.

Readers meet carnival workers, vegetable packers, bankers, murderers, and shopkeepers—just to name a few. Hinojosa's characters range from independent career women to military heroes. They are Mexican or Anglo or both, although the point of view is nearly entirely Mexican.

Even the name "Klail" was designed to signal readers of the contrasting societies in the Valley. "I wanted a very Anglo name," he explains. "The letter 'k' does not appear in the Spanish alphabet, except in foreign words like 'kilometer.' I wanted something so Anglo that it cannot be mistaken for anything else."

The writing forms vary just as much. The Klail City series includes a book of narrative poetry (*Korean Love Songs*), an epistolary collection (*Dear Rafe*), and even a detective story (*Partners in Crime*). "I will try anything that will allow me to tell the story," Hinojosa says. "Even in the detective [story] I made some changes from the genre, taking the old and still viable definition of what a novel is: something that is new."

Born Romeo Rolando Hinojosa-Smith in Mercedes, Texas, during the Depression, he grew up in the middle of two different cultures, internalizing that duality and building a career around it.

"I wanted to show the whole Texas Mexican as well as the Texas Anglo society, and you can do that in the Valley more than in any other part of Texas."

His bilingualism is so balanced that he writes some first versions in English and others in Spanish, and not all of his works are available in both languages. For him, translation is not so much a verbatim transcription but "it's more like a recreation in another language."

He has written most first versions in Spanish, however, and one of his characters hinted at a preference for the language in the following passage from *The Valley*: "Obdulio Yáñez, a relative of mine, lives in Relámpago; those who know him for what he is call him La Caballona—the he-mare. . . . The words 'shiftless' and 'lazy' used to describe him merely reveal the poverty of the English language in his case."

Such dry humor punctuates the entire series. Some chapters even read like elaborate jokes, beginning with a "there once was a fine young man . . . " flavor and ending with an ironic, one sentence conclusion. Few of the chapters exceed six pages; some are as short as 125 words. His humor even spills out of the fiction. His most recently published book, *Becky and Her Friends,* is dedicated "in particular, to everyone who has wished me ill luck. As you can see, it's brought nothing but more titles to the series. This should probably teach you a lesson, but most likely it won't."

Hinojosa has always been interested in language. In the fourth grade, he had to choose between working in the school library or being a traffic guard. He chose the library, which at the time only consisted of a four-shelf bookcase.

"My dad must have had a third-grade education, so he worked in the fields and as a policeman, and he gambled for a living, just a very hard-working guy who read a lot aloud—and my mother would read to him in Spanish." His parents, Manuel Hinojosa and Carrie Smith, gave their five children plenty of books to read.

Hinojosa was sickly as a child and missed much school, spending time at home reading Buffalo Bill stories and Guy de Maupassant. "I thought de Maupassant was Spanish," he recalls, "because I was reading French translations into Spanish." Hinojosa now reads in German, French, and Portuguese as well.

He discovered short-story magazines while attending Mercedes High School, and pored over *The New Yorker, The Atlantic,* and *Harper's.* "I would read whatever fell into my hands," he says. At fifteen his short stories were published in the high school literary journal *Creative Bits.*

Hinojosa studied Spanish at three universities after that, earning a B.S. from the University of Texas, an M.A. from New Mexico Highlands University, and a Ph.D from the University of Illinois. It was just after earning his doctorate in 1969 that he accepted a faculty position at Trinity University and decided to begin writing fiction seriously.

In 1973, Quinto Sol Publications published *Estampas del Valle y otras Obras,* a book that was released in

English ten years later. In the past two decades the Klail City series has grown to eleven books, one of which has been translated into German and published in East and West Germany.

Hinojosa has never attempted to recreate Mercedes or its residents perfectly. Instead, he uses a process he calls "telescoping," magnifying details of actual figures or events and fusing them together. One reader, a German scholar named Wolfgang Karrer, compiled a Klail City census, numbering at least a thousand characters.

Hinojosa remembers the incident clearly. "He went to Mercedes, and he went to all the places I mentioned. He went to the cemetery; he went to the bar. And he said, 'You described that perfectly.' I said, 'I guess I just close my eyes, and I know where I am.'"

He says his friends in the Valley have yet to be offended, and that although he knows of some Valley residents who read his work, his notoriety there is not due to his writing career. "I'm famous because I'm the son of Manuel Hinojosa. They say, 'Oh yeah, that's old Manuel's boy. He works up north—in Austin.'"

He feels fortunate for having known English growing up. "Those women who taught us, primarily women in grammar schools, I'm sure knew no Spanish whatsoever. So it was pretty Darwinian. . . . What people should realize is that people who come here with no knowledge of English *want* their kids to learn English. Who wants to be an underclass for ten generations?" He is also grateful that his father had a steady income. "What about those who didn't—the seasonal workers. For them to send a kid to school, that meant losing three to four dollars a day in wages."

Hinojosa went on to make teaching college-level English courses part of his career. Now an Ellen Clayton Garwood Centennial Professor of Creative Writing at the University of Texas at Austin, Hinojosa teaches fiction writing and various literature courses. He visits and corresponds with Ellen Garwood, grateful for her support.

"Wherever I go, I like to be known as the Ellen Clayton Garwood professor, because it's an honor to her. She gave the money to the university having no idea who the money was going to. So whenever I lecture someplace, whenever I publish something, I let her know."

As a professor, he also periodically teaches a course originally taught by J. Frank Dobie, Life and Literature of the Southwest.

"My question when I came here in 1981 was 'how can we teach Life and Literature of the Southwest if we don't include the sizable block of Texas Mexicans who are also writers?' . . . And now, of course, it's being taught all over."

Despite this rise in awareness of Southwest literature, Hinojosa intends to continue working with smaller

publishing houses, citing Arizona State University's Bilingual Press and Arte Público, the Houston press that has published some of his most recent works. He likes being able to review his manuscripts through phone calls with his editors. Even his cover-art suggestion for *Becky and Her Friends* was used, and Hinojosa knows the model who now appears on his book.

He also receives a good dose of scholarly review, which means more to him than any market-share predictions. A group of professors who have reviewed his work since the 70s recently published the *Rolando Hinojosa Reader*, a collection of personal interviews and criticisms of his work.

He writes all of his novels by hand, forsaking the computer he owns. After editing his handwritten versions, he types them on a manual typewriter and sends them to his publishers. Although he never worked as a journalist or professional editor, he is edited very little by the publishers. "I edit myself so well, and it's so tight, that when it's there and I make up my mind, I don't change it."

It's doubtful that we've seen the last of Klail City. He is currently finishing a Spanish translation of *Becky and Her Friends*. Hinojosa comments, "The first one [in the series] was dynamic. It was written in fragments with multiple plots and many, many characters, and I saw clearly that this whole city, this whole county, was going to be the main character." And with a creator such as Hinojosa, Belken County is likely to have a long, prosperous life ahead of it. (pp. 79–81)

Amy L. Root, "Rolando Hinojosa: A Voice of the Valley," in *Texas Libraries*, Vol. 51, No. 3, Fall, 1990, pp. 79–81.

ANTONIO C. MÁRQUEZ
(essay date 1991)

[In the following excerpt, Márquez surveys Hinojosa's treatment of *la mujer nueva*—"the Chicana who eschews traditional roles and asserts her independence and individuality"—in *Becky and Her Friends*.]

Rolando Hinojosa is one of the most eminent Chicano writers and perhaps the most prolific. His singularly ambitious project is a multivolume work called "The Klail City Death Trip Series." Like Faulkner, he has created a fictional county (Belken County), invested it with centuries of complex history, and populated it with generations of families and a host of unique characters. The Belken County saga is a rich mosaic of interrelated novels; characters, incidents, and themes overlap, and Hinojosa renders the collective social history of a Chicano community. *Becky and Her Friends* is the seventh novel in the series and the third written in English.

Hinojosa's tack in his latest novel is to dramatize how the community responds to *la mujer nueva*, the Chicano who eschews traditional roles and asserts her independence and individuality. Becky boldly announces her emancipation from an unfulfilling marriage to Ira Escobar and the country-club life-style proffered by his political and financial connections. She *decides* (the text emphasizes this "power-laden verb") to divorce Ira, to use her college education and go into business. Her actions are the catalyst for the twenty-six vignettes/monologues that make up the novel. A social kaleidoscope whirls; the multitudinous voices are individualized by ethnicity (six non-Chicano characters also speak), generation, gender, social class, profession, and status in the community.

The responses range from sympathetic espousals of liberal, progressive views supporting Becky's emancipation, to conservative denunciations of her actions and expressions of fear at the erosion of traditional values. Not surprisingly, a priest offers the most strident criticism, voicing the platitude that "women are the first bastion, the principal base and foundation of the Church family." In effect, Hinojosa's anecdotal and deceptively simple novel couches important, engaging themes: the pressing dilemmas and conflicts that beset Chicano communities as traditionalism meets modernity; the changes undergone and forthcoming as mores are questioned and traditional gender roles are challenged.

The novel does not intimate that *la mujer nueva* will also repudiate the touchstones of Chicano culture. Becky also decides to speak Spanish again, signifying her valuation of a language and culture which she had partially lost when her parents had made the "big mistake" of raising her as an Anglo girl. The conclusion suggests that she will return to the wellsprings of Chicano culture and at the same time forge her new life on her own terms. Hinojosa saves the last monologue and the last word for Becky: "I'm not a woman who was saved, redeemed. I saved myself."

Interweaving three generations of families, Hinojosa spins the story of Becky and her twenty-five friends *and* enemies with sensitivity, humor, wit, and keen insight into the history and attitudes of the people of the lower Rio Grande Valley of Texas. *Becky and Her Friends* augments the author's reputation as an acute, wise, and entertaining storyteller.

Antonio C. Márquez, in a review of "Becky and Her Friends," in *World Literature Today*, Vol. 65, No. 2, Spring, 1991, p. 303.

SOURCES FOR FURTHER STUDY

Bruce-Novoa, Juan. "Interview with Rolando Hinojosa." *Latin American Literary Review* 5, No. 10 (Spring-Summer 1977): 103–14.
Discussion of Hinojosa's literary background and philosophy, as well as of his opinions on numerous aspects of Chicano literature.

Hinojosa, Rolando. "Mexican-American Literature: Toward an Identification." *Books Abroad* 49, No. 3 (Summer 1975): 422–30.
Surveys the background and literary contributions of Mexican-American authors and urges greater critical recognition of their works.

Houston, Robert. Review of *Dear Rafe. The New York Times Book Review* (18 August 1985): 20.
Commends Hinojosa's satirical portrayal of everyday life in the fictional town of Klail City.

Morales, Alejandro. "And in the Other Texas . . . ." *The Los Angeles Times Book Review* (12 April 1987): 1, 6.
Asserts that Hinojosa creates "a beautiful, witty verbal tapestry" in *Fair Gentlemen of Belken County* which "captures the intra-history of the collective experience of the Chicano."

Ramírez, Arthur. Review of *Klail City. Hispania* 71, No. 1 (March 1988): 97–8.
Largely positive assessment of *Klail City,* praising in particular Hinojosa's effective use of multiple narrators and his compact language.

Ríos, Herminio. Introduction to *Estampas del valle y otras obras* by Rolando Hinojosa, pp. 7–9. Berkeley, Calif.: Quinto Sol Publications, 1973.
Considers Hinojosa an "intrepid humorist" whose novels will ultimately assume a prominent position in the Hispanic literary tradition.

Saldívar, José David, ed. *The Rolando Hinojosa Reader: Essays Historical and Critical.* Houston, Tex.: Arte Público Press, 1985, 190 p.
Collection of essays featuring observations by Hinojosa on the importance and function of Chicano literature, analyses of his works by other scholars, and an interview with the author.

Tatum, Charles. Review of *Fair Gentlemen of Belken County. World Literature Today* 61, No. 3 (Summer 1987): 423–24.
Asserts that *Fair Gentlemen of Belken County* is largely successful due to Hinojosa's "vivid imagination" and his

"penchant for rendering orality into the written word."

Williams, Arnold. "Belken County Revisited." *San Francisco Review of Books* X, Nos. 2–3 (Fall-Winter 1985): 10, 14.
    Commends Hinojosa's narrative experimentation in *Dear Rafe* and his unconventional treatment of the detective genre in *Partners in Crime*.

Additional coverage of Hinojosa's life and career is contained in the following sources published by Gale Research: *Dictionary of Literary Biography*, Vol. 82; and *Hispanic Writers*.

Juan Ramón Jiménez

1881–1958

(Full name Juan Ramón Jiménez Mantecón; also known as Ramón Jiménez, Juan Jiménez Mantecón, and Juan Ramón) Spanish poet, short story writer, and translator.

INTRODUCTION

*T*he winner of the 1956 Nobel Prize in Literature, Jiménez is considered one of Spain's finest and most influential modern lyric poets. His verse, known for its formal elegance, haunting beauty, and gentle sonority, addresses such fundamental themes as solitude, sorrow, death, transcendence, and the mystery of human existence. In assessing his literary status, scholars frequently perceive Jiménez as a link between such early Spanish-speaking modernists as Nicaraguan poet Rubén Darío and a younger generation of Spanish-speaking poets that includes Federico García Lorca, Rafael Alberti, and Jorge Guillén. Claudio Guillen has asserted: "No one questions the extraordinary historical importance of Jimenéz. He is not only the dean of Hispanic poets, but the pioneer and source of all those who wrote in the Spanish tongue after him."

Jiménez was born in the Andalusian town of Moguer. He studied in Cadiz and Seville in the 1890s and published his first two collections of poetry in 1900. Deeply affected by his father's death that same year, Jiménez was diagnosed with depression and hospitalized in 1901. Upon his release Jiménez devoted himself to writing, and critics note that his verse composed after this time evinces a deep melancholy and obsession with death. Jiménez moved to Madrid in 1912, actively participating in the literary life of the capital, where he founded several journals, encouraged young poets, and pursued numerous literary projects. In 1916 he traveled to New York, where he married translator Zenobia Camprubí Aymar; the couple later settled in Madrid. A sympathizer of the short-lived Spanish Republic, Jiménez, like many of his contemporaries, went into self-imposed exile in 1936. He and his wife intermittently lived in Cuba, Puerto Rico, and Florida, eventually settling in Washington, D.C. For much of his exile, Jiménez was an active figure in the Spanish-speaking literary world, traveling frequently, publishing numerous poems and prose works, and lecturing on Spanish literature. Suffering from illness and depression, Jiménez returned in 1951 to Puerto Rico, where he spent the remainder of his life. He died in 1958.

Critics generally agree that Jiménez's works can be divided into three distinct periods: modernist, purist, and metaphysical. Initially writing in the tradition of late romantic sentimentality, Jiménez gained renown as a modernist poet, successfully emulating the metrical musicality of Darío, who was a leader in the Spanish-American Modernist literary movement. Representative of Jiménez's modernist inspiration are the sentimental and ornate ballads in *Almas de violeta* (1900) and *Ninfeas* (1900). The second period, during which Jiménez strove to create a highly expressive minimalist idiom, is characterized by his use of free verse and search for pure—or "naked"—poetry in which meaning is manifested through exceedingly simple and unobtrusive formal presentation. Typical of this period is Jiménez's collection *Diario de un poeta recién casado* (1917), which relates his voyage to America for his wedding. In this work Jiménez employs the ocean as a symbol of loneliness, mutability, and emotional uncertainty. The popular *Platero y yo* (1914; *Platero and I: An Andalusian Elegy*), regarded as a modern classic, is also representative of this phase of Jiménez's career. The simple story of the poet as a boy traveling through the Andalusian landscape with his donkey, *Platero and I* focuses on the themes of death, rebirth, and salvation. In the third period of his career Jiménez turned from his quest for pure poetry to an artistic search for divine archetypes, subsequently introducing an element of religious devotion into his work. However, as critics have noted, his devotion was not directed towards God as defined by Christianity; rather, Jiménez looked for what he felt was the platonic essence underlying the poetic word. This search for the divine, Jiménez believed, was necessary, but could never be fully achieved. "Poetry," Jiménez told Ricardo Gullón, "is an attempt to approximate the absolute by means of symbols. Universality is personal—the essence of each one elevated to the absolute. . . . Poetry in its conception should be sacred, winged, and full of grace, and the proper realm of poetry is mystery and enchantment." This search for wisdom and salvation through poetry culminated in the powerful spiritual testament *Animal de fondo* (1949), an account of a voyage at sea during which Jiménez experienced what he termed a moment of divine and universal consciousness.

Jiménez has received considerable critical attention, particularly in the Spanish-speaking world. Critics have praised the graceful musicality of his poetic language and have viewed his oeuvre, rich in philosophical content and resonant with deep—yet delicately expressed—emotion, as a significant force in modern European poetry. As the poet Louis Simpson has written about Jiménez's mature work, the force of his poems "is not due to the absence of decorative language but the presence of emotion." This presence of emotion, commentators have asserted, is what reveals the fundamentally life-affirming nature of Jiménez's lifelong literary meditation on death and transfiguration.

CRITICAL COMMENTARY

AUBREY F. G. BELL

(essay date 1925)

[Bell was a Hispanist whose books include *Balstasar Gracian* (1921), *Portuguese Literature* (1922), and *Contemporary Spanish Literature* (1925). In the following excerpt from the latter, in which he briefly discusses Jiménez's place in the Spanish Modernist tradition, Bell admires the themes, imagery, and musical fluidity of Jiménez's poetical language, recognizing formal beauty as a crucial element of the poet's work.]

The chief Modernist poet of Spain, Don Juan Ramón Jiménez, evidently has the gift of infuriating some critics and of fascinating others. But studying his work impartially nearly ten years after the death of Rubén Darío, when modernism is seen to have been a passing craze, the critic finds that there is something in Señor Jiménez'

Principal Works

Almas de violeta (poetry) 1900

Ninfeas (poetry) 1900

Rimas (poetry) 1902

Arias tristes (poetry) 1903

Pastorales (poetry) 1911

Laberinto (poetry) 1913

Platero y yo (prose poem) 1914; also published as *Platero y yo; elegía andaluza, 1907–1916* [enlarged edition], 1917
[*Platero and I: An Andalusian Elegy,* 1956]

Estio (poetry) 1915; also published as *Estio: A punta de espina,* 1959

Diario de un poeta recién casado (poetry) 1917; also published as *Diario de poeta y mar,* 1955

Poesías escojidas (1899–1917) de Juan Ramón Jiménes (poetry) 1917

Sonetos espirituales (poetry) 1917; also published as *Sonetos espirituales (1914–1915),* 1957

Piedra y cielo (poetry) 1919; also published as *Piedra y cielo, 1917–1918,* 1948

Antolojía poética (poetry) 1922

Segunda antolojía poética (poetry) 1922; also published as *Segunda antolojía poética 1898–1918,* 1956

Belleza (poetry) [with Zenobia C. de Jiménez] 1923

Poesía (en verso) (poetry) [with Zenobia C. de Jiménez] 1923

Poesía en prosa y verso (poetry) 1932

Españoles de tres mundos, viejo mundo, nuevo mundo, otro mundo: Caricatura lirica, 1914–1940 (poetry) 1942

La estacion total (poetry) 1946

Animal de fondo (poetry) 1949

Fifty Spanish Poems (poetry) 1950

The Literary Collaboration and the Personal Correspondence of Rubén Darío and Juan Ramón Jiménez (letters) 1956

Antología poética (1898–1953) (poetry) 1957
[*Selected Writings,* 1957]

Three Hundred Poems, 1903–1953 (poetry) 1962

Dios deseado y deseante: Animal de fondo con numerosos poemas inéditos (poetry) 1964
[*God Desired and Desiring,* 1987]

Libros inéditos de poesía. 2 vols. (poetry) 1964–67

Historias y cuentos (short stories) 1979
[*Stories of Life and Death,* 1986]

La realidad invisible (poetry) 1983
[*Invisible Reality,* 1986]

Tiempo y espacio (autobiography) 1986
[*Time and Space: A Poetic Autobiography,* 1988]

poetry that endures. He has his mannerisms, he will introduce strange words, such as *auriluzones* (*Poesías Agrestes*) or *nictálope* (*Eternidades*), and no one has more ruthlessly cut verses in half: Luis de Leon might boldly give the *mente* of an adverb to the following line; Señor Jiménez divides *jara-mago, ama-rillo* (*Pastorales*), *se ve* or *a la presión* (*Laberinto*). He will give an epithet of colour to things of the ear and of sound to the things of sight: the wind is blue, the fragrance golden. His fondness for the adjective *malva* reminds one of the modernist painters whose insubstantial tree-trunks are a light purple and their leaves shrill yellow. We have *paisajes malvas, ángeles malvas, terciopelos malvas, paredes, penumbras, brazos, bocas, callejas, instantes, claridades:* dust, the sun, the moon, clouds, a hand, a rock, an afternoon, the grass, the sea are all *malva*. One remembers that his first volume of verse was entitled *Almas de Violeta* (1901). The epithets *rosa* and *violeta* are fairly frequent in his work. There is morbidity, too, in the recurrence of the adjectives *melancólico, romántico,* while a line such as "y en el landó forrado de viejo raso malva" is perishable stuff that will not last longer than much of the verse of Rostand, and words like *corsé* and *parterre* would be sufficiently

hideous and terrible in Spanish prose, not to speak of poetry.

Yet the occasion on which Señor Jiménez' already large body of verse sinks to earth are surprisingly few (as in the phrase *de todas clases,* which occurs in the same poem as the word *parterres,* to which exception has already been taken). As a rule it maintains an astonishingly high level. The poems in which he has employed rhyme show that his poetry might gain rather than lose by its more frequent use; for this poet, who is so careless of rhyme, and sometimes of rhythm, and goes out of his way to cut a word or a phrase in twain and introduces far sought newfangled words into his verse, is very quiet and natural in the use of rhyme, when he does use it, while the rhyme helps to shape and concentrate what might tend to be the indefinite flow of his verse. He would appear to have a keener sense of sound and colour in all their shades and subtleties than of definite shape; he is the impressionist painter rather than the sculptor, and his poetry is in fact an ever-flowing though transparent stream; it is perhaps interesting to notice that his favourite flowers are the scented flowers formed not of bold petals but of a hundred tiny flowerets: heliotrope, lilac, verbena, jasmine, whin, honeysuckle. Yet, in this minute and constant flow, how delicate is his ear for the pattern and construction of the verse!—

> Y sobre la doliente luz monótona
> del indolente sol, con trágico
> é infantil sentimiento se agudizan,
> finas, las hojas últimas
> y amarillas de un árbol
> leve
> y lánguido.

His poetry is like a nocturne of Chopin played in the twilight, full of faint sounds and rustling silences and from time to time revealing some concrete lovely presence, the gleam of a star, the note of a bird, the mellow ringing of an Angelus bell:

> Sólo turban la paz una campana, un pájaro:
> parece que los dos hablan con el ocaso.

                              (**"Silencio de Oro"**)

There is more of the concrete and the substantial in his work than one might imagine. This may be seen in the delicious prose of his *Platero y Yo*, in which poetry and reality are mingled without the omission of common things and with a charm and precision of words which produce definite pictures. That, for instance, of the autumn afternoon: "Claras tardes del otoño moguereño! Cuando el aire puro de Octubre afila los limpidos sonidos, sube del valle un alborozo idílico de balidos, de rebuznos, de risas de niños, de ladridos y de campanillas"; that of the Corpus procession, of the mocking gipsy children, the idiot boy, the boy shepherd, the orange-seller's donkey-cart stuck fast in the mud, the little girl Blanca in one of the donkey's panniers: "soft, white and pink as the flower of peach," or the pretty little unwashed daughter of the charcoal-burner. Thus we read delightedly, as in an older story, of roses and the ass; there is a certain hardness underlying the beauty, *piedra* as well as *cielo*, but the poetry is always there, even in the smallest, humblest things: Platero drinks stars and water ("dos cubos de agua con estrellas") and his hoofs in the stream break the golden moon into small pieces ("entra en el arroyo, pisa la luna y la hace pedazos").

These concrete images are not confined to Señor Jiménez' prose. In his poetry likewise, the snowy-haired old woman goes up the flowered path in spring: the sky is blue, the lark is singing and the stream murmurs in the grass, but her thoughts are of her dying little grand-daughter Estrellita (*Pastorales*); thus we have the picture of the young mother and her child with hand outstretched to reach the cherries (*Diario de un poeta recién casado*); the little *carbonerilla* burnt to death in her mother's absence (*Historias*); girls coming in decked with flowers on the hay-carts; the aged *abuela*, with a merry *copla* running in her head from times past, going along the Spring-decked path with her sad and pensive grand-daughter; the peasants driving in their cows to market in the shade of the green poplars by the roadside. It is this definiteness

and exactness which give an artistic, one might almost say an Italian finish to some of his verse. "Intelligence," he cries, "give me the exact word for each thing. May my word be the thing itself, created anew by my spirit!" (*Eternidades*).

More often, no doubt, he is the vague dreamer, whose thoughts wander between earth and heaven:

> Tesoros del azul
> que un día y otro'en vuelo repetido
> traigo a la tierra. Polvo de la tierra
> que un dia y otro llevo al cielo.

                              (*Piedra y Cielo*)

His soul is vexed with immortal longings (*afanes imposibles; anhelos de cien cosas que no fueron*); he searches for the "hidden beauty" of things; and his *poemas mágicos y dolientes* are filled with elegiac regret, until his song becomes the echo of a song rather than the song itself—or, as it were, a shadow cast before:

> Canción mía,
> canta antes de cantar.

                              (*Piedra y Cielo*)

It sings before and after, in memory and anticipation:

> ¿Soy? Seré!
> seré, hecho onda
> del río del recuerdo.

He hovers musically about the ghosts of things, the broken petals:

> O gracia rota, O sueño azul deshecho!

and feels, like Albert Samain (with whom he has been compared),

> l'infini de douceur qu'ont les choses brisées.

Much of his poetry is the

> fin sin fin de una rota armonía sin nombre,
> jamás en la idea apagada.

                              (*Laberinto*)

His song becomes

>   la rosa abierta
> de las voces todas que no hablan

or is shot through with

>   una antigua alegría
> de olores y de esencias.

Or it subtly recaptures

>   un aire
> viejo que estaba cantando
> no sé quién por otro valle;

                              (*Arias Tristes*)

>   suspiros rotos
> de coplas que se cantaron
> por las sendas, al retorno.

                              (*Pastorales*)

His senses delight in "delicate and strange intuitions" or his thought

>   se hunde

en abismos fantásticos, inmensos, e inefables.

(*Libros de Amor*)

Yet here again his art is not of things entirely insubstantial,

Light that is scarcely light, light that is scent
Of flowers, wholly peace.

Few poets have shown a more exquisite sensibility towards the moods of Nature; but if the Nature described is a reflection of the poet's spirit, the expression of the

idilio dormido
en el fondo de mi alma,

it also dwells concretely in his mind and heart. Nature, such as he sees it, and his soul are one:

the valley
Seems unto me a valley of the soul;
my heart
was like a darkening cloud
above the sunset's fire;
Hard stars and seas unplumbed,
and thoughts of other, virgin lands:
these are my soul;
In my breast lies the dawn,
and in my back the sunset:
How fearfully my life
Is rent from out the whole;
My soul is sister to the withered leaves
and to the heavens grey.
the trees their sorrows have,
the branches feel.

In the dedication of this volume (*Pastorales*) to Don Gregorio Martínez Sierra, he says that "my heart seems like a landscape." It is perhaps scarcely necessary to remark that this Nature in which the poet's soul merges itself and which merges itself in the poet's soul until they are completely identified, is not the whole of Nature but a limited if exquisite view of it. The poet may declare that the dawn is in his breast and the sunset in his back, but mountain ranges and rushing torrents and sounding forests are more discomfortable guests; the *desgarradura* would have to be even greater if they are to be harboured. These wilder aspects of Nature have no echo in his lyrics. In a storm in the mountains, he finds that "the notion of things is lost" (*Melancolía*), and the sea for him is the glancing, laughing sea of halcyon days, ...:

Mar del sur en abril, amor; O golondrinas,
breves noches con alma de auroras transparentes;
A la tarde, las brisas se tornan más divinas.
Las golondrinas van en las olas indolentes.

(*Historias*)

His Nature is confined chiefly to gardens and scenes such as Watteau painted. He himself describes the poems of *Laberinto* as "scenes and editions of a literary Watteau, a little more subjective and less optimistic than his pictures." [In *Jardines Lejanos* he] sings of the "gentle sadness of the country" and of gardens of

araucarias, magnolieros,

tílos, chopos, lilas, plátanos.

Cities, like the sea, can enter his spirit only in the distance of a dream, white as lilies or marble:

Ciudades de cristal, de azucena, de mármol,
aléjanse en un sueño de cumbres de frescura.

Señor Jiménez is not a poet to be imitated; one hopes that he will not found a school. He himself changes and develops and has now shed most of his modernist trappings. Mannerisms matter but little when there is a fundamental sincerity; Señor Jiménez is sincere and a true poet. His aim is to be simple and spontaneous, as he has recently informed us. His poetry holds a high place in the Spanish literature of the Twentieth Century and it will retain it. Señor Jiménez repeats himself, quotes himself, and imposes himself; the reader may at first be disconcerted and try to protest, but very soon he becomes fascinated, as a bird by a snake, and it is noticeable that the repetition of this poet's verse seems to increase its value, bringing out much that had escaped one on a first reading.

In reading this poet of the extreme South-west of Spain, one is reminded sometimes of Becquer and of Rubén Darío and Rosalía de Castro; at other times one thinks of Leopardi or Chénier or Heine or Baudelaire or Verlaine. He has been strongly influenced by the primitive Spanish poets, by Góngora and by the popular poetry (the *romances*). In a lyric such as **"Verde verderol"** (*Baladas de Primavera*) he is half Góngora (the early Góngora) and half popular. But as he has a true and constant lyric vein, he stands out distinct and different from all these influences.

The singular fascination of his poetry lies not in its thought or construction but in the flowing pliant numbers which every now and then concentrate and crystallize, oh, so *cristalinamente*, into a finer, more perfect poem and subtle but more definite effect:

Mañana alegre de otoño,
cielo azul, y sobre el cielo
azul las hojas de oro
de los jardines enfermos;
colores májicos del poniente enarbolado;
O plenitud de oro! Encanto verde y lleno
de pájaros! Arroyo de azul, cristal y arisa!
O soledad sonora! Mi corazōn sereno
se abre, como un tesoro, al soplo de tu brisa.

(*Elejías*)

His elegiac poetry is crowded with *nostalgias* but they are not dully abstract but of a glowing intensity: *nostalgias encendidas;* and so it abounds in concrete pregnant phrases: *la ventana se enciende, oros lentos, lento ocaso, crepúsculos líricos, auroras de tormenta, claridades plácidas, estrellas desgranadas,* the *blanco mañanero* of the frosted flowers. Often the effect is produced by suggestion, in disconnected phrases, and his art becomes softly *staccato* (one thinks again of Chopin and of one liquid note emerging distinct from a stream of melody):

Nubes blancas y estrellas. Mar de fondo. A lo lejos arde
el faro

(*Poemas Májicos y Dolientes*)

. . . . .

una alondra mañanera
subió del surco cantando
'Mañana de primavera'

(*Jardines Lejanos*)

. . . . .

Nadie. un pájaro. Dios

(*Poesías Agrestes*)

. . . . .

El campo es todo
bruma y rocío. La alondra.

(*Pastorales*)

There we have the modernist who, with the economy of a true artist but also with his loyalty to the beautiful, can convey a whole scene in four words. (pp. 208–17)

Aubrey F. G. Bell, "Lyric Poetry," in his *Contemporary Spanish Literature*, Alfred A. Knopf, 1925, pp. 193–227.

JOHN TAGLIABUE

(essay date 1958)

[Tagliabue is an Italian-born American poet and
scholar whose collections of poetry include *The Buddha Uproar* (1967) and *The Doorless Door* (1970).
In the following review of *Platero and I* and *The Selected Works of Juan Ramón Jiménez*, he offers
enthusiastic praise for the poet's work. Discerning
a magical quality in Jiménez's poems, Tagliabue
declares that "when we read them we seem to be
walking in the sky."]

Jiménez really won the Nobel Prize long before it was
officially declared in 1956; when his poems came into
time and words he began winning noble prizes all over
the universe. But only recently have [English versions of
Platero and I and *The Selected Writings of Juan Ramón
Jiménez*] become available.

Platero carried the poet early in his career around
Andalusia and carries us around the world now; what he
helped the poet and us see changes our speed, our music,
effects our happiness. Such happiness and such song and
such strength! He helped lead Jiménez stubbornly and
persistently, quietly and without lostness, rancor, clangor
or confusion to the light and the truth which we all enjoy
in *Platero y Yo* and in the poems that come after this
lovely group of prose poems. The donkey carries him as
he carried Cervantes and other princes towards the peace
that is beyond understanding; though Jiménez is also so
related to the world and a sense of transitoriness that he
never forgets the world and sorrow, the way Dante never
forgets the world when he is in Paradise.

The books that he wrote contain the space and clarity and color of the Mediterranean. "Pomegranates in the
blue sky, / Streets of the mariners, / A man always at sea,
/ And the heart in the wind!" One of his most recent
poems says, "And the beyond-the-sky was here with this
earth." In his books the shadows and songs of the world
grow. "As it grew dark, I was sitting by a lonely little Staircase of Water in Generalife, in Granada, weary from the
pleasures of an afternoon of successive paradisal delights,
sunk in a weightless shadow, without substance, in the
great growing shadow which was turning dark yet was
all shot through with celestial transparency, leaving the
stars naked in their places." The rest is not less wonderful. The silence in his poems as in the playing of Segovia is
as amazing as the sound. "Through the water I communicated with the interior of the world." So many of his poems have this motion, power, clarity, coolness; like many
streams they come to a garden, his green book, which we
can hold in our hand. "By sounding and resounding the
water refined my soul more and more to the point where
it could not hear or say, even by being what it doubtless
was or said." The songs of his progress towards purity
make the future radiant, but the now, the presence of a
song, is enough. "Transition is a complete present which
unites the past and the future in a momentary progressive
ecstasy . . . eternal moments."

"A morning skylark / Sang in the still sleeping garden." Nothing is heavy because of the knowledge of his
syllables: "The green greenfinch / Sweetens the setting
sun!" He speaks of the "flight of the river"; it too is a bird.
There are great melodies between objects as in the poem
"The Moon in the Pine Tree" and between writer and
poem and reader; "the orange trees will be swollen with
birds"; I become increasingly aware of these conversations
in the poems written after 1930; a pastoral optimism. The
birds please the sky as Platero pleases the earth as the poems please us: they enjoy each other. Such liberties this
peacemaker makes us take, such poetic or mulish license.
Jiménez says the poet is also a "good friend of space"
and the poem a "passionate form of liberty." His knowledge is at times such a dazzling kind that he closes his
eyes and the images and colors come to the poem "from
the first paradise... which the birds and flowers immensely
know." "All the night / The birds have been / Singing
me their colors." The ecstasies expand the glory of the
book or *light* which is one of its main themes as it is for
Fra Angelico (who "painted glory on his knees") until—
"we seem to be within a great honeycomb of light, the
burning center of an immense flaming rose."

Jiménez enlightened Spain and us while slowly riding Platero or walking by him or writing in his shadow.
There are many quiet, exciting annunciations and simple
holidays in the images. "Platero, as the Angelus sounds,
it seems that this quotidian life of ours loses its power and

another loftier, purer, more constant force from within makes all things rise, as fountains of grace, to the stars which are set alight among the roses . . . more roses . . . your eyes which you cannot see, Platero, which you raise submissively to heaven, are two lovely roses." The vitality is varied without being a rampage, the images surprising; the conclusion of the prose poem about a furious priest: "At the time for prayers, all is changed. The silence of Don José can be heard in the silence of the countryside. Putting on his cassock, cloak and shovel hat, he goes almost without a glance into the darkened town on his slow-moving donkey, as slow as Jesus' death." The correspondences are clear: "Platero's brilliant, lively eyes copy the whole landscape of sun and rain." And in the same happy translation which welcomes such simple everyday pleasures we hear and see "Twenty wine presses worked day and night. What madness, what dizziness, what burning optimism!" The wind falls asleep like a child after play. The humor is unforced, unpredictable as when Platero wins a race and we all win that superb "Crown of Parsley". Then there is old Darbon, Platero's doctor, "who is as large as an ox and as red as a watermelon, . . . and when he talks, some notes are missing as in old pianos." The sadness has this apparent lightness and freedom too: and if Darbon "sees a flower or a little bird, he gives a sudden laugh, opening his mouth wide in a great sustained burst of laughter which always ends in tears. Then, calm again, he looks toward the old cemetery and murmurs: 'My little girl, my poor little girl'. . . " Oddly this sense of grief is often present like a small stone.

There are days and poems when the sense of space suggests catastrophe; the poem **"Sea and Nothing"** for instance: "Nothing! Today, for me, / The word finds its place / In rigid catastrophe, / Like the corpse of a word / Which should be stretched out in its natural / Sepulchre." As in some of the early work of De Chirico and Hemingway the sense of *nada* and silence has a spacious and devastating limit.

But usually these poems of white butterflies or the games of children at dusk or the swallow or the simple child or the crazy man know the little flowers of St. Francis. Their freshness and sweetness is an evident blessing everywhere; Platero makes us humorous. The sounds and silence of the civilization of Moguer are modern enough because they are true and very beautiful. Bread and wine and poverty and innocence are anywhere and modern too. In an essay he says, "The greatest assassin of life is haste, the desire to reach things before the right time which means overreaching them." The truth always catches up to this persistent poet who in a poem from the 1949 collection says: "The southern cross is watching over me"; (that southern cross could be another name for his poems); "over my ultimate innocence, over my return to the child-god I was one day in my Moguer of Spain". This is about freedom too. "I let him do," he says of Platero but it is in a way true about the wind and stream and

song, "as he pleases." Disciplined? not like a fearful soldier. Certainly the poems do not scatter words and readers in confusion. The freest are the most disciplined: the humorous Zen masters who say "Devotion frees" and the followers of St. Francis and the sheep in Platero's dream.

As devoted as Jascha Heifetz is to his violin. That is what I call the greatest political grace. We learn about Jiménez's devotion to poetry and freedom also in his essays, and see that like another noble exile, Dante, he can be very sharp, shrewd, critical as well as gentle and ardent. "The poet has never forgotten that what is really the worst is injustice, hunger, vulgarization, hatred, crime." His economy and rejection of confusion and corruption required the political bravery of Thoreau and Gandhi, one of his heroes; but being Spanish he refers in his essays more often to the peasants, the "authentic and primitive aristocracy". "The Spanish peasant is a pantheist and a mystic and therefore delicate, fine, generous, because he loves, for mysticism and pantheism are love and love is a good sign of aristocracy." In this too his poems are part of the Spanish earth and nobility and air. His poetry is never clustered with contention or furniture, never "encrusted with opinion", which is what Eliot said of Tennyson's, nor with a sad need for Optimistic Mottoes, nor with collages of Ezra Pound, Baudelaire, bleeding newspapers, etc.; it is free in that sense too. Jiménez continuing the above political remarks says: "His unique reward is his good and beautiful life, a mountain, a hand, a star, his reward is his peaceful death." And "there is no more exquisite form of aristocracy than living out of doors." "Inebriate of air am I," his favorite American poet said.

The peasant, the poet and the Spanish poem stand erect; this singularity and strength is explained by the following poem: "I am not I. / I am he, / Who walks at my side without my seeing him, / Who at times I am about to see, / Who at times, I forget. / He, who is silent, serene when I am speaking; / He who pardons gently when I am hating; / He, who walks when I am not, / He, who shall stand erect when I am dead."

Therefore what is essential in the poem or resurrection and this in his case is shockingly almost exclusive is not a matter for historical allusions or rational or rhetorical debates. "Poetry is a state of grace, before and after culture." He likes his own poetry to seem "instinctive, terse, easy like a flower or fruit." The objects are the heroes in his momentous poems. "The moment is like a song rising from a dream and we are its heroes." Rilke reminds the young poet to stay close to objects, that they will not abandon him. And Jiménez says, "Poetry is making divine what we have at hand, the beings and things which we have the good fortune to possess, not as ideals to be pursued but as substances which contain essences." In a very early poem objects are seeking the reader: "How quiet objects are / . . . And with what ecstasy they behold / The dream we are dreaming!"

Nothing is crowded. Nothing is hurried. Their radiance takes up the comedy of our room. The books of the poet or the above translators are precious objects in any lover's house. The nameless names us. "The sky rises, departs, vanishes, now it has no name, it is not a sky but a glory." When Andalusia enters a poem you expect something like that: the objects are clear and sing. "Intelligence, give me / The exact name of things! / Let my word be / The thing itself, / Newly created by my soul. / Through me may all those / Who have forgotten things reach them; / Through me may all those / Who even love things reach them. . . / Intelligence, give me / The exact name, and yours, / and his, and mine, of things!"

The sky or glory has vanished *into his poems;* sometimes when we read them we seem to be walking in the sky. In that tranquil atmosphere the poems announce themselves luminously. (pp. 184–88)

John Tagliabue, "The Poetry of Juan Ramón Jiménez," in *Poetry*, Vol. XCII, No. 3, June, 1958, pp. 184–88.

PAUL R. OLSON

(essay date 1967)

[In the following excerpt, Olson examines fundamental religious and philosophical issues which appear in Jiménez's poetical works.]

It is clear that Jiménez's lifelong search for an ideal beauty, which in *Animal de fondo* achieves its goal and to which, once achieved, he gives the name of God, is also, at the most fundamental level, a search for essence, for the inner reality of things which, precisely because it is reality, is eternal. The reference here to 'things' means, of course, all things, and to that total essence can be given also the name of Being.

The equivalence of the two goals is made clear in a retrospective poem in which Juan Ramón compares his state following the mystic experience on his sea voyage with that of the self of former years. [In *Animal de fondo* he] realizes that nothing has changed except his own understanding of the true relation between God and the self:

Entre aquellos jeranios, bajo aquel limón,
junto a aquel pozo, con aquella niña,
tu luz estaba allí, dios deseante;
tú estabas a mi lado,
dios deseado,
pero no habías entrado todavía en mi.

Among those geraniums, under that lemon tree,
beside that well, with that girl-child,
your light was there, desiring God;
and you were at my side,

Oh God desired,
but had not entered yet in me.

Then follows an explicit reference to a poem from *Piedra y cielo*, [a memorable expression] of Jiménez's constant pursuit of beauty and of his inability ever to possess it fully. It is the poem in which beauty is a "butterfly of light," which always escapes, leaving the poet only with the "form of its flight":

El sol, el azul, el oro eran,
como la luna y las estrellas,
tu chispear y tu coloración completa,
pero yo no podía cojerte con tu esencia,
la esencia se me iba
(como la mariposa de la forma)
porque la forma estaba en mí
y al correr tras lo otro la dejaba;
tanto, tan fiel que la llevaba,
que no me parecía lo que era.

The sun, the blue, the gold all were,
as were the moon and stars,
your scintillation and color complete,
but I could not seize you with your essence,
the essence fled from me
(as did the butterfly of the form)
because the form was in me,
and running after other things I left it behind;
so much, so faithfully I bore it,
that it did not seem to me what it was.

In contrast to that former state, he is now able to declare his complete possession of that essence, which he has gained by means of a revelation which is as mysterious as it is unexpected:

Y hoy, así, sin yo saber por qué,
la tengo entera, entera.
No sé qué día fué ni con qué luz
vino a un jardín, tal vez, casa mar, monte,
y vi que era mi nombre sin mi nombre,
sin mi sombra, mi nombre,
el nombre que yo tuve antes de ser
oculto en este ser que me cansaba,
porque no era este ser que hoy he fijado

(que pude no fijar)
para todo el futuro iluminado
ilúminante,
dios deseado y deseante.
And now, just so, without my knowing why,
I have it complete, complete.
I do not know what day it was nor with what light
it came into a garden, perhaps, house, sea, mountain,
and I saw it was my name without my name,
without my shadow, my name,
one I had before I was
hidden in this being I was weary of,
because it was not this being which I now have secured
(but might never have secured)
for all the future, illuminated
and illuminating,
God, desired and desiring.

Although it was said in the first part of the poem that until the moment of revelation God had not yet entered the poet's consciousness, it becomes clear in the central section that the 'form' within is the same as the essence which he had been seeking, but the anxious search for it in things external to and beyond his own mind only carried him farther from it. The final apprehension of that essence was effected by a simple act of cognition—which appears to the seeker much like a special revelation—of the truth that the essence he had sought was within him all the while. The discovery of the Divine or Absolute Essence thus coincides with the discovery of his own essence, and he thereby realizes that in searching for one he was at the same time seeking the other.

In acknowledging the identity of the two essences, he approaches that form of mysticism which has found its fullest expression in the *Upanishads*, where that identity is proclaimed in the formula, *Tat tvam asi*, 'That art thou.' It is a formula which expresses the concept of identity between the human and the divine, the subjective and the transcendent, and between the self and Self— which is the form of identity most specifically referred to in the formula and in Hindu philosophy's concept of Divine Essence as *Atman*, the Self. Yet despite the strong probability of a direct influence from Eastern thought in Jiménez's spiritual attitudes, they can perhaps be more clearly understood in terms of recent Western philosophy's ontological analyses than of oriental mysticism, not simply because the former provides a reductionist explanation for the latter, but because Jiménez was always so rationalistic and secular in his thinking as to remain basically within the Western tradition. It is not surprising, then, if we see in his vision of a longed-for identity of self with Self an intuition similar to that of the ontological analyses of consciousness in Hegel and Sartre, for there is no European poet in whose work the immediate structure of consciousness as an anguished awareness of separation of the self from its own being, of failing to be what it is is more clearly evident; and in Jiménez's poetic version of the *Tat tvam asi* is immediately implied the goal of every

conscious subject: to coincide with its own being. For despite the distance separating it from that being, the latter is completely its own, and when we write here of an ideal identity of self with Self it must be understood that the honorific capital refers not to a being actually distinct from the 'self,' but only to the self seen as a goal which for consciousness is forever transcendent—that is, just beyond reach—and therefore ever desired, loved, and revered.

In order to understand that 'truth of being' which is the *esencia* spoken of in the central section of the poem, one must recognize the 'butterfly of the form' as an allusion to the famous poem from *Piedra y cielo*, in which beauty is a 'butterfly of light' that always eludes the poet's grasp, leaving him only with the 'form of its flight.' The evocation of this last concept makes it evident that here, too, the word 'form' and the 'essence' with which it is equated must be understood as meaning the 'form of flight.' At the end, therefore, of Jiménez's lifelong search for the inner reality of things, of himself, and of God, he perceives it, not as inert substance or as purely static being, but as dynamic form, a structure of movement.

Before the period of *Animal de fondo*, the very word 'essence' was a relatively rare one in Jiménez's poetry, being used most frequently to mean simply 'fragrance' in a flower and only secondarily referring to the whole quality of being of the flower itself. In the last book, however, the term is very clearly established as one of several equivalent names for the *dios deseado y deseante*:

Cada mañana veo la ciudad
donde te hallé del todo, dios, eséncia,
conciencia, tú, hermosura llena.

Each morning I see the city
where I found you completely, God—essence,
consciousness, you, and complete beauty.

In another poem the temporal dynamism which is the essence of God—and of man—is endued with the quietude of eternity by the poet's sense of the simultaneous presence of all objects of experience and of time as the sum total of all its successive moments:

En estas perspectivas ciudadales
que la vida suceden, como prismas,
con su sangre de tiempo en el cojido espacio,
tú, conciencia de dios, eres presente fijo,
esencia tesorera de dios mío,
con todas las edades
de colores, de músicas, de voces,
en país de países.

In perspectives like these, as though of cities
that give a prism-like successiveness to life
with its temporal blood in captured space,
you, consciousness of God, are a fixed present,
treasuring essence of my God,
with all ages
of colors, music, voices,
in a realm of realms.

It is not difficult, in this abstract image of the spectrum seen in a 'city-like' perspective, to recognize the continuing presence of the sunset scene, of inexhaustible fascination for the impressionist poet. But the ordering of every nuance of the sunset's colors into the prismatic gamut is essential for the creation from such a scene of a symbol of temporal successiveness, a creation effected with the image—poignant, but conceptually bold—of the "sangre de tiempo en el cojido espacio." The representation of successiveness by means of this symbol confers an immediate simultaneity upon each point in the series, and the space which is 'captured' in the single glance of a beholder's eye represents by analogy the whole of a temporal series likewise 'captured' in a single comtemplative moment. The 'treasuring essence' which is the 'consciousness of God' (a phrase understood here as a subjective rather than objective genitive, although the ambiguity is doubtless deliberate) accumulates and preserves within itself the content of each moment of that series in the vision of an eternal and simultaneous present which orthodox theology regards as a prime attribute of God and to which the mystic and every true believer aspire. In poetry, that vision is achieved through the spatialization of time, which in these verses is so complete as to create a realm in which are found simultaneously every age of past and future history and every sight and sound—all sense experiences—which they have contained. Such a realm is necessarily eternal—*is* eternity itself, and therefore it is a 'realm of realms,' a spatial symbol of the *saecula saeculorum*.

The temporal successiveness thus seen is, despite the simultaneity and the cumulative faculty of the vision, correlative to the successiveness which is in consciousness itself, whether human or divine. This is the concept set forth at the beginning of the second stanza, which in its first line refers again to the "perspectivas ciudadales":

Y en ellas, simultánea
creencia de fijados paraísos de fondo,
te sucedes también, conciencia y dios
intercalado de verdores nuevos,
de niñas de color solar,
de cobre retenido en adiós largo,
que componen tu sólita estación total,
tu intemporalidad tan realizada en mí.

And in them, simultaneous
belief in fixed paradises of depth,
you succeed yourself also, consciousness and God,
interpolated with new greens,
with children of the color of the sun,
with copper retained in a long farewell,
which compose your constant total season,
your timelessness so realized in me.

If the attribution of successiveness to the divine consciousness is much less 'orthodox' than was the concept of simultaneity in the divine vision, it can be immediately added that the simultaneity of summation is found as much in that subjective successiveness which is consciousness as it was in the successiveness of the object. So close, indeed, is the parallel, that, as [noted] elsewhere in *Animal de fondo*, the distinction between subject and object is virtually lost, and the divine consciousness is described as 'interpolated' successively with the new greens of returning springs, colors of children in the summer sun, and copper hues of autumn leaves and sunsets, all of which would presumably have been thought to be attributes of the natural world which is the object of consciousness, rather than of the Mind which is its subject. The implication of this virtual identification of the two poles of consciousness is that divinity is immanent in the world itself, subjectivity constituted by its objects. Therefore the successiveness of objective consciousness of time, and the summation of the temporal series is constitutive of a 'constant total season,' a timelessness realized in a consciousness which is total, and in which the poet shares.

It is, however, the final poem in the *Libros de poesía* which most explicitly proclaims dynamic temporality to be the essence of divinity and reaffirms the *panta rhei* as the ultimate truth in a world composed of pure color, light, and rhythmic successiveness. As in all the poems of *Animal de fondo*, the second person singular refers to the *dios deseado y deseante*. The first part of the prose poem was quoted earlier in this chapter, and the work ends on a note of almost pure temporality:

Sí; en masa de verdad reveladora, de sucesión
perpetua pasas, en masa de color, de luz, de ritmo;
en densidad de amor estás pasando, estás viniendo,
estás presente siempre; pasando estás en mí; eres lo
     ilimitado de mi órbita.

Y me detengo en mi alijeración, porque en el
horizonte del espacio eterno estás cayendo siempre
hasta mi imán. Tu sucesión no es fuga de lo mío, es
venida impetuosa de lo tuyo, del todo que eres tú,
eterno vividor del todo; caminante y camino a fuerza
de pasado, a fuerza de presente, a fuerza de futuro.

Yes; in a body of revealing truth, of perpetual successiveness you pass, in body of color, light, and rhythm; in density and love you pass, you come, you are ever present; and are passing within me; you are what is limitless in my orbit.

And I stop in my acceleration, because in the horizon of eternal space you are always falling to my magnet. Your own successiveness is no flight from what is mine, it is impetuous coming from what is yours, from the all which is you, eternal force of life in all; wayfarer and way by force of past, by force of present, and by force of future.

The God within is no mere static 'presence' but a constant coming from the infinitely distant horizon to the center of the poet's consciousness, and this infinite coming is what gives an immanent infinity to the orbit—

the circle—of his own life. Ultimately, however, the dynamism or 'acceleration' of that circle is superseded by the impetuous successiveness of the eternal force of life, the *vividor* which not only lives within all things but far and beyond them as well. So thoroughly is subjective consciousness absorbed into this vision of metaphysical dynamism that it now feels no anguish for the eventual loss of its own finite existence, or even any awareness that its actual absorption into the infinite implies such a loss. Only in the over-whelming dynamic presence of divine totality can Jiménez find satisfaction for what he once called his "total anhelo," 'total longing,' which here is clearly seen to be for the whole of time. For the God desired and desiring is both wayfarer—the power which moves through time and space—and way—the abiding form of movement which unites past, present, and future into a single eternal reality.

In these lines, which conclude the volume of **Libros de poesía**, we discover that the conscious awareness of this reality is identical with the consciousness of God, who in the form of wayfarer and way is the supreme manifestation of the synthesis of time and the timeless, of *éstasis dinámico*. . . . The name of God is given to that ultimate reality because the poet regards it, with love, as a Thou, which in its ontological structure so fully includes (at the same time that it transcends) the structure of conciousness, that it is itself conscious—itself an I as well as a Thou. And that structure, which is an eternal becoming, an eternal but never definitive realization of being by consciousness, is the essence for which Jiménez had always sought:

> Tú, esencia, eres conciencia; mi conciencia
> y la de otros, la de todos,
> con forma suma de conciencia;
> que la esencia es lo sumo,
> es la forma suprema conseguible,
> y tu esencia está en mí, como mi forma.

> You, essence, are consciousness, my consciousness
>   and that of others, that of everyone,
> with supreme form of consciousness;
> for essence is what is supreme,
> the highest form achievable,
> and your essence is within me, as my form.

The peril of absolute subjectivity, by which Jiménez the contemplative poet and mystic had so often been beset, is at length overcome through the universalizing and sharing of consciousness, so that his metaphysics becomes, rather, an absolute humanism—absolute and essential, for consciousness is the essence of what is human. The God of Juan Ramón is, then, the absolute and universal form of the ontological structure of man himself and of that to which he aspires, a synthesis of existence and essence, being which is at once in and for itself.

Logically, perhaps, such syntheses are either impossible or possible only if the term is taken in the etymological sense of a 'simultaneous positing,' as we have seen

in all of Jiménez's paradoxes. In [Jean-Paul Sartre's *Being and Nothingness*], for example, we find an absolute insistence upon the impossibility of synthesis as fusion between the in-itself and the for-itself, but in many ways his analysis of the ontological aspiration of human consciousness describes perfectly what Jiménez's vision seeks to achieve:

> This perpetually absent being which haunts the for-itself is itself fixed in the in-itself. It is the impossible synthesis of the for-itself and the in-itself; it would be its own foundation not as nothingness but as being and would preserve within it the necessary translucency of consciousness along with the coincidence with itself of being in-itself. It would preserve in it that turning back upon the self which conditions every necessity and every foundation.

The difficulty, according to this system of analysis, is that any fusion of the two radically separated regions of being would bring about a complete annihilation of consciousness:

> If what consciousness apprehends as the being toward which it surpasses itself were the pure in-itself, it would coincide with the annihilation of consciousness. But consciousness does not surpass itself toward its annihilation; it does not want to lose itself in the in-itself of identity at the limit of its surpassing. It is for the for-itself as such that the for-itself lays claim to being-in-itself.

But the contradictions or paradox of such a being do not prove, even for Sartre, that it does not exist, but only that it can not be realized as a fusion of the two disparate modes of being into a single Being. Poetic vision moves, however, beyond the form of synthesis which is simply a simultaneous positing of contraries to create an image of being which is absolute transcendence in absolute immanence, the God desired and desiring, consciousness desired and desiring. Ultimately it can be seen that the poetic structures which have been examined in these studies correspond to the structure of that being so closely that far from being opposed to life they are the image of life itself. The suggestions of solipsism and poetic hermeticism which we have seen structurally implied in the tendency toward symmetry and in the ever-present circle can be understood, in the context of the universalized and 'shared' consciousness which Jiménez achieves in **Animal de fondo**, to correspond to a concept of the being of human reality sufficient in itself, needing no relation to a cause as an 'excuse' for its being nor any consequence as justification for it.

The modern philosophers who have most thoroughly analyzed this being have tended to use anthropomorphic—that is, pathetic—language to refer to its immanent justification, as though only external justification (which entails a problem of infinite regress) could save it from triviality. Thus, Sartre speaks of the 'superfluity' of all being and of the 'absurdity' of human life, and even Heidegger's reference to the 'throwness' of *Dasein* into its 'there' seems to imply a negative judgment resulting from the disappointed expectation of a more deliberately purposeful delivering-over of human existence into its being.

But it is precisely the absence of that kind of pathos in Jiménez which permits him to accept and treat with the seriousness of attitude traditionally called religious the immanent justification of the being of consciousness. The attitude is fundamentally realistic and free from the sentimentality of cynicism, for it retains no normative prejudices to suffer disappointment. Doubtless this acceptance is conditioned by a tradition of religious belief which has made familiar the concept of a Being who coincides with his own being, one who is absolute, unconditioned, and sufficient to himself and at the same time conscious and present to himself. But the poet's intuition has penetrated all traditional beliefs to achieve a direct confrontation with that essence of human reality which is consciousness and life, of whose structure and intrinsic worth his art is the reflection. (pp. 217–31)

Paul R. Olson, in his *Circle of Paradox: Time and Essence in the Poetry of Juan Ramón Jiménez*, The Johns Hopkins Press, 1967, 236 p.

MICHAEL P. PREDMORE
(essay date 1970)

[Predmore is a noted Hispanist whose writings include *La Obra en prosa de Juan Ramón Jiménez* (1973), *La poesía de Juan Ramón Jiménez* (1973), and *Una España joven en la poesía de Antonio Machado* (1981). In the following essay, he analyzes Jiménez's acclaimed prose poem *Platero y Yo*, describing the work as a masterfully crafted apotheosis of life.]

As one of the most famous prose poems in twentieth-century Spanish literature, *Platero y Yo* stands as an early masterpiece in the long and distinguished career of Juan Ramón Jiménez. Translations into eight different languages and over one million copies testify to its vitality. It has always been popular, even and especially among its critics, who unite unanimously in praising the artistic qualities of the work. But much critical commentary is simply sheer eulogy, and when the commentary is good, it is always brief and never fully developed. Perhaps it is time now to subject the work to close analysis and try to discover wherein lies some of its artistic value. The purpose of this essay is to study the structure of *Platero*

y Yo— structure in the sense of underlying principle or principles which give shape to an expressive form.

It will be remembered that *Platero y Yo* does not tell a conventional story; there is no strict narrative ordering of events, no causal relationship linking one lyric chapter to the next. There are sudden shifts of scene and changes in time. We may pass directly from the lyric portrayal of a sunset to the description of a vicious cock-fight, and then to more anecdotal material relating how the mother of a family of four puppies retrieved her young after they had become separated. One looks in vain for the inner thread which must weave these chapters together. Yet, if *Platero* is a prose poem, if it is indeed an artistic masterpiece, there must be some principle of organization, some basis for poetic unity and wholeness.

Let us pursue this line of inquiry with respect to several chapters that occur early in the work. "La Púa,". . . describes a curious incident which involves the removal of a painful thorn from Platero's hoof. Why, we may ask, was this detail selected, and is there any significance to its occurrence so early in the work? Similarly, in "El Loro,". . . one of the poet's friends, a doctor, treats the wound of a hunter who accidently shot himself. And again, "La Sanguijuela,". . . recounts how the poet with the help of his friend, Raposo, pries open Platero's mouth to remove a leech. Each incident, at first glance, seems to have little to do with the lyric descriptions of nature or with the collective life of Moguer that so commonly characterize *Platero*. True, two of the incidents are expressive of the affectionate relationship between master and donkey, but why the accidental shedding of blood in all three cases? It is here, I suggest, that a significant pattern begins to emerge. For in general, it will be recalled, pain and suffering (and, in some cases, death) in *Platero* are not accidental or gratuitous, but are seen as the result of specific conditions: sickness or incapacitation at birth ("El Niño Tonto," "La Tísica," "La Niña Chica"), premeditated action ("El Potro Castrado"), repeated or habitual actions (the ragged children who torment or harass aged and infirm animals, "El Perro Sarnoso," "El Demonio," "La Yegua Blanca"), or cruel public ceremonies ("Los Gallos," "Los Toros").

Further efforts to find exceptions to the general rule, to find incidents of accidental injury or bloodletting, are rewarded, though only up to a certain point in the book. Gratuitous injury resulting in death occurs in "La Fantasma,". . . (a young girl is struck dead by lightning), in "El Perro Sarnoso,". . . (a mangy dog is killed by a guard in a burst of bad temper), and in "Lord,". . . (a pet fox terrier was bitten by a rabid dog and had to be taken away). Though there is no mention of blood in the above chapters, there are other incidents where a flow of blood occurs: in "Remanso,". . . (a human heart is pricked and blood flows; the significance of this will be dealt with later) and in "La Coz,". . . (Platero is bloodied by a kick from a colt). Finally, as if to confirm further the fact that there is something significant and mysterious about so much bloodletting during the early chapters of **Platero**, the image of blood even invades the metaphorical description of a sunset in "Paisaje Grana,". . . :"La cumbre. Ahí está el ocaso, todo empurpurado, herido por sus propios cristales, que le hacen sangre pordoquiera." In the same chapter, Platero goes to a pool of water to drink, and the reflected light from the sunset makes it appear as though he is drinking waters of blood: "Yo me quedo extasiado en el crepúsculo. Platero, granas de ocaso sus ojos negros, se va, manso, a un charquero de aguas de carmín, de rosa, de violeta; hunde suavemente su boca en los espejos, que parece que se hacen líquidos al tocarlos él; y hay por su enorme garganta como un pasar profundo de umbrías aguas de sangre." It is important to note, I think, that this description is unique in the entire work. There are no other instances in which the image of blood is associated with the countless descriptions of sunset in **Platero**.

That there is violence and misery and suffering in this **Andalusian Elegy** is well-known and has been noted on a number of occasions. What concerns us for the moment is the vein of gratuitous suffering and bloodletting in **Platero**, which does not seem to occur beyond. . . "La Coz." Thus a special pattern has been identified and located. Rather than try to relate an isolated incident like that of "La Púa" to the poetic whole, it may be easier now and more meaningful to try to relate this cluster of similar events to the totality of the poetic work.

At this point three sets of related observations can be introduced. Each one governs both the beginning and the ending of the book. The first observation is that Platero dies in the month of February. The second is that the book begins in March, passes through the cycle of a year, and ends in April. (**Platero** begins in late winter-early spring and ends in spring.) And the third observation, which reveals the significance of the first two, is that the book begins with the introduction of butterfly imagery, the "mariposas blancas". . ., and ends with a cluster of butterfly imagery. It will be remembered that.. . . Platero and his master enter the outskirts of town at nightfall. Suddenly they are challenged by a man who wants to collect a tax on provisions they may be bringing into town:

—¿Va? algo?

—Vea usted. . . Mariposas blancas. . .

El hombre quiere clavar su pincho de hierro en el seroncillo, y yo lo evito. Abro la alforja y él no ve nada. Y el alimento ideal pasa, libre y cándido, sin pagar su tributo a los Consumos. . .

Clearly "mariposas blancas" must be read on a symbolic level. Platero is carrying spiritual goods; he does not participate in the material and economic life of the village. The significance of the butterflies, which is a recurring image throughout the work, is established in five final chapters [which deal with the death, rebirth, and metamorphosis of Platero]. . . . When Platero dies at noonday in the month of February, the chapter "La Muerte" ends: "Por la cuadra en silencio, encendiéndose cada vez que pasaba por el rayo de sol de la ventanilla, revolaba una bella mariposa de tres colores. . . " Three chapters later in "Melancolía," the poet goes to visit Platero's grave and asks Platero if he still remembers his master. The answer to the question takes the following form: "Y, cual contestando a mi pregunta, una leve mariposa blanca, que antes no había visto, revolaba insistentemente, igual que un alma, de lirio en lirio. . . " Again the figure of a butterfly hovers near the dead or the buried Platero. This association, I think, is made explicit in. . . "A Platero, en el cielo de Moguer.". . . The poet goes to visit his friend's grave for the final time. The last paragraph reads: "Sí. Yo sé que, a la caída de la tarde, cuando, entre las oropéndolas y los azahares, llego, lento y pensativo, por el naranjal solitario, al pino que arrulla tu muerte, tú, Platero, feliz en tu prado de rosas eternas, me verás detenerme ante los lirios amarillos que ha brotado tu descompuesto corazón." Platero's body is part of the earth and soil that is giving birth to flowers. His death contributes to life processes and becomes part of creation. In this way, Platero like the butterfly has undergone metamorphosis. It is not essential to the argument, but highly interesting as an extrinsic factor, to learn that Jiménez had planned, in a future revised version of **Platero**, to make explicit precisely what seems to be the principal expressive value of the butterfly imagery. We learn from Ricardo Gullón ["Platero, revivido," *PSA*, 1960] that the poet, by way of revision, included the following clause (in italics) in the last paragraph of "Melancolía," already cited above: "Y, cual contestando a mi pregunta, una ["otra" appears in the Gullón version] leve mariposa blanca, que antes no había visto, *y que me pareció, metamorfoseada, la de la cuadra, el día de la muerte de Platero*, revolaba insistentemente, igual que un alma, de lirio en lirio. . . " This butterfly, recalling the butterfly that hovered near Platero's body on the day of his death, seems to fulfill the promise of metamorphosis implied in the earlier image. Thus the answer to the poet's question when he asks if Platero still remembers him is that Platero has never really died. He is still there alive in nature, a spiritual companion of the poet as always. His soul like a butterfly has undergone metamorphosis and is attending the spiritual condition of the irises just as his decomposed heart will nurture their physical being in the next chapter. Therefore, when Platero carries symbolically white butterflies. . ., he carries within him the principle of regeneration and transformation. Platero, like all plants and creatures of the natural world, participates in nature's vital processes.

Let us summarize the three observations made earlier, related now in their full significance. Platero is introduced to us in the month of March, he dies in the month of February, and is resurrected again in the season of spring—through his spiritual and physical metamorphosis into yellow irises. The underlying theme, then, of *Platero y Yo*, put in its most abstract formulation, is the theme of death and rebirth as a process of metamorphosis. And the principle of metamorphosis, linked to the seasonal cycle of nature, constitutes the key structural principle.

Now the special pattern of gratuitous violence and accidental bloodletting, identified earlier, assumes its full significance. All the incidents that belong to these categories occur during the season of spring. The last incident of gratuitous bleeding takes place in "La Coz" toward the end of May. Thus, the accounts of Platero's bleeding hoof or the hunter's bleeding arm no longer appear as unrelated to surrounding chapters as they did at first glance. Nor does the occurrence of the child struck dead by lightning nor the mangy dog shot dead at the whim of a guard seem quite as gratuitous. This is the seasonal sacrifice and the letting of blood that ensures the renovation of spring and the well-being of society. These events can be interpreted as the symbolic enactments of the rites of spring. The treatment of blood, it seems to me, makes a convincing case for a symbolic reading of these events as ritual elements in a great seasonal drama, in which Platero himself is the protagonist. In the four instances in which blood is specifically elaborated as the result of a human or animal wound ("La Púa," "El Loro," "La Sanguijuela," "La Coz"), no death occurs and the injury is a minor one. In three of the four cases, it is Platero's blood that is shed. In two of these cases, the blood is cleansed and washed away by the pure waters of a stream. In "La Púa," the poet removes the thorn and takes Platero to a stream: "me lo he llevado al pobre al arroyo de los lirios amarillos, para que el agua corriente le lama, con su larga lengua pura, la heridilla." In "La Sanguijuela," the poet disposes of the leech in the water of a stream and explains: "Para que no saque sangre a ningún burro más, la [la sanguijuela] corto sobre el arroyo, que un momento tiñe de la sangre de Platero la espumela de un breve torbellino. . . " These occurrences of Platero's blood fusing with the waters of a stream serve to point out the significance of "Paisaje Grana," where, we may recall, the bleeding sunset causes it to appear as though Platero himself is drinking waters of blood ("y hay por su enorme garganta como un pasar profundo de umbrías aguas de sangre"). How appropriate, in the season of spring, for Platero to appear to renew himself with blood from the waters of nature when he also releases, on two occasions, his own blood to the waters of nature. The passage of blood from Platero to nature is a reciprocal affair. Thus his intimate and vital intercourse with nature is enacted at the outset of the work long before the symbolic value of the butterfly reveals the meaning of his death at the end. Platero's relationship with nature begins with an exchange of vital substances (water and blood) and ends with an exchange of both substance and form (the metamorphosis of a donkey into yellow irises).

That the flow of blood from a wound is both purifying and revitalizing receives confirmation on other occasions where the image of blood is used in a metaphorical sense. In . . . "Remanso," the poet stops to contemplate a pool of water, and to reflect on its capacity to stimulate the inner imaginative world of magic at an earlier point in his life. But the poet reveals that there was something unhealthy about the excessive cultivation of inner sensations in solitude. Eventually more intimate contact with things human, with human love, punctured the unhealthy storage of inner life, released the corrupted blood, and purified the flow. The reader familiar with Jiménez's poetry will recognize in the following passage the same rejection of a modernist mode of style and feeling that is expressed in the fifth poem of *Eternidades*, "Vino, primero, puro":

> Este remanso, Platero, era mi corazón antes, Así me lo sentía, bellamente envenenado, en su soledad, de prodigiosas exuberancias detenidas... Cuando el amor humano lo hirió, abriéndole su dique, corrió la sangre corrompida, hasta dejarlo puro, limpio y fácil, como el arroyo de los Llanos, Platero, en la más abierta, dorada y caliente hora de abril.

The contemplation of the flickering flames of a fire in. . . "La Llama," offers another example of the expressive value of the blood of a wound. Fire, like blood, both warms and strengthens: "El fuego es el universo dentro de casa. Colorado e interminable, como la sangre de una herida en el cuerpo, nos calienta y nos da hierro, con todas las memorias de la sangre."

The images of blood and bloodletting, as a ritual element in the rebirth of spring, can be established convincingly, I think, if we review now all the related evidence. Platero, in the springtime, both releases and absorbs blood from the waters of nature. The blood of wounds is seen as a purifying and revitalizing agent in other contexts that do not concern Platero directly. The image of blood flowing from a wound invades metaphorically the description of a cosmic phenomenon—the setting of the sun. And this occurs only once in the entire work, most significantly in the season of early spring. Finally, in. . . "La Primavera," "la cruda primavera" of the earlier chapters gives way to spring in full bloom. It seems most expressive that nature's rebirth is described for the first time as "vida sana y nueva." The descriptive word "sana" occurs only after three instances of bloodletting have already taken place ("La Púa," "Paisaje Grana," and "El Loro"), which further supports the notion that the shedding of blood as a spring ritual contributes to the fertility of the land and helps provide for a healthy rebirth. The passage in question reads: "¡Cómo está la mañana! El sol pone en la tierra su alegría de plata y oro; mariposas de cien colores juegan por todas partes, entre las flores, por la casa—ya dentro, ya fuera—, en el manantial. Por doquiera, el campo se abre en estallidos, en crujidos, en un hervidero de vida sana y nueva."

It might be appropriate at this point to take account of what has thus far been established. The intent of this study is to analyze and make explicit the structure of *Platero*. We have chosen to approach the subject by trying to explain the meaning of an important pattern of violence (about which there is still more to be said) and to explain the meaning of important patterns of imagery. We have seen how disparate images such as those of blood and butterflies help account for the expressive organization of material in *Platero*. The occurrences of gratuitous bloodletting become comprehensible as ritual elements in the rebirth of spring. The pattern of butterfly images serves to express the underlying theme of death and rebirth in nature's annual cycle. The significance of these patterns is sufficient, I think, to allow us to define the general structural framework within which *Platero y Yo* must be read and interpreted. Events must be read on a symbolic level as well as a literal level. The clue to the expressive value of a given lyric chapter should be sought in the season (and at times even in the month) in which it occurs, whether spring, summer, autumn, or winter. What is being established in each case is the emotional climate, or the climate of feeling, of each season. Events are symbolic of meanings and feelings and rhythms that belong to the different seasons of nature and that have been preserved and maintained through ancient traditions of myth and ritual. Thus the rebirth of spring, the plenitude of summer, the decline of autumn, and the death of winter are enacted and relived through every page of *Platero*. But we must be careful not to impose too rigidly a pattern of meaning that comes from other sources. The unique structure of a literary work is always different from the structure of myth or ritual. Let us continue our study, then, with reference to the seasons of summer and autumn, which will in part confirm the above observations. Finally, we will conclude by analyzing one further significant pattern which spans all four seasons and which serves to demonstrate how a work of art, in the last analysis, conforms to its own inner logic, and not to a pattern inherited from tradition.

The season of summer is initiated significantly in. . . "Corpus," with the slow, ponderous procession of a religious ceremony. The climate of feeling that predominates in the chapters devoted to summer is expressed through the heat, the slowness, the static, timeless sense of hot summer days. What strikes the attention immediately about the section devoted to summer is its extreme brevity. It contains only twelve chapters as compared to approximately forty-eight chapters devoted to spring, forty-two devoted to autumn, and twenty-three to winter. In the treatment of each season, there is always one chapter which bears the title of the season under elaboration and which presumably establishes the completeness of its arrival. After the chapter entitled "La Primavera,"

there are thirty more that continue to treat springtime. After the chapter "El Otoño," twenty-four more chapters continue to treat autumn; after "El Invierno," fourteen more chapters deal with winter. But after "El Verano," only two chapters intervene before the arrival of September. The season of summer is hardly elaborated at all. This provides a dramatic example of what seems to be true of many other early works of Jiménez's poetic world. There is almost always a marked preference for the transitional seasons of spring and autumn. In *Platero y Yo*, the relevance to the theme of death and rebirth as a process of metamorphosis accounts, I think, for the greater elaboration of spring and autumn as opposed to summer and winter. It is only fitting that close attention is paid to visible changes of form, to the natural processes of growth and decline, of becoming and dying, and less attention to nature's more visibly static seasons of maturity and sterility.

There is one chapter in the brief treatment of summer, however, that deserves our close attention. It is, appropriately enough, . . . "El Verano," which begins by describing Platero, bleeding profusely, this time bitten by horseflies: "Platero va chorreando sangre, una sangre espesa y morada, de las picaduras de los tábanos. La chicharra sierra un pino, que nuncallega. . . Al abrir los ojos, después de un inmenso sueño instantáneo, el paisaje de arena se me torna blanco, frío en su ardor, espectral." We notice immediately that this case of bloodletting is not developed. The description passes quickly to other things. How significantly different this instance of bleeding is from the earlier occurrences in spring. A flow of blood in the middle of the summer as a result of horseflies is a natural event. There is no mention of a wound ("herida") —which is always the case in the earlier examples—and no mention of pain. Platero is not caused to limp as in the case of "La Púa," nor provoked to cough as in the case of "La Sanguijuela." This is no surprising and painful bloodletting as a ritual element of spring, but rather a painless flowing of blood which is expressive of life in its fullness in summertime—the blood as it gushes forth is a thick and deep purple. Furthermore, as if to confirm the naturalness of this event, the blood is quickly restored by the end of the chapter, distinguishing once again what happens here from earlier cases of bloodletting. Platero and the poet arrive soon afterward at an orchard and begin to eat watermelon: "Cuando llegamos a la sombra del nogal grande rajo dos sandías, que abren su escarcha grana y rosa en un largo crujido fresco. Yo me como la mía lentamente, oyendo, a lo lejos, las vísperas del pueblo. Platero se bebe la carne de azúcar de la suya como si fuese agua." Thus, soon after Platero is described as bleeding profusely, he is seen to be drinking the red flesh of a watermelon as if it were water. The release and restoration of vital substances takes place in close succession. Platero's reciprocal affair with nature achieves an even higher degree of harmony in summer.

The season of autumn, as already indicated, is treated almost as fully as the season of spring. A change in mood, a change in the climate of feeling, is revealed immediately when the month of September is first announced in. . . "Domingo": "Y el campo, un poco enfermo ya." A few chapters later in "El Vergel,". . . a specific reference is again made to the effect produced by a change of season: "En el cielo, por la masa de verdor tocado ya del mal otoño, donde el ciprés y la palmera perduran, mejor vistos, la luna amarillenta se va encendiendo, entre nubecillas rosas. . . " The sense of decline and decay that accompanies the slow and beautiful passage of summer to winter invades many of the lyric sketches now. Afternoon sunsets occur more frequently and are more deliberately elaborated. This aspect of temporality is especially developed in such chapters as "La Niña Chica," . . . "El Otoño," . . . "El Perro Atado," . . . "Tarde de Octubre," . . . "Viñeta,". . . "El Cementerio Viejo," . . . "La Plaza Vieja de Toros," . . . "La Fuente Vieja," . . . "Camino," . . . "Idilio de Noviembre," . . . —all of which convey a sense of beauty and sadness, a sense of beauty and nostalgia for things irretrievably lost.

This sense of time passing is mitigated, however, by another recurring pattern which expresses once again the central theme of death and rebirth. First of all, it is noteworthy that in none of the pages dealing with autumn is Platero injured in any way, as he was repeatedly in the springtime, by a painful thorn, a bloodsucking leech, and a kick delivered by another four-footed companion. Not only does Platero not suffer injury, but he is not involved in any way with incidents of conditioned violence which continue through most of the work. When the passing of life and the coming of death is seen to follow its natural course, and not subject to the brutal ways of men (such as when men and children beat and stone infirm animals), Platero is instructed by his master in the beautiful and mysterious ways of nature. We note in the following four examples that Platero is being directly spoken to in three of them, and the lesson in each case involves the promise of rebirth in spring. In the first example, "El Otoño,". . . Platero learns that the yellow autumn leaves are certain to turn green again:

El arado va, como una tosca arma de guerra, a la labor alegre de la paz, Platero; y en la ancha senda húmeda, los árboles amarillos, seguros de verdecer, alumbran, a un lado y otro, vivamente, como suaves hogueras de oro claro, nuestro rápido caminar.

In the next example, the poet is speaking of a turtle which has been so durable and indestructible that it seems to have the capacity to renew itself in the spring: "A veces, en primavera, se enseñorea del corral, y parece que ha echado de se seca vejez eterna y sola una rama nueva; que se ha dado a luz sí misma para otro siglo. . . " In the following example, the poet speaks to Platero about the passing away of both leaves and birds. Unlike men

and larger animals for whom burial is almost always a customary practice, the smaller creatures of nature disappear mysteriously in anticipation of spring:

¿Ves el campo, Platero, todo lleno de hojas secas? Cuando volvamos por aquí, el domingo que viene, no verás una sola. No sé dónde se mueren. Los pájaros, en su amor de la primavera, han debido de decirles el secreto de ese morir bello y oculto, que no tendremos tú ni yo, Platero. . .

Finally, in this last example, the poet explains to Platero that the yellow canary that has just died will emerge again in the spring from the heart of a white rose, in a passage that recalls the metamorphosis of Platero into yellow irises:

Oye, a la noche, los niños, tú y yo bajaremos el pájaro muerto al jardín. La luna está ahora llena, y a su pálida plata, el pobre cantor, en la mano cándida de Blanca, parecerá el pétalo mustio de un lirio amarillento. Y lo enterraremos en la tierra del rosal grande.

A la primavera, Platero, hemos de ver al pájaro salir del corazón de una rosa blanca.

While butterfly imagery is perhaps the key expressive pattern, dominating as it does both the beginning and the ending of the work, it is certainly not the only pattern of its kind. We have just seen that the treatment of autumn gives rise to a variety of metaphorical language, equally expressive of the theme of death and rebirth.

The treatment of winter offers a significant departure from the expression of seasonal moods and feelings. The first mention of winter occurs in. . . "Los Gitanos," and for the next nine chapters there seems to be appropriate expression of the feeling of winter, particularly in four chapters, "Convalecencia,". . . "El Burro Viejo,". . . "Florecillas,". . . and "Leche de Burra,". . . where incidents of sickness, old age, and death are deliberately developed. But from this point on, the climate of feeling changes. There is a whole series of chapters dominated by a sense of happiness and even exhilaration, whether it be the experience of nature on a winter day or the excitement of children at "Los Reyes Magos." Given the earlier treatment of the seasonal cycle, we might expect more elaboration of the themes of death and sterility, of life frozen and inert in nature's least productive season. Yet this does not seem to be the case. It is at this point that we must take into account one final significant pattern, which has been a constant up to now, throughout all of *Platero*. We note that the pattern of violence, both conditioned and gratuitous, seems mysteriously to disappear, precisely in the season where one might expect its greatest concentration. It will be remembered that incidents of human cruelty and human and animal misery are regularly distributed through the pages of *Platero*. They are juxtaposed repeatedly with moments of vitality and harmony in nature. It is as though the forces of violence and harmony are constant conditions that govern all life, to a greater or lesser degree, in all seasons. But after the incident of "La Yegua Blanca,". . . in which children stone to death a blind old mare, there is no further instance where human cruelty results in death. Indeed, after "La Yegua Blanca," which occurs at the end of November, there is no example of human cruelty or sordidness that is comparable to it or to the earlier chapters of "Pinito,". . . "Sarito,". . . "Los Gallos,". . . "El Demonio,". . . or "El Perro Sarnoso.". . . As the season of winter progresses, the gradual reduction of violence and sordidness becomes notable (a reduction which begins almost imperceptibly in autumn). There are still occasional references to unpleasant facts, such as "gitanos astrosos" or "niños pobres y tristes," but, with the exception of the four chapters mentioned above, the ugly side of life is not developed now. Indeed, after "Leche de Burra," eleven of the twelve chapters that immediately precede the death of Platero are ones in which the happiness and the innocence and purity of the child's world or the natural world is so insistently elaborated as to exclude almost everything else. The only incident that disturbs this innocent world of the child established at the end occurs in "Los Burros del Arenero.". . . This exception is so notable that it confirms the general observation. The poet begins to point out to Platero the unfortunate donkeys that labor under their loads of sand. This is the shortest chapter in the book and its four lines can be quoted in their entirety:

> Mira, Platero, los burros del Quemado; lentos, caídos, con su picoda y roja carga de mojada arena, en la que Bevan clarada, como en el corazón, la vara de acebuche verde coa que les pegan. . .

Precisely at the point where the poet makes explicit a detail of human cruelty ("pegan"), he breaks off. He suppresses any further elaboration, and this suppression is most significant. For Platero's death is very close now, only two chapters away, and we suddenly realize that the gradual reduction and, finally, the elimination of all instances of cruelty and violence is a deliberate attempt to purify the environment, the climate of feeling, in which Platero is to die. Just as Platero is instructed through the season of autumn in the mysterious ways of death and rebirth, so he is especially prepared in winter, even his environment is prepared, for the final event of his death. Indeed, some of the final chapters reveal this intent very clearly. Death is very near and the final words of assurance and reassurance about things, or the final words of instruction, are most expressive. For example, in "La Fábula,". . . Platero is assured that his master will always respect his language, the language of a donkey, and will never make of him the talking hero of any animal fable. Or in "Mons-Urium,". . . after the poet tells of his discovery of the Latin etymology of Moguer, he says to Platero: "Me encontré de pronto como sobre un tesoro inextinguible. Moguer, Monte de Oro, Platero; puedes vivir y morir

contento." Again in "La Torre,". . . the poet would like to take Platero up to the top of the tower of Moguer, but explains to him that he is just too big and concludes: "¡A cuántos triunfos tienes que renunciar, pobre Platero! ¿Tu vida es tan sencilla como el camino corto del Cementerio viejo!" Finally, in the last chapter before his death, the poet insistently calls Platero's attention to the flight of a butterfly, which provokes the following comments on the beauties of nature: "Hay, Platero, bellezas culminantes que en vano pretenden otras ocultar. Como en el rostro tuyo los ojos son el primer encanto, la estrella es el de la noche y la rosa y la mariposa lo son del jardín matinal."

Platero dies presumably in the month of February (at least February is the last mentioned month, in "León,". . .) and he dies at noonday, with the sun streaming through the window of his stable, illuminating a butterfly, that flutters nearby. Nature is at its most radiant moment as if to receive him in a special way, and even indicates symbolically, by illuminating the butterfly what the outcome of his death will be. Deliberate care has been taken, then, to prepare the environment surrounding Platero's death to make sure that no ugly incident or violent act contaminates the circumstances of his disappearance as a donkey. All violence is eliminated or suppressed. Final words of assurance or instruction are given. Children people the scenes in happy play either before his death at Christmas time or afterward in the country or near his grave. A cluster of butterfly imagery symbolizes the significance of his death as a process of rebirth. And finally, at the crucial moment, the sun is shining straight overhead at noon. Only in such an environment is death finally permitted to take place. It is important to note that the pain and suffering of death is not elaborated. Platero dies suddenly, presumably from something he ate. There is only sadness and the sadness is soon dispelled by the depiction of the pure and innocent conditions of the world in which rebirth is to take place.

In this way, then, the treatment of the seasonal cycle has been manipulated in the months of winter to accommodate the death of Platero. Of equal interest and importance now is to observe closely how Platero's world is introduced in early spring. The contrast with the state of the world at his release is striking. Three of the first five chapters take place at nightfall or at night, and the fourth deals with the darkening effect of the sun's eclipse. Four of the first eight chapters convey a sense of fear and shivering. A fifth chapter deals with the eerie effect of the eclipse and a sixth depicts the poet riding out of town with Platero, pursued by a taunting band of ragged gypsy children. The fear acquires proportions of ominousness and latent violence in. . . "Escalofrío." Indeed, the violence, though harmless, is made explicit in. . . "Judas," in which the townspeople of Moguer, practicing a springtime ritual, blast away with shotguns at effigies of unpopular or hated citizens of the community. These disturbances of the emotional climate, expressed in tension and fear, are further elaborated by unnatural events in the world of nature. The stars of the night acquire an ominous character. . . . Even Platero seems to become destructive as he dashes to bits the water's reflection of the moon: "Platero. . . entra en el arroyo, pisa la luna y la hace pedazos." The ominous character of these cosmic events serves to remind us of the unique description of the sunset in terms of a bleeding wound ("el ocaso. . . herido por sus propios cristales, que le hacen sangre por doquiera.") Now, in an earlier chapter, "Las Brevas,". . . we become more sensitive to a unique description of dawn, where night hides in the shadow of giant fig trees and sleeps on: "Fué el alba neblinosa y cruda. . . Aún, bajo las grandes higueras centenarias, cuyos troncos grises enlazaban en la sombra fría, como bajo una falda, sus muslos corpulentos, dormitaba la noche." The clue to these unnatural and curious events can be found in. . . "Las Golondrinas." Just as the eclipse earlier. . . disoriented the chickens and sent them scurrying prematurely to their roosts in anticipation of night, so the swallows are disoriented by the early and premature arrival of spring. It is worth quoting from this chapter at length. It makes explicit the premature arrival of spring, which, as we will try to establish, is a key factor in giving expressive form to the entire prose poem. The poet begins by pointing to one swallow in particular:

> Ahí la tienes ya Platero, negrita y vivaracha. . . Está la infeliz como asustada. Me parece que esta vez se han equivocado las pobres golondrinas, como se equivocaron, la semana pasada, las gallinas, recogiéndose en su cobijo cuando el sol de las dos se eclipsó. La primavera tuvo la coquetería de levantarse este año más temprano; pero ha tenido que guardar de nuevo, tiritando, su tierna desnudez en el lecho nublado de marzo. ¡Da pena ver marchitarse, en capullo, las rosas vírgenes del naranjal!
>
> Están ya aquí, Platero, las golondrinas, y apenas se las oye, como otros años, cuando el primer día de llegar lo saludan y lo curiosean todo, charlando sin tregua en su rizado gorjeo. . .
>
> No saben qué hacer. Vuelan mudas, desoreintadas, como andan las hormigas cuando un niño les pisotea el camino. . . .¡ Se van a morir de frío, Platero!

Thus the disorders of Platero's world, as it is first introduced to us, can be accounted for now by the untimely arrival of spring. Night lingers on at dawn; winter lingers on in spring. Disturbances and agitation ominously pervade everything. Among the first impressions are the fear produced by the dark, ugly man, . . . the pathetic games of the poor children, . . . the impoverishment of the whole village of Monguer suffered by the sun's eclipse, . . . and the ragged band of gypsy children. . . . When. . . the poet speaks these words to the poor children, "Pronto, al amanecer de vuestra adolescencia, la primavera os asustará, como un mendigo, enmascarada de invierno," he gives a fitting description to

the symbolic treatment of spring throughout the early chapters—spring comes in like a beggar, impoverished and needy, masked as winter. To treat the arrival of spring as a premature birth is especially effective since it allows the poet to elaborate at length the expressive elements that contrast clearly and significantly with those at the end of the work. The fear, the shivering, the poverty, the bloodletting, and the pain are all symbolically expressive of the prolonged labor pains of spring's rebirth. While the order, the harmony, the clarity, the youthful and healthy gaiety, and the promise of rebirth are all symbolically expressive of winter's capacity for transcendence and renewal.

Thus the symmetry of opposing forces that governs the beginning and the ending of *Platero* stands out now in full relief. The companions of rebirth are the forces of darkness and winter. The companions of death are the forces of light and spring. The experience of birth is long and painful; the experience of death is quick and painless. With this symmetry in mind, we can now make more fully explicit the structure of *Platero y Yo*. Earlier it was established that the principle of metamorphosis, linked to the seasonal cycle, constitutes the key structural principle. Now this can be modified and refined in a way that accounts, I think, for nearly all the expressive material, seen as an organic and unified whole. The organization of *Platero* into an expressive form involves the following sets of interrelated principles: the symbolic treatment of the sense and feeling of life embodied in the seasons of nature; the expressive manipulation and elaboration of the seasonal pattern to fit the special needs of Platero's death; the juxtaposition and distribution of expressive material in terms of life and death, light and darkness, violence and harmony, with the gradual reduction of death and violence and the triumph of life and harmony, reborn through the mysterious process of metamorphosis. (pp. 56–64)

Michael P. Predmore, "The Structure of 'Platero y Yo'," in *PMLA*, Vol. 85, No. 1, January, 1970, pp. 56–64.

MERVYN COKE-ENGUÍDANOS
(essay date 1981)

[In the following excerpt, Coke-Enguídanos comments on Jiménez's philosophy of poetry, identifying Jiménez's belief in the quasi-divine nature of the poetic word as the foundation of his aesthetics.]

The poet's struggle with the word, his struggle for expression, is essentially of a Romantic nature. For the Romantics, it is the imagination which provides the theatre of the battle; and it is the creative power of the imagination which, as Coleridge says in his *Biographia Literaria*, is for them the finite counterpart of the original creative act of God; significantly, of the act by which God created Himself, the divine "I Am": the Logos. The problem of taming the unpredictable and unbridled products of the Romantic imagination is especially explicit in Bécquer. His prose introduction to *Rimas* acknowledges that formal expression alone can save, order and perpetuate them. And yet the first *Rima* confesses: "Pero en vano es luchar; que no hay cifra / capaz de encerrarlo. . . " Rubén Darío too speaks of the unequal struggle of the poet with his intractable material, in his early composition, "El libro":

> Mas es en vano cantar;
> es muy grande mi flaqueza
> y del libro la belleza
> yo no podré retratar.

And in the final poem of *Prosas profanas*, he says: "Yo persigo una forma que no encuentra mi estilo /. . . Y no hallo sino la palabra que huye." The Romantic concept of the word is that of ineffability. Its attainment is believed to be an invincible impossibility.

It is at this point that Juan Ramón's own concept differs and develops beyond the Romantics. That is not to deny its source in the Romantic theory. But the important departure for Juan Ramón is that he connects once more "Intelijencia" with the imaginative search for poetic expression. In so doing, defeat need no longer be the poet's pre-ordained fate in his struggle for the word. Indeed, toward the end of his creative life, Juan Ramón can victoriously announce:

> Yo he acumulado mi esperanza
> en lengua, en nombre hablado, en nombre escrito;
> a todo yo le había puesto nombre.

For the generation of 1914, the political circumstances in Europe—and indeed the work of Ortega y Gasset himself—opened up the philosophy of the international vanguard into Spain. Much of this philosophical enquiry (by men such as Husserl, Heidegger, Wittgenstein, and others) was concerned with the value of language: specifically, the insufficiency of language to capture and convey reality. It is important to remember that Juan Ramón would have been very much alive to this climate of thinking, which formed a significant part of his background culture. It was this seemingly impossible reconciliation of language with reality which was the very goal at which he aimed. His first clear articulation of this is in his famous poem in *Eternidades*, written between 1914 and 1916, with its injunction; "¡Intelijencia, dame / el nombre exacto de las cosas!" Yet even earlier than this, in the collection entitled *La frente pensativa* written between 1911 and 1912, we have evidence of his esteem for the Word, unique to the essence that it enfolds:

> Una bella palabra
> es toda la palabra.

> Todo velo
> cubre un secreto sólo.

> Si cojo todo el cielo,
> aunque todos lo cojan, seré yo Apolo.

For Juan Ramón the Word represented not only, nor merely, an instrument for the stark naming of things, but a tool of sacred and creative significance. The Word, as conceived by Juan Ramón, was the repository of just that reality which, for instance Wittgenstein began in his *Tractatus* by denying it; of the irreducible essence of things, of emotions—in short, of all experience. The naming process for Juan Ramón was a veritable act of creation, with something of a religious rite about it: "Nombrar las cosas ¿ no es crearlas? En realidad, el poeta es un nombrador a la manera de Dios: 'Hágase, y hágase porque yo lo digo'" [*Pájinas escojidas: prosa*, 1970]. . . . The Word not only represents reality, but actually creates reality. Thus the function of the Word, in the hands of the poet, is to draw forth potentialities from their raw state of mere possibility and to realize them as actuality fulfilled: that which is "not-yet" thereby arriving at a state of Being, or permanence, in the poem. In this way, the process of poetic naming appears as a kind of religious "actus purus" of fulfilment, a creative elicitation.

The poem "**Cielo**", from *Diario de un poeta recien casado*, offers a parable of this redemptive power of the Word as "nombre-exacto-de-las-cosas". It is the Word which here restores to its reality the sky. At first, the sky is a mere hypothesis, "sin nombre", suspended between being and non-being. By the end of the poem, the sky has achieved the slow ascent to meet its name—an achievement which is inseparably accompanied and aided by the witnessing act of the poet's "mirar":

> Te tenía olvidado,
> cielo, y no eras
> más que un vago existir de luz,
> visto—sin nombre—
> por mis cansados ojos indolentes.
> Y aparecías, entre las palabras
> perezosas y desesperanzadas del viajero,
> como en breves lagunas repetidas
> de un paisaje de agua visto en sueños ...

> Hoy te he mirado lentamente,
> y te has ido elevando hasta tu nombre.

The sky has had to mount to ever greater heights in order to attain selfhood. But this has less to do with purely physical distance, than with characterizing through metaphor, the sheer asperity of the act of self-realization. It is not so much *where* realization takes place, as *how*. And this "how" of realization is the "how" of language. The concept of ascent had immemorial connections with difficulty, danger and asceticism. The "nombre", which embodies the desired self-realization, is therefore imaged in the poem as perched aloft in almost unreachable domains. The aspiration towards it will acquire all the greater virtue and glory in proportion to the hardship entailed. Thus the significance of the poet's emphasis on height and distance sheds its primary physical sense, to reveal itself as the metaphorical expression of the dignity of language. From the dignification of the "nombre", through its metaphorical elevation, we ought plainly to infer that upon that linguistic dignity is dependent our own. Finally, this metaphorical struggle to distant heights bears with it the concept of appropriation: the appropriation by which realities can linguistically be mastered. Just as the incipient sky must go forth to meet its destiny—the destiny of its "nombre"—so all language likewise must be appropriated. The naming process is one of active effort. Hence the struggle, as of parturition, in the nascent sky: and its effortfully slow procedure up to lay claim finally to that which is its own. As with the Romantics, then the concept of struggle remains, and very forcefully so. But it is struggle victorious.

To the Word, as the medium whereby the poetic act is consummated, Juan Ramón renders up his whole self. This mysterious metamorphosis through which he is subsumed into the Word, *becomes* the Word, he describes as follows: "Cuando yo escribo, desaparezco por completo; no me siento siquiera, soy todo idea o todo sentimiento, todo palabra, nombre" [Ricardo Gullón, *El último Juan Ramón Jiménez*, 1968]. Such loss of identity and such perfect oneness with the Word invites parallel with the divine mystic union of the soul with God, of the kind experienced by San Juan de la Cruz. It is of course a profane analogy; but although not explicit, it does appear that Juan Ramón is deliberately calling comparison with religious concepts, and this was common *modernista* practice. This clearly indicates the sacred nature of the poetic act as Juan Ramón conceived it, and the divine holiness of the Word. The reason for Juan Ramón's capitalization of "Palabra" is therefore apparent: it is a veritable transcript into Castilian of the Latin "Verbum" of theology. Certainly the theological conception of the Word was present in the mind of Juan Ramón. From his readings of religious texts—San Juan de la Cruz, Santa Teresa de Avila, St Augustine, Fray Luis de León, St Thomas Aquinas, Thomas á Kempis—Juan Ramón would have found constant reminders of the divinity of the "Verbum". In parenthesis, however, it should of course be remembered that such readings as these appealed to him not so much for any orthodox religious reasons, as for their aesthetic value. They were not devotional handbooks for Juan Ramón in the strictly orthodox Christian sense; because Juan Ramón's religious sense was centred around the notion of transcendence as achieved not through Christianity but by virtue of Poetic Expression. That is to say, by the Word, which thus becomes for him the profane embodiment of "The Way, The Truth and The Life". (Already, in *Cantos de vida y esperanza*, 1905, Rubén Darío had formulated this same idea, modifying the words of *The Gospel According to St John:* "El Arte puro como Cristo éxclama: / Ego sum lux et veritas et vita!" This verse was to become, in fact, a commonplace of *modernismo* and its virtual motto.) What the Divine "Verbum" is for the Christian believer, the poetic "verbum" was for Juan Ramón: the repository and the creator of Reality, just as the Word that is God, in Christian terms, is Creator, Maker and Artist of the universe. One is reminded of the often repeated statement of St Augustine in his *De Civitate Dei*, that the universe is the poem of God.

Marcello, the fictitious spokesman of Fray Luis de León, in his *De los nombres de Cristo*, tries to ascertain "qué cosa es esto que llamamos nombre. . . " In doing so, he declares that names fall into two categories: the first are what he calls "soul-words" and these derive from nature and are therefore perfect in their correlation of image and idea. The second kind consist of words which are fashioned by art and are of human invention. If we apply this analysis to the poetry of Juan Ramón, it is of course the latter class of name with which Juan Ramón is concerned. A poem entitled **"Acción"** says: "No sé con qué decirlo, / porque aún no está hechá / mi palabra." The word "hecha" and the possessive adjective "mi" suffice for proof. The Juanramonian Word is indeed a poetic artefact—"fabricated", in the sense that Fray Luis's Marcello employs; and it is invention. Juan Ramón conceives the Word as the instrument of invention and creation, that is, both *found*, objective reality; and *created*, "artificial" reality. This conception—which may be seen as an extension of the Aristotelian theory of the language of "praxis" and the language of "poiesis"—serves to affirm the existence of two worlds, paradoxically at once autonomous and confluent. The everyday world of reality, and the poetically real world. It is this which will permit Juan Ramón to transcend within the Work time, space and differentiation of identity. It is Juan Ramón's special conception of the Word which allows the existence of a "different" world wherein alone Juan Ramón can assume divine omnipotence, ignore terrestrial dimensions, and surpass all human limitations. As an example of the kind of conjuration of a new poetic world and different order of reality, of which the Word is capable, the following early poem can be cited. It comes from the third section, "Jardines dolientes", of *Jardines lejanos*, written between 1903 and 1904:

Cuando la mujer está,
todo es, tranquilo, lo que es
—la llama, la flor, la música—.
Cuando la mujer se fue
—la luz, la canción, la llama—,
!todo! es, loco, la mujer.

The structure of the poem is bi-partite to convey two different orders of reality. The first three lines display the objectively real presence of the woman in her context of the objectively real world, whose "tranquillity" is clearly consequent upon her being there. But with her physical departure, it is in the last three lines that the major potency of poetic diction comes into its own. Through the power of the Word, the return of the woman is effected, conjured home again into a new poetic reality: a kind of absent presence. With the investiture of this new order of being, and resurrected to poetic reality, so the world about likewise undergoes a transformation, made newly real and existent *within the frame of the poem*, its serenity changed to the poetic frenzy of ecstasy. Indeed, world and woman are now one—through the alchemy of the Word.

It is evident that the fact that "Palabra" and "Obra" are given capital letters by Juan Ramón is an indication that they signify much more than their usual everyday counterparts in the lower case. The capital letters operate as typographical signposts to a deeper and more mysterious meaning, a richer currency, than that normally ascribed to such familiar terms. It is necessary to establish at what point in his career Juan Ramón began to speak of his "Obra" as a total entity and to lend it this capital letter. Such an action was no mere idiosyncrasy. There is ample proof of the rigour and scrupulousness with which Juan Ramón attended to such matters of typography, print, format, colour and so on. That capitalization of the "Obra" coincided with the growth and fruition of his vision of the Work as a total Book, a *Summa*. It is the visual symbol of a whole concept.

Eternidades saw the initiation of the Work. But its roots were there from the very first. On 20 July 1931, Juan Ramón acknowledged this fact to his friend, Juan Guerrero Ruiz, who records him as follows: "Cuando habla de su Obra es después de treinta y cinco años de meditar sobre ella". The long, slow gestation of the Work does not rest there. Its realization is one of unceasing process for, in continuation, Guerrero Ruiz reports: "por eso cuando escribe no sólo está escribiendo versos, sino que está realizando su estética". (pp. 224–31)

The evolution of the Work as a unity is reflected in the evolution of the poetry itself. From *Eternidades* onward, Juan Ramón's poetry was to have for its sole true "subject", poetry itself. The poetic Word was to become the instrument of its own meditation. This self-regarding nature of the Work was, in large part, the logical development from the manner in which Juan Ramón conceived the special relationship between himself as poet and the Work created. "Yo concibo el libro como un todo orgánico", he stated, and indeed it was for him something very much akin to a living breathing creature. He believed, moreover, in the organic oneness of the poet with his Work, the latter being born of the rhythm of heart- and blood-beat and of the very pumping of the lung. "El verso", he declared [in *El trabajo gustoso*], "es como un río de agua de la tierra, río de la sangre de nuestra carne, nuestro barro; el río de esta sangre que respiramos del mar del aire y la echamos con el ritmo del corazón y del pulmón nuestros, al aire de la tierra y del mar." This conception of the organic nature of the Work is again testified by Guerrero Ruiz: "Dice que un poeta verdadero debe contener en sí toda la historia de la poesía; volver a crearla con su obra, y ser romántico en su primera juventud hasta recorrer el ciclo completo. Es—aunque sea una comparación demasiado naturalista—como el feto en el vientre de su madre, que experimenta una evolución total." A perfect illustration of this conception is to be found in the poem "**La menuda floración**" from *Dios deseado y deseante*. Here, the revolution of the poet's life is one and the same with the revolution of the poetic Work, for they are identified under the one symbol of "niñodiós", the "dios" is the "dios" of his poetic consciousness. The "niño", the child that endures with the man. Together with these, the poem synthesizes the concept of the flower, in which the early bud of childhood and the flowering of manhood parallel the blossoming of the poetic dream into its own inflorescent prime:

> El sueño no fue sueño, era distancia,
> y de ella venía la fragancia,
> la fragancia que yo, que dios en niñodiós, los dos
> le dimos en botón de primavera.
> Ella se dilató y hoy llena un mundo
> que yo ensanché para este niñodiós.

In the Work, Juan Ramón sought the superior goal of perfect beauty and, ultimately, his own God. His untiring loving meditation of this goal corresponds in a way with León Hebreo's analysis of the lover in his *Diálogos de amor*: "Del todo es ajeno de si mismo y propio del que ama y contempla, en el cual se convierte totalmente, que la esencia del ánima es su propio acto, y si se une para contemplar intimamente un objeto, se transporta en él su esencia y aquél es su propia sustancia, y no es más ánima y esencia del que ama, sino sola especie actual de la persona amada." The comparison is all the more appropriate since Juan Ramón frequently likened his poetic Work to a beautiful woman. For instance, he says [in *Pájinas escojidas: prósa*]: "Yo tengo escondida en mi casa, por su gusto y por el mio a la Poesia, como una mujer hermosa; y nuestra relación es la de los apasionados." Such is the oneness of the poet with his Work, for the Work is simultaneously both the object of his contemplation and the subject of it, since it is integral with its author. This fusion is particularly true in the case of free verse, above all other forms of poetry, according to Juan Ramón: "En el poema en verso libre, todo es del poeta. No así en otro género de composiciones, donde es la rima quien dirige y tuerce el desarrollo natural del poema" [Gullón, *Conversaciones con Juan Ramón Jiménez*, 1958]. Free verse therefore is self-generating. This raises the question of cause and effect with regard to poetry. Does the thought precede the word? Or the word engender the thought? The indication would seem to be that the spiritual state may very well be the product, rather than the premise, of the poetic creation. Turning to the text of Juan Ramón, we find evidence of this kind of mutual integration. The poem called "**Poeta y palabra**" from *La estación total* is an excellent illustration. It also exemplifies that poetry of self-reflection which I mentioned earlier. It is a poem upon poem-making, in which poet and Work are fused, both physically and spiritually. As the opening to the poem shows, it is when the poet is left in solitude, away from all social commerce, that he can be transubstantiated into the Word and become himself the Work:

> Cuando el aire, suprema compañia,
> ocupa el sitio de los que fueron,
> (. . .)
> él(. . .)
> se queda con el aire en su lugar.
> Puede olvidar, callar, gritar entonces dentro
> la palabra que llega del redondo todo,
> redondo todo solo;
> (. . .)
> la vibrante palabra muda,
> la inmanente.

Then it is that:

> La carne, el alma una de él, en su aire,
> son entonces palabra: . . .

I have spoken of the oneness of Juan Ramón with his Work. But it is necessary to identify which Juan Ramón is meant by this. For there is a clear awareness of two quite separate selves: the self of world-experience, and the literary self projected into the Work. "Yo no soy yo", he declares, in the poem of that title from *Eternidades:*

> Soy este
> que va a mi lado sin yo verlo;
> que, a veces, voy a ver,
> y que, a veces, olvido.
> El que calla, sereno, cuando hablo,
> el que perdona, dulce, cuando odio,
> el que pasea por donde no estoy,
> el que quedará en pie cuando yo muera.

The sense of such a dichotomy is of course not unique to Juan Ramón. It is expressed by Antonio Machado, by Unamuno, by Borges, in the "masks" of Yeats, and so on. In the kind of conflict between the empirical self of Juan Ramón and his lyrical self we may see that same "quarrel" of which Yeats, in his *Per amica silentia lunae* period of 1917, speaks: "We make out of the quarrel with others rhetoric, but of the quarrel with ourselves, poetry". Or, as he elsewhere says, "No mind can engender till divided into two" [*Autobiographies*]. The implications of this distinction between the empirical and lyrical self are far-reaching. For it is in precisely this distinction that Juan Ramón finds his ultimate redemption. His literary self, the self that is the Work, will prove his salvation. Death will be able to claim only the former, the insignificant Juan Ramón which is but a remnant left over from all that he has poured of his other self into the Work: ". . . toda mi alma / —vaciada ya por mi en la Obra plena— / segura para siempre" [*Poésia (en verso)*]. In this way, the Work becomes the enactment of a continuous drama between two personae: Death, and the twinned selves of Juan Ramón. An important difference emerges between

Juan Ramón's attitude to his Work and that of the majority of poets and writers who seek to embody themselves in their work. For whereas in the latter it is the life of the author that fulfils the book, with Juan Ramón it is the other way about. It is the Work which fulfils and actually creates the life of the poet. This startling inversion of the norm—the creation of Juan Ramón by and in his Work (a little like the creation of Cervantes by and in *Don Quijote*)—is expressed in a brief poem entitled **"Epitafio ideal"** from [*Poesía (en verso)*]:

> Libro acabado,
> caida carne mia,
> labrado subterráneo de mi vida!

With its suggestion of Adam, of mortality and the Fall, the terms of this poem are certainly surprising.

The significance which Juan Ramón gave to the simultaneity of growth, development and maturation of himself with the Work, within a strictly temporal dimension, is evident from a conversation with Ricardo Gullón in January 1954 in which he stated: "Yo creo que el mejor sistema para ordenar la obra es cronológico. Cada poema va así en la línea del tiempo, en el momento que apareció" [*Conversaciones con Juan Ramón Jiménez*]. In the chronological sequence thus ascribed to the Work is implicit already the idea of autobiography, of diary. However, unlike any ordinary diary, the Work is almost entirely bereft of anecdotal element, and should rather be seen as the record of a spiritual procession. It is true that Juan Ramón insisted on the need for a daily outlet, in a regular magazine or periodical, in order to disencumber himself of his day-to-day creations; and it is also true that in December 1952 he declared his intention to publish his Work chronologically: "Voy a dar, por orden cronológico, la obra total" [Gullón, *Conversaciones con Juan Ramón Jiménez*]. Nevertheless, despite these manifestations of an apparently logical and sequential time progression in the Work, they cannot be taken at strict face-value. The Work, on the contrary, cannot be "metred" in so simple a manner. Ultimately, it abides by quite other and more essential time laws. One cogent indication of this fact is Juan Ramón's own subtitle to the publication *Obra en marcha* which read. . . : "España. Sin día." That "Sin día" signified the special rhythm of Juan Ramón himself which, in his own words, "no es de reló, ni calendario, sino de tiempo verdadero". The puzzling apparent self-contradiction which this implies is one which has seriously to be taken into account. Those last two words, "tiempo verdadero", afford us the key to the truth. They refer to the chronology of the inner life; and the inner life adheres to no ordinary mundane laws of time. In this connection, it is useful to recall one of Juan Ramón's cryptically telling apothegms: "Mi vida interior, la belleza eterna, mi Obra." The Work is the inner life, and it will follow therefore only that "tiempo verdadero" which is proper to the inner life.

Only through an understanding of Juan Ramón's aesthetic of Word and Work will we begin fully to appreciate his poetry . . . In his special concept of the Word, Juan Ramón was able to combine intelligent reason with poetic faith—in the proportion that Dante-personàggio required to reach his Catholic God—in order to arrive at the "dios" of his Work. The capital letters with which he denoted Word and Work symbolize the magnitude of this undertaking and achievement. (pp. 231–36)

Mervyn Coke-Enguídanos, "Word and Work (with Capital Letters) in Juan Ramón Jiménez," in *MLN*, Vol. 96, No. 2, March, 1981, pp. 224–36.

SOURCES FOR FURTHER STUDY

Allen, Rupert C. "Juan Ramón and the World Tree: a Symbological Analysis of Mysticism in the Poetry of Juan Ramón Jiménez." *Revista Hispánica Moderna* XXXV, No. 3 (July 1969): 306–22.

    Study of the "World Tree" archetype in Juan Ramón's poetry. The critic suggests that the "World Tree" archetype serves as symbol of the transcendence of ego-consciousness in Jiménez's "secular" mysticism.

———. "Juan Ramón Jiménez: The Transcendentalist as 'Animal de Fondo de Aire'." *The Modern Language Review* 76, No. 1 (January 1981): 81–98.

    Discusses Jiménez's poem "Soy animal de fondo" within the context of the transcendentalist literary movement.

Cardwell, Richard A. *Juan R. Jiménez: The Modernist Apprenticeship 1895–1900*. Berlin: Colloquium Verlag, 1977, 323 p.

    In-depth discussion of Jiménez and the Spanish "modernist" writers, their influences on literature, and their evolution from the original style of the generation of 1898. Critical references are interspersed throughout the book, but most of the critical terminology is in Spanish.

Florit, Eugenio. Preface to *Selected Writings of Juan Ramón Jiménez*, by Juan Ramón Jiménez, translated by H. R. Hays, pp. xiii–xxxiii. New York: Farrar, Straus and Cudahy, 1957.

    Biographical and critical overview of Jiménez's life and career that discusses his achievements as a poet, prose writer, and literary mentor to contemporary Spanish poets.

Fogelquist, Donald F. "Poet and Pine." *Hispania* 54, No. 3 (September 1971): 452–58.

    Discusses the image of the pine tree in Jiménez's work.

Gullón, Ricardo. Introduction to *Juan Ramón Jiménez: Three Hundred Poems, 1903–1953*, by Juan Ramón Jiménez, translated by Eloise Roach, pp. xvii–xxxiv. Austin: University of Texas Press, 1962.

    General introduction to Jiménez's poetry and life.

Nemes, Graciela P. " Juan Ramón Jiménez." *Books Abroad* 26, No. 1 (Winter 1952): 16–19.

    Biographical discussion of Jiménez's life and career.

Olson, Paul R. "Structure and Symbol in a Poem of Juan Ramón Jiménez." *Modern Language Notes* LXXVI, No. 7 (November 1961): 636–47.

    Analysis of structure and symbolism in "Viene una música lánguida" from *Arias tristes*.

———. "Time and Essence in a Symbol of Juan Ramón Jiménez." *MLN* 78, No. 1 (January 1963): 169–93.

    Examines Jiménez's poetry and his symbolic use of the rose.

Patterson, Jack E. "The Poetry of Jiménez." *The Commonweal* LXVIII, No. 16 (18 July 1958): 400–02.

    Brief overview of Jiménez's life and career.

Predmore, Michael P. "The Structure of the *Diario de un poeta recién casado*: A Study of Hermetic Poetry." *Contemporary Literature* 13, No. 1 (Winter 1972): 53–105.

    Exhaustive study of Jiménez's acclaimed work. Predmore suggests possible interpretations of the *Diario*, with particular emphasis on the hermetic elements, traditional and new, in the poem.

Trend, J. B. "Juan Ramón Jiménez." In *Fifty Spanish Poems*, by Juan Ramón Jiménez, translated by J. B. Trend, pp. 9–25. Oxford: Dolphin Book Co., 1950.

    Thorough introduction to various biographical and literary influences on Jiménez's career. Commentary on several of Jiménez's works is included.

Wilcox, John C. "'Naked' Versus 'Pure' Poetry in Juan Ramón Jiménez, with Remarks on the Impact of W. B. Yeats." *Hispania* 66, No. 4 (December 1983): 511–21.

    Examines the influence of William Butler Yeats on Jiménez, the similarities between their work, their aims as poets, and their views on the creative process.

Young, Howard T. "Juan Ramón Jiménez (1881–1958): The Religion of Poetry." In his *The Victorious Expression: A Study of Four Contemporary Spanish Poets, Miguel de Unamuno, Antonio Machado, Juan Ramón Jiménez, Federico García Lorca*, pp. 75–135. Madison: University of Wisconsin Press, 1964.

    Provides an indepth analysis of the three phases of Jiménez's career.

———. "The Exact Names." *Modern Language Notes* 96, No. 2 (March 1981): 212–23.

    Studies various poems in Jiménez's *Eternidades*, concluding that "the open-ended creative act is the central import of Juan Ramón's *arte poética*."

Additional coverage of Jiménez's life and career is contained in the following sources published by Gale Research: *Contemporary Authors*, Vols. 104 and 131; *Hispanic Writers; Major 20-Century Writers; Poetry Criticism*, Vol. 7; and *Twentieth-Century Literary Criticism*, Vol. 4.